New 1991-92 Edition!

Sites for Tenters, Car Campers & RVers!

CALIFORNIA CAMPING

Completely updated and revised!

Find the perfect campground in CALIFORNIA CAMPING from the more than 1,500 campground descriptions with over 50,000 different sites!

"Ever want to get out of your same old place rut? Do you like to window-shop future trips or call ahead to check details or make reservations? If there is a "yes" there, California Camping might be an excellent addition to your recreation reference library. Recommended." —Sierra Club

"You won't find such useful and essential material in the usual campground atlas. Stienstra cuts through the fluff to the truth of camping." —San Diego Union

"Author Tom Stienstra includes tent, backpack, and RV campgrounds and covers such topics as hiking and foot care, fishing gear, and first aid. California Camping offers information on specific sites, along with detailed personal observations." —Sunset Magazine

"California Camping is an invaluable resource for backpackers, anglers, hunters, wilderness seekers, motor home campers or anyone eager to explore the Golden State's beautiful recreation areas. It's the most complete guide to California's outdoor areas." —Fishing & Hunting News

51695

9 780935 701289

CALIFORNIA CAMPING: 1991-92 Edition

 Foghorn Press, PO Box 77845, San Francisco, CA 94107. 415-241-9550.

Book Design and Maps ....LUKE THRASHER

Senior Research Editor .... JULIE LANCELLE

Researcher Editor .... NANCY STIENSTRA

Proofreader....................................... ANN MARIE BROWN

Cover Photo ....MATT BRADLEY

New 1991-92 Edition!

CALIFORNIA CAMPING

The Complete Guide
to California's
Recreational Areas

Tom Stienstra

Foghorn Press
San Francisco

photo by John Storey

ABOUT THE AUTHOR

Author Tom Stienstra is one of the West's most traveled outdoorsmen and most honored outdoor writers.

Tom's adventures include hiking the entire John Muir Trail, rafting 200 miles on the Klamath River, canoeing 400 miles on the Sacramento River, climbing Mt. Shasta, Mt. Whitney and Half Dome, searching for Big Foot, and travelling across the hemisphere in search of the world's bitingest fish. For this book, he explored each of the state's 58 counties.

His top awards include being named Outdoor Writer of the Year in 1990 and, in 1988, being awarded first place for the nation's best feature outdoor column. Recently, he received a Gold Medal Distinguished Service Award from the San Francisco Police Department for helping convert the therapy pool at Shriners Hospital to a trout pond for kids.

Stienstra (pronounced Steen' struh) is the outdoor columnist for the San Francisco Examiner and camping editor for Western Outdoors. He is an airplane pilot and lives in California with his wife Nancy Stienstra.

"Tom Stienstra looks like Grizzly Adams, has the outdoor sense of Marlin Perkins, the spirit of Johnny Appleseed and literally, the range of John Muir," said Charles Cooper, editor of the Houston Post and former sports editor of the San Francisco Examiner.

Dear Camper,

CALIFORNIA CAMPING is the most thorough, accurate and entertaining guidebook for campers ever published in California. Every site has been updated for the 1991-92 season. Plus, this new edition has been reorganized using a geographic grid system that provides greater detail in the maps and a fast way to pinpoint campgrounds. The book is now tabbed throughout for easy access. The main California map is highlighted with a tab running the entire length of the book. New symbols accompany each site and allow you to immediately identify the terrain or find a secluded site (look for those marked Tom Stienstra's 5 Percent Club).

We've cross-referenced activities, parks, lakes, streams, cities and special attractions in the index. This extensive index allows you to select the exact type of campground you desire. For instance, you can look for free sites, camps that allow pets or provide wheelchair access. You can discover whether your chosen campground has boat launch or laundry facilities.

So, enjoy it, use it and please keep the comments coming (use the enclosed postcard or the form at the end of this book). It always seems that the book can't get any better, until some ingenious camper writes in with a suggestion that we can't resist implementing. We are committed to making CALIFORNIA CAMPING the best outdoor book ever published. Write us at our mailing address: Foghorn Press, P.O. Box 77845, San Francisco, CA 94107.

Vicki K. Morgan

Publisher
Foghorn Press

CONTENTS

* See HOW TO LOCATE A CAMPGROUND on the next page

* HOW TO LOCATE A CAMPGROUND

1. If you have a destination in mind and want to see what campgrounds are available, use the index starting on page 673 to find the page numbers for listings. For example, June Lake in the index refers you to pages 385-387 in zone E5.

2. If you know what general area you want to go to, or want to explore new areas, use this California state map (or the larger map on pages 64-65). Locate the area of interest and turn to the corresponding tabbed section for detailed campground listings.

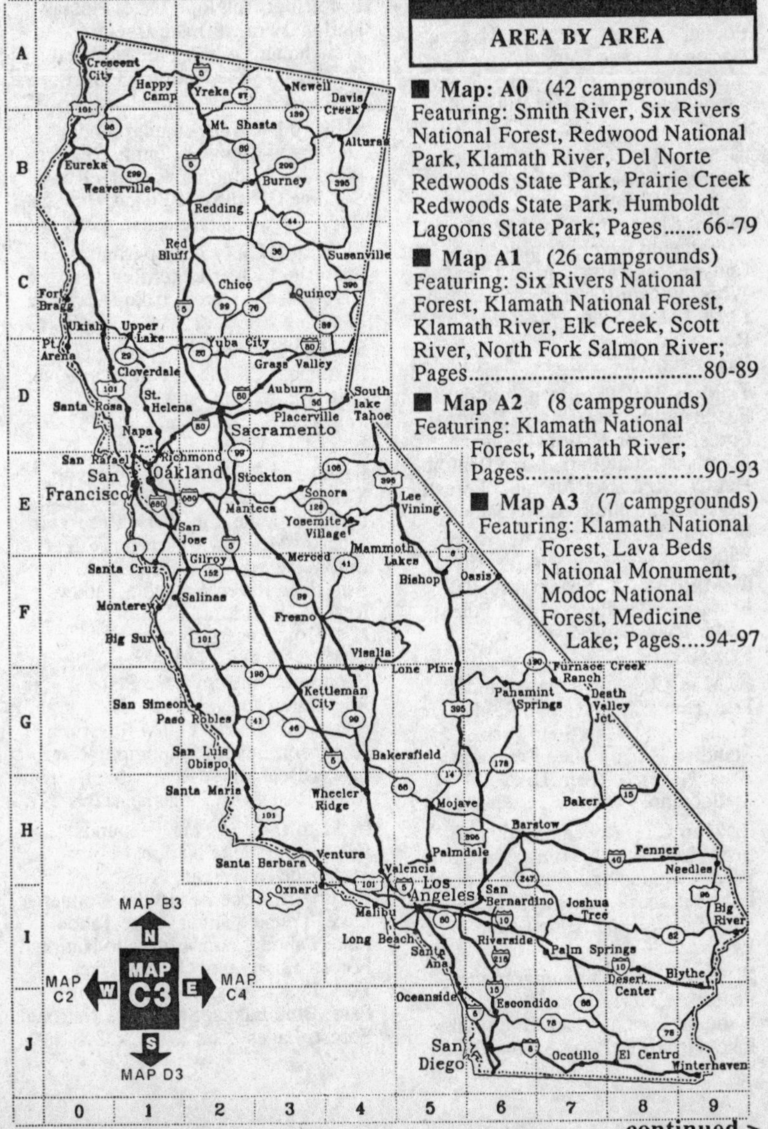

AREA BY AREA

continued >

TABLE OF CONTENTS

TABLE OF CONTENTS

continued >

* Every effort has been made to make the campgrounds as accessible, accurate and up-to-date as possible. We recommend you use the phone numbers provided for each campground for last-minute checks on campsite availability, weather and road conditions, plus the short-term effects of drought, fire or flood.

• JOINING THE FIVE PERCENT CLUB •

Going on a camping trip can be like trying to put hiking boots on an octopus. You've tried it too, eh? Instead of the relaxing, exciting sojourn it was intended, a camping trip can turn into a scenario called You Against The World. You want something easy? Try fighting an earthquake.

But it doesn't have to be that way and that's what this book is all about. If you give it a chance, this book can put the mystery, excitement and fun back into your camping vacations—and remove the fear of snarls, confusion and occasional temper explosions of volcanic proportions that keep people at home, locked away from where the action is.

Mystery? There are hundreds of hidden, rarely used campgrounds listed and mapped in this book that you have never dreamed of. Excitement? With many of them comes the sizzle with the steak, the hike to a great lookout, the big fish at the end of the line. Fun? The how-to section of the book can take the futility out of your trips so you can put the fun back in. Add it up, put it in your cash register and you can turn camping into the satisfying adventure it is meant to be, whether for just an overnight quicky or for a month-long fortune hunt.

It has been documented that 95 percent of the vacationers use only five percent of the available recreation areas. With this book, you can leave the herd to wander and be free, and join the inner circle, the five percenters who know the great, hidden areas used by so few people. To join the Five Percent Club, you should take a hard look at the maps for the areas you wish to visit, and in turn, the numbered listings for the campgrounds that follow. As you study the camps, you will start to feel a sense of excitement building, a sense that you are about to unlock a door—and catch a glimpse of a world that is rarely viewed. When you feel that excitement, act on it, parlay the energy into a great trip, so you can spend your time making memories, rather than remembering old ones.

The campground maps and guide lists can serve two ways: **1.** If you're on the road, it's late in the day and you are stuck for a spot for the night, you can likely find one nearby, or **2.** for planning in advance, you can custom tailor a vacation to fit exactly into your plans, rather than heading off, and hoping—maybe praying—it turns out all right.

For the latter, you may wish to obtain additional maps, particularly if you are venturing into areas governed by the U.S Forest Service or Bureau of Land Management. Both are federal agencies and have low-cost maps available that detail all hiking trails, lakes, streams and backcountry camps reached via logging roads. How to obtain these and other maps is described in Chapter 7. The backcountry camps are often in primitive and rugged settings, but provide the sense of isolation that many need on a trip. In addition, they can provide good jump-off points for backpacking trips, if that is your calling. These camps are also often free, and we have included hundreds of them in this book.

At the other end of the spectrum are the developed parks for motor homes, parks that offer a home away from home with everything from full hookups to a grocery store to a laundromat. These spots are just as important as the remote camps with no facilities. Instead of isolation, RV parks provide a place to shower, get outfitted for food and clean clothes, and for the motor home cruisers, spots to stay in high style while touring the area. They tend to cost from $10 to $25 per night, the amount depending on the location of the park with those in urban areas costing on the high end. An advance deposit may be necessary in summer months.

Somewhere between the two—the remote, unimproved camps and the lavish motor home parks—are hundreds and hundreds of campgrounds that provide a compromise—beautiful settings, some facilities, and a small overnight fee. Piped water, vault toilets, and picnic tables tend to come with the territory, along with a fee in the range of $6 to $15. State-operated camps set with ocean frontage, such as along Monterey Bay and along the Southern California coast, are the highest priced of camps in this range. Because state parks provide a bit of both worlds, being both rustic yet developed, this is where demand is highest. Reservations are usually advised, and during the summer season, you can expect plenty of company. This does not mean you need to abandon them in hope of a less confined environment. For one, most state parks have set up quotas so you don't feel like you've been squeezed in with a shoehorn, and for two, the same parks often provide off-season or weekday prospects when there can be virtually no use.

Prior to your trip, you will want to get organized, and that's where you will want to start putting socks on that giant octopus. The key to organization for any task is breaking it down to its key components, then solving each element independently of the others. Remember the octopus. Grab a moving leg, jam a boot on, and make sure it's on tight before reaching for another leg. Do one thing at a time, in order, and all will get done quick and right.

As a result, we have isolated the different elements of camping, and you should do the same when planning for your trip. There are separate sections on each of the primary ingredients for a successful trip: **1.** Food and cooking gear; **2.** Clothes and weather protection; **3.** Foot, leg care, and how to choose the right boots and socks; **4.** Sleeping gear and how to get your rest; **5.** Combatting bugs and some common-sense first-aid; **6.** Recreation gear and catching fish; **7.** How to obtain good maps and put them in use.

Each section has a list at the end of its respective chapter. This way you can become completely organized for your trip in just one week—spending just a little time each evening, working a different section each night. In itself, getting organized is an unnatural act for many; by splitting it up, you take the pressure out and put the fun back in.

As a full-time outdoor writer, the question I get asked more than any other is, "Where are you going this week?" All of the answers are in this book.

CHAPTER ONE

FOOD & COOKING GEAR

It was a warm, crystal clear day, the kind of day when if you had ever wanted to go sky diving, you would go sky diving. That was exactly the case for my old pal Foonsky, who had never before tried the sport. But a funny thing happened after he jumped out of the plane and pulled on the rip cord for the first time: The parachute didn't open.

In total free fall, Foonsky watched the earth below getting closer and closer. Not one to panic, he calmly pulled the rip cord on the emergency parachute. But nothing happened then either. No parachute, no nothing.

The ground was getting closer and closer, and as he tried to search out for a soft place to land, Foonsky detected a small object shooting up toward him, getting larger as it approached. It looked like a camper.

Foonsky figured this could be his last chance, so as they passed in mid-flight, he shouted, "Hey, do you know anything about parachutes?"

The other fellow just shouted back as he headed off into space, "Do you know anything about lighting camping stoves?"

Well, Foonsky got lucky and his parachute opened. But as for the other fellow, well, he's probably in orbit like a NASA weather satellite. If you've ever had a mishap lighting a camping stove, you know exactly what I'm talking about.

When it comes to camping, all things are not created equal. Nothing is more important than lighting your stove easily and having it reach full heat without feeling like you're playing with a short fuse to a miniature bomb. If your stove does not work right, your trip can turn into a disaster, regardless of how well you have planned the other elements. In addition, a bad stove will add an underlying feel of futility to your day, especially if you have carefully detailed your cooking gear and food for the trip. You will constantly have the inner suspicion that your darn stove is going to foul up on you again.

CAMPING STOVES

If you are buying a camping stove, remember this one critical rule: Do not leave the store with a new stove unless you have been shown exactly how to use it.

Know what you are getting. Many stores that specialize in outdoor recreation equipment now provide experienced campers/employees who will demonstrate the use of every stove they sell, and while they're at it, describe the respective strengths and weaknesses.

A second rule to remember is never buy a stove that uses kerosene for fuel. Kerosene is smelly and messy, provides low heat, needs priming, and in America, is virtually obsolete as a camp fuel. As a test experience, I tried using a kerosene stove once. I could scarcely boil a pot of water. In addition, some kerosene leaked out when the stove was packed, and it ruined everything it touched. The smell of kerosene never did go away. Kerosene remains popular in Europe only because the campers haven't heard much of white gas yet, and when they do, they will demand it.

That leaves white gas or butane as the best fuels, and either can be right for you, depending on your special preferences.

White gas is the most popular, because it can be purchased at most outdoor recreation stores, at many supermarkets, and is inexpensive and effective. It burns hot, has virtually no smell, and evaporates quickly if it should spill. If you get caught in wet, miserable weather and can't get a fire going, you can use it as an emergency fire starter, though its use as such should be sparing and never on an open flame.

White gas is a popular fuel both for car campers who use the large, two-burner stoves equipped with a fuel tank and a pump, or for hikers who use one of the lightweight backpacking stoves. On the latter, lighting can require priming with a gel called priming paste, which some people dislike. Another problem with white gas is that it can be extremely explosive.

As an example, I once almost burned my beard completely off in a mini-explosion while lighting one of the larger stoves styled for car camping. I was in the middle of cooking dinner when the flame suddenly shut down. Sure enough, the fuel tank was empty, and after refilling it, I pumped the tank 50 or 60 times to regain pressure. When I lit a match, the sucker ignited from three feet away. The concussion from the explosion was like a stick of dynamite going off, and immediately, the smell of burning beard was in the air. In the quick flash of an erred moment, my once thick, dark beard had been reduced to a mass of little, yellow burned curly-queues.

My error? After filling the tank, I forgot to shut the fuel cock off while pumping up the pressure in the tank. As a result, as I pumped the tank, the stove burners were slowly producing the gas/air mixture, filling the air space above the stove. The strike of a match even from a few feet away and ka-boom!

That problem can be solved by using stoves that use bottled butane fuel. On the plus side, butane requires no pouring, pumping, or priming, and stoves that use butane are the easiest to light of all camping stoves. Just turn a knob and light, that's it. On the minus side, because it comes in bottles, you never know precisely how much fuel you have left, and when a bottle is empty, you have a potential piece of litter. Never litter. Ever.

The other problem with butane as a fuel is that it just plain does not work well in cold weather, or when there is little fuel left in the cartridge. Since you cannot predict mountain weather in spring or fall, you can use more fuel than originally projected. That can be frustrating, particularly if your stove starts wheezing with several days left in your trip. In addition, with most butane cartridges, if there is any chance of the temperature falling below freezing, you often have to sleep with the cartridge to keep it warm, or otherwise forget using it come morning.

Personally, I prefer using a small, lightweight stove that uses white gas so I can closely gauge fuel consumption. My pal Foonsky uses one with a butane bottle because it lights so easily. We have contests to see who can boil a pot of water faster and the difference is usually negligible. Thus, other factors are important when choosing a stove.

Of the other elements, ease of cleaning the burner is the most important. If you camp much, especially with the smaller stoves, the burner holes will eventually become clogged. Some stoves have a built-in cleaning needle; a quick twist of a knob and you're in business. On the other hand, others require disassembling and a protracted session using special cleaning tools. If a stove is difficult to clean, you will tend to put off doing it, and your stove will sputter and pant while you get humiliated watching the cold pot of water sitting atop it.

Thus, before making a purchase, require the salesman to show you how to clean the burner head. Except in the case of the large, multi-burner family camping stoves, which rarely require cleaning, this test can do more to determine the long-term value of a stove than any other factor.

BUILDING FIRES

One summer expedition took me to the Canadian wilderness in British Columbia for a 75-mile canoe trip on the Bowron Lake Circuit, a chain of 13 lakes, six rivers, and seven portages. It is one of the true great canoe trips in the world, a loop trip that ends just a few hundred feet distant from the start. But at the first camp at Kibbee Lake, my camp stove developed a fuel leak at the base of the burner and the nuclear-like blast that followed just about turned Canada into a giant crater.

As a result, the final 70 miles of the trip had to be completed without a stove, cooking on open fires each night. The problem was compounded by the weather. It rained eight of the ten days. Rain? In Canada, raindrops the size of silver dollars fall so hard they actually bounce on the lake surface. We had to stop paddling a few times in order to empty the rain water out of the canoe. At the end of the day, we'd make camp, and then came the test. Either make a fire or go to bed cold and hungry.

With an axe, at least we had a chance for success. As soaked as all the downed wood was, I was able to make my own fire-starting tinder from the chips of splitting logs; no matter how hard it rains, the inside of a log is always dry.

In miserable weather, matches don't stay lit long enough to get the tinder started. Instead, we used either a candle or the little, wax-like, fire-starter cubes that stay lit for several minutes. From that, we could get the tinder going. Then we added small, slender strips of wood that had been axed from the interior of the logs. When the flame reached a foot high, we added the logs, with the dry interior of them facing in. By the time the inside of the logs had caught fire, the outside would be drying from the heat. It wasn't long and a royal blaze was brightening the rainy night.

That's a worst possible case scenario and perhaps you will never face anything like it. Nevertheless, being able to build a good fire and cook on it can be one of the more satisfying elements of a camping trip. At times, just looking into the flames can provide a special satisfaction at the end of a good day.

However, never expect to build a fire for every meal, or in some cases, even to build one at all. Many state and federal campgrounds have been picked clean of downed wood, or forest fire danger will force rangers to prohibit fires altogether during the fire season. In either case, you either use your camp stove or go hungry.

But when you can build a fire, and the resources are available to do so, it will add depth and a personal touch to your camping trip. Of the campgrounds listed in the directory of this book, the sites that allow for fires will likely already have fire rings available. In primitive areas where you can make your own, you should dig a ring eight inches deep, line the edges with rock, and clear all the needles and twigs in a five-foot radius. The next day, when the fire is dead, you can discard the rocks, fill over the black charcoal with dirt, then scatter pine needles and twigs over it. Nobody will even know you camped there. That's the best way I know to keep a secret spot a real secret.

When you start to build a campfire, the first thing you will notice is that no matter how good your intentions, your fellow campers will not be able to resist moving the wood around. Watch. You'll just be getting ready to add a key piece of wood at just the right spot, and your companion will stick his mitts in, quietly believing he has a better idea, shift the fire around, and undermine your best thought-out plans.

So I make a rule on camping trips. One person makes the fire and everybody else stands clear, or is involved with other camp tasks, like gathering wood, getting water, putting up tents, or planning dinner. Once the fire is going strong, then it's fair game; anyone adds logs at their discretion. But in the early, delicate stages of the campfire, it's best to leave it to one person.

Before a match is first struck, a complete pile of firewood should be gathered alongside. Then start small, with the tiniest twigs you can find, and slowly add in larger twigs as you go, criss-crossing them like a miniature tepee. Eventually, you will get to the big chunks that will produce high heat. The key is to get one piece of wood burning into another, which then burns to another, setting off what I call the chain-of-flame. Conversely, single pieces of wood, set apart from each other, will not burn.

On a dry, summer evening at a campsite where plenty of wood is available, about the only way you can blow the deal is to get impatient and try to add the big pieces too quickly. Do that and you'll just get smoke, not flames, and it won't be long before every one of your fellow campers is poking at your fire. It will drive you crazy, but they just can't help it.

COOKING GEAR

I like traveling light, and I've found all one needs is a cooking pot, small frying pan, metal pot grabber, fork, knife, cup, and matches for a cook kit. If you want to keep the price of food low and also cook customized dinners each night, a small pressure cooker can be just the ticket (see "Keeping the Price Down.") In fact, I keep all the gear in one small bag, which fits into my pack. If I'm camping out of my four-wheel drive rig, the little bag of cooking gear is easy to keep track of. Simple, not complicated, is the key to keeping a camping trip on the right track.

You can get more elaborate by purchasing complete cook kits with plates, a coffee pot, large pots, and other cookware, but what really counts is having one single pot you're happy with. It needs to be just the right size, not too big or small, and be stable enough so it won't tip over, even if it is at a slight angle on a fire, full of water at a full boil. Mine is just six inches wide and 4.5 inches deep, holds better than a quart of water, and has served well for several hundred camp dinners.

The rest of your cook kit is easy to complete. The frying pan should be small, light-gauge aluminum, teflon-coated, with a fold-in handle so it's no hassle to store. A pot grabber is a great addition, that is, a little aluminum gadget that will clamp to the edge of pots and allow you to lift them and pour water with total control and without burning your fingers. A fork, knife, and cup are at your discretion. For cleanup, take a small bottle filled with dish cleaner and a plastic scrubber, and you're in business.

A Sierra Cup, which is a wide aluminum cup with a wire handle, is ideal because you can eat out of them as well as use them for drinking. This means no plates to clean after dinner, so cleanup is quick and easy. In addition, if you go for a hike, you can clip them to your belt with the wire handle.

If you want a more formal setup, complete with plates, glasses, silverware, and the like, you can end up spending more time preparing and cleaning up from meals than you do enjoying the country you are exploring. In addition, the more equipment you bring, the more loose ends you will have to deal with and loose ends can cause plenty of frustration. If you have a choice, choose simple.

And remember what Thoreau said: "A man is rich in proportion to what he can do without."

FOOD AND COOKING TRICKS

On a trip to the Bob Marshall Wilderness in western Montana, I woke up one morning, yawned, and said, "What've we got for breakfast?"

The silence was ominous. "Well," finally came the response, "we don't have any food left."

"What!?"

"Well, I figured we'd catch trout for meals every other night."

On the return trip, we ended up eating wild berries, buds, and yes, even tried roots (not too tasty). When we finally landed the next day at a Kalispell pizza parlor, we nearly ate the wooden tables.

Running out of food on a camping trip can do more to turn reasonable people into violent grumps than any other event. There's no excuse for it, not when a system for figuring meals can be outlined with precision and little effort. You should not go out and buy a bunch of food, throw it in your rig, and head off for yonder. That leaves too much to chance. And if you've ever been in the woods and real hungry, you'll know to take a little effort to make sure a day or two of starvation will not reoccur. A three-step process offers a solution:

1. Make a general meal-by-meal plan and make sure your companions like what is on it. Never expect to catch fish for any meals.

2. Tell your companions to buy any specialty items (like a special brand of coffee) on their own and not to expect you to take care of everything.

3. Put all the food on your living room floor and literally figure every day of your trip meal-by-meal, bagging the food in plastic bags as you go. You will know exact food quotas and will not go hungry.

Fish for meals? There's a guaranteed rule for that: If you expect to catch fish for meals, you will most certainly get skunked. If you don't expect to catch fish for meals, you will probably catch so many they'll be coming out of your ears. I've seen it a hundred times.

KEEPING THE PRICE DOWN

"There must be some mistake," I said with a laugh. "Who ever paid $750 for some camp food?"

But the amount was as clear as the lit digital numbers on the cash register: $753.27.

"How is this possible?" I asked the clerk at the register.

"Just add it up," she responded, irritated.

Then I started figuring. The freeze-dried backpack dinners cost $6 apiece. A small pack of beef jerky went for $2, the beef sticks for 75 cents, Granola bars for 50 cents apiece. Then multiply it by four hungry men, including Foonsky, for 21 days. This was for a major expedition, four guys hiking 250 miles over three weeks from Mt. Whitney to Yosemite Valley.

The dinners alone cost close to $500. Add in the usual goodies, the jerky, Granola bars, the soups, dried fruit, oatmeal, Tang, candy and coffee, and I was handed a bill that felt like an earthquake.

A lot of campers have received similar shocks. In preparation for their trips, campers shop with enthusiasm. Then after hearing the price, they pay the bill in horror. Watch and you will see it.

Well, there are answers, lots of them. You can eat gourmet style in the outback without having your wallet drilled by a hole the size of Crater Lake. But it means do-it-yourself style cooking, more planning, and careful shopping. It also means transcending the push-button "I-want-it-now" philosophy that so many people try to take with them to the mountains.

The secret is to bring along a small pressure cooker. A reader, Mike Bettinger of San Francisco, passed this tip on to me. These little pressure cookers weigh about two pounds, and for backpackers and back-country campers, that may sound like a lot, but when three or four people are on the trip, it actually saves weight.

The key is that it allows campers to bring items that are difficult to be cooked at high altitudes, such as brown and white rice, red, black pinto and lima beans, and lentils. The idea for a dinner is to pick one or more for a basic staple and then add a variety of freeze dried ingredients to make a final dish. Available are packets of meat, vegetables, onions, shallots and garlic. Sun-dried tomatoes, for instance, reconstitute wonderfully in the pressure cooker. Add herbs, spices, and maybe a few rainbow trout and you will be eating better out of a backpack than most people eat in their homes.

"In the morning, I have used the pressure cooker to turn dried apricots into apricot sauce to put on the pancakes we have made with sour dough starter," Bettinger said. "The pressure cooker is also big enough to wash out cups and utensils in. The day when backpacking meant eating terrible freeze-dried food is over. It always tasted the same no matter what was on the label. It doesn't take a gourmet cook to prepare these meals, only some thought before hand."

Now when Foonsky, Mr. Furnai, Rambob and me sit down to eat such a meal, we don't call it "eating." We call it "hodgepacking," or "time to pack your hodge." After a particular long day on the trail, you can do some serious hodgepackin'.

If your trip is a shorter one, like for over a weekend, that means you can bring more fresh food to add some sizzle to the hodge. You can design a hot soup/stew mix that is good enough to make and eat at home.

You start by bringing a pot of water to a full boil, then adding pasta, ramen or macaroni. While it simmers, cut in a potato, carrot, onion and garlic clove, and let it cook for about 10 minutes. When the vegetables have been softened, add in a soup mix or two, maybe some cheese, and you are just about in business. But you can still ruin it, and turn your hodge into slodge. Make sure you read the directions on the soup mix to determine cooking time. That can vary widely. In addition, make sure you stir the whole thing up, otherwise you will get these hidden dry clumps of soup mix that can taste like garlic sawdust.

How do I know? It was up near Kearsage Pass, where feeling half-starved, I will never forget the first bite of that night's hodge. I damn near gagged to death. Foonsky laughed at me, that is, until he took his first bite, a nice big one, then turned green.

Another way to trim food costs is to make your own beef jerky, the trademark staple of campers for 200 years. But hey, a tiny, little packet of beef jerky costs $2. On that 250-mile expedition, I spent $150 on jerky alone. Never again. Now we make our own and get big strips of jerky that taste better than anything you can buy.

Foonsky settled on the following recipe, starting with a couple pieces of meat, lean top round, sirloin, or tri-tip. At home, cut it in 3/16-inch strips across the grain, trimming out the membrane, gristle, and fat. Marinate the strips for 24 hours, placing them in a glass dish. The fun begins when picking a marinade. Try two-thirds Soy Van Terriyaki, one-third Worcestershire. You can customize the recipe by adding pepper, ground mustard, bay leaf, red wine vinegar, garlic, and for the brave, Tabasco. After a day or so, squeeze each strip of meat out with a rolling pin, lay them in rows on a cooling rack over a cookie sheet, place them in an oven and dry the strips at 125 degrees for 12 hours. Thicker pieces can take as long as 18 to 24 hours.

That's it. The hardest part is cleaning the cookie sheet when you are done. The easiest part is eating your own homemade jerky while sitting at a lookout on a mountain ridge. The do-it-yourself method for jerky may take a day or so, but it is cheaper and can taste better than anything you can buy pre-made.

If all this still doesn't sound like your idea of a gourmet but low-cost camping meal, well, you are forgetting the main course: rainbow trout. The law of the wild is that if you expect to catch trout for meals, you will starve to death. However, if you plan to catch none, you will have plenty to top off each night's hodgepackin'.

Some campers go to great difficulties to cook their trout, bringing along frying pans, butter, grills, tin foil, et al, but all you really need is some seasoned salt and a campfire.

Rinse the trout off, and while still wet, sprinkle a good dose of seasoned salt on it, both inside and out. Clear any burning logs to the side of the campfire, then lay the trout right on the coals, turning it once so both sides are cooked. Sound ridiculous? Sound like you are throwing the fish away? Sound like the fish will burn up? Sound like you will have to eat the campfire ash? Wrong on all counts. The fish cooks perfectly, the ash doesn't stick, and after cooking trout this way, you may never fry a trout again.

But if you can't convince your buddies, who may insist the trout be fried, then make sure you have butter to fry them in, not oil. And also make sure you cook them all the way through, so the meat strips off the back bone in two nice, clean fillets. The fish should end up looking like Sylvester the Cat just dipped it in his mouth, leaving only the head, tail and a perfect skeleton.

You can supplement your eats with sweets, nuts, freeze-dried fruits, and drink mixes. In any case, make sure you keep the dinner menu varied. If you and your buddies look into your dinner cups and grown, "Ugh, not this again," you will soon start dreaming of cheeseburgers and french fries on your trip instead of hiking, fishing, and finding beautiful campsites.

If you are car camping and have a big ice chest, you can bring virtually anything to eat and drink. If you are on the trail, and don't mind paying the price, the new era of pre-made freeze-fried dinners provide a final option.

Some of the biggest advances in the outdoor industry have come in freeze-dried dinners now available for campers. Some of them are almost good enough to serve in restaurants. Sweet-and-sour pork over rice, tostadas, burgundy chicken . . . it sure beats the poopy goop we used to eat, like the old, soupy chili mac dinners that tasted bad and looked so unlike "food" that consumption was near impossible, even for my dog, Rebel. Foonsky managed to get it down, however, but just barely.

To provide an idea of how to plan a menu, consider what my companions and I ate while hiking 250 miles on California's John Muir Trail:

Breakfast: Instant soup, oatmeal (never get plain), one beef jerky stick, coffee or hot chocolate.

Lunch: One beef stick, two jerky sticks, one Granola bar, dried fruit, half cup of pistachio nuts, Tang, small bag of M&Ms.

Dinner: Instant soup, freeze-dried dinner, milk bar, rainbow trout.

What was that last item? Rainbow trout? Right! Lest you plan on it, you can catch them every night.

CHAPTER TWO

CLOTHING & WEATHER PROTECTION

What started as an innocent pursuit of a perfect campground had evolved into one heck of a predicament for Foonsky and me.

We had parked at the end of a logging road and then bushwhacked our way down a canyon to a pristine trout stream. And on my first cast, a little flip into the plunge pool of a waterfall, I caught a 16-inch rainbow trout, a real beauty that jumped three times. Magic stuff.

Then just across stream, we saw it. The Perfect Camping Spot. On a sandbar on the edge of the forest, there lay a flat, high and dry spot above the river. Nearby was plenty of downed wood collected by past winter storms that we could use for firewood. And, of course, this beautiful trout stream was bubbling along just 40 yards from the site.

But nothing is perfect, right? To reach it, we had to wade across the river, though it didn't appear too difficult a task. The cold water tingled a bit, and the river came up surprisingly high, just above the belt. But it would be worth it to camp at The Perfect Spot.

Once across the river, we put on some dry clothes, set up camp, explored the woods, and fished the stream, catching several nice trout for dinner. But late that afternoon, it started raining. What? Rain in the summertime? Nature makes its own rules. By next morning it was still raining, pouring like a Yosemite waterfall from a solid gray sky.

That's when we noticed The Perfect Spot wasn't so perfect. The rain had raised the river level too high for us to wade back across. We were marooned, wet, and hungry.

"Now we're in a heck of a predicament," said Foonsky, the water streaming off him.

Getting cold and wet on a camping trip with no way to get warm is not only unnecessary and uncomfortable, but it can be a fast ticket to hypothermia, the number one killer of campers in the woods. By definition, hypothermia is a condition where body temperature is lowered to the point where it causes illness. It is particularly dangerous because the afflicted are usually unaware it is setting in. The first sign is a sense of apathy, then a state of confusion, which can lead eventually to collapse (or what appears to be sleep), then death.

You must always have a way to get warm and dry in short order, regardless of any condition you may face. If you have no way of getting dry, then to prevent hypothermia you must take emergency steps. Those steps are detailed in the chapter on first-aid.

But you should never reach that point. For starters, always have different sets of clothes tucked away, so no matter how cold and wet you might get, you always have something dry. On hiking trips, I always carry a second set of clothes, sealed to stay dry, in a plastic garbage bag. I keep a third set waiting back at the truck.

If you are car camping, the vehicle can cause an illusionary sense of security. But with an extra set of dry clothes stashed safely away, there is no illusion. The security is real. And remember, no matter how hot the weather is when you start on your trip, always be prepared for the worst. Foonsky and I learned the hard way.

So both of us were soaking wet on that sandbar, and with no other choice, we tried holing up in the tent for the night. A sleeping bag with Quallofil, or another polyester fiber fill, can retain warmth too, even when wet, because the fill is hollow and retains its loft. So as miserable as it was, we made it through the night.

The rain finally stopped the next day, and the river dropped a bit, but it was still rolling big and angry. Using a stick as a wading staff, Foonsky crossed about 80 percent of the stream before he was dumped, but he made a jump for it and managed to scramble to the river bank. He waved for me to follow. "No problem," I thought.

It took me some 20 minutes to reach nearly the same spot where Foonsky had been dumped. The heavy river current was above my belt and pushing hard. Then, in the flash of an instant, my wading staff slipped on a rock. I teetered in the river current, and was knocked over like a bowling pin. I became completely submerged. I went tumbling down the river, heading right toward the waterfall. While underwater, I looked up at the river surface and can remember how close it appeared, yet how out of control I was. Right then, this giant hand appeared, and I grabbed it. It was Foonsky. If it wasn't for that hand, I would have sailed right over the nearby waterfall.

My momentum drew Foonsky right into the river, and we scrambled in the current, but I suddenly sensed the river bottom under my knees. On all fours, the two of us clambered ashore. We were safe.

"Thanks ol' buddy," I said.

"Man, we're wet," he responded. "Let's get to the rig and get some dry clothes on.

DRESSING IN LAYERS

After falling in the river, Foonsky and I looked like a couple of cold swamp rats. When we eventually reached the truck, and finally started getting into warm clothes, a strange phenomenon hit both of us. Now that we were warming up, we started shivering and shaking like an old engine trying to start. It's the body's built-in heater. Shivering is how the body tries to warm itself, producing as much heat as if you were jogging.

To retain that heat, you should dress in "layers." The interior layer, what you wear closest to your skin, and the exterior layer, what you wear to repel the weather, are the most important.

In the good ol' days, campers wore long underwear made out of wool, which was scratchy, heavy, and sometimes sweaty. Well, times have changed. You can now wear long underwear made of Polypropylene, a synthetic material that is warm, light, and wicks dampness away from your skin. It's ideal to wear in a sleeping bag on cold nights, during cool evenings after the sun goes down, or for winter snow sports. Poly shirts come in three weights: light, medium, and heavy. The medium weight is ideal for campers. The light weight clings too much to your body. We call it Indian Underwear, because it keeps creeping up on you. And the heavy weight is too warm and bulky. For most folks the medium is just right.

The next layer of clothes should be a light cotton shirt or a long-sleeve cotton/wool shirt, or both, depending on coolness of the day. For pants, many just wear blue jeans when camping, but blue jeans can be hot, tight, and once wet, they tend to stay that way. Putting on wet blue jeans on a cold morning is a torturous way to start the day. I can tell you that from experience, since I have suffered that fate a number of times. A better choice are pants made from a cotton/canvas mix, which are available at outdoor shops. They are light, have a lot of give, and dry quickly. If the weather is quite warm, shorts that have some room to them can be the best choice.

VESTS, PARKAS

In cold weather, you should take the layer system one step further with a warm vest and a parka jacket. Vests are especially useful because they provide warmth without the bulkiness of a parka.

The warmest vests and parkas are either filled with down, Quallofil, or are made with a cotton/wool mix. Each has its respective merits and problems. Downfill provides the most warmth for the amount of weight, but becomes useless when wet, taking on a close resemblance to a wet dish rag. Quallofil keeps much of its heat-retaining qualities even when wet, but is expensive. Vests made of cotton/wool mixes are the most attractive and also are quite warm, but can be as heavy as a ship's anchor when wet.

Sometimes the answer is combining the two. One of my best camping companions wears a good-looking, cotton-wool vest, and a parka filled with Quallofil. The vest never gets wet, so weight is less of a factor.

RAIN GEAR

One of the most miserable nights I ever spent in my life was on a camping trip where I didn't bring my rain gear or a tent. Hey, it was early August, the temperature had been in the 90s for weeks, and if anybody told me it was going to rain, I would have asked them to consult a brain doctor.

But rain it did. And as I got more and more wet, I kept saying to myself, "Hey, it's summer, it's not supposed to rain." Then I remembered one of the Ten Commandments of camping: Forget your rain gear and you can guarantee it will rain.

To stay dry, you need some form of water repellent shell. It can be as simple as a $5 poncho made out of plastic or as elaborate as a Gore-Tex rain jacket and pants that cost $300 a set. What counts is not how much you spend, but how dry you stay.

Some can do just fine with a cheap poncho, and note that ponchos can serve other uses in addition to a rain coat. Ponchos can be used as a ground tarp, a rain cover for supplies or a backpack, or in a pinch, can be roped up to trees to provide a quick storm ceiling if you don't have a tent. The problem with ponchos is that in a hard rain, you just don't stay dry. First your legs get wet, then they get soaked. Then your arms follow the same pattern. If you're wearing cotton, you'll find that once part of the garment gets wet, the water will spread until, alas, you are dripping wet, poncho and all. Before long you start to feel like a walking refrigerator.

One high-cost option is buying a Gore-Tex rain jacket and pants. Gore-Tex is actually not a fabric, as is commonly believed, but a laminated film that coats a breathable fabric. The result is a lightweight, water repellent, breathable jacket and pants. They are perfect for campers, but they cost a fortune.

Some hiking buddies of mine have complained that the older Gore-Tex rain gear loses some water repellent qualities over time. However, manufacturers insist that this is the result of water seeping through seams, not leaks in the jacket. At each seam, tiny needles will have pierced through the fabric, and as tiny as the holes are, water will find a way through. An application of Seam Lock, especially at major seams around the shoulders of a jacket, can usually end the problem.

If you don't want to spend the big bucks for Gore-Tex rain gear, but want more rain protection than a poncho affords, a coated nylon jacket is the middle road that many choose. They are inexpensive, have the highest water repellent qualities of any rain gear, and are warm, providing a good outer shell for your layers of clothing. But they are not without fault. These jackets don't breathe at all, and if you zip it up tight, you can sweat like an Eskimo.

My brother, Rambob, gave me a $20 nylon jacket prior to an expedition we took climbing Northern California's Mt. Shasta, one of America's most impressive peaks at 14,162 feet. I wore that $20 special all the way to the top and with no complaints; it's warm and 100 percent waterproof. The one problem with nylon is when the temperatures drop below freezing. They get so stiff it feels like you are wearing a strait jacket. But at $20, it seems like a treasure, especially compared to the $180 Gore-Tex jackets. And its value increases every time it rains.

OTHER GEAR, AND A FEW TIPS

What are the three items most commonly forgotten on a camping trip? "A cook, a dishwasher, and a fish cleaner," says my pal, the Z-Man.

C'mon now, Z-man, the real answers? A hat, sunglasses, and chapstick. A hot day is unforgiving without them.

A hat is crucial, especially when you are visiting high elevations. Without one you are constantly exposed to everything nature can give you. The sun will dehydrate you, sap your energy, sunburn your head, and in worst cases, cause sunstroke. Start with a comfortable hat. Then finish with sunglasses, chapstick, and sunscreen for additional protection. That will help protect you from extreme heat.

To guard against extreme cold, it's a good idea to keep a pair of thin ski gloves stashed away with your emergency clothes, along with a wool ski cap. The gloves should be thick enough to keep your fingers from stiffening up, but pliable enough to allow full movement, so you don't have to take them off to complete simple tasks, like lighting a stove. An option to gloves are glovelets, which look like gloves with no fingers. In any case, just because the weather turns cold doesn't mean that your hands have to.

And if you fall into a river like Foonsky and I did, well, I hope you have a set of dry clothes waiting back at your rig. Oh, and a hand reaching out to you.

CHAPTER THREE

HIKING & FOOT CARE

We had set up a nice, little camp in the woods, and my buddy, Foonsky, sitting against a big Douglas fir, was strapping on his hiking boots.

"New boots," he said with a grin. "But they seem pretty stiff."

We decided to hoof it on down the trail for a few hours, exploring the mountain wildlands that are said to hide Bigfoot and other strange creatures. These woods are quiet and secret, and after just a short while on the trail, a sense of peace and calm seemed to settle in. The forest provides the chance to be cleansed with clean air and the smell of trees, freeing you from all troubles.

But it wasn't long and the look of trouble was on Foonsky's face. And no, it wasn't from seeing Bigfoot.

"Got a hot spot on a toe," he said.

Immediately we stopped. He pulled off his right boot, then socks, and inspected the left side of his big toe. Sure enough, a blister had bubbled up, filled with fluid, but not popped. From his medical kit, Foonsky cut a small piece of moleskin to fit over the blister, then taped it to hold it in place. A few minutes later, we were back on the trail.

A half hour later, there was still no sign of Bigfoot. But Foonsky stopped again and pulled off his other boot. "Another hot spot." Another small blister had started on the little toe of his left foot, over which he taped a Band-Aid to keep it from further chafing against the inside of his new boot.

In just a few days, ol' Foonsky a big, strong guy who goes 6-foot-5, 200-plus pounds was walking around like a sore-hoofed hoss that had been loaded with a month of supplies and then ridden over sharp rocks. Well, it wasn't the distance that had done Foonsky in, it was those blisters. He had them on eight of his ten toes and was going through Band-Aids, moleskin, and tape like he was a walking emergency ward. If he used any more tape, he was going to look like a mummy from an Egyptian tomb.

If you've ever been in a similar predicament, then you know the frustration of wanting to have a good time, wanting to hike and explore the area at which you have set up a secluded camp, only to be turned gimp-legged by several blisters. No one is immune, not big, strong guys nor small, innocent-looking women. All are created equal before the blister god. You can be forced to bow to it unless you get your act together.

That means wearing the right style boots for what you have in mind and then protecting your feet with a careful selection of socks. And then, if you are still so unfortunate as to get a blister or two, it means knowing how to treat them fast so they don't turn your walk into a sore-footed endurance test.

What causes blisters? In almost all cases, it is the simple rubbing of your foot against the rugged interior of your boot. That act can be worsened by several factors:

1. A very stiff boot, that is, one in which your foot moves inside the boot as you walk, instead of the boot flexing as if it was another layer of skin.

2. Thin, holey, or dirty socks. This is the fastest route to blister death. Thin socks will allow your feet to move inside of your boots, holey socks will allow your skin to chafe directly again the boot's interior, and dirty socks will wrinkle and fold, also rubbing against your feet instead of cushioning them.

3. Soft feet. By themselves, soft feet will not cause blisters, but in combination with a stiff boot or thin socks, they can cause terrible problems. The best way to toughen up your feet is to go barefoot. In fact, some of the biggest, toughest-looking guys you'll ever see from Hells Angels to pro football players have feet that are as soft as a baby's butt. Why? Because they never go barefoot and don't hike much.

SELECTING THE RIGHT BOOTS

One summer I hiked 400 miles, including 250 miles in three weeks, along the crest of California's Sierra Nevada, and another 150 miles over several months in an earlier general training program. In that span, I got just one blister, suffered on the fourth day of the 250-miler. I treated it immediately, and suffered no more. One key is wearing the right boot, and for me, that means a boot that acts as a thick layer of skin that is flexible and pliable to my foot. I want my feet to fit snugly in them, with no interior movement.

There are three kinds of boots: mountaineering boots, hiking boots, and canvas walking shoes. Either select the right one for you or pay the consequences.

The stiffest of the lot is the mountaineering boot. These boots are often identified by mid-range tops, laces that extend almost as far as the toe area, and ankle areas that are as stiff as a board. The lack of "give" in them is what enamors them to mountaineers. The stiffness is preferred when rock climbing, walking off-trail on craggy surfaces, or hiking down the edge of stream beds where walking across small rocks can cause you to turn your ankle. Because these boots don't give on rugged, craggy terrain, they reduce ankle injuries and provide better traction.

The backlash of stiff boots is that if careful selection of socks is not made and your foot starts slipping around in them, you will get a set of blisters that would raise even Foonsky's eyebrows. But if you just want to go for a walk, or a good tromp with a backpack, then hiking shoes or backpacking boots are better designed for those respective uses.

Canvas walking shoes are the lightest of all boots, designed for day walks or short backpacking trips. Some of the newer models are like rugged tennis shoes, designed with a canvas top for lightness and a lug sole for traction. These are perfect for people who like to walk but rarely carry a backpack. Because they are flexible, they are easy to break in, and with fresh socks, rarely cause blister problems. And because they are light, general hiking fatigue is greatly reduced.

On the negative side, because they have shallow lug soles, traction can be far from good on slippery surfaces. In addition, canvas hiking shoes provide less than ideal ankle support, which can be a problem in rocky areas, such as along a stream where you might want to go trout fishing. Turn your ankle and your trip can be ruined.

My preference is for a premium backpacking boot, the perfect medium between the stiff mountaineering boots and the soft canvas hiking shoes. The deep lug bottom provides traction, high ankle coverage provides support, yet the soft, waterproof leather body gives each foot a snug fit—add it up and that means no blisters. On the negative side, they can be quite hot, weigh a ton, and, if they get wet, take days to dry.

There are a zillion styles, brands, and price ranges of boots to choose from. If you wander about, looking at them equally, you will get as confused as a kid in a toy store. Instead go into the store with your mind clear with what you want, then find it, and buy it. If you want the best, expect to spend $60 to $80 for canvas walking shoes, from $100 to $140 and sometimes more for hiking or mountaineering boots. This is one area you don't want to scrimp on, so try not to yelp about the high cost. Instead, walk out of the store believing you deserve the best, and that's exactly what you just paid for.

If you plan on using the advice of a shoe salesman for your purchase, first look at what kind of boots he is wearing. If he isn't even wearing boots, then any advice he might attempt to tender may not be worth a plug nickel. Most people I know who own quality boots, including salesmen, will wear them almost daily if their job allows, since boots are the best footwear available. However, even these well-meaning folks can offer skeptical advice. Every hiker I've ever met will tell you he wears the world's greatest boot.

Instead, enter the store with a precise use and style in mind. Rather than fish for suggestions, tell the salesman exactly what you want, try two or three different brands of the same style, and always try on the matching pair of boots simultaneously so you know exactly how they'll feel. If possible, walk up and down stairs with them. Are they too stiff?

Are your feet snug yet comfortable, or do they slip? Do they have that "right" kind of feel when you walk?

If you get the right answers to those questions, then you're on your way to blister-free, pleasure-filled days of walking.

SOCKS

The poor gent was scratching his feet like ants were crawling over them. I looked closer. Huge yellow calluses had covered the bottom of his feet, and at the ball and heel, the calluses were about a quarter of an inch thick, cracking, and sore.

"I don't understand it," he said. "I'm on my feet a lot, so I bought a real good pair of hiking boots. But look what they've done to my feet. My feet itch so much I'm going crazy."

People can spend so much energy selecting the right kind of boot, that they can virtually overlook wearing the right kind of socks. One goes with the other.

Your socks should be thick enough to provide a cushion for your foot, as well as a good, snug fit. Without good socks, you might try to get the boot laces too tight and that's like putting a tourniquet on your feet. You should have plenty of clean socks on hand, or plan on washing what you have on your trip. As socks are worn, they become compressed, dirty, and damp. Any one of those factors can cause problems.

My camping companions believe I go overboard when it comes to socks, that I bring too many, wear too many. But it works, so that's where the complaints stop. So how many do I wear? Well, would you believe three socks on each foot? It may sound like overkill, but each has its purpose, and like I said, it works.

The interior sock is thin, lightweight, and made out of Polypropylene or silk synthetic materials that actually transport moisture away from your skin. With a poly-interior sock, your foot stays dry when it sweats. Without a poly sock, your foot can get damp, mix with dirt, which in turn can cause a "hot spot" to start on your foot. Eventually you get blisters, lots of them.

The second sock is for comfort, and can be cotton, but a thin wool-based composite is ideal. Some made of the latter can wick moisture away from the skin, much like the qualities of Polypropylene. If wool itches your feet, a thick cotton sock can be suitable, though cotton collects moisture and compacts more quickly than other socks. If you're on a short hike, though, cotton will do just fine.

The exterior sock should be made of high quality, thick wool, at least 80 percent wool. It will cushion your feet, provide that "just right" snug fit in your boot, and in cold weather, give you some additional warmth and insulation. It is critical to keep the wool sock clean. If you wear a dirty wool sock over and over again, it will compact and lose its cushion, start wrinkling while you hike, and with that chain of events, your feet will catch on fire from the blisters that start popping up.

A FEW TIPS

If you are like most folks, that is, the bottom of your feet are rarely exposed and quite soft, you can take additional steps in their care. The best tip is keeping a fresh foot pad in your boot made of sponge rubber. Another cure for soft feet is to get out and walk or jog on a regular basis prior to your camping trip.

If you plan to use a foot pad and wear three socks, you will need to use these items when sizing boots. It is an unforgiving error to wear thin cotton socks when buying boots, then later trying to squeeze all this stuff, plus your feet, into your boots. There just won't be enough room.

The key to treating blisters is fast work at the first sign of a hot spot. But before you remove your socks, first check to see if the sock has a wrinkle in it, a likely cause of the problem. If so, either change socks or get them pulled tight, removing the tiny folds, after taking care of the blister. Cut a piece of moleskin to cover the offending toe, securing the moleskin with white medical tape. If moleskin is not available, small Band-Aids can do the job, but have to be replaced daily, and sometimes with even more frequency. At night, clean your feet and sleep without socks.

Two other items that can help your walking is an Ace bandage and a pair of gaiters.

For sprained ankles and twisted knees, an Ace bandage can be like an insurance policy to get you back on the trail and out of trouble. Over the years, I have had serious ankle problems and have relied on a good wrap with a four-inch bandage to get me home. The newer bandages come with the clips permanently attached, so you don't have to worry about losing them.

Gaiters are leggings made of plastic, nylon or Gore-Tex which fit from just below your knees, over your calves, and attach under your boots. They are of particular help when walking in damp areas, or places where rain is common. As your legs brush against ferns or low-lying plants, gaiters will deflect the moisture. Without them, your pants will be soaking wet in short order.

Should your boots become wet, a good tip is to never try to force dry them. Some well-meaning folks will try to speed dry them at the edge of a campfire or actually put the boots in an oven. While this may dry the boots, it can also loosen the glue that holds them together, ultimately weakening your shoe until one day they fall apart in a heap.

A better bet is to treat the leather so the boots become water repellent. Silicone-based liquids are the easiest to use and least greasy of the treatments available.

A final tip is to have another pair of lightweight shoes or moccasins that you can wear around camp, and in the process, give your feet the rest they deserve.

CHAPTER FOUR

SLEEPING GEAR

One mountain night in the pines on an eve long ago, my dad, brother, and I had rolled out our sleeping bags and were bedded down for the night. After the pre-trip excitement, a long drive, an evening of trout fishing, and a barbecue, we were like three tired doggies who had played too much.

But as I looked up at the stars, I was suddenly wide awake. The kid was still wired. A half hour later? No change—wide awake.

And as little kids can do, I had to wake up ol' dad to tell him about it. "Hey, Dad, I can't sleep."

"This is what you do," he said. "Watch the sky for a shooting star and tell yourself that you cannot go to sleep until you see at least one. As you wait and watch, you will start getting tired, and it will be difficult to keep your eyes open. But tell yourself you must keep watching. Then you'll start to really feel tired. When you finally see a shooting star, you'll go to sleep so fast you won't know what hit you."

Well, I tried it that night and I don't even remember seeing a shooting star, I went to sleep so fast.

It's a good trick, and along with having a good sleeping bag, ground insulation, maybe a tent—or a few tricks for bedding down in a pickup truck or motor home—you can get a good sleep on every camping trip.

Some 20 years later after that camping episode with my dad and brother, we made a trip to the Planetarium at the Academy of Sciences in San Francisco to see a show on Halley's Comet. The lights dimmed, and the ceiling turned into a night sky, filled with stars and a setting moon. A scientist began explaining phenomena of the heavens.

After a few minutes, I began to feel drowsy. Just then, a shooting star zipped across the Planetarium ceiling. I went into a deep sleep so fast it was like I was in a coma. I didn't wake up until the show was over, the lights were turned back on, and the people were leaving.

Drowsy, I turned to see if ol' Dad had liked the show. Oh yeah? He not only had gone to sleep too, but apparently had no intention of waking up, no matter what. Just like a camping trip.

SLEEPING BAGS

What could be worse than trying to sleep in a cold, wet sleeping bag on a rainy night without a tent in the mountains?

Answer: Trying to sleep in a cold, wet sleeping bag on a rainy night without a tent in the mountains—when your sleeping bag is filled with down.

Water will turn a down-filled sleeping bag into a mushy heap. Many campers do not like a high-tech approach, but the state-of-the-art polyfiber sleeping bags can keep you warm even when wet. That factor, along with temperature rating and weight, are key factors when selecting a sleeping bag.

A sleeping bag is a shell filled with a heat-retaining insulation. By itself, it is not warm. Your body provides the heat, and the sleeping bag's ability to retain that heat is what makes it warm or cold.

The old-styled canvas bags are heavy, bulky, cold, and, when wet, useless. With other options available, their use is limited. Anybody who sleeps outdoors or backpacks should choose otherwise. Instead, buy and use a sleeping bag filled with down or one of the quality poly-fills. Down is light, warm, and aesthetically pleasing to those who don't think camping and technology mix. If you like down bags, be sure to keep it double wrapped in plastic garbage bags on your trips in order to keep it dry. Once wet, you'll spend your nights howling at the moon.

The polyfiber-filled bags are not necessarily better than those filled with down, but can be. The one key advantage is that even when wet, some poly-fills can retain up to 80 to 85 percent of your body heat. This allows you to sleep and get valuable rest even in miserable conditions. And my camping experience is that no matter how lucky you may be, there comes a time when you will get caught in an unexpected, violent storm and everything you've got will get wet, including your sleeping bag. That's when the value of a poly-fill bag becomes priceless. You either have one and can sleep—or you don't have one and suffer. It is that simple. Of the synthetic fills, Quallofil made by Dupont is the leader of the industry.

But as mentioned, just because a sleeping bag uses a high-tech poly-fill doesn't necessarily make it a better bag. There are other factors.

The most important are a bag's temperature rating and weight. The temperature rating of a sleeping bag refers to how cold it can get before you start actually feeling cold. Many campers make the mistake of thinking, "I only camp in the summer, so a bag rated at a 30 or 40 degrees should be fine." Later, they find out it isn't so fine, and all it takes is one cold night to convince them of that. When selecting the right temperature rating, visualize the coldest weather you might ever confront, and then get a bag rated for even colder weather.

For instance, if you are a summer camper, you may rarely experience a night in the low 30s or high 20s. A sleeping bag rated at 20 degrees would thus be appropriate, keeping you snug, warm, and asleep. For most campers, I advise bags rated at zero or ten degrees.

If you buy a poly-filled sleeping bag, never leave it squished in your stuff sack between camping trips. Instead keep it on a hanger in a closet or use it as a blanket. One thing that can reduce a polyfilled bag's heat-retaining qualities is if you lose the loft out of the tiny hollow fibers that make up the fill. You can avoid this with proper storage.

The weight of a sleeping bag can also be a key factor, especially for backpackers. When you have to carry your gear on your back, every ounce becomes important. To keep your weight to a minimum, sleeping bags that weigh just three pounds are available, though expensive. But if you hike much, it's worth the price. For an overnighter, you can get away with a 4 or 4.5-pound bag without much stress. However, bags weighing five pounds and up should be left back at the car.

I have two sleeping bags: A seven-pounder that feels like I'm in a giant sponge, and a little three-pounder. The heavy duty model is for pickup truck camping in cold weather and doubles as a blanket at home. The lightweight bag is for hikes. Between the two, I'm set.

INSULATION PADS

Even with the warmest sleeping bag in the world, if you just lay it down on the ground and try to sleep, you will likely get as cold as a winter cucumber. That is because the cold ground will suck the warmth right out of your body. The solution is to have a layer of insulation between you and the ground. For this, you can use a thin Insulite pad, a light-weight Therm-a-Rest inflatable pad, or an air mattress. Here is a capsule summary of them:

Insulite pads: They are light, inexpensive, roll up quick for transport, and can double as a seat pad at your camp. The negative side is that in one night, they will compress, making you feel like you are sleeping on granite.

Therm-a-Rest pads: They are a real luxury, because they do everything an Insulite pad does, but also provide a cushion. The negative side to them is that they are expensive by comparison, and if they get a hole in them, they become worthless unless you have a patch kit.

Air mattress: OK for car campers, but their bulk, weight and the amount of effort necessary to blow them up makes them a nuisance.

A FEW TRICKS

When surveying a camp area, the most important consideration should be to select a good spot to sleep. Everything else is secondary. Ideally, you want a flat spt that is wind sheltered, on ground soft enough to drive stakes into. Yeah, and I want to win the lottery too.

Sometimes that ground will have a slight slope to it. In that case, always sleep with your head on the uphill side. If you sleep parallel to the slope, every time you roll over in your sleep, you can find yourself rolling down the hill. If you sleep with your head on the downhill side, you can get a headache that feels like an axe is embedded in your brain.

When you have found a good spot, clear it of all branches, twigs, and rocks, of course. A good tip is to dig a slight indentation in the ground where your hip will fit. Since your body is not flat, but has curves and edges, it will not feel comfortable on flat ground. Some people even get severely bruised on the sides of their hips when sleeping on flat, hard ground. For that reason alone, they learn to hate camping. Instead, bring a spade, dig a little depression in the ground for your hip, and sleep well.

After the ground is prepared, throw a ground cloth over the spot, which will keep much of the morning dew off you. In some areas, particularly where fog is a problem, morning dew can be quite heavy and get the outside of your sleeping bag quite wet. In that case, you either need a tent or some kind of roof, like that of a poncho or tarp, with its ends tied to trees.

TENTS AND WEATHER PROTECTION

All it takes is to get caught in the rain once without a tent and you will never go anywhere without one again. A tent provides protection from rain, wind, and mosquito attacks. In exchange, you can lose a starry night's view, though some tents now even provide moon roofs.

A tent can be as complex as a four-season, tubular-jointed dome with rain fly, or nothing more complicated than two ponchos snapped together and roped up to a tree. They can be as cheap as a $10 tube tent, which is nothing more than a hollow piece of plastic, or as expensive as a $500 five-person deluxe expedition dome model. They vary greatly in size, price, and put-up time. If you plan on getting a good one, then plan on doing plenty of shopping and asking lots of questions. The key ones are: Will it keep me dry? How hard is it to put up? Is it roomy enough? How much does it weigh?

With a little bit of homework, you can get the right answers to these questions.

Will it keep me dry? On many one and two-person tents, the rain fly does not extend far enough to keep water off the bottom sidewalls of the tent. In a driving rain, water can also drip from the rain fly and to the bottom sidewalls of the tent. Eventually the water can leak through to the inside, particularly through the seams where the tent has been sewed together. Water can sneak through the tiny needle holes.

You must be able to stake out your rain fly so it completely covers all of the tent. If you are tent shopping and this does not appear possible, then don't buy the tent. To prevent potential leaks, use a seam water proofer like Seam Lock, a glue-like substance, to close potential leak areas on tent seams. On the large umbrella tents, keep a patch kit handy and dig a canal around your tent to channel rain water.

Another way to keep water out of your tent is to store all wet garments outside the tent, under a poncho. Moisture from wet clothes stashed in the tent will condense on the interior tent walls. If you bring enough wet clothes in the tent, by the next morning you can feel like you're camping in a duck blind.

How hard is it to put up? If a tent is difficult to erect in full sunlight, you can just about forget it at night. Some tents can go up in just a few minutes, without you requiring help from another camper. This might be the kind of tent you want.

The way to compare put-up time of tents when shopping is to count the number of connecting points from the tent poles to the tent, and also the number of stakes required. The fewer, the better. Think simple. My tent has seven connecting points and, minus the rain fly, requires no stakes. It goes up in a few minutes. If you need a lot of stakes, it is a sure tipoff to a long put-up time. Try it at night or in the rain, and you'll be ready to cash your chips and go for broke.

Another factor is the tent poles themselves. Some small tents have poles that are broken into small sections that are connected by Bungy cords. It takes only an instant to convert it to a complete pole.

Some outdoor shops have tents on display on their showroom floor. Before buying the tent, have the salesman take the tent down and put it back up. If it takes him more than five minutes, or he says he "doesn't have time," then keep looking.

Is it roomy enough? Don't judge the size of a tent on floor space alone. Some tents small on floor space can give the illusion of roominess with a high ceiling. You can be quite comfortable in them and snug.

But remember that a one-person or two-person tent is just that. A two-person tent has room for two people plus gear. That's it. Don't buy a tent expecting it to hold more than it is intended to.

How much does it weigh? If you're a hiker, this becomes the preeminent question. If it's much more than six or seven pounds, forget it. A 12-pound tent is bad enough, but get it wet and its like carrying a piano on your back. On the other hand, weight is scarcely a factor if you camp only where you can take your car. My dad, for instance, used to have this giant canvas umbrella tent that folded down to this neat little pack that weighed about 500 pounds.

AN OPTION

If you like going solo and choose not to own a tent at all, a bivvy bag, short for bivouac bag, can provide the weather protection you require. A bivy bag is a water repellent shell in which your sleeping bag fits. They are light and tough, and for some, are a perfect option to a heavy tent. On the down side, however, there is a strange sensation when you try to ride out a rainy night in one. You can hear the rain hitting you, sometimes even feel the pounding of the drops through the bivy bag. It can be unsettling to try to sleep under such a circumstance.

PICKUP TRUCK CAMPERS

If you own a pickup truck with a camper shell, you can turn it into a self-contained campground with a little work. This can be an ideal way to go: it's fast, portable, and you are guaranteed a dry environment.

But that does not necessarily mean it is a warm environment. In fact, without insulation from the metal truck bed, it can be like trying to sleep on an iceberg. That is because the metal truck bed will get as cold as the air temperature, which is often much colder than the ground temperature. Without insulation, it can be much colder in your camper shell than it would be on the open ground.

When I camp in my rig, I use a large piece of foam for a mattress and insulation. The foam measures four inches thick, is 48 inches wide and 76 inches long. It makes for a bed as comfortable as anything one might ask for. In fact, during the winter, if I don't go camping for a few weeks because of writing obligations, I sometimes will throw the foam on the living room floor, lay down the old sleeping bag, light a fire, and camp right in my living room. It's in my blood, I tell you.

If you camp in cold areas in your pick-up truck camper shell, a Coleman catalytic heater can keep you toasty. When using a catalytic heater, it is a good idea to keep ventilation windows partially open to keep the air fresh. Don't worry about how cold it is—the heater will take the snap out of it.

MOTOR HOMES

The problems motor home owners encounter come from two primary sources: Lack of privacy and light intrusion.

The lack of privacy stems from the natural restrictions of where a "land yacht" can go. Without careful use of the guide portion of this book, motor home owners can find themselves in parking lot settings, jammed in with plenty of neighbors. Because motor homes often have large picture windows, you lose your privacy, causing some late nights, and come daybreak, light intrusion forces an early wake-up. The result is you get short on your sleep.

The answer is to always carry inserts to fit over the inside of your windows. This closes off the outside and retains your privacy. And if you don't want to wake up with the sun at daybreak, you don't have to. It will still be dark.

CHAPTER FIVE

FIRST AID & PROTECTION AGAINST INSECTS

A mountain night could not have been more perfect, I thought as I lay in my sleeping bag.

The sky looked like a mass of jewels and the air tasted sweet and smelled of pines. A shooting star fireballed across the sky, and I remember thinking, "It just doesn't get any better."

Just then, as I was drifting into sleep, this mysterious buzz appeared from nowhere and deposited itself inside my left ear. Suddenly awake, I whacked my ear with the palm of my hand about hard enough to cause a minor concussion. The buzz disappeared. I pulled out my flashlight and shined it on my palm, and there, lit in the blackness of night, lay the squished intruder. A mosquito, dead amid a stain of blood.

Satisfied, I turned off the light, closed my eyes, and thought of the fishing trip planned for the next day. Then I heard them. It was a squadron of mosquitos, flying landing patterns around my head. I tried to grab them with an open hand, but they dodged the assault and flew off. Just 30 seconds later another landed back in my left ear. I promptly dispatched the invader with a rip of the palm.

Now I was completely awake, so I got out of my sleeping bag to retrieve some mosquito repellent. But while en route, several of the buggers swarmed and nailed me in the back and arms. Later, after application of the repellent and again snug in my sleeping bag, the mosquitos would buzz a few inches from my ear. After getting a whiff of the poison, they would fly off. It was like sleeping in a sawmill.

The next day, drowsy from little sleep, I set out to fish. I'd walked but 15 minutes when I brushed against a bush and felt this stinging sensation on the inside of my arm, just above the wrist. I looked down: A tick had got his clamps into me. I ripped it out before he could embed his head into my skin.

After catching a few fish, I sat down against a tree to eat lunch, and just watch the water go by. My dog, Rebel, sat down next to me and stared at the beef jerky I was munching as if it was a T-bone steak. I finished eating, gave him a small piece, patted him on the head, and said, "Good dog." Right then, I noticed an itch on my arm where a mosquito had drilled me. I unconsciously scratched it. Two days later, in that exact spot, some nasty red splotches started popping up. Poison oak. By petting my dog and then scratching my arm, I had transferred the oil residue of the poison oak leaves from Rebel's fur to my arm.

On returning back home, Foonsky asked me about the trip.

"Great," I said. "Mosquitos, ticks, poison oak. Can hardly wait to go back."

"Sorry I missed it," he said sarcastically.

"On the next trip," I said, "We'll declare war on those buggers."

MOSQUITOS, NO-SEE-UMS, GNATS, AND HORSEFLIES

On a trip to Canada, Foonsky and I were fishing a small lake from the shore when suddenly a black horde of mosquitos could be seen moving across the lake toward us. It was like when the French Army looked across the Rhine and saw the Wehrmacht coming. There was a literal buzz in the air. We fought them off for a few minutes, then made a fast retreat to the truck and jumped in, content the buggers had been fooled. But somehow, still unknown to us, the mosquitos started gaining entry to the truck. In 10 minutes, we squished 15 of them while they attempted to plant their oil derricks in our skin. Just outside the truck, the black horde waited for us to make a tactical error, like rolling down a window. It finally took a miracle hailstorm to wipe out the attack.

When it comes to mosquitos, no-see-ums, gnats, and horseflies, there are times when there is nothing you can do. However, in most situations you can muster a defense to repel the attack.

The first key with mosquitos is to wear clothing too heavy for them to drill through. Expose a minimum of skin, wear a hat, and, around your neck, tie a bandanna, one that has preferably been sprayed with repellent. If you try to get by with just a cotton T-shirt, you will be declared a federal mosquito sanctuary.

So first your skin must be well covered, exposing only your hands and face. Second, you should have your companion spray your clothes with repellent in an aerosol can. Third, you should dab liquid repellent directly on your skin.

Taking Vitamin B1 and eating garlic are reputed to act as natural insect repellents, but I've met a lot of mosquitos that are not convinced. A better bet is to take the mystery out of the task and examine the contents of the repellent in question. The key is the percentage of the ingredient called "non-diethyl-metatoluamide." That is the poison, and the percentage of it in the container must be listed and will indicate that brand's effectiveness. Inert ingredients are just excess fluids used to fill the bottles.

At night, the easiest way to get a good sleep without mosquitos buzzing in your ear is to sleep in a bug-proof tent. If the nights are warm and you want to see the stars, new tent models are available that have a skylight covered with mosquito netting. If you don't like tents on summer evenings, mosquito netting rigged with an air space at your head can solve the problem. Otherwise prepare to get bit, even with the use of mosquito repellent.

If your problems are with no-see-ums or biting horseflies, then you need a slightly different approach.

No-see-ums are a tiny, black insect that can look like nothing more than a sliver of dirt on your skin. Then you notice something stinging—and when you rub the area, you scratch up a little no-see-um. The results are similar to mosquito bites, making your skin itch, splotch, and, when you get them bad, puffy. In addition to using the techniques described to repel mosquitos, you should go one step further.

The problem is, no-see-ums are tricky little devils. Somehow they can actually get under your socks and around your ankles where they will bite to their heart's content all night long while you sleep, itch, sleep, and itch some more. The best solution is to apply a liquid repellent to your ankles, then wear clean socks.

Horseflies are another story. They are rarely a problem, but when they get their dander up, they can cause problems you'll never forget.

One such episode occurred when Foonsky and I were paddling a canoe along the shoreline of a large lake. This giant horsefly, about the size of a fingertip, started dive bombing the canoe. After 20 minutes, it landed on his thigh. Foonsky immediately slammed it with an open hand—then let out a blood-curdling "yeeeee-ow" that practically sent ripples across the lake. When Foonsky whacked it, the horsefly had somehow turned around and bit him in the hand, leaving a huge, red welt.

In the next 10 minutes, that big fly strafed the canoe on more dive-bomb runs. I finally got ready with my canoe paddle, as if it was a baseball bat, swung, and nailed that horsefly like I'd hit a home run. It landed about 15 feet from the boat, still alive and buzzing in the water. While I was trying to figure what it would take to kill this bugger, a large rainbow trout surfaced and snatched it out of the water finally avenging the assault.

If you have horsefly or yellow jacket problems, you'd best just leave the area. One, two or a few can be dealt with. More than that and your fun camping trip will be about as fun as being roped to a tree and stung by an electric shock rod.

On most trips, you will spend time doing everything possible to keep from getting bit by mosquitos or no-see-ums. When that fails, you must know what to do next—and fast, if you are among those ill-fated campers who get big, red lumps from a bite inflicted from even a microscopic-sized mosquito.

A fluid called "After Bite," or a dab of ammonia, should be applied immediately to the bite. To start the healing process, apply a first-aid gel, not liquid, such as Campho-Phenique.

TICKS

Ticks are a nasty little vermin that will wait in ambush, jump on unsuspecting prey, and eventually crawl to a prime location before trying to fill his body with his victim's blood.

I call them the Dracula Bug, but by any name they can be a terrible camp pest. Ticks rest on grass and low plants and attach themselves to those who brush against the vegetation (dogs are particularly vulnerable). Typically, they are no more than 18 inches above ground, and if you stay on the trails, you can usually avoid them.

There are two common species of ticks. The common coastal tick is larger, brownish in color, and prefers to crawl around prior to putting the clamps on you. The latter habit can give you the creeps, but when you feel it crawling, you can just pick it off and dispatch it. Their preferred destination is usually the back of your neck, just where the hairline starts. The other species, a wood tick, is small, black, and when he puts the clamps in, it's immediately painful. When a wood tick gets into a dog for a few days, it can cause a large, red welt. In either case, ticks should be removed as soon as possible.

If you have hiked in areas infested with them, it is advisable to shower as soon as possible, discarding and washing your clothes immediately. If you just leave your clothes in a heap, a tick can crawl from your clothes and thus invade your home. They like warmth, and, one way or another, they can end up in your bed. Waking up in the middle of the night with a tick crawling across you chest can really give you the creeps.

Once a tick has the clampers on you, you must decide how long it has been there. If it has been a short time, the most painless and effective method is to just take a pair of sharp tweezers and grasp the little devil, making certain to isolate the mouth area, then pull him out. Reader Johvin Perry sent in the suggestion to coat the tick with vaseline, which will cut off its oxygen supply, after which it may voluntarily give up the hunt.

If the tick has been in longer, you may wish a doctor to extract it. Some people will burn it with a cigarette, or poison it with lighter fluid, but this is not advisable. In any case, you must take care to remove all of it, especially its claw-like mouth.

The wound, however small, should then be cleansed and dressed. This is done by applying liquid peroxide, which cleans and sterilizes the wound, and then coating a dressing with a first-aid gel such as First-Aid Cream, Campho-Phenique, or Neosporin ointment.

Lyme disease, which is rarely transmitted by the bite of the deer tick, is rare in California, but common enough to warrant some attention. To prevent tick bites, tuck your pant legs into your hiking socks and always wear a shirt, making sure it is tucked into your pants. Then spray tick repellent, called Permamone, on your pants.

The first symptom of Lyme disease is that the bite area will develop a bright-red, splotchy rash. Other early symptoms sometimes include headache, nausaea, fever and/or a stiff neck. If this happens or if you have any doubts, you should see your doctor immediately. If you do get

Lyme disease, don't panic. Doctors say it is easily treated in the early stages with simple antibiotics. If you are nervous about getting Lyme disease, carry a small plastic bag with you when you hike. If a tick manages to get his clampers into you, put it in the plastic bag after you pull it out. Then give it to your doctor for analysis, to see if the tick is a carrier of the disease. With this approach, you will never have to fret about Lyme disease again, and can enjoy your adventure without a second thought.

POISON OAK

After a nice afternoon hike, about a five-miler, I was concerned about possible exposure to poison oak, so I immediately showered and put on clean clothes. Then I settled into a chair with my favorite foamy, body-building elixir to watch the end of a baseball game. The game went 18 innings and meanwhile, my dog, tired from the hike, had gone to sleep on my bare ankles.

A few days later I had a case of poison oak. My feet looked like they had been on fire and put out with an ice pick. The lesson? Don't always trust your dog, give him a bath as well, and beware of extra-inning ball games.

You can get poison oak only from direct contact with the oil residue from the leaves. It can be passed in a variety of fashions, as direct as skin to leaf contact or as indirect as leaf to dog, dog to sofa, sofa to skin. Once you have it, there is little you can do but itch yourself to death. Applying Caladryl lotion or its equivalent can help because it contains antihistamines, which attack and dry the itch.

A tip that may sound crazy but seems to work is advised by my pal Furniss. You should expose the afflicted area to the hottest water you can stand, then suddenly immerse it in cold water. The hot water opens the skin pores and gets the "itch" out, and the cold water then quickly seals the pores.

In any case, you're a lot better off if you don't get poison oak to begin with. Remember the old Boy Scout saying: "Leaves of three, let them be." Also remember that poison oak can disguise itself. In the spring it is green, then gradually turns reddish in the summer. By fall, it becomes a bloody, ugly-looking red. In the winter, it loses its leaves altogether and appears to be nothing more than barren, brown sticks of small plant. However, at any time and in any form, skin contact can cause quick infection.

Some people are more easily afflicted than others, but if you are one of the lucky few, don't cheer too loudly. While some people can be exposed to the oil residue of poison oak with little or no effect, the body's resistance can gradually be worn down with repeated exposures. At one time, I could practically play in the stuff and the only symptom would be a few little bumps on the inside of my wrist. Now, some 15 years later, times have changed. My resistance has broken down. If I merely rub against poison oak now, in a few days the exposed area can look like it has been used for a track meet.

So regardless if you consider yourself vulnerable or not, you should take heed to reduce exposure. That can be done by staying on trails when you hike and making sure your dog does the same. Remember, the worst stands of poison oak are usually brush-infested areas just off the trail. Protect yourself also by dressing so your skin is completely covered, wearing long-sleeve shirts, long pants, and boots. If you suspect you've been exposed, immediately wash your clothes, then wash yourself with aloe vera, rinsing with a cool shower.

And don't forget to give your dog a bath as well.

SUNBURN

The most common injury suffered on camping trips is sunburn, yet some people wear it as a badge of honor, believing that it somehow enhances their virility. Well it doesn't. Neither do suntans. And too much sun can lead to serious burns or sunstroke.

It is easy enough to avoid. Use a high-level sunscreen on your skin, chapstick on your lips, and wear sunglasses and a hat. If any area gets burned, apply First-Aid Cream, which will soothe, and provide moisture for the parched, burned skin.

The best advice from Doctor Bogney is not to even get a suntan. Those that do are involved in a practice that can be eventually ruinous to their skins.

A WORD ABOUT GIARDIA

You have just hiked in to your secret backwoods fishing or hunting spot, thirsty and a bit tired, but you smile as you consider the prospects. Everything seems perfect: You have a campsite along a stream that tumbles into a nearby lake, there's not a stranger in sight, and you have nothing to do for a week but fish or hunt with your pals.

You toss down your gear, grab your cup and dip it into the stream, and take a long drink of that ice cold mountain water. It seems crystal pure and sweeter than anything you've ever tasted. It's later that you find out that it can be just like drinking a cup of poison.

By drinking what appears to be pure mountain water without treating it, you can ingest a microscopic protozoan called *Giardia lamblia*. The pain of the abdominal cramps can make you feel like your stomach and intestinal tract are in a knot, ready to explode. With that comes long-term diarrhea that is worse than even a bear could imagine.

Doctors call the disease giardiasis, or Giardia for short, but it is difficult to even diagnose. One friend of mine who contracted Giardia was first told he might have stomach cancer before the proper diagnosis was eventually made.

Drinking directly from a stream or lake does not mean you will get Giardia, but you are taking a giant chance. Yet there is no reason to take such a risk, potentially ruining your trip and enduring weeks of misery.

A lot of fishermen and hunters are taking that risk. I made a personal survey of backpackers in the Yosemite National Park Wilderness last year, and found roughly only one in 20 were equipped with some kind of water purification system. The result, according to the federal Public Health Service, is that an average of 4 percent suffer giardiasis. Across the country, the rates range from 1 percent to 20 percent, depending on the geographic location and age of the person studied, according to the Parasitic Diseases Division of the Center for Infectious Diseases.

But if you get Giardia, you are not going to care about the statistics. "When I got Giardia, I just about wanted to die," said Henry McCarthy, a California camper. "For about ten days, it was the most terrible thing I have ever experienced. And through the whole thing, I kept thinking, 'I shouldn't have drunk that water, but it seemed all right at the time."

That is the mistake most campers make. The stream might be running free, gurgling over boulders in the high country, tumbling into deep, oxygenated pools. It looks pure. Then the next day, the problems suddenly start. Drinking untreated water from mountain streams is a lot like Russian roulette. Sooner or later, the gun goes off.

If you camp, fish, and hunt in primitive settings, there are some clear-cut answers to use at your discretion. I hike about 200 miles per year, and in the process have tested them all. Here are my findings.

Katadyn Water Filter: This is the best system for screening out Giardia, as well as other microscopic bacteria more commonly found in stream and lake water that can also cause stomach problems.

This filter works by placing the nozzle in the water, then pumping the water directly from a spout at the top of the pump into a canteen. The pumping can be fairly rigorous, especially as the filter becomes plugged. On the average, it takes a few minutes to fill a canteen.

The best advantages are that the device has a highly advanced screening system (a ceramic element), and it can be cleaned repeatedly with a small brush.

The drawbacks are that the filter is expensive at $170, it can easily break when dropped because its body is made of porcelain, and if you pack very light, its weight (about two pounds) may be a factor. But those are good trade-offs when you can drink ice cold stream water without risk.

First-Need Water Purifier: This is the most cost-effective water purification system for a variety of reasons.

At $35, the unit is far less expensive than the Katadyn, yet provides much better protection than anything cheaper. They are small and lightweight, so they don't add much to the weight of your pack. And if you use some care to pump water from sediment-free sources, they easily last a week, the length of most outdoorsmen's trips.

These devices consist of a plastic pump and a hose that connects to a separate filter canister. They pump faster and with less effort than the Katadyn, but one of the reasons for that is because the filter is not as fine-screened.

The big drawback is that if you pump water from a mucky lake, the filter can clog in a few days. Therein lies the weakness. Once plugged up, it is useless and you have to replace it ($25) or take your chances.

One trick to extend the filter life is to fill your cook pot with water, let the sediment settle, then pump from there. It is also advisable to always have a spare filter canister as an insurance policy.

Boiling Water: Except for water filtration, this is the only treatment that you can use with complete confidence. According to the federal Center of Disease Control, it takes a few minutes at a rolling boil to be certain to kill *Giardia lamblia.* At high elevations, the advice is to boil for three to five minutes. A side benefit is that you'll also kill other dangerous bacteria that also live undetected in natural waters.

But to be honest, boiling water is a thorn for most people on backcountry fishing and hunting trips. For one thing, if you boil water on an open fire, what should taste like crystal-pure mountain water tastes instead like a mouthful of warm ashes. If you don't have a campfire, it wastes stove fuel. And if you are thirsty *now,* forget it. The water takes hours to cool.

The one time boiling always makes sense, however, is when you are preparing dinner. The ash taste will disappear in whatever freeze-dried dinner, soup, or hot drink you have planned.

Water purification pills are the preference for most anglers and hunters—and it can get them in trouble. The pills come cheap at just $3 to $8 per bottle, which can figure to just a few cents per canteen. In addition, they kill most of the bacteria, regardless of whether you use iodine crystals or potable aqua iodine tablets.

They just don't always kill *Giardia lamblia*, and that is the one critter worth worrying about on your trip. That makes water treatment pills unreliable and dangerous.

Another key element is the time factor. Depending on the water's temperature, organic content, and pH level, these pills can take a long time to do the job—a minimum wait of 20 minutes is prescribed. Most guys don't like waiting that long, especially when hot and thirsty after a long hike, "and what the heck, the water looks fine."

And then there is the taste. On one trip, my water filter clogged and we had to use the iodine pills instead. It doesn't take long to get tired of the iodine-tinged taste of the water. Mountain water should be one of the great-tasting beverages of the world, but the iodine kills that.

No treatment: This is your last resort and, using extreme care, can be executed with success. One of my best hiking buddies is a hydrologist for the Forest Service, Michael Furniss, and on wilderness fishing trips he has showed me the difference between "safe" and "dangerous" water sources.

At one time, just finding water running over a rock used to be a guarantee of its purity. No longer. The safe water sources are almost always small creeks or springs located in high, craggy mountain areas. The key is making sure no one has been upstream from where you drink.

He mentioned that another problem you can have if you bypass water treatment is that even in settings free of Giardia, you can still ingest other bacteria that can cause stomach problems.

The only sure way to beat the problem is to pump filter or boil the water before drinking, eating, or brushing your teeth. And the best way to prevent its spread is to be certain to bury your waste products at least eight inches deep and at least 100 feet away from natural waters.

HYPOTHERMIA

No matter how well planned your trip might be, a sudden change in weather can turn it into a puzzle for which there are few answers. Bad weather or an accident can result in a dangerous chain of events.

Such a chain of episodes occurred for my brother, Rambob, and me on a fishing trip one fall day just below the snow line. The weather had suddenly turned very cold and ice was forming along the shore of the lake. Suddenly, the canoe was placed in terrible imbalance and just that quick, it flipped. The little life vest seat cushions were useless, and using the canoe as a paddle board, we tried to kick our way back to shore where my dad was going crazy at the thought of his two sons drowning before his eyes.

It took 17 minutes in that 38-degree water, but we finally made it to the shore. When they pulled me out of the water, my legs were dead, not strong enough to even hold up my weight. In fact, I didn't feel so much cold as tired, and I just wanted to lay down and go to sleep.

I closed my eyes, and my brother-in-law, Lloyd Angal, slapped me in the face several times, then got me on my feet and pushed and pulled me about.

In the celebration over making it to shore, only Lloyd had realized that hypothermia was setting in—where the temperature of the body is lowered to the point that it causes poor reasoning, apathy, and collapse. It can look like the endangered is just tired and needs to sleep, but that sleep can be the next step to a coma.

Ultimately, my brother and I shared what little dry clothing remained. We then began hiking around to get muscle movement, creating internal warmth. Shivering is another way the body creates warmth for itself. We ate whatever munchies were available because the body produces heat by digestion. But most important, we got our heads as dry as possible. More body heat is lost through wet hair than any other single factor.

A few hours later, we were in a pizza parlor replaying the incident, talking about how only a life vest can do the job of a life vest. We decided never again to rely on those little flotation seat cushions that disappear when the boat flips.

Almost by instinct we had done everything right to prevent hypothermia: Don't go to sleep, start a physical activity, induce shivering, put dry clothes on, dry your head, and eat something. That's how you fight hypothermia. In a dangerous setting, whether you fall in a lake, a stream, or get caught unprepared in a storm, that's how you can stay alive.

After being in that ice-bordered lake for almost 20 minutes, and then finally pulling ourselves to the shoreline, a strange, eerie phenomena occurred. My canoe was flipped right-side up, and lost were almost all of its contents: tackle box, flotation cushions, and cooler. But remaining was one paddle and one fishing rod, the trout rod my grandfather had given me for my 12th birthday.

Lloyd gave me a smile. "This means that you are meant to paddle and fish again," he said with a laugh.

GETTING UNLOST

You could not have been more lost. But there I was, a guy who is supposed to know about these things, transfixed by confusion, snow, and hoof prints from a big deer.

I discovered it is actually quite easy to get lost. If you don't get your bearings, getting found is the difficult part.

This was in the Siskiyou Wilderness of northwestern California, where I'd hiked in to a remote lake called Devil's Punchbowl, and then set up a base camp for a deer hunt.

"There are some giant bucks up on that rim," confided Mr. Furnai, who lives near the area. "But it takes a mountain man to even get close to them."

That was a challenge I answered. After four-wheeling it to the trailhead, I tromped off with pack and rifle, gut-thumped it up 100 switchbacks, over the rim, then followed a creek drainage up to a small but beautiful lake. The area near the Punchbowl is stark and near-treeless, with bald granite broken only by large boulders. To keep from getting lost, I marked my route with piles of small rocks to act as directional signs for the return trip.

But at daybreak the next day, I stuck my head out of my tent and found eight inches of snow on the ground. I looked up into a gray sky filled by huge, cascading snowflakes. Visibility was about 50 yards, with fog on the mountain rim. "I better get out of here and get back to my truck," I said to myself. "If my truck gets buried at the trailhead, I'll never get out."

After packing quickly, I started down the mountain. But after 20 minutes, I began to get disoriented. You see, all the little piles of rocks I'd stacked to mark the way were now buried in snow, and I had only a smooth white blanket of snow to guide me. Everything looked the same, and it was snowing even harder now.

Five minutes later I started chewing on some jerky to keep warm, then suddenly stopped. Where was I? Where was the creek drainage? Isn't this where I was supposed to cross over a creek and start the switchbacks down the mountain?

Right then I looked down and saw the tracks of a huge deer, the kind Mr. Furnai had talked about. What a predicament: Lost, snowed in, with big hoof prints in the snow. Part of me wanted to abandon all safety and go after that deer, but a little voice in the back of my head won out; "Treat this as an emergency."

The first step in any predicament is to secure your present situation, that is, to make sure it does not get any worse. I unloaded my rifle (too easy to slip, fall and have a misfire), took stock of my food (three days worth), camp fuel (plenty), and clothes (rain gear keeping me dry). Then I wondered, "Where the hell am I?"

I took out my map, compass and altimeter, then opened the map and laid it on the snow. It immediately began collecting snowflakes. I set the compass atop the map, and oriented it to north. Because of the fog, there was no way to spot landmarks, such as prominent mountain tops, and verify my position. Then I checked the altimeter: It read 4,900 feet. Well, the elevation at Devil's Punchbowl was 5,320 feet. That was critical information.

I scanned the elevation lines on the map and was able to trace the approximate area of my position, somewhere downstream from the lake, yet close to 4,900 feet elevation. "Right here," I said, pointing to a spot on the map with a finger. "I should pick up the switchback trail down the mountain somewhere off to the left, maybe just 40, 50 yards away."

Slowly and deliberately, I pushed through the light, powdered snow. In five minutes, I suddenly stopped. To the left, across a 10-foot depression in the snow appeared a flat spot that veered off to the right. "That's it! That's the crossing."

In minutes, I was working down the switchbacks, on my way, no longer lost. I thought of the hoof prints I had seen, and now that I knew my position, wanted to head back and spend the day hunting. Then I looked up at the sky, saw it filled with falling snowflakes, and envisioned my truck buried deep in snow. Alas, this time logic won out over dreams.

In a few hours, now trudging through well more than a foot of snow, I was at my truck at a spot called Doe Flat, and next to it was a giant, all-terrain Forest Service vehicle and two rangers.

"Need any help?" I asked them.

They just laughed. "We're here to help you," one answered. "It is a good thing you filed a trip plan with our district office in Gasquet. We wouldn't have known you were out here."

"Winter has arrived," said the other. "If we don't get your truck out now, it will be stuck here until next spring. If we hadn't found you, you might have been here until the end of time."

They connected a chain from the rear axle of their giant rig to the front axle of my truck and started towing me out, back to civilization. On the way to pavement, I figured I had gotten the lessons of my life: Always file a trip plan, have plenty of food, fuel and a camp stove you can rely on. Make sure your clothes, weather gear, sleeping bag and tent will keep you dry and warm. Always carry a compass, altimeter and map with elevation lines, and know how to use them, practicing in good weather to get the feel of it.

And if you get lost and see the hoofprints of a giant deer, well, this is one time when it is best to pass them by.

C H A P T E R S I X

FISHING & RECREATIONAL EQUIPMENT

Feet tired and hot, stomachs hungry, we stopped our hike for lunch beside a beautiful little river pool that was catching the flows from a long but gentle waterfall. My brother, Rambob, passed me a piece of jerky. I took my boots off, then slowly dunked my feet into the cool, foaming water.

I was gazing at a towering peak across a canyon, when suddenly—Wham! There was sudden jolt at the heel of my right foot. I pulled my foot out of the water and incredibly, a trout had bitten it.

My brother looked at me like I had antlers growing out of my head. "Wow!" he exclaimed, "that trout almost caught himself an outdoors writer!"

It's true that in remote areas trout sometimes bite on almost anything, even feet. In California's High Sierra, I have caught limits of trout using nothing but a bare hook. The only problem is the fish will often hit the splitshot sinker instead of the hook. Of course, fishing isn't usually that easy. But it gives you an idea of what is possible.

America's wildlands are home for a remarkable abundance of fish and wildlife. Deer browse with little fear of man, bear keep an eye out for your food, and little critters like squirrels and chipmunks are daily companions. Add in the fishing and you've got yourself a camping trip.

Your camping trips will evolve into premium outdoor experiences if you can parlay in a few good fishing trips, avoid bear problems, and occasionally add a little offbeat fun with some camp games.

TROUT AND BASS

He creeps up on the stream as quiet as an old Indian, keeping his shadow off the water. With his little spinning rod, he'll zip his lure within an inch or two of its desired mark, probing along rocks, the edges of riffles, pocket water; wherever he can find a change in river habitat. It's my brother, Rambob, trout fishing, and he's a master at it.

In most cases, he'll catch a trout on his first or second cast. After that it's time to move up river, giving no spot much more than five minutes due. Stick and move, stick and move, stalking the stream like a bobcat zeroing in on a unsuspecting rabbit. He might keep a few trout for dinner, but mostly he releases what he catches. Rambob doesn't necessarily fish for food. It's the feeling that comes with it.

Fishing can give you a sense of exhilaration, like taking a hot shower after being coated with dust. On your walk back to camp, the steps come easy. You suddenly understand what John Muir meant when he talked of developing a oneness with nature, because you have it. That's what fishing can help provide.

You don't need a million dollars worth of fancy gear to catch fish. What you need is the right outlook, and that can be learned. That goes regardless if you are fishing for trout or bass, the two most popular fisheries in America. Your fishing tackle selection should be as simple and as clutter-free as possible.

At home, I've got every piece of fishing tackle you might imagine, more than 30 rods and many tackle boxes, racks, and cabinets filled with all kinds of stuff. I've got one lure that looks like a chipmunk and another that resembles a miniature can of beer with hooks. If I hear of something new, I want to try it, and usually do. It's a result of my lifelong fascination with the sport.

But if you just want to catch fish, there's an easier way to go. And when I go fishing, I take that path. I don't try to bring everything. It would be impossible. Instead, I bring a relatively small amount of gear. At home I will scan my tackle boxes for equipment and lures, make my selections, and bring just the essentials. Rod, reel, and tackle will fit into a side pocket of my backpack or a small carrying bag.

So what kind of rod should be used on an outdoor trip? For most camper-anglers, I suggest the use of a light, multi-piece spinning rod that will break down to a small size. One of the best deals on the fishing market is the six-piece Daiwa 6.5-foot pack rod, No. 6752. It retails for as low as $30 yet is made of a graphite/glass composite that gives it the quality of a much more expensive model. And it comes in a hard plastic carrying tube for protection. Other major rod manufacturers, such as Fenwick, offer similar premium rods. It's tough to miss with any of them.

The use of graphite-glass composites in fishing rods has made them lighter and more sensitive, yet stronger. The only downside to graphite as a rod material is that it can be brittle. If you rap your rod against something, it can crack or cause a weak spot. That weak spot can eventually snap when under even light pressure, like setting a hook or casting. Of course, a bit of care will prevent that from ever occurring.

If you haven't bought a fishing reel in some time, you will be surprised at the quality and price of micro spinning reels on the market. The reels come tiny and strong, with rear-control drag systems. Sigma, Shimano, Cardinal, Abu, and others all make premium reels. They also come expensive, usually $50 to $75. They're worth it. With your purchase, you've just bought a reel that will last for years and years.

The one downside to spinning reels is that after long term use, the bail spring will weaken. The result is that after casting and beginning to reel, the bail will sometimes not flip over and allow the reel to retrieve the line. You then have to do it by hand. This can be incredibly frustrating, particularly when stream fishing, where instant line pickup is essential. The solution is to have a new bail spring installed every few years. This is a cheap, quick operation for a tackle expert.

You might own a giant tackle box filled with lures, but on your fishing trip you are better off to fit just the essentials into a small container. One of the best ways to do that is to use the Plano Micro-Magnum 3414, a tiny two-sided tackle box for trout fishermen that fits into a shirt pocket. In mine, I can fit 20 lures in one side of the box and 20 flies, splitshot and snap swivels in the other. For bass lures, which are larger, you need a slightly larger box, but the same principle applies.

There are more fishing lures on the market than you can imagine, but a few special ones can do the job. I make sure these are in my box on every trip. For trout I carry: small black Panther Martin spinner with yellow spots, small gold Kastmaster, yellow Roostertail, gold Z-Ray with red spots, Super Duper, and Mepps Lightning spinner.

You can take it a step further using insider's wisdom. My old pal Ed the Dunk showed me his trick of taking a tiny Dardevle spoon, then spray painting it flat black and dabbing five tiny red dots on it. It's a real killer, particularly in tiny streams where the trout are spooky.

The best trout catcher I've ever used on rivers is a small metal lure called a Met-L Fly. On days when nothing else works, it can be like going to a shooting gallery. The problem is that the lure is near impossible to find. Rambob and I consider the few we have remaining so valuable that if the lure is snagged on a rock, a cold swim is deemed mandatory for its retrieval. These lures are as elusive to find in tackle shops as trout can be to catch without one.

For bass, you can also fit all you need into a small plastic tackle box. I have fished with many bass pros and all of them actually use just a few lures: a white spinner bait, a small jig called a Git's It, a surface plug called a Zara Spook, and plastic worms. At times, like when the bass move into shoreline areas during the spring, shad minnow imitations such as those made by Rebel or Rapala can be dynamite. For instance, my favorite is the one-inch blue-silver Rapala. Every spring, as the lakes begin to warm and the fish snap out of their winter doldrums, I like to float and paddle around small lakes in my small raft. I'll cast that little Rapala along the shoreline and catch and release hundreds of bass, bluegill, and sunfish. The fish are usually sitting close to the shoreline, awaiting my offering.

A FEW TRICKS

There's an old angler's joke about how you need to "think like a fish." But if you're the one getting zilched, you may not think it's so funny.

The irony is that it is your mental approach, what you see and what you miss, that often determines your fishing luck. Some people will spend a lot of money on tackle, lures, and fishing clothes, and that done, just saunter up to a stream or lake, cast out and wonder why they are not catching fish. The answer is their mental outlook. They are not tuning themselves to their surroundings.

You must live on nature's level, not your own. Try this and you will start to feel things you never believed even existed. Soon you will see things that will allow you to catch fish. You can get a head start by reading about fishing, but to get your degree in fishing, you must attend the University of Nature.

On every fishing trip, regardless of what you fish for, try to follow three hard-and-fast rules:

1. Always approach the fishing spot so you will be undetected.

2. Present your lure, fly or bait in a manner so it appears completely natural, as if no line was attached.

3. Stick and move, hitting one spot, working it the best you can, then move to the next.

Here's a more detailed explanation.

1. Approach: No one can just walk up to a stream or lake, cast out, and start catching fish as if someone had waved a magic wand. Instead, give the fish credit for being smart. After all, they live there.

Your approach must be completely undetected by the fish. Fish can sense your presence through sight and sound, though this is misinterpreted by most people. By sight, this rarely means the fish actually see you, but more likely, they will see your shadow on the water, or the movement of your arm or rod while casting. By sound, it doesn't mean they hear you talking, but that they will detect the vibrations of your footsteps along the shore, kicking a rock, or the unnatural plunking sound of a heavy cast hitting the water. Any of these elements can spook them off the bite. In order to fish undetected, you must walk softly, keep your shadow off the water, and keep your casting motion low. All of these keys become easier at sunrise or sunset, when shadows are on the water. At mid-day, a high sun causes high level of light penetration in the water, which can make the fish skittish to any foreign presence.

Like hunting, you must stalk the spots. When my brother Rambob sneaks up on a fishing spot, he looks like a burglar sneaking through an unlocked window.

2. Presentation: Your lure, fly, or bait must appear in the water as if no line was attached, so it appears as natural as possible. My pal Mo Furniss has skin-dived in rivers to watch what the fish see when somebody is fishing.

"You wouldn't believe it," he said. "When the lure hits the water, every trout within 40 feet, like 15, 20 trout, will do a little zig-zag. They all see the lure and are aware something is going on. Meanwhile, on-shore the guy casting doesn't get a bite and thinks there aren't any fish in the river."

If your offering is aimed at fooling a fish into striking, it must appear as part of its natural habitat, as if it is an insect just hatched or a small fish looking for a spot to hide. That's where you come in.

After you have snuck up on a fishing spot, you should zip your cast upstream, then start your retrieve as soon as it hits the water. If you let the lure sink to the bottom, then start the retrieve, you have no chance. A minnow, for instance, does not sink to the bottom then start swimming. On rivers, the retrieve should be more of a drift, as if the "minnow" was in trouble and the current was sweeping it downstream.

When fishing on trout streams, always hike and cast up river, then retrieve as the offering drifts downstream in the current. This is effective because trout will sit almost motionless, pointed upstream, finning against the current. This way they can see anything coming their direction, and if a potential food morsel arrives, all they need to do is move over a few inches, open their mouths, and they've got an easy lunch. Thus you must cast upstream.

Conversely, if you cast downstream, your retrieve will bring the lure from behind the fish, where he cannot see it approaching. And I've never seen a trout that had eyes in its tail. In addition, when retrieving a downstream lure, the river current will tend to sweep your lure inshore to the rocks.

3. Finding spots: A lot of fishermen don't catch fish and a lot of hikers never see any wildlife. The key is where they are looking.

The rule of the wild is that fish and wildlife will congregate wherever there is a distinct change in the habitat. This is where you should begin your search. To find deer, for instance, forget probing a thick forest, but look for when it breaks into a meadow, or a clear-cut has splayed a stand of trees. That's where the deer will be. Look for the change.

In a river, it can be where a riffle pours into a small pool, a rapid that plunges into a deep hole and flattens, a big boulder in the middle of a long riffle, a shoreline point, a rock pile, a submerged tree. Look for the changes. Conversely, long straight stretches of shoreline will not hold fish—the habitat is lousy.

On rivers, the most productive areas are often where short riffles tumble into small oxygenated pools. After sneaking up from the downstream side and staying low, you should zip your cast so the lure plops gently in the white water just above the pool. Starting your retrieve instantly, the lure will drift downstream and plunk into the pool. Bang! That's where the trout will hit. Take a few more casts, then head upstream to the next spot.

With a careful approach and lure presentation, and by fishing in the right spots, you have the ticket to many exciting days on the water.

OF BEARS AND FOOD

The first time you come nose-to-nose with a bear, it can make your skin quiver.

Even mild-mannered black bears, the most common bear in America (and the one you see in California) can send shock waves through your body. They range from 250 to 400 pounds and have large claws and teeth that are made to scare campers. When they bound, the muscles on their shoulders seem to roll like ocean breakers.

Bears in camping areas are accustomed to sharing the mountains with hikers and campers. They have become specialists in the food-raiding business. As a result, you must be able to make a bear-proof food hang, or be able to scare the fellow off. Many campgrounds provide bear and raccoon-proof food lockers. You can also stash your food in your vehicle, but that puts a limit on your trip.

If you are in a particularly remote area, there will be no food lockers available. Your car will not be there either. The answer is making a bear-proof food hang—suspending all of your food wrapped in a plastic garbage bag from a rope in mid-air, ten feet from the trunk of a tree and 20 feet off the ground. (Counter-balancing two bags with a rope thrown over a tree limb is very effective, but an extensive search must often be made to find an appropriate limb.)

This is accomplished by tying a rock to a rope, then throwing it over a high but sturdy tree limb. Next, tie your food bag to the rope, and hoist it up in the air. When you are satisfied with the position of the food bag, tie off the end of the rope to another tree. Nothing else will do, especially for hikers in bear-troubled areas, such as Kings Canyon, Yosemite or Sequoia National Parks. For instance, one day in Yosemite near Tuolumne Meadows, I met five consecutive teams of hikers heading the other direction who had all lost food to bears.

I've been there. On one trip, Foonsky and Rambob had left to fish, and I was stoking up an evening campfire when I felt the eyes of an intruder on my back. I turned around and this big bear was heading straight for our camp. In the next half hour, I scared the bear off twice, but then he got a whiff of something sweet in my brother's pack.

In most situations you can spook a black bear by banging on a pot and shouting like a lunatic. But some bears are on to the old banging-the-pot trick. If so, and he gets a whiff of your Tang, banging on a pot and shouting can be like trying to stop a tank with a roadblock.

In this case, the bear rolled into camp like a semi truck, grabbed my brother's pack, ripped it open and plucked out the Tang and the Swiss Miss. The bear, a 350-pounder, then sat astride a nearby log and lapped at the goodies like a thirsty dog finding water.

I took two steps toward the pack and that bear jumped off the log and galloped across the camp right at me. Scientists say a man can't outrun a bear, but they've never seen how fast I can go up a granite block with a bear on my tail. Once a bear gets his mitts on your gear, he considers it his.

Shortly thereafter, Foonsky returned while I was still perched on top of the rock, and demanded to know how I could let a bear get our Tang. But it took all three of us, Foonsky, Rambob, and myself, all charging at once and shouting like madmen to clear the bear out of the camp and send him off over the ridge. It was a lesson to never let food sit unattended again—a lesson learned the hard way.

THE GRIZZLY

When it comes to grizzlies, well, my friends, you need what we call an "attitude adjustment." Or that big ol' bear may just decide to adjust your attitude for you and make your stay at the park a short one.

Grizzlies are nothing like black bears. They are bigger, stronger, have little fear, and take what they want. Some people believe there are many different species of this critter, like Alaskan brown, silvertip, cinnamon, kodiak, but the truth is they are all grizzlies. Any difference in appearance has to do with diet, habitat, and life habits, not speciation. But by any name, they all come big. Although you won't find grizzlies in California, it is good to know what to do in case you ever do run into one.

The first thing you must do to prepare is determine if there are grizzlies in the area where you are camping. That can usually be done easily enough by asking rangers in the area. If you are heading into Yellowstone or Glacier National Park, or the Bob Marshall Wilderness of Montana, well, you don't have to ask. They're out there, and they're the biggest and potentially most dangerous critters you could run into.

One general way to figure the size of a bear is from his footprint. Take the width of the footprint in inches, add one to it -- and you'll have an estimated length of the bear in feet. For instance, a nine-inch footprint equals a 10-foot bear. Any bear that big is a grizzly, my friends. In fact, most grizzly footprints average about nine to ten inches across, and black bears (though they may be brown in color) tend to have footprints only 4.5 to six inches across.

If you are hiking in a wilderness area that may have grizzlies, then it becomes a necessity to wear bells on your pack. That way, the bear will hear you coming and likely get out of your way. Keep talking, singing, or maybe even debate the country's foreign policy, but whatever, do not fall into a silent hiking vigil. And if a breeze is blowing in your face, you must make even more noise (now a good excuse to rant and rave about the government's domestic affairs). Noise is important, because your smell will not be carried in the direction you are hiking. As a result, the bear will not smell you coming.

If a bear can hear you and smell you, they will tend to get out of the way and let you pass without your knowing they were even close by. The exception is, if you are carrying fish, lots of sweets in your pack, or are wearing heavy, sweet deodorants or makeup. All three are bear attractants.

Most encounters with grizzlies occur when hikers fall into a silent march in the wilderness with the wind in their faces—and they walk around a corner and right into a big, unsuspecting grizzly. If you do this, and see a big hump just behind its neck, well, gulp, don't think twice, it's a grizzly.

And then what should you do? Get up a tree, that's what. Grizzlies are so big that their claws cannot support their immense weight, and thus they cannot climb trees. And although their young can climb, they rarely want to get their mitts on you.

If you do get grabbed, every instinct in your body will tell you to fight back. Don't believe it. This is a time to listen to logic; not the heart. Play dead. Go limp. Let the bear throw you around a little, because after awhile you become unexciting play material, and the bear will get bored. My grandmother was grabbed by a grizzly in Glacier National Park and after a few tosses and hugs, was finally left alone to escape.

Some say it's a good idea to tuck your head under his chin, and therefore, the bear will be unable to bite your head. I'll take a pass on that one. If you are taking action, any action, it's a signal that you are a force to be reckoned with, and he'll likely respond with more aggression. And bears don't lose many wrestling matches.

What grizzlies really like to do, believe it or not, is to pile a lot of sticks and leaves on you. Just let them, and keep perfectly still. Don't fight them; don't run. And when you have a 100-percent chance (not 98 or 99) to dash up a nearby tree, that's when you let fly. Once safely in a tree, then you can hurl down insults, and let your aggression out. Remember, logic.

In a wilderness camp, there are special precautions you should take. Always hang your food at least 100 yards down wind of your camp. and get it high; 30 feet is reasonable. In addition, circle your camp with rope, and hang the bells from your pack onto it. Thus, if a bear walks into your camp, he'll run into your rope; the bells will ring, and everybody will have a chance to get up a tree before ol' griz figures out what's going on. Often, the unexpected ringing of bells is enough to send him off in search of a quieter environment.

You see, more often than not, grizzlies tend to clear the way for campers and hikers. So, be smart, and don't act like bear bait, and always have a plan if you are confronted by one.

My pal Foonsky had such a plan during a wilderness expedition in Montana's northern Rockies. On our second day of hiking, we started seeing scratch marks on the trees, like 13 to 14 feet off the ground.

"Mr. Griz made those," Foonsky said. "With spring here, the grizzlies are coming out of hibernation and using the trees like a cat uses a scratch board to stretch the muscles."

The next day, I noticed Foonsky had a pair of track shoes tied to the back of his pack. I just laughed.

"You're not going to outrun a griz," I said. "In fact, there's hardly any animals out here in the wilderness that man can outrun."

Foonsky just smiled.

"I don't have to outrun a griz," he said. "I just have to outrun you!"

FUN AND GAMES

"Now what are we supposed to do?" the young boy asked his dad.

"Yeah, dad, think of something," asked another son.

Well, 'ol dad thought hard. This was one of the first camping trips he'd taken with his sons and one of the first lessons he received was that kids don't want the philosophic release of mountain quiet. They want action, and lots of it. With a glint in his eye, dad searched around the camp and picked up 15 twigs, breaking them so each was four inches long. He laid them in three separate rows, three twigs in one row, five twigs in another, and seven in the other.

"OK, this game is called 3-5-7," said dad. "You each take turns picking up sticks. You are allowed to removed all or as few as one twig from a row, but here's the catch: You can only pick from one row per turn. Whoever picks up the last stick left is the loser."

Well, I remember this episode well because those two little boys were my brother Bobby, as in Rambobby, and me. And to this day, we still play 3-5-7 on campouts, with the winner getting to watch the loser clean the dishes. What I have learned in the span of time since that original episode is that it does not matter what your age is: campers need options for camp fun.

Some evenings, after a long hike or ride, you are likely to feel too worn-out at the end of the day to take on a serious romp downstream to fish, or a climb up to a ridge for a view. That is especially true if you have been in the outback for a week or more. At that point a lot of campers will spend their time resting and gazing at a map of the area, dreaming of the next day's adventure, or just take a seat against a rock, watching the colors of the sky and mountain panorama change minute-by-minute. But for kids in the push-button video era, and for a lot of adults too, they want more. After all, "I'm on vacation," and "I want some fun."

There are several options, like the 3-5-7 twig game, and they should be just as much a part of your pre-trip planning as arranging your gear.

For kids, plan on games, the more physicially challenging the competition, the better. One of the best games is to throw a chunk of wood into a lake, then challenge the kids to hit it by throwing rocks. It wreaks havoc on the fishing, but it can keep kids totally absorbed for some time. Target practice with a wrist-rocket style sling-shot is also all-consuming for kids, firing rocks away at small targets like pine cones set on a log.

You can also set kids off on little missions near camp: Looking for the footprints of wildlife, searching out good places to have a "snipe hunt," picking up twigs to get the evening fire started, or having them take the water purifier to a stream to pump some drinking water into a canteen. The latter is an easy, fun, yet important task that will allow kids to feel a sense of equality they often don't get at home.

For adults, the appeal should be more to the intellect. A good example is star and planet identification, and while you are staring into space, you're bound to spot a few asteroids, or shooting stars. A star chart can make it easy to locate and identify many distinctive star and constellations, such as Pleides (the Seven Sisters), Orion, and several from the zodiac, depending on the time of year. With a little research, it can add a unique perspective to your trip. You could point to Polaris, one of the most easily identified of all stars, and note that navigators in the 1400s used it to find their way. Polaris, of course, is the "North Star," and is at the end of the handle of the Little Dipper. Pinpointing Polaris is quite easy. First find the Big Dipper, then locate the outside stars of the ladle of the Big Dipper. They are called the "Pointer Stars" because they point right at Polaris.

A tree identification book can also teach you a few things about your surroundings. It is also a good idea for one member of the party to research the history of the area you have chosen and another to research the geology. With shared knowledge, you end up with a deeper love of wild places.

Another way to add some recreation into your trip is to bring a board game, a number of which have been miniaturized for campers. The most popular are chess, checkers and Cribbage. The latter comes with an equally miniature set of playing cards. And if you bring those little cards, that opens a vast set of other possibilities. With kids along, for instance, just take the Queen of Clubs out of the deck and you can instantly play Old Maid.

But there are more serious card games and they come with high stakes. Such occurred at Rae Lakes, located in the high country of the Sierra Nevada above Kings Canyon National Park, where Foonsky, Rambob and myself sat down for a late afternoon game of poker. In a game of seven-card stud, I caught a straight on the sixth card and felt like a dog licking on a T-bone. Already, I had bet several Skittles and M&M's with nuts on this promising hand.

Then I examined the cards Foonsky had face up. He was showing three sevens, and acting as happy as a grizzly with a pork chop, like he had a full house. He matched my bet of two M&M's with nuts, then raised me three SweetTarts, one Starburst and one sour apple Jelly Rancher. Rambob folded, but I matched Foonsky's bet and hoped for the best as the seventh and final card was dealt.

Just after Foonsky glanced at that last card, I saw him sneak a look at my grape stick and beef jerky stash.

"I raise you a grape stick," he said.

Rambob and I both gasped. It was the highest bet ever made, equivalent to a million dollars laid down in Las Vegas. Cannons were going off in my chest. I looked hard at my cards. They looked good, but were they good enough?

Even with a great hand like I had, a grape stick was too much to gamble, my last one with 10 days of trail ahead of us. I shook my head and folded my cards. Foonsky smiled at his victory.

But I still had my grape stick.

OLD TRICKS DON'T ALWAYS WORK

Most people are born honest, but after a few camping trips, they usually get over it.

I remember some advice I got from Rambob, normally an honest soul, on one camping trip. A giant mosquito had landed on my arm and he alerted me to some expert advice.

"Flex your arm muscles," he commanded, watching the mosquito fill with my blood. "He'll get stuck in your arm, then he'll explode."

For some unknown reason, I believed him. We both proceeded to watch the mosquito drill countless holes in my arm.

Alas, the unknowning face sabotage from their most trusted companions on camping trips, It can arise at any time, usually in the form of advice from a friendly, honest-looking face, as if to say, "What? How can you doubt me?" After that mosquito episode, I was a little more skeptical of my dear, old brother. Then, the next day, when another mosquito was nailing me in the back of the neck, out came this gem:

"Hold your breath," he commanded. I instinctively obeyed. "That will freeze the mosquito," he said, "then you can squish him."

But in the time I wasted holding my breath, the little bugger was able to fly off without my having the satisfaction of squishing him. When he got home, he probably told his family, "What a dummy I got to drill today!"

Over the years, I have been duped numerous times with dubious advice:

On a grizzly bear attack: "If he grabs you, tuck your head under the grizzly's chin, then he won't be able to bite you in the head." This made sense to me until the first time I looked face to face with a 9-foot grizzly, 40 yards away. In seconds, I was at the top of a tree, which suddenly seemed to make the most sense.

On coping with animal bites: "If a bear bites you in the arm, don't try to jerk it away. That will just rip up your arm. Instead force your arm deeper into his mouth. He'll lose his grip and will have to open it to get a firmer hold, and right then you can get away." I was told this in the Boy Scouts, and when I was 14, I had a chance to try it out when a friend's dog bit me when I tried to pet it. What happened? When I shoved my arm deeper into his mouth, he bit me about three extra times.

On cooking breakfast: "The bacon will curl up everytime in a camp frying pan. So make sure you have a bacon stretcher to keep it flat." As a 12-year-old Tenderfoot, I spent two hours looking for the bacon stretcher until I figured out the camp leader had forgotten it. It wasn't for several years until I learned that there is no such thing.

On preventing sore muscles: "If you haven't hiked for a long time and you are facing a rough climb, you can keep from getting sore muscles in your legs, back and shoulders by practicing the 'Dead Man's Walk.' Simply let your entire body go slack, and then take slow, wobbling steps. This will clear your muscles of lactic acid, which cause them to be so sore after a rough hike." Foonsky pulled this one on me. Rambob and I both bought it, then tried it while we were hiking up Mt. Whitney, which requires a 6,000-foot elevation gain in six miles. In one 45-minute period, about 30 other hikers passed us and looked at us as if we were suffering from some rare form of mental aberration.

Fish won't bite? No problem: "If the fish are not feeding or will not bite, persistent anglers can still catch dinner with little problem. Keep casting across current, and eventually, as they hover in the stream, the line will feed across their open mouths. Keep reeling and you will hook the fish right in the side of the mouth. This technique is called 'lining.' You should never worry if the fish will not bite, because you can always line 'em." Of course, heh, heh, heh, that explains why so many fish get hooked in the side of the mouth.

How to keep bears away: "To keep bears away, urinate around the borders of your campground. If there are a lot of bears in the area, it is advisable to go right on your sleeping bag." Yeah, surrrrrre.

Finding pure stream water: "To find crystal pure stream water that you can safely drink, search for fast-moving water that has a lot of bubbles. That water is naturally purified." Actually, Giardia lamblia is more likely to be suspended in fast-moving water than still water, according to hydrologist Dr. Furnai. All non-piped drinking water should be screened on camping trips.

What to do with trash: "Don't worry about packing out trash. Just bury it. It will regenerate into the earth and add valuable minerals." Bears, raccoons, skunks and other critters will dig up your trash as soon as you depart, leaving one huge mess for the next camper. Always pack out everything.

Often the advice comes without warning. That was the case after a fishing trip with my wife, Nancy, when she outcaught me two-to-one, the third such trip in a row. I explained this to a shopkeeper, and he nodded, then explained why.

"The male fish are able to detect the female scent on the lure, and thus become aroused into striking."

Of course! That explains everything!

GETTING REVENGE

I was just a lad when Foonsky pulled the old snipe-hunt trick on me. It's taken 30 years to get revenge.

You probably know about snipe hunting. That is where the victim is led out at night in the woods by a group, then is left holding a bag.

"Stay perfectly still and quiet," Foonsky explained. "You don't want to scare the snipe. The rest of us will go back to camp and let the woods settle down. Then when the snipe are least expecting it, we'll form a line and charge through the forest with sticks, beating bushes and trees, and we'll flush the snipe out right to you. Be ready with the bag. When we flush the snipe out, bag it. But until we start our charge, make sure you don't move or make a sound or you will spook the snipe and ruin everything."

I sat out there in the woods with my bag for hours, waiting for the charge. I waited, waited, and waited. Nothing happened. No charge, no snipe. It wasn't until well past midnight that I figured something was wrong. When I finally returned to camp, everybody was sleeping.

Well, I tell ya, don't get mad at your pals for the tricks they pull on you. Get revenge. Some 25 years later, on the last day of a camping trip, the time finally came.

"Let's break camp early," Foonsky suggested to Mr. Furnai and me. "Get up before dawn, eat breakfast, pack up, then be on the ridge to watch the sun come up. It will be a fantastic way to end the trip."

"Sounds great to me," I replied. But when Foonsky wasn't looking, I turned his alarm clock ahead three hours. So when the alarm sounded at the appointed 4:30 a.m. wakeup time, Mr. Furnai and I knew it was actually only 1:30 a.m.

Foonsky clambered out of his sleeping bag and whistled with a grin. "Time to break camp."

"You go ahead," I answered. "I'll skip breakfast so I can get a little more sleep. At the first sign of dawn, wake me up, and I'll break camp."

"Me too," said Mr. Furnai.

Foonsky then proceeded to make coffee, cook a breakfast and eat it, sitting on a log in the black darkness of the forest, waiting for the sun to come up. An hour later, with still no sign of dawn, he checked his clock. It now read 5:30 a.m. "Any minute now we should start seeing some light," he said.

He made another cup of coffee, packed his gear and sat there in the middle of the night, looking up at the stars, waiting for dawn. "Anytime now," he said. He ended up sitting there all night long.

Revenge is sweet. Prior to a fishing trip at a lake, I took Foonsky aside and explained that the third member of the party, Jimbobo, was hard of hearing and very sensitive about it. "Don't mention it to him," I advised. "Just talk real loud."

Meanwhile, I had already told Jimbobo the same thing. "Foonsky just can't hear very good."

We had fished less than 20 minutes when Foonsky got a nibble.

"GET A BITE?" shouted Jimbobo.

"YEAH!" yelled back Foonsky, smiling. "BUT I DIDN'T HOOK HIM!"

"MAYBE NEXT TIME!" shouted Jimbobo with a friendly grin.

Well, they spent the entire day yelling at each other from the distance of a few feet. They never did figure it out. Heh, heh, heh.

That is, I thought, until we made a trip salmon fishing. I got a strike that almost knocked my fishing rod out of the boat. When I grabbed the rod, it felt like Moby Dick was on the other end. "At least a 25-pounder," I said. "Maybe bigger."

The fish dived, ripped off line and then bulldogged. "It's acting like a 40-pounder," I announced, "Huge, just huge. It's going deep. That's how the big ones fight."

Some 15 minutes later, I finally got the "salmon" to the surface. It turned out to be a coffee can that Foonsky had clipped on the line with a snap swivel, then by maneuvering the boat, he made the coffee can fight like a big fish.

This all started with a little old snipe hunt years ago. You never know what your pals will try next. Don't get mad. Get revenge!

CHAPTER SEVEN

RESOURCE GUIDE

Now you're ready to join the Five Percent Club, that is, the five percent of campers who know the secret spots where they can camp, fish and hike, and have the time of their lives doing it.

To aid in that pursuit, there are a number of contacts, map sources, and reservation systems available for your use. These include contacts for national forests, state parks, national parks, the Bureau of Land Management, Pacific Gas & Electric, and motor home parks. For BLM camps, there is no central reservation or information service. For these camps, we have listed the appropriate district contact on a camp-by-camp basis. For information on PG&E camps, phone (916)527-0354. The state and federal agencies listed can provide detailed maps at low cost and any additional information you might require.

NATIONAL FORESTS

The Forest Service provides many secluded camps and permits camping anywhere except where it is specifically prohibited. If you ever want to clear the cobwebs and get away from it all, this is the way to go.

Many Forest Service campgrounds are quite remote and have no developed water. You don't need to check in, you don't need reservations, and there is no fee. At many Forest Service campgrounds that provide piped water, the camp fee is often only a few dollars, with payment made on the honor system. Because most of these camps are in mountain areas, they are subject to closure for snow or mud during the winter.

Dogs are permitted in National Forests with no extra charge and no hassle. Conversely, in state and national parks, dogs are not allowed on trails.

Some of the more popular camps on National Forests are on the MISTIX reservation system. The phone number to make a reservation at these camps is (800)283-CAMP, a different phone number than MISTIX uses for state park reservations. The fee to make a reservation for a campground on National Forests is usually $6, but in rare cases, such as for a group site at a premium location, can be $10.

Maps for National Forests are among the best you can get. They detail all backcountry streams, lakes, hiking trails, and logging roads for access. They cost $2 and can be obtained by writing to USDA-Forest Service, Office of Information, Pacific Southwest Region, 630 Sansome Street, San Francisco, CA 94111. For information, phone (415)705-2874. Some wilderness maps cost a bit more.

I've found the Forest Service personnel to be the most helpful of the government agencies when obtaining camping or hiking trail information. Unless you are buying a map, it is advisable to phone, not write, to get the best service. As long as you are phoning, you might also remind them that National Forests are for campers as well as timber companies. For specific information on a National Forest, write or phone the following addresses and phone numbers.

Angeles National Forest, located northeast of Los Angeles: write to 701 N. Santa Anita Avenue, Arcadia, CA 91006, or phone (818) 574-1613.

Cleveland National Forest, located east of San Diego: write to 880 Front Street, Room 5-N-14, San Diego, CA 92188, or phone (619)557-5050.

Eldorado National Forest, located east of Placerville: write to 100 Forni Road, Placerville, CA 95667, or phone (916)622-5061.

Inyo National Forest, located in the eastern Sierra Nevada: write to 873 N. Main Street, Bishop, CA 93514, or phone (619)873-5841.

Klamath National Forest, located northeast of Eureka: write to 1215 S. Main Street, Yreka, CA 96097, or phone (916)842-6131.

Lake Tahoe Basin, located west of Lake Tahoe: write to P.O.Box 731002, 870 Emerald Bay Road, South Lake Tahoe, CA 95731, or phone (916) 573-2600.

Lassen National Forest, located east of Redding: write to 707 Nevada Street, Susanville, CA 96130, or phone (916)257-2151.

Los Padres National Forest, located south of Monterey: write to 6144 Calle Real, Goleta, CA 93111, or phone (805)683-6711.

Mendocino National Forest, located northeast of Ukiah: write to 420 Laurel Street, Willows, CA 95988, or phone (916)934-3316.

Modoc National Forest, located in the northeast corner of the state: write to 441 N. Main Street, Alturas, CA 96101, or phone (916) 233-5811.

Plumas National Forest, located northwest of Lake Tahoe: write to P.O. Box 1500, Quincy, CA 95971, or phone (916)283-2050.

San Bernardino National Forest, located east of San Bernardino: write to 1824 S. Commercenter Circle, San Bernardino, CA 92408, or phone (714)383-5588.

Sequoia National Forest, located south of Sequoia National Park: write to 900 W. Grand Avenue, Porterville, CA 93257, or phone (209)784-1500.

Shasta-Trinity National Forest, located northwest of Redding: write to 2400 Washington Avenue, Redding, CA 96001, or phone (916)246-5222.

Sierra National Forest, located south of Yosemite: write to 1600 Tollhouse Road, Clovis, CA 93612, or phone (209)487-5155.

Six Rivers National Forest, located between Eureka and Crescent City: write to 500 5th Street, Eureka, CA 95501, or phone (707)442-1721.

Stanislaus National Forest, located east of Sonora: write to 19777 Greenly Road, Sonora, CA 95370, or phone (209)532-3671.

Tahoe National Forest, located northwest of Lake Tahoe: write to Highway 49, Nevada City, CA 95959, or phone (916)265-4531.
Toiyabe National Forest, located in eastern Sierra Nevada, near Bridgeport: write to P.O. Box 595, Bridgeport, CA 93517, or phone (916)932-7070.

STATE PARKS

The California State Parks system provides many popular camping spots. Reservations are often a necessity during the summer months. The camps include drive-in numbered sites, tent spaces, picnic tables, with showers and bathrooms provided nearby. Although some parks are well-known, there are still some little-known gems in the State Parks system where campers can get seclusion, even in the summer months.

Reservations can be obtained through MISTIX, which can be reached toll-free by calling (800)444-PARK from anywhere in California. MISTIX charges $3.95 for the reservation service for state parks, a separate charge from the campsite fee. Most state parks charge $7-$14 per night, with a $1 fee for pets. The most expensive camps have ocean or beach frontage, such as along Monterey Bay. For those 62 years and older, site discounts are available.

Reservations are available at state parks up to eight weeks ahead of your camp date. At parks such as Clear Lake and any along the coast, reserving your spot that far in advance can be a necessity, especially during the vacation season.

NATIONAL PARKS

The California National Parks are natural wonders, ranging from the spectacular yet crowded Yosemite Valley to the remote and rugged beauty of Lava Beds National Monument in northeastern California. At national parks, reservations, when taken, are usually made directly through the park at the following numbers. At many campgrounds at national parks, it's first come, first serve. At some camps at Yosemite, reservations can be made through Ticketron by calling (800)452-1111. Ticketron charges $4 per reservation.

The six most popular parks are:

Yosemite National Park at (209)372-0301 or (209)372-0302.
Sequoia National Park at (209)565-3341.
Kings Canyon National Park at (209)565-3341.
Death Valley National Monument at (619)786-2331.
Devils Postpile National Monument at (619)934-2289.
Point Reyes National Seashore at (415)663-1092.

The best of the rest are:

Lassen Volcanic National Park at (916)595-4444.

Lava Beds National Monument at (916)667-2282.
Whiskeytown National Recreation Area at (916)241-6584.
Joshua Tree National Monument at (619)367-7511.
Pinnacles National Monument at (408)389-4462.

MOTOR HOME PARKS

The charge for hookups at motor home parks varies from $10 to $20 per night. In populated areas, the charge often climbs to the $20 range. Many motor home parks, particularly those in rural counties, must be contacted directly by phone. Many require a deposit with a reservation, which is usually just an advance payment for your first night's stay. No reservation service is available that links privately-operated parks.

SHASTA CASCADE

The best free private source for camping information in northern California is the Shasta Cascade Wonderland Association. They provide information on Shasta, Trinity, Siskiyou, Modoc, and Tehama counties, which is an area the size of Ohio. They can be reached by writing to 1250 Parkview, Redding, CA 96001, or phoning (916)243-2643. Nice folks.

CHAPTER EIGHT

ETHICS

The perfect place to set up a base camp for a camping trip turned out to be not so perfect. In fact, according to Doug Williams of California, "it did not even exist."

Williams and his son, James, had driven deep into Angeles National Forest, prepared to set up camp and then explore the surrounding area on foot. But when they reached their destination, "no campground existed."

"I wanted a primitive camp on a national forest where I could teach my son some basics," said the senior Williams. "But when we got there, there wasn't much left of the camp and it had been closed. It was obvious that the area had been vandalized."

It turned out not to be an isolated incident. A lack of outdoor ethics practiced by a few people using the non-supervised campgrounds available on national forest land has caused the U.S. Forest Service to close a few of them, and make extensive repairs to others.

"There have been sites closed, especially on Angeles and San Bernardino national forests in Southern California," said David Flohr, regional campground coordinator for the Forest Service. "It's an urban type of thing, affecting forests near urban areas, and not just Los Angeles. They get a lot of urban users and they bring with them a lot of the same ethics they have in the city. They get drinking and they're not afraid to do things. They vandalize and run. Of course, it is a public facility, so they think nobody is getting hurt."

But somebody is getting hurt, starting with the next person who wants to use the campground. And if the ranger district budget doesn't have enough money to pay for repairs, the campground is then closed for the next arrivals. Just ask Doug and James Williams.

In an era of considerable fiscal restraint for the Forest Service, vandalized campgrounds could face closures instead of repair in the next few years. The Williams had a taste of it, but Flohr, as camping coordinator, gets a steady diet.

"It starts with behavior," Flohr said. "General rowdiness, drinking, partying and then vandalism. It goes all the way from the felt tip pen things (graffiti) to total destruction, blowing up toilet buildings with dynamite. I have seen toilets destroyed totally with shotguns. They burn up tables, burn barriers. They'll burn up signs for firewood, even the shingles right off the roofs of the bathrooms. They'll shoot anything, garbage cans, signs. It can get a little hairy. A favorite is to remove the stool out of a toilet building. We've had people fall in the open hole."

The National Park Service had a similar problem 10 years ago, especially with rampant littering. Park Director Bill Mott responded by creating an interpretive program that attempts to teach visitors the wise use of natural areas, and to have all park workers set examples by picking up litter and reminding others to do the same.

The Forest Service has responded with a similar program, with brochures available that detail the wise use of national forests. The four most popular brochures are titled: "Rules for Visitors to the National Forest," "Recreation on the National Forests," "Is the Water Safe?" and "Backcountry Safety Tips." These include details on campfires, drinking water from lakes or streams, hypothermia, safety and outdoor ethics. They are available for free by writing Public Affairs, U.S. Forest Service, 630 Sansome Street, San Francisco, CA 94111.

Flohr said even the experienced sometimes cross over the ethics line unintentionally. The most common example, he said, is when campers toss garbage into the outhouse toilet, rather than packing it out in a plastic garbage bag.

"They throw it in the vault toilet bowls, and that just fills them up," Flohr said. "That creates an extremely high cost to pump it. You know why? Because that stuff has to be picked out piece-by-piece by some poor guy. It can't be pumped."

At most backcountry sites, the Forest Service has implemented a program called, "Pack it in, pack it out," even posting signs that remind all visitors to do so. But a lot of people don't do it, and others may even uproot the sign and burn it for firewood.

On a trip to a secluded lake near Carson Pass in the Sierra Nevada, I arrived at a small, little-known camp where the picnic table had been spray-painted and garbage had been strewn about. A pristine place, the true temple of God, had been defiled.

Then I remembered back 30 years, and a story my dad told me: "There are two dogs inside of you," he said, "a good one, and a bad one. The one you feed is the one that will grow. Always try to feed the good dog."

CHAPTER NINE

CAMPING GEAR CHECK LIST

1. COOKING GEAR

- ☐ Matches bagged in different zip lock bags
- ☐ Fire-starter cubes or candle
- ☐ Camp stove
- ☐ Camp fuel
- ☐ Pot, pan, cup
- ☐ Pot grabber
- ☐ Knife, fork
- ☐ Dish soap and scrubber
- ☐ Salt, pepper, spices
- ☐ Itemized food
- ☐ Plastic spade

OPTIONAL

- ☐ Axe or hatchet
- ☐ Wood or charcoal for barbecue
- ☐ Ice chest
- ☐ Spatula
- ☐ Grill
- ☐ Tin foil
- ☐ Dust pan
- ☐ Tablecloth
- ☐ Whisk broom
- ☐ Clothespins

2. CAMPING CLOTHES

- ☐ Polypropylene underwear
- ☐ Cotton shirt
- ☐ Long sleeve cotton/wool shirt
- ☐ Cotton/canvas pants
- ☐ Vest
- ☐ Parka
- ☐ Rain jacket, pants, or poncho
- ☐ Hat
- ☐ Sunglasses
- ☐ Chapstick

OPTIONAL

- ☐ Seam lock
- ☐ Shorts
- ☐ Swimming suit
- ☐ Gloves
- ☐ Ski cap

3. HIKING AND FOOT CARE LIST

- ☐ Quality hiking boots
- ☐ Backup lightweight shoes
- ☐ Polypropylene socks
- ☐ Thick cotton socks
- ☐ 80 percent wool socks
- ☐ Strong boot laces
- ☐ Innersole or foot cushion
- ☐ Moleskin and medical tape
- ☐ Gaiters
- ☐ Water repellent boot treatment

4. GOOD NIGHT'S SLEEP LIST

- ☐ Sleeping bag
- ☐ Insulite pad or Therm-a-rest
- ☐ Ground tarp
- ☐ Tent

OPTIONAL

- ☐ Air pillow
- ☐ Mosquito netting
- ☐ Foam pad for truck bed
- ☐ Windshield light screen for RV
- ☐ Catalytic heater

5. FIRST-AID KIT

- ☐ Band-Aids
- ☐ Sterile gauze pads
- ☐ Roller gauze
- ☐ Athletic tape
- ☐ Moleskin
- ☐ Thermometer
- ☐ Aspirin
- ☐ Ace bandage
- ☐ Mosquito repellent
- ☐ After Bite or ammonia
- ☐ Campho-Phenique gel
- ☐ First-Aid cream
- ☐ Sunscreen
- ☐ Neosporin Ointment
- ☐ Caladryl
- ☐ Biodegradable soap
- ☐ Towelette

OPTIONAL

- ☐ Water purification system
- ☐ Coins for emergency phoning
- ☐ Extra set of matches
- ☐ Tweezers
- ☐ Mirror for signaling

6. FISHING/RECREATIONAL GEAR

- ☐ Fishing rod
- ☐ Fishing reel with fresh line
- ☐ Small tackle box with lures, splitshot, and snap swivels
- ☐ Pliers
- ☐ Knife

OPTIONAL

- ☐ Stargazing chart
- ☐ Tree identification hand book
- ☐ Deck of cards
- ☐ Backpacking cribbage board
- ☐ Knapsack for each person

7. MISCELLANEOUS

- ☐ Maps
- ☐ Flashlight
- ☐ Nylon rope for food hang
- ☐ Handkerchief
- ☐ Camera and film
- ☐ Plastic garbage bags
- ☐ Toilet paper
- ☐ Compass
- ☐ Watch

OPTIONAL

- ☐ Binoculars
- ☐ Notebook and pen
- ☐ Towel

THE CALIFORNIA CAMPGROUNDS

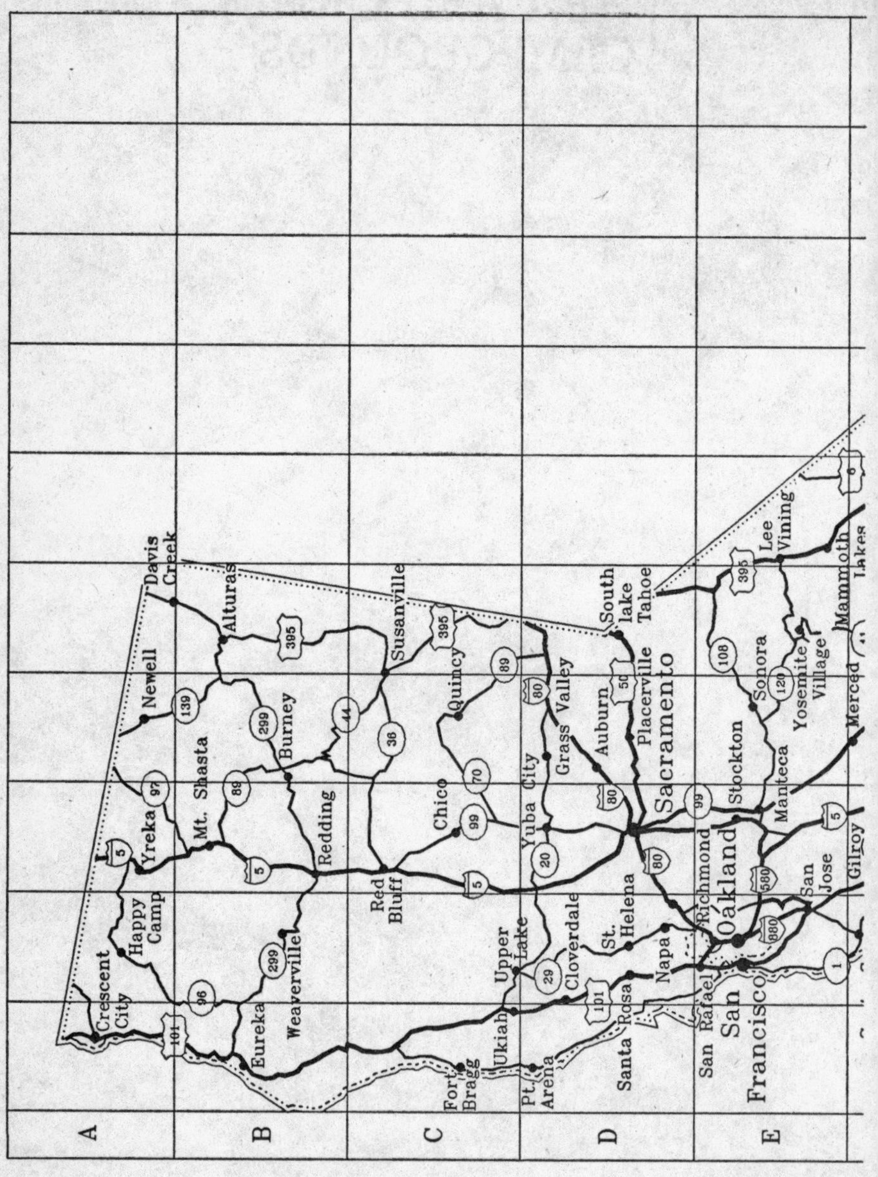
A
B
C
D
E
Crescent City
Happy Camp
Yreka
Newell
Davis Creek
Alturas
Mt. Shasta
Eureka
Weaverville
Redding
Burney
Susanville
Red Bluff
Chico
Quincy
Fort Bragg
Ukiah
Upper Lake
Yuba City
Grass Valley
Pt. Arena
Cloverdale
St. Helena
Auburn
Placerville
South lake Tahoe
Santa Rosa
Napa
Sacramento
San Rafael
San Francisco
Richmond
Oakland
Stockton
Sonora
Lee Vining
San Jose
Gilroy
Manteca
Merced
Yosemite Village
Mammoth Lakes
101
96
299
5
97
139
89
395
44
36
99
70
20
29
80
50
108
120
580
880
1

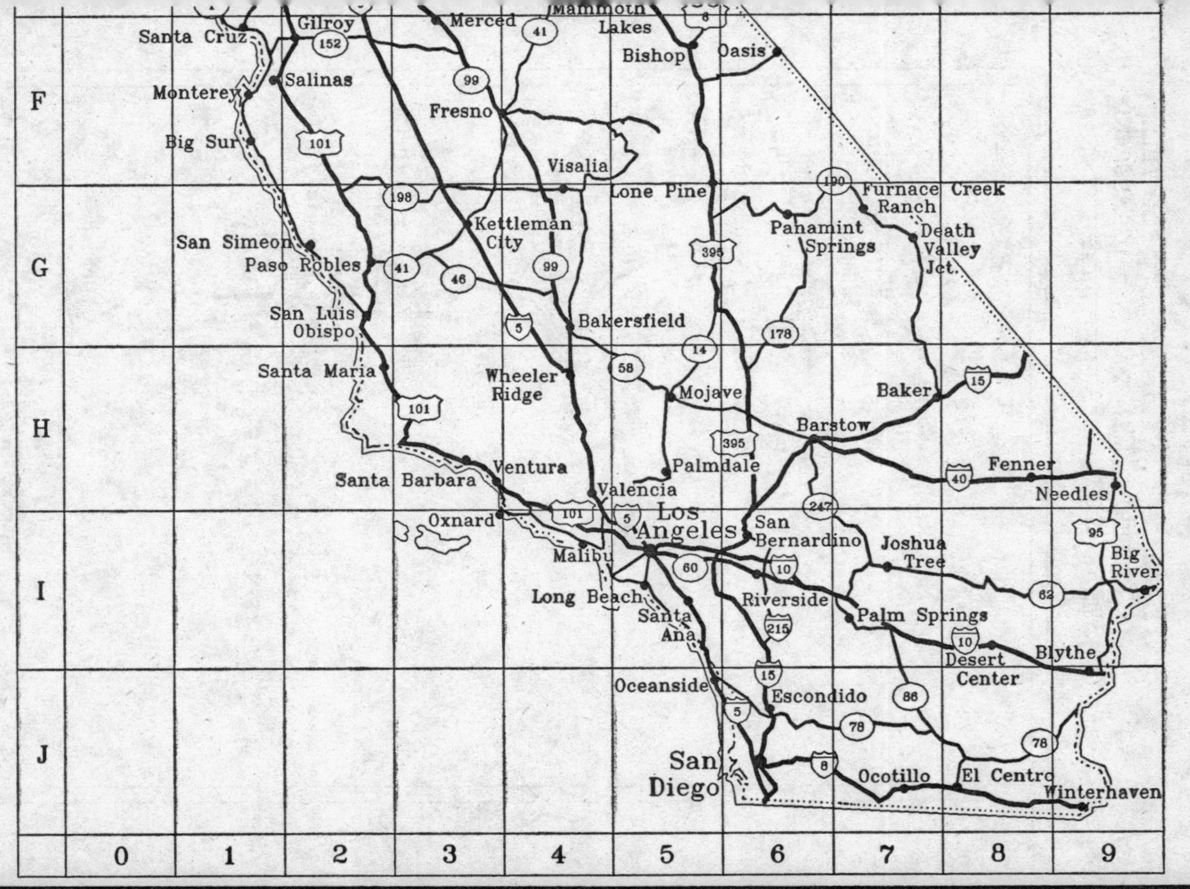
F
G
H
I
J
0
1
2
3
4
5
6
7
8
9
Santa Cruz
Gilroy
Monterey
Salinas
Big Sur
Merced
Fresno
Mammoth Lakes
Bishop
Oasis
Visalia
Lone Pine
Furnace Creek Ranch
Death Valley Jct.
Panamint Springs
San Simeon
Paso Robles
Kettleman City
San Luis Obispo
Bakersfield
Santa Maria
Wheeler Ridge
Mojave
Baker
Barstow
Santa Barbara
Ventura
Oxnard
Valencia
Palmdale
Fenner
Needles
Los Angeles
San Bernardino
Joshua Tree
Malibu
Long Beach
Santa Ana
Riverside
Palm Springs
Desert Center
Blythe
Big River
Oceanside
Escondido
Ocotillo
El Centro
Winterhaven
San Diego
152
101
99
41
198
46
5
58
14
395
178
190
15
40
247
10
60
215
62
95
86
78
8
6

◆ MAP AO ◆

BEACH
DESERT
FOOTHILL
TREES
URBAN
GRASSLAND
5% CLUB

15 MILES

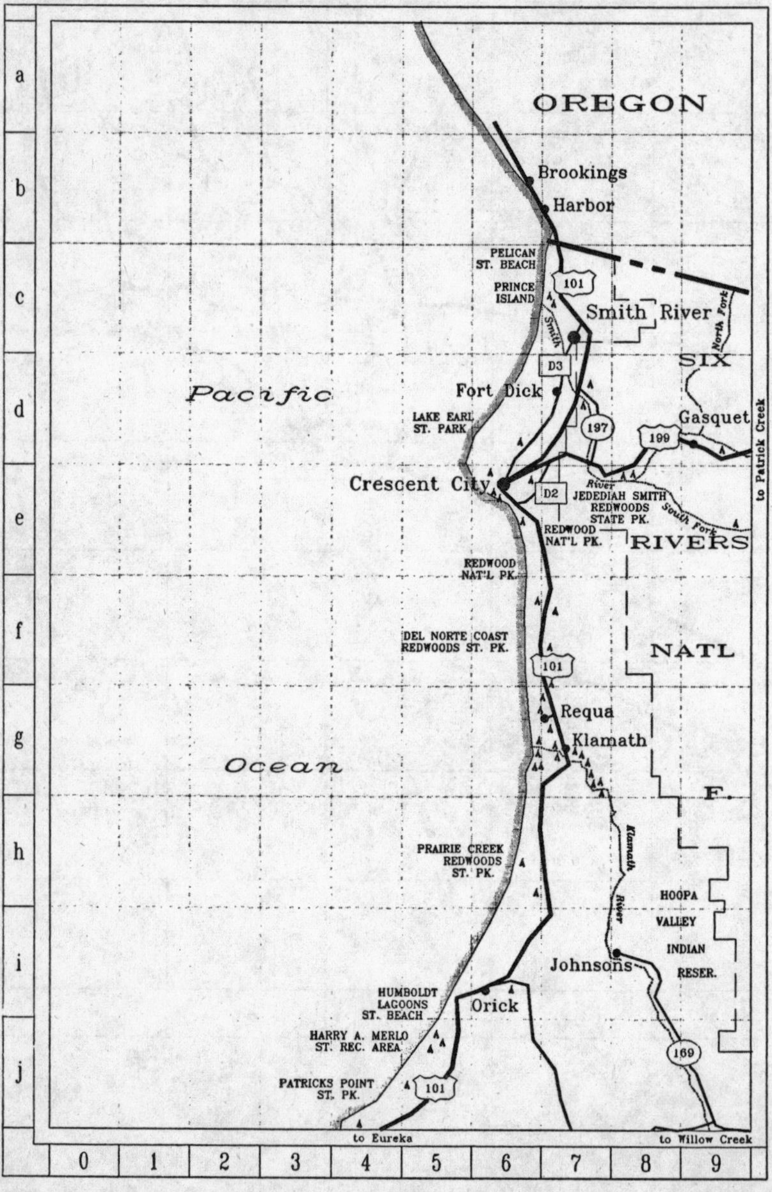

OREGON
Brookings
Harbor
PELICAN ST. BEACH
PRINCE ISLAND
101
Smith River
Smith
North Fork
SIX
D3
Fort Dick
Pacific
LAKE EARL ST. PARK
197
199
Gasquet
to Patrick Creek
Crescent City
D2
River
JEDEDIAH SMITH REDWOODS STATE PK.
South Fork
REDWOOD NAT'L PK.
RIVERS
REDWOOD NAT'L PK.
DEL NORTE COAST REDWOODS ST. PK.
NATL
101
Requa
Klamath
Ocean
F.
Klamath
PRAIRIE CREEK REDWOODS ST. PK.
River
HOOPA VALLEY INDIAN RESER.
Johnsons
HUMBOLDT LAGOONS ST. BEACH
Orick
HARRY A. MERLO ST. REC. AREA
169
PATRICKS POINT ST. PK.
101
to Eureka
to Willow Creek

a b c d e f g h i j

0 1 2 3 4 5 6 7 8 9

SALMON HARBOR RESORT
on Smith River

Map grid c7

Campsites, facilities: There are 98 campsites for tents or motor homes, 88 with full hookups and cable TV. Picnic tables, fire grills, flush toilets, showers, boat rentals, and a recreation room are provided. A laundromat, ice, gas, and a bait and tackle shop are available nearby.

Reservations, fee: Reservations accepted; $14 fee per night.

Who to contact: Phone (707)487-3341.

Location: From the town of Smith River, drive three miles north on US 101 to the mouth of the Smith River. Located at 200 Salmon Harbor Road, Smith River.

Trip note: This is a good layover spot for motor home cruisers stuck near the Oregon border. It is actually a motor home parking area with hookups, set within a mobile home park. Located at the mouth of the Smith River, it overlooks the ocean. Enjoy fishing, beachcombing, and driftwood and agate hunting.

SHIP ASHORE RV PARK
on Smith River

Map grid c7

Campsites, facilities: There are 212 motor home sites, most with full hookups, and a separate area for tents. Patios, tables, flush toilets, showers, a whirlpool, a recreation room, and a boat dock and ramp are provided. A laundromat, LP gas, marine gas, groceries, and boat rentals are available.

Reservations, fee: Reservations accepted; $14 fee per night.

Who to contact: Phone (707)487-3141.

Location: From the town of Smith River, drive three miles north on US 101.

Trip note: This is a famous spot for Smith River fishermen, where the tales get taller as the evening gets late. The park is set on five acres of land adjacent to the lower Smith River. The salmon and steelhead seem to come in one size here, giant, but they can be as elusive as Bigfoot. If you want to hear how big, just check into the Ship Ashore Restaurant any fall evening.

LAKE EARL AND TALAWA STATE PARK

Map grid d6

Campsites, facilities: There are six primitive campsites. There is **no piped water,** but picnic tables, fire rings, food lockers, and composting toilets are provided.

Reservations, fee: No reservations necessary; $7 fee per night; register at either Del Norte or Jedediah Smith State Parks and pick up the park and campground information sheet.

Who to contact: Write to Camp Lincoln at 4241 Kings Valley Road, Crescent City, CA 95531, or call (707)464-9533.

Location: From Crescent City, drive half a mile north on US 101. Turn northwest on Northcrest-Lake Earl Drive. For trail and walk-in beach access, turn west on Old Mill Road and Sand Hill Road. For the boat launch, go northwest on Lake View Road. For primitive campsites and beach access, drive west on Moorhead Road, or north on Lower Lake Road, or west on Kellogg Road. For beach access, picnicking, and bird watching, drive north on Lower Lake Road to Palo Road.

Trip note: Now don't get all panicky at the long set of directions. Once here, it's not so difficult. Lakes Earl and Talawa offer 7.5 miles of ocean frontage, more than a mile of Smith River frontage, 15 miles of horseback riding, and numerous hiking trails. Boating and fishing are available. Guided walks are offered on a regular basis during July and August. For informal walks call ahead.

Map grid **d7**

RAMBLIN' ROSE RESORT

on Smith River

Campsites, facilities: There are 110 motor home spaces, most with full hookups. Rest rooms, showers, picnic tables, and a recreation hall are provided. A gift store, groceries, ice, a laundromat, a sanitary disposal station, and firewood are also available.

Reservations, fee: Reservations accepted; $13-16 fee per night.

Who to contact: Call (707)487-4831.

Location: From the junction of US 101 and US 199, travel six miles north on US 101 to the campground. Located at 6701 US 101 North, Crescent City.

Trip note: For a motor home park, this one offers quite a bit—the Smith River to the north, the beach to the immediate west, and Six Rivers National Forest to the east.

Map grid **d7**

CRESCENT CITY REDWOODS KOA

on Smith River

Campsites, facilities: There are 44 tent spaces and 50 campsites for motor homes with full hookups. A sanitary disposal station, flush toilets, showers, picnic tables, a laundromat, fireplaces, and a playground are provided. LP gas, groceries, ice, and wood are also available. Pets are allowed.

Reservations, fee: Reservations accepted; $14-$17 per night.

Who to contact: Call (707)464-5744.

Location: From the junction of US 101 and US 199, drive one mile north to the campground.

Trip note: This is a good base camp for motor home cruisers who discover that Jedediah Smith Redwoods State Park is full up, as is par for the course during summer months. This campground is one mile from Redwood National Park and four miles from both the ocean and Smith River. There are many side trip possibilities: hiking in the redwoods, fishing in the ocean during summer and on the Smith River during winter, beachcombing, and golf.

Map grid **d9**

PANTHER FLAT

on Smith River

SIX RIVERS NATIONAL FOREST

Campsites, facilities: There are 42 campsites for tent, trailer and motor homes, some up to 22 feet long. Piped water, vault toilets, fireplaces, and picnic tables are provided. Propane gas, groceries, and a laundromat are available nearby. One campsite is wheelchair accessible. Pets are permitted on leashes or otherwise controlled.

Reservations, fee: No reservations; $6 use fee for spring and summer, $4 at other times with reduced services.

Who to contact: Write to Gasquet Ranger Station at P.O. Box 228, Gasquet, CA. 95543 or call (707)457-3131.

Location: From Gasquet, drive 2.5 miles east on US 199.

Trip note: This is an ideal alternative to the often crowded Jedediah Smith State Park. The park provides easy road access since it is set right along Highway 299, as well as the Smith River. The Redwood National Park is a short drive

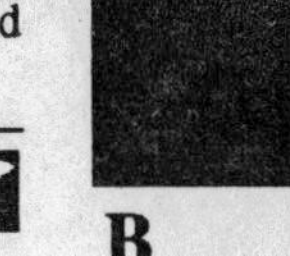

to the west. The Siskiyou Wilderness is a short drive to the southeast via Forest Roads, detailed on Forest Service maps. The wild and scenic Smith River system provides swimming, sunbathing and beautiful scenery, and in fall and winter, fishing for salmon and steelhead. The camp is open year-round.

Map grid **e6**

SUNSET HARBOR RV PARK

in Crescent City

B

Campsites, facilities: There are 70 motor home spaces with full hookups. Picnic tables, flush toilets, and showers are provided. A laundromat, grocery store and recreation room are available.

Reservations, fee: Reservations accepted; $14 per night.

Who to contact: Phone (707)464-3423.

C

Location: In Crescent City, from the intersection of King Street and US 101, drive one block east on King Street.

Trip note: You get easy access and many prime side trips in the immediate area. The ocean is a few minutes drive to the west; there are dramatic ocean views on the northwest side of town. Other possibilities are Smith River, Lake Earl, and Jedediah Smith Redwoods State Park, among others. Open year-round.

D

Map grid **e6**

NACO WEST SHORELINE CAMPGROUND

in Crescent City

E

Campsites, facilities: There are 242 campsites for tents or motor homes, 192 with hookups for electricity, water, and sewage. Piped water, picnic tables, flush toilets, and showers are provided. A laundromat and LP gas are available. The facilities are wheelchair accessible.

Reservations, fee: Reservations accepted; $11-$16 per night.

Who to contact: Phone (707)464-2473.

F

Location: In Crescent City, turn west off US 101 onto Sunset Circle. Drive one block to the campground.

Trip note: This year-round park is set up primarily for motor homes. There are many excellent side trips available in the area. Smith River, Lake Earl, Jedediah Smith Redwoods State Park, and Six Rivers National Forest are all within ten miles. And, of course, you've got the Pacific Ocean sitting about a mile away, with some remarkable beaches on the northwest side of Crescent City.

G

Map grid **e6**

HARBOR RV ANCHORAGE

in Crescent City

H

Campsites, facilities: There are 169 motor home spaces with full hookups. Picnic tables, flush toilets, showers, and a sanitary disposal station are provided. A laundromat is available. Cable T.V. is also available.

Reservations, fee: Reservations accepted; $13 per night.

Who to contact: Phone (707)464-1724.

I

Location: In Crescent City at the south end, turn west off US 101 onto Anchor Way. Turn north on Starfish Way and drive to the campground.

Trip note: This is a privately operated motor home park that overlooks the Pacific Ocean. There's good beachcombing year-round. Smith River, Jedediah Smith Redwoods State Park, and Six Rivers National Forest are all within ten miles.

J

Map grid **e6**

BAYSIDE RV PARK
in Crescent City

Campsites, facilities: There are 131 motor home spaces with full hookups. Picnic tables, patios, flush toilets, and showers are provided. A laundromat is available.

Reservations, fee: Reservations accepted; $15 per night.

Who to contact: Phone (707)464-9482.

Location: This site is located at the intersection of US 101 and Citizen Dock Road in Crescent City.

Trip note: This is a good layover for US 101 motor home cruisers. Side trips within ten miles include Smith River, Lake Earl, Jedediah Smith Redwoods State Park, and Six Rivers National Forest.

Map grid **e6**

VILLAGE CAMPER INN
in Crescent City

Campsites, facilities: There are 170 motor home spaces, most with full hookups, and a separate area for tents. Picnic tables, a sanitary disposal station, flush toilets and showers are provided. A laundromat and cable TV hookups are available.

Reservations, fee: Reservations accepted; $13-$15 per night.

Who to contact: Call (707)464-3544.

Location: In Crescent City, if you're coming from the north on US 101, take Washington Boulevard to Parkway Drive. If you're coming from the south on US 101, take a right on Parkway Drive. The park is located at 1543 Parkway Drive, Crescent City.

Trip note: The privately-operated motor home park is set on 20 acres of land near some spectacular beaches. Prime beachcombing for agates or driftwood.

Map grid **e8**

HIOUCHI HAMLET RV RESORT
near Smith River

Campsites, facilities: There are 120 campsites for tents or motor homes, most with full hookups. Flush toilets, showers, and a sanitary disposal station are provided. A laundromat, LP gas, groceries, and a golf course are available nearby. The facilities are wheelchair accessible. Pets are permitted.

Reservations, fee: Reservations accepted; $15.50 per night.

Who to contact: Call (707)458-3321.

Location: From Crescent City, drive five miles north on US 101 to Highway 199. Take Highway 199 for four miles. Follow the signs to Jedediah Smith State Park (this campground is located on the border).

Trip note: The folks that run this outfit are among the nicest you'll ever find, and hey, the fried chicken at the Hamlet is always good for a quick hit. The park is out of the wind and fog you get on the coast, and set, instead, in the heart of the forest country. It makes a good base camp for a steelhead trip in winter.

Map grid **e8**

JEDEDIAH SMITH REDWOODS STATE PARK

Campsites, facilities: There are 108 campsites for tents or motor homes up to 30 feet long. Piped water, flush toilets, showers, picnic tables, fireplaces, and a sanitary disposal station are provided. Propane gas, groceries, and a laundromat are nearby. Some facilities are wheelchair accessible. Pets are allowed.

Reservations, fee: Reserve through MISTIX by phoning (800)444-PARK ($3.95 fee); campsite fee is $12-$14.

Who to contact: Phone (707)458-3310 or (707)464-9533.

Location: From Crescent City, drive nine miles east on US 199. Or from Smith River, drive three miles south on US 101 to Highway 197. Drive seven miles south to US 199 and the park.

Trip note: This is a beautiful redwood park set along the Smith River, where you can get direct river access for fishing or a put-in spot for a drift boat, canoe or raft. The fishing is best for steelhead from mid-January through March. In summer, guided walks are available. An excellent side trip is driving along Howland Hill Road, a narrow, scenic, unpaved alternate route, through redwood forest to Crescent City. Howland Hill Road gives you access to Stout Grove and hiking trails; trailers are not recommended. Walker Road is an unpaved scenic road through redwood forest that provides access to the Smith River and short hiking trails.

Map grid e9

BIG FLAT

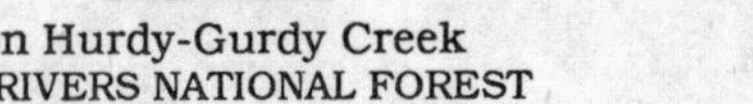

on Hurdy-Gurdy Creek

SIX RIVERS NATIONAL FOREST

5% CLUB

Campsites, facilities: There are 16 tent spaces and 14 campsites for tents or motor homes up to 22 feet long. Vault toilets, picnic tables, and fireplaces are provided. There is no water, so bring your own. Pets are permitted on leashes or otherwise controlled.

Reservations, fee: No reservations; $3-$6 fee spring/summer, depending on services available.

Who to contact: Write to Six Rivers National Forest Headquarters at 500 5th Street, Eureka, CA 95501, or call (707)442-1721.

Location: From Hiouchi on US 199, turn south onto South Fork Road and drive 15 miles to the campground.

Trip note: This camp is far enough off the highway (yet without leaving pavement) to get missed by most folks. Yet it provides an ideal setting for the few who know of it. It is set along Hurdy-Gurdy Creek, near where the creek enters the South Fork of the Smith River. It provides nearby access to old Kelsey Trail, an outstanding backpacking route. From January through March, it's an ideal base camp for a steelhead fishing trip. In the summer, it is a good layover spot for rafters or kayakers paddling the South Fork Smith River. Open year-round with limited services (like just about nothing) in the fall and winter.

Map grid f6

NICKEL CREEK

REDWOOD NATIONAL PARK

5% CLUB

Campsites, facilities: There are five tent spaces. There is **no piped water**, but picnic tables, fireplaces, and composting toilets are provided. Pets are permitted on leashes or otherwise controlled.

Reservations, fee: No reservations, no fee.

Who to contact: Write to Redwood National Park Headquarters at 1111 Second Street, Crescent City, CA 95531, or call (707)464-6101.

Location: From Crescent City, drive south for two miles on US 101. Turn onto the road to Enderts Beach and hike in one-half mile to the campground.

Trip note: This is an ideal spot for beach campers who don't actually like to set up shop on the beach and get sand in the food. This camp is set about 100 yards from the beach, perched on a grassy area on a hill overlooking the ocean. During summer months, two-hour guided tide pool and seashore walks are available. Open year-round.

Map grid **f7**

CAMP MARIGOLD MOTEL AND TRAILER PARK

on Klamath River

Campsites, facilities: There are 40 motor home spaces with full hookups and a separate area for tents. Piped water, flush toilets, showers, picnic tables, and fireplaces are provided. A laundromat is available.

Reservations, fee: Reservations accepted; $10 per night.

Who to contact: Phone (707)482-3585.

Location: From Klamath, drive 3.5 miles north of town on US 101.

Trip note: One of several motor home parks in the area, this one is popular both as a layover for folks cruising US 101 and as a base camp for fishermen during the fall salmon run on the Klamath River. Open year-round.

Map grid **f7**

DE MARTIN

REDWOOD NATIONAL PARK

Campsites, facilities: There are ten tent spaces here. Piped water, composting toilets, and caches for food storage are provided. Pets are permitted on leashes.

Reservations, fee: No reservations, no fee.

Who to contact: Write to 1111 Second Street, Crescent City, CA 95531, or call (707)464-6101.

Location: From Crescent City, drive south for approximately 18 miles on US 101. Turn east at Wilson Creek Road and hike into the campground.

Trip note: This campground is located in a grassy, prairie area overlooking the ocean along the De Martin section of the Pacific Coastal Trail. The camp, a little known spot, is located beside Wilson Creek. Open year-round.

Map grid **f7**

MILL CREEK

DEL NORTE REDWOODS STATE PARK

Campsites, facilities: There are 38 tent spaces and 107 campsites for tents or motor homes up to 31 feet long. Piped water, a sanitary disposal station, flush toilets, showers, fireplaces, and picnic tables are provided. Pets are allowed.

Reservations, fee: Reserve by phoning MISTIX at (800)444-PARK ($3.95 fee); $12-$14 camp use fee.

Who to contact: Call Del Norte Redwoods State Park at (707)464-9533.

Location: From Crescent City, drive nine miles south on US 101.

Trip note: Groves of redwoods thrive in this nurturing coastal climate and several creeks criss-cross the area. Nurturing, in this case, means rain like you wouldn't believe in the winter and lots of fog in the summer. Evening ranger programs are conducted here. Open from April to October.

Map grid **g6**

RIVERWOODS CAMPGROUND

on Klamath River

Campsites, facilities: There are 74 motor home spaces, many with full hookups, and a separate area for tents. Piped water, picnic tables, fire grills, flush toilets, showers, and a sanitary disposal station are provided. Ice and wood are available.

Reservations, fee: Reservations accepted; $9-$13 per night.
Who to contact: Phone (707)482-5591.
Location: From the junction of US 101 and Highway 169 in Klamath, drive one mile south on US 101. Turn west on Klamath Beach Road and drive two miles to the campground.
Trip note: This motor home park provides direct access to the Klamath River. The prime time for salmon is from mid-August through September. Open from April to mid-October.

Map grid **g6**

FLINT RIDGE
Hike-In
REDWOOD NATIONAL PARK

5% CLUB

Campsites, facilities: There are ten tent spaces. Piped water and composting toilets are provided. Pets are permitted on leashes.
Reservations, fee: No reservations, no fee.
Who to contact: Write to Redwood National Park Headquarters at 1111 Second Street, Crescent City, CA 95531, or call (707)464-6101.
Location: From Klamath, take Coastal Drive out of town. Park at Douglas Bridge or 2.5 miles from Douglas Bridge on Coastal Drive just beyond the Pacific Coastal Trail sign. Hike into the campground.
Trip note: This little-known camp is located in a grassy area overlooking the ocean, along the Flint Ridge section of the Pacific Coastal Trail. Oh yeah? Read on: The Pacific Coastal Trail leads from the campground and picks up again on the north bank of the Klamath River at the end of Requa Road, a good site for whale watching. Another hike leads south from Flint Ridge on the Pacific Coastal Trail into the heart of Redwood National Park, where the trail ends at Tall Trees Grove. The approximate distance from Flint Ridge to Tall Trees Grove is 18 miles with Gold Bluffs Campground at the halfway point.

Map grid **g6**

DEL'S CAMP
on Klamath River

Campsites, facilities: There are 73 motor home spaces, many with full hookups, and a separate area for tents. Picnic tables, fire grills, piped water, flush toilets, and showers are provided. Boat rentals and a dock are available.
Reservations, fee: Reservations accepted; $10-$12 fee per night.
Who to contact: Phone (707)482-4922.
Location: From the junction of Highway 169 and US 101 in Klamath, drive 2.5 miles north on US 101. Turn west on Requa Road and drive one-half mile to the campground.
Trip note: Open from May 15 to October 30. The most popular season is from mid-August through September, when the salmon are running on the Klamath River and the weather is best.

Map grid **g6**

DAD'S CAMP
on Klamath River

Campsites, facilities: There are 100 campsites for tents or motor homes, 30 with hookups for water and electricity. Piped water, flush toilets, showers, vault toilets, a sanitary disposal station, and picnic tables are provided. Ice, boat rentals, a dock, and a gift store are available.
Reservations, fee: Reservations accepted; $8-$10 per night.

Who to contact: Phone (707)482-3415.

Location: From the junction of US 101 and Highway 169 in Klamath, drive one mile south on 101. Turn west on Klamath Beach Road and drive 3. 5 miles to the campground.

Trip note: This spot is located right at the mouth of the Klamath River (on the southern side of the river). That provides unique options; you get your choice of exploring beach or river. Open May through September.

Map grid g6

KLAMATH COVE RV PARK
on Klamath River

Campsites, facilities: There are 74 motor home spaces with full hookups. Picnic tables, piped water, flush toilets, showers, laundry room, and a recreation room are provided. A boat ramp and a boat dock are available. Pets are allowed.

Reservations, fee: Reservations accepted; $14 per night.

Who to contact: Phone (707)482-3305.

Location: From the junction of US 101 and Highway 169 in Klamath, drive one mile south on US 101. Turn west on Klamath Beach Road and drive about 3.2 miles to the park.

Trip note: With all the motor home parks on California's north coast, you'd think there'd be no shortage of spots. Guess again. When the salmon start moving through the mouth of the Klamath River starting in mid-August, you should feel fortunate you have a spot.

Map grid g7

CRIVELLIS TRAILER PARK
on Klamath River

Campsites, facilities: There are 31 motor home spaces with full hookups. Flush toilets and showers are provided. A laundromat is available.

Reservations, fee: Reservations accepted; $12 per night. Seasonal leases available.

Who to contact: Phone (707)482-3713.

Location: From the junction of US 101 and Highway 169 in Klamath, drive 2.5 miles east on Highway 169.

Trip note: This motor home park is adjacent to a motel, with the Klamath River nearby. It's a good base camp for a salmon fishing trip during the fall run. A cafe and lounge are available. Open year-round.

Map grid g7

STEELHEAD LODGE
on Klamath River

Campsites, facilities: There are 51 motor home spaces with full hookups (ten with drive-through sites). Picnic tables, flush toilets and showers are provided. Ice is available. A bar, restaurant and motel are also available.

Reservations, fee: Reservations accepted; $12 per night.

Who to contact: Phone (707)482-8145.

Location: From the junction of US 101 and Highway 169 in Klamath, drive about 3.2 miles east on Highway 169. Turn south on Terwer Riffle Road and drive one block to the lodge.

Trip note: Many anglers use this park as headquarters when the salmon and steelhead get going in August. The park has grassy sites near the Klamath River. The lodge usually provides good fishing reports by telephone. Open year-round.

A0 B C D E F G H I J

REDWOOD REST
Map grid **g7**

on Klamath River

Campsites, facilities: There are 100 motor home spaces with full or partial hookups (ten with drive-through sites). Picnic tables, flush toilets, and showers are provided. Wood is available.

Reservations, fee: Reservations accepted; $10-$14 per night.

Who to contact: Phone (707)482-5033.

Location: From the junction of US 101 and Highway 169 in Klamath, drive about 3.2 miles east on Highway 169 to the park.

Trip note: This is a privately-operated motor home park set near the Klamath River. Reservations are advised during summer and a necessity when salmon fishing picks up in mid-August. Open from May through October.

TERWER PARK
Map grid **g7**

on Klamath River

Campsites, facilities: There are 98 motor home spaces with full hookups. Picnic tables, flush toilets, showers, and a swimming pool are provided. LP gas, ice, a laundromat, boat rentals, and a dock are available.

Reservations, fee: Reservations accepted; $15 per night.

Who to contact: Phone (707)482-3855.

Location: From the junction of US 101 and Highway 169 in Klamath, drive about 3.2 miles east on Highway 169. Turn south on Terwer Riffle Road and drive one-half mile to the park.

Trip note: This motor home park is situated near the Terwer Riffle, one of the better shore-fishing spots for steelhead and salmon on the lower Klamath River. You get grassy sites, river access, and some trails. Open year-round.

MYSTIC FOREST RV PARK
Map grid **g7**

on Klamath River

Campsites, facilities: There are 40 motor homes spaces, many with full hookups (15 have drive-through sites), and a separate area for tents. Picnic tables, fire rings, piped water, flush toilets, showers, and a playground are provided. A laundromat and wood are available.

Reservations, fee: Reservations accepted; $13 per night.

Who to contact: Phone (707)482-4901.

Location: From the junction of US 101 and Highway 169 in Klamath, drive about 3.2 miles north on US 101.

Trip note: This is a well-known, privately-operated motor home park with easy access from US 101. Side trips include the nearby lower Klamath River and numerous hiking trails. Open from mid-May through mid-October.

BLACKBERRY PATCH
Map grid **g7**

on Klamath River

Campsites, facilities: There are 35 motor homes spaces with full hookups in this adults-only motor home park. Flush toilets, showers, and picnic tables are provided. A laundromat is available.

Reservations, fee: Reservations accepted; $12 fee per night.

Who to contact: Phone (707)482-4782.

Location: From the junction of US 101 and Highway 169 in Klamath, drive about

3.2 miles east and south on Highway 169 (Terwer Valley Road). Turn west on Terwer Riffle Road and drive one-quarter mile.

Trip note: "Adults-only" and nothing else need be said.

Map grid g7

CAMPER CORRAL
on Klamath River

Campsites, facilities: There are 140 sites for tents or motor homes, many with full hookups. Flush toilets, showers, picnic tables, fireplaces, a recreation hall, and a playground are provided. A sanitary disposal station, LP gas, a laundromat, cable TV, ice, and a bait and tackle shop are available.

Reservations, fee: Reservations accepted; $10-$16 per night.

Who to contact: Phone (707)482-5741.

Location: From the north end of the Klamath River bridge, take the Terwer Valley Road exit on US 101. Drive west one-eighth of a mile to the campground.

Trip note: This resort has 3,000 feet of Klamath River frontage, grassy tent sites, berry picking, the ocean nearby, and hiking trails. And of course, in the fall it has salmon, the main attraction on the lower Klamath.

Map grid g7

KING SALMON RESORT
on Klamath River

Campsites, facilities: There are 70 motor home spaces, many with full hookups, and a separate area for tents. Piped water and flush toilets are provided. Showers, a laundromat, cable TV, and a dock are available.

Reservations, fee: Reservations accepted; $10-$15 per night.

Who to contact: Phone (707)482-4151.

Location: From the junction of US 101 and Highway 169 in Klamath, drive one-half mile west on Highway 169.

Trip note: This is one heck of a popular spot during the salmon run. Reservations are a must when the fishing is good (from mid-August through September).

Map grid g7

KAMP KLAMATH
on Klamath River

Campsites, facilities: There are 109 motor home spaces with full hookups. Picnic tables, fire grills, flush toilets, showers, and a recreation room are provided. Ice, a laundromat, cable TV, boat rentals, and a boat dock are available.

Reservations, fee: Reservations accepted; $10-$13 per night.

Who to contact: Write to Kamp Klamath at Box 128, Klamath, CA 95548, or call (707)482-3405.

Location: From Klamath, drive 1.5 miles north on US 101.

Trip note: This camp is level and grassy with many sites along the Klamath River, which is famous for fall salmon fishing. A bonus here is the hot tub. Open year-round (so is the camp).

Map grid g7

CHINOOK RV RESORT
on Klamath River

Campsites, facilities: There are 72 motor home spaces with full hookups. Picnic tables, fire grills, flush toilets, showers, a playground, a laundromat, and a recreation room are provided. LP gas, groceries, RV supplies, marine gas, a boat ramp, and a tackle shop are available. Pets are allowed.

Reservations, fee: Reservations accepted; $14 per night.

Who to contact: Phone (707)482-3511.
Location: From the Klamath River bridge, drive one mile north on US 101.
Trip note: Grassy RV spaces overlook the Klamath River, famous for its salmon fishing from mid-August through September. It's a pretty spot. During the prime fishing season, be sure to have a reservation.

Map grid g7

RIVERSIDE RV PARK
on Klamath River

Campsites, facilities: There are 92 motor home spaces with full hookups (30 with drive-through sites). Flush toilets, showers, and a recreation room are provided. Boat rentals and a dock are available.
Reservations, fee: Reservations accepted; $12 per night.
Who to contact: Phone (707)482-2523.
Location: From the junction of Highways 101 and 169 in Klamath, drive 1.5 miles north on US 101 to the campground.
Trip note: This is an option for motor home cruisers looking for a layover spot on a US 101 tour or a base of operations for a Klamath River fishing trip. There's good salmon fishing during the fall run on the Klamath River. Open from mid-April through October.

Map grid h6

ELK PRAIRIE
PRAIRIE CREEK REDWOODS STATE PARK

Campsites, facilities: There are 75 sites for tents or motor homes up to 27 feet long. Piped water, flush toilets, showers, picnic tables, and fireplaces are provided. The facilities are wheelchair accessible.
Reservations, fee: Reservations advised through MISTIX at (800)444-7275 ($3.95 MISTIX fee); campsite fee is $12-$14 per night; pets $1.
Who to contact: Call Prairie Creek Redwoods State Park at (707)488-2171 or (707)445-6547.
Location: From Orick, drive six miles north on US 101.
Trip note: In this remarkable park, herds of Roosevelt elk wander free. Great photograph opportunities abound, often right beside the highway. How often do you ever see a giant animal this close? For most people, the answer is never, except at a zoo. There's good hiking in the park and a scenic drive through the redwoods on unpaved Barrel Road.

Map grid h6

GOLD BLUFF BEACH
PRAIRIE CREEK REDWOODS STATE PARK

Campsites, facilities: There are 27 primitive campsites for tents or motor homes up to 20 feet long (no trailers or vehicles wider than seven feet). Piped water, flush toilets, solar showers, fireplaces, and tables are provided.
Reservations, fee: No reservations; $7-$9 fee per night; pets $1.
Who to contact: Call Prairie Creek Redwoods State Park at (707)488- 2171 or (707)445-6547.
Location: From Orick, drive three miles north on US 101. Turn west on Davison Road and drive four miles to the campground. Note: No trailers are allowed on Davison Road, which is narrow and unpaved.
Trip note: The campsites are in a sandy area with man-made windbreaks. Fern Canyon Trail, one of the best hikes in California, is located at the end of Davison Road. Hikers walk along a stream in a narrow canyon with vertical walls

covered with magnificent ferns. There are some herds of elk in the area. Open year-round. There's heavy rain in winter.

Map grid i6 ORICK RV AND MOBILE HOME PARK

in Orick

Campsites, facilities: There are 20 mobile home and 20 RV spaces with full or partial hookups. Cable TV hookups and rest rooms with showers are provided. A laundromat, LP gas, and propane are available.

Reservations, fee: Reservation accepted; $10 fee per night.

Who to contact: Phone (707)488-3501.

Location: The park is located in Orick at the north end of town on US 101.

Trip note: This is a layover for motor home drivers cruising on the Redwood Highway. It is actually an RV park within a mobile home park. Nearby Redwood Creek, also at the north end of town, provides a chance to catch steelhead from shore in the winter months.

Map grid j4 PATRICK'S POINT STATE PARK

Campsites, facilities: There are 123 campsites for tents or motor homes up to 31 feet long. Piped water, flush toilets, showers, fireplaces, and picnic tables are provided. The facilities are wheelchair accessible. Pets are permitted.

Reservations, fee: Reservations advised and available through MISTIX by phoning (800)444-7275 ($3.95 MISTIX fee); $12-$14 per night; $1 for pets.

Who to contact: Phone Patrick's Point State Park at (707)677-3570.

Location: From Trinidad, drive five miles north on US 101.

Trip note: The unique trails that probe through fern vegetation tunnels are a highlight, along with beach lookouts and common whale sightings. It's often foggy and damp, but always beautiful. In summer, count on needing reservations.

Map grid j5 STONE LAGOONS BOAT-IN

HUMBOLDT LAGOONS STATE PARK

Campsites, facilities: A primitive camp accessible by boat with six primitive tent sites. There is **no piped water**, but pit toilets, picnic tables, and fire rings are provided. No pets are allowed.

Reservations, fee: No reservations; $7-$9 fee per night.

Who to contact: Call Prairie Creek Redwoods State Park at (707)488-2171 or (707)445-6547.

Location: From the Redwood Information Center on US 101 (south of Orick), drive about three miles south on US 101 to the parking lot entrance (at mile post 115.4). The boat ramp is there, and the campground area is three-quarters of a mile away, across the lagoon. The campsites are dispersed about 300 yards from the landing area.

Trip note: This is an ideal spot for canoeists that virtually nobody knows about. The water is usually calm in the morning, but often gets choppy from afternoon winds. Translation: Get your paddling done early on Stone Lagoon. Open year-round.

Map grid **j5**

STONE LAGOON

HUMBOLDT LAGOONS STATE PARK

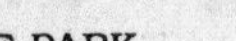

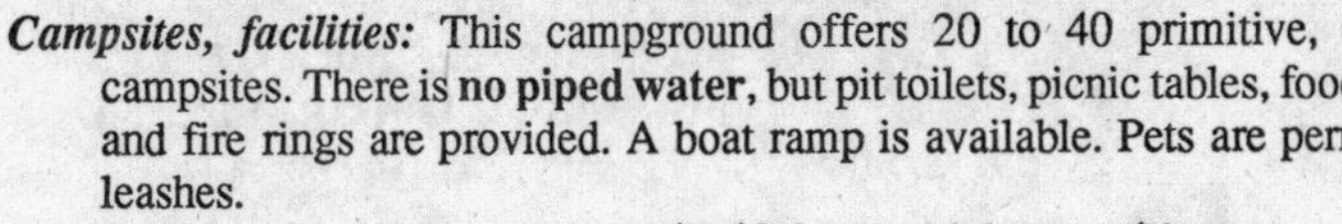

Campsites, facilities: This campground offers 20 to 40 primitive, dispersed campsites. There is **no piped water**, but pit toilets, picnic tables, food lockers, and fire rings are provided. A boat ramp is available. Pets are permitted on leashes.

Reservations, fee: No reservations; $7-$9 fee per night; pets $1.

Who to contact: Call Prairie Creek Redwoods State Park at (707)488-2171 or (707)445-6547.

Location: From the Redwood Information Center on US 101 (south of Orick), drive about 1.5 miles south on US 101 to the campground entrance at the north end of Stone Lagoon.

Trip note: This is a good spot for campers with boats. Several campsites are available along the road in; it's a take-your-pick deal. A boat ramp is available on the lagoon. It's often foggy in summer.

Map grid **j5**

DRY LAGOON

HUMBOLDT LAGOONS STATE PARK

Campsites, facilities: There are six primitive tent sites. There is **no piped water**, but pit toilets, fire rings, and picnic tables are provided. No pets are allowed.

Reservations, fee: No reservations; $7-$9 fee per night.

Who to contact: Call Prairie Creek Redwoods State Park at (707)488-2171 or (707)445-6547.

Location: From Trinidad, drive about 13 miles north on US 101 to the parking entrance at milepost 114.5.

Trip note: This is a walk-in camp, that is, you need to walk about 200 yards from the parking area to reach the campsites. Right there, this makes it a dream for members of the Five Percent Club, because most tourists are unwilling to walk at all. It is a beautiful campground set in the woods, with ocean views and beach access.

Map grid **j5**

BIG LAGOON COUNTY PARK

overlooking Pacific Ocean

Campsites, facilities: There are 22 sites for tents or motor homes. Piped water, toilets, fireplaces, and picnic tables are provided. A boat ramp is available. Pets are permitted.

Reservations, fee: No reservations; $7 fee per night; pets $1.

Who to contact: Phone Big Lagoon County Park at (707)445-7652.

Location: From Trinidad, drive seven miles north on US 101.

Trip note: This is a remarkable, huge lagoon that borders the Pacific Ocean. It provides good boating, fishing, exploring, and in winter, duck hunting. It's a good spot to paddle a canoe around on a calm day. Open year-round.

MAP A1

BEACH
TREES
5% CLUB
DESERT
URBAN
FOOTHILL
GRASSLAND

15 MILES

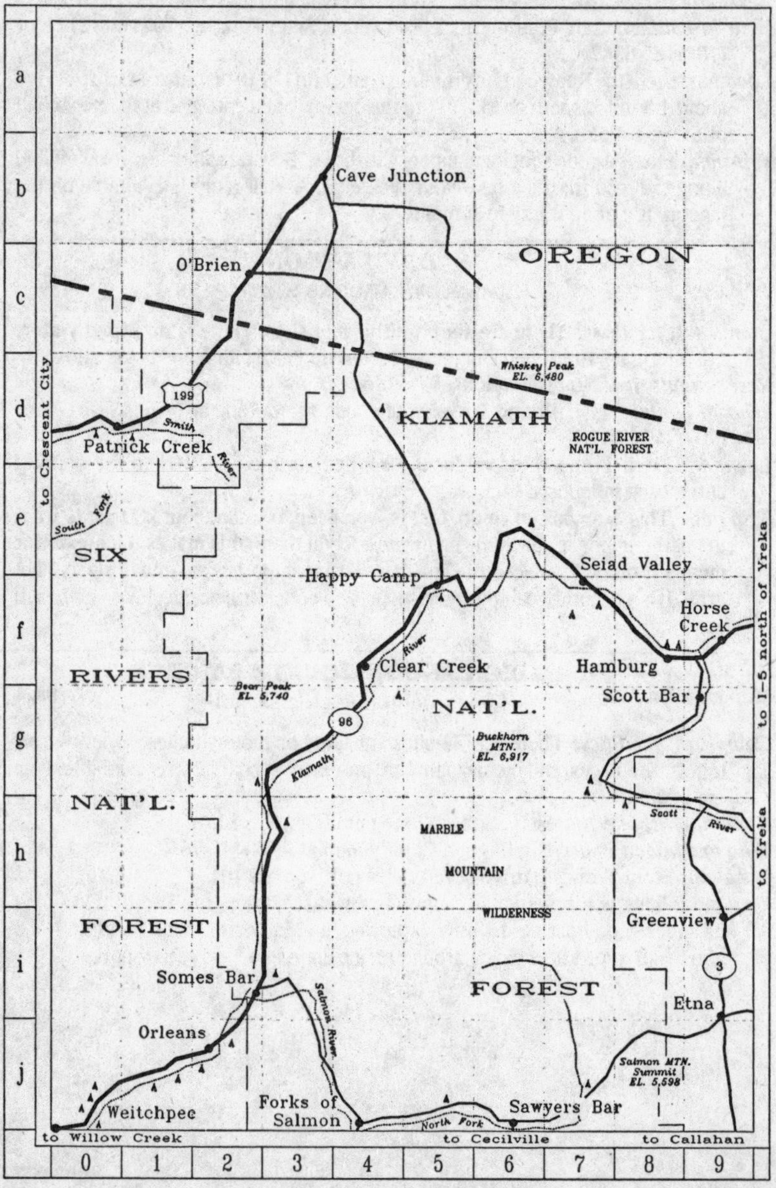

a
b
c
d
e
f
g
h
i
j

0 1 2 3 4 5 6 7 8 9

Cave Junction
O'Brien
OREGON
199
Whiskey Peak
EL. 6,480
KLAMATH
ROGUE RIVER
NAT'L. FOREST
Patrick Creek
Smith
River
to Crescent City
South Fork
SIX
Happy Camp
Seiad Valley
Horse Creek
River
Clear Creek
Hamburg
RIVERS
Bear Peak
EL. 5,740
NAT'L.
Scott Bar
96
Buckhorn
MTN.
EL. 6,917
Klamath
NAT'L.
Scott
River
MARBLE
MOUNTAIN
WILDERNESS
to 1-5 north of Yreka
to Yreka
FOREST
Greenview
3
Somes Bar
Salmon River
FOREST
Etna
Orleans
Salmon MTN.
Summit
EL. 5,598
Forks of Salmon
Sawyers Bar
Weitchpec
North Fork
to Willow Creek
to Cecilville
to Callahan

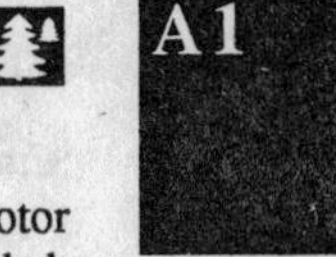

Map grid **d0**

GRASSY FLAT

on Smith River

SIX RIVERS NATIONAL FOREST

Campsites, facilities: There are eight tent spaces and 11 campsites for tents or motor homes. Piped water, vault toilets, fireplaces, and picnic tables are provided. Propane gas, groceries, and a laundromat are available nearby. The facilities are wheelchair accessible. Pets are permitted on leashes or otherwise controlled.

Reservations, fee: No reservations; $5 fee per night.

Who to contact: Write to Six Rivers National Forest Headquarters at 500 5th Street, Eureka, CA 95501, or call (707)442-1721.

Location: From Gasquet, drive five miles east on US 199.

Trip note: This is one in a series of easy-to-reach, Forest Service camps set along the beautiful Smith River. It's a classic wild river, popular in the summer for kayakers, and the steelhead come huge in the winter for the crafty few. Open from May through mid-September.

B

C

Map grid **d1**

PATRICK CREEK

SIX RIVERS NATIONAL FOREST

Campsites, facilities: There are five tent spaces and 12 campsites for tents and motor homes. Piped water, flush toilets, picnic tables, and fireplaces are provided. Pets are permitted on leashes or otherwise controlled.

Reservations, fee: No reservations; $5 fee per night.

Who to contact: Write to Six Rivers National Forest Headquarters at 500 5th Street, Eureka, CA 95501, or call (707)442-1721.

Location: From Gasquet, drive eight miles east on US 199.

Trip note: One of the prettiest spots along US 199, the camp is set along Patrick Creek, which pours into the Smith River. A short drive to the southeast provides access to the Siskiyou Wilderness, with all roads detailed on a Forest Service map (available at the nearby district office in Gasquet). Open from May through mid-September.

D

E

F

Map grid **d4**

WEST BRANCH

KLAMATH NATIONAL FOREST

Campsites, facilities: There are 15 sites for tents or motor homes. Piped water, vault toilets, picnic tables, and fireplaces provided. There are sanitary disposal stations in Happy Camp at the Elk Creek Campground and the Happy Camp Open Dump. Pack out your garbage. Pets are permitted on leashes or otherwise controlled.

Reservations, fee: No reservations, no fee.

Who to contact: Phone the Klamath National Forest Headquarters at (916)842-6131.

Location: From Happy Camp on Highway 96, turn north on Indian Creek Road and drive 14 and a half miles to the campground.

Trip note: This is a virtually unknown, no-charge camp, set in a canyon near Indian Creek, about a 20-minute drive from the town of Happy Camp. The elevation is 2,200 feet. Forest Service maps are helpful for locating the many remote hiking trails in the area. Open May through October.

G

H

I

J

Map grid **e6**

FORT GOFF

KLAMATH NATIONAL FOREST

Campsites, facilities: There are five campsites. Vault toilets, picnic tables, and fireplaces are provided, but there is **no piped water**, and you must pack out your garbage. Pets are permitted on leashes or otherwise controlled. Supplies are available in Seiad Valley.

Reservations, fee: No reservations, no fee.

Who to contact: Phone the Klamath National Forest Headquarters at (916)842-6131.

Location: From Seiad Valley, drive five miles west on Highway 96.

Trip note: Many of the most productive shore fishing spots on the Klamath River are in this area. It's a five-mile stretch of river that is both accessible and a good resting spot for steelhead on their fall and winter migratory journey. And hey, you can't beat the price.

Map grid **f5**

ELK CREEK CAMPGROUND

on Klamath River

Campsites, facilities: There are 78 motor home sites, many with full or partial hookups and a separate area for tents. Rest rooms, hot showers, recreation room, picnic tables, and fireplaces are provided. A laundromat, sanitary disposal station, ice, and wood are available.

Reservations, fee: Reservations accepted; $15 fee per night.

Who to contact: Phone (916)493-2208.

Location: From Highway 96 in the town of Happy Camp, turn south on Elk Creek Road and drive one mile to the campground.

Trip note: This is a year-round motor home park set where Elk Creek pours into the Klamath River.

Map grid **f7**

O'NEIL CREEK

KLAMATH NATIONAL FOREST

Campsites, facilities: There are 18 campsites for tents or motor homes up to 22 feet. Vault toilets, picnic tables, and fireplaces are provided, but bring your own water and pack out your garbage. Pets are permitted on leashes or otherwise controlled. Supplies can be obtained in Seiad Valley.

Reservations, fee: No reservations, no fee.

Who to contact: Phone the Klamath National Forest Headquarters at (916)842-6131.

Location: From Seiad Valley, drive five miles east on Highway 96.

Trip note: This camp is set near O'Neil Creek, and though not far from the Klamath River, access to the river is not easy. In the fall hunting season, this is a good base camp for hunters branching out into the surrounding National Forest.

Map grid **f7**

GRIDER CREEK

KLAMATH NATIONAL FOREST

Campsites, facilities: There are ten sites for tents or motor homes up to 16 feet long. Vault toilets, picnic tables, and fireplaces are provided, but there is **no piped water**, so bring your own and pack out your garbage. Pets are permitted on leashes or otherwise restrained.

Reservations, fee: No reservations, no fee.

Who to contact: Phone the Klamath National Forest Headquarters at (916)842-6131.

Location: From Seiad Valley, drive east on Highway 96 for 1.5 miles to Walker

Creek Road (46N64). Turn right on Walker Creek Road. Turn right again on Grider Creek Road and drive six miles to camp.

Trip note: This obscure little camp is known primarily by hikers who connect here with the Pacific Crest Trail. It is set at 1,700 feet elevation along Grider Creek.

Map grid f8

STEELHEAD TRAILER PARK
on Klamath River

Campsites, facilities: There are 12 motor home sites with full hookups. Rest rooms, hot showers, picnic tables, and fireplaces are provided. A laundromat is available.

Reservations, fee: Reservations accepted; $12 fee per night.

Who to contact: Phone (916)496-3256.

Location: Set at the west end of Hamburg on Highway 96.

Trip note: This privately-operated motor home park is set near the Klamath River, complete with a horseshoe pit. Open all year.

Map grid f8

SARAH TOTTEN
on Klamath River
KLAMATH NATIONAL FOREST

Campsites, facilities: There are 12 tent sites, five camp and mobile home spaces, and five group sites. The maximum length allowed for motor homes is 22 feet. Piped water, vault toilets, picnic tables, and fireplaces are provided. Pets are permitted on leashes or otherwise controlled. There's a grocery store nearby.

Reservations, fee: No reservations; $4 fee per night.

Who to contact: Phone the Klamath National Forest Headquarters at (916)842-6131.

Location: From Hamburg, drive one-half mile east on Highway 96.

Trip note: This is one of the more popular Forest Service camps on the Klamath River, and there's no mystery why. In the summer, its placement is perfect for rafters, who camp here and use it as a put-in spot. In fall and winter, fishermen arrive for the steelhead run. It's located in the "banana belt" or good weather area of the Klamath.

Map grid g2

DILLON CREEK
on Klamath River
KLAMATH NATIONAL FOREST

Campsites, facilities: There are ten tent sites and 11 motor home sites. Piped water, vault toilets, picnic tables, and fireplaces are provided. There is a sanitary disposal station in Happy Camp (25 miles north of the campground) or at Aikens Campground (13 miles west of the town of Orleans). Pets are permitted on leashes or otherwise controlled.

Reservations, fee: No reservations; $4 fee per night.

Who to contact: Phone the Klamath National Forest Headquarters at (916)842-6131.

Location: From Somes Bar, drive 15 miles north on Highway 96.

Trip note: Some of the Klamath River's best bank fishing access is along this stretch of river, especially for steelhead from September through December. It's decent all the way through March. For summer visitors, there are several good swimming holes in the vicinity. The elevation is 800 feet. Open year-round.

Map grid g4 — SULPHUR SPRINGS

on Elk Creek
KLAMATH NATIONAL FOREST

Campsites, facilities: There are several walk-in tent sites with vault toilets. Picnic tables and fireplaces are provided. But there's **no piped water,** so bring your own, and pack out your garbage. Pets are permitted on leashes.

Reservations, fee: No reservations, no fee.

Who to contact: Phone the Klamath National Forest Headquarters at (916)842-6131.

Location: From Highway 96 in Happy Camp, turn south on Elk Creek Road and drive 14 miles to the campground.

Trip note: This hidden spot is set along Elk Creek on the border of the Marble Mountain Wilderness. The camp is at a trailhead that provides access to miles and miles of trails that follow the streams into the backcountry of the Marble Mountains Wilderness. It's set at 3,100 feet elevation.

Map grid g7 — BRIDGE FLAT

KLAMATH NATIONAL FOREST

Campsites, facilities: There are eight sites for tents or motor homes up to 22 feet long. Piped water, vault toilets, fireplaces, and picnic tables are provided. Pets are permitted on leashes or otherwise restrained.

Reservations, fee: No reservations; $4 fee per night.

Who to contact: Phone Klamath National Forest Headquarters at (916)842- 6131.

Location: From Yreka, drive 16.5 miles south to Fort Jones. Turn west on Scott River Road and drive 21 miles to the campground.

Trip note: This camp is popular for whitewater rafting, fishing and bicycling. It can also be used as a departure point for backpackers heading into the adjacent Marble Mountain Wilderness. One problem here is a fence between the campground and the Scott River, required for safety since this is a bad bluff area. To get down to the river, you have to walk down to the end of the fence, around it, then finally, down. The camp is set at 2,000 feet elevation.

Map grid g7 — LOVERS CAMP

KLAMATH NATIONAL FOREST

Campsites, facilities: There are ten walk-in sites. Well water, vault toilets, fireplaces, and picnic tables are provided. There are also facilities for stock unloading and a corral. There is a Forest Service camp host in summer. Pets are permitted on leashes or otherwise restrained.

Reservations, fee: No reservations, no fee.

Who to contact: Phone the Klamath National Forest Headquarters at (916)842-6131.

Location: From Fort Jones, drive 18 miles on Scott River Road. Turn south on Forest Service Road 43N45 and drive nine miles to the campground.

Trip note: This makes an ideal beginning point for backpackers heading into the Marble Mountain Wilderness. One of the trailheads leads right out of the camp, which is set at 4,300 feet elevation. Open from June through October.

Map grid h3 — YOUNG'S RANCH RESORT

near Klamath River

Campsites, facilities: There are 44 motor home sites with full hookups, and 20 tent sites. Rest rooms, hot showers, recreation room, picnic tables, fireplaces, horeshoe pits, volleyball and basketball are provided. A laundromat, ice, and wood are available.

Reservations, fee: Reservations accepted; $11-$14 fee per night.

Who to contact: Phone (916)469-3322.

Location: From Somes Bar, drive 7.5 miles north on Highway 96.

Trip note: The lodge is set just across the road from the Klamath River. This can be a good headquarters for a steelhead or salmon fishing trip from fall through spring. Excellent fishing guides (with boats) are available at Young's Ranch. Known for reliable fishing reports.

Map grid h8

INDIAN SCOTTY

on Scott River

KLAMATH NATIONAL FOREST

Campsites, facilities: There are 32 campsites, including several group sites, for tents or motor homes up to 22 feet long. Piped water, vault toilets, fireplaces, and picnic tables are provided. Pets are permitted on leashes or otherwise restrained.

Reservations, fee: Reservations made through Scott River Ranger District: (916) 468-5351; $4 fee per night.

Who to contact: Phone the Klamath National Forest Headquarters at (916)842-6131.

Location: From Yreka, drive 16.5 miles south to Fort Jones. Turn west on Scott River Road and drive 18 miles to the campground.

Trip note: This is a popular camp that provides direct access to the Scott River. Because it is easy to reach and it's shaded, it gets a lot of use. The camp is set at 2,400 feet elevation.

Map grid i3

OAK BOTTOM ON THE SALMON RIVER

KLAMATH NATIONAL FOREST

Campsites, facilities: There are 35 campsites for tents and motor homes, and some group sites. Piped water, vault toilets, picnic tables, and fireplaces are provided. There is a sanitary disposal station at the Elk Creek Campground in Happy Camp or at Aikens Camp (13 miles west of the town of Orleans). Pets are permitted on leashes or otherwise controlled. Supplies in Somes Bar.

Reservations, fee: No reservations; $4 fee per night.

Who to contact: Phone the Klamath National Forest Headquarters at (916)842-6131.

Location: From Somes Bar on Highway 96, turn east on Somes Bar-Etna Road and drive three miles to the campground.

Trip note: This camp is just far enough off Highway 96 that it gets missed by zillions of out-of-towners every year. There's good steelhead fishing on Klamath River in the fall and winter months. One option for fishing is to head up the Salmon River, which feeds into the Klamath at Somes Bar. Open year around.

Map grid j0

BLUFF CREEK

near Klamath River

SIX RIVERS NATIONAL FOREST

Campsites, facilities: There 11 sites for tents or motor homes up to 22 feet long. Piped water, vault toilets, picnic tables, and fireplaces are provided. Pets are permitted on leashes.

Reservations, fee: No reservations; $5 fee per night.

Who to contact: Phone Six Rivers National Forest at (707)442-1721.

Location: From Orleans, drive ten miles west on Highway 96.

Trip note: This is an ideal setting on Bluff Creek near where it enters the Klamath

River, providing access to good steelhead fishing in the fall and winter. Open from mid-August to nearly November. Keep an eye for giant footprints in the 19-inch range. This is the spot where a famous Bigfoot movie was taken in 1963.

Map grid jO

BLUFF CREEK GROUP CAMP

near Klamath River
SIX RIVERS NATIONAL FOREST

Campsites, facilities: There is a large camping area for tents or motor homes up to 22 feet long. Piped water, vault toilets, and fireplaces are provided. Pets are permitted on leashes.

Reservations, fee: This campground is available to groups from mid-May to early November. Single family camping and day-use is also available. Call ahead for group reservations; $10-$20 group fee per night, depending on group size. Single families are charged $5.

Who to contact: Phone Orleans Ranger District Office at (916)627-3291 for reservations.

Location: From Orleans, drive 9.5 miles west on Highway 96.

Trip note: The camp is located in an ideal setting overlooking the Klamath River with good steelhead fishing in the fall and winter. But watch out for large, hairy creatures, eight-feet tall, 800 pounds. Bluff Creek is the site of a famous movie taken of Bigfoot trotting along the creek.

Map grid jO

AIKENS

on Klamath River
SIX RIVERS NATIONAL FOREST

Campsites, facilities: There are 29 sites for tents or motor homes up to 22 feet long. Piped water, flush toilets, picnic tables, fireplaces, and a sanitary disposal station are provided. Pets are permitted on leashes.

Reservations, fee: No reservations; $6 fee per night.

Who to contact: Phone Six Rivers National Forest at (707)442-1721.

Location: From Weitchpec, drive five miles east on Highway 96.

Trip note: The camp is set along the Klamath River, just outside the edge of the Hoopa Valley Indian Reservation. The steelhead fishing can be good in this area from mid-August through mid-December. Highway 96 is a scenic but slow cruise.

Map grid jO

FISH LAKE

SIX RIVERS NATIONAL FOREST

Campsites, facilities: There are ten sites for tents and 13 sites for tents or motor homes up to 22 feet long. Piped water, vault toilets, picnic tables, and fireplaces are provided. Pets are permitted on leashes.

Reservations, fee: No reservations; $5 fee per night, mid-May through mid-October.

Who to contact: Phone Six Rivers National Forest at (707)442-1721.

Location: From Weitchpec, drive seven miles north on Highway 96, then five more miles west on Fish Lake Road.

Trip note: This is a pretty little lake that provides good trout fishing for stocked rainbow trout from the season opener on Memorial Day weekend, on through June and July. It gets little camping pressure in other months. It's located in the heart of Bigfoot country. Open year-round.

Map grid **j1**

THE PINES CAMPGROUND
on Klamath River

Campsites, facilities: There are 25 motor home sites, all with full hookups, and a separate area for tents. Picnic tables, rest rooms, showers, and a sanitary disposal station are provided. A laundromat is available.
Reservations, fee: Reservations accepted; $10 fee per night.
Who to contact: Phone (916)627-3425.
Location: This campground is located in the town of Orleans on Highway 96.
Trip note: This is an option for motor home cruisers touring Highway 96, looking for a stopover in Orleans. The steelhead fishing is good in this area in the fall.

Map grid **j1**

MOUNTAIN VIEW RANCH
on Klamath River

Campsites, facilities: There are 25 motor home sites, all with full hookups. Rest rooms, showers, a laundromat, and a sanitary disposal station are available.
Reservations, fee: Call ahead for reservations and rates.
Who to contact: Phone (916)627-3354.
Location: From Highway 96 in Orleans, turn south onto Red Cap Road and drive 1.5 miles to the campground.
Trip note: This makes a good base camp for a Klamath River fishing trip from August to December. But what the heck, sometimes all you need to feel good is just to watch the water roll by. Open year-round.

Map grid **j2**

RIVERSIDE PARK
on Klamath River

Campsites, facilities: There are 48 motor home sites with full hookups. Picnic tables, rest rooms, showers, and a sanitary disposal station are provided. A laundromat is available.
Reservations, fee: Reservations accepted; $12 fee per night. Seasonal leases available.
Who to contact: Phone (916)627-3239.
Location: This campground is located at the west end of the town Orleans on Highway 96.
Trip note: This is one option for motor home cruisers touring Highway 96 looking for a place in Orleans to tie up the horse for the night.

Map grid **j2**

PEARCH CREEK
on Klamath River
SIX RIVERS NATIONAL FOREST

Campsites, facilities: There are nine sites for tents and two sites for tents or motor homes up to 22 feet long. Piped water, vault toilets, picnic tables, and fireplaces are provided. A grocery store, a laundromat, and propane gas are available nearby.
Reservations, fee: No reservations; $5 per night fee, mid-May through early November.
Who to contact: Phone Six Rivers National Forest at (707)442-1721.
Location: From Orleans, drive one mile east on Highway 96.
Trip note: This is one of the premium Forest Service camps on the Klamath River because of its easy access from the highway and easy access to the river. The

camp is open year-round and has fish smokers available, which is either a sign of optimism or tells you how good the fishing can be. Indeed, the fishing is excellent for one to five-pound steelhead from August through November.

Map grid **j5**

LITTLE NORTH FORK
KLAMATH NATIONAL FOREST

Campsites, facilities: There are four tent spaces with vault toilets, picnic tables, and fireplaces. But there is **no piped water,** so bring your own and pack out your garbage. Corrals are available. Pets are permitted on leashes or otherwise restrained.

Reservations, fee: No reservations, no fee.

Who to contact: Phone Klamath National Forest Headquarters at (916)842- 6131.

Location: From Etna, drive about 20 miles west on Sawyers Bar Road to Sawyers Bar. Continue past Sawyers Bar for 3.5 miles on the same road to the campground.

Trip note: What the heck, ya can't beat the price, eh? And what you get is a tiny, primitive campground, at an elevation of 2,300 feet, that can be used as a starting point for a hike into the Marble Mountain Wilderness or, in the fall, a base camp for a steelhead fishing trip on the nearby Salmon River.

Map grid **j7**

IDLEWILD
on the North Fork of Salmon River
KLAMATH NATIONAL FOREST

Campsites, facilities: There are 14 sites, including a group site, for tents or motor homes up to 22 feet long and nine tent-only campsites. Piped water, vault toilets, fireplaces, and picnic tables are provided. Pets are permitted on leashes or otherwise restrained.

Reservations, fee: No reservations, except for group sites; $4 fee per night.

Who to contact: Phone the Klamath National Forest Headquarters at (916)842-6131.

Location: From Etna, drive about 16 miles southwest on Sawyers Bar Road to the campground. (The road can be narrow and the logging trucks, which frequent the road, are big).

Trip note: This is a trailhead camp, set at 2,600 feet elevation; backpackers can start here for multi-day wilderness adventures in adjacent Marble Mountains. The North Fork of the Salmon River is a beautiful, cold, clear stream and a major tributary to the Klamath River. Open from June through October.

◆ MAP A2 ◆

BEACH
TREES
5% CLUB
DESERT
URBAN
FOOTHILL
GRASSLAND

15 MILES

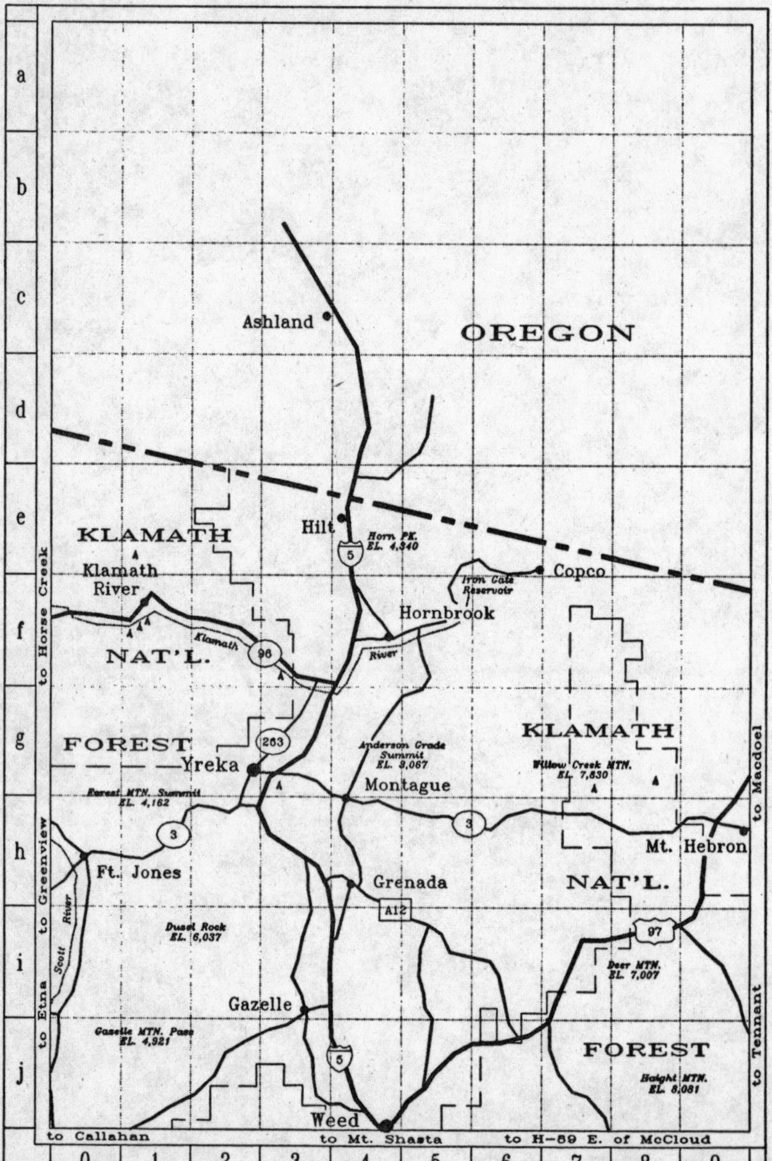

Map grid **e1**

BEAVER CREEK
KLAMATH NATIONAL FOREST

Campsites, facilities: There are eight campsites for tents or motor homes. Piped water, vault toilets, picnic tables, and fireplaces are provided. Pets are permitted on leashes or otherwise controlled.

Reservations, fee: No reservations; fees range from $4-$6 per night.

Who to contact: Phone the Klamath National Forest Headquarters at (916)842-6131.

Location: From the town of Klamath River, drive four miles north on Beaver Creek Road (follow the signs).

Trip note: This camp is set near where Beaver Creek pours into the Klamath River. It is a pretty spot with good fishing nearby in the fall. Fishing guides are available at Beaver Creek Lodge.

B

C

Map grid **f1**

KLAMATH RIVER TRAILER PARK

Campsites, facilities: There are 17 motor home sites with full hookups. Rest rooms, hot showers, and a laundromat are provided.

D

Reservations, fee: Reservations accepted; $9 fee per night.

Who to contact: Phone (916)465-2324.

Location: From the town of Klamath River, drive one mile east on Highway 96.

Trip note: This privately-operated motor home park is located in one of the prettiest areas of the Klamath River. There's a good piece of river here for summer rafters or fall steelhead fishing. Open year-round.

E

Map grid **f1**

QUIGLEY'S GENERAL STORE AND TRAILER PARK
on Klamath River

F

Campsites, facilities: There are 20 motor home sites with full hookups. Tables, rest rooms, and hot showers are provided. A store and a laundromat are available.

Reservations, fee: Reservations accepted; $12 fee per night.

Who to contact: Phone (916)465-2224.

G

Location: Set in the town of Klamath River on Highway 96.

Trip note: This year-round, privately operated park set along the Klamath River is known to provide honest fishing reports.

Map grid **f1**

THE OAK MOBILE HOME AND RV PARK
on Klamath River

H

Campsites, facilities: There are ten sites for tents and 12 sites for mobile homes or RV's with full hookups. Picnic tables, fire grills, piped water, restrooms, hot showers, satellite TV and a laundromat are available. Groceries are available in the town of Klamath River.

I

Reservations, fee: Reservations accepted; $12 fee per night.

Who to contact: Call the park at (916)465-2323.

Location: From the west take Highway 96 to the town of Klamath River. The park is across the highway from the Klamath River Post Office. From the east take Highway 5 north to the junction of Highway 96. Follow 96 west to the town of Klamath River, and look for the park entrance across from the Post Office.

J

Trip note: Fishing? Rafting? Canoeing? Hiking? This camp provides a good headquarters for all of those adventures. The Bigfoot Inn nearby provides canoe rentals and instructions and is operated by Neil Rucker, who I paddled 400 miles with while covering the entire Sacramento River. This stretch of the Klamath is ideal for boating, with summers flows perfect for rafting and canoeing. Fishing is best in the fall, when the salmon, and later, steelhead migrate through the area.

Map grid f3

TREE OF HEAVEN

KLAMATH NATIONAL FOREST

Campsites, facilities: There are ten tent sites and 11 motor home spaces for moderate sized RVs. Piped water, vault toilets, picnic tables, and fireplaces are provided. Pets are permitted on leashes or otherwise controlled. A boat ramp is available.

Reservations, fee: No reservations; $6 fee per night.

Who to contact: Phone the Klamath National Forest Headquarters at (916)842-6131.

Location: From Yreka, drive ten miles north to Highway 96. Drive two miles west on Highway 96 to the campground.

Trip note: This is another easy-to-reach camp that gets missed by most all the folks ripping up and down Interstate 5. It's just a 15 or 20-minute drive from the highway, and it's a pretty spot, set right along the river, well forested. On the drive in from the highway, you can watch the landscape turn from high chaparral country to forest. There is good steelhead fishing at the mouth of Shasta River.

Map grid g3

WALIAKA TRAILER HAVEN

Campsites, facilities: There are 52 motor home sites with full or partial hookups. Rest rooms, showers, playground, and a recreation room are provided. A laundromat and propane gas are available.

Reservations, fee: Reservations accepted; $16 fee per night.

Who to contact: Phone (916)842-4500.

Location: From Interstate 5 in Yreka, take the Fort Jones exit. Drive one block east and turn north on Fairlane Road. Drive to Sharps Road. Turn east on Sharps Road and drive one block to the motor home park.

Trip note: This is a good spot for motor home campers heading up Highway 5. A good side trip is exploring the nearby Klamath River. The river passes right under the Interstate 5 bridge and provides good steelhead fishing at the nearby mouth of the Shasta River from mid-September through March. Open all year.

Map grid g7

MARTIN'S DAIRY

KLAMATH NATIONAL FOREST

Campsites, facilities: There are eight campsites for tents or motor homes. Piped water, vault toilets, picnic tables, and fireplaces provided. Pack out your garbage. Pets are permitted on leashes or otherwise controlled.

Reservations, fee: No reservations, no fee.

Who to contact: Phone the Klamath National Forest Headquarters at (916)842-6131.

Location: From Montague just east of Yreka, drive 30 miles east on Ball Mountain Road and Little Shasta Road to the campground.

Trip note: This camp is set at 6,000 feet where the deer get big and the country seems wide open. There is good fishing in Little Shasta River, and the quaking Aspen groves are beautiful. In the fall, it makes a good base camp for hunters. Before heading into the surrounding backcountry, obtain a map of Klamath National Forest.

Map grid **g8**

JUANITA LAKE
KLAMATH NATIONAL FOREST

Campsites, facilities: There are 12 tent sites and 11 spaces for motor homes up to 32 feet. Piped water, vault toilets, picnic tables, and fireplaces provided. Boating is allowed, but no motorboats are permitted on the lake.

Reservations, fee: No reservations; $6-$8 fee per night.

Who to contact: Phone the Klamath National Forest Headquarters at (916)842-6131.

Location: From Macdoel on Highway 97, turn west on Meiss Lake-Sam's Neck Road and drive 8.5 miles to Butte Valley Road. Take Butte Valley Road to the campground.

Trip note: Small and relatively little-known, this camp is set along the shore of Juanita Lake at 5,100 feet elevation. Bass fishing can be decent in the early summer. There is a paved trail around the lake for handicapped and elderly, approximately 1.25 miles. Open May through October.

◆ MAP A3 ◆

BEACH
TREES
5% CLUB
DESERT
URBAN
FOOTHILL
GRASSLAND

15 MILES

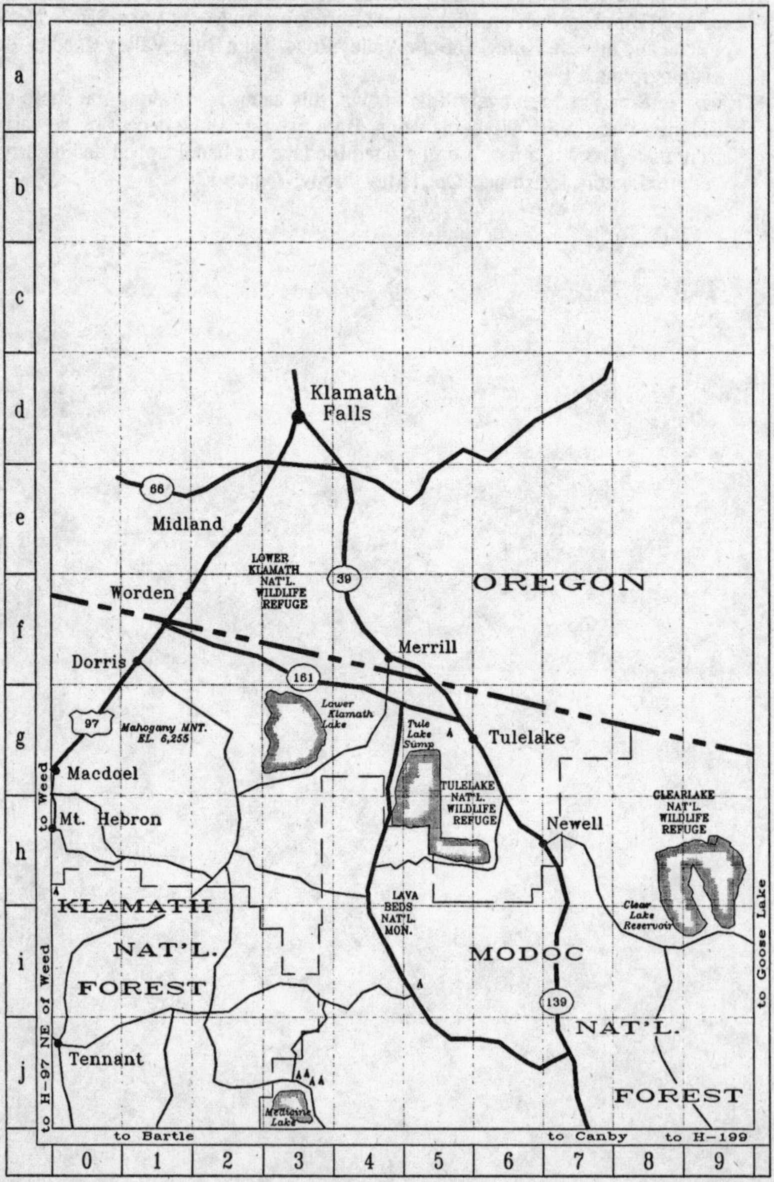

a
b
c
d
e
f
g
h
i
j

Klamath Falls
66
Midland
LOWER KLAMATH NAT'L. WILDLIFE REFUGE
39
OREGON
Worden
Merrill
Dorris
161
Lower Klamath Lake
97
Mahogany MNT. EL. 6,255
Tule Lake Sump
Tulelake
Macdoel
TULELAKE NAT'L. WILDLIFE REFUGE
CLEARLAKE NAT'L. WILDLIFE REFUGE
Mt. Hebron
Newell
KLAMATH NAT'L. FOREST
LAVA BEDS NAT'L. MON.
Clear Lake Reservoir
MODOC NAT'L. FOREST
139
Tennant
Medicine Lake
to Weed
to H-97 NE of Weed
to Goose Lake
to Bartle
to Canby
to H-199

0 1 2 3 4 5 6 7 8 9

A3

Map grid g5 — SHADY LANE TRAILER PARK

in Tulelake

Campsites, facilities: There are 30 motor home sites with full hookups. Rest rooms, showers, and patios are provided, and a laundromat is available.

Reservations, fee: Reservations accepted; $12 per night.

Who to contact: Write to Shady Lane Trailer Park, 795 Modoc Avenue, Box 297, Tulelake, CA 96134 or call (916)667-2617.

Location: From Highway 139 in Tulelake, take the south exit on East West Road to Modoc Avenue. Turn left to mid-block.

Trip note: Welp, after a long day of driving the old motor home, ya start lookin' around for a shady spot to hunker down. There isn't much shade in Modoc County, but this private park manages to provide some. Good side trips include Lava Beds National Monument and Tulelake Game Refuge.

Map grid h0 — SHAFTER

KLAMATH NATIONAL FOREST

Campsites, facilities: There are 14 sites for tents or motor homes. Vault toilets, picnic tables, and fireplaces provided, but there is **no piped water,** so bring your own and pack out your garbage. Pets are permitted on leashes or otherwise controlled.

Reservations, fee: No reservations, no fee.

Who to contact: Phone the Klamath National Forest Headquarters at (916)842-6131.

Location: From Macdoel on Highway 97, drive south for 6.5 miles to the campground.

Trip note: You get great views of Mt. Shasta as you drive south on Highway 97. It is a little-used camp with trout fishing at nearby Butte Creek. It's primitive and not well known.

Map grid i5 — INDIAN WELL

LAVA BEDS NATIONAL MONUMENT

Campsites, facilities: There are 40 sites, suitable for tents, pickup campers, or small trailers. Each site has a picnic table, fire ring, and cooking grill. During the summer season, which extends from Memorial Day to Labor Day, water and flush toilets are available. Rangers are also available during the summer to lead activities, including nightly campfire programs. During the winter, the water in the campground is turned off and only pit toilets are available. However, water and flush toilets are always available at Camp Headquarters. The town of Tulelake (30 miles north of the Headquarters) is the nearest supply station.

Reservations, fee: No reservations; winter camping is free; $6 summer fee per night.

Who to contact: Call Lava Beds National Monument at (916)667-2282.

Location: The campground at Lava Beds National Monument is situated about three-quarters of a mile from the park headquarters, 30 miles south of Tulelake off Highway 139.

Trip note: This is a one-in-a-million spot with 20 lava tube caves, a cinder cone (climbable), Mammoth Crater, Indian pictographs, and wildlife overlooks at Tule Lake. After winter's first snow, this is one of the best places in the West to photograph deer. Nearby Klamath National Wildlife Refuge is the largest bald eagle wintering area in the lower 48. If you are new to the outdoors, an interpretive center is available to explain it all to you.

B C D E F G H I J

Map grid **j3**

MEDICINE LAKE

MODOC NATIONAL FOREST

Campsites, facilities: There are 22 tent and motor home spaces. Piped water, vault toilets, picnic tables, and fireplaces provided. Pets are permitted on leashes. Supplies can be obtained in Bartle.

Reservations, fee: No reservations; $5 fee per vehicle (trailers excluded).

Who to contact: Phone the Modoc National Forest District Office at (916)667-2246.

Location: There are well-signed turnoffs from Highway 89. From McCloud, drive 17 miles east on Highway 89 to the town of Bartle. From Bartle, drive 31 miles northeast on Powder Hill Road (Forest Service Road 46) to Medicine Lake Road. Take Medicine Lake Road to the campground on the lake.

Trip note: Lakeside campsites tucked away in conifers make this camp a winner. It's a unique area. Medicine Lake was formed in a crater of an old volcano and is surrounded by sugar pine and fir trees. The lake is stocked with rainbow and brook trout in the summer, but gets quite cold in the fall. Many side trips are possible, including nearby Blanche Lake, Ice Fields (both signed, off the access road), and Lava Beds National Monument just 15 miles north of the lake. At 6,700 feet elevation, temperatures can turn cold, even in summer.

Map grid **j3**

A.H. HOGUE

on Medicine Lake

MODOC NATIONAL FOREST

Campsites, facilities: There are 24 spaces for tents or motor homes. Picnic tables, fireplaces, piped water and vault toilets are provided. Pets are permitted on leashes. Supplies can be obtained in Bartle.

Reservations, fee:No reservations; $5 fee per night.

Who to contact:Phone the Modoc National Forest District Office at (916)667-2246.

Location:There are well-signed turnoffs from Highway 89. From McCloud, drive 17 miles east on Highway 89 to the town of Bartle. From Bartle, drive 31 miles northeast on Powder Hill Road (Forest Service Road 46) to Medicine Lake Road. Take Medicine Lake Road to the campground on the lake.

Trip note: Medicine Lake Campground was divided in 1990, creating this camp in the process.

Map grid **j3**

HEMLOCK

on Medicine Lake

MODOC NATIONAL FOREST

Campsites, facilities: There are 19 tent and motor home spaces. The maximum length allowed for motor homes is 22 feet. Piped water, vault toilets, picnic tables, and fireplaces are provided. Pets are permitted on leashes. Supplies can be obtained in Bartle.

Reservations, fee: No reservations; $5 fee per vehicle (trailers excluded).

Who to contact: Phone the Modoc National Forest District Office at (916)667-2246.

Location: There are well-signed turnoffs from Highway 89. From McCloud, drive 17 miles east on Highway 89 to the town of Bartle. From Bartle, drive 31 miles northeast on Powder Hill Road (Forest Service Road 46) to Medicine Lake Road. Take Medicine Lake Road to the campground on the lake.

Trip note: This is one of three campgrounds on Medicine Lake operated by the Forest Service. Open June through October.

Map grid j3

HEADQUARTERS

on Medicine Lake

MODOC NATIONAL FOREST

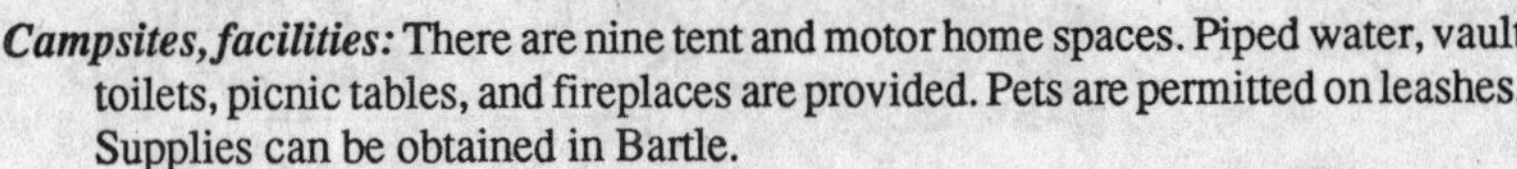

Campsites, facilities: There are nine tent and motor home spaces. Piped water, vault toilets, picnic tables, and fireplaces are provided. Pets are permitted on leashes. Supplies can be obtained in Bartle.

Reservations, fee: No reservations; $5 fee per vehicle (trailers excluded).

Who to contact: Phone Modoc National Forest District Office at (916)667-2246.

Location: There are well-signed turnoffs from Highway 89. From McCloud, drive 17 miles east on Highway 89 to the town of Bartle. From Bartle, drive 31 miles northeast on Powder Hill Road (Forest Service Road 46)to Medicine Lake Road. Take Medicine Lake Road to the campground on the lake.

Trip note: This is one of three campgrounds set beside Medicine Lake.

• MAP A4 •

BEACH
TREES
5% CLUB
DESERT
URBAN
FOOTHILL
GRASSLAND

15 MILES

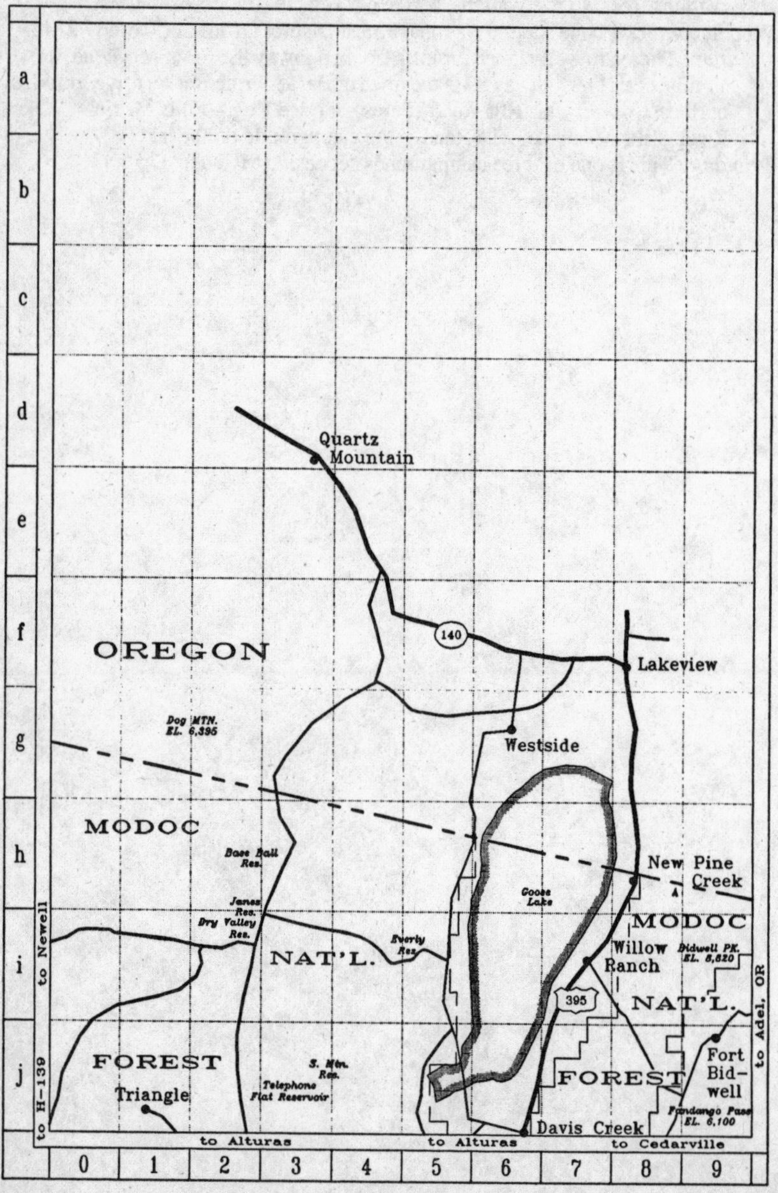

a
b
c
d
e
f
g
h
i
j

Quartz Mountain
140
OREGON
Lakeview
Westside
Dog MTN. EL. 6,395
MODOC
Base Ball Res.
Janes Res.
Dry Valley Res.
Goose Lake
New Pine Creek
MODOC
Everly Res.
NAT'L.
Willow Ranch
Bidwell PK. EL. 8,820
395
NAT'L.
to Newell
to H-139
FOREST
Triangle
S. Mtn. Res.
Telephone Flat Reservoir
FOREST
Fort Bidwell
to Adel, OR
Fandango Pass EL. 6,100
Davis Creek
to Alturas
to Alturas
to Cedarville

0 1 2 3 4 5 6 7 8 9

Map grid **h8**

CAVE LAKE

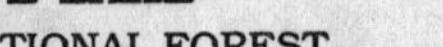

MODOC NATIONAL FOREST

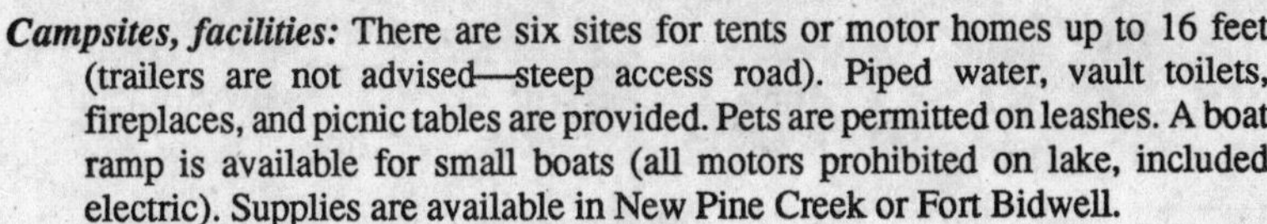

Campsites, facilities: There are six sites for tents or motor homes up to 16 feet (trailers are not advised—steep access road). Piped water, vault toilets, fireplaces, and picnic tables are provided. Pets are permitted on leashes. A boat ramp is available for small boats (all motors prohibited on lake, included electric). Supplies are available in New Pine Creek or Fort Bidwell.

Reservations, fee: No reservations, no fee.

Who to contact: Phone the Modoc National Forest District Office at (916)279-6116, or write to Box 220, Cedarville, CA 96101.

Location: From New Pine Creek (on the Oregon/California border), drive six miles east on Forest Service Road 2, off Highway 395 (a steep, dirt road—trailers are not recommended). The campground is just beyond the Lily Lake picnic area.

Trip note: Little-known, little-used, and hard-to-reach, this camp is hidden in northeastern California alongside a pretty lake that offers trout fishing and plenty of quiet time. Lily Lake picnic area is nearby. The elevation is 6,600 feet. Open from July through October.

• MAP B0 •

BEACH
TREES
5% CLUB
DESERT
URBAN
FOOTHILL
GRASSLAND
15 MILES

to Orick
to Orleans
TRINIDAD ST. BEACH
Trinidad
Weitchpec
HOOPA VALLEY INDIAN RES.
to Weitchpec
Pacific
101
LITTLE RIVER STATE BEACH
Crannell
96
Hoopa
McKinleyville
LANPHERE-CHRISTENSEN DUNES PRESERVE
299
Ocean
Arcata
Blue Lake
Korbel
Willow Creek
to Weaverville
Eureka
HUMBOLDT BAY
SIX
FT. HUMBOLDT ST. HIST. PK.
Freshwater
Fields Landing
Kneeland
Loleta
Mad River
RIVERS
Ferndale
Fernbridge
Fortuna
Rohnerville
Alton
211
Rio Dell
Carlotta
Van Duzen River
Capetown
36
GRIZZLY CREEK REDWOODS PK.
Scotia
Eel
Bridgeville
NAT'L.
Homes
101
Redcrest
Petrolia
Bull Creek
Mad R.
Mattole River
HUMBOLDT REDWOOD PK.
River
Weott
McCann
to Forest Glen
Honeydew
Myers Flat
FOREST
Miranda
Blocksburg
KING RANGE NAT'L. CONSER. AREA
Phillipsville
REDWOOD GROVE AREA
Ft. Stewart
Zenia
Redway
Briceland
Garberville
Alderpoint
Shelter Cove
to Bear Harbor
to Leggett
to Harris
to Covelo

a b c d e f g h i j
0 1 2 3 4 5 6 7 8 9

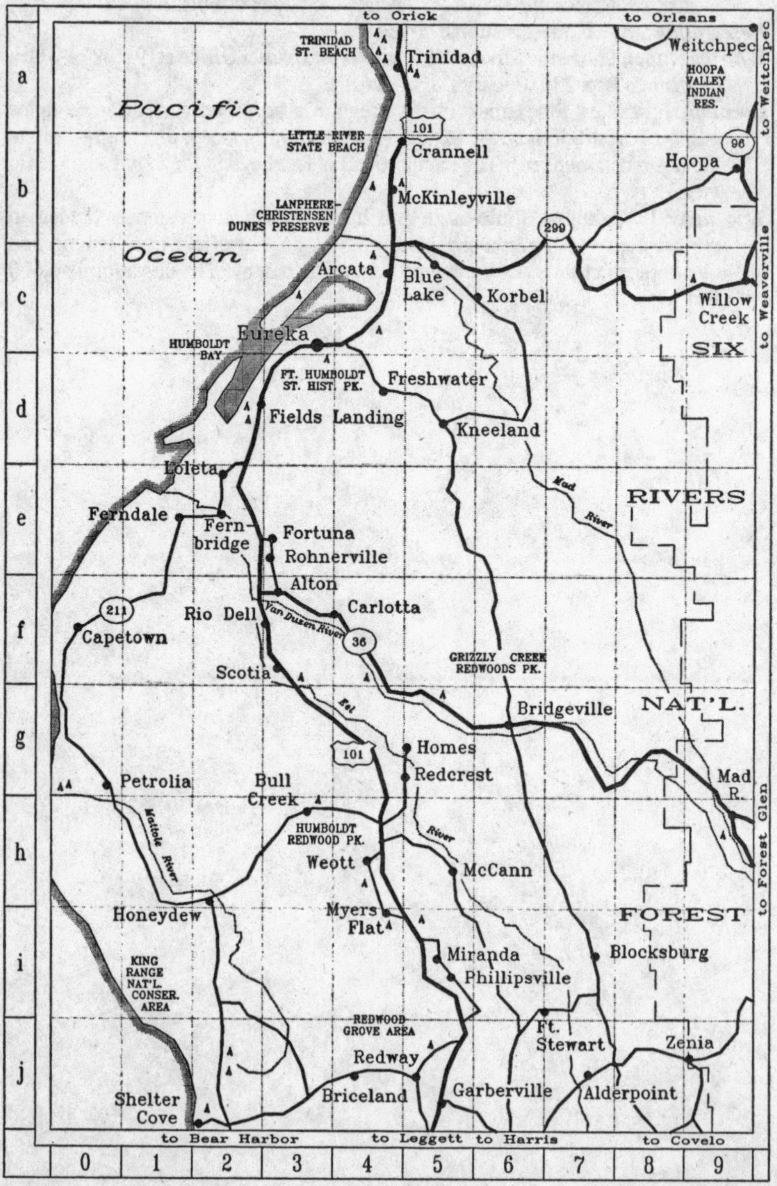

A B0 C D E F G H I J

Map grid **a4**

SOUNDS OF THE SEA
in Trinidad

Campsites, facilities: There are 52 motor home spaces with full hookups. Picnic tables, fire rings, rest rooms, showers, and a sanitary disposal station are provided. RV storage, a laundromat, a grocery store, a gift shop, RV supplies, and ice are available. The facilities are wheelchair accessible.
Reservations, fee: Reservations accepted; $14 fee per night.
Who to contact: Phone (707)677-3271.
Location: On US 101, continue north past the Trinidad exit for 2.5 miles. Turn west on Seawood Drive and drive for one-quarter mile. Turn north on Patrick's Point Drive and drive for two miles to the campground.
Trip note: This privately-operated motor home park offers whale watching, berry picking, volleyball, and horseshoes.

Map grid **a4**

SYLVAN HARBOR TRAILER PARK
in Trinidad

Campsites, facilities: There are 73 motor home spaces with full hookups. Rest rooms, showers, and a sanitary disposal station are provided. A laundromat and LP gas are available.
Reservations, fee: Reservations not accepted; $11 fee per night.
Who to contact: Phone (707)677-9988.
Location: On US 101, take the Trinidad exit. Drive one mile north on Patrick's Point Drive (west frontage road) to the campground.
Trip note: This is one of several privately-operated parks in the Trinidad area. It offers a choice of shaded or open sites near the ocean. Open year-round.

Map grid **a4**

VIEW CREST CAMPGROUND
in Trinidad

Campsites, facilities: There are 49 motor home spaces (nine with drive-through sites), many with full or partial hookups, and a separate area for tents. Picnic tables, fire rings, rest rooms, showers, a playground, and a sanitary disposal station are provided. Cable TV, RV storage, wood, and LP gas are available.
Reservations, fee: Reservations accepted; $11-$16 fee per night.
Who to contact: Phone (707)677-3393.
Location: On US 101, continue north past the Trinidad exit for 2.5 miles. Turn west on Seawood Drive for one-quarter mile. Turn north on Patrick's Point Drive for 1.75 miles to the campground.
Trip note: This spot offers everything from hiking to horseshoes and also has cottages available. The fishing for salmon and rockfish is quite good in the area, and a side trip to Patrick's Point State Park provides unique tunnel-like hikes through the fern vegetation.

Map grid **a4**

MIDWAY RV PARK
in Trinidad

Campsites, facilities: There are 65 motor home spaces with full hookups. Picnic tables, rest rooms, showers, cable TV, a club room, and a playground are provided. RV storage is available.
Reservations, fee: Reservations advised in July and August; $14 fee per night.
Who to contact: Phone (707)677-3934.

Location: On US 101, take the Trinidad exit. Drive one-half mile north on Patrick's Point Drive (west frontage road) to the RV park.

Trip note: This is one of several privately developed campgrounds in Trinidad. In summer, the salmon fishing can be excellent just off Trinidad Head. In the fall, rockfishing is the way to go, and in winter, crabbing is tops. Patrick's Point State Park provides a side trip option.

Map grid a5

HIDDEN CREEK
in Trinidad

Campsites, facilities: There are 59 motor home spaces (13 drive-through sites) with full or partial hookups and a separate area for tents. Picnic tables, patios, rest rooms, showers, a sanitary disposal station, and a recreation room are provided. LP gas is available. A laundromat and a grocery store are nearby.

Reservations, fee: Reservations advised in July and August; $11-$14 fee per night.

Who to contact: Phone (707)677-3775.

Location: On US 101, take the Trinidad exit. Drive 100 yards east on Main Street to 199 North Westhaven.

Trip note: Some of the California's best deep sea fishing for salmon, lingcod, and rockfish is available on boats out of nearby Trinidad Harbor. There's also good beachcombing for agates and driftwood. Nearby Patrick's Point State Park provides an additional side trip opportunity.

Map grid a5

DEER LODGE
in Trinidad

Campsites, facilities: There are 107 sites for tents or motor homes (two have drive-through sites), some with full or partial hookups. Picnic tables, fire rings, rest rooms, showers, and a playground are provided. A grocery store, ice, wood, and LP gas are available. Pets are permitted on leashes.

Reservations, fee: Reservations advised in July and August; $10-$15 fee per night; pets $1.

Who to contact: Phone (707)677-3554.

Location: On US 101, take the Trinidad exit. Drive 100 yards east on Main Street to the campground.

Trip note: This campground, one of several options in Trinidad, is set in nine acres of redwoods.

Map grid b4

CLAM BEACH COUNTY PARK
near McKinleyville

Campsites, facilities: There are 100 campsites for both tents and motor homes. Piped water and vault toilets are provided. Propane gas, a grocery store, and a laundromat are in McKinleyville. Pets are permitted.

Reservations, fee: No reservations; $7 fee per night; $1 for pets.

Who to contact: Phone Clam Beach County Park at (707)445-7652.

Location: From US 101 in McKinleyville, turn west at the sign for Clam Beach and drive two miles to the campground, which is adjacent to Little River State Beach.

Trip notes: This campground provides many options for anglers and clammers. The park gets its name from the good clamming that can be had, but you must come equipped with a clam gun or special clam shovel, and then be out when minus low tides arrive at daybreak. Another option is to head to the mouth of the Mad

River where the perch fishing is excellent, using sand crabs for bait, during the first two hours of incoming tide. Mad River also gets steelhead in January and February.

Map grid **b4**

WIDOW WHITE CREEK RV PARK
in McKinleyville

Campsites, facilities: There are 40 motor home spaces with full hookups and a separate area for tents. Picnic tables, rest rooms, showers, a playground, and a sanitary disposal station are provided. A laundromat is available. The facilities are wheelchair accessible.

Reservations, fee: Reservations accepted; $13 fee per night.

Who to contact: Phone (707)839-1137.

Location: From the junction of US 101 and Highway 299, continue north on US 101 for 4.5 miles to the Murray Road exit. Drive one block east on Murray Road to the campground.

Trip note: This privately-operated park provides easy access from the highway. Nearby there is stream fishing (in winter on the Mad River) and ocean fishing (during summer). The park offers horseshoes, volleyball, badminton, and get this, nearby are the "world's largest totem poles."

Map grid **c3**

SAMOA BOAT LAUNCH COUNTY PARK
on Humboldt Bay

Campsites, facilities: There are ten tent sites and 40 motor home spaces at this county park. Picnic tables, fire grills, piped water, and flush toilets are provided. A boat ramp, a grocery store, LP gas, and a laundromat are available nearby. Pets are permitted on leashes.

Reservations, fee: Reservations not required; $7 fee per night; $1 for pets.

Who to contact: Phone (707)445-7652.

Location: From US 101 in Eureka, drive west on Highway 255 across Humboldt Bay to the Samoa Peninsula.

Trip note: This park is set near the famed all-you-can-eat, logger-style Samoa Cookhouse. At the park, you get good beachcombing and clamming on low tides and a chance to see a huge variety of seabirds. There's a reason: directly across the bay is Humboldt Bay National Wildlife Refuge. Open year-round.

Map grid **c4**

MAD RIVER RAPIDS RV PARK
in Arcata

Campsites, facilities: There are 92 motor home spaces (21 drive-through) with full hookups. Patios, picnic tables, fire grills, rest rooms, showers, a sanitary disposal station, a recreation room, tennis courts, fitness room, a playground, a swimming pool, and a spa are provided. Cable TV, VCR rentals, a grocery store, and a laundromat are available. Some facilities are wheelchair accessible.

Reservations, fee: Reservations accepted; $18 fee per night.

Who to contact: Phone (707)822-7275.

Location: From the junction of US 101 and Highway 299 in Arcata, drive one-quarter mile north on US 101 to the Janes Road-Guintoli Lane exit. Turn west on Janes Road and drive two blocks west to the campground.

Trip note: Arcata is a unique town, a bit of old and a bit of the new. The influence of nearby Humboldt State College is felt in most areas. The Humboldt Bay Wildlife Refuge is a good side trip.

Map grid c4 — EUREKA KOA

Campsites, facilities: There are 25 tent sites and 140 motor home spaces (40 drive-through sites) with full or partial hookups. Group sites are available. Piped water, flush toilets, showers, fireplaces, picnic tables, a playground, and a recreation room are provided. A grocery store, a laundromat, a sanitary disposal station, LP gas, ice, and wood are available. Pets are permitted.

Reservations, fee: Reservations accepted; $16-$20 fee per night.

Who to contact: Phone Eureka KOA at (707)822-4243.

Location: From Eureka, drive four miles on US 101 to 4050 North US 101.

Trip note: This is a year-round KOA camp for US 101 cruisers looking for a layover spot in Eureka. The salmon fishing is often excellent in June, July, and August. Party boats are available just south of town at King Salmon Charters.

Map grid c4 — BOISE CREEK

SIX RIVERS NATIONAL FOREST

Campsites, facilities: There are two sites for bicyclists and hikers and 14 sites for tents or motor homes up to 22 feet long. Piped water, vault toilets, picnic tables, and fireplaces are provided. Grocery store, laundromat, propane gas are available nearby. The facilities are wheelchair accessible. Pets are permitted on leashes.

Reservations, fee: No reservations; $5 fee in spring-summer; $3 during fall-winter.

Who to contact: Phone Six Rivers National Forest at (707)442-1721, or the Lower Trinity Ranger District at (916)629-2118.

Location: From Willow Creek, drive two miles west on Highway 299.

Trip note: The nearby Trinity River provides good salmon and steelhead fishing during fall and winter, respectively, with the best access upriver at Burnt Ranch. In summer, it's a prime river to swim in. By the way, keep your eyes on lookout for giant footprints; this is Bigfoot country.

Map grid d2 — E-Z LANDING

on Humboldt Bay

Campsites, facilities: There are 55 motor home spaces (20 drive-through sites) with full hookups. Patios, flush toilets, and showers are provided. A sanitary disposal station, marine gas, ice, a laundromat, boat docks, a boat launch, party boat rentals, bait and tackle are available. Pets are permitted.

Reservations, fee: Reservations accepted; $16 fee per night.

Who to contact: Phone E-Z Landing RV Park and Marina at (707)442-1118.

Location: From Eureka, drive 2.5 miles south on US 101. Turn west on King Salmon Avenue and drive for one-half mile. Turn south on Buhne Drive and drive one-half mile to 1875 Buhne Drive.

Trip note: This is a good base camp for salmon trips in July and August when big schools of king and coho salmon often school just west of the entrance of Humboldt Bay. A boat launch is available. This spot is ideal for ocean fishing, clamming, beachcombing, and boating.

Map grid d2 — JOHNNY'S MARINA AND RV PARK

on Humboldt Bay

Campsites, facilities: There are 56 motor home spaces (four drive-through sites)

with full hookups. Patios, rest rooms, showers, and a sanitary disposal station are provided. A laundromat, a boat dock, and boat rentals are available. Pets are permitted.

Reservations, fee: Reservations accepted; $14-$16 fee per night. Seasonal leases available.

Who to contact: Phone (707)442-2284.

Location: From Eureka, drive 3.5 miles south on US 101. Turn west on King Salmon Avenue and drive one-half mile. Turn south on Buhne Drive and drive one-half mile to 1821 Buhne Drive.

Trip note: This is a good base camp for salmon fishing during the peak season in June, July, and August. Boat rentals are available along with launching and mooring for private boats. Other fun activities are beachcombing, clamming, and perch fishing from shore. Charter fishing trips are available from King Salmon Charters.

Map grid d3

EBB TIDE PARK
in Eureka

Campsites, facilities: There are 81 motor home sites (58 drive-through) with full or partial hookups. Rest rooms, showers, picnic tables, and patios are provided. A sanitary dump station, RV storage, and a laundromat are available. Pets are permitted.

Reservations, fee: Reservation accepted; $11-$17 fee per night.

Who to contact: Phone Ebb Tide Park at (707)445-2273.

Location: In Eureka, if you are traveling north, take the Mall 101 exit of US 101 and follow signs to 2600 Sixth Street. If you are traveling south on US 101, turn east on V Street and drive one block. Turn north on US 101 to Mall 101 exit and follow the signs.

Trip note: This year-round motor home park provides easy access off the highway and to stores and movie theatres. Not exactly a primitive spot for grizzled old coots.

Map grid f3

STAFFORD RV PARK
near Scotia

Campsites, facilities: There are 50 motor home sites (14 drive-through spaces) with full or partial hookups, and 30 tent sites. Group sites are available. Piped water, flush toilets, showers, fireplaces, and picnic tables are provided. A laundromat, a playground, a sanitary disposal station, satellite TV, and RV storage are available. The facilities are wheelchair accessible. Pets are permitted.

Reservations, fee: Reservations accepted; $8-$16 per night fee.

Who to contact: Phone Stafford RV Park at (707)764-3416.

Location: From Scotia, drive three miles south on US 101 to its junction with Stafford Road. Turn east on North Road and drive one-quarter mile east to 385 North Road.

Trip note: This is a privately-operated park for motor homes that provides several side trip options: A tour of the giant sawmill in Scotia, a tour of giant redwoods on the Avenue of the Giants, or access to the nearby Eel River.

Map grid f4

VAN DUZEN COUNTY PARK
on Van Duzen River

Campsites, facilities: There are 30 sites for tents or motor homes. Piped water, pit

A B C D E F G H I J

toilets, fireplaces, and picnic tables are provided. A grocery store and laundromat are available nearby. Pets are permitted.

Reservations, fee: No reservations; $7 camp fee per night; pets $1.

Who to contact: Phone (707)445-7652.

Location: From Carlotta, drive six miles east on Highway 36.

Trip note: Compared to the state parks in the area, this hidden, quiet spot is a premium alternative. It is set near the Van Duzen River, which gets a steelhead run during the winter months. There's heavy rain in the winter, but what the heck, that's why the fish are there. Open year-round, but the river is subject to fishing closures if the stream flows are low.

Map grid g0

A.W. WAY COUNTY PARK
on Mattole River

Campsites, facilities: There are 30 campsites for tents or motor homes. Piped water, flush toilets, showers, fireplaces, picnic tables, and a playground are provided. A grocery store, a laundromat, and propane gas are available nearby. Pets are permitted.

Reservations, fee: Reservations not required; $7 fee per night; pets $1.

Who to contact: Phone (707)445-7652.

Location: From Petrolia, drive 7.5 miles south on Mattole Road to the park.

Trip note: This secluded camp provides an ideal base of operations for a steelhead fishing trip. The steelhead run peaks in mid-December through March. This a heavy rain area in winter, and it's often foggy in summer. The area north of here is called the "Lost Coast," a unique and beautiful stretch of California.

Map grid g0

MOUTH OF THE MATTOLE
on the Pacific Ocean

Campsites, facilities: There are five campsites for tents or motor homes up to 15 feet long. Piped water, vault toilets, fireplaces, and tables are provided. Pets are permitted.

Reservations, fee: No reservations; no fee.

Who to contact: Phone Bureau of Land Management at (707)462-3873.

Location: From US 101, take the South Fork-Honeydew exit and drive west to Petrolia. Turn west on Lighthouse Road and drive five miles to the campground.

Trip note: This is a little-known camp set at the mouth of the Mattole River, right where it pours into the Pacific Ocean. Perch fishing is good here, and the Mattole often provides excellent steelhead fishing. Check the Department of Fish and Game regulations for closed areas. Open year-round.

Map grid g5

GRIZZLY CREEK REDWOODS STATE PARK

Campsites, facilities: There are nine tent sites and 21 sites for tents or motor homes up to 30 feet long. Piped water, flush toilets, showers, fireplaces, and picnic tables are provided. A laundromat and grocery store are available nearby. The facilities are wheelchair accessible. Pets are permitted on leashes.

Reservations, fee: Reserve through MISTIX by phoning (800)444-7275 ($3.95 MISTIX fee); $12-$14 fee per night; pets $1.

Who to contact: Phone (707)946-2311.

Location: From Bridgeville, drive eight miles west on Highway 36.

Trip note: This is in one of the more secluded state parks in California, though it's gaining in popularity since MISTIX went on line. It's in a beautiful setting in the redwoods with good hiking in the area. Open year-round.

A

Map grid **h3**

ALBEE CREEK
HUMBOLDT REDWOODS STATE PARK

B0

Campsites, facilities: There are 14 sites for tents and 20 sites for tents or motor homes up to 30 feet long. Piped water, flush toilets, showers, fireplaces, and picnic tables are provided. Pets are permitted on leashes.
Reservations, fee: Reserve through MISTIX by phoning (800)444-7275 ($3.95 MISTIX fee); $12-$14 fee per night; pets $1.
Who to contact: Phone Humboldt Redwoods State Park at (707)946-2311.
Location: From Weott, drive two miles north on US 101 to Bull Creek Flats Road. Turn west and drive six miles to the campground.
Trip note: Of the camps available in Humboldt Redwoods State Park, this is one of the smaller and more secluded, and it's worth getting your reservation in. There's good hiking in the area, and the smell of redwoods has a special magic. Open from May through September.

C

D

Map grid **h4**

BURLINGTON
HUMBOLDT REDWOODS STATE PARK

Campsites, facilities: There are 58 sites for tents or motor homes up to 33 feet long. Piped water, a sanitary disposal station, flush toilets, showers, fireplaces, and picnic tables are provided. Pets are permitted on leashes.
Reservations, fee: Reserve through MISTIX by phoning (800)444-7275 ($3.95 MISTIX fee); $12-$14 fee per night; pets $1.
Who to contact: Phone Humboldt Redwoods State Park at (707)946-2311.
Location: From Weott on US 101, turn onto Avenue of the Giants and drive two miles south to the campground.
Trip notes: This camp is often at capacity during the tourist months. You get shady campgrounds with big redwood stumps that kids can play on. There's good hiking on trails routed through the redwoods, and in winter, steelhead fishing is often good on the nearby Eel River. Open year-round.

E

F

G

Map grid **h9**

MAD RIVER
SIX RIVERS NATIONAL FOREST

Campsites, facilities: There are a total of 40 campsites, a few of which are for motor homes up to 22 feet long. Piped water, vault toilets, picnic tables, and fireplaces are provided.
Reservations, fee: No reservations; $5 fee per night, mid-May through mid-October.
Who to contact: Phone the Six Rivers National Forest at (707)442-1721.
Location: From the town of Mad River, drive five miles southeast on Lower Mad River Road to the campground.
Trip note: If you prefer the sound of a running stream to that of the sight of a quiet lake, this is the spot. It's set along the Mad River, two miles north of where it pours into Ruth Lake. The elevation is 2,500 feet. Open year-round.

H

I

Map grid **i4**

GIANT REDWOODS RV CAMP
on Eel River

J

Campsites, facilities: There are 82 motor homes sites (40 drive-through spaces), many with full or partial hookups, and 30 tent sites. Picnic tables, fire rings, rest rooms, showers, and a sanitary disposal station are provided. A store, ice, LP gas, a laundromat, a playground, and a recreation room are available. Pets are allowed.

Reservations, fee: Reservations recommended in summer; $13-$17 per night fee.

Who to contact: Phone Giant Redwoods RV Camp at (707)943-3198.

Location: This camp is in Myers Flat (on US 101) on Myers Road, just off Avenue of the Giants.

Trip note: The privately-operated park covers 23 acres, much of it fronting the Eel River. Side trip options include the scenic drive on Avenue of the Giants. Open year-round.

Map grid i5

HIDDEN SPRINGS
HUMBOLDT REDWOODS STATE PARK

Campsites, facilities: There are 50 tent sites and 105 sites for tents or motor homes up to 30 feet long. Piped water, flush toilets, showers, fireplaces, and picnic tables are provided. A grocery store, a laundromat, and LP gas are available in Myers Flat. Pets are permitted on leashes.

Reservations, fee: Reserve through MISTIX by phoning (800)444-7275 ($3.95 MISTIX fee); $12-$14 fee per night; pets $1.

Who to contact: Phone Humboldt Redwoods State Park at (707)946-2311.

Location: From Myers Flat on US 101, turn east onto Avenue of the Giants and drive less than a mile to the campground entrance.

Trip note: This camp gets heavy use from May through September, but the campgrounds have been situated in a way that offers relative seclusion. Side trips include good hiking on trails routed through redwoods and a touring drive on Avenue of the Giants.

Map grid j2

HORSE MOUNTAIN
in Kings Range

Campsites, facilities: There are nine campsites for tents or motor homes up to 20 feet long. Piped water, vault toilets, fireplaces, and tables are provided. Pets are permitted.

Reservations, fee: No reservations; $5 fee per night.

Who to contact: Phone the Bureau of Land Management at (707)462-3873.

Location: From Redway on US 101, drive 17.5 miles west on Shelter Cove Road. Turn north on Kings Peak Road and drive six miles to the campground.

Trip note: Few people know of this spot. The campground is set along the ridge at 2,000 feet elevation, about six miles from the ocean. There is good hiking in the summer, hunting in the fall, or backcountry travel for four-wheel drive cowboys. The ocean provides many side trip options. Open year-round.

Map grid j2

SHELTER COVE CAMPGROUND
overlooking Pacific Ocean

Campsites, facilities: There are 105 campsites for tents or motor homes (15 drive-through spaces), many with full hookups. Picnic tables, fire rings, rest rooms, showers, and sanitary disposal stations are provided. A laundromat, a grocery store, a deli, LP gas, RV supplies, a boat ramp, and boat rentals are available.

Reservations, fee: Reservations suggested; $12-$16 fee per night.

Who to contact: Phone (707)986-7474.

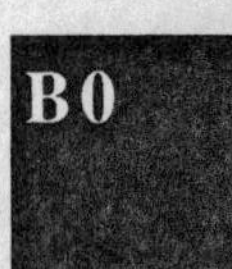

Location: From Garberville on US 101, take the Shelter Cove-Redway-Redwood Drive exit. Drive 2.5 miles west on Redwood Road. Turn west onto Briceland-Shelter Cove Road and drive 24 miles (following the truck/RV route signs). Turn south onto Upper Pacific Drive and go one-half mile.

Trip note: This is a prime oceanside spot to set up a base camp for deep sea fishing, whale watching, tide pooling, beach combing, and hiking. The salmon fishing is quite good here in July and August, crabbing in December, clamming during winter's low tides, and hiking in the Kings Mountain Range during the summer. There is heavy rain in winter. Open year-round.

Map grid j2

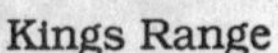

TOLKAN
in Kings Range

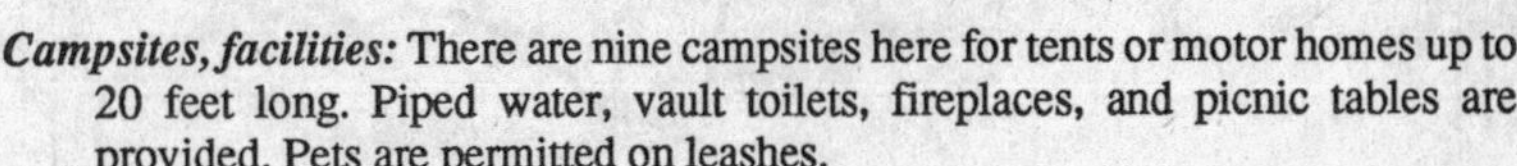

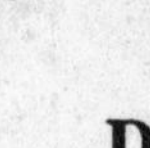

Campsites, facilities: There are nine campsites here for tents or motor homes up to 20 feet long. Piped water, vault toilets, fireplaces, and picnic tables are provided. Pets are permitted on leashes.

Reservations, fees: No reservations; $5 fee per night.

Who to contact: Phone the Bureau of Land Management at (707)462-3873.

Location: From Redway on US 101, drive 17.5 miles west on Shelter Cove Road. Turn north on Kings Peak Road and drive 3.5 miles to the campground.

Trip note: This remote camp is set at 1,840 feet elevation. For trip options, see the trip note for Horse Mountain.

Map grid j5

DEAN CREEK RESORT
on the South Fork of Eel River

Campsites, facilities: There are 40 motor home sites with full or partial hookups. Picnic tables, fire grills, rest rooms, showers, and a recreation room are provided. A laundromat, a store, RV supplies, wood, ice, a giant spa, a sauna, a sanitary dump station, and a playground are available. In summer, inner tubes and tandem bikes are available. Pets are permitted.

Reservation, fee: Reservations recommended in the summer; $12-$18 fee per night.

Who to contact: Phone Dean Creek Resort at (707)923-2555.

Location: From Garberville, drive three miles north on US 101 to the Redwood Drive exit. Follow signs from the exit.

Trip note: This year-round motor home park is set on the South Fork of the Eel River, which has good steelhead fishing in winter. An excellent side trip is to drive on Avenue of the Giants, a tour through giant redwood trees, located three miles from the park. The campground also offers volleyball, shuffleboard, badminton, and horseshoes. You get the idea.

◆ MAP B1 ◆

BEACH
TREES
5% CLUB
DESERT
URBAN
FOOTHILL
GRASSLAND

15 MILES

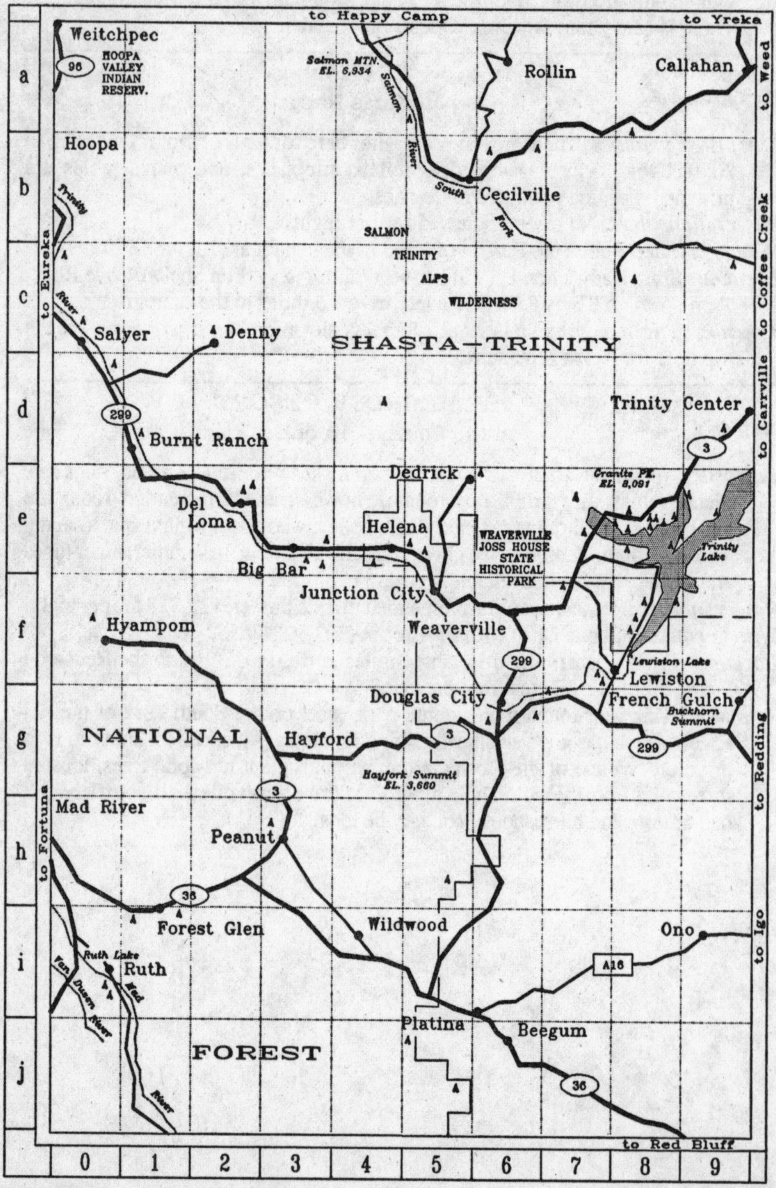

to Happy Camp
to Yreka
to Weed
to Coffee Creek
to Carrville
to Redding
to Igo
to Red Bluff
to Eureka
to Fortuna

Weitchpec
96
HOOPA VALLEY INDIAN RESERV.
Hoopa
Trinity River
Salmon MTN. EL. 6,934
Salmon River
South Fork
Rollin
Callahan
Cecilville
SALMON TRINITY ALPS WILDERNESS
SHASTA–TRINITY
Salyer
Denny
299
Burnt Ranch
Trinity Center
3
Dedrick
Granite PK. EL. 8,091
Del Loma
Helena
WEAVERVILLE JOSS HOUSE STATE HISTORICAL PARK
Trinity Lake
Big Bar
Junction City
Weaverville
Hyampom
Lewiston Lake
Lewiston
Douglas City
French Gulch
Buckhorn Summit
NATIONAL
Hayford
Hayfork Summit EL. 3,660
Mad River
Peanut
36
Forest Glen
Wildwood
Ono
Ruth Lake
Ruth
Van Duzen River
Mad River
A16
Platina
Beegum
FOREST

a b c d e f g h i j

0 1 2 3 4 5 6 7 8 9

Map grid a5

MATTHEWS CREEK
on Salmon River
KLAMATH NATIONAL FOREST

Campsites, facilities: There are seven sites for tents and seven campsites for tents or motor homes up to 16 feet long. Piped water, vault toilets, fireplaces, and picnic tables are provided. Pets are permitted on leashes or otherwise restrained.

Reservations, fee: No reservations, no fee.

Who to contact: Phone the Klamath National Forest Headquarters at (916)842-6131.

Location: From Cecilville, drive 8.5 miles northwest on Cecilville Road (narrow).

Trip note: This camp is set in a dramatic river canyon, with the beautiful South Fork of the Salmon River nearby. It's a nice spot in summer. In winter, the mountain rims shield the canyon floor from sunlight and it gets so cold you'll feel like a human glacier.

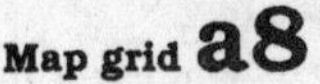

Map grid a8

TRAIL CREEK
on Salmon River
KLAMATH NATIONAL FOREST

Campsites, facilities: There are seven sites for tents or motor homes up to 22 feet long and eight tent-only sites. Piped water, vault toilets, fireplaces, and picnic tables are provided. Pets are permitted on leashes or otherwise restrained.

Reservations, fee: No reservations; $4 fee per night.

Who to contact: Phone the Klamath National Forest Headquarters at (916)842-6131.

Location: From Callahan, drive 17 miles southwest on Cecilville Road.

Trip note: This camp is set beside Trail Creek, a small tributary to the upper Salmon River, at an elevation of 4,700 feet. The Salmon River is a short distance away, providing steelhead fishing in the fall. Open from May through October.

Map grid b6

EAST FORK
on Salmon River
KLAMATH NATIONAL FOREST

Campsites, facilities: There are six tent sites and three sites for motor homes up to 16 feet long. Vault toilets, fireplaces, and picnic tables are provided. But there is no piped water, so bring your own and pack out your garbage. Pets are permitted on leashes or otherwise restrained.

Reservations, fee: No reservations, no fee.

Who to contact: Phone the Klamath National Forest Headquarters at (916)842-6131.

Location: From Cecilville, drive two miles northeast on Cecilville Road.

Trip note: This is one of the more spectacular areas in the fall when the leaves turn different shades of gold. It's a pretty spot year-round, though. It's set at 2,400 feet along the Salmon River. Note to steelhead anglers: Check the Department of Fish and Game regulations for closed areas on Salmon River.

Map grid b6

SHADOW CREEK
KLAMATH NATIONAL FOREST

Campsites, facilities: There are five tent sites and five sites for motor homes up to

16 feet long. Piped water, vault toilets, fireplaces, and picnic tables are provided. Pets are permitted on leashes or otherwise restrained.

Reservations, fee: No reservations; $4 fee per night.

Who to contact: Phone the Klamath National Forest Headquarters at (916)842-6131.

Location: From Cecilville, drive seven miles northeast on Cecilville Road.

Trip note: This tiny spot, secluded and quiet too, is along little Shadow Creek. No fishing is allowed, but that's no problem. This is the kind of place where you just lean against a tree and taste the clean air. That can be enough.

Map grid c0

TISH TANG

SIX RIVERS NATIONAL FOREST

Campsites, facilities: There are 28 sites for tents and 14 sites for tents or motor homes up to 32 feet long. Piped water, vault toilets, picnic tables, and fireplaces are provided. Pets are permitted on leashes.

Reservations, fee: No reservations; $5 fee per night.

Who to contact: Phone Six Rivers National Forest at (707)442-1721, or the Lower Trinity Ranger District at (916)629-2118.

Location: From Willow Creek, drive eight miles north on Highway 96.

Trip note: This camp is set along a twisty section of Highway 96 that connects Willow Creek to Weitchpec. The weather is quite hot during the summer. The camp is situated near several side trip possibilities: the Trinity River country along Highway 299 to the southeast, the Klamath River along Highway 96 to the northeast, and the Hoopa Valley Indian Reservation directly to the north.

Map grid c0

LAZY DOUBLE "B" RV PARK

on Trinity River

Campsites, facilities: There are 19 tent sites and 46 motor home spaces with full or partial hookups. A grocery store, a laundromat, a sanitary dump station, a playground, hot showers, free firewood, rest rooms, picnic tables, and fireplaces are provided.

Reservations, fee: Reservations accepted; $13-$15 fee per night.

Who to contact: Phone (916)629-2156.

Location: This park is in Salyer on Highway 299, 95 miles west of Redding or 46 miles east of Eureka.

Trip note: This is a privately-operated park set along the Trinity River, with easy and direct access to the river. There are sandy beaches nearby along the river, which is a good area for rafting and inner tubing. Salmon fishing here is best in the fall, steelhead fishing in the winter. There are on-site trailer rentals. Open year-round with limited winter facilities.

Map grid c2

DENNY

on New River

SHASTA-TRINITY NATIONAL FOREST

Campsites, facilities: There are ten tent sites and six campsites that will accommodate tents or motor homes up to 25 feet long. Piped water, vault toilets, picnic tables, and fireplaces are provided. Pets are permitted on leashes. Supplies are available in Salyers Bar.

Reservations, fee: No reservations, no fee.

Who to contact: Phone the Shasta-Trinity National Forest District Office at (916) 623-6106.

Location: From Salyers Bar, drive four miles east on Highway 299. Cross the river on County Road 402 (Denny Road) and drive about 14 miles on a very windy road to the campground.

Trip note: Very secluded and quiet, this site is set along New River, a designated wild and scenic river, at the base of the Trinity Alps. Access to the wilderness is available at the end of the road, four to eight miles further up. A Forest Service Map details possible options.

Map grid c8

GOLDFIELD

SHASTA-TRINITY NATIONAL FOREST

Campsites, facilities: There are six tent sites. Vault toilets, picnic tables, and fireplaces are provided, but there is **no piped water** so bring your own. Pets are permitted on leashes.

Reservations, fee: No reservations, no fee.

Who to contact: Phone the Shasta-Trinity National Forest District Office at (916) 623-2121.

Location: From the town of Coffee Creek on Highway 3 at the north end of Trinity Lake, drive 6.5 miles west on Coffee Creek Road to the campground.

Trip note: This camp is set at the head of the Boulder Creek Trail. It can be a possible jump-off point for a multi-day backpacking adventure into the adjacent Trinity Alps Wilderness. The Big Flat camp farther down the road provides a better jump-off point to reach several alpine lakes. They include Upper or Lower Caribou Lakes, a good first day trip. Elevation is 2,500 feet.

Map grid c9

BIG FLAT

on Coffee Creek

KLAMATH NATIONAL FOREST

Campsites, facilities: There are nine campsites for tents or motor homes up to 16 feet long. Vault toilets, fireplaces, and picnic tables are provided. But there is **no piped water,** so bring your own and pack out your garbage. Pets are permitted on leashes or otherwise restrained.

Reservations, fee: No reservations, no fee.

Who to contact: Phone the Klamath National Forest Headquarters at (916)842-6131.

Location: From Trinity Center at the north end of Trinity Lake, drive about nine miles north on Highway 3 to Coffee Creek Road. Turn west on Coffee Creek Road and drive about 21 miles to the campground.

Trip note: This is a good jump-off spot for a wilderness backpacking trip into the adjacent Trinity Alps. Emerald and Sapphire lakes are good destinations for anglers. A backcountry map is a must. On the drive in, you'll see evidence of past mining activity. The camp is set at 5,000 feet along Coffee Creek.

Map grid d0

GRAY'S FALLS

on Trinity River

SIX RIVERS NATIONAL FOREST

Campsites, facilities: There are 17 tent sites and 16 campsites for tents or motor homes up to 32 feet long. Piped water, flush toilets, picnic tables, and fireplaces are provided. One facility is wheelchair accessible.

Reservations, fee: No reservations; $6 fee per night.

Who to contact: Phone the Six Rivers National Forest at (707)442-1721, or the Lower Trinity Ranger District at (916)629-2118.

Location: From Salyer, drive six miles east on Highway 299.

Trip note: One of the best steelhead spots on the Trinity River is just below Gray's Falls, a short hike from the campground. That makes this camp an ideal spot for a fall camping-fishing adventure. During the summer, it's also a good spot to lay around and do absolutely nothing and revel in the pleasure of it. It is also a great put-in spot for river tubing during summer months.

Map grid **d1**

BURNT RANCH

on Trinity River

SHASTA-TRINITY NATIONAL FOREST

Campsites, facilities: There are 16 sites for tents or motor homes up to 25 feet long. Piped water, vault toilets, picnic tables, and fireplaces are provided. Pets are permitted on leashes. Supplies can be obtained in Burnt Ranch.

Reservations, fee: No reservations, no fee.

Who to contact: Phone the Shasta-Trinity National Forest District Office at (916) 623-6106.

Location: From Burnt Ranch, drive one-half mile west on Highway 299.

Trip note: Set on the Trinity River, this is a short hike from Burnt Ranch Falls and a prime steelhead spot in the late fall and winter—good enough for a fishing trip Highway 299 is a picturesque drive in summer. Open year-round.

Map grid **d4**

HOBO GULCH

on the North Fork of Trinity River

SHASTA-TRINITY NATIONAL FOREST

Campsites, facilities: There are ten sites for tents or motor homes. Vault toilets, picnic tables, and fireplaces are provided, but there's **no piped water,** so bring your own. Pets are permitted. Supplies can be obtained in Junction City.

Reservations, fee: No reservations; no fee.

Who to contact: Phone Shasta-Trinity National Forest District Office at (916) 623-6106.

Location: From Weaverville, drive 13 miles west on Highway 299 to Helena. From Helena, drive 20 miles north on Hobo Gulch Road to the campground.

Trip note: This camp is situated on the North Fork of the Trinity River on the edge of the Salmon-Trinity Alps Wilderness Primitive Area. Numerous trails lead out into the wilderness, one of which hooks up to the New River Divide Trail. For hikers, a Forest Service map is a must. The elevation is 2,900 feet.

Map grid **d9**

PREACHER MEADOW

SHASTA-TRINITY NATIONAL FOREST

Campsites, facilities: There are 45 campsites for tents or motor homes up to 32 feet long. Piped water, vault toilets, picnic tables, and fireplaces are provided. Supplies, a laundromat, and a small airport are available nearby.

Reservations, fee: No reservations; $5 fee per night.

Who to contact: Phone the Shasta-Trinity National Forest District Office at (916) 623-2121.

Location: From Trinity Center, drive two miles south on Highway 3 to the campground entrance.

Trip note: This camp provides two possibilities: an overflow camp if the camps at the lakeside at Trinity Lake are full or a jump-off point for a hiking trip. A premium one-day hike is to venture into the Salmon-Trinity Alps Primitive Area, taking the Swift Creek Trail to Swift Creek Gorge.

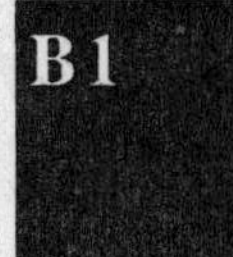

DEL LOMA VILLAGE

Map grid e2

on Trinity River

Campsites, facilities: There are 49 motor home spaces with full or partial hookups. Picnic tables, fire grills, flush toilets, hot showers, a sanitary dump station, picnic tables, and fireplaces are provided. A grocery store, RV supplies, firewood, laundromat, propane gas, a recreation room, volleyball, and horseshoe pits are available.

Reservations, fee: Reservations accepted; $13-$17 fee per night.

Who to contact: Phone (916)623-2780 or (916)623-2834.

Location: From Burnt Ranch, drive ten miles east on Highway 299 to the town of Del Loma. The campground is in the town.

Trip note: Motor home cruisers looking for a layover spot near the Trinity River will find just that at Del Loma. Shady sites and sandy beaches are available here along the Trinity. Rafting and inner tube trips are popular in this area during summer months. Salmon fishing is best in the fall, steelhead fishing in the winter. Open all year.

HAYDEN FLAT

Map grid e2

on Trinity River

SHASTA-TRINITY NATIONAL FOREST

Campsites, facilities: There are 11 tent sites and 24 campsites for tents or motor homes up to 25 feet long. Piped water, vault toilets, picnic tables, and fireplaces are provided. Pets are permitted on leashes.

Reservations, fee: No reservations; $4 fee per night.

Who to contact: Phone the Shasta-Trinity National Forest District Office at (916) 623-6106.

Location: From Burnt Ranch, drive ten miles east on Highway 299.

Trip note: This campground is split into two pieces, with most of the sites grouped in a large, shaded campground across the road from the river and a few on the river side. A beach area is available along the river. The elevation is 1,200 feet. Open year-round.

BIG FLAT

Map grid e3

on Trinity River

SHASTA-TRINITY NATIONAL FOREST

Campsites, facilities: There are ten campsites for tents or motor homes up to 25 feet long. Piped water, vault toilets, picnic tables, and fireplaces are provided. Pets are permitted on leashes.

Reservations, fee: No reservations; $4 fee per night.

Who to contact: Phone the Shasta-Trinity National Forest District Office at (916) 623-6106.

Location: From Big Bar, drive three miles east on Highway 299 to the campground.

Trip note: This level, shaded campground is set off Highway 299, just across the road from the Trinity River. The sites are close together. A trip option is to take the trail along Manzanita Ridge to Twin Sisters Mountain in the Trinity Alps; it's a good multi-day trip. See a Forest Service map for details.

Map grid **e3**

BIG BAR

on Trinity River
SHASTA-TRINITY NATIONAL FOREST

Campsites, facilities: There are three tent sites here. Piped water, vault toilets, picnic tables, and fireplaces are provided. Supplies are available nearby.
Reservations, fee: No reservations, no fee.
Who to contact: Phone the Shasta-Trinity National Forest District Office at (916) 623-6106.
Location: From Big Bar, drive one mile east on Highway 299.
Trip note: You name it, you got it: quiet, small campground, easy access, riverside setting, good fishing nearby (in the fall), and piped water. If the shoe fits . . .

Map grid **e3**

SKUNK POINT GROUP CAMP

on the South Fork of Trinity River
SHASTA-TRINITY NATIONAL FOREST

Campsites, facilities: There are two group camp units that hold up to 30 people each. Vault toilets, picnic tables, and fireplaces are provided, but there is **no piped water**, so bring your own. Pets are permitted on leashes.
Reservations, fee: Reservations required; call for fee.
Who to contact: Phone the Shasta-Trinity National Forest District Office at (916) 623-6106.
Location: From Big Bar, drive two miles east on Highway 299.
Trip note: This is an ideal site for groups like Boy Scout Troops, for instance, who want easy access, privacy, and a streamside setting. A beach on the Trinity River is near the camp. The elevation is 1,200 feet. Open year-round.

Map grid **e4**

PIGEON POINT

on Trinity River
SHASTA-TRINITY NATIONAL FOREST

Campsites, facilities: There are ten sites for tents or motor homes up to 25 feet long. Vault toilets, picnic tables, and fireplaces are provided. There's **no piped water**, so bring your own. Supplies can be obtained in Helena. Pets are permitted on leashes. The facilities are wheelchair accessible.
Reservations, fee: No reservations, no fee.
Who to contact: Phone the Shasta-Trinity National Forest District Office at (916) 623-6106.
Location: From Weaverville, drive about 15 miles west on Highway 299.
Trip note: These sites along the Trinity River are well separated and shaded . A big swimming beach makes this a good spot in the summer for families. The elevation is 1,100 feet. Open May through October.

Map grid **e5**

BIGFOOT CAMPGROUND AND RV PARK

on Trinity River

Campsites, facilities: There are 54 motor home sites here with full or partial hookups and a separate area for tent camping. From December 1 to May 1, only self-contained vehicles are allowed. Flush toilets, hot showers (for a fee), a laundromat, a grocery store, a sanitary dump station, television, propane gas, a swimming pool, and horseshoe pits are available. Some facilities are wheelchair accessible.

Reservations, fee: Reservations desirable in September and October; $14 fee per night.
Who to contact: Phone (916)623-6088.
Location: From Junction City, drive three miles west on Highway 299.
Trip note: Set along the Trinity River, the camp's shoreline access is excellent for fishing, panning for gold, or swimming. It's a good spot for motor home cruisers touring Highway 299.

Map grid e5

JUNCTION CITY CAMPGROUND

on Trinity River
SHASTA-TRINITY NATIONAL FOREST

Campsites, facilities: There are 26 campsites for motor homes up to 30 feet long. Piped water, vault toilets, picnic tables, and fire grills are provided. Groceries and propane gas are available in Junction City.
Reservations, fee: No reservations; $7 fee per night.
Who to contact: Phone the Bureau of Land Management at (916)246-5325.
Location: From Junction City, drive 1.5 miles west on Highway 299.
Trip note: Some of the Trinity River's best fall salmon fishing is in this area in September and early October, with steelhead following from mid-October into the winter. That makes it an ideal base camp for a fishing or camping trip.

Map grid e6

RIPSTEIN

5% CLUB

on Canyon Creek
SHASTA-TRINITY NATIONAL FOREST

Campsites, facilities: There are eight tent sites and two campsites for tents or motor homes. Vault toilets, picnic tables, and fireplaces are provided, but there's **no piped water,** so bring your own. Pets are permitted on leashes. Supplies can be obtained in Junction City.
Reservations, fee: No reservations, no fee.
Who to contact: Phone Shasta-Trinity National Forest District Office at (916) 623-6106.
Location: From Junction City (on Highway 299), drive 15 miles north on Canyon Creek Road to the campground.
Trip note: The trout are small but plentiful in neighboring Canyon Creek. Backpackers should consider the hike up Canyon Creek Trail to Canyon Creek Falls and beyond to the Canyon Creek Lakes, Sawtooth Mountain, and the Boulder Creek Lakes. Be sure to stay clear of the old mine sites in the area. The camp is set at 2,600 feet elevation.

Map grid e7

BRIDGE CAMP

on Stuart's Fork
SHASTA-TRINITY NATIONAL FOREST

Campsites, facilities: There are ten campsites for tents or trailers up to 12 feet long. Piped water, vault toilets, picnic tables, and fireplaces are provided. Horse corrals are available. Pets are permitted on leashes.
Reservations, fee: No reservations; $4 fee per night.
Who to contact: Phone the Shasta-Trinity National Forest District Office at (916) 623-2121.
Location: From Weaverville (on Highway 299), drive 17 miles north on Highway 3 to Trinity Alps Road. Turn on Trinity Alps Road and drive about 2.5 miles to the campground.

Trip note: This remote spot is an ideal jump-off point for backpackers. It's located at the head of Stuart's Fork Trail, about two miles from the western shore of Trinity Lake. The trail leads into the Trinity Alps Wilderness, along Stuart Fork, past Oak Flat, Morris Meadows, and up to Emerald Lake and the Sawtooth Mountains. The camp is set at 2,700 feet elevation. Open all year, but there's **no water in the winter** and it gets mighty cold up here.

Map grid e7

PINEWOOD COVE CAMPGROUND

on Trinity Lake

Campsites, facilities: There are 42 motor home spaces with full or partial hookups and 37 tent sites. Picnic tables and fire grills are provided. Rest rooms, showers, a laundromat, a sanitary disposal station, RV supplies, free movies three nights a week, a recreation room, pinball and video machines, a grocery store, ice, fishing tackle, a library, a boat dock with 32 slips, a beach, and boat rentals are available.

Reservations, fee: Reservations recommended in the summer; $13.50-$17 fee per night; pets $1.

Who to contact: Phone (916)286-2201.

Location: From Weaverville (on Highway 299), drive 14 miles north on Highway 3 to the campground entrance.

Trip note: This is a privately-operated camp with full boating facilities. If you don't have a boat, but want to get on Trinity Lake, this can be a good starting point. A reservation is advised during the peak summer season. The elevation is 2,300 feet. Open all year.

Map grid e8

RIDGEVILLE ISLAND BOAT-IN CAMP

on Trinity Lake

SHASTA-TRINITY NATIONAL FOREST

Campsites, facilities: There are three tent sites. Vault toilets, picnic tables, and fireplaces are provided. There is **no piped water,** so bring your own. Boat ramps can be found near Clark Springs Campground, Alpine View Campground or further north at Trinity Center.

Reservations, fee: No reservations, no fee.

Who to contact: Phone the Shasta-Trinity National Forest District Office at (916) 623-2121.

Location: From any of the boat ramps on Trinity Lake, travel to the Stuart Fork arm of Trinity Lake (western shore); the campground is set on a little island near the entrance to that part of the lake.

Trip note: How would you like to be on a deserted island for a week? Well, you'll learn the answer from this tiny, little-known island. The elevation is 2,500 feet.

Map grid e8

RIDGEVILLE BOAT-IN CAMP

on Trinity Lake

SHASTA-TRINITY NATIONAL FOREST

Campsites, facilities: There are 21 tent sites. Vault toilets, picnic tables, and fireplaces are provided. There is **no piped water,** so bring your own. Boat ramps can be found near Clark Springs Campground, Alpine View Campground or further north at Trinity Center.

Reservations, fee: No reservations, no fee.

Who to contact: Phone Shasta-Trinity National Forest District Office at (916) 623-2121.

Location: From any of the boat ramps on Trinity Lake, travel to the Stuart Fork arm of the lake. The campground is set on the western shore at the end of a peninsula at the entrance to that part of the lake.

Trip note: This is one of the ways to get a camping spot to call your own—go by boat. The exposed camp is set on the western shore of the lake. The early part of the season is the prime time here for boaters, prior to the furnace heat of full summer, with trout and bass both on the bite.

Map grid e8

HAYWARD FLAT

on Trinity Lake

Campsites, facilities: There are 94 campsites for tents or motor homes up to 40 feet long and four multi-family sites. Piped water, flush toilets, picnic tables, and fireplaces are provided. Supplies and a boat ramp are available nearby.

Reservations, fee: Reserve with MISTIX at (800)283-CAMP; $9-$14 fee per night plus reservation fee.

Who to contact: Phone the Shasta-Trinity National Forest District Office at (916) 623-2121.

Location: From Weaverville (on Highway 299), drive 20 miles north on Highway 3 to the campground entrance.

Trip note: This is one of the most popular Forest Service campgrounds on Trinity Lake. The reason is because the camp sits right along the shore of Trinity Lake and offers a "private" beach for Hayward Flat campers only. The elevation is 2,400 feet. Open from mid-May through mid-September.

Map grid e8

MINERSVILLE

on Trinity Lake

SHASTA-TRINITY NATIONAL FOREST

Campsites, facilities: There are 21 campsites for tents or motor homes up to 18 feet long. Piped water, flush toilets, picnic tables, and fireplaces are provided. There's a boat ramp nearby at the Clark Springs Campground.

Reservations, fee: No reservations; $7-$12 fee per night.

Who to contact: Phone the Shasta-Trinity National Forest District Office at (916) 623-2121.

Location: From Weaverville (on Highway 299), drive 18 miles north on Highway 3 to the campground entrance on the right.

Trip note: This is a popular spot for boaters and campers, particularly if Clark Springs camp is full, because the boat ramp is still nearby. The elevation is 2,500 feet. Open all year, but there's **no piped water in the winter.**

Map grid e8

STONEY POINT

on Trinity Lake

SHASTA-TRINITY NATIONAL FOREST

Campsites, facilities: There are 22 tent sites. Piped water, flush toilets, picnic tables, and fireplaces are provided. Pets are permitted on leashes.

Reservations, fee: No reservations; $5 fee per night.

Who to contact: Phone the Shasta-Trinity National Forest District Office at (916) 623-2121.

Location: From Weaverville (on Highway 299), drive 14 miles north on Highway 3 to the campground.

Trip note: This popular spot, set along the shore of Trinity Lake, has easy access. The elevation is 2,400 feet. Open all year, but **no piped water in the winter.**

Map grid **e8**

TANNERY GULCH
on Trinity Lake
SHASTA-TRINITY NATIONAL FOREST

Campsites, facilities: There are 83 campsites for tents or motor homes up to 40 feet long and four multi-family sites. Piped water, flush and vault toilets, picnic tables, and fireplaces are provided. A grocery store and boat ramp are available. Pets are permitted on leashes.

Reservations, fee: Reservations available from MISTIX at (800)283-CAMP ($6 MISTIX fee).

Who to contact: Phone the Shasta-Trinity National Forest at (916)246-5222.

Location: From Weaverville (on Highway 299) drive 13.5 miles north on Highway 3. Turn east on County Road 172 and drive 1.5 miles to the campground.

Trip note: This is one of the more popular Forest Service camps set beside huge Trinity Lake, and is set on the southwest shore. There's a nice beach near the campground, provided the infamous Bureau of Reclamation hasn't drawn the lake level down too far. The lake level can be quite low in the fall. The elevation is 2,400 feet. Open from May through October.

Map grid **e8**

STONEY CREEK GROUP CAMP

on Trinity Lake
SHASTA-TRINITY NATIONAL FOREST

Campsites, facilities: This is a group campground that can handle up to 50 people. Piped water, flush toilets, picnic tables, and fireplaces are provided. Pets are permitted on leashes.

Reservations, fee: Reservations required; $30 fee per night.

Who to contact: Phone the Shasta-Trinity National Forest District Office at (916) 623-2121.

Location: From Weaverville (on Highway 299), drive 14.5 miles north on Highway 3 to the campground.

Trip note: There's a nice swimming beach adjacent to this camp. It's on the shores of Trinity Lake with good trout fishing in early summer and smallmouth bass fishing in spring. The elevation is 2,400 feet. Open all year, but there's no piped water in the winter.

Map grid **e8**

BUSHYTAIL GROUP CAMP

on Trinity Lake
SHASTA-TRINITY NATIONAL FOREST

Campsites, facilities: This campground will accommodate tents or motor homes up to 22 feet long and hold up to 200 people. Piped water, flush toilets, picnic tables, and fireplaces are provided. Supplies and a boat ramp are available nearby.

Reservations, fee: Reservation required; $30 group fee per night.

Who to contact: Phone the Shasta-Trinity National Forest District Office at (916) 623-2121.

Location: From Weaverville (on Highway 299), drive 17 miles north on Highway 3 to the campground entrance.

Trip note: This is a huge group camp, the kind of place where you might want to have the Republican Convention. Then you could tell Richard Nixon to go jump in a lake. (Haven't you always wanted to do that?) What the heck, it's pretty enough to want to jump in yourself, and with a boat launch nearby, you get a bonus. The elevation is 2,500 feet. The camps open from May through September.

A

Map grid e8

CLARK SPRINGS

on Trinity Lake

SHASTA-TRINITY NATIONAL FOREST

B1

Campsites, facilities: There are 34 tent sites. Piped water, flush toilets, picnic tables, and fireplaces are provided. A grocery store and boat ramp are nearby.

Reservations, fee: No reservations; $5 fee per night.

Who to contact: Phone the Shasta-Trinity National Forest District Office at (916) 623-2121.

C

Location: From Weaverville (on Highway 299), drive 18 miles north on Highway 3 to the campground at Mule Creek Station.

Trip note: This used to be a day-use-only picnic area, but by popular demand, the Forest Service has opened it for camping. That makes sense because people were bound to declare it a campground anyway, with lakeside sites, a nearby boat ramp, and a beach. The elevation is 2,400 feet. Open all year, but there's **no piped water in the winter.**

D

Map grid e8

MARINERS ROOST BOAT-IN CAMP

5% CLUB

on Trinity Lake

SHASTA-TRINITY NATIONAL FOREST

E

Campsites, facilities: There are seven tent sites. Vault toilets, picnic tables, and fireplaces are provided. There is **no piped water,** so bring your own. Boat ramps can be found near Clark Springs campground, Alpine View campground or further north at Trinity Center.

Reservations, fee: No reservations, no fee.

F

Who to contact: Phone the Shasta-Trinity National Forest District Office at (916) 623-2121.

Location: From any of the boat ramps, travel to the East Fork Stuart arm of Trinity Lake; the campground is east of Ridgeville Island Boat-In Camp, on the opposite shore from Ridgeville Boat-In Camp.

G

Trip note: This camp is on the shore of the lake, but not accessible by car. The elevation is 2,400 feet.

Map grid e8

FAWN GROUP CAMP

on Trinity Lake

SHASTA-TRINITY NATIONAL FOREST

H

Campsites, facilities: This is a group campground for tents or motor homes up to 37 feet long; the maximum capacity for the campground is 300 people. Piped water, flush toilets, picnic tables, and fireplaces are provided. Pets are permitted on leashes.

I

Reservations, fee: Reservations required; $40 fee per night.

Who to contact: Phone the Shasta-Trinity National Forest District Office at (916) 623-2121.

Location: From Weaverville (on Highway 299), drive 15 miles north on Highway 3 to the campground.

J

Trip note: If you want Trinity Lake all to yourself, one way to do it is to get a group together and then reserve this camp near the shore of Trinity Lake. The elevation is 2,500 feet. Open from May through September.

Map grid **e9**

CAPTAIN'S POINT BOAT-IN CAMP

on Trinity Lake

Campsites, facilities: There are three tent sites. Vault toilets, picnic tables, and fireplaces are provided. There's **no piped water,** so bring your own. Boat ramps can be found near Clark Springs campground, Alpine View campground or further north at Trinity Center.

Reservations, fee: No reservations, no fee.

Who to contact: Phone the Shasta-Trinity National Forest District Office at (916) 623-2121.

Location: From any of the boat ramps, travel to the Trinity River arm of Trinity Lake (west shore), and it is set on the west shore of the main arm of the lake.

Trip note: There are no other campgrounds along this part of the lake. It's on the shore of the lake, but not accessible by car. The elevation is 2,400 feet.

Map grid **e9**

ALPINE VIEW

on Trinity Lake

SHASTA-TRINITY NATIONAL FOREST

Campsites, facilities: There are 66 campsites for tents or motor homes up to 32 feet long. Piped water, flush toilets, picnic tables, and fireplaces are provided. Pets are permitted on leashes. The Bowerman boat ramp is next to the camp.

Reservations, fee: No reservations; $8 fee per night.

Who to contact: Phone the Shasta-Trinity National Forest District Office at (916) 623-2121.

Location: From Trinity Center, drive six miles south on Highway 3 to Covington Mill. Turn south on Guy Covington Road and drive three miles to the camp.

Trip note: This is yet another pretty spot, set on the shore of Trinity Lake at a creek inlet. The boat ramp nearby provides a bonus. The elevation is 2,400 feet. Open from mid-May through mid-September.

Map grid **f0**

BIG SLIDE

on the South Fork of Trinity River

SHASTA-TRINITY NATIONAL FOREST

Campsites, facilities: There are four tent sites and four campsites for tents or motor homes. Piped water, vault toilets, picnic tables, and fireplaces are provided. Pets are permitted on leashes.

Reservations, fee: No reservations, no fee.

Who to contact: Phone the Shasta-Trinity National Forest District Office at (916) 628-5227.

Location: From Hayfork, drive west about 20 miles on County Road 301 to the town of Hyampom. From Hyampom, drive five miles on County Road 311 (Lower South Fork Road) to the campground.

Trip note: Bet you didn't know about this one. It's a tiny, secluded, little-visited spot set along the South Fork of the Trinity River. The elevation is 1,200 feet. Open from April through November.

Map grid **f7**

EAST WEAVER

on the East Branch of Weaver Creek

SHASTA-TRINITY NATIONAL FOREST

Campsites, facilities: There are eight tent sites and seven campsites for tents or motor homes up to 16 feet long. Piped water, vault toilets, picnic tables, and fireplaces are provided. Pets are permitted on leashes. Supplies and laundromat are available in Weaverville.

Reservations, fee: No reservations; $4 fee per night.

Who to contact: Phone Shasta-Trinity National Forest District Office at (916) 623-2121.

Location: In Weaverville, drive northeast on Highway 3. Turn north on East Weaver Road and drive 3.5 miles to the campground.

Trip note: This camp is set along East Weaver Creek. A hiking trail out of the camp leads to little East Weaver Lake, Weaver Bally Mountain, and Monument Peak. The elevation is 2,700 feet. Open all year, but there's **no piped water in the winter.**

Map grid f7

OLD LEWISTON BRIDGE TRAILER PARK

on Trinity River

Campsites, facilities: There are 52 motor home sites with full hookups and a separate area for tents. Rest rooms, hot showers, laundromat, and picnic tables are provided. Propane gas refills are available. Supplies can be obtained in Lewiston.

Reservations, fee: Call in advance for space; $15 fee per night.

Who to contact: Phone (916)778-3894.

Location: From the town of Lewiston, drive north to the junction of Rush Creek Road and Trinity Dam Road. Turn west on Rush Creek Road and drive three-quarters of a mile.

Trip note: If you don't like to catch fish, then don't come here. Because this is one of the few areas on the Trinity River where there is as much catching as there is fishing. Upstream is prime in the early summer for trout, downstream in the fall for steelhead. The campground is in a hilly area, but has level sites.

Map grid f7

TRINITY RIVER LODGE

Campsites, facilities: There are 60 RV sites, all with full hookups, and 20 tent sites. Rest rooms, hot showers, laundromat, cable TV, a recreation room with movies, a playground, propane gas, some supplies, ice, wood, furnished trailer rentals, boat and trailer storage, volleyball, horseshoes, badminton, and croquet are available. There is lake fishing nearby.

Reservations, fee: Call in advance for space; $10-$16 fee per night.

Who to contact: Phone (916)778-3791.

Location: From the town of Lewiston, drive north to the junction of Rush Creek Road and Trinity Dam Road. Turn west on Rush Creek Road and drive 1.5 miles on to the campground.

Trip note: For many, this private-operated park is located in the ideal spot. You get level, grassy sites along the Trinity River, yet it is just a short drive north to Lewiston Lake. Lake or stream, take your pick. Open year-round.

Map grid f8

ACKERMAN

on Lewiston Lake

SHASTA-TRINITY NATIONAL FOREST

Campsites, facilities: There are 66 campsites for tents or motor homes up to 27 feet long. Piped water, flush toilets, picnic tables, and fireplaces are provided. A

sanitary dump station is available. Pets are permitted on leashes.
Reservations, fee: No reservations; $7 fee per night.
Who to contact: Phone the Shasta-Trinity National Forest District Office at (916) 623-2121.
Location: From the town of Lewiston, drive eight miles north on County Route 105 (Buckeye Creek Road) to the campground on Lewiston Lake.
Trip note: This isn't the prettiest spot on Lewiston Lake (Mary Smith Camp is), but it provides the most direct access to the best fishing on the lake, the first two miles of water below Trinity Dam. When the Trinity powerhouse is running, trout fishing is excellent in this area. The elevation is 2,000 feet. Open all year, but there's **no piped water in winter.**

Map grid f8

LAKEVIEW TERRACE RESORT
on Lewiston Lake

Campsites, facilities: There are 35 motor home sites with full hookups. Rest rooms, hot showers, a laundromat, a dump station, a heated pool, propane gas, and boat rentals are available. A grocery store is nearby.
Reservations, fee: Call in advance for space; $15 fee per night.
Who to contact: Phone (916)778-3803.
Location: From the town of Lewiston, drive north to the junction of Rush Creek Road and Trinity Dam Road. Drive four miles north on Trinity Dam Road.
Trip note: This might be your Golden Pond. It's a terraced motor home park that overlooks Lewiston Lake, one of the prettiest drive-to lakes in the region. Fishing for trout is excellent from the park, and on upstream toward the dam.

Map grid f8

MARY SMITH
on Lewiston Lake
SHASTA-TRINITY NATIONAL FOREST

Campsites, facilities: There are 18 tent sites. Piped water, flush and vault toilets, picnic tables, and fireplaces are provided. Pets are permitted on leashes. Supplies and a laundromat are available in Lewiston.
Reservations, fee: No reservations; $5 fee per night.
Who to contact: Phone the Shasta-Trinity National Forest District Office at (916) 623-2121.
Location: From the town of Lewiston, drive 2.5 miles north on County Road 105 (Buckeye Creek Road) to the campground.
Trip note: This is one of the prettiest spots you'll ever see, set along the southwestern shore of Lewiston Lake. If you get here in May or early June prior to the major camping season in July and August, you'll have your pick of several prime spots as well as the best fishing of the year. The elevation is 2,000 feet. Open from April through October.

Map grid f8

COOPER GULCH
on Lewiston Lake
SHASTA-TRINITY NATIONAL FOREST

Campsites, facilities: There are nine sites for tents or motor homes up to 16 feet long. Vault toilets, picnic tables, and fireplaces are provided, but there's **no piped water,** so bring your own. Pets are permitted on leashes. Supplies and a laundromat are available in Lewiston.
Reservations, fee: No reservations, no fee.
Who to contact: Phone the Shasta-Trinity National Forest District Office at (916)

623-2121.

Location: From the town of Lewiston, drive four miles north on County Road 105 (Buckeye Creek Road) to the campground.

Trip note: Here is a nice spot along a beautiful lake. The trout fishing is good on the upper end of the lake where the current starts on upstream. Bring all of your own supplies and plan on hunkering down here for awhile.

Map grid f8

TUNNEL ROCK

on Lewiston Lake

SHASTA-TRINITY NATIONAL FOREST

Campsites, facilities: There are six tent sites. Vault toilets, picnic tables, and fireplaces are provided, but there is **no piped water,** so bring your own.

Reservations, fee: No reservations, no fee.

Who to contact: Phone the Shasta-Trinity National Forest District Office at (916) 623-2121.

Location: From the town of Lewiston, drive seven miles north on County Route 105 (Buckeye Creek Road) to the campground.

Trip note: A small, primitive option to the Ackerman camp, this camp is also set where the fishing is best in Lewiston Lake. The camp has a lakeside setting, not far from Trinity Dam, and is often passed over by folks en route farther north to Trinity Lake. The elevation is 1,900 feet. Open all year.

Map grid g6

DOUGLAS CITY

on Trinity River

Campsites, facilities: There are 19 campsites for tents or motor homes up to 30 feet long. Piped water, vault toilets, picnic tables, and fireplaces are provided. Pets are permitted on leashes or otherwise controlled. Supplies are available in Douglas City.

Reservations, fee: No reservations; $8 fee per night.

Who to contact: Phone the Bureau of Land Management at (916)246-5325.

Location: From Weaverville, drive four miles east on Highway 299 (toward Douglas City). Turn off Highway 299 on Steiner Flat Road, just west of the bridge, and drive one-half mile to the campground.

Trip note: Off the main road and set along the Trinity River, there's good bank fishing access in this area, with the prime season from mid-August on through winter. There's paved parking and a nice beach. This can be a good base camp for an off-season fishing trip on Trinity River or a lounging spot during the summer. The elevation is 2,000 feet.

Map grid g6

INDIAN CREEK TRAILER PARK

on Trinity River

Campsites, facilities: There are 12 motor home spaces with full hookups. Water, showers, flush toilets, picnic tables, and a laundromat are provided. Supplies are available in Douglas City.

Reservations, fee: Reservations accepted; $14 fee per night.

Who to contact: Phone (916)623-6332.

Location: From Weaverville, drive eight miles east on Highway 299.

Trip note: This privately-operated motor home park is set in the heart of the Trinity River country across the road from the Trinity River. The elevation is 1,650 feet. Open year-round.

Map grid g7 — STEELBRIDGE
on Trinity River

Campsites, facilities: There are eight campsites for tents or motor homes up to 30 feet long. There is **no piped water,** but pit toilets, picnic tables, and fireplaces are provided. Pets are permitted on leashes or otherwise controlled. Supplies are available in Douglas City.

Reservations, fee: No reservations, no fee.

Who to contact: Phone the Bureau of Land Management at (916)246-5325.

Location: From Weaverville, drive four miles east on Highway 299 to Douglas City. Continue past Douglas City on Highway 299 for 2.3 miles. As you are going uphill you will see Steel Bridge Road on the left. Turn on Steel Bridge Road and drive about four miles to the campground at the end of the road.

Trip note: Very few campers know of this spot, but it is a prime spot for angler-campers. It's one of the better stretches of water in the area for steelhead, with October through December being the prime time. In the summer, the shade of conifers will keep you cool. Don't forget to bring your own water. The elevation is 2,000 feet. Open year-round.

Map grid h3 — PHILPOT
on the North Fork of Salt Creek
SHASTA-TRINITY NATIONAL FOREST

Campsites, facilities: There are six sites for tents or motor homes. Piped water, vault toilets, picnic tables, and fireplaces are provided. Pets are permitted on leashes.

Reservations, fee: No reservations, no fee.

Who to contact: Phone the Shasta-Trinity National Forest District Office at (916) 628-5227.

Location: From Hayfork, drive about six miles south on Highway 3 to Peanut. Turn west on Plummer Lookout Road and drive one mile to the campground.

Trip note: It's time to join the Five Percent Club, that is, the five percent of the people who know the little-used, beautiful spots in California. This is one of those spots, set on the North Fork of Salt Creek on National Forest land. The elevation is 2,600 feet. Open from April through November. Remember: 95 percent of the people use five percent of the available areas.

Map grid h5 — DEERLICK SPRINGS
on Browns Creek
SHASTA-TRINITY NATIONAL FOREST

Campsites, facilities: There are 15 campsites for tents or motor homes up to 20 feet. Piped water, vault toilets, picnic tables, and fireplaces are provided. Pets are permitted on leashes or otherwise controlled.

Reservations, fees: No reservations; $4 fee per night.

Who to contact: Phone the Shasta-Trinity National Forest District Office at (916) 352-4211.

Location: From the Ranger Station in Platina (on Highway 36), turn north on Harrison Gulch Road. Drive ten miles to the campground.

Trip note: This quiet little spot is set along Browns Creek. There are several hiking trails available in the area, detailed on a Forest Service map. The elevation is 3,100 feet. Open May through November.

Map grid **i0**

BAILEY CANYON

on Ruth Lake
SIX RIVERS NATIONAL FOREST

Campsites, facilities: There are a total of 22 campsites, a few of which are for motor homes up to 22 feet long. Piped water, vault toilets, picnic tables, and fireplaces are provided.

Reservations, fee: No reservations; $5 group fee per night.

Who to contact: Phone the Six Rivers National Forest at (707)442-1721.

Location: From the town of Mad River (on Highway 36), drive 13 miles southeast on Lower Mad River Road.

Trip note: It's surprising how few people know of Ruth Lake, the closest major lake to Eureka. Maybe that's because it's set in remote, western Trinity County. Regardless of the reason, it's one of the major lakes you can drive to, where the crowds are small and the fishing can be good for trout or bass. The elevation is 2,800 feet. Open from mid-May through mid-October.

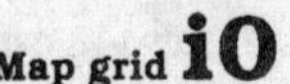

FIR COVE CAMPGROUND

on Ruth Lake
SIX RIVERS NATIONAL FOREST

Campsites, facilities: There are a total of 19 campsites, a few of which are for motor homes up to 22 feet long. Piped water, vault toilets, picnic tables, and fireplaces are provided.

Reservations, fee: The campground is available for single family camping during May, and also the week before and after each holiday; no reservations; $5 fee per night. Starting the first part of June this campground becomes a group reservation site until mid-October; reserve through the Mad River Ranger Station at (707)574-6233; $15-$20 fee per night.

Who to contact: Phone the Six Rivers National Forest at (707)442-1721.

Location: From the town of Mad River (on Highway 36), drive 12 miles southeast on Lower Mad River Road.

Trip note: This spot is situated along Ruth Lake adjacent to the Bailey Canyon campground. It's a unique setup for families only. The elevation is 2,800 feet. Open from May through October.

Map grid **i1**

HELL GATE

on the South Fork of Trinity River
SHASTA-TRINITY NATIONAL FOREST

Campsites, facilities: There are ten tent sites and seven campsites for tents or motor homes up to 15 feet long. Piped water, vault toilets, picnic tables, and fireplaces are provided. The facilities are wheelchair accessible. Supplies are available in Forest Glen. Pets are permitted on leashes. There are ten additional campsites that will take tents and motor homes up to 20 feet long, just one-half mile beyond this campground on the dirt road.

Reservations, fee: No reservations; $4 fee per night.

Who to contact: Phone the Shasta-Trinity National Forest District Office at (916) 628-5227.

Location: From Hayfork, drive south about ten miles on Highway 3 to Highway 36. Turn west (right) and travel ten miles on Highway 36 to the campground entrance on left, one mile before the town of Forest Glen.

Trip note: This is a pretty spot set along the South Fork of the Trinity River. If you want to hoof it, the South Fork National Recreation Trail begins at the campground and follows the river for many miles. Additional trails branch off and up into the South Fork Mountains. The elevation is 2,300 feet. Open from April through November.

Map grid i1

FOREST GLEN

on the South Fork of Trinity River
SHASTA-TRINITY NATIONAL FOREST

Campsites, facilities: There are 15 campsites here for tents or motor homes up to 15 feet long. Piped water, vault toilets, picnic tables, and fireplaces are provided. Pets are permitted on leashes. Supplies are available in Forest Glen.

Reservations, fee: No reservations; $4 fee per night.

Who to contact: Phone the Shasta-Trinity National Forest District Office at (916) 628-5227.

Location: From Hayfork, drive south on Highway 3 for about ten miles to Highway 36. Turn west (right) and travel ten miles to the town of Forest Glen. The campground is at the west end of town.

Trip note: If you get stuck for a spot in this region, this camp virtually always has sites open, even during three-day weekends. It is on the edge of a forest near the South Fork of the Trinity River. Open from April through November.

Map grid j5

BASIN GULCH

SHASTA-TRINITY NATIONAL FOREST

Campsites, facilities: There are 16 campsites for tents or motor homes up to 20 feet. Piped water, vault toilets, picnic tables, and fireplaces are provided. Pets are permitted on leashes or otherwise controlled.

Reservations, fees: No reservations, no fee.

Who to contact: Phone the Shasta-Trinity National Forest District Office at (916) 352-4211.

Location: From Red Bluff, drive about 45 miles west on Highway 36 to the Yolla Bolly District Ranger Office. From the Yolla Bolly District Ranger Station on Highway 36, west of the town of Platina, turn south on Stuart Gap Road and drive six miles to the campground.

Trip note: This is one of three little-known campgrounds set in the vicinity. There are many backcountry Forest Service roads in the area. Your best bet is to get a Shasta-Trinity National Forest map, which details them. The elevation is 2,600 feet. Camp is open April through November.

Map grid j5

BEEGUM GORGE

SHASTA-TRINITY NATIONAL FOREST

Campsites, facilities: There are three campsites for tents or motor homes up to 16 feet. There is **no piped water,** but vault toilets, picnic tables, and fireplaces are provided. Pets are permitted on leashes or otherwise controlled.

Reservations, fees: No reservations, no fee.

Who to contact: Phone the Shasta-Trinity National Forest District Office at (916) 352-4211.

Location: From Platina on Highway 36, turn south on Forest Service Road 29N06 and drive 6.5 miles to the campground.

Trip note: If you want to get the heck away from anything and everything, this spot should be your calling. Just make sure you bring something to drink. Side trip options include two hiking trails that start at the camp, one that follows Beegum Creek for many miles and another that heads up nearby Little Red Mountain. The elevation is 2,600 feet. Open from April through November.

MAP B2

BEACH
TREES
5% CLUB
DESERT
URBAN
FOOTHILL
GRASSLAND

to Gazelle
to Gazelle
to H-97
to Cecilville
to Weaverville
to Douglas City
to Platina
to Bartle
to Burney
to Burney
to Manzanita Lake
to Beegum
to Red Bluff
to Dales
to Mineral

Weed
Callahan
SHASTA-
MT. Eddy EL. 9,038
SHASTA-
MT. Shasta EL. 14,162
TRINITY
Mt. Shasta
Lake Siskiyou
NAT'L.
Scott MTN. Summit EL. 5,401
3
Snowmans Hill Summit EL. 4,470
FOREST
TRINITY
CASTLE CRAGS STATE PARK
5
McCloud
89
Dunsmuir
Coffee Creek
Carrville
Castella
Lake McCloud
Grizzly PK. Lookout EL. 6,253
River
NAT'L.
Trinity Lake
McCloud
Iron Canyon Reservoir
La Moine
Vollmers
Lakehead
Big Bend
WHISKEYTOWN SHASTA-TRINITY NAT'L. REC. AREA
FOREST
Wrengler
O'Brien
Montgomery Creek
Bohemotash MTN EL. 4,432
5
Shasta Lake
Hatchet MTN. Summit EL. 4,368
French Gulch
299
Round Mtn.
SHASTA NAT'L. FOREST
Whiskeytown
Project City
299
Whiskeytown Lake
Shasta
Bella Vista
Oak Run
Redding
Sacramento
Palo Cedro
Igo
Whitmore
A16
Millville
Shingle-town
Anderson
44
5
River
A17
Viola
Cottonwood
A5
A6
Manton

a
b
c
d
e
f
g
h
i
j

0 1 2 3 4 5 6 7 8 9

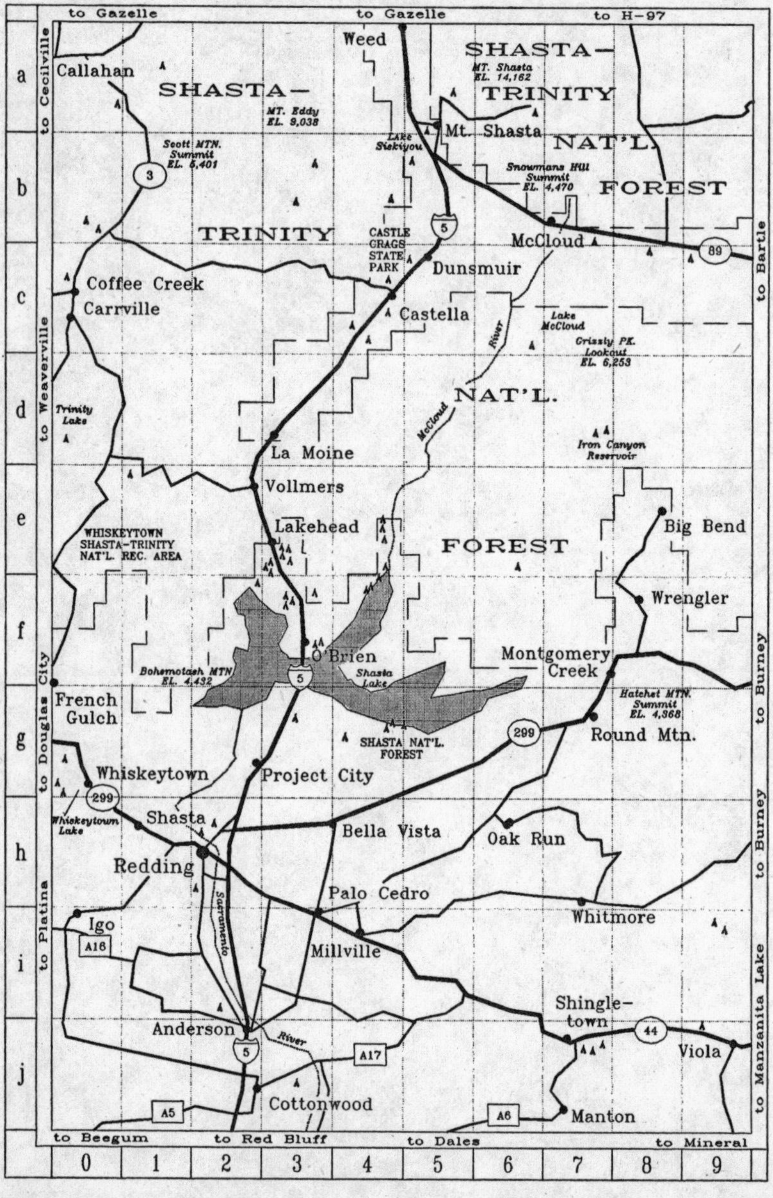

SCOTT MOUNTAIN

Map grid a0

SHASTA-TRINITY NATIONAL FOREST

Campsites, facilities: There are seven campsites. Vault toilets, picnic tables, and fireplaces are provided, but there is **no piped water**, so bring your own. Pets are permitted on leashes.

Reservations, fee: No reservations, no fee.

Who to contact: Phone the Shasta-Trinity National Forest District Office at (916) 623-2121.

Location: From Coffee Creek, drive 16 miles north on Highway 3.

Trip note: This is a prime jump-off point for hikers, with the Pacific Crest Trail passing right by the camp. If you hike southwest it leads into the Trinity Alp Wilderness. The elevation is 5,400 feet. Open all year.

KANGAROO LAKE

Map grid a1

KLAMATH NATIONAL FOREST

Campsites, facilities: There are sites for tents or motor homes. Piped water, vault toilets, fireplaces, and picnic tables are provided. Pets are permitted on leashes or otherwise restrained.

Reservations, fee: No reservations; $6 to $8 fee per night.

Who to contact: Phone the Klamath National Forest Headquarters at (916)842-6131.

Location: From Callahan, drive 18.5 northeast on Gazelle-Callahan Road.

Trip note: Here's a rarity—a high altitude lake that is easy to reach by car. Car-top boats are allowed. The elevation is 6,000 feet and there is a nice beach and a hiking trail around the lake.

KOA MT. SHASTA

Map grid a5

in Mt. Shasta

Campsites, facilities: There are 41 motor home spaces with full hookups, two camping cabins, and 89 additional spaces for tents or motor home (partial hookups). Rest rooms, showers, fireplaces, picnic tables, a playground, and a heated pool are provided. Propane gas, a grocery store, and a laundromat are available.

Reservations, fee: Reservations accepted; $14-$24 fee per night.

Who to contact: Phone (916)926-4029.

Location: In the town of Mt. Shasta at 900 North Mt. Shasta Boulevard.

Trip note: This is a good layover near Interstate 5. An excellent side trip is to the city park where you can see the source of the Sacramento River actually bubbling from the ground at a giant spring. Nearby fishing prospects are good at Lake Siskiyou.

MCBRIDE SPRINGS

Map grid a5

SHASTA-TRINITY NATIONAL FOREST

Campsites, facilities: There are six tent sites and three motor home spaces. Maximum length allowed for motor homes is ten feet. Piped water, vault toilets, picnic tables, and fireplaces provided. Supplies and laundromat are available in the town of Mt. Shasta. Pets are permitted on leashes.

Reservations, fee: No reservations; $6 fee per night.

Who to contact: Phone the Shasta-Trinity National Forest District Office at (916)

926-4511.

Location: From the town of Mt. Shasta (off Interstate 5), drive 4.5 miles northeast on Everitt Memorial Highway to the campground.

Trip note: This camp is set on the slopes of the awesome Mt. Shasta (14,162 feet), California's most majestic mountain. A good side trip is to drive to the end of Everitt Memorial Highway, which tops out above 7,000 feet. You get great lookouts to the west and a jump-off point for a Shasta expedition.

Map grid a6

PANTHER MEADOWS

SHASTA-TRINITY NATIONAL FOREST

Campsites, facilities: There are four tent sites (trailers not recommended). Vault toilets, picnic tables, and fireplaces are provided, but there is **no piped water**. Supplies are available in the town of Mt. Shasta. Pets are permitted on leashes.

Reservations, fee: No reservations, no fee.

Who to contact: Phone the Shasta-Trinity National Forest District Office at (916) 926-4511.

Location: From the town of Mt. Shasta, drive 13.5 miles on Everitt Memorial Highway to the campground. The turnoff to the campground is signed.

Trip note: This quiet site, located on the slopes of Mt. Shasta at 7,400 feet, is used primarily by hikers as a starting point for two-day climbs to the 14,162-foot summit.

Map grid b0

HORSE FLAT

on Eagle Creek

SHASTA-TRINITY NATIONAL FOREST

Campsites, facilities: There are five tent sites and 11 campsites for tents or motor homes up to 16 feet long. Vault toilets, picnic tables, and fireplaces are provided, but there is **no piped water**, so bring your own. Pets are permitted on leashes. Horse corrals available.

Reservations, fee: No reservations, no fee.

Who to contact: Phone the Shasta-Trinity National Forest District Office at (916) 623-2121.

Location: From Trinity Center at the north end of Trinity Lake, drive 16.5 miles north on Highway 3. Turn left at Eagle Creek Campground and drive two miles to the campground.

Trip note: This camp gets use by commercial pack operations, as well as horse owners preparing for trips into the Trinity Alps. The camp even has a corral, so if you don't like horses, go somewhere else. The Eagle Creek Trail leads to Salmon-Trinity Alps Primitive Area.

Map grid b0

EAGLE CREEK

SHASTA-TRINITY NATIONAL FOREST

Campsites, facilities: There are five tent sites and 12 campsites for tents or motor homes up to 27 feet long. Piped water, vault toilets, picnic tables, and fireplaces are provided. Pets are permitted on leashes.

Reservations, fee: No reservations, $5 fee per night.

Who to contact: Phone the Shasta-Trinity National Forest District Office at (916) 623-2121.

Location: From Trinity Center at the north end of Trinity Lake, drive 16 miles north on Highway 3 to the campground entrance.

Trip note: Situated at the confluence of Eagle Creek and the Trinity River, this makes a good base camp for a fishing trip. Bring a rod and reel because there is good fishing for small rainbow trout on upper Trinity River. It's open all year, but there is **no piped water in the winter.** The elevation is 2,800 feet.

Map grid b3

TOAD LAKE

SHASTA TRINITY NATIONAL FOREST

5% CLUB

Campsites, facilities: There are six tent sites. Vault toilets and picnic tables are provided, but not piped water. Pets are permitted on leashes.

Reservations, fee: No reservations, no fee.

Who to contact: Phone the Shasta-Trinity National Forest District Office at (916) 926-4511.

Location: From the town of Mt. Shasta, travel about eight miles west on Forest Service Road 26 (W.A. Barr Road) past Lake Siskiyou to South Fork Road. Turn right and follow the road up the grade, eventually reaching the rim. Take Morgan Meadow Road for ten miles—it winds all over the mountain—eventually ending just a quarter-mile hike away from the campground. A Forest Service map is advised. Four-wheel drives also advised.

Trip note: If you want the remote beauty and splendor of an alpine lake on the Pacific Crest Trail, yet don't want to walk far to get there, this is the place. Little Toad Lake is no easy trick to get to, but it's worth the effort. It's a beautiful little lake in the Mt. Eddy Range. Other alpine lakes in the area provide side trip options. Porcupine Lake is a 45-minute hike from Toad Lake, and another option is climbing to the top of Mt. Eddy, about a six-mile round trip.

Map grid b3

GUMBOOT LAKE

SHASTA TRINITY NATIONAL FOREST

Campsites, facilities: There are four campsites for tents or motor homes up to 16 feet long. Vault toilets and picnic tables are provided, but there is **no piped water**. Pets are permitted on leashes.

Reservations, fee: No reservations, no fee.

Who to contact: Phone the Shasta-Trinity National Forest District Office at (916) 926-4511.

Location: From the town of Mt. Shasta, drive 17 miles on W.A. Barr Road (Forest Service Road 26), past Lake Siskiyou, to the campground.

Trip note: This nice little spot consists of a few small camps set beside a small yet beautiful lake. The trout have been decent size the past few years and the lake is ideal for fishing from a float tube. The lake is usually iced up until mid-June. It's one of many alpine lakes accessible via Forest Service roads. If it's crowded here, the harder-to-reach Toad Lake provides a better choice, but adds a lot more time to your trip.

Map grid b4

CASTLE LAKE

SHASTA TRINITY NATIONAL FOREST

Campsites, facilities: There are six tent sites available. There is **no piped water,** but vault toilets, a picnic table, and a fireplace are provided. Pets are permitted.

Reservations, fee: No reservations, no fee.

Who to contact: Phone the Shasta-Trinity National Forest District Office at (916) 926-4511.

Location: From the town of Mt. Shasta, drive 11.5 miles southwest on W. A. Barr

A B2 C D E F G H I J

Road, past Lake Siskiyou. Turn left on Castle Lake Road and continue to the campground.

Trip note: This beautiful little spot with its lakeside camps has become much better known in the past few years. The lake is a glacial bowl filled with snowmelt, with a high rock-facing on the far side. Trout fishing is poor to fair, but the views are spectacular, especially the one of Mt. Shasta to the east, and hiking in the area is good. Open mid-May through mid-September. In winter, the area is converted to a Nordic Ski Center. The elevation is 5,450 feet.

Map grid b5

LAKE SISKIYOU CAMPGROUND

near Mt. Shasta

Campsites, facilities: There are 54 motor home spaces with full hookups and 293 additional sites for tents or RVs. Piped water, flush toilets, fireplaces, picnic tables, showers, a playground, propane, a grocery store, a laundromat, and a sanitary disposal station are all available for campers' use. There are also boat rentals.

Reservations, fee: Reservation accepted; $10-$13 camping fee per night.

Who to contact: Phone (916)926-2610.

Location: From the town of Mt. Shasta, drive five miles southwest on W. A. Barr Road (off Interstate 5).

Trip note: This gem of a lake, set virtually in the shadow of Mt. Shasta, offers good trout fishing in the spring and good bass fishing in the summer. An option is heading up the east fork of the Sacramento River or on the nearby Forest Service road to explore several alpine lakes. As one of the few lakes in California built expressly for recreation, the water level in Lake Siskiyou is maintained throughout the summer. This campground has been expanded in 1991.

Map grid b7

FOWLER'S CAMP

on McCloud River

SHASTA-TRINITY NATIONAL FOREST

Campsites, facilities: There are 39 sites for tents or motor homes up to 30 feet long. Piped water, vault toilets, picnic tables, and fireplaces are provided. Pets are permitted on leashes. The facilities are wheelchair accessible.

Reservations, fee: No reservations; $7 fee per night.

Who to contact: Phone the Shasta-Trinity National Forest District Office at (916) 964-2184.

Location: From McCloud, drive five miles east on Highway 89 to the campground entrance. Look for the signed turnoff on the right side of the road.

Trip note: This is a beautiful campground set beside the McCloud River, with good trout fishing, several waterfalls, and views of Mt. Shasta. From the camp, you can hike upstream to the base of Middle Falls, the prettiest and least-known of the three waterfalls here. Fishing can be good practically a cast away from your campsite, particularly after trout stocks by the Department of Fish and Game. Open from the opening of trout season (the last Saturday in April) through the closing of trout season in mid-November. If this camp is full, Cattle Camp and Algoma Camp offer overflow areas.

Map grid c0

TRINITY RIVER

SHASTA-TRINITY NATIONAL FOREST

Campsites, facilities: There are seven campsites for tents or motor homes up to 32

feet long. Piped water, vault toilets, picnic tables, and fireplaces are provided. Pets are permitted on leashes.

Reservations, fee: No reservations; $5 fee per night.

Who to contact: Phone the Shasta-Trinity National Forest District Office at (916) 623-2121.

Location: From Trinity Center at the north end of Trinity Lake, drive 9.5 miles north on Highway 3.

Trip note: This camp provides easy access yet is fairly secluded and provides streamside access to the upper Trinity River. It's a good base camp for a trout fishing trip when the upper Trinity is loaded with small trout. Open all year, but there is **no piped water in the winter**. The elevation is 2,500 feet.

Map grid c4

SIMS FLAT
on Sacramento River

Campsites, facilities: There are 20 campsites here for tents or motor homes up to 16 feet. Piped water, flush toilets, picnic tables, and fireplaces are provided. Pets are permitted on leashes. A grocery store is nearby. The campground is wheelchair acessible.

Reservations, fee: No reservations; $8 fee per night.

Who to contact: Phone the Shasta-Trinity National Forest District Office at (916) 926-4511.

Location: From Dunsmuir, drive 12 miles south on Interstate 5. Take the Sims Road exit and continue south on Sims Road to the campground.

Trip note: Considering how easy it is to reach this spot, it is surprisingly secluded. The campground sits beside the upper Sacramento River, providing access to some of the better spots for trout fishing, particularly from mid-May to June (prospects get a little tougher after that). A side trip option is to hike the trail along the South Fork to Tombstone Mountain or south to North Salt Creek.

Map grid c4

CRAG VIEW VALLEY CAMP
on Sacramento River

Campsites, facilities: There are 33 campsites (one drive-through) most with full hookups. There is a separate area for tents only. Picnic tables, fire grills, rest rooms, and hot showers are provided. A laundromat is available.

Reservations, fee: Reservations accepted; $10-$14 fee per night.

Who to contact: Phone (916)235-0081.

Location: From Dunsmuir, drive south on Interstate 5 to the Castella exit. Drive 3/4 mile south on the east side frontage road to the campground.

Trip note: This is one of the better motor home parks around. It's in a pretty setting, situated below nearby Castle Crags State Park, and also near both Castle Creek and the Sacramento River.

Map grid c4

CASTLE CRAGS STATE PARK
on Sacramento River

Campsites, facilities: There are 64 campsites for tents or motor homes up to 27 feet. Picnic tables, fire grills, piped water, hot showers, and flush toilets are provided. Wood is available. Facilities are wheelchair accessible. Pets are permitted.

Reservations, fee: Make reservations through MISTIX by phoning (800) 444-PARK; $12-$14 fee per night.

Who to contact: Call (916)235-2684.

Location: From Dunsmuir, drive six miles south on Interstate 5 to the entrance.

Trip note: Ancient granite spires tower 6,000 feet above the camp, and beyond them, to the north, is the giant Mt. Shasta. In the spring, Castle Creek provides good fishing for small trout, and the nearby Sacramento River provides miles of good fishing. Near the river, there are lots of oaks and maples, with a mixed conifer forest at higher altitudes. It's a popular state park. Open year-round. Only gripe is there is not direct access to Castle Creek from the campground.

Map grid c4

BEST IN THE WEST RESORT

near Dunsmuir

Campsites, facilities: There are 16 motor home sites, most with full hookups. Picnic tables are provided. Rest rooms, hot showers, a grocery store, ice, a laundromat, a playground, propane gas, and horseshoes are available.

Reservations, fee: Reservations accepted; $13 fee per night.

Who to contact: Phone at (916)235-2603.

Location: From Dunsmuir, drive 12 miles south on Interstate 5. Take the Sims Road exit and drive one block west on Sims Road to the campground.

Trip note: This is a good layover spot for motor home cruisers looking to take a break. For side trip options, see the trip note for Sims Flat.

Map grid c5

RAILROAD PARK RESORT

on Sacramento River

Campsites, facilities: There are 60 campsites, many with full hookups, and a separate area for tents only. Rest rooms, hot showers, satellite TV hookups, grocery store, ice, laundromat, recreation room, playground, and horse-shoes are available. Pets are allowed.

Reservations, fee: Deposit required with reservation; $10-$14 fee per night.

Who to contact: Phone (916)235-4440 or 235-9983.

Location: From Dunsmuir, drive one mile south on Interstate 5 to Railroad Park Road. Turn west and drive one-half mile to the campground.

Trip note: This camp is set in the spirit of the railroad, when the steam trains ruled the rails. Many good side trips are available in the area, including Castle Crags (a series of granite spires) and trout fishing on the upper Sacramento River.

Map grid c6

AH-DI-NA

on McCloud River

SHASTA-TRINITY NATIONAL FOREST

Campsites, facilities: There are 16 tent sites. Piped water, flush toilets, picnic tables, and fireplaces are provided. Pets are permitted on leashes.

Reservations, fee: No reservations; $5 fee per night.

Who to contact: Phone the Shasta-Trinity National Forest District Office at (916) 964-2184.

Location: From McCloud, drive 16.5 miles south on Forest Service Road 16 (Squaw Valley Road). Turn on an unpaved road near the southwestern shore of McCloud Lake and drive four miles south to the campground.

Trip note: This is the perfect base camp for trout fishing on Lower McCloud River, with campsites set just a cast away from one of the prettiest streams in California. Downstream of the camp is a special two-mile stretch of river governed by the Nature Conservancy, where all fish must be released, no bait is permitted, and single, barbless hooks are mandated. Wildlife is abundant in the area, and the Pacific Crest Trail passes adjacent to the camp.

A

Map grid **c8**

CATTLE CAMP
on McCloud River
SHASTA-TRINITY NATIONAL FOREST

B2

Campsites, facilities: There are 30 sites for tents or motor homes. **No piped water** is available, but vault toilets, picnic tables and fireplaces are provided. Pets are permitted on leashes.
Reservations, fee: No reservations, no fee.
Who to contact: Phone the Shasta-Trinity National Forest District Office at (916) 964-2184.
Location: From McCloud, drive 11 miles east on Highway 89. Turn right at the signed "Cattle Camp" turnoff. The campground is on left side of the Forest Service, a minute's drive off the highway.
Trip note: This primitive campground is ideal for motor home campers that want a rustic setting. There are several good side trips in the area, including fishing on the nearby McCloud River, taking a gander at the three waterfalls, or driving for 20 minutes and then exploring the north slopes of Mt. Shasta.

C

D

Map grid **c9**

ALGOMA
On McCloud River
SHASTA-TRINITY NATIONAL FOREST

E

Campsites, facilities: There are eight sites for tents or motor homes. There is **no piped water**, but vault toilets, picnic tables, and fireplaces are provided. Pets are permitted on leashes.
Reservations, fee: No reservations, no fee.
Who to contact: Phone the Shasta-Trinity National Forest District Office at (916) 964-2184.
Location: From McCloud, drive 14 miles east on Highway 89 to the signed Forest Service access road on the right.
Trip note: This little-known, undeveloped spot along the McCloud River is quite dusty in August. It is an alternative to Fowlers Camp and Cattle Camp. See the trip note for those camps for side trip options.

F

G

Map grid **d0**

JACKASS SPRING
on Trinity Lake
SHASTA-TRINITY NATIONAL FOREST

5% CLUB

H

Campsites, facilities: There 21 campsites for tents or motor homes up to 32 feet long. Piped water, vault toilets, picnic tables, and fireplaces are provided. Pets are permitted on leashes.
Reservations, fee: No reservations, no fee.
Who to contact: Phone the Shasta-Trinity National Forest District Office at (916) 623-2121.
Location: From Redding, drive 17 miles west on Highway 299 to Trinity Lake Road (just west of Whiskeytown Lake). Turn north on Trinity Lake Road and continue past the town of French Gulch for about 12 miles to the Trinity Mountain Station. Proceed north on East Side Road (a gravel road) for about 12 miles to the campground access road (dirt) on left. Turn and drive three miles to the campground.
Trip note: If you're poking around for a more secluded campsite on this end of the

I

J

lake, you'd best halt your search and pick the best spot you can find at this campground, since it's the only one in this area of Trinity Lake. The elevation is 2,500 feet. Open all year, but there's **no piped water in winter.**

Map grid **d7**

HAWKINS LANDING
on Iron Canyon Reservoir

Campsites, facilities: There are ten sites for tents or motor homes up to 16 feet long. No piped water, so bring your own. Vault toilets, picnic tables, and fire grills are provided. A boat ramp is available. Supplies can be obtained in Fall River Mills.

Reservations, fee: No reservations; $8-$9 fee per night.

Who to contact: Phone the PG&E District Office at (916)527-0354.

Location: From Burney, drive 14 miles west on Highway 299. Turn north on Big Bend Road and drive 15.2 miles to the town of Big Bend. Continue for 2.1 miles. Turn left on Road 38N11 and drive 3.3 miles to the Iron Canyon Reservoir Spillway. Turn right and drive one mile to the campground.

Trip note: Of the two camps on this remote lake, this one is the better one for boaters because the boat ramp is set nearby. It's a good lake for camping and fishing, particularly in the spring for fishing, prior to the hot summer weather.

Map grid **d7**

DEADLUN
on Iron Canyon Reservoir
SHASTA-TRINITY NATIONAL FOREST

Campsites, facilities: There are 15 tent sites and 15 campsites for tents or motor homes up to 24 feet long. No piped water, so bring your own. Vault toilets, picnic tables, and fireplaces are provided. Pets are permitted on leashes.

Reservations, fee: No reservations, no fee.

Who to contact: Phone the Shasta-Trinity National Forest District Office at (916) 275-1587.

Location: From Burney, drive 14 miles west on Highway 299. Turn north on Big Bend Road and drive 15.2 miles to the town of Big Bend. Continue north for 2.1 miles. Turn left on Road 38N11 and drive 3.3 miles to the Iron Canyon Reservoir Spillway. Turn right and drive 1.5 miles to the campground.

Trip note: This is one of the prime drive-to mountain lakes that gets overlooked by so many people. Camps are set beside Iron Canyon Reservoir, which has good trout fishing, particularly early in the season. The shoreline can be quite muddy in March and April, but that's when the big trout bite here. There are numerous trails, peaks, and creeks in the area.

Map grid **e1**

CLEAR CREEK
SHASTA-TRINITY NATIONAL FOREST

Campsites, facilities: There are two tent sites and six campsites for tents or motor homes up to 22 feet long. Vault toilets, picnic tables, and fireplaces are provided, but there is **no piped water,** so bring your own.

Reservations, fee: No reservations; no fee.

Who to contact: Phone the Shasta-Trinity National Forest District Office at (916) 623-2121.

Location: From Redding, drive 17 miles west on Highway 299 to Trinity Lake Road (just west of Whiskeytown Lake). Turn north on Trinity Lake Road and continue past the town of French Gulch for about 12 miles to the Trinity

Mountain Station. Proceed north on East Side Road (a gravel road) for about 11 miles to the campground access road (dirt) on right. Turn on the access road and drive two miles to the campground.

Trip note: This is a primitive, little-known option to the crowds at nearby Trinity Lake. It is set at 3,500 feet elevation, about five miles from the east shore of Trinity Lake on Clear Creek. A trail from the camp follows Clear Creek for about four miles. In the fall, the camp gets used by hunters.

Map grid e3

LAKESHORE VILLA RV PARK AND CAMPGROUND
on Shasta Lake

Campsites, facilities: There are 90 campsites with partial or full hookups. Picnic tables are provided. Rest rooms, hot showers, a sanitary disposal station, satellite T.V., a grocery store, a laundromat, a playground, a recreation room, and a boat dock are available. Pets are permitted.

Reservations, fee: Deposit required with reservation; $17-$19 fee per night.

Who to contact: Phone (916)238-8688.

Location: From Redding, drive 24 miles north on Interstate 5. Take the Lakeshore-Antlers Road exit off Interstate 5. Drive one-half mile south on Lakeshore Drive to the campground.

Trip note: This is a large campground with level, shaded sites for motor homes and tents. The camp is located on the upper end of Shasta Lake. If you are going late in the year, particularly August through November, call first to make sure the upper end of the lake still has water in it. The lake is subject to drawdowns, leaving some areas on the upper end of the lake high and dry late in the year.

Map grid e3

LAKESHORE RESORT AND MARINA
on Shasta Lake

Campsites, facilities: There are 28 motor home spaces with partial and full hookups. Picnic tables are provided. Rest rooms, hot showers, a swimming pool, boat rentals, a boat dock, and a small grocery store are available.

Reservations, fee: Call ahead for availability; $12-$14 fee per night.

Who to contact: Phone (916)238-2301.

Location: From Redding, drive 24 miles north on Interstate 5. Take the Lakeshore-Antlers Road exit off Interstate 5. Drive one mile south on Lakeshore Drive.

Trip note: This camp is located on the upper end of Shasta Lake. If you are going late in the year, particularly August through November, call first to make sure the upper end of the lake still has water in it. The lake is subject to drawdowns, leaving some areas on the upper end of the lake high and dry late in the year.

Map grid e3

SHASTA LAKE TRAILER RESORT AND CAMPGROUND
on Shasta Lake

Campsites, facilities: There are 21 tent sites and 53 motor home spaces with full hookups. Picnic tables and fire grills are provided. Rest rooms, hot showers, a grocery store, wood, a laundromat, a playground, and a swimming pool are available. Pets are permitted. There is also a private dock with 36 boat slips.

Reservations, fee: Deposit required with reservation; $13-$18 fee per night, $.50 for pets. Fee discounted in the off-season.

Who to contact: Phone (916)238-2370.

Location: From Redding, drive 24 miles north on Interstate 5. Take the Lakeshore-Antlers Road exit off Interstate 5. Drive south on Lakeshore Drive for 1.5 miles to the campground.

Trip note: This camp is located on the upper end of Shasta Lake. If you are going late in the year, particularly in August through November, call first to make sure the upper end of the lake still has water in it. The lake is subject to drawdowns, leaving some areas on the upper end of the lake high and dry.

Map grid e3

GREGORY CREEK

on Shasta Lake

SHASTA-TRINITY NATIONAL FOREST

Campsites, facilities: There are five tent sites and 13 campsites for tents or motor homes up to 24 feet long. Piped water, flush toilets, picnic tables, and fireplaces are provided.

Reservations, fee: No reservations; $6 fee per night.

Who to contact: Phone the Shasta-Trinity National Forest District Office at (916) 275-1587.

Location: From Lakehead, drive three miles south on Interstate 5. Take the Salt Creek exit and drive four miles north on Gregory Creek Road to the camp.

Trip note: This is one of the more secluded Forest Service campgrounds on Shasta Lake. It is located across the inlet from the Antlers campground.

Map grid e3

ANTLERS RV RESORT AND CAMPGROUND

on Shasta Lake

Campsites, facilities: There are 106 campsites, many with full hookups, and a separate area for tents. Rest rooms, hot showers, a snack bar, a grocery store, ice, a laundromat, a recreation room, a playground, shuffle board, volleyball, propane gas, boats for rent, houseboats, moorage, and a complete marina are available. Pets are permitted.

Reservations, fee: Deposit required with reservation. $17 per night fee.

Who to contact: Phone (916)238-2322.

Location: From Redding, drive 24 miles north on Interstate 5. Take the Lakeshore-Antlers Road exit off Interstate 5. Drive 1.5 miles south on Antlers Road to the campground.

Trip note: Antlers Resort is set along the Sacramento River arm of Shasta Lake at 1,215 feet. The prime time to visit is from March through June when the lake levels are highest. This is a full-service spot for campers, boaters, and anglers.

Map grid e3

LAKEHEAD CAMPGROUND

on Shasta Lake

Campsites, facilities: There are 20 tent sites and 30 motor home spaces with full or partial hookups. Picnic tables, fire grills, rest rooms, hot showers, a dump station, a store, wood, a laundromat, a swimming pool, bike rentals, and horseshoes are available. An outdoor pavillion for groups is available. Pets are permitted. There's a boat ramp less than a mile from the campground.

Reservations, fee: Reservations available with deposit; $13-$16 fee per night from Memorial Day through Labor Day, $12-$14 the rest of the year.

Who to contact: Call (916)238-2671.

Location: From Redding, drive 24 miles north on Interstate 5. Take the Lakeshore-Antlers Road exit off Interstate 5. Drive one-quarter mile north on Antlers Road to the campground.

Trip note: This is one of the many campgrounds set around Shasta Lake. This one is particularly popular for motor home or pickup truck campers with trailer boats because there's a boat launch just a few minutes from the camp. The elevation is 1,200 feet. Open year-round, but best from March through June, when lake levels are at their highest.

A

B2

C

Map grid e3

ANTLERS

on Shasta Lake

SHASTA-TRINITY NATIONAL FOREST

Campsites, facilities: There are 41 single campsites and 18 double campsites for tents or motor homes up to 30 feet long. Piped water, flush toilets, picnic tables, and fireplaces are provided. A grocery store and a laundromat are nearby.

Reservations, fee: No reservations; $8-$12 fee per night (reduced rates in winter).

Who to contact: Phone Shasta-Trinity National Forest District Office at (916) 275-1587.

Location: From Redding, drive 24 miles north on Interstate 5. Take the Lakeshore-Antlers Road exit off Interstate 5. Drive one mile south on Antlers Road to the campground.

D

Trip note: This spot is set on the northwestern inlet of giant Shasta Lake. If you are going late in the year, particularly August through November, call first to make sure the upper end of the lake still has water in it. The lake is subject to drawdowns, leaving some areas on the upper end high and dry late in the year. Open year-round, with limited winter facilities.

E

Map grid e4

ELLERY CREEK

on Shasta Lake

SHASTA-TRINITY NATIONAL FOREST

F

Campsites, facilities: There are 21 campsites for tents or motor homes up to 30 feet long. Piped water, vault toilets, picnic tables, and fireplaces are provided. The facilities are wheelchair accessible. Pets are permitted on leashes.

Reservations, fee: No reservations; $7 fee per night.

Who to contact: Phone the Shasta-Trinity National Forest District Office at (916) 275-1587.

G

Location: From Lakehead, drive three miles south on Interstate 5. Take the Gilman Road exit and drive northeast for 15 miles to the campground.

Trip note: This camp is set at a pretty spot where Ellery Creek empties into Shasta Lake. If you are making your trip late in the year, particularly August through November, call first to make sure the upper end of the lake still has water in it. The lake is subject to drawdowns, leaving some areas on the upper end of the lake high and dry late in the year.

H

Map grid e4

MOORE CREEK

on Shasta Lake

SHASTA-TRINITY NATIONAL FOREST

I

Campsites, facilities: There are 12 campsites for tents or motor homes up to 30 feet long. Piped water, vault toilets, picnic tables, and fireplaces are provided. Pets are permitted on leashes.

J

Reservations, fee: No reservations; $6 fee per night.

Who to contact: Phone the Shasta-Trinity National Forest District Office at (916) 275-1587.

Location: From Lakehead, drive three miles south on Interstate 5. Take the Gilman Road exit and drive 11 miles northeast to the campground.

Trip note: Set just inland enough to be overlooked by Interstate 5 cruisers looking for fast answers, the McCloud arm of the Shasta Lake is the one most folks miss. Well, that's where this camp is set and it plumb always gets missed by the out-of-towners. Heh, heh, heh.

Map grid e4

PINE POINT

on Shasta Lake

SHASTA-TRINITY NATIONAL FOREST

Campsites, facilities: There are 14 campsites for tents or motor homes up to 30 feet long. Piped water, vault toilets, picnic tables, and fireplaces are provided. The facilities are wheelchair accessible. Pets are permitted on leashes.

Reservations, fee: No reservations; $7 fee per night.

Who to contact: Phone the Shasta-Trinity National Forest District Office at (916) 275-1587.

Location: From Lakehead, drive three miles south on Interstate 5. Take the Gilman Road exit and drive northeast for 19.5 miles to the campground.

Trip note: Shasta Lake gets tons of visitors, more than a million every year. That means the easy-to-reach spots get filled up quickly. This one may take some extra time to reach, but it's worth it to folks who desire a little more peace and quiet than the next guy.

Map grid e4

MCCLOUD BRIDGE

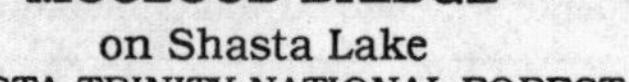

on Shasta Lake

SHASTA-TRINITY NATIONAL FOREST

Campsites, facilities: There are nine tent sites and 11 campsites for tents or motor homes up to 16 feet long. Piped water, flush and vault toilets, picnic tables, and fireplaces are provided. Pets are permitted on leashes.

Reservations, fee: No reservations; $6 fee per night, plus $6 for each additional vehicle.

Who to contact: Phone the Shasta-Trinity National Forest District Office at (916) 275-1587.

Location: From Lakehead, drive three miles south on Interstate 5. Take the Gilman Road exit and drive northeast for 19 miles to the campground.

Trip note: This is one of the more secluded camps on giant Shasta Lake. The McCloud arm of the lake has excellent fishing, especially in late summer for big brown trout. A backpacking trail from camp leads east into the backcountry.

Map grid e6

MADRONE CAMP

on Squaw Creek

SHASTA-TRINITY NATIONAL FOREST

Campsites, facilities: There are 13 campsites for tents or motor homes up to 16 feet long. There is **no piped water,** but vault toilets, picnic tables, and fireplaces are provided. Pets are permitted on leashes or otherwise controlled.

Reservations, fee: No reservations, no fee.

Who to contact: Phone the Shasta-Trinity National Forest District Office at (916) 275-1587.

Location: From Redding, drive 29 miles east on Highway 299 to the town of Montgomery Creek. Turn north (left) on Fenders Ferry Road and drive 22 miles to the camp (The road starts as a gravel road and then becomes dirt).

Trip note: Tired of people? Then you came to the right place. This remote camp is set along Squaw Creek and used primarily by backpackers as a jump-off point into the backcountry. Forest Service maps detail back roads, trails, streams, and lakes in the surrounding wildlands.

Map grid **f2**

LAKESHORE

on Shasta Lake

SHASTA-TRINITY NATIONAL FOREST

Campsites, facilities: There are 28 sites for tents or motor homes up to 24 feet long. Piped water, flush toilets, picnic tables, and fireplaces are provided. Pets are permitted on leashes. A boat ramp, grocery store, and laundromat are nearby.

Reservations, fee: No reservations; $7 fee per night.

Who to contact: Phone the Shasta-Trinity National Forest District Office at (916) 275-1587.

Location: From Lakehead, take the Lakeshore Drive exit off Interstate 5. Drive three miles southwest on Lakeshore Drive.

Trip note: If Shasta Lake is full of water, and that can be a mighty big "if" in late summer, this is one of the quieter spots. It's a nice Forest Service campground on Shasta Lake's north end. Regular sites are open from May to September. Walk-in sites are open year-round, but there's **no piped water in the winter.**

Map grid **f3**

SOLUS CAMPGROUND

on Shasta Lake

Campsites, facilities: There are 56 campsites, many with full hookups. Picnic tables and fire grills are provided. Rest rooms, hot showers, a sanitary disposal station, a grocery store, wood, a laundromat, a playground, a heated pool, horseshoes, and volleyball are available. Pets are permitted.

Reservations, fee: Deposit required with reservation; $13-$17 fee per night.

Who to contact: Phone (916)238-2451.

Location: From Redding, drive 22 miles north on Interstate 5. Take the Gilman Road-Salt Creek Road exit and follow the signs to the campground.

Trip note: There's boating, water skiing, swimming, and fishing on the upper end of Shasta Lake. Some private, shaded RV sites are available. Open all year.

Map grid **f3**

NELSON POINT

on Shasta Lake

SHASTA-TRINITY NATIONAL FOREST

Campsites, facilities: There are eight campsites here that can accommodate tents or motor homes up to 16 feet long. Piped water, vault toilets, picnic tables, and fireplaces are provided. Pets are permitted on leashes. A grocery store and a laundromat are nearby.

Reservations, fee: No reservations; $6 fee per night; $6 for each additional vehicle.

Who to contact: Phone the Shasta-Trinity National Forest District Office at (916) 275-1587.

Location: From Lakehead, drive three miles south on Interstate 5. Take the Salt Creek exit and drive one mile west to the campground.

Trip note: This is an easy-to-reach campground, only a few minutes from Interstate 5. It's set beside an inlet of Shasta Lake. Open from April through August.

Map grid **f3**

HOLIDAY HARBOR
on Shasta Lake

Campsites, facilities: There 27 motor home spaces with full hookups. Rest rooms, hot showers, picnic tables, and fire grills are provided. A grocery store, a laundromat, a playground, propane gas, and boat rentals are available.
Reservations, fee: Call ahead for availability; $14 per night.
Who to contact: Phone (916)238-2383.
Location: From the Shasta Lake Visitor Center (south of the lake), drive eight miles north on Interstate 5 to the Shasta Caverns Road exit on the right and drive three quarters of a mile. Turn right into the campground.
Trip note: This camp is one of the more popular year-round, all-service resorts on Shasta Lake. It is set on the lower McCloud arm of the lake, an ideal jump-off for boating and fishing. A good side trip is to Shasta Caverns, a privately guided adventure with a fee charged.

Map grid **f3**

TRAIL IN RV CAMPGROUND
on Shasta Lake

Campsites, facilities: There are 39 sites, some pull-through, with full hookups. Picnic tables and fire grills are provided. Rest rooms, hot showers, sanitary disposal station, a swimming pool, a grocery store, ice, wood, and a laundromat are available. The facilities are wheelchair accessible. Pets are permitted.
Reservations, fee: Deposit required with reservation; $11-$16 fee per night.
Who to contact: Phone (916)238-8533.
Location: From Redding, drive 22 miles north on Interstate 5. Take the Gilman Road-Salt Creek Road exit and drive 500 feet west on Gilman Road. Turn north on Gregory Creek Road and drive one mile to the campground.
Trip note: This is a privately-operated campground on the Salt Creek arm of giant Shasta Lake. Open, level sites are available.

Map grid **f3**

OAK GROVE
on Shasta Lake
SHASTA-TRINITY NATIONAL FOREST

Campsites, facilities: There are 43 campsites for tents or motor homes up to 16 feet long. Piped water, flush toilets, picnic tables, and fireplaces are provided. Pets are permitted on leashes. A grocery store is nearby.
Reservations, fee: No reservations; $6 fee per night.
Who to contact: Phone the Shasta-Trinity National Forest District Office at (916) 275-1587.
Location: From Lakehead, drive three miles south on Interstate 5. Take the Salt Creek exit and drive two miles west to the campground.
Trip note: This camp is on Salt Creek Inlet of Shasta Lake. Sometimes this campground is closed, so call ahead. Open from May through September.

Map grid **f3**

BAILEY COVE
on Shasta Lake
SHASTA-TRINITY NATIONAL FOREST

Campsites, facilities: There are 15 campsites for tents or motor homes up to 16 feet long. Piped water, flush and vault toilets, picnic tables, and fireplaces are provided. A boat ramp is available. The facilities are wheelchair accessible.

Supplies can be obtained in O'Brien.

Reservations, fee: No reservations; $6 fee per night.

Who to contact: Phone the Shasta-Trinity National Forest District Office at (916) 275-1587.

Location: From the Shasta Lake Visitor Center (south of the lake), drive eight miles north on Interstate 5 to the Shasta Caverns Road exit on the right and turn in.

Trip note: This campground is sometimes closed for the season, so always call ahead to check its availability. That done, you have yourself one of the quieter spots on a popular lake, with a boat ramp adjacent to the campground to boot.

Map grid f4

HIRZ BAY GROUP CAMP

on Shasta Lake

SHASTA-TRINITY NATIONAL FOREST

Campsites, facilities: There are two group campsites for motor homes up to 24 feet long. Piped water, vault toilets, picnic tables, and fireplaces are provided. Pets are permitted on leashes.

Reservations, fee: Reservations required; group fee is $40-$60 per night.

Who to contact: Phone the Shasta-Trinity National Forest District Office at (916) 275-1587.

Location: From Lakehead, drive three miles south on Interstate 5. Take the Gilman Road exit and drive ten miles northeast to the campground entrance road.

Trip note: This is the spot for your own private party, providing you get a reservation and have a motor home. The boat launch ramp is nearby. Open from May through September.

Map grid f4

HIRZ BAY

on Shasta Lake

SHASTA-TRINITY NATIONAL FOREST

Campsites, facilities: There are 38 single and double campsites for tents or motor homes up to 30 feet long. Piped water, flush toilets, picnic tables, and fireplaces are provided. A boat ramp is nearby. The facilities are wheelchair accessible. Pets are permitted on leashes.

Reservations, fee: No reservations; $8 fee per night for single sites, $12 fee for doubles. Reduced rates and services in the winter.

Who to contact: Phone the Shasta-Trinity National Forest District Office at (916) 275-1587.

Location: From Lakehead, drive three miles south on Interstate 5. Take the Gilman Road exit and drive ten miles east to the campground entrance road.

Trip note: A nearby boat ramp gives this camp a special attraction—ideal for camping boaters at Shasta Lake.

Map grid f4

DEKKAS ROCK

on Shasta Lake

SHASTA-TRINITY NATIONAL FOREST

Campsites, facilities: There are two campsites for tents or motor homes up to 16 feet long. Piped water, vault toilets, picnic tables, and fireplaces are provided. Pets are permitted on leashes. A grocery store is nearby.

Reservations, fee: Call for reservations and fee.

Who to contact: Phone the Shasta-Trinity National Forest District Office at (916) 275-1587.

Location: From Lakehead, drive three miles south on Interstate 5. Take the Gilman

Road exit and drive ten miles northeast to the campground.

Trip note: Bet you didn't know about this one. This here's the smallest campground in northern California, and it's set beside the largest lake. If you don't like neighbors, this is your calling. There's good fishing on the middle fork of Shasta Lake.

Map grid go

BRANDY CREEK
on Whiskeytown Reservoir

Campsites, facilities: There are 46 motor home spaces for self-contained vehicles up to 25 feet long. No tents permitted here. A dump station and piped water are available. Pets are permitted on six-foot leash.

Reservations, fee: Reservations accepted, no fee.

Who to contact: Phone the Whiskeytown National Recreation Area at (916)241-6584.

Location: From Redding, drive ten miles west on Highway 299. Turn left on Kennedy Memorial Drive and drive to the campground.

Trip note: This is a good base camp for motor homes or pick-up truck campers looking for a fishing trip. A boat ramp is nearby, with good fishing for kokanee salmon and rainbow trout.

Map grid go

OAK BOTTOM
on Whiskeytown Reservoir

Campsites, facilities: There are 101 walk-in (short walk) tent sites with picnic tables and fire grills, and there are 50 motor home spaces in the large parking area near the launch ramp and rest rooms. Piped water, flush toilets, cold showers, groceries, ice, wood, a sanitary dump station, a boat ramp, and boat rentals are available. Some facilities are wheelchair accessible. Pets are permitted on six-foot leashes.

Reservations, fee: Reservations required in summer and available through Ticketron; $7-$9 fee per night in summer, $5-$7 fee the rest of the year.

Who to contact: Phone Whiskeytown National Recreation Area at (916)241- 6584.

Location: From Redding, drive 15 miles west on Highway 299 to the entrance.

Trip note: The campsites are too close together here and it gets windy in the spring, but, other than that, this can be an excellent destination. The trout and kokanee salmon fishing are quite good, especially in May and June. The campground is set next to a beach area with a self-guided nature trail nearby. There are junior ranger programs for kids six to twelve years old, and evening ranger seminars at the Oak Bottom Amphitheater are available every night from mid-June through Labor Day.

Map grid go

DRY CREEK GROUP CAMP
on Whiskeytown Reservoir

Campsites, facilities: There is one large camp with piped water, pit toilets, picnic tables, and fireplaces. Pets are permitted on six-foot leashes.

Reservations, fee: Reservations required; group fee is $30-$50 per night.

Who to contact: Phone the Whiskeytown National Recreation Area at (916)241-6584.

Location: From Redding, drive ten miles west on Highway 299. Turn left on Kennedy Memorial Drive and drive to the campground.

Trip note: If you're in a group and take the time to reserve this spot, you'll be rewarded with some room and the quiet that goes along with it (compared to nearby Oak Bottom Camp). Hiking trails and horse-back riding are available.

Map grid g3 — WONDERLAND RV PARK

near Shasta Lake

Campsites, facilities: There are 36 motor home spaces, many with full hookups. Rest rooms, showers, a laundromat, a heated swimming pool, and horseshoes are available.

Reservations, fee: Reservations required with deposit; $13.50 fee per night.

Who to contact: Phone (916)275-1281.

Location: From Redding, drive 11 miles north on Interstate 5 to the Fawndale exit. Drive one-quarter mile south on Wonderland Boulevard.

Trip note: This campground is located within a mobile home park near Shasta Lake, not far from the O'Brien and Shasta Cavern tours. The city of Redding offers an extensive visitor center, the Carter House Natural History Museum in Caldwell Park, public golf courses, and the Sacramento River trails, which are paved, making them accessible for wheelchairs and bikes. Open year-round.

Map grid g4 — ROCKY RIDGE GROUP CAMP

on Shasta Lake
SHASTA-TRINITY NATIONAL FOREST

Campsites, facilities: There is one group campground with piped water, vault toilets, picnic tables, and fireplaces provided. Jones Valley Boat Ramp is three miles east of this camp. A grocery store is nearby.

Reservations, fee: Reservations required; call for fee.

Who to contact: Phone the Shasta-Trinity National Forest District Office at (916) 275-1587.

Location: From Redding, drive 7.5 miles east on Highway 299 to Bella Vista. Turn north on Dry Creek Road and drive ten miles to the campground.

Trip note: This is near Jones Valley Resort, but removed enough for a group to feel that the camp is its self-proclaimed refuge.

Map grid g4 — BEAR MOUNTAIN RV RESORT

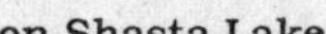

on Shasta Lake

Campsites, facilities: There are 41 tent sites and 99 motor home spaces with full or partial hookups. Piped water, flush toilets, a laundromat, a grocery store, a dump station, picnic tables, and fire rings are provided. A swimming pool, recreation hall, arcade, horseshoe pit, volleyball court, basketball court, shuffleboard court, and television are available. Nearby is a free boat launch ramp.

Reservations, fee: Reservations accepted; $9-$13 per night.

Who to contact: Phone (916)275-4728.

Location: From Redding, drive three miles north on Interstate 5 to the Oasis Road exit. Turn east on Oasis Road (Old Oregon Trail) and drive 3.5 miles. Turn northeast on Bear Mountain Road and drive 3.5 miles to the campground.

Trip note: This is a privately-operated park set up primarily for motor homes in the Jones Valley area along Shasta Lake.

Map grid **g4**

JONES INLET

on Shasta Lake

SHASTA-TRINITY NATIONAL FOREST

Campsites, facilities: There are an undesignated number of primitive campsites for tents or motor homes up to 30 feet long. There is **no piped water,** but vault toilets are provided. A boat ramp is two miles from camp. Pets are permitted on leashes.

Reservations, fee: No reservations, no fee.

Who to contact: Phone the Shasta-Trinity National Forest District Office at (916) 275-1587.

Location: From Redding, drive 7.5 miles east on Highway 299 to Bella Vista. Turn north on Dry Creek Road and drive nine miles to the camping area.

Trip note: This is one of the few primitive, free campgrounds on Shasta Lake. It is set near Jones Valley Resort, the big marina on Shasta Lake's southern shore, with a boat ramp nearby. If you head up the Pit River arm of the lake by boat, beware of submerged tree stumps. There's a side trip hike to Buck Point.

Map grid **g5**

UPPER & LOWER JONES VALLEY CAMPS

on Shasta Lake

SHASTA-TRINITY NATIONAL FOREST

Campsites, facilities: There are a total of 27 campsites for tents or motor homes up to 24 feet long in these two adjacent campgrounds. Picnic tables, fire grills, piped water, and vault toilets are provided. A boat ramp is two miles from camp. Pets are permitted on leashes.

Reservations, fee: No reservations; $6 fee per night.

Who to contact: Phone the Shasta-Trinity National Forest District Office at (916) 275-1587.

Location: From Redding, drive 7.5 miles east on Highway 299 to Bella Vista. Turn north on Dry Creek Road and drive nine miles to the camping area.

Trip note: This is one of the major resort marinas on Shasta Lake with a reputation for providing detailed fishing reports. If you're going by boat up the Pit River arm of the lake, beware of submerged tree stumps. Open year-round.

Map grid **h2**

KOA OF REDDING

Campsites, facilities: There are 124 campsites, 54 with full hookups and a separate area for tents. Piped water, flush toilets, showers, a playground, a swimming pool, a laundromat, a dump station, picnic tables, and fireplaces are provided. A grocery store and propane gas are also available. Pets are permitted.

Reservations, fee: Reservation not required; $16-$20 fee per night.

Who to contact: Phone (916)246-0101.

Location: From Redding, drive north on Interstate 5 to the Lake Boulevard (Alturas-Burney) exit. Drive one-quarter mile west on Lake Boulevard. Turn north on North Boulder Drive and drive one block to 280 North Boulder Drive.

Trip note: If you're stuck with no place to go, this large park may be your savior. But expect very hot weather in the summer. Nearby recreation options include the Sacramento River, which runs through town, Whiskeytown Lake to the west, and Shasta Lake to the north.

Map grid **h2**

TWIN VIEW TERRACE RV PARK

near Redding

Campsites, facilities: There are 48 pull-through motor home spaces with full hookups. Rest rooms, showers, laundromat, two swimming pools, and a recreation room are available.

Reservations, fee: Reservations not accepted; $15 fee per night.

Who to contact: Phone (916)243-8114.

Location: In Redding, take the Twin View exit off Interstate 5. Drive one mile south on Twin View Boulevard to the mobile home park.

Trip note: This is one of several motor home parks open year-round in the Redding area. This particular park is located within a mobile home park.

Map grid **h2**

MARINA MOTOR HOME PARK

on Sacramento River

Campsites, facilities: There are 86 tent trailer and motor home sites with full or partial hookups. Rest rooms, hot showers, a laundromat, a grocery store, a swimming pool, a whirlpool, a boat ramp, and a dump station are on park grounds. Pets are permitted.

Reservations, fee: Reservations accepted; $14-$17 fee per night.

Who to contact: Phone (916)241-4396.

Location: From the junction of Interstate 5 and Highway 299 in Redding, drive west on Highway 299 to Marina Park Drive. Turn south and drive one mile on Park Marina Drive to the park.

Trip note: The riverside setting is a highlight, with the Sacramento River providing relief from the dog days of summer. From August to October, salmon fishing is quite good on the river, with salmon averaging 10 to 25 pounds, occasionally bigger. There's a miniature golf course nearby. This park is open year-round.

Map grid **i2**

SACRAMENTO RIVER MOTOR HOME PARK

Campsites, facilities: There are 20 tent sites and 140 motor home spaces with full hookups. Rest rooms, hot showers, a grocery store, a laundromat, a dump station, a free satellite TV, a bait and tackle shop, propane gas, a launch and slips, two tennis courts, and a large swimming pool are available for campers' pleasure.

Reservations, fee: Reservations accepted; $14-$19 fee per night.

Who to contact: Phone (916)365-6402.

Location: From Redding, drive five miles south on Interstate 5 to the Knighton Road exit. Turn west and drive about 100 feet. Turn south on Riverland Drive and drive two miles to the end of the road.

Trip note: This makes a good headquarters for a fall fishing trip on the Sacramento River, where the salmon come big from August through October. The park is open year-round, and if you want to stay close to home, a three-acre pond is available at the park.

Map grid **i9**

OLD COW MEADOWS

LATOUR STATE FOREST

Campsites, facilities: There are three campsites for tents or motor homes. There is **no piped water,** but picnic tables, fireplaces, and pit toilets are provided. Pets are permitted and a horse corral is available.

Reservations, fee: No reservations, no fee.

Who to contact: Phone the Latour State Forest at (916)224-2495.

Location: From Redding, drive seven miles east on Highway 44 to Palo Cedro. Continue east for 2.5 miles on Old Oak Run Road. Drive 16 miles east on Old Oak Run Road and Whitmore Road to the town of Whitmore. From Whitmore, drive 15 miles east on Bateman Road to the campground.

Trip note: You want quiet? You don't want to be bugged by anybody? You want piped water, too? Well, two out of three ain't bad. This tiny camp, virtually unknown, is set at 5,900 feet in a wooded area along Old Cow Creek. Recreation options include fishing, off-road vehicle use, and walking the dirt roads that crisscross the area. Open June through October.

Map grid i9

SOUTH COW CREEK MEADOWS

LATOUR STATE FOREST

Campsites, facilities: There are two campsites for tents or motor homes. Non-piped water is available. There are no toilets, but picnic tables, and fireplaces are provided. Pets are allowed.

Reservations, fee: No reservations, no fee.

Who to contact: Phone the Latour State Forest at (916)224-2495.

Location: From Redding, drive seven miles east on Highway 44 to Palo Cedro. Continue east for 16 miles on Old Oak Run Road and Whitmore Road to the town of Whitmore. Drive 14 miles east on Bateman Road to the campground.

Trip note: This camp is set in a pretty wooded area next to a small meadow along South Cow Creek. It's mostly used in the fall for hunting. It's set at 5,600 feet elevation. If you want to get away from it all without leaving your vehicle, this is one way to do it. Open from June through October.

Map grid j3

READING ISLAND

on Sacramento River

Campsites, facilities: There are eight campsites for tents or motor homes up to 30 feet long. Piped water, vault toilets, picnic tables, and fireplaces are provided. A boat ramp, groceries, propane gas, and a laundromat are available nearby. The facilities are wheelchair accessible.

Reservations, fee: No reservations; $5 fee per night.

Who to contact: Phone the Bureau of Land Management at (916)246-5325.

Location: From Redding, drive 15 miles south on Interstate 5 to Cottonwood. In Cottonwood, turn east on Balls Ferry Road and drive five miles to Adobe Road. Take Adobe Road to the campground entrance.

Trip note: This prime spot along the Sacramento River is in the midst of the best stretch of river for salmon. The state-record 88-pounder was caught near here.

Map grid j7

KOA MT. LASSEN

Campsites, facilities: There are 50 sites for tents or motor homes and some pull-through sites with full or partial hookups. Picnic tables, fire grills, piped water, flush toilets, hot showers,playground, heated pool, and a dump station are provided. Groceries, ice, wood, a laundromat, and propane gas are available nearby. Pets are permitted.

Reservations, fee: Deposit required with reservation; $14-$18 fee per night.

Who to contact: Phone (916)474-3133.
Location: From Shingletown, drive four miles east on Highway 44. Or drive 14 miles west on Highway 44 from the entrance of Lassen Volcanic National Park (junction of Highways 44 and 89).
Trip note: This is a popular KOA camp set outside Lassen National Park. Open year-round.

Map grid j7

CREEKSIDE MOBILE ESTATES AND RV PARK
near Shingletown

Campsites, facilities: There are 12 sites for motor homes with full or partial hookups. Piped water, flush toilets, hot showers, and a laundromat are available.
Reservations, fee: Reservations accepted; $15 fee per night.
Who to contact: Phone (916)474-3792.
Location: From Shingletown store drive 2.5 mile east on Highway 44. Or drive 17 miles west on Highway 44 from the entrance of Lassen National Park (junction of Highways 44 and 89).
Trip note: What you get here are RV spaces set within a mobile home park.

Map grid j7

MILL CREEK PARK
near Shingletown

Campsites, facilities: There are 34 sites for tents or motor homes and some pull-through sites with full or partial hookups. Picnic tables, fire grills, piped water, flush toilets, a dump station, and a laundromat are available. A fishing pond and creek are also available. Pets permitted.
Reservations, fee: Deposit required with reservation; $10-$14 fee per night.
Who to contact: Phone (916)474-5384.
Location: From Shingletown, drive two miles east on Highway 44. Or drive 18 miles west on Highway 44 from the entrance of Lassen Volcanic National Park (junction of Highways 44 and 89).
Trip note: This year-round park is set up primarily for motor homes, but has spaces for tenters. Its elevation is 4,000 feet and it's set amid conifers on the western slopes of Mt. Lassen.

Map grid j9

MACUMBER RESERVOIR
on Macumber Reservoir

Campsites, facilities: There are ten campsites for tents or motor homes. Piped water, vault toilets, picnic tables, and fire grills are provided. Pets are permitted on leashes.
Reservations, fee: No reservations; $8 fee per night.
Who to contact: Phone the PG&E District Office at (916)527-0354.
Location: From Viola, drive four miles west on Highway 44. Turn north on Macumber Road and drive two miles to the reservoir and the campground.
Trip note: This small campground is not widely known. It's set along Macumber Reservoir at 3,500 feet elevation. Car-top boats, that is, prams, canoes, rafts, and small aluminum boats, are permitted. No gas motors .

◆ MAP B3 ◆

BEACH
TREES
5% CLUB
DESERT
URBAN
FOOTHILL
GRASSLAND

15 MILES

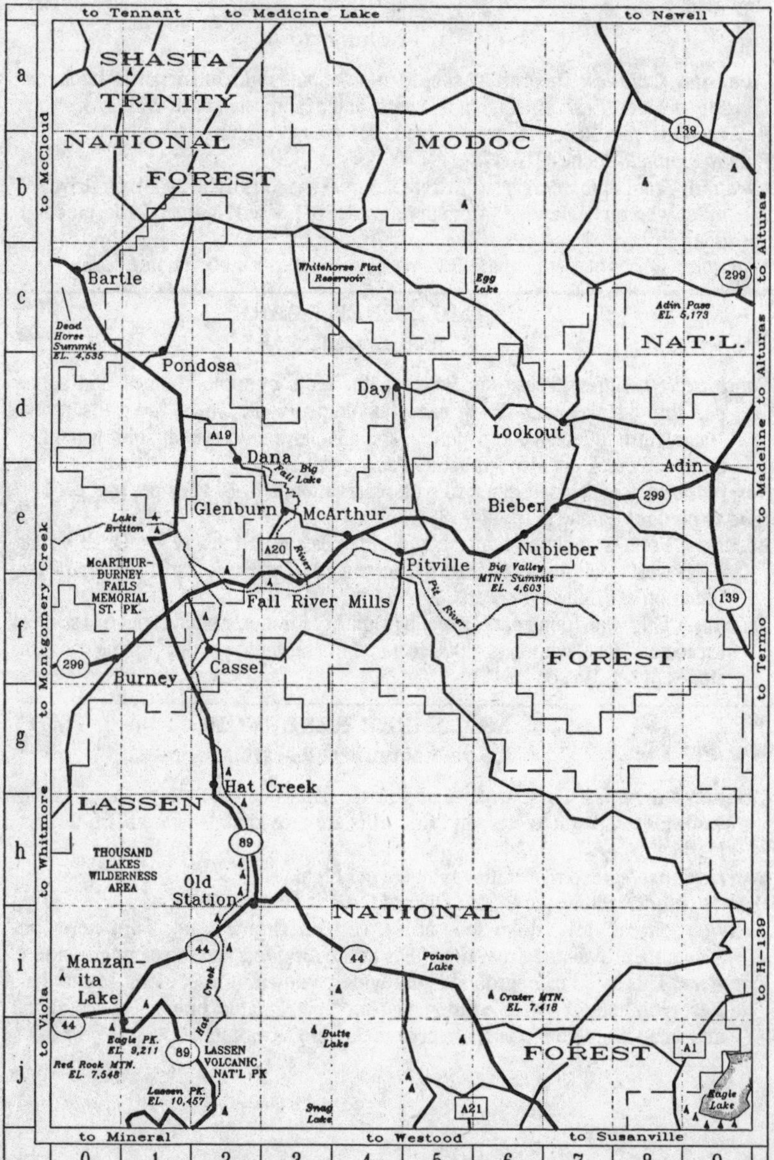

Map grid a1 — HARRIS SPRINGS

SHASTA-TRINITY NATIONAL FOREST

Campsites, facilities: There are 15 sites for tents or motor homes up to 32 feet long. Piped water, vault toilets, picnic tables, and fireplaces provided. Pets are permitted on leashes.

Reservations, fee: No reservations; no fee.

Who to contact: Phone the Shasta-Trinity National Forest District Office at (916) 964-2184.

Location: From McCloud, drive 17 miles east on Highway 89 to the town of Bartle. Turn north on Medicine Lake Road and drive 17 miles to the campground.

Trip note: This spot gets missed by a lot of folks heading to nearby Medicine Lake or Lava Beds National Monument. If those two areas have too many people for your taste, this camp is usually sparsely settled. The elevation is at 4,800 feet. The camp is open from mid-May to mid-September. Maps of the Shasta-Trinity National Forest detail the backcountry roads, hiking trails, and streams.

Map grid b5 — LAVA CAMP

MODOC NATIONAL FOREST

Campsites, facilities: There are 12 campsites for tents or motor homes up to 32 feet long. Vault toilets, tables, and fireplaces are provided. **No piped water** is available, so be certain to bring your own.

Reservations, fee: No reservation, no fee.

Who to contact: Phone the Modoc National Forest District Office at (916) 299-3215.

Location: From Adin, drive about ten miles south on Highway 299. Turn north on County Road 91 and drive seven miles to the town of Lookout. Then drive 21 miles northwest from the town of Lookout on Forest Service Roads 93, 95, or 91. (A Forest Service map is highly recommended.)

Trip note: Modoc country is "old country." It feels like it hasn't changed since the beginning of time. If that's what you are looking for, this camp is for you. It's virtually unknown, yet in a prime spot in the area, on the outskirts of Long Bell State Game Refuge. The elevation is 4,400 feet. In the fall, it's a good base camp for a hunting trip. Open from May through October.

Map grid b8 — COTTONWOOD FLAT

MODOC NATIONAL FOREST

Campsites, facilities: There are ten sites for tents of motor homes of any length. Potable spring water, vault toilets, fireplaces, and picnic tables are provided. Pets are permitted on leashes or otherwise controlled. Supplies are available in Canby.

Reservations, fee: No reservations, no fee.

Who to contact: Phone the Modoc National Forest District Office at (916)233-4611.

Location: From Canby, drive five miles south on Highway 299. Turn at the Canby River Bridge and drive eight miles west on a fair access road to the campground.

Trip note: Hunters who have deer tags for the area in the fall use this camp primarily. The elevation is 4,700 feet and the rugged setting gets very cold early or late in the season. Open from June to October.

Map grid **b9**

HOWARD'S GULCH

near Duncan Reservoir
MODOC NATIONAL FOREST

Campsites, facilities: There are 12 sites for tents or motor homes up to 22 feet long. Piped water, vault toilets, tables, and fireplaces are provided. One toilet is wheelchair accessible. Pets are permitted on leashes. Supplies are available in Canby.

Reservations, fee: No reservations, no fee.

Who to contact: Phone the Modoc National Forest District Office at (916)233-4611.

Location: From Canby, drive six miles northwest on State Highway 139.

Trip note: Duncan Reservoir, which is stocked with trout by the Department of Fish and Game, is about three miles from this camp. The elevation is 4,700 feet. Open from May through October.

Map grid **e1**

MCARTHUR-BURNEY FALLS

MEMORIAL STATE PARK

Campsites, facilities: There are 128 campsites for tents or motor homes up to 30 feet long. Piped water, flush toilets, hot showers, a sanitary dump station, picnic tables, and fireplaces are provided. The facilities are wheelchair accessible. Pets are permitted. A grocery store and boat rentals are available.

Reservations, fee: Reserve through MISTIX at (800)444-PARK ($3.95 MISTIX fee); $12-$14 fee per night; $1 pet fee.

Who to contact: Phone (916)335-2777.

Location: From Burney, drive 11 miles east on Highway 299.

Trip note: The spectacular waterfall near the park entrance gives this park its name and major attraction. But there are other options. Nearby Lake Britton offers possibilities for boating and fishing, the Pacific Crest Trail passes nearby, and Burney Spring Mountain or Long Valley Mountain can be reached by trail. A great beach for swimming is located along the shore of Lake Britton, just a short hike from the campground.

Map grid **e1**

NORTHSHORE

on Lake Britton

Campsites, facilities: There are 30 sites for tents or motor homes up to 16 feet long. Piped water, vault toilets, picnic tables, and fire grills are provided. A boat ramp is available. Supplies can be obtained in Fall River Mills.

Reservations, fee: No reservations; $8-$9 fee per night.

Who to contact: Phone the PG&E District Office at (916)527-0354.

Location: From the junction of Highways 89 and 299, drive north on Highway 89 for 9.7 miles. Turn west (left) on Old Highway Road and drive nine-tenths of a mile. Turn left and drive one mile to the campground.

Trip note: This peaceful campground set among the woodlands along the shore of Lake Britton is across the lake from McArthur-Burney Falls Memorial State Park. Water skiing, swimming, fishing, and boating are all options here. If you want to see how PG&E monopolizes the area, drive along the Pit River and check out the power stations. The best fishing on the Pit River is near Powerhouse No. 3. There is a nice hot springs place in Big Bend about a 30-minute drive from camp.

Map grid e2 — BURNEY FALLS TRAILER RESORT

Campsites, facilities: There are 28 motor home spaces with full hookups. Rest rooms, hot showers, a laundromat, horseshoes, and a swimming pool are on the premises.
Reservations, fee: Reservations accepted; $14 fee per night.
Who to contact: Phone (916)335-2781.
Location: From Burney, drive east on Highway 299 for five miles to the intersection of Highway 89. Go left and drive 4 miles to Clark Creek Road. Go left again and drive a short distance to the campground entrance.
Trip note: This is a year-round motor home park located along Clark Creek, near the Pit River, quite close to McArthur-Burney Falls Memorial State Park. Sight-seeing is spectacular with Lassen Volcanic National Park, Subway Caves, and many lakes and streams within 30 miles.

Map grid f2 — CASSEL FOREBAY
on Hat Creek

Campsites, facilities: There are 27 sites for tents or motor homes up to 20 feet long. Piped water, vault toilets, picnic tables, and fire grills are provided. Pets are permitted on leashes.
Reservations, fee: No reservations; $8-$9 fee per night.
Who to contact: Phone the PG&E District Office at (916)527-0354.
Location: From the junction of Highways 89 and 299, drive east on Highway 299 for two miles. Turn south on Cassel Road and drive 3.6 miles to the campground.
Trip note: This camp is a take-your-pick deal, with fishing on Hat Creek or nearby Baum Lake, both of which can be quite good for trout. A special Wild Trout Section of Hat Creek is nearby which has good fishing and special regulations. Baum Lake is ideal for car-top boats with electric motors.

Map grid f3 — PIT RIVER

Campsites, facilities: There are ten campsites for tents or motor homes. There is **no piped water,** but vault toilets, picnic tables, and fireplaces are provided. Pets are permitted. There are supplies and a laundromat in Fall River Mills.
Reservations, fee: No reservations, no fee.
Who to contact: Phone the Bureau of Land Management at (916)257-5381
Location: From Fall River Mills, drive 3.5 miles west on Highway 299. Turn south on the dirt road (Pit River Powerhouse Road) and follow it along the river to the campground.
Trip note: This primitive camp is often overlooked, but it can provide a good base camp for a fishing trip adventure on the nearby Pit River. The Pit is a brushy stream in many spots, but the vicinity of Powerhouse No. 3 is a premium spot for trout anglers.

Map grid g2 — HAT CREEK RANCH CAMPGROUND

Campsites, facilities: There are 30 tent sites and 40 motor home spaces with full or partial hookups. Rest rooms, hot showers, a sanitary dump station, a laundromat, a playground, and a grocery store are on the premises.

Reservations, fee: Reservations recommended; $9-$13 fee per night.

Who to contact: Phone (916)335-7171.

Location: From Burney, drive five miles east on Highway 299 to the intersection with Highway 89. Turn south on Highway 89 and drive about 13 miles to Doty Road, the entrance to the campground.

Trip note: This privately-operated campground is set in the midst of a working cattle range, so watch where you plant your Vibrams. Fishing is available in Hat Creek or in the nearby stocked trout pond. Sightseeing is excellent with Burney Falls, Lassen Volcanic National Park, and Subway Caves all within 30 miles. Open April through October.

Map grid h2

CAVE
on Hat Creek
LASSEN NATIONAL FOREST

Campsites, facilities: There are 46 campsites for tents or motor homes up to 22 feet long. Piped water, vault toilets, picnic tables, and fireplaces are provided. Supplies can be obtained in Old Station.

Reservations, fee: No reservations; $7 fee per night.

Who to contact: Phone the Lassen National Forest District Office at (916)336-5521.

Location: From Burney, drive five miles east on Highway 299 to the intersection with Highway 89. Turn south on Highway 89 and travel about 23 miles south to the campground entrance about a mile before you get to Old Station.

Trip note: This is an easy access camp along Hat Creek, with many side trip possibilities. Subway Cave and Devil's Half Acre are in the vicinity.

Map grid h2

BRIDGE
on Hat Creek
LASSEN NATIONAL FOREST

Campsites, facilities: There are 25 campsites here for tents or motor homes up to 22 feet long. Piped water, vault toilets, picnic tables, and fireplaces are provided. A grocery store and propane gas are also available nearby.

Reservations, fee: No reservations; $7 fee per night.

Who to contact: Phone the Lassen National Forest District Office at (916)336-5521.

Location: From Burney, drive five miles east on Highway 299 to the intersection with Highway 89. Turn south on Highway 89 and travel about 19 miles south to the campground entrance, about four miles before you get to the town of Old Station.

Trip note: The camp, one of four in the area, is in a pretty spot set along Hat Creek. This one is a bit downstream from the others at 3,800 feet elevation. Trout fishing is exceptional after a stock.

Map grid h2

ROCKY
on Hat Creek
LASSEN NATIONAL FOREST

Campsites, facilities: There are eight tent sites. There is **no piped water,** but vault toilets, picnic tables, and fireplaces are provided. A grocery store and propane gas are also available nearby.

Reservations, fee: No reservations, no fee.

Who to contact: Phone the Lassen National Forest District Office at (916)336-5521.

Location: From Burney, drive five miles east on Highway 299 to the intersection with Highway 89. Turn south on Highway 89 and travel about 20 miles south to the entrance, about three miles before you get to the town of Old Station.

Trip note: This is a small, primitive camp located in the Hat Creek Lava Bed area. If you want piped water, nearby Cave, Honn and Bridge camps will provide it, but expect some neighbors.

Map grid **h2**

HONN
on Hat Creek
LASSEN NATIONAL FOREST

Campsites, facilities: There are six tent sites. There is **no piped water,** but vault toilets, picnic tables and fireplaces are provided. A grocery store, a laundromat and propane gas are also available nearby.

Reservations, fee: No reservations, no fee.

Who to contact: Phone the Lassen National Forest District Office at (916)336-5521.

Location: From Burney, drive five miles east on Highway 299 to the intersection with Highway 89. Turn south on Highway 89 and travel about 15 miles south to the campground entrance, about nine miles before you get to Old Station.

Trip note: This primitive, tiny camp, set near Hat Creek, is a possible camp base for an exploration of the area. The lava bed area, a remnant of Mt. Lassen's explosions from 1914 to 1918, begins on the western edge. The elevation is 3,400 feet.

Map grid **i0**

NORTH BATTLE CREEK RESERVOIR

Campsites, facilities: There are ten campsites for tents or motor homes and five walk-in tent sites. Piped water, vault toilets, picnic tables, and fire grills are provided. Pets are permitted on leashes. A car-top boat launch is available.

Reservations, fee: No reservations; $8 fee per night.

Who to contact: Phone the PG&E District Office at (916)527-0354.

Location: From Viola, drive 3.5 miles east on Highway 44. Turn north on Road 32N17 and drive five miles. Turn east (left) on Road 32N31 and drive four miles. Turn right on Road 32N18 and drive one-half mile to the reservoir and the campground.

Trip note: This little-known reservoir is ideal for canoes, rafts, and car-top aluminum boats. Electric motors are permitted, but no gas engines. Trout fishing can be good. The camp is set at 5,600 feet elevation.

Map grid **i1**

CRAGS CAMP
LASSEN VOLCANIC NATIONAL PARK

Campsites, facilities: There are 45 campsites for tents or motor homes up to 35 feet long. Piped water, pit toilets, picnic tables, and fireplaces are provided. Pets are permitted.

Reservations, fee: No reservations; $5 fee per night.

Who to contact: Phone Lassen Volcanic National Park at (916)595-4444.

Location: From Manzanita Lake, drive 4.5 northeast on Lassen Park Road.

Trip note: This is primarily used an overflow camp in case the nearby Manzanita Lake camp fills up as it often does during peak summer periods.

Map grid i2

HAT CREEK

LASSEN NATIONAL FOREST

Campsites, facilities: There are 73 campsites for tents or motor homes up to 22 feet long. Piped water, flush toilets, a sanitary dump station, picnic tables, and fireplaces are provided. A grocery store, a laundromat, and propane gas are also available nearby.

Reservations, fee: No reservations; $7 fee per night.

Who to contact: Phone the Lassen National Forest District Office at (916)336-5521.

Location: From Burney, drive five miles east on Highway 299 to the intersection with Highway 89. Turn south on Highway 89 and travel about 24 miles south to the town of Old Station. Continue one mile south of Old Station on Highway 89-44 to the campground entrance.

Trip note: This is one of a series of Forest Service camps set beside beautiful Hat Creek, a good trout stream stocked regularly by the Department of Fish and Game. The elevation is 4,400 feet. Side trip options include Logan Lake, Devil's Half Acre, many caves, and the Pacific Crest Trail.

Map grid i2

BIG PINE CAMP

on Hat Creek

LASSEN NATIONAL FOREST

Campsites, facilities: There are 19 campsites for tents or motor homes up to 22 feet long. Two hand pumps provide water. Vault toilets, picnic tables, and fireplaces are provided. A sanitary disposal station, a grocery store, and propane gas are nearby.

Reservations, fee: No reservations; $5 fee per night.

Who to contact: Phone the Lassen National Forest District Office at (916)336-5521.

Location: From Burney, drive five miles east on Highway 299 to the intersection with Highway 89 (four corners). Turn south on Highway 89 and travel about 24 miles to the town of Old Station. Continue four miles south of Old Station on Highway 89-44 to the campground entrance.

Trip note: The campground is set beside Hat Creek, a beautiful trout stream. This particular stretch is stocked with trout by Fish and Game. Good side trips include visiting nearby Lassen National Park or hiking a bit on the Pacific Crest Trail, which passes near Big Pine.

Map grid i4

BUTTE CREEK

LASSEN NATIONAL FOREST

Campsites, facilities: There are 14 campsites for either tents or motor homes up to 22 feet long. **No piped water** is available. Vault toilets, fireplaces, and tables are provided. Pets are permitted on leashes.

Reservations, fee: No reservations, no fee charged.

Who to contact: Call the Lassen National Forest at (916)257-2151 or write to 55 South Sacramento Street, Susanville, CA 96130.

Location: From Burney, drive five miles east on Highway 299 to the intersection with Highway 89. Turn south on Highway 89 and travel about 24 miles south to the town of Old Station. Turn east on Highway 44 and drive 11 miles, then turn south on Road 18 and drive two miles to the campground.

Trip note: This prime, little-known spot is just three miles from the northern boundary of Lassen Volcanic National Park, with fishing at Butte Creek and nearby Butte Lake.

Map grid i6

CRATER LAKE
LASSEN NATIONAL FOREST

Campsites, facilities: There are 17 campsites for tents or motor homes up to 16 feet long. Well water is available. Vault toilets, fireplaces, and picnic tables are provided. Pets are permitted on leashes.

Reservations, fee: No reservations; $6 fee per night.

Who to contact: Call Lassen National Forest at (916)257-2151.

Location: From Susanville, drive 28 miles northwest on Highway 44 to the Bogard Work Center. Then drive northeast for seven miles on a Forest Service Road to the campground at the lake.

Trip note: This camp is set beside little Crater Lake at 6,800 feet elevation, not far from Crater Mountain(that's it up there to the east at 7,420 feet). Fishing can be good here and, if you're lucky enough to get a hot day, so is the swimming.

Map grid j0

MANZANITA LAKE
LASSEN VOLCANIC NATIONAL PARK

Campsites, facilities: There are 179 campsites for tents or motor homes up to 35 feet long. Piped water, flush toilets, showers, a sanitary dump station, picnic tables, fireplaces and naturalist programs are provided. Pets are permitted. Propane gas, groceries and a laundromat are also available nearby.

Reservations, fee: No reservations; $7 fee per night.

Who to contact: Phone Lassen Volcanic National Park at (916)595-4444.

Location: This campground is located just beyond the Visitor Center on Highway 44 at the western boundary of the park.

Trip note: Manzanita Lake, set at 5,890 feet, is one of the prettiest lakes in Lassen Park and has fantastic trout fishing for experienced fly fishermen. Special regulations are in effect. It makes a good base camp for a Lassen vacation. Side trips include climbing to the top of Lassen, taking backcountry hikes, or visiting the bubbling pools from the underground volcanic waterways.

Map grid j2

SUMMIT LAKE, NORTH AND SOUTH
LASSEN VOLCANIC NATIONAL PARK

Campsites, facilities: There are 94 campsites for tents or motor homes up to 30 feet long. Piped water, flush toilets, picnic tables, fireplaces and naturalist programs are provided. Pets are permitted.

Reservations, fee: No reservations; $5-$7 fee per night.

Who to contact: Phone Lassen Volcanic National Park at (916)595-4444.

Location: From Manzanita Lake, drive 12 miles southeast on Lassen Park Road.

Trip note: Summit Lake is a beautiful spot where deer commonly visit each evening and where the trout rise can be a good one at sunset. Alas, most of the fish are little dinkers, nowhere as good as Manzanita Lake (also in Lassen Park). Trails that lead to backcountry lakes and, in the spring, past lavish displays of wildflowers are accessible from this camp.

Map grid j3

BUTTE LAKE
LASSEN VOLCANIC NATIONAL PARK

Campsites, facilities: There are 98 campsites for tents or motor homes up to 30 feet

long. Piped water, flush toilets, fireplaces, and tables are provided. Pets are permitted on leashes.

Reservations, fee: No reservations; $7 fee per night.

Who to contact: Call Lassen Volcanic National Park at (916)595-4444.

Location: From Burney, drive five miles east on Highway 299 to the intersection with Highway 89. Turn south on Highway 89 and travel about 24 miles south to the town of Old Station. Turn east on Highway 44 and drive 11 miles. Turn south on Road 18 and drive seven miles to the campground.

Trip note: This camp is a prime spot set beside Butte Lake. Side trips include hiking to Cinder Cone and nearby lava beds or hiking and fishing at Snag or Horseshoe Lakes. Both provide trout fishing. Car-top boats and other non-motored crafts are allowed on Butte Lake. The camp is set at 6,000 feet.

Map grid j5

SILVER BOWL

on Silver Lake

LASSEN NATIONAL FOREST

Campsites, facilities: There are ten sites for tents or motor homes. Piped water, vault toilets, fireplaces, and picnic tables are provided. Pets are permitted on leashes.

Reservations, fee: No reservations; $6 per night fee.

Who to contact: Phone the Lassen National Forest at (916)257-2151.

Location: From Westwood, drive 12.5 miles north on County Road A21. Turn left on Silver Lake Road and drive 8.5 miles to the camp.

Trip note: This is one of two camps on Silver Lake. It is set at 6,400 feet elevation. A nearby trailhead provides access to the Caribou Wilderness and numerous alpine lakes.

Map grid j5

BOGARD

LASSEN NATIONAL FOREST

Campsites, facilities: There are 22 campsites at Bogard that can accommodate tents or motor homes up to 22 feet long. Water, vault toilets, tables, and fireplaces are provided. Pets are permitted on leashes.

Reservations, fee: No reservations; $6 per night fee.

Who to contact: Phone the Lassen National Forest at (916)257-2151 or write to 55 South Sacramento Street, Susanville, CA 96130.

Location: From Susanville, drive 28 miles northwest on Highway 44 to the campground entrance road on the left.

Trip note: This is an easy-to-reach camp set along Highway 44 at 5,600 feet elevation. A good side trip is to fish the small stream in Pine Creek Valley at the foot of Bogard Buttes (elevation 7,500 feet).

Map grid j5

ROCKY KNOLL

on Silver Lake

LASSEN NATIONAL FOREST

Campsites, facilities: There are seven tent sites and 11 campsites for motor homes up to 22 feet long. Piped water, vault toilets, fireplaces, and picnic tables are provided. Pets are permitted on leashes.

Reservations, fee: No reservations; $6 fee per night.

Who to contact: Phone the Lassen National Forest at (916)257-2151.

Location: From Westwood, drive 12.5 miles north on County Road A21. Turn left on Silver Lake Road and drive 7.5 miles to the camp.

Trip note: This small camp, set along Silver Lake at 6,400 feet elevation, is popular during summer months for swimming, boating, and fishing. A trailhead near the camp provides access to numerous lakes in the Caribou Wilderness.

Map grid **j9**

ASPEN GROVE

on Eagle Lake
LASSEN NATIONAL FOREST

Campsites, facilities: There are 26 tent sites. Picnic tables, fireplaces, piped water, and flush toilets are provided. Pets are permitted on leashes. A boat ramp is available.
Reservations, fee: No reservations; $7 fee per night.
Who to contact: Phone the Lassen National Forest at (916)257-2151.
Location: From Susanville, drive three miles west on Highway 36, then 15.5 miles northwest on County Road A1, and 1.5 miles northeast on County Road 201 to the campground.
Trip note: This is a good spot for campers, boaters, or anglers. There's a boat launch adjacent to the camp, right along Eagle Lake.

Map grid **j9**

EAGLE

on Eagle Lake
LASSEN NATIONAL FOREST

Campsites, facilities: There are 50 campsites for tents or motor homes up to 32 feet long. Piped water, flush toilets, picnic tables, and fireplaces are provided. The facilities are wheelchair accessible. There is a boat launch nearby at Aspen Grove. Pets are permitted on leashes.
Reservations, fee: Reserve through MISTIX at (800)283-CAMP ($6 MISTIX fee); $9 fee per night.
Who to contact: Phone the Lassen National Forest at (916)257-2151.
Location: From Susanville, drive three miles west on Highway 36, then 15.5 miles northwest on County Road A1, and one mile northeast on County Road 201 to the campground.
Trip tip: This is one of the most popular camps set along Eagle Lake, yet get this. The fishing isn't all that great in this area. It's far better on the northern end of the lake or off Eagle Nest.

Map grid **j9**

WEST EAGLE GROUP CAMPS

on Eagle Lake
LASSEN NATIONAL FOREST

Campsites, facilities: There are two group camps for tents and motor homes up to 22 feet long. Piped water, flush toilets, tables, and picnic areas are provided. The facilities are wheelchair accessible. Pets are permitted on leashes. A grocery store and a boat ramp are nearby. The campground capacity is limited to 100 people for camp one and 75 people for camp two.
Reservations, fee: Camping is available by reservation only; $65 fee per night for camp one; $55 fee per night for camp two.
Who to contact: Reserve through MISTIX at (800)283-CAMP ($6 MISTIX fee).
Location: From Susanville, drive three miles west on Highway 36, then 15.5 miles northwest on County Road A1, and one mile northeast on County Road 201 to the campground.
Trip note: If you are coming in a big group to Eagle Lake, obviously you better get on the horn first and reserve this camp. Then you have your own private slice

of solitude along the shore of Eagle Lake. And bring your boat. The Aspen Boat Ramp is only about a mile away.

Map grid **j9**

MERRILL

on Eagle Lake

LASSEN NATIONAL FOREST

Campsites, facilities: There are 181 campsites for tents or motor homes up to 32 feet long. Piped water, flush toilets, picnic tables, and fireplaces are provided. A sanitary disposal station is available. The facilities are wheelchair accessible. A grocery store and boat ramp are nearby.

Reservations, fee: No reservations; $9 fee per night.

Who to contact: Phone Lassen National Forest at (916)257-2151.

Location: From Susanville, drive three miles west on Highway 36, then 15.5 miles northwest on County Road A1, and one mile northwest on County Road 201 to the campground.

Trip note: This is one of the largest, most developed Forest Service campgrounds in the entire county. It is set along Eagle Lake at 5,100 feet elevation.

Map grid **j9**

CHRISTIE

on Eagle Lake

LASSEN NATIONAL FOREST

Campsites, facilities: There are 69 campsites for tents or motor homes up to 32 feet long. Piped water, flush toilets, fireplaces, and picnic tables are provided. The facilities are wheelchair accessible. A grocery store is nearby. Pets are permitted on leashes. A disposal station is two miles away at Merrill Camp.

Reservations, fee: No reservations; $9 fee per night.

Who to contact: Phone the Lassen National Forest at (916)257-2151.

Location: From Susanville, drive three miles west on Highway 36. Turn northwest on County Road A1 and drive 15.5 miles, and three miles northwest on County Road 201 to the campground.

Trip note: This camp is set along the shore of Eagle Lake at 5,100 feet elevation. The area is known for big trout (see trip note for North Eagle Camp), but also for afternoon winds, particularly during early summer.

MAP B4

BEACH
DESERT
FOOTHILL
TREES
URBAN
GRASSLAND
5% CLUB

15 MILES

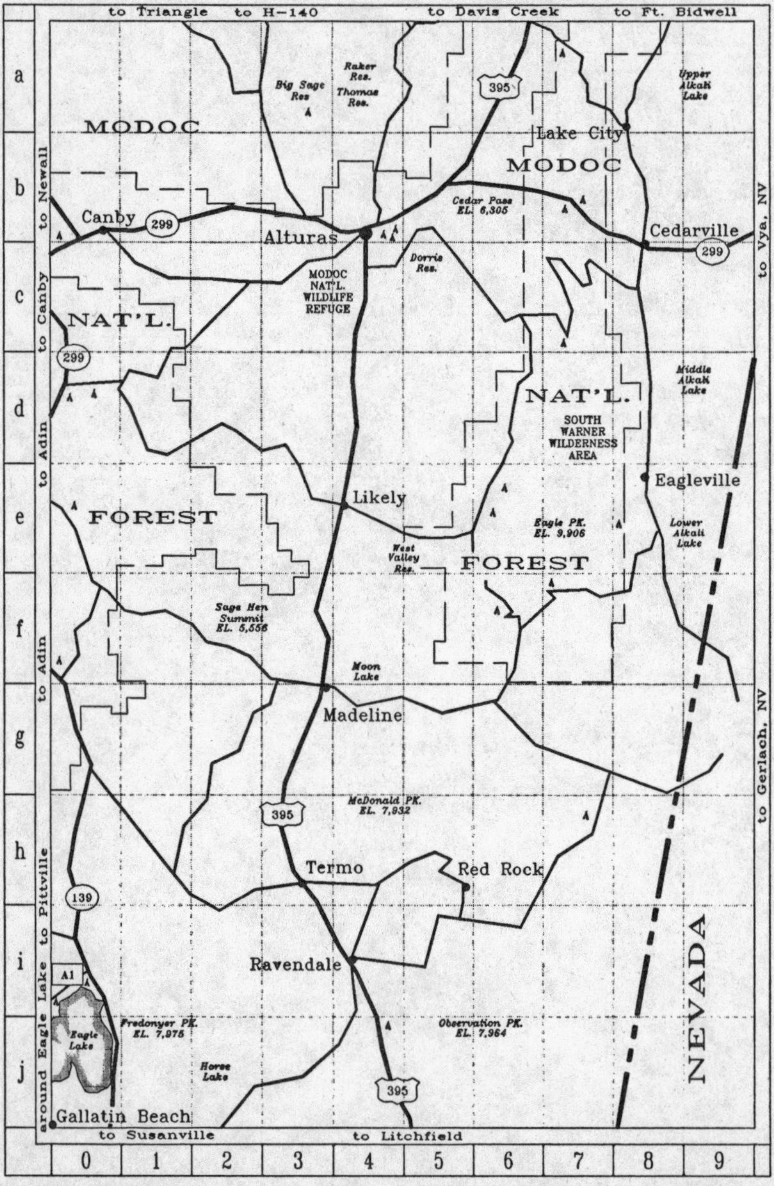

to Triangle
to H-140
to Davis Creek
to Ft. Bidwell
Big Sage Res
Raker Res.
Thomas Res.
Upper Alkali Lake
MODOC
Lake City
MODOC
Cedar Pass EL. 6,305
Canby
299
Alturas
Cedarville
299
to Newall
Dorris Res.
MODOC NAT'L. WILDLIFE REFUGE
to Canby
NAT'L.
299
Middle Alkali Lake
to Vya, NV
NAT'L.
SOUTH WARNER WILDERNESS AREA
to Adin
Eagleville
Likely
FOREST
Eagle PK. EL. 9,906
Lower Alkali Lake
West Valley Res.
FOREST
Sage Hen Summit EL. 5,556
to Adin
Moon Lake
Madeline
to Gerlach, NV
McDonald PK. EL. 7,932
395
Termo
Red Rock
139
to Pittville
NEVADA
Ravendale
A1
around Eagle Lake
Eagle Lake
Fredonyer PK. EL. 7,975
Observation PK. EL. 7,964
Horse Lake
395
Gallatin Beach
to Susanville
to Litchfield

a b c d e f g h i j

0 1 2 3 4 5 6 7 8 9

Map grid a3 — BIG SAGE RESERVOIR

MODOC NATIONAL FOREST

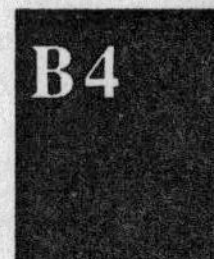

Campsites, facilities: This campground offers dispersed sites for tents or motor homes of any length. Vault toilets and picnic tables are provided. **No piped water** is available, so bring your own. Pack out your garbage. A boat ramp is available. Pets are permitted on leashes. Supplies can be obtained in Alturas.

Reservations, fee: No reservations, no fee.

Who to contact: Phone the Modoc National Forest District Office at (916) 233-4611.

Location: From Alturas, drive four miles west on Highway 299. Turn north and drive ten miles on a fair access road to the camping area.

Trip note: This is a do-it-yourself camp, that is, pick your own spot, bring your own water, and don't expect to see any Forest Service rangers. It is set along Big Sage Reservoir—that's right, sagebrush country at 4,900 feet elevation. This is one of the better bass lakes in Modoc County.

Map grid a7 — PLUM VALLEY

near the South Fork of Davis Creek

MODOC NATIONAL FOREST

Campsites, facilities: There are 15 sites for tents or motor homes up to 15 feet long. Vault toilets, fireplaces, and picnic tables are provided. **No piped water** is available. Pets are permitted on leashes. Supplies are available in Davis Creek.

Reservations, fee: No reservations, no fee.

Who to contact: Phone the Modoc National Forest District Office at (916)279-6116.

Location: From Alturas, drive about 20 miles north on US 395 to the town of Davis Creek. Turn east on Forest Service Road 11 and drive 3.5 miles to the campground.

Trip note: This secluded camp near the South Fork of Davis Creek is set at 5,600 feet elevation. It's a good headquarters for a quiet trout fishing trip.

Map grid b0 — BELLY ACRES CAMPGROUND

near Canby

Campsites, facilities: There are 22 motor home sites, some with full hookups. Picnic tables are provided. Hot showers, flush toilets, and a sanitary disposal station are available. Supplies are available in Canby.

Reservations, fee: Reservations accepted, $12 fee per night.

Who to contact: Phone (916)233-4759.

Location: From the junction of Highways 139 and 299 in Canby, drive 1.5 miles west on Highway 299, then 300 yards northeast on County Road 214.

Trip note: This privately-developed motor home park has open, level sites and is located along Highway 299. It's open May through November. The elevation is 4,200 feet.

Map grid b4 — BRASS RAIL CAMPGROUND

near Alturas

Campsites, facilities: There are 70 motor home sites, some with full hookups, and a separate tenting area. Picnic tables are provided. Hot showers, flush toilets, a sanitary disposal station, a laundromat, ice, propane gas, a playground, a tennis court and a swimmimg pool are available. Pets are permitted on leashes. Supplies can be obtained in Alturas.

Reservations, fee: Reservations accepted, $13 fee per night.
Who to contact: Phone (916)233-2906.
Location: From the junction of Highway 299 and US 395 in Alturas, drive one-half mile east on US 395 to the campground.
Trip note: This private motor home park has easy access from the highway. The altitude is 4,400 feet. Open March through October. Alturas is the biggest "small town" in Modoc County and offers a nice city park with a playground, a museum, an old time saloon, and, just south of town, the Modoc National Wildlife Refuge.

Map grid **b4**

NIFTY RV AND MOBILE HOME PARK

near Alturas

Campsites, facilities: There are 15 motor home sites with full hookups available in this mobile home park. Hot showers, flush toilets, and a laundromat are available. Supplies can be obtained in Alturas.
Reservations, fee: Reservations accepted, $10-$11 fee per night.
Who to contact: Phone (916)233-5322.
Location: From the junction of Highway 299 and US 395 in Alturas, drive three-quarters of a mile west on Highway 299, then 300 yards north on Thomason Lane.
Trip note: This camp is set for easy highway access. The elevation is 4,400 feet. For side trip options, see trip note for Bass Rail Campground.

Map grid **b4**

SULLY'S TRAILER LODGE

near Alturas

Campsites, facilities: There are 15 motor home sites, some with full hookups, available in this mobile home park. Hot showers, flush toilets, a laundromat, and horseshoe pits are available. Cable TV is available for an extra fee. Supplies can be obtained in Alturas.
Reservations, fee: Reservations accepted, $9 fee per night.
Who to contact: Phone (916)233-2253.
Location: From the junction of Highway 299 and US 395 in Alturas, drive one mile south on US 395, then one block east on County Road 56 to the campground.
Trip note: This year-round, privately-operated park is located next to the playground, the city park, and the Modoc County Museum, which details the history of the area. The Modoc National Wildlife Refuge requires only a short drive.

Map grid **b7**

STOUGH RESERVOIR CAMPGROUND

MODOC NATIONAL FOREST

Campsites, facilities: There are eight sites for tents or motor homes up to 22 feet long. Piped water, vault toilets, picnic tables, and fireplaces are provided. Pets are permitted on leashes. Supplies can be obtained in Cedarville.
Reservations, fee: No reservation, no fee.
Who to contact: Phone the Modoc National Forest District Office at (916)279-6116.
Location: From Cedarville, drive six miles west on Highway 299. Turn at the entrance sign and drive one mile to the campground.
Trip note: This camp is located just off the main road, but it's tucked in the lonely Warner Mountains, a quiet spot even in middle of summer. It's set at 6,300 feet elevation. For backpackers, the Warners are worth getting into, a unique experience that feels like entering a time machine.

Map grid **b7**

CEDAR PASS

on Cedar Pass
MODOC NATIONAL FOREST

A

Campsites, facilities: There are 17 sites for tents or motor homes up to 22 feet long. Vault toilets, picnic tables, and fireplaces are provided. **No piped water** is available, so bring your own. Pack out your garbage. Pets are permitted on leashes. Supplies can be obtained in Cedarville or Alturas.

B4

Reservations, fee: No reservations, no fee.

Who to contact: Phone the Modoc National Forest District Office at (916) 279-6116.

Location: From Cedarville, drive eight miles west on Highway 299 to the campground entrance.

C

Trip note: This spot is just off Highway 299 along Cedar Creek, and has plenty of room between the campsites. The elevation is 5,900 feet. A good side trip is to Stough Reservoir, less than three miles away.

Map grid **c7**

PEPPERDINE

MODOC NATIONAL FOREST

D

Campsites, facilities: There are five sites for tents or motor homes up to 22 feet long. Piped water, vault toilets, picnic tables, and fireplaces are provided. Corrals are available with stock watering facilities. Pack out your garbage. Pets are permitted on leashes. Supplies are available in Cedarville or Alturas.

E

Reservations, fee: No reservations, no fee.

Who to contact: Phone the Modoc National Forest District Office at (916)279-6116.

Location: From the south end of Alturas, turn east on County Road 56 and drive 13 miles to the Modoc Forest boundary. Continue for six miles on Park Creek Road, then south on the Pepperdine campground access road (the access is good for motor homes and trailers).

F

Trip note: This camp is known by virtually no one, except for backpackers who use it as a jump-off point for multi-day trips into the South Warner Wilderness. The trailhead is right at the camp. The elevation is 6,680 feet. Open from June through September.

G

Map grid **d0**

LOWER RUSH CREEK

MODOC NATIONAL FOREST

Campsites, facilities: There are five sites for tents and five sites for motor homes up to 22 feet. Piped water, vault toilets, picnic tables, and fireplaces are provided. Pets are permitted on leashes. Supplies are available in Canby or Adin.

H

Reservations, fee: No reservations, $4 fee per night.

Who to contact: Phone the Modoc National Forest District Office at (916)299-3215.

Location: From Adin, drive 7.5 miles northeast on Highway 299. Turn right on County Road 198 and drive two miles to the campground.

I

Trip note: This level campground is surrounded by a fenced area and set beside Rush Creek. This camp is better suited for trailers than the camp at Upper Rush Creek. It is little-known and little-used. It's set at 4,400 feet elevation.

Map grid **d0**

UPPER RUSH CREEK

MODOC NATIONAL FOREST

J

Campsites facilities: There are 13 sites for tents or motor homes up to 22 feet long, but Lower Rush Creek camp is better for trailers. Piped water, vault toilets, fire grills, and tables are provided. Pets are permitted on leashes. Supplies can be obtained in Adin or Canby.

Reservations, fee: No reservations, $4 fee per night.

Who to contact: Phone the Modoc National Forest District Office at (916) 299-3215.

Location: From Adin, drive 7.5 miles northeast on Highway 299. Turn right on County Road 198 and drive two miles to the campground.

Trip note: This beautiful, wooded, somewhat steep campground sits along Rush Creek. It's a very quiet spot. A trail from camp leads up 7,036-foot Manzanita Mountain, a climb of 1,800 feet. When other campgrounds in the state are jammed, like on the 4th of July, you might find only a few campers here.

Map grid e0

ASH CREEK
MODOC NATIONAL FOREST

Campsites, facilities: There are seven campsites for tents or motor homes up to 22 feet long. Vault toilets, tables, and fireplaces are provided. **No piped water** is available so bring your own. Pack out your garbage. Pets are permitted on leashes. Supplies can be obtained in Adin.

Reservations, fee: No reservations, no fee.

Who to contact: Phone the Modoc National Forest District Office at (916)299-3215, or write to Box 885, Adin, CA 96006.

Location: From Adin, drive eight miles southeast on Ash Valley Road. The campground is located off Ash Valley Road on a short, signed entrance road.

Trip note: This remote camp has stark beauty and is set along Ash Creek. It can get colder than expected, especially in early summer or fall. Stash some extra clothes, just in case. That will probably guarantee nice weather.

Map grid e6

SOUP SPRINGS
MODOC NATIONAL FOREST

Campsites, facilities: There are eight sites for tents and six level sites for tents or motor homes up to 22 feet long. Piped water, vault toilets, picnic tables, and fireplaces are provided. Pets are permitted on leashes. Corrals are available. Supplies can be obtained in Likely.

Reservations, fee: No reservations, no fee.

Who to contact: Phone the Modoc National Forest District Office at (916)279-6116.

Location: From Alturas, drive 17 miles south on US 395 to the town of Likely. Turn left on Jess Valley Road and drive nine miles to the fork. Bear left for 4.5 miles on West Warner Road. Turn right on Soup Loop Road (gravel) and drive six miles to the campground.

Trip note: This is a beautiful, quiet, wooded campground at the trailhead into the South Warner Wilderness. Soup Creek originates at Soup Springs in the meadow adjacent to the campground. The camp has been empty every time we've checked it. The elevation is 6,800 feet. Open from June to October.

Map grid e6

MILL CREEK FALLS
MODOC NATIONAL FOREST

Campsites, facilities: There are 11 sites for tents and eight sites for tents or motor homes up to 22 feet long. Piped water, vault toilets, tables, and fireplaces are provided. Pets are permitted on leashes in the campground. Supplies are available in Likely.

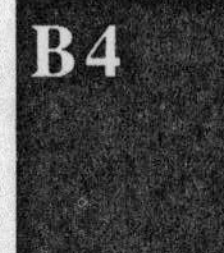

Reservations, fee: No reservation, $4 fee per night.
Who to contact: Phone the Modoc National Forest District Office at (916) 279-6116.
Location: From Alturas, drive 17 miles south on US 395 to the town of Likely. Turn left on Jess Valley Road and drive nine miles to the fork. Bear left for 2.5 miles, then turn right and proceed two miles to the campground.
Trip notes: This nice, wooded campground is a good base camp for a wilderness backpack trip into the South Warner Wilderness. The camp is set on Mill Creek, near Mill Creek Falls. Trails from the camp lead to nearby Mill Creek Falls and further to Clear Lake, a natural lake formed near the headwaters of the Pit River. Horse rentals are available at the Brooks Ranch in Jess Valley. The elevation is 5,700 feet. Open May through October.

Map grid e8

EMERSON

MODOC NATIONAL FOREST

Campsites, facilities: There are four sites for tents or RV's up to 16 feet long. Vault toilets, tables, and fireplaces are provided. **No piped water** is available, so bring your own. Pets are permitted on leashes. Supplies can be obtained in Eagleville.
Reservations, fee: No reservations, no fee.
Who to contact: Phone the Modoc National Forest District Office at (916) 279-6116.
Location: From Eagleville, drive one mile south on County Road 1, then three miles southwest on the Emerson access road. The access road is very steep and trailers are not recommended.
Trip note: This tiny, virtually unknown camp is nestled at 6,000 feet on the eastern side of the Warner Mountains. Big alkali lakes and Nevada can be seen on the other side of the highway as you drive to the entrance road to the campground. This primitive setting is used by backpackers hitting the trail to the southeastern boundary of the South Warner Wilderness. From camp, you can take a 4.5-mile trail up, up, and up to North Emerson Lake, but alas, the fishing is often lousy there. In any case, you'll know the meaning of a gut thumper.

Map grid f0

WILLOW CREEK

MODOC NATIONAL FOREST

Campsites, facilities: There are eight sites for tents or motor homes up to 32 feet long. Piped water, vault toilets, tables, and fireplaces are provided. Pets are permitted on leashes.
Reservations, fee: No reservations, $5 fee per night.
Who to contact: Phone the Modoc National Forest at (916)233-5811.
Location: From Adin, drive 16 miles southeast on Highway 139.
Trip note: This campground is on the road to Reno and gets heavy use in the summer by overnighters. Open from May through October.

Map grid f6

BLUE LAKE

MODOC NATIONAL FOREST

Campsites, facilities: There are 48 sites for tents or motor homes up to 22 feet long. Piped water, vault toilets, tables, and fireplaces are provided. A dirt and gravel boat launch is available on the lake. Pets are permitted on leashes in the campground. Supplies are available in Likely.
Reservations, fee: No reservations; $5 fee per night.
Who to contact: Phone the Modoc National Forest District Office at (916) 279-6116.

Location: From Alturas, drive 17 miles south on US 395 to the town of Likely. Turn left on Jess Valley Road and drive nine miles to the fork. Bear right for seven miles, then turn right and proceed two miles to the campground.

Trip notes: This is a wooded campground with some level sites near the shore of Blue Lake. The lake, which covers 160 acres, provides fishing for brown trout and rainbow trout. A five-mph speed limit assures quiet water for small boats and canoes. A trail circles the lake and takes less than an hour to hike around. The elevation is 6,000 feet. Open May through October.

Map grid f7

PATTERSON

MODOC NATIONAL FOREST

Campsites, facilities: There are five sites for tents or motor homes up to 20 feet long. Piped water, vault toilets, tables, and fireplaces provided. Corrals are available for public use. Pack out your garbage. Supplies are available in Likely.

Reservations, fee: No reservations, no fee.

Who to contact: Phone the Modoc National Forest District Office at (916) 279-6116.

Location: From Alturas, drive 17 miles south on US 395 to the town of Likely. Turn left on Jess Valley Road and drive nine miles to the fork. Bear right for 16 miles to the campground. There is an alternate route from Eagleville, but it is very steep.

Trip note: This quiet, wooded campground is set across the road from Patterson Meadow at 7,200 feet elevation. It's a good base camp for hikers because the trailheads for Summit Creek Trail and Emerson Lake Trail are located a short drive down the road. Fishing can be good in East Creek. Rarely open prior to July.

Map grid h7

DODGE RESERVOIR

Campsites, facilities: There are 11 tent sites. **No piped water** is available, but vault toilets, picnic tables and fireplaces are provided. Pets are permitted on leashes. There is no boat ramp.

Reservations, fee: No reservations, no fee.

Who to contact: Contact the Bureau of Land Management at (916)257-5381.

Location: Turn off US 395 at Ravendale and drive east for 25 miles, following the signs to the reservoir and the campground.

Trip note: This small spot sitting along Dodge Reservoir gets missed by the masses. It's way out there in booger country, as they say, in the stark high desert country at 5,735 feet. The weather turns cold in the spring and fall. Car-top boats, fishing, hunting, hiking (on surrounding BLM land), and swimming are recreation options.

Map grid i0

EAGLE LAKE RV PARK

Campsites, facilities: There are five tent sites and 57 motor home sites, most with full or partial hookups. There is a separate area for tents only. Picnic tables and fire grills are provided. Rest rooms, showers, a laundromat, a sanitary disposal station, a grocery store, propane gas, RV supplies, wood, a recreation room, and a boat ramp are available.

Reservations, fee: Reservations recommended; $11-$15 fee per night.

Who to contact: Phone (916)825-3133.

Location: From the junction of Highways 139 and 36 in Susanville, drive north on Highway 39 for 31 miles. Turn west on Eagle Lake Road (County Road A1) and drive nine miles. Turn east on County Road 518 and drive three miles, then one-half mile south on a paved road to Palmetto Way. Turn west and drive a short distance to the motor home park.

Trip note: This motor home park has all amenities available, including a small store. That means no special trips into town, just vacation time, lounging beside Eagle Lake, maybe catching a big trout now and then.

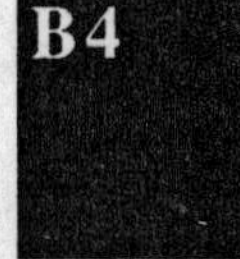

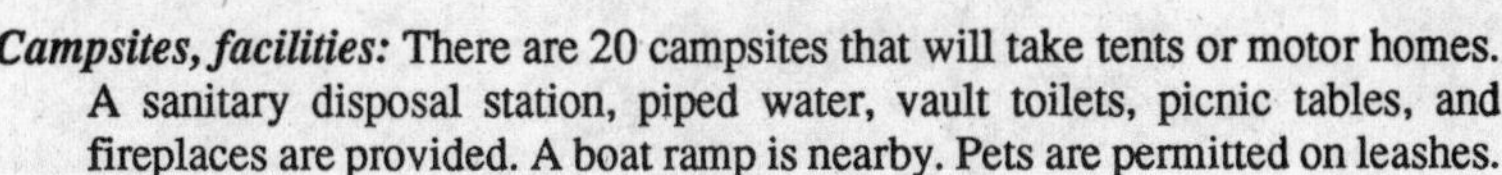

Map grid i0

NORTH EAGLE LAKE

Campsites, facilities: There are 20 campsites that will take tents or motor homes. A sanitary disposal station, piped water, vault toilets, picnic tables, and fireplaces are provided. A boat ramp is nearby. Pets are permitted on leashes.

Reservations, fee: No reservations; $6 fee per night.

Who to contact: Phone the Bureau of Land Management at (916)257-5381.

Location: From Susanville, drive 29 miles north on Highway 139. Then drive one-half mile west on County Road A1 (201).

Trip note: If you like to catch big trout, this is the best camp on Eagle Lake to do it. From shore, fish with inflated night crawlers near the lake bottom along the tules, for trout two to five pounds. By boat, troll a needlefish lure. This spot is best in the fall, when the wind is down, but it's open from Memorial Day through December 31. The elevation is 5,100 feet.

Map grid j4

RAMHORN SPRING

Campsites, facilities: There are 12 campsites for tents or motor homes up to 28 feet long. Piped water, vault toilets, picnic tables, and fireplaces are provided. Pets are permitted on leashes.

Reservations, fee: No reservations, no fee.

Who to contact: Phone the Bureau of Land Management at (916)257-5381.

Location: From Susanville, drive 50 miles north on Highway 395. Drive two miles east on Post Camp Road to the campground.

Trip note: This very remote, little-known spot has good hiking and hunting prospects (if you can get drawn for the tags). Shinn Peak (7,562 feet) is quite close. This camp is way out there in No Man's Land.

◆ MAP C0 ◆

BEACH
DESERT
FOOTHILL
TREES
URBAN
GRASSLAND
5% CLUB

15 MILES

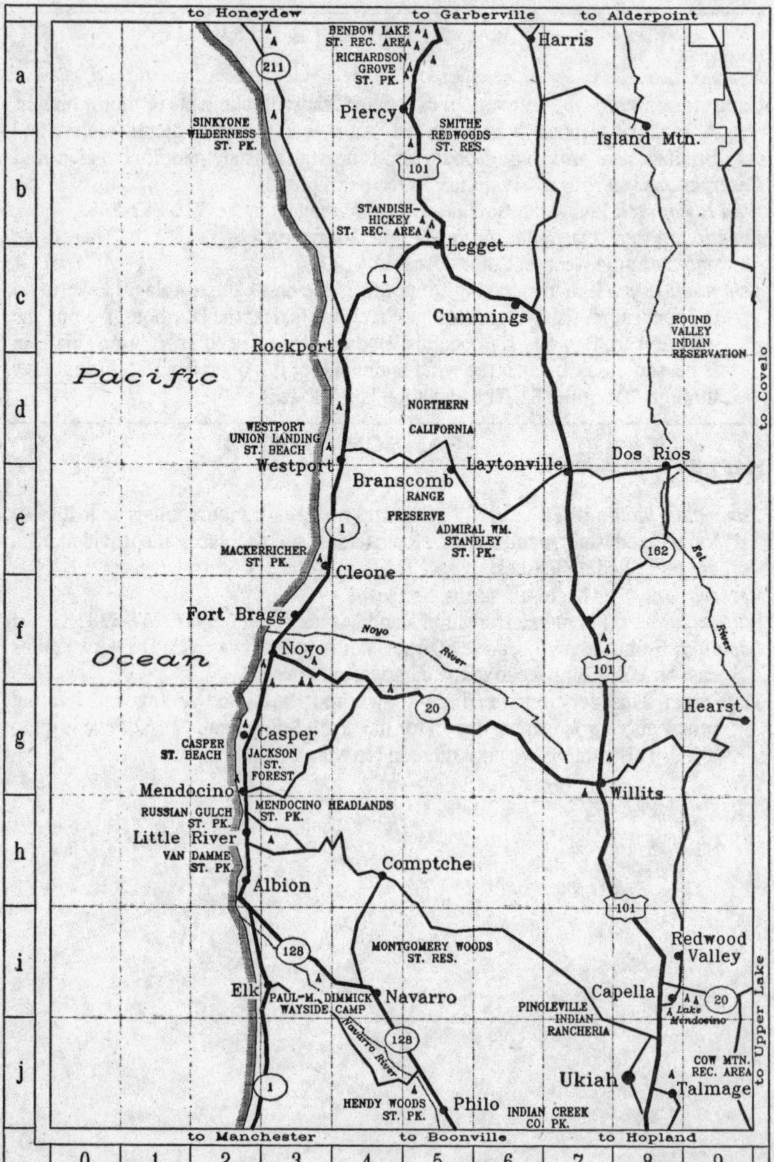

to Honeydew
to Garberville
to Alderpoint
BENBOW LAKE ST. REC. AREA
RICHARDSON GROVE ST. PK.
Harris
211
Piercy
SINKYONE WILDERNESS ST. PK.
SMITHE REDWOODS ST. RES.
Island Mtn.
101
STANDISH-HICKEY ST. REC. AREA
Legget
1
Cummings
ROUND VALLEY INDIAN RESERVATION
Rockport
Pacific
NORTHERN CALIFORNIA
WESTPORT UNION LANDING ST. BEACH
Westport
Branscomb RANGE PRESERVE
Laytonville
Dos Rios
to Covelo
ADMIRAL WM. STANDLEY ST. PK.
1
162
Eel River
MACKERRICHER ST. PK.
Cleone
Fort Bragg
Noyo
Noyo River
Ocean
101
20
Hearst
Casper
CASPER ST. BEACH
JACKSON ST. FOREST
Mendocino
Willits
MENDOCINO HEADLANDS ST. PK.
RUSSIAN GULCH ST. PK.
Little River
VAN DAMME ST. PK.
Comptche
Albion
101
MONTGOMERY WOODS ST. RES.
Redwood Valley
128
Elk
PAUL M. DIMMICK WAYSIDE CAMP
Navarro
Capella
20
Lake Mendocino
PINOLEVILLE INDIAN RANCHERIA
to Upper Lake
Navarro River
128
COW MTN. REC. AREA
Ukiah
Talmage
1
HENDY WOODS ST. PK.
Philo
INDIAN CREEK CO. PK.
to Manchester
to Boonville
to Hopland

a b c d e f g h i j

0 1 2 3 4 5 6 7 8 9

NADELOS
in Kings Range

Map grid a3

Campsites, facilities: There are four group sites, and three walk-in sites. Piped water, vault toilets, picnic tables, and fireplaces are provided. Pets are permitted.

Reservations, fee: No reservations; $5 per night fee.

Who to contact: Call the Bureau of Land Management at (707)822-7648.

Location: From Redway on US 101, drive 17 miles west on Shelter Cove Road. Turn south on Chemise Mountain Road and drive two miles to the campground.

Trip note: This camp has relatively easy access, yet it is still not well known because it's just far enough off US 101. There are good hiking opportunities in the surrounding Kings Mountain Range. The camp is set at 1,840 feet elevation.

WAILAKI
overlooking Pacific Ocean

Map grid a3

Campsites, facilities: There are 13 campsites for tents or motor homes up to 20 feet long. Piped water, vault toilets, picnic tables, and fireplaces are provided. Pets are permitted on leashes.

Reservations, fee: No reservations, $5 fee per night.

Who to contact: Phone the Bureau of Land Management at (707)462-3873.

Location: From Redway on US 101, drive 17 miles west on Shelter Cove Road. Turn south on Chemise Mountain Road and drive 2.5 miles to the campground.

Trip note: The coastal beauty of the Chemise Mountain Primitive Area and the nearby Sinkyone Wilderness State Park are the side trip highlights of this camp. There are options for hiking and off-road vehicle use for the four-wheel drive cowboys. At Shelter Cove, boaters will find a launch ramp for access to good fishing grounds. The camp is set at 1,840 feet elevation. Open year-round.

SINKYONE WILDERNESS STATE PARK

Map grid a3

Campsites, facilities: At Usal Beach there are 15 tent sites, each with a fire ring and a picnic table. There is **no piped water**, but there is plenty of water on the premises, provided you purify it. Pit toilets are provided. Between Bear Harbor and Jones Beach there are about 25 primitive campsites, some of which have tables, fire rings, and pit toilets. You can drive within three-quarters of a mile of Bear Harbor and park at Orchard Creek provided the weather is good and the gate is open at Needle Rock Ranch House.

Reservations, fee: No reservations; $12-$14 fee; pets $1.

Who to contact: Phone (707)946-2311.

Location: From Redway on US 101, drive 17 miles west on Briceland Road following the signs to Whitethorn. From Whitethorn, continue six more miles to the four corners fork. Take the middle left fork and drive four miles to the Usal Beach campground. From Leggett, drive south on Highway 1 toward Fort Bragg and drive 14.66 miles to milepost 90.88. Turn right onto County Road 431 (a dirt road, often unsigned) and drive six miles to the Usal Beach campground. From Fort Bragg, drive north on Highway 1 to Rockport. Continue north past Rockport for three more miles. Turn left onto County Road 431 and drive six miles to the Usal Beach campground.

Trip note: This is an ideal jump-off point for experienced backpackers. The area is called the "Lost Coast" because of its rugged and little-known beauty.

Beginning at Usal Beach there is a 17-mile trail north to Bear Harbor. This ocean front trail is steep and rugged, but beautiful as it takes you past sheer bluffs and fern meadows. Several primitive campsites are in this area. Wheeler Creek, Bear Harbor, and Usal Beach all provide beach access.

Map grid a5

MADRONE
RICHARDSON GROVE STATE PARK

Campsites, facilities: There are 40 sites for tents or motor homes up to 30 feet long. Piped water, flush toilets, showers, fireplaces, and picnic tables are provided. A grocery store and a sanitary disposal station are available. The facilities are wheelchair accessible. Pets are permitted.

Reservations, fee: Reservations usually necessary through MISTIX by phoning (800)444-7275 ($3.95 MISTIX fee); $12-$14 per night fee; pets $1.

Who to contact: Call Richardson Grove State Park at (707)247-3318.

Location: From Garberville, drive eight miles south on US 101 to the park entrance, which is on the east side of US 101.

Trip note: This is one of several campgrounds at Richardson Grove State Park. See the trip note for Huckleberry Camp.

Map grid a5

BENBOW LAKE STATE RECREATION AREA
on Eel River

Campsites, facilities: There are 75 campsites for tents or motor homes up to 30 feet long. Piped water, flush toilets, cold showers, fireplaces, and picnic tables are provided. A boat ramp (no motors) and boat rentals are available. Supplies and a laundromat are available in Garberville.

Reservations, fee: Reservations recommended from May through September through MISTIX by phoning (800)444-7275; camp fee $12-$14; pets $1.

Who to contact: Phone Benbow Lake State Recreation Area at (707)946-2311.

Location: From Garberville. drive two miles south on US 101 and follow the signs.

Trip note: This camp is set along the South Fork of the Eel River, with easy access from US 101. It gets heavy use in summer. The river is dammed each summer, which temporarily creates Benbow Lake, an ideal spot for swimming and light boating. In winter, this stretch of river can be quite good for steelhead fishing. The campground is closed during high water periods in the winter.

Map grid a5

BENBOW VALLEY RV PARK
on Eel River

Campsites, facilities: There are 112 paved motor home sites (60 drive-through spaces) with full hookups, lawns, trees, and picnic tables. Cable TV, rest rooms, showers, a laundromat, a grocery store, LP gas, a restaurant, a playground, a recreation room, a heated swimming pool, a jacuzzi, RV supplies, a nine-hole golf course, a boat dock, and lake boat rentals (in summer) are available. Pets are allowed on leashes.

Reservations, fee: Reservations accepted; $21 fee per night.

Who to contact: Phone Benbow Valley RV Park at (707)923-2777.

Location: From Garberville, drive two miles south on US 101. Turn north on Benbow Drive and travel a short distance to the campground.

Trip note: This is a home away from home, as they say. It's not for those who want isolation, but it is a nice spot along the Eel River with all amenities available. Open year-round.

Map grid **a5**

HUCKLEBERRY

RICHARDSON GROVE STATE PARK

Campsites, facilities: There are 36 campsites for tents or motor homes up to 30 feet. Piped water, flush toilets, showers, fireplaces, and picnic tables are provided. A grocery store and a sanitary disposal station are available. The facilities are wheelchair accessible. Pets are permitted on leashes.

Reservations, fee: Reservations a must in summer months through MISTIX by phoning (800)444-7275 ($3.95 MISTIX fee); $12-$14 per night fee; pets $1.

Who to contact: Call Richardson Grove State Park at (707)247-3318.

Location: From Garberville, drive eight miles south on US 101 to the park entrance, which is on the east side of US 101.

Trip note: This camp is set in a giant grove of coastal redwoods, the tallest trees in the world. The park is one of the prettiest and most popular state parks in the state, making reservations a necessity from Memorial Day through Labor Day. There is good hiking and sight-seeing, but it is often crowded by tourists in the summer months. It's a good base camp in the winter months for steelhead fishing in the South Fork of the Eel River.

Map grid **a5**

RICHARDSON GROVE KOA

on Eel River

Campsites, facilities: There are 105 campsites for tents or motor homes (40 drive-through sites), many with full or partial hookups. Picnic tables, fire rings, rest rooms, showers, a sanitary disposal station, a recreation room, and a playground are provided. A laundromat, a grocery store, LP gas, ice, and wood are available.

Reservations, fee: Reservations suggested; $17-$19 fee per night.

Who to contact: Phone (707)247-3380.

Location: From Garberville, drive 8.5 miles south on US 101 to the campground entrance on the west side of the highway.

Trip note: This popular KOA park is set near the Eel River. The fishing is best in winter for steelhead. Don't keep those "little trout" you might catch in summer months. They're actually baby steelhead, spending the summer growing and readying themselves to head out to sea in the winter. Open year-round.

Map grid **a5**

OAK FLAT

RICHARDSON GROVE STATE PARK

Campsites, facilities: There are 94 campsites for tents or motor homes up to 30 feet long. Piped water, flush toilets, showers, fireplaces, and picnic tables are provided. A grocery store, a sanitary disposal station, and propane gas are available nearby.

Reservations, fee: Reservations necessary in summer months through MISTIX by phoning (800)444-7275 ($3.95 MISTIX fee); $12-$14 per night fee; pets $1.

Who to contact: Call Richardson Grove State Park at (707)247-3318.

Location: From Garberville, drive eight miles south on US 101 to the park entrance, which is on the east side of US 101.

Trip note: This camp is set on the east side of the Eel River in the shade of forest and provides easy access to the river. It is one of three campgrounds in Richardson Grove State Park. For more information, see the trip note for Huckleberry camp. This one is open only in the summer.

Map grid **b5**

REDWOOD CAMPGROUND

on Eel River

STANDISH HICKEY STATE RECREATION AREA

Campsites, facilities: There are 63 campsites for tents or motor homes up to 18 feet long. Piped water, showers, flush toilets, picnic tables, and fire rings are provided. Some facilities are wheelchair accessible.

Reservations, fee: Reserve through MISTIX at (800)444-7275 ($3.95 MISTIX fee); $12-$14 fee per night; pets $1.

Who to contact: Phone Standish-Hickey State Recreation Area at (707)946- 2311.

Location: From Leggett, drive one mile north on US 101.

Trip note: If Standish and Rock Creek camps are full, this spot provides a nearby alternative. It is located just down the road and across the temporary "summer bridge." Since the bridge is up only during the summer, this camp is open only from June through September. The elevation is 800 feet.

Map grid **b5**

ROCK CREEK

on Eel River

STANDISH HICKEY STATE RECREATION AREA

Campsites, facilities: There are 36 campsites for tents or motor homes up to 27 feet long. Piped water, showers, flush toilets, picnic tables, and fire rings are provided. Some facilities are wheelchair accessible.

Reservations, fee: Reserve through MISTIX at (800)444-7275 ($3.95 MISTIX fee); $12-$14 fee per night; pets $1.

Who to contact: Phone Standish-Hickey State Recreation Area at (707)946-2311.

Location: From Leggett, drive one mile north on US 101.

Trip note: This is set adjacent to Hickey Camp, providing a nearby option. See the trip note for Hickey Camp for side trip options. This camp is set at 800 feet elevation. Open year-round.

Map grid **b5**

STANDISH

on Eel River

STANDISH HICKEY STATE RECREATION AREA

Campsites, facilities: There are 65 campsites for tents or motor homes up to 27 feet long. Piped water, showers, flush toilets, picnic tables, and fire rings are provided. A grocery store and laundromat are nearby. Some facilities are wheelchair accessible.

Reservations, fee: Reserve through MISTIX at (800)444-7275 ($3.95 MISTIX fee); $12-$14 fee per night; pets $1.

Who to contact: Phone Standish-Hickey State Recreation Area at (707)946-2311.

Location: From Leggett, drive one mile north on US 101.

Trip note: This is another pretty spot in the redwoods, set along the Eel River. It's an ideal layover spot for US 101 cruisers yearning to spend a night in the redwoods. Side trip options include exploring the Eel River and, in the winter, fishing for steelhead. The camp is set at 800 feet elevation. This is one of three camps in the immediate area.

Map grid **b5**

REDWOOD RIVER RETREAT

on Eel River

Campsites, facilities: There are nine tent sites and 27 motor home spaces (five drive-through sites) with full hookups. Rest rooms, hot showers, a heated pool, a playground, a video game room, a store, a laundromat, a dump station, and an evening campfire are among the amenities offered here. Pets are permitted.

Reservations, fee: Reservations recommended in the summer; $10-$18 fee per night.

Who to contact: Phone (707)925-6249.

Location: From Piercy, drive five miles south on US 101 to the campground.

Trip note: This motor home resort is situated in a 20-acre grove of redwoods on US 101. It's a shady place to rest, explore the redwoods, or fish in the Eel River. Steelhead fishing can be quite good on the South Fork of the Eel during the winter months. The spot is set at 700 feet elevation. Open year-round.

Map grid d3

WAGES CREEK BEACH CAMPGROUND

overlooking Pacific Ocean

Campsites, facilities: There are 250 sites for tents or motor homes. Piped water, fireplaces, picnic tables, and flush toilets are provided. Hot showers, a sanitary disposal station, wood and ice are available.

Reservations, fee: Reservations accepted; $14 fee per night.

Who to contact: Phone (707)964-2964.

Location: From Westport, drive one-half mile north on Highway 1 to the campground.

Trip note: This camp is set above the beach near the mouth of Wages Creek. Perch fishing can be good here at the start of an incoming tide. Open year-round, but fully operational only from March through November.

Map grid d4

WESTPORT UNION LANDING STATE BEACH

overlooking Pacific Ocean

Campsites, facilities: There are 130 primitive sites for tents or motor homes up to 35 feet long. Piped water, chemical toilets, fireplaces, and picnic tables are provided. Pets are permitted. A grocery store is nearby.

Reservations, fee: No reservations; $7-$9 fee per night; pets $1.

Who to contact: Phone (707)937-5804.

Location: From Westport, drive three miles north on Highway 1 to the campground.

Trip note: This is one of several beach camps set beside the Mendocino Coast, where you can have your hot dogs marinated in sand at no extra charge. The camps are actually on bluffs, far enough from the beach to keep the sand out of your food most of the time. Note that it is often foggy here in the summer, the warmest weather being in the fall. Open year-round.

Map grid e3

MACKERRICHER STATE PARK

overlooking Pacific Ocean

Campsites, facilities: There are 140 campsites for tents or motor homes up to 35 feet long. Piped water, showers, flush toilets, a dump station, picnic tables, and fireplaces are provided. Pets are permitted. The facilities are wheelchair accessible.

Reservations, fee: Reserve through MISTIX at (800)444-PARK ($3.95 MISTIX fee); $12-$14 fee per night; pets $1.

Who to contact: Phone (707)937-5804.

Location: From Fort Bragg, drive three miles north on Highway 1 to the site.

Trip notes: This is a beautiful coastal layover for those touring the coast. If you are cruising Highway 1, don't expect to drive anywhere fast during summer months because the winding two-laner has a way of getting clogged up. Once here, you'll find the hiking and the beachcombing in the park are highlights. Nearby options including sport fishing on the ocean (out of Fort Bragg) or on little Cleone Lake, which is stocked with trout by the Department of Fish and Game. The elevation is 20 feet. Open year-round.

Map grid **f3**

WILDWOOD CAMPGROUND
near Fort Bragg

Campsites, facilities: There are 65 motor home spaces, many with full or partial hookups. Rest rooms, picnic tables, fire rings, hot showers, and a sanitary disposal station are provided. A laundromat and wood are available. No pets are permitted.

Reservations, fee: Reservations accepted; $10-$14 fee per night.

Who to contact: Phone (707)964-8297.

Location: From Fort Bragg, drive to the intersection of Highways 1 and 20. Drive three miles east Highway 20 to the campground.

Trip note: This is just far enough out of Fort Bragg so you can find some coastal redwoods. That's a bonus. So are some of the area's trails.

Map grid **f3**

FORT BRAGG LEISURE TIME RV PARK

Campsites, facilities: There are 60 sites for tents or motor homes, many with full or partial hookups. Rest rooms, picnic tables, cable TV, fire rings, hot showers (coin-operated), and a sanitary disposal station are provided. A laundromat is available. The facilities are wheelchair accessible.

Reservations, fee: Reservations accepted; $10-$14 fee per night.

Who to contact: Phone (707)964-5994.

Location: From Fort Bragg, drive to the intersection of Highways 1 and 20. Drive 2.5 miles east on Highway 20 to the campground.

Trip note: The wooded setting is a highlight here for motor home campers. This is one of several camping options in the Fort Bragg area. The privately-operated park offers volleyball, horseshoes, and badminton. You get the idea.

Map grid **f3**

POMO CAMPGROUND AND MOTOR HOME PARK
in Fort Bragg

Campsites, facilities: There are ten sites for tents only and 94 motor home spaces with full or partial hookups. Rest rooms, hot showers (coin-operated), cable TV hookups, a store, wood, ice, RV supplies, propane gas, a laundromat, a sanitary disposal station, a fish cleaning table, horseshoe pits, and a large grass playing field are available. Picnic tables and fire rings are at each campsite.

Reservations, fee: Reservations recommended in the summer; $11-$17 fee per night.

Who to contact: Phone (707)964-3373.

Location: From Fort Bragg, drive south to the intersection of Highways 1 and 20. Continue for one mile south on Highway 1. Turn east on Tregoning Lane for a short distance to 17999 Tregoning Lane.

Trip note: This is one in a series of privately-operated parks in the Fort Bragg area. This park covers 17 acres near the ocean. Side trip options include the historic Skunk Train in Fort Bragg and fishing out of Noyo Harbor. In the winter, there is steelhead fishing on the Noyo River.

A

Map grid f3 WOODSIDE RV PARK AND CAMPGROUND
in Fort Bragg

Campsites, facilities: There are 18 sites for tents only and 86 sites for tents or motor homes, with full or partial hookups. Group sites are available. Picnic tables, fire rings, rest rooms, showers, a recreation room, a sauna, and a sanitary disposal station are provided. Cable TV, a store, RV supplies, ice, wood, and a fish cleaning table are available. Boating and fishing access are nearby.

B

Reservations, fee: Reservations accepted; $11-$15 fee per night.
Who to contact: Phone (707)964-3684.
Location: From the intersection of Highways 1 and 20 in Fort Bragg, drive one mile south on Highway 1 to the campground.
Trip note: This privately-operated park is set up primarily for motor homes. It covers nine acres, is somewhat wooded, and provides access to nearby Fort Bragg and the ocean.

C0

D

Map grid f3 DOLPHIN ISLE MARINA
in Fort Bragg

Campsites, facilities: There are 83 motor home spaces with full or partial hookups. Rest rooms, picnic tables, fire rings, hot showers (coin-operated), recreation room, and a sanitary disposal station are provided. A laundromat, grocery store, propane gas, a boat ramp, and a dock are available. The facilities are wheelchair accessible.

E

Reservations, fee: Reservations accepted; $12-$16 fee per night.
Who to contact: Phone (707)964-4113.
Location: From Fort Bragg, drive to the intersection of Highways 1 and 20. Drive one-quarter mile east on Highway 20. Turn north on South Harbor Drive and drive one-quarter mile north. Turn east on Basin Street and drive one mile to the campground.

F

Trip note: This motor home park is right at the marina, providing an ideal jump-off point for a fishing trip.

G

Map grid f7 HIDDEN VALLEY CAMPGROUND
north of Willits

Campsites, facilities: There are 50 sites for tents or motor homes, some with full or partial hookups. Picnic tables, fire grills, rest rooms, and showers are provided.
Reservations, fee: Reservations accepted; $14 fee per night.

H

Who to contact: Phone (707)459-2521.
Location: From Willits, drive 6.5 miles north on US 101 to the campground.
Trip note: This is a nearby option to Sleepyhollow campground. Open year-round.

I

Map grid f7 SLEEPYHOLLOW RV PARK
north of Willits

Campsites, facilities: There are six sites for tents only and 24 motor home spaces (seven are drive-through) with full or partial hookups. Picnic tables, rest rooms, showers, a playground, and a sanitary dump station are provided.
Reservations, fee: Reservation accepted; $10-$12 fee per night.

J

Who to contact: Phone (707)459-0613.
Location: From Willits, drive eight miles north on Highway 101 to the 55.5 mile marker (two-tenths of a mile beyond the Shimmins Ridge Road sign). Turn

right at the beginning of the divided four-lane highway and drive to the campground.

Trip note: This year-round, privately-operated park provides easy access off Highway 101 and a number of side trip options. The options include riding the Skunk Train in Willits, hiking in the surrounding Mendocino National Forest, and boating and fishing at Lake Pillsbury and Lake Mendocino.

Map grid g2

RUSSIAN GULCH STATE PARK

overlooking Pacific Ocean

Campsites, facilities: There are 30 campsites for tents or motor homes up to 30 feet long. Some special sites are provided for hikers and bicyclists. Piped water, showers, flush toilets, picnic tables, and fireplaces are provided. Pets are permitted. The facilities are wheelchair accessible.

Reservations, fee: Reserve through MISTIX at (800)444-PARK ($3.95 MISTIX fee); $12-$14 fee per night from Memorial Day to Labor Day; pets $1.

Who to contact: Phone (707)937-5804.

Location: From Mendocino, drive two miles north on Highway 1 to the campground.

Trip note: This camp is set beside some of California's most beautiful coastline. The sites are on a bluff, so you don't get afflicted with the old sand-in-food problem. One possible side trip is the three-mile bike trail in the park. Open mid-March to mid-October.

Map grid g2

CASPAR BEACH RV PARK

near Mendocino

Campsites, facilities: There are ten sites for tents only and 127 motor home spaces with full or partial hookups. Picnic tables, fire grills, cable TV hookups, flush and pit toilets, showers (coin-operated), and a sanitary disposal station are provided. A store, wood, a playground, and a laundromat are available.

Reservations, fee: Reservations accepted; $13-$22 fee per night.

Who to contact: Phone (707)964-3306.

Location: From Mendocino, drive three miles north on Highway 1 to the Point Cabrillo exit. Drive three-quarters of a mile west on Point Cabrillo Road to the campground.

Trip note: This privately operated park has ocean frontage and good lookouts for whale watching. Open year-round.

Map grid g4

JACKSON STATE FOREST

near Fort Bragg

Campsites, facilities: There are 18 separate campgrounds scattered throughout this large state forest, with as few as two or as many as 24 campsites. **No piped water** is available, but pit toilets, picnic tables, and fireplaces are provided. Pets are permitted on leashes. One horseback riding-equestrian campground is available.

Reservations, fee: No fee. Get a camping permit and a campground map from the State Department of Forestry office at 802 North Main Street (Highway 1) in Fort Bragg.

Who to contact: Phone (707)964-5674.

Location: This forest stretches for miles beside Highway 20 between Fort Bragg and Willits. There are no signs for the campgrounds off the road, so a map is required for newcomers. You can get the map from the Forestry Department.

Trip note: Primitive campsites set in a forest of redwoods and Douglas fir are the prime attraction here. Even though Highway 20 is a major connecting link to the coast in the summer months, these spots get bypassed. Get a map from the State Forestry Department, remember to bring your own water, and you'll be in business. Some of the trails offer self-guided tours on natural history and forest "management," which is how foresters describe cutting down trees. The elevation is 2,000 feet. Open year-round.

Map grid g7

UKIAH KOA
near Willits

Campsites, facilities: There are 21 sites for tents only and 50 motor home spaces (27 drive through) with full or partial hookups. Group sites are available. Piped water, flush toilets, showers, picnic tables, a playground, and a sanitary dump station are provided. A grocery store, RV supplies, and a laundromat are available.
Reservations, fee: Reservations accepted; $14-$19 fee per night.
Who to contact: Phone (707)459-6179.
Location: From Willits, drive 1.5 miles west on Highway 20 to the campground.
Trip note: This is an ideal spot to park your motor home if you plan on taking the Skunk Train west to Fort Bragg. A depot for the train is within walking distance from the campground. The elevation is 1,377 feet. Open year-round.

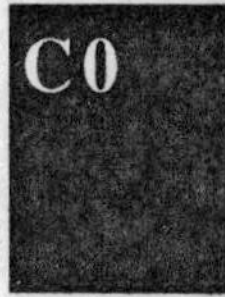

Map grid g7

QUAIL MEADOWS CAMPGROUND
in Willits

Campsites, facilities: There are 56 motor home spaces, most with full or partial hookups. There is a separate section for tents only. Patios, picnic tables, fire grills, rest rooms, showers, and a sanitary disposal station are provided. A grocery store, a laundromat, propane gas, ice, and TV hookups are available.
Reservations, fee: Reservations accepted; $10-$13 fee per night.
Who to contact: Phone (707)459-6006.
Location: From the intersection of US 101 and and Highway 20 in Willits, drive one mile north on US 101 to the campground.
Trip note: This is one of several motor home parks in the Willits area. The Skunk Train ride, a unique ride that runs through the forest and ends in Fort Bragg, is one of the main attractions here.

Map grid h3

VAN DAMME STATE PARK
near Mendocino

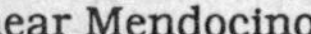

Campsites, facilities: There are 70 campsites for tents or motor homes up to 35 feet long. Piped water, flush toilets, a sanitary disposal station, showers, picnic tables, and fireplaces are provided. A grocery store, a laundromat, and propane gas are available nearby. Pets are permitted.
Reservations, fee: Reserve through MISTIX at (800)444-PARK ($3.95 MISTIX fee); $12-$14 fee per night; pets $1.
Who to contact: Phone (707)937-5804.
Location: From Mendocino, drive three miles south on Highway 1 to the park entrance road in the town of Little River.
Trip note: The many side trip possibilities make this a take-your-pick deal. Attractions in the park include a nature trail and three-mile bike trail. During winter, this makes a good base camp for steelhead fishing trips on the Noyo,

A B D E F G H I J

Navarro, Garcia, or Gualala Rivers. The elevation is 100 feet. Open year-round.

Map grid i3

PAUL M. DIMMICK WAYSIDE STATE CAMPGROUND
on Navarro River

Campsites, facilities: There are 30 campsites for tents or motor homes up to 27 feet long. Piped water, chemical toilets, fireplaces, and picnic tables are provided. Pets are permitted.

Reservations, fee: No reservations; $7-$9 fee per night; pets $1.

Who to contact: Phone (707)937-5804.

Location: From the intersection of Highways 1 and 128 on the coast, drive eight miles east on Highway 128 to the campground.

Trip note: The nearby Navarro River is the highlight here. In summer, it's a good spot for swimming or paddling a canoe around. In winter, the Navarro gets a fair steelhead run. Open year-round.

Map grid i8

CHE-KAKA
at Lake Mendocino

Campsites, facilities: There are 22 campsites for tents or motor homes up to 35 feet long. Piped water, chemical toilets, picnic tables, and fireplaces are provided. A boat ramp is nearby.

Reservations, fee: No reservations, $5 fee per night.

Who to contact: Phone the U.S. Corps of Engineers, Lake Mendocino at (707)462-7581.

Location: From the junction of US 101 and Highway 20 (north of Ukiah), drive east on Highway 20 for four miles to the lake entrance road. Follow the signs to this campground set on the southwest end of the lake.

Trip note: This campground sits beside Lake Mendocino. That's right, the lake with the catfish that bite your legs. The Russian River is quite close, providing a side trip. The elevation is 750 feet. Open from April through September.

Map grid i9

KY-EN
at Lake Mendocino

Campsites, facilities: There are 103 campsites for tents or motor homes up to 35 feet long. Rest rooms, showers, a playground (in the adjacent day-use area), a sanitary dump station, picnic tables, and fireplaces are provided. A boat ramp, boat rentals, and limited supplies are available at the nearby marina.

Reservations, fee: No reservations; $8 fee per night.

Who to contact: Phone the U.S. Corps of Engineers, Lake Mendocino at (707)462-7581.

Location: From the junction of US 101 and Highway 20 (north of Ukiah), drive east on Highway 20 for four miles to the lake entrance road. Follow the signs to this campground set on the north shore of the lake.

Trip note: This is one of three camps at Lake Mendocino. During the winter months, this camp has 30 campsites; no fee is charged in winter (after all, then the Army Corps would have to send somebody to collect it).

Map grid i9

BU-SHAY
at Lake Mendocino

Campsites, facilities: There are 164 campsites for tents or motor homes up to 35

feet long. There are three group campsites available for up to 120 people each. Rest rooms, showers, a playground (in the adjacent day-use area), a sanitary dump station, picnic tables, and fireplaces are provided. The boat ramp is about two miles from camp near Ky-en campground. Some sites are wheelchair accessible.

Reservations, fee: No reservations; $8 fee per night for family campsites; $70 per night for group sites with reservation.

Who to contact: Phone the U.S. Corps of Engineers, Lake Mendocino at (707)462-7581.

Location: From the junction of US 101 and Highway 20 (north of Ukiah), drive east on Highway 20 for four miles to the lake entrance road. Follow the signs to this campground set on the eastern shore of the lake.

Trip note: This is the lake with the man-biting catfish. That's right, the catfish actually bite the legs of swimmers and waders! Happens all the time. The lake is about three miles long and one mile wide and offers fair to middlin' fishing for bass and bluegill. There's water skiing during the hot summer months. A nearby visitor center offers exhibits of local Indian history. The elevation is 750 feet. Open from April through September.

Map grid j5

HENDY WOODS STATE PARK
near Booneville

Campsites, facilities: There are 90 campsites here for tents or motor homes up to 35 feet long. Piped water, flush toilets, showers, a sanitary disposal station, picnic tables, and fireplaces are provided. A grocery store and a propane gas station are available nearby. Pets are permitted. The facilities are wheelchair accessible.

Reservations, fee: Reserve through MISTIX at (800)444-PARK ($3.95 MISTIX fee); $12-$14 fee per night; pets $1.

Who to contact: Phone (707)937-5804.

Location: From Booneville, drive 8.5 miles northwest on Highway 128. Turn left (west) on Philo Greenwood Road and drive a short distance to the park entrance.

Trip note: This pretty and heavily forested park is set far enough off the coast to be clear of the fog for most days in the summer months. Highway 128 is a nice drive to the coast, and if you want to prolong the trip, a layover here is just what the doctor ordered. Open mid-May through late September.

Map grid j8

MANOR OAKS OVERNIGHTER PARK
in Ukiah

Campsites, facilities: There are 53 motor home spaces (15 are drive-through) with full hookups. Picnic tables, fire grills, rest rooms, showers, and a swimming pool are provided. A laundromat and ice are available. The facilities are wheelchair accessible.

Reservations, fee: No reservations; $17 fee per night.

Who to contact: Phone (707)462-0529.

Location: From US 101 in Ukiah, take the Central Ukiah-Gobbi Street exit and drive east for a short distance to 700 East Gobbi Street.

Trip note: This is a motor home park in an urban setting for Highway 101 motor-home cruisers. Nearby Lake Mendocino provides a side trip option, with boating access and average smallmouth bass and panfish fishing—but watch out for the man-biting catfish. No foolin'! Open year-round.

MAP C1

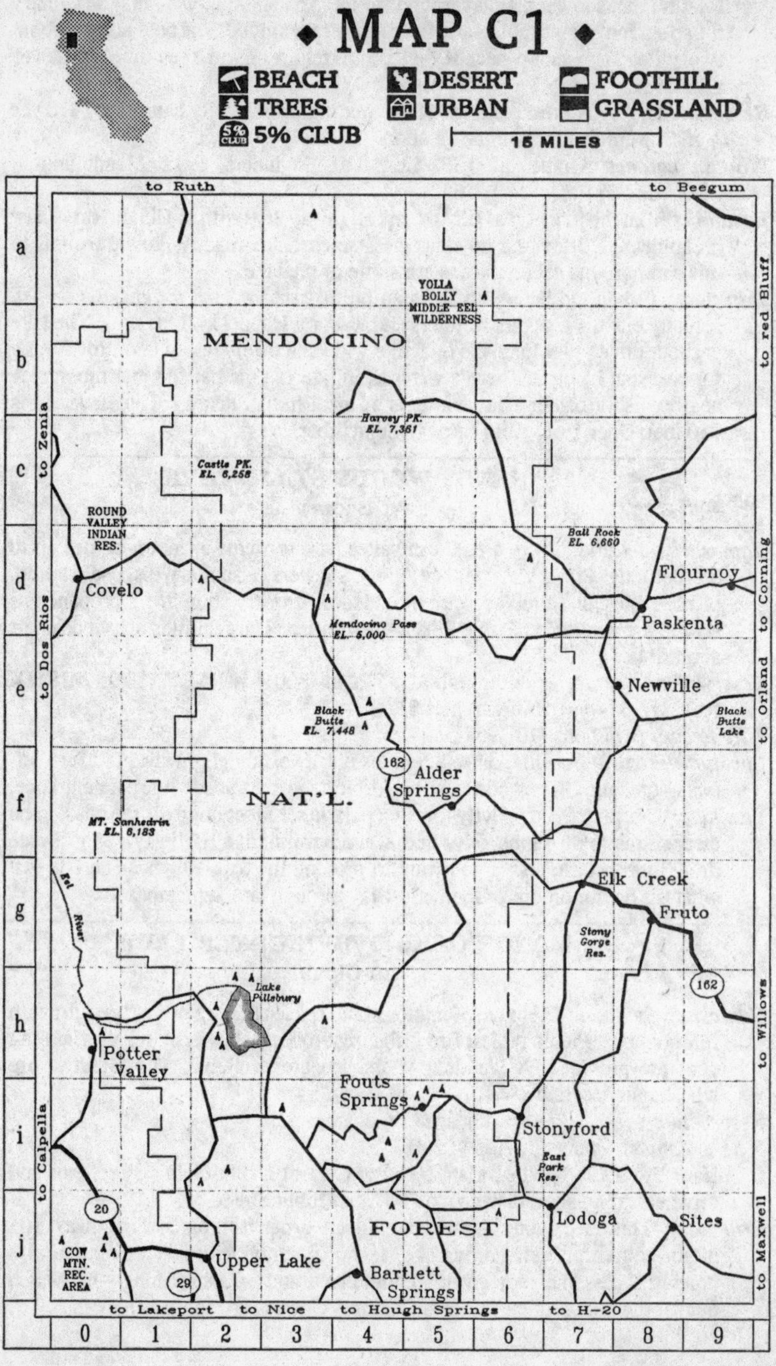

BEACH
DESERT
FOOTHILL
TREES
URBAN
GRASSLAND
5% CLUB

15 MILES

TOMHEAD SADDLE
Map grid **a3**

SHASTA-TRINITY NATIONAL FOREST

Campsites, facilities: There are five campsites for tents or motor homes. There's **no piped water,** so bring your own. Vault toilets, picnic tables, and fireplaces are provided. Pets are permitted. A horse corral is available.
Reservations, fee: No reservations, no fee.
Who to contact: Phone the Shasta-Trinity National Forest District Office at (916) 352-4211.
Location: From Red Bluff, drive 42 miles west on Reeds, Cannon, and Pettyjohn Roads to the campground. A Forest Service Map is essential.
Trip note: This one is way out there in booger country. Little known and rarely visited, it's primarily a jump-off point for backpackers. It is located on the edge of the Yolla Bolly Middle Eel Wilderness Area. The elevation is 5,700 feet.

WHITE ROCK
Map grid **a6**

SHASTA-TRINITY NATIONAL FOREST

Campsites, facilities: There are three tent sites here. Piped water, vault toilets, picnic tables, and fireplaces are provided. Pets are permitted on leashes.
Reservations, fee: No reservations, no fee.
Who to contact: Phone the Shasta-Trinity National Forest District Office at (916) 352-4211.
Location: From Red Bluff, drive about 45 miles west on Highway 36 to the Yolla Bolly Ranger Office. Continue west for about eight miles to Forest Service Road 30. Turn left and drive nine miles to Pine Root Springs. Turn left on Forest Service Road 35 (gravel) and drive nine miles to the campground.
Trip note: There's a reason that there's no charge to camp here: Usually nobody's ever here. It's primitive, little-known, and most likely empty. There's no way the Forest Service is going to waste the time to go out and collect a few bucks. If you don't want to see anybody, you found the right place.

EEL RIVER
Map grid **d2**

MENDOCINO NATIONAL FOREST

Campsites, facilities: There are 16 campsites for tents or motor homes. Piped water, vault toilets, picnic tables, and fireplaces are provided. Be prepared to pack out your garbage. Pets are permitted on leashes or otherwise controlled.
Reservations, fee: No reservations, no fee.
Who to contact: Phone the Mendocino National Forest Covelo Ranger District at (707)983-6118.
Location: From Covelo, drive 13 miles east on Highway 162 to the campground.
Trip note: This is a little-known spot, set in the oak woodlands at the confluence of the Middle Fork of the Eel River and Black Butte River. The elevation is 1,500 feet. At no cost, the price is right. Open from May through September.

WELLS CABIN
Map grid **d3**

MENDOCINO NATIONAL FOREST

Campsites, facilities: There are 25 campsites for tents or motor homes up to 22 feet long. Piped water, vault toilets, picnic tables, and fireplaces are provided. Be prepared to pack out your garbage. Pets are permitted on leashes or otherwise controlled. There is no water here in the winter.

Reservations, fee: No reservations, no fee.

Who to contact: Phone the Mendocino National Forest Covelo Ranger District at (707)983-6118.

Location: If you are coming from the west: From Covelo, drive 13 miles east on Highway 162 to the Eel River Work Center. Continue east on Forest Service Road 7 (a dusty, dirt road with logging traffic) to the road junction a short distance beyond Low Gap Guard Station. Turn north on the road to Anthony Peak and the campground. If you are coming from the east: From Paskenta, take Road 23N02 west to the junction with Anthony Peak Road. Turn north and drive about three miles to campground.

Trip note: You'll join the Five Percent Club when you reach this spot. It is situated one mile from Anthony Peak Lookout (6,900 feet), where you can get great views all the way to the Pacific Ocean on a clear day. This campground is hardly used during the summer and often provides a cool escape from the heat of the valley. The elevation is 6,300 feet. Open from July through October.

Map grid d6

WHITLOCK

MENDOCINO NATIONAL FOREST

Campsites, facilities: There are five campsites for tents or motor homes up to 22 feet long. Piped water, flush toilets, picnic tables, and fireplaces are provided. Be prepared to pack out your own garbage. Pets are permitted on leashes or otherwise controlled.

Reservations, fee: No reservations, no fee.

Who to contact: Phone the Mendocino National Forest at (916)934-3316.

Location: From Corning on Interstate 5, turn west onto County Road A9 (Corning Road) and drive 20 miles to Paskenta. Turn north on Toomes Camp Road and drive 14 miles to the campground.

Trip note: This obscure Forest Service camp is often empty or close to empty. It is set at 4,300 feet elevation, amid good deer range, and makes a good hunting base camp in the fall. It is advisable to obtain a Forest Service map of the area. Open from May through October.

Map grid e4

PLASKETT LAKES

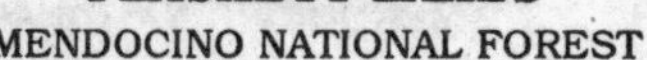
MENDOCINO NATIONAL FOREST

Campsites, facilities: There are 43 campsites available for tents or motor homes to 22 feet long. Piped water, vault toilets, fireplaces, and picnic tables are provided.

Reservations, fee: No reservations; $4 per night fee.

Who to contact: Phone the Mendocino National Forest at (916)934-3316.

Location: From the town of Elk Creek, drive four miles north on Road 306. Turn left (west) on Alder Springs Road and drive 31 miles to the campground .

Trip note: This is a little-known lakeside camp in the mountains. This is one answer, set at 6,000 feet elevation and missed by most folks. The lakes are stocked with trout. Open mid-May through mid-October.

Map grid e4

MASTERSON

near Plaskett Lakes

MENDOCINO NATIONAL FOREST

Campsites, facilities: There are 20 campsites for tents only, with piped water, vault toilets, fireplaces, and picnic tables provided. This site can accommodate 100

people maximum for group use.

Reservations, fee: Reservation required; $15 fee for group use of entire camp. A

Who to contact: Phone the Mendocino National Forest at (916)963-3128.

Location: From the town of Elk Creek, drive four miles north on Road 306. Turn left (west) on Alder Springs Road and drive 31 miles to the campground entrance on the right.

Trip note: This is a group camp only. It is set just a mile away from the Plaskett Lakes, two small lakes set at 6,000 feet and surrounded by mixed conifer forest. No swimming and no motors are permitted at either lake. It is advisable to obtain the map of Mendocino National Forest, which details nearby streams, lakes, and hiking trails. Open from mid-May through mid-October. B

Map grid h0

TROUT CREEK

near East Van Arsdale Reservoir

C1

Campsites, facilities: There are 15 campsites for tents or motor homes. Piped water, picnic tables, fireplaces, and vault toilets are provided. Pets are permitted on leashes or otherwise controlled.

D

Reservations, fee: No reservations; $8 fee per night.

Who to contact: Phone PG & E at (415)973-5552.

Location: From Ukiah, drive north to the junction of US 101 and Highway 20. Turn east on Highway 20 and drive five miles east. Turn northwest on County Road 240 (Potter Valley-Lake Pillsbury Road) toward Lake Pillsbury. From the Eel River Bridge, drive two miles to the campground entrance. E

Trip note: This is a spot that relatively few campers know of. Most others looking over this area are setting up shop at nearby Lake Pillsbury. But if you like to watch the water roll by, this could be your port of call, since it is located at the confluence of Trout Creek and Eel River (not far downstream from the East Van Arsdale Reservoir). The elevation is 1,500 feet. Open from May through October. F

Map grid h2

FULLER GROVE

on Lake Pillsbury

MENDOCINO NATIONAL FOREST

G

Campsites, facilities: There are 30 campsites for tents or motor homes. Picnic tables and fireplaces are provided. Piped water and vault toilets are available. A boat ramp is nearby. Pets are permitted on leashes or otherwise controlled.

Reservations, fee: No reservations; $5 fee per night.

Who to contact: Phone the Mendocino National Forest Upper Lake Ranger Station at (707)275-2361. H

Location: From Ukiah, drive north to the junction of US 101 and Highway 20. Turn east on Highway 20 and drive five miles. Turn northwest on County Road 240 (Potter Valley-Lake Pillsbury Road) to Lake Pillsbury. From the Eel River Information Kiosk at Lake Pillsbury, continue 2.2 miles toward the lake, then turn right and drive one-half mile to the campground. I

Trip note: This is one of several options for campers looking for a lakeside spot at Lake Pillsbury. The nearby boat ramp is a bonus and so is the surrounding National Forest country.

J

Map grid **h2**

LAKE PILLSBURY RESORT

Campsites, facilities: There are 40 spaces for RV or tent camping. A sanitary disposal station, rest rooms, showers, boat rentals, fuel, a dock, fishing supplies, a pier, and lake frontage sites are available.

Reservations, fee: Call ahead for available space and fee.

Who to contact: Phone the park at (707)743-1581.

Location: From Ukiah, drive north to the junction of US 101 and Highway 20. Turn east on Highway 20 and drive five miles. Turn north on County Road 240 (Potter Valley-Lake Pillsbury Road) and drive to the town of Potter Valley. From Potter Valley, drive 19 miles north and east continuing on County Road 240 to the campground.

Trip note: This is a pretty spot beside the shore of Lake Pillsbury in the heart of Mendocino National Forest. For some reason, the trout fishing here is never as good as most figure it could be. But with plenty of side trips available, there's no problem. A map of Mendocino National Forest will detail the surrounding area. Open from May through November.

Map grid **h2**

POGIE POINT
on Lake Pillsbury
MENDOCINO NATIONAL FOREST

Campsites, facilities: There are 50 campsites for tents or motor homes. Piped water (gravity system), picnic tables, and fireplaces are provided. Vault toilets are available. Pets are permitted on leashes or otherwise controlled.

Reservations, fee: No reservations; $5 fee per night.

Who to contact: Phone the Mendocino National Forest Upper Lake Ranger Station at (707)275-2361.

Location: From Ukiah, drive north to the junction of US 101 and Highway 20. Turn east on Highway 20 and drive five miles. Turn northwest on County Road 240 (Potter Valley-Lake Pillsbury Road) and drive 26 miles to Lake Pillsbury. The campground is on the northwest shore.

Trip note: This camp is set beside Lake Pillsbury in Mendocino National Forest, one of several camps at Pillsbury. It's a pretty lake, but the trout fishing rarely measures up to the scenery. The surrounding National Forest country offers the options of back roads, trails, lakes, and streams, detailed on the Forest Service's $2 map. If you want to branch out from Pillsbury, it's a good idea to get the map. The elevation is 1,900 feet. Open year-round.

Map grid **h2**

SUNSET CAMPGROUND
on Lake Pillsbury
MENDOCINO NATIONAL FOREST

Campsites, facilities: There are 54 campsites for tents or motor homes. Piped water (except in the winter), picnic tables, fireplaces, and vault toilets are provided. Pets are permitted on leashes or otherwise controlled. A boat ramp is nearby.

Reservations, fee: No reservations; $5 fee per night.

Who to contact: Phone the Mendocino National Forest Upper Lake Ranger Station at (707)275-2361.

Location: From Ukiah, drive north to the junction of US 101 and Highway 20. Turn east on Highway 20 and drive five miles. Turn northwest on County Road 240 (Potter Valley-Lake Pillsbury Road) and drive 26 miles to Lake Pillsbury. The campground is on the east shore of the lake.

Trip note: The adjacent, designated Nature Trail and the nearby boat ramp make this one of the more popular camps at Lake Pillsbury. The surrounding National Forest offers side trip possibilities. Open year-round.

A

Map grid h2

OAK FLAT
on Lake Pillsbury
MENDOCINO NATIONAL FOREST

B

Campsites, facilities: This is a primitive camping area with 12 campsites for tents or motor homes. There is **no piped water,** but picnic tables, fireplaces, and vault toilets are provided. Pets are permitted on leashes or otherwise controlled.

Reservations, fee: No reservations, no fee.

C1

Who to contact: Phone the Mendocino National Forest Upper Lake Ranger Station at (707)275-2361.

Location: From Ukiah, drive north to the junction of US 101 and Highway 20. Turn east on Highway 20 and drive five miles. Turn northwest on County Road 240 (Potter Valley-Lake Pillsbury Road) and drive 26 miles to Lake Pillsbury. The campground is on the north shore.

D

Trip note: This primitive camp is used primarily by riders of off-road motorcycles and as an overflow area if Lake Pillsbury's other camps are full. It is set at 1,850 feet elevation near the north shore of Lake Pillsbury in the heart of Mendocino National Forest. Trails leading into the backcountry are nearby, detailed on a Forest Service map. Open all year.

E

Map grid h3

LOWER NYE
MENDOCINO NATIONAL FOREST

Campsites, facilities: There are six campsites for tents or motor homes. There is **no piped water,** but picnic tables, fireplaces, and vault toilets are provided. Pets are permitted on leashes or otherwise controlled.

F

Reservations, fee: No reservations, no fee.

Who to contact: Phone the Mendocino National Forest Upper Lake Ranger Station at (707)275-2361.

G

Location: From the town of Upper Lake, drive 17 miles north on Forest Service Road 1N02 (Elk Mountain Road). Turn east on Forest Service Road 18N01 (Bear Creek Road) and drive seven miles. Turn north on Forest Service Road 18N04 (Rice Creek Road) and drive 14 miles to the campground.

Trip note: This is a good jump-off point for backpackers or a spot for folks to hunker down for a while who don't want to be bugged by anybody. It is set at 3,300 feet on Skeleton Creek near the Eel River. There are several trails nearby leading to various backcountry spots, all detailed on the map of Mendocino National Forest. Open from May to mid-September.

H

Map grid i2

DEER VALLEY CAMPGROUND
MENDOCINO NATIONAL FOREST

I

Campsites, facilities: There are 13 campsites for tents or motor homes. There is **no piped water,** but picnic tables, fireplaces, and vault toilets are provided. Pets are permitted on leashes or otherwise controlled.

Reservations, fee: No reservations, no fee.

J

Who to contact: Phone the Mendocino National Forest Upper Lake Ranger Station at (707)275-2361.

Location: From the town of Upper Lake, drive 12 miles north on Forest Service Road 1N02 (Elk Mountain Road). Turn right on Forest Service Road 16N01, an unimproved road about two miles past the East Fork of Middle Creek, and drive four miles to camp.

Trip note: This one is out there in booger country. It is used primarily in the fall by deer hunters. It is set at 3,700 feet elevation in Deer Valley about five miles from the East Fork of Middle Creek. Open from April through November.

Map grid i2

MIDDLE CREEK CAMPGROUND

MENDOCINO NATIONAL FOREST

Campsites, facilities: There are 12 campsites for tents or small motor homes. Piped water (gravity system), picnic tables, and fireplaces are provided. Vault toilets are available. Pets are permitted on leashes or otherwise controlled.

Reservations, fee: No reservations; $3 fee per night.

Who to contact: Phone Mendocino National Forest, Upper Lake Ranger Station at (707)275-2361.

Location: From the town of Upper Lake, drive eight miles north on Forest Service Road 1N02 (Elk Mountain Road) to the campground.

Trip note: This camp is not widely known, but it is known well enough. Sometimes there's a problem with off-road motorcycles making a lot of noise in the area. That ruins an otherwise quiet spot, which is set at 2,000 feet elevation at the confluence of the West and East Forks of Middle Creek. Open year-round.

Map grid i3

BEAR CREEK CAMPGROUND

MENDOCINO NATIONAL FOREST

Campsites, facilities: There are 16 campsites for tents or small motor homes. There is **no piped water,** but picnic tables, fireplaces, and vault toilets are provided. Pets are permitted on leashes or otherwise controlled.

Reservations, fee: No reservations, no fee.

Who to contact: Phone the Mendocino National Forest Upper Lake Ranger Station at (707)275-2361.

Location: From the town of Upper Lake, drive 17 miles north on Forest Service Road 1N02 (Elk Mountain Road). Turn east on Forest Service Road 18N01 (Bear Creek Road) and drive eight miles to the campground.

Trip note: Bet you didn't know about this one—a primitive spot out in the boondocks of Mendocino National Forest, set at 2,000 feet elevation. It's a pretty spot too, set beside Bear Creek near its confluence with Blue Slides Creek. It is advisable to obtain a National Forest map, which details all back roads, trails, and streams. Open from May to mid-October.

Map grid i4

LETTS LAKE COMPLEX

MENDOCINO NATIONAL FOREST

Campsites, facilities: There are 35 campsites here that can accommodate tents or motor homes up to 20 feet long. Piped water, vault toilets, picnic tables, and fireplaces are provided. Pets are permitted on leashes or otherwise controlled.

Reservations, fee: No reservations; $5 fee per night.

Who to contact: Phone the Mendocino National Forest Stonyford Ranger District at (916)963-3128.

Location: From Stonyford, drive eight miles west on Road M10 (Fouts Springs Road). Bear left (southwest) on Forest Service Road 18N01 and drive six miles.

Continue southeast on Forest Service Road 17NO2 for three miles to the campgrounds around the lake.

Trip note: Letts Lake, a 35-acre lake set in a mixed conifer forest, is a spot not too many folks know about. No motors are allowed, making it ideal for canoes, rafts, and float tubes. The camps are spread around the lake, so take your pick. This lake is stocked with trout in the early summer. The elevation is 4,500 feet. Open mid-April through October.

Map grid i4

MILL VALLEY

near Letts Lake

MENDOCINO NATIONAL FOREST

Campsites, facilities: There are 15 campsites for tents or motor homes up to 18 feet long. Piped water (gravity system), vault toilets, picnic tables, and fireplaces are provided. Pets are permitted on leashes or otherwise controlled.

Reservations, fee: No reservations; $3 fee per night.

Who to contact: Phone the Mendocino National Forest Stonyford Ranger District at (916)963-3128.

Location: From Stonyford, drive eight miles west on Road M10 (Fouts Springs Road). Bear left (southwest) on Forest Service Road 18N01 and drive six miles. Continue southeast on Forest Service Road 17NO2 for one mile to the campground.

Trip note: This camp is set beside the Lily Pond, a little, teeny guy, with larger Letts Lake just a mile away. The area is criss-crossed with numerous creeks and trails, making it a good base camp for hikers. It is advisable to obtain the Forest Service map. The elevation is 4,200 feet. Open from mid-April through October.

Map grid i5

MILL CREEK

MENDOCINO NATIONAL FOREST

Campsites, facilities: There are six sites for tents only. There is **no piped water,** but vault toilets, picnic tables, and fireplaces are provided. Pets are permitted on leashes or otherwise controlled.

Reservations, fee: No reservations, no fee.

Who to contact: Phone the Mendocino National Forest Stonyford Ranger District at (916)963-3128.

Location: From Stonyford, drive about eight miles west on Road M10 (Fouts Springs Road). Turn right (north) on Forest Service Road 18N03 and you'll see the campground on your right.

Trip note: This tiny, pretty, secluded camp is set beside Mill Creek near Fouts Springs. It's an ideal base camp for hikes; trails in the area lead to Letts Lake, Trout Creek, Stoney Creek, and Summit Spring. In the spring and early summer, Mill Creek is quite pretty. By late summer, the flow drops way down. In the winter months and early spring, beware of heavy motorcycle use in the area, but note that no motorized vehicles are permitted in the Snow Mountain Area (located to the west). The elevation is 1,700 feet. Open year-round.

Map grid i5

OLD MILL

near Mill Creek

MENDOCINO NATIONAL FOREST

Campsites, facilities: There are eight sites for tents only and two campsites that will accommodate tents or motor homes up to 16 feet long (however the access road to the campground is narrow). Piped water (gravity system), vault toilets, picnic tables, and fireplaces are provided. Pets are permitted on leashes or otherwise controlled.

Reservations, fee: No reservations, no fee.

Who to contact: Phone the Mendocino National Forest Stonyford Ranger District at (916)963-3128.

Location: From Stonyford, drive about six miles west on Road M10 (Fouts Springs Road). Turn left (south) on Forest Service Road M5 (John Smith Road) and drive 7.5 miles (narrow road) to the campground on your right.

Trip note: Little known and little used, this camp is set at 3,700 feet elevation amid a mature stand of pine and fir on Trough Spring Ridge. It's just a short walk from Mill Creek. Open from May through October.

Map grid i5

NORTH FORK

on Fouts Creek

MENDOCINO NATIONAL FOREST

Campsites, facilities: There are four sites for tents only. There is **no piped water,** but vault toilets, picnic tables, and fireplaces are provided. Pets are permitted on leashes or otherwise controlled.

Reservations, fee: No reservations, no fee.

Who to contact: Phone the Mendocino National Forest Stonyford Ranger District at (916)963-3128.

Location: From Stonyford, drive about eight miles west on Road M10 (Fouts Springs Road). Turn right (north) on Forest Service Road 18N03 and drive two miles to the campground.

Trip note: This quiet, primitive camp is set in a grove of oak trees on Fouts Creek. There are many hiking trails in area. See trip note for Mill Creek camp for additional information. The elevation is 1,700 feet. Open all year.

Map grid i5

FOUTS CAMPGROUND

on Fouts Creek

MENDOCINO NATIONAL FOREST

Campsites, facilities: There are ten campsites for tents or motor homes up to 16 feet long. Piped water (gravity system), vault toilets, picnic tables, and fireplaces are provided. Pets are permitted on leashes or otherwise controlled.

Reservations, fee: No reservations, no fee.

Who to contact: Phone the Mendocino National Forest Stonyford Ranger District at (916)963-3128.

Location: From Stonyford, drive about eight miles west on Road M10 (Fouts Springs Road). Turn right (north) on Forest Service Road 18N03 and drive one mile to the campground on your right.

Trip note: This camp is located in a brushy area shaded by digger pines. It is set beside Fouts Creek near Davis Flat and Fouts Springs. The several trails in the area are detailed on the Forest Service map. The elevation is 1,700 feet. Heavy motorcycle use from October to June. Open year-round.

Map grid j0

LE TRIANON RESORT

on Lower Blue Lake

Campsites, facilities: There are 400 campsites for tents or motor homes, many with water and electrical hookups. Picnic tables are provided. Flush toilets, showers, a sanitary disposal station, a video game room, a playground, a boat ramp, boat rentals, fishing supplies, a laundromat, propane gas, and a grocery store are available.

Reservations, fee: No reservations; $15 fee per night.

Who to contact: Phone the park at (707)275-2262.

Location: From the town of Upper Lake, drive seven miles northwest on Highway 20 to 5845 West Highway 20.

Trip note: This is the biggest of the camps on the Blue Lakes, the overlooked lakes not far from giant Clear Lake. This one is an angler's special with good trout fishing in spring and no water skiing permitted. This park has some lakeside campsites. Open from April through October.

Map grid **jO**

MAYACMUS
near Ukiah

Campsites, facilities: There are nine campsites for tents. Piped water, vault toilets, picnic tables, and fireplaces are provided. Pets are permitted on leashes or otherwise controlled. Fourteen days is the maximum for camping.

Reservations, fee: No reservations, no fee.

Who to contact: Phone the Bureau of Land Management, Ukiah District at (707)462-3873.

Location: From US 101 in Ukiah, turn east on Talmage Road and drive 1.5 miles. Turn right on Eastside Road and drive one-third mile. Turn left on Mill Creek Road and drive three miles. Turn left on Mendo Rock Road and drive seven miles to the campground.

Trip note: This campground sits on the slopes of Cow Mountain in the oft overlooked wild area located east of Ukiah. The primitive area is ideal for hiking and horseback riding. In the fall, it is a popular hunting area as well, for the few who know of it.

Map grid **jO**

PINE ACRES BLUE LAKE RESORT
on Upper Blue Lake

Campsites, facilities: There are 32 motor home spaces, most with full or partial hookups. Picnic tables and fire grills are provided. Flush toilets, showers, a sanitary disposal station, boat rentals, boat launching, moorings, a boat ramp, fishing supplies, and lake frontage sites are available.

Reservations, fee: Reservations accepted; $14-$17 fee per night.

Who to contact: Phone the park at (707)275-2811.

Location: From the town of Upper Lake, drive six miles northwest on Highway 20. Turn left on Irvine Street and drive two blocks. Turn right on Blue Lakes Road and drive one block to the resort.

Trip note: Because of their proximity to Clear Lake, the Blue Lakes are often overlooked. But these lovely lakes offer good fishing for trout, especially in spring and early summer, and quiet boating activities. Swimming is good here. No water skiing is permitted. Open year-round.

Map grid **jO**

NARROWS LODGE RESORT
on Upper Blue Lake

Campsites, facilities: There are 28 campsites for tents or motor homes, with full or partial hookups. Picnic tables are provided. Flush toilets, showers, a sanitary disposal station, a recreation room, boat rentals, pier, a boat ramp, boat rentals, fishing supplies, and ice are available.

Reservations, fee: Reservations accepted; $16-$18 fee per night.
Who to contact: Phone the park at (707)275-2718.
Location: From the town of Upper Lake, drive 7.5 miles northwest on Highway 20. Turn on Blue Lakes Road and drive to 5690 Blue Lakes Road.
Trip note: This is one of four campgrounds in the immediate vicinity. The Blue Lakes are often overlooked because of their proximity to Clear Lake, but they are a quiet and pretty alternative, with good trout fishing in the spring and early summer. Open year-round.

Map grid j4

CEDAR CAMP

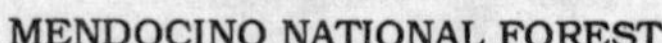
MENDOCINO NATIONAL FOREST

Campsites, facilities: There are six campsites here that can accommodate tents or small motor homes (access road is poor for trailers). There is **no piped water,** but vault toilets, picnic tables, and fireplaces are provided. Pets are permitted on leashes or otherwise controlled.
Reservations, fee: No reservations, no fee.
Who to contact: Phone the Mendocino National Forest Stonyford Ranger District at (916)963-3128.
Location: From Stonyford, drive about six miles west on M10 (Fouts Spring Road). Turn left (south) and drive 13 miles on Road M5 (John Smith Road) to the campground on your right. It's narrow going.
Trip note: This secluded area near Goat Mountain is set at 4,300 feet elevation. In mid-summer, mosquitos like it too. Open from mid-June through mid-October.

Map grid j6

DIGGER PINE FLAT

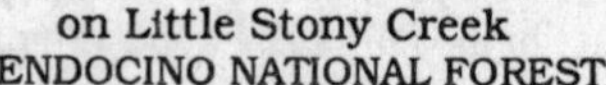
on Little Stony Creek
MENDOCINO NATIONAL FOREST

Campsites, facilities: There are seven campsites for tents or small motor homes. There is **no piped water,** but vault toilets, picnic tables, and fireplaces are provided. Pets are permitted on leashes or otherwise controlled.
Reservations, fee: No reservations, no fee.
Who to contact: Phone the Mendocino National Forest Stonyford Ranger District at (916)963-3128.
Location: From Stonyford, drive about six miles south on Lodoga-Stonyford Road. Turn right (southwest) and travel four miles on Goat Mountain Road (a rough, country road) to the campground.
Trip note: This pretty spot is set beside Little Stony Creek at 1,500 feet elevation. You might think that nobody would know about this spot, but in the off-season, from October through May, the area gets heavy motorcycle use.

◆ MAP C2 ◆

BEACH
TREES
5% CLUB
DESERT
URBAN
FOOTHILL
GRASSLAND

15 MILES

to Cottonwood
to A-17
to Manton
to Beegum
to Paskenta
to Flournoy
to Newville
to fruto
to Sites
to Mineral
to Chester
to Berry Creek
to Brownsville
to Williams
to Colusa
to Live Oak
to Marysville

a
b
c
d
e
f
g
h
i
j

0
1
2
3
4
5
6
7
8
9

A5
5
36
Paynes Creek
Dales
Morgan Summit EL. 5,750
36
W. IDE HISTORIC PARK
Red Bluff
99
STATE GAME REFUGE
LASSEN
NAT'L.
FOREST
Dairyville
A8
Dewitt PK. EL. 2,064
Proberta
Richfield
Henleyville
A11
Los Molinos
Butte Meadows
A9
Corning
WOODSON BRIDGE ST. REC. AREA
Lomo
A9
Promontory PT. EL. 3,622
Vina
Black Butte Lake
5
Kirkwood
Sacramento River
Forest Ranch
Stirling City
De Sabla
Orland
32
Nordo
BIDWELL MANSION ST. HIST. PK.
32
Magalia
Chico
Paradise
45
Artios
Ordbend
Durham
191
70
Oroville Lake
Willows
162
Berry Creek
Glenn
Nelson
99
70
Butte City
162
Richvale
Oroville
162
SACAMENTO NAT'L. WILDLIFE REFUGE
Princeton
5
162
DELEVAN NAT'L. WILDLIFE REFUGE
45
Biggs
Palermo
Maxwell
Gridley
70
Bangor

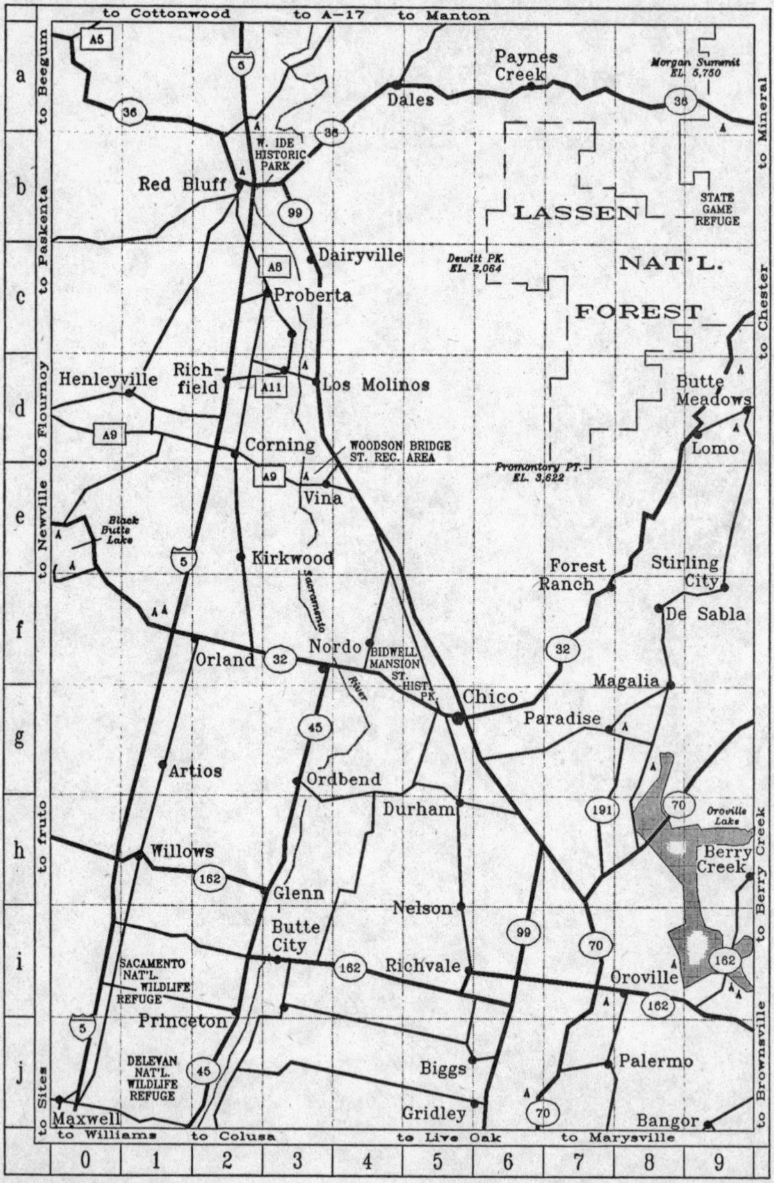

A

Map grid a2 — BEND RV PARK AND FISHING RESORT
on Sacramento River

Campsites, facilities: There are 37 spaces for motor homes with full or partial hookups. There is a separate area for tents only. Piped water, showers, flush toilets, picnic tables, and fireplaces are provided. A grocery store, bait and tackle shop, boat ramp, boat dock, laundromat, and sanitary dump station are nearby. Pets are permitted.

B

Reservations, fee: Reservations accepted; $10-$16 fee per night.

Who to contact: Phone (916)527-6289.

Location: From the junction of Interstate 5 and Highway 36 in Red Bluff, drive four miles north on Interstate 5 to the Jelly's Ferry Road exit. Drive 2.5 miles northeast on Jelly's Ferry Road to the resort.

C2

Trip note: For motor home cruisers, here's a spot to tie up your hoss for awhile. It's open year-round and set beside the Sacramento River. Salmon average 15 to 25 pounds in this area, with the best results from mid-August through October. Expect very hot weather in July and August.

D

Map grid a9 — BATTLE CREEK
on Battle Creek
LASSEN NATIONAL FOREST

E

Campsites, facilities: There are 12 sites for tents only and 38 spaces for tents or motor homes. Piped water, picnic tables, and fireplaces are provided. Flush toilets are available. Supplies can be obtained in the town of Mineral. Pets are permitted on leashes.

Reservations, fee: No reservations; $7 fee per night.

Who to contact: Phone the Lassen National Forest Almanor Ranger District Office at (916)258-2141.

F

Location: From Red Bluff, drive 41 miles east on Highway 36 to the campground, which is located two miles before you get to the town of Mineral.

Trip note: This pretty spot offers easy access and streamside camping along Battle Creek. The trout fishing can be good in May and June, when the creek is stocked by the Department of Fish and Game. The elevation is 4,800 feet. Open from May through November.

G

Map grid b2 — O'NITE PARK
near Sacramento River

H

Campsites, facilities: There are 74 motor home spaces with full hookups. Picnic tables, rest rooms, showers, and a swimming pool are provided. A laundromat, propane gas, and ice are available. Pets are permitted.

Reservations, fee: Reservations accepted; $16 fee per night.

Who to contact: Phone (916)527-5868.

I

Location: From Interstate 5 and the junction of Highways 99 and 36 (in Red Bluff), drive west on Highway 36 (Antelope Boulevard) for one block. Turn south on Gilmore Road and drive one block to the campground.

Trip notes: Easy access from the highway, nearby supermarkets and restaurants, and many nearby side trips make this spot a winner. The park is only one block from the Sacramento River, which gets a big salmon run from mid-August through October. It's about a 45-minute drive east to Lassen Park.

J

Map grid d3

HIDDEN HARBOR RV PARK
on Sacramento River near Los Molinos

Campsites, facilities: There are 500 sites for tents or motor homes without hookups and 30 spaces for motor homes with full hookups. Rest rooms, showers, picnic tables, fire grills, patios, swimming pool, a volleyball court, and a recreation room are provided. A grocery store, a laundromat, a boat dock, boat rentals and a sanitary dump station are available nearby.

Reservations, fee: Call for space available; $9-$14 fee per night.

Who to contact: Phone (916)384-1800 or write to 24680 River Road, Los Molinos, CA 96055.

Location: In Los Molinos on Highway 99, turn west onto Tehama-Vina Road (at the northern edge of town) and drive a short distance to River Road. Turn north (right) and drive one block to the campground.

Trip note: This is an ideal spot on the Sacramento River for a shad fishing base camp in June or a salmon fishing trip in September. The one bugaboo is the heat, which never seems to let up—100-degree days are common in the summer. Open year-round.

Map grid d9

SODA SPRINGS
LASSEN NATIONAL FOREST

Campsites, facilities: There are ten sites for tents or motor homes. There is **no piped water**, but picnic tables, fireplaces, and vault toilets are provided. Pets are permitted on leashes.

Reservations, fee: No reservations, no fee.

Who to contact: Phone the Lassen National Forest, Almanor Ranger District at (916)258-2141 or write to P.O. Box 767, Chester, CA 96020.

Location: From Chico, drive about 15 miles north on Highway 32 to the town of Forest Ranch. Continue on Highway 32 for another 15 miles to the campground.

Trip note: You can camp at the confluence of Cascade and Big Chico Creeks, a little-known, secluded spot. Bring a water purifier. The elevation is 3,600 feet. Open from May through September.

Map grid d9

BUTTE MEADOWS
on Butte Creek
LASSEN NATIONAL FOREST

Campsites, facilities: There are 12 campsites available for tents or motor homes. Piped water, vault toilets, fireplaces, picnic tables are provided. Pets are permitted on leashes. Supplies are available in Butte Meadows.

Reservations, fee: No reservations; $6 per night fee.

Who to contact: Phone the Lassen National Forest Almanor Ranger District at (916) 258-2141.

Location: From Chico, drive about 15 miles north Highway 32 to the town of Forest Ranch. Continue on Highway 32 for another nine miles. Turn right onto Humboldt Road and drive five miles to Butte Meadows.

Trip note: This is a pretty, summer camp situated along Butte Creek. There is some trout fishing. The elevation is 4,300 feet. Open from June through October.

ORLAND BUTTES
Map grid e0

on Black Butte Lake

Campsites, facilities: There are four sites for tents only and 31 sites that can handle tents or motor homes up to 35 feet long. Piped water, restrooms, showers, fireplaces, picnic tables, and a sanitary disposal station are provided.

Reservations, fee: No reservations; $10 per night fee.

Who to contact: Phone the U.S. Army Corps of Engineers at (916)865-4781.

Location: From Interstate 5 in Orland, take the Black Butte Lake exit. Drive west on Road 200 (Newville Road) for eight miles to the east shore of the lake.

Trip note: Black Butte Lake isn't far from Highway 5, but a lot of campers zoom right by it. The prime time is in early summer, when the bass and crappie fishing is quite good. There's a boat launch nearby. Expect very hot weather in the summer. The elevation is 500 feet. Open from March through September.

BUCKHORN
Map grid e0

on Black Butte Lake

Campsites, facilities: There are 90 campsites for tents or motor homes up to 35 feet long. Piped water, picnic tables, fireplaces, flush toilets, a sanitary dump station, showers, and a playground are provided. A boat ramp, propane gas, and a grocery store are nearby. Pets are permitted on leashes.

Reservations, fee: No reservations; $10 fee per night.

Who to contact: Phone the U.S. Corps of Engineers Black Butte Lake at (916) 865-4781.

Location: From Interstate 5 in Orland, take the Black Butte Lake exit. Drive about ten miles west on Road 200 (Newville Road) to Buckhorn Road. Turn left and drive a short distance to the campground on the north shore of the lake.

Trip note: Black Butte Lake is set in the foothills of the north valley at 500 feet elevation. The crappie fishing is often quite good here in the spring, though the size of the fish varies quite a bit from year to year. Recreation options include hiking on interpretive trails or, for dirt bikers, heading to the off-road motorcycle park available at the Buckhorn Recreation Area. Open year-round.

WOODSON BRIDGE STATE REC. AREA
Map grid e3

on Sacramento River

Campsites, facilities: There are 46 campsites for tents or motor homes up to 31 feet. Group sites are available. Piped water, picnic tables, and fireplaces are provided. Showers, flush toilets, a playground, and a boat launch are available. Some facilities are wheelchair accessible. Pets are permitted.

Reservations, fee: Reservations are advised in the summer and fall months; reserve through MISTIX by phoning (800)444-PARK ($3.95 MISTIX fee); $12-$14 fee per night; pets $1.

Who to contact: Phone (916)839-2112.

Location: From Interstate 5 in Corning, take the South Avenue exit and drive nine miles east to the campground.

Trip note: This camp is located right next to the bridge, providing an ideal spot for the boating and camping angler. The boat launch is an added bonus. The adjoining stretch of the Sacramento River is a good piece of water for shad, which arrive in large numbers in June and July. The salmon arrive in August and September.

Map grid **f1**

OLD ORCHARD RV PARK

near Orland

Campsites, facilities: There are 51 motor home sites with partial or full hookups and 40 sites for tents only. A sanitary disposal station, propane, a laundromat, and a store are available.

Reservations, fee: Call ahead.

Who to contact: Phone at (916)865-5335 or write to Route 4, Box 4037, Orland, CA 95963.

Location: From Interstate 5 at Orland, take Black Butte Lake exit, then head one block west and turn right. The park is one block down.

Trip note: Most folks use this as a layover spot while cruising the Central Valley, but there are two side trips that could have appeal for anglers. Nearby Black Butte Lake to the west, with crappie in the early summer, and the Sacramento River to the east, with salmon in the late summer and early fall, can add some spice to your trip. It's very hot in the summer.

Map grid **f1**

KOA GREEN ACRES

near Orland

Campsites, facilities: There are 68 motor home sites with partial or full hookups and 32 sites for tents only. A store, a laundromat, a sanitary dump station, barbecues, a recreation room, a swimming pool, ice, and propane gas are available.

Reservations, fee: Call ahead to be certain room is available; $14-$18 fee per night.

Who to contact: Phone KOA Green Acres at (916)865-9188 or write to Route 4, Box 4048, Orland, CA 95963.

Location: From Orland on Interstate 5, take the Highway 32 exit and drive a one-half mile west to the campground.

Trip note: This is a good layover spot located in the heart of the olive and almond country. It's a restful setting, but hot in summer. There's fishing on the Sacramento River. Mid-August through October is best for big king salmon.

Map grid **g8**

QUAIL TRAILS VILLAGE

near Paradise

Campsites, facilities: There are 22 motor home sites with full hookups. Picnic tables are provided. Rest rooms, hot showers, and a laundromat are available.

Reservations, fee: Reservations accepted; $15 fee per night.

Who to contact: Phone (916)877-6581.

Location: From Highway 191 in Paradise (at the south end of town), turn east on Pearson Road and drive two miles. Turn south on Pentz Road and drive 1.5 miles to the campground.

Trip note: This is a rural motor home campground, set near the northern end of Lake Oroville. A beach, boat launching facilities, concessions, and a picnic area are located nearby at the Lime Saddle Section of Lake Oroville Recreation Area. Open year-round.

Map grid **g8**

PINE RIDGE PARK

near Paradise

Campsites, facilities: There are 46 motor home sites with full hookups. Piped water, flush toilets, showers and a laundromat are available. Pets are permitted. No tent camping allowed here.

Reservations, fee: Reservations accepted; $15 fee per night.

Who to contact: Phone at (916)877-0677.

Location: From Highway 191 in Paradise (at the south end of town), turn east on Pearson Road and drive two miles. Turn south on Pentz Road and drive one mile to 5084 Pentz Magalia Highway.

Trip note: This privately-operated motor home park offers shaded sites in the pines and is set at 1,700 feet elevation. A good side trip is to the Lime Saddle Area, the northernmost part of the Lake Oroville Recreation Area. It offers a beach, a boat ramp, concessions, and a picnic area. Open year-round.

Map grid i7

FEATHER RIVER RV PARK
near Oroville

Campsites, facilities: There are 25 sites with full hookups for motor homes and a separate area for tents. Picnic tables are provided. Rest rooms, showers, cable TV hookups, a grocery store, and a sanitary dump station are available.

Reservations, fee: Reservations accepted; $13 fee per night.

Who to contact: Phone (916)534-0605.

Location: In Oroville at the junction of Highways 70 and 162, drive one-half mile west on Highway 162 to the RV park.

Trip note: This motor home park is popular with fishermen. A bait and tackle shop is on the premises, which is a rare bonus. The Feather River is nearby. The Afterbay Outlet Hole is a popular spot to fish for salmon in the late summer, and the river has runs of striped bass, shad, and steelhead as well.

Map grid i8

BIDWELL CANYON
on Lake Oroville

Campsites, facilities: There are 75 sites for tents or motor homes up to 31 feet long (including boat trailers), all with full hookups. Piped water, flush toilets, showers, tables, and fireplaces are provided. A laundromat, a grocery store, and propane gas are available. Pets are permitted.

Reservations, fee: Reserve through MISTIX by calling (800)444-PARK ($3.95 MISTIX fee); $20-$22 per night; $1 pet fee.

Who to contact: Call the Lake Oroville State Recreation Area at (916)538-2200.

Location: From Oroville, drive eight miles east on Highway 162. Turn north on Kelly Ridge Road and drive to the campground.

Trip note: Giant Lake Oroville is a popular destination. Recent habitat work has improved fishing prospects, especially for bass. Many campers use this spot for boating headquarters. The fishing is best in the spring and fall. It is very hot in mid-summer.

Map grid i9

LOAFER CREEK
on Lake Oroville

Campsites, facilities: There are 137 campsites for tents and motor homes up to 31 feet long (including a boat trailer). A sanitary disposal station, piped water, flush toilets, showers, fireplaces, and tables are provided. A boat ramp is available. The facilities are wheelchair accessible. Propane, groceries, and a laundromat are available. Pets are permitted.

Reservations, fee: Reservations are advised; reserve by calling MISTIX at (800) 444-PARK ($3.95 MISTIX fee); $12-$14 fee per night; $1 pet fee.

on Lake Oroville

Who to contact: Phone Lake Oroville State Recreation Area at (916)538-2200.

Location: From Oroville, drive eight miles east on Highway 162 to the campground.

Trip note: This rustic, but well-cared-for state park is set along the shore of Lake Oroville. The nearby boat launch makes this a good base camp for boating campers. The fishing is best for bass and trout in the spring and early summer. Open from mid-March through October.

Map grid i9

LOAFER CREEK GROUP CAMPS

on Lake Oroville

Campsites, facilities: There are six group camps that can accommodate up to 25 people each. The sites can be combined to accommodate up to 150 people. RV parking is limited and the maximum length is 20 feet; no trailers are permitted. Piped water, flush toilets, showers, fireplaces, and picnic tables are provided. A laundromat, a grocery store, and propane gas are available. Pets are permitted. Two large boat-in group camps are also available; call Lake Oroville Recreation Area at the number below for more information.

Reservations, fee: Reserve through MISTIX by phoning (800)444-PARK ($3.95 MISTIX fee). $37.50 fee per night for adult groups, $18.75 fee per night for youth groups; $1 pet fee.

Who to contact: Phone Lake Oroville State Recreation Area at (916)538-2200.

Location: From Oroville, drive eight miles east on Highway 162 to the campground.

Trip note: This is an ideal base camp for Boy Scout Troops or other large groups that need some privacy and a spot to call their own. The scenery includes a lakeside setting. A beach is nearby, along with a boat launching facilities. Open from April through October.

Map grid j6

DINGERVILLE USA

near Oroville

Campsites, facilities: There are 41 sites for motor homes, many with full hookups. Picnic tables and fire rings are provided. Rest rooms, showers, a swimming pool, a laundromat, a horseshoe pit and a sanitary dump station are available. Facilities are wheelchair accessible.

Reservations, fee: Reservations not required; rates on a daily, weekly, or monthly basis.

Who to contact: Call (916)533-9343 or write to Route 6, Box 2225, Oroville, CA 95965.

Location: If you are coming from the north: From Oroville, drive south on Highway 70. Turn right at the second Pacific Heights Road turnoff and continue on Pacific Heights Road to the campground. If you are coming from the south: From Highway 70, turn left at Palermo-Welsh R-1 Road and continue north on Pacific Heights Road for one-half mile to camp.

Trip note: You're right, they thought of this name all by themselves, needed no help. But for a motor home park, there are a variety of excellent side trips. It is adjacent to a wildlife area and the Feather River and close to boating and fishing. It's a clean, quiet campground with easy access from the highway.

MAP C3

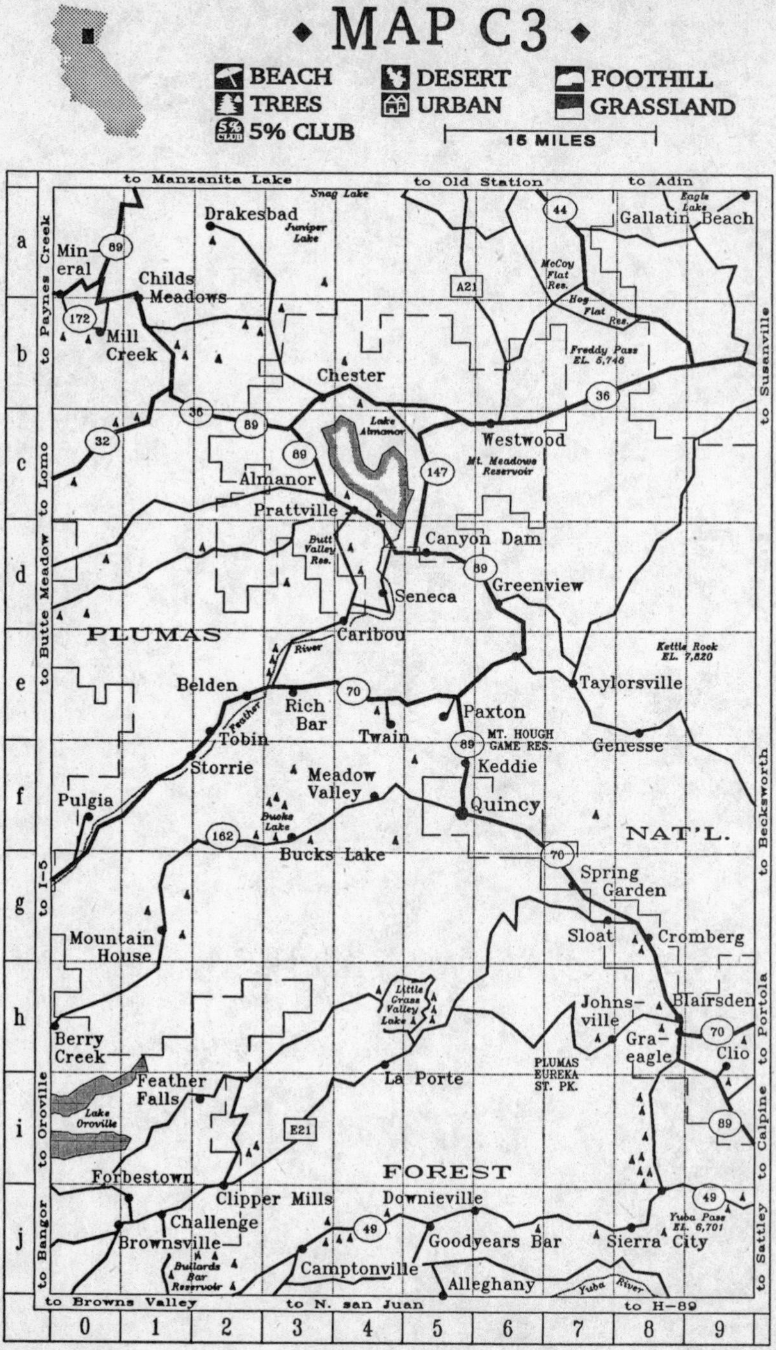

BEACH
DESERT
FOOTHILL
TREES
URBAN
GRASSLAND
5% CLUB

15 MILES

Map grid **a2**

WARNER VALLEY

on Hot Springs Creek
LASSEN VOLCANIC NATIONAL PARK

Campsites, facilities: There are 18 tent or motor home sites in Warner Valley. Piped water, pit toilets, fireplaces, and picnic tables are provided. Pets are permitted.
Reservations, fee: No reservations; $5 fee per night.
Who to contact: Phone the Lassen Volcanic National Park at (916)595-4444.
Location: From Chester on Highway 36, turn on Warner Valley Road and drive 16 miles to the campground (a dirt road).
Trip note: Lassen is one of the great national parks of the West, yet it gets surprisingly little use compared to Yosemite, Sequoia, and Kings Canyon National Parks. This camp is set along Hot Springs Creek at 5,650 feet elevation. A highlight here is a trail that leads to several lakes, as well as the unique Devil's Kitchen Geothermal Area. It's also a good horseback riding area. Open from June through September.

Map grid **a3**

BENNER CREEK

LASSEN NATIONAL FOREST

Campsites, facilities: There are eight tent sites. There is **no piped water**, but vault toilets, picnic tables, and fireplaces are provided. Pets are permitted on leashes.
Reservations, fee: No reservations, no fee.
Who to contact: Phone the Lassen National Forest Almanor Ranger District at (916) 258-2141.
Location: From Chester on Highway 36, turn on Juniper Lake Road and drive seven miles to the campground.
Trip note: This small, primitive campground is set in the vicinity of several prime fishing waters, including Lake Almanor, the North Fork of the Feather River, and Butte Lake. The elevation is 5,600 feet. Open from June through September.

Map grid **b0**

MILL CREEK RESORT

on Mill Creek
LASSEN NATIONAL FOREST

Campsites, facilities: There are 12 campsites for tents or motor homes up to 22 feet. Picnic tables, fireplaces, piped water, and vault toilets are provided. Showers and a laundromat are available. Pets are permitted.
Reservations, fee: Reservations accepted; $6 fee per night.
Who to contact: Phone concessionaire at (916)595-4449.
Location: From Chester, drive about 25 miles west on Highway 36 to the sign for Highway 172. Turn south and drive three miles to the campground.
Trip note: This is a good base camp for a trout fishing trip, with the camp set along Mill Creek at 4,700 feet elevation. There is a trail that follows Mill Creek for many miles. Open from May through mid-October.

Map grid **b0**

HOLE-IN-THE-GROUND

on Mill Creek
LASSEN NATIONAL FOREST

Campsites, facilities: There are four sites for tents only and nine sites for tents or motor homes. Piped water, vault toilets, picnic tables, and fireplaces are provided. Pets are permitted on leashes. Supplies are available in Mineral.

Reservations, fee: No reservations; $6 per night fee.

Who to contact: Phone the Lassen National Forest Almanor Ranger District Office at (916)258-2141.

Location: From Red Bluff, drive 43 miles east on Highway 36 to the town of Mineral. Turn south on Highway 172 and drive seven miles to the town of Mill Creek. Turn south onto a Forest Service Road, which is signed and drive five miles southwest to the campground.

Trip note: This is one of two campgrounds set along Mill Creek at 4,300 feet elevation. Take your pick. A big bonus is the trail that follows Mill Creek for many miles, which provides good fishing access. A trail leading into the nearby State Game Refuge is located at the end of the access road, two miles from the camp. To keep things easy, it's advisable to obtain a map of Lassen National Forest that details the recreational opportunities.

Map grid b1

GURNSEY CREEK GROUP CAMP

LASSEN NATIONAL FOREST

Campsites, facilities: There are 20 sites for any combination of tents or motor homes. The campground will accommodate up to 100 people. Piped water, vault toilets, picnic tables, and fireplaces are provided. A large community fireplace is centrally located for group use. Pets are permitted on leashes. Supplies are available in Mineral or Chester.

Reservations, fee: Reservations required; $50 fee per night and a deposit of 50% is required. The deposit is refundable if a cancellation notice is given ten days prior to the reservation date.

Who to contact: Phone the Lassen National Forest Almanor Ranger District Office at (916)258-2141.

Location: From Red Bluff, drive 55 miles east on Highway 36 to the campground (five miles east of Child's Meadow).

Trip note: This is a group-camp. It's an ideal spot for a Boy Scout troop.

Map grid b1

GURNSEY CREEK

LASSEN NATIONAL FOREST

Campsites, facilities: There are 31 sites for tents or motor homes. Piped water, vault toilets, picnic tables, and fireplaces are provided. Pets are permitted on leashes. Supplies are available in Mineral.

Reservations, fee: No reservations; $6 fee per night.

Who to contact: Phone the Lassen National Forest Almanor Ranger District Office at (916)258-2141.

Location: From Red Bluff, drive 55 miles east on Highway 36 to the campground (five miles east of Childs Meadow).

Trip note: This is a good headquarters for a summer trout fishing trip with many activity choices in the area. A map of Lassen National Forest will detail the fishing options, back roads, and hiking trails. There's easy access to the campground from the road. The elevation is 4,700 feet. Open from May through September.

A B C3 D E F G H I J

Map grid **b2**

HIGH BRIDGE

on the North Fork of Feather River
LASSEN NATIONAL FOREST

Campsites, facilities: There are 12 campsites for tents or motor homes. Non-piped water, vault toilets, picnic tables, and fireplaces are provided. Pets are permitted on leashes. Groceries and propane gas are available nearby.

Reservations, fee: No reservations, $6 fee per night.

Who to contact: Phone the Lassen National Forest Almanor Ranger District at (916) 258-2141.

Location: From Chester on Highway 36, turn on Warner Valley Road and drive five miles west to the campground.

Trip note: This is an easy-to-reach camp right along a beautiful stream, yet it gets missed by thousands of campers wishing for such a spot. They don't know about it, but you do, and if you get a Forest Service map, you'll find out about several streams, hiking trails, and back roads in the area. There's good fishing on the North Fork of the Feather River. The elevation is 5,200 feet. Open from June through September.

Map grid **b2**

DOMINGO SPRINGS

LASSEN NATIONAL FOREST

Campsites, facilities: There are nine sites for tents only and nine campsites for tents or motor homes. Piped water, vault toilets, picnic tables, and fireplaces are provided. Pets are permitted on leashes.

Reservations, fee: No reservations; $6 fee per night.

Who to contact: Phone the Lassen National Forest Almanor Ranger District at (916) 258-2141.

Location: From Chester on Highway 36, turn on Warner Valley Road and drive 8.5 miles west via Warner Valley Road and Red Bluff Road to the campground.

Trip note: This is a good base camp for a trout fishing trip because the camp is set near the North Fork of the Feather River. A trail adjacent from camp leads north into Lassen Volcanic National Park and connects to additional trails. The elevation is 5,200 feet. Open from June through September.

Map grid **b2**

WILLOW SPRINGS

on Lost Creek
LASSEN NATIONAL FOREST

Campsites, facilities: There are eight sites for tents or motor homes. There is no piped water, but vault toilets, picnic tables, and fireplaces are provided. Pets are permitted on leashes.

Reservations, fee: No reservations, no fee.

Who to contact: Phone the Lassen National Forest Almanor Ranger District Office at (916)258-2141.

Location: From Red Bluff, drive 62 miles east on Highway 36/89. Turn north on Lost Creek Road and drive four miles to the campground. Or, from Chester at Lake Almanor, drive nine miles west on Highway 36 to Lost Creek Road. Turn north and drive four miles to the campground.

Trip note: This is a primitive setting with good hiking and fishing in the area. Bring what you need, including a water pump or bottled, fresh water. The elevation is 5,100 feet. Open from June through September.

Map grid **b3**

WARNER CREEK

LASSEN NATIONAL FOREST

Campsites, facilities: There are 15 campsites for tents or motor homes up to 22 feet long. There is **no piped water**, but vault toilets, picnic tables, and fireplaces are provided. Pets are permitted on leashes.

Reservations, fee: No reservations, no fee.

Who to contact: Phone the Lassen National Forest Almanor Ranger District at (916) 258-2141.

Location: From Chester on Highway 36, turn on Warner Valley Road and drive seven miles west on Warner Valley Road to the campground.

Trip note: This primitive camp, set along Warner Creek at 5,000 feet elevation, is used primarily as an overflow camp when more developed spots in the area are full. Open from June through September.

Map grid **b4**

LAST CHANCE CREEKTREE

on Lake Almanor

Campsites, facilities: There are 12 family campsites for tents or motor homes up to 30 feet, and 13 group-camp units. Piped water, vault toilets, picnic tables, and fireplaces are provided. Pets are permitted on leashes. There's a fee for pets.

Reservations, fee: Reservations required for the group camp only; $8 fee per night for family campsites; $15 for group sites.

Who to contact: Phone PG&E at (916)527-0354.

Location: From the Fire Station in the town of Chester, drive 2.2 miles east on Highway 36. Turn left and follow the left fork for one-tenth mile. Turn right and drive three-tenths of a mile. Turn left and travel eight-tenths of a mile to the fork. Follow the left fork for nine-tenths of a mile, then turn right to the campground.

Trip note: This secluded camp is adjacent to where Last Chance Creek empties into the north end of Lake Almanor. It's not well known, in spite of the fact that it's a short, although circuitous, drive from Chester.

Map grid **b4**

NORTHSHORE CAMPGROUND

on Lake Almanor

Campsites, facilities: There are 120 sites for motor homes, many with full or partial hookups, and a separate area for tents. Piped water, picnic tables, fire grills, flush toilets, and showers are provided. RV storage, a boat ramp, and a dock are available.

Reservations, fee: Reservations accepted; $10-$12 fee per night.

Who to contact: Phone (916)258-3376.

Location: From the junction of Highways 36 and 89 south of Chester, drive six miles north on Highway 36 to the campground.

Trip note: This large, privately-developed park is primarily for motor homes on the northern shoreline of Lake Almanor. How developed? Well, they've got a volleyball net. The boat ramp is a nice bonus. Open from April through October.

Map grid **c0**

ALDER CREEK

on Deer Creek

LASSEN NATIONAL FOREST

Campsites, facilities: There are five tent sites. There is **no piped water.** Vault toilets, picnic tables, and fireplaces are provided. Pets are permitted on leashes.

Reservations, fee: No reservations, no fee.

Who to contact: Phone the Lassen National Forest Almanor Ranger District Office at (916)258-2141.

Location: From Chester, drive 12 miles west on Highway 36. Turn south onto Highway 32 and drive seven miles to the campground, four miles downriver from the Elam Creek camp.

Trip note: This is a good alternative if the other camps on Deer Creek have too many folks. It's located near where Alder Creek pours into Deer Creek.

Map grid C0

POTATO PATCH
on Deer Creek
LASSEN NATIONAL FOREST

Campsites, facilities: There are 20 sites for tents and 12 sites for tents or motor homes. Piped water, vault toilets, picnic tables, and fireplaces are provided. Pets are permitted on leashes.

Reservations, fee: No reservations; $6 fee per night.

Who to contact: Phone the Lassen National Forest Almanor Ranger District Office at (916)258-2141.

Location: From Chester, drive 12 miles west on Highway 36. Turn south onto Highway 32 and drive 11 miles to the campground.

Trip note: You get good hiking and fishing at this camp. It is set beside Deer Creek, where the trout fishing is best in May and June. The elevation is 3,400 feet. Open from May through October.

Map grid C1

ELAM CREEK
on Deer Creek
LASSEN NATIONAL FOREST

Campsites, facilities: There are 17 sites for tents or motor homes. Piped water, vault toilets, picnic tables, and fireplaces are provided. Pets are permitted on leashes.

Reservations, fee: No reservations; $6 fee per night.

Who to contact: Phone the Lassen National Forest Almanor Ranger District Office at (916)258-2141.

Location: From Chester, drive 12 miles west on Highway 36. Turn south onto Highway 32 and drive three miles to the campground.

Trip note: This is an easy-to-reach yet secluded camp set at the confluence of Elam Creek and Deer Creek. The creeks are stocked with trout in May and June by the Department of Fish and Game. A Forest Service Information Center is nearby. If the camp has too many people to suit your style, consider other more primitive camps on Deer Creek. The elevation here is 4,400 feet.

Map grid C4

LAKE ALMANOR CAMPGROUNDS

Campsites, facilities: There are 130 campsites for tents or motor homes up to 30 feet. Piped water, vault toilets, picnic tables, and fireplaces are provided. A sanitary disposal station is available. Pets are permitted on leashes. There is a fee for pets.

Reservations, fee: No reservations; $9 per night.

Who to contact: Phone PG&E at (916)527-0354.

Location: From the dam at the southern end of Lake Almanor, drive 1.5 miles north on Highway 89 to the campground entrance. The camps are located on the southwest shore of the lake.

Trip note: What you get here are a series of virtually connected campgrounds along Lake Almanor provided by PG&E as mitigation for their hydroelectric activities on the Feather River system.

Map grid c4

ALMANOR
on Lake Almanor
LASSEN NATIONAL FOREST

Campsites, facilities: There are 15 sites for tents only and 86 campsites for tents or motor homes. Piped water, vault toilets, picnic tables, and fireplaces are provided. Pets are permitted on leashes. A grocery store is nearby.

Reservations, fee: No reservations; $7 fee per night.

Who to contact: Phone the Lassen National Forest Almanor Ranger District at (916) 258-2141.

Location: From Chester on Highway 36, drive two miles south on Highway 36. Turn southeast onto Highway 89 and drive six miles. Turn east on County Road 310 and drive one mile to the campground.

Trip note: This is one of Almanor's best-known and most popular campgrounds. Lake Almanor has good smallmouth bass fishing in spring, trout and salmon in spring and fall. The elevation is 4,600 feet. Open from June through October.

Map grid d0

CHERRY HILL
on Butte Creek
LASSEN NATIONAL FOREST

Campsites, facilities: There are 13 walk-in tent spaces and 12 sites for tents or motor homes. Picnic tables, fireplaces, piped water, and vault toilets are provided. Pets are permitted on leashes. Supplies are available nearby in the town of Butte Meadows.

Reservations, fee: No reservations; $6 fee.

Who to contact: Phone the Lassen National Forest Almanor Ranger District at (916) 258-2141.

Location: From Chico, drive about 15 miles north on Highway 32 to the town of Forest Ranch. Continue on Highway 32 for another nine miles. Turn right onto Humboldt Road and drive five miles to Butte Meadows. Continue on Humboldt Road and drive three miles northeast to the campground.

Trip note: The camp is set along Butte Creek. A map of Lassen National Forest details the hiking and fishing potential of the area. A climb of 2,000 feet of elevation in four miles will take you to the Colby Mountain lookout.

Map grid d0

PHILBROOK RESERVOIR

Campsites, facilities: There are 20 campsites for tents or motor homes up to 30 feet long. Picnic tables, fireplaces, piped water, and vault toilets are provided. A car-top boat launch is available.

Reservations, fee: No reservations; $9 fee per night.

Who to contact: The campground is run by PG&E. Phone PG&E at (916)527-0354.

Location: From Paradise, drive 27 miles north on Skyway. Bear right on Humbug Summit Road and drive two miles. Turn right on Philbrook Road and drive three miles to the intersection. Turn right and drive one-half mile to the campground.

Trip note: The camp is set along the shore of Philbrook Reservoir. Trout fishing, boating, and swimming are all options here. The elevation is 5,500 feet. Open from June through September.

A

Map grid d0

WEST BRANCH
on Feather River
LASSEN NATIONAL FOREST

B

Campsites, facilities: There are eight sites for tents only and seven sites for tents or motor homes. Picnic tables, fireplaces, piped water and vault toilets are provided. Pets are permitted on leashes.
Reservations, fee: No reservations; $6 fee.
Who to contact: Phone the Lassen National Forest Almanor Ranger District at (916) 258-2141.
Location: From Paradise, drive 27 miles north on Skyway.Bear right on Humbug Summit Road. Turn right on Philbrook Road to the campground.
Trip note: This is a nice spot on the West Branch of the Feather River. The trout fishing can be good. It's advisable to obtain a map of Lassen National Forest. The elevation is 5,000 feet. Open June through September.

C3

D

Map grid d2

LITTLE GRIZZLY
LASSEN NATIONAL FOREST

5% CLUB

Campsites, facilities: There are five tent sites. There is **no piped water**, but vault toilets, picnic tables, and fireplaces are provided. Pets are permitted on leashes.
Reservations, fee: No reservations, no fee.
Who to contact: Phone the Lassen National Forest Almanor Ranger District at (916)258-2141.
Location: From Highway 89 near Lake Almanor, turn west onto Humbug Road and drive 14 miles southwest to the campground.
Trip note: This little-used, primitive camp, set at 5,800 feet elevation, is for people who don't mind bringing their own water and who want quiet. Open from June through September.

E

F

Map grid d3

YELLOW CREEK
in Humbug Valley

G

Campsites, facilities: There are ten campsites for tents or motor homes. Piped water, vault toilets, picnic tables, and fireplaces are provided. Pets are permitted on leashes. There is a fee for pets.
Reservations, fee: No reservations; $8 per night.
Who to contact: Phone PG&E at (916)527-0354.
Location: From the dam at the south end of Lake Almanor, drive 7.5 miles northwest on Highway 89. Turn southwest, following the sign to Humbug Road, and drive for 1.2 miles to the fork. Bear right (toward Longville) and drive 5.4 miles. Turn left at the Humbug Valley intersection and drive 1.2 miles to the fork. Bear right and go three-tenths of a mile to camp.
Trip note: Yellow Creek is one of Cal Trout's pet projects. It's a beautiful stream for fly fishermen only, demanding the best from skilled anglers. The camp is set near the creek in Humbug Valley at 4,400 feet elevation. Some of the area was logged in the summer of 1989 by PG&E. Open from May through October.

H

I

J

Map grid d4

PONDEROSA FLAT
on Butt Valley Reservoir

Campsites, facilities: There are 63 campsites for tents or motor homes. Piped water, vault toilets, picnic tables, and fireplaces are provided. A boat ramp is available. Pets are permitted on leashes. There is a fee for pets.

Reservations, fee: No reservations; $9 per night.

Who to contact: Phone PG&E at (916)527-0354.

Location: From the dam at the southern end of Lake Almanor, drive six miles northwest on Highway 89. Turn southwest onto Butt Valley Road and drive 3.2 miles to the campground.

Trip note: This camp is set at the north end of Butt Valley Reservoir at 4,150 feet elevation. Butt Reservoir often gets missed in the shadow of its nearby big sister, Lake Almanor, but the rainbow trout seem to get much bigger here at Butt. When the Powerhouse is running, cast a Rapala into the adjacent channel; that's where the big ones are. Open from May through October.

Map grid d4

COOL SPRINGS
on Butt Valley Reservoir

Campsites, facilities: There are 25 campsites for tents or motor homes. Piped water, vault toilets, picnic tables, and fireplaces are provided. A boat ramp is available. Pets are permitted on leashes. There is a fee for pets.

Reservations, fee: No reservations; $9 fee per night.

Who to contact: Phone PG&E at (916)527-0354.

Location: From the dam at the southern end of Lake Almanor, drive six miles northwest on Highway 89, turn southwest onto Butt Valley Road, and drive six miles to the campground.

Trip note: This is one of two camps at Butt Valley Reservoir. Butt is known for its big rainbow trout; however, they can be elusive when the Powerhouse is not running. It's on the eastern shoreline and open from May through October.

Map grid e3

QUEEN LILY
on the North Fork of Feather River
PLUMAS NATIONAL FOREST

Campsites, facilities: There are 12 sites for tents only and one campsite for tents or motor homes up to 16 feet long. Piped water, flush toilets, fireplaces, and picnic tables are provided. Pets are permitted on leashes. A grocery store and a laundromat are nearby.

Reservations, fee: No reservations; $6 fee per night.

Who to contact: Phone Plumas National Forest Headquarters at (916)283-2050.

Location: From Belden on Highway 70, drive four miles northeast on Caribou Road to the campground.

Trip note: This is a prime little hideaway with good fishing on the North Fork of the Feather River. It is one of three campgrounds along the river off Caribou Road, which runs along the stream all the way north to Butt Dam. Open from April through September.

Map grid e3

NORTH FORK FEATHER RIVER
PLUMAS NATIONAL FOREST

Campsites, facilities: There are seven sites for tents only and 13 campsites for tents or motor homes up to 32 feet long. Piped water, flush toilets, showers, fireplaces, and picnic tables are provided. Pets are permitted on leashes. A grocery store and a laundromat are nearby.

Reservations, fee: No reservations; $6 fee per night.

Who to contact: Phone Plumas National Forest Headquarters at (916)283-2050.

Location: From Belden on Highway 70, drive four miles northeast on Caribou Road to the campground.

Trip note: The camp, one of the three in the area, is situated on the North Fork of the Feather River at 2600 feet. Take your pick; all could be good base camps for a fishing trip. Trout fishing is often best here in late May after the river clears. Open from April through September.

Map grid e3

GANSNER BAR
on the North Fork of Feather River
PLUMAS NATIONAL FOREST

Campsites, facilities: There are 14 campsites for tents or motor homes up to 32 feet long. Piped water, flush toilets, showers, fireplaces, and picnic tables are provided. Pets are permitted on leashes. A grocery store and a laundromat are nearby.

Reservations, fee: No reservations; $6 fee per night.

Who to contact: Phone Plumas National Forest Headquarters at (916)283-2050.

Location: From Belden on Highway 70, drive two miles northeast on Caribou Road to the campground.

Trip note: This is one of the three camps on the North Fork of the Feather River that provides direct access to the river for anglers. All three often get missed by cruisers on Highway 70 who are hoping that just such a spot jumps up and bites them. The elevation is 2,300 feet. Open from April through October.

Map grid e4

HALLSTED
on the North Fork of Feather River
PLUMAS NATIONAL FOREST

Campsites, facilities: There are five sites for tents only and 15 campsites for tents or motor homes up to 22 feet long. Piped water, flush toilets, picnic tables, and fireplaces are provided. Pets are permitted on leashes. A grocery store is nearby.

Reservations, fee: No reservations required, however sites can be reserved through MISTIX at (800)283-CAMP ($6 MISTIX fee); $6 fee per night.

Who to contact: Phone Plumas National Forest Headquarters at (916)283-2050.

Location: From Quincy, drive about 20 miles north and west on Highway 70 to the campground.

Trip note: Easy access and streamside campsites highlight Hallsted Camp. It is set along the East Branch of the North Fork of the Feather River at 2,800 feet elevation. Got that? Open from May through September.

Map grid f2

GRIZZLY CREEK
near Bucks Lake
PLUMAS NATIONAL FOREST

Campsites, facilities: There are eight campsites for tents or motor homes up to 22 feet long. There is **no piped water**, but vault toilets, picnic tables, and fireplaces are provided. Pets are permitted on leashes. A grocery store and laundromat are nearby.

Reservations, fee: No reservations, no fee.

Who to contact: Phone Plumas National Forest Headquarters at (916)283-2050.

Location: From Quincy on Highway 70, turn west onto Bucks Lake Road and drive 16.5 miles to the town of Bucks Lake. Turn on Oroville-Quincy Road and drive three miles south and west.

Trip note: This is an alternative to the more developed, more crowded campgrounds at Bucks Lake. Bucks Lake provides good trout fishing, especially in May. The elevation is 5,400 feet. Open from June through October.

Map grid f3

HASKINS VALLEY
on Bucks Lake

Campsites, facilities: There are 65 campsites for tents or motor homes. Piped water, vault toilets, picnic tables, and fireplaces are provided. A sanitary disposal station and a boat ramp are available. Pets are permitted on leashes. There is a fee for pets.

Reservations, fee: No reservations; $9 fee per night.

Who to contact: Phone PG&E at (916)527-0354 or (800)552-4743.

Location: From Quincy on Highway 70, turn west onto Bucks Lake Road and drive 16.5 miles to the campground.

Trip note: This is the biggest and most popular of the campgrounds at Bucks Lake. The close proximity to the boat launch is a big plus here. The camp is set at 5,200 feet elevation. Open from May through October.

Map grid f3

SILVER LAKE
PLUMAS NATIONAL FOREST

Campsites, facilities: There are seven tent sites. There is **no piped water**, but vault toilets, picnic tables, and fireplaces are provided. Pets are permitted on leashes.

Reservations, fee: No reservations, no fee.

Who to contact: Phone Plumas National Forest Headquarters at (916)283-2050.

Location: From Quincy, drive about seven miles west on Bucks Lake Road to Spanish Ranch. Turn north onto Silver Lake Road and drive seven miles to the campground.

Trip note: This is one of the more secluded, lesser-known spots that you can drive to, and yet get lakeside camping. No power boats (or swimming) are allowed on Silver Lake, which makes it ideal for canoes and rafts. Detailed fishing reports are available from the Sportsmen's Den in Quincy. The elevation is 5,800. Open from May through October.

Map grid f3

WHITEHORSE
near Bucks Lake
PLUMAS NATIONAL FOREST

Campsites, facilities: There are 20 campsites for tents or motor homes up to 22 feet long. Piped water, vault toilets, fireplaces, and picnic tables are provided. A grocery store and laundromat are nearby.

Reservations, fee: No reservations; $8 fee per night.

Who to contact: Phone Plumas National Forest Headquarters at (916)283-2050.

Location: From Quincy on Highway 70, turn west onto Bucks Lake Road and drive 14.5 miles to the campground.

Trip note: This campground is set along Whitehorse Creek about a mile from the boat ramps and south shore concessions at Bucks Lake. The trout fishing can be quite good at Bucks Lake, particularly on early summer evenings. The elevation is 5,200 feet. Open from June through October.

Map grid **f3**

SUNDEW
on Bucks Lake
PLUMAS NATIONAL FOREST

Campsites, facilities: There are 19 campsites for tents or motor homes up to 22 feet long. Piped water, vault toilets, fireplaces, and picnic tables are provided. Pets are permitted on leashes. There is a boat ramp two miles north of the camp near the Mill Creek campground.

Reservations, fee: No reservations; $8 fee per night.

Who to contact: Phone Plumas National Forest Headquarters at (916)283-2050.

Location: From Quincy on Highway 70, turn west onto Bucks Lake Road and drive 16.5 miles to the town of Bucks Lake. Turn north on Bucks Lake Dam Road and drive six miles to the campground.

Trip note: This camp, set at 5,200 feet elevation near Bucks Lake, has many activity options, including good trout fishing, particularly in early summer. A network of backcountry roads takes off from the lake, providing many side trips. It's advisable to obtain a map of Plumas National Forest.

Map grid **f3**

MILL CREEK
at Bucks Lake
PLUMAS NATIONAL FOREST

Campsites, facilities: There are ten campsites for tents or motor homes up to 22 feet long and two walk-in sites. Piped water, flush toilets, fireplaces, and picnic tables are provided. Groceries are available within five miles. Pets are permitted on leashes.

Reservations, fee: No reservations; $8 fee per night.

Who to contact: Phone Plumas National Forest Headquarters at (916)283-2050.

Location: From Quincy on Highway 70, turn west onto Bucks Lake Road and drive 16.5 miles to the town of Bucks Lake. Turn north on Bucks Lake Road and travel six miles to the campground.

Trip note: This small, pretty spot is set where Mill Creek empties into Bucks Lake. It's one of several camping options at Bucks Lake.

Map grid **f3**

HUTCHINS MEADOW GROUP CAMP
near Bucks Lake
PLUMAS NATIONAL FOREST

Campsites, facilities: There are three group sites for tents or motor homes. Piped water, vault toilets, picnic tables, and fireplaces are provided. A sanitary disposal station and a boat ramp are available. Pets are permitted on leashes. There is a fee for pets.

Reservations, fee: Reservations required; $25 fee per night.

Who to contact: Phone the Plumas National Forest Oroville Ranger District at (916) 534-6500.

Location: From Quincy on Highway 70, turn west onto Bucks Lake Road and drive 17 miles to the dam at Bucks Lake. Follow the road past the dam, and turn right onto the road just west of the dam. Drive one-half mile, cross the stream to the intersection, and continue straight for one-half mile to the campground.

Trip note: This is a prime spot for a Boy Scout outing or any other trip that has a large group and would like a pretty spot. It is set at 5,200 feet elevation between Bucks and Lower Bucks Lakes. Open from May through October.

Map grid **f4**

DEANES VALLEY
on Rock Creek
PLUMAS NATIONAL FOREST

Campsites, facilities: There are seven sites for tents or motor homes. There is **no piped water**, but vault toilets, picnic tables, and fireplaces are provided. There is a dump station nearby.
Reservations, fee: No reservations, no fee.
Who to contact: Phone Plumas National Forest Headquarters at (916)283-2050.
Location: From Quincy, drive 3.5 miles west on Bucks Lake Road. Turn south and drive seven miles to the campground.
Trip note: Most out-of-towners don't have a clue about this one. It's set on the South Fork of Rock Creek, remote, quiet, primitive. A Forest Service map details the back roads and hiking trails. Open April through October.

Map grid **f5**

SNAKE LAKE
PLUMAS NATIONAL FOREST

Campsites, facilities: There are six tent sites. There is **no piped water**, but vault toilets, picnic tables, and fireplaces are provided. Pets are permitted on leashes.
Reservations, fee: No reservations, no fee.
Who to contact: Phone Plumas National Forest Headquarters at (916)283-2050.
Location: From Quincy, drive five miles west on Bucks Lake Road. Turn north and drive five miles to Snake Lake.
Trip note: This little-known, drive-to camp is primitive and offers good trout fishing in early summer. The elevation is 4,200 feet. Open from April through October.

Map grid **f7**

BRADY'S CAMP
on Pine Creek
PLUMAS NATIONAL FOREST

Campsites, facilities: There are four tent sites. There is **no piped water** or toilets, but picnic tables and fireplaces are provided.
Reservations, fee: No reservations, no fee.
Who to contact: Phone Plumas National Forest Headquarters at (916)283-2050.
Location: From Quincy, drive four miles east on Highway 89/70. Turn east onto Squirrel Creek Road and drive eight miles to the campground.
Trip note: This is a tiny, little-known and primitive camp along Pine Creek at 7,200 feet elevation. A good side trip is to hike up Argentine Rock (7,209 feet). Don't expect any company. Open from May through October.

Map grid **g1**

ROGERS COW CAMP
PLUMAS NATIONAL FOREST

Campsites, facilities: There are five sites for tents or motor homes. Tables, fireplaces, and vault toilets are provided, but **no piped water** is available. Pets are permitted on leashes.
Reservations, fee: No reservation, no fee.
Who to contact: Phone Plumas National Forest at (916)283-2050.
Location: In Oroville at the junction of Highways 70 and 162, drive east and then north on Highway 162 (Oroville-Quincy Highway) for 26.5 miles to the town of Brush Creek. Continue northeast for eight miles on Forest Service Road 27562 (narrow, curving, paved, then dirt) for eight miles to the campground.

Trip note: This one is way out there in No Man's Land, set in National Forest at 4,100 feet elevation. You want quiet, you get it. You want water, you bring it yourself. It's advisable to obtain a map of Plumas National Forest, which details all backcountry roads, trails, streams, and lakes.

Map grid g1

MILSAP BAR

on the Middle Fork of Feather River
PLUMAS NATIONAL FOREST

5% CLUB

Campsites, facilities: There are 20 sites for tents or motor homes up to 16 feet long. Tables, fireplaces, piped water, and vault toilets are provided. Pets are permitted on leashes.

Reservations, fee: No reservation; $6 fee per night.

Who to contact: Phone the Plumas National Forest at (916)283-2050.

Location: In Oroville at the junction of Highways 70 and 162, drive east and then north on Highway 162 (Oroville-Quincy Highway) for 26.5 miles to the town of Brush Creek. Turn south on Bald Rock Road and drive for about half a mile to Forest Service Road 22N62 (Milsap Bar Road). Go left and follow for eight miles to campground (narrow, steep, mountainous dirt road).

Trip note: You join the Five Percent Club if you get here, an out-of-the-way spot that 95 percent of the people miss. It is set along the Middle Fork of the Feather River, a designated Wild and Scenic River. Swimming, fishing, and hiking are among the options. The elevation is 1,600 feet.

Map grid g1

LITTLE NORTH FORK

on the Middle Fork of Feather River
PLUMAS NATIONAL FOREST

5% CLUB

Campsites, facilities: There are eight campsites for tents or motor homes up to 16 feet long. There is **no piped water**, but vault toilets, tables, and fireplaces are provided. Pets are permitted on leashes.

Reservations, fee: No reservations, no fee.

Who to contact: Phone Plumas National Forest Headquarters at (916)283-2050.

Location: From Quincy on Highway 70, turn west onto Bucks Lake Road and drive 16.5 miles to the town of Bucks Lake. Turn on Oroville-Quincy Road and travel about 15 miles south. The road is gravel for most of the way. An alternate route: From Lake Oroville on Highway 162, drive to Brush Creek. Continue 15 miles northeast on Oroville-Quincy Road. The route to the site is a long, rough, single lane, dirt road. Having a map is a must, either way.

Trip note: Guaranteed quiet? You got it. This is a primitive camp in the outback that few know of. It is set along the Little North Fork of the Middle Fork of the Feather River at 2,700 feet elevation. Open from May through October.

Map grid g8

GOLDEN COACH TRAILER RESORT

near Feather River

Campsites, facilities: There are fifty RV sites with full hookups. Rest rooms, showers, picnic tables, and fireplaces are provided. A laundromat, wood, and LP gas are also available. Adults only.

Reservations, fee: Reservations recommended; $15 fee per night; group rates are available.

Who to contact: Phone (916)836-2426.

Location: From Blairsden, drive 6.5 miles north on Highway 70 to the motor home park.

Trip note: This is a good layover spot for RV cruisers looking to hole up for the night. This park is wooded, set near the Feather River. Open May through mid-September.

Map grid **g8**

JACKSON CREEK
near Feather River
PLUMAS NATIONAL FOREST

Campsites, facilities: There are 15 campsites for tents or motor homes up to 22 feet long. Piped water, flush toilets, picnic tables, and fireplaces are provided. A grocery store is nearby. Pets are permitted on leashes.
Reservations, fee: No reservations; $6 fee per night.
Who to contact: Phone Plumas National Forest Headquarters at (916)283-2050.
Location: From Blairsden, drive six miles north on Highway 70 to campground entrance.
Trip note: This is a pretty spot with easy access, a good combination for most campers. It is set at 4,500 feet elevation on Jackson Creek near the Feather River. Mt. Jackson (6,565 feet) looms nearby. Open May through October.

Map grid **h4**

BLACK ROCK
on Little Grass Valley Reservoir
PLUMAS NATIONAL FOREST

Campsites, facilities: There are 14 campsites for tents or motor homes up to 22 feet long. Piped water, flush toilets, picnic tables, and fireplaces are provided. A sanitary dump station, boat ramp, and grocery store are nearby. Pets are permitted on leashes.
Reservations, fee: No reservations; $8 fee per night.
Who to contact: Phone Plumas National Forest Headquarters at (916)283-2050.
Location: From La Porte, drive 1.5 miles north on Quincy-La Porte Road to Little Grass Valley Road. Turn north (left) and drive 2.5 miles to the campground.
Trip note: This is the only campground on the west shore of Little Grass Valley Reservoir. If you don't like the company, there are four other camps to choose from at the lake. The elevation is 5,000 feet. Open from June through October.

Map grid **h5**

RUNNING DEER
on Little Grass Valley Reservoir
PLUMAS NATIONAL FOREST

Campsites, facilities: There are 40 campsites for tents or motor homes. Piped water, flush toilets, picnic tables, and fireplaces are provided. A boat ramp, grocery store, and sanitary dump station are nearby. Pets are permitted on leashes.
Reservations, fee: No reservations; $8 fee per night.
Who to contact: Phone Plumas National Forest Headquarters at (916)283-2050.
Location: From La Porte, drive 1.5 miles north on Quincy-La Porte Road to Little Grass Valley Road. Turn north (left) and drive four miles to the campground.
Trip note: This is a fairly large campground set along the shore of Little Grass Valley Reservoir at an elevation of 5,000 feet. It's one of five campgrounds on the lake. Open from June through September.

Map grid h5

WYANDOTTE

on Little Grass Valley Reservoir
PLUMAS NATIONAL FOREST

Campsites, facilities: There are 32 sites for tents only and two campsites for tents or motor homes up to 22 feet long. Piped water, flush toilets, picnic tables, and fireplaces are provided. A sanitary dump station, boat ramp, and grocery store are nearby. Pets are permitted on leashes.
Reservations, fee: No reservations; $8 fee per night.
Who to contact: Phone Plumas National Forest Headquarters at (916)283-2050.
Location: From La Porte, drive 1.5 miles north on Quincy-La Porte Road to Little Grass Valley Road. Turn north (left) and drive 2.5 miles to the campground.
Trip note: Of the five camps on Little Grass Valley Lake, this is the favorite. It is set on a small peninsula that extends into the lake. If it fills up, four other camps are available at the lake.

Map grid h5

LITTLE BEAVER

on Little Grass Valley Reservoir
PLUMAS NATIONAL FOREST

Campsites, facilities: There are 121 campsites for tents or motor homes. Piped water, flush toilets, picnic tables, and fireplaces are provided. A grocery store, sanitary dump station, and boat ramp are nearby. Pets are permitted on leashes.
Reservations, fee: No reservations; $8 fee per night.
Who to contact: Phone Plumas National Forest Headquarters at (916)283-2050.
Location: From La Porte, drive 1.5 miles north on Quincy-La Porte Road to Little Grass Valley Road. Turn north (left) and drive 3.5 miles to the campground.
Trip note: This is one of five campgrounds on Little Grass Valley Reservoir, set at 5,000 feet elevation. Take your pick. The trout fishing is good in the early summer, and backpackers can use the area as a jump-off point. A trailhead for the Pacific Crest Trail is located at the northeast end of the lake. Open from June through October.

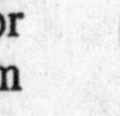

Map grid h5

RED FEATHER GROUP CAMP

on Little Grass Valley Reservoir
PLUMAS NATIONAL FOREST

Campsites, facilities: There are 60 campsites for tents or motor homes up to 22 feet long. This campground has group camp areas. Piped water, flush toilets, picnic tables, and fireplaces are provided. A sanitary dump station, boat ramp, and grocery store are nearby. Pets are permitted on leashes.
Reservations, fee: Reservations requested; sites can be reserved through MISTIX at (800)283-CAMP ($6 MISTIX fee); $10 fee per night.
Who to contact: Phone Plumas National Forest Headquarters at (916)283-2050.
Location: From La Porte, drive 1.5 miles north on Quincy-La Porte Road to Little Grass Valley Road. Turn north (left) and drive four miles to the campground.
Trip note: If you have a large group and Little Grass Valley Reservoir is your destination, then reserve the group camping areas here so you don't have to split up. The elevation is 5,000 feet.Open from June through October.

Map grid **h7** PLUMAS-EUREKA STATE PARK

near Graeagle

Campsites, facilities: There are ten sites for tents only and 27 motor home sites for motor homes up to 30 feet long. Piped water, showers, flush toilets, a sanitary dump station, picnic tables, and fireplaces are provided. A grocery store, laundromat, and propane gas are available in Graeagle.

Reservations, fee: Reserve through MISTIX at (800)444-PARK ($3.95 MISTIX fee); $12-$14 fee per night; pets $1.

Who to contact: Phone (916)836-2380.

Location: From Blairsden, drive one mile south on Highway 89 to Graeagle. Turn onto County Road A14 and drive five miles west to the park.

Trip note: Because this is a popular park, reservations are required. Expect company. It provides a taste of what Plumas County is all about. There are hiking trails, lakes, streams, and forest, as well as historic mining ruins and a museum. The elevation is 5,200 feet. Open May through September.

Map grid **h8** LITTLE BEAR RV PARK

on Feather River

Campsites, facilities: There are 89 motor home sites, most with full hookups. Rest rooms, showers, picnic tables, and fireplaces are provided. A laundromat, a grocery store, ice, and a club room are also available.

Reservations, fee: Reservations accepted; $14-$17 fee per night.

Who to contact: Phone (916)836-2774.

Location: From Blairsden, drive one mile north on Highway 70. Turn south on Little Bear Road and drive a short distance to the campground.

Trip note: This is a privately-operated motor home park beside the Feather River that is open March through October.

Map grid **h8** MOVIN' WEST TRAILER RANCH

near Graeagle

Campsites, facilities: There are 45 motor homes spaces with full or partial hookups. Piped water, picnic tables, fire grills, flush toilets, showers and a laundromat are provided. Propane gas is available nearby.

Reservations, fee: Reservations accepted; $18 fee per night.

Who to contact: Phone (916)836-2614.

Location: From Blairsden, drive one mile south on Highway 89 to Graeagle. Turn onto County Road A14 and drive one-half mile northwest to the campground.

Trip note: This RV area is set within a mobile home park. If that's what you want, you found it. The trout fishing is excellent on the Middle Fork of the Feather River, but a rugged hike-in is required. The elevation is 4,300 feet. Open May through October.

Map grid **h9** SIERRA SPRINGS TRAILER RESORT

Campsites, facilities: There are 30 motor homes sites with full hookups and ten sites with no hookups. Piped water, showers, flush toilets, picnic tables, and fireplaces are provided. A sanitary dump station, a laundromat, cable TV, a playground, a recreation room, and a volleyball court are available.

Reservations, fee: Reservations accepted; $16.50 fee per night.

Who to contact: Phone (916)836-2747.
Location: From Blairsden, drive three and a half miles southeast on Highway 70.
Trip note: This year-round, privately-operated park provides all amenities. Possible side trips include the Feather River Park, located four miles away in the town of Blairsden. The elevation is 5,000 feet.

Map grid **i2**

STRAWBERRY

on Sly Creek Reservoir
PLUMAS NATIONAL FOREST

Campsites, facilities: There are 15 sites for tents, trailers, or motor homes. Piped water, vault toilets, picnic tables, and fireplaces are provided. A car-top boat launch is available on Sly Creek Reservoir.
Reservations, fee: No reservation; $6 fee per night.
Who to contact: Phone the Plumas National Forest at (916)283-2050.
Location: From the town of Strawberry Valley on County Road E21, drive west on Lewis Road to the campground along the shore of Sly Creek Reservoir.
Trip note: This is a good option to the previous camp. Take your pick at Sly Creek Reservoir north of Lake Oroville.

Map grid **i2**

SLY CREEK

on Sly Creek Reservoir
PLUMAS NATIONAL FOREST

Campsites, facilities: There are 14 sites for tents, trailers, or motor homes. Piped water, vault toilets, picnic tables, and fireplaces are provided. A car-top boat launch is available on Sly Creek Reservoir.
Reservations, fee: No reservation; $6 fee per night.
Who to contact: Phone the Plumas National Forest at (916)283-2050.
Location: From the town of Strawberry Valley on County Road E21, drive west on Lewis Road to the campground along the shore of Sly Creek Reservoir.
Trip note: This is one of two campgrounds on Sly Creek Reservoir, a lake set due north of Lake Oroville and often lost in giant Oroville's shadow. But this is a good option, especially for campers with car-top boats or canoes. You get quiet water and decent fishing.

Map grid **i8**

DIABLO

5% CLUB

on Packer Creek
TAHOE NATIONAL FOREST

Campsites, facilities: This is an undeveloped, designated camping area for tents and self-contained motor homes. There is **no piped water**, but vault toilets are provided. Pets are permitted if they are quiet and on leashes or otherwise controlled. Supplies are available in Bassetts and Sierra City.
Reservations, fee: No reservations, no fee.
Who to contact: Phone Tahoe National Forest Headquarters at (916)265-4531.
Location: From Sierra City, drive 4.5 miles north on Highway 49. Turn left on Gold Lake Highway and travel 1.5 miles. Turn left on Packer Lake Road and drive 1.5 to the camping area on the right.
Trip note: This primitive camping area, set on Packer Creek, is about two miles from Packer Lake. At the lake, the Forest Service has provided a day-use picnic area with tables and barbecue pits, but there are no campsites. In any case, bring your own water or a water purifier.

Map grid **i8**

SALMON CREEK
TAHOE NATIONAL FOREST

Campsites, facilities: There are 31 campsites for tents or motor homes up to 22 feet long. Piped water, vault toilets, picnic tables, and fireplaces are provided. Pets are permitted if they are quiet and on leashes or otherwise controlled. Supplies and a laundromat are available in Sierra City.

Reservations, fee: No reservations; $6 fee per night.

Who to contact: Phone Tahoe National Forest Headquarters at (916)265-4531.

Location: From Sierra City, drive 4.5 miles north on Highway 49. Turn west on Gold Lake Highway and drive two miles to the campground, which is near Salmon Creek.

Trip note: It doesn't take much poking around to find a spectacular view of the crags that rise above the Yuba River Valley. The camp is set at the confluence of Packer and Salmon Creeks at 5,800 feet. Open from June through October.

Map grid **i8**

PACKSADDLE
near Packer Lake
TAHOE NATIONAL FOREST

Campsites, facilities: This is an undeveloped, designated camping area for tents and self-contained motor homes. There is **no piped water**, but vault toilets are provided. Pack and saddle stock are permitted. Hitching rails are available. Pets are permitted if they are quiet and on leashes or otherwise controlled. Supplies are available in Bassetts and Sierra City.

Reservations, fee: No reservations, no fee.

Who to contact: Phone Tahoe National Forest Headquarters at (916)265-4531.

Location: From Sierra City, drive 4.5 miles north on Highway 49. Turn left on Gold Lake Highway and travel 1.5 miles. Turn left on Packer Lake Road and drive 2.5 miles to the camping area on the right.

Trip note: This is a primitive camping area with no designated campsites. The camp is set fairly close to Packer Creek, and the Forest Service has provided a day-use picnic area with tables and barbecue pits at Packer Lake, which is about a half-mile away. Bring your own water.

Map grid **i8**

BERGER CREEK
TAHOE NATIONAL FOREST

Campsites, facilities: There are ten undesignated campsites for tents or motor homes up to 16 feet long. There is **no piped water**, but vault toilets, picnic tables, and fireplaces are provided. Pets are permitted if they are quiet and on leashes or otherwise controlled. Supplies are available in Bassetts and Sierra City.

Reservations, fee: No reservations, no fee.

Who to contact: Phone Tahoe National Forest Headquarters at (916)265-4531.

Location: From Sierra City, drive 4.5 miles north on Highway 49. Turn left on Gold Lake Highway and travel 1.5 miles. Turn left on Packer Lake Road and drive two miles to the campground on the left.

Trip note: This camp is set in the midst of several alpine lakes that provide good trout fishing and excellent hiking opportunities. Your choices in side trips include Packer Lake, the Sardine Lakes, the Tamarack Lakes, and others. It's a primitive camp, so bring what you need, including water. The elevation is 5,900 feet. Open from June through October.

Map grid **i8**

SNAG LAKE TREE

TAHOE NATIONAL FOREST

5% CLUB

Campsites, facilities: There are 16 undesignated campsites for tents or motor homes up to 16 feet long. There is **no piped water**, but vault toilets, picnic tables, and fireplaces are provided. Only hand-off boat launching is allowed. Pets are permitted if they are quiet and on leashes or otherwise controlled. Supplies are available in Bassetts and Sierra City.

Reservations, fee: No reservations, no fee.

Who to contact: Phone Tahoe National Forest Headquarters at (916)265-4531.

Location: From Sierra City, drive 4.5 miles north on Highway 49. Turn left on Gold Lake Highway and travel five miles to the campground on the left.

Trip note: This is an ideal area for camping anglers with car-top boats, particularly canoes. The fishing is decent at Snag Lake and at several other nearby lakes. There are no boat ramps, but it's a good deal for car-toppers who launch by hand. If you don't own a boat, rentals are available at Salmon Lake Lodge. It's a primitive camp, so bring what you need, including water. The elevation is 6,600 feet. Open from June through October.

Map grid **i8**

LAKES BASIN GROUP CAMP

PLUMAS NATIONAL FOREST

Campsites, facilities: There is one group camp (capacity 25 people) for tents and small motor homes. Piped water, vault toilets, picnic tables, and fireplaces are provided. Pets are permitted on leashes or otherwise controlled. Supplies are available in Graeagle.

Reservations, fee: Reserve through MISTIX at (800)283-CAMP ($6 MISTIX fee); $25 group fee per night.

Who to contact: Phone the Plumas National Forest Beckwourth Ranger District at (916)836-2575.

Location: From Blairsden, turn south on Highway 89 and drive 2.5 miles to Gold Lake Highway. Turn southwest and drive five miles to the campground.

Trip note: This is a Forest Service group camp that provides an option to the previous camp. It's ideal for the Boy or Girl Scouts (that is, providing they don't arrive at the same time).

Map grid **i8**

LAKES BASIN

PLUMAS NATIONAL FOREST

Campsites, facilities: There are 24 sites for tents or small motor homes. (Trailers are not recommended.) Piped water, vault toilets, picnic tables, and fireplaces are provided. Pets are permitted on leashes. Supplies are available in Graeagle.

Reservations, fee: No reservations; $6 fee per night.

Who to contact: Phone the Plumas National Forest Beckwourth Ranger at (916) 836-2575.

Location: From Blairsden, turn south on on Highway 89 and drive 2.5 miles. Turn southwest onto Gold Lake Highway and drive five miles to the campground.

Trip note: Time to join the Five Percent Club. The Gold Lakes Basin is a great area for camping and hike-in fishings. The Plumas mountain country is beautiful and offers many relatively easy, short day-hikes to the glacial lakes scattered throughout the area. A Forest Service map details the trails, streams, and lakes. The camp elevation is 6,400 feet. Open June through October.

Map grid i8

SARDINE LAKE
TAHOE NATIONAL FOREST

Campsites, facilities: There are 29 campsites for tents or motor homes up to 22 feet long. Piped water, vault toilets, picnic tables, and fireplaces are provided. Pets are permitted if they are quiet and on leashes or otherwise controlled. Limited supplies are available at Sardine Lake Lodge.

Reservations, fee: No reservations; $6 fee per night.

Who to contact: Phone Tahoe National Forest Headquarters at (916)265-4531.

Location: From Sierra City, drive 4.5 miles north on Highway 49. Turn west on Gold Lake Highway and drive 1.5 miles. Turn on Sardine Lake Road and drive one-half mile southwest to the campground.

Trip note: Lower Sardine Lake is one in a series of small alpine lakes in the area, this one set at 5,800 feet elevation. Anglers have several options, including fishing on the creek leading from the nearby Sardine Lakes or renting a boat at the Sardine Lake Lodge. If you want to swim, the best bet is at nearby Sand Pond. There is an interpretive trail at Sand Pond. Open from June through October.

Map grid i9

CLIO'S RIVER'S EDGE
on Feather River

Campsites, facilities: There are 172 motor homes sites with full hookups. Piped water, showers, flush toilets, a laundromat, cable TV and fireplaces are provided. A grocery store is nearby.

Reservations, fee: Reservations accepted; $15 fee per night.

Who to contact: Phone (916)836-2375.

Location: From Blairsden, drive south on Highway 89 for 4.5 miles to the campground.

Trip note: This is a giant motor home park. You bring everything, including the kitchen sink. Possible side trips include trout fishing on the Feather River, swimming at Feather River Park in Blairsden, or hiking in the Plumas-Eureka State Park. Open from May through September.

Map grid j1

BURNT BRIDGE
near Bullards Bar Reservoir
PLUMAS NATIONAL FOREST

Campsites, facilities: There are 18 sites for tents only and 13 campsites for tents or motor homes. Picnic tables, fireplaces, and vault toilets are provided. There is no piped water. Pets are permitted if they are quiet and on leashes or otherwise controlled. Supplies are available in North San Juan, Camptonville, and Dobbins.

Reservations, fee: No reservations; $3 fee per night, phone ahead to be sure it's open.

Who to contact: Phone the Plumas National Forest Ranger Station at (916)675-2462.

Location: From Camptonville, drive 2.5 miles south on Highway 49. Turn west on Marysville Road and drive four miles to the campground on the right. Or, from Marysville, drive 11 miles east on Highway 20. Turn north on Marysville Road and travel 21 miles north past Browns Valley and Dobbins to the reservoir. When you get to Bullards Bar Dam at the south end of the reservoir, turn north on Challenge Road (Oregon Hill Road) and drive five miles to the campground.

Trip note: Note: This campground was temporarily closed in the 1990-91 winter season. This camp provides an overflow area if the camps at nearby Bullards Bar Reservoir are full. It is located at 2,200 feet elevation, about seven miles from a county-run, two-lane, concrete boat ramp at the west end of Bullards Bar Dam.

Map grid j2

GARDEN POINT

boat-in on Bullards Bar Reservoir

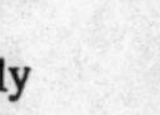

Campsites, facilities: There are 12 single-family campsites and four double-family campsites, accessible by boat only. There is **no piped water,** but picnic tables, fireplaces, and vault toilets are provided. Burnable refuse should be burned and the rest packed out. Pets are permitted if they are quiet and on leashes or otherwise controlled. Supplies are available in North San Juan, Camptonville, and Dobbins.

Reservations, fee: Reservations required; $7.50 fee per night.

Who to contact: Managed by the Emerald Cove Resort and Marina for the Yuba County Water Agency; phone (916)692-2166 or (916)741-6278.

Location: From Camptonville, drive 2.5 miles south on Highway 49. Turn west on Marysville Road and drive four miles to the campground on the right. Or, from Marysville, drive 11 miles east on Highway 20. Turn north on Marysville Road and travel 21 miles north past Browns Valley and Dobbins to the reservoir. Drive north for less than a mile to the boat ramp at Dark Day Picnic Area. From the boat ramp, drive one mile northwest to the campground on the north side of the reservoir. Open all year with limited winter facilities.

Trip note: Bullards Bar Reservoir is one of the few lakes in the Sierra Nevada to offer boat-in camping. Take your pick, there are several available. The lake is a favorite with campers since the water level is often higher here than at other area lakes. The steep shoreline drop-offs should be noted by all swimmers.

Map grid j2

FRENCHY POINT

boat-in on Bullards Bar Reservoir

Campsites, facilities: There are seven single-family campsites and one double-family campsite, accessible by boat only. There is **no piped water,** but picnic tables, fireplaces, and vault toilets are provided. Burnable refuse should be burned and the rest packed out. Pets are permitted if they are quiet and on leashes or otherwise controlled. Supplies are available in North San Juan, Camptonville, Dobbins and at the marina.

Reservations, fee: Reservations required; $7.50 fee per night.

Who to contact: Managed by the Emerald Cove Resort and Marina for the Yuba County Water Agency; phone (916)692-2166 or (916)741-6278.

Location: From Camptonville, drive 2.5 miles south on Highway 49. Turn west on Marysville Road and drive four miles to the campground on the right. Or, from Marysville, drive 11 miles east on Highway 20. Turn north on Marysville Road and travel 21 miles north past Browns Valley and Dobbins to the reservoir. Travel north for less than a mile to the boat ramp. From the boat ramp, drive three miles northwest to the campground on the east side of the reservoir.

Trip note: This is one of several camps at Bullards Bar Reservoir, this one being a unique boat-in camp. The elevation is 2,000 feet. Open all year with limited winter facilities.

Map grid **j2**

MADRONE COVE

boat-in on Bullards Bar Reservoir

Campsites, facilities: There are ten single-family campsites, accessible by boat only. There is **no piped water,** but picnic tables, fireplaces, and vault toilets are provided. Burnable refuse should be burned and the rest packed out. Pets are permitted if they are quiet and on leashes or otherwise controlled. Supplies are available in North San Juan, Camptonville, Dobbins and at the marina.

Reservations, fee: Reservations required; $7.50 fee per night.

Who to contact: Managed by Emerald Cove Resort and Marina for the Yuba County Water Agency; call (916)692-2166 or (916)741-6278.

Location: From Camptonville, drive 2.5 miles south on Highway 49. Turn west on Marysville Road and drive four miles to the campground on the right. Or, from Marysville, drive 11 miles east on Highway 20. Turn north on Marysville Road and travel 21 miles north past Browns Valley and Dobbins to the reservoir. The campground is on the southeast side of the reservoir. Travel north for less than a mile to the boat ramp at Dark Day Picnic Area. From the boat ramp, drive five miles northwest to the campground on the west side of the reservoir.

Trip note: This is one of several boat-in campgrounds at Bullards Bar Reservoir; it's a take-your-pick deal. The elevation is 2,000 feet.

Map grid **j2**

SCHOOLHOUSE

on Bullards Bar Reservoir

TAHOE NATIONAL FOREST

Campsites, facilities: There are 34 sites for tents only and 33 campsites for tents or motor homes. Picnic tables, fireplaces, piped water, and flush and vault toilets are provided. A boat ramp is nearby. Pets are permitted if they are quiet and on leashes or otherwise controlled. Supplies are available in North San Juan, Camptonville, Dobbins, and at the marina.

Reservations, fee: No reservations; $6 fee per night.

Who to contact: Phone the Tahoe National Forest at (916)265-4531.

Location: From Camptonville, drive 2.5 miles south on Highway 49. Turn west on Marysville Road and drive four miles to the campground on the right. Or, from Marysville, drive 11 miles east on Highway 20. Turn north on Marysville Road and travel 21 miles north past Browns Valley and Dobbins to the reservoir. The campground is on the southeast side of the reservoir.

Trip note: Bullards Bar Reservoir is one of the better lakes in the Sierra Nevada for camping, primarily because the lake levels tend to be higher here than at many other lakes. It is known for good fishing and water skiing, but swimmers should beware of steep shoreline drop-offs. A three-line concrete boat ramp is available at Dark Day Picnic Area, which is located less than a mile from the camp. Boaters should consider the three special boat-in camps at the lake. The elevation is 2,200 feet. Open all year with limited winter facilities.

Map grid **j3**

FIDDLE CREEK

on North Yuba River

TAHOE NATIONAL FOREST

Campsites, facilities: There are 13 tent sites. There is **no piped water**, but vault toilets, picnic tables, and fireplaces are provided. Pets are permitted if they are quiet and on leashes or otherwise controlled. Limited supplies are available nearby at the Indian Valley Outpost.

Reservations, fee: No reservations, no fee.
Who to contact: Phone Tahoe National Forest Headquarters at (916)265-4531.
Location: From Camptonville, travel nine miles north on Highway 49 to the campground.
Trip note: This camp is situated on the North Yuba River in a quiet, primitive area. Fiddle Bow Trail leads out from the camp to Halls Ranch Station or Indian Rock, take your pick. Bring your own water. It's set at 2,200 feet elevation. Open year-round.

Map grid j3

CARLTON FLAT
on North Yuba River
TAHOE NATIONAL FOREST

Campsites, facilities: There are two undeveloped, designated camping areas. There is **no piped water**, but vault toilets are provided. Pets are permitted if they are quiet and on leashes or otherwise controlled. Some supplies are available at the Indian Valley Outpost nearby.
Reservations, fee: No reservations, no fee.
Who to contact: Phone Tahoe National Forest Headquarters at (916)265-4531.
Location: From Camptonville, drive nine miles north on Highway 49. The camping area at Lower Carlton Flat is located one mile northeast of the Highway 49 bridge at Indian Valley. The camping area at Upper Carlton Flat is located behind the Indian Valley Outpost on the Cal Ida Road.
Trip note: You can join the Five Percent Club at these spots, which are little-known, primitive, and quiet. Lower Carlton Flat is on the North Yuba River, and Upper Carlton Flat is across the road.

Map grid j4

ROCKY REST
on North Yuba River
TAHOE NATIONAL FOREST

Campsites, facilities: This is an undeveloped, designated camping area. There is **no piped water**, but vault toilets are provided. Pets are permitted if they are quiet and on leashes or otherwise controlled. Limited supplies are available at the Indian Valley Outpost nearby.
Reservations, fee: No reservations, no fee.
Who to contact: Phone Tahoe National Forest Headquarters at (916)265-4531.
Location: From Camptonville travel ten miles north on Highway 49.
Trip note: This is one in a series of campgrounds set at streamside on the North Yuba River. This one is on the North Yuba. Primitive and undeveloped, it is used primarily as an overflow camp if the other campgrounds in the area that have piped water are filled.

Map grid j4

RAMSHORN
on North Yuba River
TAHOE NATIONAL FOREST

Campsites, facilities: There are 16 campsites for tents or motor homes up to 22 feet long. Piped water, vault toilets, picnic tables, and fireplaces are provided. Pets are permitted if they are quiet and on leashes or otherwise controlled. Supplies available in Downieville.
Reservations, fee: No reservations; $6 fee per night.
Who to contact: Phone Tahoe National Forest Headquarters at (916)265-4531.
Location: From Camptonville, travel 15 miles north on Highway 49.

Trip note: This camp is set on Ramshorn Creek, just across the road from the North Yuba River. It's one in a series. A side trip option is to hike the trail that leads out of the campground up to St. Charles Hill. The camp's elevation is 2,600 feet. Open year-round.

Map grid j4

INDIAN VALLEY

on North Yuba River

TAHOE NATIONAL FOREST

Campsites, facilities: There are 17 campsites for tents or motor homes up to 22 feet long. Piped water, vault toilets, picnic tables, and fireplaces are provided. Pets are permitted if they are quiet and on leashes or otherwise controlled. Limited supplies are available nearby at the Indian Valley Outpost.

Reservations, fee: No reservations; $6 fee per night.

Who to contact: Phone Tahoe National Forest Headquarters at (916)265-4531.

Location: From Camptonville, travel ten miles north on Highway 49 to the campground.

Trip note: This is an easy-to-reach spot set at 2,200 feet elevation beside the North Yuba River. Highway 49 runs adjacent to the Yuba for miles eastward, providing easy access to the river in many areas. Open year-round.

Map grid j6

UNION FLAT

on North Yuba River

TAHOE NATIONAL FOREST

Campsites, facilities: There are 14 campsites for tents or motor homes up to 22 feet long. Piped water, vault toilets, picnic tables, and fireplaces are provided. Pets are permitted if they are quiet and on leashes or otherwise controlled. Supplies are available in Downieville.

Reservations, fee: No reservations; $6 fee per night.

Who to contact: Phone Tahoe National Forest Headquarters at (916)265-4531.

Location: From Downieville, travel six miles east on Highway 49.

Trip note: This pretty, streamside campground has easy access from Highway 49. The camp is set near Quartz Point and Granite Mountain and has a nice swimming hole next to it if you can stand the cold. Recreation mining is also an attraction here. The elevation is 3,400 feet. Open from May through October.

Map grid j7

LOGANVILLE

on North Yuba River

TAHOE NATIONAL FOREST

Campsites, facilities: There are 20 campsites for tents or motor homes up to 22 feet long. Piped water, vault toilets, and picnic tables are provided. Pets are permitted if they are quiet and on leashes or otherwise controlled. Supplies and a laundromat are available in Sierra City.

Reservations, fee: No reservations; $4 fee per night.

Who to contact: Phone Tahoe National Forest Headquarters at (916)265-4531.

Location: From Sierra City, travel two miles west on Highway 49.

Trip note: This is one in a series of popular Forest Service campgrounds set along the North Yuba River and Highway 49. The elevation is 3,800 feet. Open from May through October.

A

Map grid **j8**

WILD PLUM

on Haypress Creek
TAHOE NATIONAL FOREST

Campsites, facilities: There are 47 campsites for tents or motor homes up to 22 feet long. Piped water, vault toilets, picnic tables, and fireplaces are provided. Pets are permitted if they are quiet and on leashes or otherwise controlled. Supplies and a laundromat are available in Sierra City.

B

Reservations, fee: No reservations; $6 fee per night.

Who to contact: Phone Tahoe National Forest Headquarters at (916)265-4531.

Location: From Sierra City, travel one mile east on the Wild Plum Road along Haypress Creek.

C3

Trip note: This popular Forest Service camp is set on Haypress Creek at 4,400 feet elevation. There's a scenic hike up the Haypress Trail. It goes past a waterfall, to Haypress Valley. Nearby side trips include the Kentucky Mine and Sierra County Historic Park. Open from May through October.

D

Map grid **j9**

CHAPMAN CREEK

on North Yuba River
TAHOE NATIONAL FOREST

Campsites, facilities: There are 29 campsites for tents or motor homes up to 22 feet long. Piped water, showers, vault toilets, picnic tables, and fireplaces are provided. Pets are permitted if they are quiet and on leashes or otherwise controlled. Supplies are available in Bassetts.

E

Reservations, fee: No reservations; $4 fee per night.

Who to contact: Phone Tahoe National Forest Headquarters at (916)265-4531.

Location: From Sierra City, drive eight miles north on Highway 49 to the campground.

F

Trip note: This is a popular camp set along Chapman Creek at 6,000 feet, just across the highway from the North Yuba River. A good side trip is to hike the Chapman Creek Trail, which leads out of camp to Beartrap Meadow or to Haskell Peak. Open from June through October.

G

Map grid **j9**

SIERRA

on North Yuba River
TAHOE NATIONAL FOREST

Campsites, facilities: There are nine sites for tents only and seven campsites for tents or motor homes up to 22 feet long. There is **no piped water**, but vault toilets, picnic tables, and fireplaces are provided. Pets are permitted if they are quiet and on leashes or otherwise controlled. Supplies are available in Bassetts.

H

Reservations, fee: No reservations, no fee.

Who to contact: Phone Tahoe National Forest Headquarters at (916)265-4531.

Location: From Sierra City, drive seven miles north on Highway 49 to the campground.

I

Trip note: This is a quiet, primitive, and easy-to-reach spot along the North Yuba River. The elevation is 5,600 feet. Open from June through October.

J

◆ MAP C4 ◆

BEACH
DESERT
FOOTHILL
TREES
URBAN
GRASSLAND
5% CLUB

15 MILES

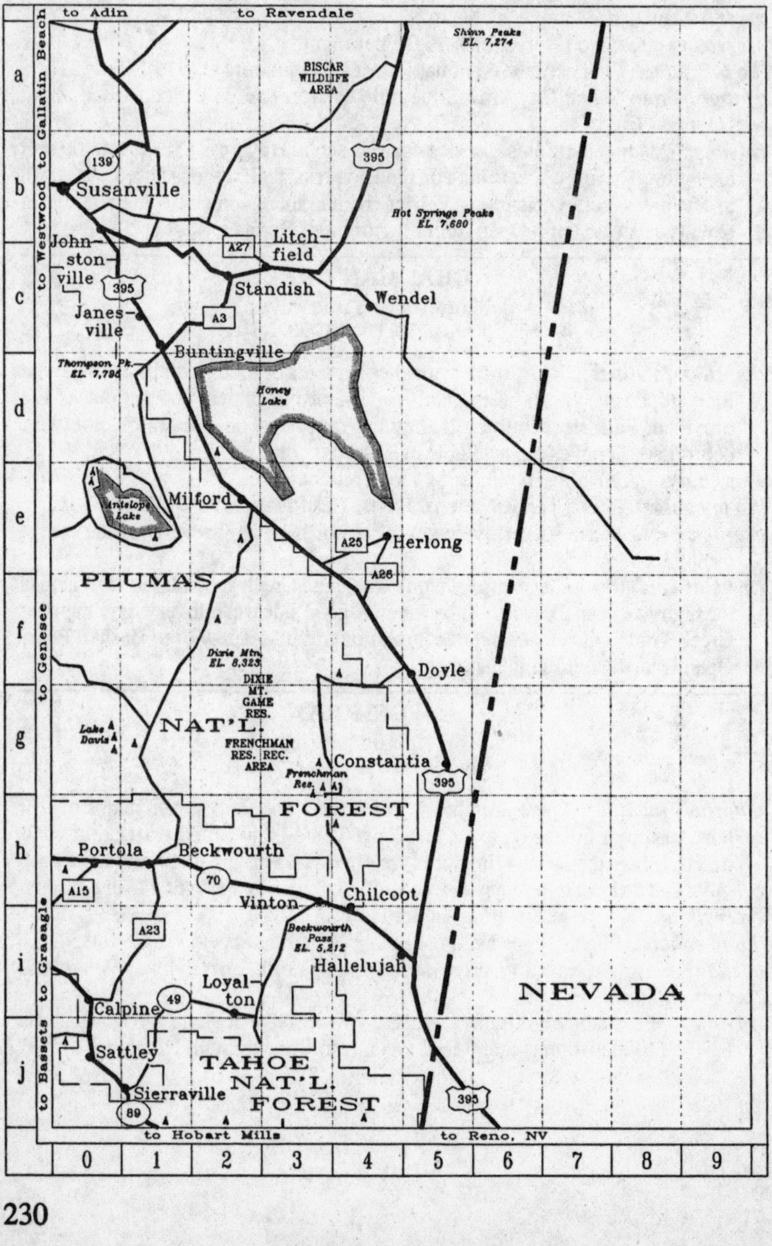

to Adin
to Ravendale
to Westwood to Gallatin Beach
to Genesee
to Bassets to Graeagle
to Hobart Mills
to Reno, NV

a
b
c
d
e
f
g
h
i
j

0 1 2 3 4 5 6 7 8 9

Shinn Peaks
EL. 7,274
BISCAR WILDLIFE AREA
395
139
Susanville
Hot Springs Peaks
EL. 7,680
A27
Litchfield
Johnstonville
395
Standish
Wendel
Janesville
A3
Buntingville
Thompson Pk.
EL. 7,795
Honey Lake
Antelope Lake
Milford
A25
Herlong
A26
PLUMAS
Dixie Mtn.
EL. 8,323
DIXIE MT. GAME RES.
Doyle
Lake Davis
NAT'L.
FRENCHMAN RES. REC. AREA
Constantia
Frenchman Res.
395
FOREST
Portola
Beckwourth
A15
70
Vinton
Chilcoot
A23
Beckwourth Pass
EL. 5,212
Hallelujah
NEVADA
Loyalton
49
Calpine
Sattley
TAHOE NAT'L. FOREST
Sierraville
89
395

Map grid **d2**

HONEY LAKE CAMPGROUND

near Milford

A

Campsites, facilities: There are 54 campsites for tents or motor homes, some with full or partial hookups. Picnic tables are provided. Rest rooms, showers, a laundromat, a sanitary disposal station, propane gas, a grocery store, ice, wood, and a game room are available.

B

Reservations, fee: Reservations accepted; $11-$13 fee per night.

Who to contact: Phone (916)253-2508.

Location: From Milford, drive two miles north on US 395; or drive 69 miles north of Reno on US 395; or 23 miles south of Susanville on US 395.

C4

Trip note: For newcomers, Honey Lake is a strange looking place; it's a vast, flat lake with not much around it. It sits in a huge basin that, from a distance, looks almost moon-like. The campground is set at 4,300 feet elevation and covers 27 acres, most of it overlooking the lake. There is a lot of chaparral, junipers, and scraggly-looking aspens in the area.

D

Map grid **e0**

BOULDER CREEK

at Antelope Lake

PLUMAS NATIONAL FOREST

Campsites, facilities: There are 70 campsites for tents or motor homes. Piped water, vault toilets, picnic tables, and fireplaces are provided. A sanitary dump station, boat ramp, and grocery store are nearby. Pets are permitted on leashes.

E

Reservations, fee: No reservations required; however, sites can be reserved through MISTIX by phoning (800)283-CAMP ($6 MISTIX fee); $8-$10 fee per night.

Who to contact: Phone Plumas National Forest Headquarters at (916)283-2050.

Location: From Taylorsville, drive 24 miles northeast on Beckwourth and Indian Creek Roads to Antelope Lake. Turn left at the dam and drive one mile to camp.

F

Trip note: All that a lot of campers want is a pretty spot along a lake, and Antelope Lake provides that. This spot is set along the north shore of the lake at 5,000 feet elevation. Open from May through October.

G

Map grid **e0**

LONE ROCK

at Antelope Lake

PLUMAS NATIONAL FOREST

Campsites, facilities: There are 86 campsites for tents or motor homes up to 22 feet long. Piped water, vault toilets, picnic tables, and fireplaces are provided. A sanitary dump station, boat ramp, and grocery store are nearby. Pets are permitted on leashes.

H

Reservations, fee: No reservations required; however, sites can be reserved through MISTIX by phoning (800)283-CAMP ($6 MISTIX fee); $8-$10 fee per night.

Who to contact: Phone Plumas National Forest Headquarters at (916)283-2050.

I

Location: From Taylorsville, drive 24 miles northeast on Beckwourth and Indian Creek Roads to Antelope Lake. Turn left at the dam and drive one mile to camp.

Trip note: This camp provides an option to nearby Boulder Creek Camp, also set along the shore of Antelope Lake. The elevation is 5,000 feet. Open from May through October.

J

Map grid e1

LONG POINT

at Antelope Lake
PLUMAS NATIONAL FOREST

Campsites, facilities: There are 38 campsites for tents or motor homes up to 32 feet long. Piped water, vault toilets, picnic tables, and fireplaces are provided. A grocery store, boat ramp, and sanitary dump station are nearby. Pets are permitted on leashes.

Reservations, fee: No reservations required; however, sites can be reserved through MISTIX by phoning (800)283-CAMP ($6 MISTIX fee); $8-$10 fee per night.

Who to contact: Phone Plumas National Forest Headquarters at (916)283-2050.

Location: From Taylorsville, drive 24 miles northeast on Beckwourth and Indian Creek Roads to Antelope Lake. Turn right at the dam and drive two miles to camp.

Trip note: One of several campgrounds on the lake, this nice vacation spot lies along the shore of Antelope Lake. A map of Plumas National Forest details backcountry roads, trails, and streams. Open from May through October.

Map grid e2

LAUFMAN

PLUMAS NATIONAL FOREST

Campsites, facilities: There are eight campsites here for tents or motor homes up to 22 feet long. There is no piped water, but vault toilets, tables, and fireplaces are provided. Pets are permitted on leashes. A grocery store and laundromat are nearby.

Reservations, fee: No reservations; no fee.

Who to contact: Call the Plumas National Forest at (916)283-2050 or write to 159 Lawrence Street, Quincy, CA 95971.

Location: From Milford on US 395, turn southeast on Milford Grade Road and drive three miles to the campground.

Trip note: This is one of two camps in the area, and let me tell ya, there ain't a whole lot else. There's a stark kind of beauty in the high desert up here, kind of like you're in a time machine and it's 1840. A side trip to the Dixie Mountain State Game Refuge is only about five miles away. The camp is at 5,100 feet elevation.

Map grid f2

CONKLIN PARK

on Willow Creek
PLUMAS NATIONAL FOREST

Campsites, facilities: There are nine campsites for tents or motor homes up to 22 feet long. There is **no piped water**, but vault toilets, picnic tables, and fireplaces are provided. Pets are permitted on leashes.

Reservations, fee: No reservations, no fee.

Who to contact: Phone Plumas National Forest Headquarters at (916)283-2050.

Location: From Milford on US 395, turn south on Highway 336 and drive three miles to the ranger station. Continue south on a dirt grade road for six miles up over the mountain. At the paved road, turn left and drive three miles to camp.

Trip note: This camp is located on Willow Creek in a State Game Refuge, but alas, a fire burned much of the surrounding area during the summer of 1989. The campground is little-known, primitive, and rarely-used and not likely to change any time soon. The elevation is 5,900 feet. Open from May through October.

MEADOW VIEW

Map grid **f4**

near Last Chance Creek
PLUMAS NATIONAL FOREST

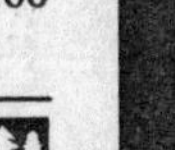

Campsites, facilities: There are six sites for tents or motor homes. There is **no piped water**, but vault toilets, picnic tables, and fireplaces are provided. Pets are permitted on leashes.

Reservations, fee: No reservations, no fee.

Who to contact: Phone Plumas National Forest Headquarters at (916)283-2050.

Location: From Doyle on US 395, turn west on Doyle Grade Road and drive 7.5 miles to the campground. Doyle Road is a dirt road for most of the way.

Trip note: This is a fairly remote, primitive camp near the border of the Dixie Mountain State Game Refuge. Bring your own water. The elevation is 6,100 feet. Open May through October.

LIGHTNING TREE

Map grid **g0**

on Lake Davis
PLUMAS NATIONAL FOREST

Campsites, facilities: There are 38 campsites for self-contained motor homes only. There is **no piped water** or toilets available. A sanitary dump station and a car-top boat launch are nearby. Pets are permitted on leashes.

Reservations, fee: No reservations, no fee.

Who to contact: Phone Plumas National Forest Headquarters at (916)283-2050.

Location: From Portola, drive two miles east on Highway 70. Turn north on Grizzly Road and drive about six miles to Lake Davis Road. Continue north for four miles to the campground.

Trip note: The camp is set at Davis Lake and is one of the better fishing spots in the region. The trout fishing is quite good in the spring and early summer. Largemouth bass have had a big population boost in recent years. The southern end of the lake is bordered by a State Game Refuge.

GRIZZLY

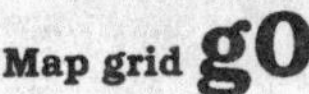

Map grid **g0**

on Lake Davis
PLUMAS NATIONAL FOREST

Campsites, facilities: There are 55 campsites for tents or motor homes up to 32 feet long. Piped water, flush toilets, picnic tables, and fireplaces are provided. A boat ramp, a grocery store, and a sanitary dump station are nearby. Pets are permitted on leashes.

Reservations, fee: No reservations; $8 fee per night.

Who to contact: Phone Plumas National Forest Headquarters at (916)283-2050.

Location: From Portola, drive two miles east on Highway 70. Turn north on Grizzly Road and drive about six miles to Lake Davis Road. Continue north for less than a mile to the campground.

Trip note: This is one of the better developed campgrounds at Lake Davis and is a popular spot for camping anglers. Open May through October.

GRASSHOPPER FLAT

Map grid **g0**

on Lake Davis
PLUMAS NATIONAL FOREST

Campsites, facilities: There are 70 campsites for tents or motor homes up to 32 feet

long. Piped water, flush toilets, picnic tables, and fireplaces are provided. A boat ramp, grocery store,, and sanitary dump station are nearby. Pets are permitted on leashes.

Reservations, fee: No reservations; $8 fee per night.

Who to contact: Phone Plumas National Forest Headquarters at (916)283-2050.

Location: From Portola, drive two miles east on Highway 70. Turn north on Grizzly Road and drive about six miles to Lake Davis Road. Continue north for less than a mile to the campground.

Trip note: This is a lakeside spot at Davis Lake with an elevation of 5,800 feet. The nearby boat ramp makes this a good base camp for anglers. The mouth of Freeman Creek is good for fly-fishing from a float tube or trolling for trout in early summer. Open from May through October.

Map grid g1

CROCKER

PLUMAS NATIONAL FOREST

Campsites, facilities: There are six sites for tents only and nine campsites for tents or motor homes up to 32 feet long. There is **no piped water**, but pit toilets, picnic tables, and fireplaces are provided. Pets are permitted on leashes.

Reservations, fee: No reservations, no fee.

Who to contact: Phone Plumas National Forest Headquarters at (916)283-2050.

Location: From Portola, drive four miles east on Highway 70 to the town of Beckwourth. Turn north on Beckwourth-Genessee Road and drive seven miles to the campground.

Trip note: This camp is just two miles from Antelope Lake, an alternative to the campgrounds there. The elevation is 5,800 feet. Open from May through October.

Map grid g3

FRENCHMAN

on Frenchman Lake

PLUMAS NATIONAL FOREST

Campsites, facilities: There are 25 sites for tents only and 37 campsites for tents or motor homes. Piped water, vault toilets, picnic tables, and fireplaces are provided. A sanitary dump station and a boat ramp are nearby. Pets are permitted on leashes.

Reservations, fee: No reservations required; however, sites can be reserved through MISTIX by phoning (800)283-CAMP ($6 MISTIX fee); $8 fee per night.

Who to contact: Phone Plumas National Forest Headquarters at (916)283-2050.

Location: From the junction of US 395 and Highway 70, drive west for five miles to the town of Chilcoot. Turn north on Frenchman Lake Road (Highway 284) and drive nine miles to the campground.

Trip note: This is a good option at Frenchman Lake. For side trip options, see the trip note for Cottonwood Springs Group Camp. The elevation is 5,100 feet. Open from May through October.

Map grid g3

COTTONWOOD GROUP CAMP

near Frenchman Lake

PLUMAS NATIONAL FOREST

Campsites, facilities: There are 28 family campsites for tents or motor homes up to 22 feet long. Piped water, flush toilets, picnic tables, and fireplaces are provided. A boat ramp and sanitary dump station are nearby. There are also two group camps available. Pets are permitted on leashes.

Reservations, fee: To reserve, phone MISTIX at (800)283-CAMP ($6-$10 MISTIX fee); $8 family fee per night; $50 group fee per night.
Who to contact: Phone Plumas National Forest Headquarters at (916)283-2050.
Location: From the junction of US 395 and Highway 70, drive west for five miles to the town of Chilcoot. Turn north on Frenchman Lake Road (Highway 284) and drive nine miles to the lake. Turn left to the campground.
Trip note: The fishing is usually pretty good at this lake, but it often gets missed by most folks who head to Davis Lake. Options include fishing Last Chance Creek, a good trout stream, especially below the Frenchman Lake Dam, or exploring the wildlife area located northwest of the lake. A side trip to Reno is often irresistible. The elevation is 5,700 feet. Open from May through October.

Map grid g3

BIG COVE
at Frenchman Lake
PLUMAS NATIONAL FOREST

Campsites, facilities: There are 38 campsites for tents or motor homes up to 32 feet long. Two of the sites are set up for handicapped users. Piped water, flush toilets, picnic tables, and fireplaces are provided. A boat ramp, sanitary dump station, grocery store, and propane gas are available nearby. Pets are permitted.
Reservations, fee: No reservations; $8-$12 fee per night.
Who to contact: Phone Plumas National Forest Headquarters at (916)283-2050.
Location: From the junction of US 395 and Highway 70, drive west for five miles to the town of Chilcoot. Turn north on Frenchman Lake Road (Highway 284) and drive ten miles to the campground.
Trip note: This well-developed camp lies along the edge of Frenchman Lake at an elevation of 5,100 feet. See the trip note for Cottonwood Springs. Open from May through September.

Map grid g4

SPRING CREEK
on Frenchman Lake
PLUMAS NATIONAL FOREST

Campsites, facilities: There are 39 campsites for tents or motor homes up to 22 feet long. Piped water, vault toilets, picnic tables, and fireplaces are provided. A boat ramp and sanitary dump station are nearby. Pets are permitted on leashes.
Reservations, fee: No reservations required; however, sites can be reserved through MISTIX by phoning (800)283-CAMP ($6 MISTIX fee); $8 fee per night.
Who to contact: Phone Plumas National Forest Headquarters at (916)283-2050.
Location: From the junction of US 395 and Highway 70, drive west for five miles to the town of Chilcoot. Turn north on Frenchman Lake Road (Highway 284) and drive nine miles to the campground.
Trip note: In many ways, Frenchman Lake is a prime spot, ideally situated. You get good trout fishing in the lake, a pretty stream (Last Chance Creek) south of the lake, a State Game Refuge along the northwestern end of the lake, and it's a short drive via US 395 to Reno. Add that up and put it in your cash register.

Map grid h0

FEATHER RIVER KOA

Campsites, facilities: There are 30 motor homes sites with full hookups and 25 sites for tents only. Piped water, showers, flush toilets, picnic tables, and fireplaces are provided. A grocery store, laundromat, sanitary dump station, heated pool, recreation room, and a playground are available.

on Last Chance Creek

Reservations, fee: Reservations accepted; $14-$17 fee per night.
Who to contact: Phone Feather River KOA at (916)836-2688.
Location: From Blairsden, drive five miles east on Highway 70. Or, from US 395, drive 24 miles west on Highway 70.
Trip note: This is a good layover spot for motor home cruisers; there are many side trip options. Historic Johnsville and its museum are nearby along with Plumas-Eureka State Park. The elevation is 4,954 feet.Open from May through October.

Map grid h4

CHILCOOT
on Last Chance Creek
PLUMAS NATIONAL FOREST

Campsites, facilities: There are five sites for tents only and 35 campsites for tents or motor homes up to 22 feet long. Piped water, flush toilets, picnic tables, and fireplaces are provided. A boat ramp, grocery store, and sanitary dump station are nearby. Pets are permitted on leashes.
Reservations, fee: No reservations; $8 fee per night.
Who to contact: Phone Plumas National Forest Headquarters at (916)283-2050.
Location: From the junction of US 395 and Highway 70, drive west for five miles to the town of Chilcoot. Turn north on Frenchman Lake Road (Highway 284) and drive six miles to the campground.
Trip note: This camp is located about three miles from Frenchman Lake on Last Chance Creek at 5,400 feet elevation. The trout fishing is good just below the dam, casting a small Panther Martin spinner. Open May through October.

Map grid j0

YUBA PASS
TAHOE NATIONAL FOREST

Campsites, facilities: There are 20 campsites for tents or motor homes up to 22 feet long. Piped water, vault toilets, picnic tables, and fireplaces are provided. Pets are permitted if they are quiet and on leashes or otherwise controlled. Supplies are available in Bassetts.
Reservations, fee: No reservations; $4 fee per night.
Who to contact: Phone Tahoe National Forest Headquarters at (916)265-4531.
Location: From Sierra City, drive 11 miles east on Highway 49 to the campground. From Sierraville, drive 11 miles west on Highway 49 to this campground at Yuba Pass.
Trip note: This unique area is right at Yuba Pass at an elevation of 6,700 feet. In the winter, the surrounding area is a ski park, which gives it an unusual look in summer months. Open June through November.

Map grid j1

COTTONWOOD CREEK
TAHOE NATIONAL FOREST

Campsites, facilities: There are 21 sites for tents only and 28 campsites for tents or motor homes up to 22 feet long. Piped water, vault toilets, picnic tables, and fireplaces are provided. Pets are permitted if they are quiet and on leashes or otherwise controlled. Supplies are available in Sierraville.
Reservations, fee: No reservations; $7 fee per night.
Who to contact: Phone Tahoe National Forest Headquarters at (916)265-4531,or California Land Management at (916)582-0120.
Location: From Sierraville, drive 4.5 miles southeast on Highway 89 to the campground on your left.

Trip note: This camp is set along the Cottonwood Creek at 5,800 feet. Side trip options include an interpretive trail that starts at the camp and the nearby Campbell Hot Springs. Open from May through October.

Map grid **j2**

BEAR VALLEY

on Bear Valley Creek
TAHOE NATIONAL FOREST

Campsites, facilities: There are ten tent sites. Piped water, vault toilets, picnic tables and fireplaces are provided. Pets are permitted if they are quiet and on leashes or otherwise controlled. Supplies are available in Sierraville.
Reservations, fee: No reservations, no fee.
Who to contact: Phone Tahoe National Forest Headquarters at (916)265-4531.
Location: From Sierraville, drive eight miles east on Lemon Canyon Road. (This road is not recommended for trailers.)
Trip note: This pretty little spot is just difficult enough to reach so that it gets missed by a lot of folks. The camp is situated on the headwaters of Bear Valley Creek. The elevation is 6,700. Open from June through October.

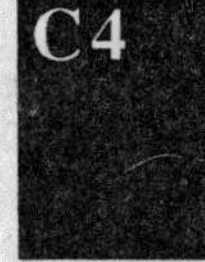

Map grid **j4**

LOOKOUT

TOIYABE NATIONAL FOREST

Campsites, facilities: There are 22 campsites for tents or motor homes up to 22 feet long and a group campsite with a maximum capacity of 16 people. Piped water, pit toilets, picnic tables, and fireplaces are provided. Pets are permitted on leashes or otherwise restrained. Another group camp may be opening near this site soon. Call ahead for information.
Reservations, fee: Reservations through MISTIX at (800)283-CAMP ($6 MISTIX fee); $6 fee per night; group site fee is $12 per night.
Who to contact: Phone Toiyabe National Forest Headquarters, Carson Ranger District at (702)882-2766.
Location: From Reno, Nevada, drive northwest on Interstate 80. Take the Verdi exit and follow Old Dog Valley Road for about 11 miles to the campground entrance sign.
Trip note: This camp is set in relatively remote country at 6,700 feet elevation. The highlight here is a quartz crystal mine a short distance from the camp, where you can try a little mining if you want. Side trips to Boca and Stampede Lakes, both about ten miles away, can be taken. Open from June through September.

◆ MAP D0 ◆

BEACH
TREES
5% CLUB
DESERT
URBAN
FOOTHILL
GRASSLAND

15 MILES

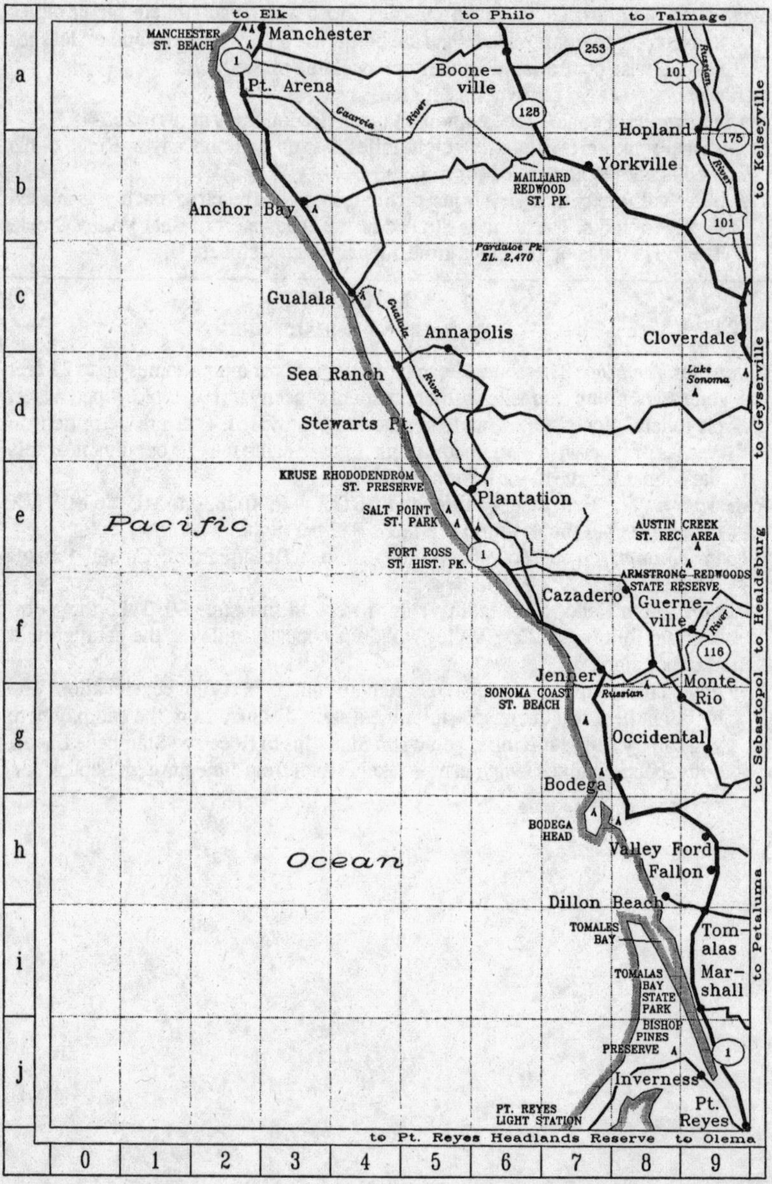

to Elk
to Philo
to Talmage
MANCHESTER ST. BEACH
Manchester
1
253
101
Russian
Pt. Arena
Boone-ville
Garcia River
128
Hopland
175
Yorkville
River
MAILLIARD REDWOOD ST. PK.
Anchor Bay
101
to Kelseyville
Pardaloe Pk. EL. 2,470
Gualala
Gualala River
Annapolis
Cloverdale
Sea Ranch
Lake Sonoma
Stewarts Pt.
to Geyserville
KRUSE RHODODENDROM ST. PRESERVE
Plantation
SALT POINT ST. PARK
Pacific
AUSTIN CREEK ST. REC. AREA
FORT ROSS ST. HIST. PK.
1
ARMSTRONG REDWOODS STATE RESERVE
Cazadero
Guerne-ville
River
116
to Healdsburg
Jenner
SONOMA COAST ST. BEACH
Russian
Monte Rio
Occidental
to Sebastopol
Bodega
BODEGA HEAD
Valley Ford
Ocean
Fallon
Dillon Beach
TOMALES BAY
Tom-alas
Mar-shall
to Petaluma
TOMALAS BAY STATE PARK
BISHOP PINES PRESERVE
1
Inverness
PT. REYES LIGHT STATION
Pt. Reyes
to Pt. Reyes Headlands Reserve
to Olema

a
b
c
d
e
f
g
h
i
j

0 1 2 3 4 5 6 7 8 9

Map grid **a2**

MANCHESTER STATE BEACH

near Point Arena

Campsites, facilities: There are 48 campsites for tents or motor homes up to 30 feet long. Piped water, chemical toilets, picnic tables, and fireplaces are provided. A sanitary dump station is at the campground.

Reservations, fee: Reserve through MISTIX at (800)444-PARK ($3.95 MISTIX fee); $7-$9 fee per night; pets $1.

Who to contact: Phone (707)937-5804.

Location: From Point Arena, drive 1.5 miles on Highway 1 to Manchester Beach. Turn west on Kinney Road and drive three-quarters of a mile to the campground.

Trip note: This is a popular state beach. The town of Point Arena provides a nearby supply point, the adjacent beach provides recreational opportunities, and, to the south, the Garcia River provides fair steelhead fishing during winter months. Open year-round.

Map grid **a2**

MANCHESTER BEACH KOA

near Point Arena

Campsites, facilities: There are 73 sites for tents or motor homes with full or partial hookups. Group sites are available. Rest rooms, showers, a heated pool, a hot tub and spa, a recreation room, a playground, a dump station, picnic tables, and fireplaces are provided. A grocery store, RV storage, ice, wood, laundromat, and propane gas are available. Pets are permitted. There are also 12 cabins available.

Reservations, fee: Reservations accepted; $20-$26 fee per night. Cabins are $30-$32 per night.

Who to contact: Phone (707)882-2375.

Location: From Point Arena, drive 1.5 miles on Highway 1 to Manchester Beach. Turn west on Kinney Road and drive one-quarter mile to the campground.

Trip note: This is a privately-operated motor home park beside Highway 1 and the sandy beach. Low tides are good for beachcombing. In the winter months, nearby Garcia River provides steelhead fishing, but that can be a longshot.

Map grid **a2**

ROLLERVILLE JUNCTION

near Point Arena

Campsites, facilities: There are 55 sites for tents or motor homes (four are drive-through), many with full or partial hookups. Rest rooms, hot showers, a hot tub, a recreation room, a playground, cable T.V. hook-ups, a sanitary dump station, picnic tables, and fireplaces are provided. A laundromat and propane gas are available.

Reservations, fee: Reservations accepted; $15-$19 fee per night.

Who to contact: Phone (707)882-2440.

Location: From Point Arena, drive two miles north on Highway 1 to the campground.

Trip note: This is a quiet section of California coast. Manchester State Beach and the Garcia River provide side trip possibilities. The park, set at 220 feet elevation, has horseshoes, volleyball, and badminton, so we're not exactly talking about the Five Percent Club here. Open year-round.

Map grid **b3** ANCHOR BAY CAMPGROUND

near Gualala

Campsites, facilities: There are 76 sites for tents or motor homes, many with water and electrical hookups. Rest rooms, hot showers, a sanitary dump station, picnic tables, and fireplaces are provided.

Reservations, fee: Reservations accepted; $18-$20 fee per night.

Who to contact: Phone (707)884-4222.

Location: From Gualala, drive four miles north on Highway 1 to the campground.

Trip note: This is a quiet and beautiful stretch of California coast. In winter, the nearby Gualala River attracts large but elusive steelhead. The campground is set at 60 feet elevation. Open year-round.

Map grid **c4** GUALALA POINT

SONOMA COUNTY REGIONAL PARK

Campsites, facilities: There are 19 sites for tents and motor homes up to 28 feet long and six walk-in sites. Rest rooms, a sanitary dump station, picnic tables, and fireplaces are provided. Wood is available. The facilities are wheelchair accessible.

Reservations, fee: No reservations; $3 per person for walk-in sites, $10 fee per night for other sites.

Who to contact: Phone (707)785-2377.

Location: From Highway 1 in Gualala, go east. Campground is right there, just off the highway. A day-use area is west of the highway.

Trip note: This is a dramatic spot right on the ocean, adjacent to the mouth of the Gualala River. A trail beside the bluff provides a great side trip and other access trails to several beaches are available. There is a wide diversity of birds in the area. Open year-round.

Map grid **d9** DUTCHER CREEK RV PARK AND CAMPGROUND

near Lake Sonoma

Campsites, facilities: There are 12 sites for tents only and 15 motor home spaces (two are drive-through) with full or partial hookups. Picnic tables are provided. Flush toilets, showers, a sanitary disposal station, and a laundromat are available.

Reservations, fee: Reservations accepted; $13 fee per night.

Who to contact: Phone the park at (707)894-4829.

Location: From US 101 just south of Cloverdale, take the Dutcher Creek exit. Turn west on Theresa Road. Drive one-half mile to the camp at 230 Theresa Drive.

Trip note: This privately-operated camp provides easy access and close vicinity to the north end of Lake Sonoma, which is off limits to waterskiers and provides quiet water for canoes. From the park, however, there is no direct access to the lake.

Map grid **d9** LAKE SONOMA RECREATION AREA

near Cloverdale

Campsites, facilities: There are three types of camping facilities available here: There are 103 primitive sites scattered around the lake in 15 separate areas and 113 developed sites and two group sites located 2.5 miles from the lake. Picnic tables, fire grills, and portable toilets are provided at the primitive sites, but **no piped water** is available. Piped water, flush toilets, solar-heated showers, and a sanitary disposal station are available in the developed area. A boat ramp, and boat rentals are available in the marina area. Saturday night campfire talks are held at the two amphitheaters during the summer..

Reservations, fee: No reservations necessary; no fee for primitive sites, but permit required from visitor center; $6 fee per night for developed sites; group sites by reservation only.

Who to contact: Phone the U.S. Corps of Engineers, Lake Sonoma at (707)433-9483.

Location: From Santa Rosa, drive north on US 101 to the Dry Creek Road exit in Healdsburg. Turn left and drive about eleven miles northwest to the Lake Sonoma Visitor Center.

Trip note: This is one of the newest lakes in California and it is also one of the best. The developed campground is fine for car campers, but the boat-in sites are ideal for folks wanting a quiet, pretty lakeside setting. The waterskiers vs. fishermen conflict has been solved by limiting high-speed boats to specified areas and the laws are strictly enforced. The best fishing is in the protective coves of the Warm Springs and Dry Creek arms of the lake; use live minnows for bass. No trout are stocked, which is one of the few disappointments here. The visitor center is adjacent to a public fish hatchery. Salmon and steelhead come to spawn from the Russian River between October and March. The lake is surrounded by 18,000 acres of parkland in its natural state. Open year-round.

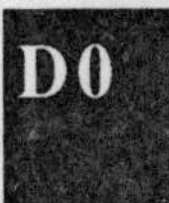

Map grid e5

SALT POINT STATE PARK

Campsites, facilities: There are 110 campsites for tents or motor homes up to 31 feet long and one campground with a walk-in site. Picnic tables, fireplaces, and piped water are provided. Flush and pit toilets and a sanitary disposal station are available. The picnic areas and some hiking trails are wheelchair accessible.

Reservations, fee: Reserve through MISTIX at (800)444-PARK ($3.95 MISTIX fee); $12-$14 fee per night.

Who to contact: Phone the park at (707)847-3221.

Location: From Jenner, drive 20 miles north on Highway 1 to the campground entrance.

Trip note: In the early winter, this is the headquarters for abalone divers; it is one of the best spots in California. In the summer, it takes a reservation to get a spot since it's a prime layover for visitors touring Highway 1. Because it is set beside the ocean, you get good beachcombing and classic sunsets.

Map grid e5

OCEAN COVE CAMPGROUND
near Fort Ross

Campsites, facilities: There are 80 campsites for tents or motor homes. Piped water, picnic tables, fireplaces, and chemical toilets are provided. A boat launch, a grocery store, fishing supplies, and diving gear rentals are available. Pets are permitted.

Reservations, fee: No reservations; $10 fee per vehicle per night, $5 day use fee; pets $1.

Who to contact: Phone the campground store at (707)847-3422.

Location: From the town of Jenner, drive 17 miles north on Highway 1 (five miles north of Fort Ross) to the campground entrance.

Trip note: The highlights here are the sites overlooking the ocean. Alas, it can be foggy during the summer. Regardless, it still offers quite a view. Good ocean access makes the camp popular for abalone divers and fishermen. Open from April through November.

Map grid **e6** **STILLWATER COVE REGIONAL PARK** 
near Fort Ross

Campsites, facilities: There are 23 campsites for tents or motor homes up to 35 feet long. Picnic tables, fireplaces, and piped water are provided. Flush toilets, showers, and a sanitary disposal station are available. Pets are permitted. Supplies can be obtained in Ocean Cove (one mile north) and Fort Ross. The facilities are wheelchair accessible.
Reservations, fee: No reservations; $10 fee per night; pets $1.
Who to contact: Phone the park at (707)847-3245.
Location: From the town of Jenner, drive 16 miles north on Highway 1 (four miles north of Fort Ross) to the park entrance.
Trip note: This campground is on the picturesque northern California coast. It's quite popular with abalone divers because of its good ocean access. A good side trip is to take the one-mile loop trail, which is routed through a canyon lined with ferns, redwoods, and has a creek running through. Open all year.

Map grid **e9** **AUSTIN CREEK RECREATION AREA** 
near Russian River

Campsites, facilities: There are 24 campsites for tents or small motor homes up to 20 feet long. No trailers of any kind are allowed. (The access road is very narrow.) Picnic tables, fireplaces, piped water, and flush toilets are provided. Pets are permitted on leashes in the main campground. There are also four primitive, backcountry campsites with tables, fire rings, and pit toilets, but **no piped water** is available and no pets are permitted. The camps are 2.5 to four miles from the main campground. Obtain a backcountry camping permit from the office.
Reservations, fee: No reservations; $7-$12 fee per night; pets $1.
Who to contact: Phone the park at (707)869-2015.
Location: From Guerneville on Highway 116, turn north on Armstrong Woods Road and drive three miles to the Armstrong Woods State Park entrance. Continue 3.5 miles from the entrance to the campground.
Trip note: Here is another take-your-pick deal with many side trip possibilities. The Russian River is only five miles away; it's popular in the summer for canoeing and sunbathing and in the winter for steelhead fishing. Another activity option is the nearby Armstrong Redwoods State Park, which provides picnic areas and hiking trails among the redwoods.

Map grid **e9** **RING CANYON CAMPGROUND** 
near Russian River

Campsites, facilities: There are 45 sites for tents or motor homes up to 31 feet long, two with full hookups. Picnic tables and fire grills are provided. Piped water, flush toilets, showers and a sanitary disposal station are available.
Reservations, fee: Reservations accepted; $13 fee per night.
Who to contact: Phone the park at (707)869-2746.
Location: From Highway 116 in Guerneville, turn north on Armstrong Woods Road and drive 1.8 miles to the campground.

Trip note: This popular, privately-operated campground near Guerneville is in close proximity to the Russian River and Armstrong Redwoods State Park.

A

Map grid f8 CASINI RANCH FAMILY CAMPGROUND

on Russian River

Campsites, facilities: There are 225 campsites for tents and motor homes (28 drive-through), many with full or partial hookups. Picnic tables and fire grills are provided. Flush toilets, showers, a playground, a sanitary disposal station, a laundromat, cable TV, a video arcade, a game arcade, boat and canoe rentals, propane gas, and a grocery store are available. Some facilities are wheelchair accessible.

B

Reservations, fee: Reservations recommended; $13-$18 fee per night.

C

Who to contact: Phone (707)865-2255, or 1-800-451-8400 toll free for reservations.

Location: From Highway 116 in Duncan Mills, turn southeast on Moscow Road and drive one-half mile to the campground.

Trip note: Take your pick: this campground offers campsites in the sun or shade beside the shores of the Russian River. A variety of side trip options are available, including canoeing, exploring nearby Armstrong Redwoods State Park, or driving out to the coast beside the Russian River. Open year-round.

D0

Map grid g7 BODEGA DUNES CAMPGROUND

SONOMA COAST STATE BEACH

E

Campsites, facilities: There are 98 campsites for tents or motor homes up to 31 feet long. Picnic tables, fireplaces, and piped water are provided. Flush toilets, showers, and a sanitary disposal station are available. Pets are permitted. A laundromat, supplies, and horse rentals are also available nearby.

Reservations, fee: Reserve through MISTIX at (800)444-PARK ($3.95 MISTIX fee); $12-$14 fee per night; pets $1.

F

Who to contact: Phone the Sonoma Coast State Beach at (707)875-3483 or (707)865-2391.

Location: From the town of Bodega Bay on Highway 1, drive one-half mile north to the campground entrance.

G

Trip note: This is quite a spot for beach campers. It is set at the end of a beach that stretches miles. Beyond that, the coast becomes rugged. Nearby Bodega Bay offers a full marina, fishing facilities, and restaurants. Salmon fishing is best in June and July, rockfish and lingcod are tops in the fall.

Map grid g7 WRIGHTS BEACH CAMPGROUND

SONOMA COAST STATE BEACH

H

Campsites, facilities: There are 30 campsites for tents or motor homes up to 27 feet long. Picnic tables, fireplaces, piped water, and flush toilets are provided. Pets are permitted.

I

Reservations, fee: Reserve through MISTIX at (800)444-PARK ($3.95 MISTIX fee); $12-$14 fee per night; pets $1.

Who to contact: Phone the Sonoma Coast State Beach at (707)875-3483 or (707)865-2391.

Location: From the town of Bodega Bay, drive six miles north on Highway 1 to the campground.

J

Trip note: This campground is at the north end of a beach that stretches south for several miles. The coast north of this campground becomes steep and rugged.

Keep in mind that it is often cold and foggy on this part of the California coast in the summer, but it is nice during the fall and spring.

Map grid **h7**

WESTSIDE REGIONAL PARK
on Bodega Bay

Campsites, facilities: There are 47 campsites for tents or motor homes. Piped water, picnic tables, and fire grills are provided. Flush toilets, showers, a sanitary disposal station, and a boat ramp are available. Pets are permitted. Supplies can be obtained in the town of Bodega Bay.

Reservations, fee: No reservations; $11 fee per night; pets $1.

Who to contact: Phone the County Parks Department at (707)875-3540.

Location: From the town of Bodega Bay, drive north a short distance. You will see a sign for Westside Park and Eastshore Road. Turn southwest at the sign on Bay Flat Road and travel two miles (looping around the bay) to the campground.

Trip note: This campground, on the west shore of Bodega Bay, is a prime spot to hole up for awhile. One of the better boat launches on the coast is near here, providing access to prime fishing waters. Salmon fishing is excellent from mid-June through August. A small, protected beach (for kids to dig in the sand and wade) is available at the end of the road beyond the campground.

Map grid **h8**

DORAN REGIONAL PARK
on Bodega Bay

Campsites, facilities: There are ten sites for tents only and 128 campsites for tents or motor homes. Picnic tables, fireplaces, and piped water are provided. Flush toilets, showers, sanitary disposal stations, and a boat ramp are available. Pets are permitted. Supplies can be obtained in Bodega Bay.

Reservations, fee: No reservations; $11 fee per night; pets $1.

Who to contact: Phone the County Parks Department at (707)875-3540.

Location: From the town of Bodega Bay, drive one mile south on Highway 1 to Doran Beach Road and the entrance to campground.

Trip note: This campground is set beside Doran Beach on Bodega Bay, which offers complete fishing and marina facilities. It's a good headquarters for a deep sea fishing trip. In season, it's a popular clamming and crabbing spot. Salmon fishing is often excellent during the summer months at the whistle buoy offshore from Bodega Head, and rockfishing is good year-round at Cordell Bank. Fishing is available off the rock jetty in the park. Open all year.

Map grid **j8**

TOMALES BAY STATE PARK

Campsites, facilities: A few campsites are available for bicyclists traveling along the coast. Piped water and tent sites are provided. No pets allowed.

Reservations, fee: No reservations; $3 fee; day use fee is $5 per vehicle.

Who to contact: Phone Tomales Bay State Park at (415)669-1140.

Location: From Inverness, drive four miles on Sir Francis Drake Boulevard and Pierce Point Road.

Trip note: Few know of this tiny campground, not even the many bicyclists touring Highway 1 who are looking for exactly such a spot. It is a pretty, secluded park on Tomales Bay with good hiking, picnicking, and, during low tides, clamming (make sure you have a fishing license).

◆ MAP D1 ◆

BEACH
DESERT
FOOTHILL
TREES
URBAN
GRASSLAND
5% CLUB

15 MILES

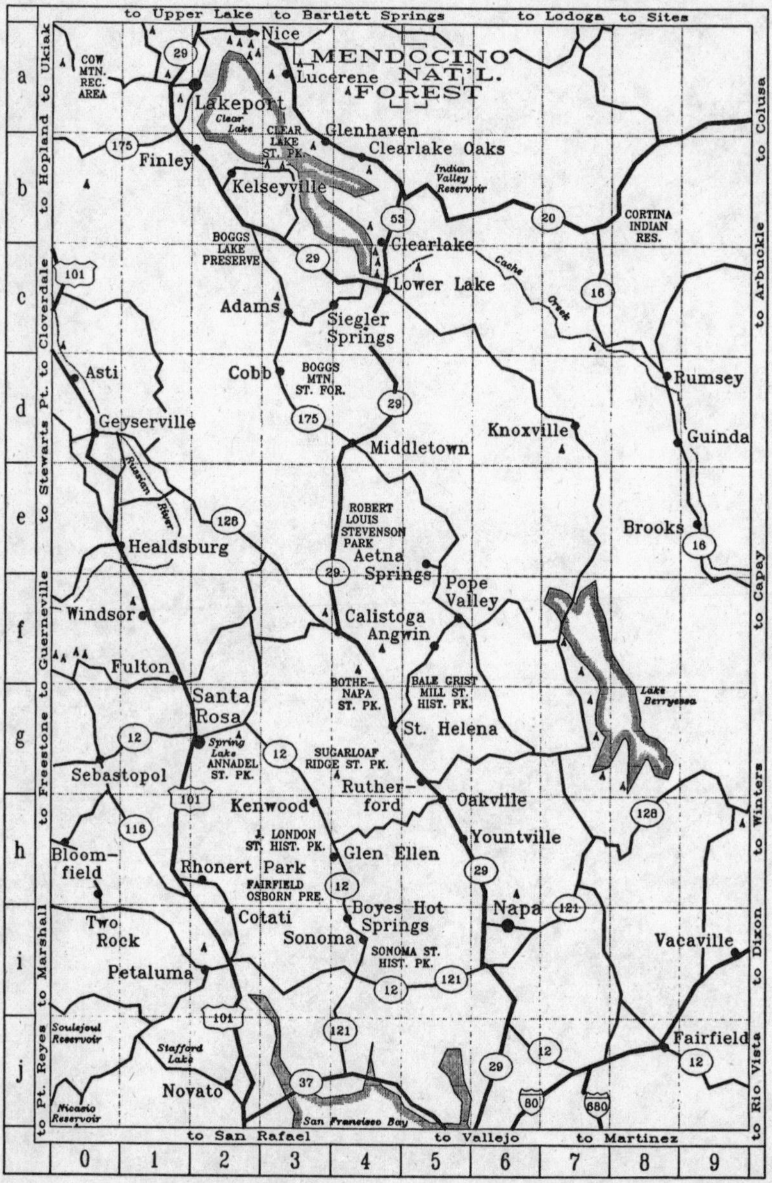

Map grid **a0**

RED MOUNTAIN
near Ukiah

A

Campsites, facilities: There are eight campsites for tents. Piped water, vault toilets, picnic tables, and fireplaces are provided. Pets are permitted on leashes or otherwise controlled.

B

Reservations, fee: No reservations, no fee.

Who to contact: Phone the Bureau of Land Management, Ukiah District at (707)462-3873.

Location: From US 101 in Ukiah, turn east on Talmage Road and drive 1.5 miles. Turn right on Eastside Road and drive one-third mile. Turn left on Mill Creek Road and drive nine miles to the campground.

C

Trip note: Like Mayacmus campground, this camp is also set in the Cow Mountain Area east of Ukiah, but be forewarned: This is a popular spot for off-road motorcycles. If you don't like bikes, go to the other camp. Besides motorcycle trails, there are opportunities for hiking, horseback riding, and hunting.

D1

Map grid **a1**

KELLY'S KAMP
on Scotts Creek near Clear Lake

Campsites, facilities: There are 75 sites for tents or motor homes, many with full or partial hookups. Picnic tables and fire grills are provided. Flush toilets, showers, a sanitary disposal station, a laundromat, ice, and a small camp store are available.

E

Reservations, fee: Call ahead for available space and fee.

Who to contact: Phone the park at (707)263-5754.

Location: From the town of Upper Lake, drive five miles northwest on Highway 20. Turn south on Scotts Valley Road and drive to 8220 Scotts Valley Road.

F

Trip note: This privately-operated park is set beside Scotts Creek, not far from the Blue Lakes. Recreation options include swimming and fishing. Closed November through March.

Map grid **a1**

U-WANNA CAMP
near Clear Lake

G

Campsites, facilities: There are 30 sites for tents or motor homes (four drive-through), with full or partial hookups. Picnic tables, fire grills, rest rooms, showers, a sanitary disposal station, a laundromat, a playground, and a recreation room are provided.

H

Reservations, fee: Reservations accepted; $11 fee per night.

Who to contact: Phone the park at (707)263-6745.

Location: From Highway 29 in Lakeport, turn west on Scotts Valley Road (11th Street) and drive one-half mile. Turn left on Riggs Road and drive three-quarters of a mile. Turn right on Scotts Creek Road and drive three-quarters of a mile to the campground at 2699 Scotts Creek Road.

I

Trip note: Whether U-Wanna or not, this could be where you end up. It is set about two miles from Clear Lake and is fairly secluded and has a small fishing pond for kids. Open year-round.

Map grid **a1**

WILL-O-POINT RESORT
on Clear Lake

J

Campsites, facilities: There are 125 sites for tents or motor homes, and nine motor home spaces with full hookups. Rest rooms, showers, a boat ramp, a fuel dock, a laundromat, a games room, jet ski rentals, fishing supplies, propane gas, a restaurant, and a small grocery store are available.

Reservations, fee: Reservations required; $15-$17 fee per night. Pets $2.

Who to contact: Phone the park at (707)263-5407.

Location: The campground is located in Lakeport (on the northwest shore of Clear Lake) at the corner of Highway 29 and First Street.

Trip note: A good lookin' spot, with a public park nearby with picnic facilities and a children's playground. There are two beaches within walking distance of the campsites. Tent cabins are available. Possible side trips include visiting the Chateau du Lac/Kendall-Jackson Winery. Open year-round.

Map grid a2

TIKI TIKI RV PARK
on Clear Lake

Campsites, facilities: There are 30 motor home spaces, many with full or partial hookups. Picnic tables, fire grills, rest rooms, showers, a boat ramp, a guest dock, and a sanitary disposal station are provided. A laundromat and horseshoes are available.

Reservations, fee: Reservations accepted; $16-$18 fee per night.

Who to contact: Phone the park at (707)274-2576.

Location: In the town of Nice, take Highway 20 to 3967 East Highway 20.

Trip note: This is one of the several parks in the town of Nice, which is pronounced "neese." Say it wrong and they'll say, "There's another tourist from the Bay Area." Closed November through February.

Map grid a2

SANDPIPER SHORES
on Clear Lake

Campsites, facilities: There are 30 motor home spaces with full or partial hookups. Picnic tables, rest rooms, showers, and a boat ramp are provided. Moorings, a pier, a laundromat, and propane gas are available.

Reservations, fee: Reservation accepted; $13 fee per night.

Who to contact: Phone the park at (707)274-4448.

Location: From Highway 20 in the town of Nice, turn south on Hammond Avenue and drive one-half mile. Turn east on Lakeshore Boulevard and drive to 2630 Lakeshore Boulevard.

Trip note: This is one of several options in the area, but they all fill up on three-day weekends. Catfishing is good outside the mouth of Rodman Slough from a boat, and in the slough itself from the shore. For bass, cast spinner baits beside the old submerged pilings in this area. Several suntanning areas are available at the north end of the lake.

Map grid a2

CALICO CAT TRAILER RESORT
on Clear Lake

Campsites, facilities: There are 30 motor home spaces, most with full hookups. Picnic tables and patios are provided. Rest rooms, showers, a boat ramp, and a boat dock are available.

Reservations, fee: Reservations accepted; $16 fee per night.

Who to contact: Phone the park at (707)274-1950.

Location: In the town of Nice (on the north shore of Clear Lake), take Highway 20 to 3297 East Highway 20.

Trip note: This area is noted for its lovely beaches dotted with large live oak, redbud, and pepperwood trees. Catfishing is excellent at Rodman Slough and just offshore Rodman Slough; a public boat launch is available west of the town of Nice (pronounced "neese"). Catfish George, the legend of Clear Lake, lived in Nice and caught thousands of catfish every year at the lake's north end.

A

B

C

D1

E

F

G

H

I

J

Map grid **a2**

NORTH SHORE RESORT AND MARINA
on Clear Lake

Campsites, facilities: There are 31 motor home spaces, many with full or partial hookups. Picnic tables and fire grills are provided. Rest rooms, showers, a laundromat, a small grocery store, ice, propane gas, marine gas, boat rentals, complete marina facilities, fishing supplies, and a snack bar are available.
Reservations, fee: Reservations accepted; $14 fee per night.
Who to contact: Phone the park at (707)274-7771.
Location: From Highway 20 in the town of Nice, turn south on Hammond Avenue and drive one-half mile. Turn west on Lakeshore Boulevard and drive to 2345 Lakeshore Boulevard.
Trip note: This is one of a half-dozen privately-run parks in the immediate vicinity.

Map grid **a2**

HOLIDAY HARBOR RV PARK
on Clear Lake

Campsites, facilities: There are 30 motor home spaces with full or partial hookups. Picnic tables, rest rooms, showers, a recreation room, a boat ramp, and a sanitary disposal station are provided. A laundromat and ice are available.
Reservations, fee: Reservations accepted; $15 fee per night.
Who to contact: Phone the park at (707)274-1136.
Location: This camp is located in the town of Nice on Highway 20.
Trip note: A popular resort, this private park is, and one of the reasons is its full-service marina. For anglers casting beside old docks and submerged pilings with spinner baits or plastic worms, the bass fishing is excellent in this area in the spring and early summer.

Map grid **a3**

BAMBOO HOLLOW MOBILE HOME PARK
on Clear Lake

Campsites, facilities: There are 39 motor home spaces with full hookups. Rest rooms, showers, a laundromat, a boat ramp, moorings, and lake frontage sites are available. A grocery store, boat rentals, fishing supplies, and propane gas are nearby.
Reservations, fee: Call ahead for available space and fee.
Who to contact: Phone the park at (707)274-7751.
Location: In Lucerne, drive to 5877 Lake Street off Highway 20.
Trip note: Lucerne is noted for its harbor and its long stretch of well-kept, public beaches with barbecue facilities.

Map grid **a3**

ARROW TRAILER PARK
on Clear Lake

Campsites, facilities: There are 24 sites for tents or motor homes, many with full or partial hookups. Rest rooms, showers, a laundromat, boat rentals, moorings, fishing supplies, a boat ramp, a grocery store, beer and wine, ice and RV supplies are available.
Reservations, fee: Reservations accepted; $14-$18.50 per night, depending on the

season.

Who to contact: Phone the park at (707)274-7715.

Location: The campground is located in the town of Lucerne at 6720 East Highway 20.

Trip note: Lucerne is known for its harbor and its long stretch of well-kept, public beaches along the shore of Clear Lake. The town offers a shopping district, restaurants, and cafes. In summer months, crappie fishing is good at night from the boat docks, as long as there are bright lights to attracts gnats, which in turn attract minnows, the prime food for crappie.

Map grid a4

LAKEVIEW CAMPGROUND

near Clear Lake

MENDOCINO NATIONAL FOREST

Campsites, facilities: There are nine campsites for tents or motor homes. There is **no piped water,** but picnic tables, fireplaces, and vault toilets are provided. Pets are permitted on leashes or otherwise controlled.

Reservations, fee: No reservations, no fee.

Who to contact: Phone the Mendocino National Forest Upper Lake Ranger Station at (707)275-2361.

Location: From the town of Lucerne, drive north on Highway 20 for two miles. Turn east on Forest Service Road 8 (Bartlett Springs Road) and drive five miles. Turn southwest on Forest Service Road 15N09 (High Valley Road) and drive three miles to the camp.

Trip note: When Clear Lake is packed to the rafters with campers, this spot offers a perfect alternative, if you don't mind roughing it a bit. It is set at 3,400 feet (above the town of Lucerne) overlooking the lake. A trail from camp leads down to the town; it's a two-mile hike, but most folks wouldn't want to make the uphill, return trip, especially on a hot summer day. Open from May to mid-October.

Map grid b0

SHELDON CREEK

near Hopland

Campsites, facilities: There are six sites for tents only. Piped water, vault toilets, picnic tables, and fireplaces are provided. Pets are permitted on leashes or otherwise controlled.

Reservations, fee: No reservations, no fee.

Who to contact: Phone the Bureau of Land Management, Ukiah District at (707)462-3873.

Location: From US 101 in Hopland (south of Ukiah), turn east on Highway 175 and drive three miles. Turn right (south) on Old Toll Road and drive eight miles to the campground.

Trip note: Only the locals know about this spot, and hey, there aren't a lot of locals around. The camp is set amid rolling hills, grasslands, and oaks. It is pretty and quiet in the spring, but hot in the summer. Recreational possibilities are hiking, horseback riding (bring your own horse, podner), and in the fall, hunting.

Map grid b3

GLENHAVEN BEACH CAMPGROUND AND MARINA

on Clear Lake

Campsites, facilities: There are 21 spaces for motor homes up to 26 feet long, with full or partial hookups. Picnic tables, fire grills, rest rooms, showers, and recreation room are provided. A boat ramp, and boat rentals are available.

Reservations, fee: Reservations accepted; $14 fee per night.

Who to contact: Phone the park at (707)998-3406.

Location: From the town of Clearlake Oaks, drive four miles northwest on Highway 20 to 9625 East Highway 20.

Trip note: This makes a good base camp for fishermen. The privately-operated park is set on a peninsula on the eastern shore of Clear Lake. Bass fishing is good in this area; the fish are often in the very shallow water beside old docks and in coves. Open from February through November.

Map grid b3 — CLEAR LAKE STATE PARK

Campsites, facilities: There are 147 campsites for tents or motor homes, located in four campgrounds. Picnic tables, fire grills, rest rooms, showers, a sanitary disposal station, and a boat ramp are available. A grocery store, a laundromat, and propane gas are nearby. Pets are permitted. The boat ramp, picnic area, and some campsites are wheelchair accessible.

Reservations, fee: Reserve through MISTIX at (800)444-PARK ($3.95 MISTIX fee); $12-$14 fee per night. Pets $1.

Who to contact: Phone the park at (707)279-4293.

Location: From Highway 29 in Kelseyville, take the Kelseyville exit and turn north on Main Street. Continue north on Gaddy Lane for about two miles. Turn right on Soda Bay Road and drive one-half mile to the park.

Trip note: This is one of California's beautiful, inexpensive, and popular state parks, set on the western shore of Clear Lake. Reservations are a necessity in summer months. That stands to reason, with excellent bass fishing from boats beside tule-lined shoreline near the park and good catfishing in the sloughs that run through park. Some campsites have water frontage. Rangers here are friendly, helpful, and provide reliable fishing information.

Map grid b3 — EDGEWATER RESORT AND RV PARK on Clear Lake

Campsites, facilities: There are 69 motor home spaces with full hookups. Picnic tables, fire grills, rest rooms, showers, a recreation room, and a boat ramp are provided. A laundromat and wood are available.

Reservations, fee: Reservations accepted; $18 fee per night.

Who to contact: Phone the park at (707)279-0208.

Location: From Highway 29 in Kelseyville, take the Kelseyville exit and turn north on Main Street. Continue north on Gaddy Lane for about two miles. Turn right on Soda Bay Road and drive three miles to the resort.

Trip note: This is a popular vacation spot for motor home cruisers looking for a spot to tie up up the "horse" for a while. Clear Lake, of course, is one of the best bass fishing lakes in America, providing year-round shallow-water action. The lake record was caught in early 1990 and weighed more than 15 pounds. Fishing for catfish, crappie, and bluegill is also often quite good, and the lake is big enough to keep the waterskiers off the backs of the anglers.

Map grid **b4**

M & M CAMPGROUNDS
on Clear Lake

Campsites, facilities: There are 37 motor home spaces for self-contained vehicles. Flush toilets, showers, and a boat ramp are provided. Boat rentals and a grocery store are nearby. Pets are allowed.

Reservations, fee: Reservations required; $10 fee per night.

Who to contact: Phone the park at (707)998-9943.

Location: From Highway 20 in Clearlake Oaks, turn on Island Drive and go two blocks to 13050 Island Drive.

Trip note: This park has a unique setting. It is located on an island in the shaded lagoons and waterways that lead from Clear Lake into the town of Clearlake Oaks. Fishing for bass and catfish is good in the immediate area. The boat launch is a bonus. Open all year.

Map grid **b4**

AUSTIN'S CAMPGROUND AND MARINA
on Clear Lake

Campsites, facilities: There are 26 motor home spaces with water and electrical hookups. Flush toilets, showers, a sanitary disposal station, a pier, a boat ramp, a recreation room, a laundromat, propane gas and a small grocery store are available.

Reservations, fee: Reservations recommended during peak times; $13 fee per night.

Who to contact: Phone the park at (707)994-7623.

Location: In the town of Clearlake, turn off Highway 53 on Olympic Drive (toward the lake) and follow it to the end. You'll see the campground entrance signs on the other side of Lakeshore Drive.

Trip note: This camp is set on the shore of Clear Lake, the largest natural lake in California. The privately-operated park has lake frontage sites available. The lake is known for tremendous fishing in the spring for largemouth bass and for catfish in the summer. There are also big crappie and tons of bluegill. There are 100 miles of shoreline with plenty of room for waterskiers and anglers. Open year-round.

Map grid **c0**

CLOVERDALE KOA
near Russian River

Campsites, facilities: There are 58 sites for tents only and 104 motor home spaces (six are drive-through), most with full hookups. Picnic tables and fire grills are provided. Flush toilets, showers, a swimming pool, a playground, a sanitary disposal station, a laundromat, a recreation room, propane gas, and a grocery store are available. Pets are permitted.

Reservations, fee: Reservations accepted; $16-20 fee per night.

Who to contact: Phone the park at (707)894-3337.

Location: In Cloverdale on US 101, turn east on First Street and drive one mile. Turn south on River Road and drive four miles to 26460 River Road.

Trip note: This campground is just above the Russian River in the Alexander Valley wine country. In the summer, visitors primarily swim and sit around in the sun. The fishing is best in the winter when steelhead migrate through the area. Open year-round.

LOCH LOMOND PARK

Map grid C3 near Middletown

Campsites, facilities: There are 37 motor home spaces with full or partial hookups. Picnic tables, fire grills, rest rooms, and showers are provided. There is a swimming pool and grocery store across the street. No pets are permitted.
Reservations, fee: Reservations accepted but not necessary; $8-$10 fee per night.
Who to contact: Phone the park at (707)928-5044.
Location: From Middletown, drive 12 miles north on Highway 175. The park entrance is on the left.
Trip note: This park is located midway between Clear Lake and the Napa Valley and is favored primarily by seniors with motor homes. The valley setting is pretty in the spring when everything is still green, but it can get hot in the summer. Open year around.

SHAW'S SHADY ACRES

Map grid C4 on Cache Creek

Campsites, facilities: There are 16 campsites for tents or motor homes, many with partial or full hookups. Picnic tables and fire grills are provided. Rest rooms, showers, a sanitary disposal station, a pier, boat rentals, a boat ramp, a laundromat, a swimming pool, a recreation room, a beer and wine bar, fishing supplies, and a grocery store are available. Pets must be on leashes and may not be left unattended in camp.
Reservations, fee: Reservations suggested in summer; $14 fee per night; pets $.50.
Who to contact: Phone the park at (707)994-2236.
Location: From the town of Lower Lake, drive north on Highway 53 for 1.3 miles. Turn left at the Old Highway 53 turnoff. Turn back on the frontage road and drive one-quarter mile to the entrance road into park.
Trip note: This is one of three privately-operated campgrounds set beside Cache Creek, just south of Clear Lake. The catfishing is often quite good on summer nights in the creek.

END O' THE RAINBOW

Map grid C4 on Cache Creek

Campsites, facilities: There are ten motor home spaces beside the river with full hook-ups and a grassy area for tents or motor homes. Picnic tables, fire grills, and shade umbrellas are provided. Rest rooms, showers, a laundromat, a playground, a game room, fishing supplies, and a small store are available.
Reservations, fee: Reservations required on holidays; $11-$13 fee per night.
Who to contact: Phone the park at (707)994-3282.
Location: From the town of Lower Lake, drive north on Highway 53 for one mile. The campground is at the intersection of Highway 53 and Old Highway 53.
Trip note: This is one of several resorts on Cache Creek, the outlet stream that pours south from Clear Lake. Catfishing can be quite good at night from the dock at this resort. Crawdads are often available for bait from the proprietors. The nearby town of Lower Lake is one of the oldest towns in Lake County and offers numerous historic sites.

Map grid **c4**

GARNERS' RESORT
on Clear Lake

Campsites, facilities: There are 25 sites for tents only and 40 motor home spaces with full hookups. Flush toilets, showers, a sanitary disposal station, boat rentals, a pier, a boat ramp, a recreation room, a swimming pool, a wading pool, fishing supplies, a laundromat, and a grocery store are available.

Reservations, fee: Reservations accepted; $12-$13 fee per night.

Who to contact: Phone the park at (707)994-6267.

Location: From the town of Lower Lake, drive north on Highway 53 for one mile. Turn off Highway 53 on Old Highway 53 toward the lake and drive 1.5 miles to the resort.

Trip note: This is one of two privately-operated parks in the immediate area. This park offers space for tents as well as RVs. Mt. Konocti looms to the west of big, beautiful Clear Lake. Open all year.

Map grid **c5**

AZTEC RV PARK
on Cache Creek

Campsites, facilities: There are 35 motor home spaces with full or partial hookups. Rest rooms, showers, a pier, a ramp, a laundromat, and river frontage sites are available. Propane gas is available nearby. No pets are permitted.

Reservations, fee: Call ahead for availability; $15 per night.

Who to contact: Phone the park at (707)994-4377.

Location: From the town of Lower Lake, drive about 3.5 miles north on Highway 29 toward Clear Lake. Turn right on Dam Road. Drive to Tish-a-Tang Road and the campground at 16150 Tish-a-Tang Road.

Trip note: This is one of the options for motor home campers looking for a parking place beside Cache Creek, the stream that runs south out of Clear Lake. See the trip note for Garners' Resort.

Map grid **c7**

CACHE CREEK CANYON REGIONAL PARK
near Rumsey

Campsites, facilities: There are 30 campsites for tents or motor homes. Picnic tables, fireplaces, and piped water are provided. Flush toilets and a sanitary disposal station are available. Pets are permitted.

Reservations, fee: No reservations; $8-$10 fee per night; $1 for pets.

Who to contact: Phone the park at (916)666-8115.

Location: From Interstate 5, take the Highway 16 exit and drive west for about 25 miles to the town of Rumsey. From Rumsey, continue west on Highway 16 for five miles to the park entrance.

Trip note: This is the best campground in Yolo County, yet it's known by few out-of-towners. It is set beside Cache Creek, which is the closest river to the Bay Area that provides white water rafting opportunities. Catfishing can be good too. Open year-round.

Map grid **d7**

LOWER HUNTING CREEK
near Lake Berryessa

Campsites, facilities: There are five campsites for tents or motor homes. Piped water, picnic tables, fireplaces, shade shelters, and vault toilets are provided. Pets are permitted on leashes or otherwise controlled.

Reservations, fee: No reservations; No fee.
Who to contact: Phone the Bureau of Land Management at (707)462-3873.
Location: From Highway 29 in the town of Lower Lake (near Clear Lake), turn on Morgan Valley Road (Berryessa-Knoxville Road) and drive 15 miles southeast. Turn south on Devilhead Road and drive two miles to the campground.
Trip note: This little-known camp might seem like it's out in the middle of nowhere for the folks who wind up here accidentally (we did). If you plan on a few days here, it's advisable to get information or a map of the surrounding area from the Bureau of Land Management prior to your trip. In the fall, this makes a good base camp for hunters. Open year-round.

Map grid f0

MIRABEL TRAILER PARK AND CAMPGROUND
on Russian River

Campsites, facilities: There are 125 sites for tents or motor homes, many with full or partial hookups. Picnic tables and fire grills are provided. Flush toilets, showers, an indoor sports area, a playground, a laundromat, a sanitary disposal station, and canoe rentals are available.
Reservations, fee: Reservations suggested; $14-$16 fee per night.
Who to contact: Phone the park at (707)887-2383.
Location: From US 101 north of Santa Rosa, take the River Road exit. Drive eight miles west to 7600 River Road.
Trip note: The big attraction here during the summer is swimming. This privately-operated park is set near the Russian River. In summer, the "river" is actually a series of small lakes, with temporary dams stopping most of the water flow. In winter, out come the dams, up comes the water, and in come the steelhead, migrating upstream past this area. Armstrong Redwoods State Park provides a nearby trip option. Open from March through October.

Map grid f0

SCHOOLHOUSE CANYON CAMPGROUND
near Russian River

Campsites, facilities: There are 29 sites for tents or motor homes. Picnic tables and fire grills are provided. Piped water, flush toilets, showers, and wood are available.
Reservations, fee: Reservations accepted; $15 fee per night.
Who to contact: Phone the park at (707)869-2311.
Location: From Highway 116 in Guerneville, turn east on River Road (Main Street) and drive four miles to the campground.
Trip note: This is one of several options in the Guerneville area. By the way, pronounce it "Gernville" and not "Gurneyville," and the locals won't look at you like you have antlers growing out of your head. The shaded campgrounds and close proximity to the Russian River are bonuses. Closed October through April.

Map grid f0

BURKE'S RESORT AND CANOE TRIPS
on Russian River

Campsites, facilities: There are 60 sites for tents or motor homes. Picnic tables and fire grills are provided. Flush toilets, showers, wood, and canoe rentals are available. Pets not permitted.
Reservations, fee: Reservations suggested; $10 fee per night.

Who to contact: Phone the park at (707)887-1222.

Location: From US 101 north of Santa Rosa, take the River Road exit. Drive 8.3 miles west to the campground. Or take Highway 116 west to Forestville and make a right on Mirabel Road (at stop sign across street).

Trip note: This camp makes a prime jump-off spot for a canoe trip, since the folks here provide rentals and shuttle service. The Russian River is a lazy river during the summer, fine for making the canoe trip with kids or newcomers. More experienced paddlers will want to make the trip in the spring, when the flows are still high enough to cause some excitement. Open year-round, with limited facilities in the winter.

Map grid f0

RIVER BEND CAMPGROUND
on Russian River

Campsites, facilities: There are 108 sites for tents or motor homes, many with full hookups (including cable TV). Picnic tables and fire rings are provided. Piped water, flush toilets, showers, a playground, a laundromat, a recreation room, a dog walking area, canoe and tube rentals, a volleyball court, propane gas (on Fridays), and a grocery store are available. Pets are permitted in the RV section of the campground only.

Reservations, fee: Reservations accepted; $18-$30 fee per night.

Who to contact: Phone the park at (707)887-7662.

Location: From US 101 north of Santa Rosa, take the River Road-Guerneville exit west. Drive 11 miles on River Road to the campground (on the left after the bridge).

Trip note: This privately-owned campground offers grassy sites beside the Russian River. For most folks, that's enough right there, but you can also use it as a home base for side trips to the coast or nearby Armstrong Redwoods State Park.

Map grid f1

WINDSORLAND RV PARK
near Santa Rosa

Campsites, facilities: There are ten sites for tents only and 55 motor home spaces with full hookups. Patios are provided. Flush toilets, showers, a swimming pool, a sanitary disposal station, a laundromat, a recreation room, a swimming pool, and a playground are available.

Reservations, fee: Reservations not needed; $22 fee per night.

Who to contact: Phone the park at (707)838-4882.

Location: From Santa Rosa, drive nine miles north on US 101. Take the Windsor exit and drive one-quarter mile north to 9290 Old Redwood Highway.

Trip note: Location is always the key. The Russian River and Lake Sonoma are near this campground, which is a developed park set up primarily for motor homes. Open all year.

Map grid f3

NAPA COUNTY FAIRGROUNDS
in Calistoga

Campsites, facilities: There are 50 drive-through campsites with water and electrical hookups and a lawn area for tents. Group sites are available by reservation only. Rest rooms, showers, and a sanitary disposal station are available. No fires are permitted. A nine-hole golf course is adjacent to the campground area.

Reservations, fee: No reservations (except for groups); $10-12 fee per night.

Who to contact: Phone the campground at (707)942-5111.

Location: From Route 29 in Calistoga, turn on Lincoln Avenue (the main street through town). Drive four blocks to Fairway and turn left. Drive to the end.

Trip note: What this really is, folks, is just the county fairground, converted to a motor home park for 11 months each year. It is closed to camping from mid-June through mid-July, but what the heck, you can stick around and try to win a stuffed animal. Surrounding attractions include health spas, mud baths, and the wine country.

A B C D1 E F G H I J

Map grid **f4**

CALISTOGA RANCH CAMPGROUND
near Calistoga

Campsites, facilities: There are 60 sites for tents only and 84 motor home spaces with full or partial hookups. Picnic tables and fire grills provided. Flush toilets, showers, a sanitary disposal station, a laundromat, a lake, a swimming pool, and a snack bar are available.

Reservations, fee: Reservations accepted; $16 to $20 fee per night.

Who to contact: Phone the park at (707)942-6565.

Location: From Highway 29 between Calistoga and St. Helena, turn east onto Larkmead Lane and then left (north) on Silverado Trail. Drive 200 yards before turning right on Lommel Road. It's a quarter mile to the campground.

Trip note: This is a large, privately-run camp set in the heart of the wine country, near the famous Calistoga spas and mud baths. And if you think it feels weird to sink into a hot tub of ooze, well, you're right. Open year-round.

Map grid **f4**

BOTHE-NAPA VALLEY STATE PARK
near Calistoga

Campsites, facilities: There are nine sites for tents only and 49 campsites for tents or motor homes up to 31 feet long. Picnic tables, fireplaces, and piped water are provided. Flush toilets, showers, a sanitary disposal station, and a swimming pool (in the summer) are available. The facilities are wheelchair accessible. Pets are permitted. Supplies can be obtained in Calistoga or St. Helena.

Reservations, fee: Reserve through MISTIX at (800)444-PARK ($3.95 MISTIX fee); $12-$14 fee per night; pets $1.

Who to contact: Phone the park at (707)942-4575.

Location: From St. Helena, drive four miles north on Highway 29 to the park entrance on the left. From Calistoga, drive four miles south on Highway 29 to the park entrance on the right.

Trip note: Finding Bothe-Napa State Park often comes as a major surprise for folks touring the Napa Valley wine-and-mud-bath country. Though the campsites are grouped, the park itself is relatively secluded compared to the nearby valley. The park offers some good hiking trails. Besides the obvious, side trips include visiting the restored Bale Grist Mill Historical Park nearby. Open year-round.

Map grid **f7**

RANCHO MONTICELLO RESORT
on Lake Berryessa

Campsites, facilities: There are 200 campsites for tents or motor homes, some with full hookups. Picnic tables, fireplaces, and piped water are provided. Rest rooms, showers, a snack bar, complete marina facilities, ice, propane gas, and groceries are available.

Reservations, fee: Reservations suggested; $17-$19 fee per night.

Who to contact: Phone (707)966-2188.

on Lake Berryessa

Location: From Vallejo, drive north on Interstate 80 to the Suisun Valley Road exit. Take Suisun Valley Road to Highway 121. Turn north on Highway 121 and drive five miles. Turn north (left) on Highway 128 and drive five miles. Turn north (right) onto Berryessa-Knoxville Road and drive ten miles to 6590 Knoxville Road.

Trip note: This is a fully-developed, privately-operated park set on the shore of Lake Berryessa. Berryessa is the third largest manmade lake in Northern California, smaller than only Shasta and Oroville. It is a popular spot for water skiing and fishing.

Map grid f7

PUTAH CREEK PARK
on Lake Berryessa

Campsites, facilities: There are 130 sites for tents or motor homes, many with full or partial hookups. Rest rooms, showers, a sanitary disposal station, a laundromat, a boat ramp, rowboat rentals, a snack bar, a restaurant, propane gas, ice, and groceries are available.

Reservations, fee: Reservations suggested; $13-$17 fee per night.

Who to contact: Phone the park at (707)966-2116.

Location: From Vallejo, drive north on Interstate 80 to the Suisun Valley Road exit. Take Suisun Valley Road to Highway 121. Turn north on Highway 121 and drive five miles. Turn north (left) on Highway 128 and drive five miles. Turn north (right) onto Berryessa-Knoxville Road and drive 13 miles to 7600 Knoxville Road.

Trip note: This campground is set on the northern end of Lake Berryessa. The Putah Creek arm provides very good bass fishing in the spring, and trout trolling in the summer. In the fall, usually by mid-October, the trout come to the surface and provide excellent fishing at the mouth of Pope Creek or Putah Creek for anglers drifting live minnows. This resort also has cabin rentals. Open all year.

Map grid g2

SPRING LAKE REGIONAL PARK
in Santa Rosa

Campsites, facilities: There are three sites for tents only and 28 campsites for tents or motor homes of any length. Picnic tables, fireplaces, and piped water are provided. Flush toilets, showers, a sanitary disposal station, a boat ramp (no motorboats), boat rentals, and bike paths are available. Pets are permitted with proof of rabies vaccination. A grocery store, a laundromat, and propane gas are available nearby.

Reservations, fee: Reservations accepted; $11 fee per night; pets $1.

Who to contact: Phone the park at (707)539-8082.

Location: From US 101 in Santa Rosa, drive east on Highway 12 until it becomes Hoen Avenue. Turn left on New Angle Avenue and drive to the park at the end of the road.

Trip note: Spring Lake is one of the few lakes in the greater Bay Area that provides lakeside camping. Not only that, Spring Lake is stocked twice each month with rainbow trout by the Department of Fish and Game, providing water temperatures are cool enough. Open from mid-May through mid-September and on weekends and holidays during the off-season.

Map grid g4 — SUGARLOAF RIDGE STATE PARK

near Santa Rosa

Campsites, facilities: There are 50 campsites for tents or motor homes up to 27 feet long. Picnic tables, fireplaces, piped water, and flush toilets are provided. Pets are permitted.

Reservations, fee: Reserve through MISTIX at (800)444-PARK ($3.95 MISTIX fee); $12-$14 fee per night; pets $1.

Who to contact: Phone the park at (707)833-5712.

Location: From US 101 in Santa Rosa, drive seven miles east on Highway 12. Turn north on Adobe Canyon Road and drive three miles (the last mile is on a steep and winding road) to the campground.

Trip note: This is a pretty state park set in the hills east of Santa Rosa, and one that gets missed by a lot of out of towners. Hiking is the primary attraction, with many trails through the surrounding wildlands (detailed on the park brochure). Summer and fall can be quite hot. Open year-round.

Map grid g7 — LAKE BERRYESSA MARINA RESORT

Campsites, facilities: There are 70 sites for tents only and 52 motor home spaces with water and electrical hookups. Flush toilets, showers, a sanitary disposal station, a recreation room, a laundromat, propane gas, a snack bar, complete marina facilities, RV supplies, and groceries are available.

Reservations, fee: Reservations recommended; $14 fee per night.

Who to contact: Phone (707)966-2161.

Location: From Vallejo, drive north on Interstate 80 to the Suisun Valley Road exit. Take Suisun Valley Road to Highway 121. Turn north on Highway 121 and drive five miles. Turn north (left) on Highway 128 and drive five miles. Turn north (right) onto Berryessa-Knoxville Road and drive nine miles to 5800 Knoxville Road.

Trip note: This is one of several campgrounds set on the shore of Lake Berryessa. Open all year.

Map grid g7 — STEELE PARK RESORT

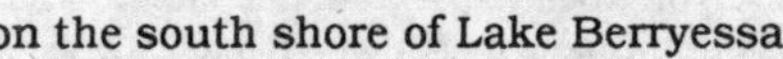

on the south shore of Lake Berryessa

Campsites, facilities: There are 250 sites for tents or motor homes, a few with full or partial hookups. Picnic tables and fire grills are provided. Rest rooms, showers, playground, a sanitary disposal station, a laundromat, a boat ramp, boat rentals, a water skiing school, and a grocery store are available.

Reservations, fee: Reservations recommended; $16 fee per night.

Who to contact: Phone (707)966-2123.

Location: From Vallejo, drive north on Interstate 80 to the Suisun Valley Road exit. Take Suisun Valley Road to Highway 121. Turn north on Highway 121 and drive 5.5 miles. Turn left on Highway 128 and drive 200 yards. Turn right onto Steele Canyon Road and drive five miles to the resort.

Trip note: This is one of the more developed parks at Lake Berryessa, complete with private patrol, store, and apartment rentals with lake views. I met some nice folks here. During the spring evenings, the bass fishing is often good along the shore for anglers in boats; cast toward the dock areas.

Map grid g7 SPANISH FLAT RESORT

on Lake Berryessa

Campsites, facilities: There are 123 campsites for tents or motor homes, a few with partial hookups. Picnic tables, fireplaces, and piped water are provided. Flush toilets, showers, a boat launch, complete marina facilities, boat rentals, and groceries are available. A laundromat, restaurant, post office, and RV supplies are nearby.

Reservations, fee: Reservations accepted; $12-$14 fee per night.

Who to contact: Phone (707)966-7700.

Location: From Vallejo, drive north on Interstate 80 to the Suisun Valley Road exit. Take Suisun Valley Road to Highway 121. Turn north on Highway 121 and drive ten miles. Turn north (left) on Highway 128 and drive five miles. Turn north (right) onto Berryessa-Knoxville Road and drive four miles to 4290 Knoxville Road.

Trip note: This is one of several lakeside camps at Lake Berryessa. Berryessa, considered the Bay Area's backyard fishing hole, is the third largest man-made lake in Northern California (Shasta and Oroville lakes are bigger). It is a popular lake for power boating, water skiing, and fishing. Trout fishing is good, trolling deep in the summer or drifting with minnows in fall and winter. Open all year.

Map grid g8 PLEASURE COVE RESORT

on Lake Berryessa

Campsites, facilities: There are 105 campsites for tents or motor homes (20 sites have water and electrical hookups). Picnic tables and fireplaces are provided. Rest rooms, showers, ice, a restaurant, a bar, a boat ramp, propane gas, and groceries are available. Pets are permitted.

Reservations, fee: Reservations accepted $12-15 fee per night for camping, plus $7 entrance fee; pets $2.

Who to contact: Phone (707)966-2172.

Location: From Vallejo, drive north on Interstate 80 to the Suisun Valley Road exit. Take Suisun Valley Road to Highway 121. Turn north on Highway 121 and drive ten miles. Turn southeast (right) on Highway 128 and drive four miles to Wragg Canyon Road. Turn north (left) to the resort on the south shore.

Trip note: This family-oriented park would make a good base camp for a camping, boating, or fishing adventure. The trout fishing is good in the southern arms of the lake, either trolling 40 to 50 feet deep in summer or, in fall or winter, drifting with live minnows.

Map grid h6 NAPA TOWN AND COUNTRY FAIRGROUNDS

in Napa

Campsites, facilities: There are 100 designated motor home spaces, many with electrical and water hookups, and an open area with space for 500 self-contained units. Rest rooms, showers, and a sanitary disposal station are provided. A laundromat, grocery store, and restaurant are within walking distance. Pets are permitted on leashes.

Reservations, fee: No reservations except for groups of 15 or more; $15 fee per night.

Who to contact: For group reservations phone (707)253-4900. For information phone (707)253-4905.

Location: From Highway 29 in Napa, take the Napa-Lake Berryessa exit and drive to Third street. Turn right and drive to Burnell Street and you will see the entrance to the campground.

Trip note: This privately-operated motor home park is located in Napa, providing easy access for shopping needs. It is open year-round, with the notable exception of Memorial Day Weekend and a period in early August. Call ahead to confirm availability.

Map grid h9 **LAKE SOLANO COUNTY PARK**
near Lake Berryessa

Campsites, facilities: There are 50 sites for tents or motor homes up to 35 feet long. Piped water, fireplaces, and tables are provided. A sanitary disposal station, flush toilets, showers, a boat ramp, and boat rentals are available. A grocery store is nearby. Some facilities are wheelchair accessible. Pets accepted with proof of vaccination.

Reservations, fee: Reservations accepted; $10-$12 fee per night; pets $1.

Who to contact: Phone Lake Solano County Park at (916)795-2990.

Location: From Winters on Interstate 505, turn west on Highway 128 and drive 4.5 miles. Turn south (left) on Pleasant Valley Road and drive to the park at 8685 Pleasant Valley Road.

Trip note: Lake Solano provides a little-known option to nearby Lake Berryessa. Some folks prefer it. It can also be used as an overflow area. This long, narrow lake gets quite hot weather in the summer and is stocked with fish in the spring. Open year-round.

Map grid i2 **SAN FRANCISCO NORTH/PETALUMA KOA**
near Petaluma

Campsites, facilities: There are 312 sites for tents or motor homes (161 drive-through), many with full or partial hookups. Picnic tables and fire grills are provided. Flush toilets, showers, cable TV hookups, a sanitary disposal station, a playground, recreation rooms, a swimming pool, a jacuzzi, a petting zoo, shuffleboard, a laundromat, propane gas, and a grocery store are available. Some facilities are wheelchair accessible. Pets are permitted.

Reservations, fee: Reservations recommended; $20-25 fee per night.

Who to contact: Phone park at (707)763-1492.

Location: From US 101 in Petaluma, take the Penngrove exit and drive west for one-quarter mile on Petaluma Boulevard. Turn north on Stony Point Road, then west on Rainsville Road and drive to 20 Rainsville Road.

Trip note: This campground is less than a mile from US 101, yet it has a rural feel to it. It's an okay layover spot for folks who need a day of mental preparation before heading south to the Bay Area or to the nearby wineries, redwoods, and the Russian River. Open year-round.

◆ MAP D2 ◆

BEACH
TREES
5% CLUB
DESERT
URBAN
FOOTHILL
GRASSLAND

15 MILES

to Maxwell
to Princeton
to Gridley
to Oroville
to Bangor
to Williams
to Rumsey
to Brooks
to Napa
to Fairfield
to Oregon House
to Smartville
to Newcastle
to Cameron Park
to Plymouth
to Birds Landing
to Walnut Grove
to Galt

COLUSA SACRAMENTO RIVER ST. REC. AREA
Colusa
COLUSA NAT'L. WILDLIFE REF.
Williams
Live Oak
Honcut
Feather River
Meridian
Sycamore
Sutter
Browns Valley
Yuba City
Marysville
Yuba River
Smartville
Grimes
Sacramento River
Arbuckle
Linda
Olivehurst
BEALE AIR FORCE BASE
SPENCEVILLE WILDLIFE MNGMT. AND REC. AREA
Tudor
Rio Oso
Wheatland
Dunnigan
Kirkville
Sheridan
Nicolaus
Zamora
Lincoln
Knights Landing
Verona
Capay
Madison
Yolo
Pleasant Grove
Loomis
Woodland
Roseville
Rio Linda
Rock-lin
Winters
MCCLELLAN A.F.B.
Carmichael
Folsom
Lake Natoma
American River
Davis
Rancho Cordova
Sacramento
MATHER A.F.B.
Dixon
Florin
Sloughhouse
Elmira
Clarksburg
Hood
Elk Grove
TRAVIS AIR FORCE BASE
Courtland
Clay

45, 99, 20, 5, 45, 70, 113, 99, 65, 193, E4, E10, 99, 16, 5, 113, E8, 80, 80, E7, 80, 505, 50, E9, 16, 80, E2, 5, 160, J8, 99, 104

a b c d e f g h i j

0 1 2 3 4 5 6 7 8 9

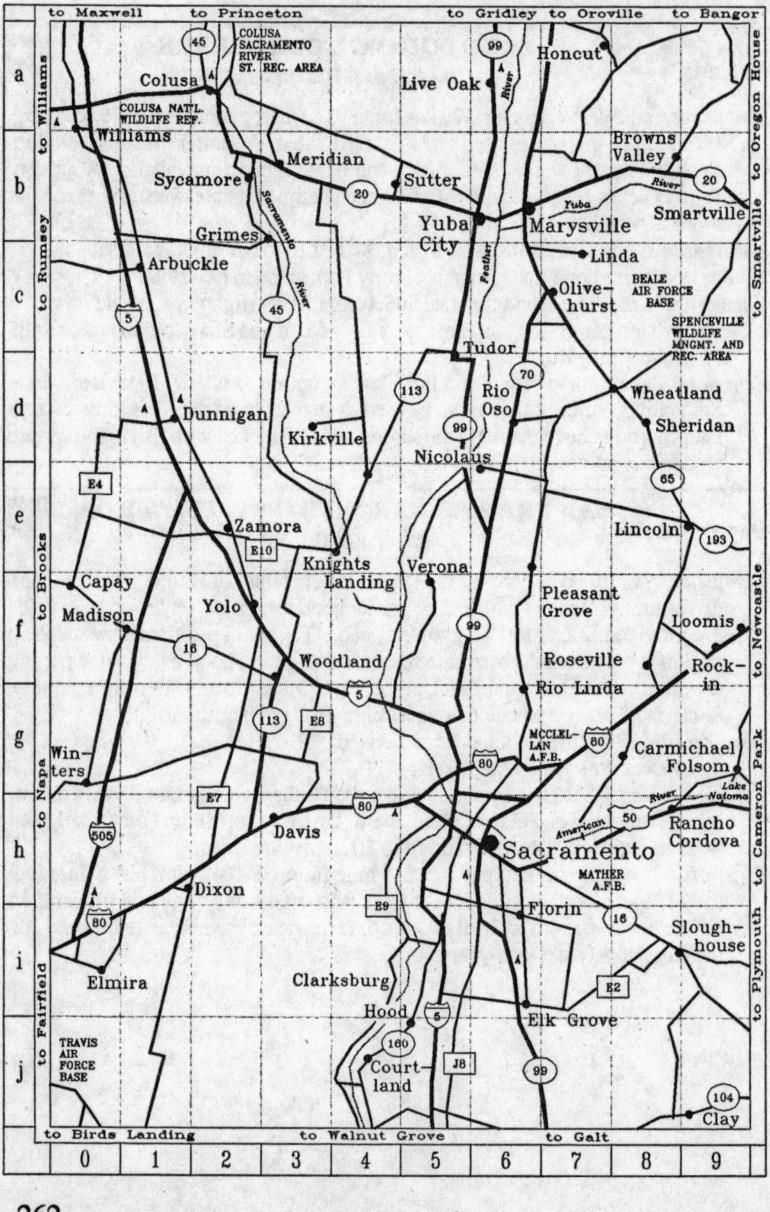

Map grid a0 ALMOND GROVE MOBILE HOME PARK

in Williams

A

Campsites, facilities: This is a mobile home park with one tent site and 16 motor home spaces with full hookups. Picnic tables, rest rooms, and showers are provided. A laundromat is available. Pets are permitted. A store is nearby.

B

Reservations, fee: Reservations accepted; $11 fee per night.

Who to contact: Phone (916)473-5620.

Location: From Interstate 5 in Williams, take the Williams exit and drive one mile west on E Street. Turn left on 12th Street and drive three blocks to the mobile home park at 880 12th Street.

C

Trip note: This is a good overnight spot for motor home cruisers in the Central Valley. Williams is known for its outstanding delicatessen (Granzella's), its Italian restaurant (Louie Cairo's), and the Sacramento Valley Museum. Open year-round.

Map grid a2 COLUSA-SACRAMENTO RIVER STATE RECREATION AREA

near Colusa

D2

Campsites, facilities: There are 20 campsites for tents or motor homes up to 27 feet long. Rest rooms, hot showers, a sanitary dump station, picnic tables, and fireplaces are provided. A grocery store and laundromat are nearby. A boat ramp is available.

E

Reservations, fee: Reserve through MISTIX at (800)444-PARK ($3.95 MISTIX fee); $12-$14 fee per night; pets $1 each.

Who to contact: Phone (916)458-4927.

Location: From the junction of Interstate 5 and Highway 20 near Williams, drive east on Highway 20 for ten miles to the town of Colusa. Drive north on 10th street for a short distance to the park.

F

Trip note: This is a good base camp in the winter for hunting. There is excellent duck in the Colusa Basin, in particular at Delevan National Wildlife Refuge. In summer months, the nearby Sacramento River is a bonus because of the good shad fishing in June and July, the salmon fishing from August through October, and the sturgeon fishing in the winter. Open year-round.

G

Map grid a6 LIVE OAK PARK

near Yuba City

H

Campsites, facilities: There are 12 campsites for tents or motor homes up to 30 feet long. Picnic tables, piped water, and portable toilets are provided. A grocery store, a laundromat, and propane gas are available in the town of Live Oak. Pets are permitted.

Reservations, fee: No reservations, no fee.

I

Who to contact: Phone the park at (916)741-7405.

Location: From Yuba City, drive 8.5 miles north on Highway 99. At Live Oak, turn east on Pennington Road and drive one mile to 1100 Pennington Road.

Trip note: This is the only game in town, so if you're looking for a spot to get some shuteye for the night, you'd best pick this one--the only campground in the county. It is set adjacent to the Grey Lodge Wildlife Refuge, which attracts a wide variety of waterfowl. The Sutter Buttes to the immediate south are a dramatic sight on clear, spring days.

J

Map grid **d1**

CAMPERS INN
near Dunnigan

Campsites, facilities: There are 13 sites for tents only and 59 motor home spaces (44 drive-through) with full or partial hookups and picnic tables. Flush toilets, showers, a heated pool, a clubhouse, a game room, horseshoes, a nine hole golf course, a laundromat, propane gas, ice, and groceries are available. The facilities are wheelchair accessible.

Reservations, fee: Reservations accepted; $16 fee per night.

Who to contact: Phone the park at (916)724-3350.

Location: From Interstate 5, take the Dunnigan exit (near the Interstate 505 cut-off). Drive west on County Road E-4 for one mile. Turn north on County Road 88 and drive for 1.5 miles.

Trip note: This private park's rural atmosphere makes it a good layover spot before hitting the Bay Area. The Sacramento River, located to the east, is the closest body of water. There are no nearby lakes. Driving the county roads in the area makes for a possible side trip. Open all year.

Map grid **d1**

HAPPY TIME RV PARK
near Dunnigan

Campsites, facilities: There are eight sites for tents only and 30 motor home spaces (18 drive-through) with full hookups and picnic tables. Flush toilets, showers, a playground, a laundromat, a small pool and propane gas are available.

Reservations, fee: Reservations accepted; $15 fee per night.

Who to contact: Phone (916)724-3336.

Location: From Interstate 5 near the Interstate 505 intersection, take the County Road 8 exit. Drive east on County Road 8 for a short distance to Road 99W. Turn left (north) and drive one block to the campground.

Trip note: This is a good layover spot for highway cruisers who need to take a deep breath before hitting the Bay Area or Sacramento. The Sacramento River is nearby, to the east. The State Historical Park and the Railroad Museum are in Sacramento, one-half hour away. Open year-round.

Map grid **h0**

NEIL'S VINEYARD RV PARK
near Vacaville

Campsites, facilities: There are ten sites for tents only and 90 motor home sites (20 drive-through), many with full or partial hookups and picnic tables. Flush toilets, showers, a swimming pool, a laundromat, a sanitary disposal station, a recreation room, and ice are available. Pets are permitted.

Reservations, fee: Reservations recommended; $16-$18 fee per night.

Who to contact: Phone (707)447-8797 or write to 4985 Midway Road, Vacaville, CA 95688.

Location: From the junction of Interstate 80 and Interstate 505, drive three miles north on Interstate 505. Turn east on Midway Road and travel one-half mile to the campground.

Trip note: This is one of two privately-operated parks set up primarily for motor homes.

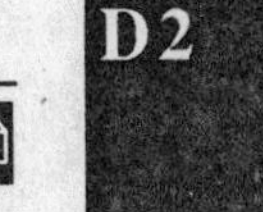

Map grid **h0**

GANDY DANCER

near Vacaville

Campsites, facilities: There are 20 sites for tents only and 70 motor home sites (46 drive-through), many with full or partial hookups and picnic tables. Flush toilets, showers, a swimming pool, a children's pool, a laundromat, a sanitary disposal station, ice, and wood are available. Pets are permitted.

Reservations, fee: Reservations recommended; $16 fee per night.

Who to contact: Phone (707)446-7679 or write to 4933 Midway Road, Vacaville, CA 95688.

Location: From the junction of Interstate 80 and Interstate 505, drive three miles north on Interstate 505. Turn east on Midway Road and travel one-quarter mile to the campground.

Trip note: This layover spot for motor home cruisers is set near the Nut Tree, a famous restaurant for travelers. Marine World U.S.A. in Vallejo is located within a half-hour's drive. This is one of two motor home parks in the area. Open year-round.

Map grid **h4**

SACRAMENTO-METRO KOA

Campsites, facilities: There are 49 sites for tents only and 95 motor home spaces with full hookups. Flush toilets, showers, a playground, a swimming pool, a recreation room, a laundromat, propane gas, and groceries are available. Pets are permitted.

Reservations, fee: Reservations recommended; $18-$22 fee per night.

Who to contact: Phone the park at (916)371-6771.

Location: From Interstate 80 in Sacramento, take the West Capitol Avenue exit. Drive one block south on Enterprise Road. Turn left on Lake Road and drive to 4851 Lake Road.

Trip note: This is the choice of car and motor home campers touring California's capital, looking for a layover spot. It is located in downtown Sacramento near the Capitol and the railroad museum. Open year-round.

Map grid **h5**

STILLMAN TRAILER PARK

in Sacramento

Campsites, facilities: There are 50 motor home spaces with full hookups. Flush toilets, showers, laundromat, a recreation room, and a swimming pool are available. Adults only.

Reservations, fee: Call for available space; $20 fee per night.

Who to contact: Phone the park at (916)392-2820.

Location: From Highway 99 in Sacramento, take the 47th Avenue West exit and go to the first light. Take a right and the park will be just ahead (On Martin Luther King Blvd.).

Trip note: This is an adults-only motor home park located in downtown Sacramento near the Capitol and the railroad museum. It's a popular layover spot in summer months.

Map grid **i6**

99 TRAILER PARK

near Sacramento

Campsites, facilities: There are 23 motor home spaces with full hookups including phone, plus two sites with partial hookups. There are no separate rest room facilities. Weekly residents preferred. A grocery store, a laundromat, and propane gas are available nearby.

Reservations, fee: Call ahead for available space and fee.

Who to contact: Phone the park at (916)423-4078.

Location: From Sacramento, drive south on Highway 99. Take the Sheldon Road exit. Drive west to Stockton Boulevard (frontage road). Turn right and drive one-tenth of a mile to the park.

Trip note: This is a popular motor home park for folks touring Sacramento because it's about a five-minute drive from the city. Most of the spaces are tree shaded, and it's a good thing, because Sacramento does a good job of imitating a furnace in summer. Maybe it's all the hot air emanating from the mouths of politicians. Side trips include all the sights of California's capital city, of course, and the nearby Consumnes River.

• MAP D3 •

BEACH
TREES
5% CLUB
DESERT
URBAN
FOOTHILL
GRASSLAND

15 MILES

to Brownsville to Camptonville to Goodyears Bar

Bullards Bar Res.
River
Alleghany
Graniteville
Oregon House
Dobbins
N. San Juan
Collins Lake
MALAKOFF DIGGINS ST. HIST. PK.
Bowman Lake
Jackson Meadow Reservoir
N. Columbia
N. Bloomfield
TAHOE
Yuba
49
Washington
Englebright Lake
Rough and Ready
Nevada City
20
Lake Spalding
Fordyce Lake
80
20
Emigrant Gap
Cisco Grove
Grass Valley
Penn Valley
EMPIRE MINE ST. HIST. PK.
SPENCEVILLE WILDLIFE MANAGEMENT AND REC. AREA
174
NAT'L.
River
American
Colfax
49
Iowa Hill
80
Fork
FOREST
Weimar
Forest-hill
Michigan Bluff
Meadow Vista
Applegate
French Meadows Reservoir
North
Bowman
Hell Hole Res.
Volcanoville
New-castle
193
ELDORADO
Auburn
Green-wood
George-town
193
Wentworth Springs
Loon Lake
Pilot Hill
Garden Valley
193
Loomis
Robbs PK. EL. 6,686
49
FOLSOM ST. REC. AREA
South
Lotus
NAT'L.
Union Valley Res.
Kelsey
Folsom Lake
MARSHALL GOLD DISCOVERY ST. PK.
Fork
American
River
Pollock Pines
Placer-ville
Camino
River-ton
Ice House Reservoir
Cameron Park
Pacific House
50
50
El Dorado Hills
Clarks-ville
Shingle Springs
Diamond Springs
Jenkinson Lake
E16
Somerset
49
Latrobe
Grizzly Flats
16
River Pines
E16
Fiddletown
FOREST
Plymouth
Drytown
Amador City
INDIAN GRINDING ROCK ST. HIST. PK.
Volcano
88
104
124
Pioneer
Salt Springs Reservoir

to Ione to Jackson

to Browns Valley
to Rockin to Lincoln
to El Dorado
to Clay to Sloughhouse
to H-89
to Soda Springs
to Twin Bridges
to Kit Carson

a b c d e f g h i j

0 1 2 3 4 5 6 7 8 9

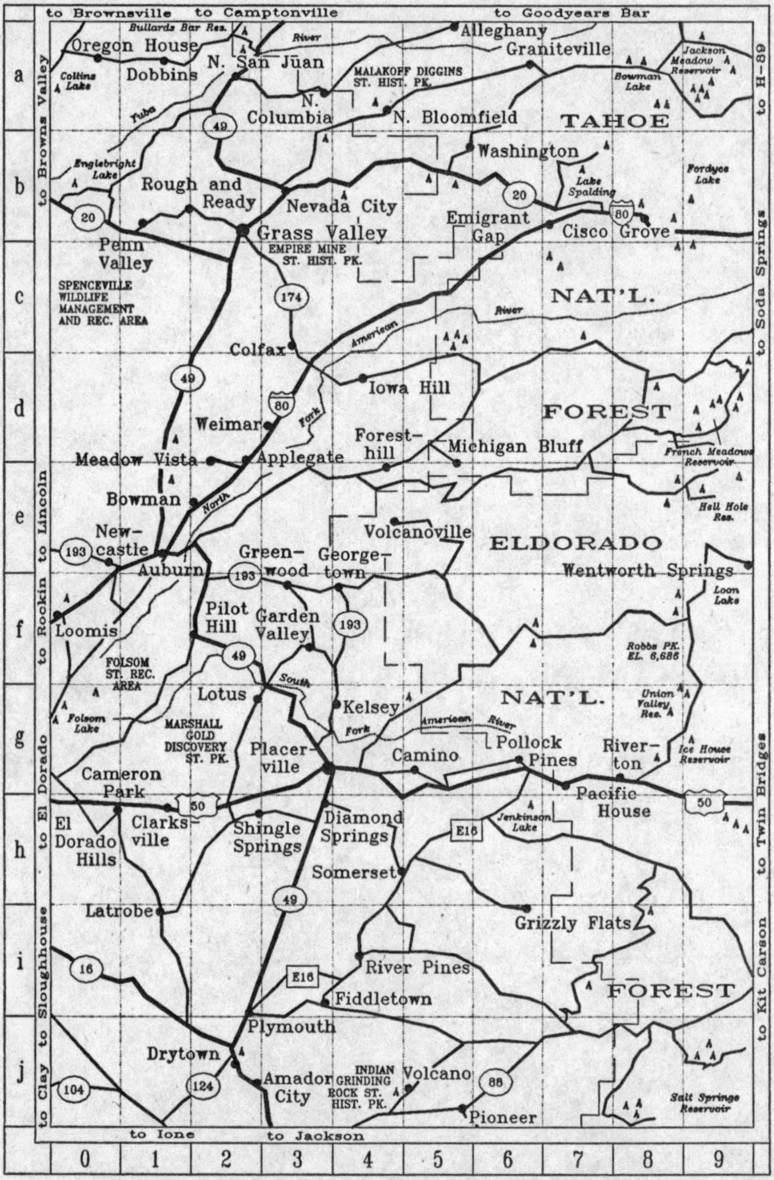

Map grid **a0**

COLLINS LAKE RECREATION AREA
near Marysville

Campsites, facilities: There are 210 campsites for tents or motor homes (20 sites are drive-through), many with full or partial hookups. Picnic tables, fireplaces, and piped water are provided. Flush toilets, sanitary disposal station, showers (fee charged), a boat ramp, boat rentals, a sandy swimming beach, a marina, a grocery store, wood, ice, and propane gas are available.

Reservations, fee: Reservations recommended; $10-$15 fee per night.

Who to contact: Phone the campground at (916)692-1600.

Location: From the intersection of Highways 70 and 20 in Marysville, drive 12 miles east on Highway 20. Turn north and drive ten miles on Marysville Road to the entrance to the recreation area.

Trip note: Collins Lake is 1600 acres and premium water for anglers. It is known especially for good trout fishing in the spring and early summer, with a sprinkling of black bass and catfish a bonus. Water skiing and swimming are also options. Open year-round.

Map grid **a2**

MOONSHINE CAMPGROUND
on Yuba River near Bullards Bar Reservoir

Campsites, facilities: There are 25 campsites for tents or motor homes. Picnic tables, fire rings, electrical connections, and piped water are provided. Vault toilets, ice, and firewood are available. A grocery store and propane gas are available in North San Juan.

Reservations, fee: Reservations required; $14-$19 fee per night.

Who to contact: Phone the campground at (916)288-3585.

Location: From Nevada City, drive 14 miles north on Highway 49 through North San Juan. After crossing the bridge over the Middle Fork of the Yuba River, turn left on Moonshine Road and drive three-quarters of a mile to the campground.

Trip note: The campground offers shady sites and a nice swimming hole on the Middle Fork of the Yuba River. It is near Bullards Bar Reservoir, about seven miles from a three-lane concrete boat ramp operated by the Forest Service at Dark Day Picnic Area.

Map grid **a2**

HORNSWOGGLE GROUP CAMP
on Bullards Bar Reservoir
TAHOE NATIONAL FOREST

Campsites, facilities: There are four 25-person group campsites and one 50-person group campsite. Picnic tables, fireplaces, piped water, and flush and vault toilets are provided. Central parking and a campfire circle are also provided. A boat ramp is nearby. Pets are permitted if they are quiet and on leashes or otherwise controlled. Supplies are available in North San Juan, Camptonville, Dobbins, and at the marina.

Reservations, fee: Reservations requested; contact MISTIX at (800)283-CAMP ($6 MISTIX fee); $25-$50 fee per night per group.

Who to contact: Phone the Tahoe National Forest Ranger Station at (916)288-3231.

Location: From Camptonville, drive 2.5 miles south on Highway 49. Turn west on Marysville Road and drive four miles to the campground on the right. Or, from Marysville, drive 11 miles east on Highway 20. Turn north on Marysville Road and travel 21 miles north past Browns Valley and Dobbins to the reservoir. This campground is across the road from Schoolhouse camp.

Trip note: This camp is designed for group use. It's about two miles from the three-lane concrete boat ramp at the Dark Day Picnic Area. Options include boat-in camping at the lake. The elevation is 2,300 feet. Open all year.

Map grid a4

MALAKOFF DIGGINS STATE HISTORICAL PARK

Campsites, facilities: There are 30 campsites for tents or motor homes up to 24 feet long. Piped water, flush toilets, picnic tables, and fireplaces are provided. There is a small grocery store nearby. Pets are permitted.

Reservations, fee: Reserve through MISTIX at (800)444-PARK ($3.95 MISTIX fee); $12-$14 camping fee per night; pets $1.

Who to contact: Phone (916)265-2740.

Location: From Nevada City, drive eight miles north on Highway 49 to the junction of Tyler Foote Crossing Road. Turn right and drive for 16 miles to the park. The last few miles are over a steep gravel road.

Trip note: This camp is set near a small lake in the park, but the main attraction of the area is the history. The area was formerly a gold mining center, and there are tours available during summer months to the numerous historic sites. The elevation is 3,400 feet. Open year-round.

Map grid a8

JACKSON CREEK

near Bowman Lake

TAHOE NATIONAL FOREST

Campsites, facilities: There are 14 tent sites. There is **no piped water,** but vault toilets, picnic tables, and fireplaces are provided. Pack out your garbage. Pets are permitted if they are quiet and on leashes or otherwise controlled.

Reservations, fee: No reservations, no fee.

Who to contact: Phone the Tahoe National Forest Headquarters at (916)265-4531.

Location: The most direct access is to start from Nevada City and drive 22 miles on Highway 20 to Bowman Road. Turn north and travel 16 miles (the last ten miles are gravel) to the campground. However the Forest Service recommends that passenger vehicles and trailers start in Nevada City and take Highway 49 north for eight miles to the junction of Tyler Foote Crossing Road. Turn east and drive for 29.5 miles (past Malakoff Diggins State Park) and you'll see the camp on your left.

Trip note: This primitive campground is located adjacent to Jackson Creek. Numerous recreation options are available at Jackson Creek and Bowman Lake. A nearby trail leads to smaller lakes to the south. The elevation is 5,600 feet. Open from June through October.

Map grid a8

BOWMAN LAKE

TAHOE NATIONAL FOREST

Campsites, facilities: There are seven unimproved tent sites. There is **no piped water,** but vault toilets are provided. Pack out your garbage. Pets are permitted if they are quiet and on leashes or otherwise controlled.

Reservations, fee: No reservations, no fee.

Who to contact: Phone the Tahoe National Forest Headquarters at (916)265-4531.

Location: The most direct access is to start from Nevada City and drive 22 miles on Highway 20 to Bowman Road. Turn north and travel 16 miles (the last ten miles are gravel) to the campground. However the Forest Service recommends that passenger vehicles and trailers start in Nevada City and take Highway 49 north for eight miles to the junction of Tyler Foote Crossing Road. Turn east and drive for 28 miles (past Malakoff Diggins State Park) to the campground.

Trip note: This is a small, primitive camp set at Bowman Lake at 5,650 feet elevation. It's a good spot for trout fishing and boating. If you want to get initiated into the Five Percent Club, a good side trip is to hike the trail to Pyramid Peak (6,000 feet) for a great lookout. The nearest supplies are available along Interstate 80 or in Nevada City. Be sure to bring your own water.

Map grid a8

FAUCHERIE LAKE GROUP CAMP

near Bowman Lake

TAHOE NATIONAL FOREST

Campsites, facilities: There is one large group camp for tents or motor homes up to 22 feet long. There is **no piped water,** but vault toilets, picnic tables, and fireplaces are provided. Pack out your garbage. Pets are permitted if they are quiet and on leashes or otherwise controlled.

Reservations, fee: Reservations required; contact MISTIX at (800)283-CAMP ($6 MISTIX fee); $25 fee per night.

Who to contact: Phone the Tahoe National Forest Headquarters at (916)265-4531.

Location: The most direct access is to start from Nevada City and drive 22 miles east on Highway 20 to Bowman Road. Turn north and travel 16 miles (the last ten miles are gravel) to the campground. However the Forest Service recommends that passenger vehicles and trailers start in Nevada City and take Highway 49 north for eight miles to the junction of Tyler Foote Crossing Road. Turn east and drive for 33 miles (past Malakoff Diggins State Park) to the campground on Faucherie Lake. (Crossing Prairie Creek can be tough for cars and trailers.)

Trip note: This is a relatively remote group camp set along Faucherie Reservoir at an elevation of 6,100 feet. It is advisable to obtain a map of Tahoe National Forest, which details back roads, lakes, streams, and hiking trails. Open from June through October.

Map grid a8

CANYON CREEK

near Faucherie Reservoir

TAHOE NATIONAL FOREST

Campsites, facilities: There are nine sites for tents only and 11 campsites for motor homes up to 22 feet long. There is **no piped water,** but vault toilets, picnic tables, and fireplaces are provided. Pack out your garbage. Pets are permitted if they are quiet and on leashes or otherwise controlled.

Reservations, fee: No reservations, no fee.

Who to contact: Phone the Tahoe National Forest Headquarters at (916)265-4531.

Location: The most direct access is to start from Nevada City and drive 22 miles on Highway 20 to Bowman Road. Turn north and travel 16 miles (the last ten miles are gravel) to the campground. However the Forest Service recommends that passenger vehicles and trailers start in Nevada City and take Highway 49 north for eight miles to the junction of Tyler Foote Crossing Road. Turn east and drive for 32 miles (past Malakoff Diggins State Park) to the campground. (Crossing Prairie Creek can be tough for cars and trailers.)

Trip note: This is a fairly remote spot for a drive-to camp. It is situated on Canyon

Creek, one mile downstream from Faucherie Reservoir. Many other small lakes in the area provide side trip options. The camp is set at 6,000 feet elevation. Open from June through October.

Map grid **a9**

SILVER TIP GROUP CAMP

at Jackson Meadow Reservoir
TAHOE NATIONAL FOREST

Campsites, facilities: There are two 25-person group campsites for tents or motor homes up to 22 feet long. Piped water, vault toilets, picnic tables, and fireplaces are provided. Pets are permitted if they are quiet and on leashes. Supplies are available in Truckee or Sierraville. A boat ramp is nearby.

Reservations, fee: Reserve through MISTIX by calling (800)283-CAMP ($10 MISTIX fee); $25 group fee per night.

Who to contact: Phone California Land Management at (916)582-0120, or Tahoe National Forest District Office at (916)994-3401; or write to Box 95, Sierraville, CA 96126.

Location: From Truckee, drive 17.5 miles north on Highway 89. Turn west on Forest Service Road 07 and drive 16 miles west to Jackson Meadow Reservoir. The campground is on the southwest shore of the reservoir.

Trip note: If you are bringing a group of Boy Scouts or Girl Scouts up here (hopefully not at the same time), this is the spot to reserve. It is set at the lakeside at Jackson Meadow Reservoir, with a swimming beach nearby at Woodcamp Picnic Site. The elevation is 6,100 feet. Open from June through November.

Map grid **a9**

WOODCAMP

at Jackson Meadow Reservoir
TAHOE NATIONAL FOREST

Campsites, facilities: There are ten sites for tents only and ten campsites for tents or motor homes up to 22 feet long. Piped water, flush toilets, picnic tables, and fireplaces are provided. Pets are permitted if they are quiet and on leashes or otherwise controlled. Supplies are available in Truckee or Sierraville. A concrete boat ramp is adjacent to the camp.

Reservations, fee: Reservations required; $8 fee per night.

Who to contact: Phone Tahoe National Forest Headquarters at (916)265-4531, or California Land Management at (916)582-0120.

Location: From Truckee, drive 17.5 miles north on Highway 89. Turn west on Forest Service Road 07 and drive 16 miles west to Jackson Meadow Reservoir. The campground is on the west shore of the reservoir.

Trip note: This is a good spot for the boater because there's a boat ramp available adjacent to the camp. Options include a good swimming beach nearby at Woodcamp Picnic Site and the Woodcamp Creek Interpretive Trail, just a half-mile hike, which guides walkers past examples of the area's unique natural features. The elevation is 6,100 feet. Open from June through November.

Map grid **a9**

PASS CREEK

at Jackson Meadow Reservoir
TAHOE NATIONAL FOREST

Campsites, facilities: There are 15 sites for tents only and 15 sites that can accommodate motor homes up to 22 feet long. Piped water, a sanitary dump station, vault toilets, picnic tables, and fireplaces are provided. There is a boat ramp nearby. Pets are permitted if they are quiet and on leashes or otherwise controlled. Supplies are available in Truckee or Sierraville.

Reservations, fee: Reservations required; $8 fee per night.

Who to contact: Phone Tahoe National Forest Headquarters at (916)265-4531, or California Land Management at (916)582-0120.

Location: From Truckee, drive 17.5 miles north on Highway 89. Turn west on Forest Service Road 7 and drive 16 miles west to Jackson Meadow Reservoir. The campground is on northeast shore of the reservoir.

Trip note: This is one in a series of campgrounds set along the Jackson Meadow Reservoir. Take your pick. The highlights here include a swimming beach at Aspen Creek Picnic Site, a concrete boat ramp nearby, and the Pacific Crest Trail. The latter passes near this camp and provides a unique side trip option. The elevation is 6,100 feet. Open from June through October.

Map grid a9

FIR TOP
at Jackson Meadow Reservoir
TAHOE NATIONAL FOREST

Campsites, facilities: There are 11 single-family campsites and one two-family campsite for tents or motor homes up to 22 feet long. Piped water, a sanitary dump station, flush toilets, picnic tables, and fireplaces are provided. Pets are permitted if they are quiet and on leashes or otherwise controlled. Supplies are available in Truckee or Sierraville. A boat ramp is nearby.

Reservations, fee: Reservations required; $8 fee per night.

Who to contact: Phone Tahoe National Forest Headquarters at (916)265-4531, or California Land Management at (916)582-0120.

Location: From Truckee, drive 17.5 miles north on Highway 89. Turn west on Forest Service Road 07 and drive 16 miles west to Jackson Meadow Reservoir. The campground is on the west shore of the reservoir.

Trip note: This is one of several campgrounds set along Jackson Meadow Reservoir. There is good fishing in early summer. The elevation is 6,200 feet. Open from June through November.

Map grid a9

FINDLEY
at Jackson Meadow Reservoir
TAHOE NATIONAL FOREST

Campsites, facilities: There are 12 single-family sites and three two-family sites for tents or motor homes up to 22 feet long. Piped water, flush toilets, picnic tables, and fireplaces are provided. Pets are permitted if they are quiet and on leashes or otherwise controlled. Supplies are available in Truckee or Sierraville. A boat ramp is nearby.

Reservations, fee: Reservations required; $8 fee per night.

Who to contact: Phone Tahoe National Forest Headquarters at (916)265-4531, or California Land Management at (916)582-0120.

Location: From Truckee, drive 17.5 miles north on Highway 89. Turn west on Forest Service Road 07 and drive 16 miles west to Jackson Meadow Reservoir. The campground is on the west shore of the reservoir.

Trip note: This is one of the prettier spots at Jackson Meadow Reservoir, and it often has good fishing, too. It is set at 6,200 feet near where Findley Creek pours into the lake. Open from June through November.

Map grid **a9**

JACKSON POINT

boat-in at Jackson Meadow Reservoir
TAHOE NATIONAL FOREST

Campsites, facilities: There are ten tent sites. There is **no piped water**, but vault toilets, picnic tables, and fireplaces are provided. Supplies are available in Truckee or Sierraville.

Reservations, fee: Reservations required; no fee.

Who to contact: Phone Tahoe National Forest Headquarters at (916)265-4531, or California Land Management at (916)582-0120.

Location: From Truckee, drive 17.5 miles north on HIghway 89. Turn west on Forest Service Road 07 and drive 16 miles west to Jackson Meadow Reservoir. The Pass Creek boat ramp is on the northeast shore of the reservoir; the campground is one-half mile southwest of the boat ramp (accessible by boat only).

Trip note: This is one of the few boat-in camps available in the Sierra Nevada. This pretty spot is situated on the end of a peninsula that extends from the east shore of Jackson Meadow Reservoir. Small and primitive, it's the one spot at the lake where you can gain entry into the Five Percent Club. The elevation is 6,100 feet. Open from June through October.

Map grid **a9**

EAST MEADOW

at Jackson Meadow Reservoir
TAHOE NATIONAL FOREST

Campsites, facilities: There are 46 campsites for tents or motor homes up to 22 feet long. Piped water, flush toilets, a sanitary dump station, picnic tables, and fireplaces are provided. There is a boat ramp nearby. Pets are permitted if they are quiet and on leashes or otherwise controlled. Supplies are available in Truckee or Sierraville.

Reservations, fee: Reservations required; $8 fee per night.

Who to contact: Phone Tahoe National Forest Headquarters at (916)265-4531, or California Land Management at (916)582-0120.

Location: From Truckee, drive 17.5 miles north on HIghway 89. Turn west on Forest Service Road 07 and drive 16 miles west to Jackson Meadow Reservoir. The campground is on east shore of the reservoir.

Trip note: This is one of several camps at Jackson Meadow Reservoir. The Pacific Crest Trail passes near this campsite. The elevation is 6,100 feet. Open from June through November.

Map grid **a9**

ASPEN GROUP CAMP

at Jackson Meadow Reservoir
TAHOE NATIONAL FOREST

Campsites, facilities: There are two 25-person group campsites and one 50-person group campsite for tents or motor homes up to 22 feet long. Piped water, vault toilets, a sanitary dump station, picnic tables, fireplaces, and a campfire circle are provided. There is a boat ramp nearby on Jackson Meadow Reservoir. Pets are permitted if they are quiet and on leashes or otherwise controlled. Supplies are available in Truckee or Sierraville.

Reservations, fee: Reserve through MISTIX by calling (800) 283-CAMP ($10 MISTIX fee); $25-$50 group fee per night.

Who to contact: For information phone the Tahoe National Forest District Office at (916)994-3401, or California Land Management at (916)582-0120.

Location: From Truckee, drive 17.5 miles north on Highway 89. Turn west on Forest Service Road 07 and drive 16 miles west to Jackson Meadow Reservoir. The campground is on the northeast shore of the reservoir.

Trip note: This is one of several campgrounds at Jackson Meadow Reservoir, a popular drive-to destination with alpine lake camping. The trout fishing is often good in early summer. A swimming beach and boat ramp adjacent to the campground make this spot quite attractive. The elevation is 6,100 feet. Open from June through October.

Map grid b0

ENGLEBRIGHT LAKE

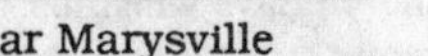

near Marysville

Campsites, facilities: There are 100 boat-in campsites along the shores of Englebright Lake, which stretches 11 miles up the narrow Yuba River Canyon. Picnic tables, fireplaces, and pit toilets are provided. Two boat ramps are available on either side of Skippers Cove. Boat rentals (including houseboats), mooring, a fuel dock, and groceries are also available.

Reservations, fee: No reservations, no fee.

Who to contact: Phone the U.S. Corps of Engineers, Englebright Lake at (916)639-2342, or call the concessionaire at Skippers Cove at (916)639-2272.

Location: From Marysville, drive east on Highway 20 to Mooney Flat Road just the other side of Smartville. Head north for three miles to the lake and boat ramps at Skippers Cove.

Trip note: Englebright Lake was formed by the damming of a section of the Yuba River, filling a steep narrow canyon. It is one of the few lakes in California that seems designed expressly for the boat-in camper, angler, and water skier.

Map grid b3

SOUTH YUBA TRAIL

near Yuba River

Campsites, facilities: There are 17 campsites for tents or motor homes up to 30 feet long. Piped water, pit toilets, picnic tables, and fireplaces are provided. Pets are permitted on leashes.

Reservations, fee: No reservations; $3 fee per night.

Who to contact: Phone the Bureau of Land Management at (916)985-4474.

Location: Vehicles with trailers should start from Nevada City and drive eight miles north on Highway 49. Turn right on Tyler Foote Crossing Road and drive to Grizzly Hills Road. Turn right on Grizzly Hills Road. Turn left on North Bloomfield Road and drive to the campground. Vehicles without trailers can start from Nevada City and drive ten miles north on North Bloomfield Road to the campground. The road gets rough toward the end.

Trip note: This camp is set near the upper Yuba River, where some great swimming holes can be searched out. A good side trip is to nearby Malakoff Diggins State Park and the town of North Bloomfield, which is being completely restored to its 1850s character. Hopefully that will not include the food. The elevation is 2,600 feet. Open March through October.

Map grid b4

SCOTTS FLAT LAKE RECREATION AREA

Campsites, facilities: There are 169 campsites for tents or motor homes up to 35 feet long. Rest rooms, showers, and a sanitary dump station are provided. A general store, a coffee shop, a bait and tackle shop, boat rentals, a boat ramp, and a playground are also available. Pets are permitted on leashes. Most facilities are wheelchair accessible.

Reservations, fee: Reservations accepted and strongly recommended May through September; $12 fee per night; pets $2.

Who to contact: Phone (916)265-5302.

Location: From Nevada City, drive five miles east on Highway 20. Turn south on Scotts Flat Road and drive four miles south (two miles are paved and two miles are gravel) to the campground at 23333 Scotts Flat Road.

Trip note: Scotts Flat Reservoir is known for providing good trout fishing, especially in May and June on days when the wind isn't blowing too hard. When the surface temperature heats up in summer, water skiing and boating are more popular. The camp is set at 3,000 feet elevation. Open year-round, weather permitting.

Map grid b5

SKILLMAN

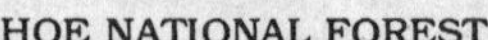
TAHOE NATIONAL FOREST

Campsites, facilities: There are 16 campsites for tents or motor homes up to 22 feet long. Piped water, vault toilets, picnic tables, and fireplaces are provided.Pets are permitted if they are quiet and on leashes or otherwise controlled.

Reservations, fee: No reservations; $4 fee per night.

Who to contact: Phone the Tahoe National Forest Headquarters at (916)265-4531.

Location: From Nevada City, drive 15 miles east on Highway 20 to the campground entrance on your right. Or take the Highway 20 exit off Interstate 80 and travel 13 miles west on Highway 20 to the campground entrance on your left.

Trip note: This is a Sierra Nevada camp at 4,400 feet elevation with easy access. If that sounds like it might fit, then try it on for size. Open from May through October.

Map grid b5

WHITE CLOUD

TAHOE NATIONAL FOREST

Campsites, facilities: There are 46 campsites for tents or motor homes up to 22 feet long. Piped water, vault and flush toilets, picnic tables, and fireplaces are provided. Pets are permitted if they are quiet and on leashes or otherwise controlled.

Reservations, fee: No reservations; $6 fee per night.

Who to contact: Phone the Tahoe National Forest Headquarters at (916)265-4531.

Location: From Nevada City, drive 12 miles east on Highway 20 to the campground entrance on your right. Or take the Highway 20 exit off Interstate 80, and travel 14 miles west on Highway 20 to the campground entrance on your left.

Trip note: You get easy-access, mountain-style camping here. It's advisable to get a map of Tahoe National Forest, which details backcountry options in the area. The elevation is 4,200 feet. Open from May through October.

Map grid b7

FULLER LAKE

TAHOE NATIONAL FOREST

Campsites, facilities: There are 9 tent spaces, with **no piped water,** but vault toilets, picnic tables, and fireplaces are provided. Pack out your garbage. Pets are permitted if they are quiet and on leashes or otherwise controlled.

Reservations, fee: No reservations, no fee.

Who to contact: Phone the Tahoe National Forest Headquarters at (916)265-4531.

Location: From Interstate 80, take the Highway 20 exit and drive west for 3.5 miles. Turn north on Bowman Road and drive four miles to the campground.
Trip note: This primitive, quiet campsite is set on Fuller Lake at 5,600 feet elevation. If the trout aren't biting at Fuller, nearby Rucker and Spaulding Lakes provide alternatives. Open May through October.

A

Map grid **b7**

GROUSE RIDGE

near Bowman Lake
TAHOE NATIONAL FOREST

B

Campsites, facilities: There are nine campsites for tents or motor homes up to 16 feet long. Piped water, vault toilets, picnic tables, and fireplaces are provided. Pack out your garbage. Pets are permitted if they are quiet and on leashes or otherwise controlled.
Reservations, fee: No reservations, no fee.
Who to contact: Phone the Tahoe National Forest Headquarters at (916)265-4531.
Location: From Interstate 80, take the Highway 20 exit and drive west for 3.5 miles. Turn north on Bowman Road and drive five miles. Turn right on Grouse Ridge Road and drive six miles to the campground.
Trip note: This is a good base camp for a backpacking trip because a trail leads out of camp into the Grouse Lakes area. There are numerous alpine lakes in the area; plan on hiking to reach them. There is ample parking at the campground and the trailhead. Grouse Ridge Lookout is a suggested side trip. The elevation is 7,400 feet. Open from June through October.

C

D3

E

Map grid **b8**

WOODCHUCK

on Rattlesnake Creek
TAHOE NATIONAL FOREST

F

Campsites, facilities: There are eight campsites for tents or motor homes up to 16 feet long. There is **no piped water,** but vault toilets, picnic tables, and fireplaces are provided. Pets are permitted if they are quiet and on leashes or otherwise controlled. A grocery store and propane gas are also available nearby.
Reservations, fee: No reservations; no fee.
Who to contact: Phone the Tahoe National Forest Headquarters at (916)265-4531.
Location: From Interstate 80, take the Cisco Grove exit north. Turn left on the frontage road and then right on Rattlesnake Road (just before Thousand Trails). Drive three miles to the campground. The road is steep and winding and trailers are not recommended.
Trip note: This is just tough enough to reach so that most folks either don't know about it or pass it by. The camp is set on Rattlesnake Creek at 6,300 feet elevation. A map of Tahoe National Forest details backcountry roads for access and side trip possibilities. Open from June through October.

G

H

Map grid **b8**

INDIAN SPRINGS

near Yuba River
TAHOE NATIONAL FOREST

I

Campsites, facilities: There are 35 campsites for tents or motor homes up to 25 feet long. Piped water, vault toilets, picnic tables, and fireplaces are provided. Pets are permitted if they are quiet and on leashes or otherwise controlled. A grocery store and propane gas are also available nearby.
Reservations, fee: Reservations available through MISTIX (800)283-CAMP($6 MISTIX fee); $8 fee per night.

J

Who to contact: Phone the Tahoe National Forest Headquarters at (916)265-4531.

Location: From Interstate 80, take the Eagle Lakes exit (about seven miles east of Emigrant Gap) and drive north for one-half mile to the campground.

Trip note: The camp is easy to reach from Interstate 80. It is set at 5,600 feet elevation, adjacent to the South Fork of the Yuba River. There are several lakes in the vicinity. Open from May through October.

Map grid b9

LAKE STERLING

TAHOE NATIONAL FOREST

Campsites, facilities: There are six campsites. There is **no piped water,** but vault toilets, picnic tables, and fireplaces are provided. Pack out your garbage. Pets are permitted if they are quiet and on leashes or otherwise controlled.

Reservations, fee: No reservations, no fee.

Who to contact: Phone the Tahoe National Forest Headquarters at (916)265-4531.

Location: From Interstate 80, take the Cisco Grove exit north. Turn left on the frontage road and then right on Rattlesnake Road (just before Thousand Trails). Drive 6.5 miles to the campground. The road is steep and winding; trailers are not recommended.

Trip note: This is a remote and primitive camp set along Sterling Lake at 7,000 feet elevation. There are good hiking trails. Open from June through October.

Map grid c5

FORBES CREEK GROUP CAMP

on Sugar Pine Reservoir

TAHOE NATIONAL FOREST

Campsites, facilities: There are two 50-person campsites for tents or motor homes up to 30 feet long. Piped water, vault toilets, picnic tables, and fireplaces are provided. All facilities are wheelchair accessible. A campfire circle, central parking area, sanitary dump station, and boat ramp are also available nearby. Pets are permitted if they are quiet and on leashes or otherwise controlled. Supplies can be obtained in Foresthill.

Reservations, fee: Reserve through MISTIX by calling (800)283-CAMP ($10 MISTIX fee); $40 fee per night.

Who to contact: For information, phone the concessionaire at (801)226-3564 or write to L & L Inc., 899 South Orem Boulevard, Orem, UT 84058. You can also phone the Tahoe National Forest District Office at (916)367-2224.

Location: From Foresthill, drive eight miles north on Foresthill Road to Sugar Pine Road. Turn west and drive for seven miles to Sugar Pine Reservoir. This campground is on the southeast shore.

Trip note: This is a special group camp, ideal for Boy Scout troops. The boat launch is nearby, but note: a ten-mile per hour speed limit is the law. That makes for quiet water, perfect for anglers and canoeists and other small boats. A paved trail circles the lake.

Map grid c5

GIANT GAP CAMPGROUND

on Sugar Pine Reservoir

TAHOE NATIONAL FOREST

Campsites, facilities: There are 30 campsites for tents or motor homes up to 30 feet long. Piped water, vault toilets, picnic tables, and fireplaces are provided. All facilities are wheelchair accessible. A sanitary dump station and a boat ramp are available on the south shore. Pets are permitted if they are quiet and on leashes or otherwise controlled. Supplies can be obtained in Foresthill.

Reservations, fee: No reservations; $6 fee per night.

Who to contact: For information, phone the concessionaire at (801)226-3564 or write to L & L Inc., 899 South Orem Boulevard, Orem, UT 84058. You can also phone the Tahoe National Forest District Office at (916)367-2224.

Location: From Foresthill, drive north for eight miles on Foresthill Road to Sugar Pine Road. Turn west and drive for seven miles to Sugar Pine Reservoir. This campground is on the north shore.

Trip note: This is a lakeside spot along the north shore of Sugar Pine Reservoir at 3,500 feet elevation. For boaters, there is a ramp on the south shore. Note that a ten-mile per hour speed limit is the law, making this lake ideal for anglers in search of quiet water. Other recreation notes: There's a paved trail around the lake, a beach nearby at Manzanita Picnic Area on the north shore, and several streams nearby in the surrounding National Forest.

Map grid c5

BIG RESERVOIR CAMPGROUND-MORNINGSTAR LAKE RESORT

on Big Reservoir
TAHOE NATIONAL FOREST

Campsites, facilities: There are 100 campsites for tents or motor homes up to 25 feet long. Piped water, vault toilets, picnic tables, and fireplaces are provided. Firewood is limited. Pets are permitted if they are quiet and on leashes or otherwise controlled. Supplies are available in Foresthill.

Reservations, fee: Reservations accepted; $8 fee per night.

Who to contact: For information call DeAnza Placer Gold Mining Company at (916)367-2129, or phone Tahoe National Forest Headquarters at (916)265-4531.

Location: From Foresthill, drive eight miles northeast on Foresthill Divide Road to the Big Reservoir turn. Turn and travel north for five miles to the campground.

Trip note: Here's a quiet lake where no motors are allowed on boats. That makes it ideal for canoeists, rowboaters, and tube floaters who don't like the idea of having to dodge waterskier traffic. A nice beach is available, not far from the resort. The elevation is 5,400 feet. Open from May through October.

Map grid c5

SHIRTTAIL CREEK

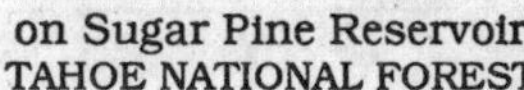

on Sugar Pine Reservoir
TAHOE NATIONAL FOREST

Campsites, facilities: There are 30 campsites for tents or motor homes up to 30 feet long (double and triple sites are available). Piped water, vault toilets, picnic tables, and fireplaces are provided. All facilities are wheelchair accessible. A sanitary dump station and a boat ramp are available on the south shore. Pets are permitted if they are quiet and on leashes or otherwise controlled. Supplies can be obtained in Foresthill.

Reservations, fee: No reservations; $6 fee per night.

Who to contact: For information, phone the concessionaire at (801)226-3564 or write to L & L Inc., 899 South Orem Boulevard, Orem, UT 84058. You can also phone the Tahoe National Forest District Office at (916)367-2224.

Location: From Foresthill, drive north on Foresthill Road for eight miles to Sugar Pine Road. Turn west and drive for seven miles to Sugar Pine Reservoir. This campground is on the north shore.

Trip note: This is one of the options at Sugar Pine Reservoir. There's boating, hiking, and swimming.

A B C D3 E F G H I J

Map grid **c7**

SECRET HOUSE

on the North Fork of American River
TAHOE NATIONAL FOREST

Campsites, facilities: There are two tent sites. There is **no piped water,** but vault toilets, picnic tables, and fireplaces are provided. Pack out your garbage. Pets are permitted if they are quiet and on leashes or otherwise controlled. Supplies are available in Foresthill.

Reservations, fee: No reservations, no fee.

Who to contact: Phone the Tahoe National Forest Headquarters at (916)265-4531.

Location: From Foresthill, drive 19 miles north on Foresthill Divide Road. This narrow, winding road is unpaved and not recommended for trailers.

Trip note: This is a remote, forested area with this tiny campground set along the North Fork of the American River. In early summer, this can be your personal base camp for a trout fishing trip. The elevation is 5,400 feet. Open from May through October.

Map grid **c7**

NORTH FORK

on the North Fork of American River
TAHOE NATIONAL FOREST

Campsites, facilities: There are 17 campsites for tents or motor homes up to 16 feet long. Piped water, vault toilets, picnic tables, and fireplaces are provided. Pets are permitted if they are quiet and on leashes or otherwise controlled. Supplies are available at the Nyack exit of Emigrant Gap, Cisco Grove and Soda Springs.

Reservations, fee: Reservations accepted through MISTIX at (800)283-CAMP($6 MISTIX fee); $8 fee per night.

Who to contact: Phone the Tahoe National Forest Headquarters at (916)265-4531.

Location: From Interstate 80, take the Emigrant Gap exit and drive six miles southeast on Texas Hill Road to the campground.

Trip note: This is just far enough from the highway to get missed by out-of-town cruisers. The campground is fairly remote and pretty and is set adjacent to the North Fork of the North Fork of the American River (got that?). The elevation is 4,400. Open from May through October.

Map grid **c7**

TUNNEL MILL

on the North Fork of American River
TAHOE NATIONAL FOREST

Campsites, facilities: There are two group campsites for tents or motor homes up to 16 feet long. There is **no piped water,** but vault toilets, picnic tables, and fireplaces are provided. Pets are permitted if they are quiet and on leashes or otherwise controlled. Supplies are available at Nyack exit of Emigrant Gap.

Reservations, fee: Reservations required; phone MISTIX at (800)283-CAMP ($10 MISTIX fee) $30 fee for group.

Who to contact: Phone the Tahoe National Forest Headquarters at (916)265-4531, or California Land Management at (916)582-0120.

Location: From Interstate 80, take the Emigrant Gap exit and drive 7.5 miles southeast to campground.

Trip note: This is a good spot for a Boy Scout camp-out. It's a rustic, quiet, group camp set all by itself along the (take a deep breath) North Fork of the North Fork of the American River (whew). The elevation is 4,400 feet. Open from June through October.

Map grid **c8**

BIG BEND

on Yuba River
TAHOE NATIONAL FOREST

Campsites, facilities: There are 15 campsites for tents or motor homes up to 16 feet long. Piped water, vault toilets, picnic tables, and fireplaces are provided. Pets are permitted if they are quiet and on leashes or otherwise controlled. A grocery store, a restaurant, and propane gas are available nearby.

Reservations, fee: Reservations available through MISTIX (800)283-CAMP ($6 MISTIX fee); $8 fee per night.

Who to contact: Phone the Tahoe National Forest Headquarters at (916)265-4531, or California Land Management at (916)582-0120.

Location: Eastbound on Interstate 80, take the Big Bend exit and continue east for one-quarter mile to the campground. Westbound, take the Rainbow Road exit and continue west for 1.5 miles to the campground.

Trip note: The camp offers easy access from Interstate 80, sites adjacent to South Fork of the Yuba River, and trails nearby to venture to high-elevation lakes. A Visitor Information Center here provides what you need to know. The elevation is 5,900 feet. Open from May through October.

Map grid **c9**

HAMPSHIRE ROCKS

on Yuba River
TAHOE NATIONAL FOREST

Campsites, facilities: There are 31 campsites for tents or motor homes up to 22 feet long. Piped water, vault toilets, picnic tables, and fireplaces are provided. Pets are permitted if they are quiet and on leashes or otherwise controlled. A grocery store, restaurant, and propane gas are available nearby.

Reservations, fee: Reservations available through MISTIX (800)283-CAMP ($6 MISTIX fee); $8 fee per night.

Who to contact: Phone the Tahoe National Forest Headquarters at (916)265-4531.

Location: Eastbound on Interstate 80, take the Big Bend exit and continue east for 1.5 mile to the campground (on the southern frontage road). Westbound, take the Rainbow Road exit and continue west for one-half mile to the campground.

Trip note: This camp sits along the South Fork of the Yuba River, providing easy access from the highway. Any questions? A Visitor Information Center is available. Nearby hiking trails provide access to backcountry lakes. The elevation is 5,900 feet. Open from May through October.

Map grid **d1**

BEAR RIVER RV CAMPGROUND

near Auburn

Campsites, facilities: There are 45 campsites with full hookups. There is a separate section for tents only. Picnic tables, fire grills, flush toilets, showers, and a sanitary dump station are provided. A playground, horseshoes, a laundromat, ice, and propane gas are available.

Reservations, fee: Reservations accepted; $18 fee per night for two people.

Who to contact: Phone (916)269-1121.

Location: From Auburn, travel north on Highway 49 for 8.5 miles to the campground.

Trip note: This privately-operated park is set up primarily for motor home cruisers getting ready to jump-off into the mountain country. It's in the foothills near the Bear River. Open year-round.

Map grid **d8**

ROBINSON FLAT

near French Meadows Reservoir
TAHOE NATIONAL FOREST

Campsites, facilities: There are five tent sites. There is **no piped water,** but vault toilets, picnic tables, and fireplaces are provided. Pack out your garbage. Pets are permitted if they are quiet and on leashes or otherwise controlled. Supplies are available in Foresthill.

Reservations, fee: No reservations, no fee.

Who to contact: Phone the Tahoe National Forest Headquarters at (916)265-4531.

Location: From Foresthill, drive 27 miles north on Foresthill Divide Road. This narrow, winding road is unpaved and not recommended for trailers.

Trip note: This camp, set at 6,800 feet elevation, is a good jump-off point for a hiking or backpacking adventure. Two trails lead from the camp: southeast for eight miles to French Meadows Reservoir and southwest into the backcountry. For lookouts, hike to Duncan Peak and Bald Mountain. A creek runs near the camp. Open from May through October.

Map grid **d9**

POPPY

on French Meadows Reservoir
TAHOE NATIONAL FOREST

Campsites, facilities: There are 12 tent sites at this campground, accessible by boat or by a one-mile foot trail from McGuire Picnic Site. There is **no piped water,** but vault toilets, picnic tables, and fireplaces are provided. Pets are permitted on leashes or otherwise controlled. Supplies are available in Foresthill.

Reservations, fee: No reservations; no fee.

Who to contact: Phone the Tahoe National Forest District Office at (916)367-2224, or L&L Inc. at (801)226-3564, or write 899 S. Orem Boulevard, Orem, VT. 84058.

Location: From Foresthill, drive 36 miles east on Mosquito Ridge Road to French Meadows Reservoir. Continue to the northwest shore of the reservoir to the McGuire Picnic Site, where there is a trailhead and boat ramp.

Trip note: French Meadows Reservoir is a popular spot, but you can still get some privacy at this boat-in or hike-in (one mile) campground. Piped water is available at the McGuire Picnic Site.

Map grid **d9**

FRENCH MEADOWS

on French Meadows Reservoir
TAHOE NATIONAL FOREST

Campsites, facilities: There are 75 campsites for tents or motor homes up to 22 feet long. Piped water, flush toilets, picnic tables, and fireplaces are provided. A concrete boat ramp is nearby. Pets are permitted if they are quiet and on leashes or otherwise controlled. Supplies are available in Foresthill.

Reservations, fee: No reservations; $8 fee per night.

Who to contact: Phone the Tahoe National Forest District Office at (916)367-2224, or L&L Inc. at (801)226-3564, or write 899 S. Orem Boulevard, Orem, VT. 84058.

Location: From Foresthill, drive 36 miles east on Mosquito Ridge Road to French Meadows Reservoir. The campground is on the south shore.

Trip note: The nearby boat launch makes this the choice for boating campers. The camp is on French Meadows Reservoir at 5,300 feet elevation. A four-wheel drive trail leads up the ridge behind the camp. See the trip notes for Poppy and Lewis for other side trip option details. Open from June through October.

Map grid d9

GATES GROUP CAMP
on North Fork American River
TAHOE NATIONAL FOREST

Campsites, facilities: There are three group campsites (two-25 person, one-75 person) for tents or motor homes up to 22 feet long. Piped water, vault toilets, picnic tables, fireplaces, central parking and a campfire circle are provided. Pets are permitted if they are quiet and on leashes or otherwise controlled. Supplies are available in Foresthill.

Reservations, fee: Reservations required; reserve through MISTIX at (800)283-CAMP ($10 MISTIX fee); $25-$50 fee per night.

Who to contact: For information, phone the concessionaire at (801)226-3564, or write L&L Inc., 899 S. Orem Boulevard, Orem, VT. 84058. You can also phone the Tahoe National Forest Headquarters at (916)265-4531.

Location: From Foresthill, drive 36 miles east on Mosquito Ridge Road to French Meadows Reservoir. Continue to the campground on the east shore of the reservoir.

Trip note: In this pretty spot, the camp is set on the North Fork of the American River near French Meadows Reservoir. There are many activity options in this area. Open from June through October.

Map grid d9

COYOTE GROUP CAMP
on French Meadows Reservoir
TAHOE NATIONAL FOREST

Campsites, facilities: There are three 25-person campsites and one 50-person campsite for tents or motor homes up to 22 feet long. Piped water, vault toilets, picnic tables, and fireplaces are provided. A campfire circle and central parking area are also provided. Pets are permitted if they are quiet and on leashes or otherwise controlled. Supplies are available in Foresthill.

Reservations, fee: Reservations required; reserve through MISTIX at (800)283-CAMP ($10 MISTIX fee); $25-$50 fee per night.

Who to contact: For information, phone the concessionaire at (801)226-3564 or write to L&L Inc., 899 S. Orem Boulevard, Orem, VT. 84058. You can also phone the Tahoe National Forest District Office at (916)367-2224.

Location: From Foresthill, drive 36 miles east on Mosquito Ridge Road to French Meadows Reservoir. Continue to the campground on the northeast shore of the reservoir.

Trip note: This is a prime base camp for many adventures. It is set on French Meadows Reservoir at 5,300 feet elevation. It is a good lake for boating, fishing, and swimming, and not far from the North Fork of the American River. For hikers, two trails lead out from the reservoir. One trail goes up and along Star Ridge (or beyond to Robinson's Flat), and the other follows the American River through Picayune Valley and beyond. Open from June through October.

Map grid d9

AHART
near French Meadows Reservoir
TAHOE NATIONAL FOREST

Campsites, facilities: There are 12 campsites for tents or motor homes up to 22 feet long. There is **no piped water,** but vault toilets, picnic tables, and fireplaces are provided. Pets are permitted if they are quiet and on leashes or otherwise controlled. Supplies are available in Foresthill.

Reservations, fee: No reservations; $7 fee per night.

Who to contact: Phone the Tahoe National Forest District Office at (916)367-2224, or L&L Inc. at (801)226-3564, or write to 899 S. Orem Boulevard, Orem, VT. 84058.

Location: From Foresthill, drive 36 miles east on Mosquito Ridge Road to French Meadows Reservoir. Continue just past the reservoir to the campground.

Trip note: This camp is located near the northeastern end of French Meadows Reservoir and set beside the Middle Fork of the American River. Between the lake and the stream, you have many options. It's a pretty, primitive spot used for overflow traffic from the lake. Open from June through October.

Map grid d9

LEWIS

on French Meadows Reservoir

TAHOE NATIONAL FOREST

Campsites, facilities: There are 40 campsites for tents or motor homes up to 22 feet long. Piped water, vault toilets, picnic tables, and fireplaces are provided. A concrete boat ramp is nearby. Pets are permitted if they are quiet and on leashes or otherwise controlled. Supplies are available in Foresthill.

Reservations, fee: No reservations; $8 fee per night.

Who to contact: Phone the Tahoe National Forest District Office at (916)367-2224, or L&L Inc. at (801)226-3564, or write 899 S. Orem Boulevard, Orem, VT. 84058

Location: From Foresthill, drive 36 miles east on Mosquito Ridge Road to French Meadows Reservoir. The campground is on the north shore of the reservoir.

Trip note: Lakeside camping is available here. This spot is set on the north shore of French Meadows Reservoir at 5,300 feet elevation. The nearby boat launch is a bonus. A side trip option is to take the hiking trail out of camp to Star Ridge and beyond into Robinson Valley. Open from May through October.

Map grid d9

TALBOT

near French Meadows Reservoir

TAHOE NATIONAL FOREST

Campsites, facilities: There are five tent sites. There is **no piped water,** but vault toilets, picnic tables, and fireplaces are provided. Pets are permitted if they are quiet and on leashes or otherwise controlled. Supplies are available in Foresthill. The camp is within a state game refuge so no firearms are permitted.

Reservations, fee: No reservations, no fee.

Who to contact: Phone the Tahoe National Forest District Office at (916)367-2224.

Location: From Foresthill, drive 36 miles east on Mosquito Ridge Road to French Meadows Reservoir. Continue past the reservoir for five miles to the campground.

Trip note: You join the Five Percent Club by visiting this spot. It is set at 5,600 feet elevation along the Middle Fork of the American River. It's a good jump-off spot for backpackers because the trailhead for a trip to Picayune Valley and the Granite Chief Wilderness area is here. There are ten stalls for trailer parking for horses and pack stock. Hitching rails are available at trailhead. A possible side trip is to French Meadows Reservoir, five miles away. Right, you saw it coming in. Open from June through October.

AUBURN KOA

Map grid e1

Campsites, facilities: There are 66 campsites with full, partial, or no hookups, and there is a separate section for tents only (ten sites). Picnic tables, fire grills, flush toilets, showers, and a sanitary dump station are provided. A playground, a swimming pool, a recreation room, a fishing pond, badminton, horseshoes, volleyball, a grocery store, a laundromat, and propane gas are available.

Reservations, fee: Reservations accepted; $15-$20 fee per night.

Who to contact: Phone (916)885-0990.

Location: From Auburn, drive north on Highway 49 for 3.5 miles to Rock Creek Road. Turn right and follow the signs to 3550 KOA Way.

Trip note: This year-round KOA park is set at 1,250 feet elevation and has all the amenities. What the heck, it even has a swimming pool!

MIDDLE MEADOWS GROUP CAMP

on Long Canyon Creek

ELDORADO NATIONAL FOREST

Map grid e8

Campsites, facilities: There are two group campsites for tents or small motor homes. Piped water, vault toilets, and picnic tables are provided. Supplies can be obtained in Foresthill. Pets are permitted on leashes or otherwise controlled.

Reservations, fee: Reserve through MISTIX at (800)283-CAMP ($6 MISTIX fee); $25 fee per night.

Who to contact: Phone the Eldorado National Forest Georgetown Ranger District at (916)333-4312.

Location: From Foresthill, drive 36 miles east via Mosquito Ridge and French Meadows Roads to the southern end of French Meadows Reservoir. Turn on Forest Service Road 48 (a gravel road) and drive nine miles to the campground.

Trip note: This group camp is set in the midst of some good adventures. The camp is right along Long Canyon Creek, five miles from Hell Hole Reservoir, and not far from French Meadows Reservoir. Open from June through September.

BIG MEADOWS

near Hell Hole Reservoir

ELDORADO NATIONAL FOREST

Map grid e8

Campsites, facilities: There are 55 campsites for tents or motor homes up to 22 feet long. Piped water, vault and flush toilets, picnic tables, and fireplaces are provided. Pets are permitted on leashes or otherwise controlled. Supplies are available in Foresthill.

Reservations, fee: Some sites can be reserved through MISTIX at (800)283-CAMP ($6 MISTIX fee); $6 fee per night.

Who to contact: Phone the Eldorado National Forest Georgetown Ranger District at (916)333-4312.

Location: From Foresthill, drive 36 miles east via Mosquito Ridge and French Meadows Roads to the southern end of French Meadows Reservoir. Turn on Forest Service Road 48 (a gravel road) and drive ten miles to the campground.

Trip note: This camp sits on the ridge above Hell Hole Reservoir (which is about two miles away). The lake provides good trout fishing in early summer but is subject to drawdowns later in the year. If you want another option, French Meadows Reservoir is only ten miles away. Open from May through November.

Map grid e9

HELL HOLE

near Hell Hole Reservoir
ELDORADO NATIONAL FOREST

Campsites, facilities: There are ten campsites for tents or motor homes. Piped water, vault toilets, picnic tables, and fireplaces are provided. Supplies can be obtained in Foresthill. Pets are permitted on leashes or otherwise controlled. A boat launch is available nearby at the reservoir.

Reservations, fee: No reservations; $6 fee per night.

Who to contact: Phone the Eldorado National Forest Georgetown Ranger District at (916)333-4312.

Location: From Foresthill, drive 36 miles east via Mosquito Ridge and French Meadows Roads to the southern end of French Meadows Reservoir. Turn on Forest Service Road 48 (a gravel road) and drive 12 miles to the campground.

Trip note: This is the closest drive-to camp at Hell Hole Reservoir; the lake is just a mile away with a boat launch and four-wheel drive road nearby. Several trails start nearby the camp and head into the surrounding backcountry, detailed on a Forest Service map. If the fish aren't biting, French Meadows Reservoir is only ten miles away. The elevation is 5,200 feet.

Map grid e9

UPPER HELL HOLE

on Hell Hole Reservoir
ELDORADO NATIONAL FOREST

Campsites, facilities: There are 15 tent sites, accessible by trail or boat only. There is **no piped water,** but pit toilets, picnic tables, and fireplaces are provided. Pets are permitted on leashes or otherwise controlled. A boat launch is available at the reservoir. Supplies can be obtained in Foresthill.

Reservations, fee: No reservations, no fee.

Who to contact: Phone the Eldorado National Forest Georgetown Ranger District at (916)333-4312.

Location: From Foresthill, drive 36 miles east via Mosquito Ridge and French Meadows Roads to the southern end of French Meadows Reservoir. Turn on Forest Service Road 48 (a gravel road) and drive 13 miles south to the boat launch on Hell Hole Reservoir. The trail to the campground begins at the end of the road, one mile beyond the boat launch.

Trip note: This is the most secluded spot in the area, and what the heck, that's what you would expect—it can only be reached by boat or by foot. It is set on the south shore at the upper end of Hell Hole Reservoir. Some of the best fishing is often in this area. Open from May through October.

Map grid f0

LOOMIS KOA

in Loomis

Campsites, facilities: There are 74 campsites with full, partial or no hookups, and a separate section for tents only. Picnic tables, fire grills, flush toilets, showers, and a sanitary dump station are provided. A playground, a swimming pool, a recreation room, volleyball, horseshoes, a grocery store, a laundromat, and propane gas are available.

Reservations, fee: Reservations accepted; $17-$21 fee per night for two people

Who to contact: Phone (916)652-6737.

Location: From the junction of Interstate 80 and Sierra College Boulevard in Loomis, drive north on Sierra College Boulevard for one-half mile. Turn east on Taylor Road and drive one-half block to the campground.

Trip note: This KOA park is set in the Sierra foothills, which are known for hot summer weather. The sites are on level gravel and some are shaded. The elevation is 400 feet.

Map grid f6

BLACK OAK GROUP CAMP

on Stumpy Meadows Lake

ELDORADO NATIONAL FOREST

Campsites, facilities: There are four group campsites for tents or motor homes up to 16 feet long. Piped water, vault toilets, picnic tables, and fireplaces are provided. Pets are permitted on leashes or otherwise controlled. A boat ramp is nearby.

Reservations, fee: Reserve through MISTIX at (800)283-CAMP ($6 MISTIX fee); $25 group use fee.

Who to contact: Phone the Eldorado National Forest Georgetown Ranger District at (916)333-4312.

Location: From Georgetown on Highway 193, turn east on Georgetown-Wentworth Springs Road and drive 20 miles to the campground.

Trip note: A boat ramp two miles from the camp is a bonus for this group camp. It is set at Stumpy Meadows Lake at 4,400 feet elevation. This is one of two camps to choose from at the lake. Open from April through November.

Map grid f6

STUMPY MEADOWS

on Stumpy Meadows Lake

ELDORADO NATIONAL FOREST

Campsites, facilities: There are 40 campsites for tents or motor homes up to 16 feet long (there is one two-family site). Piped water, vault toilets, picnic tables, and fireplaces are provided. Pets are permitted on leashes or otherwise controlled. A boat ramp is nearby.

Reservations, fee:Reserve through MISTIX (800)283-CAMP $6 MISTIX fee); $7 fee per night; $12 for two-family site.

Who to contact: Phone the Eldorado National Forest Georgetown Ranger District at (916)333-4312.

Location: From Georgetown on Highway 193, turn east on Georgetown/Wentworth Springs Road and drive 20 miles to the campground.

Trip note: This is the camp of choice for visitors to Stumpy Meadows Lake. This camp is set at 4,400 feet elevation. Open from April through November.

Map grid f8

GERLE CREEK

on Gerle Creek Reservoir

ELDORADO NATIONAL FOREST

Campsites, facilities: There are 50 campsites for tents or motor homes up to 22 feet long. Piped water, vault toilets, picnic tables, and fireplaces are provided. Pets are permitted on leashes or otherwise controlled.

Reservations, fee: Reserve through MISTIX (800)283-CAMP ($6 MISTIX fee); $7 fee per night.

Who to contact: Phone the Eldorado National Forest Pacific Ranger District at (916)644-2349.

Location: From Riverton on US 50, turn north on Ice House Road (Soda Springs-Riverton Road) and drive about 31 miles to the campground entrance.

Trip note: This small lake is ideal for canoes or other small boats because no motors are permitted. That makes for quiet water. If the fishing isn't good here, several other lakes are in the area. Hikers should obtain a Forest Service map, which details the backcountry trails. The camp is set at 5,300 feet elevation. Open from June through October.

Map grid **f8**

SOUTH FORK

on the South Fork of Rubicon River
ELDORADO NATIONAL FOREST

Campsites, facilities: There are 17 campsites for tents or motor homes up to 22 feet long. There is **no piped water,** but vault toilets, picnic tables, and fireplaces are provided. Pets are permitted on leashes or otherwise controlled.

Reservations, fee: No reservations, no fee.

Who to contact: Phone the Eldorado National Forest Pacific Ranger District at (916)644-2349.

Location: From Riverton on US 50, drive 26 miles north on Soda Springs-Riverton Road. Turn west on the campground access road and drive one mile to the campground.

Trip note: This is a good base camp, set beside the South Fork of the Rubicon River take-your-pick vacation site. You can stay put, watch the water roll by, maybe catch a few trout, or consider other adventures. Loon Lake is six miles away, Union Valley Reservoir is eight miles away, and Gerle Creek Reservoir is four miles away. Bring your own water. Open from June through October.

Map grid **g0**

PENINSULA

FOLSOM LAKE STATE RECREATION AREA

Campsites, facilities: There are 100 campsites for tents or motor homes. Picnic tables, fireplaces, and piped water are provided. Flush toilets, showers, and a bike path are available. There are boat rentals, moorings, a snack bar, ice, and bait and tackle available at the Folsom Lake Marina. Pets are permitted.

Reservations, fee: Reserve through MISTIX by phoning (800)444-PARK ($3.95 MISTIX fee); $12-$14 fee per night; pets $1.

Who to contact: Phone the Folsom Lake State Recreation Area at (916)988-0205.

Location: From Pilot Hill on Highway 49, drive nine miles southwest on Rattlesnake Bar Road to the campground.

Trip note: This is one of the big camps at Folsom Lake. Set on the northeast shore, it is somewhat more remote than the other camps at the lake. Fishing for bass and trout is often quite good in spring and early summer, and water skiing is popular in the hot summer months.

Map grid **g0**

NEGRO BAR

FOLSOM LAKE STATE RECREATION AREA

Campsites, facilities: There are 20 campsites for tents or motor homes up to 31 feet long. Picnic tables, fireplaces, and piped water are provided. Flush toilets, shower, and a bike path are available. A grocery store and a laundromat are nearby. There are boat rentals, moorings, a snack bar, ice, and bait and tackle available at the Folsom Lake Marina.

Reservations, fee: Phone MISTIX at (800)444-PARK ($3.95 MISTIX fee); $12-$14 fee per night.

Who to contact: Phone the Folsom Lake State Recreation Area at (916)988-0205.

Location: From Folsom, drive one-half mile northwest on Greenback Lane.

Trip note: This camp is set along the shore of Lake Natoma. A bonus at this camp is the two group camps, each with a capacity of up to 50 people. That makes it good headquarters for a scout outing.

Map grid g0

BEAL'S POINT

FOLSOM LAKE STATE RECREATION AREA

Campsites, facilities: There are 49 campsites for tents or motor homes up to 31 feet long. Picnic tables, fireplaces, and piped water are provided. Flush toilets, showers, a dump station, a bike path, and horseback riding facilities are available. The camping, picnicking, and fishing areas are wheelchair accessible. There are boat rentals, moorings, a snack bar, ice, bait and tackle available at the Folsom Lake Marina. Pets are permitted.

Reservations, fee: Phone MISTIX at (800)444-PARK ($3.95 MISTIX fee); $12-$14 fee per night; pets $1.

Who to contact: Phone the Folsom Lake State Recreation Area at (916)988-0205.

Location: From Folsom, drive three miles north on Folsom-Auburn Road.

Trip note: Folsom Lake is the most popular getaway spot for Sacramento area campers, fishermen, and sunbathers. In spring, the bass and trout fishing is quite good. By summer, it's usually pretty much kaput, and the waterskiers take over after 10 a.m. Open year-round.

Map grid g5

FINNON LAKE RESORT

Campsites, facilities: There are 35 campsites for tents or motor homes. There are no electrical hookups. Piped water, chemical toilets, picnic tables, and fireplaces are provided. Pets are permitted.

Reservations, fee: No reservations; $5 fee per night.

Who to contact: Phone the county park at (916)622-9314.

Location: From Placerville, drive eight miles north on Highway 193. Turn right (east) on Rock Creek Road and drive eight miles to the lake.

Trip note: Like most county parks, few folks other than the local residents have a clue that it exists. But it does and it has lakeside camping and access for fishing and swimming. It is set at 2,200 feet elevation. Open year-round.

Map grid g8

SILVER CREEK

near Ice House Reservoir

ELDORADO NATIONAL FOREST

Campsites, facilities: There are 11 tent spaces. There is **no piped water,** but vault toilets, picnic tables, and fireplaces are provided. Pets are permitted on leashes or otherwise controlled.

Reservations, fee: No reservations, no fee.

Who to contact: Phone the Eldorado National Forest Pacific Ranger District at (916)644-2349.

Location: From Riverton on US 50, turn north on Soda Springs-Riverton Road and drive nine miles to the campground, across from Ice House Resort.

Trip note: This primitive and pretty spot along Silver Creek is about two miles from Ice House Reservoir. It is often used as an overflow area if the camps at the lake are filled. The elevation is 5,200 feet. Open from June through October.

Map grid **g8**

YELLOWJACKET
on Union Valley Reservoir
ELDORADO NATIONAL FOREST

Campsites, facilities: There are 40 campsites for tents or motor homes up to 22 feet long. Piped water, vault and flush toilets, picnic tables, and fireplaces are provided. Pets are permitted on leashes or otherwise controlled. A boat ramp is nearby.

Reservations, fee:Reserve through MISTIX (800)283-CAMP($6 MISTIX fee); $7 fee per night.

Who to contact: Phone the Eldorado National Forest Pacific Ranger District at (916)644-2349.

Location: From Riverton on US 50, turn north on Soda Springs-Riverton Road and drive 21 miles. Turn left on the campground entrance road at the north end of lake and drive two miles to the campground.

Trip note: The camp, set at 4,900 feet, is located on the north shore of the reservoir. A boat launch adjacent to the camp makes this an ideal destination for trout-angling campers with boats. Union Valley Reservoir, a popular weekend destination for campers from the Central Valley, is stocked with trout by the Department of Fish and Game. Open from June through October.

Map grid **g8**

SUNSET
on Union Valley Reservoir
ELDORADO NATIONAL FOREST

Campsites, facilities: There are 131 campsites for tents or motor homes up to 22 feet long. Two of the campsites are big enough for two families each. Piped water, vault toilets, picnic tables, and fireplaces are provided. A boat ramp and sanitary disposal station are also available. Pets are permitted on leashes or otherwise controlled.

Reservations, fee: Reserve through MISTIX (800)283-CAMP($6 MISTIX fee) $8 fee per night; $13 for two-family sites.

Who to contact: Phone the Eldorado National Forest Pacific Ranger District at (916)644-2349.

Location: From Riverton on US 50, turn north on Soda Springs-Riverton Road and drive 15 miles. Turn left on the entrance road to the campground and drive 1.5 miles.

Trip note: One of three camps at Union Valley Reservoir, this one located on the tip of the east peninsula. A nice picnic area and a beach are available near the campground. The elevation is 4,900 feet. Open from June through October.

Map grid **g9**

ICE HOUSE
on Ice House Reservoir
ELDORADO NATIONAL FOREST

Campsites, facilities: There are 17 sites for tents only and 66 campsites for tents or motor homes up to 22 feet long. Three campsites are paved, with facilities designed for wheelchairs. Piped water, vault toilets, picnic tables, and fireplaces are provided. A boat ramp and sanitary disposal station are also available. Pets are permitted on leashes or otherwise controlled.

Reservations, fee: No reservations; $8 fee per night.

Who to contact: Phone the Eldorado National Forest Pacific Ranger District at (916)644-2349.

Location: From Riverton on US 50, turn north on Soda Springs-Riverton Road and drive eleven miles. Turn right on the Ice House Reservoir access road and drive one mile to campground.

Trip note: Along with Loon Lake and Union Valley Reservoir, this is a popular fishing spot in early summer for Sacramento area anglers. The reservoir is well stocked in early June by the Department of Fish and Game. The elevation is 5,500 feet. Open from June though October.

Map grid **g9**

WENCH CREEK

on Union Valley Reservoir

ELDORADO NATIONAL FOREST

Campsites, facilities: There are 100 campsites for tents or motor homes up to 22 feet long. There are also two group campsites. Piped water, flush toilets, vault toilets, picnic tables, and fireplaces are provided. Pets are permitted on leashes or otherwise controlled. A boat ramp is three miles away at the Yellowjacket campground.

Reservations, fee: No reservations for family sites; $7 fee per night; reserve group sites through MISTIX at (800)283-CAMP ($6 MISTIX fee); $25 group camp fee.

Who to contact: Phone the Eldorado National Forest Pacific Ranger District at (916)644-2349.

Location: From Riverton on US 50, turn north on Soda Springs-Riverton Road and drive about 19 miles to the campground.

Trip note: This camp, one of three at the lake, is located on the east shore of Union Valley Reservoir, which is known for its good early-summer trout fishing. The elevation is 4,900 feet. Open from June through October.

Map grid **h6**

SLY PARK RECREATION AREA

on Jenkinson Lake

Campsites, facilities: There are 185 campsites for tents or motor homes up to 32 feet long. No hookups are available. Picnic tables, fire grills, piped water, pit toilets, and two boat ramps are provided. Pets are permitted. Some facilities and campgrounds are wheelchair accessible. There are also six group campsites that can accommodate 50-100 people. A grocery store, snack bar, bait, and propane gas are available nearby.

Reservations, fee: Reservations for group sites only; $9 fee per night for single sites; starts at $75 for group sites; $1.50 for pets.

Who to contact: Phone (916)644-2545.

Location: From Pollock Pines on Highway 50 take the Sly Park Road exit and drive five miles to the campground.

Trip note: A prime spot for Sacramento-area vacationers looking for a weekend trip. Jenkinson Lake is known for good trout fishing, both for stocked rainbow and occasional large brown trout. But the trip is not limited to fishing. The area has several good hiking trails, and the lake is a good one for swimming and water skiing. A group camp is available for visitors with horses, complete with riding trails, hitching posts, and corrals. One horse trail circles the lake. The camp is set at 3,500 feet elevation. Open year-round.

Map grid **h9**

SILVER FORK

on American River
ELDORADO NATIONAL FOREST

Campsites, facilities: There are 35 campsites for tents or motor homes up to 22 feet long and five double-family sites. One of the sites is paved, with facilities designed for wheelchair use. Piped water, vault toilets, picnic tables, and fireplaces are provided. Pets are permitted on leashes or otherwise controlled.

Reservations, fee: No reservations; $7 fee per night; $14 for double-family sites.

Who to contact: Phone the Eldorado National Forest Placerville Ranger District at (916)644-2324.

Location: From Placerville, drive 29 miles east on US 50 to Kyburz Resort. Turn south on Silver Fork Road and drive eight miles to the campground.

Trip note: If you like streamside camping at developed sites, this camp provides the answer. This section of the stream is often stocked with trout, but the fishing can be quite slow if you hit it "in-between" stocks, as they say. The elevation is 5,500 feet. Open from May through October.

Map grid **h9**

SAND FLAT

on the South Fork of American River
ELDORADO NATIONAL FOREST

Campsites, facilities: There are 29 campsites for tents or motor homes up to 22 feet long. Piped water, vault toilets, picnic tables, and fireplaces are provided. Pets are permitted on leashes or otherwise controlled. Groceries, a restaurant, and gas are available nearby.

Reservations, fee: No reservations; $7 fee per night.

Who to contact: Phone the Eldorado National Forest Placerville Ranger District at (916)644-2324.

Location: From Placerville, drive 28 miles east on US 50 to the campground on right.

Trip note: This first-come, first-served campground often gets filled up by US 50 traffic. And why not? You get easy access, a well-signed exit, and a nice setting on the South Fork of the American River. The elevation is 3,900 feet. Open year-round.

Map grid **h9**

CHINA FLAT

on the Silver Fork of American River
ELDORADO NATIONAL FOREST

Campsites, facilities: There are 23 campsites for tents or motor homes up to 22 feet long. Piped water, vault toilets, picnic tables, and fireplaces are provided. Pets are permitted on leashes or otherwise controlled.

Reservations, fee: No reservations; $7 fee per night.

Who to contact: Phone the Eldorado National Forest Placerville Ranger District at (916)644-2324.

Location: From Placerville, drive 29 miles east on US 50 to Kyburz Resort. Turn south on Silver Fork Road and drive three miles to the campground.

Trip note: This is just far enough off the highway to get missed by the US 50 cruisers. It's a nice spot beside the Silver Fork at 4,800 feet elevation. It's one of several Forest Service campgrounds set in the American River country. Open from May through October.

A B C D3 E F G H I J

Map grid i7 — PI PI

on the Middle Fork of Consumnes River
ELDORADO NATIONAL FOREST

Campsites, facilities: There are 51 campsites for tents or motor homes up to 22 feet long (three double-family sites). Piped water, vault toilets, picnic tables, and fireplaces are provided. Pets are permitted on leashes or otherwise controlled. There is wheelchair access to camping areas, rest rooms, and pathways.

Reservations, fee: No reservations; $7 fee per night.

Who to contact: Phone the Eldorado National Forest Amador Ranger District at (209)295-4251.

Location: From Pioneer, drive nine miles northeast on Highway 88. Turn left (northwest) on Omo Ranch Road and drive one mile. Turn right (north) on North-South Road and drive 5.5 miles to the campground.

Trip note: This is far enough out of the way to get missed by most campers, but not you. It is set along the Middle Fork of the Consumnes River at 3,900 feet elevation. There are some good swimming holes in the area, but the water is cold in early summer (after all, it's snowmelt). New in 1991 is a nature trail/boardwalk that is wheelchair accessible along the river. Open from May through November.

Map grid i8 — CAPPS CROSSING

5% CLUB

on the North Fork of Consumnes River
ELDORADO NATIONAL FOREST

Campsites, facilities: There are 11 tent spaces. There is piped water, vault toilets, picnic tables, and fireplaces are provided. Pets are permitted on leashes or otherwise controlled.

Reservations, fee: No reservations; $6 fee per night.

Who to contact: Phone the Eldorado National Forest Placerville Ranger District at (916)644-2324.

Location: From Placerville, drive 12 miles east on Highway 50 to the Sly Park Road exit. Drive about six miles south on Sly Park Road. Turn left (east) on Mormon Emigrant Trail and drive about 13 miles. Turn right (south) on North South Road and drive about six miles to the campground.

Trip note: Here's a candidate for the Five Percent Club. It's set out in the middle of nowhere along the North Fork of the Consumnes River, a primitive spot that doesn't get much use. A Forest Service map that details roads, streams, and trails is advisable. The elevation is 5,200 feet. Open from June through October.

Map grid j2 — FAR HORIZONS 49ER TRAILER VILLAGE

near Jackson

Campsites, facilities: There are 329 motor home spaces with full hookups. Flush toilets, a sanitary disposal station, showers, a playground, two swimming pools, a jacuzzi, a recreation room, a pool room, a TV lounge, a beauty shop, a laundromat, a deli, propane gas, and a general store are available. Pets are permitted.

Reservations, fee: Reservations recommended; $24 fee per night.

Who to contact: Phone the park at (209)245-6981.

Location: From State Highway 99 in Stockton, turn east on Highway 88 and drive 40 miles to Jackson. Turn north on Highway 49 and drive 12 miles north to the campground.

Trip note: This is the granddaddy of RV parks, set in the heart of the gold country 40 miles east of Stockton and Sacramento. Open year-round.

Map grid **j4**

INDIAN GRINDING ROCK STATE HISTORICAL PARK

near Jackson

Campsites, facilities: There are 23 campsites for tents or motor homes up to 27 feet long. Picnic tables, fireplaces, and piped water are provided. Flush toilets are available. Pets are permitted.

Reservations, fee: Phone MISTIX at (800)444-PARK ($3.95 MISTIX fee); $12-$14 fee per night; pets $1.

Who to contact: Phone the park at (209)296-7488.

Location: From Jackson, drive 11 miles northeast on Highway 88. Turn on Pine Grove-Volcano Road and drive 1.5 miles to the park.

Trip note: This park, about three miles from Sutter Creek, is like entering a time machine. It offers a reconstructed Miwok village with petroglyphs, bedrock mortars, a cultural center, and interpretive talks for groups by reservation. Set at 2,500 feet elevation. Open year-round.

Map grid **j8**

WHITE AZALEA

on Mokelumne River
ELDORADO NATIONAL FOREST

Campsites, facilities: There are six tent sites. Picnic tables and fireplaces are provided. Vault toilets are available. There is **no piped water,** so bring your own. Pets are permitted on leashes or otherwise controlled.

Reservations, fee: No reservations, no fee.

Who to contact: Phone the Eldorado National Forest Amador Ranger District at (209)295-4251.

Location: From Stockton on Highway 99, turn east on Highway 88 and drive approximately 78 miles to Ellis Road (across from Lumberyard Ranger Station). Turn right and drive 12 miles (seven miles paved, five miles gravel) to Mokelumne campground. Continue past it for three-quarters. The road is steep, narrow, and winding in spots and is not good for large RVs.

Trip note: This is a take-your-pick deal. It's one of the three primitive camps set on the North Fork of the Mokelumne River. It's a pretty spot—just remember to bring your own drinking water or a water purifying system that will screen *Giardia*. It gets very hot here in mid-summer.The elevation is 3,500 feet. Open from May to November.

Map grid **j8**

MOORE CREEK

on Mokelumne River
ELDORADO NATIONAL FOREST

Campsites, facilities: There are eight campsites for tents or motor homes. Picnic tables and fireplaces are provided. Vault toilets are available. There is **no piped water,** so bring your own. Pets are permitted on leashes or otherwise controlled.

Reservations, fee: No reservations, no fee.

Who to contact: Phone the Eldorado National Forest Amador Ranger District at (209)295-4251.

Location: From Stockton on Highway 99, turn east on Highway 88 and drive approximately 78 miles to Ellis Road (across from Lumberyard Ranger Station). Turn right and drive 12 miles (seven miles paved, five miles gravel) to the Mokelumne campground. Continue past it for a short distance to the bridge. Cross the bridge to the campground. The road is steep, narrow, and winding in spots and is not good for large RVs.

Trip note: This is one of three camps set beside the Mokelumne River. The other two are White Azalea and Mokelumne. So if you don't like the company or the surroundings, you can keep on the move until you find one that has the right feel. The elevation is 3,200 feet. Very hot here in mid-summer. Open from May to November.

Map grid j8

MOKELUMNE

on Mokelumne River

ELDORADO NATIONAL FOREST

Campsites, facilities: There are eight tent sites. Picnic tables and fireplaces are provided. Vault toilets are available. There is **no piped water,** so bring your own. Pets are permitted on leashes or otherwise controlled.

Reservations, fee: No reservations, no fee.

Who to contact: Phone the Eldorado National Forest Amador Ranger District at (209)295-4251.

Location: From Stockton on Highway 99, turn east on Highway 88 and drive approximately 78 miles to Ellis Road (across from Lumberyard Ranger Station). Turn right and drive 12 miles (seven miles paved, five miles gravel) to the campground on the river. The road is steep, narrow, and winding in spots and is not good for large RVs.

Trip note: This primitive spot set beside the Mokelumne River, is pretty, quiet, and there's rarely anybody else here. There are some good swimming holes nearby. Fishing is fair, with the trout on the small side. This is one in a series of camps on the Mokelumne. The elevation is 3,200 feet. It gets very hot here in mid-summer. Open from May to November.

Map grid j9

SOUTH SHORE

on Lower Bear River Reservoir

ELDORADO NATIONAL FOREST

Campsites, facilities: There are 13 sites for tents only and nine campsites for tents or motor homes. There are four two-family sites. Picnic tables, fireplaces, piped water, and vault toilets are provided. A boat ramp is available at nearby resort. A grocery store, boat rentals, and propane gas are nearby.

Reservations, fee: Reserve through MISTIX at (800)283-CAMP ($6 MISTIX fee); $7 fee per night; $14 per night for two-family sites.

Who to contact: Phone the Eldorado National Forest Amador Ranger District at (209)295-4251.

Location: From Stockton on Highway 99, drive approximately 80 miles east on Highway 88 to the well-signed campground turn-off on the right. Turn and drive four miles over the dam. The campground entrance is on the right.

Trip note: This pretty mountain lake has provided much improved trout fishing in the past few years. It is set at 5,900 feet elevation, so the lake frees of ice earlier in the year than the relatively nearby lakes, Silver and Caples, which are at higher elevations. Open from June to November.

Map grid **j9**

BEAR RIVER GROUP CAMP

on Bear River Reservoir
ELDORADO NATIONAL FOREST

Campsites, facilities: There are three group campsites for tents or motor homes. Picnic tables, fireplaces, and piped water are provided. Vault toilets are available. A grocery store, a boat ramp, boat rentals, and propane gas are available nearby.

Reservations, fee: Reservations required; fee varies with site.

Who to contact: Contact the Eldorado National Forest Amador Ranger District at (209)295-4251.

Location: From Stockton on Highway 99, drive approximately 80 miles east on Highway 88 to the well-signed Bear River turnoff on the right. Turn and drive five miles over the dam. The campground entrance is on the left.

Trip note: This camp is set near the shore of Bear River Reservoir, a pretty lake that provides power boating and trout fishing. Open from June to November.

Map grid **j9**

BEAR RIVER LAKE RESORT

on Bear River Reservoir

Campsites, facilities: There are 127 campsites for tents or motor homes, many with partial hookups. Picnic tables, fireplaces, and piped water are provided. Rest rooms, showers, a sanitary disposal station, a boat ramp, boat rentals, firewood, ice, propane gas, a laundromat, a post office, a telephone, and a grocery store are available. Pets are permitted.

Reservations, fee: Reservations recommended; $18.50 fee per night.

Who to contact: Phone the resort at (209)295-4868.

Location: From Stockton on Highway 99, drive approximately 80 miles east on Highway 88 to the well-signed campground entrance on the right. Turn and drive four miles to the resort.

Trip note: This is the largest and most developed of three camps on pretty Bear River Reservoir. Trout fishing is excellent in early summer, with bonus stocks of large trout supplementing plants from the Department of Fish and Game. The elevation is 6,000 feet. Open year-round.

◆ MAP D4 ◆

BEACH
DESERT
FOOTHILL
TREES
URBAN
GRASSLAND
5% CLUB

15 MILES

to Sierraville
to Loyalton
to Hallelujah Jct.
to Sutcliffe, NV
to Graniteville
to Cisco Grove
to Pioneer
to Pacific House
to Fernley, NV
to Silver Springs, NV
to Smith, NV
to Lake Alpine
to Coleville

Webber Lake
TAHOE
Stampede Res.
Verdi
Sparks
Independence Lake
Donner Summit EL. 7,239
Hobart Mills
Prosser Creek Res.
Boca Res.
Floriston
Soda Springs
Donner Lake
Truckee
Martis Creek Reservoir
NAT'L.
Crystal Bay
Tahoe Vista
Incline Village
Virginia City
Washoe Lake
Silver City
Dayton
Tahoe City
FOREST
Lake Tahoe
Marlette Lake
River
Homewood
Tahoma
Carson City
Wentworth Springs
Meeks Bay
Glenbrook
Stewart
Loon Lake
Zephyr Cove
Carson
ELDO-RADO
Stateline
Genoa
Mineral Pk. EL. 8,319
Camp Richardson
South Lake Tahoe
Minden
Gardnerville
Lake Aloha
Echo Lake
Echo Summit EL. 7,382
Meyers
TOIYABE
Kyburz
Twin Bridges
NAT'L.
NEVADA
Picketts Jct.
Luther Pass EL. 7,740
Woodfords
East Fork
HOPE VALLEY
Kit Carson
NAT'L.
Carson Pass EL. 8,573
Markleeville
FOREST
Topaz Lake
Monitor Pass EL. 8,314
Mt. Reba EL. 8,758
Pacific Grade Summit EL. 8,050
STANIS-LAUS NAT'L. F.
FOREST
Topaz

89 80 395 267 431 341 89 28 28 342 50 50 395 89 88 50 89 88 395 89 208 89 4

a b c d e f g h i j
0 1 2 3 4 5 6 7 8 9

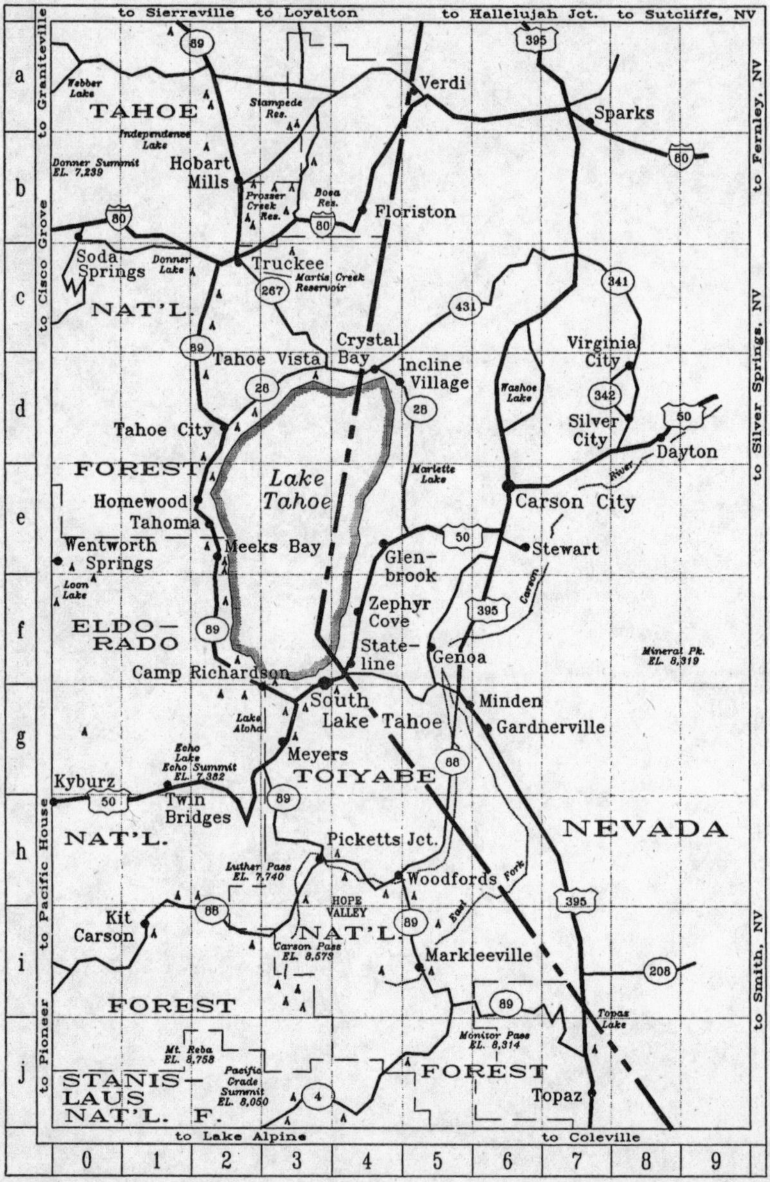

COLD CREEK

Map grid a1

TAHOE NATIONAL FOREST

Campsites, facilities: There are 13 campsites for tents or motor homes up to 22 feet long. Piped water, vault toilets, picnic tables, and fireplaces are provided. Pets are permitted if they are quiet and on leashes or otherwise controlled. Supplies are available in Sierraville.

Reservations, fee: No reservations; $7 fee per night.

Who to contact: Phone Tahoe National Forest Headquarters at (916)265-4531, or California Land Management at (916)582-0120.

Location: From Sierraville, drive five miles southeast on Highway 89 to the campground on your right.

Trip note: This is a pretty, easy-to-reach mountain campsite set along Cold Creek at 5,800 feet elevation. A bonus here is the nearby Campbell Hot Springs. Open from May through October.

UPPER LITTLE TRUCKEE

Map grid a2

at Stampede Reservoir
TAHOE NATIONAL FOREST

Campsites, facilities: There are 26 campsites for tents or motor homes up to 22 feet long. Piped water, vault toilets, picnic tables, and fireplaces are provided. Pets are permitted if they are quiet and on leashes or otherwise controlled. Supplies are available in Sierraville.

Reservations, fee: No reservations; $7 fee per night.

Who to contact: Phone Tahoe National Forest Headquarters at (916)265-4531, or California Land Management at (916)582-0120.

Location: From Sierraville, drive nine miles southeast on Highway 89 to the campground on the right.

Trip note: This one is set along the Little Truckee River at 6,100 feet elevation, two miles from Stampede Reservoir. Open from May through October.

LOWER LITTLE TRUCKEE

Map grid a2

near Stampede Reservoir
TAHOE NATIONAL FOREST

Campsites, facilities: There are 15 campsites for tents or motor homes up to 22 feet long. Piped water, vault toilets, picnic tables, and fireplaces are provided. Pets are permitted if they are quiet and on leashes or otherwise controlled. Supplies are available in Sierraville.

Reservations, fee: No reservations; $7 fee per night.

Who to contact: Phone Tahoe National Forest Headquarters at (916)265-4531,or California Land Management at (916)582-0120.

Location: From Sierraville, drive nine miles southeast on Highway 89 to the campground on the right.

Trip note: This pretty camp is set along the Little Truckee River at 6,000 feet, about two miles from Stampede Reservoir. Open from May through October.

LOGGER

Map grid a3

at Stampede Reservoir
TAHOE NATIONAL FOREST

Campsites, facilities: There are 252 campsites for tents or motor homes up to 32 feet long. Piped water, a sanitary dump station, flush toilets, picnic tables, and fireplaces are provided. A concrete boat ramp is available one mile from camp. A grocery store is nearby.

Reservations, fee: For reservations phone MISTIX at (800)283-CAMP ($6 MISTIX fee); $9 fee per night.

Who to contact: Phone California Land Management at (916)582-0120.

Location: From Truckee, drive seven miles east on Interstate 80. Take the Boca-Hirschdale ramp and drive eight miles north to the Stampede Reservoir Dam. Turn west and drive one mile to the campground.

Trip note: This is one of the Forest Service's largest and most popular campgrounds in the region. It's easy to see why. The campground is set along the south side of Stampede Reservoir at 5,900 feet elevation, about a mile east of a good boat ramp. Ideal for campers, boaters, and anglers. Open from May through October.

Map grid a3

EMIGRANT GROUP CAMP

at Stampede Reservoir
TAHOE NATIONAL FOREST

Campsites, facilities: There are two 25-person campsites and two 50-person campsites for tents or motor homes up to 32 feet long. Piped water, a sanitary dump station, vault toilets, picnic tables, and fireplaces are provided. Bring your own firewood. A three-lane concrete boat ramp is available.

Reservations, fee: Reservations required; phone MISTIX at (800)283-CAMP ($6 MISTIX fee); $25-$50 group fee per night.

Who to contact: Phone California Land Management at (916) 582-0120.

Location: From Truckee, drive seven miles east on Interstate 80. Take the Boca-Hirschdale ramp and drive eight miles north to the Stampede Reservoir Dam. Turn west and drive one-half mile to the campground.

Trip note: This camp is ideal for groups, like Boy Scouts, for a weekend expedition. The campsite is set along Stampede Reservoir, with a boat ramp nearby. The elevation is 6,000 feet. Open from May through September.

Map grid b2

PROSSER GROUP CAMPGROUND

on Prosser Reservoir
TAHOE NATIONAL FOREST

Campsites, facilities: There is one large campsite that will accommodate up to 50 people. Five picnic tables, three fire rings, one large barbecue, and a large parking area that can accommodate 40 trailers are provided. Piped water and vault toilets are available. A concrete boat ramp is nearby on Prosser Reservoir. Pets are permitted if they are quiet and on leashes or otherwise controlled.

Reservations, fee: Reservations required through MISTIX (800)283-CAMP ($10 MISTIX fee); $35 fee per night.

Who to contact: Phone the Tahoe National Forest Truckee Ranger District at (916)587-3558, or write to P.O. Box 399, Truckee, CA 95734.

Location: From Truckee, travel three miles north on Highway 89. Turn east to the west-shore peninsula of Prosser Reservoir and drive to the campground.

Trip note: This is one of the few camps at Prosser Reservoir that provides piped water. That's a bonus for the big groups that reserve this spot. A possible side trip is visiting the Donner Camp Historic and Picnic Site; just bring your own munchies. It is located across the highway, a half mile south of the camp on the southwest shore of Prosser Reservoir. There is also a short interpretive trail here. The elevation is 5,800 feet. Open from June through October.

Map grid **b2**

SAGE HEN CREEK
TAHOE NATIONAL FOREST

A

Campsites, facilities: There are ten undeveloped campsites for tents or motor homes up to 16 feet long. There is **no piped water,** but vault toilets are provided. Pack out your garbage. Pets are permitted if they are quiet and on leashes or otherwise controlled.

B

Reservations, fee: No reservations, no fee.

Who to contact: Phone the Tahoe National Forest Headquarters at (916)265-4531.

Location: From Truckee, drive nine miles north on Highway 89. Turn west on Sagehen Summit Road and drive two miles to the campground.

Trip note: This small, primitive camp gets missed by virtually all the out-of-towners. It is set beside little Sage Hen Creek at 6,500 feet elevation. Open from June through October.

C

Map grid **b2**

PROSSER
on Prosser Reservoir
TAHOE NATIONAL FOREST

D4

Campsites, facilities: There are 29 campsites for tents or motor homes up to 22 feet long. Piped water, vault toilets, picnic tables, and fireplaces are provided. A concrete boat ramp is nearby on Prosser Reservoir. Pets are permitted if they are quiet and on leashes or otherwise controlled.

E

Reservations, fee: No reservations; $8 fee per night.

Who to contact: Phone the Tahoe National Forest Headquarters at (916)265-4531.

Location: From Truckee, travel three miles north on Highway 89. Turn east to the west-shore peninsula of Prosser Reservoir and drive to the campground.

Trip note: This is one of several campgrounds set along the shore of Prosser Reservoir. A boat ramp is nearby. The elevation is 5,800 feet. Open from June through October.

F

Map grid **b2**

LAKESIDE
on Prosser Reservoir
TAHOE NATIONAL FOREST

G

Campsites, facilities: There are 30 undesignated campsites for tents or motor homes up to 33 feet long. There is **no piped water,** but vault toilets are provided. Pets are permitted if they are quiet and on leashes or otherwise controlled. A boat ramp is available nearby.

H

Reservations, fee: No reservations, no fee.

Who to contact: Phone the Tahoe National Forest Headquarters at (916)265-4531.

Location: From Truckee, travel a short distance north on Highway 89 to the Prosser Reservoir turn-off on your right. Drive four miles northwest to the campground.

Trip note: This is a primitive campsite set along the northern shore of Prosser Reservoir at 5,700 feet elevation. The shore here is good for hand-launching boats, and a concrete boat ramp is nearby. The trout fishing is often quite good after the ice breaks up in late spring. Open from June through October.

I

Map grid **b3**

ANNIE McCLOUD
on Prosser Reservoir
TAHOE NATIONAL FOREST

J

Campsites, facilities: There are ten campsites for tents or motor homes up to 16 feet long. There is **no piped water.** Chemical toilets are provided at the campground, and vault toilets are provided across the road from the campground entrance.

Reservations, fee: No reservations, no fee.

Who to contact: Phone the Tahoe National Forest Headquarters at (916)265-4531.

Location: From Interstate 80, drive one-half mile north on Highway 89 to Prosser Dam Road. Turn right and travel 4.5 miles, past the dam to the campground.

Trip note: This primitive camp is set beside Prosser Reservoir at 5,800 feet elevation. It's ideal for car-top boats, especially canoes. Side trip options include hiking on the Overland Emigrant Trail. Open from June through October.

Map grid b3

BOYINTON MILL

near Boca Reservoir

TAHOE NATIONAL FOREST

Campsites, facilities: There are ten campsites for tents or motor homes up to 32 feet long. There is **no piped water,** but vault toilets and picnic tables are provided. Pets are permitted if they are quiet and on leashes or otherwise controlled.

Reservations, fee: No reservations, no fee.

Who to contact: Phone the Tahoe National Forest Headquarters at (916)265-4531.

Location: From Truckee, travel seven miles east on Interstate 80. Take the Boca-Hirschdale exit. Drive past Boca Reservoir, four miles north of the dam to the campground.

Trip note: If the campsites at Boca Reservoir are full or you don't like the company, this nearby camp provides an alternative. It is set about four miles north of the lake in a pretty spot along the Little Truckee River. The elevation is 5,700 feet. Open from May through October.

Map grid b3

BOCA REST CAMPGROUND

on Boca Reservoir

TAHOE NATIONAL FOREST

Campsites, facilities: There are 25 campsites for tents or motor homes up to 22 feet long. Piped water, vault toilets, picnic tables, and fireplaces are provided. Pets are permitted if they are quiet and on leashes or otherwise controlled. A concrete boat ramp is three miles away on the southwest shore of Boca Reservoir. Truckee is the nearest place for telephones and supplies.

Reservations, fee: No reservations, no fee.

Who to contact: Phone the Tahoe National Forest Headquarters at (916)265-4531.

Location: From Truckee, drive seven miles east on Interstate 80. Take the Boca-Hirschdale exit and drive to the dam at Boca Reservoir. Continue for two miles to the campground on the northeast shore of Boca Reservoir.

Trip note: This camp is one of the options for campers at Boca Reservoir. The elevation is 5,700 feet. Open from May through October.

Map grid b3

BOCA CAMPGOUND

on Boca Reservoir

TAHOE NATIONAL FOREST

Campsites, facilities: There are 20 campsites for tents or motor homes up to 16 feet long. There is **no piped water,** but portable toilets and fireplaces are provided. Pets are permitted if they are quiet and on leashes or otherwise controlled. A concrete boat ramp is north of the campground on Boca Reservoir. Truckee is the nearest place for telephones and supplies.

Reservations, fee: No reservations, no fee.

Who to contact: Phone the Tahoe National Forest Headquarters at (916)265-4531.

Location: From Truckee, drive seven miles east on Interstate 80. Take the Boca-Hirschdale exit and drive to the southwest shore of Boca Reservoir to the campground.

Trip note: Boca Reservoir is known for being a "big fish factory"; it definitely has a surprising number of large rainbow trout and brown trout, however elusive they can sometimes prove to be. The lake is set at 5,700 feet elevation. Open from May through October.

A B C D4 E F G H I J

Map grid c2

DONNER MEMORIAL STATE PARK

on Donner Lake

Campsites, facilities: There are 154 campsites for tents or motor homes up to 28 feet long. Piped water, flush toilets, showers, picnic tables, and fireplaces are provided. Pets are permitted. Supplies are available in Truckee.

Reservations, fee: Reserve through MISTIX at (800)444-PARK ($3.95 MISTIX fee); $12-$14 fee per night; pets $1.

Who to contact: Phone (916)587-3841.

Location: From Truckee, drive two miles west on Donner Pass Road to the park.

Trip note: Are you getting hungry? Hey, stop looking at my arm that way. Yep, this is the site of the ill-fated Donner Party, and there are some exhibits here that detail the sordid tale. The camp is set at 5,900 feet along the lake, of course, which provides boating and fishing. In winter, a good cross-country ski trail is available. Just bring plenty of food.

Map grid c2

GOOSE MEADOW

on Truckee River

TAHOE NATIONAL FOREST

Campsites, facilities: There are 25 campsites for tents or motor homes up to 30 feet long. There is **no piped water,** but vault toilets, fire grills, and picnic tables are provided. Pets are permitted if they are quiet and on leashes or otherwise controlled. Supplies are available in Truckee and Tahoe City.

Reservations, fee: No reservations; $8 fee per night.

Who to contact: Phone the Tahoe National Forest District Office at (916)587-3558, or California Land Management at (916)582-0120.

Location: From Truckee, drive four miles south on Highway 89 to the campground entrance on the river side of the highway.

Trip note: This is one in a series of primitive, easy-access camps set beside the Truckee River. There is good trout fishing and rafting. The elevation is 5,800 feet. Open from May through October.

Map grid c3

MARTIS CREEK LAKE

near Truckee

Campsites, facilities: There are 25 campsites for tents or motor homes up to 30 feet long. Piped water, vault toilets, picnic tables, and fireplaces are provided. Supplies are available in Truckee.

Reservations, fee: No reservations, no fee.

Who to contact: Phone the U.S. Corps of Engineers, Martis Creek Lake at (916)639-2342.

Location: From Truckee, drive 2.5 miles southeast on Highway 267 to the entrance to the lake. Turn in and drive another 2.5 miles to the campground at the end of the road.

Trip note: The camp is set along the north shore of Martis Lake, which is fast becoming a fisherman's paradise thanks to special catch-and-release rules that are allowing the trout to grow to full-adult size. The law mandates the use of fishing with flies and lures only, or with single barbless hooks. Only non-motorized boating is allowed. The elevation is 5,800 feet. Open from May through October.

Map grid d2

WILLIAM KENT

near Lake Tahoe

LAKE TAHOE BASIN

Campsites, facilities: There are 55 tent spaces and 40 campsites for motor homes up to 24 feet long. Piped water, flush toilets, a sanitary dump station, picnic tables, and fireplaces are provided. Pets are permitted. A grocery store, a laundromat, and propane gas are available nearby.

Reservations, fee: Reserve through MISTIX at (800)283-CAMP ($6 MISTIX fee); $10 fee per night.

Who to contact: Phone California Land Management at (916)544-5994, or phone the campground direct at (916)573-3642.

Location: From Tahoe City, drive three miles south on Highway 89.

Trip note: Set at 6,300 feet elevation near the shore of Lake Tahoe, this is one of several camps at the giant, old lake. Open from June through September.

Map grid d2

LAKE FOREST CAMPGROUND

on Lake Tahoe

Campsites, facilities: There are 21 campsites for tents or motor homes up to 20 feet long. Piped water, flush toilets and picnic tables are provided. A boat ramp is available. Pets are permitted. A grocery store, a laundromat, and propane gas are available nearby.

Reservations, fee: No reservations; $10 fee per night.

Who to contact: Phone (916)583-5544.

Location: From Tahoe City, drive two miles north on Highway 28.

Trip note: Lake Tahoe is world-reknowned for its beauty. Its deep aquamarine blues are set in a giant pocket of trees and rock in the Sierra mountain country. This is one of several camps along its shore. The bonus here is a nearby boat launch. The elevation is 6,200 feet. Open from April through October.

Map grid d2

SILVER CREEK

on Truckee River

TAHOE NATIONAL FOREST

Campsites, facilities: There are 25 sites for tents or motor homes up to 40 feet long. Piped water, vault toilets, picnic tables, and fireplaces are provided. Pets are permitted if they are quiet and on leashes or otherwise controlled. Supplies are available in Truckee and Tahoe City.

Reservations, fee: Reservations accepted through MISTIX at (800)283-CAMP ($6 MISTIX fee); $8 fee per night.

Who to contact: Phone the Tahoe National Forest District Office at (916)587-3558.

Location: From Truckee, drive six miles south on Highway 89 to the campground entrance on the river side of the highway.

Trip note: This pretty campground is set near where Deer Creek enters the Truckee

River. The trout fishing is often good in this area, and side trips include a hike up the good trail that runs along Deer Creek. The elevation is 5,800 feet. Open from June through September.

Map grid **d2**

TAHOE STATE RECREATION AREA

on Lake Tahoe

Campsites, facilities: There are 39 campsites for tents or motor homes up to 21 feet long. Piped water, showers, flush toilets, picnic tables, fireplaces, a playground, a pier, and a boat ramp are provided. Pets are permitted. Firewood, other supplies, and a laundromat are available nearby.

Reservations, fee: Reserve through MISTIX at (800)444-PARK ($3.95 MISTIX fee); $12-$14 camp use fee; $1 for pets.

Who to contact: Phone (916)583-3074.

Location: From Tahoe City, drive one-quarter mile north on Highway 28.

Trip note: This is a popular summer-only campground at Lake Tahoe. It is quite close to facilities at Tahoe City, with recreation options that include a nearby fishing pier, horseback riding, boating, and rafting down the Truckee River.

Map grid **d3**

SANDY BEACH CAMPGROUND

on Lake Tahoe

Campsites, facilities: There are 50 campsites with full or partial hookups for tents or motor homes up to 35 feet long. Piped water, showers, flush toilets, picnic tables, and fireplaces are provided. A boat ramp is available and pets are permitted. A grocery store, a laundromat, and propane gas are available nearby.

Reservations, fee: Reservations accepted; fees vary according to site.

Who to contact: Phone (916)546-7682.

Location: From Tahoe City, drive eight miles north on Highway 28 to the campground.

Trip note: This is one of several options along the shore of magnificent Lake Tahoe, one of California's true natural wonders. The nearby boat launch is a bonus here. Fishing for rainbow trout is often quite good in this area. For the bigger mackinaws, you must be on the water at dawn and troll 120 feet and deeper off the Tahoe underwater ledge. The elevation is 6,200 feet. Open from April through October.

Map grid **e0**

WENTWORTH SPRINGS

near Loon Lake

ELDORADO NATIONAL FOREST

Campsites, facilities: There are eight tent sites. Two of the sites will accommodate two families each. There is **no piped water,** but vault toilets, picnic tables, and fireplaces are provided. Access recommended for motorcycles or four-wheel drive vehicles only. Pets are permitted on leashes or otherwise controlled.

Reservations, fee: No reservations, no fee.

Who to contact: Phone the Eldorado National Forest Pacific Ranger District at (916)644-2349.

Location: From Riverton on US 50, drive 23 miles north on Soda Springs-Riverton Road. Turn right on Ice House Road (toward Loon Lake) and drive four miles to the fork in the road at Loon Lake. Bear left and drive five miles to the campground. (The access road is suitable for four-wheel drive vehicles or motorcycles).

Trip note: This is a good spot for four-wheel drive cowboys to set up a base camp. Loon Lake, about a mile away, has good trout fishing in early summer, and the area supports abundant wildlife populations. This camp is set at 6,200 feet elevation. Open from June through October.

Map grid **e2**

SUGAR PINE POINT STATE PARK

on Lake Tahoe

Campsites, facilities: There are 175 campsites for tents or motor homes up to 30 feet long. Piped water, showers, flush toilets, a sanitary dump station, picnic tables, and fireplaces are provided. A grocery store, laundry facilities, and propane gas are available nearby. There is wheelchair access to picnic areas. Pets are permitted.

Reservations, fee: Reserve through MISTIX at (800)444-PARK ($3.95 MISTIX fee); $12-$14 camp use fee; $1 for pets.

Who to contact: Call (916)525-7982.

Location: From the junction of Highway 89 and US 50 in South Lake Tahoe, drive about 18 miles north on Highway 89.

Trip note: This is one of three beautiful and popular state parks set on the southwest shore of Lake Tahoe. This one is located just north of Meeks Bay on General Creekwith almost two miles of lake frontage. The elevation is 6,200 feet. Open all year, but no showers are available during winter.

Map grid **e2**

MEEKS BAY

on Lake Tahoe

Campsites, facilities: There are 40 campsites for tents or motor homes up to 24 feet long. Piped water, flush toilets, picnic tables, and fireplaces are provided. Laundry facilities and groceries are available nearby. Pets are permitted.

Reservations, fee: No reservations; $10 fee per night.

Who to contact: Phone California Land Management at (916)544-5994, or Lake Tahoe Basin Management Unit at (916)573-2600.

Location: From the junction of Highway 89 and US 50 in South Lake Tahoe, drive about 17 miles north on Highway 89.

Trip note: This beautiful spot is set along the southwest edge of Lake Tahoe. If you are stuck in the Tahoe Basin without a place to camp, this camp always provides hope, since no reservations are accepted. But get there early. The elevation is 6,300 feet. Open from May through October.

Map grid **e2**

KASPIAN

on Lake Tahoe

LAKE TAHOE BASIN

Campsites, facilities: There are ten tent spaces. Piped water, flush toilets, picnic tables, and fireplaces are provided. Pets are permitted if they are quiet and on leashes or otherwise controlled. A grocery store, a laundromat, and propane gas are available nearby.

Reservations, fee: No reservations; $4 fee per night.

Who to contact: Phone California Land Management at (916)544-5994.

Location: From Tahoe City, drive four miles south on Highway 89.

Trip note: Nearby Lake Tahoe and the Truckee River make this a take-your-pick deal for a quality vacation. The elevation is 6,300 feet. Open from May through September.

MEEKS BAY RESORT

Map grid e2

Campsites, facilities: There are 28 campsites for motor homes of any length. Full hookups, showers, flush toilets, picnic tables, and fireplaces are provided. Laundry facilities and groceries are available nearby. A boat ramp is available. No pets are allowed.

Reservations, fee: Reservations accepted; $12 fee per night; $3-$5 day use fee.

Who to contact: Phone (916)525-7242.

Location: From the junction of Highway 89 and US 50 in South Lake Tahoe, drive about 17 miles north on Highway 89.

Trip note: This is a relatively small, privately-operated campground set along the edge of Lake Tahoe. You'd best plan on a reservation if you want to stay here. The elevation is 6,300 feet. Open from June through September.

PLEASANT

on Loon Lake
ELDORADO NATIONAL FOREST

Map grid f0

Campsites, facilities: There are ten tent sites. There is **no piped water,** but pit toilets, picnic tables, and fireplaces are provided. The camp is accessible by boat or trail only. Pets are permitted on leashes or otherwise controlled.

Reservations, fee: No reservations, no fee.

Who to contact: Phone the Eldorado National Forest Pacific Ranger District at (916)644-2349.

Location: From Riverton on US 50, drive 32 miles north to end of Ice House-Loon Lake road to the boat ramp and trailhead, near Loon Lake campground. The distance from the boat ramp to the campground is 2.5 to three miles. It's the same distance by trail to the campground on the east shore of the lake.

Trip note: This premium Sierra Nevada campground can be reached only by boat or by foot. It is set alongside Loon Lake in classic Sierra Nevada mountain country. The trout fishing is good at the lake. Hikers might consider this a warm-up trip for backpacking through the nearby Desolation Wilderness area to numerous smaller lakes. The elevation is 6,500 feet. Open from June through October.

LOON LAKE

ELDORADO NATIONAL FOREST

Map grid f0

Campsites, facilities: There are 34 campsites for tents or motor homes up to 22 feet long. Piped water, vault toilets, picnic tables, and fireplaces are provided. Pets are permitted on leashes or otherwise controlled. A boat ramp and swimming beach are nearby.

Reservations, fee: Reserve through MISTIX (800)283-CAMP ($6 MISTIX fee); $7 fee per night.

Who to contact: Phone the Eldorado National Forest Pacific Ranger District at (916)644-2349.

Location: From Riverton on US 50, drive 32 miles north to the end of Ice House-Loon Lake road.

Trip note: This is the most popular campground at Loon Lake, and it's easy to see why. A picnic area and a beach (with a small unit to change in) are adjacent to camp, and a trail from camp loops around and through the Desolation

Wilderness area. The trout fishing is often quite good at the lake, especially in early summer. The elevation is 6,500 feet. Open from June through September.

Map grid **f2**

EMERALD BAY STATE PARK
on Lake Tahoe

Campsites, facilities: There are 100 campsites for tents or motor homes up to 25 feet long. Piped water, showers, flush toilets, picnic tables, and fireplaces are provided. Pets are permitted. There are also 20 boat-in campsites available on the north side of the bay with water and toilets provided.

Reservations, fee: Reserve through MISTIX at (800)444-PARK ($3.95 MISTIX fee); $12-$14 camp use fee; $1 for pets. No reservations for boat-in sites; fee is $8 per night.

Who to contact: Call (916)541-3030.

Location: From the junction of Highway 89 and US 50 in South Lake Tahoe, drive eight miles north on Highway 89.

Trip note: Along with nearby Bliss State Park, this is one of the most beautiful and popular state parks in California. It is set on the southwest shore of Lake Tahoe in Emerald Bay. There are several scenic hiking trails and the boat-in campsites here provide a bonus option. The elevation is 6,800 feet.Open from June through September.

Map grid **f2**

D.L. BLISS STATE PARK
on Lake Tahoe

Campsites, facilities: There are 168 campsites for tents or motor homes up to 15 feet long. Piped water, showers, flush toilets, picnic tables, and fireplaces are provided. Pets are permitted.

Reservations, fee: Reserve through MISTIX at (800)444-PARK ($3.95 MISTIX fee); $12-$14 camp use fee; $1 for pets.

Who to contact: Call (916)525-7277.

Location: From the junction of Highway 89 and US 50 in South Lake Tahoe, drive 11 miles north on Highway 89.

Trip note: This is one of the state's most popular and beautiful parks, as is Emerald Bay State Park. It's set on the southwest shore of Lake Tahoe and you don't really need to do much here to enjoy yourself, other than just leaning against a tree and watching the water lap at the beach. The elevation is 6,700 feet. Open from June through Labor Day.

Map grid **f3**

CAMP RICHARDSON RESORT
on Lake Tahoe

Campsites, facilities: There are 300 campsites for tents or motor homes of any length, some with full or partial hookups. Piped water, showers, flush toilets, a sanitary dump station, a playground, a recreation hall, picnic tables, and fireplaces are provided. A boat ramp, boat rentals, laundry facilities, groceries, and propane gas are also available. Pets permitted.

Reservations, fee: Reservations accepted; $15-$22 fee per night.

Who to contact: Phone (916)541-1801.

Location: From the junction of Highway 89 and US 50 in South Lake Tahoe, drive two miles north on Highway 89.

Trip note: This is one of the few Forest Service campgrounds that is privately operated. In turn, they offer "planned recreation activities" like horseshoes, badminton, and volleyball. It's not exactly a Five Percenters spot, but it's a nice place with public beaches, horseback riding, and a bicycle path nearby. The elevation is 6,300 feet. Open from June through October.

Map grid g0

WRIGHT'S LAKE
ELDORADO NATIONAL FOREST

Campsites, facilities: There are 35 sites for tents only and 36 campsites for tents or motor homes up to 22 feet long. Piped water, vault toilets, picnic tables, and fireplaces are provided. Pets are permitted on leashes or otherwise controlled.

Reservations, fee: Reserve through MISTIX at (800)283-CAMP ($6 MISTIX fee); $8 fee per night.

Who to contact: Phone the Eldorado National Forest Pacific Ranger District at (916)644-2349.

Location: From Placerville, drive 34 miles east on US 50. Turn north on Wrights Lake Road and drive eight miles to the campground.

Trip note: This high-mountain lake (7,000 feet) has shoreline camping, good fishing, and hiking, yet it is in a spot that often gets missed by the huddled masses. No boats with motors are allowed on the lake, a guarantee of quiet water, which makes it ideal for canoeists and small boats. Trails lead out from the camp in several directions, including two which lead to several lakes in the Desolation Wilderness area. Open from June through October.

Map grid g2

FALLEN LEAF CAMPGROUND
LAKE TAHOE BASIN

Campsites, facilities: There are 75 sites for tents only and 131 campsites for tents or motor homes up to 40 feet long. Piped water, flush toilets, picnic tables, and fireplaces are provided. A boat ramp, laundromat, and supplies are available nearby.

Reservations, fee: Reserve through MISTIX at (800)283-CAMP ($6 MISTIX fee); $10 fee per night.

Who to contact: Phone the U.S. Forest Service Tahoe Basin Management Unit at (916)544-5994.

Location: From the junction of Highway 89 and US 50 in South Lake Tahoe, drive two miles north on Highway 89 to the Fallen Leaf Lake turnoff. Turn left and drive 1.5 miles to the campground.

Trip note: This is a large "tent city" near the shores of Fallen Leaf Lake and set at 6,300 feet elevation. There are many recreation options here, including horseback riding nearby. A visitor center, located just north of the Fallen Leaf Lake turnoff on Highway 89, can provide more details. Lake Tahoe is just a few miles away to the north along with Kiva Picnic Area, Baldwin Beach, and Pope Beach on Highway 89. Open from May through October.

Map grid g2

CAMP SHELLEY
near Lake Tahoe
LAKE TAHOE BASIN

Campsites, facilities: There are 26 campsites for tents or motor homes up to 26 feet long. Piped water, flush toilets, showers, picnic tables, and fireplaces are provided. A boat ramp, groceries, and propane gas are available nearby at Camp Richardson. Pets are permitted on leashes and or otherwise controlled.

Reservations, fee: Reserve through the Livermore Area Recreation and Park District at (415)373-5700; $7.50 fee per night.

Who to contact: Phone the Ranger Office at (916)541-6985.

Location: From the junction of Highway 89 and US 50 in South Lake Tahoe, drive two miles north on Highway 89 to Camp Richardson. Continue past Camp Richardson on Highway 89 for 1.3 miles to the Mt. Tallac sign. Turn left and follow the signs to the campground.

Trip note: This privately-owned campground is set near Lake Tahoe and is nice for families. Bicycling, fishing, swimming, volleyball, and horseback riding are all nearby recreation options. Open from mid-June through Labor Day.

Map grid g3

CHRIS HAVEN MOBILE HOME AND RV PARK

near South Lake Tahoe

Campsites, facilities: There are 57 motor home spaces with full hookups. Patios, rest rooms, showers, and laundry facilities are provided.

Reservations, fee: Reservations recommended; $19 fee per night.

Who to contact: Phone (916)541-1895.

Location: From the junction of Highway 89 and US 50 in South Lake Tahoe, drive one-half mile south on US 50. Turn east on E Street and drive one block to the park.

Trip note: This is an RV-only park that is actually set within the boundaries of a mobile home park. If that excites you, go for it. Open all year.

Map grid g3

KOA SOUTH LAKE TAHOE CAMPGROUND

Campsites, facilities: There are 16 sites for tents only and 52 campsites with full hookups that will accommodate motor homes up to 30 feet long. Picnic tables, fire grills, rest rooms, showers, a sanitary dump station, a recreation room, a swimming pool, and a playground are on the premises. Laundry facilities, groceries, RV supplies, and propane gas are also available. Pets are permitted.

Reservations, fee: Reservations recommended; $18-$24 fee per night; $1.50 for pets.

Who to contact: Call (916)577-3693.

Location: From South Lake Tahoe, drive five miles south on US 50.

Trip note: The Tahoe area has it all, including gambling, fishing, hiking, bike rentals, and, in winter, good skiing. For motor home campers, this is a good spot to gamble on. The camp is set at 6,300 feet elevation. Open from April through December.

Map grid g3

TAHOE VALLEY CAMPGROUND

near Lake Tahoe

Campsites, facilities: There are 110 sites for tents only and 290 sites for motor homes of any length with full hookups. Rest rooms, a sanitary dump station, picnic tables, fireplaces, laundry facilities, a heated pool, a playground, a grocery store, RV supplies, propane gas, ice, firewood, and a recreation room are all provided on the premises. Pets are permitted.

Reservations, fee: Reservations recommended; $16-$23 fee per night, $1.50 for pets.

Who to contact: Phone (916)541-2222.

Location: From the junction of Highway 89 and US 50 in South Lake Tahoe, drive one-quarter mile south on US 50 to the entrance.

Trip note: This giant, privately-operated park near Lake Tahoe is a good one for motor home cruisers who want to hole up for awhile. The nearby attractions include five golf courses, horseback riding, the casinos, and, of course, "The Lake." Open mid-April through mid-October.

Map grid g4

EL DORADO RECREATION AREA

near Lake Tahoe

Campsites, facilities: There are 170 campsites for tents or motor homes up to 32 feet long. Piped water, flush toilets, showers, a sanitary dump station, a playground, picnic tables, and fireplaces are provided. A boat ramp is also available. Supplies and laundry facilities are available nearby. Pets are permitted.

Reservations, fee: Reservations accepted; $14.25 fee per night with a 2 night minimum; $1 for pets.

Who to contact: Call (916)573-2039 or (916)541-4611.

Location: From US 50 in South Lake Tahoe, drive a short distance south on Rufus Allen Boulevard to the campground.

Trip note: This city-operated campground is open from May through September and set near Lake Tahoe at 6,200 feet elevation. It's a good spot to park your RV while on a tour of Tahoe.

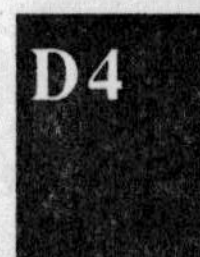

Map grid h1

KIRKWOOD LAKE

ELDORADO NATIONAL FOREST

Campsites, facilities: There are 12 tent sites. Piped water, vault toilets, picnic tables, and fireplaces are provided. Pets are permitted on leashes or otherwise controlled.

Reservations, fee: No reservations; $7 fee per night.

Who to contact: Phone the Eldorado National Forest Amador Ranger District at (209)295-4251.

Location: From Jackson, drive 60 miles east on Highway 88 to the campground entrance road on left. The actual entrance is one-half mile west of the Kirkwood Ski Resort Sign.

Trip note: Most people forget about this spot in the summer—it's a popular ski area in winter. But lakeside camping and the quiet waters of Kirkwood Lake make this a good choice for a short vacation. No boats with motors are allowed, which guarantees quiet water. The lake is stocked regularly with trout, and Kirkwood Ski Resort offers many summer activities, including horseback riding. The elevation is 7,600 feet. Open from June through October.

Map grid h2

CAPLES LAKE

ELDORADO NATIONAL FOREST

Campsites, facilities: There are 20 sites for tents only and 15 sites for tents or motor homes up to 22 feet long. Piped water, vault toilets, picnic tables, and fireplaces are provided. Groceries, propane gas, a boat ramp, and boat rentals are available nearby. Pets are permitted on leashes.

Reservations, fee: Reserve through MISTIX at (800)283-CAMP ($6 MISTIX fee); $7 use fee.

Who to contact: Phone the Eldorado National Forest Amador Ranger District at (209)295-4251.

Location: From Stockton on Highway 99, drive east on Highway 88 for about 107 miles (or east of Jackson for 63 miles). The campground is on the left across the road from the lake and the resort.

Trip note: Caples Lake, set in the high country at 7,800 feet elevation, is one of the best trout-fishing lakes for many miles, yet it also provides easy highway access. Fishing is best just after ice out, when the trout are practically saying "catch me." The surrounding National Forest provides numerous side trips, with back roads and trails detailed on the $2 map of Eldorado Forest. Open from June through October.

Map grid h3

HOPE VALLEY

near Carson River

TOIYABE NATIONAL FOREST

Campsites, facilities: There are 20 campsites for tents or motor homes up to 22 feet long. Piped water, vault toilets, picnic tables, and fireplaces are provided. Pets are permitted on leashes.

Reservations, fee: Reserve through MISTIX at (800)283-CAMP ($6 MISTIX fee); $7 fee per night.

Who to contact: Phone the Toiyabe National Forest Ranger District at (702)882-2766.

Location: From Carson Pass traveling east on Highway 88, drive 6.5 miles to Blue Lakes Road. Turn south and drive 1.5 miles to the campground. From the junction of Highways 89 and 88 traveling west, drive 2.5 miles on Highway 88. Turn south (left) on Blue Lakes Road and drive 1.5 miles to the campground.

Trip note: The valley here is one of California's prettiest settings. It's not widely known, yet it's easy to reach. The West Fork of the Carson River runs down the center of the valley, with Highway 88 providing easy access. Nearby side trip options include Red Lake Creek, Blue Lakes, ten miles away, or Tamarack Lake. The elevation is 7,300 feet. Open from June through October.

Map grid h4

KIT CARSON

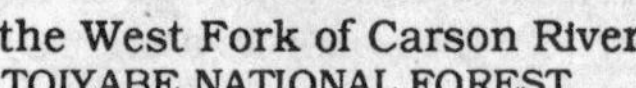

on the West Fork of Carson River

TOIYABE NATIONAL FOREST

Campsites, facilities: There are 12 campsites for tents or motor homes up to 22 feet long. Piped water, vault toilets, picnic tables, and fireplaces are provided. Pets are permitted on leashes.

Reservations, fee: Reservations not required; $7 fee per night.

Who to contact: Phone the Toiyabe National Forest Ranger District at (702)882-2766.

Location: From Woodfords, drive five miles west on Highway 88 to the campground.

Trip note: This is one in a series of pristine, high Sierra camps set alongside the West Fork of the Carson River. There's good trout fishing, thanks to regular stocks from the Department of Fish and Game. The elevation is 6,600 feet. Open from mid-May through mid-September.

Map grid h4

CRYSTAL SPRINGS

on the West Fork of Carson River

TOIYABE NATIONAL FOREST

Campsites, facilities: There are 20 campsites for tents or motor homes up to 22 feet long. Piped water, vault toilets, picnic tables, and fireplaces are provided. Pets are permitted on leashes.

Reservations, fee: Reservations not required; $7 fee per night.

Who to contact: Phone the Toiyabe National Forest Ranger District at (702)882-2766.

Location: From Woodfords, drive one mile west on Highway 88 to the campground.

Trip note: For many, this camp is ideal. Set at 6,000 feet right alongside the West Fork of the Carson River, this stretch is stocked with trout by the Department of Fish and Game. It is easy to reach, just off Highway 88, and supplies can be obtained in nearby Woodfords. Open from April through September.

Map grid h4

SNOWSHOE SPRINGS

on the West Fork of Carson River

TOIYABE NATIONAL FOREST

Campsites, facilities: There are 13 tent sites. Piped water, vault toilets, picnic tables, and fireplaces are provided. Pets are permitted on leashes.

Reservations, fee: Reservations not required; $7 fee per night.

Who to contact: Phone the Toiyabe National Forest Ranger District at (702)882-2766.

Location: From Woodfords, drive four miles west on Highway 88 to the campground.

Trip note: Take your pick of this or the other camps set at the streamside of the West Fork of the Carson River. This one is at 6,600 feet elevation. Trout are plentiful, but rarely large. Open from June through October.

Map grid h5

TURTLE ROCK PARK

near Woodfords

Campsites, facilities: There are 25 campsites for tents or motor homes up to 30 feet long. Piped water, pit toilets, picnic tables, and fireplaces are provided. Laundry facilities, groceries, and propane gas are available nearby.

Reservations, fee: Reservations not required; $6-$8 fee per night.

Who to contact: The camp is administered by Alpine County Parks. For information call (916)694-2255.

Location: From Woodfords, drive 3.5 miles south on Highway 89 to the park entrance.

Trip note: This pretty, wooded campground, set at 6,000 feet, gets missed by a lot of folks. That's because it is administered at the county level and also because most vacationers want the more pristine beauty of the nearby camps along the Carson River. Open from May through September.

Map grid i1

EAST SILVER LAKE

ELDORADO NATIONAL FOREST

Campsites, facilities: There are 28 sites for tents only and 34 campsites for tents or motor homes. Picnic tables, fireplaces, and piped water are provided. Vault toilets and a boat ramp are available. A grocery store, boat rentals, and propane gas are nearby. Pets are permitted on leashes.

Reservations, fee: Reserve through MISTIX at (800)283-CAMP ($6 MISTIX fee); $7 fee per night.

Who to contact: Phone the Eldorado National Forest Amador Ranger District at (209)295-4251.

Location: From Stockton on Highway 99, turn east on Highway 88. Drive approximately 96 miles (52 miles east of Jackson) to the well-signed campground entrance on the far side of the dam on Silver Lake.

Trip note: Silver Lake is an easy-to-reach alpine lake set at 7,200 feet elevation, which provides a beautiful setting and good trout fishing in early summer. The fishing gets boosted by stocks of rainbow trout from the Department of Fish and Game. Open from June to November.

Map grid i2

WOODS LAKE
ELDORADO NATIONAL FOREST

Campsites, facilities: There are 25 tent sites. Piped water, vault toilets, picnic tables, and fireplaces are provided. Pets are permitted on leashes. Groceries and propane gas are available nearby.

Reservations, fee: Reservations not required; $7 fee per night.

Who to contact: Phone the Eldorado National Forest Amador Ranger District at (209)295-4251.

Location: From Stockton on Highway 99, drive east on Highway 88 for about 114 miles (or east of Jackson for 70 miles). Turn when you see the big sign for Woods Lake on your right and drive two miles to the campground.

Trip note: This is a beautiful, quiet lake in the granite backdrop of the high Sierra, set at 8,200 feet elevation near Carson Pass. No boats with motors are permitted, making it ideal for canoes and row boats. Open from July through October.

Map grid i3

LOWER BLUE LAKE
near Carson Pass

Campsites, facilities: There are 16 campsites for tents. Piped water, vault toilets, picnic tables, and fireplaces are provided. Pets are permitted on leashes.

Reservations, fee: Reservations not required; $10 fee per night.

Who to contact: The camp is managed by PG&E. For information call (415) 973-5552 or (415)973-8250.

Location: From Carson Pass traveling east on Highway 88, drive 6.5 miles east to Blue Lakes Road. Turn south (right) and drive 14 miles (seven paved, seven gravel) to the campground. From the junction of Highways 89 and 88 traveling west, drive 2.5 miles west on Highway 88. Turn south (left) on Blue Lakes Road and drive 14 miles to the campground.

Trip note: This camp, set at 8,100 feet beside Lower Blue Lake, is a classic high Sierra lakeside amid the mountain country's natural granite scenery. Trout fishing is often quite good in late May and June. Nearby Upper Blue Lake provides an option. Open from June through September.

Map grid i3

MIDDLE CREEK
near Carson Pass and Blue Lakes

Campsites, facilities: There are five campsites for tents. Piped water, vault toilets, picnic tables, and fireplaces are provided. Pets are permitted on leashes.

Reservations, fee: Reservations not required; $10 fee per night.

Who to contact: The camp is managed by PG&E. For information call (415) 973-5552 or (415)973-8250.

Location: From Carson Pass traveling east on Highway 88, drive 6.5 miles east to Blue Lakes Road. Turn south (right) and drive 13 miles (seven paved, six gravel) to the campground. From the junction of Highways 89 and 88 traveling west, drive 2.5 miles west on Highway 88. Turn south (left) on Blue Lakes

Road and drive 13 miles to the campground.

Trip note: This is a tiny, captivating spot set along the creek that connects Upper and Lower Blue Lakes, providing a take-your-pick deal for anglers. The elevation is 8,200 feet. Open from June through September.

Map grid i3

UPPER BLUE LAKE
near Carson Pass

Campsites, facilities: There are 32 campsites for tents. Piped water, vault toilets, picnic tables, and fireplaces are provided. Pets are permitted on leashes.

Reservations, fee: Reservations not required; $10 fee per night.

Who to contact: The camp is managed by PG&E. For information call (415) 973-5552 or (415)973-8250.

Location: From Carson Pass traveling east on Highway 88, drive 6.5 miles to Blue Lakes Road. Turn south (right) and drive 15 miles (seven paved, eight gravel) to the campground. From the junction of Highways 89 and 88 traveling west, drive 2.5 miles on Highway 88. Turn south (left) on Blue Lakes Road and drive 15 miles to the campground.

Trip note: This is one of two camps set along Upper Blue Lake and one of four camps in the immediate area. The trout fishing is usually quite good here in early summer. The elevation is 8,200 feet. Open from June through September.

Map grid i3

UPPER BLUE LAKE DAM
near Carson Pass

Campsites, facilities: There are 25 campsites for tents. Piped water, vault toilets, picnic tables, and fireplaces are provided. Pets are permitted on leashes.

Reservations, fee: Reservations not required; $10 fee per night.

Who to contact: Camp is managed by PG&E. For information call (415)973-5552 or (415)973-8250.

Location: From Carson Pass traveling east on Highway 88, drive 6.5 miles to Blue Lakes Road. Turn south (right) and drive 12 miles (seven paved, five gravel) to the campground. From the junction of Highways 89 and 88 traveling west, drive 2.5 miles on Highway 88. Turn south (left) on Blue Lakes Road and drive 12 miles to the campground.

Trip note: This high-mountain lake provides the flavor of a backpacking trip, yet is easily accessed by car. Upper Blue Lake is set at 8,200 feet elevation near Carson Pass and provides good trout fishing in late May and June. Most years, the camp opens in June and is open through September (depending on snowfall).

Map grid i4

GROVER HOT SPRINGS STATE PARK
near Markleeville

Campsites, facilities: There are 26 sites for tents only, 13 sites for motor homes, and 37 campsites for tents or motor homes up to 27 feet long. Piped water, flush toilets, showers (except in the winter), a hot springs pool with wheelchair access, a swimming pool, picnic tables, and fireplaces are provided. A grocery store and a laundromat are nearby. Pets are permitted.

Reservations, fee: Reserve through MISTIX at (800)444-PARK ($3.95 MISTIX fee); $10-$14 fee per night; $1 for pets.

Who to contact: Call (916)694-2248.

Location: From Markleeville, drive four miles west on Hot Springs Road to the camp.

Trip note: This is a famous spot for folks who like the rejuvenating powers of a hot spring. Some say they feel a glow about them for weeks. Side trip options include a nature trail or the nearby the Carson River where the water is a might cooler. The elevation is 5,800 feet. Open year-round.

Map grid **i5**

MARKLEEVILLE

on Carson River
TOIYABE NATIONAL FOREST

Campsites, facilities: There are ten campsites for tents or motor homes up to 16 feet long. Piped water, vault toilets, picnic tables, and fireplaces are provided. A laundromat and a grocery store are nearby.

Reservations, fee: Reservations not required; $7 fee per night.

Who to contact: Phone the Toiyabe National Forest Ranger District at (702)882-2766.

Location: From Woodfords, drive south on Highway 89 to Markleeville. Continue south on Highway 89 for one-half mile to the campground.

Trip note: This is a pretty, streamside camp set at 5,500 feet along Markleeville Creek, one mile from the East Fork of the Carson River. The trout here are willing, but alas, are "dinkers." They are not exactly of the Brobdingnagian variety. The hot springs in Markleeville provide a good side trip. Open from April through September.

Map grid **i5**

INDIAN CREEK RESERVOIR

near Woodfords

Campsites, facilities: There are ten sites for tents only and 19 campsites for tents or motor homes up to 24 feet long. Piped water, showers, flush toilets, a sanitary disposal station, picnic tables, and fireplaces are provided. Groceries and propane gas are available nearby.

Reservations, fee: Reservations not required; $4-$6 fee per night.

Who to contact: The camp is administered by the Bureau of Land Management. For information call (702)882-1631.

Location: From Woodfords, drive three miles south on Highway 89 to Airport Boulevard. Turn left and drive to the campground.

Trip note: Because of the popularity of the camps on the nearby Carson River, this spot is often overlooked. It is set at 6,000 feet elevation beside Indian Creek Reservoir, a pretty spot. The lake is small, so after dry winters it is advisable to call ahead and ask about the water levels. Open from May through September.

Map grid **j3**

PACIFIC VALLEY

overlooking Pacific Creek
STANISLAUS NATIONAL FOREST

Campsites, facilities: There are several dispersed campsites for tents. There is **no piped water,** but vault toilets are provided. Pets are permitted on leashes.

Reservations, fee: No reservations, no fee.

Who to contact: Phone the Stanislaus National Forest Calaveras Ranger District at (209)795-1381.

Location: From Arnold, drive 29 miles east on Highway 4 to Lake Alpine. Continue past Lake Alpine on Highway 4 for about eight miles to the entrance road.

Trip note: This is a do-it-yourself special—more of a camping area than a campground. But it's pretty, set at 7,600 feet elevation along Pacific Creek, and surrounded by National Forest country. Open from July through September.

Map grid j3 — HERMIT VALLEY

STANISLAUS NATIONAL FOREST

Campsites, facilities: There are several dispersed campsites for tents. There is **no piped water,** but vault toilets are provided. Pets are permitted on leashes.

Reservations, fee: No reservations, no fee.

Who to contact: Phone the Stanislaus National Forest Calaveras Ranger District at (209)795-1381.

Location: From Arnold, drive 29 miles east on Highway 4 to Lake Alpine. Continue past Lake Alpine for 10.5 miles on Highway 4 (five miles west of Ebetts Pass) to the campground entrance.

Trip note: This tiny, remote, little-known spot is set near the border of the Mokelumne Wilderness near Grouse Creek at 7,500 feet elevation. It's a good jump-off spot for backpackers. The backcountry trails are detailed on Forest Service and topographical maps of the area. Open from June through September.

Map grid j4 — BLOOMFIELD

STANISLAUS NATIONAL FOREST

Campsites, facilities: There are ten campsites for tents or motor homes. There is **no piped water,** but vault toilets, picnic tables, and fireplaces are provided. A grocery store, propane gas, and a laundromat are available nearby.

Reservations, fee: No reservations, no fee.

Who to contact: Phone the Stanislaus National Forest Calaveras Ranger District at (209)795-1381.

Location: From Arnold, drive 29 miles east on Highway 4 to Lake Alpine. Continue past Lake Alpine for 14.5 miles on Highway 4 (one mile west of Ebetts Pass) to the campground entrance road on the right. Turn and drive one mile to the campground.

Trip note: This primitive camp, set in the high country at 8,000 feet elevation, is not far from Ebbett's Pass. A few backpack trails are in the area. The best starts at nearby little Highland Lake and leads downstream adjacent to Highland Creek. Use of a Forest Service map is advised. Open from June through September.

Map grid j5 — SILVER CREEK

TOIYABE NATIONAL FOREST

Campsites, facilities: There are 22 campsites for tents or motor homes up to 22 feet long. Piped water, vault toilets, picnic tables, and fireplaces are provided.

Reservations, fee: Reserve through MISTIX at (800)283-CAMP ($6 MISTIX fee); $7 fee per night.

Who to contact: Phone the Toiyabe National Forest Ranger District at (702)784-5331.

Location: From Markleeville, drive 16 miles south on Highway 4 to the campground.

Trip note: This pretty spot, set beside Silver Creek, has easy access from Highway 4 and good fishing in early summer for small trout. They just don't seem to grow big here, but no matter, it's still a good time. The elevation is 6,800 feet. Open from June through October.

Map grid j7

TOPAZ LAKE TRAILER PARK

near Markleeville

Campsites, facilities: There are 54 motor home spaces with full hookups and picnic tables. Rest rooms, showers, a laundromat, propane gas, and a boat ramp are available. Pets are permitted.

Reservations, fee: Reservations accepted; $15 fee per night.

Who to contact: Phone the park at (916)495-2357.

Location: From the intersection of Highway 89 and US 395, drive north on US 395 for about three miles to the park; or drive 45 miles north of Bridgeport on US 395.

Trip note: Topaz Lake, set at 5,000 feet elevation, is one of the hidden surprises for California anglers, providing much larger trout than most other mountain lakes. If you don't have a boat, no problem, because nearby Topaz Lake Marina offers boat rentals, as well as a tackle shop and a snack bar. Good lake swimming in the summer. Open from March to October.

A

B

C

D4

E

F

G

H

I

J

◆ MAP E0 ◆

BEACH
DESERT
FOOTHILL
TREES
URBAN
GRASSLAND
5% CLUB

15 MILES

Map grid **a9**

SKY CAMP

POINT REYES NATIONAL SEASHORE

A

Campsites, facilities: There are 12 sites available in a primitive walk-in setting with piped water and pit toilets. Fire grills are provided for use with charcoal, but no wood fires are permitted in the park. No vehicles or pets are permitted.

B

Reservations, fee: Reservations required; no fee; four-day maximum stay.

Who to contact: Call the park headquarters at (415)663-1092.

Location: Part of the Point Reyes National Seashore, Sky Camp is located on the western side of Mt. Wittenberg, 2.5 miles from the Bear Valley trailhead.

Trip note: Bring your backpacking gear, including a lightweight camping stove, for this trip. A short hike gives you a campground on the wildlands of Point Reyes National Seashore, one of the few pristine places left in the Bay Area. One in a series of hike-in camps here. No open fires and no pets are permitted. This place is secluded on weekdays. For free maps, write to Superintendent, Point Reyes National Seashore, Point Reyes, CA 94956.

C

D

Map grid **a9**

COAST CAMP

POINT REYES NATIONAL SEASHORE

Campsites, facilities: There are 14 primitive hike-in sites, with piped water and pit toilets. Fire grills are provided for use with charcoal, but no wood fires are permitted in the park. Fires are permitted on the beach providing you can find enough driftwood. No vehicles or pets are permitted.

E0

Reservations, fee: Reservations required; no fee; four-day maximum stay.

Who to contact: Call park headquarters at (415)663-1092.

Location: This camp is set on a grassy bluff 650 feet above ocean, an eight-mile hike from the Bear Valley trailhead on the Point Reyes National Seashore.

F

Trip note: This is a classic ocean bluff setting, but it takes eight miles of hiking to get here, so come prepared for the hike. Expect few trees, few people, and the possibility of wind in the spring and fog in the summer. It is often clear, calm, and warm in late summer and fall. Obtain a map prior to the trip.

G

Map grid **a9**

WILDCAT CAMP

POINT REYES NATIONAL SEASHORE

Campsites, facilities: There are 12 primitive, hike-in sites, with piped water and pit toilets. There are also 4 group sites, which can hold 25 people each. Fire grills are provided for use with charcoal, but no wood fires are permitted in the park. Fires are permitted on the beach providing you can find enough driftwood. No vehicles or pets are permitted.

H

Reservations, fee: Reservations required; no fee; four-day maximum stay.

Who to contact: Phone park headquarters at(415)663-1092.

Location: Hike in six miles from the Bear Valley trailhead on the Point Reyes National Seashore.

I

Trip note: This camp sits in a grassy meadow near a small stream that flows to the ocean. It is an environmentally sensitive area that mandates a minimum-impact camping style. No fires, camp in only designated areas, and pick up your litter—keep a beautiful place beautiful.

J

Map grid **a9**

GLEN CAMP

POINT REYES NATIONAL SEASHORE

Campsites, facilities: There are 12 primitive, hike-in sites with piped water and pit toilets. Fire grills are provided for use with charcoal, but no wood fires are permitted in the park. No vehicles or pets are permitted.

Reservations, fee: Reservations required; no fee; four-day maximum stay.

Who to contact: Phone park headquarters at (415)663-1092.

Location: Hike in five miles from the Bear Valley trailhead in the Point Reyes National Seashore.

Trip note: Glen Camp is set in a small, secluded valley, very quiet and well worth the five-mile hike. Backpackers only. Get a map, a reservation, and bring everything you need.

◆ MAP E1 ◆

BEACH
DESERT
FOOTHILL
TREES
URBAN
GRASSLAND
5% CLUB

15 MILES

to Tomales
to Navato
to Napa
to Fairfield
Olema
Ignacio
San Pablo Bay
Vallejo
Suisun Bay
PT. REYES NAT'L. MON.
Fairfax
Alpine Lake
San Rafael
Rodeo
Pinole
Bolinas
Martinez
Richmond
Pittsburg
MUIR WOODS NAT'L. MON.
Sausalito
Tiburon
Concord
Briones Reservoir
GOLDEN GATE NAT'L. REC. AREA
ANGEL IS. ST. PK.
Berkeley
Lafayette
Clayton
Walnut Creek
Moraga
SEAL ROCK BEACHES
San Francisco
Oakland
MT. DIABLO ST. PARK
Danville
THORNTON ST. BEACH
S. San Francisco
San Ramon
Lake Chabot
San Bruno
San Leandro
Castro Valley
Pacifica
Millbrae
Hayward
GRAY WHALE COVE STATE BEACH
San Francisco Bay
Pleasanton
MONTARA ST. BEACH
San Mateo
Princeton
Sunol
Belmont
Half Moon Bay
HALF MOON BAY STATE BEACH
San Carlos
Newark
Fremont
Redwood City
Menlo Park
Palo Alto
Milpitas
San Gregorio
SAN GREGORIO STATE BEACH
Mtn. View
Sunnyvale
POMPONIO ST. BEACH
La Honda
Santa Clara
Pescadero
San Jose
Campbell
Saratoga
Big Basin
BIG BASIN REDWOODS ST. PARK
Los Gatos
Coyote
Boulder Creek
Scott's Valley
Ben Lomond
Madrone
to Santa Cruz
to Gilroy
to Byron
to Antioch
to Tracy
to Henry Coe St. Pk.
to Patterson

a b c d e f g h i j

0 1 2 3 4 5 6 7 8 9

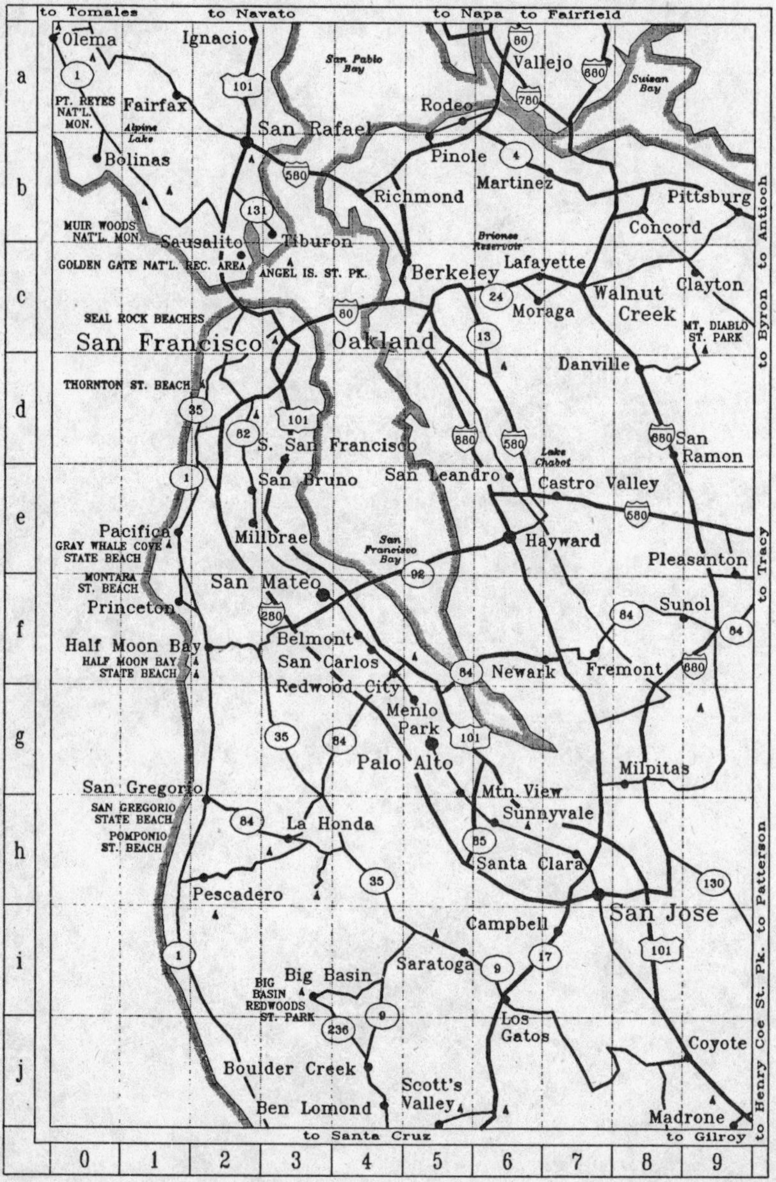

A

SAMUEL P. TAYLOR STATE PARK

Map grid **a0**

near San Rafael

Campsites, facilities: There are 25 sites for tents only and 35 sites for tents or motor homes up to 24 feet long. Piped water, fireplaces, tables, flush toilets, showers, and food lockers are provided. There is a small store two miles away in Lagunitas. Two campsites are wheelchair accessible. Pets are permitted on leashes in the campground only; pets are not permitted on trails.

B

Reservations, fee: Reserve through MISTIX by phoning (800)444-PARK ($3.95 MISTIX fee); $12-$14 per night fee. $1 pet fee.

Who to contact: Phone (415)488-9897.

Location: From US 101 in San Rafael, take the Central San Rafael exit. Follow Third Street west for about two miles until it runs into Sir Francis Drake Boulevard. Bear right onto Sir Francis Drake Boulevard. Drive about 13 miles on Sir Francis Drake Boulevard to the park entrance.

C

Trip note: This is a beautiful Marin park set among the redwoods, complete with babbling brook. Hikers will find 20 miles of hiking trails. Many side trips are possible, with Muir Woods, Mt. Tamalpais, Alpine Lake, and Point Reyes all in the vicinity. Open year-round.

D

OLEMA RANCH CAMPGROUND

Map grid **a0**

E1

Campsites, facilities: There are 200 sites for tents or motorhomes, some with full or partial hookups. Picnic tables are provided. Piped water, restrooms, showers, a sanitary disposal station, a laundromat, and a recreation hall are available.

Reservations, fee: Reservations accepted; $15-$22 fee per night.

Who to contact: Phone (415)663-8001.

F

Location: From US 101 in San Rafael, take the Central San Rafael exit and drive one mile west on Third Street. Continue west on Red Hill Boulevard for two miles to Sir Francis Drake Boulevard. Continue west for 17 miles to Highway 1. Turn right and drive one-half mile to the campground.

Trip note: If you like rest and relaxation in the country, but still want to be within driving distance of the amenities of civilization, then this is a good choice.

G

PANTOLL CAMPGROUND

Map grid **b1**

MOUNT TAMALPAIS STATE PARK

Campsites, facilities: There are 16 walk-in sites for tents. Piped water, flush toilets, fireplaces, and tables provided. Pets are permitted.

H

Reservations, fee: No reservations; $12-$14 fee per night; $1 pet fee.

Who to contact: Phone (415)388-2070.

Location: From Highway 101, take the Highway 1 North exit. Turn left (west) at the first light onto Highway 1 and drive 2.5 miles. At the top of the ridge, take the Muir Woods-Mt. Tamalpais (Panoramic Highway) turnoff to the right and continue 5.5 miles to the ranger station and campground.

I

Trip note: Mt. Tamalpais is a magnificent mountain, some say a place of special power, and it provides excellent hiking along with some of the most outstanding lookout points in California. Trails to the west provide great views of the ocean. A strongly advised side trip is to drive up to the East Peak lookout, where with a 15-minute hike, you are rewarded with a fantastic view of San Francisco Bay.

J

Map grid b1 — STEEP RAVINE ENVIROMENTAL CAMPSITES

MOUNT TAMALPAIS STATE PARK

Campsites, facilities: There are six walk-in sites for tents. Pit toilets, fireplaces, and tables are provided. Piped water is nearby and wood is also available. No pets are permitted.

Reservations, fee: Reserve through MISTIX at (800)444-PARK ($3.95 MISTIX fee); $7-$9 fee per night.

Who to contact: Phone (415)388-2070.

Location: The campground is located one mile south of Stinson Beach on Highway 1. You will see an entrance gate with a sign on the ocean side of the highway. Complete directions are included with your reservation confirmation.

Trip note: These are little-known campsites that require some planning for a stay, but in return you get a quiet, relatively remote spot with Pacific Ocean lookouts. After a while, you'll feel like you're a million miles from civilization.

Map grid b2 — MARIN RV PARK

near San Rafael

Campsites, facilities: There are 165 motor home spaces with full hookups. Showers, a laundromat, a swimming pool, a sauna, RV supplies, and a grocery store are available. Pets are permitted.

Reservations, fee: Phone for reservations, deposit required; $29 fee per night.

Who to contact: Phone at (415)461-5199.

Location: From US 101 just south of San Rafael, take the Lucky Drive exit and drive a short distance on the eastern frontage road (Redwood Highway) to 2130 Redwood Highway.

Trip notes: For out-of-towners with motor homes, this can make an ideal base camp for Marin County adventures. To the west is Mt. Tamalpais, Muir Woods, and East Peak. To the east is the Loch Lomond Marina, where bay fishing trips can be arranged for striped bass and sturgeon—phone (415)456-0321. The park offers complete sight-seeing information, and easy access to buses and ferry service to San Francisco.

Map grid c3 — SAN FRANCISCO RV PARK

Campsites, facilities: There are 200 sites with full hookups for motor homes. Water, barbecues, and tables are provided. A dump station, showers, a laundromat, and a game room are available. Pets are permitted.

Reservations, fee: Reservations required; $28-$32 per night fee.

Who to contact: Phone (415)986-8730 or write to 250 King Street, San Francisco, CA 94107.

Location: Drive into San Francisco across the Bay Bridge on Highway 80. Take the Fifth Street exit and make a left to Fourth Street. Turn right and you'll see the RV park. Traveling north into San Francisco, take the Fourth Street exit from US 101. Turn right on Fourth Street. Drive four blocks to King Street. Turn left on King Street and drive one-half block to the RV "park".

Trip note: San Francisco's only "campground," is strictly for motor homes. It consists of a long parking area set beneath a freeway structure. City buses leave from the park regularly.

Map grid c3 ANGEL ISLAND STATE PARK

Campsites, facilities: Limited space at this campground with piped water, toilets, and tables provided. No pets are permitted. Food service is available on the island.

Reservations, fee: Reservations a must through MISTIX by phoning (800)444-PARK ($3.95 MISTIX fee); $12-$14 fee per night.

Who to contact: Phone Angel Island State Park at (415)435-1915.

Location: Angel Island is in northern San Francisco Bay and reached by ferry leaving from Pier 43 in San Francisco—schedule information call (415)546-2896—and Tiburon—schedule information call (415)435-2131.

Trip note: This is one of the more unique campgrounds in California, reachable only by ferry. It requires reservations far in advance, but it's well worth it. A short walk to the top of Mt. Livermore (elevation 671 feet) will provide a spectacular lookout toward the Golden Gate Bridge to the west, the San Francisco skyline to the south, and the Bay and its ships in the foreground.

Map grid c9 MOUNT DIABLO STATE PARK

Campsites, facilities: There are three different campgrounds with a total of 48 sites for tents or motor homes up to 24 feet long. All have piped water, vault or flush toilets, fireplaces, and tables.

Reservations, fee: Reserve through MISTIX at (800)444-PARK ($3.95 MISTIX fee); $12-$14 fee per night; pets $1.

Who to contact: Phone Mt. Diablo State Park at (415)837-2525.

Location: From Highway 680 in Danville, take the Diablo Road exit and Diablo Road. Turn on Black Hawk Road and drive four miles. Turn left on South Gate Road and drive four miles to the park entrance.

Trip note: Mt. Diablo, elevation 3,849 feet, can provide one of the best lookouts in America. On crystal-clear days, you can see the Sierra Nevada and its white, snowbound crest, and with binoculars, some claim to have seen Half Dome in Yosemite. Winter and spring are good times to visit, when the weather is still cool enough for good hiking trips. In late summer, the park is sometimes closed to campers due to fire danger. No alcohol is permitted in the park.

Map grid d2 NEW SAN FRANCISCO TRAILER PARK in Daly City

Campsites, facilities: There are 90 motor home sites with full hookups. Rest rooms, showers, a sanitary dump station, and a laundromat are available. A grocery store is nearby.

Reservations, fee: Reservations recommended; $15 fee per night.

Who to contact: Phone (415)755-5850.

Location: Driving north: From Interstate 280, take the Daly City-Mission Street exit. Drive about one mile to 6925 Mission Street in Daly City. Driving south: From Interstate 280, take the Daly City exit at Seton Hospital. Turn left and drive over the freeway to Mission Street. Turn left on Mission Street and drive four blocks to the trailer park.

Trip note: This is an okay spot for a layover while on a Bay Area tour with a motor home. It's just a short hop to San Francisco and close to the BART station.

Map grid d6 — ANTHONY CHABOT REGIONAL PARK

near Castro Valley

Campsites, facilities: There are ten walk-in sites, eight motor home spaces with sewer and water hookups, and 23 sites for tents or motor homes. Fireplaces and picnic tables are provided. Piped water, toilets, showers and sanitary disposal station are available. Pets are permitted.

Reservations, fee: Reservations accepted April through October; $10 fee per night; pets $1.

Who to contact: For brochure, call East Bay Regional Park District at (415)531-9300 or Chabot Park at (415)881-1833. Reservations can be made through Ticketron at (800)452-1111.

Location: From Interstate 580 in Castro Valley, take the Redwood Road exit west and drive four miles to the park.

Trip note: This is the centerpiece of the East Bay Regional Park system—a 5,000-acre park with a fish-filled lake and 31 miles of trails. Trout fishing is outstanding during the winter by boat or shore. Huge largemouth bass are often caught during the spring (the NorCal record bass was caught here in 1989). The National Skyline Scenic Trail passes through the park, including through Bort Meadow. There's only one major nit: No launching of private boats.

Map grid e1 — PACIFIC PARK

in Pacifica

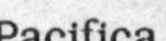

Campsites, facilities: There are 260 motor home sites with full hookups. Rest rooms, showers, a heated pool, a spa, and a recreation room are provided. Cable TV, a grocery store, a laundromat, and propane gas are available.

Reservations, fee: Reservations recommended; $27-$30 fee per night.

Who to contact: Phone (415)355-2112.

Location: On Highway 1 in Pacifica, take the Manor-Palmetto exit. Drive to 700 Palmetto Avenue.

Trip note: This is one of the newest and best motor home parks in the Bay Area. It is set on the bluffs just above the Pacific Ocean, complete with beach access and dramatic ocean sunsets, only 20 miles from San Francisco. A golf course is nearby. Another bonus is the nearby Pacifica Pier, where salmon can be caught from mid-June through August.

Map grid f2 — HALF MOON BAY STATE BEACH

Campsites, facilities: There are 51 sites for tents or motor homes up to 36 feet long. Piped water, fireplaces, and tables are provided. A sanitary disposal station and toilets are available.

Reservations, fee: Reservations advisable for weekends; book well in advance for holidays; reserve through MISTIX at (800)444-PARK ($3.95 MISTIX fee); $12-$14 fee per night.

Who to contact: Phone (415)726-6238.

Location: From the intersection of Highways 1 and 92 in Half Moon Bay, drive about one mile south on Highway 1. Turn west on Kelly Avenue and drive about two miles to the park.

Trip note: During summer months, this park often fills to capacity. It has level, grassy sites for tents, a clean parking area for motor homes, and the beach just a short walk away. Side trips include Princeton, seven miles north, and Pillar Point Marina, where trips for fishing and whale watching are available. A

Map grid **f2**

PELICAN POINT RV PARK
in Half Moon Bay

Campsites, facilities: There are 75 spaces for motor homes, with full hookups and patios. Picnic tables, rest rooms, showers, a laundromat, propane gas, a small store, a recreation room, and a sanitary disposal station are provided. B
Reservations, fee: Call for available space; $25 per night fee.
Who to contact: Phone (415)726-9100.
Location: From the intersection of Highways 1 and 92 in Half Moon Bay, drive 2.5 miles south on Highway 1. Turn west on Miramontes Point Road and drive for a short distance to the park. C
Trip note: This park is in a rural setting near bluffs overlooking the ocean, just south of Half Moon Bay. All facilities are available nearby. A good side trip is ten miles north to Princeton and the surrounding Pillar Point Marina for fine restaurants, fishing boats, and whale watching trips. Open year-round. D

Map grid **f5**

TRAILER VILLA
in Redwood City

Campsites, facilities: There are 50 motor home sites with full hookups. Rest rooms, showers, a laundromat, and a sanitary disposal station are available. E1
Reservations, fee: Reservations recommended; $20 fee per night.
Who to contact: Phone (415)366-7880.
Location: From Highway 101 in Redwood City, take the Seaport Boulevard exit east. Drive a short distance and turn right on East Bayshore Road. Drive one mile to 3401 East Bayshore Road. F
Trip note: This is a good holdover spot for motor home drivers; it's located about 20 miles south of San Francisco. The nearby Circle Star Theatre attracts many class acts and can provide some evening entertainment. Open year-round.

Map grid **g9**

SUNOL REGIONAL WILDERNESS

G

Campsites, facilities: There are four tent sites. Piped water, tables, fireplaces, and vault toilets are provided.
Reservations, fee: Reservations accepted; $10 fee per night.
Who to contact: Phone the East Bay Regional Park District at (415)531-9300; for reservations call (415)636-1684. H
Location: From San Jose, drive north on Highway 680 to the Calaveras Road-Highway 84 exit. Turn right on Calaveras and drive about five miles. Continue on Geary to the park.
Trip note: This little-known Bay Area park can provide a quiet setting or nice hiking area for the few car campers who know of it. One of the better hikes is to Little Yosemite, and though it really doesn't look anything like Yosemite Valley, it still is a pretty, secluded spot. Alameda Creek runs down the center of the Little Yosemite's granite-cut valley. I

Map grid **h3**

MEMORIAL COUNTY PARK
near La Honda

J

Campsites, facilities: There are 132 sites for tents or motor homes. Fireplaces, picnic tables, piped water, and flush toilets are provided. Showers and a sanitary disposal station are available from May through October. No pets allowed.

Reservations, fee: Call for available space; $8 fee per night.

Who to contact: Phone Memorial Park at (415)879-0212, or (415)363-4021.

Location: From the intersection of Highways 1 and 92 in Half Moon Bay, drive 15 miles south on Highway 1 to the Pescadero Road exit. Turn east on Pescadero Road and drive about ten miles to the park entrance.

Trip note: This beautiful redwood park is on the Peninsula in the Santa Cruz Mountains. Its highlights are the 50 miles of hiking trails and the Pescadero Creek headwaters. In the spring, you can actually see steelhead spawn (no fishing permitted, of course). The camp is often filled on summer weekends, but the camps are spaced so it won't cramp your style. Open all year.

Map grid h3

PORTOLA STATE PARK

near Skyline Ridge

Campsites, facilities: There are 52 sites for tents or motor homes up to 27 feet long. Piped water, fireplaces, and tables are provided. Toilets and showers are available. There are no motor home hookups. Pets are permitted.

Reservations, fee: Reserve through MISTIX at (800)444-PARK ($3.95 MISTIX fee); $12-$14 fee per night; $1 pets fee.

Who to contact: Phone (415)948-9098.

Location: From the intersection of Highways 1 and 92 in Half Moon Bay, drive ten miles south on Highway 1 to the La Honda Road (San Gregorio) exit. Turn east on La Honda Road and drive about eight miles. Turn south (right) onto Alpine Road and drive five miles. Turn right onto Portola State Park Road and drive about four miles to the campground.

Trip note: This park is surprisingly secluded for a Bay Area parkland. It offers 14 miles of trails in addition to a four-mile trek that connects it to Memorial Park (with 50 more miles of trail). One of the more popular trails is routed along Pescadero Creek. No fishing: those "little trout" are actually steelhead smelts.

Map grid h6

MOBILAND MANOR

in Sunnyvale

Campsites, facilities: There are 50 motor home sites with full hookups. A swimming pool and laundromat are available. A small shopping center is one block away. No pets. Seniors only.

Reservations, fee: Call for available space; $25 fee per night.

Who to contact: Phone (408)773-1210, or write to 780 N. Fair Oaks Avenue, Sunnyvale, CA 94086.

Location: From US 101 in Sunnyvale, take the Fair Oaks Avenue exit and drive west for two blocks to the mobile home park.

Trip note: This is not exactly a park-like setting, but it's a viable layover spot in the area. The Great America amusement park provides a recreation side trip.

Map grid i2

BUTANO STATE PARK

near Pescadero

Campsites, facilities: There are 30 sites for tents only and ten sites for tents or motor homes. Piped water, fireplaces, and picnic tables are provided. Toilets are available. Pets are permitted.

Reservations, fee: Reservations advised during summer season; reserve through

MISTIX at (800)444-PARK ($3.95 MISTIX fee); $12-$14 fee per night; pets $1.

Who to contact: Phone (415)879-0173.

Location: From the intersection of Highways 1 and 92 in Half Moon Bay, drive 15 miles south on Highway 1 to the Pescadero Road exit. Turn east on Pescadero Road and drive past the town of Pescadero. Turn right (south) on Cloverdale Road and follow the sign indicating a left turn into the park.

Trip note: This secluded, beautiful park has many hikes routed through redwoods. One hike, which starts near the park entrance on the south side of the entrance road, leads to a great lookout of Ano Nuevo Island and the Pacific Ocean. Others connect to an 11-mile loop that circles the park.

Map grid i3

BIG BASIN REDWOODS STATE PARK
near Santa Cruz

Campsites, facilities: There are 188 sites for tents or motor homes up to 27 feet long. Yosemite-style tent cabins are also available by reservation. Piped water, tables, and fireplaces are provided. Rest rooms, showers, a sanitary disposal station, and groceries are available. Some campsites and facilities are wheelchair accessible.

Reservations, fee: Reserve through MISTIX by phoning (800)444-PARK ($3.95 MISTIX fee); $12-$14 per night fee; Tent cabins are $29 per night - reserve through MISTIX also.

Who to contact: Phone Big Basin State Park at (408)338-6132.

Location: From Santa Cruz, drive north on Highway 9 for 12 miles. Turn west on Highway 236 and drive nine miles to the campground.

Trip note: This is one of the Bay Area's best parklands, a beautiful redwood shrine with many excellent hiking trails. The best hike is the two-hour walk to Berry Creek Falls, a 70-foot waterfall that is dramatic from winter into early summer. There is also a loop trail near the park headquarters in the valley floor that is routed past several mammoth redwoods.

Map grid j5

CARBONERO CREEK TRAILER PARK
near Scotts Valley

Campsites, facilities: There are ten sites for tents only and 104 motor home spaces with full or partial hookups and picnic tables. Rest rooms, showers, cable TV, a laundromat, a recreation room, a hot tub, and a swimming pool are available. Pets are permitted on leashes.

Reservations, fee: Reservations advised; $17-$22 fee per night.

Who to contact: Phone (408)438-1288.

Location: From Highway 17 four miles north of Santa Cruz, take the Mount Hermon-Big Basin exit. Drive to Scotts Valley Drive and turn north (right). Drive to Disc Drive and go east (right). The park is at 917 Disc Drive (a dead end road).

Trip note: This camp is just a short hop from Monterey Bay; there are many side trip options, making this a prime location. Several quality restaurants are available in the area; deep sea and salmon fishing trips are offered out of Santa Cruz, and there are good hiking trails through redwoods at nearby state parks.

Map grid **j6**

SCOTTS VALLEY RV PARK

near Scotts Valley

Campsites, facilities: There are 100 RV sites with full hookups. Picnic tables are provided. Rest rooms, showers, a recreation room, and a swimming pool are available.

Reservations, fee: Call ahead for available space; $20 fee per night.

Who to contact: Phone (408)438-1600.

Location: From Santa Cruz, drive five miles north on Highway 17. Turn east on Granite Creek Road and drive a short distance to Santa's Village Road. Turn and drive to 100 Santa's Village Road.

Trip note: This is an okay layover spot for RV cruisers looking for a spot to tie up the pony for the night. Side trips include touring Highway 9, which is routed through the Santa Cruz Mountains, and the Santa Cruz boardwalk, which has been cleaned up in recent years.

Map grid **j9**

PARKWAY LAKES RV PARK

near Morgan Hill

Campsites, facilities: There are 113 motor home spaces with electricity and piped water. Rest rooms, showers, a sanitary disposal station, a laundromat, and a recreation room are available.

Reservations, fee: Call ahead for available space; $20 fee per night.

Who to contact: Phone (408)779-0244.

Location: From US 101 in Morgan Hill, take the Cochrane-Monterey Road exit and drive west for one mile. Turn right (north) on Monterey Road and drive three miles to the RV park.

Trip note: Nearby Parkway Lakes is the Bay Area's famous pay-to-fish lake where for $10 you get a chance to catch rainbow trout up to ten pounds in the winter and spring and to fish for catfish and sturgeon in the summer. Other lakes in the area include Coyote, Anderson, Chesbro, Uvas, and Calero. For up-to-date tips, call Coyote Discount Bait and Tackle at (408)463-0711.

MAP E2

BEACH
TREES
5% CLUB
DESERT
URBAN
FOOTHILL
GRASSLAND

15 MILES

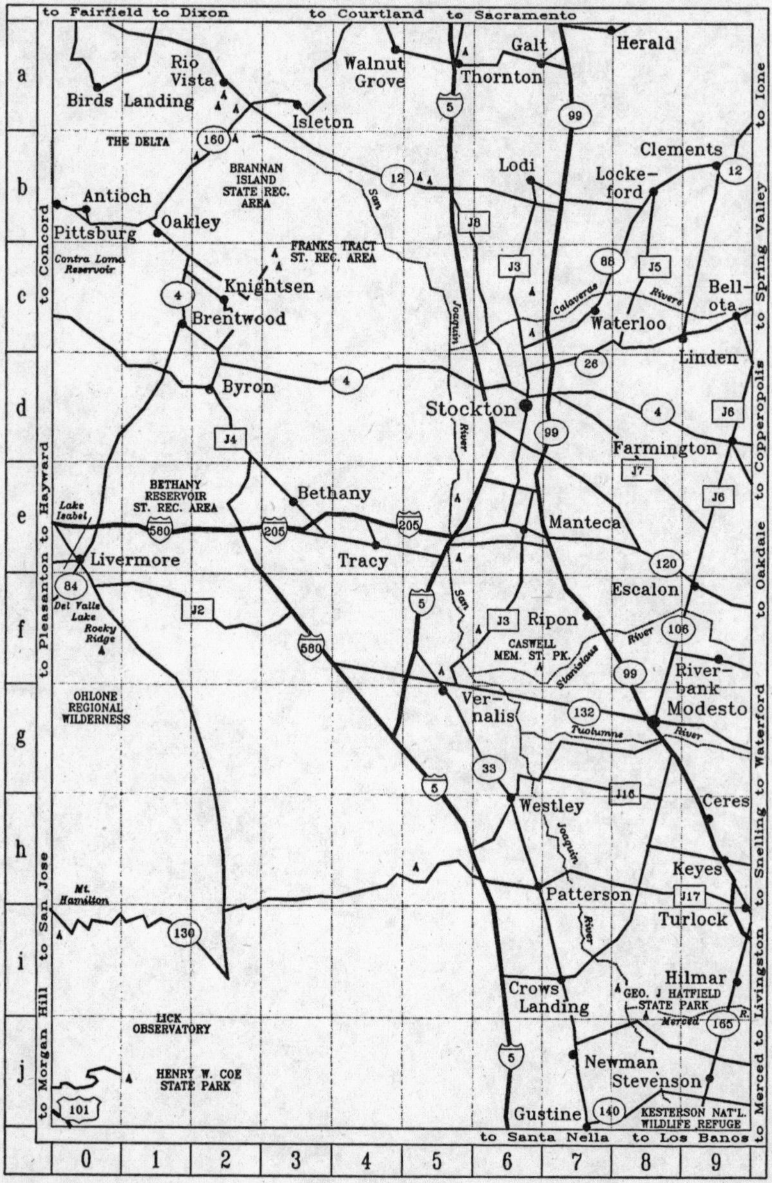

to Fairfield to Dixon
to Courtland to Sacramento
to Ione
to Spring Valley
to Copperopolis
to Oakdale
to Waterford
to Snelling
to Livingston
to Merced
to Concord
to Pleasanton to Hayward
to Morgan Hill to San Jose
to Santa Nella to Los Banos

a
b
c
d
e
f
g
h
i
j

0 1 2 3 4 5 6 7 8 9

Rio Vista
Birds Landing
Walnut Grove
Thornton
Galt
Herald
Isleton
THE DELTA
160
5
99
BRANNAN ISLAND STATE REC. AREA
12
Lodi
Clements
Lockeford
12
Antioch
Pittsburg
Oakley
San
J8
Contra Loma Reservoir
FRANKS TRACT ST. REC. AREA
J3
88
J5
Knightsen
4
Calaveras
River
Bellota
Brentwood
Joaquin
Waterloo
Linden
26
Byron
4
Stockton
4
J6
River
99
J4
Farmington
J7
BETHANY RESERVOIR ST. REC. AREA
Bethany
Lake Isabel
580
205
205
Manteca
J6
Tracy
Livermore
120
84
Escalon
Del Valle Lake
J2
San
5
J3
Ripon
Rocky Ridge
580
CASWELL MEM. ST. PK.
River
106
Stanislaus
99
Riverbank
OHLONE REGIONAL WILDERNESS
Vernalis
132
Modesto
Tuolumne
River
33
5
J16
Westley
Ceres
Joaquin
Keyes
Mt. Hamilton
Patterson
J17
Turlock
130
River
Hilmar
Crows Landing
GEO. J HATFIELD STATE PARK
Merced R.
165
LICK OBSERVATORY
5
Newman
Stevenson
HENRY W. COE STATE PARK
101
Gustine
140
KESTERSON NAT'L. WILDLIFE REFUGE

Map grid **a2**

SANDY BEACH COUNTY PARK

on Sacramento River

Campsites, facilities: There are 42 campsites for tents or motor homes. Picnic tables, fireplaces, and piped water are provided. Flush toilets, showers, a playground, and a sanitary disposal station and a boat ramp are available. The facilities are wheelchair accessible. Supplies can be obtained nearby. Pets are permitted.
Reservations, fee: No reservations; $10 fee per night; pets $1.
Who to contact: Phone the park (707)374-2097.
Location: From Highway 12 in Rio Vista, turn southeast on Main Street and drive a short distance to Second Street. Turn right and drive one-half mile to Beach Drive. Continue on Beach Drive to the park.
Trip note: This is a surprisingly little-known park, especially considering it provides beachside access to the Sacramento River. It is a popular spot for sunbathers in hot summer months, but in winter, it is one of the few viable spots one can fish from the shore for sturgeon. Open year-round.

Map grid **a2**

DUCK ISLAND RV PARK

on Sacramento River

Campsites, facilities: There are 51 motor home spaces with full hookups. Picnic tables are provided. A recreation room with a kitchen (fee charged) is available. A boat ramp is available at Brannan Island State Park, a short drive from the RV park. Supplies and a laundromat are available in Rio Vista. The facilities are wheelchair accessible. Adults only.
Reservations, fee: Reservations accepted; reservation and deposit required for groups; $17 fee per night.
Who to contact: Phone (916)777-6663.
Location: From Interstate 5, take the Highway 12 exit drive 14 miles west to Rio Vista. At the flashing light before the bridge, turn left onto Highway 160. Drive seven-eighths of a mile to the RV park. If coming from the west on Highway 12 in Rio Vista, cross the bridge and turn right on Highway 160. Drive seven-eighths of a mile to the RV park.
Trip note: This pleasant rural park, set up for motor homes, has riverside access that provides an opportunity for bank fishing on the Sacramento River.

Map grid **a2**

DELTA MARINA YACHT HARBOR

on Sacramento River Delta

Campsites, facilities: There are 25 motor home spaces with full hookups. Picnic tables and fire grills are provided. Rest rooms, showers, a sanitary disposal station, a laundromat, a playground, a boat ramp, ice, and propane gas are available.
Reservations, fee: Reservations accepted; $14-$22 fee per night.
Who to contact: Phone (707)374-2315.
Location: From Highway 12 in Rio Vista, turn southeast on Main Street. Drive a short distance to Second Street. Turn right and drive to the harbor.
Trip note: This is a prime spot for boat campers to use as headquarters. Summers are hot and breezy, and water skiing is popular on the nearby Sacramento River. From November to March, the striped bass fishing is quite good, as close, sometimes, as just a half-mile upriver at the Rio Vista Bridge. The boat launch at the harbor is a bonus. Open year-round.

Map grid **a5**

NEW HOPE LANDING

on Mokelumne River north of Stockton

Campsites, facilities: There are 25 sites for tents or motor homes. Piped water, electrical connections, and some sewer hookups are provided. Rest rooms, showers, a sanitary disposal station, a grocery store, propane gas, and a full service marina are available.

Reservations, fee: No reservations; $15-$18 fee per night.

Who to contact: Phone the camp at (209)794-2627.

Location: From Stockton, drive 25 miles north on Interstate 5. Take the Walnut Grove Road (Thornton) exit and go west. Drive 3.3 miles west on Walnut Grove Road. The entrance to the grounds is on the right.

Trip note: A privately-operated resort set along the Mokelumne River in the upper San Joaquin Delta. This is a good base of operations for boaters. There's a marina available, which gives you access to 1,000 miles of Delta waterways via the Mokelumne River.

Map grid **b2**

EDDO'S BOAT HARBOR

on San Joaquin River Delta

Campsites, facilities: There are 33 campsites for tents or motor homes. Picnic tables and piped water are provided. Flush toilets, hot showers, a launch ramp, boat storage, fuel dock, a dump station, a laundromat, and a grocery store are available.

Reservations, fee: Call ahead for available space and fee.

Who to contact: Phone the campground at (415)757-5314.

Location: From Rio Vista, drive south on Highway 160 to Sherman Island Levee Road. Turn left toward the river. The camp is on the river opposite Light 21.

Trip note: This is an ideal spot for campers with boats since Eddo's is set on the San Joaquin River on the edge of 1,000 miles of Delta waterways. In summer, it is a popular water skiing area. In the winter months, however, striped bass migrate into the immediate area, as well as to the nearby False River, which can provide excellent fishing.

Map grid **b2**

BRANNAN ISLAND STATE RECREATION AREA

on Sacramento River

Campsites, facilities: There are 102 sites for tents or motor homes up to 31 feet long. Picnic tables and fire grills are provided. Rest rooms, showers (at the boat launch site), a sanitary disposal station, and a boat launch are available. There are also several sites within walking distance of the boat launch, which provide a berth as well as a campsite. The campground facilities are wheelchair accessible. Supplies can be obtained in Rio Vista. Pets are permitted.

Reservations, fee: Reserve through MISTIX at (800)444-PARK ($3.95 MISTIX fee); $12-$14 fee per night; pets $1.

Who to contact: Phone (707)777-6671.

Location: From Interstate 5, take the Highway 12 exit and drive 14 miles west to Rio Vista. At the flashing light before the bridge, turn left onto Highway 160. If coming from the west on Highway 12 in Rio Vista, cross the bridge and turn right on Highway 160. then drive three miles to the park.

Trip note: This prime state park for boaters is set in the heart of the Delta's vast waterway. You get year-round adventure: water skiing and catfishing are popular in summer and in winter, the immediate surrounding area is often good for striped bass. The proximity of the campgrounds to the boat launch deserves a medal.

A

Map grid b5 — TOWER PARK MARINA AND RESORT

near Stockton

B

Campsites, facilities: There are 500 campsites for tents or motor homes, many with full hookups. Picnic tables and BBQs are provided. Rest rooms, showers, a sanitary disposal station, a recreation room, boat rentals, overnight boat slips, an elevator boat launch, a playground, a laundromat, a grocery store, and propane gas are available.

C

Reservations, fee: Reservations recommended; $12-$24 fee per night.

Who to contact: Phone the park at (209)369-1041.

Location: From the junction of Highway 4 and Interstate 5 in Stockton, drive 14 miles north on Interstate 5. Take the Highway 12 exit west and drive about five miles to 14900 Highway 12.

D

Trip note: This huge resort is ideal for boat-in campers who desire all the amenities. It is set on Little Potato Slough near the Mokelumne River. A band plays in the restaurant-lounge at the resort on most weekends. Open year-round.

Map grid b5 — WESTGATE LANDING PARK

in San Joaquin River Delta near Stockton

E2

Campsites, facilities: There are seven campsites for tents or motor homes. Piped water, BBQs, and picnic tables are provided. Flush toilets are available. Groceries and propane gas are nearby. Pets are permitted. There are 18 boat slips available also.

F

Reservations, fee: Reservations accepted; $7 fee per night; boat slips $5; pets $1.

Who to contact: Phone the County Parks Department at (209)953-8800.

Location: From the junction of Highway 4 and Interstate 5 in Stockton, drive 14 miles north on Interstate 5. Take the Highway 12 exit west and drive about five miles to Glasscock Road. Turn right (north) and drive about a mile to the park.

G

Trip note: This low-demand county park is set on the South Fork of the Mokelumne River in the San Joaquin Delta country. In the summer, catfishing can be good at night in this area. Open all year.

Map grid c3 — ISLAND PARK

on San Joaquin River Delta

H

Campsites, facilities: There are 59 sites for motor homes with full hookups. Rest rooms, showers, a laundromat, a recreation room, and a swimming pool are available.

Reservations, fee: No reservations; $17.50 per night for two people.

I

Who to contact: Phone (415)684-2144.

Location: From Highway 4 in Oakley, take Cypress Road east to the Bethel Island Bridge. Cross the bridge and drive north one-half mile to Gateway Road. Turn right (east) and continue one-half mile to Island Park.

Trip note: This privately-operated motor home park is set on the edge of the San Joaquin Delta's boating paradise with more than 1,000 miles of waterways. There's good striper fishing from November through March and catfishing and water skiing in summer.

J

Map grid **c3**

DELTA RESORT
on San Joaquin River Delta

Campsites, facilities: There are 80 motor home sites with full hookups. Rest rooms, showers, propane gas, a playground, a boat ramp and a full restaurant and bar are available.

Reservations, fee: Reservations required; mail 50 percent of fee as a deposit; $18 fee per night.

Who to contact: Phone (415)684-2122 or write to P.O. Box 718, Bethel Island, CA 94511.

Location: From Highway 4 in Oakley, take Cypress Road east to the Bethel Island Bridge. Cross the bridge and drive north one-half mile to Gateway Road. Turn right (east) and continue to River View Road. Turn left and drive to the park, located at 6777 River View Road.

Trip note: This park, set on Bethel Island in the heart of the Delta, is accessible to more than 1,000 miles of waterways for boaters. In the fall and winter, the area often provides good striper fishing at nearby Frank's Tract, False River, and San Joaquin River. Catfishing in surrounding slough areas is good year-round. The Delta Sportsman shop at Bethel Island has reliable fishing information.

Map grid **c6**

SAHARA MOBILE PARK
in Stockton

Campsites, facilities: There are 28 paved motor home spaces with full hookups. Rest rooms, showers, a recreation room, a heated pool, and a laundromat are available. A playground, a grocery store, and a donut shop are nearby. Small pets are permitted.

Reservations, fee: No reservations; $15 fee per night.

Who to contact: Phone the park at (209)464-9392.

Location: From Highway 99 in central Stockton, take the Cherokee exit west. Drive about three miles to Sanguinetti Lane. Turn right and drive one mile to 2340 Sanguinetti Lane.

Trip note: They play Bingo every Tuesday night here, and that should tell you everything you need to know about this spot.

Map grid **c6**

STOCKTON-LODI KOA
in Stockton

Campsites, facilities: There are 102 sites for tents or motor homes, many with full hookups. Picnic tables are provided. Rest rooms, showers, a sanitary disposal station, a grocery store, propane gas, a laundromat, a recreation room, a swimming pool, and a playground are available. Pets are permitted.

Reservations, fee: No reservations; $16-$20 fee per night.

Who to contact: Phone the park at (209)941-2573 or 334-0309.

Location: From Stockton, drive five miles north on Interstate 5. Take the Eight Mile Road exit east and drive five miles to the campground at 2851 East Eight Mile Road.

Trip note: This KOA camp is in the heart of the San Joaquin Valley, located about ten miles from the Calaveras River. Open year-round.

Map grid **e5**

DOS REIS PARK
on San Joaquin River near Stockton

A

Campsites, facilities: There are 26 motor home spaces with full hookups and a separate section for tents only. Picnic tables and fireplaces are provided. Rest rooms, showers, and a boat ramp are available. A grocery store, a laundromat, and propane gas can be found nearby. Pets are permitted on leashes.

B

Reservations, fee: Reservations accepted; $11 fee per night; pets $1.

Who to contact: Phone the County Parks at (209)953-8800.

Location: From Interstate 5 south of Stockton, take the Lathrop exit. Drive northwest for one mile to Dos Reis Road. The park is along the east side of San Joaquin River.

C

Trip note: This is a 90-acre county park that has a quarter-mile of San Joaquin River frontage—a nice touch. Open year-round.

Map grid **e5**

OAKWOOD LAKE RESORT
near Stockton

D

Campsites, facilities: There are 87 sites for tents only, 116 sites for tents or motor homes, and 194 motor home spaces. Picnic tables are provided. Piped water, electrical connections, and sewer hookups are provided at most sites. Rest rooms, showers, a dump station, a grocery store, a laundromat, propane gas, a swim lagoon, water slides, rampage ride, paddle boats, organized activities, and a stocked 75-acre lake are available. The facilities are wheelchair accessible.

E2

Reservations, fee: Reservations accepted; $18-$24 fee per night.

Who to contact: Phone the park at (209)239-9566.

Location: From the intersection of Interstate 5 and Highway 120 in Manteca, drive two miles east on Highway 120. Turn south on Airport Way and drive one-half mile. Turn right on Woodward Way and drive two miles to the park entrance.

F

Trip note: This huge, privately-operated "water theme" park covers 375 acres. A wide array of water-related recreation activities are available. Open year-round.

Map grid **f0**

DEL VALLE PARK
near Livermore

G

Campsites, facilities: There are 110 sites for tents or motor homes, 21 with full hookups. Piped water, fireplaces, and picnic tables are provided. A sanitary disposal station, toilets, showers, a full marina, and a boat launch are available. Pets are permitted.

H

Reservations, fee: Reserve through Ticketron from February through October (800)452-1111; $10 fee per night; pets $1.

Who to contact: Phone the East Bay Regional Park District at (415)531-9300 or for campsite availability, call the park directly at (415)443-4110.

I

Location: From Oakland, drive east on Highway 580 to Livermore. Take the North Livermore Avenue exit. Drive south through town on South Livermore Road (same as North Livermore Road) which becomes Tesla. Turn right onto Mines Road and drive three miles. Turn right on Del Valle Road and drive to the park.

Trip note: This park is fast turning into one of the best year-round spots for adventure in the Bay Area. A long, narrow lake fills the canyon, and during the winter months, it provides exceptional trout fishing near the boat launch. Some good hikes are available as well, including the one on the 29-mile Ohlone Wilderness

J

Trail. It's quite hot in the summer.

Map grid **f5**

ORCHARD RV PARK

near Stockton

Campsites, facilities: There are 20 sites for tents only and 88 drive-through motor home spaces with full hookups. Picnic tables and fireplaces are provided. Rest rooms, showers, a laundromat, a sanitary disposal station, a swimming pool, a restaurant, and horseshoe pits are available. The facilities are wheelchair accessible. Groceries, propane gas, and a weekend flea market can be found nearby.

Reservations, fee: Reservations accepted; $20 fee per night.

Who to contact: Phone the park at (209)836-2090.

Location: From Interstate 5 near Vernalis, drive three miles east on Highway 132 to the town of Vernalis. The park is at 2701 East Highway 132.

Trip note: This privately-operated park is set up primarily for motor homes. Considering how hot the weather gets here in the summer, you might want to take them up on their huge swimming pool and water slides.

Map grid **f6**

DURHAM FERRY STATE REC. AREA

near Stockton

Campsites, facilities: There are 75 sites for tents or motor homes, some with full hookups. Picnic tables and fireplaces are provided. Rest rooms, showers, and a sanitary dump station are available. Groceries and propane gas can be obtained nearby. Pets are permitted on leashes.

Reservations, fee: Reservations accepted; $9 fee per night; pets $1.

Who to contact: Phone the County Parks Department at (209)953-8800.

Location: From Interstate 5 in Manteca, turn east onto Highway 132 and drive to County Road J3 (Airport Way). Turn right (south) and drive six miles (road jogs left) on County Road J3 to the park entrance.

Trip note: This 176-acre park offers almost two miles of San Joaquin River shoreline. Catfishing can be good, and striped bass are also caught here, but rarely. Other options include bird watching or just watching the water roll by.

Map grid **f6**

CASWELL MEMORIAL STATE PARK

on Stanislaus River near Stockton

Campsites, facilities: There are 65 campsites for tents or motor homes up to 24 feet long. Piped water, fireplaces, and picnic tables are provided. Flush toilets, showers, wood, and a nature trail and exhibits are available. The exhibits are wheelchair accessible.

Reservations, fee: Phone MISTIX at (800)444-PARK ($3.95 MISTIX fee); $12-$14 fee per night.

Who to contact: Phone the park at (209)599-3810 or (209)874-2056.

Location: From the intersection of Highways 120 and 99 in Manteca, drive 1.5 miles south on Highway 99. Take the Austin Road exit south and drive four miles on Austin Road to the park.

Trip note: Caswell Memorial State Park is set along the Stanislaus River and covers 250 acres. The nature trail and visitor center provide recreation options. Open year-round.

Map grid h5 FRANK RAINES REGIONAL PARK
near Modesto

Campsites, facilities: There are 34 tent or motor home spaces. Fireplaces, picnic tables, piped water, electrical connections, and sewer hookups are provided. Rest rooms, showers, and a playground are available. Pets are permitted.

Reservations, fee: No reservations; $14 fee per night; pets $2; rough terrain vehicles $2.

Who to contact: Phone the park at (408)897-3127.

Location: From Interstate 5 near Modesto, take the Patterson exit. Drive west on Del Puerto Canyon Road for 16 miles to the park.

Trip note: This is a pretty park in the spring when the foothills are still green and many wildflowers are blooming. In summer, it gets hotter than a branding iron and the park becomes a popular spot for dirt-bike motorcyclists who take advantage of the rough-terrain riding course. A side trip option is to visit Minniear Park, located directly to the east, which is a day-use wilderness park with hiking trails and a creek. Open year-round.

Map grid i0 JOSEPH GRANT COUNTY PARK
near San Jose

Campsites, facilities: There are 20 sites for tents or motor homes up to 28 feet long. Fireplaces and tables are provided. Piped water and toilets are available. Pets are permitted.

Reservations, fee: Phone for available space; $8 fee per night; pets $1.

Who to contact: Phone the Grant County Park at (408)274-6121.

Location: From Interstate 280 in San Jose, drive east. The highway becomes Interstate 680. Take the Alum Rock exit. Drive east for four miles. Turn right (south) onto Mt. Hamilton Road and drive about seven miles to the park.

Trip note: If you want a unique perspective of the Santa Clara Valley, continue the trip on winding Mount Hamilton Road until you reach Lick Observatory. From your quiet lookout point, the distant valley far below will appear to be wall-to-wall with people, concrete, and cars. Yet looking to the rolling hills to the east, you likely won't see a soul. Expect hot weather in summer months.

Map grid i8 FISHERMAN'S BEND RIVER CAMPGROUND
on San Joaquin River

Campsites, facilities: There are ten sites for tents only and 38 motor home spaces with full hookups. Picnic tables and fire grills are provided. Piped water, rest rooms, showers, a sanitary disposal station, a laundromat, a boat ramp, a fish cleaning station, a swimming pool, a playground and horseshoe pits are available.

Reservations, fee: Reservations accepted; $14-$18 fee per night.

Who to contact: Phone the park at (209)862-3731.

Location: From Interstate 5, take the exit for Newman. Drive 6.5 miles east on County Road J18 (Stuhr Road). Turn left on Hills Ferry Road and drive one mile. Turn left on River Road and drive to 26836 River Road.

Trip note: This spot, on the outside edge of the San Joaquin Delta country, offers shady campsites along the San Joaquin River. Catfishing can be good on summer nights. Open from April to December.

Map grid i8 — GEORGE J. HATFIELD STATE RECREATION AREA

near Newman

Campsites, facilities: There are 21 family campsites and one large group campsite for tents or motor homes up to 32 feet long. Picnic tables, fireplaces, and piped water are provided. Flush toilets are available. Supplies can be obtained in Newman.

Reservations, fee: Call ahead for group reservations and fees; $12 fee for family sites.

Who to contact: Phone the Four Rivers district office at (209)826-1196.

Location: From Interstate 5 near Newman, take the Stuhr Road exit and drive east to Newman. Turn right (south) on Highway 33 and drive a short distance. Turn left (east) on Hills Ferry Road and drive five miles to the park entrance.

Trip note: This is a small state park set in the heart of the San Joaquin Valley near the confluence of the Merced River and San Joaquin River. Some folks say if you eat enough catfish from this spot, you'll glow in the dark after a few years. It's advisable to throw them back. Open year-round.

Map grid j1 — HENRY W. COE STATE PARK

near Gilroy

Campsites, facilities: There are seven sites for tents only and 13 sites for tents or motor homes. Piped water, pit toilets, fireplaces, and tables are provided. Pets are permitted on leashes.

Reservations, fee: Reserve through MISTIX by phoning (800)444-PARK ($3.95 MISTIX fee); $7-$9 per night fee; pets $1.

Who to contact: Phone state park rangers at (408)779-2728.

Location: From US 101 in Morgan Hill, take the East Dunne Avenue exit and drive 15 miles east on East Dunne Avenue to the park.

Trip note: This is the Bay Area's backyard wilderness—70,000 acres of wildlands with 70 lakes and ponds. You can get great backcountry fishing for bass, bluegill, and crappie, but anglers must hike or mountain bike 7 to 11 miles for the best of it. Coit Lake, Hoover Lake, and Paradise Lake are the best for bass. Expect hot weather in summer; spring and early summer are the prime times. Bring a water purifier for hikes because there is no piped water in the outback.

◆ MAP E3 ◆

BEACH
DESERT
FOOTHILL
TREES
URBAN
GRASSLAND
5% CLUB

15 MILES

to Drytown
to Pioneer
Ione
Jackson
Pine Grove
West Point
STANISLAUS
88
Lake Amador
26
Buena Vista
Pardee Res.
Mokelumne Hill
Camanche Res.
Valley Springs
CALAVERAS BIG TREES ST. PK.
4
Wallace
12
San Andreas
Burson
New Hogan Res.
Sheep Ranch
Arnold
26
49
Jenny Lind
Murphys
NAT'L.
Milton
Altaville
Vallecito
Angels Camp
Lyons Lake
J14
COLUMBIA ST. HIST. PK.
Mi-Wuk Village
Copperopolis
NEW MELONES LAKE US BUREAU OF RECLAMATION
Melones
Columbia
4
4
108
Twain Harte
Tuttletown
Eugene
New Melones Lake
Sonora
J14
Soulsbyville
Jamestown
Woodward Res.
Tulloch Res.
Tuolumne
Knights Ferry
River
Chinese Camp
Stanislaus
120
108
F.
Oakdale
49
J59
Groveland
Bucks Meadow
Big Oak Flat
120
Don Pedro Res.
Waterford
Modesto Res.
132
Toulemne
La Grange
River
Coulterville
Hickman
TURLOCK LAKE ST. REC. AREA Turlock Lake
Lake McClure
J16
J59
BAGBY REC. AREA
Turlock
J17
Snelling
Merced River
Bear Valley
Delhi
59
Merced Falls
J16
99
MC CONNELL ST. REC. AREA
Hornitos
49
Mt. Bullion
Livingston
J7
Cathey's Valley
Winton
Mariposa
140
140
Mormon Bar
Atwater
to Merced
to Raymond
to Clements
to Bellota
to Farmington
to Escalon
to Modesto
to Turlock
to Stevenson
to Bear Valley
to Long Barn
to Crane
to Nipinnawasse

a
b
c
d
e
f
g
h
i
j

0
1
2
3
4
5
6
7
8
9

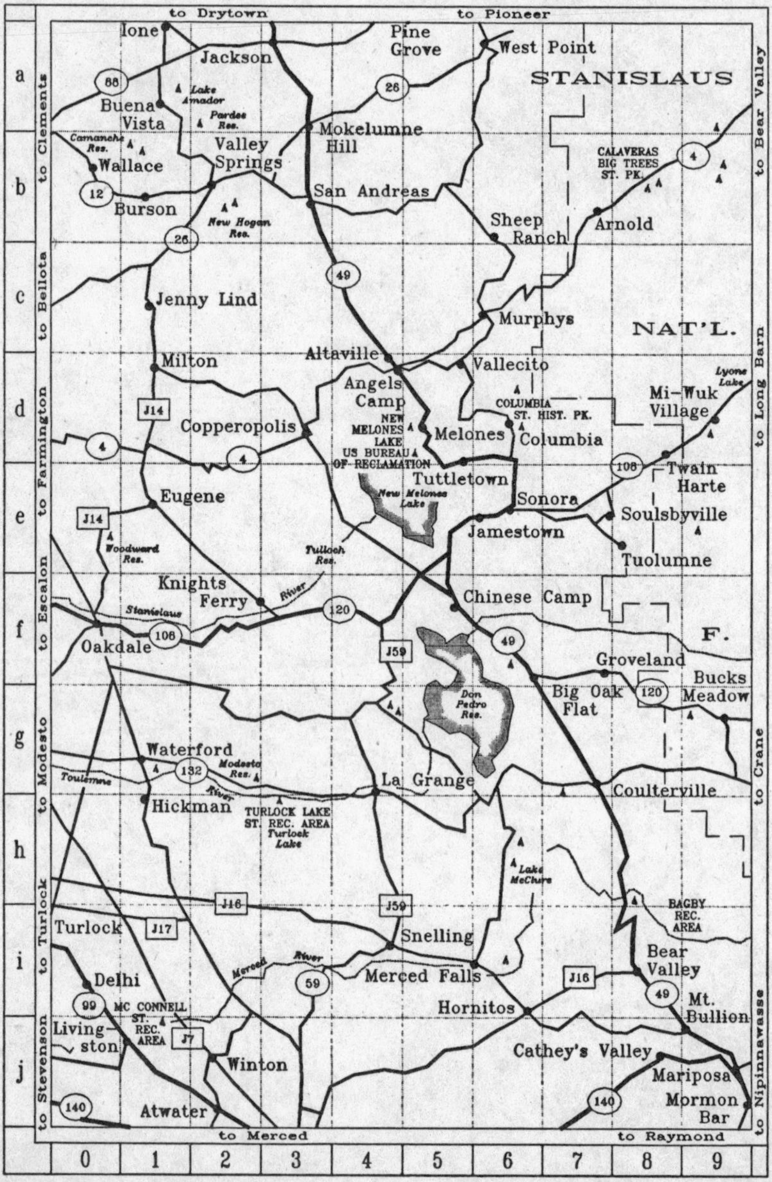

Map grid **a1** **LAKE AMADOR RECREATION AREA**
near Stockton

A

Campsites, facilities: There are 150 campsites for tents or motor homes, 72 sites with full hookups, and 12 group sites. Picnic tables and fire grills are provided. Piped water, rest rooms, showers, a sanitary disposal station, a boat ramp, boat rentals, a grocery store, propane gas, a swimming pond, and a playground are available. Pets are permitted on leashes.

B

Reservations, fee: Reservations accepted; $12-$18 fee per night.

Who to contact: Phone the resort at (209)274-4739.

Location: From Highway 99 in Stockton, drive 35 miles east on Highway 88. Turn right on well-signed Jackson Valley Road and drive four miles (through the intersection). Turn right on Lake Amador Drive and drive over the dam to the campground office.

C

Trip note: This is the Central Valley's "Big Bass Factory," known for producing many huge largemouth bass in the eight to 15-pound class every year. This is ironic because it is the smallest of the four reservoirs in the area and because many people prefer to fish for trout at Amador instead of bass. Water skiing is prohibited.

D

Map grid **a2** **PARDEE RECREATION AREA**
on Pardee Reservoir

E3

Campsites, facilities: There are 99 sites for tents or motor homes and 112 motor home spaces with full hookups. Picnic tables, fireplaces, and piped water are provided. Rest rooms, showers in the motor home section, a sanitary disposal station, a boat ramp, boat rentals, a laundromat, a grocery store, propane gas, RV and boat storage, and a swimming pool are available. Pets are permitted on leashes.

F

Reservations, fee: Reservations accepted for motor home spaces only; $3 entrance fee; $9-$14 fee for campsites; $1 for dogs.

Who to contact: Phone the resort at (209)772-1472.

Location: From Highway 99 in Stockton, drive about 35 miles east on Highway 88. Turn right on the well-signed Jackson Valley Road and drive three miles to the first stop sign. Turn right on Vista Road and drive to Stony Creek Road. Turn left and drive one-quarter mile to the campground.

G

Trip note: The reservoir is the choice of the area for trout fishermen, with very high catch rates for rainbow trout and kokanee salmon. A bonus is the quiet water because water skiing is prohibited (so is swimming). Pardee covers 2,257 acres, has 37 miles of shoreline, and the resort is known for providing reliable fishing reports, including water levels and temperatures. Open from mid-February through November.

H

Map grid **a9** **GOLDEN TORCH RV RESORT AND CAMPGROUND**
near Arnold

I

Campsites, facilities: There are 49 sites for tents only and 63 motor home spaces with full hookups. Fireplaces and picnic tables are provided. Piped water, rest rooms, showers, a sanitary disposal station, a recreation room, a swimming pool, and a playground are available. A grocery store, a laundromat, and propane gas are nearby. Pets are permitted.

J

Reservations, fee: Reservations recommended in the summer; $11-$17 fee per night.
Who to contact: Phone the campground at (209)795-2820.
Location: From Angels Camp on Highway 49, drive 22 miles north on Highway 4 to Arnold. Continue five miles past Arnold Golden Torch Drive.
Trip note: This is a privately-operated park designed primarily for motor homes. Many side trips provide options, including the Calaveras Big Trees State Park, the North Fork of the Stanislaus River, and the surrounding Stanislaus National Forest. The elevation is 5,800 feet. Open year-round.

Map grid b1

SOUTH CAMANCHE SHORE
on Camanche Reservoir

Campsites, facilities: There are 500 campsites for tents or motor homes, 300 with full hookups. Picnic tables, fireplaces, and piped water are provided. Rest rooms, showers, a sanitary disposal station, a boat ramp, boat rentals, a laundromat and a grocery store are available. Pets are permitted on leashes.
Reservations, fee: Reservations urged; call ahead for fees.
Who to contact: Phone resort at (209)763-5178.
Location: From Highway 99 in Stockton, turn east on Highway 88 and drive 24 miles to Clements. From Clements, drive east on Highway 12 for six miles to the resort entrance.
Trip note: This privately-operated park changed management in 1989 and all the changes have been good. It is one of the better lakes for fishing and camping in the Mother Lode country, particularly in the late spring, prior to the barn-burner heat of summer. It is one of two campgrounds on Camanche Reservoir. Open year-round.

Map grid b1

CAMANCHE NORTHSHORE RESORT
on Camanche Reservoir

Campsites, facilities: There are 400 campsites for tents or motor homes. Picnic tables, fireplaces, and piped water are provided. Rest rooms, showers, a sanitary disposal station, a boat ramp, boat rentals, a laundromat, a grocery store, riding stables, and a playground are available. Pets are permitted on leashes.
Reservations, fee: No reservations required; call ahead for fees.
Who to contact: Phone the resort at (209)763-5121.
Location: From Highway 99 in Stockton, turn east on Highway 88 and drive approximately 25 miles. Take the well-signed Liberty Road exit and drive east to the resort.
Trip note: This is one of two campgrounds at Camanche Reservoir. Camanche Reservoir is one of the best lakes in the Central Valley for fishing; the trout and bass prospects are good in spring, and the crappie, bluegill, and catfish are good in summer. With 63 miles of shoreline, there is enough room for anglers and waterskiers to co-exist without hassle. Water skiing is permitted in specified areas only. Open year-round.

Map grid b2

ACORN
at New Hogan Reservoir

Campsites, facilities: There are 130 campsites for tents or motor homes. Fireplaces and picnic tables are provided. Piped water, flush toilets, showers, a four-lane concrete boat ramp, and a sanitary dump station are available. Groceries and propane gas are nearby. Pets are permitted.

Reservations, fee: No reservations; call for fees.
Who to contact: Phone New Hogan Reservoir at (209)772-1343.
Location: From Stockton, drive about 35 miles east on Highway 26 to Valley Springs. Turn southeast on Hogan Dam Road and drive three miles to the campground.
Trip note: Of the four reservoirs in the area—Amador, Camanche, Pardee, and New Hogan—this is the best one for waterskiers, with 50 miles of shoreline providing plenty of room. The fishing has improved in the past few years, thanks to weekly trout plants. Bass fishing is good in the spring. Some big, but elusive striped bass provide a wild card option for anglers. An interpretive trail below the dam provides a possible side trip.

Map grid b2

OAK KNOLL
at New Hogan Reservoir

Campsites, facilities: There are 53 campsites for tents or motor homes. Fireplaces and picnic tables are provided. Piped water and vault toilets are available. Groceries, propane gas, a sanitary dump station, and a four lane boat ramp are available nearby. There is also a small campsite area, accessible only by boat, on the south shore of the lake.
Reservations, fee: No reservations; call for fees.
Who to contact: Phone New Hogan Reservoir at (209)772-1343.
Location: From Stockton, drive about 35 miles east on Highway 26 to Valley Springs. Turn southeast on Hogan Dam Road and drive three miles to the campground. Oak Knoll camp is nearby Acorn.
Trip note: This is one of two camps at New Hogan Reservoir. The reservoir was created by an Army Corps of Engineers dam project on the Calaveras River. Open from April to October.

Map grid b8

NORTH GROVE
CALAVERAS BIG TREES STATE PARK

Campsites, facilities: There are 36 sites for tents only, 13 sites for small motor homes up to 18 feet long, 24 sites for motor homes up to 30 feet long, five environmental walk-in sites and one site designed for wheelchair use. A group campground is also available. Fireplaces and picnic tables are provided. Piped water, flush toilets, showers, and a sanitary disposal station are available. Firewood is for sale. The nature trail (at the entrance station) and exhibits are wheelchair accessible. No bicycles are allowed on the paths, but they are permitted on fire roads. Pets are permitted on leashes, but not on the nature trails.
Reservations, fee: Call MISTIX at (800)444-PARK ($3.95 MISTIX fee); $7-$14 fee per night; $150 per night group site fee; pets $1.
Who to contact: Phone the Calaveras Big Trees State Park at (209)795-2334.
Location: From Angels Camp on Highway 49, drive 22 miles north on Highway 4 to Arnold. Continue four miles past Arnold to the park.
Trip note: This is one of the two campgrounds at Calaveras Big Trees State Park.

Map grid b8

OAK HOLLOW
CALAVERAS BIG TREES STATE PARK

Campsites, facilities: There are 31 sites for tents only, 21 sites for small motor homes up to 18 feet long, and five sites for motor homes up to 30 feet long.

Fire rings and picnic tables are provided. Piped water, flush toilets, a sanitary disposal station, and showers are available. Supplies can be purchased in Dorrington. The nature trail (at the entrance station) and exhibits are wheelchair accessible. Dogs are permitted on leashes, but not allowed on walking trails.

Reservations, fee: Call MISTIX at (800)444-PARK ($3.95 MISTIX fee); $12-$14 fee per night; pets $1.

Who to contact: Phone the Calaveras Big Trees State Park at (209)795-2334.

Location: From Angels Camp on Highway 49, drive 22 miles north on Highway 4 to Arnold. Continue four miles past Arnold on Highway 4 to the park.

Trip note: At this popular state park, reservations are often necessary. It is set at 4,800 feet elevation, close to the Stanislaus River, where trout are planted in summer months. Nearby Beaver Creek (three miles away) is also stocked, providing an option for fishermen. A visitor center with an herbarium, nature exhibits, and slide show on the history of the area is available near the park entrance. Guided tours through the Big Trees are offered during the peak periods. Open year-round.

Map grid b9

BOARDS CROSSING

on the North Fork of Stanislaus River

STANISLAUS NATIONAL FOREST

Campsites, facilities: There are five tent sites. There is **no piped water,** but picnic tables are provided. Vault toilets are available. Groceries and propane gas can be purchased nearby. Pets are permitted on leashes.

Reservations, fee: No reservations, no fee.

Who to contact: Phone the Stanislaus National Forest Calaveras Ranger District at (209)795-1381.

Location: From Angels Camp on Highway 49, turn north on Highway 4 and drive to Dorrington. Turn south on Boards Crossing Road and drive four miles to the campground.

Trip note: This is a small, primitive camp that isn't difficult to reach and is rarely used. No piped water is a minus, but not for folks with water purifiers. That's because the North Fork of the Stanislaus River runs beside the camp. Possible side trips include a visit to nearby Calaveras Big Trees State Park. The elevation is 3,800 feet. Open from April to October.

Map grid b9

SOURGRASS

on the North Fork of Stanislaus River

STANISLAUS NATIONAL FOREST

Campsites, facilities: There are six campsites for tents or motor homes up to 16 feet long. Piped water, fireplaces, and picnic tables are provided. Vault toilets are available. Supplies can be obtained in Dorrington. Pets are permitted on leashes.

Reservations, fee: No reservations; $4 fee per night.

Who to contact: Phone the Stanislaus National Forest Calaveras Ranger District at (209)795-1381.

Location: From Angels Camp on Highway 49, turn north on Highway 4 and drive to Dorrington. Turn south on Boards Crossing Road and drive four miles to the campground.

Trip note: This is just far enough off the main drag to get overlooked by many campers. It is a wooded site set along the North Fork of the Stanislaus River. A nearby state game refuge provides a possible side adventure. The elevation is 3,900 feet. Open from May through October.

Map grid **d5**

TUTTLETOWN RECREATION AREA
at New Melones Lake

Campsites, facilities: There are 95 campsites for tents or motor homes. Picnic tables and fire grills are provided. Piped water, flush toilets, a sanitary dump station, showers, a playground, and a boat ramp are available.
Reservations, fee: No reservations necessary; $10 fee per night.
Who to contact: Phone the US Department of Reclamation at (209)984-5248.
Location: From Sonora, drive eight miles north on Highway 49 to the campground.
Trip note: This is one of two camps on Lake New Melones in the Sierra Nevada foothills. This lake covers 12,250 acres and offers 100 miles of shoreline and good fishing. Water skiing is permitted in specified areas. The lake provides excellent bass fishing along the protected coves of the lake's arms. Trollers will find the trout fishing is best in the lake's main body. The lake level often drops dramatically in the fall. Open all year.

Map grid **d5**

GLORY HOLE
at New Melones Lake

Campsites, facilities: There are 144 campsites for tents or motor homes. Picnic tables and fire grills are provided. Piped water, flush toilets, a sanitary dump station, showers, a marina, boat rentals, a volleyball court, a baseball diamond, and a playground are available.
Reservations, fee: No reservations necessary; $10 fee per night.
Who to contact: Phone the US Department of Reclamation at (209)984-5248.
Location: From Sonora, drive 16 miles north on Highway 49 to the campground.
Trip note: This is one of two camps on Lake New Melones in the Sierra Nevada foothills. Open year-round.

Map grid **d6**

MARBLE QUARRY RESORT
near Columbia

Campsites, facilities: There are two sites for tents only and 85 sites for motor homes, 35 of which are full hookup. Piped water, picnic tables, electrical hookups, and, for some sites, sewer hookups are provided. Rest rooms, showers, a swimming pool, a laundromat, a store, a sanitary dump station, two clubhouses, a lounge, two full kitchens, satellite TV, and propane gas are available. Some facilities are wheelchair accessible.
Reservations, fee: Reservations accepted; $19-$22 camp use fee.
Who to contact: Phone (209)532-9539.
Location: From Columbia, drive one-half mile east on Yankee Hill Road to the campground at 11551 Yankee Hill Road.
Trip note: It's just a short walk to the Columbia Historic State Park from this camp, and New Melones Lake is nearby to the west. Set at 2,100 feet elevation in the Mother Lode country. It's open year-round.

Map grid **d6**

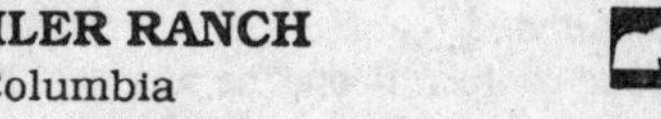

49ER TRAILER RANCH
near Columbia

Campsites, facilities: There are 45 sites for tents and motor homes, all with full hookups. Piped water, picnic tables, and fireplaces are provided. Rest rooms, hot showers, a laundromat, a store, a sanitary dump station, propane gas, and a large barn for group activities are available.

Reservations, fee: Reservations accepted; $17.50 fee per night.
Who to contact: Phone (209)532-9898.
Location: From Columbia, drive one mile north on Italian Bar Road to the campground; or from Columbia State Historic Park follow camping signs to campground.
Trip note: This privately-operated park is set up primarily for motor homes. Side trip possibilities include Columbia State Historic Park and New Melones Lake. Open year-round.

Map grid **d9**

RIVER RANCH CAMPGROUND
on Tuolumne River

Campsites, facilities: There are 55 campsites for tents or motor homes. Piped water, fireplaces, and picnic tables are provided. Rest rooms and showers are available. A grocery store, laundromat, and propane gas are nearby.
Reservations, fee: Call ahead for available space; $14 fee per night.
Who to contact: Phone (209)928-3708.
Location: From the town of Tuolumne, drive five miles northeast on Buchanan Road to the campground.
Trip note: You don't like roughing it at the Forest Service camps in this area that have no piped water? This privately-operated campground provides an option. It is set at the confluence of Basin Creek and the Tuolumne River, which is stocked by the Department of Fish and Game in early summer. Set at 2,700 feet elevation.

Map grid **d9**

SUGARPINE RV PARK
in Sugarpine

Campsites, facilities: There are 12 sites for motor homes. Piped water, picnic tables, electrical connections, cable TV, and sewer hookups are provided. Rest rooms, showers, a playground, a swimming pool, a laundromat and a store are available.
Reservations, fee: Reservations accepted; $15 fee per night.
Who to contact: Phone (209)586-4631.
Location: From Sonora, drive 14 miles east on Highway 108.
Trip note: This is a good mountain layover spot along Highway 108 for motor home drivers. Note: Heading east out of Twain Harte, beware of the unannounced horseshoe turn at the town of Confidence. Many drivers of motor homes can't keep their rigs between the white lines here.

Map grid **e0**

WOODWARD RESERVOIR COUNTY PARK

Campsites, facilities: There are 90 campsites for tents or motor homes. Piped water, fireplaces, and picnic tables are provided. Flush toilets, showers, a sanitary disposal station, groceries, propane gas, boat ramp, mooring, boat rentals, bait, and fishing licenses are available.
Reservations, fee: No reservations; $12 fee per night.
Who to contact: Phone the park at (209)847-3304 or (209)525-4107.
Location: From Highway 120 in Oakdale, turn north on County Road J14 (26 Mile Road) and drive five miles to 14528 26 Mile Road.
Trip note: This is one of the three lakes in the Central Valley foothills in this area that is popular with waterskiers in the summer. The lake is fullest in early

spring. Open year-round.

Map grid f6

MOCCASIN POINT
at Don Pedro Reservoir

Campsites, facilities: There are 65 sites for tents only and 15 sites for motor homes with full hookups. Picnic tables and barbecue units are provided at all sites. Piped water, rest rooms, showers, a store, a sanitary dump station, propane gas, ice, a snack bar, a boat ramp, motorboat and houseboat rentals, fuel, moorings, and bait and tackle are available. No pets are permitted at the developed facilities at Don Pedro Lake.
Reservations, fee: Reservations accepted; $12-$16 fee per night.
Who to contact: Phone (209)852-2396.
Location: From Chinese Camp, drive six miles east on Highway 49 and Highway 120 to the park.
Trip note: This camp is at the north end of Don Pedro Reservoir. Bass fishing can be excellent in the spring, with good fishing for salmon (believe it or not) and trout in early summer. Houseboating and water skiing are popular in the summer. The lake is set at 850 feet elevation. Open year-round.

Map grid g1

BIG BEAR PARK
near Modesto

Campsites, facilities: There are 42 sites for tents only and 116 motor home spaces, most with full hookups. Piped water, rest rooms, showers, a sanitary disposal station, a laundromat, propane gas, ice, a small store and a playground. A miniature train ride, and a water slide are available from May to September.
Reservations, fee: Reservations accepted; $15-$19 fee per night.
Who to contact: Phone the park at (209)874-1984.
Location: From Modesto, drive 12 miles east on Highway 132, through the town of Waterford to 13400 Yosemite Boulevard (Highway 132).
Trip note: This family-oriented park is located near the Tuolumne River, just at the start of the valley's foothill country. Open year-round.

Map grid g2

MODESTO RESERVOIR REGIONAL PARK

Campsites, facilities: There are 92 campsites for tents or motor homes. Piped water, fireplaces, and picnic tables are provided. Flush toilets, dump station, showers, two boat ramps, water skiing, fishing, a marina and a store are available. Propane gas is available nearby.
Reservations, fee: No reservations; $10-$12 fee per night.
Who to contact: Phone the park at (209)874-9540.
Location: From Modesto, drive 16 miles east on Highway 132, through the town of Waterford. Turn left (north) on Reservoir Road and drive to the campground at 18139 Reservoir Road.
Trip note: This is a popular lake for waterskiers. The camp is set right along the shoreline. The weather at Modesto Reservoir can be quite hot in the summer and foggy in the winter. Open year-round.

Map grid g4

FLEMING MEADOWS
on Don Pedro Reservoir

Campsites, facilities: There are 152 sites for tents or motor homes and 89 motor

A B C D E3 F G H I J

home sites with full hookups. Picnic tables are provided at all sites. Rest rooms, showers, and a sanitary dump station are available. A laundromat, a store, ice, a snack bar, a restaurant, tackle and bait, motorboat and houseboat rentals, a boat ramp, berths, engine repairs, and propane gas are nearby. No pets are permitted at the developed facilities at Don Pedro Lake.

Reservations, fee: Reservations accepted; $12-$16 fee per night.

Who to contact: Phone (209)852-2396.

Location: From Highway 132 in La Grange, turn north onto County Road J59 (La Grange Road) and drive five miles. Turn right on Bonds Flat Road and drive two miles to the campground.

Trip note: Of the several developed campgrounds at Don Pedro Reservoir, this one is designed more for motor homes than any of the areas. That can be good or bad, depending on your viewpoint. Open year-round.

Map grid g4

BLUE OAKS
at Don Pedro Reservoir

Campsites, facilities: There are 197 campsites for tents and motor homes. Piped water, picnic tables, and BBQ units are provided. Flush toilets, showers and a sanitary disposal station are available. A grocery store, a laundromat, a boat ramp, and propane gas are located nearby. No pets are permitted at the developed facilities at Don Pedro Lake.

Reservations, fee: Reservations accepted; $12-$16 fee per night.

Who to contact: Phone (209)852-2389.

Location: From Highway 132 in La Grange, turn north onto County Road J59 and drive five miles. Turn right on Bonds Flat Road and drive one mile to the campground.

Trip note: One of the several camps at Don Pedro Reservoir, this is larger than most. Bass fishing is good in the spring; trout and salmon go on the bite in early summer. Houseboat rentals are available.

Map grid g7

HORSESHOE BEND RECREATION AREA
on Lake McClure

Campsites, facilities: There are 90 sites for tent or motor home spaces, some with water and electricity. Picnic tables and fireplaces are provided. Rest rooms, showers, a sanitary disposal station, and a boat ramp are available. Nearby are a grocery store and a laundromat. Pets are permitted on leashes.

Reservations, fee: Call for available space; $10-$13 night; pets $2.

Who to contact: Phone (800)468-8889.

Location: From Coulterville, drive five miles west on Highway 132 to the campground entrance.

Trip note: Lake McClure is a unique, horseshoe-shaped lake in the foothill country west of Yosemite. It's one of four lakes in the immediate area; the others are Don Pedro Reservoir to the north and Modesto Reservoir and Turlock Lake to the west. The elevation is 900 feet. Camp and marina open all year.

Map grid g9

THE PINES
near Tuolumne River
STANISLAUS NATIONAL FOREST

Campsites, facilities: There are 12 campsites for tents or motor homes up to 22 feet long. Piped water, picnic tables, and fireplaces are provided. Vault toilets are available. A grocery store is nearby.

Reservations, fee: No reservations; $7 fee per night; $30 fee per night per group.

Who to contact: Phone the Stanislaus National Forest Groveland Ranger District at (209)962-7825.

Location: From Groveland, drive eight miles east on Highway 120 (about a mile past the County Road J20 turnoff). Turn right (south) onto the campground entrance road and drive a short distance to the camp.

Trip note: This campground is located 1.5 miles from the Tuolumne River, but on a hot summer day, you might wish it was about 1.5 miles closer. The elevation is 3,200 feet. Open all year.

Map grid h3

TURLOCK LAKE STATE RECREATION AREA

Campsites, facilities: There are 62 campsites for tents or motor homes up to 27 feet long. Piped water, fireplaces, and picnic tables are provided. Flush toilets, showers, a boat ramp, moorings, ice, a grocery store, a bait shop, and a snack bar are available. The boat facilities, grocery store, and snack bar are wheelchair accessible.

Reservations, fee: Phone MISTIX at (800)444-PARK ($3.95 MISTIX fee); $12-$14 fee per night.

Who to contact: Phone the park at (209)874-2008 or (209)874-2056.

Location: From Modesto, drive east on Highway 132 for 11 miles to Waterford. Continue east on Highway 132 for eight miles. Turn right (south) on Roberts Ferry Road and drive one mile. Turn left (east) on Lake Road and drive three miles to the park.

Trip note: This camp is set along Turlock Lake and provides fishing and water skiing opportunities. The lake is one of the three popular water skiing lakes in the area; the others are Modesto Reservoir and Woodward Reservoir.

Map grid h6

BARRETT COVE RECREATION AREA on Lake McClure

Campsites, facilities: There are 275 sites for tents or motor homes. Piped water, electrical connections, and sewer hookups are provided at some sites. Picnic tables and fireplaces are provided at all sites. Rest rooms, showers, boat ramps, a dump station, a swimming lagoon, and a playground are available. Nearby are a grocery store, a laundromat, boat and houseboat rentals, and propane gas. Pets are permitted on leashes.

Reservations, fee: Call for available space; $10-$13 fee per night; pets $2.

Who to contact: Phone (800)468-8889 for information.

Location: From Coulterville, drive 10.5 miles west on Highway 132. Turn south on Merced Falls Road and drive about five miles to the campground entrance.

Trip note: This is the largest in a series of camps on Lake McClure, a horseshoe-shaped lake popular with waterskiers and bass fishermen. Open year-round.

Map grid h6

McCLURE POINT RECREATION AREA on Lake McClure

Campsites, facilities: There are 100 sites for tents or motor homes up to 40 feet long. Piped water, electrical connections, and sewer hookups are provided at many sites. Picnic tables and fireplaces are provided at all sites. Rest rooms, showers, a boat ramp, and a laundromat are available. A grocery store is nearby. Pets are permitted on leashes.

Reservations, fee: Call for available space; $10-$13 fee per night; pets $2.

Who to contact: Phone (800)468-8889.

Location: From Coulterville, drive 10.5 miles west on Highway 132. Turn south on Merced Falls Road and drive 13 miles to the intersection of Lake McClure Road. Go left and drive six miles to the campground.

Trip note: This camp, a take-your-pick deal, is one of three camps on Lake McClure. It's an ideal lake for boaters with many miles of shoreline to explore. There are three other lakes in the immediate area. Camp and marina open all year.

Map grid h8

BAGBY RECREATION AREA
on Lake McClure

Campsites, facilities: There are 25 sites for tents only. Piped water, pit toilets and a boat ramp are available. Pets are permitted on leashes.

Reservations, fee: Call for available space; $10 fee per night; pets $2.

Who to contact: Phone (800)468-8889.

Location: From Coulterville, drive about 15 miles south on Highway 49 to the camp.

Trip note: Set well up along the Merced River, these are the most secluded camps available on Lake McClure. Trout fishing can be good in this area during early summer. The nearby Vista Point, located on the west side of Highway 49 from the camp, is a good side trip. Open from March through mid-October.

Map grid i6

LAKE McSWAIN RECREATION AREA
near McSwain Dam on Merced River

Campsites, facilities: There are 76 sites for tents or motor homes up to 40 feet long. Piped water and electrical connections are provided at most sites. Picnic tables and fireplaces are provided at all sites. Rest rooms, showers, a boat ramp, boat rentals, a laundromat, a playground, and a dump station are available. A grocery store, boat rentals, and propane gas are nearby. Pets are permitted on leashes.

Reservations, fee: Call for available space; $10 -$13 fee per night; pets $2.

Who to contact: Phone (800)468-8889.

Location: From Coulterville, drive 10.5 miles west on Highway 132. Turn south on Merced Falls Road and drive 13 miles to the intersection of Lake McClure Road. Go left and drive about a half mile to the campground.

Trip note: Lake McSwain is actually the afterbay for adjacent Lake McClure, with this camp located near the McSwain Dam on the Merced River. It you have a canoe or car-top boat, this lake is preferable to Lake McClure because water skiing is not allowed. Open from March to mid-October.

Map grid j1

McCONNELL STATE RECREATION AREA
on Merced River

Campsites, facilities: There are 17 family campsites for tents or motor homes up to 24 feet long and one group campsite for tents only. Piped water, fireplaces, and picnic tables are provided. Flush toilets and hot showers are available. Supplies can be obtained in Delhi.

Reservations, fee: Call ahead for group reservations and fees; $12 fee per night for family sites.

Who to contact: Phone the Four Rivers district office at (209)826-1196.

Location: From Highway 99 at Delhi, take the El Capitan Way exit (well marked) and drive five miles east. Turn right on Pepper Street and drive to the park.

Trip note: The weather gets as hot as a branding iron around these parts in the summer months, and a lot of out-of-towners would pay a bunch for a little shade and a river to sit next to. That's what this park provides, along with occasional mermaids on the beach. In high-water years, the Merced River attracts salmon (in the fall). Open from March through September.

◆ MAP E4 ◆

BEACH
TREES
5% CLUB
DESERT
URBAN
FOOTHILL
GRASSLAND
15 MILES

to Markleeville
Lake Alpine
Bear Valley
4
Ebbetts Pass
EL. 8,730
Coleville
NV
Walker
395
to Arnold
STANISLAUS
TOIYABE
Dardanelle
Donnell Lake
108
Devils Gate Summit
EL. 7,519
Kennedy Meadows
Sonora Pass
EL. 9,624
Beardsley Res.
Pinecrest
Pinecrest Lake
395
NAT'L.
Relief Pk.
EL. 10,808
Hanna Mtn.
EL. 11,846
Eagle Pk.
EL. 11,845
Long Barn
to Mi-Wuk Village
to Bridgeport
Twin Lakes
NAT'L.
Excelsior Mtn.
EL. 12,446
Cherry Lake
Lake Eleanor
YOSEMITE
FOREST
TO H-395
GRAND CANYON
OF THE TUOLUMNE
Tuolumne River
Hetch Hetchy Reservoir
Mather
120
Aspen Valley
Tuolumne Meadows
Tioga Pass
EL. 9,945
to Lee Vining
to Buck Meadows
Amelia Earhart
EL. 11,952
Crane Flat
Yosemite Village
Mirror Lake
NAT'L.
INYO
FOREST
Merced River
El Portal
Half Dome
140
YOSEMITE VALLEY
Glacier Pt.
EL. 7,214
Chinquapin
Mt. Lyell
EL. 13,114
NAT'L.
Briceburg
SIERRA
Badger Pass
EL. 7,300
Mt. Ansel Adams
EL. 11,760
41
Midpines
PARK
FOREST
Merced Pk.
EL. 11,726
Mt. Ritter
EL. 13,157
Wawona
NAT'L.
49
MARIPOSA GROVE
OF BIG TREES
DEVILS
POSTPILE
NAT'L.
MON.
to Mariposa
Fish Camp
FOREST
to Mammoth Lakes
to Oakhurst

a b c d e f g h i j
0 1 2 3 4 5 6 7 8 9

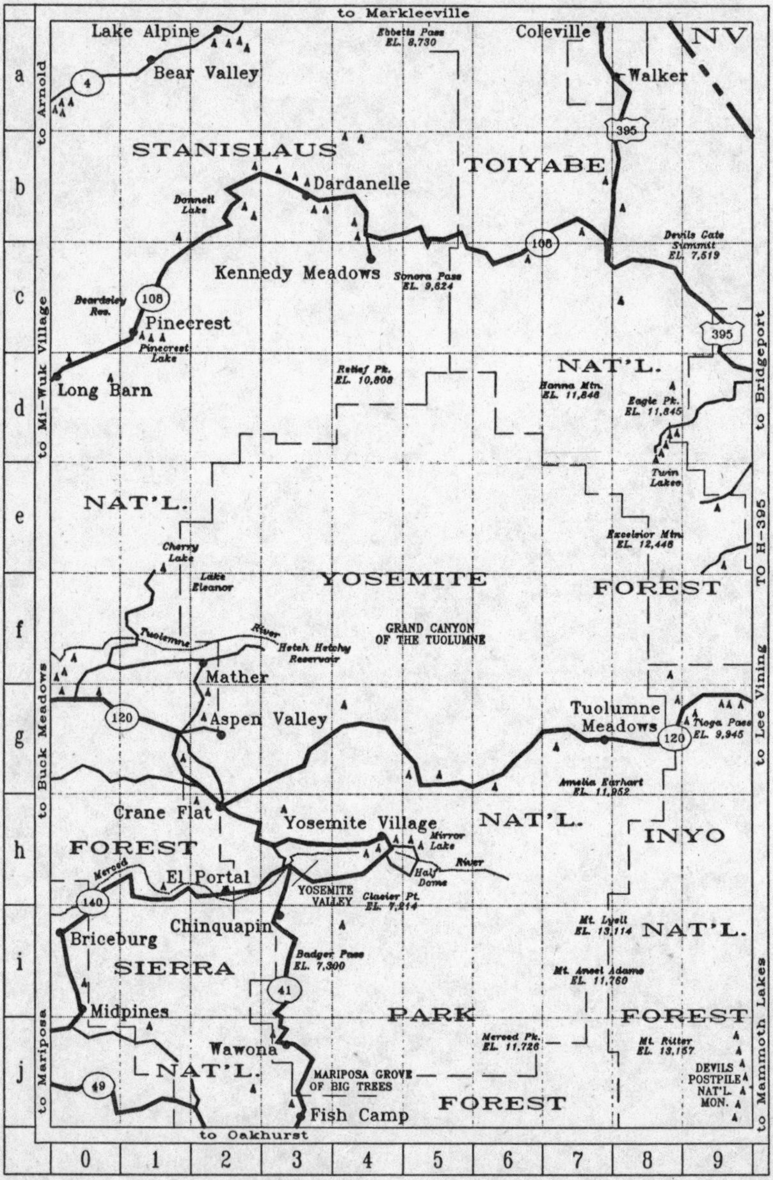

Map grid aO

BIG MEADOWS GROUP CAMP

STANISLAUS NATIONAL FOREST

Campsites, facilities: There is one group campsite for tents or motor homes. Piped water, picnic tables, and fireplaces are provided. Vault toilets are available. Groceries, a laundromat, and propane gas are nearby. Pets are permitted on leashes.

Reservations, fee: Reservations requested; $30 fee per group per night.

Who to contact: Phone the Stanislaus National Forest Calaveras Ranger District at (209)795-1381.

Location: From Angels Camp on Highway 49, turn north on Highway 4 and drive about 30 miles to the campground on the right. From Lake Alpine, drive nine miles south on Highway 4 to the campground.

Trip note: This is a spot for groups that need a large area to call their own. The nearby vicinity of the North Fork of the Stanislaus River, about a mile distant, is a bonus. The elevation is 6,500 feet. Open from May to October.

Map grid aO

SAND FLAT

on Stanislaus River

STANISLAUS NATIONAL FOREST

Campsites, facilities: There are four tent sites. Fireplaces are provided and vault toilets are available. There is **no piped water,** so bring your own. Pets are permitted on leashes.

Reservations, fee: No reservations, no fee.

Who to contact: Phone the Stanislaus National Forest Calaveras Ranger District at (209)795-1381.

Location: From Angels Camp on Highway 49, turn north on Highway 4 and drive about 30 miles to the campground on the right. From Lake Alpine, drive nine miles south on Highway 4 to Big Meadows Group Camp. Turn south and drive two miles on a steep, unimproved road (four-wheel drive required).

Trip note: This one is for four-wheel drive cowboys who want to carve out a piece of the Sierra Nevada wildlands for themselves. Set along the North Fork of the Stanislaus River, this is a tiny, primitive camp where you won't get bugged by anyone. You are strongly advised to obtain a National Forest map, which details all the back roads. The elevation is 5,800 feet. Open from June to September.

Map grid aO

STANISLAUS RIVER

STANISLAUS NATIONAL FOREST

Campsites, facilities: There are 25 campsites for tents or motor homes up to 16 feet long. Fireplaces and picnic tables are provided. Piped water and vault toilets are available. Pets are permitted on leashes. Tamarack has supplies.

Reservations, fee: No reservations; $4 fee per night.

Who to contact: Phone the Stanislaus National Forest Calaveras Ranger District at (209)795-1381.

Location: From Angels Camp on Highway 49, turn north on Highway 4 and drive about 30 miles to Big Meadow Group Camp. Continue on Highway 4 for 1.5 miles to Spicer Reservoir Road. Turn right (south) and drive four miles to the campground. From Lake Alpine, drive seven miles south on Highway 4, just past the town of Tamarack. Turn south on Spicer Reservoir Road and drive four miles to campground.

Trip note: This is a good base camp for fishermen. It is a timbered site set along the North Fork of the Stanislaus River. Both Utica and Union Reservoirs are in the vicinity for possible side trips, and Alpine Lake to the north and Spicer Meadow Reservoir to the southeast provide additional options.

Map grid a0

BIG MEADOWS

near Stanislaus River

STANISLAUS NATIONAL FOREST

Campsites, facilities: There are 68 campsites for tents or motor homes. Piped water, fireplaces, and picnic tables are provided and vault toilets are available. Groceries, laundromat, and propane gas are nearby. Pets are permitted.

Reservations, fee: No reservations; $7 fee per night.

Who to contact: Phone the Stanislaus National Forest Calaveras Ranger District at (209)795-1381.

Location: From Angels Camp on Highway 49, turn north on Highway 4 and drive about 30 miles to the campground on the right. From Lake Alpine, drive nine miles southwest on Highway 4 to the campground.

Trip note: This is an easy-access mountain camp, set at 6,500 feet elevation in the Sierra. It's all National Forest up here with numerous back roads (detailed on the Forest Service map). The closest side trip is to the North Fork of the Stanislaus River, about a mile away. Open from May through October.

Map grid a2

PINE MARTEN

on Lake Alpine

STANISLAUS NATIONAL FOREST

Campsites, facilities: There are 33 campsites for tents or motor homes up to 22 feet long. Piped water, flush toilets, picnic tables, and fireplaces are provided. A boat ramp is available. A grocery store, propane gas, and a laundromat are nearby. Pets are permitted on leashes.

Reservations, fee: No reservations; $8 fee fee per night.

Who to contact: Phone the Stanislaus National Forest Calaveras Ranger District at (209)795-1381.

Location: From Arnold, drive 29 miles east on Highway 4 to Lake Alpine.

Trip note: This is one of four camps at Lake Alpine. For details, see Alpine camp. The elevation is 7,400 feet. Open from June to September.

Map grid a2

SILVER VALLEY

on Lake Alpine

STANISLAUS NATIONAL FOREST

Campsites, facilities: There are 25 campsites for tents or motor homes up to 22 feet long. Piped water, flush toilets, picnic tables, and fireplaces are provided. A boat launch is available. Facilities are wheelchair accessible. A grocery store, propane gas, and a laundromat are nearby. Pets are permitted on leashes.

Reservations, fee: No reservations; $8 fee per night.

Who to contact: Phone the Stanislaus National Forest Calaveras Ranger District at (209)795-1381.

Location: From Arnold, drive 29 miles east on Highway 4 to Lake Alpine.

Trip note: This is one of four camps at Lake Alpine. See the trip note for Alpine camp. The elevation is 7,500 feet. Open from June through September.

Map grid **a2**

LAKE ALPINE CAMPGROUND
on Lake Alpine
STANISLAUS NATIONAL FOREST

A

Campsites, facilities: There are five campsites for tents only and 22 sites for motor homes up to 22 feet long. Piped water, flush toilets, showers, picnic tables, fireplaces, and a boat launch are provided. A grocery store, propane gas, and a laundromat are nearby. Pets are permitted on leashes.

B

Reservations, fee: No reservations; $8 fee per night.
Who to contact: Phone the Stanislaus National Forest Calaveras Ranger District at (209)795-1381.
Location: From Arnold, drive 29 miles east on Highway 4 to Lake Alpine.

C

Trip note: This is one of the Sierra Nevada's prettiest lakes, and it has lots of jumping trout during early summer evenings. Two short hikes are accessible: a one-mile, easy hike on a marked trail to Duck Lake or a moderately difficult 1.5-mile hike on an unmarked trail that starts at the south end of the lake and is routed to Inspiration Point. Backpackers might consider this as a jump-off point, with a trail that starts at the lake and leads all the way into the Emigrant Wilderness. The elevation is 7,400 feet. Open from June through October.

D

Map grid **a2**

SILVER TIP
near Lake Alpine
STANISLAUS NATIONAL FOREST

E4

Campsites, facilities: There are 23 campsites for tents or motor homes up to 22 feet long. Piped water, flush toilets, picnic tables, and fireplaces are provided. A boat launch is about a mile away. A grocery store, propane gas, and a laundromat are nearby. Pets are permitted on leashes.

F

Reservations, fee: No reservations; $8 fee per night.
Who to contact: Phone the Stanislaus National Forest Calaveras Ranger District at (209)795-1381.
Location: From Arnold, drive 28 miles east on Highway 4 to Lake Alpine.
Trip note: This camp is at Lake Alpine. See the trip note for Alpine camp.

G

Map grid **b1**

CASCADE CREEK
STANISLAUS NATIONAL FOREST

Campsites, facilities: There are three undesignated campsites for tents or motor homes up to 22 feet long. Picnic tables and vault toilets are provided. There is **no piped water.** Pets are permitted on leashes. Dardanelle has supplies.

H

Reservations, fee: No reservations, no fee.
Who to contact: Phone the Stanislaus National Forest Summit Ranger District at (209)965-3434.
Location: From Strawberry, drive nine miles north on Highway 108.

I

Trip note: This tiny, rarely-used spot along Cascade Creek is located at 6,000 feet elevation. It is a do-it-yourself special, so don't forget to bring your own drinking water or a water purifier. Open from June through October.

Map grid **b2**

NIAGARA CREEK OFF-HIGHWAY VEHICLE CAMP
STANISLAUS NATIONAL FOREST

J

Campsites, facilities: There are ten campsites for tents or motor homes up to 22 feet long. Fireplaces and picnic tables are provided. Vault toilets are available. There is **no piped water,** so bring your own. (A spring is nearby). Pets are permitted on leashes. Supplies can be purchased in Dardanelle.

Reservations, fee: No reservations, no fee.

Who to contact: Phone the Stanislaus National Forest Summit Ranger District at (209)965-3434.

Location: From Dardanelle, drive about eight miles west on Highway 108 to the campground entrance road. Continue past Niagara Creek campground on Eagle Meadows Road for two miles to the campground.

Trip note: Several backcountry roads make for prime off-highway vehicle use. A Forest Service map is advisable. The camp is set beside Niagara Creek at 6,200 feet elevation. Open from July through October.

Map grid b2

NIAGARA CREEK

near Donnells Reservoir

STANISLAUS NATIONAL FOREST

Campsites, facilities: There are five campsites for tents or motor homes up to 22 feet long. Fireplaces and picnic tables are provided. Vault toilets are available. There is **no piped water,** so bring your own. Pets are permitted on leashes. Supplies can be purchased in Dardanelle.

Reservations, fee: No reservations, no fee.

Who to contact: Phone the Stanislaus National Forest Summit Ranger District at (209)965-3434.

Location: From Dardanelle, drive about eight miles west on Highway 108 to the campground entrance road. Drive one mile to the campground.

Trip note: This small, primitive camp is set beside little Niagara Creek. A trail from the camp leads to nearby Donnell Vista picnic area, which offers a spectacular view overlooking Donnells Reservoir. The elevation is 6,200 feet. Donnells is a paradox of lake, very tough to reach, almost impossible to get a canoe into, but it has big rainbow trout. Open from July through October.

Map grid b2

FENCE CREEK

near the Middle Fork of Stanislaus River

STANISLAUS NATIONAL FOREST

Campsites, facilities: There are 12 campsites for tents or motor homes up to 22 feet long. Fireplaces and picnic tables are provided. Vault toilets are available. There is **no piped water,** so bring your own. Pets are permitted on leashes. Supplies can be purchased in Dardanelle.

Reservations, fee: No reservations, no fee.

Who to contact: Phone the Stanislaus National Forest Summit Ranger District at (209)965-3434.

Location: From Dardanelle, drive three miles west on Highway 108. Turn north on Clark Fork Road and drive one mile to the campground.

Trip note: This small, primitive camp is far enough off the highway to get missed by most folks. It is set along Fence Creek, a feeder stream to the Middle Fork of the Stanislaus River. The elevation is 5,600 feet. Open May through October.

Map grid b3

PIDGEON FLAT

on the Middle Fork of Stanislaus River

STANISLAUS NATIONAL FOREST

Campsites, facilities: There are six walk-in tent sites. Fireplaces and picnic tables are provided, and vault toilets are available. There is **no piped water,** so bring your own. Pets are permitted. Supplies can be purchased in Dardanelle. A

Reservations, fee: No reservations, no fee.

Who to contact: Phone the Stanislaus National Forest Summit Ranger District at (209)965-3434.

Location: From Dardanelle, drive two miles east on Highway 108 to the campground. B

Trip note: This small, primitive spot gets quite a bit of attention since the short trail to Columns of the Giants starts here. The Stanislaus River rolls on past as well. The trout are plentiful enough it seems, but they just don't seem to have much size. The elevation is 6,000 feet. Open May through October.

C

Map grid b3

EUREKA VALLEY

on the Middle Fork of Stanislaus River

STANISLAUS NATIONAL FOREST

Campsites, facilities: There are 28 campsites for tents or motor homes up to 22 feet long. Piped water, fireplaces, and picnic tables are provided. Vault toilets are available. Pets are permitted. Supplies can be purchased in Dardanelle. D

Reservations, fee: No reservations; $5 fee per night.

Who to contact: Phone the Stanislaus National Forest Summit Ranger District at (209)965-3434.

Location: From Dardanelle, drive three miles east on Highway 108.

E4

Trip note: This take-your-pick deal is one in a series of Forest Service campgrounds set along the Stanislaus River. The stream is stocked with trout by the Department of Fish and Game in early summer. A side trip to the unusual geologic formation called Columns of the Giants is accessible by a one-quarter mile trail leading out of the Pidgeon Flat campground, located one mile west. The elevation is 6,000 feet. Open from May through October. F

Map grid b3

BOULDER FLAT

on the Middle Fork of Stanislaus River

STANISLAUS NATIONAL FOREST

G

Campsites, facilities: There are 20 campsites for tents or motor homes up to 22 feet long. Fireplaces and picnic tables are provided. Vault toilets are available. There is **no piped water,** so bring your own. Pets are permitted on leashes. Supplies can be purchased in Dardanelle.

Reservations, fee: No reservations; $5 fee per night.

Who to contact: Phone the Stanislaus National Forest Summit Ranger District at (209)965-3434. H

Location: From Dardanelle, drive 1.5 miles west on Highway 108 to the campground.

Trip note: You want camping on the Stanislaus River? This is one in a series of campgrounds that provides exactly that. Boulder Flat is set at 5,600 feet elevation. Easy access is a bonus, but no piped water is a minus. Donnells Reservoir provides a possible side trip, but it is difficult to reach and almost impossible to get a boat in. Open from May through September. I

Map grid b3

BRIGHTMAN FLAT

on the Middle Fork of Stanislaus River

STANISLAUS NATIONAL FOREST

J

Campsites, facilities: There are 29 campsites for tents or motor homes up to 22 feet

long. Fireplaces and picnic tables are provided. Vault toilets are available. There is **no piped water,** so bring your own. Pets are permitted on leashes. Supplies can be purchased in Dardanelle.

Reservations, fee: No reservations, no fee.

Who to contact: Phone the Stanislaus National Forest Summit Ranger District at (209)965-3434.

Location: From Dardanelle, drive one mile west on Highway 108 to the campground.

Trip note: This camp is located on the Middle Fork of the Stanislaus River and set at 5,600 feet elevation. It's one in a series of free, easy-access camps along the Stanislaus River and Highway 108. Open from May through September.

Map grid b3

DARDANELLE

on the Middle Fork of Stanislaus River
STANISLAUS NATIONAL FOREST

Campsites, facilities: There are 28 campsites for tents or motor homes up to 22 feet long. Piped water, fireplaces, and picnic tables are provided. Vault toilets are available. Pets are permitted on leashes. Supplies can be purchased in Dardanelle.

Reservations, fee: No reservations; $6 fee per night for single sites; $12 fee per night for double sites.

Who to contact: Phone the Stanislaus National Forest Summit Ranger District at (209)965-3434.

Location: The camp is in the town of Dardanelle on Highway 108.

Trip note: This is one of the more popular Forest Service camps in the area. It is set near both the Stanislaus River and an unusual geologic formation called Columns of the Giants. The latter can be reached via a one-quarter mile trail leading out of the Pidgeon Flat campground, 1.5 miles east. Open from May through October.

Map grid b4

SAND FLAT

on the Clark Fork of Stanislaus River
STANISLAUS NATIONAL FOREST

Campsites, facilities: There are 53 campsites for tents or motor homes up to 32 feet long. Fireplaces and picnic tables are provided. Piped water and vault toilets are available. Pets are permitted on leashes. Supplies can be purchased in Dardanelle.

Reservations, fee: No reservations; $4 fee per night.

Who to contact: Phone the Stanislaus National Forest Summit Ranger District at (209)965-3434.

Location: From Dardanelle, drive three miles west on Highway 108. Turn north on Clark Fork Road and drive seven miles to the campground.

Trip note: This is an optional jump-off spot for backpackers; trails lead to Carson-Iceberg Wilderness to the north. This camp is located along the Clark Fork of the Stanislaus River at 6,200 feet elevation. Open May through September.

Map grid b4

BAKER

on the Middle Fork of Stanislaus River
STANISLAUS NATIONAL FOREST

Campsites, facilities: There are 44 campsites for tents or motor homes up to 22 feet long. Piped water, fireplaces, and picnic tables are provided. Vault toilets are available. Pets are permitted. Supplies can be purchased in Dardanelle.

Reservations, fee: No reservations; $6 fee per night.
Who to contact: Phone the Stanislaus National Forest Summit Ranger District at (209)965-3434.
Location: From Dardanelle, drive five miles east on Highway.
Trip note: This camp, one in a series of streamside camps, is located on the Stanislaus River. It is set at 6,200 feet elevation. Open from May through October.

A B C D E4 F G H I J

Map grid **b4**

CLARK FORK
on the Clark Fork of Stanislaus River
STANISLAUS NATIONAL FOREST

Campsites, facilities: There are 88 campsites for tents or motor homes up to 22 feet long. Fireplaces and picnic tables are provided. Piped water, flush or vault toilets, and a sanitary disposal station are available. Wheelchair accessible sites are available. Pets are permitted on leashes. Supplies can be purchased in Dardanelle.
Reservations, fee: No reservations; $5-$6 fee per night.
Who to contact: Phone the Stanislaus National Forest Summit Ranger District at (209)965-3434.
Location: From Dardanelle, drive three miles west on Highway 108. Turn north on Clark Fork Road and drive six miles to the campground.
Trip note: This is one of the big, well-known Forest Service camps that is especially popular for backpackers. Trails from camp lead to the Carson-Iceberg Wilderness to the north. The camp is set at 6,200 feet elevation on the Clark Fork of the Stanislaus River. Open May through September.

Map grid **b4**

DEADMAN
on the Middle Fork of Stanislaus River
STANISLAUS NATIONAL FOREST

Campsites, facilities: There are 17 campsites for tents or motor homes up to 22 feet long. Piped water, fireplaces, and picnic tables are provided. Vault toilets are available. Pets are permitted. Supplies can be purchased in Dardanelle.
Reservations, fee: No reservations; $6 fee per night.
Who to contact: Phone the Stanislaus National Forest Summit Ranger District at (209)965-3434.
Location: From Dardanelle, drive six miles east on Highway 108 to the campground.
Trip note: This is a popular trailhead camp and an ideal jump-off point for backpackers. A trail leaves nearby Kennedy Meadows and heads into the backcountry of the Emigrant Wilderness. The trail forks east to Kennedy Lake and south to Relief Reservoir and beyond, to many small alpine lakes. Need a bonus? The camp is set along the Stanislaus River and also has piped water.

Map grid **b7**

SONORA BRIDGE
near Walker River
TOIYABE NATIONAL FOREST

Campsites, facilities: There are 23 campsites for tents or motor homes up to 30 feet long. Piped water, fireplaces, and picnic tables are provided. Pit toilets are available. Pets are permitted on leashes.
Reservations, fee: Reservations available through MISTIX at (800)283-CAMP ($6 MISTIX fee); $6 fee per night.
Who to contact: Phone the Toiyabe National Forest District Office at (619)932-7070.

Location: From Bridgeport, drive 14 miles north on US 395. Turn west on Highway 108 and drive two miles to the campground.

Trip note: If you don't like the company at the campgrounds along the West Walker River, this spot provides an option. It's just a half-mile from the Walker, so it's not too much trouble to make your side trips. The elevation is 6,600 feet. Open from May to October.

Map grid **b7**

CHRIS FLAT
on Walker River
TOIYABE NATIONAL FOREST

Campsites, facilities: There are 15 campsites for tents or motor homes up to 22 feet long. Piped water, fireplaces, and picnic tables are provided. Pit toilets are available. Pets are permitted on leashes.

Reservations, fee: No reservations; $7 fee per night.

Who to contact: Phone the Toiyabe National Forest District Office at (619)932-7070.

Location: From Coleville, drive 15 miles south on US 395.

Trip note: This is one in a series of campgrounds set along Highway 395 next to the West Walker River. Considering the easy access, the trout fishing is often surprisingly good on the Walker, particularly in early summer and fall. The elevation is 6,600 feet. Open from May to October.

Map grid **b8**

BOOTLEG
on Walker River
TOIYABE NATIONAL FOREST

Campsites, facilities: There are 63 paved campsites for tents or motor homes. Piped water, fireplaces, and picnic tables are provided. Flush toilets are available. Pets are permitted on leashes.

Reservations, fee: Reservations available through MISTIX at (800)283-CAMP ($6 MISTIX fee); $7 fee per night.

Who to contact: Phone the Toiyabe National Forest headquarters at (619)932-7070.

Location: From Coleville, drive 13 miles south on US 395.

Trip note: Here, the location is the key, with the West Walker River running along the other side of US 395. The elevation is 6,600 feet. Open from May to October.

Map grid **c1**

MEADOW VIEW
near Pinecrest Lake
STANISLAUS NATIONAL FOREST

Campsites, facilities: There are 100 campsites for tents or motor homes up to 22 feet long. Piped water, fireplaces, and picnic tables are provided. Flush toilets and equestrian facilities are available. A grocery store, a laundromat, a boat ramp, and propane gas are nearby.

Reservations, fee: No reservations; $10 fee per night.

Who to contact: Phone the Stanislaus National Forest Summit Ranger District at (209)965-3434.

Location: From Strawberry, drive one mile south on Highway 108 to Dodge Ridge Road. Turn and drive one mile to the campground.

Trip note: This camp is located one mile from Pinecrest Lake, a popular weekend vacation area that provides fishing for small trout. The speed limit of 20 mph is strictly enforced on the lake. A side trip option is to hike the Pinecrest National Recreation Trail, which circles the lake and also branches off to Catfish Lake.

Map grid **c1**

PIONEER TRAIL GROUP CAMP

near Pinecrest Lake
STANISLAUS NATIONAL FOREST

Campsites, facilities: There are three group campsites here. Piped water, picnic tables, and fireplaces are provided. Vault toilets are available. A grocery store, a laundromat, a boat ramp, and propane gas are nearby.

Reservations, fee: Reserve through MISTIX at (800)283-CAMP ($6 MISTIX fee); $35-$50 group fee per night.

Who to contact: Phone the Stanislaus National Forest Summit Ranger District at (209)965-3434.

Location: From Strawberry, drive one mile south on Highway 108 to Dodge Ridge Road. Turn and drive 1.5 miles to the campground.

Trip note: If you're going to Pinecrest Lake with a Boy Scout troop, this is the spot since it is set up specifically for groups.

Map grid **c1**

PINECREST

on Pinecrest Lake
STANISLAUS NATIONAL FOREST

Campsites, facilities: There are 200 sites for tents or motor homes up to 22 feet long. Piped water, picnic tables, and fireplaces are provided. Vault toilets are available. Pets are permitted on leashes. A grocery store, a laundromat, equestrian facilities, a boat ramp, and propane gas are nearby.

Reservations, fee: Reserve through MISTIX at (800)283-CAMP ($6 MISTIX fee); $10.50 fee per night.

Who to contact: Phone the Stanislaus National Forest Summit Ranger District at (209)965-3434.

Location: From Strawberry, drive one mile south on Highway 108 to Dodge Ridge Road. Turn and drive one mile to the campground entrance road.

Trip note: This monster-sized Forest Service camp is set at Pinecrest Lake. In early summer, there is good fishing for stocked rainbow trout. A launch ramp is available, but a 20-mph speed limit on the lake is enforced. A trail circles the lake and also branches off to nearby Catfish Lake. Several lesser-known camps are to the east along the Stanislaus River. The elevation is 5,800 feet.

Map grid **c6**

LEAVITT MEADOWS

on Walker River
TOIYABE NATIONAL FOREST

Campsites, facilities: There are 16 campsites for tents or motor homes up to 22 feet long. Piped water, fireplaces, and picnic tables are provided. Pit toilets are available. Pets are permitted on leashes.

Reservations, fee: No reservations; $6 fee per night.

Who to contact: Phone the Toiyabe National Forest District Office at (619)932-7070.

Location: From Bridgeport, drive 14 miles north on US 395. Turn west on Highway 108 and drive seven miles to the campground.

Trip note: This is a prime spot for either a base camp for trout fishing or a backpacking jump-off point. A trail that starts near the camp is routed into the upper West Walker drainage, an area which has been recommended as an addition to the Hoover Wilderness. The camp is set at 7,000 feet elevation adjacent to the West Walker River. Open from May to October.

Map grid **c8**

OBSIDIAN
on Molybdenite Creek
TOIYABE NATIONAL FOREST

Campsites, facilities: There are 14 campsites for tents or motor homes up to 30 feet long. Fireplaces and picnic tables are provided. Pit toilets are available. There is **no piped water,** so bring your own. Pets are permitted on leashes.
Reservations, fee: No reservations, no fee—until piped water is put in.
Who to contact: Phone the Toiyabe National Forest District Office at (619)932-7070.
Location: From Bridgeport, drive about 12 miles north on US 395. Turn left (west) on the improved dirt road (the sign says "Forest Service Campground") just before Sonora Junction. Drive four miles to the campground.
Trip note: This is used primarily as a jump-off point for backpackers; a nearby trail is routed up the Molybdenite Creek drainage and into the Hoover Wilderness. Set at 7,800 feet elevation. Open from May to October.

Map grid **d0**

FRASER FLAT
on South Fork of the Stanislaus River
STANISLAUS NATIONAL FOREST

Campsites, facilities: There are 38 sites for tents or motor homes up to 22 feet. Piped water, picnic tables, and fireplaces are provided. Vault toilets are available. A grocery store and propane gas are nearby. A camping and fishing site for handicapped use are provided.
Reservations, fee: No reservations; $7 fee per night.
Who to contact: Phone the Stanislaus National Forest Mi-Wuk Ranger District at (209)586-3234.
Location: From Long Barn, drive about six miles north on Highway 108 to the entrance road on your left. Turn and drive 1.5 miles to the campground.
Trip note: This camp is set along the South Fork of the Stanislaus River. It can be an overflow area if Pinecrest Lake is filled up. Open from June through October.

Map grid **d0**

HULL CREEK
STANISLAUS NATIONAL FOREST

Campsites, facilities: There are 11 for campsites for tents or motor homes up to 22 feet long. Picnic tables and fireplaces are provided. Vault toilets are available. There is **no piped water,** so bring your own.
Reservations, fee: No reservations; $3 fee per night.
Who to contact: Phone the Stanislaus National Forest Mi-Wuk Ranger District at (209)586-3234.
Location: From Long Barn on Highway 108, drive nine miles east on Hull Meadow Road to the campground.
Trip note: Far enough off the highway to get missed by plenty of campers who yearn for exactly such a spot, this small, quiet camp is set along little Hull Creek. The elevation is 5,600 feet. Open from June through October.

Map grid **d8**

HONEYMOON FLAT
on Robinson Creek
TOIYABE NATIONAL FOREST

Campsites, facilities: There are 47 campsites for tents or motor homes up to 22 feet

long. Piped water, fireplaces, and picnic tables are provided. Pit toilets are available. Pets are permitted on leashes.

Reservations, fee: Reservations available through MISTIX at (800)283-CAMP ($6 MISTIX fee); $6 fee per night.

Who to contact: Phone the Toiyabe National Forest Ranger Station at (619)932-7070.

Location: From Bridgeport, drive eight miles southwest on Twin Lakes Road to the campground.

Trip note: This camp is often used as an overflow area if the camps at Twin Lakes are filled or noisy. But Honeymoon Flat isn't a bad choice all on its own. It's set beside little Robinson Creek at 7,000 feet elevation, just three miles from Twin Lakes. Open from May to October.

Map grid d8

PAHA

near Twin Lakes

TOIYABE NATIONAL FOREST

Campsites, facilities: There are 22 paved campsites for tents or motor homes up to 22 feet long. Piped water, fireplaces, and picnic tables are provided. Flush toilets are available. A boat launch, a store, and a laundromat are available nearby. Pets are permitted on leashes.

Reservations, fee: Reservations available through MISTIX at (800)283-CAMP ($6 MISTIX fee); $8 fee per night.

Who to contact: Phone the Toiyabe National Forest Ranger Station at (619)932-7070.

Location: From Bridgeport, drive about ten miles southwest on Twin Lakes Road to the campground.

Trip note: This is one in a series of camps near Robinson Creek and Twin Lakes. The elevation is 7,000 feet. Open from May to October.

Map grid d8

ROBINSON CREEK

near Twin Lakes

TOIYABE NATIONAL FOREST

Campsites, facilities: There are 54 paved campsites for tents or motor homes up to 30 feet long. Piped water, fireplaces, and picnic tables are provided. Flush toilets are available. Pets are permitted on leashes.

Reservations, fee: Reservations available through MISTIX at (800)283-CAMP ($6 MISTIX fee); $8 fee per night.

Who to contact: Phone the Toiyabe National Forest Ranger Station at (619)932-7070.

Location: From Bridgeport, drive about ten miles southwest on Twin Lakes Road to the campground entrance road.

Trip note: This campground, one in a series in the area, is set at 7,000 feet elevation on Robinson Creek, not far from Twin Lakes. For recreation options, see the trip note for Lower Twin Lakes camp.

Map grid d8

BUCKEYE

near Buckeye Creek

TOIYABE NATIONAL FOREST

Campsites, facilities: There are 65 paved campsites for tents or motor homes up to 30 feet long. There are also some group sites available. Piped water, fireplaces, and picnic tables are provided. Flush toilets are available. Pets are permitted on leashes.

Reservations, fee: Group reservations available through MISTIX at (800)283-CAMP ($6 MISTIX fee); $7 fee per night.

Who to contact: Phone the Toiyabe National Forest Ranger Station at (619)932-7070.

Location: From Bridgeport, drive seven miles southwest on Twin Lakes Road. Turn north on Buckeye Road (dirt) and drive 3.5 miles to the campground. (The road is impassable when wet).

Trip note: At first glance, this camp might seem to be out in the middle of nowhere. Just the opposite is true. The Buckeye Hot Springs, an undeveloped hot springs, is just two miles from camp. If you have something more rugged in mind, backpackers will find the trail near camp is routed through Buckeye Canyon and into the Hoover Wilderness. And it's only a six-mile drive to Twin Lakes. The elevation is 7,000 feet. Open from May to October.

Map grid d8

SAWMILL

near Twin Lakes

TOIYABE NATIONAL FOREST

Campsites, facilities: There are eight campsites for tents or motor homes up to 22 feet long. Piped water, fireplaces, and picnic tables are provided. Vault toilets are available. A boat launch, store, and laundromat are available nearby. Pets are permitted on leashes.

Reservations, fee: No reservations; $6 fee per night.

Who to contact: Phone the Toiyabe National Forest Ranger Station at (619)932-7070.

Location: From Bridgeport, drive 11 miles southwest on Twin Lakes Road to the campground.

Trip note: Sawmill is one in a series of camps near Twin Lakes, known for good trout fishing and an occasional monster-sized brown trout. Boat ramps are available at each of the lakes, but boaters must adhere to the posted speed limit. There is a major trailhead at Mono Village that serves the Hoover Wilderness and accesses the northern portion of Yosemite National Park.

Map grid d8

LOWER TWIN LAKE

TOIYABE NATIONAL FOREST

Campsites, facilities: There are 15 paved campsites for tents or motor homes up to 35 feet long. Piped water, fireplaces, and picnic tables are provided. Flush toilets are available. A boat launch, a store, and a laundromat are available nearby. Pets are permitted on leashes.

Reservations, fee: Reservations available through MISTIX at (800)283-CAMP ($6 MISTIX fee); $8 fee per night.

Who to contact: Phone the Toiyabe National Forest Ranger Station at (619)932-7070.

Location: From Bridgeport, drive 11 miles southwest on Twin Lakes Road.

Trip note: Some huge brown trout roam wild in Lower Twin Lake—the lake record weighed 26 pounds, five ounces—and ten-pounders are caught every month during the summer. Most of the fish are the planters, though. Boat ramps are available at each of the lakes, so take your pick (the speed limit is posted). At Mono Village, backpackers will find a major trail that heads into the Hoover Wilderness and eventually reaches the northern portion of Yosemite National Park. The camp is set at 7,000 feet elevation near Robinson Creek. Open from

May through October.

Map grid **e1**

CHERRY VALLEY

on Cherry Lake

STANISLAUS NATIONAL FOREST

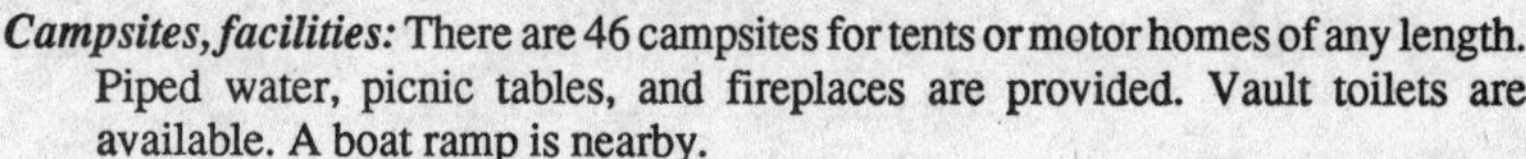

Campsites, facilities: There are 46 campsites for tents or motor homes of any length. Piped water, picnic tables, and fireplaces are provided. Vault toilets are available. A boat ramp is nearby.

Reservations, fee: No reservations; $8 fee per night; $16 for double sites.

Who to contact: Phone the Stanislaus National Forest Groveland Ranger District at (209)962-7825.

Location: From Buck Meadows on Highway 120, drive about four miles east on Highway 120. Turn left (north) onto Cherry Valley Road and drive 18 miles to the campground.

Trip note: Not many folks know about Cherry Lake, but it can provide good trout fishing, especially in early summer. Backpackers will find this a good jump-off spot as well. The trail that starts here is routed into the Emigrant Wilderness to the north. However, come prepared—there is no water available for the first 15 miles of trail, and it is steep and rocky. Cherry Lake is set at 4,700 feet. Open from May through October.

Map grid **e9**

TRUMBULL LAKE

TOIYABE NATIONAL FOREST

Campsites, facilities: There are 45 campsites for tents or motor homes up to 22 feet long. There are some group sites available. Piped water, fireplaces, and picnic tables are provided. Pit toilets are available. Pets are permitted on leashes. A store is nearby at the resort.

Reservations, fee: Reservations available through MISTIX at (800)283-CAMP ($6 MISTIX fee); $6 fee per night.

Who to contact: Phone the Toiyabe National Forest Ranger Station at (619)932-7070.

Location: From Bridgeport, drive 13.5 miles south on US 395. Turn west on Virginia Lakes Road and drive 6.5 miles to the campground entrance road.

Trip note: This high-mountain camp (9,500 feet) is set beside Trumbull Lake. There are many other small lakes in the vicinity accessible by foot (in the Hoover Wilderness) or by auto. If you don't want to rough it, Virginia Lakes Resort is down the road and offers cabins, boat rentals, and a restaurant. Open from June to October.

Map grid **e9**

GREEN CREEK

TOIYABE NATIONAL FOREST

Campsites, facilities: There are 11 campsites for tents or motor homes up to 22 feet long. Piped water, fireplaces, and picnic tables are provided. Vault toilets are available. Pets are permitted.

Reservations, fee: No reservations; $5 fee per night.

Who to contact: Phone the Toiyabe National Forest Ranger Station at (619)932-7070.

Location: From Bridgeport, drive about six miles south on US 395. Turn west on Green Lakes Road (dirt) and drive seven miles to the campground.

Trip note: An ideal jump-off point for backpackers who want to get some good trout fishing. The camp is adjacent to Green Creek at 7,500 feet elevation near a trailhead that is routed into the Hoover Wilderness and several high mountain lakes, including Green Lake, West Lake, and East Lake. The ambitious can cross the northeastern border of Yosemite. Open from May to October.

Map grid fO

LUMSDEN

on Tuolumne River

STANISLAUS NATIONAL FOREST

Campsites, facilities: There are 11 sites for tents only. Picnic tables and fireplaces are provided. Vault toilets are available. There is **no piped water.**

Reservations, fee: No reservations, no fee.

Who to contact: Phone the Stanislaus National Forest Groveland Ranger District at (209)962-7825.

Location: From Groveland, drive about 7.5 miles east on Highway 120 (one-half mile past the turn for County Road J20). Turn left (north) and drive one mile. Turn right onto a dirt road and drive six miles to the campground.

Trip note: This campground is located on the Tuolumne River, along its designated Wild-and-Scenic-River stretch between Hetch Hetchy Reservoir and Don Pedro Reservoir. The sun gets hotter than a branding iron in the summer around these parts, but rafters get the better of it. The camp is set at 1,500 feet elevation. Open from April through November.

Map grid fO

LUMSDEN BRIDGE

on Tuolumne River

STANISLAUS NATIONAL FOREST

Campsites, facilities: There are nine sites for tents only. Picnic tables and fireplaces are provided. Vault toilets are available. There is **no piped water.**

Reservations, fee: No reservations, no fee.

Who to contact: Phone the Stanislaus National Forest Groveland Ranger District at (209)962-7825.

Location: From Groveland, drive about 7.5 miles east on Highway 120 (one-half mile past the turn for County Road J20. Turn left (north) and drive one mile. Turn right onto a dirt road and drive 7.5 miles to the campground.

Trip note: This camp is a particular favorite for rafters because some of the best stretches of whitewater in California are found in this area of the Tuolumne River. The elevation is 1,500. Open from April through November.

Map grid fO

SOUTH FORK

on Tuolumne River

STANISLAUS NATIONAL FOREST

Campsites, facilities: There are eight sites for tents only. Picnic tables and fireplaces are provided. Vault toilets are available. There is **no piped water.**

Reservations, fee: No reservations, no fee.

Who to contact: Phone the Stanislaus National Forest Groveland Ranger District at (209)962-7825.

Location: From Groveland, drive about 7.5 miles east on Highway 120 (one-half mile past the turn for County Road J20). Turn left (north) and drive one mile. Turn right onto a dirt road and drive 6.5 miles to the campground.

Trip note: This is a popular spot for rafters. The campground is located on the Tuolumne River along its designated Wild-and-Scenic stretch between Hetch Hetchy Reservoir and Don Pedro Reservoir. It's one of several primitive camps in the area. The elevation is 1,500 feet. Open from April through November.

A

Map grid f8

SADDLEBAG LAKE

INYO NATIONAL FOREST

Campsites, facilities: There are 22 campsites for tents or motor homes up to 22 feet long. Piped water, fireplaces, and picnic tables are provided. Flush toilets and a boat launch are available. A grocery store is nearby.

B

Reservations, fee: No reservations; $7 fee per night.

Who to contact: Phone the Inyo National Forest District Office at (619)647-6525.

Location: From Lee Vining, drive ten miles west on Highway 120. Turn north on Saddlebag Lake Road and drive about two miles to the campground.

Trip note: This camp in the high country is set at 10,000 feet elevation along beautiful Saddlebag Lake and nearby Lee Vining Creek. A good spot to hunker down for a while or go for broke with a backpack. The trail near the camp is routed to several lakes in the Hoover Wilderness. Open from June to mid-October.

C

Map grid g0

LOST CLAIM

near Tuolumne River

STANISLAUS NATIONAL FOREST

D

Campsites, facilities: There are ten sites for tents or small motor homes. Picnic tables and fireplaces are provided. Vault toilets and hand-pumped well water are available. A grocery store is nearby.

E4

Reservations, fee: No reservations; $6 fee per night.

Who to contact: Phone the Stanislaus National Forest Groveland Ranger District at (209)962-7825.

Location: From Groveland, drive 11 miles east on Highway 120.

Trip note: This is one in a series of easy-access camps off Highway 120 near the Tuolumne River. The trout don't seem to come too big on the Tuolumne, but at least they seem to bite on quiet summer evenings where fast water tumbles into pools. The elevation is 3,100 feet. Open from April until November.

F

Map grid g0

SWEETWATER

near South Fork of Tuolumne River

STANISLAUS NATIONAL FOREST

G

Campsites, facilities: There are ten sites for tents or motor homes up to 22 feet. Piped water, picnic tables, and fireplaces are provided. Vault toilets are available. A grocery store is nearby.

Reservations, fee: No reservations; $8 fee per night.

H

Who to contact: Phone the Stanislaus National Forest Groveland Ranger District at (209)962-7825.

Location: From Buck Meadows, drive four miles east on Highway 120 to the campground.

Trip note: This camp is set at 3,300 feet elevation, which is high enough for the trees to turn to pine and the air to have that mountain sweetness. The Middle Fork of the Tuolumne River runs near the camp, Highway 120 provides easy access, and the river is stocked in early summer by the Department of Fish and Game. Open from April through November.

I

J

Map grid **g1**

HODGDON MEADOW

on North Crane Creek
YOSEMITE NATIONAL PARK

Campsites, facilities: There are 105 family campsites for tents or motor homes up to 30 feet long. There are also four group campsites for up to 30 people and a few walk-in camps for tents only. Piped water, fireplaces, and picnic tables are provided. Flush toilets are available. A grocery store and propane gas are nearby. Pets are permitted on leashes.

Reservations, fee: Reserve family sites up to eight weeks in advance (or group sites up to 12 weeks in advance) by writing to Ticketron, PO Box 617516, Chicago, IL 60661-7516 or by calling (800)452-1111; $10 fee per night from May through October; $7 per night the rest of the year; call for group campsite fee.

Who to contact: Phone the Yosemite National Park Headquarters at (209)372-0302.

Location: From Buck Meadows, drive 13 miles east on Highway 120 (Big Oak Flat Road) to the campground.

Trip note: This is one of the few Yosemite National Park camps that has space available. It is located on North Crane Creek near the South Fork of the Tuolumne River in Yosemite. The Tuolumne Big Tree Grove is three miles southeast and the Yosemite Valley is 25 miles from the camp. The elevation is 4,900 feet. Open year-round.

Map grid **g2**

MIDDLE FORK

on the Midle Fork of Tuolumne River
STANISLAUS NATIONAL FOREST

Campsites, facilities: There are 25 sites for tents or motor homes up to 16 feet. Picnic tables and fireplaces are provided. Vault toilets are available. There is **no piped water,** so bring your own. A grocery store is nearby.

Reservations, fee: No reservations, no fee.

Who to contact: Phone the Stanislaus National Forest Groveland Ranger District at (209)962-7825.

Location: From Buck Meadows, drive about 13 miles east on Highway 120 to Evergreen Road. Turn north (left) and drive five miles to the campground.

Trip note: This primitive but pretty spot along the Middle Fork of the Tuolumne River is far enough out-of-the-way to get missed by out-of-town cruisers every time. The elevation is 3,100 feet. Open from April through December.

Map grid **g2**

CARLON

on South Fork of Tuolomne River
STANISLAUS NATIONAL FOREST

Campsites, facilities: There are 18 sites for tents or motor homes up to 16 feet. Picnic tables and fireplaces are provided. Vault toilets and hand-pumped well water are available. A grocery store is nearby.

Reservations, fee: No reservations, no fee.

Who to contact: Phone the Stanislaus National Forest Groveland Ranger District at (209)962-7825.

Location: From Buck Meadows, drive about 13 miles east on Highway 120 to Evergreen Road. Turn left and drive one-half mile to the campground.

Trip note: This is one in a series of campgrounds set along the South Fork of the Tuolumne River, just off Highway 120. This one sits at 4,600 feet elevation and is surrounded by Stanislaus National Forest. Open from April (snowmelt permitting) through November.

A

Map grid **g4**

WHITE WOLF
YOSEMITE NATIONAL PARK

Campsites, facilities: There are 88 campsites for tents or motor homes up to 30 feet long. Piped water, fireplaces, and picnic tables are provided. Flush toilets, hot showers, horseback riding, and evening ranger programs are available. A grocery store is nearby. Pets are permitted on leashes.

Reservations, fee: No reservations; $7 fee per night.

Who to contact: Phone the Yosemite National Park Headquarters at (209)372-0302.

Location: From Buck Meadows, drive about 20 miles east on Highway 120 (Big Oak Flat Road) to Tioga Pass Road. Bear left and drive 15 miles to White Wolf Road (entrance road to campground).

Trip note: This is one of Yosemite National Park's prime mountain camps for people who like to hike for a day or more. Several trails start near White Wolf. One heads east to Lukens Lake and beyond to Grant Lakes. Another, actually a dirt road, goes northwest to Harden Lake. Once you arrive at Harden Lake, the trail branches northwest to Smith Peak along a ridge overlooking Hetch Hetchy Reservoir and northeast into the Grand Canyon of the Tuolumne. Get a map of the area for more details. The elevation is 7,900 feet. Open from June through October.

B C D E4

Map grid **g5**

YOSEMITE CREEK
YOSEMITE NATIONAL PARK

Campsites, facilities: There are 75 campsites for tents. Fireplaces and picnic tables are provided. Pit toilets are available. There's **no piped water,** so bring your own. No pets are permitted.

Reservations, fee: No reservations; $4 fee per night.

Who to contact: Phone the Yosemite National Park Headquarters at (209)372-0302.

Location: From Buck Meadows, drive about 20 miles east on Highway 120 (Big Oak Flat Road) to Tioga Pass Road. Bear left and drive 16 miles to the campground entrance road (just past the entrance to the White Wolf campground). Turn right and drive about five miles to the campground.

Trip note: One of Yosemite's few primitive drive-to camps. It's a pretty spot, well out of the popular valley, set along little Yosemite Creek. Come prepared—bring your own water.

F G H

Map grid **g5**

PORCUPINE FLAT
near Yosemite Creek
YOSEMITE NATIONAL PARK

Campsites, facilities: There are 52 campsites for tents or motor homes up to 30 feet long. There is limited RV space. Fireplaces and picnic tables are provided. Pit toilets are available. There is **no piped water,** so bring your own. No pets are permitted.

Reservations, fee: No reservations; $4 fee per night.

Who to contact: Phone the Yosemite National Park Headquarters at (209)372-0302.

Location: From Tuolumne Meadows, drive 16 miles west on Tioga Pass Road (Highway 120) to the campground entrance.

Trip note: This is one of Yosemite National Park's lesser-known, drive-to camps,

I J

a first-come, first-serve, do-it-yourself number that just might have a space available. Trails from the camp lead west to Yosemite Creek or east to Snow Creek. The elevation is 8,100. Open from June to October.

Map grid **g6**

TENAYA LAKE WALK-IN

at Tenaya Lake

YOSEMITE NATIONAL PARK

Campsites, facilities: There are 50 walk-in campsites for tents. Fireplaces and picnic tables are provided. Piped water and flush toilets are available. No pets.

Reservations, fee: No reservations; $7 fee per night.

Who to contact: Phone the Yosemite National Park Headquarters at (209)372-0302.

Location: From Tuolumne Meadows, drive about nine miles west on Tioga Pass Road to the campground.

Trip note: Tenaya Lake is one of the prettiest lakes in California and this camp provides a unique chance to spend some time next to it. It's in Yosemite's high country, and though it's a walk-in camp, it fills quickly. It can get surprisingly cold in spring and fall. The fish don't bite much, but that's okay. You probably will just want to sit there and look.

Map grid **g7**

TUOLUMNE MEADOWS

YOSEMITE NATIONAL PARK

Campsites, facilities: There are 314 spaces for tents or motor homes up to 27 feet long. Piped water, flush toilets, picnic tables, fire grills, and a dump station are provided, but no hookups. Pets are permitted. Showers and groceries are available nearby. There are also 25 walk-in spaces available for backpackers, and eight group sites that can accommodate 30 people each.

Reservations, fee: Reserve up to 12 weeks in advance by writing to Ticketron, PO Box 617516, Chicago, IL 60661-7516 or by calling (800)452-1111; $10 fee per night family sites; $2 fee per night walk-in sites; $34 fee per night group sites.

Who to contact: Phone the Yosemite National Park Headquarters at (209)372-0302.

Location: From Yosemite Valley take Highway 120 east for 46 miles to the entrance to Tuolomne Meadows.

Trip note: This is Yosemite's biggest camp, but unlike the camps in the valley, there is usually plenty of room. It is set in the high country, 8,600 feet elevation, and can be used as a base camp for fishing, hiking and horseback riding, or a jumpoff point for a backpacking trip (wilderness permits required). Lyell Fork is an excellent stream for brook trout, though the fish are rarely large. A great hike is through Tuolumne Meadows via the John Muir Trail to the top of Donohue Pass. Warning: Lots of food-raiding bears patrol this area. Open June through mid-October.

Map grid **g8**

JUNCTION

near Ellery and Tioga Lakes

INYO NATIONAL FOREST

Campsites, facilities: There are ten campsites for tents or motor homes up to 22 feet long. Fireplaces and picnic tables are provided. Vault toilets are available. There is **no piped water,** so bring your own.

Reservations, fee: No reservations, no fee.

Who to contact: Phone the Inyo National Forest District Office at (619)647-6525.

Location: From Lee Vining, drive ten miles west on Highway 120.

Trip note: Despite direct access off Highway 120, this is a relatively little-known camp in a beautiful area of the high Sierra. The camp is located near Ellery and Tioga Lakes and surrounded by wild, rugged country, including the Hall Natural Area to the northeast. The Tioga Tarns Nature Trail is nearby and offers a side trip. The elevation is 9,600 feet. Open from June to October.

Map grid g9

LEE VINING CREEK CAMPGROUNDS

near Lee Vining

Campsites, facilities: There are 129 campsites for tents or motor homes up to 24 feet long in four separate campgrounds located next to each other. Pit toilets are available. There is **no piped water,** so bring your own. Pets are permitted on leashes. Supplies can be purchased in Lee Vining.

Reservations, fee: No reservations; $7 fee per night.

Who to contact: Phone the Mono County Parks Department at (619)934-6876.

Location: From Lee Vining, drive four to five miles west on Highway 120. These campgrounds are all set in a row along Highway 120.

Trip note: It's hard to believe that Mono County actually charges for this camp when they don't even offer piped water. What the heck, at least it's a place to throw down your sleeping bag, and it's pretty at that. The four different camping areas are set along Lee Vining Creek. Mono Lake is a must-go side trip. Open from May through October.

Map grid g9

BIG BEND

on Lee Vining Creek
INYO NATIONAL FOREST

Campsites, facilities: There are 18 campsites for tents or motor homes up to 22 feet long. Piped water, fireplaces, and picnic tables are provided. Flush toilets are available. A grocery store is nearby.

Reservations, fee: No reservations; $7 fee per night.

Who to contact: Phone the Inyo National Forest District Office at (619)647-6525.

Location: From Lee Vining, drive seven miles west on Highway 120.

Trip note: This is one in a series of sparse, yet beautiful camps on the eastern side of the Sierra crest that gets overlooked. It is located along Lee Vining Creek at 7,800 feet elevation. Open from May to mid-October.

Map grid g9

ASPEN GROVE

on Lee Vining Creek

Campsites, facilities: There are 58 campsites for tents or motor homes up to 20 feet long. There is **no piped water,** so bring your own. Pit toilets are available. Pets are permitted on leashes. Supplies can be purchased in Lee Vining.

Reservations, fee: No reservations; $7 fee per night.

Who to contact: Phone the Mono County Parks Department at (619)934-6876.

Location: From Lee Vining, drive six miles west on Highway 120.

Trip note: This high-country, primitive camp is set along Lee Vining Creek at 8,000 feet elevation. A side trip to moon-like Mono Lake is a must. Open from May through October.

Map grid g9

TIOGA LAKE

INYO NATIONAL FOREST

Campsites, facilities: There are 13 tent sites. Piped water, picnic tables and fireplaces

are provided. Flush toilets are available.
Reservations, fee: No reservations; $7 fee per night.
Who to contact: Phone the Inyo National Forest District Office at (619)647-6525.
Location: From Lee Vining, drive ten miles west on Highway 120.
Trip note: Highway 120 is a dramatic road, leading east from Yosemite and providing dramatic views of Mono Lake. If Tuolumne Meadows in Yosemite is full, the camps on Highway 120 provide good overflow areas. This one, little Tioga Lake, makes for a pretty camp in the eastern Sierra high country. It's set at 9,700 feet elevation. Open from June to October.

Map grid g9

ELLERY LAKE

INYO NATIONAL FOREST

Campsites, facilities: There are three sites for tents only and ten campsites for tents or motor homes up to 22 feet long. Piped water, fireplaces, and picnic tables are provided. Flush toilets are available. A grocery store is nearby.
Reservations, fee: No reservations; $7 fee per night.
Who to contact: Phone the Inyo National Forest District Office at (619)647-6525.
Location: From Lee Vining, drive nine miles west of Lee Vining on Highway 120.
Trip note: This is another in a series of small, pretty camps along Highway 120. It's set beside Ellery Lake at 9,500 feet elevation, a short distance from Tioga Lake and two miles from Saddlebag Lake. Open from June to mid-October.

Map grid h1

INDIAN FLAT

on Merced River
SIERRA NATIONAL FOREST

Campsites, facilities: There are 14 tent sites and three campsites for tents or motor homes up to 22 feet long. Piped water, fireplaces, and picnic tables are provided, and vault toilets are available. A grocery store is nearby.
Reservations, fee: No reservations, but this camp usually fills by noon on Fridays; $9 fee per night.
Who to contact: Phone the Sierra National Forest Mariposa Ranger District at (209)683-4665.
Location: From El Portal, drive four miles south on Highway 140. From Mariposa, drive 24 miles north on Highway 140 to the campground.
Trip note: This pretty camp is set beside the Merced River at 1,500 feet elevation with easy access from Highway 140. Some excellent swimming holes can be found in this area. Open from June to September.

Map grid h2

CRANE FLAT

near Tuolumne Grove
YOSEMITE NATIONAL PARK

Campsites, facilities: There are 141 campsites for tents or motor homes up to 35 feet long. Piped water, fireplaces, and picnic tables are provided. Flush toilets, groceries, propane gas, and evening ranger programs are available. A gas station is nearby.
Reservations, fee: Reserve family sites up to eight weeks in advance by writing to Ticketron, PO Box 617516, Chicago, IL 60661-7516 or by calling (800)452-1111; $10 fee per night from May through October.
Who to contact: Phone the Yosemite National Park Headquarters at (209)372-0302.
Location: From Buck Meadows, drive 20 miles east on Highway 120 (Big Oak Flat Road) to the campground.

Trip note: This is a viable option for Yosemite campers who want to avoid the over-peopled valley. The campground is set at 6,200 feet elevation and located near the Tuolumne Groves of Big Trees. Yosemite Valley is about a 20-mile drive. Open from May through October.

Map grid **h3**

TAMARACK FLAT

on Tamarack Creek

YOSEMITE NATIONAL PARK

5% CLUB

Campsites, facilities: There are 52 campsites for tents or small motor homes. Fireplaces and picnic tables are provided. Pit toilets are available. **No piped water is available, so bring your own.** No pets are permitted.

Reservations, fee: No reservations; $4 fee per night.

Who to contact: Phone the Yosemite National Park Headquarters at (209)372-0302.

Location: From Buck Meadows, drive 21 miles east on Highway 120 (Big Oak Flat Road) to Tioga Pass Road. Continue east on Tioga Pass Road for about three miles to the campground entrance road on the right. Drive 2.5 miles to the campground.

Trip note: This is one of the few little-known camps in Yosemite National Park that you can reach by car. It's primitive and with Yosemite Valley 23 miles away, you won't see the Curry Company out here. Open from June through October.

Map grid **h4**

LOWER PINES

in Yosemite Valley

YOSEMITE NATIONAL PARK

Campsites, facilities: There are 173 campsites for tents or motor homes up to 30 feet long. Fireplaces and picnic tables are provided. Piped water and flush toilets are available. A grocery store, a laundromat, propane gas, a recycling center, and horse, raft, bike, and cross-country ski rentals are available nearby.

Reservations, fee: Reserve up to eight weeks in advance by writing to Ticketron, PO Box 617516, Chicago, IL 60661-7516 or by calling (800)452-1111; $12 fee per night.

Who to contact: Phone the Yosemite National Park Headquarters at (209)372-0302.

Location: After driving into Yosemite Valley, drive 1.5 miles past Yosemite Village to the campground near Camp Curry.

Trip note: This is one of the several most popular campgrounds this side of the galaxy. That's right, Yosemite Valley, the glacial-cut granite valley framed by El Capitan, Cathedral Rocks, and Half Dome, and lit up by silver-tasseled waterfalls. Reservations are a necessity. Open year-round.

Map grid **h4**

UPPER RIVER

in Yosemite Valley

YOSEMITE NATIONAL PARK

Campsites, facilities: There are 124 campsites for tents only. Fireplaces and picnic tables are provided. Piped water and flush toilets are available. A grocery store, a laundromat, propane gas, a recycling center, and horse, raft and bike rentals are available nearby. Pets are permitted on leashes in campground, but not on trails.

Reservations, fee: Reserve up to eight weeks in advance by writing to Ticketron, PO Box 617516, Chicago, IL 60661-7516 or by calling (800)452-1111. Or phone the Yosemite National Park Headquarters at (209)372-0302. 12$ fee per night.

Location: After driving into Yosemite Valley, drive one mile past Yosemite Village. Turn left at the intersection near Camp Curry to the campground entrance.
Trip note: It's no easy deal to get a campsite in Yosemite Valley, and then when you get one, you might find yourself yearning for the remote, high country of the park. This camp is the former, not the latter, set in the dramatic Yosemite Valley, the natural showpiece of the world. Open from May to mid-October.

Map grid h4

LOWER RIVER
in Yosemite Valley
YOSEMITE NATIONAL PARK

Campsites, facilities: There are 139 campsites for tents or motor homes up to 30 feet long. Fireplaces and picnic tables are provided. Piped water, flush toilets, and a sanitary disposal station are available. A grocery store, a laundromat, propane gas, a recycling center, a visitor center, and horse, raft, bike, and cross-country ski rentals are available nearby.
Reservations, fee: Reserve up to eight weeks in advance by writing to Ticketron, PO Box 617516, Chicago, IL 60661-7516 or by calling (800)452-1111; $12 fee per night.
Who to contact: Phone the Yosemite National Park Headquarters at (209)372-0302.
Location: After driving into Yosemite Valley, drive one mile past Yosemite Village. Turn left at the intersection near Camp Curry to the campground entrance.
Trip note: It looks something like Tent City in summer months, but the surroundings make it worth the price. It's located in Yosemite Valley, the world's scenic showpiece. Reservations are a must. Open from May to October.

Map grid h5

UPPER PINES
in Yosemite Valley
YOSEMITE NATIONAL PARK

Campsites, facilities: There are 240 campsites for tents or motor homes up to 30 feet long. Fireplaces and picnic tables are provided. Piped water, flush toilets and a sanitary disposal station are available. A grocery store, laundromat, propane gas, recycling center, and horse, raft, bike, and cross-country ski rentals are available nearby. Pets are permitted on leashes in campground, but not on trails.
Reservations, fee: Reserve up to eight weeks in advance by writing to Ticketron, PO Box 617516, Chicago, IL 60661-7516 or by calling (800)452-1111; $12 fee per night.
Who to contact: Phone the Yosemite National Park Headquarters at (209)372-0302.
Location: After driving into Yosemite Valley, drive two miles past Yosemite Village (past Camp Curry) to the campground.
Trip note: Plan on a reservation and plan on plenty of company if you want a campsite in Yosemite Valley. People come from all over the world to camp here. Sometimes it appears they are from other worlds as well. The elevation is 4,000 feet. Open from April to November.

Map grid h5

NORTH PINES
in Yosemite Valley
YOSEMITE NATIONAL PARK

Campsites, facilities: There are 86 campsites for tents or motor homes up to 30 feet long. Piped water, fireplaces, and picnic tables are provided. Flush toilets are available. A grocery store, laundromat, recycling center, propane gas, and horse, raft and bike rentals are available nearby. No pets are allowed.

Reservations, fee: Reserve up to eight weeks in advance by writing to Ticketron, PO Box 617516, Chicago, IL 60661-7516 or by calling (800)452-1111; $12 fee per night.

Who to contact: Phone the Yosemite National Park Headquarters at (209)372-0302.

Location: After driving into Yosemite Valley, drive two miles past Yosemite Village (past Camp Curry) to the campground.

Trip note: This is one in the series of camps that are in the dramatic Yosemite Valley, part of the most popular park in our solar system. It's easy to see why, with the high granite walls of Yosemite Valley framing nature's most beautiful picture. Obviously, reservations are a must. The elevation is 4,000 feet. Open from May to October.

Map grid i0

YOSEMITE-MARIPOSA KOA CAMPGROUND

near Mariposa

Campsites, facilities: There are 40 sites for tents only, 30 motor home spaces with full hookups, and ten sites for tents or motor homes. Picnic tables and fireplaces are provided. Rest rooms, showers, a sanitary disposal station, a laundromat, a store, propane gas, a recreation room, a swimming pool, and a playground are available.

Reservations, fee: Call for available space; $18-$25 fee per night.

Who to contact: Phone the park at (209)966-2201.

Location: From Mariposa, drive seven miles northeast on Highway 140 to 6323 Highway 140.

Trip note: This KOA camp is located 28 miles from the entrance to Yosemite National Park and provides campers with an alternative if Yosemite is packed to the rafters. The Merced River is a good side trip, located along Highway 140 east of Briceburg. Open year-round.

Map grid i4

BRIDALVEIL CREEK

YOSEMITE NATIONAL PARK

Campsites, facilities: There are 110 campsites for tents or motor homes up to 30 feet long and one group campsite. Piped water, fireplaces, and picnic tables are provided, and flush toilets are available. Pets are permitted on leashes in the campground but not on trails. There are also some stock handling facilities for camping with pack animals; call for further information.

Reservations, fee: No reservations for family camping; $7 fee per night. For group campsite, write to Bridalveil Creek Group Reservations, Wawona District Office, Box 2027, Yosemite National Park, CA 95389; $34 fee per night.

Who to contact: Phone the Yosemite National Park Headquarters at (209)372-0302.

Location: From Yosemite Valley, drive to the Glacier Point Road. Turn and drive about eight miles to the campground.

Trip note: One of Yosemite's first-come, first-served campgrounds that can be overlooked because it isn't right in the Yosemite Valley. Yet this camp has many features: it's set along Bridalveil Creek and provides a head start to one of Yosemite's great side trips—the drive to the incredible lookout at Glacier Point. The elevation is 7,200 feet. Open from June through September.

Map grid **j1**

JERSEYDALE

SIERRA NATIONAL FOREST

Campsites, facilities: There are eight tent sites and two sites for tents or motor homes up to 22 feet long. Piped water, fireplaces, and picnic tables are provided. Vault toilets are available. A grocery store is nearby.

Reservations, fee: No reservations, no fee.

Who to contact: Phone the Sierra National Forest Mariposa Ranger District at (209)683-4665.

Location: From Mariposa, drive north on Highway 140 for about five miles to Acorn Lodge. Turn right (east) onto Triangle Road and drive about six miles to Darrah. Turn left (north) and drive three miles to the campground adjacent to the Jerseydale Ranger Station.

Trip note: Here's the kind of spot a lot of campers are looking for: little-known with a variety of side trips. A dirt road from the camp is routed east for many miles into the Chowchilla Mountains. If you continue north on the main road past the Jerseydale Ranger Station to its end (about six miles) you will come to a trailhead that provides access east for miles along the South Fork of the Merced River—some of Merced's better fishing. Open from May through November.

Map grid **j2**

SUMMIT CAMP

SIERRA NATIONAL FOREST

Campsites, facilities: There are ten tent sites. Piped water, fireplaces, and picnic tables are provided. Vault toilets are available.

Reservations, fee: No reservations, no fee.

Who to contact: Phone the Sierra National Forest Mariposa Ranger District at (209)683-4665.

Location: The camp is about five miles northwest of Oakhurst off of Forest Road at Fish Camp. From Oakhurst take Highway 41 northwest to Fish Camp. Go west on Forest Road (at Fish Camp) and follow for about five miles to the campground.

Trip note: It is only five miles from Wawona in Yosemite National Park, yet this camp is often overlooked. It is located in the Chowchilla Mountains at 5,800 feet elevation, about three miles from Big Creek. It's a good southern alternative when Yosemite is packed. Open from June to November.

Map grid **j3**

SUMMERDALE

on the South Fork of Merced River

SIERRA NATIONAL FOREST

Campsites, facilities: There are 21 sites for tents only and nine campsites for tents or motor homes up to 22 feet long. Piped water, fireplaces, and picnic tables are provided. Vault toilets are available. A grocery store is nearby.

Reservations, fee: No reservations, but this camp usually fills by noon on Fridays; $9 fee per night.

Who to contact: Phone the Sierra National Forest Mariposa Ranger District at (209)683-4665.

Location: From Fish Camp (just two miles from the southern entrance to Yosemite National Park), drive one mile north on Highway 41 to the campground.

Trip note: This is a pretty spot in its own right set along the South Fork of the Merced River, yet it's used primarily as an overflow area for Yosemite Park campers.

The southern entrance station is a few minutes away. Some good swimming holes are in this area. The elevation is 5,000 feet. Open from May to October.

Map grid j3

WAWONA

on Merced River
YOSEMITE NATIONAL PARK

Campsites, facilities: There are 100 campsites for tents or motor homes up to 30 feet long and one group campsite. Piped water, fireplaces, and picnic tables are provided. Flush toilets are available. A grocery store, propane gas, and horseback riding facilities are available nearby. Pets are permitted on leashes in the campground, but not on trails. There are also some stock handling facilities for camping with pack animals; call for further information.

Reservations, fee: No reservations for family camping; $7 fee per night. For a group campsite, write to Wawona Group Reservations, Wawona District Office, Box 2027, Yosemite National Park, CA 95389; $34 fee per night.

Who to contact: Phone the Yosemite National Park Headquarters at (209)372-0302.

Location: From Wawona, drive one mile north on Highway 41 to the campground.

Trip note: The nearby Mariposa Grove of Giant Sequoias, the classic mountain redwood, is one feature attraction of Wawona. The Merced River is the other, offering some of the park's better fishing, although the trout tend to be small. The camp is set at 4,000 feet elevation, just inside the southern entrance to Yosemite. Open year-round.

Map grid j9

MINARET FALLS

on San Joaquin River
INYO NATIONAL FOREST

Campsites, facilities: There are 27 campsites for tents or motor homes up to 22 feet long. Piped water, fireplaces, and picnic tables are provided. Flush toilets and horseback riding facilities are available. Supplies can be purchased in Mammoth Lakes. Pets are permitted on leashes.

Reservations, fee: No reservations; $6 fee per night.

Who to contact: Phone the Inyo National Forest District Office at (619)934-2505.

Location: From Lee Vining, drive 26 miles south on US 395 to Mammoth Junction. Turn west on Highway 203 (Minaret Summit Road) to the town of Mammoth Lakes and drive 16 miles to the campground.

Trip note: This is another in the series of camps on the beautiful upper San Joaquin and is set at 7,600 feet elevation near Minaret Creek. Devil's Postpile National Monument is less than a mile from camp. The Pacific Crest Trail and John Muir Trail pass nearby. Open from June to October.

Map grid j9

DEVIL'S POSTPILE NATIONAL MONUMENT

near San Joaquin River

Campsites, facilities: There are 21 campsites for tents or motor homes. Piped water, fireplaces, and picnic tables are provided. Flush toilets are available.

Reservations, fee: No reservations; $6-$8 fee per night.

Who to contact: Phone the National Park Service at (619)934-2289.

Location: From Lee Vining, drive 26 miles south on US 395 to Mammoth Junction. Turn west on Highway 203 (Minaret Summit Road) to the town of Mammoth Lakes and drive 17 miles to the campground.

Trip note: Devil's Postpile is a spectacular and rare example of hexagonal, columnar rock. The camp, set at 7,600 feet elevation, is very near to the upper San Joaquin

River, Pacific Crest Trail and John Muir Trail. Open from mid-June to mid-October.

Map grid **j9**

RED'S MEADOW
INYO NATIONAL FOREST

Campsites, facilities: There are 54 campsites for tents or motor homes up to 22 feet long. Piped water, fireplaces, and picnic tables are provided, and flush toilets, showers, and horseback riding facilities are available. Supplies can be purchased in Mammoth Lakes. Pets are permitted on leashes.

Reservations, fee: No reservations; $6 fee per night.

Who to contact: Phone the Inyo National Forest District Office at (619)934-2505.

Location: From Lee Vining, drive 26 miles south on US 395 to Mammoth Junction. Turn west on Highway 203 (Minaret Summit Road) to the town of Mammoth Lakes and drive 18 miles to the campground.

Trip note: This is a choice spot for small groups. Horse rentals are available, providing great trips into the beautiful surrounding National Forest. Crystal Falls is one of the best destinations for short horseback riding trips. Other destinations include Red's Meadow Hot Springs, Scotcher Lake, and for overnighters, a series of lakes on the Pacific Crest Trail. Open from June to October.

Map grid **j9**

PUMICE FLAT
on San Joaquin River
INYO NATIONAL FOREST

Campsites, facilities: There are 17 campsites for tents or motor homes up to 22 feet long. Piped water, fireplaces, and picnic tables are provided. Flush toilets and horseback riding facilities are available. Supplies in Mammoth Lakes. Pets are permitted on leashes.

Reservations, fee: No reservations; $6 fee per night.

Who to contact: Phone the Inyo National Forest District Office at (619)934-2505.

Location: From Lee Vining, drive 26 miles south on US 395 to Mammoth Junction. Turn west on Highway 203 (Minaret Summit Road) to the town of Mammoth Lakes and drive 16 miles to the campground.

Trip note: This is a beautiful spot along the upper San Joaquin River located at 7,700 feet elevation. The Pacific Crest Trail runs right by the camp and the Devil's Postpile National Monument is just two miles south. You can hunker down for a while here and do just fine. Another option is strapping on some hiking boots and hoofing it into the Ansel Adams Wilderness, where there are many gorgeous high Sierra lakes. Open from June to October.

Map grid **j9**

UPPER SODA
on San Joaquin River
INYO NATIONAL FOREST

Campsites, facilities: There are 28 campsites for tents or motor homes up to 22 feet long. Piped water, fireplaces, and picnic tables are provided. Flush toilets and horseback riding facilities are available. Supplies can be purchased in Mammoth Lakes. Pets are permitted on leashes.

Reservations, fee: No reservations; $4 fee per night.

Who to contact: Phone the Inyo National Forest Headquarters at (619)873-5841.

Location: From Lee Vining, drive 26 miles south on US 395 to Mammoth Junction. Turn west on Highway 203 (Minaret Summit Road) to the town of Mammoth Lakes and drive 15 miles to the campground.

Trip note: This premium location has a huge variety of side trips available. The camp is set along the upper San Joaquin River, a pretty site where the trout fishing is often good. But that's not all, not by a long shot. Devil's Postpile National Monument, a massive formation of ancient columnar rock, is only three miles to the south. That's still not all. The Pacific Crest Trail passes right by the camp, providing a trailhead for access to numerous lakes in the Ansel Adams Wilderness. The elevation is 7,700 feet. Open from June to October.

Map grid j9

AGNEW MEADOWS

INYO NATIONAL FOREST

Campsites, facilities: There are 24 campsites for tents or motor homes up to 22 feet long. A group camp is also available (reservations required for group camp). Piped water, fireplaces, and picnic tables are provided. Flush toilets and horseback riding facilities are available. Supplies can be obtained in Mammoth Lakes. Pets are permitted on leashes.

Reservations, fee: No reservations; $6 fee per night. Reservations required for group camp; $30 fee per night.

Who to contact: Phone the Inyo National Forest District Office at (619)934-2505.

Location: From Lee Vining, drive 26 miles south on US 395 to Mammoth Junction. Turn west on Highway 203 (Minaret Summit Road) to the town of Mammoth Lakes and drive 14 miles to the campground.

Trip note: You can use this camp as a launching pad for a backpacking trip. It is set alongside the Pacific Crest Trail at 8,400 feet elevation. From the famed PCT, you can get to numerous lakes in the nearby Ansel Adams Wilderness (formerly the Minarets Wilderness). A detailed Forest Service map is essential. Open from June to October.

Map grid j9

PUMICE FLAT GROUP CAMP

on San Joaquin River

INYO NATIONAL FOREST

Campsites, facilities: There are four group campsites for tents or motor homes up to 22 feet long. Piped water, fireplaces, and picnic tables are provided. Flush toilets and horseback riding facilities are available. Supplies can be purchased in Mammoth Lakes. Pets are permitted on leashes.

Reservations, fee: No reservations; $30 fee per night per group.

Who to contact: Phone the Inyo National Forest District Office at (619)934-2505.

Location: From Lee Vining, drive 26 miles south on US 395 to Mammoth Junction. Turn west on Highway 203 (Minaret Summit Road) to the town of Mammoth Lakes and drive 16 miles to the campground.

Trip note: There are five premium-located camps on the San Joaquin River in this area. This one is just a mile from Devil's Postpile National Monument. The Pacific Crest Trail passes right through camp. A short trail to Scotcher Lake leaves from camp. The camp elevation is 7,700 feet. Open from June to October.

◆ MAP E5 ◆

BEACH
TREES
5% CLUB
DESERT
URBAN
FOOTHILL
GRASSLAND

15 MILES

to Wellington, NV
TOIYABE
NAT'L.
FOREST
Sweetwater Summit EL. 7,120
182
Hawthorne
Bridgeport Lake
Bridgeport
Powell Mtn. EL. 9,545
BRODIE ST. HIST. PK.
Brodie
270
Conway Summit EL. 8,138
395
167
NEVADA
Mono Lake
Mono Lake
Paoha Island
INYO
Lee Vining
NAT'L.
Tioga Pass EL. 9,945
FOREST
120
158
INYO
Deadman Summit EL. 8,041
June Lakes
Crestview
Benton
Benton Hot Springs
NAT'L.
203
INYO
Mammoth Lakes
NAT'L.
6
FOREST
Crowley lake
FOREST
to Bishop
to Walker
to Tuolumne Meadows
to Devils Postpile Nat'l. Mon.

a b c d e f g h i j

0 1 2 3 4 5 6 7 8 9

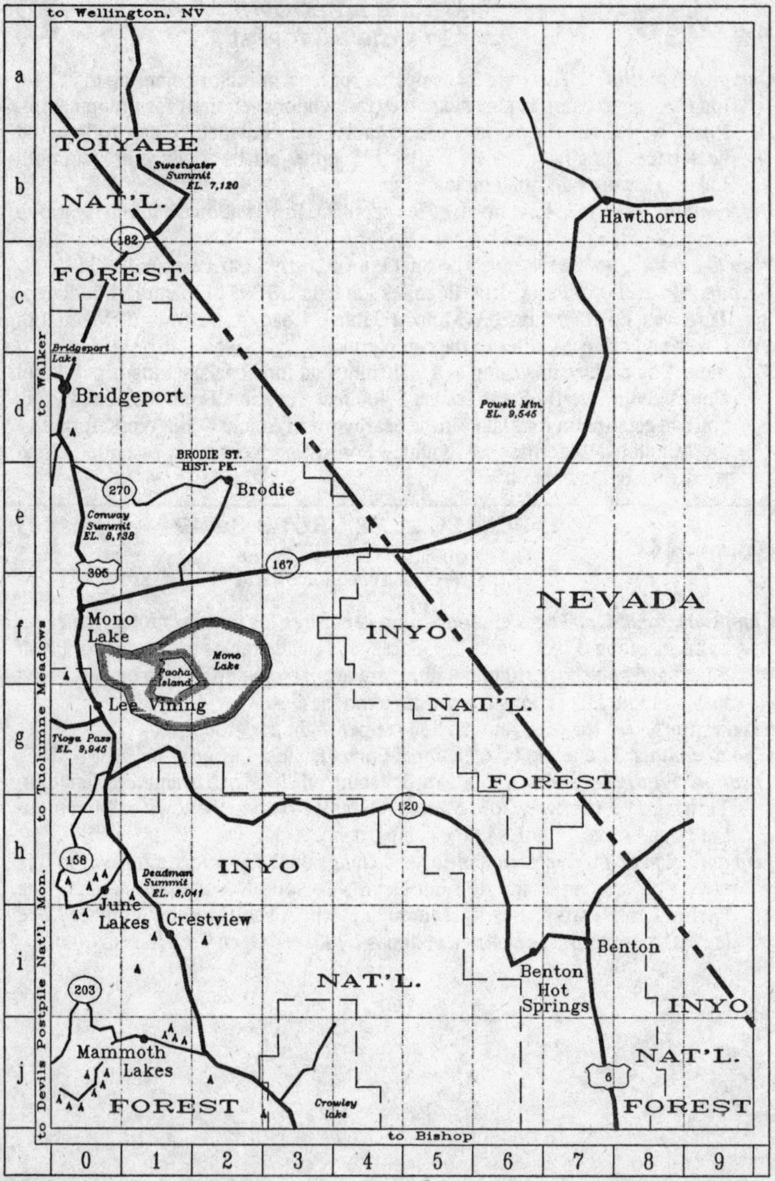

Map grid d0 — WILLOW SPRINGS TRAILER PARK

near Bridgeport

Campsites, facilities: There are 20 motor home spaces with picnic tables and full hookups. Rest rooms, showers, and a laundromat are available.

Reservations, fee: Call for available space; $14 fee per night.

Who to contact: Phone the park at (619)932-7725.

Location: From Bridgeport, drive five miles south on US 395.

Trip note: This is a good layover spot for Highway 395 cruisers. It's set at 6,800 feet elevation near Virginia Creek. Side trips include driving east to the ghost town of Bodie on nearby Highway 270 or north to Bridgeport Lake on Highway 182. Open from May to October.

Map grid f0 — LUNDY CREEK

near Mono Lake

Campsites, facilities: There are 51 campsites for tents or motor homes up to 24 feet long. Pit toilets are available. There is **no piped water,** so bring your own. Pets are permitted on leashes. Supplies can be purchased in Lee Vining.

Reservations, fee: No reservations; $7 fee per night.

Who to contact: Phone the Mono County Parks Department at (619)934-6876.

Location: From Lee Vining, drive about five miles north on US 395 to the campground entrance road, which is across the highway from Mono Lake.

Trip note: It's kind of like a moonscape out here. Even unique Mono Lake, one of the world's largest breeding areas for gulls, looks like a giant crater. This camp is set at 8,000 feet along Lundy Lake, not far from Mono Lake. Open from May through October.

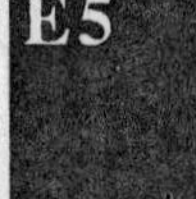

Map grid h0 — PINE CLIFF RESORT

near June Lake

Campsites, facilities: There are 20 sites for tents only, 25 sites for tent or motor homes, and 154 motor home spaces. Fire rings, picnic tables, piped water, electrical connections, and sewer hookups are provided at most sites. Rest rooms, showers, a laundromat, a store, a sanitary disposal station, and propane gas are available. A boat ramp, boat and tackle rentals, and fuel are available nearby. Pets are permitted on leashes

Reservations, fee: Reservations recommended; $9-$14 camp use fee.

Who to contact: Phone the park at (619)648-7558.

Location: From Lee Vining, drive 11 miles south on US 395 to June Lake Junction. Turn south on Highway 158 and drive one mile to June Lake. Turn north on Ridge Road and drive one mile to the campground.

Trip note: This privately-operated camp on June Lake provides a more developed option to the Forest Service camps on June Lake, Silver Lake, Grant Lake, and Gull Lake. The elevation is 7,800 feet. Open mid-April through October.

Map grid h0 — SILVER LAKE

INYO NATIONAL FOREST

Campsites, facilities: There are 65 campsites for tents or motor homes up to 22 feet long. Piped water, fireplaces, and picnic tables are provided. Flush toilets and horseback riding facilities are available. A grocery store, a laundromat, motorboat rentals, a boat ramp, bait, a snack bar, boat fuel, and propane gas are available nearby.

Reservations, fee: No reservations; $8 fee per night.

Who to contact: Phone the Inyo National Forest District Office at (619)647-6525.

Location: From Lee Vining, drive 11 miles south on US 395 to June Lake Junction. Turn south on Highway 158 and drive six miles to the campground.

Trip note: This is an ideal spot for folks either wanting to set on down for a spell or hoof it in to the backcountry. The camp is set along pretty Silver Lake near Alger Creek. A trail near camp heads uphill into the Ansel Adams Wilderness and intersects with the Pacific Crest Trail. This is some of the prettiest country in California. The camp's elevation is 7,200 feet. Open from May to October.

Map grid h0

JUNE LAKE
INYO NATIONAL FOREST

Campsites, facilities: There are 22 campsites for tents or motor homes up to 22 feet long. Piped water, fireplaces, and picnic tables are provided. Flush toilets and a boat ramp are available. A grocery store, a laundromat, boat and tackle rentals, moorings, and propane gas are available nearby.

Reservations, fee: No reservations; $8 fee per night.

Who to contact: Phone the Inyo National Forest District Office at (619)647-6525.

Location: From Lee Vining, drive 11 miles south on US 395 to June Lake Junction. Turn south on Highway 158 and drive two miles to June Lake.

Trip note: This premium vacationland area is known as the "June Lake Loop," and it is ideal for anglers who want variety. June Lake, Silver Lake, Grant Lake, and Gull Lake all provide lakeside camping. This camp is set at 7,600 feet elevation along June Lake. Backpacking is good in the surrounding Inyo National Forest. Open from mid-April to November.

Map grid h0

OH! RIDGE
on June Lake
INYO NATIONAL FOREST

Campsites, facilities: There are 148 campsites for tents or motor homes up to 32 feet long. Piped water, fireplaces, and picnic tables are provided. Flush toilets and a playground are available. A grocery store, a laundromat, a boat ramp, boat and tackle rentals, moorings, and propane gas are available nearby.

Reservations, fee: Reservations available through MISTIX at (800)283-CAMP ($6 MISTIX fee); $8 camping fee per night.

Who to contact: Phone the Inyo National Forest District Office at (619)647-6525.

Location: From Lee Vining, drive 11 miles south on US 395 to June Lake Junction. Turn south on Highway 158 and drive two miles to June Lake. Turn right (northwest) on Oh! Ridge Road and drive one mile to the campground.

Trip note: This large Forest Service camp is set along the shore of June Lake, which is one of the four lakes on Highway 158, the "June Lake Loop." It is a popular destination for summer campers looking for good fishing. The elevation is 7,600 feet. Open from mid-April to November.

Map grid h1

HARTLEY SPRINGS
INYO NATIONAL FOREST

Campsites, facilities: There are 21 campsites for tents or motor homes up to 22 feet long. Fireplaces and picnic tables are provided. Vault toilets are available. There is **no piped water,** so bring your own.

Reservations, fee: No reservations, no fee.
Who to contact: Phone the Inyo National Forest District Office at (619)647-6525.
Location: From Lee Vining, drive 11 miles south on US 395. Continue on US 395 for two miles past June Lake Junction. Turn right on an improved dirt road and drive 1.5 miles to camp.
Trip note: This is a primitive setting that most folks don't have a clue about. It is set at 8,400 feet elevation near Hartley Springs. Once here, check out Obsidian Dome, located 1.5 miles from camp. Open from June to mid-September.

Map grid i0

REVERSED CREEK
INYO NATIONAL FOREST

Campsites, facilities: There are 17 campsites for tents or motor homes up to 22 feet long. Piped water, fireplaces, and picnic tables are provided. Flush toilets are available. A grocery store, a laundromat, and propane gas are nearby. Boating is available at nearby Silver Lake, two miles away.
Reservations, fee: No reservations; $8 fee per night.
Who to contact: Phone the Inyo National Forest District Office at (619)647-6525.
Location: From Lee Vining, drive 11 miles south on US 395 to June Lake Junction. Turn south on Highway 158 and drive three miles to the campground, which is across the road from Gull Lake.
Trip note: This can be an option to nearby Gull Lake. The camp is set on Reversed Creek at 7,600 feet elevation. There are two good trips for ambitious hikers. A trail near camp leads up to Reversed Peak (three miles). Or you can go for broke and hoof it to Silver Lake (two miles). Open from May to October.

Map grid i0

GULL LAKE
INYO NATIONAL FOREST

Campsites, facilities: There are ten campsites for tents or motor homes up to 22 feet long. Piped water, fireplaces, and picnic tables are provided, and flush toilets are available. A grocery store, a laundromat, a boat ramp, and propane gas are available nearby.
Reservations, fee: No reservations; $8 fee per night.
Who to contact: Phone the Inyo National Forest District Office at (619)647-6525.
Location: From Lee Vining, drive 11 miles south on US 395 to June Lake Junction. Turn south on Highway 158 and drive three miles to the campground.
Trip note: This one is the smallest and most overlooked on the "June Lake Loop." Gull Lake, set at 7,600 feet elevation, is often lost in the shadow of its bigger siblings, June Lake, Silver Lake, and Grant Lake. Open from May to November.

Map grid i1

GLASS CREEK
INYO NATIONAL FOREST

Campsites, facilities: There are 50 campsites for tents or motor homes up to 22 feet long. Fireplaces and picnic tables are provided. Vault toilets are available. There is **no piped water,** so bring your own.
Reservations, fee: No reservations, no fee.
Who to contact: Phone the Inyo National Forest District Office at (619)647-6525.
Location: From Lee Vining, drive about 16.5 miles south on US 395. Turn right (west) at the little town of Crestview and drive one mile to the campground.
Trip note: Bet you didn't know about this one. The camp is set along Glass Creek at 7,600 feet elevation, making it a good jump-off spot for hikers. A trail heads

along Glass Creek, past Glass Creek Meadow to the foot of San Joaquin Mountain. Open from mid-May to November.

Map grid i1

DEADMAN

on Deadman Creek
INYO NATIONAL FOREST

Campsites, facilities: There are 30 campsites for tents or motor homes up to 22 feet long. A group camp is also available (reservations required). Fireplaces and picnic tables are provided. Vault toilets are available. There is **no piped water.**

Reservations, fee: No reservations, no fee. Reservations required for group camps.

Who to contact: Phone the Inyo National Forest District Office at (619)647-6525.

Location: From Lee Vining, drive about 17 miles south on US 395 (one-half mile past the town of Crestview). Turn right on an improved dirt road and drive about 2.5 miles to the campground.

Trip note: This little-known camp is set at 7,800 feet elevation along little Deadman Creek (and don't ask how it got its name). Deer Mountain is adjacent to the camp. It's advisable to get a Forest Service map, which costs $2 and details the area's backcountry. Open from June to mid-October.

Map grid i2

BIG SPRINGS

on Deadman Creek
INYO NATIONAL FOREST

Campsites, facilities: There are 24 campsites for tents or motor homes up to 22 feet long. Fireplaces and picnic tables are provided. Vault toilets are available. There is **no piped water,** so bring your own.

Reservations, fee: No reservations, no fee.

Who to contact: Phone the Inyo National Forest District Office at (619)647-6525.

Location: From Lee Vining, drive about 21 miles south on US 395. Turn left onto Owens River Road and drive two miles to the campground.

Trip note: This is one of two camps along Deadman Creek, and both have quiet settings. This one is set at 7,300 feet elevation. Open from June to October.

Map grid j0

HORSESHOE LAKE GROUP CAMP

INYO NATIONAL FOREST

Campsites, facilities: There are eight campsites for tents or motor homes up to 22 feet long. Piped water, fireplaces, and picnic tables are provided. Flush toilets are available. Supplies can be purchased in Mammoth Lakes. Pets are permitted on leashes.

Reservations, fee: Reservations required; $20-$45 per night group fee.

Who to contact: Phone the Inyo National Forest District Office at (619)934-2505.

Location: From Lee Vining, drive 26 miles south on US 395 to Mammoth Junction. Turn west on Highway 203 (Minaret Summit Road) and drive four miles. Turn left (south) onto Lake Mary Road and drive seven miles to the campground.

Trip note: This prime-time group camp is located along Horseshoe Lake at 8,900 feet elevation. That's right, this is the high country. A bonus for backpackers is a trailhead near the camp which accesses the Pacific Crest Trail and the John Muir Wilderness. Open from mid-June to mid-October.

Map grid jO

TWIN LAKES
INYO NATIONAL FOREST

Campsites, facilities: There are 23 sites for tents only and 72 sites for tents or motor homes up to 22 feet long. Picnic tables, fireplaces, and piped water are provided. Flush toilets and horseback riding facilities are available. A grocery store, a laundromat, and propane gas are nearby. Pets are permitted on leashes.
Reservations, fee: No reservations; $7 fee per night.
Who to contact: Phone the Inyo National Forest District Office at (619)934-2505.
Location: From Lee Vining, drive 26 miles south on US 395 to Mammoth Junction. Turn west on Highway 203 (Minaret Summit Road) and drive four miles. Turn left (south) on Lake Mary Road and drive three miles to the campgound.
Trip note: There are several campgrounds set beside little Twin Lakes and this is one in that series. Trout fishing is best in early summer. The elevation is 8,700 feet. Open from mid-June to mid-October.

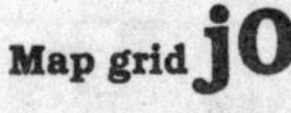

LAKE GEORGE
INYO NATIONAL FOREST

Campsites, facilities: There are 16 campsites for tents or motor homes up to 16 feet long. Piped water, fireplaces, and picnic tables are provided. Flush toilets and horseback riding facilities are available. A grocery store, a laundromat, and propane gas are available nearby. Pets are permitted on leashes.
Reservations, fee: No reservations; $7 fee per night.
Who to contact: Phone the Inyo National Forest District Office at (619)934-2505.
Location: From Lee Vining, drive 26 miles south on US 395 to Mammoth Junction. Turn west on Highway 203 and drive four miles. Turn left (south) onto Lake Mary Road and drive four miles to the campground entrance road (goes around Lake Mary).
Trip note: There are several secluded campgrounds in the area next to small lakes. Take your pick, podnah. This one, at 9,000 feet elevation, is on the shore of Lake George, near several other lakes. A trail near the camp goes up to Mammoth Crest. Open from mid-June to mid-October.

Map grid jO

LAKE MARY
INYO NATIONAL FOREST

Campsites, facilities: There are 43 campsites for tents or motor homes up to 22 feet long. Piped water, fireplaces, and picnic tables are provided. Flush toilets and horseback riding facilities are available. A grocery store, a laundromat, and propane gas are nearby. Pets are permitted on leashes.
Reservations, fee: No reservations; $7 fee per night.
Who to contact: Phone the Inyo National Forest District Office at (619)934-2505.
Location: From Lee Vining, drive 26 miles south on US 395 to Mammoth Junction. Turn west on Highway 203 (Minaret Summit Road) and drive four miles. Turn left (south) onto Lake Mary Road and drive three miles to the campground entrance road.
Trip note: This is a prime spot to launch a backpacking trek or to stay put for a while. It is located on the shore of Lake Mary. The camp is set at 8,900 feet elevation. Open from mid-June to mid-October.

Map grid **jO**

PINE CITY

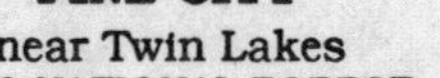

near Twin Lakes

INYO NATIONAL FOREST

Campsites, facilities: There are 11 campsites for tents or motor homes up to 22 feet long. Piped water, fireplaces, and picnic tables are provided. Flush toilets and horseback riding facilities are available. A grocery store, a laundromat, and propane gas are available nearby. Pets are permitted on leashes.

Reservations, fee: No reservations; $7 fee per night.

Who to contact: Phone the Inyo National Forest District Office at (619)934-2505.

Location: From Lee Vining, drive 26 miles south on US 395 to Mammoth Junction. Turn west on Highway 203 (Minaret Summit Road) and drive four miles. Turn left (south) onto Lake Mary Road and drive about four miles to the campground.

Trip note: There are several other small lakes in the area so this camp is a take-your-pick deal. It's set near Twin Lakes at 8,900 feet elevation. Open from mid-June to mid-October.

Map grid **jO**

COLDWATER

on Coldwater Creek

INYO NATIONAL FOREST

Campsites, facilities: There are 77 campsites for tents or motor homes up to 22 feet long. Piped water, fireplaces, and picnic tables are provided. Flush toilets and horseback riding facilities are available. Supplies can be purchased in Mammoth Lakes. Pets are permitted on leashes.

Reservations, fee: No reservations; $7 fee per night.

Who to contact: Phone the Inyo National Forest District Office at (619)934-2505.

Location: From Lee Vining, drive 26 miles south on US 395 to Mammoth Junction. Turn west on Highway 203 (Minaret Summit Road) and drive four miles. Turn left (south) onto Lake Mary Road and drive 3.5 miles to the campground entrance road.

Trip note: This classic Forest Service camp sits by little Coldwater Creek near Lake Mary. A trailhead adjacent to the camp accesses the Pacific Crest Trail, John Muir Wilderness, and several high mountain lakes. The elevation is 8,900 feet. Open from mid-June to mid-October.

Map grid **j1**

MAMMOTH MOUNTAIN RV PARK

near Mammoth Creek

Campsites, facilities: There are 130 sites for motor homes with piped water, electricity, picnic tables, and fireplaces provided. Rest rooms, hot showers, cable TV hookups, a sanitary disposal station, a laundromat, a swimming pool, and a jacuzzi are available. The facilities are wheelchair accessible. Supplies can be obtained in Mammoth Lakes.

Reservations, fee: Reservations accepted; $19-$24 fee per night.

Who to contact: Phone the park at (619)934-3822.

Location: From Casa Diablo on US 395, turn west on Highway 203 and drive about three miles to the park.

Trip note: This motor home park is ideally situated; it's set just across the street from the Forest Service Visitors Center. Got a question? They got an answer. Open from April through mid-November.

Map grid **j1**

PINE GLEN
INYO NATIONAL FOREST

A

Campsites, facilities: There are seven family campsites and 12 group campsites for tents or motor homes up to 22 feet long. Piped water, fireplaces, and picnic tables are provided. Flush toilets and a sanitary disposal station are available. The group facilities are wheelchair accessible. A grocery store, a laundromat, propane gas, and horseback riding facilities are nearby in Mammoth Lakes. Pets are permitted on leashes.

B

Reservations, fee: Reservations required; $7 fee per night for family sites; $20-$35 fee for group sites.

Who to contact: Phone the Inyo National Forest District Office at (619)934-2505.

C

Location: From Mammoth Junction on US 395, turn west on Highway 203 and drive three miles to the Mammoth Visitor Center. Turn right and drive a short distance to the campground.

Trip note: This is a well-located base camp for several side trips, including Devil's Postpile National Monument (shuttle available in Mammoth). The elevation is 7,800 feet. Open from June to September.

D

Map grid **j1**

NEW SHADY REST
INYO NATIONAL FOREST

E5

Campsites, facilities: There are 97 campsites for tents or motor homes up to 22 feet long. Piped water, fireplaces, and picnic tables are provided. Flush toilets, a dump station, a playground, and horseback riding facilities are available. A grocery store, a laundromat, and propane gas are nearby. Supplies can be obtained in Mammoth Lakes. Pets are permitted on leashes.

Reservations, fee: No reservations; $7 fee per night.

F

Who to contact: Phone the Inyo National Forest District Office at (619)934-2505.

Location: From Mammoth Junction on US 395, turn west on Highway 203 and drive three miles to the Mammoth Visitor Center. Turn right and drive to the campground.

Trip note: This easy-to-reach camp is set at 7,800 feet elevation, not far from the Mammoth Visitor Center. The surrounding Inyo National Forest provides many side trip opportunities, including Devil's Postpile National Monument (shuttles available from Mammoth), upper San Joaquin River, and the Inyo National Forest backcountry trails, streams, and lakes. Open from May to October.

G

Map grid **j1**

OLD SHADY REST
INYO NATIONAL FOREST

H

Campsites, facilities: There are 51 campsites for tents or motor homes up to 22 feet long. Piped water, fireplaces, and picnic tables are provided. Flush toilets, a dump station, a playground, and horseback riding facilities are available. A grocery store, a laundromat, and propane gas are nearby. Supplies can be obtained in Mammoth Lakes. Pets are permitted on leashes.

I

Reservations, fee: No reservations; $7 fee per night.

Who to contact: Phone the Inyo National Forest District Office at (619)934-2505.

Location: From Mammoth Junction on US 395, turn west on Highway 203 and drive three miles to the Mammoth Visitor Center. Turn right and drive a short distance to the campground.

J

Trip note: Names like "Old Shady Rest" are usually reserved for mom-and-pop motor home parks, but the Forest Service has proved it is capable of all sorts of shenanigans. Like "New Shady Rest," this camp is also located near the Mammoth Visitor Center with the same side trips available. The elevation is 7,800 feet.

Map grid j2

SHERWIN CREEK
INYO NATIONAL FOREST

Campsites, facilities: There are 87 campsites for tents or motor homes up to 22 feet long. Piped water, fireplaces, and picnic tables are provided. Flush toilets are available. Horseback riding facilities are nearby. Supplies are available in Mammoth Lakes. Pets are permitted on leashes.

Reservations, fee: No reservations; $6 fee per night.

Who to contact: Phone the Inyo National Forest District Office at (619)934-2505.

Location: From Mammoth Junction on US 395, turn west onto Highway 203 and drive three miles. Turn south on Old Mammoth Road and drive about 1 mile to Sherwin Creek Road. Turn south and drive three miles to the campground.

Trip note: This is a quality jump-off camp for backpacking into the Inyo National Forest. The camp is set at 7,600 feet elevation along Sherwin Creek with trailheads a mile from camp that head for Sherwin Lakes, Lost Lake, and Valentine Lake in the John Muir Wilderness. Open from May through October.

Map grid j3

CONVICT LAKE
INYO NATIONAL FOREST

Campsites, facilities: There are 88 campsites for tents or motor homes up to 22 feet long. Piped water, fireplaces, and picnic tables are provided. Flush toilets, a dump station, a boat ramp, and horseback riding facilities are available. Pets are permitted on leashes.

Reservations, fee: No reservations; $8 fee per night.

Who to contact: Phone the Inyo National Forest District Office at (619)934-2505.

Location: From the junction of US 395 and Highway 203, drive south on US 395 for 4.5 miles to Convict Lake Road. Turn west and drive three miles to the campground.

Trip note: A popular spot for campers and fishermen, Convict Lake (7,600 feet elevation) is gaining a reputation as a top spot for trout fishing. Its popularity has increased quite a bit in the past few years due, in part, to a decline in the fishing success at nearby giant Crowley Lake. A trailhead near camp provides access to several lakes in the John Muir Wilderness. Open from April to October.

A

B

C

D

E5

F

G

H

I

J

◆ MAP F1 ◆

BEACH
TREES
5% CLUB
DESERT
URBAN
FOOTHILL
GRASSLAND

15 MILES

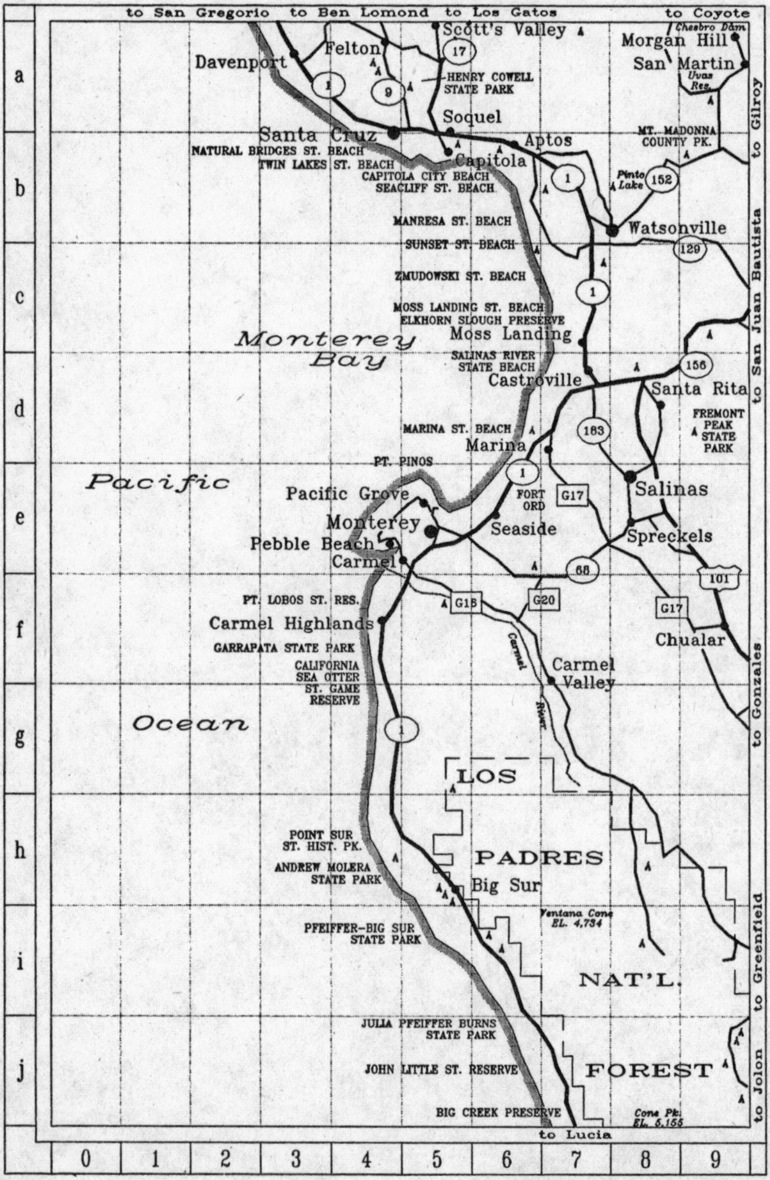

Map grid a4 — COTILLION GARDENS RV PARK
near Santa Cruz

Campsites, facilities: There are two sites for tents and 78 for motor homes, many with full hookups. Picnic tables and fireplaces are provided. Rest rooms, showers, cable TV hookups, a recreation room, a swimming pool, and a small store are available.

Reservations, fee: Reservations advised; $18-$25 fee per night.

Who to contact: Phone (408)335-7669, or write 300 Old Big Trees, Felton, CA. 95018.

Location: From Highway 17 five miles north of Santa Cruz, take the Felton-Scotts Valley exit. Drive 3.5 miles to Felton. Turn left (south) on Highway 9 and drive 1.5 miles to the campground.

Trip note: This camp may have the dumbest name of all time, but it's a pretty place with several possible side trips. It is set on the edge of the Santa Cruz Mountain redwoods, near Henry Cowell Redwoods State Park and the San Lorenzo River. Monterey Bay is only about a ten-minute drive from the park.

Map grid a4 — SMITHWOODS RESORT
near Santa Cruz

Campsites, facilities: There are 150 RV sites with full hookups. Picnic tables and fireplaces are provided. Rest rooms, showers, a recreation room, a swimming pool, a playground, and a small store are available.

Reservations, fee: Call for available space; $24 per night fee.

Who to contact: Phone (408)335-4321.

Location: From Highway 17 five miles north of Santa Cruz, take the Felton-Scotts Valley exit. Drive 3.5 miles to Felton. Turn left (south) on Highway 9 and drive about 1.5 miles to the campground.

Trip note: You get a pretty redwood setting at this privately-operated park with its many side trip possibilities. Henry Cowell Redwoods State Park (good) and Big Basin Redwoods State Park (better) are two nearby parks that provide hiking opportunities. The narrow-gauge train ride through the area is fun too.

Map grid a5 — HENRY COWELL REDWOODS STATE PARK
near Santa Cruz

Campsites, facilities: There are 112 sites for tents or motor homes up to 35 feet long. Piped water, fireplaces, and tables are provided. A sanitary disposal station, showers, and toilets are available. Pets are permitted. Some facilities are wheelchair accessible.

Reservations, fee: Reservations are advisable; reserve through MISTIX at (800) 444-PARK ($3.95 MISTIX fee); $14-$16 per night fee; pets $1.

Who to contact: Phone (408)335-4598 or (408)438-2396.

Location: From Highway 1 in Santa Cruz, take the Ocean Street-Central Santa Cruz exit. Turn inland on Graham Hill Road towards Felton. Drive about three miles uphill to the park. The entrance is on the left.

Trip note: This is a quality redwood state park near Santa Cruz with good hiking, including one trail to a great lookout over Santa Cruz and the Pacific Ocean. The San Lorenzo River runs near the park and provides steelhead fishing in winter months on Wednesdays and weekends. The fishing prospects are much improved due to the private stocking program of a local sportsmen's club. This campground is open year-round.

Map grid **a9**

UVAS CANYON COUNTY PARK

near Morgan Hill

Campsites, facilities: There are 15 sites for tents only and 15 spaces for tents or motor homes up to 28 feet long. Fireplaces and tables are provided. Piped water and toilets are available. Pets are permitted.

Reservations fee: No reservations; $8 per night fee; pets $1.

Who to contact: Call Uvas Canyon County Park at (408)779-9232.

Location: From Business 101 (Monterey Road) in Morgan Hill, turn west onto Llagas Road and drive to Oak Glen Avenue. Turn right (north) and drive to Uvas Road. Turn left (south) and drive to Croy Road. Turn right (west) and drive to the park.

Trip note: Over the years, Uvas Reservoir has provided some of the better black bass and crappie fishing in the Bay Area among the 40 public access lakes. Best by far during the spring, when it is also stocked with rainbow trout. Call Coyote Discount Bait and Tackle at (408)463-0711 for the latest fishing tips. Low water is sometimes a problem. Call first for lake levels.

Map grid **a9**

OAK DELL

on Anderson Lake

Campsites, facilities: There are 42 motor home spaces, most with full hookups. Picnic tables, rest rooms, showers, and a sanitary disposal station are provided. Pets are permitted on leashes.

Reservations, fee: Call for available space. $18 per night.

Who to contact: Phone (408)779-7779 or write to 12790 Watsonville Road, Morgan Hill, CA 95037.

Location: From US 101 in Morgan Hill, take the Tennant Road exit and drive west for one mile to Monterey Road. Turn left (south) onto Monterey Road and drive a short distance to Watsonville Road. Turn right (west) on Watsonville Road and drive 3.5 miles to the RV park.

Trip note: The first thing you should ask is, "How much water is in Lake Anderson?" The answer may be the key to the success of your trip. When Anderson has plenty of water, it has the capacity to be a large, beautiful lake providing water skiing, fishing for bass, bluegill, crappie and catfish, swimming, and general relief on the hot summer days here. But in 1987, '88, and '90, it has only been about 25 percent full.

Map grid **b5**

NEW BRIGHTON STATE BEACH

near Santa Cruz

Campsites, facilities: There are ten sites for tents only and 105 spaces for tents or motor homes up to 31 feet. Piped water, fireplaces, and picnic tables are provided. A sanitary disposal station, toilets, showers, propane gas, groceries, and a laundromat are available. Pets are permitted.

Reservations, fee: Reservations advised; reserve through MISTIX by phoning (800)444-PARK ($3.95 MISTIX fee); $14-$16 fee per night; pets $1.

Who to contact: Call the state park at (408)475-4850.

Location: From Santa Cruz, drive south on Highway 1 for about five miles to the Capitola-New Brighton Beach exit. The park is just off the highway.

Trip note: This is one in a series of camps set on the bluffs overlooking Monterey

Bay. They are among the most popular and in-demand state campgrounds in California. Reservations are a necessity. Alas, the summer months are often foggy, especially in the morning. Beachcombing and surf fishing for perch provide recreation options along with skiff rentals at the nearby Capitola Wharf. The San Lorenzo River enters the ocean nearby. A

Map grid **b6**

SEACLIFF STATE BEACH
near Santa Cruz

B

Campsites, facilities: There are 91 sites with hookups for motor homes up to 40 feet. Fireplaces and tables are provided. Rest rooms and showers are available. Propane gas, groceries, and a laundromat are available nearby.

Reservations, fee: Reservations advised; reserve through MISTIX by phoning (800)444-PARK ($3.95 MISTIX fee); $20-$27 fee per night for motor homes during the peak season. C

Who to contact: Call the state park rangers at (408)688-3241, or Seacliff State Beach at (408)688-3222 (phone sometimes unattended).

Location: From Santa Cruz, drive about six miles to the Seacliff Beach exit. Turn west and drive to the park entrance. D

Trip note: This is a popular layover in summer months, but the best weather is from mid-August to early October. The spot is pretty and set on bluffs overlooking Monterey Bay. The "old cement ship" nearby provides some of the best shore-fishing in the bay. E

Map grid **b7**

SANTA CRUZ KOA
near Watsonville

Campsites, facilities: There are 20 sites for tents only and 213 motor home spaces with full or partial hookups. There are also 20 camping cabins. Picnic tables and fireplaces are provided. Rest rooms, showers, a sanitary disposal station, a swimming pool, a jacuzzi, a wading pool, a playground, a recreation room, a store, and propane gas are available. F1

Reservations, fee: Reservations accepted; $20-$30 per night.

Who to contact: Phone (408)722-0551.

Location: From Santa Cruz, drive 12 miles southeast on Highway 1. Take the Larkin Valley Road exit. Head southwest and drive 3.5 miles to 1186 San Andreas Road. G

Trip note: This popular layover spot for motor home cruisers is not far from Manresa and Sunset State Beaches. Pinto Lake provides nearby trout fishing from winter to early summer. Open year-round. H

Map grid **b8**

PINTO LAKE COUNTY PARK
near Watsonville

Campsites, facilities: There are motor home sites at Pinto Lake Park. There are a few tent sites at an adjacent campground at the lake. Picnic tables, piped water, sewer hookups, and electricity are provided. A boat ramp and boat rentals are available. I

Reservations, fee: Reservations accepted; $15 feet per night.

Who to contact: Phone the park at (408)722-8129.

Location: From Santa Cruz, drive 17 miles south on Highway 1 to the Watsonville-Highway 152 exit. At the first intersection, turn left on Green Valley Road and drive two miles to the lake. J

Trip note: Pinto Lake is the only one of the seven lakes in the nine Bay Area counties that offers lakeside camping. For the few who know about it, it's an offer that can't be refused. From winter to early summer, the Department of Fish and Game stocks the lake twice a month with rainbow trout. The lake also has a crappie population that cycles up and down over the years, with some summers providing outstanding fishing.

Map grid b9 **MOUNT MADONNA COUNTY PARK**

near Gilroy

Campsites, facilities: There are 117 sites for tents or motor homes. Piped water, fireplaces, and tables are provided. Toilets are available. Pets are permitted on leashes.

Reservations, fee: No reservations; $8 fee per night; pets $1.

Who to contact: Call Mount Madonna County Park at (408)842-2341.

Location: From US 101 in Gilroy, take the Hecker Pass Highway (Highway 152) exit west. Drive about seven miles west to the park entrance. From Highway 1 in Watsonville, turn east onto Highway 152 and drive about 12 miles to the park entrance.

Trip note: It's a twisty son-of-a-gun road to reach the top of Mount Madonna, but the views are worth it. On clear days, visitors get great vistas of Monterey Bay to the west and Santa Clara Valley to the east. Recreation opportunities include horseback rentals and hiking trails.

Map grid c6 **SUNSET STATE BEACH**

near Watsonville

Campsites, facilities: There are 90 spaces for tents or motor homes up to 31 feet long. Rest rooms, showers, fireplaces, picnic tables, and recreation room are provided.

Reservations, fee: Reservations suggested; reserve through MISTIX by phoning (800)444-PARK ($3.95 MISTIX fee); $14-$16 fee per night.

Who to contact: Phone the park rangers at (408)724-1266.

Location: From Highway 1 near Watsonville, take the San Andreas Road exit and follow the signs to the beach.

Trip note: On clear evenings, the sunsets look like they are imported from Hawaii. The camp is set on a bluff overlooking Monterey Bay, a good spot for Pismo clams during minus low tides. The best weather is in late summer and fall. Spring can be windy here, early summer is often foggy.

Map grid c7 **LOMA LINDA TRAVEL PARK**

near Salinas

Campsites, facilities: There are 50 motor home spaces with full hookups. Picnic tables, rest rooms, and showers are provided. A sanitary disposal station and propane gas are available. The facilities are wheelchair accessible. A golf course is nearby.

Reservations, fee: Reservations are required; $17 fee per night.

Who to contact: Phone the park at (408)722-9311.

Location: Drive two miles south of Watsonville on Highway 1 to Salinas Road. Turn east and drive one mile to 890 Salinas Road.

Trip note: Location is everything, they say, and this motor home park's proximity to Monterey and Carmel gives RV cruisers what they're looking for. A possible side trip for trout anglers is too often overlooked at Pinto Lake near Watsonville. Open all year.

A

Map grid c9

MONTEREY VACATION RV PARK
near San Juan Bautista

B

Campsites, facilities: There are 88 campsites for motor homes with full hookups. Flush toilets, showers, a jacuzzi, a swimming pool, a laundromat, and propane gas are available. Pets are permitted on leashes.

Reservations, fee: Reservations suggested for three-day holiday weekends; $18 fee per night.

Who to contact: Phone the park at (408)757-8098.

C

Location: On US 101 between Gilroy and Salinas drive to 1400 Highway 101 (two miles south of the Highway 156-San Juan Bautista exit).

Trip note: This motor home park is conveniently located. It's a ten-minute drive to San Juan Bautista, 30 minutes to the Monterey Bay Aquarium, and 40 minutes to Monterey's Fisherman's Wharf.

D

Map grid d6

MARINA DUNES RV PARK
near Monterey Bay

Campsites, facilities: There are 65 motor home sites, many with full or partial hookups. Piped water and picnic tables are provided. Rest rooms, showers, a laundromat, cable TV, a recreation room, and groceries are available. Pets are permitted.

E

Reservations, fee: Reservations requested; $22-$27 fee per night; pets $1.

Who to contact: Phone the park at (408)384-6914.

Location: From US 101 in Marina, take the Reservation Road exit and drive one block west. Turn north onto Dunes Drive and drive to 3330 Dunes Drive.

F1

Trip note: This is a popular motor home park for RV cruisers who are touring Highway 1 and want a layover spot near Monterey. This spot fills the bill, being open all year and located in Marina, a short drive from the sights in Monterey and Carmel.

G

Map grid d8

CABANA HOLIDAY
near Salinas

Campsites, facilities: There are 96 motor home spaces with full or partial hookups and some tent sites. Picnic tables and fireplaces are provided. Rest rooms, showers, a recreation room, a swimming pool, a playground, a laundromat, and a store are available. Pets are permitted.

H

Reservations, fee: Reservations suggested; $23 fee per night.

Who to contact: Phone the park at (408)663-2886.

Location: From Salinas, drive north on US 101 for nine miles to the junction with Highway 156. This park is at that intersection at 8710 Prunedale North Road.

I

Trip note: If Big Sur, Monterey, and Carmel are packed, this spot provides some overflow space. It's about a half-hour's drive from the Monterey area. Limited facilities available in the winter.

Map grid d9

FREMONT PEAK STATE PARK
near San Juan Bautista

J

Campsites, facilities: There are 25 primitive campsites for tents or motor homes. Picnic tables, fire rings, and piped water are provided. Pit toilets are available.

Pets are permitted on leashes.

Reservations, fee: No reservations; $7-$9 fee per night; pets $1.

Who to contact: Phone the park at (408)623-4255.

Location: From Highway 156 in San Juan Bautista, turn south on San Juan Canyon Road and drive 11 miles to the park.

Trip note: Fremont Peak State Park is just far enough "out there" to get missed by a lot of folks. It is located on a ridge (2,900 feet elevation) with great views of Monterey Bay available on the trail going up Fremont Peak. An observatory at the park is open to the public on specified Saturdays. There is no access from this park to the adjacent Hollister State Vehicular Recreation Area.

Map grid e6

LAGUNA SECA RECREATION AREA

near Monterey

Campsites, facilities: There are 183 campsites for tents or motor homes, many with partial hookups. Picnic tables and fireplaces are provided. Rest rooms, showers, a sanitary disposal station, a recreation room, a ten-acre lake, a rifle and pistol range, and group camping facilities are available.

Reservations, fee: Reservations accepted; $11-$16 fee per night.

Who to contact: Phone the park at (408)422-6138.

Location: From Monterey, drive seven miles east on Highway 68 to the entrance.

Trip note: This campground is just minutes away from the sights in Monterey and Carmel. It is situated in oak woodlands overlooking the world famous Laguna Seca Raceway.

Map grid f5

RIVERSIDE RV PARK

near Carmel

Campsites, facilities: There are 35 motor home spaces with full hookups and cable TV. Rest rooms, showers, a recreational cabana, a barbecue area, horseshoes, and a river beach are available. A grocery store, a laundromat, and propane gas are nearby. Pets are permitted.

Reservations, fee: Reservations accepted; $26 fee per night; pets $1.

Who to contact: Phone the park at (408)624-9329.

Location: From Carmel, drive 4.5 miles southeast on Carmel Valley Road to Schulte Road. Turn right and drive to 827 Schulte Road.

Trip note: Location, location, location. That's what vacationers want to know. Well, this park is set near the Carmel River, minutes away from Carmel, Cannery Row, the Monterey Aquarium, golf courses, and the beach. Open year-round.

Map grid g5

BOTTCHER'S GAP

LOS PADRES NATIONAL FOREST

Campsites, facilities: There are nine sites for tents only and 11 campsites for tents or motor homes. Piped water, picnic tables, and fireplaces are provided. Vault toilets are available. Pets are permitted on leashes.

Reservations, fee: No reservations; $5 fee per night.

Who to contact: Phone Los Padres National Forest at (805)683-6711.

Location: From Carmel, drive south on Highway 1 for about ten miles to Palo Colorado Road. Turn left (east) and drive nine miles to the campground.

Trip note: Here is a surprise for all the Highway 1 cruisers who never leave the highway. Just inland is this little-known camp, set in beautiful Palo Colorado (redwood) Canyon. It's a good jump-off spot for a hiking trip—the trail leading out of camp is routed all the way into the Ventana Wilderness. The elevation is 2,100 feet. Open all year.

A

Map grid **h4**

ANDREW MOLERA STATE PARK
on Big Sur

Campsites, facilities: There are several primitive, walk-in campsites here with fire rings and picnic tables. Piped water and chemical toilets are available. Bring your own wood.

B

Reservations, fee: No reservations; $3 per night.
Who to contact: Phone the park at (408)667-2315,
Location: From Carmel, drive 21 miles south on Highway 1 to the park.
Trip note: Considering the grandeur of Big Sur, some campers might find it hard to believe that any primitive campgrounds are available. Believe it. This park offers walk-in campsites amid some beautiful country. A trail from the parking area leads one mile to a beautiful beach, complete with sea otters playing on the edge of kelp beds.

C

D

Map grid **h5**

FERNWOOD PARK
in Big Sur

Campsites, facilities: There are 16 sites for tents only and 49 motor home spaces, some with water and electrical hookups. Fireplaces and picnic tables are provided. Rest rooms and showers are available. A grocery store is nearby. Pets are permitted on leashes.

E

Reservations, fee: Reservations accepted; $16-$18 fee per night; $3 pet fee.
Who to contact: Phone the park at (408)667-2422.
Location: From Carmel, drive 28 miles south on Highway 1 to the campground.
Trip note: This motor home park is set in the redwoods of the beautiful Big Sur coast. You can crown your trip with a first-class dinner at Nepenthe or the Ventana Inn (bring your bank with you).

F1

Map grid **h5**

BIG SUR CAMPGROUND
in Big Sur

G

Campsites, facilities: There are 40 sites for tents only, 40 motor home spaces with water and electrical hookups, and 45 campsites for tents or motor homes. Piped water, fireplaces, and picnic tables are provided. Rest rooms, showers, a dump station, a playground, a small store, and a laundromat are available.
Reservations, fee: Reservations recommended; $16-$20 fee per night.

H

Who to contact: Phone the park at (408)667-2322.
Location: From Carmel, drive 27 miles south on Highway 1 to the campground.
Trip note: Big Sur is a nationally famous area that offers the best of all worlds. Campers can stay near redwoods, use great trails through the forest, or explore nearby Pfeiffer Beach.

I

Map grid **h5**

RIVERSIDE CAMPGROUND
in Big Sur

Campsites, facilities: There are 46 sites for tents or motor homes, some of which have water and electrical hookups. Picnic tables and fireplaces are provided. Rest rooms, showers and a playground are available. Pets are permitted.

J

Reservations, fee: Reservations suggested; $18 fee per night; pets $1.
Who to contact: Phone the campground at (408)667-2414.

Location: From Carmel, drive 27 miles south on Highway 1 to the campground.

Trip note: This is one in a series of privately-operated camps set up for Highway 1 cruisers touring the Big Sur area. This camp is set amid redwoods. Side trips include expansive beaches with sea otters playing on the edge of kelp beds (Andrew Molera State Park), redwood forests and waterfalls (Julia Pfeiffer-Burns State Park), and several quality restaurants (Nepenthe, Ventana Inn). Open from March through December.

Map grid h8

WHITE OAKS

near Anastasia Creek

LOS PADRES NATIONAL FOREST

Campsites, facilities: There are eight tent sites. Piped water, picnic tables, and fireplaces are provided. Vault toilets are available. Pets are permitted on leashes.

Reservations, fee: No reservations; $3 fee per night.

Who to contact: Phone Los Padres National Forest at (805)683-6711.

Location: From Highway 1 in Carmel, turn east on Carmel Valley Road and drive about 22 miles. Turn right (south) on Tassajara Road and drive eight miles to the campground.

Trip note: You can get some unexpected adventures in this area. I kept asking these bald guys about the hiking possibilities, and they just shook their heads. Turns out they were from a religious cult and on a one week vigil of silence. Either that, or they wanted to keep their favorite hikes secret. There's a good one that starts about a mile from the camp which is routed into the Ventana Wilderness. Several backcountry campsites are available on the way. The camp is set at 4,200 feet elevation, near Anastasia Creek.

Map grid i6

VENTANA CAMPGROUNDS

in Big Sur

Campsites, facilities: There are 75 campsites for tents and RVs up to 22 feet, but no hookups. Piped water, fireplaces, and tables are provided. A rest room and showers are available. A small grocery store is nearby. Pets must be on leashes.

Reservations, fee: Call for reservations; $19 fee per night.

Who to contact: Phone the campground at (408)667-2331.

Location: From Carmel, drive 29 miles south on Highway 1 to the campground in Big Sur.

Trip note: This rustic camp for tenters has wooded sites and an ideal location. Many premium side trips are available, from the beautiful beach at Andrew Molera State Park (a one-mile hike is necessary) to the redwoods and waterfalls in Julia Pfeiffer-Burns State Park. Open all year.

Map grid i6

PFEIFFER BIG SUR STATE PARK

in Big Sur

Campsites, facilities: There are 217 campsites for tents or motor homes up to 32 feet long. Piped water, picnic tables, and fireplaces are provided. Rest rooms, showers, a laundromat, groceries, and propane gas are available. Campgrounds, rest rooms, the grocery store, and food services are wheelchair accessible. Pets are permitted.

Reservations, fee: Phone MISTIX at (800)444-PARK ($3.95 MISTIX fee); $12-$14 fee per night; pets $1.

Who to contact: Phone the park headquarters at (707)667-2315.
Location: From Carmel, drive 29 miles south on Highway 1.
Trip note: This is one of the most popular state parks in California, and it's easy to see why. You can have it all: fantastic coastal vistas (Highway 1), redwood forests and waterfalls (Julia Pfeiffer-Burns State Park), expansive beaches with sea otters playing on the edge of kelp beds (Andrew Molera State Beach), great restaurants (Nepenthe, Ventana Inn), and private, patrolled campsites. Reservations are a necessity. Open year-round.

A B

Map grid i8

CHINA CAMP
LOS PADRES NATIONAL FOREST

Campsites, facilities: There are eight sites for tents only and five campsites for tents or motor homes. Piped water, picnic tables, and fireplaces are provided. Vault toilets are available. Pets are permitted on leashes.
Reservations, fee: No reservations; $3 fee per night.
Who to contact: Phone Los Padres National Forest at (805)683-6711.
Location: From Highway 1 in Carmel, turn east onto Carmel Valley Road and drive about 22 miles. Turn right (south) on Tassajara Road and drive ten miles to the campground.
Trip note: A lot of folks might find it difficult to believe that a spot that feels so remote can be so close to the over-manicured Carmel Valley. But here it is, one of two camps on Tassajara Road. This one has a trail out of camp that is routed into the Ventana Wilderness. Tassajara Hot Springs is seven miles away at the end of Tassajara Road, and keep a lookout for the gents with shaved heads. The elevation is 4,300 feet. Open from April to December.

C D E F1

Map grid j9

ARROYO SECO
LOS PADRES NATIONAL FOREST

Campsites, facilities: There are 51 campsites for tents or motor homes. Piped water, picnic tables, and fireplaces are provided. Vault toilets are available. Supplies can be obtained in the town of Arroyo Seco. Pets are permitted on leashes.
Reservations, fee: No reservations; $8 fee per night; $12 fee per night for multi-family sites.
Who to contact: Phone Los Padres National Forest at (805)683-6711.
Location: From US 101 in the town of Greenfield, turn west on Greenfield-Arroyo Seco Road (County Roads G16 and 3050) and drive 19 miles to the camp.
Trip note: This pretty spot near Arroyo Seco Creek, (900 feet elevation) is just outside the northern border of Ventana Wilderness. Open all year.

G H

Map grid j9

ARROYO SECO GROUP CAMP
LOS PADRES NATIONAL FOREST

Campsites, facilities: There is one group campsite for tents or motor homes. Piped water, picnic tables, and fireplaces are provided. Vault toilets are available. Supplies can be obtained in the nearby town of Arroyo Seco. Pets are permitted on leashes.
Reservations, fee: Reservations requested; $35 group fee per night.
Who to contact: Phone Los Padres National Forest at (805)683-6711.
Location: From US 101 at the town of Greenfield, turn west on Greenfield-Arroyo Seco Road (County Roads G-16 and 3050) and drive 19 miles to the campground.

I J

Trip note: If you have a larger group, give the folks Arroyo Seco a break and use this adjoining spot instead. That way you'll get the privacy you all desire. This camp is in a pretty spot, set near Arroyo Seco Creek near the northern border of the Ventana Wilderness. Open year-round.

Map grid **j9**

MEMORIAL PARK

LOS PADRES NATIONAL FOREST

Campsites, facilities: There are eight tent sites. Piped water, picnic tables, and fireplaces are provided. Vault toilets are available. Pets are permitted on leashes.

Reservations, fee: No reservations; $5 fee per night.

Who to contact: Phone Los Padres National Forest at (805)683-6711.

Location: From US 101 in King City, turn south on County Route G14 and drive 18 miles to the town of Jolon. From there, turn north on Mission Road and drive six miles. Turn left on Del Venturi-Milpitas Road (Indian Road) and drive 16 miles to the campground.

Trip note: This is one of two backcountry camps in the area. The camp has a trailhead that provides access to the Ventana Wilderness trail network. The elevation is 2,000 feet, which gives hikers a nice head start on the climb. Open year-round.

Map grid **j9**

ESCONDIDO

LOS PADRES NATIONAL FOREST

Campsites, facilities: There are nine tent sites. Piped water, picnic tables, and fireplaces are provided. Vault toilets are available. Pets are permitted on leashes.

Reservations, fee: No reservations; $5 fee per night.

Who to contact: Phone Los Padres National Forest at (805)683-6711.

Location: From US 101 in the town of Greenfield, turn west on Greenfield-Arroyo Seco Road and drive 19 miles to Indians Road. Turn south and drive seven miles on Indians Road (a narrow, winding, dirt road) to the campground.

Trip note: This is prime jump-off spot for backpackers heading into the Ventana Wilderness. The camp is set at 900 feet at a trailhead that connects to a network of other trails. The only catch is you have to plan on walking up. Open from April to December.

◆ MAP F2 ◆

BEACH
DESERT
FOOTHILL
TREES
URBAN
GRASSLAND
5% CLUB

15 MILES

to Coyote
to Patterson
to Stevenson
Anderson Reservoir
HENRY W. COE STATE PARK
San Martin
Coyote Res.
Gilroy Hot Springs
Gustine
KESTERSON NATIONAL WILDLIFE REFUGE
SAN LUIS NATIONAL WILDLIFE REFUGE
SAN LUIS RES. ST. REC. AREA
San Luis Reservoir
Gilroy
Bells Station
Santa Nella
Volta
Los Banos
San Juan Bautista
Hollister
Laveaga Pk. EL. 3,801
FREMONT PEAK STATE PARK
Tres Pinos
Paicines
Mt. Johnson EL. 3,453
Mercey Hot Springs
Gonzales
Panoche
PINNACLES NAT'L. MONUMENT
Soledad
Paraiso Springs
Greenfield
New Idria
Clear Creek Summit EL. 4,500
San Benito Mtn. EL. 5,248
LOS PADRES NAT'L. FOREST
Junipero Serra Pk. EL. 5,844
King City
to Watsonville
to Monterey
to Salinas
South to Jolon to Carmel Valley
to Red Top
to Firebaugh
to South on I-5
to San Lucas
to Priest Valley
to Coalinga

5, 33, 165, 152, 25, 156, G1, J1, 101, 146, G17, G15, G13, 198

a b c d e f g h i j

0 1 2 3 4 5 6 7 8 9

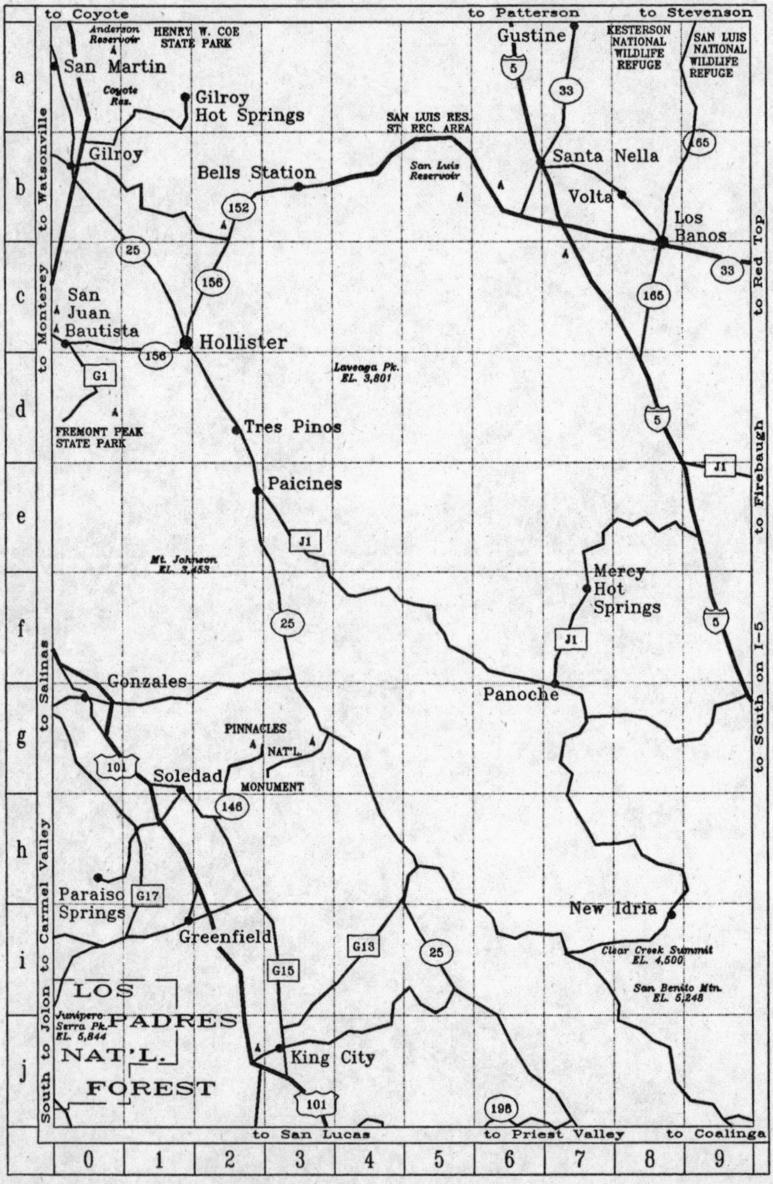

A

COYOTE LAKE COUNTY PARK

Map grid a0

near Gilroy

Campsites, facilities: There are 74 sites for tents or motor homes up to 24 feet long. Tables and fireplaces are provided. Piped water, toilets, and a boat ramp are available.

Reservations, fee: No reservations; $8 fee.

Who to contact: Phone for available space at (408)842-7800.

Location: From US 101 in Gilroy, drive east via Leavesley Road (to New Avenue, to Roop Road, then to Coyote Lake Road) for a total of 5.5 miles to the park.

Trip note: All you need is a lake full of water for this to be a pretty spot, but because of severe drawndowns that occur in some years, campers are advised to call ahead for lake levels. When the lake is full, trout stocks are made in spring months and bass fishing can be good. In summer, it can be hot and dry. Call Coyote Discount Bait and Tackle at (408)463-0711 for a free map of the lakes in Santa Clara Valley. As 1991 opened, this lake was virtually empty and the camp abandoned.

CASA DE FRUTA TRAVEL PARK

Map grid b2

near Pacheco Pass

Campsites, facilities: There are 300 motor home spaces, all with water and electric hookups. Picnic tables and fireplaces are provided. Also available are flush toilets, showers, a sanitary disposal station, Cable TV, satellite TV, a laundromat, a playground, a swimming pool, a wading pool, a recreation room, an outdoor dance floor, horseshoes, volleyball courts, baseball diamonds, a wine and cheese tasting room, a candy factory, a gift shop, and a grocery store. Pets are permitted.

Reservations, fee: Reservations accepted; $20 fee per night.

Who to contact: Phone the park at (408)842-9316.

Location: From Gilroy, drive 13 miles east, or from Los Banos, drive 28 miles west on Highway 152 to 10031 Pacheco Pass Highway.

Trip note: This 80-acre park has a festival-like feel to it with country music and dancing on summer weekends and barbecues on Sundays. It's a good thing, because there isn't a whole lot else to do around these parts. Huge but sparse San Luis Reservoir, 20 miles to the east, provides a possible side trip.

BASALT

Map grid b5

on San Luis Reservoir

Campsites, facilities: There are 79 campsites for tents or motor homes. Piped water, fireplaces, and picnic tables are provided. Flush toilets, showers, a dump station, and boat ramp are available. A grocery store, a laundromat, and propane gas are nearby. The facilities are wheelchair accessible.

Reservations, fee: Phone MISTIX at (800)444-PARK ($3.95 MISTIX fee); $9-$14 fee per night.

Who to contact: Phone the San Luis Reservoir State Recreation Area at (209) 826-1196.

Location: From Los Banos, drive 12 miles west on Highway 152 to the entrance road on left.

Trip note: San Luis Reservoir is a huge, man-made lake that is a storage facility along the California Aqueduct. When the Delta water pumps take the water,

B C D E F2 G h I J

they also take the fish, filling this lake up with both. Striped bass fishing is best in the fall when the stripers chase schools of baitfish on the lake surface (indicated by the diving birds—birds never lie). Spring and early summer can be quite windy, but that makes for good sailboarding. The elevation is 575 feet. Open year-round.

Map grid **b6**

MADEIROS
on San Luis Reservoir

Campsites, facilities: There are 350 primitive campsites for tents or motor homes. Some shaded ramadas with fireplaces and picnic tables are available. Tanked water and chemical toilets are available. A boat ramp is nearby. Pets are permitted on leashes.

Reservations, fee: No reservations; $7-$9 fee per night.

Who to contact: Phone the San Luis Reservoir State Recreation Area at (209) 826-1196.

Location: From Los Banos, drive 12 miles west on Highway 152 to the intersection of Highway 33. Turn north on Highway 33 and drive a short distance to the campground entrance.

Trip note: This campground, one of two on the vast, sparse expanse of San Luis Reservoir, gets windy in the spring, hot in the summer, and low on water in the fall. Striped bass fishing is best in the fall when the wind is down and stripers will corral schools of baitfish near the lake surface. The elevation is 225 feet. Open year-round.

Map grid **c0**

MISSION FARM RV PARK
near San Juan Bautista

Campsites, facilities: There are 25 sites for tents only and 165 motor home spaces with full hookups and picnic tables. Flush toilets, showers, a barbecue area, a sanitary disposal station, a laundromat, a recreation room, propane gas, and groceries are available. Pets are permitted on leashes; a dog run is available.

Reservations, fee: Reservations suggested; $20 per night for full hookup; discount for seniors.

Who to contact: Phone the park at (408)623-4456.

Location: From US 101, drive three miles east on Highway 156. Turn right at the blinking yellow light. Turn left at the big sign for the park and drive one-quarter mile down the road to 400 San Juan-Hollister Road.

Trip note: The close proximity to San Juan Bautista—it's within easy walking distance—is the main attraction of this privately-operated park. The park is set beside a walnut orchard, and in the fall, you can pick walnuts for free and keep them.

Map grid **c0**

SAN JUAN BAUTISTA KOA
near San Juan Bautista

Campsites, facilities: There are 17 sites for tents only, 27 campsites with partial hookups for tents or motor homes, and 14 motor home spaces with full hookups. Picnic tables and fire grills are provided. Flush toilets, showers, a sanitary disposal station, a recreation room, a swimming pool, a laundromat, propane gas, and groceries are available. Some facilities are wheelchair accessible. Pets are permitted on leashes.

Reservations, fee: Reservations accepted; $14-$18 fee per night.

Who to contact: Phone the park at (408)623-4263.

Location: From US 101, take the Highway 129 exit west and drive 100 feet. Turn left onto Searle Road (frontage road) and drive to the stop sign. Turn left again on Anza and drive under the freeway to 900 Anza Road.

Trip note: Well, at least they have some spots for tenters; they are the only privately-operated park in the immediate area that does. Its proximity to Mission San Juan Bautista is a highlight, and it is also a short drive to the Monterey-Carmel area.

A B C D E F2 G H I J

Map grid c7 — LOS BANOS CREEK RESERVOIR

near Los Banos

Campsites, facilities: There are 25 campsites for tents or motor homes up to 30 feet long. Fireplaces and picnic tables are provided. Pit toilets and a boat ramp are available. There is **no piped water,** so bring your own.

Reservations, fee: No reservations; $7-$9 fee per night.

Who to contact: Phone the San Luis Reservoir State Recreation Area at (209) 826-1196.

Location: From Los Banos, drive five miles west on Highway 152. Turn south on Volta Road and drive about one mile. Turn left (east) on Pioneer Road and drive one mile. Turn south (right) onto Canyon Road and drive about five miles to the park.

Trip note: Los Banos Creek Reservoir is a small lake set amid surrounding pastureland and is relatively little-known compared to the nearby San Luis Reservoir. In summer and fall, it's a good spot for canoes or car-top boats (there's an enforced 5-mph speed limit). In spring, it can be quite windy and is a popular spot for sailboarding. The elevation is 400 feet. Open year-round.

Map grid d0 — HOLLISTER HILLS STATE VEHICULAR RECREATION AREA

near Hollister

Campsites, facilities: There are 125 campsites for tents or motor homes. Some group sites are available. Picnic tables, fireplaces, and piped water are provided. Flush toilets, showers, and a grocery store are available. Dogs are permitted on leashes.

Reservations, fee: Reservations accepted; $5 fee per night; pets $1.

Who to contact: Phone the park at (408)637-3874.

Location: From Highway 25 in Hollister, turn south on Cienga Road and drive eight miles to the park.

Trip note: This unique park was designed for off-road vehicle enthusiasts. It provides 80 miles of trails for motorcycles and 40 miles of trails for four-wheel drive vehicles. All trails close at sunset. There is no direct access to the Fremont Peak State Park, bordering directly to the west. Open year-round.

Map grid g2 — PINNACLES NATIONAL MONUMENT

5% CLUB

Campsites, facilities: There are 23 walk-in tent sites. There are two wheelchair accessible sites near wheelchair accessible rest rooms. Picnic tables, fireplaces, and piped water are provided. Vault toilets are available. Pets are permitted on leashes.

Reservations, fee: No reservations; $6 fee per night.

Who to contact: Phone the park at (408)389-4526.

Location: From US 101 in Soledad, drive 11 miles northeast on Highway 146 to the campground.

Trip note: The Pinnacles National Monument is like a different planet. It's a 16,000-acre park with volcanic clusters and strange caves, all great for exploring. This is one of two campgrounds at the Pinnacles, and don't get the two mixed up. This is the more primitive of the two, and far less visited. Does the shoe fit? If so, come prepared for hot weather, the chance of meeting up with a rattlesnake, and with plenty of ice in a cooler to keep your drinks cold. Closed on weekends from mid-February to June 1st.

Map grid g3

PINNACLES CAMPGROUND

near Pinnacles National Monument

Campsites, facilities: There are 125 campsites for tents or motor homes. Picnic tables and fireplaces are provided. Piped water, electricity, flush toilets, sanitary disposal station, showers, a store, and a swimming pool are available. Bring your own firewood or purchase it at the campground. Pets are permitted on leashes.

Reservations, fee: Reservations accepted for group sites, all others on first-come first-served basis; $6 fee per night per person for a family site; $5 fee per night per person for a group site with a $50 minimum.

Who to contact: Phone the campground at (408)389-4462.

Location: From Hollister, drive 32 miles south on Highway 25. Turn at the sign for the Pinnacles (Highway 146) and drive about 2.5 miles to the campground.

Trip note: This is one of two camps at the Pinnacles National Monument. This private one gets a lot more traffic—it has more facilities, the road in is in better shape, and the campground is closer to Bear Gulch Caves, a prime destination. The jagged pinnacles, for which the park was named, were formed by the erosion of an ancient volcanic eruption. If you are planning to stay over the weekend in the spring, arrive early on Friday evening to be sure you get a campsite. Beware of temperatures in the 90s and 100s in the summer.

Map grid j2

SAN LORENZO REGIONAL PARK

in King City

Campsites, facilities: There are 119 campsites for tents or motor homes with partial hookups. Tables and fireplaces are provided. A dump station, rest rooms, and showers are available.

Reservations, fee: Call ahead for available space and fee.

Who to contact: Phone the park at (408)385-5964.

Location: Drive on US-101 to King City. The park is at 1160 Broadway.

Trip note: A lot of folks cruising Highway 101, underestimating the time it takes to travel the state, can get caught out near King City, and it can feel like No Man's Land to a visitor. Well, don't sweat it because this park offers a spot to overnight. It's set near the Salinas River, which isn't exactly the Mississippi, but it'll do. Open year-round.

◆ MAP F3 ◆

BEACH
TREES
5% CLUB
DESERT
URBAN
FOOTHILL
GRASSLAND

15 MILES

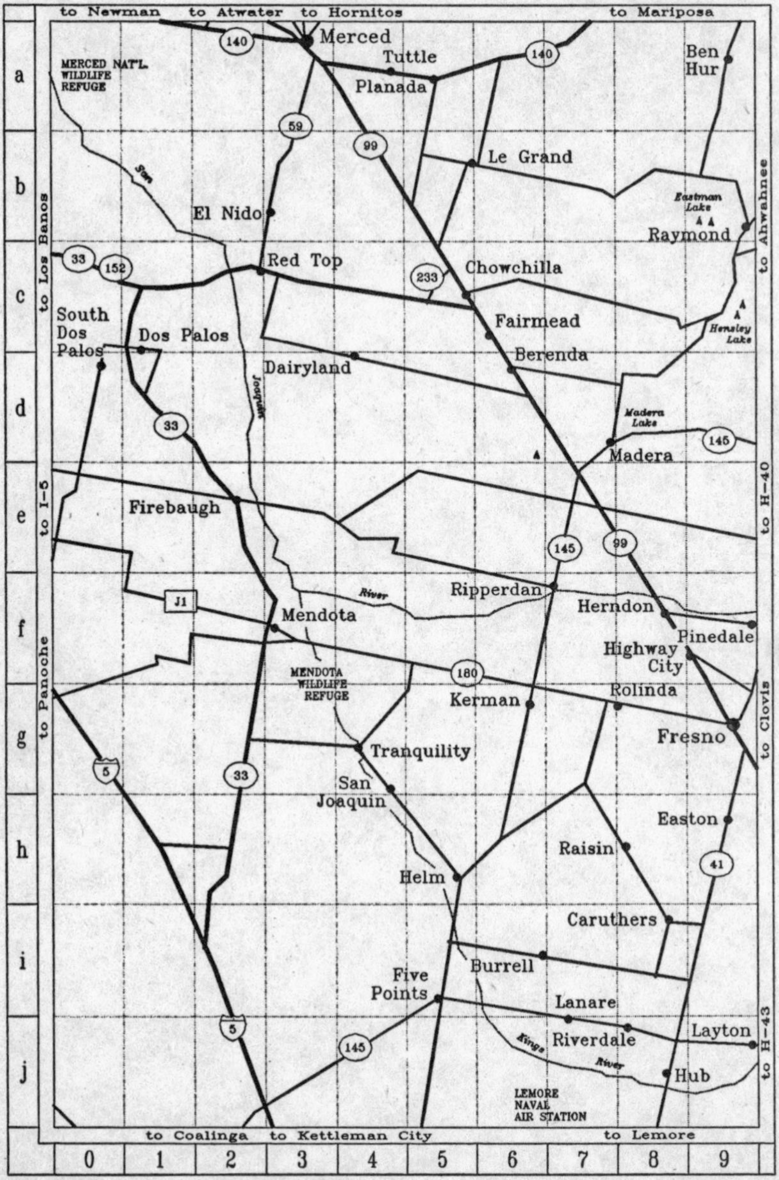

to Newman to Atwater to Hornitos to Mariposa

to Los Banos
to I-5
to Panoche
to Ahwahnee
to H-40
to Clovis
to H-43

to Coalinga to Kettleman City to Lemore

a b c d e f g h i j

0 1 2 3 4 5 6 7 8 9

MERCED NAT'L. WILDLIFE REFUGE
Merced
140
Tuttle
Planada
Ben Hur
59
99
Le Grand
Eastman Lake
Raymond
El Nido
Red Top
33
152
233
Chowchilla
Hensley Lake
South Dos Palos
Dos Palos
Fairmead
Berenda
Dairyland
Joaquin
Madera Lake
145
Madera
Firebaugh
J1
River
Ripperdan
Herndon
Mendota
Pinedale
Highway City
MENDOTA WILDLIFE REFUGE
180
Kerman
Rolinda
Fresno
Tranquility
5
San Joaquin
Easton
Raisin
41
Helm
Caruthers
Burrell
Five Points
Lanare
Riverdale
Layton
Kings River
Hub
LEMORE NAVAL AIR STATION

Map grid **b9**

CORDORNIZ RECREATION AREA
on Eastman Lake

Campsites, facilities: There are 62 campsites for tents or motor homes. Group sites are also available. Piped water, fireplaces, and picnic tables are provided. Flush toilets, showers, a dump station, a playground, and a boat ramp are available.
Reservations, fee: No reservations; $8 fee per night.
Who to contact: Phone the U.S. Corps of Engineers, Eastman Lake at (209) 689-3255.
Location: From Chowchilla on Highway 99, take the Avenue 26 exit. Drive 17 miles east on Avenue 26. Turn north on County Road 29 and drive eight miles to the lake.
Trip note: Eastman Lake, a typical federal reservoir, was created for agricultural use by damming the Chowchilla River. But on a 105-degree summer day, it can seem like a nice tub to cool off in. Ideal for water skiing, swimming, or just getting a quick dunk. Bass fishing is best in the spring, before the summer sun starts branding everything in sight. The elevation is 600 feet. Open all year.

Map grid **b9**

WILDCAT RECREATION AREA
on Eastman Lake

Campsites, facilities: There are 19 campsites for tents or motor homes. Piped water, fireplaces, and picnic tables are provided. Vault toilets, a dump station, and a playground are available. A boat ramp is nearby.
Reservations, fee: No reservations, no fee.
Who to contact: Phone the U.S. Corps of Engineers, Eastman Lake at (209) 689-3255.
Location: From Chowchilla on Highway 99, take the Avenue 26 exit. Drive 17 miles east on Avenue 26. Turn north on County Road 29 and drive eight miles to the lake.
Trip note: Eastman Lake was created by Buchanan Dam on the Chowchilla Reservoir. This is the smaller of the camps on the lake. Not exactly a pristine setting, but water is water, and during the 100-degree days of summer in the valley that means plenty. Ideal for water skiing. Open year-round.

Map grid **c9**

HENSLEY GROUP SITE
on Hensley Lake

Campsites, facilities: There are 25 campsites for tents or motor homes. Piped water, fireplaces, and picnic tables are provided. Flush toilets, showers, a dump station, a playground, and a boat ramp are available.
Reservations, fee: Reservations requested; $35 group fee per night.
Who to contact: Phone the U.S. Corps of Engineers, Hensley Lake at (209)673-5151.
Location: From Madera, drive northeast on Highway 145 for about six miles. Bear left on County Road 400 and drive 11 miles to the campground at the reservoir.
Trip note: Hensley Lake is one of the two lakes that is a short drive east of Madera. (The other is Millerton Reservoir). Hensley is the smaller of the two and has a smaller access road as well and fewer people to compete with for boating space. The reservoir was created by a dam on the Fresno River. The elevation is 500 feet. Open year-round.

Map grid **c9**

HIDDEN VIEW CAMPGROUND
on Hensley Lake

Campsites, facilities: There are 52 campsites for tents or motor homes. Piped water, fireplaces, and picnic tables are provided. Flush toilets, showers, a dump station, and a boat ramp are available. Pets are permitted on leashes.

Reservations, fee: No reservations; $10 fee per night.

Who to contact: Phone the U.S. Corps of Engineers, Hensley Lake at (209)673-5151.

Location: From Madera, drive northeast on Highway 145 for about six miles. Bear left on County Road 400 and drive 12 miles to the campground at the reservoir.

Trip note: This is the other camp at Hensley Lake, set in the foothills northeast of Madera. It is most popular with waterskiers in the summer. Because Millerton Lake is closer and easier to reach for Fresno boaters, this lake often gets overlooked. Open all year.

Map grid **d6**

COUNTRY LIVING RV PARK
in Madera

Campsites, facilities: There are 49 motor home spaces. Picnic tables, piped water, electrical connections, and sewer hookups are provided. Rest rooms, showers and a laundromat are available. A swimming pool and jacuzzi are available in the summer only. A store is nearby.

Reservations, fee: Call ahead for available space; $15 fee per night.

Who to contact: Phone the park at (209)674-5343.

Location: From Madera, drive two miles north on Highway 99 to the Avenue 16 exit. Drive to 24833 Avenue 16.

Trip note: It can be a dry piece of life driving this country on a hot summer afternoon, ready to stop, but knowing of nowhere to go. This RV park gives you an option. Open year-round.

• MAP F4 •

BEACH
TREES
5% CLUB
DESERT
URBAN
FOOTHILL
GRASSLAND

15 MILES

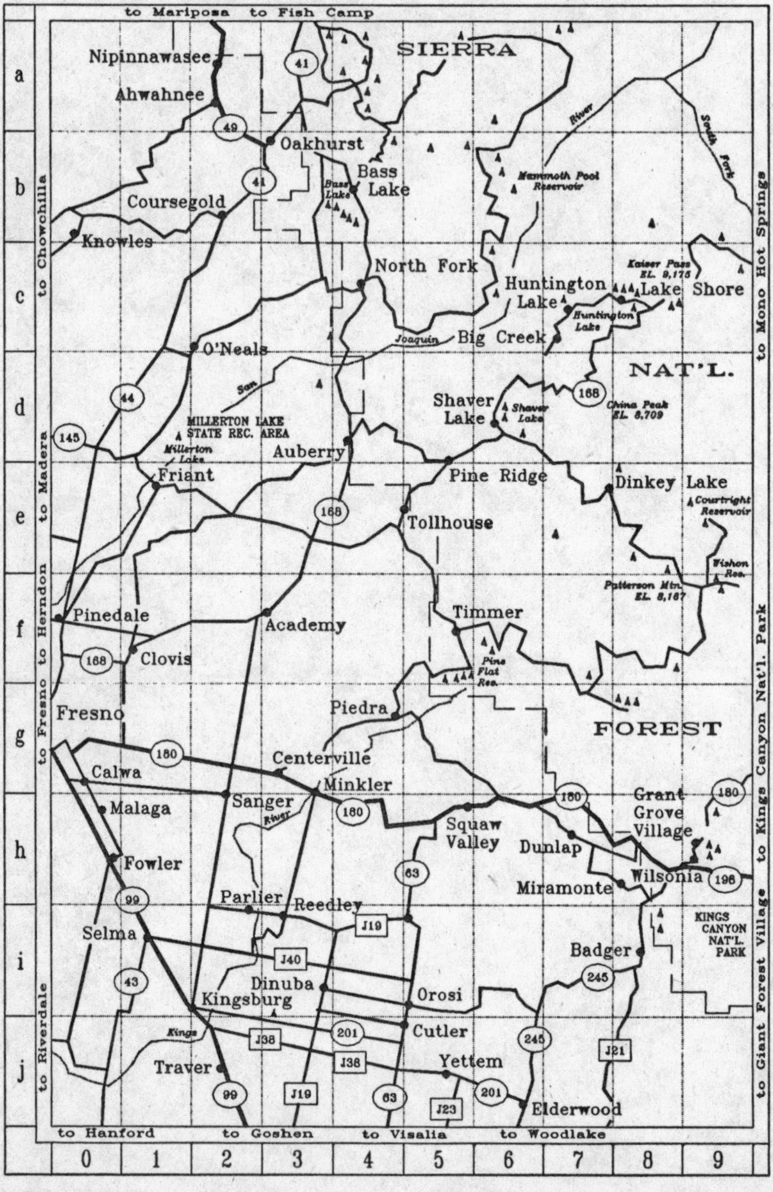

to Mariposa
to Fish Camp
SIERRA
NAT'L.
FOREST
Nipinnawasee
Ahwahnee
49
41
Oakhurst
Bass Lake
Bass Lake
Coursegold
Knowles
North Fork
Mammoth Pool Reservoir
River
South Fork
Kaiser Pass EL. 9,175
Huntington Lake
Huntington Lake
Lake Shore
Big Creek
Joaquin
San
O'Neals
44
145
MILLERTON LAKE STATE REC. AREA
Millerton Lake
168
Shaver Lake
Shaver Lake
China Peak EL. 8,709
Auberry
Friant
Pine Ridge
Dinkey Lake
Courtright Reservoir
Tollhouse
Wishon Res.
Patterson Mtn. EL. 8,167
Pinedale
Academy
Timmer
Clovis
Pine Flat Res.
Fresno
Piedra
180
Centerville
Calwa
Minkler
Grant Grove Village
Malaga
Sanger
River
Squaw Valley
Dunlap
Fowler
63
Wilsonia
198
Miramonte
99
Parlier
Reedley
J19
KINGS CANYON NAT'L. PARK
Selma
J40
Badger
43
Dinuba
Orosi
245
Kingsburg
Kings
J38
201
Cutler
J21
Traver
Yettem
J23
Elderwood
to Chowchilla
to Madera
to Fresno to Herndon
to Riverdale
to Mono Hot Springs
to Kings Canyon Nat'l. Park
to Giant Forest Village
to Hanford
to Goshen
to Visalia
to Woodlake
a b c d e f g h i j
0 1 2 3 4 5 6 7 8 9

Map grid **a3**

BIG SANDY

on Big Creek
SIERRA NATIONAL FOREST

A

Campsites, facilities: There are ten sites for tents only and 11 sites for tents or motor homes up to 16 feet long. Picnic tables and fireplaces are provided. Vault toilets are available. There is **no piped water,** so bring your own. Pets are permitted on leashes.

B

Reservations, fee: No reservations, no fee.

Who to contact: Phone the Sierra National Forest Mariposa Ranger District at (209)683-4665.

Location: From Oakhurst on Highway 41 drive about five miles north to Sky Ranch Road. Go northeast for approximately 14 miles to the campgound.

C

Trip note: It's only six miles from the highway, but this camp gets overlooked by hundreds of thousands of campers heading to the nearby southern entrance of Yosemite National Park. If you want quiet, this is a better choice. It's a pretty camp set on Big Creek in the Sierra National Forest and just eight miles from the southern entrance to Yosemite National Park. It is one of two camps in the immediate area. The elevation is 5,800 feet. Open from May to November.

D

Map grid **a4**

GREYS MOUNTAIN

on Willow Creek
SIERRA NATIONAL FOREST

E

Campsites, facilities: There are 12 tent sites. Picnic tables and fireplaces are provided. Pit toilets are available. Pets are permitted on leashes. **No piped water** is available, so bring your own.

Reservations, fee: No reservations, no fee.

F4

Who to contact: Phone the Sierra National Forest Mariposa Ranger District at (209)683-4665.

Location: From Fresno, drive 46 miles north on Highway 41 to Oakhurst. From there continue north on Highway 41 to Sky Ranch Road (about five miles). Turn right (east) and follow this road for about ten miles to the campground.

G

Trip note: This is a small, little-known, primitive campground where you can just about guarantee solitude. Yet it is located on Willow Creek, only a 15-minute drive from Bass Lake. The series of campgrounds along Willow Creek don't get much traffic. The elevation is 5,200 feet. Open from June to November.

H

Map grid **a4**

SOQUEL

on the North Fork of Willow Creek
SIERRA NATIONAL FOREST

Campsites, facilities: There are 14 campsites for tents or motor homes up to 22 feet long. Fireplaces and picnic tables are provided. Vault toilets are available. There is **no piped water,** so bring your own. Pets are permitted on leashes.

I

Reservations, fee: No reservations, no fee.

Who to contact: Phone the Sierra National Forest Mariposa Ranger District at (209)683-4665.

Location: From Fresno, drive about 52 miles north on Highway 41 to Sky Ranch Road (before Fish Camp, and five miles north of Oakhurst). Turn east and follow for about eight miles to campground.

J

Trip note: Located at 5,400 feet elevation on the North Fork of Willow Creek, this is one of the several primitive, relatively isolated campgrounds in the area. It would be handy to have a map of the Sierra National Forest that details the back roads, trails, and streams in the area. Open from June to November.

Map grid **a4**

LITTLE SANDY

on Big Creek

SIERRA NATIONAL FOREST

Campsites, facilities: There are ten tent sites. Picnic tables and fireplaces are provided. Vault toilets are available. There is **no piped water,** so bring your own. Pets are permitted on leashes.

Reservations, fee: No reservations, no fee.

Who to contact: Phone the Sierra National Forest Mariposa Ranger District at (209)683-4665.

Location: From Oakhurst drive about five miles north to Sky Ranch Road. Go northeast for approximately 15 miles to the campground.

Trip note: This quiet little spot is only nine miles from the southern entrance to Yosemite National Park. Like the camp, Big Sandy, it is set along Big Creek in the Sierra National Forest. If Yosemite is packed, this can be an ideal option. The elevation is 6,100 feet. Open from May to November.

Map grid **a4**

NELDER GROVE

SIERRA NATIONAL FOREST

Campsites, facilities: There are ten campsites for tents or motor homes up to 22 feet long. Fireplaces and picnic tables are provided. Vault toilets are available. There is **no piped water,** so bring your own. Pets are permitted on leashes.

Reservations, fee: No reservations, no fee.

Who to contact: Phone the Sierra National Forest Mariposa Ranger District at (209)683-4665.

Location: From Fresno, drive 46 miles north on Highway 41 to the town of Oakhurst. From there continue north on Highway 41 for five miles to Sky Ranch Road. Follow this road for about 8 miles northeast to the campground.

Trip note: A fantastic spot, set amid the Nelder Grove of Giant Sequoias, the majestic mountain redwoods. It's surprising more people don't know about it. But since the southern entrance to Yosemite National Park is just ten miles away, folks get sidetracked. The elevation is 5,300 feet. Open from May to October.

Map grid **a4**

TEXAS FLAT GROUP CAMP

on the North Fork of Willow Creek

SIERRA NATIONAL FOREST

Campsites, facilities: There are four campsites for tents or motor homes up to 22 feet long. Fireplaces and picnic tables are provided. Vault toilets and stock handling facilities are available. There is **no piped water,** so bring your own.

Reservations, fee: No reservations; no fee.

Who to contact: Phone the Sierra National Forest Mariposa Ranger District at (209)683-4665 from January 1st through May 13th, and at (209)642-3214 from May 14th through Labor Day.

Location: From Fresno, drive about 47 miles north on Highway 41 to Oakhurst. Go approximately five miles further north (on Highway 41) to Sky Ranch Road. Turn right (east) and follow for about 12 miles to campground.

Trip note: If you are on your honeymoon, this definitely ain't the place. Unless you like the smell of horses, that is. It's a pretty enough spot, set along the North Fork of Willow Creek, but it is primarily designed for groups with horses. Side trip options: it is 15 miles from the south entrance of Yosemite National Park and 15 miles north of Bass Lake. The elevation is 5,500 feet. Open from March (snow permitting) through November.

A

Map grid **a4**

FRESNO DOME
on Big Creek
SIERRA NATIONAL FOREST

B

Campsites, facilities: There are six sites for tents only and six sites for tents or motor homes up to 16 feet long. Picnic tables and fireplaces are provided. Pit toilets are available. There is **no piped water,** so bring your own. Pets are permitted on leashes.

Reservations, fee: No reservations, no fee.

C

Who to contact: Phone the Sierra National Forest Mariposa Ranger District at (209)683-4665.

Location: From Oakhurst on Highway 41 drive north for five miles to Sky Ranch Road. Follow this road northeast for about 12 miles to campground.

Trip note: This is one in a series of primitive, backcountry Forest Service camps in the area, and hey, the price is right. Free. This one is set along Big Creek at 6,400 feet elevation. A map of Sierra National Forest details backcountry roads, hiking trails, and streams. Because Yosemite National Park is close and borders the National Forest, this little camp gets overlooked plenty.

D

E

Map grid **a4**

KELTY MEADOW
on Willow Creek
SIERRA NATIONAL FOREST

Campsites, facilities: There are 12 campsites for tents or motor homes up to 16 feet long. Fireplaces and picnic tables are provided. Vault toilets and stock handling facilities are available. There is **no piped water,** so bring your own.

Reservations, fee: No reservations, no fee.

Who to contact: Phone the Sierra National Forest Mariposa Ranger District at (209)683-4665.

Location: From Oakhurst on Highway 41, drive five miles north to Sky Ranch Road (before Fish Camp). Follow Sky Ranch Road for about ten miles northeast to the campground.

G

Trip note: This primitive campground located by Willow Creek has sites available for campers with horses. Nearby Fresno Dome and the Nelder Grove of Giant Sequoias provide possible side trips. The elevation is 5,800 feet. Open from May to November.

H

Map grid **a5**

UPPER CHIQUITO
on Chiquito Creek
SIERRA NATIONAL FOREST

Campsites, facilities: There are ten sites for tents only and ten sites for tents or motor homes up to 22 feet long. Picnic tables and fireplaces are provided. Vault toilets are available. There is **no piped water,** so bring your own. Pets are permitted on leashes.

I

Reservations, fee: No reservations, no fee.

Who to contact: Phone the Sierra National Forest Minarets Ranger District at (209)877-2218.

J

Location: From Fresno, drive 50 miles north on Highway 41 to Yosemite Forks. Turn right (east) onto County Road 222 and drive six miles to the town of Bass

Lake. Turn left (north) onto Beasore Road and drive 16 miles to the campground.

Trip note: This is one in a series of primitive, Forest Service camps set along Chiquito Creek. This one, set at 6,800 feet elevation, is quite a bit easier to reach than the others. A map of the Sierra National Forest details the surrounding backcountry, roads, trails, and streams. Open from May to October.

Map grid a6

LOWER CHIQUITO

on Chiquito Creek

SIERRA NATIONAL FOREST

Campsites, facilities: There are seven campsites for tents or motor homes up to 22 feet long. Fireplaces and picnic tables are provided. Vault toilets are available. There is **no piped water,** so bring your own. Pets are permitted on leashes.

Reservations, fee: No reservations, no fee.

Who to contact: Phone the Sierra National Forest Minarets Ranger District at (209)877-2218.

Location: From the town of North Fork (south of Bass Lake), drive east and south on Mammoth Pool Road (County Road 225) to Minarets Road. Turn left (north) on Minarets Road (Road 4S81). The drive is a total distance of about 38 miles from North Fork. Turn left onto Forest Service Road 6S71 and drive three miles to the campground.

Trip note: This is a BOW-BOW camp: that is, "Bring your Own Water," said twice just for good measure. It gets hot up in this country and there's no piped water at the camp. It is small, little-known, and about eight miles from Mammoth Pool Reservoir. The elevation is 4,900 feet. Open from May to October.

Map grid a7

CLOVER MEADOW

on Granite Creek

SIERRA NATIONAL FOREST

Campsites, facilities: There are seven campsites for tents or motor homes up to 16 feet long. Picnic tables are provided. Piped water and vault toilets are available. Pets are permitted on leashes.

Reservations, fee: No reservations; $3 fee per night.

Who to contact: Phone the Sierra National Forest Minarets Ranger District at (209)877-2218.

Location: From the town of North Fork (south of Bass Lake), drive east and south on Mammoth Pool Road (County Road 225) to Minarets Road. Turn left (north) on Minarets Road (Road 4S81) and drive to the campground entrance road. The camp is adjacent to the Clover Meadow Ranger Station. The total distance from North Fork to the entrance road is about 43 miles—20 miles north of Mammoth Pool Reservoir on Minarets Road.

Trip note: This one of the better jump-off camps in the area for backpackers. A trail from the camp leads into the Ansel Adams Wilderness where there are many beautiful high Sierra lakes. The camp is set at 7,000 feet elevation, adjacent to the Clover Meadow Ranger Station. Open from June to October.

Map grid a7

GRANITE CREEK

SIERRA NATIONAL FOREST

Campsites, facilities: There are ten tent sites. Picnic tables and fireplaces are provided. Pit toilets are available. There is **no piped water,** so bring your own.

Pets are permitted on leashes.

Reservations, fee: No reservations, no fee.

Who to contact: Phone the Sierra National Forest Minarets Ranger District at (209)877-2218.

Location: From the town of North Fork (south of Bass Lake), drive east and south on Mammoth Pool Road (County Road 225) to Minarets Road. Turn left (north) on Minarets Road (Road 4S81) and drive to the campground entrance road, which goes to the Clover Meadow Ranger Station. (Total distance from North Fork to the entrance road is about 41 miles—18 miles north of Mammoth Pool Reservoir on Minarets Road.) Drive 3.5 miles to the campground.

Trip note: This camp can be a jump-off point for backpackers, with a trail from camp leading north to numerous lakes in the Ansel Adams Wilderness. The preceding camp may be more desirable because it has both piped water to tank up your canteens and a ranger station to obtain the latest trail information. The elevation is 6,900 feet. Open from May to October.

Map grid b3

FORKS
on Bass Lake
SIERRA NATIONAL FOREST

Campsites, facilities: There are 25 sites for tents only and six campsites for tents or motor homes up to 16 feet long. Fireplaces and picnic tables are provided. Piped water and flush toilets are available. Pets are permitted on leashes. A laundromat and a grocery store are nearby.

Reservations, fee: From Memorial Day through Labor Day, reserve through MISTIX at (800)283-CAMP ($6 MISTIX fee); $12 fee per night.

Who to contact: Phone the Sierra National Forest Mariposa Ranger District at (209)683-4665.

Location: From Fresno, drive 50 miles north on Highway 41 to Yosemite Forks. Turn right (east) onto County Road 222 and drive six miles to the campground on Bass Lake.

Trip note: Bass Lake is set in a canyon. It's a long, narrow, deep lake that is popular for fishing in the spring and water skiing in the summer. It's a pretty spot, set at 3,400 feet elevation in the Sierra National Forest. It's one of several camps at the lake. Boats must be registered at the Bass Lake observation tower after launching. The only camp on Bass Lake that is open year around is the Lupine-Cedar camp. Open from May through September.

Map grid b4

CHILCOOT
near Bass Lake
SIERRA NATIONAL FOREST

Campsites, facilities: There are seven sites for tents or motor homes up to 16 feet long. Picnic tables and fireplaces are provided. Vault toilets are available, but there is **no piped water,** so bring your own. Pets are permitted on leashes. Groceries and a laundromat are available nearby.

Reservations, fee: No reservations, no fee.

Who to contact: Phone the Sierra National Forest Mariposa Ranger District at (209)683-4665.

Location: From Fresno, drive 50 miles north on Highway 41 to Yosemite Forks. Turn right (east) onto County Road 222 and drive six miles to the town of Bass Lake. Turn left (north) onto Beasore Road and drive 4.5 miles to the campground.

Trip note: A lot of people have heard of Bass Lake, but only a handful know about Chilcoot Creek. That's where this camp is located, but it's just two miles from Bass Lake. It provides a primitive option to use either as an overflow area for Bass Lake or for folks who don't want to get jammed into one of the Bass Lake campgrounds on a popular weekend. Open from May to September.

Map grid **b4** **CRANE VALLEY GROUP & YOUTH GROUP** 

on Bass Lake

SIERRA NATIONAL FOREST

Campsites, facilities: There are four campsites that hold 30-50 people each at Youth Group Camp and seven campsites that hold 30-50 people each at Crane Valley Camp. Fireplaces and picnic tables are provided. Piped water and flush toilets are available; (there is no water at Crane Valley Camp). Pets are permitted on leashes. A grocery store is nearby.

Reservations, fee: Reserve through MISTIX (800)283-CAMP ($6 MISTIX fee); $20-$50 fee per night.

Who to contact: Phone the Sierra National Forest Mariposa Ranger District at (209)683-4665.

Location: From Fresno, drive 50 miles north on Highway 41 to Yosemite Forks. Turn right (east) onto County Road 222 and drive six miles to Bass Lake.

Trip note: Bass Lake is a long, narrow, mountain lake set in the Sierra foothills at 3,400 feet elevation. It's especially popular in the summer for waterskiers.

Map grid **b4** **LUPINE-CEDAR** 

on Bass Lake

SIERRA NATIONAL FOREST

Campsites, facilities: There are 12 sites for tents only, 101 sites for tents or motor homes up to 40 feet long, and several double-family sites. Picnic tables and fireplaces are provided. Piped water and flush toilets are available. Some facilities are wheelchair accessible. Pets are permitted on leashes. Groceries and a boat ramp are available nearby.

Reservations, fee: Reserve through MISTIX at (800)283-CAMP ($6 MISTIX fee); $12 fee per night; $24 per night for double-family sites.

Who to contact: Phone the Sierra National Forest Mariposa Ranger District at (209)683-4665.

Location: From Fresno, drive 50 miles north on Highway 41 to Yosemite Forks. Turn right (east) onto County Road 222 and drive six miles to the campground on Bass Lake.

Trip note: This is *the* camping headquarters at Bass Lake and the only camp open year-round. Bass Lake is a popular vacation spot, especially for weekends or three-day holidays. Fishing is best in the spring for rainbow trout and large-mouth bass, and by mid-June, waterskiers have usually taken over. Boats must be registered at the Bass Lake observation tower after launching.

Map grid **b4** **SPRING COVE** 

on Bass Lake

SIERRA NATIONAL FOREST

Campsites, facilities: There are 54 sites for tents only and 11 sites for tents or motor homes up to 22 feet long. Picnic tables and fireplaces are provided. Piped water and flush toilets are available. Pets are permitted on leashes. Groceries and a boat ramp are available nearby.

Reservations, fee: From Memorial Day through Labor Day, reserve through MISTIX at (800)283-CAMP ($6 MISTIX fee); $12 fee per night.

Who to contact: Phone the Sierra National Forest Mariposa Ranger District at (209)683-4665.

Location: From Fresno, drive 50 miles north on Highway 41 to Yosemite Forks. Turn right (east) onto County Road 222 and drive six miles to the campground on Bass Lake.

Trip note: This is one of the several camps set beside Bass Lake, a long, narrow reservoir set in the Sierra foothill country. Expect hot weather in the summer. Boats must be registered at the Bass Lake observation tower after launching. The elevation is 3,400 feet. Open from May to September.

Map grid b4

WISHON POINT
on Bass Lake
SIERRA NATIONAL FOREST

Campsites, facilities: There are 13 sites for tents only, 11 motor home spaces, 26 sites for tents or motor homes up to 22 feet long, and several double-family sites. Picnic tables, fireplaces and piped water are provided. Flush toilets are available. Pets are permitted on leashes. Groceries and a boat ramp are nearby.

Reservations, fee: From Memorial Day through Labor Day, reserve through MISTIX at (800)283-CAMP ($6 MISTIX fee); $12 fee per night; $24 per night for double-family sites.

Who to contact: Phone the Sierra National Forest Mariposa Ranger District at (209)683-4665.

Location: From Fresno, drive 50 miles north on Highway 41 to Yosemite Forks. Turn right (east) onto County Road 222 and drive six miles to the campground on Bass Lake.

Trip note: This is the smallest, and many say the prettiest as well, of the camps at Bass Lake. It's located on Wishon Point. The elevation is 3,400 feet. Open from May to November.

Map grid b5

GAGGS CAMP
SIERRA NATIONAL FOREST

Campsites, facilities: There are nine campsites for tents or motor homes up to 16 feet long. Picnic tables are provided. Pit toilets are available. There is **no piped water,** so bring your own. Pets are permitted on leashes.

Reservations, fee: No reservations, no fee.

Who to contact: Phone the Sierra National Forest Minarets Ranger District at (209)877-2218.

Location: From North Fork (south of Bass Lake), drive 4.5 miles north on Mallum Ridge Road (Road 274). Turn right onto Central Camp Road (a narrow, winding road) and drive 11.5 miles to the campground

Trip note: The masses are not exactly beating a hot trail to this camp. It's a little spot, set along a little creek for campers who will have no trouble taking their pick of the campsites here. It is set at 5,800 feet in the Sierra National Forest, with Bass Lake about 15 miles away. Open from May to November.

Map grid b5

SODA SPRINGS
on Chiquito Creek
SIERRA NATIONAL FOREST

Campsites, facilities: There are 18 campsites for tents or motor homes up to 22 feet

A B C D E F4 G H I J

long. Fireplaces and picnic tables are provided. Vault toilets are available. There is **no piped water,** so bring your own. Pets are permitted on leashes. A grocery store and a boat ramp are nearby.

Reservations, fee: No reservations, no fee.

Who to contact: Phone the Sierra National Forest Minarets Ranger District at (209)877-2218.

Location: From the town of North Fork (south of Bass Lake), drive east and south on Mammoth Pool Road (County Road 225) to Minarets Road. Turn left (north) on Minarets Road (Road 4S81) and drive to the campground. The total distance from North Fork is about 37 miles on narrow, winding roads.

Trip note: This camp, one in a series on Chiquito Creek, is on the West Fork, about five miles from Mammoth Pool Reservoir and is used primarily as an overflow area if the more developed camps with piped water have filled up. The elevation is 4,400 feet. Open from April to November.

Map grid b6

MAMMOTH POOL

on Mammoth Pool Reservoir

SIERRA NATIONAL FOREST

Campsites, facilities: There are 18 sites for tents only, 29 sites for tents or motor homes up to 22 feet long, and five multi-family sites. Picnic tables and fireplaces are provided. Piped water and vault toilets are available. A grocery store and a boat ramp are nearby.

Reservations, fee: No reservations; $5 fee per night.

Who to contact: Phone the Sierra National Forest Minarets Ranger District at (209)877-2218.

Location: From the town of North Fork (south of Bass Lake), drive east and south on Mammoth Pool Road (County Road 225) to Minarets Road. Turn left (north) on Minarets Road (Road 4S81) and drive to the campground. The total distance from North Fork is about 42 miles on narrow, winding roads.

Trip note: You can plan on company here. Even though Mammoth Pool Reservoir is not widely known, those that know of it, like it. They'll be your neighbors, since the camp fills quickly on the weekends. Trout fishing can be good in the spring and early summer, with water skiing dominant during warm weather. Get this: Lake use is restricted from May 1 to June 15 due to deer migrating across it—that's right, swimming—but the campgrounds here are still open. Open May to November.

Map grid b6

PLACER

near Mammoth Pool Reservoir

SIERRA NATIONAL FOREST

Campsites, facilities: There are seven tent sites. Picnic tables are provided. Piped water and vault toilets are available. Pets are permitted on leashes.

Reservations, fee: No reservations; $3 fee per night.

Who to contact: Phone the Sierra National Forest Minarets Ranger District at (209)877-2218.

Location: From the town of North Fork (south of Bass Lake), drive east and south on Mammoth Pool Road (County Road 225) to Minarets Road. Turn left (north) on Minarets Road (Road 4S81) and drive to the campground. The total distance from North Fork is about 39 miles on narrow, winding roads.

Trip note: This little camp is located just three miles from Mammoth Pool Reservoir. With piped water and a pretty setting along Chiquito Creek, it is one of the better campgrounds that is used as an overflow area for Mammoth Pool visitors. The elevation is 4,100 feet. Open from April to November.

A

Map grid **b6**

SWEETWATER
near Mammoth Pool Reservoir
SIERRA NATIONAL FOREST

B

Campsites, facilities: There are five sites for tents only and five sites for tents or motor homes up to 16 feet long. Picnic tables and fireplaces are provided. Vault toilets are available. There is **no piped water,** so bring your own. Pets are permitted on leashes. A grocery store and a boat ramp are nearby.

Reservations, fee: No reservations, no fee.

Who to contact: Phone the Sierra National Forest Minarets Ranger District at (209)877-2218.

C

Location: From the town of North Fork (south of Bass Lake), drive east and south on Mammoth Pool Road (County Road 225) to Minarets Road. Turn left (north) on Minarets Road (Road 4S81) and drive to the campground. The total distance from North Fork is about 41 miles on narrow, winding roads.

D

Trip note: It's small and primitive, but if the camp at Mammoth Pool Reservoir is filled up, this spot provides an alternative. It is set on Chiquito Creek, just a mile from the lake. The elevation is 3,800 feet. Open from May to November.

Map grid **b8**

SAMPLE MEADOWS
on Kaiser Creek
SIERRA NATIONAL FOREST

5% CLUB

E

Campsites, facilities: There are 16 campsites for tents or small motor homes. Fireplaces and picnic tables are provided. Vault toilets are available. There is **no piped water,** so bring your own. Pets are permitted on leashes.

F4

Reservations, fee: No reservations, no fee.

Who to contact: Phone the Sierra National Forest Pine Ridge Ranger District at (209)841-3311.

Location: From the town of Shaver Lake, drive 21 miles north on Highway 168 to the town of Lakeshore. From Lakeshore, turn northeast on Kaiser Pass Road (Forest Service Road 4S01) and drive for nine miles. Turn north onto the entrance road (dirt) and drive five miles to the campground.

G

Trip note: This is a pretty, secluded spot set at 7,800 feet elevation along Kaiser Creek, with nearby trailheads available for backpackers. One trail accesses several lakes in the Kaiser Wilderness and another heads north and follows Kaiser Creek all the way to Mammoth Pool Reservoir (about 13 miles). West Kaiser campground is just off that trail near the confluence of West Kaiser Creek and Kaiser Creek. Open from June to October.

H

Map grid **b9**

PORTAL FOREBAY
on Forebay Lake
SIERRA NATIONAL FOREST

I

Campsites, facilities: There are nine campsites for tents or small motor homes. Picnic tables and fireplaces are provided. Vault toilets are available. There is **no piped water** is available. Pets are permitted on leashes.

Reservations, fee: No reservations, no fee.

J

Who to contact: Phone the Sierra National Forest Pine Ridge Ranger District at (209)841-3311.

Location: From the town of Shaver Lake, drive 21 miles north on Highway 168 to the town of Lakeshore. From Lakeshore, drive northeast on Kaiser Pass Road (Forest Service Road 4S01) for about 13.5 miles to the campground entrance.

Trip note: This small, primitive camp set along the shore of Forebay Lake at 7,200 feet elevation is a good jump-off spot for hikers. Trails lead into the surrounding backcountry, including Edison Lake. Open from June to October.

Map grid C3

SMALLEY COVE

on Kerckhoff Reservoir near Madera

Campsites, facilities: There are five campsites for tents or motor homes. Piped water, fireplaces, picnic tables, and vault toilets are provided. Pets are permitted. Supplies can be purchased in Auberry.

Reservations, fee: No reservations; $8 fee per night.

Who to contact: Phone PG&E at (209)263-5234.

Location: From Highway 99 in Madera, drive 19 miles east on Highway 145. Turn right (south) on Road 206 to the town of Friant. From Friant, drive 19 miles northeast on Millerton Road and Auberry Road to Auberry. From Auberry, drive 8.5 miles north on Powerhouse Road to the campground.

Trip note: If you really want to get away from it all, this campground is a bit further than Squaw Leap camp. Yet it is not quite as primitive since it does have piped water. There's access to the San Joaquin River for fishing. Open year-round.

Map grid C6

ROCK CREEK

SIERRA NATIONAL FOREST

Campsites, facilities: There are 18 campsites for tents or motor homes up to 32 feet long. Fireplaces and picnic tables are provided. Piped water and vault toilets are available. Pets are permitted on leashes.

Reservations, fee: No reservations; $5 fee per night.

Who to contact: Phone the Sierra National Forest Minarets Ranger District at (209)877-2218.

Location: From the town of North Fork (south of Bass Lake), drive east and south on Mammoth Pool Road (County Road 225) to Minarets Road. Turn left (north) on Minarets Road (Road 4S81) and drive to the campground. (Total distance from North Fork is about 27 miles.)

Trip note: Piped water is the big bonus here. It's a heck of a lot easier to live with than the no-water situation at the Fish Creek camp. It is also why this camp tends to fill up on weekends. A trail out of camp leads southeast for one mile and then connects with a trail that goes to Mammoth Pool Reservoir, five miles north. There is another campground at Mammoth Pool (but you can drive there). The elevation is 4,300 feet. Open from April to November.

Map grid C6

FISH CREEK

SIERRA NATIONAL FOREST

Campsites, facilities: There are seven sites for tents only and four sites for tents or motor homes up to 16 feet long. Picnic tables and vault toilets are available. There is **no piped water.** Pets are permitted on leashes.

Reservations, fee: No reservations, no fee.

Who to contact: Phone the Sierra National Forest Minarets Ranger District at (209)877-2218.

Location: From the town of North Fork (south of Bass Lake), drive east and south on Mammoth Pool Road (County Road 225) to Minarets Road. Turn left (north) on Minarets Road (Road 4S81) and drive to the campground. (Total distance from North Fork is about 23 miles.)

A

Trip note: This small, primitive camp isn't difficult to reach, yet is overlooked by many folks heading to Mammoth Pool Reservoir. It is set along Fish Creek at 4,600 feet elevation in the Sierra National Forest. A trail near the camp leads to Mammoth Pool, six miles north, where there are two popular campgrounds. Of course, you could also drive there. Open from April to November.

B

Map grid c7

BILLY CREEK

on Huntington Lake
SIERRA NATIONAL FOREST

Campsites, facilities: There are 20 sites for tents only and 24 sites for tents or motor homes up to 22 feet long. Picnic tables, fireplaces, and piped water are provided. Vault toilets are available. Pets are permitted on leashes. A small grocery store is nearby.

C

Reservations, fee: Reserve through MISTIX at (800)283-CAMP ($6 MISTIX fee); $10 fee per night.

D

Who to contact: Phone the Sierra National Forest Pine Ridge Ranger District at (209)841-3311.

Location: From the town of Shaver Lake, drive 21 miles north on Highway 168 to the town of Lakeshore. Turn left on County Road M2710 and drive about five miles west to the campground.

E

Trip note: With a half dozen camps available at Huntington Lake, vacationers can usually find a campsite to their liking. And if you don't like the company, just keep looking. The elevation is 7,000 feet. Open from June to October.

Map grid c8

CATAVEE

on Huntington Lake
SIERRA NATIONAL FOREST

F4

Campsites, facilities: There are 16 sites for tents only and 11 sites for tents or motor homes up to 22 feet long. Picnic tables, fireplaces, and piped water are provided. Vault toilets are available. Pets are permitted on leashes. Horseback riding facilities, a laundromat, and a small grocery store are nearby.

G

Reservations, fee: Reserve through MISTIX at (800)283-CAMP ($6 MISTIX fee); $10 fee per night.

Who to contact: Phone the Sierra National Forest Pine Ridge Ranger District at (209)841-3311.

H

Location: From the town of Shaver Lake, drive 21 miles north on Highway 168 to the town of Lakeshore. Turn left (west) on County Road M2710 and drive one-half mile to the campground.

Trip note: This is one of the several camps set on the shore of Huntington Lake, a scenic, high country lake at 7,200 feet elevation, where you can enjoy fishing, hiking, and sailing. Sailboat regattas take place regularly during the summer. Nearby resorts offer boat rentals and guest docks. Tackle rentals and bait are also available. A trailhead near camp accesses the Kaiser Wilderness. Open from June through October.

I

Map grid c8

BADGER FLAT GROUP CAMP

on Rancheria Creek
SIERRA NATIONAL FOREST

J

Campsites, facilities: This campground will accommodate groups of up to 100 people in tents or motor homes up to 22 feet long. Fireplaces and picnic tables are provided. Vault toilets and horseback riding facilities are available. **No piped water** is available so bring your own. Pets are permitted on leashes. A grocery store is nearby.

Reservations, fee: Reserve through MISTIX at (800)283-CAMP ($6 MISTIX fee); $100 fee per night per group.

Who to contact: Phone the Sierra National Forest Pine Ridge Ranger District at (209)841-3311, or (209)893-2111.

Location: From the town of Shaver Lake, drive 21 miles north on Highway 168 to the town of Lakeshore. From Lakeshore, turn northeast on Kaiser Pass Road (Forest Service Road 4S01) and drive for six miles to the campground.

Trip note: Badger Flat is a nearby option to other camps in the area. It's a primitive site along Rancheria Creek at 8,200 feet elevation. A trail that passes through camp serves the Kaiser Wilderness to the north and Dinkey Lakes Wilderness to the south. Open from June through October.

Map grid c8

RANCHERIA

near Huntington Lake

SIERRA NATIONAL FOREST

Campsites, facilities: There are 89 sites for tents only and 70 sites for tents or motor homes up to 22 feet long. Picnic tables, fireplaces, and piped water are provided. Vault toilets are available. Pets are permitted on leashes. A grocery store and propane gas are available nearby.

Reservations, fee: Reserve through MISTIX at (800)283-CAMP ($6 MISTIX fee); $10 fee per night.

Who to contact: Phone the Sierra National Forest Pine Ridge Ranger District at (209)841-3311.

Location: From the town of Shaver Lake, drive 20 miles north on Highway 168 toward the town of Lakeshore.

Trip note: This is the granddaddy of the camps at Huntington Lake, and some say the best in the area. One reason is the nearby Rancheria Falls National Recreation Trail, which provides access to beautiful Rancheria Falls. The elevation is 7,100 feet elevation. Open year-round.

Map grid c8

BADGER FLAT

on Rancheria Creek

SIERRA NATIONAL FOREST

Campsites, facilities: There are ten campsites for tents or motor homes up to 22 feet long. Fireplaces and picnic tables are provided. Vault toilets and horseback riding facilities are available. **No piped water** is available, so bring your own. Pets are permitted on leashes.

Reservations, fee: No reservations, no fee.

Who to contact: Phone the Sierra National Forest Pine Ridge Ranger District at (209)841-3311.

Location: From the town of Shaver Lake, drive 21 miles north on Highway 168 to the town of Lakeshore. From Lakeshore, turn northeast on Kaiser Pass Road (Forest Service Road 4S01) and drive for seven miles to the campground.

Trip note: This camp is a good launching pad for backpackers. It is set at 8,200 feet elevation along Rancheria Creek. The trail leading out of the camp is routed into the Kaiser Wilderness to the north and Dinkey Lakes Wilderness to the south. Open from June to October.

Map grid **c8**

KINNIKINNICK
on Huntington Lake
SIERRA NATIONAL FOREST

Campsites, facilities: There are 16 sites for tents only and 16 sites for tents or motor homes up to 22 feet long. Picnic tables, fireplaces, and piped water are provided. Vault toilets and horseback riding facilities are available. Pets are permitted on leashes. A grocery store is available nearby.

Reservations, fee: Reserve through MISTIX at (800)283-CAMP ($6 MISTIX fee); $10 fee per night.

Who to contact: Phone the Sierra National Forest Pine Ridge Ranger District at (209)841-3311.

Location: From the town of Shaver Lake, drive 21 miles north on Highway 168 to the town of Lakeshore. Turn left (west) on County Road M2710 and drive one-half mile to the campground.

Trip note: Flip a coin; there are a half-dozen camps at Huntington Lake. The elevation is 7,000. Open from June to October.

Map grid **c8**

DEER CREEK
on Huntington Lake
SIERRA NATIONAL FOREST

Campsites, facilities: There are 15 sites for tents only and 14 sites for tents or motor homes up to 22 feet long. Picnic tables, fireplaces and piped water are provided. Vault toilets and horseback riding facilities are available. Pets are permitted on leashes. A grocery store, and propane gas are nearby.

Reservations, fee: Reserve through MISTIX at (800)283-CAMP ($6 MISTIX fee); $10 fee per night.

Who to contact: Phone the Sierra National Forest Pine Ridge Ranger District at (209)841-3311.

Location: From the town of Shaver Lake, drive 21 miles north on Highway 168 to the town of Lakeshore. Turn left (west) on County Road M2710 and drive one-half mile to the campground.

Trip note: This is another in the series of camps at Huntington Lake, a pretty mountain lake set at 7,000 feet elevation. It's a popular vacation destination for hunkering down for a while or strapping on a backpack and taking off on the nearby trail routed into the Kaiser Wilderness. Open from June to October.

Map grid **c8**

COLLEGE
on Huntington Lake
SIERRA NATIONAL FOREST

Campsites, facilities: There are 11 campsites for tents or motor homes up to 22 feet long. Piped water, fireplaces, and picnic tables are provided. Vault toilets are available. Pets are permitted on leashes. Horseback riding facilities, grocery store and propane gas are available nearby.

Reservations, fee: Reserve through MISTIX at (800)283-CAMP ($6 MISTIX fee); $10 fee per night.

Who to contact: Phone the Sierra National Forest Pine Ridge Ranger District at (209)841-3311.

Location: From the town of Shaver Lake, drive 21 miles north on Highway 168 to the town of Lakeshore. Turn left (west) on County Road M2710 and drive one-half mile to the campground.

Trip note: This is a take-your-pick deal, one of six camps along the north shore of Huntington Lake. The elevation is 7,000. Open from June to October.

Map grid c9

BOLSILLO

on Bolsillo Creek

SIERRA NATIONAL FOREST

Campsites, facilities: There are four tent sites. Piped water, picnic tables, and fireplaces are provided. Vault toilets are available. Pets are permitted on leashes. Supplies can be purchased in Mono Hot Springs.

Reservations, fee: No reservations, no fee.

Who to contact: Phone the Sierra National Forest Pine Ridge Ranger District at (209)841-3311.

Location: From the town of Shaver Lake, drive 21 miles north on Highway 168 to the town of Lakeshore. From Lakeshore, turn northeast on Kaiser Pass Road (Forest Service Road 4S01) and drive for 15 miles to the campground entrance on the right.

Trip note: This is a tiny, virtually unknown camp, yet there are several bonuses, including piped water. It is set at 7,400 feet along Bolsillo Creek. Side trip options include a hike on a trail that passes through the camp and goes north for two miles to Mono Hot Springs and south for 2.5 miles to Corbett Lake. Open from June to October.

Map grid d1

MILLERTON LAKE STATE RECREATION AREA

near Madera

Campsites, facilities: There are 131 sites for tents or motor homes up to 31 feet long, and two group sites available. Fireplaces and picnic tables are provided. Piped water, showers, flush toilets, sanitary disposal station and boat ramps are available. Some facilities are wheelchair accessible. Pets are permitted on leashes. Supplies can be purchased in Friant.

Reservations, fee: From March 10 through September 10, reserve through MISTIX at (800)444-PARK ($3.95 MISTIX fee); $12-$14 fee per night; pets $1.

Who to contact: Phone (209)822-2332.

Location: From Highway 99 in Madera, drive 22 miles east on Highway 145 (six miles past intersection with Highway 41) to the campground.

Trip note: As the temperature gauge goes up in the summer, the value of Millerton Lake increases at the same rate. A beach area is available at the day-use park across the lake from the campground. By mid-summer, waterskiers take over the lake. Fishing can be good in spring, but by fall, the water level has usually dropped quite a bit in the attempt to quench the unsatiable thirst of valley farms. A good side trip is to take the trail from camp to a lookout over the lake. Open year-round.

Map grid d3

SQUAW LEAP

on San Joaquin River near Madera

Campsites, facilities: There are five family campsites and two group campsites for tents. All are walk-in sites. Fireplaces and picnic tables are provided. Vault toilets and a hitching post are available. There is **no piped water,** so bring your own. Pets are permitted. Supplies can be purchased in Auberry.

Reservations, fee: No reservations, no fee.

Who to contact: Phone the Bureau of Land Management, Hollister Resource Area at (408)637-8183.

Location: From State Highway 99 in Madera, drive 19 miles east on Highway 145. Turn right (south) on Road 206 to the town of Friant. From Friant, drive 19 miles northeast on Millerton Road and Auberry Road to Auberry. From Auberry, drive two miles north on Powerhouse Road. Turn left at the Squaw Leap Management Area sign at Smalley Road. Drive four miles to the campground.

Trip note: Not many folks know about this spot. It's a primitive setting, but it has some bonuses. For one thing, there's access to the San Joaquin River if you drive to the fishing access trailhead at the end of the road. For another, there is a three-quarter mile trail from the camp to the river. Open year-round.

Map grid d6

SWANSON MEADOW

near Shaver Lake

SIERRA NATIONAL FOREST

Campsites, facilities: There are nine campsites for tents or motor homes up to 22 feet long. Fireplaces and picnic tables are provided. Vault toilets are available. There is **no piped water** at this site, so bring your own. Pets are permitted on leashes. A grocery store is nearby.

Reservations, fee: No reservations, no fee.

Who to contact: Phone the Sierra National Forest Pine Ridge Ranger District at (209)841-3311.

Location: From Highway 168 just south of the town of Shaver Lake, drive three miles east on Dinkey Creek Road.

Trip note: This smallest and most primitive of the camps near Shaver Lake is used primarily as an overflow area if lakeside camps are full. It is located about two miles from the Shaver Lake. The elevation is 5,400 feet. Open from May to November.

Map grid d6

DORABELLE

on Shaver Lake

SIERRA NATIONAL FOREST

Campsites, facilities: There are 20 sites for tents only, 33 motor home spaces, and 15 sites for tents or motor homes up to 22 feet long. Picnic tables, fireplaces, and piped water are provided. Vault toilets are available. Pets are permitted on leashes. A grocery store is nearby.

Reservations, fee: Reserve through MISTIX at (800)283-CAMP ($6 MISTIX fee); $8 fee per night.

Who to contact: Phone the Sierra National Forest Pine Ridge Ranger District at (209)841-3311.

Location: From Highway 168 south of the town of Shaver Lake, turn east onto County Road N257 and drive one-half mile to the campground.

Trip note: This is one of the few Forest Service camps in the state that is set up more for motor homes than for tenters. It's a popular lake for vacationers and well stocked with trout during summer months. Boat rentals and bait and tackle are available at the nearby marina. This is also a popular snow-play area in the winter. The elevation is 5,400 feet. Open from May to November.

Map grid **d6**

CAMP EDISON
on Shaver Lake

Campsites, facilities: There are 252 campsites for tents or motor homes up to 22 feet long. Forty four of these sites are for full hookups. Piped water, electrical connections, fireplaces, and picnic tables are provided. Flush toilets, showers, a sanitary disposal station, cable T.V., a laundromat, and a boat ramp are available. Pets are permitted on leashes. Some facilities are wheelchair accessible.

Reservations, fee: Call for available space; $14-$22 fee per night.

Who to contact: Phone the park at (209)841-3444.

Location: From the town of Shaver Lake, drive one mile north on Highway 168 to the campground entrance road.

Trip note: Here is a series of camps along popular Shaver Lake. Boat rentals and bait and tackle are available at the nearby marina. You can expect company. The elevation is 5,400 feet. Open year-round with limited winter facilities.

Map grid **e7**

BRETZ
on Big Creek
SIERRA NATIONAL FOREST

Campsites, facilities: There are ten campsites for tents or motor homes up to 22 feet long. Picnic tables and fireplaces are provided. Vault toilets are available. There is **no piped water,** so bring your own. Pets are permitted on leashes.

Reservations, fee: No reservations, no fee.

Who to contact: Phone the Sierra National Forest Kings River Ranger District at (209)855-8321.

Location: From Trimmer, drive nine miles east on Trimmer Springs Road. Turn north on Big Creek Road and drive 15 miles to the campground.

Trip note: This is a small, little-known Forest Service camp set along Big Creek at 3,300 feet elevation. You can't beat the price. Open from May to November.

Map grid **e8**

BUCK MEADOW
on Dear Creek
SIERRA NATIONAL FOREST

Campsites, facilities: There are ten campsites for tents or motor homes up to 22 feet long. Picnic tables and vault toilets are available. There is **no piped water,** so bring your own. Pets are permitted on leashes.

Reservations, fee: No reservations, no fee.

Who to contact: Phone the Sierra National Forest Kings River Ranger District at (209)855-8321.

Location: From Highway 168 just south of Shaver Lake, turn east on Dinkey Creek Road and drive about 12 miles. Turn right on McKinley Grove Road and drive eight miles to the campground.

Trip note: This is one of the three little-known, primitive camps in the area. This one is set at 6,800 feet elevation along Deer Creek. It's about seven miles from Wishon Reservoir, a more popular destination. Open from May to October.

Map grid **e8**

GIGANTEA

on Dinkey Creek
SIERRA NATIONAL FOREST

Campsites, facilities: There are 11 campsites for tents or motor homes up to 16 feet long. Picnic tables are provided. Vault toilets are available. There is **no piped water** at this site. Pets are permitted on leashes. Supplies can be purchased in Dinkey Creek.

Reservations, fee: No reservations, no fee.

Who to contact: Phone the Sierra National Forest Kings River Ranger District at (209)855-8321.

Location: From Highway 168 just south of Shaver Lake, turn east on Dinkey Creek Road and drive about 12 miles. Turn right on McKinley Grove Road and drive six miles to the campground.

Trip note: Backpackers use this primitive camp along Dinkey Creek as a mountain access point. A trail passes through camp that follows the creek south for many miles and going north, follows Dinkey Creek up to the town of Dinkey Creek, where convenience and horseback riding facilities can be found. The elevation is 6,500 feet. Open from May to October.

Map grid **e8**

DINKEY CREEK

SIERRA NATIONAL FOREST

Campsites, facilities: There are 136 campsites for tents or motor homes up to 22 feet long. Piped water, fireplaces, and picnic tables are provided. Flush toilets and horseback riding facilities are available. Pets are permitted on leashes. Supplies can be purchased in Dinkey Creek.

Reservations, fee: From Memorial Day through Labor Day, reserve through MISTIX at (800)283-CAMP ($6 MISTIX fee); $6 fee per night.

Who to contact: Phone the Sierra National Forest Kings River Ranger District at (209)855-8321.

Location: From Highway 168 just south of the town of Shaver Lake, turn east on Dinkey Creek Road and drive 14 miles to the campground.

Trip note: This is a huge Forest Service camp set along Dinkey Creek at 5,700 feet elevation. It serves both backpackers and folks who want to call it home for awhile. A trail passes through the camp that follows Dinkey Creek south for many miles. Taken north, the trail follows Dinkey Creek past Dinkey Dome up to Swamp Meadow, then along a dirt road for about 2.5 miles to a trailhead that leads to numerous lakes in the Dinkey Lakes Wilderness. Open from May to October.

Map grid **e9**

TRAPPER SPRINGS

on Courtright Reservoir
SIERRA NATIONAL FOREST

Campsites, facilities: There are 46 campsites for tents or motor homes up to 22 feet long. Piped water, fireplaces, and picnic tables are provided. Vault toilets are available. Pets are permitted on leashes. A boat ramp is nearby. This campground is wheelchair accessible.

Reservations, fee: No reservations; $8 fee per night.

Who to contact: Phone PG&E at (209)263-5234 or the Sierra National Forest Kings River Ranger District at (209)855-8321.

Location: From Highway 168 just south of the town of Shaver Lake, turn east onto

Dinkey Creek Road and drive 12 miles. Turn right (east)on McKinley Grove Road and drive 14 miles. Turn north onto Courtright Reservoir Road and drive 12 miles to the campground.

Trip note: This is one of the two camps on Courtright Lake, a pretty high mountain lake at 8,200 feet elevation.

Map grid **e9**

MARMOT ROCK

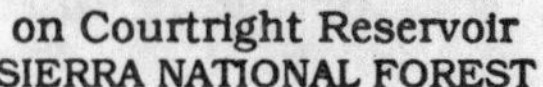

on Courtright Reservoir

SIERRA NATIONAL FOREST

Campsites, facilities: There are 11 sites for tents only and three campsites for tents or motor homes up to 22 feet long. Piped water, fireplaces, and picnic tables are provided. Vault toilets and a boat ramp are available. Pets are permitted on leashes.

Reservations, fee: No reservations; $8 fee per night.

Who to contact: Phone PG&E at (209)263-5234 or the Sierra National Forest Kings River Ranger District at (209)855-8321.

Location: From Highway 168 just south of the town of Shaver Lake, turn east onto Dinkey Creek Road and drive 12 miles. Turn right (east) on McKinley Grove Road and drive 14 miles. Turn north on Courtright Reservoir Road and drive ten miles to the campground on the south shore.

Trip note: Courtright Reservoir is in the high country at 8,200 feet. It is a pretty Sierra lake that provides options for boaters and hikers. Trout fishing can be good here. Boaters must observe a 15-mph speed limit, which makes for quiet water. Hikers should consider the trail on the western side of the lake, which is routed into the Dinkey Lakes Wilderness or the trail on the eastern side of the lake that heads into the John Muir Wilderness. Open from June to October.

Map grid **f5**

DEER CREEK POINT GROUP SITE

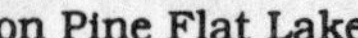

on Pine Flat Lake

Campsites, facilities: There are two group campsites (one for 20 people and one for 50 people) that will accommodate tents or motor homes. Piped water, fireplaces, and picnic tables and vault toilets are provided. Pets are permitted on leashes. Boat rentals are available within five miles of camp.

Reservations, fee: Reservations required; $25 per night per group.

Who to contact: Phone the U.S. Corps of Engineers at (209)787-2589.

Location: From Piedra, drive northeast on Trimmer Springs Road for eight miles. Turn right at the signed entrance road and drive one-half mile to campground.

Trip note: This is one of the better camps at Pine Flat Lake. The relative smallness, and the good location, are pluses. The best time to visit is in the spring when the lake levels are highest and the fishing for trout and bass is at its peak. When full, Pine Flat is 21 miles long and has 67 miles of shoreline, but it is subject to drawdowns in late summer when the water gets delivered for irrigation. The elevation is 1,000 feet. Open year-round.

Map grid **f5**

PINE FLAT RECREATION AREA

on Pine Flat Lake

Campsites, facilities: There are 52 campsites for tents or motor homes. Piped water, fireplaces, and picnic tables are provided. Flush toilets, a dump station, a playground, and a handicap fishing area are available. A grocery store, a laundromat, and propane gas are nearby.

Reservations, fee: No reservations; $9 fee per night.
Who to contact: Phone the park at (209)488-3004.
Location: In Piedra on Trimmer Springs Road, drive three miles on Pine Flat Road.
Trip note: This is a county park that is open all year and offers lakeside access to Pine Flat Lake. The lake can be subject to drawdowns due to irrigation demands, which makes spring the best time to visit. Hey, the fishing is best in the spring anyway, and by summer, waterskiers often monopolize the lake. There are several resorts on the lake that offer boat and ski rentals, bait, and tackle.

Map grid f5

ISLAND PARK
on Pine Flat Lake

Campsites, facilities: There are 52 designated campsites for tents or motor homes and 50 overflow sites with picnic tables available. Piped water, fireplaces, and picnic tables are provided at designated sites. Flush toilets, showers, a boat ramp, fish cleaning stations, and a dump station are available. Some facilities are wheelchair accessible. Pets are permitted on leashes. There is a store at the campground entrance. Boat rentals are available within five miles.
Reservations, fee: No reservations; $8 fee per night.
Who to contact: Phone the U.S. Corps of Engineers at (209)787-2589.
Location: From Piedra, drive east on Trimmer Springs Road for eight miles. Turn right at the signed entrance road and drive one-quarter mile to campground.
Trip note: This is one of the several campgrounds available at Pine Flat Lake, a popular lake set in the foothill country. The elevation is 1,000 feet.

Map grid f5

SUNNYSLOPE CAMPGROUNDS
near Pine Flat Lake

Campsites, facilities: There are 97 campsites for tents or motor homes. Piped water, electrical connections, and picnic tables are provided. Rest rooms, hot showers, a laundromat, a playground, a grocery store, ice, and propane gas are available. Boat rentals and marinas are available at Pine Flat Reservoir. Pets are permitted.
Reservations, fee: Reservations accepted; $12 fee per night.
Who to contact: Phone the park at (209)787-2730.
Location: From Piedra, drive three miles northeast on Trimmer Springs Road. Turn right onto Sunnyslope Road and drive 100 yards to the campground.
Trip note: This campground overlooks Pine Flat Lake, a pretty lake (when full of water) set in the foothill country. There are several resorts on the lake that offer boat and water ski rentals, bait, and tackle.

Map grid f6

SYCAMORE FLAT NO .2
on Pine Flat Lake
SIERRA NATIONAL FOREST

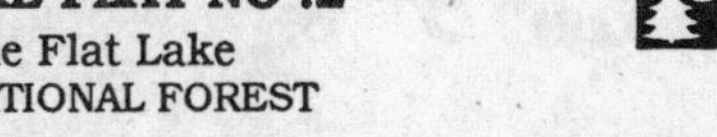

Campsites, facilities: There are 20 campsites for tents or motor homes up to 22 feet long. Fireplaces and picnic tables are provided. Vault toilets are available. There is **no piped water**, so bring your own. Pets are permitted on leashes.
Reservations, fee: No reservations, no fee.
Who to contact: Phone the Sierra National Forest Kings River Ranger District at (209)855-8321.
Location: From Trimmer, drive six miles east on Trimmer Springs Road.
Trip note: This is the other of the two large, primitive group camps on the northeast shore of Pine Flat Lake. Several other camps at Pine Flat Lake are available.

A B C D E F4 G H I J

Map grid **f6**

SYCAMORE FLAT NO .1

on Pine Flat Lake
SIERRA NATIONAL FOREST

Campsites, facilities: There is one group site that will accommodate up to 50 people with tents or motor homes up to 22 feet long. Fireplaces and picnic tables are provided. Vault toilets are available. Pets are permitted on leashes. There is **no piped water,** so bring your own.

Reservations, fee: Reservations required; call the Trimmer Ranger Station at (209)855-8321; no fee.

Who to contact: Phone the Sierra National Forest Kings River Ranger District at (209)855-8321.

Location: From Trimmer, drive five miles east on Trimmer Springs Road.

Trip note: This is a big group camp set on the northeast shore of Pine Flat Lake, a popular lake when it's full of water. Alas, it is subject to drawdowns in order to feed farms, which have an unquenchable thirst. The lake is best visited in the spring, when water levels are highest (creating 67 miles of shoreline) and fishing for bass and trout is at its peak. There are several resorts on the lake that offer boat, water ski rentals and bait, and tackle. Since this is set in the San Joaquin Valley's foothill country, the weather can get quite hot in the summer.

Map grid **f7**

KIRCH FLAT

on Kings River
SIERRA NATIONAL FOREST

Campsites, facilities: There are 25 campsites for tents or motor homes up to 22 feet long and one group camp that will accommodate up to 50 people. Fireplaces and picnic tables are provided. Vault toilets are available. There is **no piped water,** so bring your own. Pets are permitted on leashes.

Reservations, fee: No reservations, no fee for family camping; to reserve group site call Trimmer Ranger Station at (209)855-8321; group campground fee is $1 per person per night, 25 person minimum.

Who to contact: Phone the Sierra National Forest Kings River Ranger District at (209)855-8321.

Location: From Trimmer, drive 18 miles east on Trimmer Springs Road.

Trip note: In the summer, it can feel like you're camping on a branding iron. It is set in the foothill country and is adjacent to Kings River. Pine Flat Lake, six miles away, provides another option. The elevation is 1,100 feet.

Map grid **f8**

BLACK ROCK

on Black Rock Reservoir
SIERRA NATIONAL FOREST

Campsites, facilities: There are ten campsites for tents or motor homes up to 16 feet long. Piped water, fireplaces, and picnic tables are provided. Vault toilets are available. Pets are permitted on leashes.

Reservations, fee: No reservations; $8 fee per night.

Who to contact: Phone PG&E at (209)263-5238 or Sierra National Forest Kings River Ranger District at (209)855-8321.

Location: From Trimmer, drive east on Trimmer Springs Road for about 20 miles. Turn northwest onto Black Road and drive ten miles to the campground.

Trip note: This relatively little-known spot is set at Black Rock Reservoir on the North Fork of the Kings River. Exploring the Kings River Geological Area could be a possible side trip. The elevation is 4,200 feet. Open year-round; limited services in winter.

Map grid **f9**

LILY PAD

on Wishon Reservoir
SIERRA NATIONAL FOREST

Campsites, facilities: There are four sites for tents only and 11 campsites for tents or motor homes up to 16 feet long. Piped water, picnic tables, and fireplaces are provided. Vault toilets are available. Pets are permitted on leashes. Groceries, boat rentals, a boat ramp, and propane gas are available nearby. This campground is wheelchair accessible. There is also a group campsite available nearby called Upper Kings River; it will accommodate up to 50 people.

Reservations, fee: No reservations for single sites; $8 fee per night; reserve group site by phoning (209)263-5238; $75 group fee per night.

Who to contact: Phone PG&E at (209)263-5238 or the Sierra National Forest Kings River Ranger District at (209)855-8321.

Location: From Highway 168 south of the town of Shaver Lake, turn east onto Dinkey Creek Road and drive 12 miles. Turn right (east) on McKinley Grove Road and drive 16 miles to the campground.

Trip note: This is the smaller of the two camps at Wishon Reservoir. It is set along the southwest shore at 6,500 feet elevation.

Map grid **f9**

WISHON VILLAGE

on Wishon Reservoir

Campsites, facilities: There are 25 sites for tents only and 97 motor home spaces. Picnic tables, piped water, electrical connections, and sewer hookups are provided. Rest rooms, showers, a laundromat, a store, ice, a boat ramp, motorboat rentals, bait, tackle, and propane gas are available.

Reservations, fee: Reservations recommended; $17 fee per night.

Who to contact: Phone the park at (209)841-5361.

Location: From Highway 168 just south of the town of Shaver Lake, turn east onto Dinkey Creek Road and drive 12 miles. Turn right on McKinley Grove Road and drive 15 miles to 54890 McKinley Grove Road.

Trip note: This privately-operated mountain park is set on the north fork of the Kings River near the shore of Wishon Reservoir. Trout stocks often make for good fishing in early summer, but anglers with boats should heed the 15-mph speed limit. Backpackers should head to nearby Coolidge Meadow, where a trailhead awaits that is routed to the Woodchuck Creek drainage and numerous lakes in the John Muir Wilderness. The elevation is 6,500 feet. Open May to November.

Map grid **g8**

MILL FLAT

on Kings River
SEQUOIA NATIONAL FOREST

Campsites, facilities: There are five campsites for tents or motor homes up to 16 feet long. Picnic tables and fireplaces are provided. Vault toilets are available. No piped water is available, so bring your own. Pets are permitted on leashes.

Reservations, fee: No reservations, no fee.

Who to contact: Phone the Sequoia National Forest Headquarters at (209)784-1500, or the Hume Lake Ranger District at (209)338-2251.

Location: From Trimmer, drive about 17 miles east on Trimmer Springs Road

(Forest Service Road 11S12). Cross the river and drive one mile along the south side of the Kings River on Davis Road (Forest Service Road 12S01), parallel to the Keller Ranch. At the junction with the second bridge, turn right onto a dirt road and drive about 2.5 miles to the campground.

Trip note: This spot is on the Kings River at the confluence of Mill Flat Creek. It's a very small, primitive spot and very hot in the summer. It's set upstream from Pine Flat Lake. Open year-round.

Map grid **g8**

CAMP 4
on Kings River
SEQUOIA NATIONAL FOREST

Campsites, facilities: There are five campsites for tents or motor homes up to 16 feet long. Picnic tables and fireplaces are provided. Vault toilets are available. There is **no piped water,** so bring your own. Pets are permitted on leashes.

Reservations, fee: No reservations, no fee.

Who to contact: Phone the Sequoia National Forest Headquarters at (209)784-1500, or the Hume Lake Ranger District at (209)338-2251.

Location: From Trimmer, drive about 17 miles east on Trimmer Springs Road (Forest Service Road 11S12). Cross the river and drive one mile along the south side of the Kings River on Davis Road (Forest Service Road 12S01), parallel to the Keller Ranch. At the junction with the second bridge, turn right onto a dirt road and drive about 1.5 miles to the campground.

Trip note: This is one in the series of camps set on the Kings River, upstream from Pine Flat Lake. The weather gets hot, so bring a cooler. A map of the Sequoia National Forest details the backcountry roads. Open year-round.

Map grid **g8**

CAMP 4 & 1/2
on Kings River
SEQUOIA NATIONAL FOREST

Campsites, facilities: There are five campsites for tents or motor homes up to 16 feet long. Picnic tables and fireplaces are provided. Vault toilets are available. There is **no piped water,** so bring your own. Pets are permitted on leashes.

Reservations, fee: No reservations, no fee.

Who to contact: Phone the Sequoia National Forest Headquarters at (209)784-1500, or the Hume Lake Ranger District at (209)338-2251.

Location: From Trimmer, drive about 17 miles east on Trimmer Springs Road (Forest Service Road 11S12). Cross the river and drive one mile along the south side of the Kings River on Davis Road (Forest Service Road 12S01), parallel to the Keller Ranch. At the junction with the second bridge, turn right onto a dirt road and drive about three-quarters of a mile to the campground.

Trip note: We found five campsites here, not "4 and a half," though it's not easy to tell. It is one in the series of camps located just east of Pine Flat Lake along the Kings River. It's small, primitive, and usually hot. Open year-round.

Map grid **h9**

SUNSET
KINGS CANYON NATIONAL PARK

Campsites, facilities: There are 184 campsites for tents or motor homes up to 30 feet long. Piped water, fireplaces, and picnic tables are provided. Flush toilets, evening ranger programs, and horseback riding facilities are available. A grocery store and a laundromat are nearby. Showers are available in Grant Grove. Pets are permitted on leashes.

Reservations, fee: No reservations; $8 fee per night.
Who to contact: Phone the Kings Canyon National Park at (209)565-3341.
Location: From Wilsonia in Kings Canyon National Park, drive one-half mile north on Highway 180.
Trip note: This is the biggest of the camps that are located just inside the Kings Canyon National Park boundaries at Wilsonia. The Grant Grove of Giant Sequoias is the main attraction and close by. The elevation is 6,600 feet. Open May to October.

A B C D E F4 G H I J

Map grid **h9**

AZALEA

KINGS CANYON NATIONAL PARK

Campsites, facilities: There are 118 campsites for tents or motor homes up to 30 feet long. Piped water, fireplaces, and picnic tables are provided. Flush toilets, a dump station, evening ranger programs, and horseback riding facilities are available. The campgrounds and rest room facilities are wheelchair accessible. A grocery store and a laundromat are nearby. Showers are avaiable in Grant Grove. Pets are permitted on leashes.
Reservations, fee: No reservations; $8 fee per night.
Who to contact: Phone the Kings Canyon National Park at (209)565-3341.
Location: From Wilsonia in Kings Canyon National Park, drive three-quarters of a mile north on Highway 180.
Trip note: This camp is tucked just inside the western border of Kings Canyon National Park. It is set at 6,600 feet elevation near the Grant Grove of Giant Sequoias. Sequoia Lake is nearby, just west of the camp. There's a side trip to the north on Highway 180: re-enter the park at Cedar Grove, set near the spectacular canyon of Kings River, one of the deepest gorges in North America. Open year-round.

Map grid **h9**

CRYSTAL SPRINGS

KINGS CANYON NATIONAL PARK

Campsites, facilities: There are 67 campsites for tents or motor homes. Piped water, fireplaces, and picnic tables are provided. Flush toilets, a dump station, horseback riding facilities, and evening ranger programs are available. Showers are available in Grant Grove. Groceries and propane gas are nearby. Pets are permitted on leashes.
Reservations, fee: No reservations; $8 fee per night.
Who to contact: Phone the Kings Canyon National Park at (209)565-3341.
Location: From Wilsonia in Kings Canyon National Park, drive three-quarters of a mile north on Highway 180.
Trip note: Kings Canyon National Park has protected one of the deepest gorges in North America. This camp offers a pretty spot, which is set at 6,600 feet elevation. The giant Sequoias in the area are inspiring. As winter approaches, beware of bad road and snow conditions. Open from May to October.

Map grid **h9**

PRINCESS

on Indian Creek

SEQUOIA NATIONAL FOREST

Campsites, facilities: There are 50 tent sites and 40 sites for tents or motor homes up to 22 feet long. Picnic tables, fireplaces, and piped water are provided. Flush toilets and a dump station are available. Pets are permitted on leashes. A grocery store is nearby.

Reservations, fee: No reservations; $6 fee per night.
Who to contact: Phone the Sequoia National Forest Headquarters at (209)784-1500.
Location: From Wilsonia in Kings Canyon National Park, drive six miles north on Highway 180 to the campground entrance road.
Trip note: This mountain camp is set beside Indian Creek at 5,900 feet elevation. It is popular because of its close proximity to both Lake Hume and Kings Canyon National Park. Lake Hume is just four miles from the camp and the Grant Grove entrance to Kings Canyon National Park is only six miles away. Open from May to October.

Map grid i3

ROYAL OAK RESORT
on Kings River near Kingsburg

Campsites, facilities: There are 94 motor home spaces. Picnic tables, piped water, and full or partial hookups are provided. Rest rooms, showers, a laundromat, a recreation room, a store, a dump station, ice, firewood, boat gas, and propane gas are available.
Reservations, fee: Call for available space; $8-$12 fee per night.
Who to contact: Phone the park at (209)897-2441.
Location: From Highway 99 in Kingsburg, drive three miles east on Highway 201 to Road 28. Follow the signs to 39700 Road 28.
Trip note: Location, location, location. Nothing else really matters. For RV drivers, this place has a bonus, with the Kern River Park and the Kings River Golf Course nearby. It's 30 miles to Fresno, that hotbed of activity, and 55 miles to Sequoia National Park. Open year-round with all facilities provided from May through September.

Map grid i8

ESHOM
on Eshom Creek

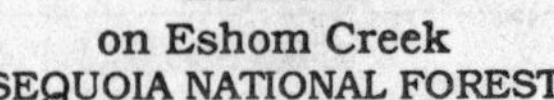

SEQUOIA NATIONAL FOREST

Campsites, facilities: There are 17 campsites for tents or motor homes up to 22 feet long. Piped water, picnic tables, and fireplaces are provided. Vault toilets are available. A grocery store is nearby. Pets are permitted on leashes.
Reservations, fee: No reservations; $3 fee per night; $6 fee per night for multi-family units.
Who to contact: Phone the Sequoia National Forest at (209)784-1500, and the Hume Lake Ranger District at (209)338-2251.
Location: From Highway 99, drive east on Highway 198 through Visalia to Highway 245. Turn left (north) on Highway 245 and drive to Badger. From Badger, drive eight miles northeast on Red Hill Road.
Trip note: With everybody heading to nearby Sequoia National Park, this is the kind of spot that is often overlooked. Or you can use it if that park is too crowded. It is set just two miles from park boundaries along Eshom Creek at 4,800 feet elevation. Open from May to November.

Map grid i8

SIERRA LAKES CAMPGROUND
near Visalia

Campsites, facilities: There are ten sites for tents only and 25 motor home spaces. Picnic tables, fireplaces, piped water, electrical connections (in most cases), and sewer hookups are provided. Rest rooms, showers, a laundromat, a store, a dump station, and propane gas, and a full service restaurant are available.

Reservations, fee: Call ahead for available space and fee.
Who to contact: Phone the park at (209)337-2520.
Location: From Highway 99, drive east on Highway 198 through Visalia to Lemon Cove. Turn left on Highway 216 and go one-half mile. Turn right (north) on County Road J21 and drive 16 miles to Mountain Road 453 (Stagecoach Road). Turn right and drive 1.5 miles to the campground.
Trip note: This secluded, privately-managed, 106-acre park offers a ten-acre lake stocked with trout. The park is about a 30-minute drive from Kings Canyon and Sequoia National Parks and has three restaurants within three miles of the camp. Open year-round.

◆ MAP F5 ◆

BEACH
DESERT
FOOTHILL
TREES
URBAN
GRASSLAND
5% CLUB

15 MILES

to Mammoth Lakes
to Benton
Tom's Place
Sherwin Summit EL. 7,000
White Mtn. Pk. EL. 14,246
6
INYO
SIERRA
Lake Thomas Edison
Mt. Morgan EL. 12,748
395
Mono Hot Springs
to Lake Shore
Rovana
S. Fork of the San Joaquin River
Florence Lake
Laws
Bishop
168
INYO
to Oasis
NAT'L.
Lake Sabrina
Black Mtn. EL. 9,083
Courtright Res.
South Lake
168
KINGS
Big Pine
NAT'L.
Glacier Lodge
Whishon Reservoir
395
Palisade Glacier
CANYON
Tinemaha Reservoir
Burnt Mtn. EL. 10,608
Aberdeen
NAT'L.
NAT'L.
FOREST
180
Hume Lake
Cedar Grove
Hume
to Wilsonia
FOREST
PARK
Independence
Palmer Mtn. EL. 11,250
Jct. Pk. EL. 13,888
198
395
Alta Pk. EL. 11,204
Barton Pk. EL. 10,350
FOREST
SEQUOIA
Giant Forest Village
Owenyo
Generals Highway EL. 6,000
NAT'L.
Highest Pt. Mt. Whitney EL. 14,494
Whitney-Portal Road Summit EL. 8,371
Lone Pine
PARK
to Three Rivers
to Cartago

a
b
c
d
e
f
g
h
i
j

0 1 2 3 4 5 6 7 8 9

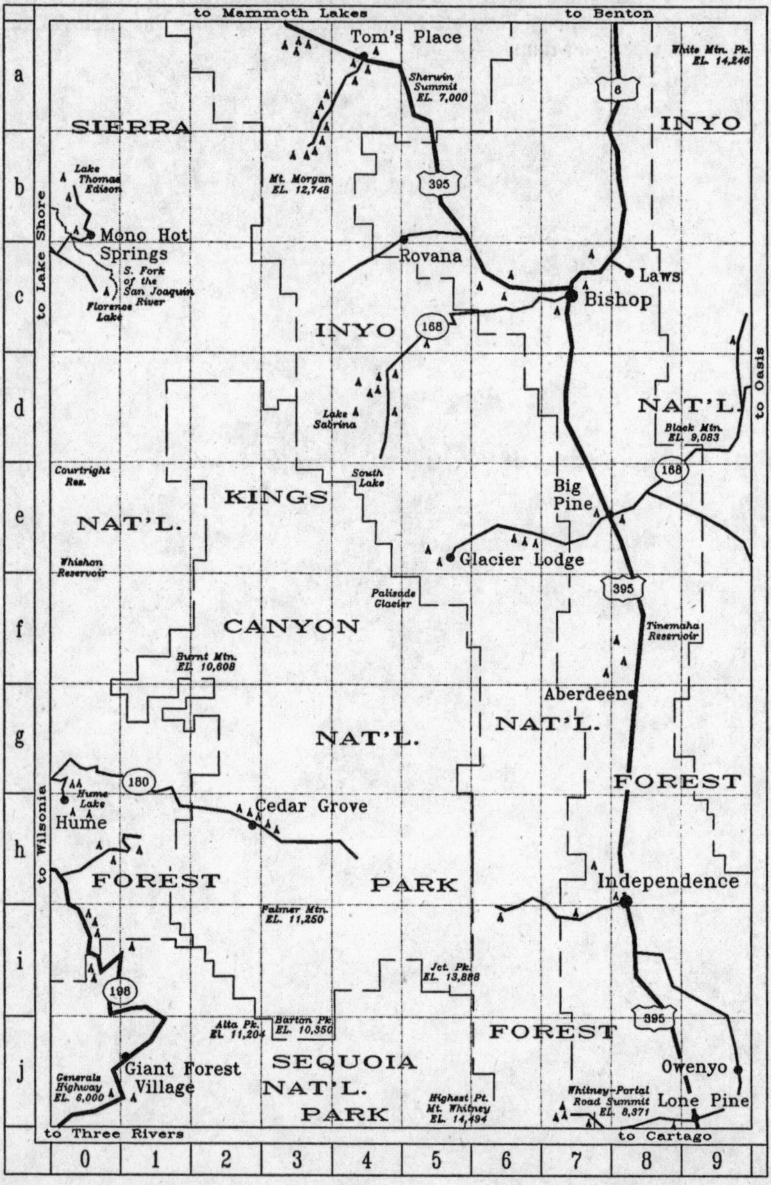

Map grid **a3**

IRIS MEADOWS

near Lake Crowley
INYO NATIONAL FOREST

A

Campsites, facilities: There are 14 campsites for tents or motor homes up to 22 feet long. Piped water, fireplaces, and picnic tables are provided. Flush toilets are available. Supplies can be purchased in Tom's Place. Pets are permitted on leashes.

B

Reservations, fee: No reservations; $7 fee per night.

Who to contact: Phone the Inyo National Forest District Office at (619)873-4207.

Location: From the junction of US 395 and Highway 203 (the Mammoth Lakes turnoff), drive 15 miles south on US 395 to Tom's Place. Turn south on Rock Creek Road and drive three miles to the campground.

C

Trip note: This Forest Service camp, at the base of Reds Mountain, is another in the series of camps on Rock Creek. It is a popular layover area for campers visiting Lake Crowley. The elevation is 8,100 feet. Open from May to October.

D

Map grid **a3**

McGEE CREEK RV PARK

near Lake Crowley
INYO NATIONAL FOREST

Campsites, facilities: There are 35 campsites for tents or motor homes, many with partial or full hookups. Piped water, fireplaces, and picnic tables are provided. Flush toilets and hot showers are available.

E

Reservations, fee: Reservations accepted; $11-$13 fee per night.

Who to contact: Phone the park at (619)935-4233.

Location: From the junction of US 395 and Highway 203 (the Mammoth Lakes turn off), drive south on US 395 for 6.5 miles to a turnoff to the frontage road that runs along the west side of US 395 and parallel to it. Continue south on that road for about 1.5 miles to McGee Creek Road. Turn onto McGee Creek Road and you'll see the park entrance.

F5

Trip note: This is a popular layover spot for folks visiting giant Lake Crowley. Lake Crowley once offered outstanding trout fishing, but as we've approached the 1990s, it's been closer to "fair to good." That means there are days where you need a Jaws of Life to get a trout to open its mouth. Convict Lake provides a nearby side trip option. The elevation is 7,000 feet. Open April to October.

G

Map grid **a3**

McGEE CREEK

INYO NATIONAL FOREST

H

Campsites, facilities: There are 28 campsites for tents or motor homes up to 22 feet long. Piped water, fireplaces, and picnic tables are provided. Flush toilets are available. Pets are permitted on leashes.

Reservations, fee: Reserve through MISTIX (800)283-CAMP ($6 MISTIX fee); $7 fee per night.

I

Who to contact: Phone the Inyo National Forest District Office at (619)873-4207.

Location: From the junction of US 395 and Highway 203 (the Mammoth Lakes turn off), drive south on US 395 for 6.5 miles to a turn off for the frontage road that runs along the west side of US 395 and parallel to it. Continue south for about two miles to McGee Creek Road. Turn right (southwest) and drive 1.5 miles to the campground.

J

Trip note: This Forest Service camp, set along little McGee Creek, is often used as a base camp for backpackers. A trailhead is available up the road that provides access along McGee Creek and is routed to the John Muir Wilderness. The elevation is 7,600 feet. Open from May through October.

Map grid **a3**

LAKE CROWLEY

Campsites, facilities: There are 47 campsites for tents or motor homes. Piped water, fireplaces, and picnic tables are provided. Pit toilets and a sanitary disposal station are available. A grocery store and a boat ramp are nearby on Lake Crowley.

Reservations, fee: No reservations; $4 fee per night.

Who to contact: Phone the Bureau of Land Management Bishop Resource Area at (619)872-4881.

Location: From the junction of US 395 and Highway 203 (the Mammoth Lakes turnoff), drive 15 miles south on US 395 to Tom's Place. Turn north on Crowley Lake Drive and drive 5.5 miles to the campground.

Trip note: This large BLM-managed camp is across US 395 from the south shore of Lake Crowley. Crowley, once the capital of trout fishing in the eastern Sierra, has lost some of its luster in recent years, and many anglers are fishing smaller mountain lakes instead. The elevation is 7,000 feet. Open from May to October.

Map grid **a3**

BIG MEADOW

near Lake Crowley
INYO NATIONAL FOREST

Campsites, facilities: There are five sites for tents only and six sites for tents or motor homes up to 22 feet long. Picnic tables, fireplaces, and piped water are provided. Flush toilets are available. Supplies can be purchased in Tom's Place. Pets are permitted on leashes.

Reservations, fee: No reservations; $7 fee per night.

Who to contact: Phone the Inyo National Forest District Office at (619)873-4207.

Location: From the junction of US 395 and Highway 203 (the Mammoth Lakes turnoff), drive 15 miles south on US 395 to Tom's Place. Turn south on Rock Creek Road and drive four miles to the campground.

Trip note: This is a smaller, quieter camp in the series of camps that are set along Rock Creek. Nearby giant Lake Crowley and tiny Rock Creek Lake provide side trips. The elevation is 8,600 feet. Open from May to October.

Map grid **a3**

PALISADE

near Lake Crowley
INYO NATIONAL FOREST

Campsites, facilities: There are two sites for tents only and three sites for tents or motor homes up to 22 feet long. Picnic tables, fireplaces, and piped water are provided. Flush toilets and horseback riding facilities are available. Supplies can be purchased in Tom's Place. Pets are permitted on leashes.

Reservations, fee: No reservations; $7 fee per night.

Who to contact: Phone the Inyo National Forest District Office at (619)873-4207.

Location: From the junction of US 395 and Highway 203 (the Mammoth Lakes turnoff), drive 15 miles south on US 395 to Tom's Place. Turn south on Rock Creek Road and drive five miles to the campground.

Trip note: This shoe might just fit. Considering how popular the Lake Crowley area has become, a tiny little spot like this one on Rock Creek could be just what the doctor ordered. The elevation is 8,600 feet. Open from May to October.

Map grid **a3**

EAST FORK
near Lake Crowley
INYO NATIONAL FOREST

Campsites, facilities: There are 133 sites for tents or motor homes up to 22 feet long. Picnic tables, fireplaces, and piped water are provided. Flush toilets and horseback riding facilities are available. Supplies can be purchased in Tom's Place. Pets are permitted on leashes.

Reservations, fee: Reservations accepted; $7 fee per night.

Who to contact: Phone the Inyo National Forest District Office at (619)873-4207.

Location: From the junction of US 395 and Highway 203 (the Mammoth Lakes turnoff), drive 15 miles south on US 395 to Tom's Place. Turn south on Rock Creek Road and drive five miles to the campground.

Trip note: If you like plenty of company, this big Forest Service camp will provide it. This is a popular campground near Lake Crowley. It is set at 9,000 feet elevation along Rock Creek. For more solitude, you might consider a side trip to little Rock Creek Lake. Open from May to November.

Map grid **a4**

ASPEN GROUP CAMP
near Lake Crowley
INYO NATIONAL FOREST

Campsites, facilities: There are five campsites for tents or motor homes up to 16 feet long. Piped water, fireplaces, and picnic tables are provided. Flush toilets are available. Supplies can be purchased in Tom's Place. Pets are permitted on leashes.

Reservations, fee: Reserve through MISTIX (800)283-CAMP ($6 MISTIX fee); $30 per night group fee.

Who to contact: Phone the Inyo National Forest District Office at (619)873-4207.

Location: From the junction of US 395 and Highway 203 (the Mammoth Lakes turnoff), drive 15 miles south on US 395 to Tom's Place. Turn south on Rock Creek Road and drive three miles to the campground.

Trip note: This small, group campsite set on Rock Creek, is used primarily as a base camp for fishermen and campers heading to Lake Crowley. The elevation is 8,100 feet. Open from May to October.

Map grid **a4**

F M D HOLIDAY
near Lake Crowley
INYO NATIONAL FOREST

Campsites, facilities: There are 33 campsites for tents or motor homes up to 22 feet long. Piped water, fireplaces, and picnic tables are provided. Vault toilets are available. Groceries are available nearby. Pets are permitted on leashes.

Reservations, fee: No reservations; $5 fee per night.

Who to contact: Phone the Inyo National Forest District Office at (619)873-4207.

Location: From the junction of US 395 and Highway 203 (the Mammoth Lakes turnoff), drive 15 miles south on US 395 to Tom's Place. Turn south on Rock Creek Road and drive one-half mile to the campground on the left.

Trip note: During peak weekends, this campground is used as an overflow area, as needed. It is set near Rock Creek, not far from Lake Crowley. The elevation is 7,500 feet.

Map grid **a4**

FRENCH CAMP

on Rock Creek near Lake Crowley

INYO NATIONAL FOREST

Campsites, facilities: There are six sites for tents only and 80 sites for tents or motor homes up to 22 feet long. Picnic tables, fireplaces, and piped water are provided. Flush toilets are available. Groceries are available nearby. Pets are permitted on leashes.

Reservations, fee: No reservations; $8 fee per night.

Who to contact: Phone the Inyo National Forest District Office at (619)873-4207.

Location: From the junction of US 395 and Highway 203 (the Mammoth Lakes turnoff), drive 15 miles south on US 395 to Tom's Place. Turn south on Rock Creek Road and drive one-quarter mile to the campground, on the right.

Trip note: This is a good alternative to nearby Lake Crowley. It's a pretty spot along Rock Creek, with side trip opportunities that include boating and fishing on giant Crowley and a westward drive on Rock Creek Road to little Rock Creek Lake ten miles away. The elevation is 7,500 feet. Open from April to October.

Map grid **a4**

TUFF

near Lake Crowley

INYO NATIONAL FOREST

Campsites, facilities: There are 15 sites for tents only and 19 sites for tents or motor homes up to 22 feet long. Picnic tables, fireplaces, and piped water are provided. Flush toilets are available. Pets are permitted on leashes.

Reservations, fee: No reservations; $7 fee per night.

Who to contact: Phone the Inyo National Forest District Office at (619)873-4207.

Location: From the junction of US 395 and Highway 203 (the Mammoth Lakes turnoff), drive 15.5 miles south on US 395 just beyond Tom's Place.

Trip note: If the Owens Valley is packed with campers, knowing every available spot can come in handy. This is one of the several camps on Rock Creek, not far from Lake Crowley. The elevation is 7,000 feet.

Map grid **b0**

VERMILLION

on Lake Edison

SIERRA NATIONAL FOREST

Campsites, facilities: There are 30 tent sites. Piped water, picnic tables, and fireplaces are provided. Vault toilets are available. Pets are permitted on leashes. A boat ramp and horseback riding facilities are nearby. Supplies can be purchased in Mono Hot Springs.

Reservations, fee: Reserve through MISTIX (800)283-CAMP ($6 MISTIX fee); $6 fee per night.

Who to contact: Phone the Sierra National Forest Pine Ridge Ranger District at (209)841-3311.

Location: From the town of Shaver Lake, drive 21 miles north on Highway 168 to the town of Lakeshore. From Lakeshore, drive northeast on Kaiser Pass Road (Forest Service Road 4S01). Kaiser Pass Road becomes Edison Lake Road at Mono Hot Springs. Continue north for five miles past the town to the campground on the west shore of Lake Edison.

Trip note: Lake Edison is a premium vacation destination. The 15-mph speed limit on the lake guarantees quiet water. Trout fishing is often quite good in early summer. A side trip option is to hike the trail from the camp, which travels along the north shore of Lake Edison for five miles to Quail Meadows, where it intersects with the Pacific Crest Trail in the John Muir Wilderness. The elevation is 7,700 feet. Open from June through October.

A

Map grid bO

MONO HOT SPRINGS

on San Joaquin River

SIERRA NATIONAL FOREST

B

Campsites, facilities: There are 20 six-person campsites with horse pastures across from the campground. Picnic tables, fireplaces are provided. Piped water and vault toilets are available. Pets are permitted on leashes. Supplies can be purchased in Mono Hot Springs. There is also a no fee campground at the Mono Creek Trail head for overnight horse camping for people heading into the wilderness.

C

Reservations, fee: Reserve through MISTIX (800)283-CAMP ($6 MISTIX fee; $6 fee per night.

Who to contact: Phone the Sierra National Forest Pine Ridge Ranger District at (209)841-3311.

D

Location: From the town of Shaver Lake, drive 21 miles north on Highway 168 to the town of Lakeshore. From Lakeshore, turn northeast on Kaiser Pass Road (Forest Service Road 4S01). Kaiser Pass Road becomes Edison Lake Road at Mono Hot Springs. Continue north about three miles until you see the campground entrance sign on the left.

E

Trip note: This is a popular spot for the few folks that know of it. It is set in the Sierra at 6,500 feet elevation along the San Joaquin River, directly adjacent to Mono Hot Springs Resort. Don't be surprised if you meet Mr. Ed at this camp. It's used primarily by horses, not people, to carry vacationers into the adjacent backcountry. There is a trail from the camp that forks to Lake Edison or into the backcountry of Ansel Adams Wilderness. It's a good idea to bring an apple along with you. Horsies like that. Open May through October.

F5

Map grid bO

MONO CREEK

near Lake Edison

SIERRA NATIONAL FOREST

G

Campsites, facilities: There are 18 sites for tents only and two sites for tents or small motor homes. Picnic tables, fireplaces, and piped water are provided. Vault toilets are available. Pets are permitted on leashes. Horseback riding facilities and a boat ramp are nearby. Supplies can be purchased in Mono Hot Springs.

H

Reservations, fee: Reserve through MISTIX (800)283-CAMP ($6 MISTIX fee); $6 fee per night.

Who to contact: Phone the Sierra National Forest Pine Ridge Ranger District at (209)841-3311.

I

Location: From the town of Shaver Lake, drive 21 miles north on Highway 168 to the town of Lakeshore. Then drive northeast on Kaiser Pass Road (Forest Service Road 4S01). Kaiser Pass Road becomes Edison Lake Road at Mono Hot Springs. Continue north for three miles past the town to the campground.

Trip note: Here's a beautiful spot along Mono Creek that offers a good alternative to nearby Lake Edison. The camp, set at 7,400 feet, is about a mile upstream from the dam at Lake Edison and has good evening trout fishing upstream from the camp. The Mono Hot Springs Resort is three miles away and there are numerous trails nearby that access the backcountry. Open from June to October.

J

Map grid **b3**

PINE GROVE

near Lake Crowley
INYO NATIONAL FOREST

Campsites, facilities: There are five sites for tents only and six sites for tents or motor homes up to 22 feet long. Picnic tables, fireplaces, and piped water are provided. Flush toilets and horseback riding facilities are available. Supplies can be purchased in Tom's Place. Pets are permitted on leashes.

Reservations, fee: No reservations; $7 fee per night.

Who to contact: Phone the Inyo National Forest District Office at (619)873-4207.

Location: From the junction of US 395 and Highway 203 (the Mammoth Lakes turnoff), drive 15 miles south on US 395 to Tom's Place. Turn south on Rock Creek Road and drive seven miles to the campground.

Trip note: This is one of the smaller camps in a series of spots along Rock Creek. The elevation is 9,300 feet. Open from May to October.

Map grid **b3**

MOSQUITO FLAT

on Rock Creek
INYO NATIONAL FOREST

Campsites, facilities: There are 14 tent sites. Picnic tables, fireplaces, vault toilets, and piped water are provided.

Reservations, fee: No reservations; $8 fee per night.

Who to contact: Phone the Inyo National Forest District Office at (619)873-4207.

Location: From the junction of US 395 and Highway 203 (the Mammoth Lakes turnoff), drive 15 miles south on US 395 to Tom's Place. Turn south on Rock Creek Road and drive eight miles to the campground.

Trip note: This one is in the high country at 10,000 feet (wait until you see how your engine runs). A short distance further, from the end of Rock Creek Road, is a small trailhead camp with ten walk-in sites (no piped water, no fee). From there it is a short distance to numerous alpine lakes in the John Muir Wilderness. Open June through October.

Map grid **b3**

ROCK CREEK LAKE

INYO NATIONAL FOREST

Campsites, facilities: There are 28 sites for tents or motor homes up to 22 feet long. Picnic tables, fireplaces, flush toilets, and piped water are provided. Supplies can be purchased in Tom's Place. Pets are permitted on leashes.

Reservations, fee: No reservations; $8 fee per night.

Who to contact: Phone the Inyo National Forest District Office at (619)873-4207.

Location: From the junction of US 395 and Highway 203 (the Mammoth Lakes turnoff), drive 15 miles south on US 395 to Tom's Place. Turn south on Rock Creek Road and drive seven miles to the campground.

Trip note: Considering how many people flock to Lake Crowley, this nearby alternative might end up being more what you're looking for. The elevation is 9,600 feet. Open from June through October.

Map grid **b3**

ROCK CREEK LAKE GROUP CAMP

INYO NATIONAL FOREST

Campsites, facilities: There is one group site for tent camping that can accomodate 20-50 people. Picnic tables, fireplaces, flush toilets, and piped water are provided. Supplies can be purchased in Tom's Place. Pets are permitted on leashes.

Reservations, fee: Reserve through MISTIX (800)283-CAMP ($6 MISTIX fee); $35 fee per night.

Who to contact: Phone the Inyo National Forest District Office at (619)873-4207.

Location: From the junction of US 395 and Highway 203 (the Mammoth Lakes turnoff), drive 15 miles south on US 395 to Tom's Place. Turn south on Rock Creek Road and drive seven miles to the campground.

Trip note: This is a group camp and an option to Rock Creek Lake. It is also set on Rock Creek Lake at 9,700 feet elevation. Open from mid-June through October.

Map grid **c0**

JACKASS MEADOW

on Florence Lake

SIERRA NATIONAL FOREST

Campsites, facilities: There are 15 campsites for tents or small motor homes. Picnic tables and fireplaces are provided. Vault toilets and piped water are available. Pets are permitted on leashes.

Reservations, fee: Reserve through MISTIX (800)283-CAMP ($6 MISTIX fee); $6 fee per night.

Who to contact: Phone the Sierra National Forest Pine Ridge Ranger District at (209)841-3311.

Location: From the town of Shaver Lake, drive 21 miles north on Highway 168 to the town of Lakeshore. From Lakeshore, turn northeast on Kaiser Pass Road (Forest Service Road 4S01) and drive to Florence Lake Road (two miles south of the town of Mono Hot Springs). Turn south on Florence Lake Road and drive five miles to the campground.

Trip note: Jackass Meadow is a pretty spot set adjacent to Florence Lake, near the upper San Joaquin River. There are good canoeing, rafting and float-tubing possibilities—high Sierra style. The elevation is 7,200 feet.

Map grid **c5**

BIG TREES

on Bishop Creek

INYO NATIONAL FOREST

Campsites, facilities: There are nine campsites for tents or motor homes. Piped water, flush toilets, fireplaces, and picnic tables are provided. Horseback riding facilities are available. Supplies can be purchased in Bishop. Pets are permitted on leashes.

Reservations, fee: No reservations; $5 fee per night.

Who to contact: Call the Inyo National Forest White Mountain Ranger District at (619)873-4207.

Location: From Bishop on US 395, drive 11 miles south on Highway 168 to the campground entrance. Continue southwest on a dirt road to the campground.

Trip note: This is a small Forest Service camp set on Bishop Creek at 7,500 feet elevation. Both South Lake and Sabrina Lake are about ten miles away (see preceding camps). Open from Memorial Day to Labor Day.

Map grid **c6**

HORTON CREEK

near Bishop

5% CLUB

Campsites, facilities: There are 54 campsites for tents or motor homes. Fireplaces and picnic tables are provided. Pit toilets are available. There is **no piped water,** so bring your own. Pets are permitted on leashes. Pack out your garbage.

Reservations, fee: No reservations, no fee.
Who to contact: Phone the Bureau of Land Management at (619)872-4881.
Location: From Bishop, drive 8.5 miles north on US 395. Turn west on Round Valley Road and drive five miles to the campground.
Trip note: This is a little-known, primitive BLM camp set along Horton Creek, northwest of Bishop. It is a popular base camp for hunters in the fall, with wild, rugged country to the west. The Inyo Mono Ecology Center is nearby. The elevation is 5,000 feet. Open from May to October.

Map grid c6

MILLPOND CAMPGROUND

near Bishop

Campsites, facilities: There are 60 campsites for tents or motor homes, many with water and electrical hookups. Piped water, fireplaces, and picnic tables are provided. Flush toilets, showers, and a laundromat are available. Pets are permitted on leashes.
Reservations, fee: Reservations accepted; $8-$10 fee per night.
Who to contact: In the winter, phone the campground at (619)872-6911, and in the summer, (619)873-5342.
Location: From Bishop, drive six miles north on US 395. Turn west at the Millpond Recreation Area sign and drive one mile to the campground.
Trip note: This privately-operated camp is adjacent to the Millpond Recreation Area which offers ball fields, playgrounds, and a swimming lake. Open from March through November.

Map grid c6

PLEASANT VALLEY COUNTY PARK

near Pleasant Valley Reservoir

Campsites, facilities: There are 200 campsites for tents or motor homes. Fireplaces and picnic tables are provided. Piped water and pit toilets are available. Pets are permitted on leashes.
Reservations, fee: No reservations; $5 fee per night.
Who to contact: Phone the County Parks Department at (619)878-2411, extension 2272.
Location: From Bishop, drive 5.5 miles north on US 395. Turn right (northeast) on the campground entrance road; or seven miles northwest of Bishop (on US 395) turn north on Pleasant Valley Road and drive one mile to the campground.
Trip note: This county park is set near long, narrow Pleasant Valley Reservoir, created by the Owens River. The elevation is 4,200 feet. Open year-round.

Map grid c7

SHADY REST TRAILER PARK

in Bishop

Campsites, facilities: There are 25 campsites for tents or motor homes. Piped water, full hookups, fireplaces, and picnic tables are provided. Flush toilets, showers, and a laundromat are available. Pets are permitted on leashes.
Reservations, fee: Reservations suggested; $15 fee per night.
Who to contact: Phone the park at (619)873-3430.
Location: In Bishop, drive to 399 East Yaney Street.
Trip note: This is an option for folks who want to find a layover in the Bishop area without going to much trouble to find it. Possible side trips include visiting the Indian Cultural Center in Bishop and the Pleasant Valley Reservoir. The latter takes about a 15-minute drive to reach. Open year-round.

Map grid **C7**

HIGHLANDS RV PARK
near Bishop

Campsites, facilities: There are 103 motor home spaces with full hookups. Piped water and picnic tables are provided. Flush toilets, showers, a dump station, cable TV, propane gas and a laundromat are available. Groceries are nearby.
Reservations, fee: Reservations suggested; $16 fee per night.
Who to contact: Phone the park at (619)873-7616.
Location: From Bishop, drive two miles north on US 6 to 2275 North Sierra Highway.
Trip note: This is a privately-operated motor home park near Bishop that is set up for Highway 395 cruisers. Possible side trips include visiting the Indian Cultural Center in Bishop or Pleasant Valley Reservoir, about ten miles northwest. The elevation is 4,300 feet. Open year-round.

Map grid **C7**

BROWN'S TOWN SCHOBER LANE CAMPGROUND
near Bishop

Campsites, facilities: There are 150 campsites for tents or motor homes, many with water and electrical hookups. Piped water, fireplaces, and picnic tables are provided. Flush toilets, showers, cable TV, a museum, a store, and a snack bar are available. Pets are permitted on leashes.
Reservations, fee: Reservations accepted; $10-$12 fee per night.
Who to contact: In the winter, phone the campground at (619)872-6911 or, in the summer, at (619)873-8522.
Location: From Bishop, drive one mile south on US 395.
Trip note: This privately-operated campground, one of several in the vicinity of Bishop, is the only one in the area that accepts tents. It's all shade and grass and next to the golf course. Open from March through November.

Map grid **C9**

GRANDVIEW
near Big Pine
INYO NATIONAL FOREST

5% CLUB

Campsites, facilities: There are 26 campsites for tents or motor homes up to 22 feet long. Fireplaces and picnic tables are provided. Vault toilets are available. There is **no piped water,** so bring your own. Pets are permitted on leashes.
Reservations, fee: No reservations, no fee.
Who to contact: Call the Inyo National Forest White Mountain Ranger District at (619)873-4207.
Location: From Big Pine on US 395, turn east on Highway 168 and drive 13 miles. Turn north on Road 4S01 (White Mountain Road) and drive 5.5 miles to the campground.
Trip note: This is a primitive and little-known camp, and the folks who visit this area earn it. It is located in the high country of the eastern Sierra at 8,600 feet elevation, along White Mountain Road. The road borders the Ancient Bristle Cone Forest to the east and leads north to jump-off spots for hikers heading up Mt. Barcroft (13,023 feet) or White Mountain (14,246 feet). A trail leads out of the camp up to an old mining site. Open from May through October.

Map grid **d4**

SABRINA
near Lake Sabrina
INYO NATIONAL FOREST

Campsites, facilities: There are 18 campsites for tents or motor homes. There is no piped water, but vault toilets, fire grills, and picnic tables are provided. A boat ramp and boat rentals are available. Supplies can be purchased in Bishop. Pets are permitted on leashes.

Reservations, fee: No reservations, no fee.

Who to contact: Call the Inyo National Forest White Mountain Ranger District at (619)873-4207.

Location: From Bishop on US 395, drive 17 miles south on Highway 168 to the campground.

Trip note: You get the best of both worlds at this camp. Set at 9,000 feet on Bishop Creek, the trails that are available here are routed into the high country of the John Muir Wilderness, and you're also just one-half mile from Lake Sabrina. Take your pick. Whatever your choice, it's a good one. Open from May to October.

Map grid **d4**

FORKS
near South Lake
INYO NATIONAL FOREST

Campsites, facilities: There are nine campsites for tents or motor homes. Piped water, flush toilets, fireplaces, and picnic tables are provided. Horseback riding facilities are available at North Lake. Supplies can be purchased in Bishop. Pets are permitted on leashes.

Reservations, fee: No reservations; $5 fee per night.

Who to contact: Call the Inyo National Forest White Mountain Ranger District at (619)873-4207.

Location: From Bishop on US 395, drive 13 miles south on Highway 168 to the campground.

Trip note: This camp is located at the fork in the road, which gives you two options. You can turn south on South Lake Road and hunker down there for a spell, or keep driving on Highway 168 to Sabrina Lake, where hikers will find a trailhead that accesses the John Muir Wilderness. The elevation is 7,800 feet. Open from May to October.

Map grid **d4**

HABEGGAR'S RESORT & TRAILER PARK
on the South Fork of Bishop Creek

Campsites, facilities: There are four sites for tents only and 44 campsites for motor homes with full or partial hookups. Piped water, flush toilets, hot showers, a laundromat, grocery store, fish cleaning facilities, and propane gas are available. Pets are permitted.

Reservations, fee: Deposit required with reservation; $14-$20 fee per night; pets $1.

Who to contact: Phone the park at (619)873-4483.

Location: From Bishop on US 395, drive 15 miles south on Highway 168. Turn south on South Lake Road and drive two miles to the campground.

Trip note: This privately-operated park in the high country is set up primarily for motor homes. A lot of folks are surprised to find it here. North, Sabrina, and South Lakes are in the area. The elevation is 8,400 feet. Open from May to

October.

Map grid d4

BISHOP PARK CAMP
near Lake Sabrina
INYO NATIONAL FOREST

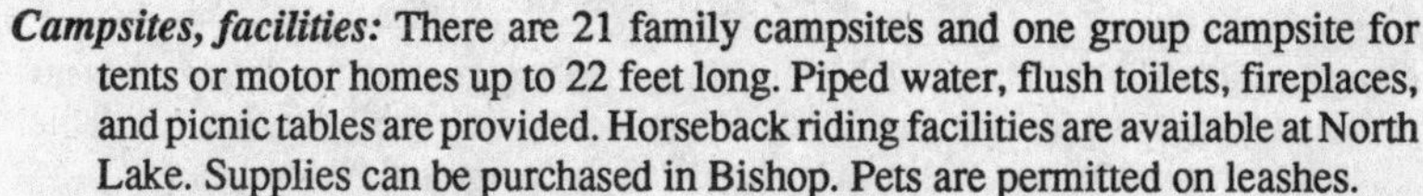

Campsites, facilities: There are 21 family campsites and one group campsite for tents or motor homes up to 22 feet long. Piped water, flush toilets, fireplaces, and picnic tables are provided. Horseback riding facilities are available at North Lake. Supplies can be purchased in Bishop. Pets are permitted on leashes.

Reservations, fee: No reservations; $7 fee per night; $25 fee per night for group campsite.

Who to contact: Call the Inyo National Forest White Mountain Ranger District at (619)873-4207.

Location: From Bishop on US 395, drive 15 miles south on Highway 168 to the campground.

Trip note: This camp is one in a series of camps in the immediate area that are located along Bishop Creek. This one is about two miles from Lake Sabrina, and an ideal area for starting a backpacking expedition into the John Muir Wilderness. The elevation is 7,500 feet. Open from May through October.

Map grid d4

INTAKE
on Sabrina Creek
INYO NATIONAL FOREST

Campsites, facilities: There are eight walk-in sites for tents only and nine campsites for tents or motor homes. Piped water, flush toilets, fireplaces, and picnic tables are provided. Supplies can be purchased in Bishop. Pets are permitted on leashes.

Reservations, fee: No reservations; $5 fee per night.

Who to contact: Call the Inyo National Forest White Mountain Ranger District at (619)873-4207.

Location: From Bishop on US 395, drive 14 miles south on Highway 168 to the campground entrance.

Trip note: This small camp, set at 7,500 feet elevation, on an equally small reservoir on Bishop Creek, is about three miles from Lake Sabrina. The trailhead at Lake Sabrina leads into the John Muir Wilderness. Nearby North Lake and South Lake provide side trip options. Open from April through October.

Map grid d4

FOUR JEFFREY
near South Lake
INYO NATIONAL FOREST

Campsites, facilities: There are 106 campsites for tents or motor homes up to 22 feet long. Piped water, flush toilets, fireplaces, and picnic tables are provided. Supplies can be purchased in Bishop. Pets are permitted on leashes.

Reservations, fee: No reservations; $7 fee per night.

Who to contact: Call the Inyo National Forest White Mountain Ranger District at (619)873-4207.

Location: From Bishop on US 395, drive 13 miles south on Highway 168 to the campground entrance. Turn south on South Lake Road and drive one-half mile to the campground.

Trip note: This is by far the largest of the Forest Service camps in the vicinity. There are three lakes in the area: North Lake, Sabrina Lake, and South Lake. The camp is set on the South Fork of Bishop Creek at 8,100 feet elevation, about four miles from South Lake. Open from mid-April through October.

Map grid **d4**

NORTH LAKE

on Bishop Creek near North Lake
INYO NATIONAL FOREST

Campsites, facilities: There are 11 tent sites. Piped water, vault toilets, fireplaces, and picnic tables are provided. Horseback riding facilities are available. Supplies can be purchased in Bishop. Pets are permitted on leashes.

Reservations, fee: No reservations; $7 fee per night.

Who to contact: Call the Inyo National Forest White Mountain Ranger District at (619)873-4207.

Location: From Bishop on US 395, drive 17 miles south on Highway 168. Turn north on Road 8S02 and drive for two miles to the campground.

Trip note: This prime trailhead camp set in the high country (9,500 feet elevation) takes care of a lot of the "up" hikers have to contend with when entering the nearby John Muir Wilderness. The camp is set on the North Fork of Bishop Creek near North Lake and close to a trailhead that accesses numerous lakes in the John Muir Wilderness and eventually connects with the Pacific Crest Trail. Open from July through September.

Map grid **e5**

BIG PINE CREEK

INYO NATIONAL FOREST

Campsites, facilities: There are five sites for tents only and 25 campsites for tents or motor homes. Piped water, fireplaces, and picnic tables are provided. Vault toilets are available. Pets are permitted on leashes.

Reservations, fee: No reservations; $7 fee per night.

Who to contact: Call the Inyo National Forest White Mountain Ranger District at (619)873-4207.

Location: From US 395 in Big Pine, turn west onto Glacier Lodge Road and drive nine miles to the campground.

Trip note: This is another good spot for backpackers to launch a multi-day trip. The camp is set along Big Pine Creek at 7,700 feet, with trails near the camp that are routed to the numerous lakes in the high country of the John Muir Wilderness. A Forest Service map is essential, of course. Open from May to mid-October.

Map grid **e5**

FIRST FALLS HIKE-IN CAMP

INYO NATIONAL FOREST

Campsites, facilities: There are five tent sites. Fireplaces and picnic tables are provided. Pit toilets are available. There is **no piped water.**

Reservations, fee: No reservations, no fee.

Who to contact: Call the Inyo National Forest White Mountain Ranger District at (619)873-4207.

Location: From US 395 in Big Pine, turn west onto Glacier Lodge Road and drive 8.5 miles. Park and hike two miles to the campground.

Trip note: This high country, hike-in camp is the first step for backpackers heading into the John Muir Wilderness. It is set at 8,300 feet elevation on the South Fork of Big Pine Creek. Open from May to mid-October.

Map grid **e6**

PALISADE GROUP CAMP

on Big Pine Creek
INYO NATIONAL FOREST

Campsites, facilities: There are two group campsites for tents or motor homes. Piped water, fireplaces, and picnic tables are provided. Vault toilets are available. Pets are permitted on leashes.

Reservations, fee: Reserve through MISTIX (800)283-CAMP ($6 MISTIX fee); $20 fee per night.

Who to contact: Call the Inyo National Forest White Mountain Ranger District at (619)873-4207.

Location: From US 395 in Big Pine, turn west onto Glacier Lodge Road and drive 8.5 miles to the campground.

Trip note: This trailhead camp, set at 7,600 feet elevation, is popular for groups planning to rock climb the Palisades. The latter is for experienced mountaineers only; it's a dangerous expedition where risk of life is included in the bargain. Safer options include exploring the surrounding John Muir Wilderness. Open from May to mid-October.

Map grid **e6**

SAGE FLAT

on Big Pine Creek near Big Pine
INYO NATIONAL FOREST

Campsites, facilities: There are 28 campsites for tents or motor homes. Piped water, fireplaces, and picnic tables are provided. Vault toilets are available. Pets are permitted on leashes.

Reservations, fee: Reserve through MISTIX (800)283-CAMP ($6 MISTIX fee); $7 fee per night.

Who to contact: Call the Inyo National Forest White Mountain Ranger District at (619)873-4207.

Location: From US 395 in Big Pine, turn west onto Glacier Lodge Road and drive 8.5 miles to the campground.

Trip note: It just depends what route you want to take. This camp, like the others in the immediate vicinity, is set up for backpackers to start multi-day expeditions into the nearby John Muir Wilderness. It's a steep climb that starts at 7,400 feet elevation. The camp is set along Big Pine Creek. Open from mid-April to mid-November.

Map grid **e6**

UPPER SAGE FLAT

on Big Pine Creek
INYO NATIONAL FOREST

Campsites, facilities: There are 21 campsites for tents or motor homes. Piped water, fireplaces, and picnic tables are provided. Vault toilets are available. Pets are permitted on leashes.

Reservations, fee: Reserve through MISTIX (800)283-CAMP ($6 MISTIX fee); $7 fee per night.

Who to contact: Call the Inyo National Forest White Mountain Ranger District at (619)873-4207.

Location: From US 395 in Big Pine, turn west onto Glacier Lodge Road and drive 8.5 miles to the campground.

Trip note: This is one in a series of Forest Service camps in the area set up primarily for backpackers to start wilderness expeditions. Several trails are available near the camp that head into the John Muir Wilderness. Even starting at 7,600 feet elevation, expect a steep climb. Open from May to mid-October.

Map grid **e7**

BAKER CREEK COUNTY PARK

near Big Pine

Campsites, facilities: There are 70 campsites for tents or motor homes. Fireplaces and picnic tables are provided. Pumped water and pit toilets are available. Pets are permitted on leashes. Supplies can be purchased in Big Pine.

Reservations, fee: No reservations; $4 fee per night.

Who to contact: Phone the County Parks Department at (619)878-2411, extension 2272.

Location: From Big Pine, drive one-half mile north on US 395. Turn west on Baker Creek Road and drive one mile to the campground.

Trip note: A lot of cruisers touring the eastern Sierra on US 395 probably wish they knew of this spot. It's ideal for a quick overnighter, with easy access from Big Pine. It's set along Baker Creek at 4,000 feet elevation.

Map grid **e8**

BIG PINE TRIANGLE COUNTY PARK

near Big Pine

Campsites, facilities: There are 40 campsites for tents or motor homes. Piped water, fireplaces, and picnic tables are provided. Flush toilets are available. Pets are permitted on leashes. Supplies can be purchased in Big Pine.

Reservations, fee: No reservations; $4 fee per night.

Who to contact: Phone the County Parks Department at (619)878-2411, extension 2272.

Location: From Big Pine, drive one-half mile north on US 395 to the campground.

Trip note: This is one of two county camps near the town of Big Pine, providing US 395 cruisers with two options. The camp is set along the Big Pine Canal at 3,900 feet elevation. Open from April to October.

Map grid **f7**

GOODALE CREEK

near Independence

Campsites, facilities: There are 62 campsites for tents or motor homes. Fireplaces and picnic tables are provided. Pit toilets are available. There is **no piped water,** so bring your own. Pack out your garbage. Pets are permitted on leashes.

Reservations, fee: No reservations, no fee.

Who to contact: Call the Bureau of Land Management at (619)872-4881.

Location: From Independence, drive 12 miles north on US 395. Turn west on Aberdeen Road and drive two miles to the campground.

Trip note: This obscure BLM camp is set along little Goodale Creek at 4,100 feet elevation. It's good layover spot for US 395 cruisers. Open May to October.

Map grid **f8**

TINEMAHA CREEK

near Big Pine

Campsites, facilities: There are 55 campsites for tents or motor homes. Fireplaces and picnic tables are provided. Pit toilets are available. There is **no piped water,** so bring your own. Pets are permitted on leashes.

Reservations, fee: No reservations; $4 fee per night.

Who to contact: Phone the County Parks Department at (619)878-2411, extension 2272.

Location: From Independence, drive 19.5 miles north on US 395. Turn west (left) onto Fish Springs Road and drive one-half mile. Turn right onto Tinemaha Road and drive two miles to the campground.

Trip note: This primitive, little-known (to out-of-towners) county park is located on Tinemaha Creek at 4,400 feet elevation. Side trip possibilities include Tinemaha Reservoir, about five miles away. Open year-round.

Map grid f8

TABOOSE CREEK
near Big Pine

Campsites, facilities: There are 55 campsites for tents or motor homes. Fireplaces and picnic tables are provided. Pumped water and pit toilets are available. Supplies can be purchased in Big Pine or Independence. Pets are permitted on leashes.

Reservations, fee: No reservations; $4 fee per night.

Who to contact: Phone the County Parks Department at (619)878-2411, extension 2272.

Location: From Big Pine, drive 11 miles south on US 395. Turn west at Taboose Creek and drive for one mile to the campground.

Trip note: The eastern Sierra is stark country, but this little spot provides a stream (Taboose Creek) and some trees in the vicinity of the campground. The easy access is a bonus. The elevation is 3,900 feet. Open year-round.

Map grid g0

HUME LAKE
SEQUOIA NATIONAL FOREST

Campsites, facilities: There are 40 tent sites and 34 sites for tents or motor homes up to 16 feet long. Picnic tables, fireplaces, and piped water are provided. Flush toilets are available. Pets are permitted on leashes. A grocery store is nearby.

Reservations, fee: No reservations; $8 fee per night.

Who to contact: Phone the Sequoia National Forest Headquarters at (209)784-1500, and the Hume Lake Ranger District (209)338-2251.

Location: From Wilsonia in Kings Canyon National Park, drive six miles north on Highway 180 to the Hume Lake Road junction. Turn south and drive three miles to Hume Lake.

Trip note: This is the best of the camps in the area because it is set on Hume Lake. The lake offers good trout fishing, especially in the spring and early summer. Entrances to Kings Canyon National Park are nearby. One note: the central theme at the entrance to the park is that of a religious retreat. The elevation is 5,200 feet. Open from May to October.

Map grid g0

ASPEN HOLLOW
near Hume Lake
SEQUOIA NATIONAL FOREST

Campsites, facilities: There is a group campsite for up to 75 people with picnic tables, fireplaces, and piped water provided. Vault toilets are available. Pets are permitted on leashes. A grocery store is nearby.

Reservations, fee: Reserve through MISTIX (800)283-CAMP ($6 MISTIX fee); $10 deposit; $40 fee per night.

Who to contact: Phone the Sequoia National Forest Headquarters at (209)784-1500, and the Hume Lake Ranger District at (209)338-2251.

Location: From Wilsonia in Kings Canyon National Park, drive six miles north on

Highway 180 to the Hume Lake Road junction. Turn south and drive three miles to Hume Lake.

Trip note: This large group camp is set at 5,200 feet elevation, near Hume Lake. Trout fishing is excellent near the dam, using Power Bait under a bobber. Entrances to Kings Canyon National Park are nearby. Open from May to October. Note that a religious retreat is at the park entrance.

Map grid **hO**

UPPER TEN MILE

on Ten Mile Creek
SEQUOIA NATIONAL FOREST

Campsites, facilities: There are five campsites for tents or motor homes up to 22 feet long. Picnic tables and fireplaces are provided. Vault toilets are available. There is **no piped water,** but a grocery store is nearby. Pets are permitted on leashes.

Reservations, fee: No reservations, no fee.

Who to contact: Phone the Sequoia National Forest Headquarters at (209)784-1500, and the Hume Lake Ranger District at (209)338-2251.

Location: From Wilsonia in Kings Canyon National Park, drive six miles north on Highway 180 to the Hume Lake Road junction. Turn south and drive eight miles around Hume Lake and up Ten Mile Road to the campground.

Trip note: This is one of the three small, primitive campgrounds set along Ten Mile Creek above Lake Hume. This one is about four miles from the lake.The elevation is 5,800 feet. Open from May to October.

Map grid **hO**

LOGGER FLAT

on Ten Mile Creek
SEQUOIA NATIONAL FOREST

Campsites, facilities: This is a group campsite for 50 people with picnic tables and fireplaces provided. Vault toilets are available. There is **no piped water,** so bring your own. Pets are permitted on leashes. A grocery store is nearby.

Reservations, fee: Reserve through MISTIX (800)283-CAMP ($6 MISTIX fee); $30 fee per night.

Who to contact: Phone the Sequoia National Forest Headquarters at (209)784-1500, and the Hume Lake Ranger District at (209)338-2251.

Location: From Wilsonia in Kings Canyon National Park, drive six miles north on Highway 189 to the Hume Lake Road junction. Turn south and drive 6.5 miles around Hume Lake and up Ten Mile Road to the campground.

Trip note: This is the group site alternative to the Landslide camp. See the trip note for that camp for details.

Map grid **hO**

LANDSLIDE

on Ten Mile Creek
SEQUOIA NATIONAL FOREST

Campsites, facilities: There are four sites for tents only and two campsites for tents or motor homes up to 16 feet long. Picnic tables and fireplaces are provided. Vault toilets are available. There is **no piped water,** so bring your own. Pets are permitted on leashes. A grocery store is nearby.

Reservations, fee: No reservations, no fee.

Who to contact: Phone the Sequoia National Forest Headquarters at (209)784-1500, and the Hume Lake Ranger District at (209)338-2251.

Location: From Wilsonia in Kings Canyon National Park, drive six miles north on

Highway 180 to the Hume Lake Road junction. Turn south and drive seven miles around Hume Lake and up Ten Mile Road to the campground.

Trip note: If you want quiet, you got it. Few folks know about this camp. If you want a stream nearby, you got it. Ten Mile Creek runs right beside the camp. If you want a lake nearby, you got it. Lake Hume is about two miles away. If you want a national park nearby, you got it. It's not far from the entrances to Kings Canyon National Park. Add it up: You got it. Set at 5,800 feet elevation. Open from May to October.

Map grid **h0**

BUCK ROCK

near Big Meadows Creek

SEQUOIA NATIONAL FOREST

Campsites, facilities: There are five campsites for tents or motor homes up to 16 feet long. Picnic tables and fireplaces are provided. Vault toilets are available. There is **no piped water,** so bring your own. Pets are permitted on leashes.

Reservations, fee: No reservations, no fee.

Who to contact: Phone the Sequoia National Forest at (209)784-1500, and the Hume Lake Ranger District at (209)338-2251.

Location: From Wilsonia in Kings Canyon National Park, drive seven miles southeast on Generals Highway. Turn left on Big Meadows Road and drive four miles to the camp.

Trip note: This is a good spot for the four-wheelers. There's a four-wheel drive road (Forest Service Road 14S47) forking off to the right about two miles north of the camp. Obtain a Forest Service map from the Big Meadows Ranger Station (one mile east). The elevation is 7,500 feet. Open from June to October.

Map grid **h1**

BIG MEADOWS

on Big Meadows Creek

SEQUOIA NATIONAL FOREST

Campsites, facilities: There are 15 sites for tents only and ten campsites for tents or motor homes up to 22 feet long. Picnic tables and fireplaces are provided. Vault toilets are available. There is **no piped water,** so bring your own. Pets are permitted on leashes.

Reservations, fee: No reservations, no fee.

Who to contact: Phone the Sequoia National Forest at (209)784-1500, and the Hume Lake Ranger District at (209)338-2251.

Location: From Wilsonia, drive seven miles southeast on Generals Highway. Turn left on Big Meadows Road and drive five miles to the camp.

Trip note: This primitive, high mountain camp (7,600 feet elevation) is set beside little Big Meadows Creek. Backpackers can use this as a launching pad, with the nearby trail (starting at Fox Meadow) leading southeast to the Jennie Lake Wilderness. Kings Canyon National Park is a nearby side trip, only a 12-mile drive to the entrance. Open from June to October.

Map grid **h2**

SENTINEL

KINGS CANYON NATIONAL PARK

Campsites, facilities: There are 83 campsites for tents or motor homes. Piped water, fireplaces, and picnic tables are provided. Flush toilets, showers, a dump station, bike rentals, and horseback riding facilities are available. Some facilities are wheelchair accessible. A grocery store and laundromat are nearby. Pets are permitted on leashes.

A B C D E F5 G H I J

Reservations, fee: No reservations; $8 fee per night.
Who to contact: Phone the Kings Canyon National Park at (209)565-3341.
Location: From Cedar Grove in Kings Canyon National Park, drive west on Highway 180 to the campground.
Trip note: This camp provides a nearby alternative to Sheep Creek camp. They both tend to fill up quickly in the summer. It's a short walk to Cedar Grove, the center of activity in the park. The elevation is 4,600 feet. Open from April through October (depending on road and snow conditions).

Map grid h2 — SHEEP CREEK

KINGS CANYON NATIONAL PARK

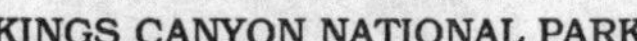

Campsites, facilities: There are 111 campsites for tents or motor homes. Piped water, fireplaces, and picnic tables are provided. Flush toilets, showers, a dump station, horseback riding facilities, and evening ranger programs are available. A grocery store, bike rentals, and a laundromat are available nearby. Pets are permitted on leashes.
Reservations, fee: No reservations; $8 fee per night.
Who to contact: Phone the Kings Canyon National Park at (209)565-3341.
Location: From Cedar Grove in Kings Canyon National Park, drive one-half mile west on Highway 180.
Trip note: This is one of the camps that always fills up fast on summer weekends. It's a pretty spot and just a short walk from Cedar Grove. The camp is set along Sheep Creek at 4,600 feet elevation. Open from June to October.

Map grid h2 — CANYON VIEW GROUP CAMP

KINGS CANYON NATIONAL PARK

Campsites, facilities: There are four campsites for tents or motor homes. Piped water, fireplaces, and picnic tables are provided. Flush toilets, showers, a dump station, bike rentals, and horseback riding facilities are available. A grocery store and a laundromat are nearby. Pets are permitted on leashes.
Reservations, fee: Call ahead for reservations and fee.
Who to contact: Phone the Kings Canyon National Park at (209)565-3341.
Location: From Cedar Grove in Kings Canyon National Park, drive east on Highway 180 to the campground, one-half mile past the ranger station.
Trip note: If you are in a large group, just plain forget trying to find a campground in Kings Canyon National Park where you can all be together—except for this spot. Reservations are required. The elevation is 4,600. Open from April to September (depending on road and snow conditions).

Map grid h3 — CANYON VIEW

KINGS CANYON NATIONAL PARK

Campsites, facilities: There are 37 campsites for tents or motor homes. Piped water, fireplaces, and picnic tables are provided. Flush toilets, showers, a dump station, bike rentals, and horseback riding facilities are available. A grocery store and a laundromat are nearby. Pets are permitted on leashes.
Reservations, fee: No reservations; $8 fee per night.
Who to contact: Phone the Kings Canyon National Park at (209)565-3341.
Location: From Cedar Grove in Kings Canyon National Park, drive east on Highway 180 to the campground, one-half mile past the ranger station.
Trip note: This is another of the several camps in the Cedar Grove area of the park.

The road leads into the river canyon, where dramatic views of the deep Kings River Canyon are available. Kings River Canyon is one of the deepest gorges in North America. The elevation is 4,600 feet. Open from June to September (depending on road and snow conditions).

A

Map grid **h3**

MORAINE
KINGS CANYON NATIONAL PARK

B

Campsites, facilities: There are 120 campsites for tents or motor homes. Piped water, fireplaces, and picnic tables are provided. Flush toilets, showers, a dump station, bike rentals, and horseback riding facilities are available. A grocery store and a laundromat are nearby. Pets are permitted on leashes.
Reservations, fee: No reservations; $8 fee per night.
Who to contact: Phone the Kings Canyon National Park at (209)565-3341.
Location: From Cedar Grove in Kings Canyon National Park, drive east on Highway 180 to the campground, one mile past the ranger station.
Trip note: This is the last in the series of camps in the Cedar Grove area of Kings Canyon National Park. Hikers should drive past the Cedar Grove Ranger Station to the end of the road at Copper Creek—this is a prime jump-off point for a hike with spectacular lookouts. The elevation is 4,600. Open from June to October (depending on road and snow conditions).

C

D

Map grid **h7**

OAK CREEK
INYO NATIONAL FOREST

E

Campsites, facilities: There are 24 campsites for tents or motor homes. Piped water, fireplaces, and picnic tables are provided. Flush toilets are available. Supplies and a laundromat are available in Independence. Pets are permitted on leashes.
Reservations, fee: No reservations; $6 fee per night.
Who to contact: Call Inyo National Forest Mt. Whitney Ranger District at (619)876-5542.
Location: From Independence, drive two miles north on US 395. Turn left (west) onto North Oak Creek Drive and drive three miles to the campground.
Trip note: This is one in a series of little-known camps located west of Independence that provide jump-off spots for backpackers. Caution: Plan on a steep climb up to the Sierra crest. This camp is set at 5,000 feet, with a trail from camp that is routed west (and up) into the California Bighorn Sheep Zoological Area, a rugged, stark country well above the tree line. Camp is open year-round.

F5

G

Map grid **h8**

INDEPENDENCE CREEK
in Independence

H

Campsites, facilities: There are 25 campsites for tents or motor homes. Piped water and picnic tables are provided. Pit toilets are available. Some facilities are wheelchair accessible. Supplies and a laundromat are available in Independence. Pets are permitted on leashes.
Reservations, fee: No reservations; $4 fee per night.
Who to contact: Phone the County Parks Department at (619)878-2411, extension 2272.
Location: From US 395 in Independence, drive one-half mile west on Market Street to the campground.
Trip note: This is an oft-overlooked camp for US 395 cruisers because it is an

I

J

unpublicized county park. It is set at 3,900 feet elevation along Independence Creek. Open year-round.

Map grid **i0**

DORST

on Dorst Creek

SEQUOIA NATIONAL PARK

Campsites, facilities: There are 219 campsites for tents or motor homes. Piped water, fireplaces, and picnic tables are provided. Flush toilets, a dump station, and evening ranger programs are available. A grocery store and a laundromat are nearby. Pets are permitted on leashes.

Reservations, fee: No reservations; $8 fee per night.

Who to contact: Phone the Sequoia National Park at (209)565-3341.

Location: From Giant Forest Village in Sequoia National Park, drive 14 miles northwest on Generals Highway.

Trip note: This is one in a series of big, popular camps in Sequoia National Park. The camp is set on Dorst Creek at 6,700 feet elevation, near a trail that is routed into the backcountry and through Muir Grove. Open from June to September.

Map grid **i0**

DORST GROUP CAMP

SEQUOIA NATIONAL PARK

Campsites, facilities: There is one group campsite for tents or motor homes. Piped water, fireplaces, and picnic tables are provided. Flush toilets, a dump station, and evening ranger programs are available. A grocery store and a laundromat are nearby. Pets are permitted on leashes.

Reservations, fee: Call for reservations and fee.

Who to contact: Phone the Sequoia National Park at (209)565-3341.

Location: From Giant Forest Village in Sequoia National Park, drive 14 miles northwest on Generals Highway.

Trip note: If you're coming in a large group, this is your spot—there is little chance of winding up together at any other camp in this area of Sequoia National Park. It is set on Dorst Creek at an elevation of 6,700 feet near a trailhead that accesses the backcountry and Muir Grove. Open from June to September (depending on weather and road conditions).

Map grid **i0**

STONY CREEK

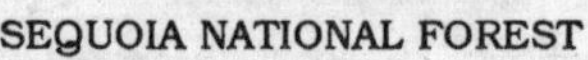

SEQUOIA NATIONAL FOREST

Campsites, facilities: There are 29 campsites for tents, and 20 sites for motor homes up to 22 feet long. Piped water, fireplaces, and picnic tables are provided. Vault toilets are available. A grocery store, propane gas and a laundromat are nearby. Pets are permitted on leashes.

Reservations, fee: Reservations available through MISTIX at (800)283-CAMP ($6 MISTIX fee); $8 fee per night, plus $6 reservation fee.

Who to contact: Phone the Sequoia National Forest at (209)784-1500, and the Hume Lake Ranger District at (209)338-2251.

Location: From Wilsonia in Kings Canyon National Park, drive 13 miles southeast on Generals Highway.

Trip note: Take your pick. One in a series of camps set along Stony Creek in the immediate area, this one is just a mile from the Kaweah River and provides a northern border to Sequoia National Park. The elevation is 6,400 feet. Open from June to October.

Map grid **i0**

FIR GROUP CAMPGROUND

on Stony Creek
SEQUOIA NATIONAL FOREST

A

Campsites, facilities: There is a group campsite for up to 100 people with piped water, picnic tables, and fireplaces provided. Vault toilets are available. A grocery store and a laundromat are nearby. Pets are permitted on leashes.

B

Reservations, fee: Reservations required; reserve through MISTIX at (800)283-CAMP ($6 MISTIX fee); $1 per person with $25 minimum, plus $10 reservation fee.

Who to contact: For general information phone Sequoia National Forest at (209) 784-1500.

C

Location: From Wilsonia in Kings Canyon National Park, drive 14 miles southeast on Generals Highway.

Trip note: This is the second of the two large group camps in the immediate vicinity set along Stony Creek. It is only two miles from the Kaweah River and provides a northern border to Sequoia National Park. Open from June to October.

D

Map grid **i0**

COVE GROUP CAMP

near Stony Creek
SEQUOIA NATIONAL FOREST

Campsites, facilities: There is a group campsite for up to 50 people. Piped water, picnic tables, and fireplaces are provided. Vault toilets are available. A grocery store and laundromat are available nearby. Pets are permitted on leashes.

E

Reservations, fee: Reservations required; reserve through MISTIX at (800)283-CAMP ($6 MISTIX fee); $1 per person with $25 minimum, plus $10 reservation fee.

F5

Who to contact: For general information phone Sequoia National Forest at (209) 784-1500.

Location: From Wilsonia in Kings Canyon National Park, drive 14 miles southeast on Generals Highway.

Trip note: This large group camp is located beside Stony Creek, two miles from the Kaweah River, and provides a northern border to Sequoia National Park. Obtain a Forest Service map, which will detail back roads, trails, lakes, and streams. The elevation is 6,500 feet. Open from May to October.

G

Map grid **i1**

LODGEPOLE

on the Marble Fork of Kaweah River
SEQUOIA NATIONAL PARK

H

Campsites, facilities: There are 260 campsites for tents or motor homes. Piped water, fireplaces, and picnic tables are provided. Flush toilets, showers, a dump station, horseback riding facilities, a gift shop, and evening ranger programs are available. A grocery store, propane gas, and a laundromat are nearby. The campgrounds and rest room facilities are wheelchair accessible. Pets are permitted on leashes.

I

Reservations, fee: Reserve through Ticketron; call (800)452-1111; $8-$10 fee per night.

Who to contact: Phone the Sequoia National Park at (209)565-3341.

J

Location: From Giant Forest Village in Sequoia National Park, drive five miles northeast on Generals Highway.

Trip note: This is a giant but pretty camp set on the Marble Fork of the Kaweah

River. Plan on plenty of company. To escape, one option is to strap on your hiking boots and hoof it on the trails near the camp leading into the backcountry of Sequoia National Park. The elevation is 6,700 feet. Open year-round.

Map grid **i6**

ONION VALLEY

INYO NATIONAL FOREST

Campsites, facilities: There are 29 tent sites. There are no motor home or trailer spaces. Piped water, flush toilets, fireplaces, and picnic tables are provided. Pets are permitted on leashes.

Reservations, fee: No reservations; $6 fee per night.

Who to contact: Call the Inyo National Forest Mt. Whitney Ranger District at (619)876-5542.

Location: From US 395 in Independence, drive 14 miles west on Onion Valley Road to the campground.

Trip note: A $2 Forest Service map and a free wilderness permit are your passports to the high country from this camp. Several trails leading out from the camp are routed deep into the John Muir Wilderness and Sequoia National Park and connect to the Pacific Crest Trail. It is set at 9,200 feet elevation, which means there's a lot of the "up" that's behind you. Open from mid-June through September.

Map grid **i7**

GRAY'S MEADOW

on Independence Creek

INYO NATIONAL FOREST

Campsites, facilities: There are 52 campsites for tents or motor homes. Piped water, fireplaces, and picnic tables are provided. Flush toilets are available. Supplies and a laundromat in Independence. Pets are permitted on leashes.

Reservations, fee: No reservations; $7 fee per night.

Who to contact: Call Inyo National Forest Mt. Whitney Ranger District at (619)876-5542.

Location: From US 395 in Independence, turn west on Onion Valley Road and drive five miles to the campground.

Trip note: This stark but pretty spot, set in the eastern Sierra along Independence Creek, is just far enough off US 395 to get missed by a lot of folks. Open from April to October.

Map grid **j0**

POTWISHA

on the Marble Fork of Kaweah River

SEQUOIA NATIONAL PARK

Campsites, facilities: There are 44 campsites for tents or motor homes up to 16 feet long. Piped water, picnic tables, and fireplaces are provided. Flush toilets, a dump station, and evening ranger programs are available. The campgrounds and rest room facilities are wheelchair accessible. Pets are permitted on leashes.

Reservations, fee: No reservations; $8 fee per night.

Who to contact: Phone the Sequoia National Park at (209)565-3341.

Location: From Visalia, drive east on Highway 198 to the town of Ash Mountain. From Ash Mountain, drive three miles northeast on Generals Highway.

Trip note: This pretty spot on the Marble Fork of the Kaweah River is one of Sequoia National Park's smaller drive-to campgrounds. From Buckeye Flat, located east of the camp a few miles, there is a trail that runs along Paradise Creek. Open year-round.

Map grid **j1**

BUCKEYE FLAT

on the Middle Fork of Kaweah River
SEQUOIA NATIONAL PARK

Campsites, facilities: There are 28 tent sites. Picnic tables, fireplaces, and piped water are provided. Flush toilets are available. Pets are permitted on leashes.
Reservations, fee: No reservations; $8 fee per night.
Who to contact: Phone the Sequoia National Park at (209)565-3341.
Location: From Giant Forest Village, drive 11 miles south on Generals Highway. Turn left at the Hospital Rock Ranger Station and drive to the campground.
Trip note: In any big, popular national park like Sequoia, the smaller the campground, the better. Well, this is one of the smaller ones here. It is set on the Middle Fork of the Kaweah River. Just south of camp is a trail that runs beside pretty Paradise Creek. Open from April to October (depending on road and weather conditions).

Map grid **j7**

LONE PINE

near Mt. Whitney
INYO NATIONAL FOREST

Campsites, facilities: There are 43 campsites for tents or motor homes. Piped water, vault toilets, fireplaces, and picnic tables are provided. Supplies are available in Lone Pine. Pets are permitted on leashes.
Reservations, fee: No reservations; $7 fee per night.
Who to contact: Call the Inyo National Forest Mt. Whitney Ranger District at (619)876-5542.
Location: From Lone Pine, drive seven miles west on Whitney Portal Road.
Trip note: This is an alternative for campers preparing to hike Mt. Whitney or start the John Muir Trail. It is set at 6,000 feet, 2,000 feet below Whitney Portal (the jump-off spot for hikers), providing a lower elevation spot for hikers to acclimate themselves to the altitude for a day. The camp is set on Lone Pine Creek and has a limited stay policy (14 days). Open year-round.

Map grid **j7**

WHITNEY PORTAL GROUP CAMP

INYO NATIONAL FOREST

Campsites, facilities: There are three group campsites for tents or motor homes up to 16 feet long. Piped water, flush toilets, fireplaces, and picnic tables are provided. Supplies are available in Lone Pine.
Reservations, fee: Reserve through MISTIX (800)283-CAMP ($6 MISTIX fee); $25 fee per group per night.
Who to contact: Call the Inyo National Forest Mt. Whitney Ranger District at (619)876-5542.
Location: From Lone Pine, drive 13 miles west on Whitney Portal Road.
Trip note: This is the spot for groups planning to hike to the top of Mt. Whitney. Permits and reservations are required to camp and climb. The elevation is 8,100 feet. Open from mid-May to mid-October.

Map grid **j7**

WHITNEY TRAILHEAD

INYO NATIONAL FOREST

Campsites, facilities: There are ten tent sites at this walk-in campground. Piped water, pit toilets, fireplaces, and picnic tables are provided. Supplies are available in Lone Pine. Stays are limited to one night only.

Reservations, fee: No reservations; $5 fee per night.

Who to contact: Call the Inyo National Forest Mt. Whitney Ranger District at (619)876-5542.

Location: From Lone Pine, drive 13 miles west on Whitney Portal Road, then hike.

Trip note: If Whitney Portal is packed to the rafters, this camp provides a hike-in option (elevation 8,000 feet). The trailhead to the Mt. Whitney summit (14,495 feet) is nearby. Mt. Whitney is the beginning of the 211-mile John Muir Trail, which ends in Yosemite Valley. Open from mid-May to mid-October.

Map grid j7

WHITNEY PORTAL

near Mt. Whitney

INYO NATIONAL FOREST

Campsites, facilities: There are 44 campsites for tents or motor homes up to 16 feet long. Piped water, flush toilets, fireplaces, and picnic tables are provided. Supplies are available in Lone Pine.

Reservations, fee: No reservations; $10 fee per night.

Who to contact: Call the Inyo National Forest Mt. Whitney Ranger District at (619)876-5542.

Location: From Lone Pine, drive 13 miles west on Whitney Portal Road.

Trip note: The trailhead at this camp is one of the most popular jump-off spots for backpackers in America. The trail is routed up to the top of Mt. Whitney (14,495 feet) and forks off at Trail Crest to the Pacific Crest Trail-John Muir Trail. A maximum seven-day stay is enforced. Hikers must have a wilderness permit, available at the Forest Service office in Lone Pine, to climb Whitney. The camp is set at 8,000 feet. Open from mid-May to mid-October.

Map grid j8

PORTAGEE JOE

near Lone Pine

Campsites, facilities: There are 15 campsites for tents or motor homes. Piped water, pit toilets, fireplaces, and picnic tables are provided. Supplies and a laundromat are available in Lone Pine. Pets are permitted on leashes.

Reservations, fee: No reservations; $5 fee per night.

Who to contact: Phone the County Parks Department at (619)878-2411, extension 2272.

Location: From Lone Pine, drive one mile west on Whitney Portal Road. Turn south and drive a short distance to the campground.

Trip note: This small, little-known camp provides an option for both Mt. Whitney hikers or US 395 cruisers. It is located about five miles from Diaz Lake camp and set on a small creek at 3,750 feet elevation. Open year-round.

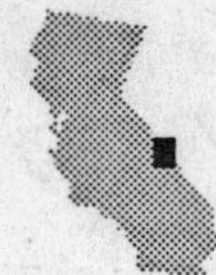

MAP F6

BEACH
TREES
5% CLUB
DESERT
URBAN
FOOTHILL
GRASSLAND

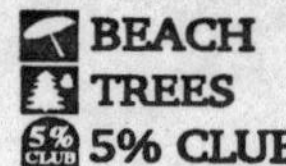

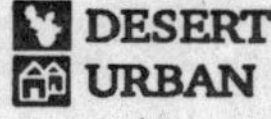

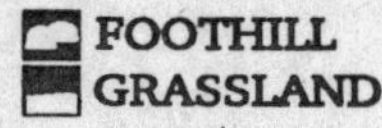

15 MILES

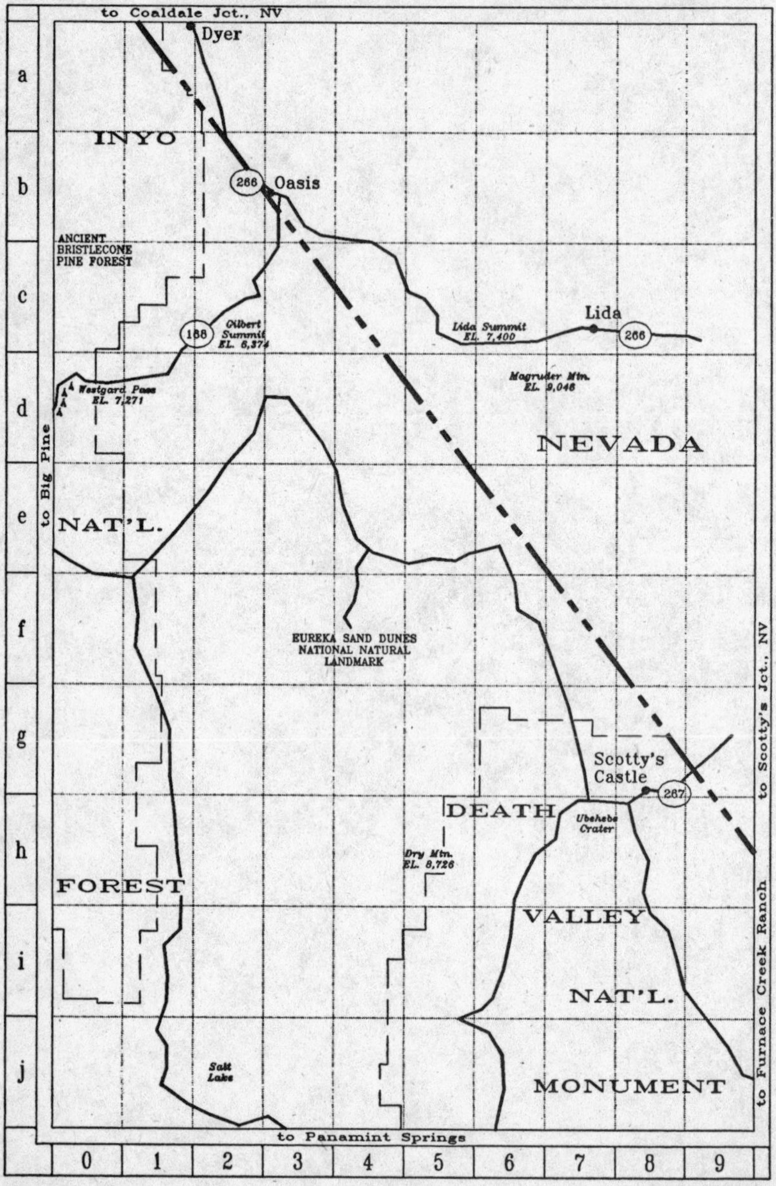

to Coaldale Jct., NV
Dyer
INYO
266
Oasis
ANCIENT BRISTLECONE PINE FOREST
168
Gilbert Summit EL. 6,374
Lida Summit EL. 7,400
Lida
266
Westgard Pass EL. 7,271
Magruder Mtn. EL. 9,046
NEVADA
to Big Pine
NAT'L.
EUREKA SAND DUNES NATIONAL NATURAL LANDMARK
Scotty's Castle
267
DEATH
Ubehebe Crater
Dry Mtn. EL. 8,726
FOREST
VALLEY
NAT'L.
Salt Lake
MONUMENT
to Panamint Springs
to Scotty's Jct., NV
to Furnace Creek Ranch
a
b
c
d
e
f
g
h
i
j
0
1
2
3
4
5
6
7
8
9

Map grid **dO**

PINYON GROUP CAMP

near Big Pine
INYO NATIONAL FOREST

Campsites, facilities: There are eight campsites for tents or motor homes. Picnic tables and vault toilets are provided. There is **no piped water,** so bring your own. Pets are permitted on leashes.

Reservations, fee: Reserve through MISTIX (800)283-CAMP ($6 MISTIX fee); $15 group fee per night.

Who to contact: Call the Inyo National Forest White Mountain Ranger District at (619)873-4207.

Location: From Big Pine on US 395, turn east on Highway 168 and drive 13 miles to the campground.

Trip note: This is one in a series of camps in the immediate area. For side trip details, see the trip note for Fossil Group Camp.

Map grid **dO**

POLETA GROUP CAMP

near Big Pine
INYO NATIONAL FOREST

Campsites, facilities: There are eight campsites for tents or motor homes. Picnic tables and vault toilets are provided. There is **no piped water,** so bring your own. Pets are permitted on leashes.

Reservations, fee: Reservations requested; $15 group fee per night.

Who to contact: Call the Inyo National Forest White Mountain Ranger District at (619)873-4207.

Location: From Big Pine on US 395, turn east on Highway 168 and drive 13 miles to the campground.

Trip note: This is one of the four camps in the immediate area, so take your pick. For side trip possibilities, see the trip note for Fossil Group Camp.

Map grid **dO**

JUNIPER GROUP CAMP

near Big Pine
INYO NATIONAL FOREST

Campsites, facilities: There are five campsites for tents or motor homes. Picnic tables and vault toilets are provided. There is **no piped water,** so bring your own. Pets are permitted on leashes.

Reservations, fee: Reservations requested; $15 fee per group per night.

Who to contact: Call the Inyo National Forest White Mountain Ranger District at (619)873-4207.

Location: From Big Pine on US 395, turn east on Highway 168 and drive 13 miles to the campground.

Trip note: A nearby option to the preceding spot for group campers. See the trip note for Fossil Group Camp for side trip details.

Map grid **dO**

FOSSIL GROUP CAMP

near Big Pine
INYO NATIONAL FOREST

Campsites, facilities: There are 11 campsites for tents or motor homes. Picnic tables and vault toilets are provided. There is **no piped water,** so bring your own. Pets are permitted on leashes.

Reservations, fee: Reservations requested; $15 group fee per night.
Who to contact: Call the Inyo National Forest White Mountain Ranger District at (619)873-4207.
Location: From Big Pine on US 395, turn east on Highway 168 and drive 13 miles to the campground.
Trip note: This is a primitive and little-known Forest Service camp set at 7,220 feet elevation. Ambitious visitors have several side trip options. From nearby Cedar Flat, a trail leads west to Black Mountain (9,083 feet). Deep Spring Lake is ten miles from camp via Highway 168 and primitive roads; a Forest Service map is a necessity. Another option is to drive north on White Mountain Road, which is routed through the Ancient Bristle Cone Pine Forest.

A

B

C

D

E

F6

G

H

I

J

◆ MAP G1 ◆

BEACH
DESERT
FOOTHILL
TREES
URBAN
GRASSLAND
5% CLUB
15 MILES

to Big Sur
Lucia
LOS
PADRES
Pacific
Gorda
NAT'L.
CAPE SAN MARTIN
FOREST
Ocean
1
RAGGED POINT
to Jolon
to San Simeon

a b c d e f g h i j

0 1 2 3 4 5 6 7 8 9

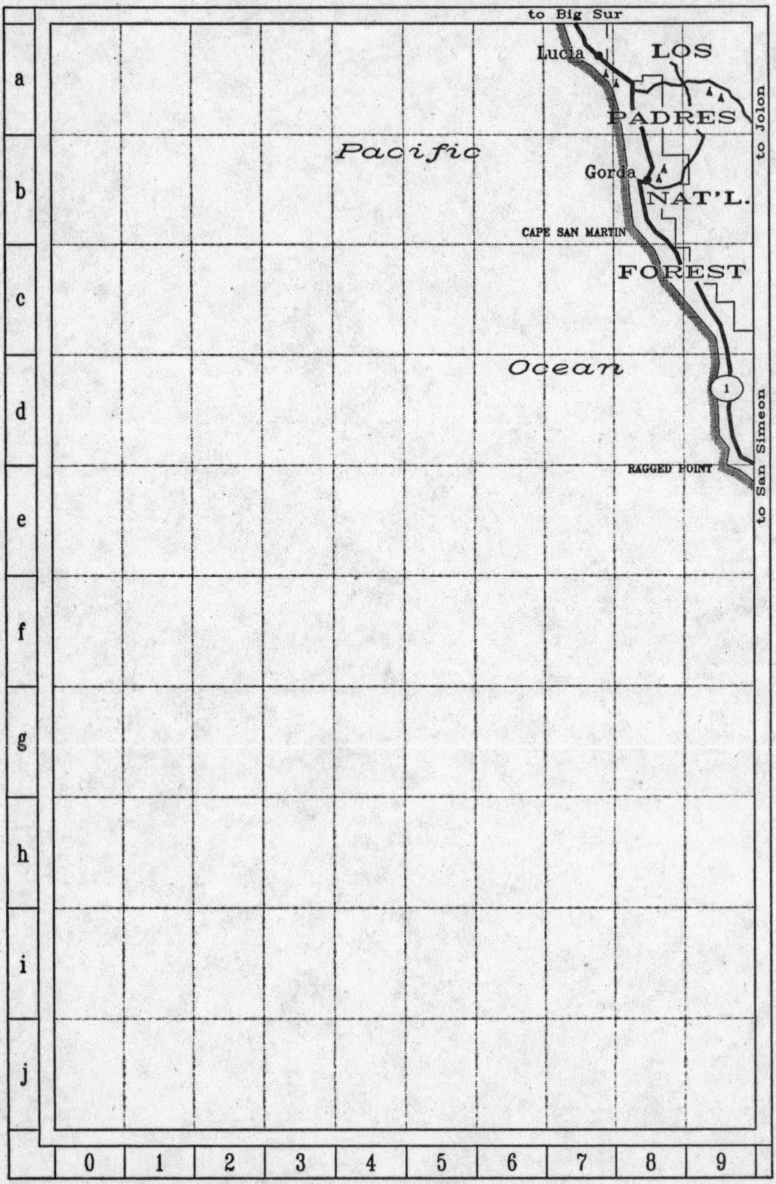

Map grid **a7**

LIMEKILN BEACH REDWOODS

on Pacific Ocean

A

Campsites, facilities: There are five sites for tents only and 50 motor home spaces with piped water provided. Rest rooms, showers, a dump station, a grocery store, bait, and firewood are available.

B

Reservations, fee: Call ahead for available space and fee.

Who to contact: Phone the park at (408)667-2403.

Location: From Big Sur, drive 26 miles south on Highway 1.

Trip note: This is a Highway 1 layover spot, set up primarily for motor homes. Drive-in campsites are set up both near the beach and the redwoods, take your pick. Several hiking trails are available, including one that is routed past some historic lime kilns.

C

Map grid **a8**

KIRK CREEK

near Pacific Ocean

LOS PADRES NATIONAL FOREST

D

Campsites, facilities: There are 33 campsites for tents or motor homes. Piped water, picnic tables, and fireplaces are provided. Vault toilets are available. Pets are permitted on leashes.

Reservations, fee: No reservations; $10 fee per night, $2 fee per night for bicyclists.

Who to contact: Phone Los Padres National Forest at (805)683-6711.

E

Location: From the little town of Lucia on Highway 1, drive four miles south on Highway 1 to the campground.

Trip note: This pretty camp is set along Kirk Creek near where it empties into the Pacific Ocean. A trail from camp branches north through the Ventana Wilderness, which is dotted with backcountry campsites. Open year-round.

F

Map grid **a9**

PONDEROSA

LOS PADRES NATIONAL FOREST

Campsites, facilities: There are 23 campsites for tents or motor homes up to 32 feet long. Piped water, picnic tables, and fireplaces are provided. Vault toilets are available. Pets are permitted on leashes.

G1

Reservations, fee: No reservations; $5 fee per night.

Who to contact: Phone Los Padres National Forest at (805)683-6711.

Location: From US 101 in King City, drive 18 miles south on County Route G14 to the town of Jolon. From Jolon, turn north on Mission Road and drive four miles. Turn left on Nacimiento-Fergusson Road and drive 12 miles to the campground.

H

Trip note: Not many folks know about this spot that's just far enough off the main track to get missed. It's set at 1,500 feet elevation in Los Padres National Forest, not far from the Ventana Wilderness (good hiking) and Hunter Liggett Military Reservation (wild pig hunting with permit). Open year-round.

I

Map grid **a9**

NACIMIENTO

LOS PADRES NATIONAL FOREST

Campsites, facilities: There are nine sites for tents only and eight campsites for tents or motor homes. Piped water, picnic tables, and fireplaces are provided. Vault toilets are available. Pets are permitted on leashes.

J

Reservations, fee: No reservations; $3 fee per night.

Who to contact: Phone Los Padres National Forest at (805)683-6711.

Location: From the little town of Lucia on Highway 1, drive 9.5 miles south on Highway 1 to Nacimiento Road. Turn east and drive about eight winding miles to the campground. Or from the town of Jolon, drive 15 miles northwest on Nacimiento-Fergusson Road.

Trip note: This little-known spot near the Nacimiento River at 1,600 feet elevation makes for a good jump-off spot for a backpack or hunting trip. The camp is set in Los Padres National Forest near the Ventana Wilderness and Hunter Liggett Military Reservation. The latter provides good hunting for wild pigs (check headquarters for all permits and dates of hunts). Open year-round.

Map grid b8

PLASKETT CREEK

overlooking Pacific Ocean
LOS PADRES NATIONAL FOREST

Campsites, facilities: There are 43 campsites for tents or motor homes. Piped water, picnic tables, and fireplaces are provided. Flush toilets are available. Pets are permitted on leashes.

Reservations, fee: No reservations; $10 fee per night; $15 multi-family sites; $2 for bicyclists.

Who to contact: Phone Los Padres National Forest at (805)683-6711.

Location: From the town of Lucia, drive 9.5 miles south on Highway 1 to the campground.

Trip note: This is a premium coastal camp for Highway 1 cruisers, set at 200 feet elevation along little Plaskett Creek above the Pacific Ocean. A little cafe in Lucia provides open-air dining with a dramatic lookout down the coast. Open all year.

Map grid b8

PLASKETT CREEK GROUP CAMP

overlooking Pacific Ocean
LOS PADRES NATIONAL FOREST

Campsites, facilities: There are three group campsites for tents or motor homes. Piped water, picnic tables, and fireplaces are provided. Vault toilets are available. Pets are permitted on leashes.

Reservations, fee: Reserve through MISTIX (800)283-CAMP ($6 Mistix fee); $45 group fee per night.

Who to contact: Phone Los Padres National Forest at (805)683-6711.

Location: From the little town of Lucia, drive 9.5 miles south on Highway 1 to the campground.

Trip note: This is one of two prime, coastal camps in this immediate area along Highway 1, which is one of the prettiest drives in the West. This camp is for small groups and is set beside little Plaskett Creek. A great little cafe that overlooks the coast is available in Lucia. Open year-round.

MAP G2

BEACH
TREES
5% CLUB
DESERT
URBAN
FOOTHILL
GRASSLAND
15 MILES

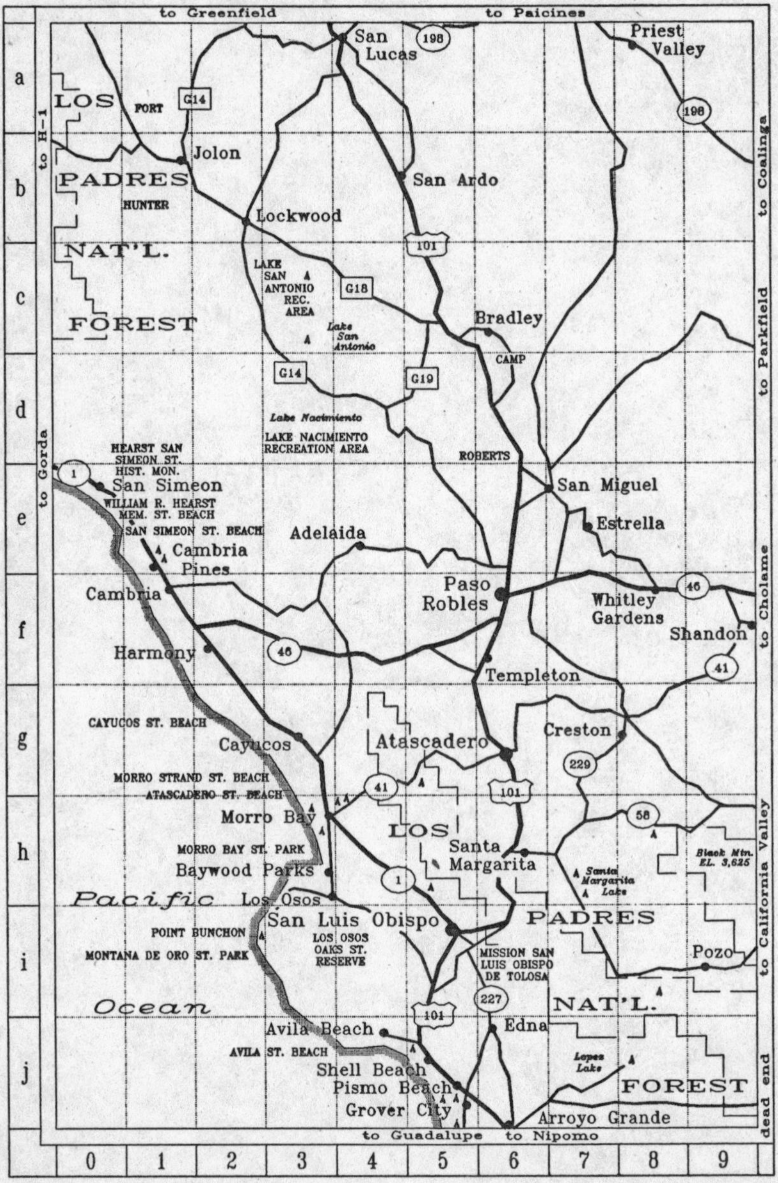

Map grid **c3**

NORTH SHORE
on Lake San Antonio

A

Campsites, facilities: There are 236 campsites for tents or motor homes, some with full or partial hookups. Piped water, fireplaces, and tables are provided. A dump station, rest rooms, showers, a boat ramp, boat rentals, stables, a playground, a recreation room, a laundromat, and a grocery store are available. Pets are permitted.

B

Reservations, fee: Reservations accepted for groups; $9-$17 fee per night; pets $1.

Who to contact: Phone the resort at (805)472-2311.

Location: From King City on US 101, turn south onto County Road G18 and drive 24 miles to the Lockwood intersection. Continue straight on County Road G18 (Jolon Road) and drive about ten miles to the campground entrance road.

C

Trip note: Lake San Antonio is a year-round spot for adventure. It is a narrow, 16-mile long reservoir that provides fishing for bass in the spring, water skiing in the summer, and one-of-a-kind bald eagle tours in the winter. It's a good spot for boaters and campers.

D

Map grid **c3**

SOUTH SHORE
on Lake San Antonio

Campsites, facilities: There are three campgrounds with a total of 458 campsites for tents or motor homes, many with full or partial hookups. Piped water, fireplaces, and tables are provided. A dump station, rest rooms, showers, a boat ramp, boat rentals, a playground, a recreation room, a laundromat, and a grocery store are available. Pets are permitted.

E

Reservations, fee: Reservations accepted; $9-$17 fee per night; pets $1.

Who to contact: Phone the resort at (805)472-2311.

F

Location: From King City, drive 29 miles south on US 101. Take the County Road G19 (Nacimiento Lake Road) exit and drive 12 miles to County Road G14 (Interlake Road). Turn right and drive nine miles to the campground entrance road (San Antonio Road).

Trip note: Harris Creek, Redondo Vista, and Lynch are the three campgrounds set near each other along the south shore of Lake San Antonio, a 16-mile reservoir that provides good bass fishing in the spring and water skiing in the summer. In the winter months, the Monterey County Department of Parks offers a unique eagle watch program, which includes boat tours. Open all year.

G2

Map grid **e1**

WASHBURN
SAN SIMEON STATE BEACH

H

Campsites, facilities: There are 70 campsites for tents or motor homes up to 31 feet long. Fireplaces and picnic tables are provided. Piped water and chemical toilets are available. A grocery store, a laundromat, and propane gas can be found nearby in Cambria. Pets are permitted.

I

Reservations, fee: Reserve through MISTIX at (800)444-PARK ($3.95 MISTIX fee); $7-$9 fee per night; pets $1.

Who to contact: Phone the state beach at (805)927-2038.

Location: From Cambria, drive three miles north on Highway 1 to the park entrance. This campground is just beyond San Simeon Creek Campground on the park entrance road.

J

Trip note: This camp is primarily used as an overflow area if the San Simeon Creek campground is jammed to the rafters. It sits on the hill above the other camp and offers an ocean view, but it is less developed. That's good or bad depending on your viewpoint. Open year-round.

Map grid **e1**

SAN SIMEON CREEK

SAN SIMEON STATE BEACH

Campsites, facilities: There are 134 campsites for tents or motor homes up to 35 feet long. Two of the sites are set up for wheelchair access. Fireplaces and picnic tables are provided. Piped water, flush toilets, showers, and a dump station are available. A grocery store, a laundromat, and propane gas can be found nearby in Cambria. Pets are permitted.

Reservations, fee: Reserve through MISTIX at (800)444-PARK ($3.95 MISTIX fee); $12-$14 fee per night; pets $1.

Who to contact: Phone the state beach at (805)927-2038.

Location: From Cambria, drive three miles north on Highway 1 to the park entrance.

Trip note: Hearst Castle is only five miles northeast, so this spot is a natural for visitors planning to take the tour. For a tour reservation phone MISTIX. The camp is set across the highway from the ocean, with easy access under the highway to the beach. San Simeon Creek, while not exactly the Mississippi, runs through the campground and adds a nice touch. Open year-round.

Map grid **g5**

CERRO ALTO

LOS PADRES NATIONAL FOREST

Campsites, facilities: There are eight walk-in tent sites and 16 campsites for tents or motor homes up to 19 feet long. Piped water, fireplaces, and picnic tables are provided. Vault toilets are available. Pets are permitted on leashes.

Reservations, fee: No reservations; $5 fee per night.

Who to contact: Phone the Los Padres National Forest Santa Lucia District at (805)925-9538.

Location: From Morro Bay, drive eight miles northeast on Highway 41. Turn on the campground entrance road and drive 1.5 miles to campground.

Trip note: This is just obscure enough to get missed by a lot of folks. It is set near Morro Creek in the Santa Lucia Mountain Range at 1,000 feet elevation. A map of Los Padres National Forest details back roads and trails. Open all year.

Map grid **h3**

MORRO BAY STATE PARK

Campsites, facilities: There are 20 motor home spaces with water and electrical connections and 115 campsites for tents or motor homes up to 31 feet long. Some sites are wheelchair accessible. Fireplaces and picnic tables are provided. Piped water, flush toilets, showers, a dump station, museum exhibits, nature walks and programs are available. A laundromat, a grocery store, propane gas, a boat ramp, mooring, rentals, and food service are available in Morro Bay. The picnicking, museum, and food service areas are wheelchair accessible. Pets are permitted.

Reservations, fee: Reserve through MISTIX at (800)444-PARK ($3.95 MISTIX fee); $12-$18 fee per night; pets $1.

Who to contact: Phone the park at (805)772-2560.

Location: On Highway 1, drive to the south end of Morro Bay to the park entrance.

Trip note: Reservations are strongly advised. This is one of the premium stopover spots for folks cruising north on Highway 1 out of the L.A. area. The park offers a wide range of activities and exhibits covering the natural and cultural history of the area. Side trips include fishing in Morro Bay, touring Hearst Castle, or visiting the Morro Bay Wildlife Refuge.

A

Map grid **h3**

MORRO STRAND STATE BEACH
near Morro Bay

B

Campsites, facilities: There are 23 sites for tents only and 81 motor home spaces for motor homes up to 24 feet long. Piped water, fireplaces, and picnic tables are provided. Flush toilets and cold, outdoor showers are available. Supplies and a laundromat are available in Morro Bay. Pets are permitted.

Reservations, fee: Reserve through MISTIX at (800)444-PARK ($3.95 MISTIX fee); $12-$14 fee per night; pets $1.

C

Who to contact: Phone the state beach at (805)772-2560.

Location: From the town of Morro Bay, drive three miles north on Highway 1.

Trip note: A ton of Highway 1 cruisers plan to stay overnight at this state park. And why not? It is set along the ocean near Morro Bay, a pretty spot year-round. Side trip options include the Morro Bay Wildlife Refuge, Museum of Natural History, or an ocean fishing trip out of Morro Bay.

D

Map grid **h4**

RANCHO COLINA RV PARK
in Morro Bay

E

Campsites, facilities: There are 57 motor home spaces with full hookups. Picnic tables are provided. Rest rooms, showers, a laundromat, and a recreation room are available. Supplies can be found nearby.

Reservations, fee: Call ahead for available space; $18 fee per night.

Who to contact: Phone the park at (805)772-8420.

F

Location: From Morro Bay on Highway 1, drive one mile east on Atascadero Road (Highway 41) to 1045 Atascadero Road.

Trip note: This is a privately-operated motor home park, one of several camping options in the Morro Bay area.

Map grid **h4**

MORRO DUNES TRAILER PARK AND CAMPGROUND
in Morro Bay

G2

Campsites, facilities: There are 43 sites for tents only and 139 motor home spaces. Picnic tables, fireplaces, piped water, electrical connections, and, in most cases, sewer hookups are provided. Rest rooms, showers, a laundromat, a store, wood, ice, and a dump station are available. Propane gas can be obtained nearby.

H

Reservations, fee: Call ahead for available space; $12-$20 fee per night.

Who to contact: Phone the park at (805)772-2722.

Location: From Highway 1 in Morro Bay, drive west on Atascadero Road (Highway 41) for one-half mile to 1700 Atascadero.

I

Trip note: The many side trip possibilities make this an attractive destination. Available trips include deep sea fishing and clamming out of Morro Bay, the Hearst Castle tour, Montana de Oro State Park, the Museum of Natural History, and the Morro Bay Wildlife Refuge. Open year-round.

J

Map grid h5 EL CHORRO REGIONAL PARK
near San Luis Obispo

Campsites, facilities: There are 25 primitive, undesignated sites for tents or motor homes. Fireplaces and picnic tables are provided. Piped water, flush toilets, and a playground are available. Supplies and a laundromat are nearby in San Luis Obispo. Pets are permitted on leashes.
Reservations, fee: No reservations; $10 fee per night; pets $1.50.
Who to contact: Phone the park at (805)549-5219.
Location: From San Luis Obispo, drive seven miles north on Highway 1 to the park entrance on the east side of the highway.
Trip note: Despite easy access just off Highway 1, this park is often overlooked for one reason: It isn't in the state park or MISTIX reservation systems. That means there are times when coastal state parks can be jammed full and this regional park may still have space. Morro Bay, located six miles away, provides many possible side trips.

Map grid h7 RINCONADA CAMPGROUND
near Santa Margarita Lake

Campsites, facilities: There are 60 campsites for tents or motor homes, many with full or partial hookups. Picnic tables and fireplaces are provided. Flush toilets, showers, and a dump station are available. A grocery store, a laundromat, and propane gas are available nearby. Pets are permitted on leashes.
Reservations, fee: Call for available space; $9-$11 fee per night.
Who to contact: Phone the park at (805)438-5479.
Location: From Santa Margarita, drive east on Highway 58 for two miles. Turn south on Pozo Road and drive seven miles to the campground.
Trip note: This camp's nearby proximity to Santa Margarita Lake is a highlight. It's a pretty lake, especially in spring when the surrounding hills are green and the lake is at its fullest. Open year-round.

Map grid h7 SANTA MARGARITA LAKE CAMPGROUND

Campsites, facilities: There are 54 sites for tents or motor homes. Picnic tables, fireplaces, piped water, and, in some cases, electrical connections and sewer hookups are provided. Rest rooms, showers, a swimming pool, a playground, a laundromat, a store, a dump station, and propane gas are available. Pets are permitted on leashes.
Reservations, fee: Call for available space; $12 fee per night; pets $3.
Who to contact: Phone the camp at (805)438-5618.
Location: From San Luis Obispo, drive eight miles north on US 101. Turn east on Highway 58 and drive four miles (two miles past Santa Margarita). Turn southeast on Pozo Road and drive for seven miles to Santa Margarita Lake Road. Follow this road for two miles to the campground at 4765 Santa Margarita Lake Road.
Trip note: Santa Margarita Lake is set in the coastal oak woodlands east of San Luis Obispo, just below the Santa Lucia Mountains. It is a long narrow lake that has good fishing for bass in the spring but slows in late summer. Open year-round.

Map grid **h8**

BLACK MOUNTAIN RV RESORT
near Santa Margarita Lake

A

Campsites, facilities: There are 20 tent sites and 25 motor home spaces. Picnic tables and fireplaces are provided. Rest rooms, showers, a swimming pool, a laundromat, a store, a tavern, a sanitary disposal station, ice, a recreation room with a large barbecue, and propane gas are available. Pets are permitted on leashes.

B

Reservations, fee: Reservations suggested; $10 fee per night.

Who to contact: Phone the campground at (805)438-3778.

Location: From Santa Margarita, drive ten miles east on Highway 58 to the signed entrance to the park.

Trip note: This year-round, privately-operated park in the mountains is set up primarily for motor home cruisers who want to get off the main drag. Its proximity to nearby Santa Margarita Lake to the south is a bonus.

C

Map grid **i2**

MONTANA DE ORO STATE PARK
near Morro Bay

D

Campsites, facilities: There are 50 campsites for tents or motor homes up to 24 feet long. Fireplaces and picnic tables are provided. Pit toilets and a nature trail are available. There is **no piped water,** so bring your own. Supplies and a laundromat are nearby.

Reservations, fee: Reserve through MISTIX at (800)444-PARK ($3.95 MISTIX fee); $7-$9 fee per night; pets $1.

E

Who to contact: Phone the park at (805)528-0513.

Location: From Morro Bay, drive two miles south on Highway 1. Turn on South Bay Boulevard and drive four miles to Los Osos. Turn right (west) on Pecho Valley Road and drive five miles to the park.

F

Trip note: This primitive, sprawling chunk of land includes coastline, 7,300 acres of foothills, and Valencia Peak, elevation 1,345 feet. There's no water—that stops a lot of people.

Map grid **i8**

HI MOUNTAIN
LOS PADRES NATIONAL FOREST

G2

Campsites, facilities: There are 11 campsites for tents or motor homes up to 16 feet long (trailers not recommended). Piped water, fireplaces, and picnic tables are provided. Vault toilets are available. Pets are permitted on leashes.

Reservations, fee: No reservations; $5 fee per night.

H

Who to contact: Phone the Los Padres National Forest Santa Lucia District at (805)925-9538.

Location: From San Luis Obispo, drive eight miles north on US 101. Turn east on Highway 58 and drive four miles (two miles past Santa Margarita). Turn southeast on Pozo Road and drive for 16 miles to the town of Pozo. Turn on Hi Mountain Road and drive two miles to the campground.

I

Trip note: At an elevation of 2,800 feet, this is the highest point in the Santa Lucia Wilderness. It's a trailhead camp with two trails starting here leading into the Garcia Mountain area to two other camps. In fall, it makes a good base camp for hunters. Open year-round (road may be closed during heavy rains).

J

Map grid j5 AVILA HOT SPRINGS SPA AND RV PARK

on San Luis Obispo Bay

Campsites, facilities: There are 25 sites for tents only and 50 motor home spaces, many with full or partial hookups. Picnic tables and some fireplaces are provided. Rest rooms, showers, a swimming pool, a hot mineral pool, a spa, cable TV, a dump station, a recreation room, an arcade, and group barbecue pits are available. A grocery store, a laundromat, propane gas, a golf course, and riding stables are nearby.

Reservations, fee: Call ahead for available space and fee.

Who to contact: Phone the park at (805)595-2359.

Location: From San Luis Obispo, drive eight miles south on US 101 to the Avila Beach Drive exit. Drive to 250 Avila Beach Drive.

Trip note: The hot mineral pool here is a featured attraction. Not exactly a fountain of youth, but it'll give you a glow for a few days. Nearby recreation options include Avila State Beach and Pismo State Beach. Open year-round.

Map grid j5 PISMO COAST VILLAGE

in Pismo Beach

Campsites, facilities: There are 400 motor home spaces with full hookups, picnic tables, and fireplaces. Rest rooms, showers, playgrounds, swimming pools, a laundromat, a store, firewood, ice, a recreation room, propane gas, recreation programs, a restaurant, and a miniature golf course are available.

Reservations, fee: Call for available space; $17-$30 fee per night.

Who to contact: Phone the park at (805)773-1811.

Location: In Pismo Beach drive to 165 South Dolliver Street (Highway 1).

Trip note: This big time motor home park gets a lot of use by Highway 1 cruisers. Its location is a plus, being set near the ocean. Open year-round.

Map grid j5 NORTH BEACH

PISMO STATE BEACH

Campsites, facilities: There are 100 campsites for tents or motor homes up to 31 feet long. Fireplaces and picnic tables are provided. Piped water, flush toilets and a dump station are available. Horseback riding facilities, a grocery store, a laundromat, and propane gas are nearby. Pets are permitted on leashes.

Reservations, fee: Reserve through MISTIX at (800)444-PARK ($3.95 MISTIX fee); $12-$14 fee per night; pets $1.

Who to contact: Phone the park at (805)489-2684.

Location: From Pismo Beach, drive one mile south on Highway 1.

Trip note: Plan on a reservation and plenty of company. This is an exceptionally popular state beach, as an ultimate destination as well as for folks just wanting a stopover while cruising Highway 1. The adjacent dune area makes for great walks, or, for kids, great rolls.

Map grid j5 LE SAGE RIVIERA

near Pismo State Beach

Campsites, facilities: There are 87 motor home spaces. Picnic tables, piped water, electrical connections, and sewer hookups are provided. Rest rooms, showers, and a laundromat are available. Stores, restaurants, and golf courses are nearby. Pets are permitted on leashes.

Reservations, fee: Call for available space; $18-$20 fee per night.
Who to contact: Phone the park at (805)489-2103.
Location: From Pismo Beach, drive two miles south on Grand Avenue or Dolliver Street to 319 North Highway 1.
Trip note: This is a year-round motor home park that can provide headquarters for visits to several nearby attractions. They include nearby Pismo State Beach and Lopez Lake, ten miles to the east. Open year-round.

A B C D E F G2 H I J

Map grid j8

LOPEZ LAKE RECREATION AREA

near Arroyo Grande

Campsites, facilities: There are 354 sites for tents or motor homes of any length, many with full or partial hookups. Picnic tables and fireplaces are provided. Rest rooms, showers, a playground, a laundromat, a store, ice, a snack bar, a boat ramp, mooring, boat fuel, propane gas, tackle, boat rentals, and a water slide are available. Pets are permitted on leashes.
Reservations, fee: Reservations accepted; Call (805)489-8019; $10-$16 fee per night; pets $1.50.
Who to contact: Phone the park at (805)489-1122.
Location: From Arroyo Grande on US 101, take the Grand Avenue exit. Turn east and drive through Arroyo Grande. Turn northeast on Lopez Drive and drive ten miles to the park.
Trip note: Lopez Lake is set amid oak woodlands southeast of San Luis Obispo. The lake is shaped something like a horseshoe, and in the spring, maybe it brings good luck to fishermen. By summer, waterskiers take over. Side trips include hiking or horseback riding, with a number of trails looping through the area. Open year-round.

◆ MAP G3 ◆

BEACH
TREES
5% CLUB
DESERT
URBAN
FOOTHILL
GRASSLAND

15 MILES

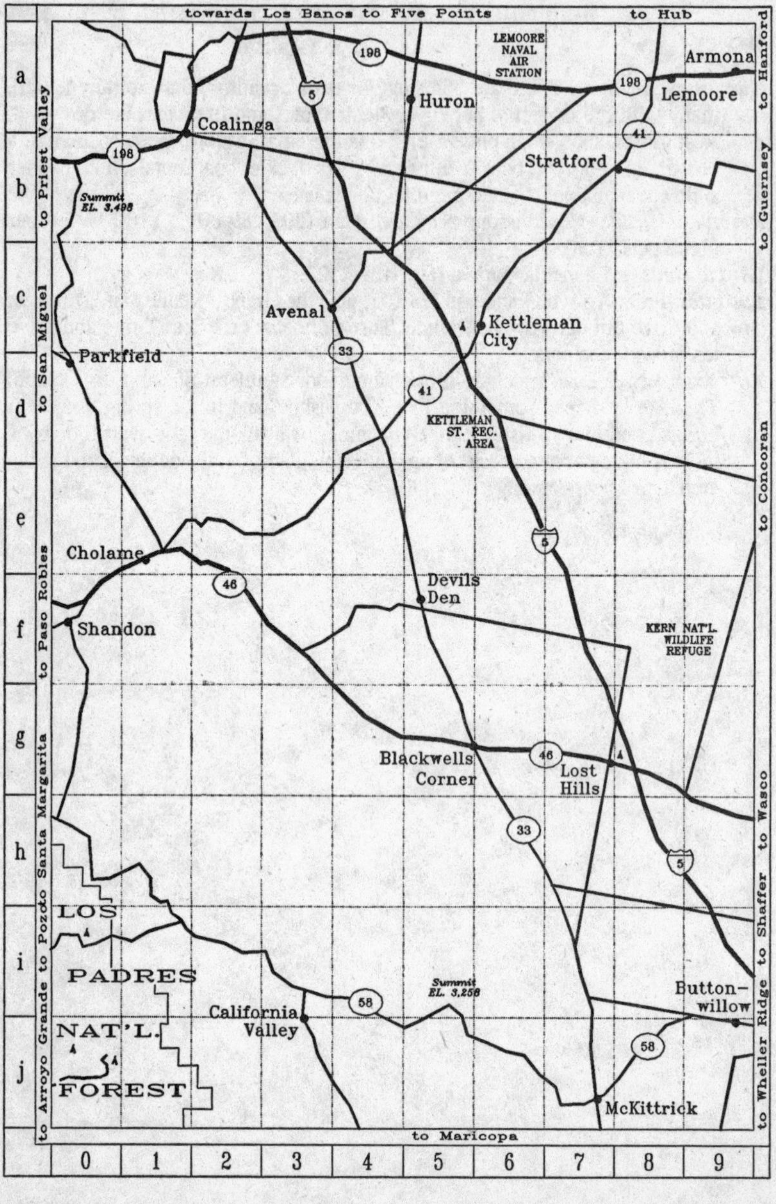

towards Los Banos to Five Points
to Hub
to Hanford
to Guernsey
to Concoran
to Wasco
to Shaffer
to Wheller Ridge
to Maricopa
to Priest Valley
to San Miguel
to Paso Robles
to Arroyo Grande to Pozo to Santa Margarita

198
5
LEMOORE NAVAL AIR STATION
Armona
Lemoore
Huron
Coalinga
41
Stratford
Summit EL. 3,498
Avenal
Kettleman City
33
Parkfield
KETTLEMAN ST. REC. AREA
Cholame
46
Devils Den
Shandon
KERN NAT'L. WILDLIFE REFUGE
Blackwells Corner
Lost Hills
LOS PADRES NAT'L. FOREST
Summit EL. 3,258
58
Button-willow
California Valley
McKittrick

a b c d e f g h i j

0 1 2 3 4 5 6 7 8 9

Map grid c5 — KETTLEMAN CITY RV PARK

near Kettleman City

Campsites, facilities: There are 65 motor home spaces, and unlimited tent sites. Picnic tables, piped water, and full or partial hookups are provided. Rest rooms, showers, playgrounds, a laundromat, a store, a dump station, a dog run, a restaurant, a snack bar, horseback riding facilities, and propane gas are available.

Reservations, fee: Call ahead for available space; $7-$15 fee per night.

Who to contact: Phone the park at (209)386-4000.

Location: From Interstate 5 near Kettleman City, take the Highway 41 exit. Drive one-half mile north on Highway 41. Turn left (west) on Hubert Way, then right on Cyril Place to 452 Cyril Place.

Trip note: Being stuck in Kings County looking for a place to park a motor home is no picnic. Unless, that is, you are lucky enough to have this book and know about Kettleman City RV Park. It's literally the "only game in town;" in fact, it's the only camp in the entire county. Visitors will find access to miles of open paths and roads for hiking or running. Open year-round.

Map grid g8 — LOST HILLS KOA

near Kern National Wildlife Refuge

Campsites, facilities: There are ten sites for tents only and 80 motor home spaces. Picnic tables, piped water, satellite TV, and full hookups are provided. Rest rooms, showers, a swimming pool, a laundromat, a store, a video room, and propane gas are available. Some facilities are wheelchair accessible. Restaurants are nearby.

Reservations, fee: Call ahead for available space and fee.

Who to contact: Phone the park at (805)797-2719.

Location: Drive to the junction of Interstate 5 and Highway 46.

Trip note: The pickings can get slim around these parts if you're cruising north on Interstate 5, so if it's late, don't be too quick to pooh-pooh a KOA camp. The nearby Kern National Wildlife Refuge, about a 15-minute drive away, offers a side trip possibility. It's a waterfowl reserve that attracts a lot of ducks and geese in the fall and winter months. Open year-round.

Map grid i0 — LA PANZA

LOS PADRES NATIONAL FOREST

Campsites, facilities: There are 16 campsites for tents or motor homes up to 16 feet long. Fireplaces and picnic tables are provided. Vault toilets are available. The availability of potable water is not guaranteed.

Reservations, fee: No reservations; $3 fee per night during deer season.

Who to contact: Phone the Los Padres National Forest Santa Lucia District at (805)925-9538.

Location: From San Luis Obispo, drive eight miles north on US 101. Turn east on Highway 58 and drive four miles (two miles past Santa Margarita). Turn southeast on Pozo Road and drive for 16 miles to the town of Pozo. Continue 11.5 miles east past Pozo on County Road M3093 to the campground.

Trip note: This primitive spot is located at 2,400 feet in the La Panza Range, an oak woodland area which is crisscrossed by numerous trails and streams. This is a nearby option to the Hi Mountain campground. Open year-round.

Map grid **jO**

AGUA ESCONDIDO
LOS PADRES NATIONAL FOREST

Campsites, facilities: There are two campsites for tents. Fireplaces and picnic tables are provided. Vault toilets and a horse trough are available. Open only in the early summer to late fall, during deer season. There is **no piped water,** so bring your own. Pets are permitted on leashes.

Reservations, fee: No reservations, no fee.

Who to contact: Phone the Los Padres National Forest Santa Lucia District at (805)925-9538.

Location: From Arroyo Grande on US 101, take the Grand Avenue exit. Turn east and drive through Arroyo Grande. Turn northeast on Lopez Drive and drive 1.5 miles. Turn right on Huasna Road and drive 11 miles east. Continue east on County Road M2023 (Arroyo Seco/Huasna Road) for ten miles. Turn north (left) on Forest Service Road 30S02 and drive two miles to the campground.

Trip note: This gets the award as the smallest official campground in Southern California. There's not much here; it's a small and obscure hunting camp, that gets some rare use in the fall. A map of Los Padres National Forest will give details about the surrounding area. The elevation is 2,200 feet. Open only in the early summer to late fall, during deer season.

Map grid **jO**

STONY CREEK
LOS PADRES NATIONAL FOREST

Campsites, facilities: There are six campsites for tents. Fireplaces and picnic tables are provided. Vault toilets are available. There is **no piped water,** so bring your own. Pets are permitted on leashes.

Reservations, fee: No reservations, no fee.

Who to contact: Phone the Los Padres National Forest Santa Lucia District at (805)925-9538.

Location: From Arroyo Grande on US 101, take the Grand Avenue exit. Turn east and drive through Arroyo Grande. Turn northeast on Lopez Drive and drive 1.5 miles. Turn right on Huasna Road and drive 11 miles east. Continue east on County Road M2023 (Arroyo Seco/Huasna Road) for ten miles. Turn north (left) on Forest Service Road 30S02 and drive 2.5 miles. Turn left on Forest Service Road 31S09 and drive 1.5 miles to the campground.

Trip note: Just about nobody goes out here. It is a small, primitive spot set along little Stony Creek at 1,800 feet elevation, deep in the Los Padres National Forest. You're not going to see Bigfoot here, but you won't likely see any other folks either. Open year-round.

A

B

C

D

E

F

G3

H

I

J

◆ MAP G4 ◆

BEACH
TREES
5% CLUB
DESERT
URBAN
FOOTHILL
GRASSLAND

15 MILES

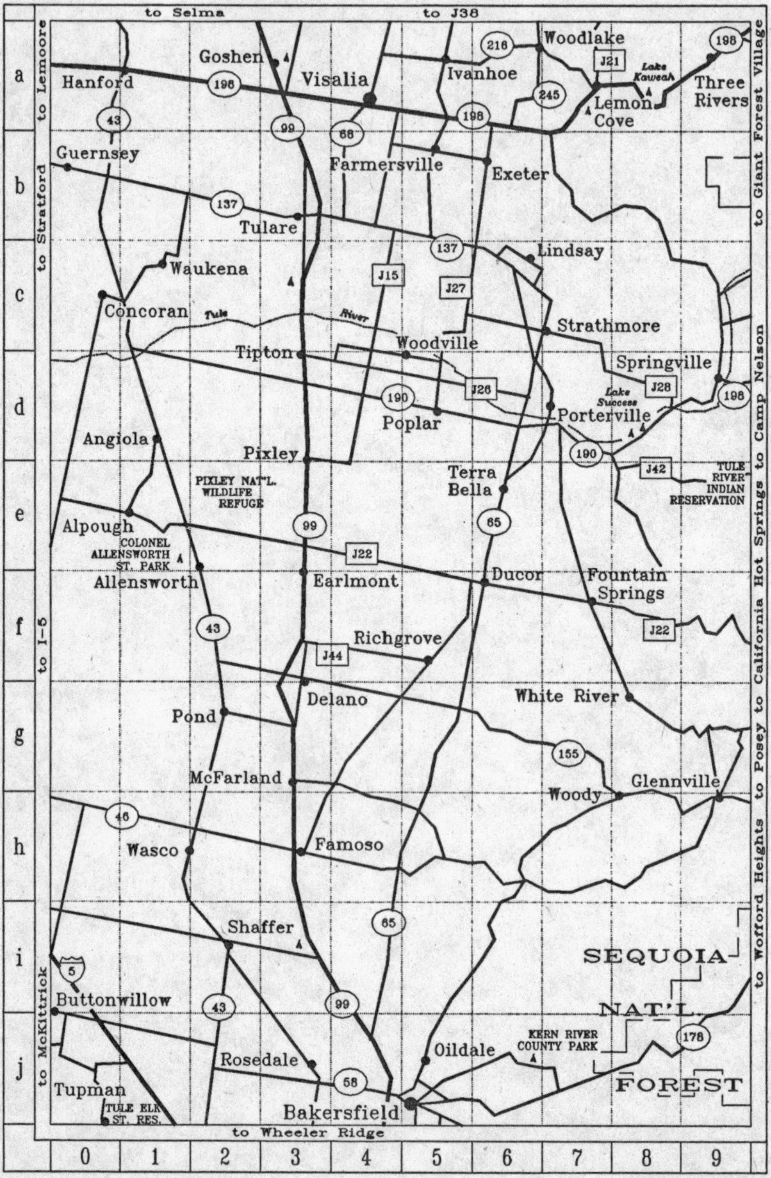

to Selma
to J38
to Lemoore
to Stratford
to I-5
to McKittrick
to Giant Forest Village
to Camp Nelson
to Posey to California Hot Springs
to Wofford Heights
to Wheeler Ridge

a b c d e f g h i j

0 1 2 3 4 5 6 7 8 9

Goshen
Visalia
Ivanhoe
Woodlake
Lake Kaweah
Three Rivers
Hanford
Lemon Cove
Guernsey
Farmersville
Exeter
Tulare
Lindsay
Waukena
Concoran
Tule River
Strathmore
Tipton
Woodville
Springville
Lake Success
Porterville
Poplar
Angiola
Pixley
Terra Bella
PIXLEY NAT'L. WILDLIFE REFUGE
TULE RIVER INDIAN RESERVATION
Alpough
COLONEL ALLENSWORTH ST. PARK
Allensworth
Earlmont
Ducor
Fountain Springs
Richgrove
Delano
White River
Pond
McFarland
Woody
Glennville
Wasco
Famoso
Shaffer
SEQUOIA NAT'L. FOREST
Buttonwillow
KERN RIVER COUNTY PARK
Oildale
Rosedale
Tupman
TULE ELK ST. RES.
Bakersfield

198 216 245 43 99 68 137 J21 J15 J27 J26 J28 190 J42 65 J22 J44 155 46 5 43 99 58 178

GOSHEN-VISALIA KOA

Map grid a3

Campsites, facilities: There are ten sites for tents only, 48 motor home spaces, and 38 sites for tents or motor homes. Piped water and full or partial hookups are provided. Rest rooms, showers, a swimming pool, a laundromat, a playground, a recreation room, a store, a dump station, and propane gas are available.

Reservations, fee: Call for available space; $14-$18 fee per night.

Who to contact: Phone the park at (209)651-0544 or (800)322-2336 in California.

Location: From Visalia, drive five miles west to 7480 Avenue 308; or drive one mile east of Highway 99; or drive one mile north of Highway 198.

Trip note: This is a layover spot for Highway 99 cruisers. If you're looking for a spot to park your rig for the night, don't get too picky around these parts. Open all year.

LEMON COVE-SEQUOIA KOA

near Lake Kaweah

Map grid a7

Campsites, facilities: There are 55 sites for tents or motor homes. Picnic tables, fireplaces, piped water, and full or partial hookups are provided. Rest rooms, showers, a playground, a swimming pool, a laundromat, a recreation room, cable TV, a store, a dump station, and propane gas are available.

Reservations, fee: Call for available space; $12-$16 fee per night.

Who to contact: Phone the park at (209)597-2346.

Location: From Visalia, drive east on Highway 198 to its intersection with Highway 65. Continue for eight miles on Highway 198 to the campground.

Trip note: This year-round KOA camp provides an option for campers who want a spot near Lake Kaweah.

HORSE CREEK RECREATION AREA

on Lake Kaweah

Map grid a8

Campsites, facilities: There are 80 campsites for tents or motor homes. Piped water, fireplaces, and picnic tables are provided. Flush toilets, showers, a paved boat ramp, and a dump station are available. Some facilities are wheelchair accessible. Nearby are a grocery store, laundromat, boat and water ski rentals, ice, a snack bar, and propane gas.

Reservations, fee: No reservations; $8-$10 fee per night.

Who to contact: Phone the U.S. Corps of Engineers at (209)597-2301.

Location: From Visalia, drive 25 miles east on Highway 198 to Lake Kaweah's south shore.

Trip note: The sun brands everything in sight around this part of the valley. Lake Kaweah is the spot folks go for a quick dunk. The camp is set on the southern shore of the lake. Waterskiers tend to monopolize the lake, but in spring, before it gets too hot, trout and bass fishing are decent. The water level drops a great deal during late summer, as thirsty farms suck up every drop they can get. The elevation is 300 feet.

SUN AND FUN RV PARK

near Tulare

Map grid c3

Campsites, facilities: There are 87 motor home spaces. Picnic tables, fireplaces, piped water, and full hookups are provided. Rest rooms, showers, a dump station, a playground, a swimming pool, a spa, a laundromat, a store, a recreation room with color TV and billiard tables, a dog run, a restaurant, and propane gas are available. Some facilities are wheelchair accessible. A golf course is nearby.

Reservations, fee: Call ahead for available space; $18.50 fee per night.

Who to contact: Phone the park at (209)686-5779.

Location: From Tulare, drive three miles south Highway 99 to the Avenue 200 exit west. Drive a short distance to 1000 Avenue 200.

Trip note: We figured somebody should give the swimming pool a lifesaver award, so what the heck, we did. This motor home park is just off Highway 99, exactly halfway between San Francisco and Los Angeles. Are you having fun yet?

Map grid d8

PORTERVILLE-YOKUT KOA
near Success Lake

Campsites, facilities: There are 250 sites for tents or motor homes, 50 with full or partial hookups. Picnic tables and, in some cases, fire grills are provided. Rest rooms, showers, a recreation room, a playground, a swimming pool, a laundromat, a store, a dump station, firewood, a dog-walking area, and propane gas are available. Pets are permitted on leashes, but they must be attended at all times and they are not allowed in the office or the rest rooms; noisy or dangerous pets not permitted at all.

Reservations, fee: Call for available space; $15-$18 fee per night. Group rates can be arranged.

Who to contact: Phone the park at (209)784-2123.

Location: From Porterville on Highway 65, turn east on Highway 190 and drive five miles to 27798 Highway 190.

Trip note: This campground is set in a parklike setting with trees and flowers. It is two miles from Success Lake. A small, stocked fishing pond is available, and pet geese and ducks are often wandering around. Get this: Their names are Heckel, Jeckel, and Hansel, and Heckel and Jeckel like to chase Hansel. Open all year.

Map grid d8

TULE RECREATION AREA
on Success Lake

Campsites, facilities: There are 104 campsites for tents or motor homes up to 30 feet long. Piped water, fireplaces, and picnic tables are provided. Flush toilets, a dump station, and a playground are available. Nearby are a grocery store, a boat ramp, boat and water ski rentals, bait, tackle, and propane gas. Pets are permitted on leashes.

Reservations, fee: No reservations; $10 fee per night for regular camping; several primitive no fee sites are available.

Who to contact: Phone the U.S. Corps of Engineers at (209)784-0215.

Location: From Porterville, drive eight miles east on Highway 190 to Success Lake.

Trip note: Success Lake is a popular spot for San Joaquin Valley waterskiers. The lake is set in the foothill country, where 100-degree weather is common in the summer. Fishing is best in the spring and so is the hiking. The wildlife area along the west side of the lake is worth exploring. In the fall, pheasant hunting is permitted here. Another option is to hike the nature trail below the dam, which passes through groves of sycamores. The elevation is 655 feet.

Map grid **e1**

ALLENSWORTH STATE HISTORIC PARK
near Earlimart

A

Campsites, facilities: There are 15 campsites for tents or motor homes up to 35 feet long. Piped water, fireplaces, and picnic tables are provided. Vault toilets, dump station and visitor center are available. A grocery store is nearby. Pets are permitted on leashes.

B

Reservations, fee: Reserve through MISTIX at (800)444-PARK ($3.95 MISTIX fee); $12 fee per night; pets $1.

Who to contact: Phone the park at (805)849-3433.

Location: From Earlimart on Highway 99, drive nine miles west on Avenue 56. Turn left on Highway 43 and drive to the park.

C

Trip note: What you have here is the old town (Allensworth) that has been restored as an historical park dedicated to the African American pioneers who founded it with Colonel Allen Allensworth, the highest ranking army chaplin of his time. One museum is available at the school here and another at the Colonel's house with a 30-minute movie on the history of Allensworth. Open year-round.

D

Map grid **i3**

KOA BAKERSFIELD

Campsites, facilities: There are 12 tent sites and 62 motor home spaces. Picnic tables, piped water, and full or partial hookups are provided. Rest rooms, showers, a swimming pool, a recreation room, a laundromat, a store, a dump station, and propane gas are available.

E

Reservations, fee: Call for space available; $18 fee per night.

Who to contact: Phone the park at (805)399-3107.

Location: From Bakersfield, drive 12 miles north on Highway 99 to the Shafter-Lerdo Highway exit. Drive one mile west on Lerdo Way to 32569 Lerdo Way.

F

Trip note: If you're stuck in the southern valley and the temperature feels like you're sitting in a cauldron, well, this spot provides a layover for the night, near the town of Shafter. It's not exactly a hotbed of excitement. Open year-round.

G4

Map grid **j6**

KERN RIVER COUNTY PARK
at Lake Ming

Campsites, facilities: There are 50 campsites for tents or motor homes. Picnic tables, fireplaces, and piped water are provided. Flush toilets, showers, a dump station, a playground, and a boat ramp are available. Pets are permitted on leashes. Nearby is a grocery store.

H

Reservations, fee: No reservations; $10 fee per night; pets $2.

Who to contact: Phone the County Parks Department at (805)861-2345 or (805)872-3179.

I

Location: From Bakersfield, drive east on Highway 178. Turn left (north) on Alfred Harrell Highway and follow the signs to Lake Ming. Then follow the signs.

Trip note: This is a popular spot for southern valley residents, since it is only a 15-minute drive from Bakersfield. Water skiing is permitted on Lake Ming, and dominates summer activity. Recreation options include Hart Park and the Foss-Kern River County Golf Course. The elevation is 450 feet. Open all year.

J

◆ MAP G5 ◆

BEACH
TREES
5% CLUB
DESERT
URBAN
FOOTHILL
GRASSLAND

15 MILES

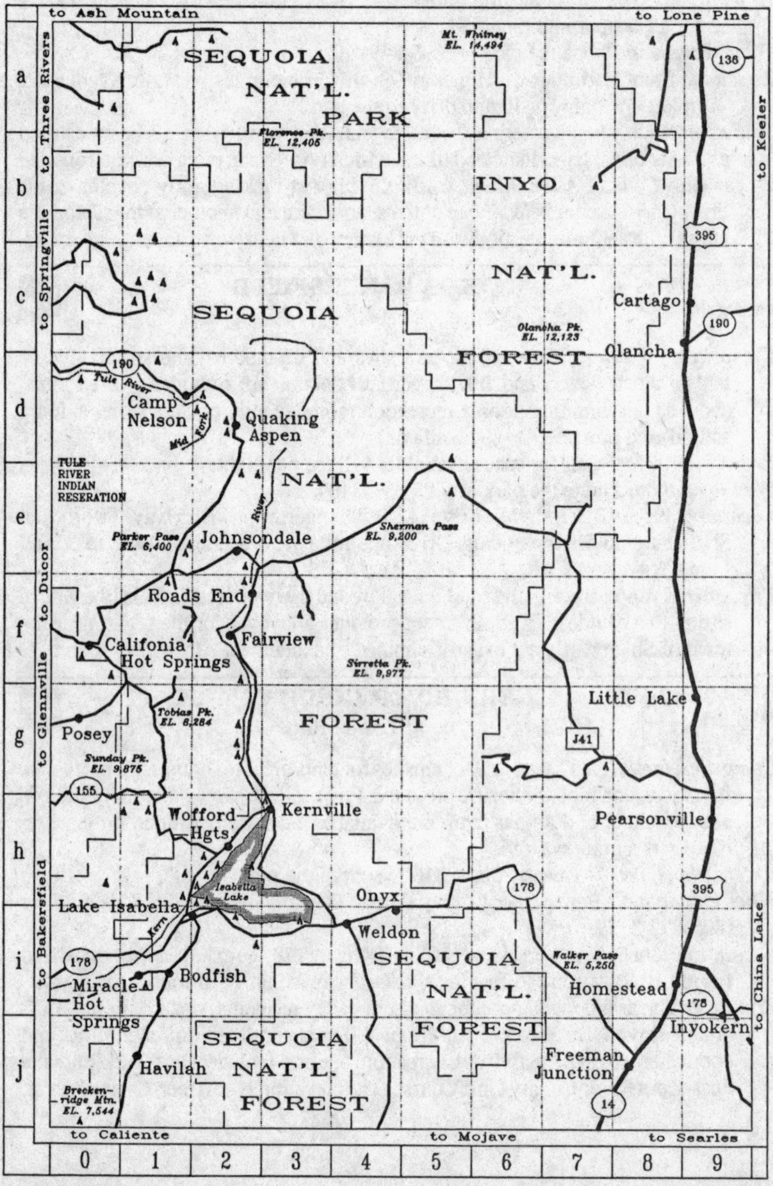

to Ash Mountain
to Lone Pine
to Three Rivers
to Springville
to Keeler
to Ducor
to Glennville
to Bakersfield
to China Lake

SEQUOIA NAT'L. PARK
Mt. Whitney EL. 14,494
Florence Pk. EL. 12,405
INYO NAT'L. FOREST
Olancha Pk. EL. 12,123
SEQUOIA NAT'L. FOREST
136
395
190
Cartago
Olancha
Camp Nelson
Tule River
Mid Fork
Quaking Aspen
TULE RIVER INDIAN RESERATION
River
Parker Pass EL. 6,400
Johnsondale
Sherman Pass EL. 9,200
Roads End
Fairview
Califonia Hot Springs
Sirretta Pk. EL. 9,977
Tobias Pk. EL. 8,284
Posey
Sunday Pk. EL. 9,875
155
Little Lake
J41
Kernville
Wofford Hgts
Pearsonville
Isabella Lake
Lake Isabella
Onyx
178
Weldon
Kern
Bodfish
Miracle Hot Springs
Walker Pass EL. 5,250
Homestead
Inyokern
Havilah
Freeman Junction
14
Brecken-ridge Mtn. EL. 7,544

to Caliente
to Mojave
to Searles

a b c d e f g h i j

0 1 2 3 4 5 6 7 8 9

Map grid a0

SOUTH FORK

on the South Fork of Kaweah River
SEQUOIA NATIONAL PARK

Campsites, facilities: There are 13 tent sites. Picnic tables, fireplaces, and piped water are provided. Pit toilets are available. Pets are permitted on leashes. There is no piped water in the winter.

Reservations, fee: No reservations; $4 fee per night.

Who to contact: Phone the Sequoia National Park at (209)565-3341.

Location: From Visalia, drive to Three Rivers on Highway 198. In Three Rivers, turn east on South Fork Road and drive 23 miles to the campground.

Trip note: The smallest developed camp in Sequoia National Park might just be what you're looking for. It is set at 3,650 feet elevation on the South Fork of the Kaweah River, just inside the southwestern border of Sequoia National Park. The ranger station here has maps and information. A trail heads east from the camp and traverses Dennison Ridge, eventually leading to Hocket Lakes and connecting to other backcountry trails.

Map grid a1

ATWELL MILL

on Atwell Creek
SEQUOIA NATIONAL PARK

Campsites, facilities: There are 23 tent sites. Picnic tables, fireplaces, and piped water are provided. Pit toilets are available. A grocery store is nearby. Pets are permitted on leashes.

Reservations, fee: No reservations; $4 fee per night.

Who to contact: Phone the Sequoia National Park at (209)565-3341.

Location: From Visalia, take Highway 198 to Three Rivers. Continue north for three miles on Highway 198. Turn right (east) on Mineral King Road and drive 20 miles to the campground.

Trip note: This small, pretty camp in Sequoia National Park is located on Atwell Creek near the East Fork of the Kaweah River. Trails near camp provide access to the backcountry. The elevation is 6,650 feet. Open from May to September (depending on road and weather conditions).

Map grid a2

COLD SPRINGS

on the East Fork of Kaweah River
SEQUOIA NATIONAL PARK

Campsites, facilities: There are 37 tent sites. Picnic tables, fireplaces, and piped water are provided. Pit toilets are available. A grocery store is nearby. Pets are permitted on leashes.

Reservations, fee: No reservations; $4 fee per night.

Who to contact: Phone the Sequoia National Park at (209)565-3341.

Location: From Visalia, take Highway 198 to Three Rivers. Continue to drive three miles north on Highway 198. Turn right (east) on Mineral King Road and drive 25 miles to the campground.

Trip note: This high country camp at Sequoia National Park is set at 7,500 feet elevation on the East Fork of the Kaweah River. A trail is routed south of camp to a network of backcountry trails, including those to Mosquito Lakes (that sounds like fun, eh?), Eagle Lake, and, for the ambitious, White Chief Lake. Open from May to September.

Map grid **a8**

TUTTLE CREEK
near Mt. Whitney

Campsites, facilities: There are 84 campsites for tents or motor homes. There is no piped water, but pit toilets, fire grills, and picnic tables are provided. Supplies are available in Lone Pine. Pets are permitted on leashes. Pack out your garbage.
Reservations, fee: No reservations, no fee.
Who to contact: Phone the Bureau of Land Management at (619)872-4881.
Location: From Lone Pine, drive 3.5 miles west on Whitney Portal Road. Turn south on Horseshoe Meadow Road and drive 1.5 miles. Turn west on Tuttle Creek Road (a winding, dirt road) and drive to the campground.
Trip note: This primitive, BLM camp is set at the base of Mt. Whitney along Tuttle Creek at 5,100 feet elevation. It is often used as an overflow area if the camps farther up Whitney Portal Road are full. Open from May through October.

Map grid **a9**

DIAZ LAKE
near Lone Pine

Campsites, facilities: There are 200 campsites for tents or motor homes. Piped water, fireplaces, and picnic tables are provided. Flush toilets, showers, and a boat ramp are available. Supplies and a laundromat are available in Lone Pine. Pets are permitted on leashes.
Reservations, fee: No reservations; $6 fee per night.
Who to contact: Phone the County Parks Department at (619)878-2411, extension 2272.
Location: From Lone Pine, drive two miles south on US 395 to the entrance.
Trip note: A lot of people don't even know this place exists. It's a small lake near Lone Pine, 3,800 feet elevation, providing an opportunity for boating, water skiing, and trout fishing. A 20-foot limit is enforced for boats. Open year-round.

Map grid **b1**

HIDDEN FALLS
on Tule River
MOUNTAIN HOME STATE FOREST

Campsites, facilities: There are eight sites for tents only. Picnic tables, fireplaces, and piped water are provided. Pit toilets are available. Pets are permitted on leashes.
Reservations, fee: No reservations, no fee.
Who to contact: Phone the Mountain Home State Forest at (209)539-2855.
Location: From Porterville, drive 19 miles east on Highway 190 (one mile past the town of Springville). Turn left (north) onto Balch Park Road and drive 30 miles to the campground. Alternate route: After driving three miles on Balch Park Road, turn right (east) on Bear Creek Road and drive 25 miles to the campground. This is not a good road for trailers and motor homes.
Trip note: One of the prettier camps in Mountain Home State Forest, this small, quiet camp is set along the Tule River, near Hidden Falls, at 6,000 feet elevation. Open from June to October.

Map grid **b1**

MOSES GULCH
on Tule River
MOUNTAIN HOME STATE FOREST

Campsites, facilities: There are four campsites for tents and seven for motor homes.

Piped water, fireplaces, and picnic tables are provided. Vault toilets are available. Pets are permitted on leashes.

Reservations, fee: No reservations, no fee.

Who to contact: Phone the Mountain Home State Forest at (209)539-2855.

Location: From Porterville, drive 19 miles east on Highway 190 (one mile past the town of Springville). Turn left (north) onto Balch Park Road and drive 31 miles to the campground. Alternate route: After driving three miles on Balch Park Road, turn right (east) on Bear Creek Road and drive 26 miles to the campground. This is not a good road for trailers and motor homes.

Trip note: This is another in the series of camps in the remote Mountain Home State Forest, so take your pick. And you can't beat the price.

Map grid **b7**

ROADS END

near John Muir Wilderness

INYO NATIONAL FOREST

Campsites, facilities: There are 15 campsites for tents or motor homes. Vault toilets and horseback riding facilities are available. There is **no piped water,** so bring your own. Pets are permitted on leashes.

Reservations, fee: No reservations, no fee.

Who to contact: Call the Inyo National Forest Mt. Whitney Ranger District at (619)876-5542.

Location: From Lone Pine, drive 3.5 miles west on Whitney Portal Road. Turn left on Horseshoe Meadows Road and drive 19 miles to the end of the road.

Trip note: This is an alternative for backpackers who want to avoid the mob climbing Mt. Whitney. The camp is set at 9,400 feet elevation on the border of the John Muir Wilderness. Open from mid-May through mid-November.

Map grid **c0**

SUNSET POINT

MOUNTAIN HOME STATE FOREST

Campsites, facilities: There are two campsites for tents and two sites for motor homes. Picnic tables, fireplaces, and piped water are provided. Vault toilets are available. Pets are permitted on leashes.

Reservations, fee: No reservations, no fee.

Who to contact: Phone the Mountain Home State Forest at (209)539-2855.

Location: From Porterville, drive 19 miles east on Highway 190 (one mile past the town of Springville). Turn left (north) onto Balch Park Road and drive 35 miles to the campground. Alternate route: After driving three miles on Balch Park Road, turn right (east) on Bear Creek Road and drive 18 miles to campground). However, this is not a good road for trailers and motor homes.

Trip note: This is the smallest and least used of the eight camps at Mountain Home State Forest. A good side trip option is to explore the nearby creek for Indian bathtubs and grinding holes (bedrock mortars). Open June to October.

Map grid **c1**

FRAZIER MILL

MOUNTAIN HOME STATE FOREST

Campsites, facilities: There are 46 campsites for tents or motor homes. Piped water, fireplaces, and picnic tables are provided. Vault toilets are available. Pets are permitted on leashes.

Reservations, fee: No reservations, no fee.

Who to contact: Phone the Mountain Home State Forest at (209)539-2855.

Location: From Porterville, drive 19 miles east on Highway 190 (one mile past the town of Springville). Turn left (north) onto Balch Park Road and drive 35 miles to the campground. Alternate route: After driving three miles on Balch Park Road, turn right (east) on Bear Creek Road and drive 17 miles to the campground. However, this is not a good road for trailers and motor homes.

Trip note: The prime attraction here is the many old-growth giant Sequoias. A Forest Information Trail and the trailhead leading into the Golden Trout Wilderness are nearby. The Wishon Fork of the Tule River is the largest of the several streams that pass through this forest. And hey, you can't beat the price. Open from June to October.

Map grid c1

SHAKE CAMP
MOUNTAIN HOME STATE FOREST

Campsites, facilities: There are 11 campsites for tents or motor homes. Piped water, fireplaces, and picnic tables are provided. Vault toilets are available, and a public pack station with corrals is available nearby. Pets are permitted on leashes.

Reservations, fee: No reservations, no fee.

Who to contact: Phone the Mountain Home State Forest at (209)539-2855.

Location: From Porterville, drive 19 miles east on Highway 190 (one mile past the town of Springville). Turn left (north) onto Balch Park Road and drive 36 miles to the campground. Alternate route: After driving three miles on Balch Park Road, turn right (east) on Bear Creek Road and drive 21 miles to the campground. This is not a good road for trailers and motor homes.

Trip note: This is a rare spot for horseback riding. Horses can be rented for the day, hour or night. This is a popular spot for backpackers. It is set at 6,500 feet elevation and there's a trailhead here for a hiking trip into the Golden Trout Wilderness. The Balch Park Pack Station, a commercial outfitter, is located nearby, so you can expect horse traffic on the trail. Open from June to October.

Map grid c1

BALCH COUNTY PARK
MOUNTAIN HOME STATE FOREST

Campsites, facilities: There are 70 campsites for tents or motor homes up to 35 feet long. Piped water, fireplaces, and picnic tables are provided. Flush toilets are available. Pets are permitted on leashes.

Reservations, fee: No reservations; $5 fee per night; $1 fee for pets.

Who to contact: Phone the park at (209)733-6612.

Location: From Porterville, drive 19 miles east on Highway 190 (one mile past the town of Springville). Turn left (north) onto Balch Park Road and drive three miles to Bear Creek Road. Turn east (right) and drive 15 miles to the campground (trailers not recommended). Alternate route: After turning north onto Balch Park Road, drive 40 miles to the park.

Trip note: Secluded, hard-to-reach? Yes, and that's just what folks want here. Mountain Home State Forest has eight campgrounds, all surrounded by state land and Sequoia National Forest. Nearby there's a grove of giant Sequoias that's an attraction. The elevation is 6,500 feet. Open from May to October.

Map grid c1

METHUSELAH GROUP CAMP
MOUNTAIN HOME STATE FOREST

Campsites, facilities: There are campsites for tents or motor homes. Fireplaces and picnic tables are provided. Vault toilets are available. Pets are permitted on leashes. There is **no piped water,** so bring your own.

Reservations, fee: Reservations required (20 to maximum of 100 people); no fee.

Who to contact: Phone the Mountain Home State Forest at (209)539-2855.

Location: From Porterville, drive 19 miles east on Highway 190 (one mile past the town of Springville). Turn left (north) onto Balch Park Road and drive three miles to Bear Creek Road. Turn east (right) and drive 15 miles to the campground (trailers not recommended). Alternate route: After turning north onto Balch Park Road, drive 40 miles to the campground.

Trip note: This is one of the few free group camps available anywhere in California. Remember to BOW. The elevation is 5,900 feet. Open from June to October.

Map grid c1

HEDRICK POND
MOUNTAIN HOME STATE FOREST

Campsites, facilities: There are 14 campsites for tents or motor homes. Piped water, fireplaces, and picnic tables are provided. Vault toilets are available. Pets are permitted on leashes.

Reservations, fee: No reservations, no fee.

Who to contact: Phone the Mountain Home State Forest at (209)539-2855.

Location: From Porterville, drive 19 miles east on Highway 190 (one mile past the town of Springville). Turn left (north) onto Balch Park Road and drive 35 miles to the campground. Alternate route: After driving three miles on Balch Park Road, turn right (east) on Bear Creek Road and drive 16 miles to the campground. However, this is not a good road for trailers and motor homes.

Trip note: Take your pick of the eight camps at Mountain Home State Forest at about 6,300 feet elevation. The beautiful country is highlighted by the giant Sequoias and Hedrick Pond provides a fishing opportunity, being stocked occasionally with rainbow trout. Open from June through October.

Map grid d0

COFFEE CAMP
on the Middle Fork of Tule River
SEQUOIA NATIONAL FOREST

Campsites, facilities: There are 18 tent sites. Picnic tables, fireplaces, and piped water are provided. Vault toilets are available. Propane gas can be found nearby. Pets are permitted on leashes.

Reservations, fee: No reservations; $5 fee per night.

Who to contact: Phone the Sequoia National Forest Tule River Ranger District at (209)539-2607.

Location: From Porterville, drive 23 miles east on Highway 190 to the campground.

Trip note: Sometimes you might just want to watch the water roll by. Not here. You'll want to jump in. The camp is set along the Middle Fork of the Tule River. The elevation is 2,000 feet. Right, the foothill country.

Map grid d1

WISHON
on Tule River
SEQUOIA NATIONAL FOREST

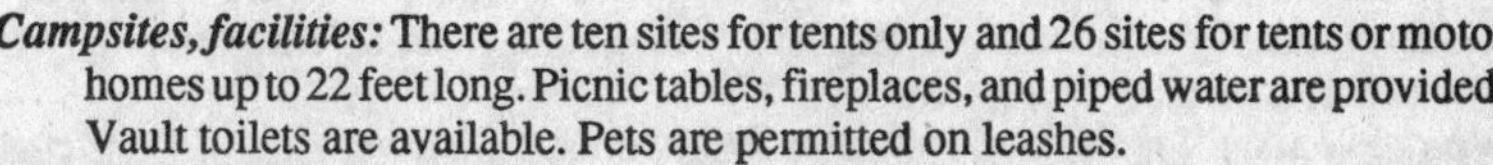

Campsites, facilities: There are ten sites for tents only and 26 sites for tents or motor homes up to 22 feet long. Picnic tables, fireplaces, and piped water are provided. Vault toilets are available. Pets are permitted on leashes.

Reservations, fee: No reservations; $5 fee per night; $8 fee per night for multi-family units.

Who to contact: Phone the Sequoia National Forest Tule River Ranger District at (209)539-2607.

Location: From Porterville, drive 25 miles east on Highway 190. Turn north (left) on Forest Service Road 208 (Wishon Drive) and drive 3.5 miles.

Trip note: There is a trail routed northeast out of the camp along the Middle Fork that heads to Mountain Home State Forest. The elevation is 4,000 feet. Open from April to October.

Map grid d2

COY FLAT
SEQUOIA NATIONAL FOREST

Campsites, facilities: There are 20 campsites for tents or motor homes up to 22 feet long. Piped water, fireplaces, and picnic tables are provided. Vault toilets are available. Pets are permitted on leashes.

Reservations, fee: No reservations; $5 fee per night.

Who to contact: Phone the Sequoia National Forest Tule River Ranger District at (209)539-2607.

Location: From Porterville, drive 34 miles east on Highway 190 to Camp Nelson. Turn right (south) on Forest Service Road 21S94 and drive one mile.

Trip note: This is just far enough off the beaten path to get missed by most vacationers. It is set on Coy Creek at 5,000 feet elevation. For hikers, there is a trail that is routed through Belknap Camp Grove and then south along Slate Mountain. Open from March to October.

Map grid d2

BELKNAP
on the South Middle Fork of Tule Creek
SEQUOIA NATIONAL FOREST

Campsites, facilities: There are 15 campsites for tents or motor homes up to 16 feet long. Trailers are not recommended in this area. Piped water, fireplaces, picnic tables, and vault toilets are available. A grocery store is nearby. Pets are permitted on leashes.

Reservations, fee: No reservations; $6 fee per night.

Who to contact: Phone the Sequoia National Forest Tule River Ranger District at (209)539-2607.

Location: From Porterville, drive 34 miles east on Highway 190 to Camp Nelson. Turn right (east) on Nelson Drive and drive one mile to the campground.

Trip note: This quiet spot is set on the South Middle Fork of Tule Creek near McIntyre Grove and Belknap Camp Grove. A trail leads out of camp past Wheel Meadow Grove and winds through the backcountry. The elevation is 5,000 feet. Open from April to October.

Map grid d2

QUAKING ASPEN GROUP CAMP
near Freeman Creek
SEQUOIA NATIONAL FOREST

Campsites, facilities: There are three campsites for 12, 15, or 50 people suitable for tents or motor homes up to 22 feet long. Piped water, fireplaces, picnic tables, and vault toilets are available. A grocery store is nearby. Pets are permitted.

Reservations, fee: Reservations requested with $10 deposit; $8-$40 group fee per night, depending on the campsite.

Who to contact: Phone the Sequoia National Forest Tule River Ranger District at (209)539-2607.

Location: From Porterville, drive 34 miles east on Highway 190 to Camp Nelson.

Continue about 11 miles east on Highway 190 to the campground.

Trip note: This is a group camp option to Peppermint camp. See that trip note for side trips. The elevation is 7,000 feet. Open from May to October.

A

Map grid **d2**

QUAKING ASPEN

SEQUOIA NATIONAL FOREST

B

Campsites, facilities: There are 32 campsites for tents or motor homes up to 22 feet long. Piped water, fireplaces picnic tables, and vault toilets are available. A grocery store is nearby. Pets are permitted on leashes.

Reservations, fee: No reservations; $6 fee per night.

Who to contact: Phone the Sequoia National Forest Tule River Ranger District at (209)539-2607.

C

Location: From Porterville drive 34 miles east on Highway 190 to Camp Nelson. Continue 11 miles east of Camp Nelson on Highway 190.

Trip note: A pretty spot, especially in the fall, set at 7,000 feet elevation near the head of Freeman Creek. A trail passes through camp that accesses other trails leading into the backcountry. Open from May to October.

D

Map grid **d5**

TROY MEADOW

on Fish Creek

SEQUOIA NATIONAL FOREST

Campsites, facilities: There are ten sites for tents only and 63 campsites for tents or motor homes up to 22 feet long. Piped water, fireplaces, and picnic tables are provided. Vault toilets are available. A grocery store is nearby. Pets are permitted on leashes.

E

Reservations, fee: No reservations, no fee.

Who to contact: Phone the Sequoia National Forest Cannell Meadow Ranger District at (619)376-3781.

F

Location: From the town of Brown on Highway 14, drive four miles north. Turn left (west) on Nine Mile Canyon Road and drive 31 miles northwest (road becomes Kennedy Meadow Road) to the campground.

Trip note: Obscure? Yes, but what the heck, it gives you an idea of what is possible out in the boondocks. The camp is set at 7,800 feet elevation right along Fish Creek. An information station is available two miles northwest. You are advised to stop there prior to any backcountry trips. Open from June to November.

G5

Map grid **e1**

LONG MEADOW

SEQUOIA NATIONAL FOREST

H

Campsites, facilities: There are six campsites for tents or motor homes up to 16 feet long. Fireplaces and picnic tables are provided. Vault toilets are available. There is **no piped water,** so bring your own. Pets are permitted on leashes.

Reservations, fee: No reservations, no fee.

Who to contact: Phone the Sequoia National Forest Hot Springs Ranger District at (805)548-6503.

I

Location: From Highway 99 in Earlimart, take the County Road J22 (Avenue 56) exit and drive east for 39 miles to the town of California Hot Springs. Turn north (left) on County Road M50 (Parker Pass Road) and drive 15 miles. Turn left on Western Divide Highway and drive four miles to the entrance.

J

Trip note: This is a nearby option to the Redwood Meadow camp, where the Trail of the Hundred Giants is an attraction. The elevation is 6,500 feet. Open from June to September.

Map grid **e1**

REDWOOD MEADOW

near Parker Meadow Creek
SEQUOIA NATIONAL FOREST

Campsites, facilities: There are 15 campsites for tents or motor homes up to 16 feet long. Piped water, fireplaces, and picnic tables are provided. Vault toilets are available. Pets are permitted on leashes.

Reservations, fee: No reservations; $5 fee per night.

Who to contact: Phone the Sequoia National Forest Hot Springs Ranger District at (805)548-6503.

Location: From Highway 99 in Earlimart, take the County Road J22 (Avenue 56) exit and drive east for 39 miles to the town of California Hot Springs. Turn north (left) on County Road M50 (Parker Pass Road) and drive 15 miles. Turn left on Western Divide Highway and drive three miles to the entrance.

Trip note: The highlight here is the half-mile Trail of the Hundred Giants, which is routed through a grove of giant Sequoias. It is usable by wheelchair hikers. The camp is set near Parker Meadow Creek. The elevation is 6,500 feet. If this camp is full, the Long Meadow camp provides a nearby option. Open from June to September.

Map grid **e2**

PEPPERMINT

on Peppermint Creek
SEQUOIA NATIONAL FOREST

Campsites, facilities: There are 19 campsites for tents or motor homes up to 22 feet long. Fireplaces and picnic tables are provided. Vault toilets are available. There is **no piped water,** so bring your own. A grocery store is nearby. Pets are permitted on leashes.

Reservations, fee: No reservations, no fee.

Who to contact: Phone the Sequoia National Forest Tule River Ranger District at (209)539-2607.

Location: From Porterville, drive 34 miles east on Highway 190 to Camp Nelson. Continue about 15 miles southeast on Highway 190 to the entrance road.

Trip note: This is one of the two primitive camps at Peppermint Creek, but the two are not directly connected by a road. Several backcountry roads are in the area, detailed on a Forest Service map, and can make for some self-styled fortune hunts. For the ambitious, hiking the trail at the end of Forest Service Road 32E22 can lead to a fantastic lookout at The Needles (8,245 feet). The camp elevation is 7,100 feet. Open from May to October.

Map grid **e2**

LOWER PEPPERMINT

SEQUOIA NATIONAL FOREST

Campsites, facilities: There are 17 campsites for tents or motor homes up to 16 feet long. Piped water, fireplaces, and picnic tables are provided. Vault toilets are available. Pets are permitted on leashes.

Reservations, fee: No reservations; $5 fee per night.

Who to contact: Phone the Sequoia National Forest Hot Springs Ranger District at (805)548-6503.

Location: From the town of Lake Isabella, drive 35 miles north on Burlando Road and Sierra Way to the town of Johnsondale. Turn right (north) on Forest Service

Road 22S82 (Lloyd Meadow Road) and drive about 14 miles on a paved road to the campground.

Trip note: This is a little-known camp in the Sequoia National Forest, set along Peppermint Creek at 5,300 feet elevation. Many backcountry roads are available in the area, which are detailed on a Forest Service map. Open from June to October.

A

B

Map grid **e2**

LIMESTONE
on Kern River
SEQUOIA NATIONAL FOREST

Campsites, facilities: There are 12 sites for tents only and ten campsites for tents or motor homes up to 22 feet long. Fireplaces, and picnic tables are provided. Vault toilets are available. There is **no piped water,** so bring your own. Pets are permitted on leashes. Supplies and a laundromat are available in Kernville.

Reservations, fee: No reservations, no fee.

Who to contact: Phone the Sequoia National Forest Cannell Meadow Ranger District at (619)376-3781.

Location: From Kernville, drive 19 miles north on Kern River Highway-Sierra Way Road.

Trip note: This is a small camp along the Kern River, set deep in the Sequoia National Forest at 3,800 feet elevation. It is advisable to obtain a Forest Service map, which details the back roads. A mile to the west, South Creek Falls provides a possible side trip. Open from May to October.

C

D

E

Map grid **e5**

FISH CREEK
SEQUOIA NATIONAL FOREST

Campsites, facilities: There are 40 campsites for tents or motor homes up to 22 feet long. Piped water, fireplaces, and picnic tables are provided. Vault toilets are available. A grocery store is nearby.

Reservations, fee: No reservations, no fee.

Who to contact: Phone the Sequoia National Forest Cannell Meadow Ranger District at (619)376-3781.

Location: From the town of Brown on Highway 14, drive four miles north. Turn left (west) on Nine Mile Canyon Road and drive 28 miles northwest (the road becomes Kennedy Meadows Road) to the campground.

Trip note: This is a pretty spot set at the confluence of Fish Creek and Jackass Creek. They provide piped water, yet don't charge campers for its use. The elevation is 7,400 feet. Open from June to November.

F

G5

H

Map grid **f0**

LEAVIS FLAT
on Deer Creek
SEQUOIA NATIONAL FOREST

Campsites, facilities: There are five sites for tents only and four campsites for motor homes up to 16 feet long. Piped water, fireplaces, and picnic tables are provided. Vault toilets are available. A grocery store, a laundromat, and propane gas can be found nearby. Pets are permitted on leashes.

Reservations, fee: No reservations; $5 fee per night.

Who to contact: Phone the Sequoia National Forest Hot Springs Ranger District at (805)548-6503.

Location: From Highway 99 in Earlimart, take the County Road J22 (Avenue 56) exit and drive east for 39 miles to the campground. Or from Highway 65 follow

I

J

the California Hot Springs resort signs from Ducor.

Trip note: This is an easy-to-reach camp set on the western border of Sequoia National Forest along Deer Creek. The elevation is 3,100 feet. Open year around.

Map grid f0

WHITE RIVER

SEQUOIA NATIONAL FOREST

Campsites, facilities: There are twelve campsites for motor homes up to 16 feet long. Piped water, fireplaces, and picnic tables are provided. Vault toilets are available. Pets are permitted on leashes.

Reservations, fee: No reservations; $5 fee per night.

Who to contact: Phone the Sequoia National Forest Hot Springs Ranger District at (805)548-6503.

Location: From Highway 155 just west of Glennville, turn north on Linns Valley Road and drive about 5.5 miles. Turn right and drive two miles through Idyllwild. Continue northeast on Forest Service Road 24S05 for six more miles.

Trip note: This relatively obscure spot gets missed by plenty of folks who wished they knew about it. The camp is set at 4,000 feet elevation along the White River. It is advisable to obtain a Forest Service map.Open from May to October.

Map grid f1

HOLEY MEADOW

on Double Bunk Creek

SEQUOIA NATIONAL FOREST

Campsites, facilities: There are ten campsites for tents or motor homes up to 16 feet long. Piped water, fireplaces, and picnic tables are provided. Vault toilets are available. Pets are permitted on leashes.

Reservations, fee: No reservations; $5 fee per night.

Who to contact: Phone the Sequoia National Forest Hot Springs Ranger District at (805)548-6503.

Location: From Highway 99 in Earlimart, take the County Road J22 (Avenue 56) exit and drive east for 39 miles to the town of California Hot Springs. Turn north (left) on County Road M50 (Parker Pass Road) and drive 15 miles. Turn left on Western Divide Highway and drive one-half mile to the entrance.

Trip note: This is a shaded, quiet spot to hunker down for awhile, maybe to lean against a tree, watch the water roll by, and not be bugged by anything. It's set along Double Bunk Creek on the slopes of Holey Meadow. The elevation is 6,400 feet. Open from June to October.

Map grid f1

FROG MEADOW

SEQUOIA NATIONAL FOREST

Campsites, facilities: There are ten campsites for tents or motor homes up to 16 feet long. Piped water, fireplaces, and picnic tables are provided. Vault toilets are available. Pets are permitted on leashes.

Reservations, fee: No reservations, no fee.

Who to contact: Phone the Sequoia National Forest Hot Springs Ranger District at (805)548-6503.

Location: From Highway 155 just west of Glennville, turn north on Linns Valley Road and drive about 5.5 miles. Turn right and drive five miles to the Pozo Park junction. Continue northeast on County Road M3 (to Guernsey Mill) for eight miles. Turn right on Forest Service Road 24S06 and drive six miles to the campground (paved all the way). Continue two miles past Panorama camp to the intersection with Frog Meadow Road (Forest Service Road 24S50). Take the left fork and follow the signs for about six miles.

Trip note: This small, primitive camp, set near Tobias Creek at 7,500 feet elevation, is used primarily by hunters in the fall. Several trails, sometimes used by motorcyclists, lead out from the camp. Open from June to October.

Map grid **f2**

FAIRVIEW
on Kern River
SEQUOIA NATIONAL FOREST

Campsites, facilities: There are 55 campsites for tents or motor homes up to 22 feet long. Piped water, fireplaces, and picnic tables are provided. Vault toilets are available. Pets are permitted on leashes. Supplies and a laundromat are available in Kernville.

Reservations, fee: No reservations; $5 fee per night.

Who to contact: Phone the Sequoia National Forest Cannell Meadow Ranger District at (619)376-3781.

Location: From Kernville, drive 16 miles north on Kern River Highway-Sierra Road to the town of Fairview. The campground is at north end of town.

Trip note: Easy-to-reach, easy-to-like, this Forest Service camp is set on the Kern River. The elevation is 3,500 feet. Open from May to October.

Map grid **f2**

GOLD LEDGE
on Kern River
SEQUOIA NATIONAL FOREST

Campsites, facilities: There are 37 campsites for tents or motor homes up to 22 feet long. Piped water, fireplaces, and picnic tables are provided. Vault toilets are available. Pets are permitted on leashes. Supplies and a laundromat are available in Kernville.

Reservations, fee: No reservations; $5 fee per night.

Who to contact: Phone the Sequoia National Forest Cannell Meadow Ranger District at (619)376-3781.

Location: From Kernville, drive ten miles north on Kern River Highway-Sierra Way Road to the campground.

Trip note: This is another in the series of camps on the Kern River, north of Isabella Reservoir. This one is set at 3,200 feet elevation. Open from May to October.

Map grid **f3**

HORSE MEADOW
on Salmon Creek
SEQUOIA NATIONAL FOREST

5% CLUB

Campsites, facilities: There are 18 sites for tents only and 15 campsites for tents or motor homes up to 23 feet long. Piped water, fireplaces, and picnic tables are provided. Vault toilets are available. Pets are permitted on leashes. Pack out your garbage.

Reservations, fee: No reservations, no fee.

Who to contact: Phone the Sequoia National Forest Cannell Meadow Ranger District at (619)376-3781.

Location: From Kernville, drive north on Sierra Way for about 20 miles to the sign that says "Highway 395-Black Rock Ranger Station." Make a sharp right on Sherman Pass Road and drive about 6.5 miles to Cherry Hill Road (there is a green gate with a sign that says "Horse Meadow-Big Meadow"). Turn right and drive for about four miles. The road becomes dirt, and continues for about another three miles (follow the signs) to the campground entrance road.

Trip note: This is a virtually unknown spot set along Salmon Creek at 7,600 feet elevation. It is a very pretty area of big meadows, forests, and backcountry roads. A trail starts at the camp and follows along Salmon Creek to Salmon Creek Falls, a good side trip. Open from June to November.

Map grid g1

PANORAMA
SEQUOIA NATIONAL FOREST

Campsites, facilities: There are ten campsites for tents or motor homes up to 16 feet long. Fireplaces and picnic tables are provided. Vault toilets are available. There is **no piped water,** so bring your own. Pets are permitted on leashes.

Reservations, fee: No reservations, no fee.

Who to contact: Phone the Sequoia National Forest Hot Springs Ranger District at (805)548-6503.

Location: From Highway 155 just west of Glennville, turn north on Linns Valley Road and drive about 5.5 miles. Turn right and drive five miles to the Pozo Park junction. Continue northeast on County Road M3 (to Guernsey Mill) for eight miles. Turn right on Forest Service Road 24S06 and drive six miles to the campground (paved all the way).

Trip note: This pretty spot, set near the end of an old logging spur, is the kind of place not many folks have a clue exists. Nearby Portuguese Pass provides a lookout and Portuguese Meadow a spot for lunch. The elevation is 7,000 feet. Open from June to September.

Map grid g2

HOSPITAL FLAT
on the North Fork of Kern River
SEQUOIA NATIONAL FOREST

Campsites, facilities: There are 28 sites for tents only and 12 campsites for tents or motor homes up to 22 feet long. Piped water, fireplaces, and picnic tables are provided. Vault toilets are available. Pets are permitted on leashes. Supplies and a laundromat are available in Kernville.

Reservations, fee: No reservations; $5 fee per night.

Who to contact: Phone the Sequoia National Forest Cannell Meadow Ranger District at (619)376-3781.

Location: From Kernville, drive seven miles north on Kern River Highway-Sierra Way Road to the campground.

Trip note: It's kind of like the old shell game, trying to pick the best of the camps set along the North Fork of the Kern River. This one is set seven miles north of Lake Isabella. The elevation is 2,800 feet. Open from May to October.

Map grid g2

HEADQUARTERS
on the North Fork of Kern River
SEQUOIA NATIONAL FOREST

Campsites, facilities: There are 44 campsites for tents or motor homes up to 22 feet long. Piped water, fireplaces, and picnic tables are provided. Vault toilets and horseback riding facilities are available. Supplies and a laundromat are available in Kernville.

Reservations, fee: No reservations; $5 fee per night.

Who to contact: Phone the Sequoia National Forest Cannell Meadow Ranger District at (619)376-3781.

Location: From Kernville, drive three miles north on Sierra Way to the campground.

Trip note: As you head north from Lake Isabella on Sierra Way, this is the first in a series of Forest Service campgrounds that you have your pick of, all of them set along the North Fork of the Kern River. The North Fork is known for offering prime kayaking water. The elevation is 2,700 feet. Open from May to October.

Map grid g2

CAMP 3

on Kern River

SEQUOIA NATIONAL FOREST

Campsites, facilities: There are 52 campsites for tents or motor homes up to 27 feet long. Piped water, fireplaces, and picnic tables are provided. Vault toilets are available. Pets are permitted on leashes. Supplies and a laundromat are available in Kernville.

Reservations, fee: No reservations; $5 fee per night.

Who to contact: Phone the Sequoia National Forest Cannell Meadow Ranger District at (619)376-3781.

Location: From Kernville, drive five miles northwest on Kern River Highway-Sierra Way Road to the campground.

Trip note: This is one in a series of camps located along the Kern River, north of Lake Isabella (this camp is five miles north). These camps provide excellent put-in and take-out spots for kayakers. If you don't like this spot, the next camp is just two miles upriver. The elevation is 2,800 feet. Open from May to October.

Map grid g6

LONG VALLEY

near Dome Land Wilderness Area

5% CLUB

Campsites, facilities: There are 13 tent sites. Piped water, fireplaces, and picnic tables are provided. Pit toilets are available. Pack out your garbage.

Reservations, fee: No reservations, no fee.

Who to contact: Phone the Bureau of Land Management at (805)861-4236.

Location: From the town of Brown on Highway 14, drive four miles north. Turn left (west) on Nine Mile Canyon Road and drive 11 miles to the BLM Ranger Station. Turn left on the dirt road opposite the station and drive 14 more miles.

Trip note: This one is way out there in booger country. It's set in Long Valley, a good spot for backpackers to take a leap into the surrounding wildlands. A trail from camp leads 2.5 miles west to the South Fork of the Kern River and the Dome Land Wilderness Area. The elevation is 5,200 feet. Open year-round.

Map grid g7

CHIMNEY CREEK

on Pacific Crest Trail

5% CLUB

Campsites, facilities: There are 36 campsites for tents or motor homes up to 25 feet long. Piped water, fireplaces, and picnic tables are provided. Pit toilets are available. Please pack out your own garbage.

Reservations, fee: No reservations, no fee.

Who to contact: Phone the Bureau of Land Management at (805)861-4236.

Location: From the town of Brown on Highway 14, drive four miles north. Turn left (west) on Nine Mile Canyon Road and drive 11 miles to the BLM Ranger Station. Turn left on the dirt road opposite the station and drive three miles.

Trip note: This is one of the premium launching pads for a first-class backpacking trip. The Pacific Crest Trail runs right through camp, providing the ideal trailhead. Set at 5,900 feet elevation on Chimney Creek. Open year-round.

Map grid **h0**

EVANS FLAT
SEQUOIA NATIONAL FOREST

Campsites, facilities: There are 16 campsites for tents or motor homes up to 16 feet long. Fireplaces and picnic tables are provided. Vault toilets are available. There is **no piped water** at this site, so bring your own.

Reservations, fee: No reservations, no fee.

Who to contact: Phone the Sequoia National Forest Greenhorn District at (805)871-2223.

Location: From Greenhorn Summit on Highway 155, turn south on Rancheria Road (paved, then dirt) and drive 8.3 miles to the campground.

Trip note: You have to earn this one, but if you want solitude, Evans Flat can provide it. It is set at 6,200 feet, with Woodward Peak located one-half mile to the east (an obvious side trip). Open from May to October.

Map grid **h1**

HUNGRY GULCH
on Isabella Lake

Campsites, facilities: There are 78 campsites for tents or motor homes. Piped water, fireplaces, and picnic tables are provided. Flush toilets, showers and a playground are available. Pets are permitted on leashes. Supplies and a laundromat are available in the town of Lake Isabella.

Reservations, fee: No reservations; $8 fee per night.

Who to contact: Phone the U.S. Corps of Engineers at (619)379-2742.

Location: From the town of Lake Isabella, drive four miles north on Highway 155 to the campground.

Trip note: This camp is located just across from Boulder Gulch camp, on Lake Isabella. For details, see that trip note. Open from March through September.

Map grid **h1**

PIONEER POINT
on Isabella Lake

Campsites, facilities: There are 78 campsites for tents or motor homes up to 30 feet long. Piped water, fireplaces, and picnic tables are provided. Flush toilets, showers, a playground, and a fish cleaning station are available. A boat ramp is three miles from camp. Some facilities are wheelchair accessible. Pets are permitted on leashes. Supplies and a laundromat are available in the town of Lake Isabella.

Reservations, fee: No reservations; $8 fee per night from March through September.

Who to contact: Phone the U.S. Corps of Engineers at (619)379-2742.

Location: From the town of Lake Isabella, drive 2.5 miles on Highway 155 to the campground.

Trip note: Pioneer Point is one of the two camps in the immediate area near the main dam at Isabella Lake. For details, see the trip note for the French Gulch, Boulder Gulch, or Eastside camps. The elevation is 2,650. Open all year.

Map grid **h1**

ALDER CREEK
SEQUOIA NATIONAL FOREST

Campsites, facilities: There are 13 campsites for tents or motor homes up to 20 feet long. Fireplaces and picnic tables are provided. Vault toilets are available. There is **no piped water,** so bring your own. Pets are permitted on leashes.

Reservations, fee: No reservations, no fee.

Who to contact: Phone the Sequoia National Forest Greenhorn Ranger District at (805)871-2223. A

Location: From Glennville, drive about eight miles east on Highway 155. Turn right (south) on Alder Creek Road and drive three miles to the campground.

Trip note: This primitive camp is set just a quarter-mile upstream from where Alder Creek meets Slick Rock Creek. There is a trail that runs north two miles along Slick Rock Creek. The elevation is 3,900 feet. Open from May to November. B

Map grid h1

GREENHORN MOUNTAIN PARK

near Shirley Meadows

Campsites, facilities: There are 91 campsites for tents or motor homes up to 24 feet long. Piped water, fireplaces, and picnic table are provided. Flush toilets and showers are available. Pets are permitted on leashes. C

Reservations, fee: No reservations; $6 fee per night; pets $2.

Who to contact: Phone the County Parks Department at (805)861-2345 or (805)872-3179.

Location: From Wofford Heights (on the west shore of Lake Isabella), drive ten miles west on Highway 155 to the park. D

Trip note: This county campground is open all year and is near the Shirley Meadows ski area (open on weekends during the snow season). There are numerous back roads that can provide some side trips, all detailed on a Forest Service map.

E

Map grid h1

CEDAR CREEK

SEQUOIA NATIONAL FOREST

Campsites, facilities: There are seven sites for tents and four campsites for motor homes up to 16 feet long. Piped water, picnic tables, and fireplaces are provided and vault toilets are available. Pets are permitted on leashes. F

Reservations, fee: No reservations, no fee.

Who to contact: Phone the Sequoia National Forest Greenhorn Ranger District at (805)871-2223.

Location: From Glennville on Highway 155, drive nine miles east on Highway 155 to the campground. Or from Wofford Heights (on the west shore of Lake Isabella), drive 11 miles west on Highway 155 to the campground. G5

Trip note: This is a little-used Forest Service camp set along Cedar Creek, with easy access off "Highway" 155. Greenhorn Summit and Alder Creek provide alternatives. The elevation is 4,200 feet. Open from May to October.

Map grid h2

FRENCH GULCH GROUP CAMP

on Isabella Lake

H

Campsites, facilities: There is one large group campsite for up to 100 people with tents or motor homes. Picnic tables, fireplaces, and piped water are provided. Flush toilets and solar-heated showers are available. Rest rooms are wheelchair accessible. A grocery store, a laundromat, and propane gas are nearby. I

Reservations, fee: Reservations requested; $60 group fee per night from March through September; no fee the rest of the year.

Who to contact: Phone the U.S. Corps of Engineers at (619)379-2742.

Location: From the town of Lake Isabella, drive 2.5 miles on Highway 155 to the campground entrance on the right. J

Trip note: Take your pick from another in the series of camps along Lake Isabella. Rental boats are available at one of several marinas nearby. Side trips include the town of Keysville, the first of the gold rush towns on the Kern River. The County Boat Permit Station is nearby. The elevation is 2,700 feet.

Map grid **h2**

BOULDER GULCH
on Isabella Lake

Campsites, facilities: There are 79 campsites for tents or motor homes up to 30 feet long. Piped water, fireplaces, and picnic tables are provided. Flush toilets, showers, a playground, and a fish cleaning station are available. Some facilities are wheelchair accessible. Pets are permitted on leashes. Supplies and a laundromat available in the town of Lake Isabella.

Reservations, fee: No reservations; $8 fee per night.

Who to contact: Phone the U.S. Corps of Engineers at (619)379-2742.

Location: From the town of Lake Isabella, drive four miles north on Highway 155.

Trip note: Boulder Gulch is set on the western shore of Lake Isabella, across the road from Hungry Gulch camp. Take your pick. Isabella is the biggest lake for many miles and a prime destination point for Bakersfield area residents. Fishing for trout and bass is best in the spring. By the dog days of summer, when people are bowwowin' at the heat, waterskiers take over, along with folks just lookin' to cool off. Like a lot of lakes in the valley, Isabella is subject to drawdowns. The elevation is 2,650 feet. Open from March through September.

Map grid **h2**

MAIN DAM
on Isabella Lake

Campsites, facilities: There are 82 campsites for tents or motor homes up to 30 feet long. Piped water, fireplaces, and picnic tables are provided. Flush toilets, showers, a dump station, and a boat ramp are available. Pets are permitted on leashes with proof of shots. Supplies and a laundromat are available in the town of Lake Isabella.

Reservations, fee: No reservations, $8 fee per night.

Who to contact: Phone the U.S. Corps of Engineers at (619)379-2742.

Location: From the town of Lake Isabella, drive 1.5 miles northwest on Highway 155.

Trip note: This camp is scheduled for re-opening in 1991 from April to September. It's located on the south shore of Lake Isabella.

Map grid **h2**

EASTSIDE
on Isabella Lake

Campsites, facilities: There are 109 primitive campsites for tents or motor homes. Piped water, flush toilets, a sanitary disposal station, a boat launch, and a fish cleaning station are available. Supplies and a laundromat are available nearby. Pets are permitted on leashes.

Reservations, fee: No reservations, no fee.

Who to contact: Phone the U.S. Corps of Engineers at (619)379-2742.

Location: From Kernville, drive five miles south on Sierra Way to the north shore of Isabella Lake and the campground entrance.

Trip note: This campground is primitive and sparsely covered, but has several bonus features. It is set along the shore of Lake Isabella, known for good boating, water skiing (in summer), and fishing (in the spring). Other options include great kayaking waters along the North Fork of the Kern River (located north of the lake), a good bird-watching area at the South Fork Wildlife Area (along the northeast corner of the lake), and an off-road motorcycle park across the road from this campground. The elevation is 2,650 feet.

A

Map grid **h2**

TILLIE CREEK
on Isabella Lake

Campsites, facilities: There are 159 family campsites and four group sites for tents or motor homes up to 30 feet long. Piped water, fireplaces, and picnic tables are provided. Flush toilets, showers, a sanitary disposal station, a playground, an amphitheater, and a fish cleaning station are available. Four sites are wheelchair accessible. Pets are permitted on leashes. Supplies and a laundromat are nearby in Wofford Heights.

B

Reservations, fee: No reservations; $8 fee per night for family sites; $40 per night for group sites.

C

Who to contact: Phone the U.S. Corps of Engineers at (619)379-2742.

Location: From Wofford Heights on the west side of Lake Isabella, drive one mile southwest on Highway 155.

Trip note: This is one of the two camps located along Tillie Creek, near Lake Isabella. See the trip note for the Eastside camp. Open from March through September.

D

Map grid **h2**

LIVE OAK
on Isabella Lake

Campsites, facilities: There are 150 family campsites and one group site for tents or motor homes up to 30 feet long. Piped water, fireplaces, and picnic tables are provided. Flush toilets, showers, and a fish cleaning station are available. Supplies and a laundromat are available nearby.

E

Reservations, fee: No reservations; $8 fee per night for family site; $40 fee per night for group site.

F

Who to contact: Phone the U.S. Corps of Engineers at (619)379-2742.

Location: From Wofford Heights on the west side of Lake Isabella, drive one-half mile south on Highway 155 to the campground entrance road on your right.

Trip note: This is the second of the camps set along Tillie Creek, on Lake Isabella's northwest side. For details on the area, see the trip note for the Eastside camp. The elevation is 2,600 feet. Open from March through September.

G5

Map grid **h2**

AUXILLIARY DAM
on Isabella Lake

Campsites, facilities: There are a number of primitive, undesignated campsites for tents or motor homes. Piped water, flush toilets, showers, and a dump station are available. Pets are permitted on leashes. Supplies and a laundromat are available in the town of Lake Isabella.

H

Reservations, fee: No reservations, no fee.

Who to contact: Phone the U.S. Corps of Engineers at (619)379-2742.

Location: From the town of Lake Isabella, drive a mile northeast on Highway 178.

I

Trip note: This is a primitive Army Corps camp that is designed to be an overflow area if other camps at Lake Isabella are packed. It's not exactly paradise, but if you're stuck for a spot, it'll do for the night.

Map grid **h3**

RIVERNOOK CAMPGROUND
on the North Fork of Kern River

J

Campsites, facilities: There are 23 tent sites and 166 motor home spaces. Picnic tables, piped water, and full or partial hookups are provided. Rest rooms, showers, a dump station, and cable TV hookups are available.

Reservations, fee: Call for space available; $12-$14 fee per night.

Who to contact: Phone the park at (619)376-2705.

Location: From Kernville, drive one-half mile north to 14001 Sierra Way.

Trip note: This is a large, privately-operated park set near Lake Isabella. Boat rentals are available at one of the nearby marinas. Take a side trip to the town of Keysville, the first town to spring up on the Kern River during the gold rush days. The elevation is 2,665 feet. Open year-round.

Map grid i1

HOBO
on Kern River
SEQUOIA NATIONAL FOREST

Campsites, facilities: There are 25 campsites for tents or motor homes up to 16 feet long. Fireplaces and picnic tables are provided. Water is provided some of the time. Vault toilets, showers, and a dump station are available.

Reservations, fee: No reservations; $5 per night; no fee when there is no water.

Who to contact: Phone the Sequoia National Forest Greenhorn Ranger District at (209)871-2223.

Location: From the town of Lake Isabella, drive five miles south west on Highway 178. Turn left on Borel Road and drive south for about one-third mile to the intersection of Old Kern Road. Turn right and drive about two miles to campground on your right.

Trip note: Because this camp is overshadowed by nearby Lake Isabella to the north, it is often overlooked. It is a small campground set along the Kern River, about two miles off Highway 178. A new campground is in the works about a mile north of this campground at Sandy Flat; it will probably open in 1992. The elevation is 2,300 feet. Open from May to October.

Map grid i2

PARADISE COVE
on Isabella Lake

Campsites, facilities: There are 138 campsites for tents or motor homes, some with picnic tables and fireplaces provided. Flush toilets, showers, and a fish cleaning station are available. The rest rooms are wheelchair accessible. Pets are permitted on leashes. Supplies and a laundromat are available in the town of Lake Isabella.

Reservations, fee: No reservations; $8 fee per night.

Who to contact: Phone the U.S. Corps of Engineers at (619)379-2742.

Location: From the town of Lake Isabella, drive six miles northeast on Highway 178.

Trip note: Paradise Cove is on the south shore of Lake Isabella. The elevation is 2,600 feet. For details on the area, see the trip note for the Eastside, Boulder Gulch, and French Gulch campgrounds. Open all year.

Map grid i2

MOUNTAIN MESA TRAILER COURT
on Isabella Lake

Campsites, facilities: There are 45 motor home spaces with full hookups. Rest rooms, showers, a swimming pool, a recreation room, cable TV hookups, and a laundromat are available. Pets are permitted on leashes.

Reservations, fee: Reservations accepted; $12-$13.50 fee per night.

Who to contact: Phone the park at (619)379-2046.

Location: From the town of Lake Isabella, drive six miles northeast on Highway 178.

Trip note: This quiet, privately-operated park is set up for motor homes at Lake Isabella. It is one of many camps at the lake. Plan on plenty of company. For details on the area, see the trip note for the Eastside, Boulder Gulch, and French Gulch camps. The elevation is 2,600 feet. Open all year.

Map grid i3

KOA LAKE ISABELLA

Campsites, facilities: There are 104 campsites for tents or motor homes. Picnic tables, piped water, and full or partial hookups are provided. Rest rooms, showers, a playground, a swimming pool, a laundromat, a store, a dump station, and propane gas are available. Pets are permitted on leashes.

Reservations, fee: Call for available space; $16-$20 per night.

Who to contact: Phone the park at (619)378-2001.

Location: From the town of Lake Isabella, drive ten miles east on Highway 178.

Trip note: If the camps around Lake Isabella are jam-packed, the KOA camp provides an alternative. It is set in South Fork Valley (elevation is 2,600 feet).

Map grid j0

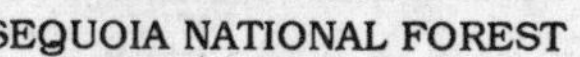

BRECKENRIDGE

SEQUOIA NATIONAL FOREST

Campsites, facilities: There are eight tent sites. Picnic tables and fireplaces are provided and vault toilets are available. There is **no piped water,** so bring your own. Pets are permitted on leashes.

Reservations, fee: No reservations, no fee.

Who to contact: Phone the Sequoia National Forest Greenhorn Ranger District at (209)861-4212.

Location: From the town of Lake Isabella on Highway 178, turn south on Caliente Bodfish Road and drive about 12 miles to the town of Havilah. Continue south on Caliente Bodfish Road for two more miles. Turn right (west) on Forest Service Road 28S06 (dirt road) and drive ten miles to the campground.

Trip note: You join the One Percent Club by visiting this camp. In other words, *nobody* knows about it. It is a tiny, primitive camp set at 7,100 feet elevation near Breckenridge Mountain (a good lookout here) in a little-traveled sector of the Sequoia National Forest. There are no other camps in the immediate area. Open from May to October.

◆ MAP G6 ◆

BEACH DESERT FOOTHILL
TREES URBAN GRASSLAND
5% CLUB 5% CLUB

15 MILES

to Big Pine
to Scotty's Castle
to Lone Pine
to Olancha
to Furnace Creek
to Homestead
to Johannesburg

DEATH
VALLEY
NAT'L.
MON.

Stovepipe Wells
Cerro Gordo EL. 9,217
Keeler
Owens Lake
136
190
Panamint Springs
Darwin
Towne Pass EL. 4,956
Pinto Pk. EL. 7,450
Emigrants Pass EL. 5,318
Wildrose
Telescope Pk. EL. 11,049
Sentinel Pk. EL. 9,480
Ballarat
Dry Lake
Naval Weapons Center Area
Argus Pk. EL. 6,562
Pioneer Point
China Lake
Trona
178
Westend
Searles Lake
China Lake
395
Ridgecrest
NATIONAL NATURAL LANDMARK
Naval Weapons Center

a b c d e f g h i j

0 1 2 3 4 5 6 7 8 9

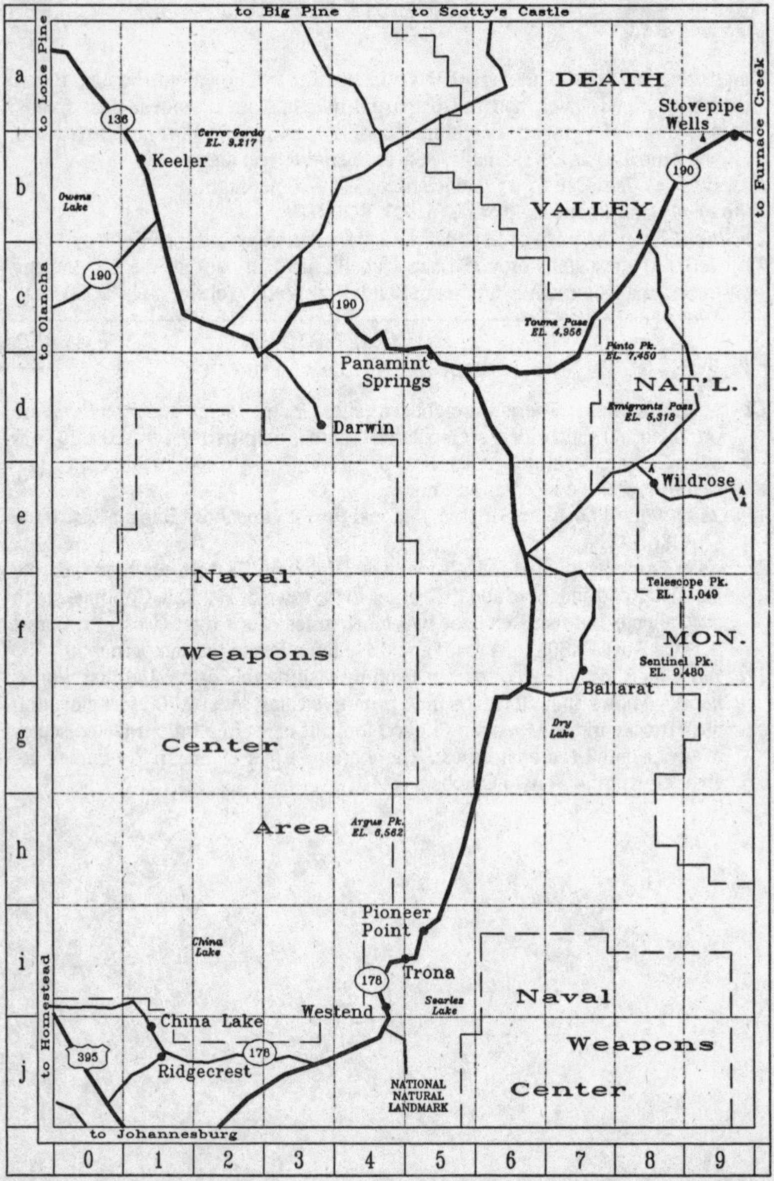

A

Map grid **b8**

EMIGRANT

DEATH VALLEY NATIONAL MONUMENT

Campsites, facilities: There are ten campsites for tents or motor homes. Piped water, fireplaces, and picnic tables are provided. Flush toilets are available. Pets are permitted on leashes.

Reservations, fee: No reservations, no fee.

Who to contact: Phone the Death Valley National Monument at (619)786-2331.

Location: In Stovepipe Wells Village, drive nine miles southwest on Highway 190.

Trip note: The key here is the elevation, and Emigrant camp, at 2,000 feet elevation, is out of the forbidding sub-zero elevations of Death Valley. That makes it one of the more habitable camps when others at Death Valley National Monument are like furnaces. Open May through October.

B C

Map grid **b9**

STOVEPIPE WELLS

DEATH VALLEY NATIONAL MONUMENT

Campsites, facilities: There are ten sites for tents only and 200 campsites for tents or motor homes. Piped water is provided and there are fire grills at the tent sites only. Flush toilets, a dump station, a swimming pool, a camp store, gasoline, and evening ranger programs are available. The rest rooms are wheelchair accessible.

Reservations, fee: No reservations; $4 fee per night.

Who to contact: Phone the Death Valley National Monument at (619)786-2331.

Location: In Stovepipe Wells Village, drive to the north end of town on Highway 190.

Trip note: This is a good base camp for four-wheel drive cowboys because it is set near a rugged road that is routed into Cottonwood and Marble. (No cross-country vehicle travel is permitted in the park). The elevation is at sea level, on the edge of dropping off into never-never land. Open from November through April.

D E F

Map grid **e8**

WILDROSE

DEATH VALLEY NATIONAL MONUMENT

Campsites, facilities: There are 30 campsites for tents or motor homes. Fireplaces and picnic tables are provided. Piped water and pit toilets are available. Pets are permitted on leashes.

Reservations, fee: No reservations, no fee.

Who to contact: Phone the Death Valley National Monument at (619)786-2331.

Location: From Stovepipe Wells Village, drive 30 miles south on Highway 190 and Panamint Valley or Emigrant Canyon Roads to Wildrose Canyon Road. Note: Emigrant Canyon Road is steep, narrow, winding, and not recommended for vehicles over 25 feet long.

Trip note: The nearby Wildrose Ranger Station is the highlight at this camp, providing a chance to get the latest info on trail and road conditions. It is set on the road that heads out to the primitive country, eventually to Telescope Peak, the highest point in Death Valley National Monument (11,049 feet). The elevation is 4,100 feet. Open year-round.

G6 H I J

Map grid **e9**

MAHOGANY FLAT

DEATH VALLEY NATIONAL MONUMENT

Campsites, facilities: There are ten campsites for tents or motor homes. Picnic tables and pit toilets are available. There is **no piped water,** so bring your own. The campground is accessible by foot or four-wheel drive.

Reservations, fee: No reservations; no fee.

Who to contact: Phone the Death Valley National Monument at (619)786-2331.

Location: From Stovepipe Wells Village, drive 38 miles south on Highway 190 and Panamint Valley Road or Emigrant Canyon Road to Wildrose Canyon Road. Drive to the end of the road. Note: Emigrant Canyon Road is steep, narrow, winding, and not recommended for vehicles over 25 feet long.

Trip note: This is one of two primitive, hard-to-reach camps set in Death Valley National Monument's high country. The trail that is routed to Bennett and Telescope Peaks leads out from camp. Only the ambitious and well-conditioned should attempt the climb. The elevation is 8,200 feet. Open from April through October.

Map grid **e9**

THORNDIKE

DEATH VALLEY NATIONAL MONUMENT

Campsites, facilities: This backcountry campground is accessible by foot or four-wheel drive and has eight campsites for tents or motor homes. Picnic tables and pit toilets are available. There is **no piped water,** so bring your own. Pets are permitted on leashes.

Reservations, fee: No reservations, no fee.

Who to contact: Phone the Death Valley National Monument at (619)786-2331.

Location: From Stovepipe Wells Village, drive 37 miles south on Highway 190 and Panamint Valley Road or Emigrant Canyon Road to Wildrose Canyon Road. Drive to the end of the road. Note: Emigrant Canyon Road is steep, narrow, winding, and not recommended for vehicles over 25 feet long.

Trip note: This is one of Death Valley National Monument's little-known camps. It is set in the high country at 7,500 feet elevation. It's free, of course. Otherwise they'd have to actually send somebody out to tend to the place. Nearby are century-old charcoal kilns that were built by Chinese laborers and tended by Shoshone Indians. The trailhead that serves Telescope Peak (11,049 feet), the highest point in Death Valley, can be found in nearby Mahogany Flat campground. It is a strenuous all-day hike. Open from March to October.

A

B

C

D

E

F

G6

H

I

J

MAP G7

BEACH
DESERT
FOOTHILL
TREES
URBAN
GRASSLAND
5% CLUB

15 MILES

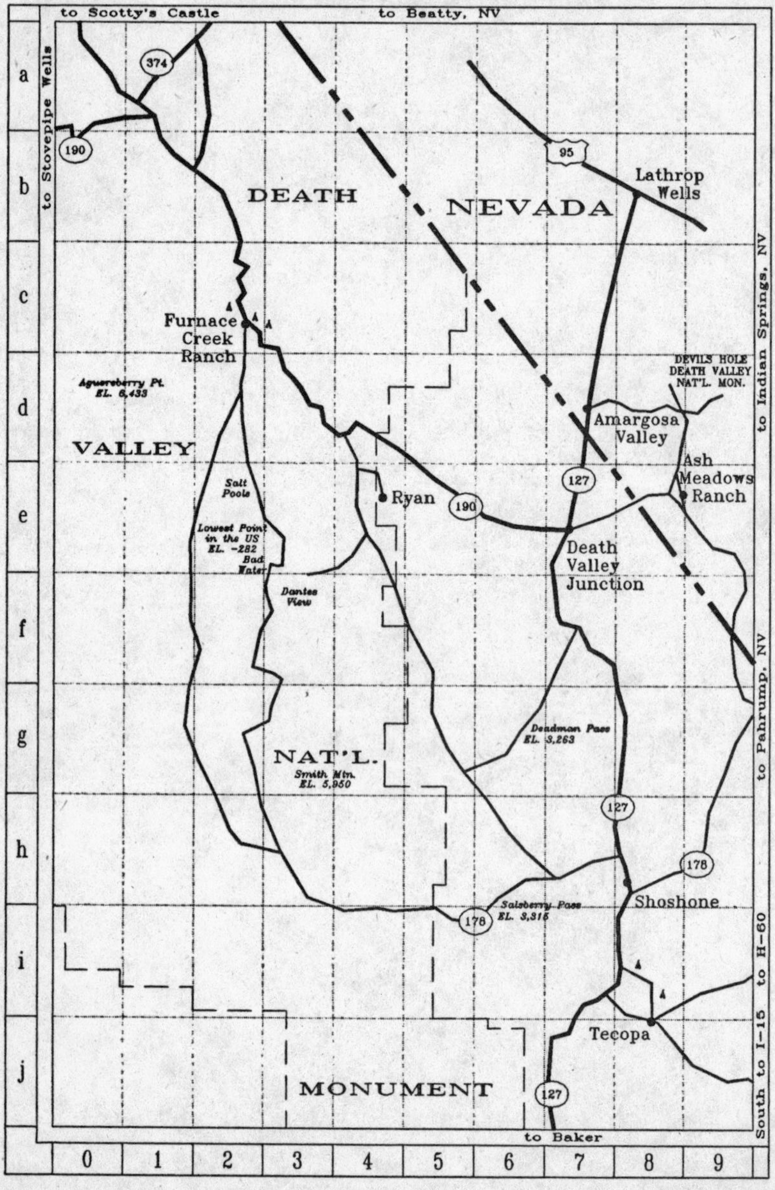

to Scotty's Castle
to Beatty, NV
to Stovepipe Wells
to Indian Springs, NV
to Pahrump, NV
South to I-15 to H-60
to Baker

374
190
95
127
178

DEATH VALLEY NAT'L. MONUMENT
NEVADA

Lathrop Wells
Furnace Creek Ranch
Aguereberry Pt. EL. 6,433
DEVILS HOLE DEATH VALLEY NAT'L. MON.
Amargosa Valley
Ash Meadows Ranch
Salt Pools
Ryan
Lowest Point in the US EL. -282 Bad Water
Death Valley Junction
Dantes View
Deadman Pass EL. 3,263
Smith Mtn. EL. 5,950
Shoshone
Salsberry Pass EL. 3,315
Tecopa

a
b
c
d
e
f
g
h
i
j

0 1 2 3 4 5 6 7 8 9

FURNACE CREEK

Map grid **c2** 

DEATH VALLEY NATIONAL MONUMENT

Campsites, facilities: There are 136 campsites for tents or motor homes. Picnic tables, fireplaces, and piped water are provided. Flush toilets, a dump station and evening ranger programs, are available. The rest rooms are wheelchair accessible.

Reservations, fee: No reservations; $8 fee per night.

Who to contact: Phone the Death Valley National Monument at (619)786-2331.

Location: From Furnace Creek Ranch, drive one mile north on Highway 190.

Trip note: This is a well developed national park site that provides a good base camp for exploring Death Valley, especially for newcomers. The nearby Visitor's Center and Death Valley Museum offer maps and suggestions for hikes and drives in this unique wildland. The elevation is 190 feet below sea level.Open all year, but keep in mind that the summer temperatures commonly exceed 100 degrees.

SUNSET

Map grid **c2** 

DEATH VALLEY NATIONAL MONUMENT

Campsites, facilities: There are 1,000 campsites for tents or motor homes. Piped water and picnic tables are provided. Flush toilets, a dump station and evening ranger programs are available. There are 16 wheelchair accessible campsites near accessible rest rooms.

Reservations, fee: No reservations; $4 fee per night.

Who to contact: Phone the Death Valley National Monument at (619)786-2331.

Location: From Furnace Creek Ranch, drive one-quarter mile east.

Trip note: This is one of several options for campers in the Furnace Creek area. Newcomers should check out the Visitor's Center for maps and suggested hikes and drives. Don't forget your canteen—and if you're backpacking, never set up a wilderness camp near water in Death Valley. A thirsty animal may think it has to fight you in order to get a drink. It'll probably win. The elevation is 190 feet below sea level. Open from November through April.

TEXAS SPRING

Map grid **c3** 

DEATH VALLEY NATIONAL MONUMENT

Campsites, facilities: There are 93 campsites for tents or motor homes. There are also two group campsites, each accommodating 70 people and ten vehicles. Piped water, fireplaces, and picnic tables are provided. Flush toilets, a dump station and evening ranger programs are available.

Reservations, fee: No reservations; $5 fee per night.

Who to contact: Phone the Death Valley National Monument at (619)786-2331.

Location: From Furnace Creek Ranch, drive one-half mile east on Highway 190.

Trip note: Death Valley is kind of like an ugly dog that you love. After awhile, you can't help it. This campground, like the others near Furnace Creek Ranch, offers a good headquarters to get a feel for Death Valley. The nearby Visitors Center and Death Valley Museum offer maps and suggestions for hikes and drives. Open from November to April.

Map grid i8 TECOPA HOT SPRINGS RESORT
near Death Valley

Campsites, facilities: There are 92 motor home sites with full hookups. A mesa is available for tent campers. Rest rooms with hot showers, mineral bath spas, a grocery store, and a laundromat are available. Propane gas can be found nearby.
Reservations, fee: Reservations are recommended during the winter; $8 fee per night.
Who to contact: Phone (619)852-4373.
Location: From Interstate 15, take Highway 127 north for 48 miles to Tecopa. Turn east (right) on Old Spanish Trail and drive to Tecopa Hot Springs Road Road. Turn left and drive 1.5 miles to the park.
Trip note: This is the fanciest place in Tecopa, where folks enjoy the mineral hot springs in personal spas and say they feel a glow about them for days. Death Valley, located nearby to the west, provides a possible side trip. But what do you really want to know? Right, it's 80 miles to Las Vegas!

Map grid i8 TECOPA HOT SPRINGS COUNTY PARK

Campsites, facilities: There are 300 campsites for tents or motor homes. Piped water, fireplaces, picnic tables, and, in some cases electrical connections are provided. Flush toilets, showers, a dump station, a store, a laundromat, and propane gas are available. Some facilities are wheelchair accessible.
Reservations, fee: No reservations; $5.50 fee per night.
Who to contact: Phone the County Parks Department at (619)852-4264.
Location: From Death Valley Junction, drive about 35 miles south on State Highway 127 to the park entrance.
Trip note: This one is out there in No Man's Land, and if it wasn't for the hot springs, all you'd see around here is a few skeletons. Regardless, it's quite an attraction in the winter, when the warm climate is a plus, and the nearby mineral baths are worth taking a dunk in. The elevation is 1,500 feet. Open all year.

◆ MAP H2 ◆

BEACH
DESERT
FOOTHILL
TREES
URBAN
GRASSLAND
5% CLUB

15 MILES

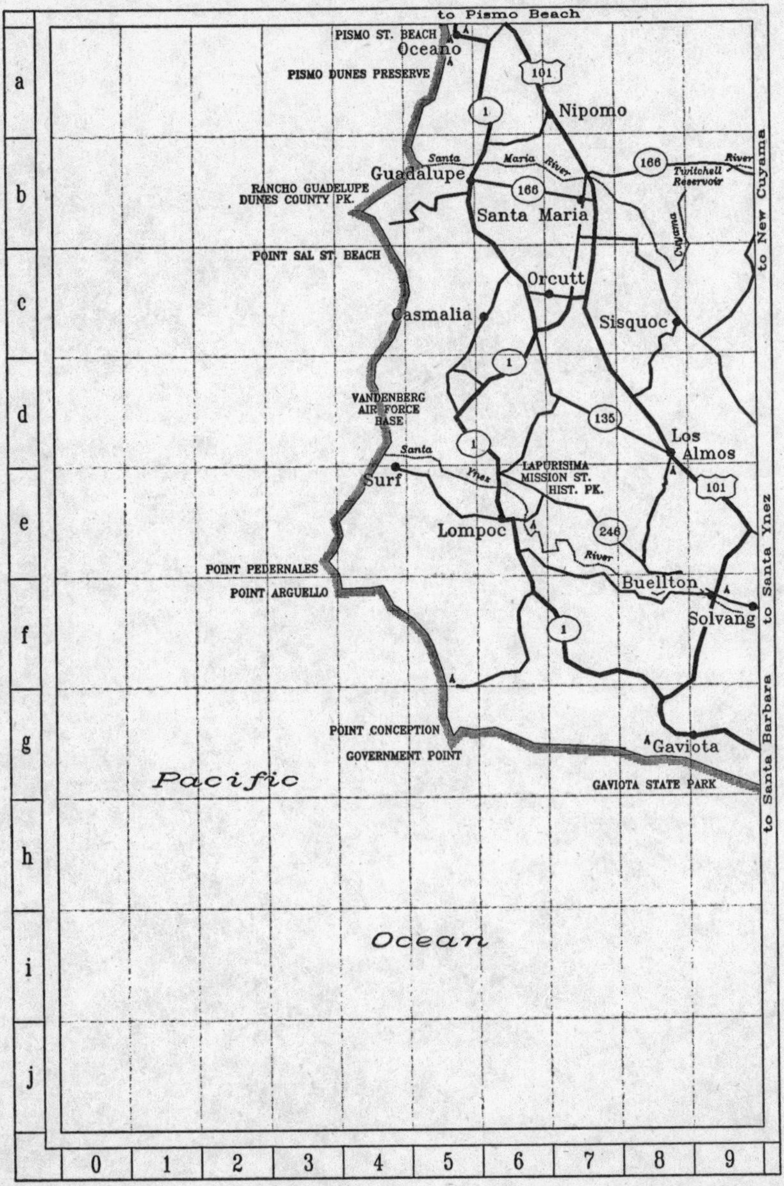

A

Map grid **a5**

OCEANO COUNTY CAMPGROUND

near Arroyo

Campsites, facilities: There are 24 campsites for motor homes with full hookups. Fireplaces and picnic tables are provided. Flush toilets, showers, and a sanitary disposal station are available. A playground, a laundromat, a grocery store, and propane gas are available nearby. Pets are permitted on leashes.

B

Reservations, fee: No reservations; $16 fee per night; fee for pets.

Who to contact: Phone the park at (805)549-5219.

Location: From Pismo Beach, drive south on US 101. Take the Arroyo-Grand Avenue exit west to Highway 1. Turn south for a short distance and turn left on Airpark. The campground is at 414 Airpark Drive.

C

Trip note: This county park often gets overlooked because it isn't on the state reservation system. That's other folks' loss, your gain. The location is a bonus, set near Pismo State Beach. Open from April through September.

Map grid **a5**

PISMO DUNES STATE RECREATION AREA

D

Campsites, facilities: There are 500 primitive campsites here for off-road vehicles. Vault toilets are provided. There is **no piped water,** so bring your own Horseback riding facilities, a grocery store, a laundromat, and propane gas are available nearby. Pets are permitted on leashes.

E

Reservations, fee: Reserve through MISTIX at (800)444-PARK ($3.95 MISTIX fee); $5 fee per night.

Who to contact: Phone the park at (805)549-3433.

Location: Northbound on US 101, take the Grand Avenue exit. Make a left at the signal. If you don't have reservations, continue westbound on Grand Avenue for about eight miles until the road ends at the beach. If you have reservations, continue westbound on Grand Avenue. Turn left at the last traffic light on Highway 1. Drive about 1.5 miles south to Pier Avenue. Turn right and follow the road to the dead end. Southbound on US 101, take the Pismo Beach Exit and continue straight to the fourth traffic light. If you don't have reservations, turn right on Grand Avenue and drive to the end. If you have reservations continue straight on Highway 1 for 1.5 miles to Pier Avenue. Turn right and drive to the end.

F

G

Trip note: This is "National Headquarters for All-Terrain Vehicles." You know, those three and four-wheeled motorcycles that turn otherwise normal people into lunatics. They roam wild on the dunes here, that's the law, so don't go planning a quiet stroll. If you don't like 'em, you are strongly advised to go elsewhere. Open year-round.

H2

Map grid **a5**

OCEANO

PISMO STATE BEACH

I

Campsites, facilities: There are 80 sites for tents only and 40 motor home spaces with water and electrical hookups for RVs up to 36 feet long. Picnic tables and fireplaces are provided. Piped water, rest rooms, showers, and a dump station are available. Horseback riding facilities, a grocery store, a laundromat, and propane gas are nearby.

J

Reservations, fee: Reserve through MISTIX at (800)444-PARK ($3.95 MISTIX fee); $12-$18 fee per night.

Who to contact: Phone the park at (805)489-2684.

Location: From Pismo Beach, drive one mile south on Highway 1 to the campground entrance.

Trip note: This is the other campground at Pismo State Beach. With a world-famous beach, dunes, and all, plan on plenty of company. Open year-round.

Map grid e6

RIVER PARK
in Lompoc

Campsites, facilities: There 34 motor home spaces with full hookups and a large open area for tents. Piped water, flush toilets, a dump station, a fishing pond and a playground are available. Supplies and a laundromat are nearby. Pets are permitted on leashes.

Reservations, fee: No reservations; $6-$10 fee per night; hikers and bikers $2 fee per night. $1 pet fee.

Who to contact: Phone the park at (805)736-6565.

Location: In Lompoc, drive to the junction of Highway 246 and Sweeney Road at the southwest edge of town.

Trip note: Before checking in here, you'd best get a lesson in how to pronounce Lompoc. It's "Lom-Poke." If you arrive and say, "Hey, it's great to be in Lom-Pock," they might just tell ya to get on back to Nebraska with the other cowpokes. It is set near the lower Santa Ynez River, which looks quite a bit different than it does up in Los Padres National Forest. There is a small fishing lake within the park which is stocked regularly with trout. Side trip possibilities include the nearby La Purisima Mission State Historical Park.

Map grid f5

JALAMA BEACH COUNTY PARK
near Lompoc on the Pacific Ocean

Campsites, facilities: There are 100 campsites for tents or motor homes up to 35 feet long. Piped water, fireplaces, and picnic tables are provided. Flush toilets, showers, a dump station, a grocery store, a laundromat. and propane gas are available. Pets are permitted on leashes.

Reservations, fee: No reservations, except for groups; $10 fee per night; pets $1.

Who to contact: Phone the park at (805)736-6316.

Location: From Lompoc, drive south on Highway 1. Turn southwest on Jalama Road and drive 15 miles to the park.

Trip note: This is a pretty spot set where Jalama Creek empties into the ocean, about five miles north of Point Conception and just south of Vandenberg Air Force Base. The area is known for its beachcombing (occasional lost missiles) and sunsets.

Map grid f9

FLYING FLAGS TRAVEL PARK
near Solvang

Campsites, facilities: There are 100 sites for tents and 200 motor home spaces with full or partial hookups. Picnic tables and fireplaces are provided. Rest rooms with wheelchair access, showers, a playground, a swimming pool, two hot therapy pools, a laundromat, a store, a dump station, ice, a recreation room, an arcade, three clubhouses, a putting green, and propane gas are available. Pets are permitted on leashes. A nine hole golf course is next door.

Reservations, fee: Call for available space; $13-$18 fee per night.

Who to contact: Phone the park at (805)688-3716.

Location: From Santa Barbara, drive 45 miles north on US 101 to its intersection with Highway 246.

Trip note: This is one of the few privately-operated parks that welcomes tenters as well as motor homes. Nearby side trips include the Santa Ynez Mission, located just east of Solvang.

Map grid g8

GAVIOTA STATE PARK
near Santa Barbara

Campsites, facilities: There are 18 sites for tents only and 36 sites for motor homes up to 27 feet long. Fireplaces and picnic tables are provided at tent sites only. Piped water, flush toilets, showers, and a boat hoist are available. A grocery store is nearby. Pets are permitted on leashes.

Reservations, fee: No reservations; $14-$16 fee per night; pets $1.

Who to contact: Phone the park at (805)968-1033.

Location: From Santa Barbara, drive 33 miles north on US 101 to park entrance.

Trip note: This is the granddaddy, the biggest of the three state beaches along Highway 1 northwest of Santa Barbara. The park covers 2,800 acres, providing both trails for hiking and horseback riding as well as a mile-long stretch of beautiful beach frontage. The ambitious can hike the beach to get more seclusion.

• MAP H3 •

BEACH
DESERT
FOOTHILL
TREES
URBAN
GRASSLAND
5% CLUB

16 MILES

to California Valley
to McKittrick
to Buttonwillow
to Sisquoc to Santa Maria
to Buellton
to Caviota
to Maricopa to I-5
to Frazier Park
connects
to Camarillo to Santa Paula

Derby Acres
LOS
Fellows
119
Ford City
Taft
Cuyama River
166
Manzanita Mtn. EL. 3,125
PADRES
New Cuyama
Cuyama
Crocer Grade EL. 2,968
McPhearson Pk. EL. 5,947
33
RAFAEL
WILDERNESS
Ventucopa
Los Olivos
154
NAT'L.
Cuyama Pk. EL. 5,875
Solvang
246
Santa Ynez
Santa Ynez River
Lake Cachuma
FOREST
154
San Marcos Pass EL. 2,225
Pine Mtn. Summit EL. 5,084
Monte Arido EL. 6,003
101
REFUGIO ST. BEACH
EL CAPITAN ST. BEACH
192
Goleta
Santa Barbara
Montecito
Summerland
Wheeler Springs
33
Carpinteria
CARPINTERIA ST. BEACH
150
Lake Casitas
Pacific
Oak View
101
33
Ocean
EMMA K. WOOD ST. BEACH
Ventura

a
b
c
d
e
f
g
h
i
j

0 1 2 3 4 5 6 7 8 9

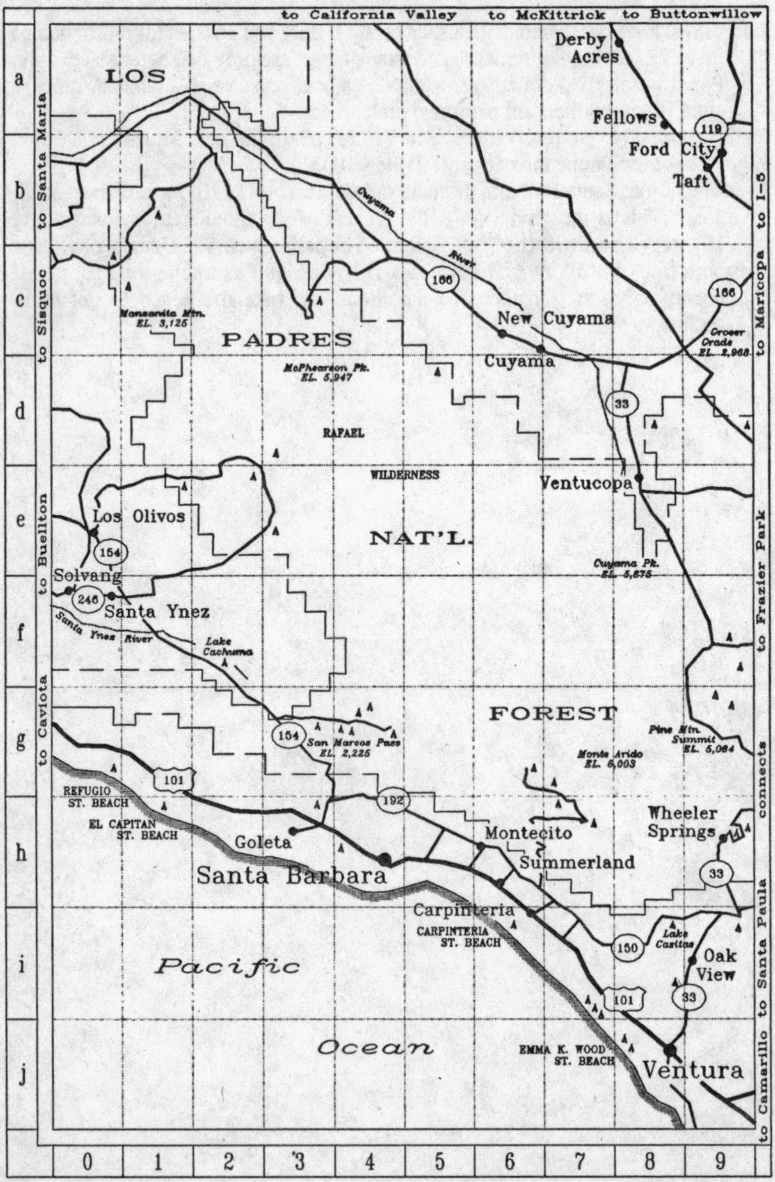

Map grid **b1**

WAGON FLAT

on the North Fork of La Brea Creek
LOS PADRES NATIONAL FOREST

Campsites, facilities: There are five campsites for tents. Fireplaces and picnic tables are provided. Vault toilets are available. There is **no piped water,** so bring your own. Pets are permitted on leashes.

Reservations, fee: No reservations, no fee.

Who to contact: Phone the Los Padres National Forest Santa Lucia District at (805)925-9538.

Location: From Santa Maria, drive southeast on Foxen Canyon Road for eight miles to the town of Garey. Continue southeast on Santa Maria Mesa Road for four miles. Turn left on Tepusqet Road and drive 6.5 miles. Turn right on Colson Canyon Road (Forest Service Road 11N04) and drive ten more miles.

Trip note: Not many folks know about this obscure spot, and if it's a hot, late summer day, they're probably better off for it. In the late fall, winter, and spring, however, it makes for a good base camp for a hiking trip. It is set at 1,400 feet elevation, with a trail out of camp leading up Kerry Canyon. Open all year.

Map grid **c0**

COLSON

LOS PADRES NATIONAL FOREST

Campsites, facilities: There are eight tent sites. Fireplaces and picnic tables are provided. Vault toilets are available. Pets are permitted on leashes. Piped water is only sometimes available.

Reservations, fee: No reservations, no fee.

Who to contact: Phone the Los Padres National Forest Santa Lucia District at (805)925-9538.

Location: From Santa Maria on US 101, take the Betteravia Road exit. Drive eight miles southeast on Foxen Canyon Road. Bear left at the fork and continue southeast on Santa Maria Mesa Road. Turn left on Tepuset Road and drive 6.5 miles. Turn right on Colson Canyon Road (Forest Service Road 11N04) and drive four miles to the campground.

Trip note: This area has two seasons to it, spring and fall. In the spring, it's beautiful. In the fall, it's hot and dry and with no water and is scarcely fit for habitation. The camp is deep in the Los Padres National Forest, with trails leading out of camp for ambitious hikers. The elevation is 2,100 feet. Open year-round.

Map grid **c1**

BARREL SPRINGS

LOS PADRES NATIONAL FOREST

Campsites, facilities: There are six tent sites. Piped water, fireplaces, and picnic tables are provided. Vault toilets are available. Pets are permitted on leashes.

Reservations, fee: No reservations, no fee.

Who to contact: Phone the Los Padres National Forest Santa Lucia District at (805)925-9538.

Location: From Santa Maria on US 101, take the Betteravia Road exit. Drive eight miles southeast on Foxen Canyon Road. Bear left at the fork and continue southeast on Santa Maria Mesa Road. Turn left on Tepuset Roadand drive 6.5 miles. Turn right on Colson Canyon Road (Forest Service Road 11N04) and drive eight miles to the campground. (The road is dirt and impassable when wet).

Trip note: This small, little-known camp is used primarily by backpackers starting wilderness expeditions. It is set at 1,000 feet elevation along La Brea Creek and shaded by the oaks in La Brea Canyon. A trail near the camp is routed into the backcountry and into the San Rafael Wilderness, with more campgrounds spaced every ten miles along the trail. Open year-round.

Map grid c3

BATES CANYON
LOS PADRES NATIONAL FOREST

Campsites, facilities: There are six tent sites. Fireplaces and picnic tables are provided. Vault toilets are available. Pets are permitted on leashes. There is **no piped water,** so bring your own.

Reservations, fee: No reservations, no fee.

Who to contact: Phone the Los Padres National Forest Santa Lucia District at (805)925-9538.

Location: From Santa Maria, drive 50 miles east on Highway 166. Turn right on Cottonwood Canyon Road and drive 7.5 miles southwest to the campground.

Trip note: This camp is located in the Sierra Madre Mountains, not far from the panoramic Bates Ridge Lookout. As with the other camps in this area, a Los Padres National Forest map will open up the area to you. The elevation is 2,900 feet. Open year-round.

Map grid d3

NIRA
on Manzana Creek
LOS PADRES NATIONAL FOREST

Campsites, facilities: There are ten sites for tents and two spaces for motor homes up to 16 feet long. Fireplaces and picnic tables are provided. Vault toilets and horse hitching posts are available. There is piped water. Pets are permitted on leashes.

Reservations, fee: No reservations, no fee.

Who to contact: Phone the Los Padres National Forest Santa Lucia District at (805)925-9538.

Location: From US 101 in Santa Barbara, drive 22 miles northeast on Highway 154. Turn right on Armour Ranch Road and drive 1.5 miles. Turn right on Happy Canyon Road and drive 11 miles to Cachuma Saddle. Continue straight (north) on Sunset Valley/Cachuma Road (Forest Service Road 8N09) for six miles to the campground.

Trip note: This premium jump-off spot for backpackers is set at 2,100 feet elevation along Manzana Creek on the border of the San Rafael Wilderness. A primary trailhead for the San Rafael Wilderness is located here and connects to numerous trails and backcountry camps. All are detailed on a Forest Service map. Today's history lesson? This camp was originally an NRA (National Recovery Act) camp during the Depression, hence the name Nira. Wow! Open year-round.

Map grid d5

ALISO PARK
LOS PADRES NATIONAL FOREST

Campsites, facilities: There are 11 campsites for tents or motor homes up to 22 feet long. Fireplaces and picnic tables are provided. Vault toilets are available. There is **no piped water,** so bring your own. Pets are permitted on leashes.

Reservations, fee: No reservations, no fee.

Who to contact: Phone the Los Padres National Forest Mt. Pinos District at (805)245-3731.

Location: From Santa Maria, drive 59 miles east on Highway 166. Turn right on Aliso Canyon Road and drive six miles south to the campground.

Trip note: This primitive, quiet park is set at the foot of the Sierra Madres Mountains at 3,200 feet elevation, directly below McPherson Peak (5,747 feet elevation). Open year-round.

Map grid d8

BALLINGER
LOS PADRES NATIONAL FOREST

5% CLUB

Campsites, facilities: There are 12 campsites for tents or motor homes up to 32 feet long. Fireplaces and picnic tables are provided. Pit toilets are available. There is **no piped water,** so bring your own. Pets are permitted on leashes.

Reservations, fee: No reservations, no fee.

Who to contact: Phone the Los Padres National Forest Mount Pinos Ranger District at (805)245-3731.

Location: From the junction of Highways 166 and 33 in Maricopa, drive 14 miles south on Highway 33. Where Highway 33 separates from Highway 166, turn left (south) on Highway 33 and drive 5.5 miles to Ballinger Canyon Road. Turn left (east) and drive three miles to the campground.

Trip note: Hope you like four-wheel drives and dirt bikes. Why? Because that's the kind of company campers keep around this area. Off-road vehicles use the nearby Hungry Valley Recreation Area, which is near the boundary of Los Padres National Forest. Open year-round.

Map grid d9

VALLE VISTA
LOS PADRES NATIONAL FOREST

5% CLUB

Campsites, facilities: There are seven campsites for tents or motor homes up to 32 feet long. Fireplaces and picnic tables are provided. Vault toilets are available. There is **no piped water,** so bring your own. Pets are permitted on leashes.

Reservations, fee: No reservations, no fee.

Who to contact: Phone the Los Padres National Forest Mount Pinos Ranger District at (805)245-3731.

Location: From the junction of Highways 166 and 33 in Maricopa, drive about nine miles south on Highway 166. Turn east (left) on Cerro Noroeste Road and drive 12 miles to the campground.

Trip note: The view of Bakersfield Valley is the highlight of this primitive camp. It is set at 4,800 feet elevation, near the boundary of Los Padres National Forest. Visitors can usually spot a few buzzards circling around. If you don't bring your own water, they might just start circling you. Open year-round.

Map grid e1

FIGUEROA
LOS PADRES NATIONAL FOREST

Campsites, facilities: There are 27 campsites for tents and six spaces for motor homes up to 22 feet long. Piped water, fireplaces, and picnic tables are provided. Vault toilets are available. Pets are permitted on leashes.

Reservations, fee: Groups may reserve through MISTIX at (800)283-CAMP ($10 MISTIX fee); $5 fee per night; reservations available for groups of up to 56 people; $50 for groups.

Who to contact: Phone the Los Padres National Forest Santa Lucia District at

A B C D E F G H3 I J

(805)925-9538.

Location: From Highway 154 in Los Olivos, turn northeast on Figueroa Mountain Road and drive 12.5 miles to the campground.

Trip note: This is one of the more attractive camps in Los Padres National Forest. Set at 4,000 feet beneath a unique stand of oak and huge manzanita trees, the camp offers a view of Santa Inez Valley. Several trailheads in the area provide access for hikers to the San Rafael Wilderness. The nearby Pino Alto Picnic Area offers a panoramic view of the adjacent wildlands and has a wheelchair accessible nature trail. Open all year.

Map grid e2

DAVY BROWN
on Davy Brown Creek
LOS PADRES NATIONAL FOREST

Campsites, facilities: There are ten campsites for tents and three spaces for motor homes up to 18 feet long. Fireplaces and picnic tables are provided. Vault toilets are available. There is **no piped water,** so bring your own. Pets are permitted on leashes.

Reservations, fee: No reservations; $5 fee per night.

Who to contact: Phone the Los Padres National Forest Santa Lucia District at (805)925-9538.

Location: From US 101 in Santa Barbara, drive 22 miles northeast on Highway 154. Turn right on Armour Ranch Road and drive 1.5 miles. Turn right on Happy Canyon Road and drive 11 miles to Cachuma Saddle. Continue straight (north) on Sunset Valley/Cachuma Road (Forest Service Road 8N09) for four miles.

Trip note: This is a pretty spot, either to hunker down for awhile or to strap on a backpack and hoof it. Davy Brown Creek runs almost all year, a big bonus. It is set at 4,000 feet, deep in Los Padres National Forest, near the border of the San Rafael Wilderness. A trail from the camp leads into the adjacent wildlands. Open year-round.

Map grid e3

CACHUMA
near Cachuma Creek
LOS PADRES NATIONAL FOREST

Campsites, facilities: There are six tent sites. Fireplaces and picnic tables are provided. Vault toilets are available. There is **no piped water,** so bring your own. Pets are permitted on leashes.

Reservations, fee: No reservations, no fee.

Who to contact: Phone the Los Padres National Forest Santa Barbara District at (805)967-3481.

Location: From US 101 in Santa Barbara, drive 22 miles northeast on Highway 154. Turn right on Armour Ranch Road and drive 1.5 miles. Turn right on Happy Canyon Road and drive 9.5 miles to the campground.

Trip note: Yes, Cachuma is the sound you make when sneezing. The stream here, which runs seven miles from camp downstream to Lake Cachuma, was named after an explorer known for his vociferous sneezing. A dirt road south of the camp follows the creek to the lake. The elevation is 2,200. Open year-round.

Map grid f2

LAKE CACHUMA
near Santa Barbara

Campsites, facilities: There are 500 campsites for tents or motor homes, some with full hookups. Fireplaces and picnic tables are provided. Flush toilets, showers, a playground, a general store, propane gas, a swimming pool, a boat ramp, mooring, boat fuel, boat rentals, bicycle rentals, ice, and a snack bar are available. Craft under ten feet prohibited.

Reservations, fee: Reservations not necessary; $12-$16 fee per night.

Who to contact: Phone the park at (805)688-4658.

Location: From Santa Barbara, drive 18 miles north on Highway 154 to the campground entrance.

Trip note: The climate is not only perfect for weekend vacationers, but for bass as well. Some monsters are known to swim in this lake along with plenty of little brothers. Premium weather and good fishing makes Lake Cachuma a popular destination for vacationers because of the fish. Note: No water-skiing is permitted. It is set at 600 feet in the foothill oaks-grassland country. Open year-round.

Map grid f9

REYES CREEK
LOS PADRES NATIONAL FOREST

Campsites, facilities: There are 30 sites for tents only and six campsites for tents or motor homes up to 22 feet long. Piped water, fireplaces, and picnic tables are provided. Vault toilets are available. Pets are permitted on leashes.

Reservations, fee: No reservations; $5 fee per night; $12 multi-family fee per night.

Who to contact: Phone the Los Padres National Forest Mount Pinos Ranger District at (805)245-3731.

Location: From Ojai, drive 36 miles north on Highway 33. Turn right (east) on Lockwood Valley Road and drive about three miles to the campground entrance on your right.

Trip note: This developed camp is set at the end of an old spur, Forest Service Road 7N11. The trail leading out of camp goes south and connects to several backcountry camps set along small streams. The camp is set at 4,000 feet elevation along Reyes Creek, which is stocked with trout in early summer. Open year-round.

Map grid f9

OZENA
LOS PADRES NATIONAL FOREST

Campsites, facilities: There are 12 campsites for tents or motor homes up to 22 feet long. Fireplaces and picnic tables are provided. Vault toilets are available. There is **no piped water,** so bring your own. Groceries and propane gas can be purchased nearby. Pets are permitted on leashes.

Reservations, fee: No reservations, no fee.

Who to contact: Phone the Los Padres National Forest Mount Pinos Ranger District at (805)245-3731.

Location: From Ojai, drive 36 miles north on Highway 33. Turn right (east) on Lockwood Valley Road and drive 1.5 miles to the campground.

Trip note: This roadside campground has a trail out of camp that leads south along Boulder Canyon to Pine Mountain and Reyes Peak. The elevation is 3,600 feet. Open year-round.

Map grid g0

REFUGIO STATE BEACH
near Santa Barbara

Campsites, facilities: There are 85 campsites for tents or motor homes up to 30 feet long. Fireplaces and picnic tables are provided. Piped water, flush toilets, showers, a grocery store and food service are available. The campground, food service area, and grocery store are wheelchair accessible. Pets are permitted on leashes.

Reservations, fee: Reserve through MISTIX at (800)444-PARK ($3.95 MISTIX fee); $14-$16 fee per night; pets $1.

Who to contact: Phone the park at (805)968-1033.

Location: From Santa Barbara, drive 23 miles northwest on US 101.

Trip note: This is the smallest of the three beautiful state beaches located along Highway 1 north of Santa Barbara. The others are El Capitan to the east and Gaviota to the west. Open year-round.

Map grid g3

FREMONT

on Santa Ynez River
LOS PADRES NATIONAL FOREST

Campsites, facilities: There are 15 campsites for tents or motor homes up to 16 feet long. Piped water, fireplaces, and picnic tables are provided. Flush toilets are available. Groceries and propane gas are nearby. Pets are permitted on leashes.

Reservations, fee: No reservations; $6 fee per night.

Who to contact: Phone the Los Padres National Forest Santa Barbara District at (805)967-3481.

Location: From Santa Barbara, drive about ten miles northwest on Highway 154. Turn right on Paradise Road and drive 2.5 miles to the campground.

Trip note: It's a take-your-pick deal for campers who find their way to the Santa Ynez River. There are several camps set along the stream. This one is set at 900 feet elevation. The eastern shore of Lake Cachuma is six miles away. Open from April to October.

Map grid g4

SANTA YNEZ

on Santa Ynez River
LOS PADRES NATIONAL FOREST

Campsites, facilities: There are 34 campsites for tents or motor homes up to 22 feet long. Piped water, fireplaces, and picnic tables are provided. Vault toilets are available. Horseback riding facilities are nearby. Pets are permitted on leashes.

Reservations, fee: No reservations; $6 fee per night.

Who to contact: Phone the Los Padres National Forest Santa Barbara District at (805)967-3481.

Location: From Santa Barbara, drive ten miles north on Highway 154. Turn right on Paradise Road and drive eight miles to the campground.

Trip note: Drive around, look around, then take your pick. This is one in a series of camps along the Santa Ynez River. The elevation is 1,100 feet elevation. Open from April to November.

Map grid g4

LOS PRIETOS

on Santa Ynez River
LOS PADRES NATIONAL FOREST

Campsites, facilities: There are 38 campsites for tents or motor homes up to 22 feet long. Piped water, fireplaces, and picnic tables are provided. Flush toilets are available. Pets are permitted on leashes.

Reservations, fee: No reservations; $6 fee per night.

Who to contact: Phone the Los Padres National Forest Santa Barbara District at (805)967-3481.

Location: From Santa Barbara, drive ten miles north on Highway 154. Turn right on Paradise Road and drive 3.8 miles to the campground.

Trip note: If you're coming here to hike, you are better off at the Sage Hill camp, which is closer to the San Rafael Wilderness than Los Prietos. In fact, the trail out of this camp will lead hikers past other camps en route to the backcountry. It is set at 1,000 feet, and like the others in the area, is located next to the Santa Ynez River. Open April to October.

Map grid **g4**

UPPER OSO
near Santa Ynez River
LOS PADRES NATIONAL FOREST

Campsites, facilities: There are 27 campsites for tents or motor homes up to 22 feet long. Piped water, fireplaces, horse corrals and picnic tables are provided. Flush toilets are available. Pets are permitted on leashes.

Reservations, fee: No reservations; $6 fee per night.

Who to contact: Phone the Los Padres National Forest Santa Barbara District at (805)967-3481.

Location: From Santa Barbara, drive about ten miles north on Highway 154. Turn right on Paradise Road and drive 5.5 miles. Turn left on Camuesa Drive (Forest Service Road 5N15) and drive 1.5 miles to the campground.

Trip note: This is the most remote of the seven Forest Service campgrounds located in the immediate area. It is set in Oso Canyon at 1,100 feet, not far from the Santa Ynez River. A trailhead into the San Rafael Wilderness is nearby, and once on the trail, there are many primitive campsites set in the backcountry. Open year-round.

Map grid **g4**

PARADISE
on Santa Ynez River
LOS PADRES NATIONAL FOREST

Campsites, facilities: There are 15 campsites for tents or motor homes up to 22 feet long. Piped water, fireplaces, and picnic tables are provided. Flush toilets are available. Pets are permitted on leashes. Horseback riding facilities, groceries, and propane gas can be found nearby.

Reservations, fee: Reservations requested; reserve through MISTIX at (800)283-CAMP ($6 MISTIX fee); $6 fee per night.

Who to contact: For information phone Los Padres National Forest Santa Barbara District at (805)967-3481.

Location: From Santa Barbara, drive about ten miles north on Highway 154. Turn right on Paradise Road and drive three miles.

Trip note: This is a more developed option among the camps set along the Santa Ynez River. Side trips include west to Vista Point on Highway 154, which provides a nice lookout of Lake Cachuma. The lake itself is only six miles from the camp. Or drive east deep into the backcountry. Open year-round.

Map grid **g4**

SAGE HILL GROUP CAMP
on Santa Ynez River
LOS PADRES NATIONAL FOREST

Campsites, facilities: There are five loops with spaces for tents or motor homes up to 32 feet long. Piped water, fireplaces, picnic tables and flush toilets are available. Horse corrals are located in Loop 5. Pets are permitted on leashes.

Reservations, fee: Reservations requested; reserve through MISTIX at (800)283-

CAMP ($10 MISTIX fee); $35-$45 fee per group per night.

Who to contact: For information phone Los Padres National Forest Santa Barbara District at (805)967-3481.

Location: From Santa Barbara, drive ten miles north on Highway 154. Turn right on Paradise Road and drive five miles to the ranger station. Turn left (north) and drive about one mile to the campground.

Trip note: This is another in the series of camps located along the Santa Ynez River in Los Padres National Forest. This one is set at 2,000 feet elevation and designed for large groups. A trail from the camp is routed into the San Rafael Wilderness, where numerous primitive campsites are available along the trails. Open year-round.

Map grid g6

MONO

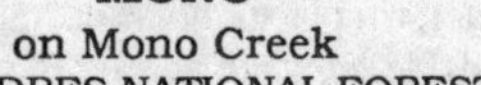

LOS PADRES NATIONAL FOREST

Campsites, facilities: There are seven tent sites. Fireplaces and picnic tables are provided. Vault toilets are available. There is **no piped water,** so bring your own. Pets are permitted on leashes.

Reservations, fee: No reservations, no fee.

Who to contact: Phone the Los Padres National Forest Santa Barbara District at (805)967-3481.

Location: From US 101 in Santa Barbara, drive eight miles north on Highway 154. Turn east (right) on East Camino Cielo (paved most of the way) and drive 22 miles to Juncal Camuesa Road (a dirt road). Turn north (left) and drive 13.1 miles to the campground.

Trip note: Not many folks know about this spot. It is set beside Mono Creek, a feeder stream to Gibraltar Reservoir. The lake is small and narrow with no direct access. The camp is small and primitive. The elevation is 1,500 feet. Open year-round.

Map grid g7

P-BAR FLAT

on Santa Ynez River

LOS PADRES NATIONAL FOREST

Campsites, facilities: There are four tent sites. Fireplaces and picnic tables are provided. Vault toilets are available. There is **no piped water,** so bring your own. Pets are permitted on leashes.

Reservations, fee: No reservations, no fee.

Who to contact: Phone the Los Padres National Forest Santa Barbara District at (805)967-3481.

Location: From US 101 in Santa Barbara, drive eight miles north on Highway 154. Turn east (right) on East Camino Cielo (paved most of the way) and drive 22 miles to Juncal Camuesa Road (a dirt road). Turn north (left) and drive 9.8 miles to the campground.

Trip note: This is one of the three smallish, primitive and little-known camps set along the Santa Ynez River between Gibraltar Reservoir to the west and little Jameson Lake to the east. The elevation is 1,800 feet. Open all year.

Map grid g9

PINE MOUNTAIN

LOS PADRES NATIONAL FOREST

Campsites, facilities: There are six tent sites. Fireplaces and picnic tables are provided. Vault toilets are available. There is **no piped water,** so bring your own. Pets are permitted on leashes.

Reservations, fee: No reservations, no fee.

Who to contact: Phone the Los Padres National Forest Ojai Ranger District at (805)646-4348.

Location: From Ojai, drive 33 miles north on Highway 33. Turn right (east) on Reyes Peak Road and drive 2.5 miles to the campground.

Trip note: This is the kind of place a lot folks have no idea even exists. It's a tiny, primitive camp in a pretty area with a few trailheads in the area. The half-mile hike to Raspberry Spring (a backcountry camp is available there) is an easy trip, with the trailhead located immediately to the east of this camp. Immediately to the west is a trail that is routed along Boulder Canyon leading four or five miles north to Ozena Camp, where piped water is available. It's advisable to obtain a Forest Service map. The elevation is 6,700 feet. Open from April to December.

Map grid g9

REYES PEAK
LOS PADRES NATIONAL FOREST

Campsites, facilities: There are six tent sites. Fireplaces and picnic tables are provided. Vault toilets are available. There is **no piped water,** so bring your own. Pets are permitted on leashes.

Reservations, fee: No reservations; no fee.

Who to contact: Phone the Los Padres National Forest Ojai Ranger District at (805)646-4348.

Location: From Ojai, drive 33 miles north on Highway 33. Turn right (east) on Reyes Peak Road and drive three miles to the campground.

Trip note: This camp is just down the road from Lion's Canyon camp. For hiking options, see the trip note for the Pine Mountain camp. The elevation is 6,800 feet. Open from April to November.

Map grid h1

EL CAPITAN STATE BEACH
near Santa Barbara

Campsites, facilities: There are 140 campsites for tents or motor homes up to 30 feet long. Fireplaces and picnic tables are provided. Piped water, flush toilets, showers, a dump station, food service, and a grocery store are available. Pets are permitted on leashes. The campground, food service area, picnic grounds, and grocery store are wheelchair accessible.

Reservations, fee: Reserve through MISTIX at (800)444-PARK ($3.95 MISTIX fee); $14-$16 fee per night; pets $1.

Who to contact: Phone the park at (805)968-1033.

Location: From Santa Barbara, drive 20 miles northwest on US 101.

Trip note: This is one in a series of beautiful state beaches along the Santa Barbara coast. The water is warm, the swimming good, and folks, the park ranger asks that you "Please keep your bathing suits on."

Map grid h3

EL PATIO CAMPER VILLAGE
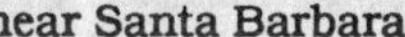
near Santa Barbara

Campsites, facilities: There are 92 motor home spaces with full hookups and private patios. Rest rooms, showers, cable TV, a laundromat, and propane gas delivery are available. Stores, restaurants, a bowling alley, a golf course, a beach, and deep sea fishing are nearby.

Reservations, fee: Reservations accepted; $22 fee per night.

Who to contact: Phone the park at (805)687-7614.

Location: From the junction of US 101 and Highway 154 in Santa Barbara, drive north on US 101 to 4040 Calle Real (follow the signs).

Trip note: The coast highway is one of the most popular roads in the world and the number of privately-operated parks along it, from San Diego to Crescent City, attests to that. This one fills the bill nicely. It is five miles from El Presidio de Santa Barbara State Historical Park, a possible side trip. Open year-round.

Map grid h4

SANTA BARBARA SUNRISE RV PARK

near Santa Barbara

Campsites, facilities: There are 33 motor home spaces with full hookups and patios. Rest rooms, showers, cable TV, and a laundromat are available. A grocery store, golf course, tennis courts, and propane gas are nearby.

Reservations, fee: Call ahead for available space and fee.

Who to contact: Phone the park at (805)966-9954, or (800)345-5018.

Location: In Santa Barbara on US 101, take the Salinas Street exit going north or the Milpas Street exit going south and follow the blue camper signs.

Trip note: Motor home cruisers get a little of two worlds here. For one thing, it's close to the beach, and for another, the downtown shopping area isn't too far distant either. Open year-round.

Map grid h7

JUNCAL

on Santa Ynez River

LOS PADRES NATIONAL FOREST

Campsites, facilities: There are six tent sites. Fireplaces and picnic tables are provided. Vault toilets are available. There is **no piped water,** so bring your own. Pets are permitted on leashes.

Reservations, fee: No reservations, no fee.

Who to contact: Phone the Los Padres National Forest Santa Barbara District at (805)967-3481.

Location: From US 101 in Santa Barbara, drive eight miles north on Highway 154. Turn east (right) on East Camino Cielo (paved most of the way) and drive 22 miles to Juncal Camuesa Road (a dirt road). Turn north (left) and drive one-quarter mile to the campground.

Trip note: We never did discover who Mr. Juncal was, but he got this campground, a road, and the dam at Jameson Lake named after him. As long as he wasn't a politician, that's okay with us. The camp is set on the Santa Ynez River at 1,800 feet elevation. Open year-round.

Map grid h7

MIDDLE SANTA YNEZ

on Santa Ynez River

LOS PADRES NATIONAL FOREST

Campsites, facilities: There are nine tent sites. Fireplaces, and picnic tables are provided. Vault toilets are available. Pets are permitted on leashes. There's **no piped water.**

Reservations, fee: No reservations, no fee.

Who to contact: Phone the Los Padres National Forest Santa Barbara District at (805)967-3481.

Location: From US 101 in Santa Barbara, drive eight miles north on Highway 154. Turn east (right) on East Camino Cielo (paved most of the way) and drive 22 miles to Juncal Camuesa Road (a dirt road). Turn north (left) and drive 8.8 miles to the campground.

Trip note: There are three camps set on the Santa Ynez River between Gibraltar Reservoir to the west and little Jameson Lake to the east. Look 'em over and pick the one you like. The elevation is 1,500 feet. Open year-round.

Map grid h9

HOLIDAY GROUP CAMP
on Matilija Creek
LOS PADRES NATIONAL FOREST

Campsites, facilities: There are three campsites for tents or motor homes up to 22 feet long. Piped water, fireplaces, and picnic tables are provided. Vault toilets are available. Pets are permitted on leashes.

Reservations, fee: Reservations required; $30 group fee per night.

Who to contact: Phone the Los Padres National Forest Ojai Ranger District at (805)646-4348.

Location: From Ojai, drive nine miles northwest on Highway 33 to the entrance.

Trip note: This group site, set at 2,000 feet elevation, is very near the North Fork of the Matilija. Wheeler Gorge provides a nearby option. A trailhead is located a half-mile down the road to the southwest, allowing hikers to thump up into the headwaters of Tule Creek. Open from April to December.

Map grid h9

WHEELER GORGE
on Matilija Creek
LOS PADRES NATIONAL FOREST

Campsites, facilities: There are 73 campsites for tents or motor homes up to 16 feet long. Piped water, fireplaces, and picnic tables are provided. Flush toilets are available. Pets are permitted on leashes.

Reservations, fee: Reserve through MISTIX at (800)283-CAMP; $8 fee per night.

Who to contact: Phone the Los Padres National Forest Ojai Ranger District at (805)646-4348 or park concessionaire at (805)646-3428.

Location: From Ojai, drive 8.5 miles northwest on Highway 33.

Trip note: This developed Forest Service camp is set at 2,000 feet and is one of the more popular spots in the area. The North Fork of the Matilija runs beside the camp and provides some fair trout fishing in the spring and good swimming holes in early summer. A trailhead is located less than a mile down the road, providing access for hikers who want to make the trip to the headwaters of Tule Creek. Nearby Matilija Reservoir provides a side trip option. Open year-round.

Map grid i6

CARPINTERIA STATE BEACH
near Santa Barbara

Campsites, facilities: There are 100 sites for tents and 162 campsites for motor homes up to 30 feet long. Piped water, fireplaces, picnic tables, and, in some cases, full hookups are provided. Flush toilets, coin-operated showers and a dump station are available. Pets are permitted on leashes. A grocery store, a laundromat, and propane gas are nearby. The campground and picnic areas are wheelchair accessible.

Reservations, fee: Reserve through MISTIX at (800)444-PARK ($3.95 MISTIX fee); $14-$23 fee per night.

Who to contact: Phone the park at (805)684-2811.

Location: From Santa Barbara, drive ten miles south on US 101. Take the Casitas Pass exit and drive west to the campground (less than one mile).

Trip note: First, plan on reservations, then, plan on plenty of neighbors. This state beach is one pretty spot and a lot of folks cruising up the coast like the idea of taking off their cowboy boots here for awhile. Open year-round.

Map grid **i7**

RINCON PARKWAY

on Pacific Ocean north of Ventura

Campsites, facilities: There are 100 motor home spaces for self-contained vehicles up to 34 feet long. A sanitary disposal station is available. Supplies are available nearby. No pets allowed.

Reservations, fee: No reservations; $9 fee per night.

Who to contact: Phone the County Parks Department at (805)654-3951.

Location: From Ventura, drive six miles northwest on US 101.

Trip note: This is basically a motor home park located near the ocean. Emma Wood State Beach, San Buenaventura State Beach, and McGrath State Beach are all within ten miles. Open year-round.

Map grid **i7**

HOBSON COUNTY PARK

on Pacific Ocean north of Ventura

Campsites, facilities: There are 31 campsites for tents or motor homes up to 34 feet long. Piped water, fireplaces, and picnic tables are provided. Flush toilets, showers, and a grocery store are available. Pets are permitted on leashes.

Reservations, fee: Reservations accepted; $14 fee per night, during the summer, $9 in the winter; pets $1.

Who to contact: Phone the County Parks Department at (805) 654-3951.

Location: From Ventura, drive nine miles northwest on US 101.

Trip note: This county park is located at the end of Rincon Parkway with easy access to the beach and offers many side-trip possibilities. Emma Wood State Beach, San Buenaventura State Beach, and McGrath State Beach are all within 11 miles of the park. Open year-round.

Map grid **i7**

FARIA COUNTY PARK

on Pacific Ocean north of Ventura

Campsites, facilities: There are 42 campsites for tents or motor homes up to 34 feet long. Piped water, fireplaces, and picnic tables are provided. Flush toilets, a playground, showers, and a grocery store are available. Pets are permitted.

Reservations, fee: No reservations; $14 fee per night during the summer, and $9 during the winter; pets $1.

Who to contact: Phone the County Parks Department at (805)654-3951.

Location: From Ventura, drive seven miles northwest on US 101.

Trip note: This county park provides a possible base of operations for beach trip adventures. It is set along the ocean, with Emma Wood State Beach, San Buenaventura State Beach, and McGrath State Beach all within ten miles of the park. Open year-round.

Map grid **i8**

FOSTER COUNTY PARK

north of Ventura

Campsites, facilities: There are 50 campsites for tents or motor homes up to 34 feet long. Piped water, fireplaces, and picnic tables are provided. Flush toilets and a playground are available. Supplies and a laundromat are nearby. Pets are permitted on leashes.

Reservations, fee: Reservations accepted; $10 fee per night; pets $1.
Who to contact: Phone the County Parks Department at (805)654-3951. A
Location: From Ventura, drive six miles northeast on Highway 33. Turn left on Casitas Vista-Santa Ana Road and drive a short distance to the park.
Trip note: This is the kind of place that the locals take for granted and an out-of-towner stuck for the night might get on his knees and beg for. Well, there's no need to be a prisoner of prayer, not with this hilly county park B
providing year-round camping and a variety of good trails in the surrounding foothills.

Map grid i8

LAKE CASITAS RECREATION AREA
north of Ventura C

Campsites, facilities: There are 450 campsites for tents or motor homes up to 40 feet long. Piped water, fireplaces, and picnic tables are provided. Flush toilets, showers, a dump station, a playground, a grocery store, ice, a snack bar, bait, boat ramps, and propane gas are available. Boat rentals, slips, fuel, and tackle
are nearby. Pets are permitted on leashes. D
Reservations, fee: No reservations; $10 fee per night; pets $1.
Who to contact: Phone the park at (805) 649-2233.
Location: From Ventura, drive 11 miles north on Highway 33. Turn left (west) on Highway 150 and drive about four miles to the campground entrance.
Trip note: Known as southern California's world-class fish factory, Lake Casitas E
holds the state record for largemouth bass (21 pounds, 3 ounces) and also produces big catfish. The ideal climate in the foothill country (560 feet elevation) gives the fish a nine-month growing season. The lake is managed primarily for anglers and only boats between 11 and 24 feet are allowed on the lake. Swimming and water skiing are prohibited. Open year-round.

F

Map grid i9

CAMP COMFORT COUNTY PARK
on San Antonio Creek

Campsites, facilities: There are 43 campsites for tents or motor homes up to 34 feet long. Fireplaces, picnic tables, and in some cases electrical connections are G
provided. Piped water, flush toilets, showers, and a playground are available. Supplies and a laundromat are nearby. Pets are permitted on leashes.
Reservations, fee: Reservations accepted; $9-$11 fee per night; pets $1.
Who to contact: Phone the County Parks Department at (805)654-3951.
Location: From Ventura, take Highway 33 to Highway 150. Turn right (west) on Highway 150 and drive three miles to Creek Road. Turn right and drive one H3
mile to the park.
Trip note: This county park gets missed by thousands of wannabees because it's not on the MISTIX ticket system. That's their loss, your gain. It's a pretty spot, set in the foothill country at 1,000 feet elevation along San Antonio Creek in the Ojai Valley. Lake Casitas Recreation Area is ten miles away. I

Map grid j8

EMMA WOOD COUNTY PARK
on Pacific Ocean near Ventura

Campsites, facilities: There are 95 campsites including group areas for tents or motor homes up to 40 feet long. Picnic tables and fireplaces are provided. J
chemical toilets and a dump station are available. There's **no piped water**, so bring your own. All conveniences are within one mile of the campground. Pets

are permitted on leashes.

Reservations, fee: Reservations accepted for groups; $9 fee per night; pets $1.

Who to contact: Phone the County Parks Department at (805)654-3951.

Location: From Ventura, drive three miles northwest on US 101.

Trip note: This is one of the most popular county parks around, but you'd expect that with beachfront campsites set within such close driving range of Highway 101. Open year-round.

Map grid j8

EMMA WOOD STATE BEACH

on Pacific Ocean north of Ventura

Campsites, facilities: There are four group campsites for tents that can accommodate groups of 30-50 people. There are some additional sites for hikers and bicyclists. Picnic tables and fireplaces are provided. Piped water, pit toilets, and cold showers are available. Supplies and a laundromat are nearby.

Reservations, fee: Reserve through MISTIX at (800)444-PARK ($3.95 MISTIX fee); $45-$75 fee per night for group site.

Who to contact: Phone the park at (805)654-4611 or (805)643-7532.

Location: From Ventura, drive two miles north on US 101.

Trip note: Plan on a reservation or don't plan on an overnight stay here. That's the way it is at popular state beaches, especially here. It is set along the ocean, a pretty spot with tidepools full of all kinds of little marine critters. It is also just a short drive to the town of Ventura and the Mission San Buenaventura. Open year-round.

◆ MAP H4 ◆

BEACH
DESERT
FOOTHILL
TREES
URBAN
GRASSLAND
5% CLUB

15 MILES

to Buttonwillow to Shaffer to Rosedale to Bakersfield

to Ford City to Cuyama to H-166 to Ventucopa to H-33 to Oak View to Ventura

to Bodfish to Tehachapi to H-14 to Vincent

to Camarillo to Simi Valley to Burbank

a b c d e f g h i j

0 1 2 3 4 5 6 7 8 9

Tupman
TULE ELK ST. RES.
Edison
119
99
204
Lake Webb
Old River
Lamont
58
Caliente
Buena Vista Lake
Weed Patch
33
Arvin
223
Bear Mtn. EL. 6,895
99
Keene
Maricopa
5
184
166
202
Cummings Mtn. EL. 7,753
Wheeler Ridge
LOS
FT. TEJON ST. HIST. PK.
Mt. Abel EL. 8,286
Mt. Pinos EL. 8,831
Frazer Park
Lebec
PADRES
Tejon Pass EL. 4,144
Gorman
Summit EL. 5,516
Frazier Mtn. EL. 8,026
138
Reyes Pk. EL. 7,510
N2
NATIONAL
ANGELES
Thorn Pt. EL. 6,935
Pyramid Lake
Sawtooth Mtn. EL. 5,175
33
NAT'L.
Topatopa Mtn. EL. 6,210
Green Valley
FOREST
Ojai
Lake Piru
Castaic Lake
FOREST
150
Castaic
5
Fillmore
Piru
126
126
Santa Paula
23
Saugus
Saticoy
Valencia
Montalvo
Santa Clarita
118
Moorpark
14

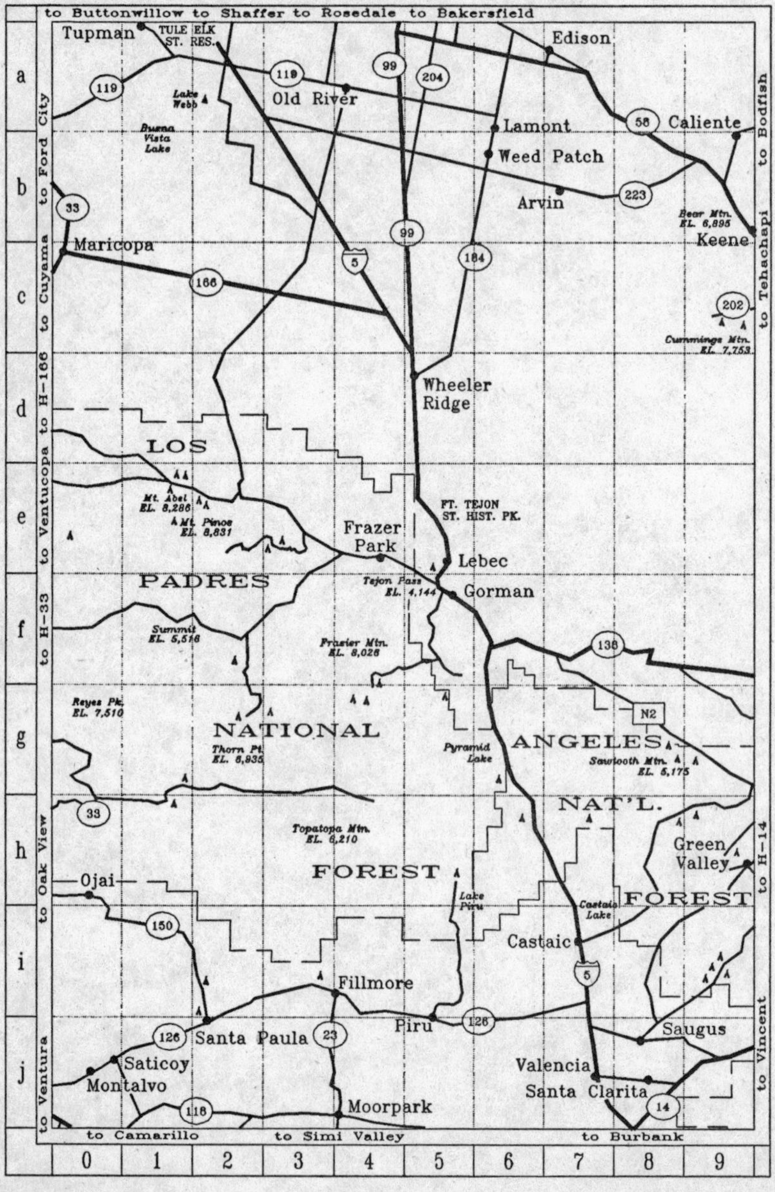

Map grid **a2**

BUENA VISTA AQUATIC RECREATION AREA

near Bakersfield

Campsites, facilities: There are 112 campsites for tents or motor homes, many with full hookups. Picnic tables and fireplaces are provided. Rest rooms, showers, a playground, three boat ramps, a store, a dump station, and propane gas are available. Pets are permitted on leashes.

Reservations, fee: No reservations; $12-$18 fee per night; pets $2.

Who to contact: Phone the park at (805)763-1526.

Location: From Interstate 5 near Bakersfield, drive two miles west on Highway 119. Turn left (south) on Enos Lane and drive three miles to the campground.

Trip note: Lake Evans and Lake Webb are the highlights at this county park, providing separate lakes for fishing and boating. A public golf course is also nearby. The elevation is 330 feet. Open year-round.

Map grid **c9**

INDIAN HILL RANCH CAMPGROUND

near Tehachapi

Campsites, facilities: There are 225 sites for tents or motor homes, some with water and electrical hookups. Picnic tables and fireplaces are provided. Rest rooms, showers, a dump station, and five stocked fishing ponds are available.

Reservations, fee: Reservations accepted; $10-$12 fee per night.

Who to contact: Phone the park at (805)822-6613.

Location: From Highway 58 near Tehachapi, take the Highway 202 exit. Head west on Highway 202 for 3.5 miles to Banducci Road. Turn left and drive one mile to Indian Hill (Arosa) Road. Turn left and drive 1.5 miles to the campground.

Trip note: The five ponds here are stocked with trout and catfish which makes this a unique park. The campground is open all year and offers spacious, private campsites with oak trees and a view of Brite Valley.

Map grid **c9**

BRITE VALLEY RECREATION AREA

at Brite Lake

Campsites, facilities: There are several campsites for tents or motor homes up to 30 feet long, some with water and electrical hookups. Fireplaces and picnic tables are provided. Rest rooms, showers, a dump station, a playground, three pavilions with electricity and tables, and a fish cleaning station are available. Supplies are available nearby. Pets are permitted on leashes.

Reservations, fee: No reservations; $7-$10 fee per night.

Who to contact: Phone the park at (805)822-3228.

Location: From Highway 58 near Tehachapi, take the Highway 202 exit. Head west on Highway 202 for 3.5 miles to Banducci Road. Turn left on Banducci Road and follow the signs for about a mile to the park.

Trip note: The highlight here is Brite Lake; it provides fishing for trout in the spring and catfish in the summer. No gas motors are permitted on the lake. The camp is near Tehachapi Mountain Park. Open from May to October.

Map grid **e0**

NETTLE SPRING

LOS PADRES NATIONAL FOREST

Campsites, facilities: There are nine sites for tents only and four campsites for tents or motor homes up to 22 feet long. Fireplaces and picnic tables are provided.

Vault toilets are available. There is **no piped water,** so bring your own. Pets are permitted on leashes.

Reservations, fee: No reservations, no fee.

Who to contact: Phone the Los Padres National Forest Mount Pinos Ranger District at (805)245-3731.

Location: From the junction of Highways 166 and 33 in Maricopa, drive 14 miles south on Highway 33. Where Highway 33 separates from Highway 166, turn left (south) on Highway 33 and drive about 13 miles to Apache Canyon Road. Turn left (east) and drive about ten miles to the campground.

Trip note: This is a good headquarters for four-wheel drive cowboys. A rough road (for four-wheel drive vehicles only) leads northeast from camp and then forks after two miles. The fork that heads east is a winner, connecting two miles later with a primitive camp (Mesa Spring). From there, a trail leads into the backcountry. A Forest Service map is most advisable. In the fall, this campground is frequently used by hunters. The elevation is 4,400. Open all year.

Map grid e1

CAMPO ALTO

LOS PADRES NATIONAL FOREST

Campsites, facilities: There are 17 campsites for tents or motor homes up to 22 feet long. Fireplaces and picnic tables are provided. Vault toilets are available, but there is **no piped water.**

Reservations, fee: No reservations, no fee.

Who to contact: Phone the Los Padres National Forest Mount Pinos District at (805)245-3731.

Location: From Interstate 5, take the Frazier Park exit (just south of Lebec) and drive west on Lockwood Valley Road to Lake of the Woods. Turn right on Cuddy Valley Road and continue 15 miles west on Cuddy Valley Road (which becomes Mil Potrero Highway). Turn south on Cerro Noroeste Road and drive nine miles to the campground.

Trip note: It's primitive, little known, and little used, but a visit makes you an honorary member of the five Percent Club. The camp is set high (8,200 feet elevation) on Cerro Noroeste (Mt. Abel) in Los Padres National Forest. Don't show up thirsty. Open from May to November.

Map grid e1

MARIAN

LOS PADRES NATIONAL FOREST

Campsites, facilities: There are five campsites for tents or motor homes up to 16 feet long. Fireplaces and picnic tables are provided and vault toilets are available. There is **no piped water** at this site. Pets are permitted on leashes.

Reservations, fee: No reservations, no fee.

Who to contact: Phone the Los Padres National Forest Mount Pinos District at (805)245-3731.

Location: From Interstate 5, take the Frazier Park exit (just south of Lebec) and drive west on Lockwood Valley Road to Lake of the Woods. Turn right on Cuddy Valley Road and continue 15.5 miles west on Cuddy Valley Road (which becomes Mil Potrero Highway) to the campground entrance. Proceed up the dirt entrance road one mile past the Caballo campground to this camp.

Trip note: This camp is a little higher (6,600 feet elevation), a little farther up the road, and a little more primitive than the other nearby sites in Los Padres National Forest. Side trip options include heading to the top of several mountains in the area, including Abel Mountain (8,286 feet), Mt. Pinos (8,831 feet), and Frazier Mountain (8,026 feet). All are detailed on Forest Service maps. Open from May to November.

A

Map grid **e1**

TOAD SPRING

LOS PADRES NATIONAL FOREST

B

Campsites, facilities: There are four sites for tents only and three campsites for tents or motor homes up to 16 feet long. Fireplaces and picnic tables are provided and vault toilets are available. There is **no piped water,** so bring your own. Pets are permitted on leashes.

Reservations, fee: No reservations, no fee.

Who to contact: Phone the Los Padres National Forest Mount Pinos District at (805)245-3731.

C

Location: From Interstate 5, take the Frazier Park exit (just south of Lebec) and drive west on Lockwood Valley Road to Lake of the Woods. Turn right on Cuddy Valley Road and continue 15.5 miles west on Cuddy Valley Road (which becomes Mil Potrero Highway) to the campground entrance.

D

Trip note: This is one in a series of camps near Abel Mountain. Come prepared. The elevation is 5,700 feet. Open from May to November.

Map grid **e1**

CABALLO

LOS PADRES NATIONAL FOREST

E

Campsites, facilities: There are five campsites for tents or motor homes up to 16 feet long. Fireplaces and picnic tables are provided. Vault toilets are available. There is **no water,** so bring your own. Pets are permitted on leashes.

Reservations, fee: No reservations, no fee.

Who to contact: Phone the Los Padres National Forest Mount Pinos District at (805)245-3731.

F

Location: From Interstate 5, take the Frazier Park exit (just south of Lebec) and drive west on Lockwood Valley Road to Lake of the Woods. Turn right on Cuddy Valley Road and continue 15.5 miles west on Cuddy Valley Road (which becomes Mil Potrero Highway) to the campground entrance on the right.

G

Trip note: As one of several primitive camps in this immediate area, it is a take-your-pick offer. But it's an offer not many folks even know about. Caballo is set at 5,800 feet, not far from Abel Mountain (8,286 feet elevation). Open from May to November.

Map grid **e2**

HAPPY GULCH

near Mt. Pinos

H4

Campsites, facilities: There are 17 campsites for tents. Fireplaces and picnic tables are provided. Pit toilets are available, but there is **no piped water,** so bring your own. Pets are permitted on leashes.

I

Reservations, fee: No reservations; $6 fee per night; pets $2.

Who to contact: Phone the County Parks Department at (805)861-2345.

Location: From Interstate 5, take the Frazier Park exit (just south of Lebec) and drive west on Lockwood Valley Road to Lake of the Woods. Turn right on Cuddy Valley Road and continue 15 miles west on Cuddy Valley Road (which becomes Mil Potrero Highway) to the campground entrance road.

J

Trip note: This primitive county park is surrounded by National Forest. Mt. Pinos offers a side trip in the summer, and Camp Alto Ski Tow provides winter recreation possibilities. The elevation is 6,300 feet. Open year-round.

Map grid **e2**

MIL POTRERO PARK

near Mt. Pinos

Campsites, facilities: There are ten sites for tents only and 33 campsites for tents or motor homes. Fireplaces and picnic tables are provided. Piped water, flush toilets, showers, and horse corrals are available. Pets are permitted on leashes.

Reservations, fee: Reservations required; $8 fee per night.

Who to contact: Phone the park at (805)763-4246.

Location: From Interstate 5, take the Frazier Park exit (just south of Lebec) and drive west on Lockwood Valley Road to Lake of the Woods. Turn right on Cuddy Valley Road and continue 11 miles west on Cuddy Valley Road (which becomes Mil Potrero Highway) to the campground entrance.

Trip note: This quiet camp is set in the pines, but there are no lakes anywhere in the area. Instead, nearby Mt. Pinos is the highlight here with its dramatic 360-degree views. Also nearby are the Big Trees of Pleito Canyon. The elevation is 5,300 feet. Open year-round (except for occasional holidays—not exactly a brilliant business decision).

Map grid **e3**

MT. PINOS

LOS PADRES NATIONAL FOREST

Campsites, facilities: There are 19 campsites for tents or motor homes up to 16 feet long. Piped water, fireplaces, and picnic tables are provided. Vault toilets and horseback riding facilities are available. Pets are permitted on leashes. A note of caution: The water wells have been known to run dry in summer, so bring your own water at that time.

Reservations, fee: No reservations; $5 fee per night.

Who to contact: Phone the Los Padres National Forest Mount Pinos Ranger District at (805)245-3731.

Location: From Interstate 5, take the Frazier Park exit (just south of Lebec) and drive west on Lockwood Valley Road to the town of Lake of the Woods. Turn right on Cuddy Valley Road and drive about seven miles. Turn left (south) on Mt. Pinos Road and drive about six miles to the campground.

Trip note: A lot of folks have no idea about the high country in southern California, but this camp provides a good clue to what is available. Set at 7,800 feet elevation high on the slopes of Mt. Pinos (8,831 feet), it's a good place to watch for several varieties of raptors. Open from June to October.

Map grid **e3**

McGILL

near Mt. Pinos

LOS PADRES NATIONAL FOREST

Campsites, facilities: There are 73 family campsites and two group sites for tents or motor homes up to 16 feet long. Piped water, fireplaces, and picnic tables are provided. Vault toilets are available. Pets are permitted on leashes. A note of caution: The water wells have been known to run dry in summer, so bring your own water at that time.

Reservations, fee: Reservations required for group sites; $5 fee per night for family sites; $35-$50 fee for a group site.

Who to contact: Phone the Los Padres National Forest Mount Pinos District at (805)245-3731.

Location: From Interstate 5, take the Frazier Park exit (just south of Lebec) and drive west on Lockwood Valley Road to the town of Lake of the Woods. Turn right on Cuddy Valley Road and drive about seven miles. Turn left on Mt. Pinos Road and drive about six miles to the campground.

Trip note: If you wanted a great panoramic lookout, you came to the right place. The camp is set at 7,400 feet—it's an easy drive to the top of nearby Mt. Pinos—where you get a spectacular 360-degree view of the high Sierra, the San Joaquin Valley, the Channel Islands, and Antelope Valley. Frazier Mountain Park, which is about seven miles from camp, provides a nearby side trip. Open from June to October.

Map grid e5

FORT TEJON TENT & RV CAMPGROUND
near Lebec

Campsites, facilities: There are 37 sites for tents only and 58 motor home spaces, many with full or partial hookups. Picnic tables and fire grills are provided. Rest rooms, showers, a small playground, a swimming pool, a laundromat, a store, a dump station, and propane gas are available. Pets are permitted on leashes.

Reservations, fee: Reservations recommended in the summer; $12-$15 fee per night.

Who to contact: Phone the park at (805)248-6145.

Location: Driving north on Interstate 5, take the Lebec exit and cross the freeway. Go north on the frontage road for 1.5 miles to the campground. Driving south, take the Fort Tejon-Highway Patrol exit. Drive 1.5 miles south on the frontage road to the campground.

Trip note: The camp gets its name from the nearby Fort Tejon State Historical Park, headquarters for the United States Army's 1st Dragoon and Camel Corps from 1854-1864. Frazier Mountain Park, located eight miles south and west via Lebec Road and Mt. Pinos Way, respectively, provides a good side trip. This isn't exactly nosebleed country (39 feet elevation) but it is open year-round.

Map grid f2

PINE SPRINGS
near San Guillermo Mountain
LOS PADRES NATIONAL FOREST

Campsites, facilities: There are ten campsites for tents or motor homes up to 22 feet long. Fireplaces and picnic tables are provided. Vault toilets are available. There is **no piped water,** so bring your own. Pets are permitted on leashes.

Reservations, fee: No reservations, no fee.

Who to contact: Phone the Los Padres National Forest Mount Pinos Ranger District at (805)245-3731.

Location: From Interstate 5, take the Frazier Park exit (just south of Lebec) and drive west on Lockwood Valley Road to the town of Lake of the Woods. Continue southwest (take the left fork) on Lockwood Valley Road and drive about 12 miles to the campground entrance road on your left.

Trip note: This primitive camp is set at 5,800 feet elevation at the foot of San Guillermo Mountain (6,600 feet). It is one of the camps in the area that is easier to reach. Open from May to October.

Map grid f4

KING'S CAMP
near Piru Creek
LOS PADRES NATIONAL FOREST

5% CLUB

Campsites, facilities: There are three sites for tents only and four campsites for tents or motor homes up to 16 feet long. Fireplaces and picnic tables are provided. Vault toilets are available. There is **no piped water,** so bring your own. Pets are permitted on leashes.

Reservations, fee: No reservations, no fee.

Who to contact: Phone the Los Padres National Forest Mount Pinos Ranger District at (805)245-3731.

Location: From Interstate 5, take the Gorman-Hungry Valley Road exit. Drive 13 miles south on Hungry Valley Road to the campground.

Trip note: This is a primitive, but well-placed camp for four-wheelers. It is set near Piru Creek, five miles from the four-wheeler capital of Ventura County, the Hungry Valley State Vehicular Recreation Area. The elevation is 4,200 feet. Open year-round.

Map grid **g1**

LION'S CANYON

on Sespe Creek
LOS PADRES NATIONAL FOREST

Campsites, facilities: There are 30 campsites for tents or motor homes up to 16 feet long. Piped water, fireplaces, and picnic tables are provided. Vault toilets and horseback riding facilities are available. Pets are permitted on leashes.

Reservations, fee: No reservations; $6 fee per night.

Who to contact: Phone the Los Padres National Forest Ojai Ranger District at (805)646-4348.

Location: From Ojai, drive about 15 miles north on Highway 33. Turn right (east) on Sespe River Road and drive seven miles to the campground.

Trip note: Hikers might consider this spot, set on Sespe Creek at 3,000 feet elevation. If you continue driving east on Forest Service Road 6N31, it will dead end at a trailhead for a hike that is routed east along Sespe Creek. It's about five miles to Willett Hot Springs at Tan Sycamore Flat. Open from April to December.

Map grid **g2**

THORN MEADOWS

on Piru Creek
LOS PADRES NATIONAL FOREST

Campsites, facilities: There are five sites for tents only or motor homes up to 16 feet long. Fireplaces and picnic tables are provided. There is **no piped water,** so bring your own. Vault toilets are available. Pets are permitted on leashes.

Reservations, fee: No reservations, no fee.

Who to contact: Phone the Los Padres National Forest Mount Pinos Ranger District at (805)245-3731.

Location: From Interstate 5, take the Frazier Park exit (just south of Lebec) and drive west on Lockwood Valley Road to the town of Lake of the Woods. Continue southwest (take the left fork) on Lockwood Valley Road and drive about 12 miles. Turn left on Mutau Flat Road (Forest Service Road 7N03) and drive seven miles to the campground entrance on your right.

Trip note: This is sure way out there in No Man's Land. It is tough to reach, but the reward is a small, quiet spot along Piru Creek at 5,000 feet, deep in Los Padres National Forest. A trail out of camp leads right up to Thorn Peak, a magnificent 6,935-foot lookout. Worth the effort. Open from May to October.

Map grid **g3**

HALF MOON

near Piru Creek
LOS PADRES NATIONAL FOREST

Campsites, facilities: There are 12 campsites for tents or motor homes up to 22 feet long. Fireplaces and picnic tables are provided. Vault toilets are available. There is **no piped water,** so bring your own. Pets are permitted on leashes.

Reservations, fee: No reservations, no fee.

Who to contact: Phone the Los Padres National Forest Mount Pinos Ranger District at (805)245-3731.

Location: From Interstate 5, take the Frazier Park exit (just south of Lebec) and drive west on Lockwood Valley Road to the town of Lake of the Woods. Continue southwest (take the left fork) on Lockwood Valley Road and drive about 12 miles. Turn left on Mutau Flat Road (Forest Service Road 7N03) and drive eight miles to the campground entrance on your left.

Trip note: This obscure camp, along with Thorn Meadows (about three miles southwest), is way out there in booger country. It is tough to reach and four-wheel drive is advisable, but in return, you get a quiet spot along little Piru Creek. The elevation is 4,700 feet. Open from May to November.

Map grid **g4**

TWIN PINES

on Alamo Mountain
LOS PADRES NATIONAL FOREST

Campsites, facilities: There are five tent sites. Fireplaces and picnic tables are provided. Vault toilets are available, but there is **no piped water,** so bring your own. Pets are permitted on leashes.

Reservations, fee: No reservations, no fee.

Who to contact: Phone the Los Padres National Forest Mount Pinos Ranger District at (805)245-3731.

Location: From Interstate 5, take the Gorman-Hungry Valley Road exit (it's the northern exit for the Hungry Valley Recreation Area). Drive about 21 miles south on Hungry Valley Road and Alamo Mountain Road (a rough, dirt road) to the campground.

Trip note: You'd best get a Forest Service map if you plan on exploring this area. Alamo Mountain is the jump-off spot to a network of back roads, with many primitive camps sprinkled along the way. The elevation is 6,600 feet. Open from May to October.

Map grid **g4**

DUTCHMAN

at Alamo Mountain
LOS PADRES NATIONAL FOREST

Campsites, facilities: There are eight campsites for primitive camping. Fire grills are available, but there is **no piped water,** so bring your own. Pets are permitted on leashes.

Reservations, fee: No reservations, no fee.

Who to contact: Phone the Los Padres National Forest Mount Pinos Ranger District at (805)245-3731.

Location: From Interstate 5, take the Gorman-Hungry Valley Road exit (it's the northern exit for the Hungry Valley Recreation Area). Drive about 23 miles south on Hungry Valley Road and Alamo Mountain Road (a rough, dirt road) to the campground.

Trip note: This do-it-yourself camp is set near the top of Alamo Mountain at 6,800 feet elevation. Nearby options are Twin Pines, Sunset, and Cottonwood. A Forest Service map, which details the back roads in the area, is heartily advised. Open from May to October.

Map grid **g5**

HARDLUCK

on the Smith Fork of Piru Creek
LOS PADRES NATIONAL FOREST

Campsites, facilities: There are 24 campsites for tents or motor homes up to 22 feet long. Fireplaces and picnic tables are provided. Vault toilets are available. There is **no piped water,** so bring your own. Pets are permitted on leashes.

Reservations, fee: No reservations; no fee.

Who to contact: Phone the Los Padres National Forest Mount Pinos Ranger District at (805)245-3731.

Location: From Interstate 5, take the Gorman-Hungry Valley Road exit (it's the northern exit for the Hungry Valley Recreation Area). Drive about ten miles south on Hungry Valley Road. Turn left on Canada del los Alamos and drive three miles to the campground entrance on your right. Turn right and drive three miles to the campground.

Trip note: This may be the spot you're looking for. It's a developed Forest Service camp set on the Smith Fork of Piru Creek. It is just three miles upstream of popular Pyramid Reservoir, but since there are no direct roads to the lake, you won't be bugged by the heavy traffic there. Meanwhile the Hungry Valley State Vehicular Recreation Area, the popular four-wheel drive area, is just a mile north of camp. The elevation is 2,800 feet. Open from April to November.

Map grid **g6**

LOS ALAMOS

near Pyramid Lake
ANGELES NATIONAL FOREST

Campsites, facilities: There are 93 family campsites for tents or motor homes and several group sites. Piped water, fire pits, flush toilets, and picnic tables are provided. A boat ramp is nearby at the Emigrant Landing Picnic Area. Pets are permitted on leashes.

Reservations, fee: No reservations; $5 fee per night.

Who to contact: Phone the Angeles National Forest Saugus Ranger District at (805)296-9710 or concessionaire at (805)248-6575.

Location: From Gorman, drive eight miles south on Interstate 5. Take the Hungry Valley Road exit. Drive west and follow the signs to the campground.

Trip note: Oak Flat is near the southwestern border of Angeles National Forest at 2,800 feet elevation. It is a short drive north to Pyramid Lake, about ten miles to the recreation area at Emigrant Landing. Open year around.

Map grid **g8**

SAWMILL MEADOWS

on Pacific Crest Trail
ANGELES NATIONAL FOREST

Campsites, facilities: There are eight tent sites. Picnic tables and fire pits, vault toilets are provided. There is **no piped water,** so bring your own. Pets are permitted on leashes.

Reservations, fee: No reservations, no fee.

Who to contact: Phone the Angeles National Forest Saugus District Office at (805)296-9710.

Location: From Castaic, turn northeast on Lake Hughes Road and drive 27 miles to the town of Lake Hughes. Turn left on Elizabeth Lake Road and drive to Sawmill Mountain (northwest) on Sawmill Mountain-Liebre Ridge Road and drive about ten miles to the campground.

Trip note: This is one of the more appealing camps that hikers will find in the Angeles National Forest because it is set on the Pacific Crest Trail and is also one mile from the Burnt Peak Canyon trailhead into the backcountry. Take your pick. The elevation is 5,200 feet. Open from May to November.

Map grid g8

UPPER SHAKE

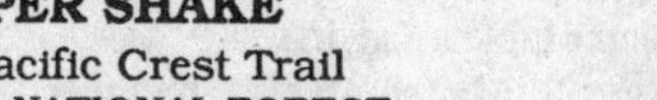

near Pacific Crest Trail
ANGELES NATIONAL FOREST

Campsites, facilities: There are 13 campsites for tents or motor homes up to 22 feet long. Fire pits, vault toilets, and picnic tables are provided. There is **no piped water,** so bring your own.

Reservations, fee: No reservations, no fee.

Who to contact: Phone the Angeles National Forest Saugus District Office at (805)296-9710.

Location: From Castaic, turn northeast on Lake Hughes Road and drive 27 miles to the town of Lake Hughes. Turn left (northwest) on County Road N2 (Pine Canyon Road) and drive about 5.5 miles to the entrance road on the left.

Trip note: This is a nearby option to Lower Shake camp. This camp is set a bit higher at 4,300 feet, with easy access and the Pacific Crest Trail, which passes nearby. Open from May to November.

Map grid g9

LOWER SHAKE

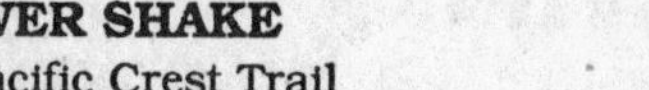

near Pacific Crest Trail
ANGELES NATIONAL FOREST

Campsites, facilities: There are five tent sites. Picnic tables fire pits, and vault toilets are provided. There is **no piped water,** so bring your own. Groceries and laundry facilities can be found nearby.

Reservations, fee: No reservations, no fee.

Who to contact: Phone the Angeles National Forest Saugus District Office at (805)296-9710.

Location: From Castaic, turn northeast on Lake Hughes Road and drive 27 miles to the town of Lake Hughes. Turn left (northwest) on County Road N2 (Pine Canyon Road) and drive about five miles to the entrance road on the left.

Trip note: Easy access is a bonus here. The camp is set near the road and the Pacific Crest Trail passes within a half mile of the camp. The elevation is 4,120 feet. Open from May to November.

Map grid h1

ROSE VALLEY FALLS

LOS PADRES NATIONAL FOREST

Campsites, facilities: There are nine campsites for tents or motor homes up to 16 feet long. Piped water, fireplaces, and picnic tables are provided. Vault toilets and horseback riding facilities are available. Pets are permitted on leashes.

Reservations, fee: No reservations; $4 fee per night.

Who to contact: Phone the Los Padres National Forest Ojai Ranger District at (805)646-4348.

Location: From Ojai, drive about 15 miles north on Highway 33. Turn right (east) on Sespe River Road and drive 5.5 miles to the campground entrance.

Trip note: Rose Valley Falls is one of the scenic highlights in this section of Los Padres National Forest, especially in winter and spring, when the stream flow is highest. It is just a short hike from the camp to the falls. The camp is set at 3,400 feet elevation next to Rose Valley Creek, about two miles from Sespe Creek.

Map grid **h5**

LAKE PIRU RECREATION AREA

Campsites, facilities: There are 247 campsites for tents or motor homes. Fireplaces, picnic tables, and, in some cases, electrical hookups are provided. Piped water, flush toilets, showers, a dump station, a snack bar, ice, bait, a boat ramp, temporary mooring, boat fuel, rentals for motorboats, and tackle are available. Pets are permitted on leashes.

Reservations, fee: No reservations; $11-$14 fee per night; pets $1.

Who to contact: Phone the park at (805)521-1500.

Location: From Ventura, drive east on Highway 126 for about 30 miles to the Piru Canyon Road exit. Follow this road northeast for about 6 miles to the campground.

Trip note: Lake Piru is monopolized by power boats and waterskiers. In fact, the lake is designated for motorboats over 12 feet long; all others are prohibited. The lake is shaped kind of like a tear drop and was created by Santa Paula Dam on the Piru River. Bass fishing can be quite good in the spring, before the waterskiers take over. Open all year.

Map grid **h6**

OAK FLAT
near Pyramid Lake
ANGELES NATIONAL FOREST

Campsites, facilities: There are 27 campsites for tents or motor homes up to 32 feet long. Piped water (sometimes), fire pits, vault toilets and picnic tables are provided.

Reservations, fee: No reservations; $5 fee per night; no fee when there's **no piped water.**

Who to contact: Phone the Angeles National Forest Saugus Ranger District at (805)296-9710.

Location: From Castaic, drive six miles north on Interstate 5. Turn left on Templin Highway and go under the freeway. Drive northwest for three more miles.

Trip note: Oak Flat is near the southwestern border of Angeles National Forest at 2,800 feet elevation. It is a short drive north to Pyramid Lake, about ten miles to the recreation area at Emigrant Landing. Open year-round.

Map grid **h7**

CIENEGA
at Redrock Mountain
ANGELES NATIONAL FOREST

Campsites, facilities: There are eight sites for tents only and 14 campsites for tents or motor homes up to 18 feet long. Fire pits, vault toilets, and picnic tables are provided. There is **no piped water,** so bring your own.

Reservations, fee: No reservations, no fee.

Who to contact: Phone the Angeles National Forest Saugus District Office at (805)296-9710.

Location: From Castaic, drive six miles north on Interstate 5. Turn right on Templin Highway and drive three miles. At the bottom of the road, cross the concrete bridge. The road becomes dirt. Drive one-eighth of a mile on the dirt road. Turn left and drive two miles to the campground. The road is closed in winter.

Trip note: This primitive, Forest Service trailhead camp is set at 2,000 feet elevation. A trail is routed into the backcountry surrounding Redrock Mountain. A Forest Service map is strongly advised. Open from April to November.

Map grid h8

PROSPECT
on Elizabeth Lake Canyon Creek
ANGELES NATIONAL FOREST

Campsites, facilities: There are 22 tent sites. Piped water (sometimes), picnic tables, fire pits, and vault toilets are provided. Pets are permitted on leashes.

Reservations, fee: No reservations; $5 fee per night; no fee when there is **no piped water.**

Who to contact: Phone the Angeles National Forest Saugus District Office at (805)296-9710. This camp was temporarily closed in 1990 by the Forest Service. Call first to determine availability.

Location: From Castaic, turn northeast on Lake Hughes Road and drive 17 miles to the campground.

Trip note: This is one of two camps in the area. This one is set along Elizabeth Lake Canyon Creek. It is set at 2,200 feet elevation near the base of Warm Springs Mountain. A good side trip is to drive two miles further on Lake Hughes Road, park, and then hike to Necktie Basin Lookout (look for the trailhead on the right side of the road). Open year around.

Map grid h9

COTTONWOOD
on Elizabeth Lake Canyon Creek
ANGELES NATIONAL FOREST

Campsites, facilities: There are 22 campsites for tents or motor homes up to 22 feet long. Piped water (sometimes), fire pits, vault toilets, and picnic tables are provided. Groceries are nearby. Pets are permitted on leashes.

Reservations, fee: No reservations; $5 fee per night; no fee if there is **no piped water.**

Who to contact: Phone the Angeles National Forest Saugus District Office at (805)296-9710.

Location: From Castaic, turn northeast on Lake Hughes Road and drive 21 miles.

Trip note: This is a quiet spot in Elizabeth Lake Canyon Creek with a small stream running by the camp. A nearby option on the same road is Prospect camp. It is better for hikers. The elevation is 2,680 feet. Open year-round.

Map grid h9

SOUTH PORTAL
on South Portal Creek
ANGELES NATIONAL FOREST

Campsites, facilities: There are eight tent sites. Picnic tables fire pits, and vault toilets are provided. There is **no piped water,** so bring your own. There is a grocery store in Green Valley. Pets are permitted on leashes.

Reservations, fee: No reservations, no fee.

Who to contact: Phone the Angeles National Forest Saugus District Office at (805)296-9710.

Location: From Castaic, drive south on Interstate 5 to the Valencia Boulevard exit, and drive east to Valencia Boulevard. Turn left and drive about two miles to San Francisquito Canyon-South Portal Road. The entrance is 20 more miles.

Trip note: Small and primitive, this little camp along South Portal Creek might be what you are looking for. If you don't like crowds, take the do-it-yourself approach. This spot can provide a place where you won't be bugged by anything. The elevation is 2,800 feet. Open year-round.

Map grid i2

STECKEL COUNTY PARK
on Santa Paula Creek

Campsites, facilities: There are 75 campsites for tents or motor homes. Fireplaces, picnic tables, and, in most cases, electrical connections are provided. Piped water, flush toilets, and a playground are available. Some facilities are wheelchair accessible. Supplies and a laundromat are nearby. Pets are permitted on leashes.

Reservations, fee: No reservations; $10 fee per night; pets $1.

Who to contact: Phone the County Parks Department at (805)654-3951.

Location: From Ventura, drive south on US 101 to the Highway 126 turnoff. Travel 14 miles northeast on Highway 126. Turn northwest on Highway 150 and drive four miles to the park.

Trip note: You either know about this spot or you don't. You either have this book or you don't. Other than the locals, this park is not well known. It is a pretty spot set along little Santa Paula Creek in the foothill country. Open year-round.

Map grid i2

MOUNTAIN VIEW RV PARK
in Santa Paula

Campsites, facilities: There are 33 motor home spaces with full hookups. TV and a swim spa are available. A laundromat, a restaurant, and a shopping center are nearby.

Reservations, fee: Call for available space; $18 fee per night.

Who to contact: Phone the park at (805)933-1942.

Location: From Ventura, drive south on US 101 to the Highway 126 turnoff. Travel 11 miles northeast on Highway 126. Take the Peck Drive exit and drive a short distance to Harvard Boulevard. Turn right and drive to 714 West Harvard Boulevard.

Trip note: The town of Santa Paula is known for its excellent weather and nearby recreation options. They include Steckel County Park, Los Padres National Forest, and the beaches at Ventura. Open year-round.

Map grid i3

KENNY GROVE COUNTY PARK
near Fillmore

Campsites, facilities: There are 40 campsites for tents or motor homes, some with electrical hookups. Fireplaces and picnic tables are provided. Piped water, flush toilets, and a playground are available. Supplies and a laundromat are nearby. Pets are permitted on leashes.

Reservations, fee: Reservations accepted; $9-$11 fee per night; pets $1.

Who to contact: Phone the County Parks Department at (805)654-3951 or (805)524-0750.

Location: From Ventura, drive south on US 101 to the Highway 126 turnoff. Travel 22 miles northeast on Highway 126. Take the Old Telegraph Road exit near the town of Fillmore and turn left. Drive to Seventh Street and turn right and drive two miles to the park.

Trip note: A lot of folks miss this spot. It is a county park set among the orchards and eucalyptus groves. It's just far enough off the highway to get some privacy. It is 12 miles from the Sespe Condor Sanctuary in Los Padres National Forest.

A

Map grid **i9**

BOUQUET
on Bouquet Canyon Creek
ANGELES NATIONAL FOREST

B

Campsites, facilities: There are four tent sites. Picnic tables fire pits, and vault toilets are provided. There is **no piped water.** Pets are permitted on leashes.
Reservations, fee: No reservations, no fee.
Who to contact: Phone the Angeles National Forest Saugus District Office at (805)296-9710.
Location: From Castaic, drive six miles south on Interstate 5 to the Magic Mountain Parkway exit. Take the exit and drive east to Valencia Boulevard. Turn left and drive about two miles to Bouquet Canyon Road. Turn north on Bouquet Canyon Road and drive about 12 miles to the campground.

C

Trip note: This camp and Streamside are the best of the camps in this immediate area. This camp is set in Bouquet Canyon along Bouquet Canyon Creek, which is stocked with trout when stream flows are sufficient. There are no hiking trails in the immediate area, but Bouquet Reservoir to the north provides a good side trip, but do not drink the water! Open year-round.

D

Map grid **i9**

BIG OAK
on Bouquet Canyon Creek
ANGELES NATIONAL FOREST

E

Campsites, facilities: There are nine tent sites. Piped water (sometimes), picnic tables, fire pits, and vault toilets are provided. Pets are permitted on leashes.
Reservations, fee: No reservations; $5 fee per night; no fee if there is **no piped water.**

F

Who to contact: Phone the Angeles National Forest Saugus District Office at (805)296-9710.
Location: From Castaic, drive six miles south on Interstate 5 to the Magic Mountain Parkway exit. Take the exit and drive east to Valencia Boulevard. Turn left and drive about two miles to Bouquet Canyon Road. Turn north on Bouquet Canyon Road and drive about 13 miles to the campground.

G

Trip note: This is one of the three camps set right in a line in this area along Bouquet Canyon Creek. Do not drink the water from Bouquet Canyon Creek under any circumstances. The elevation is 2,340 feet. Open all year.

H4

Map grid **i9**

STREAMSIDE
on Bouquet Canyon Creek
ANGELES NATIONAL FOREST

Campsites, facilities: There are nine tent sites. Piped water (sometimes), picnic tables, fire pits, and vault toilets are provided. Pets are permitted on leashes.

I

Reservations, fee: No reservations; $5 fee per night; no fee if there's **no piped water.**
Who to contact: Phone the Angeles National Forest Saugus District Office at (805)296-9710.
Location: From Castaic, drive six miles south on Interstate 5 to the Magic Mountain Parkway exit. Take the exit and drive east to Valencia Boulevard. Turn left and drive about two miles to Bouquet Canyon Road. Turn north on Bouquet Canyon Road and drive about 14 miles to the campground.

J

on Bouquet Canyon Creek

Trip note: This is a nearby option to Bouquet camp. For details, see the trip note for that camp. Do not drink the water from Bouquet Canyon Creek under any circumstances. The elevation is 2,300 feet. Open from April to October.

Map grid i9

ZUNI

on Bouquet Canyon Creek
ANGELES NATIONAL FOREST

Campsites, facilities: There are ten tent sites. Piped water, picnic tables, fire pits, and vault toilets are provided. Pets are permitted on leashes.
Reservations, fee: No reservations; $5 fee per night.
Who to contact: Phone the Angeles National Forest Saugus District Office at (805)296-9710. Call to confirm availability.
Location: From Castaic, drive six miles south on Interstate 5 to the Magic Mountain Parkway exit. Take the exit and drive east to Valencia Boulevard. Turn left and drive about two miles to Bouquet Canyon Road. Turn north on Bouquet Canyon Road and drive about seven miles to the campground.
Trip note: If you are heading north out of Saugus on Bouquet Canyon Road, this is the first camp you come to, set just inside the southern border of Angeles National Forest, at 1,700 feet elevation. Do not drink the water from Bouquet Canyon Creek that runs nearby under any circumstances.

MAP H5

BEACH
TREES
5% CLUB
DESERT
URBAN
FOOTHILL
GRASSLAND
15 MILES

to Havilah
to Weldon
to Freeman Junction
to Bakersfield
to Randsburg
to Boron
to I-5
to Santa Clarita
to Saugus
to Victorville
to Pasadena
to Wrightwood

SEQUOIA NAT'L. FOREST
Harper Pk. EL. 5,784
Twin Oaks
Butterbread Pk. EL. 6,000
Black Mtn. EL. 5,259
RED ROCK CANYON ST. PK.
Garlock
Koehn Lake
Keene
Cross Mtn. EL. 6,192
Cantil
Cache Pk. EL. 6,708
Tehachapi
Monolith
Tehachapi Summit EL. 4,064
Double Mtn. EL. 7,988
California City
Mojave
North Edwards
Willow Springs
Edwards
Edwards Air Force Base
Rosamond
Rosamond Dry Lake
Rogers Dry Lake
Fairmont
Lake Hughes
Lancaster
Quartz Hill
Green Valley
Bouquet Lake
SADDLEBACK BUTTE ST. PK.
ANGELES NAT'L. FOREST
Palmdale
Soledad Pass EL. 3,178
Littlerock
El Mirage
Pearblossom
Acton
Vincent
Ravenna
Valyermo

14
58
202
138
18
N2
N3
N4
N5
N6

a b c d e f g h i j

0 1 2 3 4 5 6 7 8 9

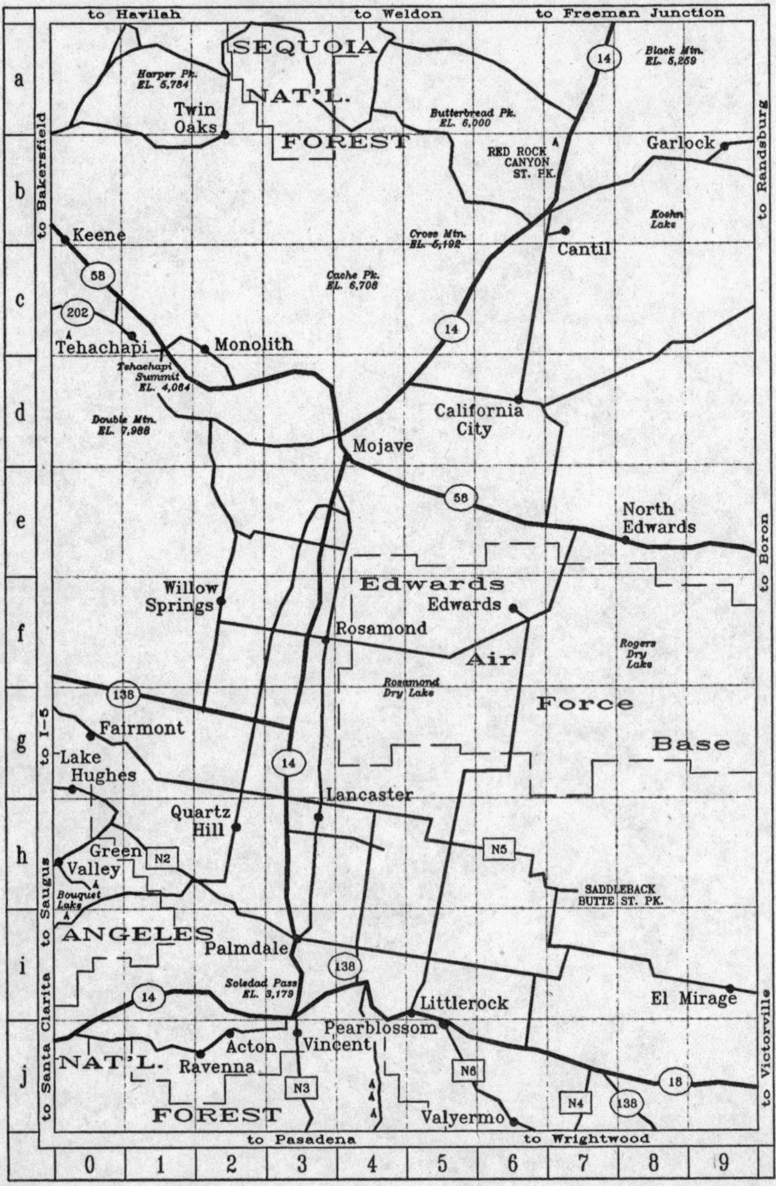

Map grid **b7**

REDROCK CANYON STATE PARK
near Mojave

A

Campsites, facilities: There are 50 campsites for tents or motor homes up to 30 feet long. Piped water, fireplaces, and picnic tables are provided. Pit toilets, a dump station, exhibits, and a nature trail are available. Two campgrounds are wheelchair accessible. Pets are permitted on leashes.

B

Reservations, fee: No reservations; $7-$9 fee per night; pets $1.
Who to contact: Phone the park at (805)942-0662.
Location: From Highway 58 in the town of Mojave, turn northeast on Highway 14 and drive 25 miles to the park.
Trip note: Easy access makes this a prime attraction, along with the chance to see colorful rock formations. A side trip for geologically-oriented visitors or rock-hounds is the drive up Jawbone Canyon Road in order to explore Jawbone and Last Chance Canyons. The elevation is 2,600 feet. Open year-round.

C

Map grid **c0**

TEHACHAPI MOUNTAIN PARK

D

Campsites, facilities: There are 65 campsites for tents or motor homes up to 24 feet long. Piped water, showers, fireplaces, and picnic tables are provided. Pit toilets and overnight corral facilities for equestrian groups are available. Pets are permitted.

E

Reservations, fee: No reservations; $6 fee per night; pets $2.
Who to contact: Phone the County Parks Department at (805)822-4632.
Location: From Tehachapi, drive eight miles southwest on Water Canyon Road.
Trip note: This is the kind of place that out-of-towners don't have a clue about, yet it is the most delightful spot to be found for many miles in the area. It is set on the slopes of the Tehachapi Mountains and covers 570 acres. The elevation is 7,000 feet. Winter sports are available during the snow season. Open year-round.

F

Map grid **h0**

SPUNKY
near Bouquet Reservoir
ANGELES NATIONAL FOREST

G

Campsites, facilities: There are ten campsites for tents or motor homes. Piped water, fire pits, vault toilets, and picnic tables are provided. A grocery store is nearby. Pets are permitted on leashes.

H5

Reservations, fee: No reservations; $5 fee per night.
Who to contact: Phone the Angeles National Forest Saugus District Office at (805)296-9710. This camp was temporarily closed in 1990. Call the Forest Service for availability.
Location: From Castaic, drive six miles south on Interstate 5 to the Valencia Boulevard exit. Take the exit and drive east to Valencia Boulevard. Turn left and drive about two miles. Turn on Bouquet Canyon Road and drive 15 miles. Turn left on Spunky Canyon Road and drive four miles to the campground.

I

Trip note: This is a good spot for hikers or anglers. The camp is set at 3,760 feet elevation and has two prime side trip options. For hikers, the Pacific Crest Trail passes a mile east of camp, and is a good backcountry adventure. For anglers, Bouquet Reservoir is only two miles south and is stocked with rainbow trout in the spring and early summer. Open from April to October.

J

Map grid i0

THE FALLS

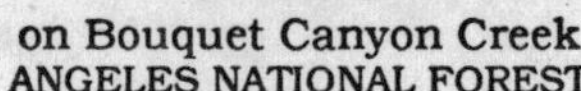

ANGELES NATIONAL FOREST

Campsites, facilities: There are 14 tent sites. Piped water (sometimes), picnic tables, fire pits, and vault toilets are provided. Pets are permitted on leashes.

Reservations, fee: No reservations; $5 fee per night; no fee if there's **no piped water.**

Who to contact: Phone the Angeles National Forest Saugus District Office at (805)296-9710.

Location: From Castaic, drive six miles south on Interstate 5 to the Valencia Boulevard exit. Drive east to Valencia Boulevard. Turn left and drive about two miles to Bouquet Canyon Road. Drive 18 miles to the campground.

Trip note: This is the premium camp among the three that are in the immediate area. It is set at 2,560 feet elevation along Bouquet Canyon Creek, which is stocked with rainbow trout in early summer. If they aren't biting, you can head north two miles to Bouquet Reservoir instead. Do not drink the water from Bouquet Canyon Creek under any circumstances. Open from April to October.

Map grid j4

BASIN

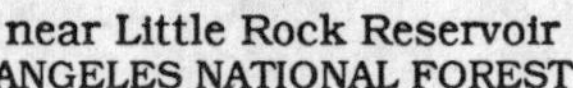

ANGELES NATIONAL FOREST

Campsites, facilities: There are 15 campsites for tents or motor homes up to 20 feet long. Piped water, fire pits, vault toilets, and picnic tables are provided. A grocery store is nearby on the reservoir. Pets are permitted on leashes.

Reservations, fee: No reservations; $9 fee per night.

Who to contact: Phone the Angeles National Forest Valyermo District Office at (805)944-2187.

Location: From Highway 14 near Palmdale, turn east onto Highway 138 and continue past the stoplight at the intersection. Turn right on Cheeseboro Road and continue six miles to the campground.

Trip note: If the camps at nearby Little Rock Reservoir (one mile to the north) are full, this camp provides an ideal alternative. It is set along Little Rock Creek at 3,400 feet elevation, just south of a designated Off-Road Vehicle Area. Campsites are assigned at the entrance to Little Rock during the summer months. Open year-round.

Map grid j4

LAKESIDE

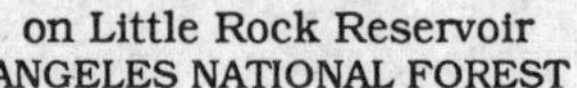

ANGELES NATIONAL FOREST

Campsites, facilities: There are six campsites for tents or motor homes up to 18 feet long. Piped water, fire pits, vault toilets, and picnic tables are provided. Pets are permitted on leashes.

Reservations, fee: No reservations; $7 fee per night.

Who to contact: Phone the Angeles National Forest Valyermo District Office at (805)944-2187.

Location: From Highway 14 near Palmdale, turn east on Highway 138 and continue past the stoplight at the intersection. Turn right on Cheeseboro Road and drive four miles to the campground at the reservoir.

Trip note: This is the smaller of the two camps at Little Rock Reservoir. During the summer months, campsites are assigned at the entrance to Little Rock. A designated Off-Road Vehicle Area is located southeast of the lake. The elevation is 3,330 feet.

Map grid **j4**

JUNIPER GROVE

on Little Rock Reservoir

ANGELES NATIONAL FOREST

Campsites, facilities: There are seven tent sites. Piped water, picnic tables, fire pits, and vault toilets are provided. Pets are permitted on leashes.

Reservations, fee: No reservations; $7 fee per night.

Who to contact: Phone the Angeles National Forest Valyermo District Office at (805)944-2187.

Location: From Highway 14 near Palmdale, turn east on Highway 138 and continue past the stoplight at the intersection. Turn right on Cheeseboro Road and continue 4.5 miles to the campground on the reservoir.

Trip note: There are two camps set on Little Rock Reservoir, a little-known lake located just inside the northern border of Angeles National Forest. The lake is stocked with trout in early summer, but the water level gets low in the late summer. Juniper Grove camp is on the west side of the lake, mid-way from the ends. Campsites are assigned at the entrance to Little Rock during the summer months. The elevation is 3,400 feet. Open year-round.

◆ MAP H6 ◆

BEACH
TREES
5% CLUB
DESERT
URBAN
FOOTHILL
GRASSLAND

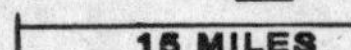

to Inyokern
to Westland
to Garlock
to California City
to North Edwards
to Lancaster
to Littlerock
to Fort Irwin
to Baker
to Newberry Springs
to San Bernardino
to Lucerne Valley

a
b
c
d
e
f
g
h
i
j

0 1 2 3 4 5 6 7 8 9

395
Searles
178
U. S. Naval Weapons Center
Randsburg
Joahnnesburg
Red Mountain
Atolia
Fort Irwin Mil. Res.
Cuddeback Lake
395
Fremont Pk. EL. 4,584
Opal Mtn. EL. 3,950
58
Boron
Harper Lake
RAINBOW NAT'L. NATURAL LANDMARK
EDWARDS AIR FORCE BASE
58
Hinkley
Barstow
Lenwood
15
Yermo
Daggett
Hodge
Helendale
40
15
395
El Mirage
Oro Grande
GEORGE AIR FORCE BASE
247
Adelanto
Victorville
18
18
Apple Valley

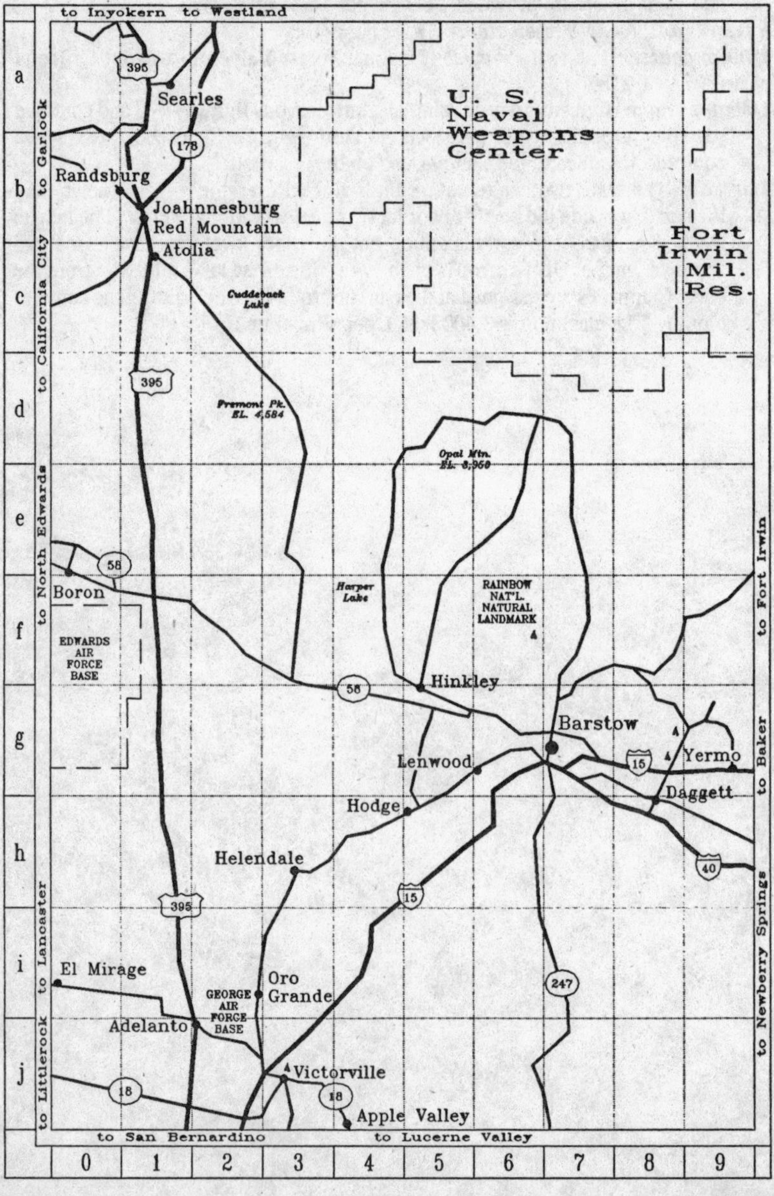

Map grid f6 — OWL CANYON
near Barstow

Campsites, facilities: There are 31 campsites for tent or motor homes. Fireplaces, picnic tables, and vault toilets are provided. There is limited piped water so bring your own. Pets are permitted on leashes.

Reservations, fee: No reservations; $4 fee per night.

Who to contact: Phone the Bureau of Land Management at (714)276-6394.

Location: From Barstow on Highway 58, drive eight miles north on Camp Irwin Road. Turn on Fossil Beds Road and drive two miles west.

Trip note: The sparse BLM land out here is kind of like an ugly pet. After awhile, you love it anyway. It is best visited in the winter, of course, when hiking allows a new look at what appears, at first, to be a wasteland. The beauty is in the detail of it, tiny critters and tiny flowers seen against the unfenced vastness. The elevation is 2,600 feet.

Map grid g8 — BARSTOW CALICO KOA
near Barstow

Campsites, facilities: There are 80 campsites for tents or motor homes, many with full or partial hookups. Picnic tables and fireplaces are provided. Piped water, flush toilets, showers, a sanitary dump station, a playground, a swimming pool, a recreation room, a grocery store, propane gas, ice, and a laundromat are available. Pets are permitted on leashes. Some facilities are wheelchair accessible.

Reservations, fee: Reservations accepted; $12-$18 fee per night.

Who to contact: Call (619)254-2311.

Location: From Barstow, drive seven miles east on Interstate 15 North. Take the Ghost Town Road exit and drive west a short distance to the campground.

Trip note: Don't blame us if you end up way out here. But as long as you're here, you might as well take a side trip to the Calico Ghost Town, located about ten miles to the northeast at the foot of the Calico Mountains. The elevation is 1,900 feet. Open year-round.

Map grid g8 — CALICO GHOST TOWN REGIONAL PARK
near Barstow

Campsites, facilities: There are 114 campsites for tents or motor homes, some with partial hookups. Piped water and fireplaces are provided. Piped water, flush toilets, showers, a sanitary dump station, and a playground are available. Groceries, propane gas, and laundry facilities are available nearby. Pets are permitted on leashes.

Reservations, fee: Reservations requested; $9-$15 fee per night; pets $1.

Who to contact: Phone the park at (619)254-2122.

Location: From Barstow, drive seven miles northeast on Interstate 5. Take the Ghost Town Road exit and drive north for three miles to the park.

Trip note: Let me tell you about this ghost town—there's probably more people here now than there's ever been. In the 1880s and 1890s, it was a booming silver mine town and there are still remnants of that. Alas, it now has lots of restaurants and shops. Recreation options include riding on a narrow gauge railroad, touring a silver mine, or watching an old-style play with villains and heros. Open year-round.

Map grid **j3**

SHADY OASIS VICTORVILLE KOA

near Victorville

Campsites, facilities: There are 136 campsites for tents or motor homes, many with full or partial hookups. Piped water, picnic tables, and fireplaces are provided. Rest rooms, showers, a recreation room, a swimming pool, a playground, a grocery store, propane gas, and a laundromat are available. Some facilities are wheelchair accessible. Pets are permitted on leashes.

Reservations, fee: Reservation accepted; $18-$22 fee per night.

Who to contact: Call (619)245-6867.

Location: From Victorville, drive north on Interstate 15 to Stoddard Wells Drive. Turn south and drive a short distance to the campground at 16530 Stoddard Wells Drive.

Trip note: Keep your eyes open, Roy Rogers (the real one, not the rock star) might just ride by. He lives just minutes away from this park, where he sits happily in his living room with his horse, Trigger, which he stuffed. Open year-round.

• MAP H7 •

BEACH
DESERT
FOOTHILL
TREES
URBAN
GRASSLAND
5% CLUB

15 MILES

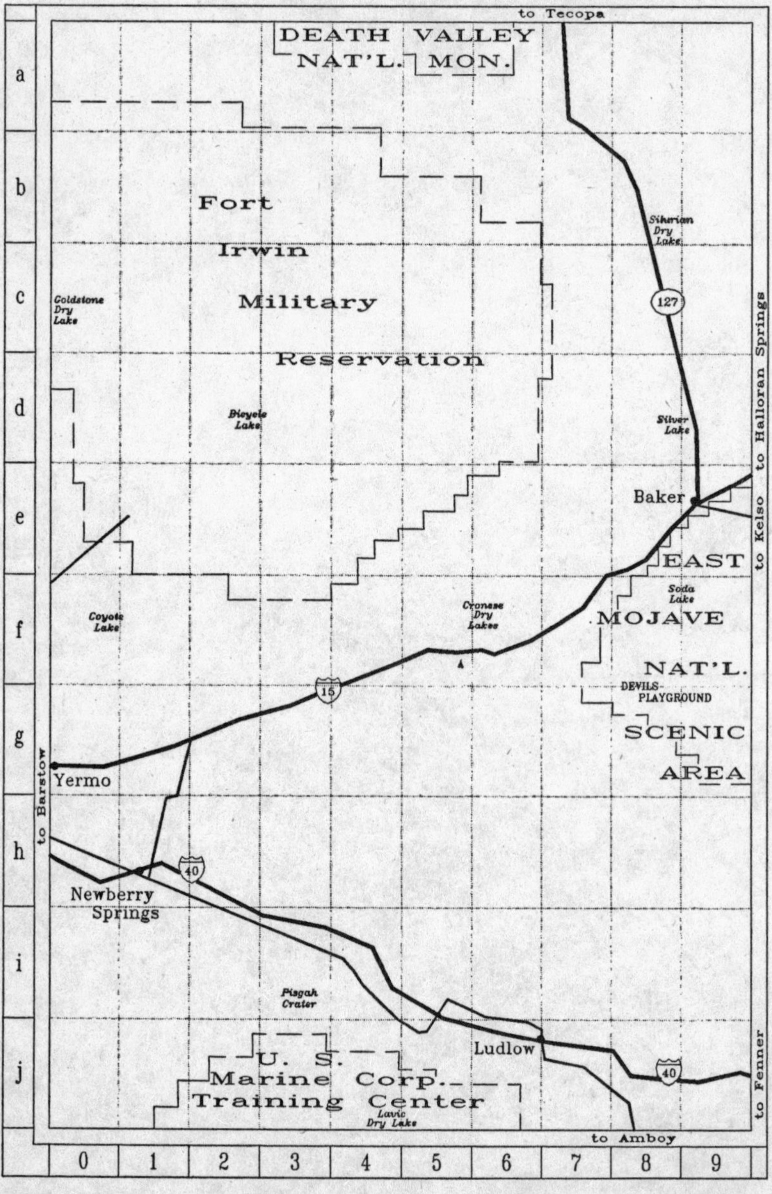

to Tecopa

DEATH VALLEY NAT'L. MON.

Fort Irwin Military Reservation

Silurian Dry Lake

127

Goldstone Dry Lake

Bicycle Lake

Silver Lake

Baker

to Kelso

to Halloran Springs

EAST MOJAVE NAT'L. SCENIC AREA

Soda Lake

Coyote Lake

Cronese Dry Lakes

DEVILS PLAYGROUND

15

Yermo

to Barstow

40

Newberry Springs

Pisgah Crater

Ludlow

U. S. Marine Corp. Training Center

Lavic Dry Lake

40

to Fenner

to Amboy

a b c d e f g h i j

0 1 2 3 4 5 6 7 8 9

Map grid **f5**

AFTON CANYON

near Barstow
EAST MOJAVE NATIONAL SCENIC AREA

Campsites, facilities: There are 22 campsites for tents or motor homes. Fireplaces, picnic tables, vault toilets are provided. There is limited piped water so bring your own. Pets are permitted on leashes.

Reservations, fee: No reservations; $4 fee per night.

Who to contact: Phone the Bureau of Land Management at (714)276-6394.

Location: From Barstow, drive 40 miles east on Interstate 15. Drive three miles south on Afton Canyon Road.

Trip note: This camp is set in a desert riparian habitat along the Mojave River. Remember, rivers in the desert are not like rivers in the cooler climates. There are lots of Tamarisk trees and no fish worth eating. This is one of several Bureau of Land Management areas in the East Mojave National Scenic Area.

◆ MAP H8 ◆

BEACH
DESERT
FOOTHILL
TREES
URBAN
GRASSLAND
5% CLUB

15 MILES

to Tecopa
to Sandy—Cold Springs, NV
Sandy
Kingston Pk. EL. 7,323
Jean
Mesquite Lake
15
NEVADA
Clark Mtn. EL. 7,929
Ivanpah Dry Lake
Mtn. Pass EL. 4,730
15
Nipton
164
Halloran Springs
EAST
to Baker
Ivanpah
MOJAVE
Cima
dead end to Searchlight, NV
Kelso Pk. EL. 4,757
Table Mtn. EL. 6,176
NAT'L.
DEVILS
Kelso
Hackberry Mtn. EL. 5,390
PLAYGROUND
PROVIDENCE MTNS. ST. REC. AREA
SCENIC
to Goffs
AREA
40
Fenner
40
to Ludlow
to Needles
to Amboy
to Essex

a b c d e f g h i j
0 1 2 3 4 5 6 7 8 9

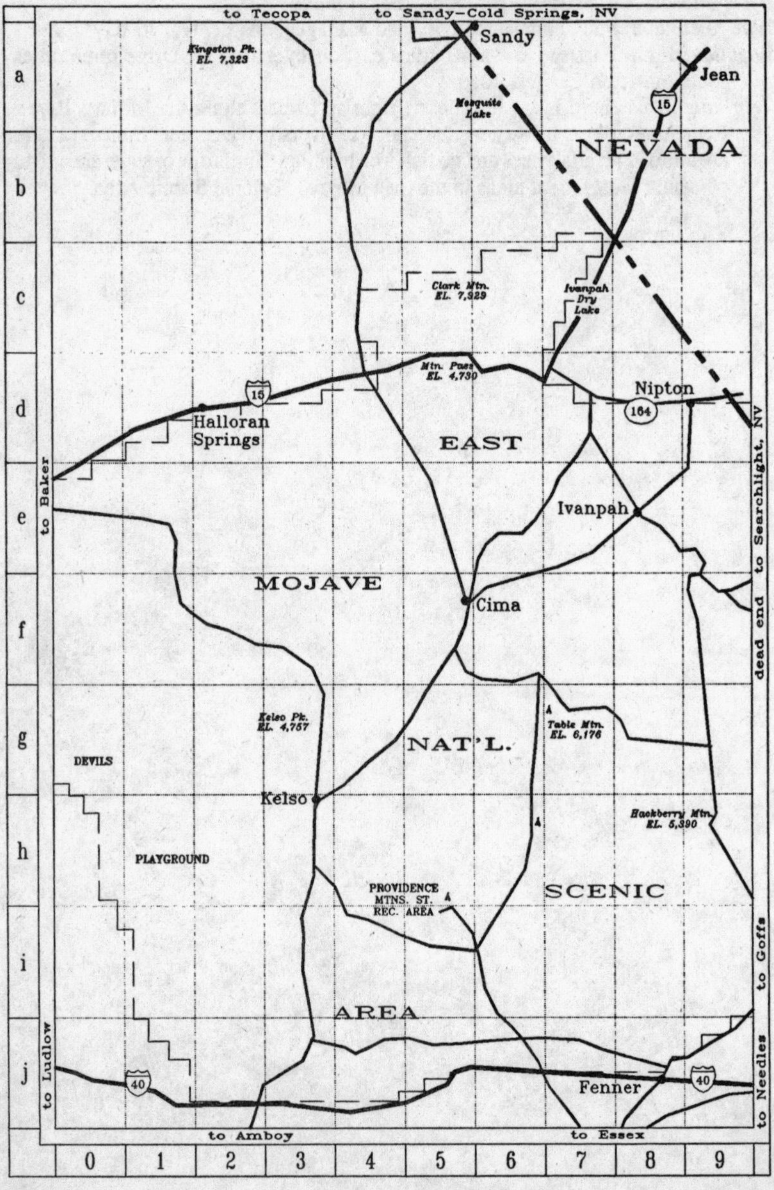

MID HILLS

Map grid g7

EAST MOJAVE NATIONAL SCENIC AREA

Campsites, facilities: There are 20 campsites for tents or motor homes. Fireplaces, picnic tables and vault toilets are provided. There is limited piped water so bring your own. Pets are permitted on leashes.

Reservations, fee: No reservations; $4 fee per night.

Who to contact: Phone the Bureau of Land Management at (714)276-6394.

Location: From Interstate 40 near Essex, take the Essex Road exit and drive 16 miles north to Black Canyon Road. Turn north on Black Canyon Road and drive 19 miles, following the signs to the campground.

Trip note: This is a nice campground set among the junipers and pinyon trees in a mountainous area. It is one in a series of little-known camps that are sprinkled about the vast desert that is managed by the Bureau of Land Management. The elevation is 5,500 feet. Open all year.

PROVIDENCE MOUNTAINS STATE RECREATION AREA

Map grid h5

near Mitchell Caverns

Campsites, facilities: There are six campsites for tents. Motor homes up to 32 feet long can park in the parking lot. Fireplaces, pit toilets, and picnic tables are provided. There is limited piped water so bring your own. Pets are permitted on leashes.

Reservations, fee: No reservations; $7 fee per night; pets $1.

Who to contact: Phone (619)389-2281.

Location: From Interstate 40 near Essex, drive 17 miles northwest on Essex Road to the park.

Trip note: This desert park offers guided tours of Mitchell Caverns from mid-September through early summer. It is a unique and remote park set at 4,300 feet elevation.

HOLE-IN-THE-WALL

Map grid h6

EAST MOJAVE NATIONAL SCENIC AREA

Campsites, facilities: There are 24 campsites for tents or motor homes. Fireplaces, picnic tables, vault toilets, and limited piped water are available, so bring your own. Pets are permitted on leashes.

Reservations, fee: No reservations; $4 fee per night.

Who to contact: Phone the Bureau of Land Management at (714)276-6394. This campground was scheduled to be renovated in 1990; call ahead for availability.

Location: From Highway 40 near Essex, take the Essex Road exit and drive 16 miles north to Black Canyon Road. Turn north on Black Canyon Road and drive 12 miles, following the signs to the campground.

Trip note: An option to the previously-listed camp, Mid Hills is located about five miles away. This is the tiniest and least known of the camps in the vast Mojave National Scenic Area. They even truck in water here, a big bonus. An interesting side trip is the Mitchell Caverns and Winding Stair Caverns in the nearby Providence Mountains State Recreation Area. To get there, go back to Essex Road, turn right and continue northeast for about six miles to the end of Essex Road. The elevation is 5,000 feet. Open year-round.

MAP H9

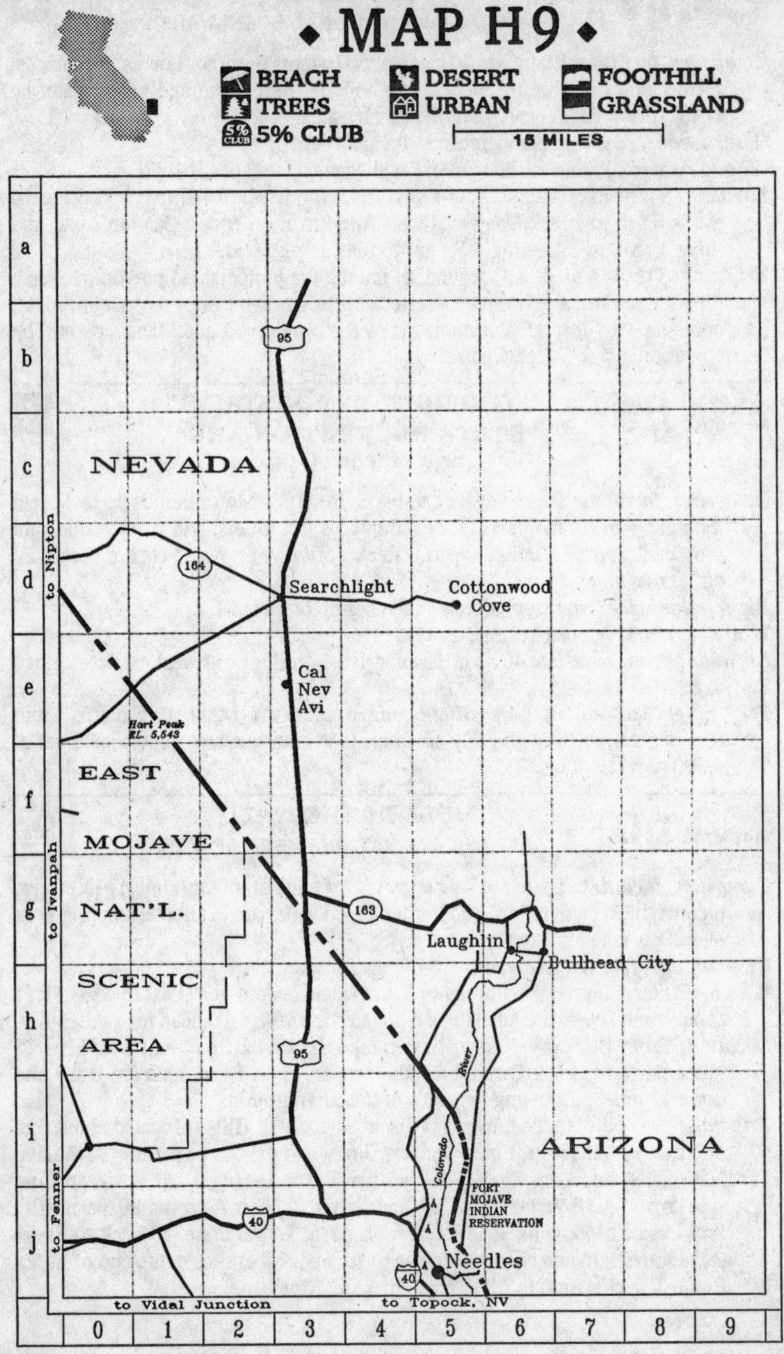

BEACH
DESERT
FOOTHILL
TREES
URBAN
GRASSLAND
5% CLUB
15 MILES

Map grid **j5**

NEEDLES KOA
near Colorado River

Campsites, facilities: There are 90 campsites for tents or motor homes, most with full or partial hookups. Flush toilets, showers, a recreation room, a swimming pool, a playground, a grocery store, propane gas, and a laundromat are available. Pets are permitted on leashes.

Reservations, fee: Reservations accepted; $13-$16 fee per night.

Who to contact: Call the Needles KOA at (619)326-4207.

Location: In Needles on Interstate 40, take the River Road exit and drive 1.5 northwest on Old National Trails Highway.

Trip note: Now quit your yelpin'. So it's hot. So it's ugly. So you're on your way home from Las Vegas after getting cleaned out. At least you've got the Needles KOA, complete with swimming pool, where you can get a new start. Side trips include heading north to Lake Mead. Open year-round.

Map grid **j5**

NEEDLES MARINA PARK
on Colorado River

Campsites, facilities: There are 190 spaces for motor homes with full hookups and picnic tables. Rest rooms with showers, a heated pool, jacuzzi, a recreation room, a swimming pool, a playground, a boat ramp, boat slips, a grocery store, gas, and a laundromat are available.

Reservations, fee: Reservations accepted; $17-$19 fee per night.

Who to contact: Call the Needles Marina Park at (619)326-2197.

Location: From Highway 40 in Needles, take the "J" Street exit to Broadway. Turn left, then turn right on River Road and drive one-half mile to the park.

Trip note: The campsites are on a stretch of the Colorado River that is smooth enough for water skiing. An 18-hole golf course is adjacent to the camp. Compared to the surrounding desert, why it's almost a goldarn paradise.

Map grid **j5**

RAINBO BEACH RESORT
on Colorado River

Campsites, facilities: There are 70 motor home spaces with full hookups and picnic tables. Rest rooms with showers, a laundromat, a recreation room (in the winter), a swimming pool, a store, and a marina are available. A restaurant is available in the summer.

Reservations, fee: Call ahead for available space; $15 fee per night.

Who to contact: Phone the Rainbo Beach Resort and Marina at (619)326-3101.

Location: From Interstate 40 in Needles, drive 1.5 miles north on River Road.

Trip note: The big bonus at this resort beside the Colorado River is the full marina, making this a boat and waterskier's headquarters. Open year-round.

MAP I3

BEACH
TREES
5% CLUB
DESERT
URBAN
FOOTHILL
GRASSLAND

15 MILES

to Ventura
Oxnard
Port Hueneme
to Oxnard
SANTA CRUZ ISLAND
SANTA ROSA ISLAND
ANACAPA ISLAND
CHANNEL ISLANDS NATIONAL PARK
Pacific
Ocean
CHANNEL ISLANDS NATIONAL PARK
SANTA BARBARA ISLAND
SAN NICHOLAS ISLAND

a b c d e f g h i j

0 1 2 3 4 5 6 7 8 9

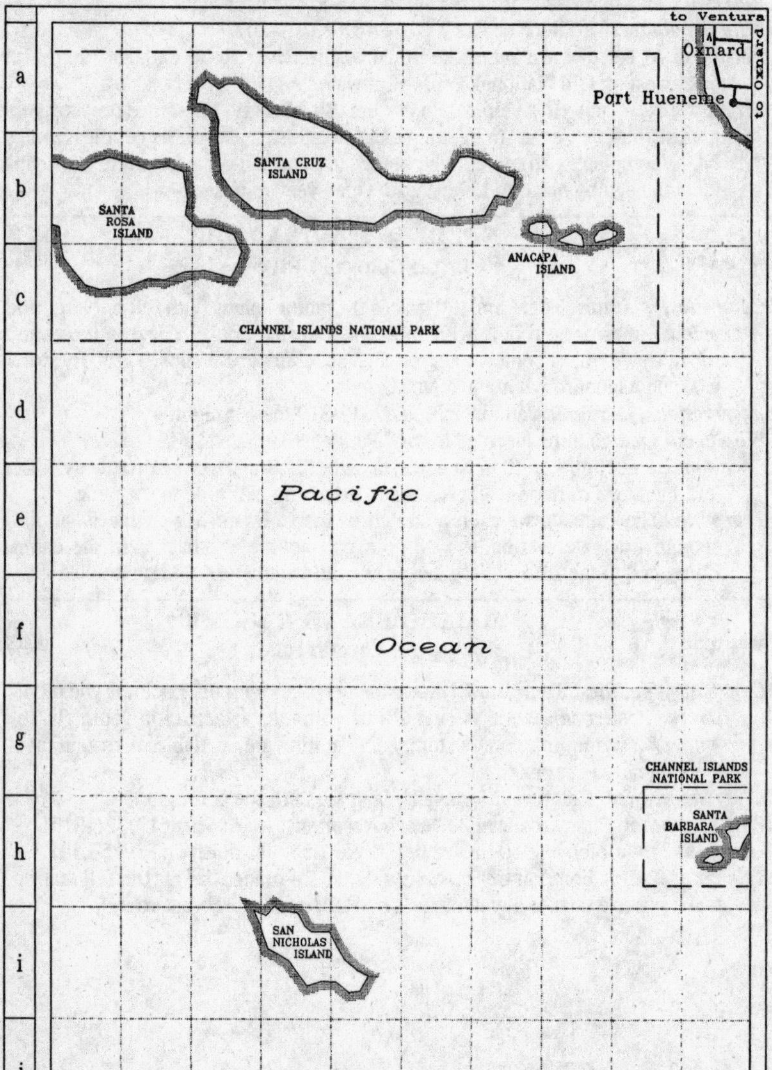

Map grid a9

McGRATH STATE BEACH

on Pacific Ocean south of Ventura

Campsites, facilities: There are 174 campsites for tents or motor homes up to 34 feet long. Piped water, fireplaces, and picnic tables are provided. Flush toilets, showers, a dump station, horseshoes and a visitor center are available. Supplies and a laundromat are nearby. Pets are permitted on leashes in the camping area only, not on the beach.

Reservations, fee: Reserve through MISTIX at (800)444-PARK ($3.95 MISTIX fee); $14-$16 fee per night; pets $1.

Who to contact: Phone the park at (805)654-4611 or (805)654-4744.

Location: From Ventura, drive south on US 101. Take the Seaward Avenue/Harbor Boulevard exit and drive four miles on Harbor Boulevard to the park.

Trip note: This is a pretty spot just south of Pierpoint Bay. The north tip of the park borders the Santa Clara River Estuary Natural Preserve and is close to Ventura Harbor and the Channel Islands National Park Visitor Center. Plan on a reservation or don't make a plan. Open year-round.

◆ MAP I4 ◆

BEACH
TREES
5% CLUB
DESERT
URBAN
FOOTHILL
GRASSLAND

15 MILES

to Ventura
to Moorpark
to Valencia
to Port Hueneme
to Pasadena
to E. Los Angeles
to Downey
to Long Beach

Oxnard
Camarillo
Simi Valley
San Fernando
Burbank
Thousand Oaks
Woodland Hills
Agoura
SANTA MONICA MTNS. NAT'L. REC. AREA
POINT MUGU
LEO CARRILLO ST. BEACH
EL PESCADOR ST. BEACH
LA PIEDRA ST. BEACH
EL MATADOR ST. BEACH
POINT DUME
Malibu
LAS TUNAS ST. BEACH
WILL ROGERS ST. BEACH
SANTA MONICA ST. BEACH
WILL ROGERS ST. PARK
Pacific Palisades
Beverly Hills
Venice
Los Angeles
Culver City
Marina Del Rey
DOCKWEILER ST. BEACH
Inglewood
El Segundo
Hawthorne
MANHATTAN ST. BEACH
Torrance
Redondo Beach
KING HARBOR
REDONDO ST. BEACH
Palos Verdes Estate
PALOS VERDES POINT
San Pedro
ROYAL PALMS ST. BEACH
POINT FERMIN PARK
CABRILLO BEACH AND REC. AREA
LONG BEACH NAVAL SHIP-YARD
Pacific Ocean
Two Harbors
CATALINA ISLAND
Avalon

34 · 34 · 1 · 101 · 23 · 23 · 118 · 5 · 27 · 27 · 405 · 210 · 170 · 5 · 101 · 134 · 101 · 1 · 10 · 42 · 1 · 110 · 91 · 405 · 1

a b c d e f g h i j

0 1 2 3 4 5 6 7 8 9

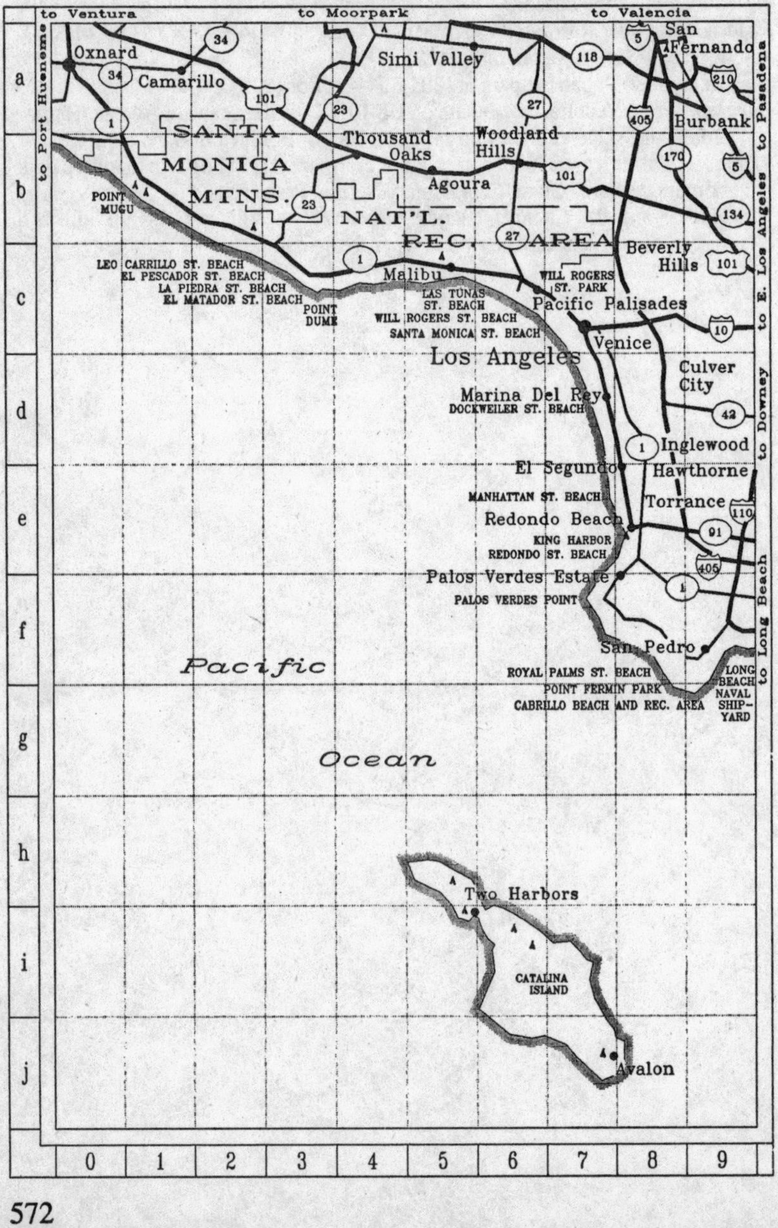

Map grid **a4**

OAK COUNTY PARK
near Moorpark

A

Campsites, facilities: There are 20 sites for tents only and 35 sites for motor homes. Fireplaces, picnic tables, and, in some cases, electrical hookups are provided. Piped water, flush toilets, a dump station, and a playground are available. Supplies and a laundromat are nearby.

B

Reservations, fee: Reservations accepted; $9-$11 fee per night; pets $1.

Who to contact: Phone the County Parks Department at (805)654-3951.

Location: From Ventura, drive south on US 101 to the Highway 126 turnoff. Travel six miles northeast on Highway 126 to Highway 118 (Los Angeles Avenue). Drive east for about 15 miles to the town of Moorpark. Continue east on Highway 118 for one mile to the park.

C

Trip note: This is an oft-overlooked county park set in the foothill country of Simi Valley. The park has many trails, offering good hiking possibilities. The camp is somewhat secluded, more so than you might expect.

D

Map grid **a8**

LOS ANGELES-SAN FERNANDO VALLEY KOA

Campsites, facilities: There are 95 tent sites and 126 motor home spaces. Piped water, electrical connections, and, at some sites, sewer hookups are provided. Rest rooms, showers, a playground, a swimming pool, a recreation room, and a sanitary dump station are available. Supplies and laundry facilities are nearby. Pets are permitted on leashes.

E

Reservations, fee: Reservations accepted; $26 fee per night.

Who to contact: Phone the camp at (818)362-7785.

Location: From San Fernando, drive 2.5 miles northwest on San Fernando Road to 15900 Olden Street.

F

Trip note: This KOA camp is located on the northern outskirts of the Los Angeles basin. The Angeles National Forest, to the immediate northeast, can be accessed by Little Tujunga Road out of San Fernando. To the south about 20 miles is Hollywood. Open year-round.

G

Map grid **b1**

BIG SYCAMORE
POINT MUGU STATE PARK

Campsites, facilities: There are 54 campsites for tents or motor homes up to 31 feet long. Picnic tables and fire grills are provided. Piped water, flush toilets, and a sanitary disposal station are available. Supplies are available nearby. There is wheelchair access to trails, exhibits, picnic areas, and Sycamore Canyon campground. Pets are permitted on leashes.

H

Reservations, fee: Reserve through MISTIX at (800)444-PARK ($3.95 MISTIX fee); $14-$16 fee per night; pets $1.

I4

Who to contact: Phone the Point Mugu State Park at (818)706-1310 or (805)987-3303.

Location: From Oxnard, drive 16 miles south on Highway 1.

Trip note: This camp is set across the highway from the ocean, but is also part of Point Mugu State Park, which covers 14,980 acres in all. That gives you plenty of options. It is a popular surfing area. If that doesn't grab you, you can always just lay there in the sun and pretend you're a large, beached, marine mammal.

J

Or you can head into the interior of the park by trail to explore the foothills of the Santa Monica Mountains. A recent fire has left its mark. Open year-round.

Map grid **b1**

THORNHILL BROOME STATE BEACH

POINT MUGU STATE PARK

Campsites, facilities: There are 88 primitive campsites for tents or motor homes up to 31 feet long. Picnic tables are provided. Piped water and pit toilets are available. Supplies are available nearby. Pets are permitted on leashes.

Reservations, fee: Reserve through MISTIX at (800)444-PARK ($3.95 MISTIX fee); $7-$9 fee per night; pets $1.

Who to contact: Phone the Point Mugu State Park at (818)706-1310 or (805)987-3303.

Location: From Oxnard, drive 15 miles south on Highway 1.

Trip note: This camp is set along the ocean, but it is also a chunk of Point Mugu State Park, covering 14,980 acres in all. That gives you plenty of options. It is a popular surfing area, or hey, you can always just lay there in the sun and pretend you're a beached whale. Or you can head into the interior of the park, exploring by trail the foothills of the Santa Monica Mountains. Open year-round.

Map grid **b2**

LEO CARILLO STATE BEACH

north of Malibu

Campsites, facilities: There are 136 campsites for tents or motor homes up to 31 feet long. Picnic tables and fireplaces are provided. Piped water, flush toilets, showers, and a dump station are available. Some facilities are wheelchair accessible. Supplies are available nearby. Pets are permitted on leashes.

Reservations, fee: Reserve through MISTIX at (800)444-PARK ($3.95 MISTIX fee); $14-$16 fee per night; pets $1.

Who to contact: Phone the park at (805)706-1310 or (805)987-3303.

Location: From Santa Monica, drive 28 miles north on Highway 1 to the park. Or from Oxnard, drive 20 miles south on Highway 1 to the park.

Trip note: There are two camping areas, one along the beach, near the ocean and another in an adjacent canyon—good either way. Reservations are essential.

Map grid **c5**

MALIBU BEACH RV PARK

Campsites, facilities: There are 40 tent sites and 125 motor home spaces with full or partial hookups. Picnic tables and BBQ grills are provided. Rest rooms, showers, a playground, a laundromat, propane gas, ice, cable TV, a sanitary dump station, and a grocery store are available. Some facilities are wheelchair accessible. Pets are permitted on leashes.

Reservations, fee: Reservations accepted; $25-$35 fee per night; pets $1.

Who to contact: Phone the camp at (213)456-6052.

Location: From Malibu, drive four miles north on Highway 1.

Trip note: This is one of the few privately-developed RV parks that provides some spots for tent campers as well. It's one of the nicer spots in the area, set on a bluff overlooking the Pacific Ocean, near both Malibu Pier (for fishing) and Paradise Cove. And Hollywood is ten miles to the east. Open year-round.

Map grid e8 — DOCKWEILER BEACH RV PARK
on Pacific Ocean near Manhattan Beach

Campsites, facilities: There are 118 campsites for motor homes up to 35 feet long; 83 with full hookups. Picnic tables and BBQ grills are provided. Flush toilets, a sanitary disposal station, and a laundromat are available. Supplies are available nearby. Pets are permitted on leashes.

Reservations, fee: Reserve through MISTIX at (800)444-PARK ($3.95 MISTIX fee); $12-$20 camp use fee.

Who to contact: Phone the County Parks at (213)305-9545.

Location: From Santa Monica, drive 12 miles south on Interstate 405 to the Imperial West Highway exit. Drive about four miles west to Vista del Mar and the park.

Trip note: This layover spot for coast cruisers is just a hop from the beach and the Pacific Ocean. Open year-round.

Map grid h5 — PARSON'S LANDING
on Catalina Island

Campsites, facilities: There are no assigned sites, but the campground will hold about 200 campers. Pit toilets, fire rings, barbecue pits, and limited water are available. Pets are not permitted. Firewood, charcoal, and lighter fluid must be obtained on the island, as US Coast Guard regulations prohibit combustible materials in passenger vehicles when crossing the channel.

Reservations, fee: Reservations required; $6 fee per person per night; check in at the visitor information booth to validate your camping permit. An adult round-trip pass on the ferry costs $30.

Who to Contact: For ferry information or camp reservations phone (213)510-2800 or (213)510-0303.

Location: From Redondo, San Diego, San Pedro, Newport, or Long Beach a ferry is available that will take you to Two Harbors. From Two Harbors travel by shoreboat (check schedule) to Emerald Bay. Hike one mile to the campground.

Trip Note: This primitive campground, one of five on Catalina Island, is set on the island's northern end, seven miles from the island's isthmus and the village of Two Harbors. Primitive as it is, it can really fill up on a holiday weekend.

Map grid i5 — TWO HARBORS
on Catalina Island

Campsites, facilities: There no are designated sites, but there is room for 250 people. Flush toilets, cold showers, fire rings, barbecues, picnic tables, sun shades, and telephones are provided. A general store, a restaurant and saloon, a snack bar, tennis courts, volleyball, a laundromat, and hot showers are available in the town of Two Harbors. Firewood, charcoal, and lighter fluid must be obtained on the island, as US Coast Guard regulations prohibit combustible materials in passenger vehicles when crossing the channel. Pets are not permitted.

Reservations, fee: Reservations requested; $6 fee per person per night; check in at the visitor information booth to validate your camping permit. An adult round-trip pass on the ferry costs $30.

Who to Contact: For ferry information or camp reservations phone (213)510-2800 or (213)510-0303.

Location: From San Diego, San Pedro, Newport, Long Beach or Redondo a ferry is available that will take you directly to Two Harbors. If you are on the island

A B C D E F G H

J

at Avalon, take the bus to Two Harbors. Hike approximately one-quarter mile from the village of Two Harbors to the campground.

Trip Note: This campground is only one-quarter mile away from the village of Two Harbors. Nearby attractions include the Two Harbors Dive Station with snorkeling equipment and paddleboard rentals, and scuba tank fills to 3000 psi. There are guided tours of the island and a scheduled bus service between Two Harbors and Avalon; the bus stops at all the interior campgrounds.

Map grid i6

BLACK JACK
on Catalina Island

Campsites, facilities: There are accommodations for 75 campers. Water, chemical toilets, fire rings, barbecue pits, and a public phone are available. Firewood, charcoal, and lighter fluid must be obtained on the island, as US Coast Guard regulations prohibit you from carrying any combustible materials in passenger vehicles when crossing the channel. Pets are not permitted.

Reservations, fee: Reservations preferred; $5 fee per per person per night; $.50 fee per night for children 14 and under. An adult round-trip pass on the ferry costs $30.

Who to Contact: Phone (213)510-0688 for reservations. This camp is operated by the Los Angeles County Department of Parks and Recreation; for information you can also phone (213)510-1520.

Location:From San Diego, San Pedro, Newport, Long Beach, or Redondo a ferry is available that can take you to Avalon or Two Harbors. From either Avalon or Two Harbors take the shuttle bus to Black Jack Junction. Then hike one mile in from the junction to the campground.

Trip Note: This camp, named after Mount Black Jack (2,008 feet), is a great place to hunker down for a spell. It's also the site of the old Black Jack Mine. The camp is set at 1,500 feet elevation. If you stand in just the right spot you can see the mainland.

Map grid i6

LITTLE HARBOR
on Catalina Island

Campsites, facilities: This camp can hold 150 people. Chemical toilets, cold showers, barbecue pits, fire rings, picnic tables, and phone and shuttle bus service are available. Firewood, charcoal, and lighter fluid must be obtained on the island, as US Coast Guard regulations prohibit you from carrying any combustible materials in passenger vehicles when crossing the channel. Pets are not permitted.

Reservations, fee: Reservations preferred; $5 fee per person per night, $.50 for children 14 and under. An adult round-trip pass on the ferry costs $30.

Who to Contact: Phone (213)510-0688 for reservations. This camp is operated by the Los Angeles County Department of Parks and Recreation; for information you can also phone (213)510-1520.

Location: From San Diego, San Pedro, Newport, Long Beach, or Redondo a ferry is available that can take you to Two Harbors. You then hike seven miles to the campground.

Trip Note: Some folks consider this camp to be the pick of the campgrounds on the island. It is a gorgeous place; small wonder that some of the big Hollywood flicks have been shot here. There is plenty to do: You can swim, dive, fish, or go for day hikes. It's also set plunk on top of an historic Indian site.

Map grid j7

HERMIT GULCH
on Catalina Island

A

Campsites, facilities: There are 75 campsites. Piped water, hot showers, flush toilets, picnic tables, fire rings, barbecue pits, and a public phone are available. Firewood, charcoal, and lighter fluid must be obtained on the island, as US Coast Guard regulations prohibit you from carrying any combustible materials in passenger vehicles when crossing the channel. Pets are not permitted.

B

Reservations, fee: Reservations requested; $6 fee per person per night; children under five free. An adult round-trip pass on the ferry costs $30.

Who to Contact: Phone (213)510-0688 for reservations. This camp is operated by the Los Angeles County Department of Parks and Recreation; for information you can also phone (213)510-1520.

C

Location: From San Diego, San Pedro, Newport, Long Beach, or Redondo a ferry is available that can take you to Avalon. From Sumner Avenue in Avalon, walk up Avalon Canyon. Follow the sign that says "Avalon Canyon Road" and walk one mile. The camp is across from the picnic grounds.

D

Trip Note: This is the closest campground to the town of Avalon, the gateway to Catalina. Explore Avalon's underwater city park, play the nine-hole golf course, or visit the famous Casino. Of course, there is fishing for a variety of fish, including sea bass, sheepshead, and the challenging marlin.

E

F

G

H

J

◆ MAP 15 ◆

BEACH
TREES
5% CLUB
DESERT
URBAN
FOOTHILL
GRASSLAND
15 MILES

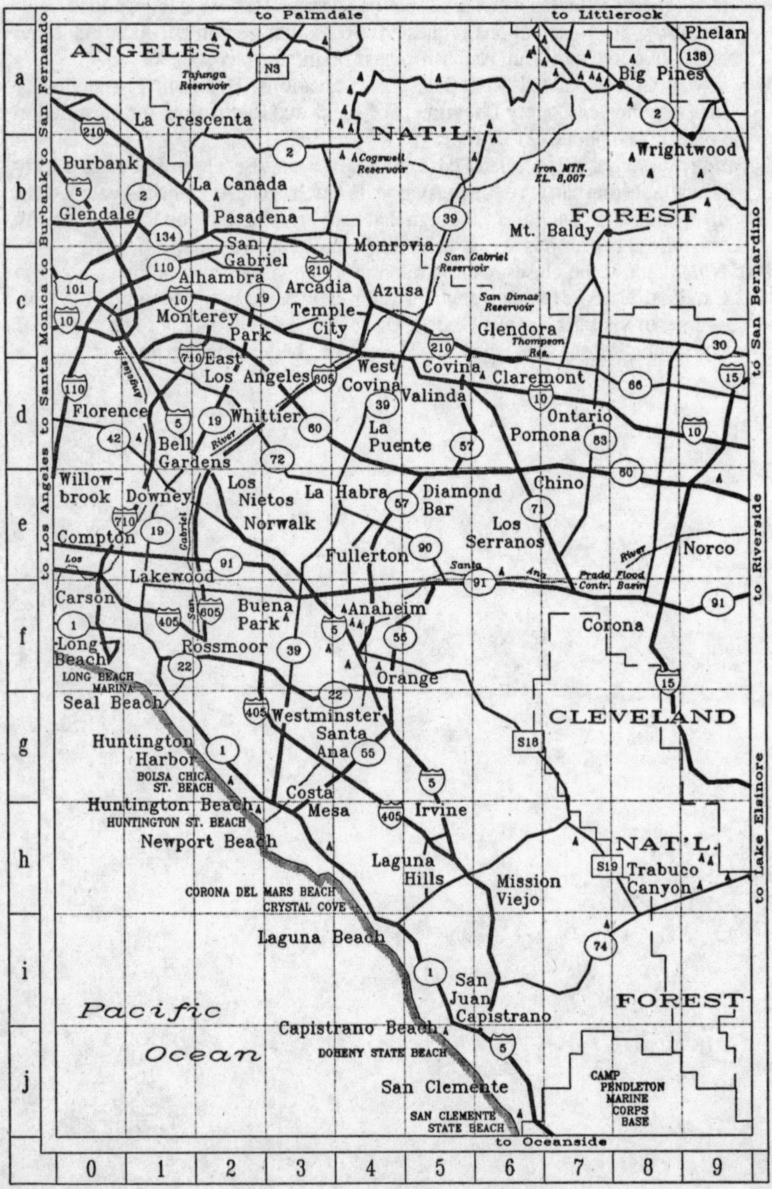

to Palmdale
to Littlerock
to Los Angeles to Santa Monica to Burbank to San Fernando
to San Bernardino
to Riverside
to Lake Elsinore
to Oceanside

ANGELES NAT'L. FOREST
Tujunga Reservoir
Cogswell Reservoir
Iron MTN. EL. 8,007
Phelan
Big Pines
Wrightwood
Mt. Baldy
La Crescenta
Burbank
La Canada
Glendale
Pasadena
San Gabriel
Monrovia
San Gabriel Reservoir
San Dimas Reservoir
Alhambra
Arcadia
Azusa
Monterey Park
Temple City
Glendora
Thompson Res.
East Los Angeles
West Covina
Covina
Valinda
Claremont
Florence
Whittier
La Puente
Ontario
Pomona
Bell Gardens
Willowbrook
Downey
Los Nietos
Norwalk
La Habra
Diamond Bar
Chino
Compton
Fullerton
Los Serranos
Norco
Lakewood
Carson
Santa Ana River
Prado Flood Contr. Basin
Buena Park
Anaheim
Corona
Long Beach
Rossmoor
LONG BEACH MARINA
Seal Beach
Orange
CLEVELAND NAT'L. FOREST
Westminster
Santa Ana
Huntington Harbor
BOLSA CHICA ST. BEACH
Huntington Beach
HUNTINGTON ST. BEACH
Costa Mesa
Irvine
Newport Beach
Laguna Hills
Mission Viejo
Trabuco Canyon
CORONA DEL MARS BEACH
CRYSTAL COVE
Laguna Beach
San Juan Capistrano
Pacific Ocean
Capistrano Beach
DOHENY STATE BEACH
San Clemente
SAN CLEMENTE STATE BEACH
CAMP PENDLETON MARINE CORPS BASE

a b c d e f g h i j
0 1 2 3 4 5 6 7 8 9

Map grid **a2**

MOUNT PACIFICO

on Pacific Crest Trail

ANGELES NATIONAL FOREST

Campsites, facilities: There are ten tent sites. Picnic tables and fire pits, vault toilets are provided. There is **no piped water,** so bring your own. Pets are permitted on leashes.

Reservations, fee: No reservations, no fee.

Who to contact: Phone the Angeles National Forest Arroyo Seco District Office at (818)790-1151.

Location: From Interstate 210 north of Pasadena, take the Angeles Crest Highway (Highway 2) exit and drive north for nine miles. Turn left onto Angeles Forest Highway (County Road N3) and drive about 12 miles to the intersection with Santa Clara Divide Road at Three Points (there is a sign). Turn left and drive about six miles to the signed gate. Turn left and then take the dirt road for four miles to the campground. The gate is locked in the winter when the road is impassable; walk in at that time.

Trip note: Backpackers can use Mt. Pacifico as the launching pad for a multi-day trip. That is because the Pacific Crest Trail actually intersects with the camp. Being at 7,100 feet elevation means hikers can start the hike by going down instead of up. Open from April to October.

Map grid **a2**

LIGHTNING POINT GROUP CAMP

near Mt. Gleason

ANGELES NATIONAL FOREST

Campsites, facilities: There are several group campsites here. Piped water, picnic tables, and fire pits are provided. Flush toilets are available. Pets are permitted on leashes.

Reservations, fee: Reservations requested; $30 group fee per night.

Who to contact: Phone the Angeles National Forest Tujunga District Office at (818)899-1900.

Location: From Interstate 210 north of Pasadena, take the Angeles Crest Highway (Highway 2) exit and drive north for nine miles. Turn left onto Angeles Forest Highway (County Road N3) and drive about 12 miles to the Santa Clara Divide Road intersection. Turn left and drive ten miles to the entrance road on the left.

Trip note: This group camp is out in the middle of nowhere. If you want to climb Mt. Gleason, trailheads are located at the Messenger Flats camp and also three miles to the east on Forest Service Road 3N32 (left side of the road). The elevation is 6,200 feet. Open from April to November.

Map grid **a2**

MESSENGER FLATS

near Mt. Gleason

ANGELES NATIONAL FOREST

Campsites, facilities: There are ten tent sites. Piped water, picnic tables, fire pits, and vault toilets are provided. Pets are permitted on leashes.

Reservations, fee: No reservations; $5 fee per night.

Who to contact: Phone the Angeles National Forest Tujunga District Office at (818)899-1900.

Location: From Interstate 210 north of Pasadena, take the Angeles Crest Highway (Highway 2) exit and drive nine miles north. Turn left onto Angeles Forest Highway (County Road N3) and drive about 12 miles to the intersection with

Santa Clara Divide Road. Turn left and continue 11 miles to the campground.

Trip note: The Pacific Crest Trail is routed right past this camp, which makes it a good jump-off spot both for backpackers starting a multi-day trip or hikers looking to climb Mt. Gleason, about a half-mile trip to the east. The elevation is 5,900 feet. Open from April to November.

Map grid a3

MONTE CRISTO

on Mill Creek

ANGELES NATIONAL FOREST

Campsites, facilities: There are 19 campsites for tents or motor homes up to 32 feet long. Piped water, fire pits, vault toilets, and picnic tables are provided. Pets are permitted on leashes.

Reservations, fee: No reservations; $5 fee per night.

Who to contact: Phone the Angeles National Forest Tujunga District Office at (818)899-1900.

Location: From Interstate 210 north of Pasadena, take the Angeles Crest Highway (Highway 2) exit and drive north for nine miles. Turn left onto Angeles Forest Highway (County Road N3) and drive about nine miles to the campground.

Trip note: This is a developed Forest Service camp set on Mill Creek at 3,600 feet elevation, just west of Iron Mountain. A target shooting area is located about two miles away: Drive south on Forest Service Road FH59, then turn north on the road that parallels the Middle Fork of Mill Creek. Open all year.

Map grid a4

BANDIDO GROUP CAMP

near Pacific Crest Trail

ANGELES NATIONAL FOREST

Campsites, facilities: There are 25 campsites for tents or motor homes up to 16 feet long. The camp will accommodate up to 120 people. Piped water, fire pits, vault toilets, and picnic tables are provided. Pets are permitted on leashes. Corrals and a water trough are available.

Reservations, fee: Reservations requested; $50 fee per night.

Who to contact: Phone the Angeles National Forest Concessionaire at (818)578-1079 or (818)449-1749.

Location: From Interstate 210 north of Pasadena, take the Angeles Crest Highway (Highway 2) exit and drive north for nine miles. Turn left onto Angeles Forest Highway (County Road N3) and drive about 12 miles to the intersection with Santa Clara Divide Road at Three Points (there is a sign). Turn left and drive two miles to the campground.

Trip note: This is a base camp for groups preparing to hike off into the surrounding wilderness. A trail out of the camp heads north and intersects with the Pacific Crest Trail a little over one mile away at Three Points. Any questions? Rangers at the nearby Chilao Visitor Station (a mile to the west) can answer them. The elevation is 5,100 feet. Open from April to December.

Map grid a4

HORSE FLATS

near San Gabriel Wilderness

ANGELES NATIONAL FOREST

Campsites, facilities: There are 25 campsites for tents or motor homes up to 22 feet long. Piped water, fire pits, vault toilets, and picnic tables are provided. A grocery store is nearby. Pets are permitted on leashes.

Reservations, fee: No reservations; $8 fee per night.

Who to contact: Phone the Angeles National Forest Arroyo Seco District Office at (818)790-1151.

Location: From Interstate 210 north of Pasadena, take the Angeles Crest Highway (Highway 2) exit and drive north for nine miles. Turn left onto Angeles Forest Highway (County Road N3) and drive about 12 miles to the intersection with Santa Clara Divide Road at Three Points (there is a sign). Turn left and drive three miles to the signed campground.

Trip note: This is one of the four options in the immediate area—Bandido, Chilao, and Coulter are the other three. Horse Flats is set at 5,500 feet elevation along a national recreation trail and is close to the Chilao Visitor Center. Several trails into the San Gabriel Wilderness are nearby. Open from May to November.

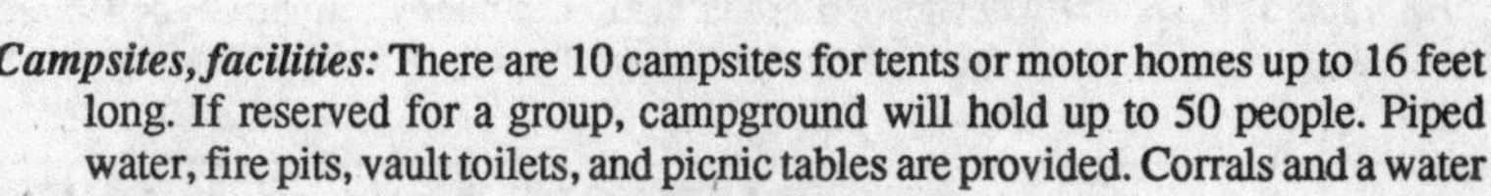

Map grid a4

SULPHUR SPRINGS GROUP CAMP

near Pacific Crest Trail

ANGELES NATIONAL FOREST

Campsites, facilities: There are 10 campsites for tents or motor homes up to 16 feet long. If reserved for a group, campground will hold up to 50 people. Piped water, fire pits, vault toilets, and picnic tables are provided. Corrals and a water trough are available. Pets are permitted on leashes.

Reservations, fee: No reservations for individual sites; reservations requested for groups; $5 single camp fee per night; $50 group fee per night.

Who to contact: Phone the Angeles National Forest Concessionaire at (818)578-1079 or (818)449-1749.

Location: From Interstate 210 north of Pasadena, take the Angeles Crest Highway (Highway 2) exit and drive north for nine miles. Turn left onto Angeles Forest Highway (County Road N3) and drive about 12 miles to the intersection with Santa Clara Divide Road at Three Points (there is a sign). Turn left and drive five miles to the campground entrance road on the right (it will seem like the continuation of the road you're on).

Trip note: Set in the pines along the Pacific Crest Trail, this makes a good base camp for groups preparing to hike off into the surrounding wilderness. Any questions? Rangers at the nearby Chilao Visitor Station can answer them. The elevation is 5,100 feet. Open from April to December.

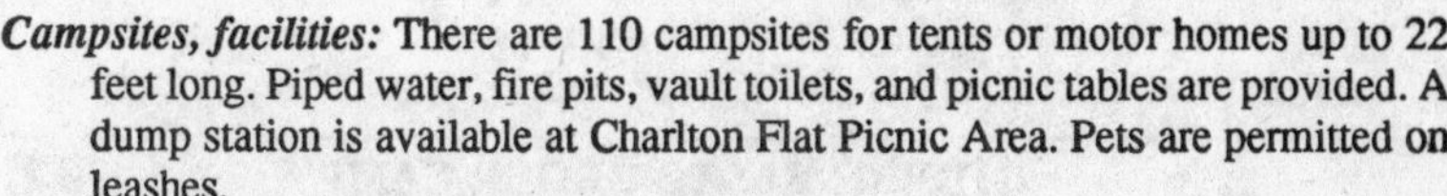

Map grid a4

CHILAO

near San Gabriel Wilderness

ANGELES NATIONAL FOREST

Campsites, facilities: There are 110 campsites for tents or motor homes up to 22 feet long. Piped water, fire pits, vault toilets, and picnic tables are provided. A dump station is available at Charlton Flat Picnic Area. Pets are permitted on leashes.

Reservations, fee: No reservations; $8 fee per night.

Who to contact: Phone the Angeles National Forest Arroyo Seco District Office at (818)790-1151.

Location: From Interstate 210 north of Pasadena, take the Angeles Crest Highway (Highway 2) exit and drive 26 miles northeast to the signed campground entrance road on the left.

Trip note: This popular trailhead camp gets a lot of use. And it's easy to see why, with the Chilao Visitor Center (any questions?) located nearby and a national recreation trail running right by the camp. Access to the Pacific Crest Trail is two miles north at Three Points, with parking available there. The elevation is 5,200 feet. Open from May to November.

Map grid **a4**

COULTER GROUP CAMP

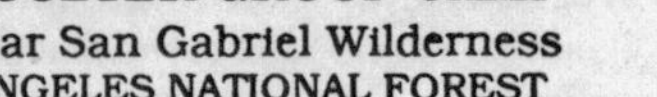

near San Gabriel Wilderness

ANGELES NATIONAL FOREST

Campsites, facilities: There is one large campsite that will accommodate up to 50 people. No motor homes are permitted. Piped water, picnic tables, fire pits, and vault toilets are provided. Pets are permitted on leashes.

Reservations, fee: Reservations requested; $45 group fee per night.

Who to contact: Phone the Angeles National Forest Concessionaire at (818)449-1749 or (818)578-1079.

Location: From Interstate 210 north of Pasadena, take the Angeles Crest Highway (Highway 2) exit and drive north for 25 miles to the signed campground.

Trip note: This specially designated group camp is actually set within the Chilao camp. For details see the trip note for Chilao. The elevation is 5,300 feet. Open from May to November.

Map grid **a5**

BUCKHORN

near Kratka Ridge

ANGELES NATIONAL FOREST

Campsites, facilities: There are 40 campsites for tents or motor homes up to 16 feet long. Piped water, fire pits, vault toilets, and picnic tables are provided. Pets are permitted on leashes.

Reservations, fee: No reservations; $10 fee per night.

Who to contact: Phone the Angeles National Forest Arroyo Seco District Office at (818)790-1151.

Location: From Interstate 210 north of Pasadena, take the Angeles Crest Highway (Highway 2) and drive 35 miles northeast to the signed campground entrance.

Trip note: This is a prime jump-off spot for backpackers in Angeles National Forest. The camp is set among huge pine and cedar trees, along a small creek near Mt. Waterman (8,038 feet elevation). The High Desert National Recreational Trail leads northward from the camp into the backcountry, over Burkhart Saddle, west around Devil's Punchbowl County Park to the South Fork campground. Then it heads south into the Islip trailhead, east past Eagle's Roost and Ridgecrest picnic areas, and south again for the last mile back to Buckhorn camp. It's a 20-mile hike, with the South Fork camp situated perfectly ten miles out to make it a weekend trip. A shorter trip to popular Cooper Canyon is 1.5 miles from Buckhorn and is accessible by trail. Open from May to October.

Map grid **a6**

DEER FLATS GROUP CAMP

near Crystal Lake

ANGELES NATIONAL FOREST

Campsites, facilities: There are nine group campsites which will accommodate up to 300 people. Piped water, picnic tables, fire pits, and vault toilets are provided. A grocery store and a visitor information center are nearby. Pets are permitted on leashes.

Reservations, fee: Reservations required; fee varies by site.

Who to contact: Phone the Angeles National Forest Mt. Baldy District Office at (818)335-1251.

Location: From Interstate 210, take the Azuza Canyon exit. Drive 25 miles north on San Gabriel Canyon Road (Highway 39) to the Crystal Lake Recreation Area.

A

Trip note: This is good spot to bring a Boy or Girl Scout. It is located about a mile from Crystal Lake at 6,300 feet. A nearby trail leads north from camp and in two miles, intersects with the Pacific Crest Trail. From there, you could go to Mexico or Canada, though it might take six months or so. Open from May to October.

B

Map grid a6

SOUTH FORK GROUP CAMP

on Big Rock Creek
ANGELES NATIONAL FOREST

C

Campsites, facilities: There is one group campsite here which will accommodate up to 50 people. Piped water, picnic tables, fire pits, and vault toilets are provided. A grocery store is nearby. Pets are permitted on leashes.

Reservations, fee: Reservations requested; $40 fee per night.

Who to contact: Phone the Angeles National Forest District Office at (805)944-2187.

D

Location: From Highway 138 in Pearblossom, turn south on Longview Road. Turn left on Valyermo Road and drive past the ranger station. Turn right on Big Rock Road and continue up the canyon. Turn right at the signed dirt road.

Trip note: This designated group camp is right next to the South Fork camp. For details, see that trip note. Open from May to November.

E

Map grid a6

SOUTH FORK

on Big Rock Creek
ANGELES NATIONAL FOREST

F

Campsites, facilities: There are 20 campsites for tents or motor homes up to 15 feet long. Piped water, fire pits, vault toilets, and picnic tables are provided. Pets are permitted on leashes.

Reservations, fee: No reservations; $7 fee per night.

Who to contact: Phone the Angeles National Forest Valyermo District Office at (805)944-2187.

G

Location: From Highway 138 in Pearblossom, turn south on Longview Road. Turn left on Valyermo Road and drive past the ranger station. Turn right on Big Rock Road and continue up the canyon. Turn right at the signed dirt road.

Trip note: This is an ideal jump-off point for backpackers. It is set at 4,600 feet elevation along the South Fork of Big Rock Creek at the intersection of three trails. If you head west, the trail leads into Devil's Punchbowl County Park. If you head east, the trail goes to the edge of the Sheep Mountain Wilderness and intersects with the Pacific Crest Trail. Open from May to November.

H

Map grid a7

JACKSON FLAT GROUP CAMP

near Pacific Crest Trail
ANGELES NATIONAL FOREST

15

Campsites, facilities: There are five group campsites here which will accommodate 40 to 50 people each. Piped water, picnic tables, fire pits, and vault toilets are provided. Pets are permitted on leashes.

Reservations, fee: Reservations requested; call for fee.

J

Who to contact: Phone the Angeles National Forest Concessionaire at (619)249-3483.

Location: From Interstate 15 near Cajon, take Highway 138 west. Turn left (west) on Angeles Crest Highway and drive five miles to Wrightwood. Continue for three miles to Big Pines. Bear left and continue on Angeles Crest Highway for two miles. Turn right, opposite the sign for Grassy Hollow Campground, and drive one mile to the campground.

Trip note: This is a good spot for a group to overnight, assess themselves, and get information prior to heading out into the surrounding wildlands. The camp is set in the Angeles National Forest high country at 7,500 feet elevation, near the Grassy Hollow Visitor Center. The Pacific Crest Trail passes just north of camp and is reached by a short connecting link trail. Open June to October.

Map grid **a7**

GRASSY HOLLOW

on Pacific Crest Trail
ANGELES NATIONAL FOREST

Campsites, facilities: There are 15 campsites for tents or motor homes up to 18 feet long. Piped water, fire pits, vault toilets, and picnic tables are provided. Pets are permitted on leashes.

Reservations, fee: No reservations; $10 fee per night.

Who to contact: Phone the Angeles National Forest Valyermo District Office at (805)944-2187.

Location: From Interstate 15 near Cajon, take Highway 138 west. Turn left (west) on Angeles Crest Highway and drive five miles to Wrightwood. Continue for three miles to Big Pines. Bear left and continue on Angeles Crest Highway for two miles. Turn left at the signed campground entrance.

Trip note: This ideal jump-off camp for backpackers is set right along the Pacific Crest Trail at 7,400 feet elevation. That means a lot of the "up" has already been taken care of. The Sheep Mountain Wilderness is located directly to the south. There is a trail that traces Vincent Gulch, located two miles to the west at Lamel Spring. Want more? Got more: Inspiration Point is located less than a mile to the east, just off the road. This campground may convert to a visitor center in 1991. Open from May to November.

Map grid **a7**

APPLE TREE

near Jackson Lake
ANGELES NATIONAL FOREST

Campsites, facilities: There are eight tent sites and one group site for up to 50 people. Piped water, picnic tables, fire pits, and vault toilets are provided. Pets are permitted on leashes.

Reservations, fee: No reservations for individual sites; reservations necessary for group site (call number below); $10 fee per night.

Who to contact: Phone the Angeles National Forest Valyermo District Office at (805)944-2187. For group camp information and reservations, call (619)249-3483.

Location: From Interstate 15 near Cajon, take Highway 138 west. Turn left (west) on Angeles Crest Highway and drive five miles to Wrightwood. Continue for three miles to Big Pines. Bear right on Big Pines Highway (County Road N4) and drive two miles to the campground.

Trip note: This is one of the four camps set on Big Pines "Highway" near Jackson Lake, a small lake located about one-half mile up the road. Any questions? Rangers can answer them at the nearby Big Pines Visitor Information Center and Ski Complexes. The elevation is 6,200 feet. Open from April to November.

Map grid **a7**

MOUNTAIN OAK

near Jackson Lake
ANGELES NATIONAL FOREST

Campsites, facilities: There are 17 campsites for tents or motor homes up to 18 feet long. Piped water, fire pits, and picnic tables are provided. Flush toilets are available. Groceries and propane gas are nearby. Pets are permitted on leashes.
Reservations, fee: No reservations; $10 fee per night.
Who to contact: Phone the Angeles National Forest Valyermo District Office at (805)944-2187.
Location: From Interstate 15 near Cajon, take Highway 138 west. Turn left (west) on Angeles Crest Highway and drive five miles to Wrightwood. Continue for three miles to Big Pines. Bear right on Big Pines Highway (County Road N4) and drive three miles to the campground.
Trip note: This is one of four camps within a mile, set to the west of Jackson Lake on Big Pines Highway. The others are Lake, Peavine, and Apple Tree. The elevation is 6,200 feet. Open from May to October.

Map grid **a7**

BIG ROCK

on Big Rock Creek
ANGELES NATIONAL FOREST

5% CLUB

Campsites, facilities: There are eight campsites for tents. Fire pits, vault toilets, and picnic tables are provided. There is **no piped water,** so bring your own. Pets are permitted on leashes.
Reservations, fee: No reservations, no fee.
Who to contact: Phone the Angeles National Forest Valyermo District Office at (805)944-2187.
Location: From Highway 138 in Pearblossom, turn south on Longview Road. Turn left on Valyermo Road and drive past the ranger station. Turn right on Big Rock Road and continue up the canyon past the South Fork camp turn and past Camp Fenner to the campground entrance road on the right.
Trip note: This is a good spot for four-wheel drive cowboys. It is a primitive Forest Service Camp set at the head of Fenner Canyon along Big Rock Creek. Forest Service Road 4N11 to the southeast is a four-wheel drive road that connects to a network of backcountry roads and hiking trails. A Forest Service map is essential. The elevation is 5,550 feet. Open from June to October.

Map grid **a7**

SYCAMORE FLAT

on Big Rock Creek
ANGELES NATIONAL FOREST

Campsites, facilities: There are 11 campsites for tents or motor homes up to 22 feet long. Piped water, fire pits, vault toilets, and picnic tables are provided. Pets are permitted on leashes.
Reservations, fee: No reservations; $7 fee per night.
Who to contact: Phone the Angeles National Forest Valyermo District Office at (805)944-2187.
Location: From Highway 138 in Pearblossom, turn south on Longview Road. Drive to Valyermo Road and turn left. Drive past the ranger station. Turn right on Big Rock Road and drive about two miles up the canyon to the campground.
Trip note: This is a developed camp set just inside the northern boundary of Angeles National Forest. No trails lead out from the camp; the nearest trailhead is located

at the South Fork camp, which is a little over one mile to the north. The elevation is 4,300 feet. Open year-round.

Map grid **a7**

LAKE

on Jackson Lake

ANGELES NATIONAL FOREST

Campsites, facilities: There are eight campsites for tents or motor homes up to 18 feet long. Piped water, fire pits, vault toilets, and picnic tables are provided. Pets are permitted on leashes.

Reservations, fee: No reservations; $10 fee per night.

Who to contact: Phone the Angeles National Forest Valyermo District Office at (805)944-2187.

Location: From Interstate 15 near Cajon, take Highway 138 west. Turn left (west) on Angeles Crest Highway and drive five miles to Wrightwood. Continue for three miles to Big Pines. Bear right on Big Pines Highway (County Road N4) and drive 2.5 miles to the campground.

Trip note: This is a pretty setting set on the southeast shore of little Jackson Lake. Of the four camps within a mile this is the only one set right along the lake. The elevation is 6,100 feet. Open from May to November.

Map grid **a7**

PEAVINE

near Jackson Lake

ANGELES NATIONAL FOREST

Campsites, facilities: There are four tent sites. Piped water, picnic tables, fire pits, and vault toilets are provided. A grocery store and propane gas are nearby. Pets are permitted on leashes.

Reservations, fee: No reservations; $8 fee per night.

Who to contact: Phone the Angeles National Forest Valyermo District Office at (805)944-2187.

Location: From Interstate 15 near Cajon, take Highway 138 west. Turn left (west) on Angeles Crest Highway and drive five miles to Wrightwood. Continue for three miles to Big Pines. Bear right on Big Pines Highway (County Road N4) and drive 2.5 miles to the campground.

Trip note: This tiny camp, one of the four in the immediate area, is set at 6,100 feet elevation. Little eight-acre Jackson Lake is located just a half mile to the west. Open from May to November.

Map grid **a8**

TABLE MOUNTAIN

ANGELES NATIONAL FOREST

Campsites, facilities: There are 115 campsites for tents or motor homes up to 22 feet long. Piped water, fire pits, vault toilets, and picnic tables are provided. Pets are permitted on leashes.

Reservations, fee: No reservations; $10 fee per night.

Who to contact: Phone the Angeles National Forest Valyermo District Office at (805)944-2187.

Location: From Interstate 15 near Cajon, take Highway 138 west. Turn left (west) on Angeles Crest Highway and drive five miles to Wrightwood. Continue for three miles to Big Pines. Turn right on Table Mountain Road and drive one mile to the campground.

Trip note: This is a base camp for campers with four-wheel drive rigs because there are several rugged and remote roads in the area. In fact, it takes a four-wheeler to reach this camp. The nearby Big Pine Visitor Information Center, located one mile to the south, can provide maps and information on road conditions. The elevation is 7,200 feet. Open from May to October.

A

Map grid **a8**

BLUE RIDGE

on Pacific Crest Trail
ANGELES NATIONAL FOREST

B

Campsites, facilities: There are eight campsites for tents or motor homes up to 16 feet long. Fire pits, vault toilets, and picnic tables are provided. There is **no piped water,** so bring your own. Pets are permitted on leashes.

Reservations, fee: No reservations, no fee.

Who to contact: Phone the Angeles National Forest Valyermo District Office at (805)944-2187.

C

Location: From Interstate 15 near Cajon, take Highway 138 west. Turn left (west) on Angeles Crest Highway and drive five miles to Wrightwood. Continue for three miles to Big Pines. Bear left and continue on Angeles Crest Highway for 1.5 miles. Turn left (opposite Inspiration Point) on Blue Ridge Road and drive three miles to the campground.

D

Trip note: Set high in Angeles National Forest at 8,000 feet, this makes an ideal jump-off spot for a multi-day backpacking trip. The Pacific Crest Trail runs right alongside the camp. Guffy camp, also located aside the PCT, provides an option two miles to the southeast, but it takes a four-wheel drive vehicle to get there. Open from June to October.

E

Map grid **b2**

MILLARD

near Millard Falls
ANGELES NATIONAL FOREST

F

Campsites, facilities: There are five tent sites. Piped water, picnic tables, fire pits, and vault toilets are provided. Pets are permitted on leashes.

Reservations, fee: No reservations, no fee.

Who to contact: Phone the Angeles National Forest Arroyo Seco District Office at (818)790-1151.

G

Location: From Interstate 210 north of Pasadena, take the Lake Avenue exit north to Loma Alta Drive. Turn west (left) on Loma Alta Drive and drive to the Chaney Trail (at the flashing yellow light). Follow the signs to the campground.

Trip note: This tiny camp can be used as a launching point for some excellent hikes. One trail out of camp leads to Inspiration Point and continues farther to San Gabriel Peak. Millard Falls, best viewed in late winter and early spring, is within a mile of the campground. The camp is set near a creek in oak and alder woodlands. The elevation is 1,200 feet. Open year-round.

H

Map grid **b4**

WEST FORK WALK-IN

on the West Fork of San Gabriel River
ANGELES NATIONAL FOREST

I5

Campsites, facilities: There are seven tent sites. Picnic tables, fire pits, and vault toilets are provided. There is **no piped water,** so bring your own.

Reservations, fee: No reservations, no fee.

Who to contact: Phone the Angeles National Forest Arroyo Seco District Office at (818)790-1151.

J

Location: From Interstate 210 north of Pasadena, take the Angeles Crest Highway (Highway 2) and drive about 14 miles to the Red Box Ranger Station. Park in the lot there, walk in through the gate (on Red Box-Rincon Road) to the dirt road (not the paved one), and walk-in about three miles to the campground.

Trip note: It takes a circuitous drive and a three-mile hike to reach this camp, but for backpackers it is worth it. It is set along the West Fork of the San Gabriel River amid pine woodlands, with two national recreational trails intersecting just south of the camp. The elevation is 3,000 feet. Open from April to November.

Map grid b4

VALLEY FORGE

on San Gabriel River

ANGELES NATIONAL FOREST

Campsites, facilities: There are 17 tent sites. Piped water, picnic tables, fire pits, and vault toilets are provided. **No piped water.**

Reservations, fee: No reservations; no fee.

Who to contact: Phone the Angeles National Forest Arroyo Seco District Office at (818)790-1151.

Location: From Interstate 210 north of Pasadena, take the Angeles Crest Highway (Highway 2) and drive about 14 miles to the Red Box Ranger Station. Follow the signs to the campground.

Trip note: This is a good camp for fishermen or hikers. For fishermen, the adjacent West Fork of the San Gabriel River is stocked with trout in the early summer. For hikers, a national recreation trail passes close to the camp. If the gate is locked so that you can't drive through, just walk in. The elevation is 3,500 feet. Open from April to November.

Map grid b6

CRYSTAL LAKE

ANGELES NATIONAL FOREST

Campsites, facilities: There are 176 campsites for tents or motor homes up to 22 feet long. Piped water, fire pits, and picnic tables are provided. Flush toilets are available. A grocery store and a visitor information center are nearby. Pets are permitted on leashes.

Reservations, fee: No reservations; $8 fee per night.

Who to contact: Phone the Angeles National Forest Mt. Baldy District Office at (818)335-1251.

Location: From Interstate 210, take the Azuza Canyon exit. Drive 25 miles north on San Gabriel Canyon Road (Highway 39) to the Crystal Lake Recreation Area.

Trip note: The few folks who know of this spot love it. It is a pretty camp nestled near little Crystal Lake at 5,800 feet in the Angeles National Forest. The lake is stocked with rainbow trout on a seasonal basis. Open year-round.

Map grid b6

COLDBROOK

on the North Fork of San Gabriel River

ANGELES NATIONAL FOREST

Campsites, facilities: There are 25 campsites for tents or motor homes up to 22 feet long. Piped water, fire pits, vault toilets, and picnic tables are provided. Pets are permitted on leashes.

Reservations, fee: No reservations; $8 fee per night.

Who to contact: Phone the Angeles National Forest Mt. Baldy District Office at (818)335-1251.

Location: From Interstate 210, take the Azuza Canyon exit. Drive 18 miles north on San Gabriel Canyon Road (Highw

Trip note: This is one of the prime spots in t Fork of the San Gabriel River. The strea early summer. About one-quarter mile fr backpacking trip into the San Gabriel Wilden Open year-round.

Map grid b8

LUPINE
on Prairie Fork Creek
ANGELES NATIONAL FORE

Campsites, facilities: There are 11 tent sites. Picnic tables and fi Vault toilets are available. There is **no piped water,** so brin are permitted on leashes.

Reservations, fee: No reservations; no fee.

Who to contact: Phone the Angeles National Forest Valyermo Distric (805)944-2187.

Location: From Interstate 15 near Cajon, take Highway 138 west. Turn left on Angeles Crest Highway and drive five miles to Wrightwood. Continue for three miles to Big Pines. Bear left and continue on Angeles Crest Highway for 1.5 miles. Turn left (opposite Inspiration Point) on Blue Ridge Road (it's a rough, dirt road after the first three miles)and drive ten miles to the campground.

Trip note: This is a little-known, hard-to-reach camp, set at 6,500 feet elevation along Prairie Fork Creek. There's a fantastic hike that starts here. The trail is routed from the camp over Pine Mountain Ridge and then eventually to the east up Dawson Peak. Open from June to October.

Map grid b8

CABIN FLAT
5% CLUB
on Prairie Creek
ANGELES NATIONAL FOREST

Campsites, facilities: There are 12 tent sites. Picnic tables, fire pits, and vault toilets are provided. There is **no piped water,** so bring your own. Pets are permitted on leashes.

Reservations, fee: No reservations, no fee.

Who to contact: Phone the Angeles National Forest Valyermo District Office at (805)944-2187.

Location: From Interstate 15 near Cajon, take Highway 138 west. Turn left (west) on Angeles Crest Highway and drive five miles to Wrightwood. Continue for three miles to Big Pines. Bear left and continue on Angeles Crest Highway for 1.5 miles. Turn left (opposite Inspiration Point) on Blue Ridge Road and drive 12 miles to the campground (the road becomes a rough, dirt road after the first three miles).

Trip note: It takes a four-wheel drive to get here, but that done, you're guaranteed solitude along little Prairie Creek, deep in the Angeles National Forest. To get here, you will pass several other camps, including Guffy and Lupine. A short trail runs beside the stream for about one-quarter mile. The elevation is 5,400 feet. Open from May to October.

Map grid b9

GUFFY

on Pacific Crest Trail
ANGELES NATIONAL FOREST

Campsites, facilities: There are six tent sites. Picnic tables and fire pits are provided.

...e. There is **no piped water,** so bring your own. Pets ...es.

...eservations, no fee.

...ne the Angeles National Forest Valyermo District Office at ...

...Interstate 15 near Cajon, take Highway 138 west. Turn left (west) ...es Crest Highway and drive five miles to Wrightwood. Continue for ...miles to Big Pines. Bear left and continue on Angeles Crest Highway for ...miles. Turn left (opposite Inspiration Point) on Blue Ridge Road and drive ...x miles to the campground (it's a rough, dirt road after the first three miles).

...note: A short trail right out of this camp connects with the Pacific Crest Trail, and from there you can hike to Canada if you want. You say you don't want to? Anyway, it takes a four-wheel drive to reach this camp. The elevation is 8,300 feet. Open from June to October.

Map grid b9

MANKER FLATS

near Mt. Baldy
ANGELES NATIONAL FOREST

Campsites, facilities: There are 22 campsites for tents or motor homes up to 16 feet long. Piped water, flush toilets, picnic tables, and fireplaces are provided. Pets are permitted on leashes.

Reservations, fee: No reservations; $6 fee per night.

Who to contact: Phone the Angeles National Forest Mount Baldy Ranger District at (818)335-1251.

Location: From Ontario, drive six miles north on Highway 83 to Mt. Baldy Road. Drive nine miles north on Mt. Baldy Road to the campground.

Trip note: The camp is set between the Cucamonga Wilderness to the south and Sheep Mountain Wilderness to the west. There is a trail out of camp that leads to San Antonio Falls, a good side trip.

Map grid d1

DEL RIO MOBILE HOME AND RV PARK

in Los Angeles

Campsites, facilities: There are 49 motor home spaces. Piped water, electrical connections, and sewer hookups are provided. A swimming pool, a jacuzzi, propane gas, and laundry facilities are available.

Reservations, fee: Call ahead for available space and fee.

Who to contact: Phone the park at (213)560-2895.

Location: From Interstate 710 (Long Beach Freeway), take the Florence Avenue exit. Drive west on Florence Avenue to 5246 East Florence Avenue.

Trip note: This privately-operated, urban motor home park is located about 15 minutes from downtown Los Angeles and 20 minutes from Long Beach.

Map grid d6

EAST SHORE RV PARK

at Puddingstone Lake

Campsites, facilities: There are 25 walk-in tent sites and 426 motor home spaces. Piped water, electrical connections, and sewer hookups are provided at most motor home sites. Rest rooms, showers, a recreation room, a swimming pool, a grocery store, propane gas, and a laundromat are available. Pets are permitted on leashes.

Reservations, fee: Reservations accepted; $20-$23 fee per night; walk-in tent sites

$8 per person per night; pets $2.

Who to contact: Phone the camp at (714)599-8355.

Location: From Pomona, drive five miles west on Interstate 10. Take the Fairplex exit north to the first traffic light. Turn left on Via Verde and drive to the first stop sign. Turn right on Campers View and drive into the park.

Trip note: Puddingstone Lake is bigger than most folks expect any body of water in the Los Angeles basin to be and it provides all water sport activities, including boating, fishing, jet skiing, and water skiing. Side trip options include venturing north of Azusa on San Gabriel Canyon Road to Morris and San Gabriel reservoirs or farther in Angeles National Forest. Open year-round.

Map grid e6

FEATHERLY REGIONAL PARK

near Santa Ana River

Campsites, facilities: There are 120 campsites for tents or motor homes up to 40 feet long. Fireplaces and picnic tables are provided. Piped water, flush toilets, showers, a dump station, and a playground are available. A grocery store, a laundromat, and propane gas are nearby. Pets are permitted on leashes.

Reservations, fee: No reservations; $10 fee per night; pets $1.

Who to contact: Phone the park at (714)637-0210.

Location: From Interstate 5 north of Anaheim, take the Gypsum Canyon Road exit. Drive 18 miles east on Highway 91 to the park entrance.

Trip note: In the mad rush to find a spot to park an RV in the area, this regional park is often overlooked. It is located near the Santa Ana River. Side trip possibilities include Chino Hills State Park to the north, Cleveland National Forest to the south, and Lake Mathews to the southeast. Open year-round.

Map grid e9

RANCHO JURUPA COUNTY PARK

near Riverside

Campsites, facilities: There are 80 campsites for tents or motor homes. Electrical connections, piped water, fireplaces, and picnic tables are provided. Flush toilets, showers, and a dump station are available. Pets are permitted on leashes.

Reservations, fee: No reservations; $12 fee per night; pets $1.

Who to contact: Phone the park at (714)684-7032.

Location: From Interstate 15 in Riverside, turn west on Highway 60 for about three miles. Turn left on Rubidoux Boulevard and drive one-half mile. Turn left on Mission Boulevard and drive about one mile to Crestmore Boulevard. Turn right and drive 1.5 miles to the park.

Trip note: Lord, it gets hot here in the summertime. If you want a lake to jump into, you have your pick of Lake Mathews or Lake Perris, each about a 20-minute drive. In the cooler weather during spring, this county park stocks a fishing pond. That is also the best time to explore the park's modest hiking trails. The elevation is 780 feet. Open year-round.

Map grid f3

VACATIONLAND

at Disneyland

Campsites, facilities: There are 73 sites for tents and 406 spaces for motor homes, with picnic tables and full hookups provided. Rest rooms, showers, a playground, a swimming pool, a laundromat, a store, ice, a dump station, a recreation room, and propane gas are available.

Reservations, fee: Call for available space; $22-$27 fee per night.

Who to contact: Phone the park at (714)533-7270.

Location: From Interstate 5 in Anaheim, take the Harbor Boulevard exit and drive one block north. Turn left on Ball Road and drive one quarter of a mile. Turn left on West Street to 1343 S. West Street.

Trip note: When we advise calling for available space, we mean it. This camp is within walking distance of Disneyland and that is something nobody else offers. Sometimes "Vacationland" looks like an RV sales lot, but the kids will have fun. Open year-round.

Map grid f3

ANAHEIM VACATION PARK

near Knott's Berry Farm

Campsites, facilities: There are 222 motor home spaces with full hookups. Rest rooms, showers, a playground, a swimming pool, a laundromat, a store, a recreation room, and propane gas are available. A grocery store is nearby. Pets are permitted on leashes.

Reservations, fee: Reservations accepted; $24 fee per night.

Who to contact: Phone the park at (714)821-4311.

Location: From Highway 91 in Anaheim, drive one mile south on Highway 39 to 311 N. Beach Boulevard (Highway 39).

Trip note: Some of the most popular motor home parks in America are in this area, and it's easy to see why. Disneyland is nearby, and Knott's Berry Farm is within walking distance. Plus, where else are you going to park your rig?

Map grid f4

TRAVELERS WORLD RV PARK

near Disneyland

Campsites, facilities: There are 335 sites for tents or motor homes with full hookups, picnic tables, and fireplaces provided. Rest rooms, showers, a playground, a swimming pool, a laundromat, a store, a dump station, ice, a recreation room and propane gas are available. Pets are permitted on leashes.

Reservations, fee: Call for available space; $19-$23 fee per night; pets $2.50.

Who to contact: Phone the park at (714)991-0100.

Location: From Interstate 5 in Anaheim, take the Harbor Boulevard exit and drive one block north. Turn left on Ball Road and drive one block to 333 West Ball Road.

Trip note: This is one of the premium and most popular motor home parks you can find anywhere. It is easy to see why, being located just a half-mile from Disneyland, with a shuttle-tour bus option—the park bus will deliver you to Knott's Berry Farm, Wax Museum, Universal Studios, Marineland, and the Queen Mary. Open year-round.

Map grid f4

ANAHEIM JUNCTION CAMPGROUND

near Disneyland

Campsites, facilities: There are 124 sites for motor homes with full hookups and picnic tables provided. Rest rooms, showers, a playground, a swimming pool, a recreation room, a laundromat, and a small store are available. Pets are permitted on leashes.

Reservations, fee: Call for available space; $21-$26 fee per night; pets $ .50.

Who to contact: Phone the park at (714)533-0641.

Location: From Interstate 5 in Anaheim, take the Harbor Boulevard exit and drive one block north. Turn left on Ball Road and drive one-half mile. Turn left on

West Street to 1230 S. West Street.

Trip note: Location is the key here: just off Highway 5 and just a short distance from Disneyland. It is one of several RV parks in the immediate area. Open year-round.

Map grid **f4**

C C CAMPERLAND
near Disneyland

Campsites, facilities: There are 90 sites for tents or motor homes. Picnic tables and in many cases full hookups are provided. Rest rooms, showers, a video arcade, a swimming pool, a laundromat, a store, a dump station, ice, and a recreation room are available.

Reservations, fee: Call ahead for available space and fee.

Who to contact: Phone the park at (714)750-6747.

Location: From Interstate 5 in Garden Grove, drive south on Harbor Boulevard to 12262 Harbor Boulevard.

Trip note: Camperland is located nine blocks south of Disneyland, and that right there is the number one appeal. Other side trip options include Knott's Berry Farm. Open year-round.

Map grid **f4**

ANAHEIM KOA
near Disneyland

Campsites, facilities: There are 221 sites for motor homes with full hookups, picnic tables, and fireplaces provided. Rest rooms, showers, a playground, a swimming pool, a jacuzzi, a wading pool, a recreation room, a grocery store, and propane gas are available. Pets are permitted on leashes.

Reservations, fee: Call for available space; $27-$33 fee per night.

Who to contact: Phone the park at (714)533-7720.

Location: From Interstate 5 in Anaheim, take the Harbor Boulevard exit and drive one block north. Turn left on Ball Road and drive one-half mile. Turn left on West Street to 1221 S. West Street.

Trip note: This is another option for RV cruisers. Open year-round.

Map grid **f4**

ORANGELAND RECREATIONAL VEHICLE PARK
near Disneyland

Campsites, facilities: There are 212 sites for motor homes with picnic tables, fireplaces and full hookups provided. Rest rooms, showers, a playground, a video game arcade, a swimming pool, a therapy pool, a laundromat, a store, a carwash, a shuffleboard court, a dump station, ice, a recreation room, and propane gas are available. Pets are permitted on leashes.

Reservations, fee: Call for available space; $24 fee per night; pets $1.

Who to contact: Phone the park at (714)633-0414.

Location: From Interstate 5 in Orange, drive two miles north on Freeway 57. Turn east onto Katella Avenue and drive one-half mile to 1600 W. Struck Avenue.

Trip note: This park is located about five miles east of Disneyland. If the RV parks on West Street near Disneyland are filled, this spot provides a viable alternative. Open year-round.

Map grid **g2**

BOLSA CHICA STATE BEACH

near Huntington Beach

Campsites, facilities: This is an en route campsite. En route campsites are parking areas during the day. Self-contained motor homes can park for one night stays, but they must leave by 12 p.m. The beach park provides fire rings, dressing rooms, cold showers, picnic area, food service, a bicycle trail and a paved ramp for wheelchair access to the beach.

Reservations, fee: Reserve through MISTIX (800)444-CAMP ($3.95 MISTIX fee); $14-$16 fee per night.

Who to contact: Phone the park at (714)846-3460.

Location: From Huntington Beach, drive three miles up the coast on Highway 1.

Trip note: This is basically a parking lot, but a popular one. Motor home drivers can park for the night, then say adios the next morning. Open year-round.

Map grid **h2**

SUNSET VISTA

on Pacific Ocean

Campsites, facilities: There are 160 sites for motor homes up to 30 feet long. Piped water and fireplaces are provided. Flush toilets and a dump station are available. Supplies available nearby.

Reservations, fee: Call for available space; $12 fee per night.

Who to contact: Phone the park at (714)536-5280.

Location: From Interstate 405 in Huntington Beach, take the Beach Boulevard exit and drive to Highway 1 (Pacific Coast Highway). Turn north and drive to the intersection with Lake Street.

Trip note: This is the other of the two popular beach-side camps in the immediate area, both prime layovers for Highway 1 cruisers. Bolsa Chica State Beach camp provides an option. Open year-round.

Map grid **h3**

NEWPORT DUNES

near Newport Beach

Campsites, facilities: There are 600 sites for tents or motor homes, all with full hookups. Picnic tables and fireplaces are provided. Rest rooms, showers, a pool area and spa, a playground, a laundromat, a store, ice, a recreation room, a boat ramp, and boat rentals are available. Some facilities are wheelchair accessible.

Reservations, fee: Call ahead for available space and fee.

Who to contact: Phone the park at (714)729-3863.

Location: From Highway 55, drive two miles south on Interstate 405. Turn on Jamboree Road and drive southwest for five miles. Turn west (right) onto Back Bay Drive and drive a short distance to 1131 Back Bay Drive.

Trip note: This privately-operated park is set in a nice spot on the bay, with a beach, boat ramp, and storage area providing bonuses. Corona Del Mar State Beach to the west and Crystal Cove State Park to the south provide possible side trips. Open year-round.

Map grid **h7**

O'NEILL REGIONAL PARK

near Cleveland Forest

Campsites, facilities: There are 150 campsites for tents or motor homes up to 35 feet long. Piped water, fireplaces, and picnic tables are provided. Flush toilets, showers, a playground, and a dump station are available. A grocery store is nearby. Pets are permitted on leashes.

Reservations, fee: No reservations; $10 fee per night; pets $1.

Who to contact: Phone the park at (714)858-9365.

Location: From Interstate 5 in Laguna Hills, take the County Road S18 (El Toro Road) exit and drive east (past El Toro) for 13 miles. Turn right onto Live Oak Canyon Road (County Road S19) and drive about three miles to the park.

Trip note: This park is just far enough off the main drag to get missed by the Highway 5 cruisers. It is set near Trabuco Canyon, adjacent to Cleveland National Forest to the east. Several roads near this park lead to trailheads into the Cleveland National Forest. The elevation is 1,000 feet. Open year-round.

Map grid h9

UPPER SAN JUAN

CLEVELAND NATIONAL FOREST

Campsites, facilities: There are 18 campsites for tents or motor homes up to 18 feet long. Fireplaces and picnic tables are provided. Piped water and vault toilets are available. Pets are permitted on leashes.

Reservations, fee: No reservations; $7 fee per night.

Who to contact: Phone the Cleveland National Forest Headquarters at (619)557-5050.

Location: From Interstate 5 in San Juan Capistrano, drive 21 miles northeast on Highway 74 (Ortega Highway).

Trip note: This is the best camp for hikers in this region of Cleveland National Forest. It is set among the oaks, with trailheads for hikes south into San Mateo Canyon Wilderness and north into the Santa Ana Mountains. The elevation is 1,800 feet. Open from April to October.

Map grid h9

FALCON GROUP CAMP

in Santa Ana Mountains

CLEVELAND NATIONAL FOREST

Campsites, facilities: There are three campsites for tents or motor homes up to 16 feet long. Piped water, fireplaces, and picnic tables are provided. Vault toilets are available. A grocery store is nearby. Pets are permitted on leashes.

Reservations, fee: Reserve through MISTIX at (800)283-CAMP ($6 MISTIX fee); $35-$70 fee per group per night.

Who to contact: Phone the Cleveland National Forest Headquarters at (619)557-5050.

Location: From Interstate 15 in Lake Elsinore, take the Highway 74 exit and drive 12 miles west. Turn right (north) on Forest Service Road 6S05 and drive about seven miles to the campground entrance on your left.

Trip note: If you're planning a group outing, this camp provides an option to Blue Jay camp. The campground is at the trailheads for the San Juan Trail and the Chiquito Trail, both of which lead into the backcountry wilderness, and the Santa Ana Mountains. Open from May to September.

Map grid h9

BLUE JAY

in Santa Ana Mountains

CLEVELAND NATIONAL FOREST

Campsites, facilities: There are eight sites for tents only and 43 campsites for tents or motor homes up to 22 feet long. Piped water, fireplaces, and picnic tables are provided. Chemical toilets are available and a grocery store is nearby. Pets are permitted on leashes.

Reservations, fee: Some sites by reservation only; phone MISTIX at (800)283-CAMP ($6 MISTIX fee); $7 fee per night.

Who to contact: Phone the Cleveland National Forest Headquarters at (619)557-5050.

Location: From Interstate 15 at Lake Elsinore, take the Highway 74 exit and drive 12 miles west. Turn right (north) on Forest Service Road 6S05 and drive about seven miles to the campground entrance on your left.

Trip note: The few hikers who know of this spot like it and keep coming back. It is one of three camps in the immediate area, located deep in the Santa Ana Mountains. The trailheads to the San Juan Trail and the Chiquito Trail, both of which lead into the backcountry wilderness and the Santa Ana Mountains, are adjacent to the camp. A Forest Service map is strongly advised. The elevation is 3,300 feet. Open year-round.

Map grid h9

EL CARISO CAMPGROUNDS

near Lake Elsinore
CLEVELAND NATIONAL FOREST

Campsites, facilities: There are 43 campsites for tents or motor homes up to 22 feet long. Piped water, fireplaces, and picnic tables are provided. Vault toilets are available. Pets are permitted on leashes.

Reservations, fee: No reservations; $7 fee per night.

Who to contact: Phone the Cleveland National Forest Headquarters at (619)557-5050.

Location: From Interstate 5 in San Juan Capistrano, drive 24 miles northeast on Highway 74 (Ortega Highway). Or from Interstate 15 in Lake Elsinore, drive 12 miles west on Highway 74 to the campground.

Trip note: This pretty, shaded spot at 3,000 feet is just inside the border of Cleveland National Forest with Lake Elsinore to the east. Hikers should head west to the Upper San Juan campground. Open from April through November.

Map grid i7

CASPERS REGIONAL PARK

on San Juan River

Campsites, facilities: There are 42 campsites for tents or motor homes. Fireplaces and picnic tables are provided. Piped water, flush toilets, showers, a dump station, and a playground are available. No one under eighteen is allowed to camp here.

Reservations, fee: No reservations; $10 fee per night.

Who to contact: Phone the park at (714)831-2174.

Location: From San Juan Capistrano, drive eight miles northeast on Highway 74 to the park entrance.

Trip note: Highway 74 provides easy access to this regional park, which is bordered to the south by the San Juan River and to the east by the Cleveland National Forest and the San Mateo Canyon Wilderness. Open year-round.

Map grid j5

DOHENY STATE BEACH

on Dana Point Harbor

Campsites, facilities: There are 121 campsites for tents or motor homes. No hookups provided. Fireplaces and picnic tables are provided. Flush toilets, showers, a dump station, exhibits, and food service (summer only) are available. Propane gas is nearby. Camping, picnicking, food service, and exhibit areas are wheelchair accessible. Pets are permitted on leashes in campground only, not on the beach.

Reservations, fee: Reserve through MISTIX at (800)446-PARK ($3.95 MISTIX fee); $14-$19 fee per night; pets $1.

Who to contact: Phone the park at (714)496-6172.

Location: From San Juan Capistrano, drive three miles south on Interstate 5 to the Coast Highway 1-Doheny State Beach exit. Turn left at 2nd light onto Dana Point Harbor Drive. Drive one block and go left onto Park Lantern. The park entrance is one block away.

Trip note: It's right in town but you should still plan on a reservation or don't make a plan. It is set at the entrance to Dana Point Harbor, a pretty spot, with easy access off the highway. San Juan Capistrano provides a nearby side trip. That's too many good things not to expect a lot of folks to want to stay here for the night. Open year-round.

Map grid j6

SAN CLEMENTE STATE BEACH

near San Clemente

Campsites, facilities: There are 160 campsites for tents or motor homes up to 32 feet long, 72 with full hookups. Fireplaces and picnic tables are provided. Flush toilets and showers are available. A grocery store, a laundromat, and propane gas are nearby. The camping area is wheelchair accessible.

Reservations, fee: Reserve through MISTIX at (800)444-PARK ($3.95 MISTIX fee); $14-$18 fee per night.

Who to contact: Phone the park at (714)492-3156.

Location: From Interstate 5 in San Clemente, take the Avenida Califa exit. Drive west for a short distance to the park entrance.

Trip note: In the series of three state beaches that provide easy access and beachfront camping, this one offers full hookups. The others are Doheny State Beach to the north, and San Onofre State Beach to the south. Open year-round.

◆ MAP 16 ◆

BEACH
TREES
5% CLUB
DESERT
URBAN
FOOTHILL
GRASSLAND

15 MILES

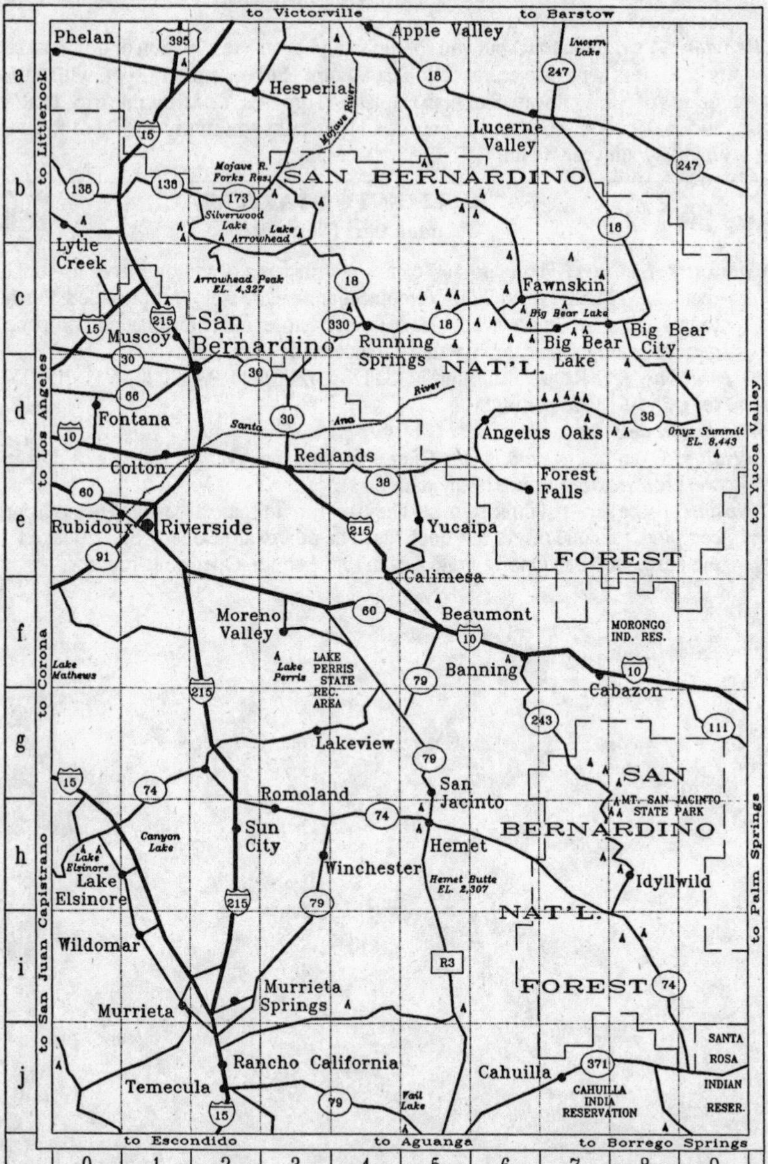

to Victorville
to Barstow
to Littlerock
to Los Angeles
to Corona
to San Juan Capistrano
to Yucca Valley
to Palm Springs
to Escondido
to Aguanga
to Borrego Springs

a b c d e f g h i j

0 1 2 3 4 5 6 7 8 9

Phelan
Apple Valley
Lucern Lake
Hesperia
Mojave River
Lucerne Valley
Mojave R. Forks Res.
SAN BERNARDINO
Silverwood Lake
Lake Arrowhead
Lytle Creek
Arrowhead Peak EL. 4,327
Fawnskin
Big Bear Lake
Big Bear City
Muscoy
San Bernardino
Running Springs
NAT'L.
Fontana
Santa Ana River
Angelus Oaks
Onyx Summit EL. 8,443
Colton
Redlands
Forest Falls
Rubidoux
Riverside
Yucaipa
FOREST
Calimesa
Beaumont
Moreno Valley
MORONGO IND. RES.
Lake Mathews
Lake Perris
LAKE PERRIS STATE REC. AREA
Banning
Cabazon
Lakeview
San Jacinto
SAN BERNARDINO
MT. SAN JACINTO STATE PARK
Romoland
Sun City
Canyon Lake
Hemet
Lake Elsinore
Winchester
Hemet Butte EL. 2,307
Idyllwild
NAT'L.
Wildomar
FOREST
Murrieta Springs
Murrieta
Rancho California
Temecula
Vail Lake
Cahuilla
CAHUILLA INDIA RESERVATION
SANTA ROSA INDIAN RESER.

395 15 138 138 173 18 247 247 18 18 330 18 15 215 30 30 66 30 10 38 38 60 215 91 60 10 10 79 243 111 215 79 15 74 74 79 215 R3 74 371 79 15

Map grid **a1**

DESERT WILLOW RV PARK
in Hesperia

Campsites, facilities: There are 176 motor home spaces with full hookups. Rest rooms, hot showers, cable TV hookups, a convenience store, groceries, ice, laundry, propane gas, a swimming pool, an indoor spa, a recreation room, a library, an adult lounge, and cable TV are on the premises. Some facilities are wheelchair accessible. Pets are permitted on leashes.

Reservations, fee: Reservations accepted; $18 fee per night.

Who to contact: Call (619)949-0377.

Location: In Hesperia on Interstate 15, take the Main Street exit and drive west to 12624 Main Street West.

Trip note: This is a motor home park for Interstate 15 cruisers looking to make a stop. Silverwood Lake, 16 miles to the south, provides a side trip option. The elevation is 3,200 feet. Open year-round, with limited winter facilities.

Map grid **a4**

MOJAVE NARROWS REGIONAL PARK
on Mojave River

Campsites, facilities: There are 110 campsites for tents or motor homes. Picnic tables and BBQ grills are provided. Piped water, flush toilets, showers, a sanitary dump station, a snack bar, a bait house, boat rentals, horse rentals, and horseback riding facilities are available. A grocery store, propane gas, and a laundromat are available three miles from campground. Pets are permitted on leashes.

Reservations, fee: Reservations not required; $9 fee per night; $1 pets.

Who to contact: This a county park; call (619)245-2226 for information.

Location: From Interstate 15 south of Victorville, take the Bear Valley exit and drive west for six miles. Turn left on Ridgecrest and drive three more miles.

Trip note: Just about nobody but the locals know about this little county park. It is set at 2,000 feet and provides a few recreation options, including fishing in a stocked pond, horseback riding facilities, and trails. The "river level fluctuates," according to the ranger, which means that sometimes it just about disappears. Open year-round.

Map grid **b0**

APPLE WHITE
near Lytle Creek
SAN BERNARDINO NATIONAL FOREST

Campsites, facilities: There are 44 campsites for tents or motor homes up to 22 feet long. Piped water, vault toilets, picnic tables, and fireplaces are provided. A grocery store is nearby.

Reservations, fee: No reservations; $10 fee per night, $15 for multi-family sites.

Who to contact: Phone the San Bernardino National Forest District Office at (714)887-2576.

Location: From Los Angeles, take Interstate 10 to Ontario. Continue past Ontario on Interstate 10 to the Interstate 15 North interchange. Drive 11 miles north on Interstate 15. Take the Sierra Avenue exit. Turn left, go under the freeway, and continue north for about nine miles to the campground.

Trip note: Nothing like a little inside know-how. You can reach the Middle Fork of Lytle Creek by driving north from Fontana via Serra Avenue to the Lytle Creek cabin area. To get to the stretch of water that is stocked with trout by the Department of Fish and Game, turn west on the first dirt road past South Fork Road. The first mile upstream is stocked in early summer. The elevation is 3,300 feet. Open year-round.

Map grid **b1**

WEST FORK GROUP CAMPS TENT
on Silverwood Lake

Campsites, facilities: There are three group camps here with piped water, flush toilets, showers, a sanitary dump station, picnic tables, and fireplaces provided. Picnic areas, fishing, hiking, swimming, boating, food service and a grocery store are available. Pets are permitted on leashes.

Reservations, fee: Reserve through MISTIX at (800)444-PARK ($3.95 MISTIX fee); $150 group camp fee per night; $1 for pets.

Who to contact: Phone the Silverwood Lake State Recreation Area at (619)389-2303.

Location: From San Bernardino, drive north on Interstate 215. Continue north on Interstate 15 to the Silverwood Lake exit in Cajon. Drive 13 miles east on Highway 138 to the park.

Trip note: This is a group camping option at Silverwood Lake. Open from March through October.

Map grid **b1**

MESA CAMPGROUND
on Silverwood Lake

Campsites, facilities: There are 128 campsites for tents or motor homes up to 34 feet long. Piped water, flush toilets, showers, a sanitary dump station, picnic tables, and fireplaces are provided. There's wheelchair access to the campground facilities, picnic areas, fishing, hiking paths, exhibits, swimming areas, boating, food service, and grocery store. Boat ramp and rentals available.

Reservations, fee: Reservations through MISTIX at (800)444-PARK ($3.95 fee); $12-$14 fee; $1 for pets.

Who to contact: Phone the Silverwood Lake State Recreation Area at (619)389-2303.

Location: From San Bernardino, drive north on Interstate 215. Continue north on Interstate 15 to the Silverwood Lake exit in Cajon. Drive 13 miles east on Highway 138 to the park.

Trip note: This is a popular lake set at 3,355 feet elevation and surrounded by National Forest land. Fishing is best for trout and bass in the spring, before the heat of summer and waterskiers take over. The park is located on the west side of the lake and offers both nature and bicycle trails. Open year-round.

Map grid **b2**

CAMP SWITZERLAND
on Lake Gregory

Campsites, facilities: There are ten campsites for tents and 30 spaces for motor homes with full hookups. Piped water, flush toilets, showers, and picnic tables are provided. Propane gas is available nearby. Pets are permitted on leashes.

Reservations, fee: Reservations accepted; $19 fee per night; $1 for pets.

Who to contact: Call Camp Switzerland at (714)338-2731.

Location: From San Bernardino, drive 12 miles north on Highway 18 to the town of Crestline. Drive north for a short distance on Highway 138. Turn right (east) on Lake Drive and drive two miles to the campground at Lake Gregory.

Trip note: Well, it really doesn't look anything like Switzerland, unless maybe you compare it to downtown Los Angeles. But it is pretty enough, set at 4,500 feet along little Lake Gregory. The lake is surrounded by San Bernardino National Forest. Open year-round.

A

Map grid **b3** **MOJAVE RIVER FORKS REGIONAL PARK**
near Silverwood Lake

B

Campsites, facilities: There are 30 sites for tents only, 25 motor home spaces with full hookups, and 25 campsites for tents or motor homes. An equestrian camping area and three group sites are also available. Picnic tables and fire grills are provided. Piped water, flush toilets, showers, a laundromat, and a sanitary dump station are available. A convenience store and a recreation room are available in the summer. Pets are permitted on leashes with proof of shots and/or current license.

C

Reservations, fee: Reservations accepted; $9-$14 fee per night; pets $2.

Who to contact: Call the park at (619)389-2322.

Location: From San Bernardino, drive north on Interstate 215. Continue north on Interstate 15 to the Silverwood Lake exit. Drive nine miles east to Highway 173. Stay to the left and drive seven miles to the park. From Hesperia on Interstate 15, take the Hesperia exit and drive four miles east to Hesperia. Continue southeast on Highway 173 (Arrowhead Lake Road) for nine miles to the park entrance.

D

Trip note: The bonus here is the full hookups for motor homes and the park's close proximity to Silverwood Lake, which is 15 minutes away and does not have any spaces with hookups available. The sites are well spaced. The nearby "river" is usually dry. The elevation is 3,000 feet. Open all year.

E

Map grid **b3** **DOGWOOD**
near Lake Arrowhead
SAN BERNARDINO NATIONAL FOREST

F

Campsites, facilities: There are 93 campsites for tents or motor homes up to 22 feet long. Piped water, flush toilets, a sanitary dump station, picnic tables, and fireplaces are provided. The facilities are wheelchair accessible. A grocery store and a laundromat are nearby.

G

Reservations, fee: Reserve through MISTIX (800)283-CAMP ($6 MISTIX fee); $12 fee per night; $18 for multi-family units.

Who to contact: Phone the San Bernardino National Forest District Office at (714)337-2444.

H

Location: From San Bernardino, drive about 15 miles north on Highway 18 to the Arrowhead Ranger Station. Continue east on Highway 18 for two-tenths of a mile to Dailey Canyon Road. Turn left on Dailey Canyon Road and then right on the Dailey Canyon access road into campground.

Trip note: This popular Forest Service camp is located along the outlet to Lake Arrowhead, about a mile from the lake. Got a question? The rangers at the Arrowhead Ranger Station, located about a half-mile down the road to the west, can answer it. Lake Arrowhead is stocked regularly in the late spring and early summer and can provide good trout fishing. The elevation is 5,600 feet. Open from May through October.

I6

J

Map grid **b3**

NORTH SHORE

on Lake Arrowhead

SAN BERNARDINO NATIONAL FOREST

Campsites, facilities: There are 27 campsites for tents or motor homes up to 22 feet long. Piped water, flush toilets, picnic tables, and fireplaces are provided. The facilities are wheelchair accessible. A grocery store and a laundromat are nearby. Pets are permitted on leashes. This site is for weekend camping only: Friday through Monday 2p.m.-2p.m.

Reservations, fee: Reservations not required; $10 fee per night.

Who to contact: Call San Bernardino National Forest Headquarters at (714)383-5588.

Location: From San Bernardino, drive about 15 miles north on Highway 18 to the Arrowhead Ranger Station. Continue east on Highway 18 for 1.8 miles. Turn left on Highway 173 and drive north for 1.6 miles to the traffic light. Turn right (still on Highway 173) and drive 2.9 miles to Hospital Road. Turn right and go one-tenth mile to the top of the small hill. Turn left just past the hospital entrance and you will see the campground.

Trip note: This is the preferable camp of the two at Lake Arrowhead. It is set near the northeastern shore of the lake, which provides good trout fishing in the spring and early summer. A trail starts at the camp and is routed east in National Forest and connects to the Pacific Crest Trail. The elevation is 5,300 feet. Open from May through September.

Map grid **b5**

BIG PINE HORSE CAMP

SAN BERNARDINO NATIONAL FOREST

Campsites, facilities: There is one group camp that can accommodate up to 60 people and 15 cars. Piped water, vault toilets, picnic tables, and fireplaces are provided.

Reservations, fee: Reservation required; $20 group fee per night.

Who to contact: Phone the San Bernardino National Forest District Office at (714)866-3437.

Location: From San Bernardino, take Highway 30 (the sign says "Mountain Resorts") to Highway 330. Drive about 35 miles on Highway 330 to the dam on Big Bear Lake. Take the left fork (Highway 38) and drive about four miles to the town of Fawnskin. Turn left on Rim of the World Road (it becomes Forest Service Road 3N14, a dirt road, after one-half mile) and drive seven miles. Turn left on Forest Service Road 3N16 and drive one mile to the campground on the left.

Trip note: You might want to bring an apple or a carrot, or maybe some nose plugs. That's because this is a camp for the horse packers located adjacent to the Big Pine Ranger Station. The elevation is 6,700 feet.

Map grid **b5**

HORSE SPRINGS

SAN BERNARDINO NATIONAL FOREST

Campsites, facilities: There are 17 tent sites. There is **no piped water.** Vault toilets, picnic tables, and fireplaces are provided. Pack out your garbage.

Reservations, fee: No reservations, no fee.

Who to contact: Phone the San Bernardino National Forest District Office at (714)866-3437.

Location: From San Bernardino, take Highway 30 (the sign says "Mountain Resorts") to Highway 330. Drive about 35 miles on Highway 330 to the dam on Big Bear Lake. Take the left fork (Highway 38) and drive about four miles to the town of Fawnskin. Turn left on Rim of the World Road (it becomes Forest Service Road 3N14, a dirt road, after one-half mile) and drive six miles to Big Pine Flat Station. Continue straight on Forest Service Road 3N14 for about six more miles to the campground entrance, Road 3N17.

Trip note: Horse Springs is way out there in booger country. It is set just southeast of Rattlesnake Mountain next to the headwaters of a small creek. If you want to be alone, this is the place. The elevation is 5,800 feet. Opens and closes according to road conditions; call Forest Service for the latest.

Map grid b6

IRONWOOD GROUP CAMP

SAN BERNARDINO NATIONAL FOREST

Campsites, facilities: There is one group camp that can accommodate up to 25 people and five cars (no trailers or motor homes). There is **no piped water.** Vault toilets, picnic tables, and fireplaces are provided.

Reservations, fee: Reservation required; $20 fee per night for group.

Who to contact: Phone the San Bernardino National Forest District Office at (714)866-3437.

Location: From San Bernardino, take Highway 30 (the sign says "Mountain Resorts") to Highway 330. Drive about 35 miles on Highway 330 to the dam on Big Bear Lake. Take the left fork (Highway 38) and drive about four miles to the town of Fawnskin. Turn left on Rim of the World Road (it becomes Forest Service Road 3N14, a dirt road, after one-half mile) and drive six miles. Turn left at the Forest Service Road 3N97 sign and go one mile to the campground.

Trip note: This nearby option to Hanna Flat camp is a bit more isolated and in higher country. The camp is set in a wooded area near a meadow, and the rough road going in scares a lot of folks off. The elevation is 6,700 feet. Open from June through September.

Map grid b6

BIG PINE FLATS

SAN BERNARDINO NATIONAL FOREST

Campsites, facilities: There are 15 sites for tents only and four campsites for tents or motor homes up to 22 feet long. Piped water, vault toilets, picnic tables, and fireplaces are provided.

Reservations, fee: No reservations; $7 fee per night.

Who to contact: Phone the San Bernardino National Forest District Office at (714)866-3437.

Location: From San Bernardino, take Highway 30 (the sign says "Mountain Resorts") to Highway 330. Drive about 35 miles on Highway 330 to the dam on Big Bear Lake. Take the left fork (Highway 38) and drive about four miles to the town of Fawnskin. Turn left on Rim of the World Road (it becomes Forest Service Road 3N14, a dirt road, after one-half mile) and drive seven miles to Big Pine Flat Station and the campground on the right.

Trip note: This pretty spot, set at 6,800 feet in the National Forest, is popular with the folks who know about it. You get a little of both worlds; you are surrounded by wildlands near Redondo Ridge, yet you're not a long drive from Big Bear Lake to the south. Any questions? The rangers at Big Flat Ranger Station, just across the road, can answer them. Open from mid-May to mid-November.

Map grid **c1** **SAN BERNARDINO-CABLE CANYON KOA**
near Silverwood Lake

Campsites, facilities: There are 153 tent and motor home sites with full or partial hookups and picnic tables. Piped water, flush toilets, showers, a laundromat, a playground, a swimming pool, a recreation room, a grocery store, and propane gas are available. Some facilities are wheelchair accessible. Pets are permitted on leashes.

Reservations, fee: Reservation accepted; $16-$18 fee per night.

Who to contact: Call (714)887-4098.

Location: From San Bernardino, drive 16 miles north on Interstate 215. Take the Devore exit and drive a short distance to Cable Canyon Road. Turn right and drive to 1707 Cable Canyon Road.

Trip note: This KOA camp provides space for tents as well as motor homes. It is set at 2,200 feet and virtually surrounded by National Forest. Silverwood Lake to the east provides a nearby side trip. Open year-round.

Map grid **c4** **CANYON PARK**
near Big Bear Lake

Campsites, facilities: There are 30 campsites for tents and 5 mobile home sites with full or partial hookups. Piped water, flush toilets, showers, picnic tables, and fireplaces are provided. Horses can be boarded here.

Reservations, fee: Call ahead for this information.

Who to contact: Call (714)867-2090.

Location: From San Bernardino, take Highway 30 (the sign says "Mountain Resorts"). Follow the road about four or five miles until it ends. Turn left on Highway 330 and drive 13 miles. Turn left on Highway 18 and drive to Running Springs School Road. Go right and drive to the park at 2840 Running Springs School Road.

Trip note: A quiet, privately-operated park with dirt roads, right smack in between Big Bear Lake to the east and Lake Arrowhead to the west; they are each about 15 miles away.

Map grid **c5** **CRAB FLATS**
near Crab Creek
SAN BERNARDINO NATIONAL FOREST

Campsites, facilities: There are 29 campsites for tents or motor homes up to 22 feet long. Piped water, vault toilets, picnic tables, and fireplaces are provided.

Reservations, fee: No reservations; $7 fee per night.

Who to contact: Phone the San Bernardino National Forest District Office at (714)337-2444.

Location: From San Bernardino, travel about 15 miles north on Highway 18 to the Arrowhead Ranger Station. Continue east on Highway 18 for 12 miles (past the town of Running Springs). Turn north (left) on Green Valley Road and drive three miles to Forest Service Road 3N16 (a dirt road) on the left. Turn left and drive four miles. You will cross two creeks which vary in depth depending on season. High clearance is recommended, but it is not necessary if you are careful. After four miles you will come to an intersection. Bear left and you'll see the entrance on your right.

Trip note: This is a developed Forest Service camp set at a fork in the road, with

Tent Peg camp located just a half mile to the west on Forest Service Road 3N34 (a hiking trail is available there). The elevation is 6,200 feet. Open from mid-May through October.

A

Map grid **c5**

GREEN VALLEY

near Green Valley Lake
SAN BERNARDINO NATIONAL FOREST

B

Campsites, facilities: There are 36 campsites for tents or motor homes up to 22 feet long. Piped water, flush toilets, picnic tables, and fireplaces are provided. A grocery store and a laundromat are nearby.
Reservations, fee: No reservations; $10 fee per night; $16 for multi-family sites.
Who to contact: Phone the San Bernardino National Forest District Office at (714)337-2444.

C

Location: From San Bernardino, drive 15 miles north on Highway 18 to the Arrowhead Ranger Station. Continue east on Highway 18 for 12 miles to Green Valley Road. Turn north (left) and go four miles up the road to the campground (one mile past town of Green Valley Lake).

D

Trip note: This is a pretty spot along Green Valley Creek. Little Green Valley Lake is located a mile to the west. The lake is stocked with trout by the Department of Fish and Game and is also a good spot to take a flying leap and belly flop. The elevation is 7,000 miles. Open from May through October.

E

Map grid **c5**

TENT PEG GROUP CAMP

near the Pacific Crest Trail
SAN BERNARDINO NATIONAL FOREST

Campsites, facilities: There is one group camp that will accommodate 10-30 people and five cars. There is **no piped water.** Vault toilets, picnic tables, and fireplaces are provided. A grocery store and a laundromat are nearby.

F

Reservations, fee: Reservations requested; $30 camp fee per night.
Who to contact: Call San Bernardino National Forest District Office at (714)337-2444.
Location: From San Bernardino, travel about 15 miles north on Highway 18 to the Arrowhead Ranger Station. Continue east on Highway 18 for 12 miles (past the town of Running Springs). Turn north (left) on Green Valley Road and drive three miles to Forest Service Road 3N16 (a dirt road) on the left. Turn left and drive four miles. You will cross two creeks which vary in depth depending on season. High clearance is recommended, but not necessary if you are careful. After four miles you will come to an intersection. Bear left on Forest Service Road 3N34, drive west for one mile, and the campground is on your left.

G

H

Trip note: This camp would be a lot easier to reach with a helicopter than a vehicle. But that's why it gets little use. It's a primitive camp used by groups hiking the Pacific Crest Trail which is located just a mile away. The trail from this camp links up with the PCT. In early summer, nearby Holcomb Creek provides fishing for small trout. The elevation is 5,400 feet. Open May through October.

I6

Map grid **c5**

FISHERMAN'S HIKE-IN GROUP CAMP

on Deep Creek
SAN BERNARDINO NATIONAL FOREST

J

Campsites, facilities: There is one group camp that will accommodate 10-30 people. Vault toilets, picnic tables, and fireplaces are provided. There is **no piped** water, so bring in your own. Pack out your garbage. Pets are permitted on leashes.

Reservations, fee: Reservations required; $10 camp fee per night.

Who to contact: Call San Bernardino National Forest District Office at (714)337-2444.

Location: From San Bernardino, travel about 15 miles north on Highway 18 to the Arrowhead Ranger Station. Continue east on Highway 18 for 12 miles (past the town of Running Springs). Turn north (left) on Green Valley Road and drive three miles to Forest Service Road 3N16 (a dirt road) on the left. Turn left and drive four miles. You will cross two creeks which vary in depth depending on season. High clearance is recommended, but not necessary if you are careful. After four miles you will come to an intersection. Bear left on Forest Service Road 3N34, drive west for 1.3 miles to Forest Service Trail 2W07 on your left. Follow this hiking trail southwest for 2.5 miles and you will come to Deep Creek. The campground is on the other side of the creek.

Trip note: Get here and you join the Five Percent Club. It's a beautiful, secluded, and wooded campground set deep in San Bernardino National Forest. Deep Creek runs alongside, providing stream trout fishing. It's worth the hike. The elevation is 5,400 feet.

Map grid C5

SHADY COVE GROUP CAMP

near Children's Forest

SAN BERNARDINO NATIONAL FOREST

Campsites, facilities: There is one camp that accommodates up to 75 people and 15 cars (no trailers or motor homes). Piped water, vault toilets, picnic tables, and fireplaces are provided.

Reservations, fee: Reservations required; special Forest Service arrangements are necessary; $40 plus $1 for each person over 25 people.

Who to contact: Phone the San Bernardino National Forest District Office at (714)337-2444.

Location: From San Bernardino, drive about 15 miles north on Highway 18 to the Arrowhead Ranger Station. Continue east on Highway 18 for nine miles (past the town of Running Springs). Turn south (right) on Keller Peak Road and drive four miles to the Children's Forest (just past Deer Lake Fire Station). Bear left for the parking area (it requires a key to enter). The campsites are 100 yards from parking area. Contact the district office for information.

Trip note: The highlight here is the short looped trail that is routed through the National Children's Forest. The camp is excellent for Boy Scout and Girl Scout troops. The elevation is 7,500 feet. Open from May through September.

Map grid C6

HANNA FLAT

near Big Bear Lake

SAN BERNARDINO NATIONAL FOREST

Campsites, facilities: There are 69 sites for tents and 19 campsites for tents or motor homes up to 15 feet long. Piped water, vault toilets, picnic tables, and fireplaces are provided.

Reservations, fee: Reservations not required; $9 fee per night.

Who to contact: Phone the San Bernardino National Forest District Office at (714)866-3437.

Location: From San Bernardino, take Highway 30 (the sign says "Mountain Resorts") to Highway 330. Drive about 35 miles on Highway 330 to the dam on Big Bear Lake. Take the left fork (Highway 38) and drive about four miles to the town of Fawnskin. Turn left on Rim of the World Road (it becomes Forest Service Road 3N14, a dirt road, after one-half mile), and drive about three miles to the campground on the left.

Trip note: This is the largest, best maintained, and most popular of the Forest Service camps set in the Big Bear Lake district. All the trees and vegetation provide seclusion for individual sites. It is set at 7,000 feet elevation, just under three miles from Big Bear Lake, which provides good trout fishing. The Pacific Crest National Scenic Trail passes by, one mile north of the camp. Open from May through September.

Map grid c6

GRAY'S PEAK GROUP CAMP

near Big Bear Lake

SAN BERNARDINO NATIONAL FOREST

Campsites, facilities: There is one group camp that will accommodate up to 40 people and eight cars (limited use of trailers and motor homes). There is **no piped water.** Vault toilets, picnic tables, and fireplaces are provided.

Reservations, fee: Reservation requested; $25 group fee per night.

Who to contact: Phone the San Bernardino National Forest District Office at (714)866-3437.

Location: From San Bernardino, take Highway 30 (the sign says "Mountain Resorts") to Highway 330. Drive about 35 miles on Highway 330 to the dam on Big Bear Lake. Take the left fork (Highway 38) and drive about four miles to the town of Fawnskin. Turn left on Rim of the World Road (it becomes Forest Service Road 3N14, a dirt road, after one-half mile) and drive about two miles to Forest Service Road 2N68. Turn left and drive about one mile to campground on the right.

Trip note: This primitive group camp is set at 7,200 feet elevation, about two miles northwest of Big Bear Lake. The name "Gray's Peak Camp" is a bit of a misnomer, since Gray's Peak (7,952 feet) is located about a mile south of the camp. Open from June through September.

Map grid c6

SIBERIA CREEK HIKE-IN GROUP CAMP

SAN BERNARDINO NATIONAL FOREST

Campsites, facilities: There is one group camp that will accommodate up to 40 people. Fire rings are provided, but that's all. There is **no piped water,** so bring your own, and pack out your garbage.

Reservations, fee: Reservations requested; no fee.

Who to contact: Phone the San Bernardino National Forest District Office at (714)866-3437.

Location: From San Bernardino, take Highway 30 (the sign says "Mountain Resorts") to Highway 330. Drive about 33 miles on Highway 330 (two miles BEFORE reaching the dam on Big Bear Lake). There is a turnout on the south (right) side of the highway. Take Forest Service Road 2N15 and follow this road for about two miles to the trailhead. Follow Glory Ridge Trail for about a mile to the junction with Siberia Creek Trail. The trail is steep and continues for three to four miles to the campground.

Trip note: This is a primitive area that requires a fairly steep four-mile hike. Your reward is solitude at a camp that will hold up to 40 people. The camp is set near the confluence of Siberia Creek and larger Bear Creek. The latter is the major feeder stream into Big Bear Lake. The elevation is 4,800 feet.

Map grid **c6**

BLUFF MESA GROUP CAMP

near Big Bear Lake
SAN BERNARDINO NATIONAL FOREST

Campsites, facilities: There is one group camp that will accommodate up to 40 people and eight cars (no trailers or motor homes). There is **no piped water.** Pit toilets, picnic tables, and fireplaces are provided.

Reservations, fee: Reservations requested; $25 group fee per night.

Who to contact: Phone the San Bernardino National Forest District Office at (714)866-3437.

Location: From San Bernardino, take Highway 30 (the sign says "Mountain Resorts") to Highway 330. Drive about 35 miles on Highway 330 to the dam on Big Bear Lake. Bear right at the dam on Highway 18 and drive about four miles. Turn right on Mill Creek Road and drive about 1.5 miles to the sign at the top of the hill. Turn right on Forest Service Road 2N10 and drive three miles on the dirt road. Turn right on Road 2N86 and drive one-quarter mile to the campground.

Trip note: This is one of the several camps located south of Big Bear Lake. Many Forest Service roads are available nearby for self-planned side trips. Maps are available at the ranger station in Fawnskin on the north side of the lake. The elevation is 7,600 feet. Open from June through September.

Map grid **c6**

BOULDER GROUP CAMP

near Big Bear Lake
SAN BERNARDINO NATIONAL FOREST

Campsites, facilities: There is one group camp that will accommodate up to 40 people and eight cars (limited use of trailers and motor homes). There is **no piped water.** Pit toilets, picnic tables, and fireplaces are provided. A grocery store and a laundromat are nearby.

Reservations, fee: Reservations required; $25 group fee per night.

Who to contact: Phone the San Bernardino National Forest District Office at (714)866-3437.

Location: From San Bernardino, take Highway 30 (the sign says "Mountain Resorts") to Highway 330. Drive about 35 miles on Highway 330 to the dam on Big Bear Lake. Bear right at the dam on Highway 18 and drive about four miles to Mill Creek Road. Turn right on Forest Service Road 2N10 and drive about two miles. Turn right on Road 2N10B and drive a short distance to campground.

Trip note: This is a primitive camp, just far enough away from some prime attractions to make you wish the camp was in a slightly different spot. The headwaters of Metcalf Creek are hidden in the forest on the other side of the road, little Cedar Lake is about a half-mile drive north, and Big Bear Lake is about two miles north. You get the idea. The elevation is 7,500 feet. Open from June through September.

Map grid **c6**

COLDBROOK

near Big Bear Lake
SAN BERNARDINO NATIONAL FOREST

Campsites, facilities: There are 32 sites for tents only and four campsites for tents or motor homes up to 16 feet long. Piped water, vault toilets, picnic tables, and fireplaces are provided. A grocery store and a laundromat are nearby.

Reservations, fee: Reservations not required; $7 fee per night.
Who to contact: Phone the San Bernardino National Forest District Office at (714)866-3437.
Location: From San Bernardino, take Highway 30 (the sign says "Mountain Resorts") to Highway 330. Drive about 35 miles on Highway 330 to the dam on Big Bear Lake. Bear right at the dam on Highway 18 and drive about four miles to Mill Creek Road. Turn right on Forest Service Road 2N10 and drive two miles to the campground entrance road on the right.
Trip note: No camps are set along the southern shoreline of Big Bear Lake, but this one comes the closest, about a mile distant. It is a pretty spot, set on Metcalf Creek at 6,800 feet elevation. Open from May through November.

Map grid c6

HOLLOWAY'S MARINA AND RV PARK
on Big Bear Lake

Campsites, facilities: There are 66 motor home spaces with full or partial hookups. Picnic tables and fire grills are provided. Piped water, flush toilets, showers, a sanitary dump station, cable TV, a convenience store, ice, propane gas, a laundromat, a playground, and a full marina with boat rentals are on the premises.
Reservations, fee: Reservations suggested; $22 fee per night.
Who to contact: Call Holloway's Marina and RV Park at (714)866-5706.
Location: From San Bernardino, take Highway 30 (the sign says "Mountain Resorts") and follow the road about four or five miles until it ends. Turn left on Highway 330 and drive 35 miles to the dam. Bear right on Highway 18 and drive three miles. Turn left at the Log Cabin Restaurant on Edgemoor Road and drive to the park.
Trip note: Big Bear Lake is a large, popular lake set at 6,500 feet in the San Bernardino National Forest. There are tons of campgrounds to pick from here. Big Bear has good trout fishing in the spring and is well stocked. In the summer, a bonus is that a breeze off the lake keeps the temperature in the mid-80s.

Map grid c6

GROUT BAY
on Big Bear Lake
SAN BERNARDINO NATIONAL FOREST

Campsites, facilities: There are 21 sites for tents only and two campsites for tents or motor homes up to 16 feet long. Piped water, flush toilets, picnic tables, and fireplaces are provided.
Reservations, fee: Reservations not required; $7 fee per night.
Who to contact: Phone the San Bernardino National Forest District Office at (714)866-3437.
Location: From San Bernardino, take Highway 30 (the sign says "Mountain Resorts") to Highway 330. Drive about 35 miles on Highway 330 to the dam on Big Bear Lake. Take the left fork (Highway 38) and drive about three miles (just short of Fawnskin) to the campground on the right.
Trip note: This is one of the two camps set right along the shore of Big Bear Lake. It is located on the north shore of the lake on Grout Bay. If you think it can be hard to get a campground here, you are right. It's first-come, first-served, so it is a good idea to make a phone call ("Any spaces available at Grout Bay?"), then plan on getting there prior to the weekenders. If the camp is full, there are several alternatives in the National Forest north of the lake; the closest is Hanna Flat. The elevation is 6,800 feet. Open from May through November.

Map grid **c7**

HOLCOMB VALLEY
near Pacific Crest Trail
SAN BERNARDINO NATIONAL FOREST

Campsites, facilities: There are 19 campsites for tents or motor homes up to 15 feet long. There is **no piped water.** Pit toilets, picnic tables, and fireplaces are provided. Pack out your garbage.

Reservations, fee: No reservations, no fee.

Who to contact: Phone the San Bernardino National Forest District Office at (714)866-3437.

Location: From San Bernardino, take Highway 30 (the sign says "Mountain Resorts") to Highway 330. Drive about 35 miles on Highway 330 to the dam on Big Bear Lake. Take the left fork (Highway 38) and drive about ten miles. Turn left on Van Dusen Canyon Road (3N09) and drive (dirt road) for three miles. Turn left 3N16 and the campground is on the right.

Trip note: This primitive camp, set north of Big Bear Lake, is ideal for an overflow area if the Grout Bay camp at Big Bear is full. The camp is set near the Holcomb Valley Historic Area and two miles north of the Pacific Crest Trail. The elevation is 7,400 feet. Open year-round, depending on the weather.

Map grid **c7**

MEADOWS EDGE GROUP CAMP
on Big Bear Lake
SAN BERNARDINO NATIONAL FOREST

Campsites, facilities: There is one group camp that will accommodate up to 60 people and 12 recreational vehicles (but only 12). There is **no piped water.** Vault toilets, picnic tables, and fireplaces are provided.

Reservations, fee: Reservation requested; call for fee.

Who to contact: Phone the San Bernardino National Forest Big Bear District at (714)866-3437.

Location: From San Bernardino, take Highway 30 (the sign says "Mountain Resorts") to Highway 330. Drive about 35 miles on Highway 330 to the dam on Big Bear Lake. Take the left fork (Highway 38) and drive about six miles to the campground entrance on the right.

Trip note: This is the other camp that is set right on Big Bear Lake. It is a group camp located on the northern shore on the upper end of the lake. Grout Bay is the only other camp set on the lake. Any questions? The nearby Big Bear Ranger Station, located a half mile to the east, can provide the answers.

Map grid **c7**

PINEKNOT
near Big Bear Lake
SAN BERNARDINO NATIONAL FOREST

Campsites, facilities: There are 49 sites for tents only and three campsites for tents or motor homes up to 15 feet long. Piped water, flush toilets, picnic tables, and fireplaces are provided. Facilities are wheelchair accessible. A grocery store and a laundromat are nearby.

Reservations, fee: Reservations not required; $7 fee per night.

Who to contact: Phone the San Bernardino National Forest District Office at (714)866-3437.

Location: From San Bernardino, take Highway 30 (the sign says "Mountain Resorts") to Highway 330. Drive about 35 miles on Highway 330 to the dam on Big Bear Lake. Bear right at the dam on Highway 18 and drive about six miles to Summit Boulevard. Turn right and drive through the parking area and make a left into the campground just before the gate to the slopes.

Trip note: This popular, developed Forest Service camp is set just east of Big Bear Lake Village, about two miles from Big Bear Lake. The elevation is 7,000 feet. Open from mid-May through September.

Map grid c7

BUTTERCUP GROUP CAMP

near town of Big Bear Lake

SAN BERNARDINO NATIONAL FOREST

Campsites, facilities: There is one group camp that will accommodate up to 40 people and eight cars (limited use of trailers or motor homes). Piped water, pit toilets, picnic tables, and fireplaces are provided. A grocery store and a laundromat are nearby.

Reservations, fee: Reservation requested; $25 group fee per night.

Who to contact: Phone the San Bernardino National Forest Headquarters at (714) 383-5588.

Location: From San Bernardino, take Highway 30 (the sign says "Mountain Resorts") to Highway 330. Drive about 35 miles on Highway 330 to the dam on Big Bear Lake. Bear right at the dam on Highway 18 and drive about six miles to Summit Boulevard. Turn right and drive through the parking area and make a left into the campground, just before the gate to the ski slopes.

Trip note: This is a forested camp, set up for large groups looking for a developed site near Big Bear Lake. The elevation is 7,000 feet. Open from June through September.

Map grid c7

TANGLEWOOD GROUP CAMP

on Pacific Crest Trail

SAN BERNARDINO NATIONAL FOREST

Campsites, facilities: There is one group camp that will accommodate up to 40 people and eight cars (limited use of trailers or motor homes). There is **no piped water.** Pit toilets, picnic tables, and fireplaces are provided.

Reservations, fee: Reservation required; $25 group fee per night.

Who to contact: Phone the San Bernardino National Forest District Office at (714)866-3437.

Location: From San Bernardino, take Highway 30 (the sign says "Mountain Resorts") to Highway 330. Drive about 35 miles on Highway 330 to the dam on Big Bear Lake. Take the left fork (Highway 38) and drive about ten miles. Turn left on Van Dusen Canyon Road (Forest Service Road 3N09) and drive the dirt road for three miles. Turn right on Forest Service Road 3N16 and drive about two miles. Turn right on Forest Service Road 3N79 to the campground.

Trip note: This primitive group camp is set off an old spur road. The Pacific Crest Trail is accessible immediately to the south. It is set at 7,400 feet elevation in a flat, but wooded area, with Big Bear Lake three miles to the southeast by road. Open from June through September.

Map grid d7

COUNCIL GROUP CAMP

near San Gorgonio Wilderness

SAN BERNARDINO NATIONAL FOREST

Campsites, facilities: There is one group camp that will accommodate up to 50 people and ten cars (no trailers or motor homes). Piped water, vault toilets, picnic tables, and fireplaces are provided.

Reservations, fee: Reserve through MISTIX at (800)283-CAMP ($6 MISTIX fee); call for per night fees.

Who to contact: Phone the San Bernardino National Forest District Office at (714)794-1123.

Location: On Interstate 10 in Redlands, drive 26 miles east on Highway 38 to the campground on the left.

Trip note: This site is next to Holcomb Valley camp. Campers who are not in large groups should consider the following camp. See the trip note for details.

Map grid d7

SOUTH FORK
on Lost Creek
SAN BERNARDINO NATIONAL FOREST

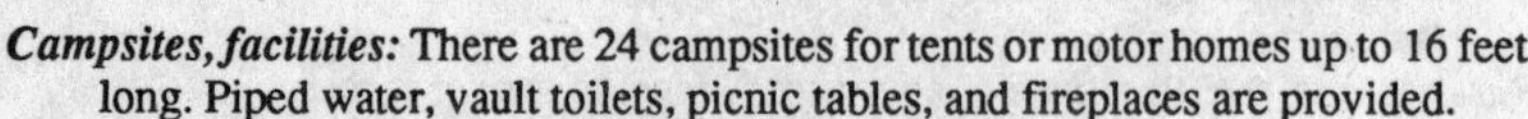

Campsites, facilities: There are 24 campsites for tents or motor homes up to 16 feet long. Piped water, vault toilets, picnic tables, and fireplaces are provided.

Reservations, fee: No reservations; $6 fee per night.

Who to contact: Phone the San Bernardino National Forest District Office at (714)794-1123.

Location: From Interstate 10 in Redlands, drive 29.5 miles east on Highway 38 to the campground on the right.

Trip note: This easy access Forest Service camp, just off Highway 38, is set at 6,400 feet elevation on Lost Creek. It is part of the series of camps in the immediate area, just north of the San Gorgonio Wilderness. See the trip note for Barton Flats for more details. Open from mid-May through mid-October.

Map grid d7

OSO GROUP CAMP
near San Gorgonio Wilderness
SAN BERNARDINO NATIONAL FOREST

Campsites, facilities: There are sites that will accommodate up to 100 people and 20 cars. Piped water, flush toilets, picnic tables, and fireplaces are provided.

Reservations, fee: Reserve through MISTIX at (800)283-CAMP ($6 MISTIX fee); call ahead for fees.

Who to contact: Phone the San Bernardino National Forest District Office at (714)794-1123.

Location: From Interstate 10 in Redlands, drive 29 miles east on Highway 38 to the campground entrance road on the left.

Trip note: This camp is set directly next to Lobo camp. The elevation is 6,600 feet. Open from May through October.

Map grid d7

LOBO GROUP CAMP
near Santa Ana River
SAN BERNARDINO NATIONAL FOREST

Campsites, facilities: There are 15 sites which will accommodate up to 75 people and 15 cars (limited use of trailers and motor homes). Piped water, flush toilets, picnic tables, and fireplaces are provided.

Reservations, fee: Reserve through MISTIX at (800)283-CAMP ($6 MISTIX fee); call for fees.

Who to contact: Phone the San Bernardino National Forest District Office at (714)794-1123.

Location: From Interstate 10 in Redlands, drive 29 miles east on Highway 38 to the campground entrance road on the left.

Trip note: Lobo is right next to Oso camp and is just north of the San Gorgonio

Wilderness. The camp is about three-quarters of a mile from the Santa Ana River, which frequently has low flows in summer months. The elevation is 6,600 feet. Open from May through September.

A

Map grid **d7**

BARTON FLATS

near San Gorgonio Wilderness
SAN BERNARDINO NATIONAL FOREST

B

Campsites, facilities: There are 23 sites for tents only, 24 motor home spaces, and two campsites for tents or motor homes up to 21 feet long. Piped water, vault toilets, picnic tables, and fireplaces are provided. The facilities are wheelchair accessible.

C

Reservations, fee: Reserve through MISTIX at (800)283-CAMP ($6 MISTIX fee); $6 fee per night.

Who to contact: Phone the San Bernardino National Forest District Office at (714)794-1123.

Location: On Interstate 10 in Redlands, drive 26.5 miles east on Highway 38 to the campground on the left.

D

Trip note: This is one of the more developed Forest Service camps in southern California. It's set up to be 50-50 between tenters and motor homes. The camp is set at 6,300 feet elevation near Barton Creek—the "creek" part is a misnomer because there's rarely any water in it. The San Gorgonio Wilderness is located one mile to the south and is accessible via Forest Service roads to the trailhead. A wilderness permit and a Forest Service map are required and can be picked up on your way in from Redlands at the Mill Creek Ranger Station on Highway 38. Open from mid-May through October.

E

Map grid **d7**

SAN GORGONIO

near San Gorgonio Wilderness
SAN BERNARDINO NATIONAL FOREST

F

Campsites, facilities: There are 37 tent sites, 23 motor home spaces and two campsites for tents or motor homes up to 24 feet long. Piped water, vault toilets, picnic tables, and fireplaces are provided.

G

Reservations, fee: Reserve through MISTIX at (800)283-CAMP ($6 MISTIX fee); $6 camp fee per night, $12 for multi-family units.

Who to contact: Phone the San Bernardino National Forest District Office at (714)794-1123.

Location: From Interstate 10 in Redlands, drive 28 miles east on Highway 38 to the campground on the left.

H

Trip note: This is another in the series of developed Forest Service camps in the immediate area. See the trip note for Barton Flats for details.

Map grid **d8**

HEART BAR EQUESTRIAN GROUP CAMP

SAN BERNARDINO NATIONAL FOREST

I6

Campsites, facilities: There is one group camp with ten sites that will accommodate up to 75 people and 25 cars (limited use of trailers and motor homes). Piped water, vault toilets, picnic tables, and fireplaces are provided.

Reservations, fee: Reserve through MISTIX at (800)283-CAMP ($6 MISTIX fee) call for fees.

J

Who to contact: Phone the San Bernardino National Forest District Office at (714)794-1123.

Location: From Interstate 10 in Redlands, drive 32.5 miles east on Highway 38 to the campground entrance road (Forest Service Road 1N02) on the right. Turn in and drive 1.5 miles to the campground.

Trip note: You might not meet Mr. Ed here, but bring an apple anyway. It's a horse camp, located less than a mile east of Heart Bar Group Camp. A good trail that leads east into the San Gorgonio Wilderness starts four miles down the road at Coon Creek. The elevation is 7,000 feet. Open from May through November.

Map grid d8 HEART BAR and SKYLINE GROUP CAMP

SAN BERNARDINO NATIONAL FOREST

Campsites, facilities: There are 94 campsites for tents or motor homes up to 30 feet long and one group site that will accommodate up to 25 people. Piped water, vault toilets, picnic tables, and fireplaces are provided.

Reservations, fee: Reservations through MISTIX (800)283-CAMP ($6 MISTIX fee); $8 fee per night for single family site; $14 for multi-family sites; $35 for group site.

Who to contact: Phone the San Bernardino National Forest District Office at (714)794-1123.

Location: From Interstate 10 in Redlands, drive 32.5 miles east on Highway 38 to the campground entrance road (Forest Service Road 1N02) on the right. Turn and drive one mile to the campground.

Trip note: It's a good thing there is piped water at this camp. Why? Because Heart Bar Creek often isn't much more than a trickle and can't be relied on for water The camp is set at 6,900 feet elevation near Big Meadows, the location of the Heart Bar Ranger Station. A great trail that is routed along Wildhorse Creek to Sugarloaf Mountain (9,952 feet) starts just off the main road, about one-half mile away to the north, midway between the camp and the ranger station. Open from May through November.

Map grid d8 GREEN CANYON GROUP CAMP

near Green Springs

SAN BERNARDINO NATIONAL FOREST

Campsites, facilities: There is one group camp that will accommodate 40 people and eight cars (no trailers or motor homes). There is **no piped water.** Pit toilets, picnic tables, and fireplaces are provided.

Reservations, fee: Reservation required; $25 group fee.

Who to contact: Phone the San Bernardino National Forest District Office at (714)866-3437.

Location: From Interstate 10 in Redlands, drive about 45 miles east on Highway 38 (1.5 miles past the town of Lake Williams) to the campground entrance on the left (Forest Service Road 2N93). Turn left and then make another immediate left and follow the road for one-half mile and you'll see the campground sign on your left.

Trip note: This primitive group camp provides an overflow area for Big Bear Lake campers that can't find a spot closer. It is set at 7,200 feet elevation, with a trail located to the southwest just off the road (look for the gate) that is routed along Green Canyon to Wild Horse Creek. There it intersects with a great trail that goes west to Sugar Loaf Mountain, 9,952 feet elevation. Open from June through September.

A

Map grid **d9**

COON CREEK CABIN GROUP CAMP

on Pacific Crest Trail
SAN BERNARDINO NATIONAL FOREST

Campsites, facilities: There is one group camp with ten sites that will accommodate up to 40 people and ten cars (no trailers or motor homes). There is **no piped water.** Vault toilets, picnic tables, and fireplaces are provided.

B

Reservations, fee: Reserve through MISTIX at (800)283-CAMP ($6 MISTIX fee) call for fees.

Who to contact: Phone the San Bernardino National Forest District Office at (714)794-1123.

C

Location: From Interstate 10 in Redlands, drive 32.5 miles east on Highway 38 to the campground entrance road (Forest Service Road 1N02) on the right. Turn in and drive five miles to the campground.

Trip note: This is a good jump-off spot for ambitious backpackers. The camp is set beside the Pacific Crest Trail at 8,200 feet elevation, near Coon Creek. Hikers should not count on getting water out of the creek; it often runs dry by early summer. Open all year.

D

Map grid **d9**

JUNIPER SPRINGS GROUP CAMP

SAN BERNARDINO NATIONAL FOREST

E

Campsites, facilities: There is one group camp that will accommodate up to 40 people and eight cars (limited use of trailers and motor homes). Piped water, pit toilets, picnic tables, and fireplaces are provided.

Reservations, fee: Reservation required; $25 fee per night.

Who to contact: Phone the San Bernardino National Forest District Office at (714)866-3437.

F

Location: From Interstate 10 in Redlands, drive about 40 miles east on Highway 38 (1.5 miles past Onyx Summit) to the campground entrance road (Forest Service Road 2N01) on the right. Turn in on the dirt road and drive three miles. Make a right (opposite the sign that says 2N04, on your left) and drive into the campground.

G

Trip note: This is a little-known group camp, set at 7,700 feet in a desert-like area, about ten miles east of Big Bear Lake. The reason it is little known is because there are not a lot of reasons to camp here. You need to be creative. Watch the features of the land change colors as the day passes. Open from June through September.

H

Map grid **f3**

LAKE PERRIS STATE RECREATION AREA

Campsites, facilities: There are 161 sites for tents only, 245 sites for tents or motor homes up to 31 feet long, seven primitive horse camps with corrals, and several group camps (by reservation only). Picnic tables, fireplaces, electrical connections, and piped water are provided. Flush toilets, showers, a dump station, a playground, a grocery store, horseback riding facilities, boat launch, mooring, and rentals are available. The exhibits, pathways, campgrounds, and picnic areas are wheelchair accessible. Pets are permitted on leashes.

I6

J

Reservations, fee: Reserve through MISTIX at (800)444-PARK ($3.95 MISTIX fee); $12-$18 fee per night; pets $1.

Who to contact: Phone the park at (714)657-9000.

Location: From Riverside, drive about 11 miles south on Interstate 215 to the Ramona Expressway exit. Turn east and drive about two miles to Lake Perris Drive. Turn left and drive right into the park.

Trip note: This is a giant recreation area with many options, but the few elusive but giant spotted bass are the highlight. Some world-class level fish have been caught here. Spring months are best, when their cousins, the largemouth bass, provide the most consistent fishing of the year. By summer, the waterskiers take over, and if you can't beat 'em, join 'em. An Indian Museum features artifacts and handicrafts and is open Wednesdays and weekends. The elevation is 1,600 feet. Open year-round.

Map grid f5

BOGART COUNTY PARK
in Cherry Valley

Campsites, facilities: There are 40 campsites for tents or motor homes. Fireplaces and picnic tables are provided. Piped water, flush toilets, and a playground are available. Supplies available in Beaumont. Pets are permitted on leashes.

Reservations, fee: No reservations; $7 fee per night.

Who to contact: Phone the county parks at (714)845-3818.

Location: From Interstate 10 in Beaumont, drive four miles north on Beaumont Avenue to 14th and Cherry Avenue; park is at 9600 Cherry Ave.

Trip note: A lot of Interstate 10 cruisers overlook this county park because they flat don't know it exists. But it does, and it is as pretty as it gets for this area. Some hiking trails provide a recreation option during the cooler months. The elevation is 2,800 feet. Open year-round.

Map grid f6

BANNING TRAVEL PARK
in Banning

Campsites, facilities: There are 115 sites for tents or motor homes, many with full hookups. Picnic tables and fireplaces are provided. Cable TV, rest rooms, showers, a playground, a swimming pool, a laundromat, a store, a dump station, ice, a recreation room, horseshoes, a video arcade, and propane gas are available. Pets are permitted on leashes.

Reservations, fee: Reservations accepted; $11-$16 fee per night.

Who to contact: Phone the park at (714)849-7513.

Location: From Interstate 10 in Banning, take the Highway 243 exit and drive one block south on 8th Avenue. Turn left on Lincoln and drive two blocks. Turn right on San Gorgonio and drive one mile to 1455 South San Gorgonio Avenue.

Trip note: Banning is not exactly a hotbed of civilization, but for folks on Interstate 10 praying for a layover spot on the outskirts of the Los Angeles basin, it will do just fine. It is set at 2,400 feet elevation, 22 miles from Palm Springs. A good side trip is to head south on curving "Highway" 240 up to Vista Point in the San Bernardino National Forest. Open year-round.

Map grid g7

BLACK MOUNTAIN GROUP CAMP
near Mt. San Jacinto
SAN BERNARDINO NATIONAL FOREST

Campsites, facilities: There are two group camps here for tents or motor homes up to 22 feet long. Each has a capacity of 50 people and 16 vehicles. Piped water, vault toilets, picnic tables, and fireplaces are provided.

Reservations, fee: Reserve through MISTIX (800)283-CAMP ($6 MISTIX fee);

$50 fee per night.

Who to contact: Phone the San Bernardino National Forest District Office at (714)659-2117. A

Location: From Idyllwild, drive nine miles north on Highway 243. Turn right on Forest Service Road 4S01 and drive eight miles to the campground.

Trip note: This is a beautiful scenic area, particularly north on the edge of the San Jacinto Wilderness and east in Mt. San Jacinto State Park. The camp is set at 7,500 feet elevation and has a trail routed out from the camp north into the National Forest and east into Mt. San Jacinto State Park. Open from May to October. B

Map grid g7

BOULDER BASIN

near San Jacinto Wilderness

SAN BERNARDINO NATIONAL FOREST

C

Campsites, facilities: There are 34 campsites for tents or motor homes up to 22 feet long (trailers are not recommended). Piped water, vault toilets, fireplaces, and picnic tables are provided. D

Reservations, fee: No reservations; $7 fee per night.

Who to contact: Phone the San Bernardino National Forest District Office at (714)659-2117.

Location: From Idyllwild, drive nine miles north on Highway 243. Turn right on Forest Service Road 4S01 and drive six miles to the campground. E

Trip note: Located near the San Jacinto Wilderness (to the northeast), this is an ideal trailhead camp for hikers. A trail heads west into a designated scenic area, starting at Black Mountain Lookout. The elevation is 7,300 feet. Open from May to mid-October.

Map grid g8

DARK CANYON

in San Jacinto Mountains

SAN BERNARDINO NATIONAL FOREST

F

Campsites, facilities: There are 22 campsites for tents or motor homes up to 22 feet long. Piped water, vault toilets, fireplaces, and picnic tables are provided. Pets are permitted on leashes. G

Reservations, fee: No reservations; $7-$8 fee per night.

Who to contact: Phone the San Bernardino National Forest District Office at (714)659-2117.

Location: From Idyllwild, drive seven miles north on Highway 243. Turn right on Forest Service Road 4S02 and drive three more miles on a narrowing road. H

Trip note: This pretty setting is on the slopes of the San Jacinto Mountain. Hikers will find a trailhead at the end of Forest Service Road 4S02, less than a mile north of the camp. The trail leads east into Mt. San Jacinto State Park to Deer Springs, where it intersects with a major trail. The elevation is 5,800 feet. Open from mid-April to mid-October. I6

Map grid h0

ELSINORE WEST MARINA

near Lake Elsinore

Campsites, facilities: There are 271 motor home spaces with full hookups and picnic tables provided. Rest rooms, showers, a sanitary dump station, clubhouse, convenience store, laundromat, telephone hookups, cable TV hookups, and a boat ramp are available. J

Reservations, fee: Reservations accepted; $12-$18 fee per night.

Who to contact: Phone the park at (714)678-1300 or (800)328-6844.

Location: From Interstate 15 in Lake Elsinore, take Highway 74 and drive four miles west to 32700 Riverside Drive.

Trip note: This is one of two privately-operated motor home parks located adjacent to each other, just a half mile from Lake Elsinore. The Roadrunner camp provides a nearby option.

Map grid h0 — LAKE ELSINORE STATE RECREATION AREA

Campsites, facilities: There are 175 campsites for tents or motor homes up to 40 feet long. Piped water, electrical connections, fireplaces, and picnic tables are provided. Flush toilets, showers, dump station, playground, boat launch, laundromat and a grocery store are available. Pets are permitted on leashes. The camping and picnicking areas are wheelchair accessible.

Reservations, fee: No reservations; $11.50 fee per night; pets $2.

Who to contact: Phone the park at (714)674-3177.

Location: From Interstate 15 in Lake Elsinore, drive three miles west on Highway 74 to the park entrance.

Trip note: This is a pretty spot set along the northern shore of Lake Elsinore, a popular lake for water skiing. The elevation is 1,250 feet. Open year-round.

Map grid h5 — CASA DEL SOL RV RESORTS in Hemet

Campsites, facilities: There are 358 motor home spaces. Picnic tables, piped water, electrical connections, and sewer hookups are provided. Rest rooms, showers, a swimming pool, a recreation room, a billiard room, a jacuzzi, a putting green, and a laundromat are available. Pets are permitted on leashes.

Reservations, fee: Reservations accepted; $20 fee per night.

Who to contact: Phone the park at (714)925-2515.

Location: From Interstate 215 south of Perris, turn east on Highway 74 and drive about 14 miles to Hemet (the highway becomes Florida Avenue in Hemet). Turn north on Kirby drive to the campground on the corner of Kirby and Acacia at 2750 West Acacia Avenue.

Trip note: Hemet is a retirement town, so if you want excitement, the three lakes in the area are the best place to look for it: Lake Perris to the northwest, Lake Skinner to the south, and Lake Hemet to the east. Open year-round.

Map grid h5 — MOUNTAIN VALLEY RECREATIONAL VEHICLE PARK in Hemet

Campsites, facilities: There are 170 motor home spaces. Piped water, cable TV, electrical connections and sewer hookups are provided. Rest rooms, showers, a swimming pool, an enclosed jacuzzi, a laundromat, a recreation room, shuffleboard, and telephone hookups are available. A grocery store and propane gas are available nearby. Pets are permitted on leashes.

Reservations, fee: Call ahead for available space and fee.

Who to contact: Phone the park at (714)925-5812.

Location: From Interstate 215 south of Perris, turn east on Highway 74 and drive about 14 miles to Hemet (the highway becomes Florida Avenue in Hemet). Turn south (right) on Lyon Avenue and drive to 235 South Lyon Avenue.

Trip note: This is one of two motor home parks in the Hemet area. Three lakes in the area provide side trip possibilities: Lake Perris to the northwest, Lake Skinner to the south, and Lake Hemet to the east. Open year-round.

A

Map grid h7

IDYLLWILD COUNTY PARK
near San Bernardino National Forest

B

Campsites, facilities: There are 90 campsites for tents or motor homes up to 34 feet long (30 for motor homes). Fireplaces and picnic tables are provided. Flush toilets and showers are available. Pets are permitted on leashes. A grocery store, a laundromat and propane gas are available nearby.

Reservations, fee: Reservations accepted; $10 fee per night; pets $1.

Who to contact: Phone the park at (714)659-2656.

C

Location: From Highway 243 in Idyllwild, drive one-half mile west on Riverside County Playground Road (follow the signs) to the campground.

Trip note: Mt. San Jacinto State Park, San Jacinto Wilderness, and the San Bernardino National Forest lands surround this park. That provides plenty of options for visitors. A trail from the State Park Headquarters nearby leads into the backcountry and connects with the Pacific Crest National Scenic Trail. The elevation is 5,300 feet. Open year-round.

D

Map grid h8

STONE CREEK
MOUNT SAN JACINTO STATE PARK

E

Campsites, facilities: There are ten tent sites and 40 campsites for tents or motor homes up to 24 feet long. Fireplaces and picnic tables are provided. Piped water and pit toilets are available. Pets are permitted on leashes. Supplies and a laundromat are nearby.

Reservations, fee: Reserve through MISTIX at (800)444-PARK ($3.95 MISTIX fee); $7-$9 fee per night; pets $1.

F

Who to contact: Phone the Mt. San Jacinto State Park at (714)659-2607.

Location: From Idyllwild, drive six miles north on Highway 243 to the entrance.

Trip note: This is a wooded camp located off the main road along Stone Creek, less than a mile from the Fern Basin camp and less than three miles from Dark Canyon camp. The elevation is 5,900 feet. Open year-round.

G

Map grid h8

IDYLLWILD
MOUNT SAN JACINTO STATE PARK

Campsites, facilities: There are 11 sites for tents only and 22 campsites for tents or motor homes up to 24 feet long. Fireplaces and picnic tables are provided. Piped water, flush toilets and showers are available. Pets are permitted on leashes. Supplies and a laundromat are nearby.

H

Reservations, fee: Reserve through MISTIX at (800)444-PARK ($3.95 MISTIX fee); $12-$14 fee per night; pets $1.

Who to contact: Phone the Mt. San Jacinto State Park at (714)659-2607.

I6

Location: In Idyllwild, drive to the north end of town on Highway 243 to the entrance.

Trip note: This is a prime spot for hikers and one of the better jump-off points in the area. A trail leading from the camp goes into the backcountry of Mt. San Jacinto State Park and San Jacinto Wilderness and connects with the Pacific Crest National Scenic Trail. The elevation is 5,400 feet. Open year-round.

J

Map grid h8 FERN BASIN

near Mt. San Jacinto State Park
SAN BERNARDINO NATIONAL FOREST

Campsites, facilities: There are 22 campsites for tents or motor homes up to 15 feet long. Piped water, vault toilets, fireplaces, and picnic tables are provided.

Reservations, fee: No reservations; $7 fee per night.

Who to contact: Phone the San Bernardino National Forest District Office at (714)659-2117.

Location: From Idyllwild, drive seven miles north on Highway 243. Turn right on Forest Service Road 4S02 and drive one mile to the campground.

Trip note: This is a nearby option to Black Mountain camp. It is located a little over one mile south of Dark Canyon camp. Backpackers should head north on Forest Service Road 4S02 for two miles until it dead ends at a trailhead. That trail is routed east into Mt. San Jacinto State Park, where it connects to a network of other trails. The elevation is 6,300 feet. Open from mid-April to October.

Map grid h8 MARION MOUNTAIN

SAN BERNARDINO NATIONAL FOREST

Campsites, facilities: There are 24 campsites for tents or motor homes up to 15 feet long. Piped water, vault toilets, fireplaces, and picnic tables are provided.

Reservations, fee: No reservations; $7 fee per night.

Who to contact: Phone the San Bernardino National Forest District Office at (714)659-2117.

Location: From Idyllwild, drive seven miles north on Highway 243. Turn right on Forest Service Road 4S02 and drive two miles to the campground.

Trip note: You get good nearby lookouts and a developed campground at this spot. The nearby trails head up the slopes to Marion Mountain and east into adjacent San Jacinto State Park. The elevation is 6,400 feet. Open from mid-April to mid-October.

Map grid i4 LAKE SKINNER RECREATION AREA

Campsites, facilities: There are 257 sites for tents or motor homes, many with full hookups. Picnic tables and fireplaces are provided. Rest rooms, showers, a playground, a grocery store, ice, bait, a dump station, a swimming pool (in the summer), a boat ramp, mooring, boat rentals, and propane gas are available. Pets are permitted on leashes.

Reservations, fee: Reservations requested; $10-$14 fee per night; pets $1.

Who to contact: Phone this county park at (714)926-1541 or (714)684-0196 for reservations.

Location: From Interstate 15 in Temecula, take the Rancho California exit and drive nine miles northeast to the park entrance.

Trip note: Lake Skinner is a piece of water in the middle of some very dry, hot country. That's why it gets hit hard by boaters and sunbathers. However, note that no swimming or water skiing is permitted here, and that non-motorized boats under 10 feet are prohibited. There is good fishing in the spring. The elevation is 1,500 feet. Open year-round.

Map grid **i5**

TUCALOTA SPRINGS RV PARK
near Lake Skinner

Campsites, facilities: There are 35 tent sites and 102 motor home spaces with full hookups. Picnic tables and fireplaces are provided. Rest rooms, showers, a playground, a swimming pool, a laundromat, a store, a dump station, ice, a recreation room, and propane gas are available. Fishing and boating access are nearby. Pets are permitted on leashes.
Reservations, fee: Reservations accepted; $14-$16 fee per night.
Who to contact: Phone the park at (714)925-3183.
Location: From Interstate 215 south of Perris, turn east on Highway 74 and drive about 14 miles to Hemet. From Hemet, drive 13 miles south on State Street to the town of Sage. Turn left on Benton Road to 41601 Benton Road.
Trip note: Lake Skinner, located to the west of Sage, has no campgrounds, so this is the closest alternative. It is set in foothill country at 2,400 feet elevation. The bonus feature is a small fishing pond. Open year-round.

Map grid **i8**

HURKEY CREEK COUNTY PARK
near Lake Hemet

Campsites, facilities: There are 105 family campsites and 104 group sites for tents or motor homes up to 35 feet long. Fireplaces and picnic tables are provided. Piped water, flush toilets, and showers are available. A dump station is available for a fee at Lake Hemet campground nearby. Pets are permitted on leashes.
Reservations, fee: Reservations required; $10 fee per night; pets $1.
Who to contact: Phone the park at (714)659-2050.
Location: From Palm Desert, drive about 32 miles southwest on Highway 74 to the campground entrance on your right.
Trip note: This large county park is located just east (across the road) from Lake Hemet, beside Hurkey Creek (which runs in winter and spring). The highlight, of course, is the nearby lake, known for good fishing in the spring. No swimming is permitted. The elevation is 4,800 feet. Open year-round.

Map grid **i8**

LAKE HEMET

Campsites, facilities: There are 500 campsites for tents or motor homes. Piped water, fireplaces, picnic tables, and, in some cases, electrical connections are provided. Flush toilets, showers, a dump station, a playground, a boat ramp, boat rentals, a grocery store, and propane gas are available.
Reservations, fee: No reservations; $7 fee per night.
Who to contact: Phone the camp at (714)659-2680.
Location: From Palm Desert, drive 32 miles on Highway 74 to the entrance.
Trip note: Hemet is a long, narrow lake, set on the South Fork of the San Jacinto River. It's a popular place for trout fishing, particularly in the spring. Boats under ten feet or over 18 feet are prohibited and no swimming either. The elevation is 4,300 feet. Open June through November.

Map grid **j0**

TENAJA
on Tenaja Creek
CLEVELAND NATIONAL FOREST

Campsites, facilities: There are five campsites. Picnic tables and fireplaces are provided. Piped water and vault toilets are available. Pets are permitted on leashes.

Reservations, fee: No reservations; $7 fee.

Who to contact: Phone the Cleveland National Forest Headquarters at (619)557-5050.

Location: From Interstate 5 in Murietta, drive 12 miles west on Tenaja Road (a dirt road) to the campground.

Trip note: This is a tiny, oft-overlooked camp set along little Tenaja Creek. The trailhead for a hike into the San Mateo Canyon Wilderness is three miles further up the dirt road. The elevation is 2,000 feet. Open year-round.

Map grid j5

DRIPPING SPRINGS

near Agua Tibia Wilderness
CLEVELAND NATIONAL FOREST

Campsites, facilities: There are 26 campsites for tents or motor homes up to 32 feet long. Piped water, fireplaces, and picnic tables are provided. Vault toilets are available. Pets are permitted on leashes. A grocery store is nearby.

Reservations, fee: No reservations; $5 fee per night.

Who to contact: Phone the Cleveland National Forest Headquarters at (619)557-5050.

Location: From Interstate 15 in Temecula, drive 11 miles east on Highway 79 to the campground.

Trip note: This is one of the premium Forest Service camps, set just inside the northern border above Vail Lake and adjacent to the Agua Tibia Wilderness. The Dripping Springs Trail is routed south out of camp, starting at 1,500 feet elevation and climbing near the peak of Agua Tibia Mountain, which is 4,779 feet. Open from April to November.

Map grid j8

KAMP ANZA KAMP-GROUND

near Anza

Campsites, facilities: There are 106 sites for tents or motor homes, many with full hookups. Picnic tables and fireplaces are provided. Rest rooms, showers, a playground, a fishing pond, a swim spa, horseshoe pits, a laundromat, a store, a dump station, ice, a recreation room, and propane gas are available.

Reservations, fee: Reservations accepted; $12-$15 fee per night.

Who to contact: Phone the park at (714)763-4819.

Location: From Palm Desert, drive west on Highway 74 for 24 miles. Turn left on Highway 371 and drive west to the town of Anza. Turn left on Kirby Road and drive one mile. Turn left on Wellman Road and drive one mile. Turn right on Terwilliger Road and drive to 41560 Terwilliger Road.

Trip note: This is a year-round motor home park set at 4,100 feet elevation, with many nearby recreation options. Lake Hemet is 11 miles away, with hiking, motorbiking, and jeep trails nearby in San Bernardino National Forest.

◆ MAP I7 ◆

BEACH
TREES
5% CLUB
DESERT
URBAN
FOOTHILL
GRASSLAND

15 MILES

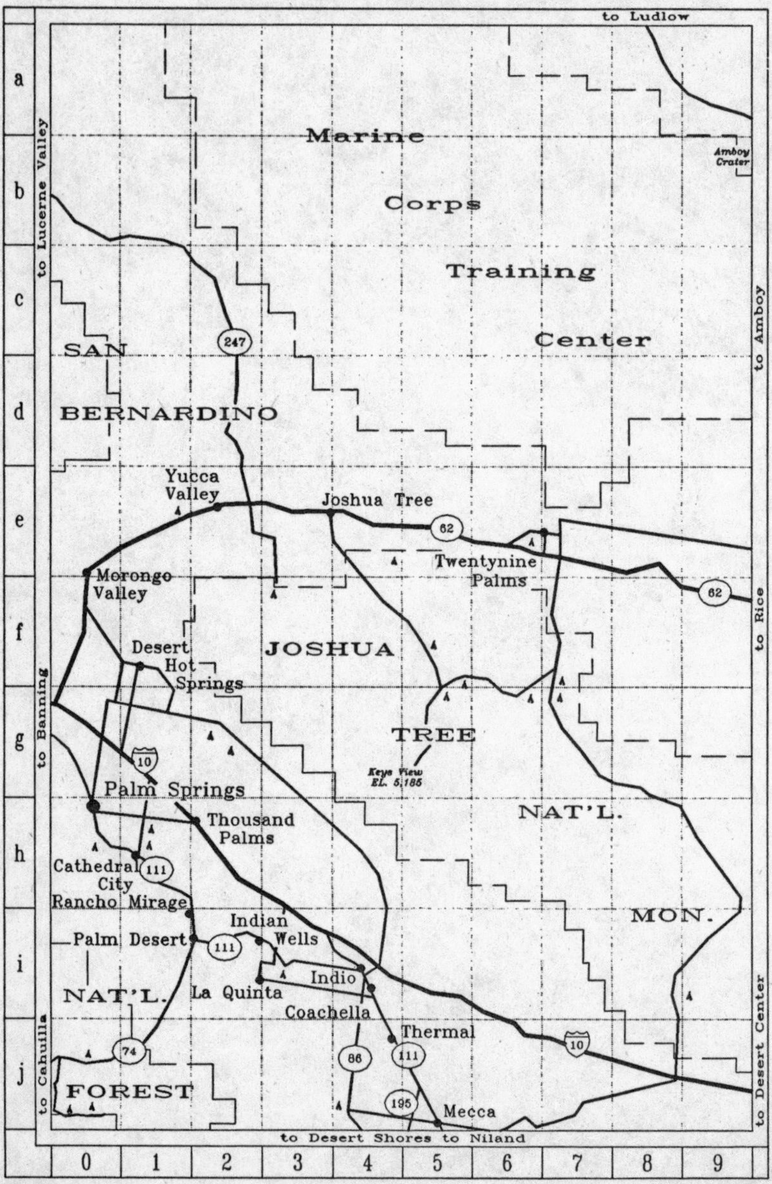

Map grid **e1**

MORONGO PARK

near Joshua Tree National Monument

A

Campsites, facilities: There are six campsites that can accommodate tents or motor homes. There is **no piped water,** but pit toilets, picnic tables, and fireplaces are provided. Supplies can be purchased in Morongo Valley. Pets are permitted on leashes.

B

Reservations, fee: No reservations, no fee..

Who to contact: This is a city park. For information call (619)363-6454.

Location: From Yucca Valley, drive five miles west on Highway 62.

Trip note: Not many folks use this camp. It's basically for desperate overnighters, stuck for a spot. So ya really can't whine too much about the no piped water. No nuthin', in fact. If it's summer, you'd best bring your own drinks or risk dying of dehydration. The elevation is 3,000 feet.

C

Map grid **e4**

INDIAN COVE CAMPGROUND

JOSHUA TREE NATIONAL MONUMENT

D

Campsites, facilities: There are 111 campsites for tents or motor homes to 32 feet long. Adjacent to this campground is a group camp with 13 sites for tents only that will accommodate 30-70 people each. Drinking water is available at the Indian Cove Ranger Station. Pit toilets, picnic tables, and fireplaces are provided. Gas, groceries, and laundry services are in town, which is about ten miles from camp. Pets are permitted on leashes and not on backcountry trails.

E

Reservations, fee: No reservations, no fee; reserve group sites through Ticketron by calling (800)452-1111.

Who to contact: Phone the Joshua Tree National Monument at (619)367-7511.

Location: From Joshua Tree, drive about nine miles east on Highway 62 to Indian Cove Road. Turn right and drive three miles to the campground.

F

Trip note: This is one of the campgrounds that is near the northern border of Joshua Tree National Monument. The vast desert park, covering 870 square miles, is best known for its unique granite formations and scraggly-looking trees. If you had to withstand the summer heat here, you'd look scraggly too. Drinking water is available at the Indian Cove Ranger Station.

G

Map grid **e6**

KNOTT SKY PARK

near Joshua Tree National Monument

Campsites, facilities: There are 80 sites for tents or motor homes, some with water and electrical hookups. Picnic tables and fireplaces are provided. Piped water, flush toilets, showers, a sanitary dump station, and a playground are available. Supplies and a laundromat are available nearby.

H

Reservations, fee: No reservations; $7.50 fee per night.

Who to contact: Phone the County Parks at (619)367-9669.

I7

Location: From Twentynine Palms, drive one mile west on Highway 62 to the park entrance.

Trip note: What the heck, unlike the camps in the nearby national monument to the south, this one has showers. And if you've spent any degree of time at Joshua Tree, you're probably in need in one. Whoo-eee! So turn that water on and dive in. The elevation is 2,000 feet. Open all year.

J

Map grid **f3**

BLACK ROCK CAMPGROUND

JOSHUA TREE NATIONAL MONUMENT

Campsites, facilities: There are 100 campsites for tents or motor homes to 32 feet long. Picnic tables and fireplaces are provided. Piped water, flush toilets, and a sanitary disposal station are available. Pets are permitted on leashes, but not on backcountry trails. Some sites are wheelchair accessible.

Reservations, fee: Reserve through Ticketron at (800)452-1111; $10 fee per night (plus reservation fee).

Who to contact: Phone the Joshua Tree National Monument at (619)367-7511.

Location: From the junction of Interstate 10 and Highway 62, drive about 22.5 miles north on Highway 62 to Yucca Valley. Turn south (right) on Joshua Lane and drive about five miles to the campground.

Trip note: This is the fanciest darn campground this side of the galaxy. Why they actually have piped water. Course, they charge you for it. It is set at the mouth of Black Rock Canyon, which provides good winter hiking possibilities amid unique (in other words, weird) rock formations. Show up in summer and you'll trade your gold for a sip of water. The elevation is 4,000 feet. Open October through May.

Map grid **f5**

HIDDEN VALLEY

JOSHUA TREE NATIONAL MONUMENT

Campsites, facilities: There are 62 campsites here for tents or motor homes up to 27 feet long. Picnic tables and fireplaces are provided. Pit toilets are available. There is **no piped water,** so bring plenty along. Pets are permitted on leashes.

Reservations, fee: No reservations, no fee.

Who to contact: Phone the Joshua Tree National Monument at (619)367-7511.

Location: From Joshua Tree on Highway 62, turn south on Park Boulevard and drive 14 miles southwest to the campground.

Trip note: Set at 4,200 feet elevation in the high desert country, this is one of several camping options in the area. Open year-round.

Map grid **f5**

SHEEP PASS GROUP CAMP

JOSHUA TREE NATIONAL MONUMENT

Campsites, facilities: There are six campsites here for tents. Picnic tables and fireplaces are provided. Pit toilets are available. There is **no piped water,** so bring plenty along. Pets are permitted on leashes.

Reservations, fee: Reserve through Ticketron at (800)452-1111; no fee except to Ticketron.

Who to contact: Phone the Joshua Tree National Monument at (619)367-7511.

Location: From Twentynine Palms, drive south on Utah Trail for about 16 miles to the campground on the south (left) side of the road.

Trip note: There are several camps located in this stretch of high desert. Ryan Camp is just one mile down the road and provides a nearby option. For details on the area, see the trip note for White Tank and Jumbo Rocks. Temperatures are routinely over 100 degrees in the summer months. Open year-round.

Map grid **f7**

BELLE

JOSHUA TREE NATIONAL MONUMENT

Campsites, facilities: There are 20 campsites here for tents or motor homes up to

27 feet long. Picnic tables and fireplaces are provided. Pit toilets are available. There is **no piped water,** so bring your own. Pets are permitted on leashes.

Reservations, fee: No reservations, no fee.

Who to contact: Phone the Joshua Tree National Monument at (619)367-7511.

Location: From Twentynine Palms, drive eight miles south on Utah Trail to the intersection with Cottonwood Springs Road. Turn south (bear left) on Cottonwood Road (goes to Interstate 10) and drive about 1.5 miles to the campground.

Trip note: This camp is at 3,800 feet elevation. It is one of the six camps in the immediate area. For details, see the trip note for White Tank.

Map grid g2

SAM'S FAMILY SPA

near Palm Springs

Campsites, facilities: There are 180 RV spaces, with full hookups and picnic tables. There is a separate area with fire grills. Rest rooms, showers, a playground, swimming pool, a wading pool, hot mineral pools, a sauna, a laundromat, a store, and a restaurant are available. Pets are permitted on leashes.

Reservations, fee: Call ahead for available space and fee.

Who to contact: Phone the park at (619)329-6457.

Location: From Interstate 10, take the Palm Drive exit north and drive three miles north on Palm Drive. Turn east (right) on Dillon Road and drive 4.5 miles to 70-875 Dillon Road.

Trip note: Hot mineral pools attract tons of winter vacationers to the Palm Springs area. This spot, being set ten miles outside of Palm Springs, provides an alternative to the more crowded spots. The elevation is 1,000 feet. Open year-round.

Map grid g2

SKY VALLEY EAST

near Palm Springs

Campsites, facilities: There are 360 motor home spaces. Picnic tables, piped water, electrical connections, and sewer hookups are provided. Rest rooms, showers, a swimming pool, five natural hot mineral pools, a laundromat, a large recreation room, a social director, shuffleboard, tennis, horseshoes, a crafts room, and walking trails are available. A grocery store and propane gas are nearby. Some facilities are wheelchair accessible.

Reservations, fee: Reservations accepted; $25 fee per night.

Who to contact: Phone the park at (619)329-2909.

Location: From Interstate 10, take the Palm Drive exit north and drive three miles north on Palm Drive. Turn east (right) on Dillon Road and drive 8.5 miles to 74-711 Dillon Road.

Trip note: A great spot for family fun and relaxation.

Map grid g5

RYAN

JOSHUA TREE NATIONAL MONUMENT

Campsites, facilities: There are 27 campsites here for tents or motor homes up to 27 feet long. Picnic tables and fireplaces are provided. Pit toilets are available. There is **no piped water,** so bring plenty along. Hitching posts are available at the campground (bring water for the horses).

Reservations, fee: No reservations, no fee.

Who to contact: Phone the Joshua Tree National Monument at (619)367-7511.

Location: From Joshua Tree on Highway 62, turn south on Park Boulevard and drive 17 miles southwest to the campground.

Trip note: This is one of the high desert camps in the immediate area (see Jumbo Rocks camp). Joshua Tree National Monument is a forbidding paradise, huge, hot, and waterless (most of the time). The unique rock formations look like some great artist made them with a chisel. The elevation is 4,300 feet.

Map grid g6

JUMBO ROCKS
JOSHUA TREE NATIONAL MONUMENT

Campsites, facilities: There are 130 camp sites here for tents or motor homes up to 27 feet long. Picnic tables and fireplaces are provided. Pit toilets are available. There is **no piped water,** so bring plenty along. Pets are permitted on leashes.

Reservations, fee: No reservations, no fee.

Who to contact: Phone the Joshua Tree National Monument at (619)367-7511.

Location: From Twentynine Palms, drive south on Utah Trail for about 12 miles to the campground on the south (left) side of the road.

Trip note: Joshua Tree National Monument covers more than 870 square miles. It is striking high desert with unique granite formations that seem to change color at different times of the day. This camp is one of the higher ones in the Monument at 4,400 feet elevation. Open all year.

Map grid g7

WHITE TANK
JOSHUA TREE NATIONAL MONUMENT

Campsites, facilities: There are 20 campsites here for tents or motor homes up to 27 feet long. Picnic tables and fireplaces are provided. Pit toilets are available, but there is **no piped water,** so bring plenty along. Pets are permitted on leashes.

Reservations, fee: No reservations, no fee.

Who to contact: Phone the Joshua Tree National Monument at (619)367-7511.

Location: From Twentynine Palms, drive eight miles south on Utah Trail to the intersection with Cottonwood Springs Road. Turn south (bear left) on Cottonwood Road (goes to Interstate 10) and drive three miles to the campground.

Trip note: Joshua Tree National Monument is a unique area where the high and low desert meet. It looks kind of like high plains country. Winter is a good time to explore the beautiful boulder piles and rock formations amid scraggly Joshua trees. There are several trails in the area, but don't even think about hiking in summer. The elevation is 3,800 feet.

Map grid h0

HAPPY TRAVELER RECREATIONAL VEHICLE PARK
in Palm Springs

Campsites, facilities: There are 139 motor home spaces with full hookups and picnic tables. Rest rooms, showers, a recreation room, a swimming pool, a jacuzzi, and a laundromat are available. Pets are permitted on leashes.

Reservations, fee: Reservations; $22 fee per night.

Who to contact: Phone the park at (619)325-8518.

Location: In Palm Springs, drive one mile south on Palm Canyon Drive. Turn right on Mesquite Avenue to 211 West Mesquite Avenue.

Trip note: Are we having fun yet? They are at "Happy Traveler," which is within walking distance of Palm Springs shopping areas. Open year-round.

Map grid **h1**

OUTDOOR RESORTS
near Palm Springs

A

Campsites, facilities: There are 1,213 motor home spaces with full hookups. Rest rooms, showers, swimming pools, tennis courts, a health club with saunas, jacuzzis, a 27-hole golf course, a club house, a snack bar, a laundromat, a store, shuffleboard, and planned activities are available. Some facilities are wheelchair accessible. Pets are permitted on leashes.

B

Reservations, fee: Reservations accepted; $35-$40 fee per night.

Who to contact: Phone the park at (619)324-4005.

Location: From Cathedral City, drive two miles north on Date Palm Drive to Ramon Road. Turn and drive to 69-411 Ramon Road.

C

Trip note: This is the motor home park that was voted the "Most Likely To Succeed As a City." It's huge, it's flat, and it offers many activities. If you still can't think of anything to do, you can always compare tires. The park is located four miles from Palm Springs. Open year-round.

D

Map grid **h1**

DE ANZA PALM SPRINGS OASIS RV RESORT
near Palm Springs

Campsites, facilities: There are 140 motor home spaces with full hookups. Rest rooms, showers, cable TV hookups, a swimming pool, a jacuzzi, a putting green, a laundromat, a store, and propane gas are available. Pets are permitted on leashes.

E

Reservations, fee: Reservations accepted; $16-$24 fee per night.

Who to contact: Phone the park at (619)328-4813.

Location: In Cathedral City, drive to 36-100 Date Palm Drive.

F

Trip note: This popular wintering spot is for motor home cruisers looking to hole up in the Palm Springs area for awhile. Palm Springs is only six miles away. Open all year.

Map grid **i3**

INDIAN WELLS RV ROUNDUP
in Indio

G

Campsites, facilities: There are 381 motor home spaces, most with full hookups. Picnic tables and fireplaces are provided. Rest rooms, showers, cable TV hookups, three swimming pools, two therapy pools, a fitness room, shuffleboard courts, a putting green, planned activities, ice, a dog run, a barbecue, and a laundromat are available.

H

Reservations, fee: Call ahead for available space and fee; adults only.

Who to contact: Phone the park at (619)347-0895.

Location: In Indio on Interstate 10, take the Monroe Street exit and drive 1.5 miles south. Turn west (right) on Highway 111 and drive two miles. Turn left on Jefferson Street and drive to 47-340 Jefferson Street.

I7

Trip note: Indio is a good-size town located midway between the Salton Sea to the south and Palm Springs to the north. In the summer, it is one of the hottest places in America.

J

Map grid **i9**

COTTONWOOD
JOSHUA TREE NATIONAL MONUMENT

Campsites, facilities: There are 62 campsites here for tents or motor homes up to

27 feet long. There is a group campground adjacent to this one (Cottonwood Group Camp) that has three group sites for up to 30 people each. Piped water, picnic tables, and fireplaces are provided. Flush toilets are available. Pets are permitted on leashes.

Reservations, fee: No reservations for family sites; $6 fee per night; reserve group sites through Ticketron at (800)452-1111; $13 group fee per night plus reservation fee.

Who to contact: Phone the Joshua Tree National Monument at (619)367-7511.

Location: From Indio, drive 26 miles east on Interstate 10. Take the Twentynine Palms exit (near Chiriaco Summit) and drive ten miles north on the park entrance road to the campground.

Trip note: If you enter Joshua Tree National Monument at its southern access point, this is the first camp you come to. The park visitor center, with maps available, is a mandatory stop. The Monument is a vast, high desert, highlighted by unique rock formations, occasional scraggly trees, and vegetation that manages to survive the bleak, roasting summers. This camp is set at 3,000 feet elevation. Open year-round.

Map grid jO

TOOL BOX SPRINGS

SAN BERNARDINO NATIONAL FOREST

Campsites, facilities: There are six tent sites. Vault toilets, fireplaces, and picnic tables are provided. **No piped water** is provided. Pets are permitted on leashes.

Reservations, fee: No reservations, no fee.

Who to contact: Phone the San Bernardino National Forest District Office at (714)659-2117.

Location: Traveling southeast just past Lake Hemet on Highway 74, you'll see Forest Service Road 6S13 (paved, then dirt) on the right. Turn right (west) and drive about four miles. Turn left on Forest Service Road 5S13 and drive 4.5 miles to the camping area.

Trip note: This alternative to Thomas Mountain camp is located two miles southwest, also on the flank of Thomas Mountain. The difference is this camp has a little creek that runs by, though it turns into a trickle in summer, and a trail that runs right through the camp. If it is winter, call for road conditions to determine accessibility. The elevation is 6,500 feet.

Map grid jO

THOMAS MOUNTAIN

SAN BERNARDINO NATIONAL FOREST

Campsites, facilities: There are six tent sites. There is **no piped water,** but vault toilets, fireplaces, and picnic tables are provided. Pets are permitted on leashes.

Reservations, fee: No reservations, no fee.

Who to contact: Phone the San Bernardino National Forest District Office at (714)659-2117.

Location: Traveling southeast just past Lake Hemet on Highway 74 you'll see Forest Service Road 6S13 (paved, then dirt) on the right. Turn right (west) and drive about four miles. Turn left on Forest Service Road 5S13 and drive three miles.

Trip note: If you don't want to be bugged by anything but a few bugs, this is the place. It's a small, primitive camp set just on the eastern flank of Thomas Mountain, 6,800 feet elevation. There are no trails, no streams, no nuthin' in the immediate area. After you have purged your soul out here, you might consider a side trip to Lake Hemet, located four nautical miles (and a heck of a lot longer by car) to the north. Accessibility depends on weather conditions.

Map grid **j0**

PINYON FLATS

near Bighorn Sheep Lookout
SAN BERNARDINO NATIONAL FOREST

Campsites, facilities: There are 18 campsites for tents or motor homes up to 22 feet long. Piped water, vault toilets, fireplaces, and picnic tables are provided. The facilities are wheelchair accessible. Pets are permitted on leashes.

Reservations, fee: No reservations; $5 fee per night.

Who to contact: Phone the San Bernardino National Forest District Office at (714)659-2117.

Location: From Palm Desert, drive 14 miles southwest on Highway 74 to the camp.

Trip note: The Bighorn Sheep Lookout is just two miles east of the camp and provides a good, easy side trip. If you want to work harder at it, a trail that leads deep into the National Forest to the southeast starts less than one mile away. To get there, drive one mile south on Forest Service Road 7S01 and look for the trailhead on the left side of the road. The elevation is 4,000 feet. Open year-round. Have fun!

Map grid **j4**

LAKE CAHUILLA COUNTY PARK

near Indio

Campsites, facilities: There are 61 campsites for tents and 71 sites for motor homes up to 30 feet long, some with water and electrical hookups. Fireplaces and picnic tables are provided. Rest rooms, showers, a dump station, a playground, a swimming beach, and an unpaved boat ramp are available. Pets are permitted on leashes.

Reservations, fee: Reservations accepted; $7-$12 fee per night; pets $1.

Who to contact: Phone the park at (619)564-4712 or (714)684-0196 for reservations.

Location: From Interstate 10 in Indio, drive south on Washington Street for three miles. Turn left (or east) on Highway 111 and drive two miles. Turn right on Jefferson and drive eight miles to the park.

Trip note: Boaters beware. Even though Lake Cahuilla doesn't look big enough to cause much of a fuss, it can be quite dangerous when the Santa Ana winds are blowing. If the winds are moderate, the lake is good for sailboarding. In the summer it gets so hot here the lake starts to look like a sun spot until, in an attempt to keep from getting grilled alive, you jump in.

◆ MAP I8 ◆

BEACH
DESERT
FOOTHILL
TREES
URBAN
GRASSLAND
5% CLUB

15 MILES

to I-40
to Fenner
Essex
to Ludlow
Danby
Amboy
Amboy Crater
Chambless
Bristol Lake
Cadiz
Marine Corps Train. Center
Cadiz Lake
to Twentynine Palms
Danby Lake
62
to Rice
JOSHUA TREE NAT'L. MONUMENT
177
R2
Palen Lake
Hayfield Lake
Desert Center
10
to Indio
to Blythe

a
b
c
d
e
f
g
h
i
j

0 1 2 3 4 5 6 7 8 9

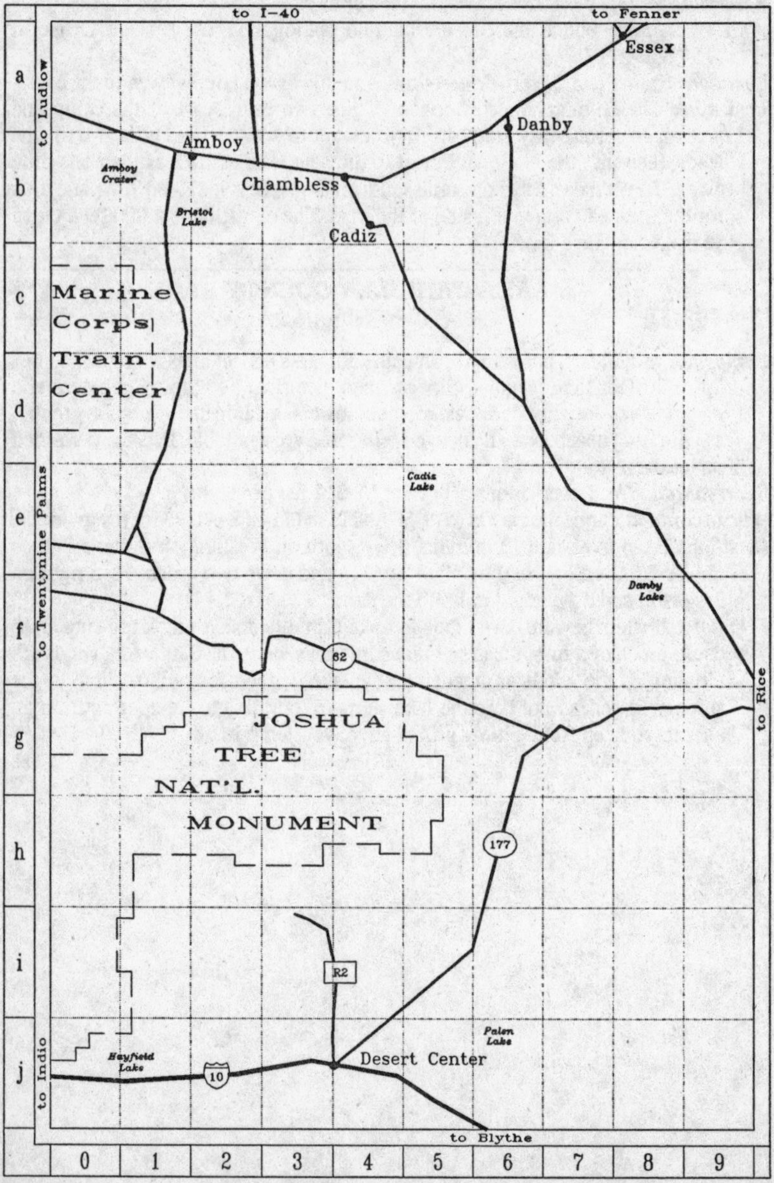

(no campgrounds)

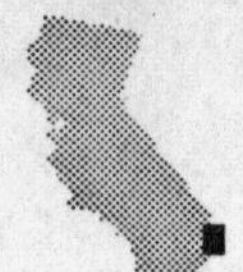

◆ MAP 19 ◆

BEACH
TREES
5% CLUB
DESERT
URBAN
FOOTHILL
GRASSLAND

15 MILES

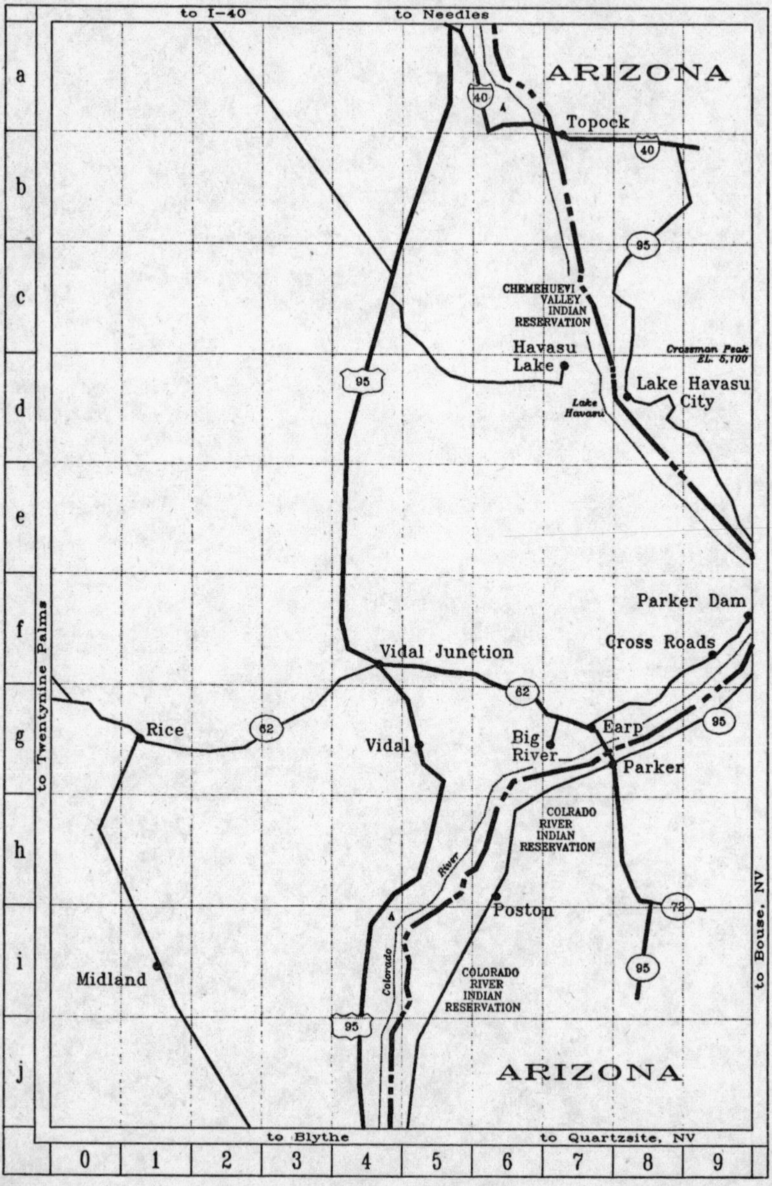

to I-40
to Needles
ARIZONA
40
Topock
40
95
CHEMEHUEVI VALLEY INDIAN RESERVATION
Havasu Lake
Crossman Peak EL. 5,100
95
Lake Havasu City
Lake Havasu
Parker Dam
Cross Roads
Vidal Junction
62
Earp
95
Big River
Parker
Rice
62
Vidal
COLORADO RIVER INDIAN RESERVATION
River
Poston
72
95
Colorado
COLORADO RIVER INDIAN RESERVATION
Midland
95
ARIZONA
to Twentynine Palms
to Bouse, NV
to Blythe
to Quartzsite, NV
a
b
c
d
e
f
g
h
i
j
0
1
2
3
4
5
6
7
8
9

Map grid **a6**

MOABI REGIONAL PARK

on Colorado River

Campsites, facilities: There are over 600 campsites for tents or motor homes, some with full or partial hookups. Picnic tables and fireplaces are provided at most sites. Flush toilets, showers, a laundromat, a store, ice, a playground, a sanitary dump station, and a boat ramp are available. Pets are permitted on leashes.
Reservations, fee: Reservations accepted; $10-$15 fee per night; pets $1.
Who to contact: Phone the Moabi Regional Park at (619)326-3831.
Location: From Needles, drive 11 miles east on Interstate 40. Turn north on Park Moabi Road and drive one-half mile to the park.
Trip note: The adjacent Colorado River provides the main attraction, with the beach and boat ramp a bonus. This is a popular boating area, with lots of wild and crazy types having the times of their lives on the water. Open year-round.

◆ MAP J5 ◆

BEACH
DESERT
FOOTHILL
TREES
URBAN
GRASSLAND
5% CLUB
15 MILES

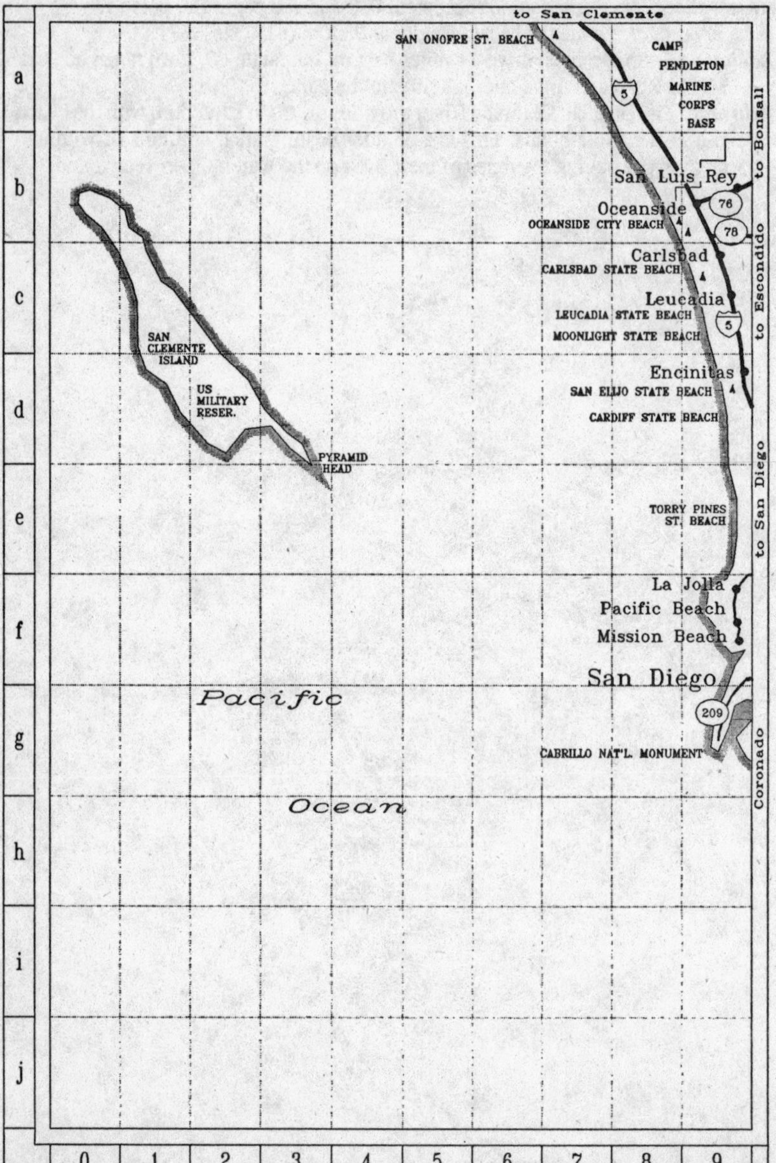

to San Clemente
SAN ONOFRE ST. BEACH
5
CAMP PENDLETON MARINE CORPS BASE
to Bonsall
San Luis Rey
76
Oceanside
OCEANSIDE CITY BEACH
78
Carlsbad
CARLSBAD STATE BEACH
Leucadia
LEUCADIA STATE BEACH
5
MOONLIGHT STATE BEACH
to Escondido
SAN CLEMENTE ISLAND
US MILITARY RESER.
Encinitas
SAN ELIJO STATE BEACH
CARDIFF STATE BEACH
PYRAMID HEAD
TORRY PINES ST. BEACH
to San Diego
La Jolla
Pacific Beach
Mission Beach
San Diego
Pacific
209
CABRILLO NAT'L. MONUMENT
Coronado
Ocean

a b c d e f g h i j

0 1 2 3 4 5 6 7 8 9

Map grid **a7**

SAN ONOFRE STATE BEACH
near San Clemente

Campsites, facilities: There are 230 campsites for tents or motor homes. Piped water, fireplaces, and picnic tables are provided. Cold showers and flush toilets are available. A grocery store, a laundromat, and propane gas are nearby. Pets are permitted on leashes.

Reservations, fee: Reserve through MISTIX at (800)444-PARK ($3.95 MISTIX fee); $12-$16 fee per night; pets $1.

Who to contact: Phone the campground at (714)492-4872.

Location: From San Clemente, drive three miles south on Interstate 5. Take the Basilone exit and drive to the park.

Trip note: Located just off the busy interstate highway, this park is one of three set along the beach near San Clemente. The others are San Clemente State Beach and Doheny State Beach, both located to the north. This area was one of the most popular areas in California for surfing and sits in the shadow of the San Onofre Nuclear Power Plant.

Map grid **b8**

PARADISE BY THE SEA RV PARK
in Oceanside

Campsites, facilities: There are 102 motor home spaces with full hookups. Flush toilets, showers, cable TV hookups, a swimming pool, a jacuzzi, a clubhouse, a banquet room, laundry, RV supplies, a telephone, and a mini-store are available. Boat rentals can be found nearby. Pets are permitted on leashes.

Reservations, fee: Call for available space; $22-$27 fee per night; pets $1.

Who to contact: Phone the park at (619)439-1376.

Location: From Interstate 5 in Oceanside, take the Highway 78-Vista Way exit. Drive west for one-half mile. Turn right on Hill Street to 1537 South Hill Street.

Trip note: This is a classic ocean-front motor home park, but no tenters need apply. It's an easy walk to the beach. For boaters, Oceanside Marina to the immediate north is the place to go. Camp Pendleton, a huge marine corps training complex, is located to the north. Open year-round.

Map grid **b9**

CASITAS RV PARK
in Oceanside

Campsites, facilities: There are 140 motor home spaces with full hookups, picnic tables and patios provided. Flush toilets, showers, cable TV hookups, a playground, a laundromat, a recreation room, a swimming pool, a jacuzzi, a billiard room, propane gas, and a grocery store are available.

Reservations, fee: Reservations recommended; $22-$30 fee per night.

Who to contact: Phone the park at (619)722-4404.

Location: From Interstate 5, in Oceanside, take the Oceanside Blvd. exit. Drive west for one-half mile. Turn right on Hill Street to 1510 South Hill Street.

Trip note: There are three options for motor home cruisers in the Oceanside area. This is one of them. For details on the area, see the trip note for Paradise By the Sea. Open year-round, a short distance to the beach.

Map grid **c9**

SOUTH CARLSBAD STATE BEACH
near Carlsbad

Campsites, facilities: There are 224 campsites for tents or motor homes up to 35 feet long. Picnic tables and fireplaces are provided. Piped water, flush toilets, showers, and a dump station are available. Some facilities are wheelchair accessible. Supplies and a laundromat are available in Carlsbad. Pets are permitted on leashes.

Reservations, fee: Reserve through MISTIX at (800)444-PARK ($3.95 MISTIX fee); $14-$19 fee per night; pets $1.

Who to contact: Phone the park at (619)438-3143.

Location: From Carlsbad, drive four miles south on County Road S21 to the entrance.

Trip note: No reservation? Then likely you can forget about staying here. This is a beautiful state beach and as big as it is, the sites go fast to the coastal cruisers who used the MISTIX reservation system. Open year-round.

Map grid d9

SAN ELIJO STATE BEACH

in Cardiff by the Sea

Campsites, facilities: There are 171 campsites for tents or motor homes up to 35 feet long. Picnic tables and fireplaces are provided. Piped water, flush toilets, showers, a dump station, and a small store are available. Some of the campground and the store are wheelchair accessible. Pets are permitted on six foot leashes in the campground, but not on the beach.

Reservations, fee: Reserve through MISTIX at (800)444-PARK ($3.95 MISTIX fee); $14-$21 fee per night; pets $1.

Who to contact: Phone the park at (619)753-5091.

Location: From Cardiff by the Sea, drive one-half mile northwest on County Road S21 to the park entrance.

Trip note: This is another in the series of popular state beaches along the San Diego County coast. This one is located along a beautiful beach just north of the small town of Cardiff by the Sea. Like at all state beaches, reservations are usually required to get a spot between Memorial Day weekend and Labor Day weekend. Open year-round.

◆ MAP J6 ◆

BEACH
TREES
5% CLUB
DESERT
URBAN
FOOTHILL
GRASSLAND

15 MILES

to Murrieta
to Temecula
to Cahuilla
to Oceanside
to Encinitas
to Cabrillo Nat'l. Mon.
to Borrego Springs
to Ocotillo Wells
to Agua Caliente
to Boulevard

CAMP PENDLETON MARINE CORPS BASE
Fallbrook
Bonsall
Vista
San Marcos
Escondido
Rancho Santa Fe
Del Mar
Pala
Pauma Valley
Rincon Springs
Center Valley
PALOMAR MTN. ST. PK.
Palomar Mtn.
ANZA–BORREGO DESERT STATE PARK
LOS COYOTES IND. RES.
Warner Springs
Lake Henshaw
CLEVELAND NAT'L. FOREST
Santa Ysabel
Julian
Rancho Bernardo
Ramona
Poway
San Vicente Lake
CAPTAIN GRANDE IND. RES.
El Capitan Lake
CUYAMACA RANCHO ST. PARK
Lakeside
Santee
Lake Murray
El Cajon
Alpine
Descanso
Guatay
Mt. Laguna
La Mesa
San Diego
Coronado
National City
Sweetwater Reservoir
Jamul
Pine Valley
Laguna Jct. EL. 4,055
Chula Vista
Barrett Lake
Lake Morena
Tecate Divide EL. 4,140
Lower Otay Lake
Dulzura
Morena Village
Otay
Imperial Beach
San Ysidro
Barrett Junction
Potrero
MANZANITA INDIAN RES.
Campo
Tijuana
Tecate
MEXICO
Pacific Ocean
Rosarito

S13, 76, 78, 15, S6, S7, 79, S2, S22, 805, 52, 163, 5, 8, 67, 94, 54, 75, S1, 1, 2, 3

a b c d e f g h i j

0 1 2 3 4 5 6 7 8 9

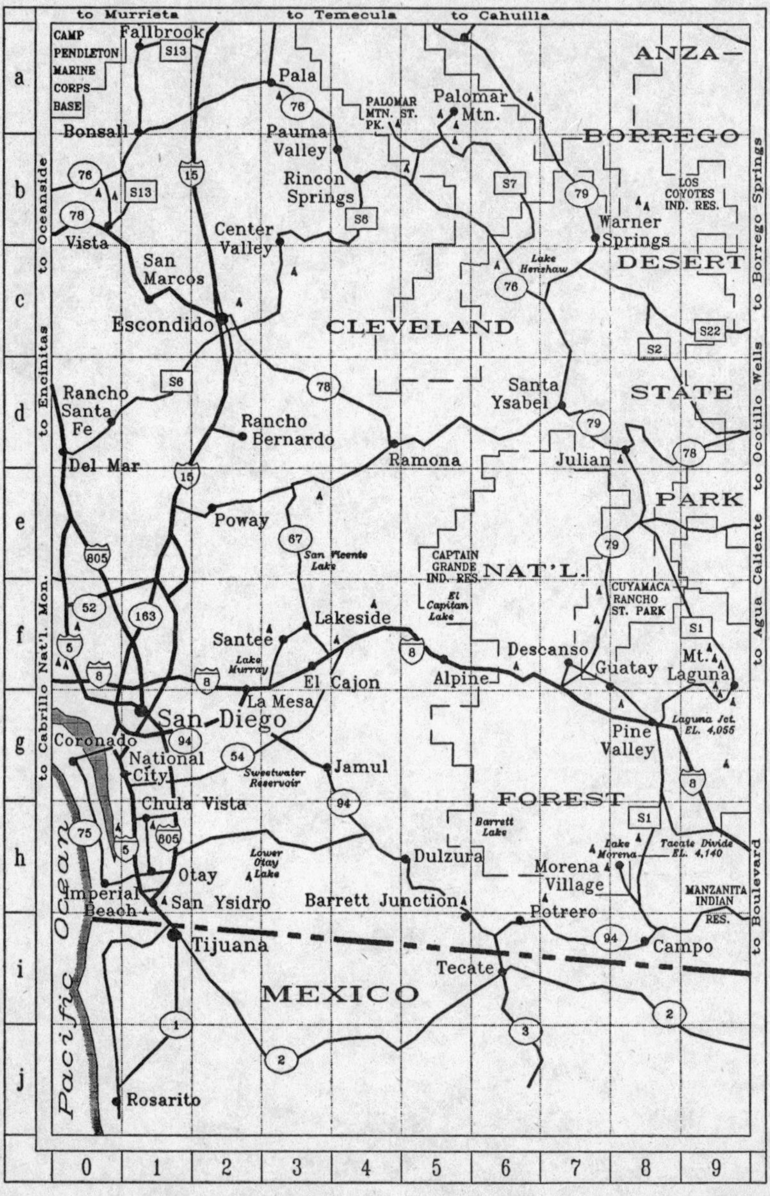

RANCHO CORRIDO

Map grid **a3**

near Pala Mission

Campsites, facilities: There are 120 campsites for tents or motor homes. Picnic tables, fireplaces, electrical connections, piped water, and, in some cases, sewer connections are provided. Flush toilets, showers, a dump station, a playground, cable T.V., a small store, a rifle range, propane gas, and a laundromat are available. Pets are permitted on leashes.

Reservations, fee: Reservations accepted; $17 fee per night.

Who to contact: Phone the park at (619)742-3755.

Location: From Interstate 15, take the Highway 76 exit and drive east to the town of Pala. Continue east on Highway 76 for four miles to 14715 Highway 76.

Trip note: This motor home layover spot is located ten miles east of the main drag, Interstate 15. It is a short drive to Pala Indian Reservation and the Pala Mission to the east. The Palomar Observatory is 20 miles to the east, another possible side trip. Open year-round.

PALOMAR MOUNTAIN STATE PARK

Map grid **a4**

near Palomar Observatory

Campsites, facilities: There are 21 sites for tents only and ten sites for motor homes up to 22 feet long. Fireplaces and picnic tables are provided. Piped water, flush toilets, and showers are available. Some facilities are wheelchair accessible. Pets are permitted on leashes.

Reservations, fee: Reserve through MISTIX at (800)444-PARK ($3.95 MISTIX fee); $12-$14 fee per night; pets $1.

Who to contact: Phone the park at (619)742-3462 or 765-0755.

Location: From Interstate 15, turn east on Highway 76 and drive about 20 miles to County Road S6 (goes up to Palomar Mountain). Turn left (north) and drive 6.5 miles. Turn left on County Road S7 and drive 4.5 miles to the campground.

Trip note: This developed state park is a short drive from Palomar Observatory. It offers hiking trails and some fishing in Doane Pond. There are four other campgrounds in the immediate area that are a short distance from Palomar Observatory. The elevation is 4,700 feet. Open year-round.

FRY CREEK

Map grid **a5**

near Palomar Observatory

CLEVELAND NATIONAL FOREST

Campsites, facilities: There are 12 tent sites and eight campsites for tents or motor homes. Piped water, fireplaces, and picnic tables are provided. Vault toilets are available. A grocery store is nearby.

Reservations, fee: No reservations; $7 fee per night.

Who to contact: Phone the Cleveland National Forest at (619)557-5050.

Location: From Interstate 15, turn east on Highway 76 and drive about 20 miles to County Road S6 (goes up to Palomar Mountain). Turn left (north) and drive about nine miles to the campground entrance on the left.

Trip note: On a clear night, you can see forever from Palomar Mountain. Literally. That's because Palomar Observatory, just a short distance from this forested camp, houses America's largest telescope. The elevation is 5,200 feet. Open from May to November.

Map grid **a5**

OBSERVATORY

near Palomar Observatory

CLEVELAND NATIONAL FOREST

Campsites, facilities: There are 42 campsites for tents or motor homes up to 22 feet long. Fireplaces and picnic tables are provided, and piped water. Pit toilets are available. Pets are permitted on leashes.

Reservations, fee: No reservations; $7 fee per night.

Who to contact: Phone the Cleveland National Forest at (619)557-5050.

Location: From Interstate 15, turn east on Highway 76 and drive about 20 miles to County Road S6 (goes up to Palomar Mountain). Turn left (north) and drive about 8.5 miles to the campground entrance on the right.

Trip note: This popular Forest Service camp is used primarily as a layover spot for campers visiting the nearby Palomar Observatory, housing the largest telescope in America. There are four other camps in the immediate area. The elevation is 4,800 feet. Open from May to November.

Map grid **a6**

OAK GROVE

near Temecula Creek

CLEVELAND NATIONAL FOREST

Campsites, facilities: There are 81 campsites for tents or motor homes. Piped water, fireplaces, and picnic tables are provided. Flush toilets are available. Propane gas and groceries are nearby. Pets are permitted on leashes.

Reservations, fee: No reservations; $7 fee per night.

Who to contact: Phone the Cleveland National Forest at (619)557-5050.

Location: From Aguanga, drive 6.5 miles southeast on Highway 79.

Trip note: Easy access from Highway 79 makes this a popular camp. It is set at 2,800 feet elevation. Vail Lake, located about 15 miles to the northwest, provides good bass fishing in the spring. A boat ramp and boat rentals are available there. Open year-round.

Map grid **b0**

SUNRISE TERRACE RV PARK

near Vista

Campsites, facilities: There are 30 motor home spaces with full hookups. Flush toilets, showers, laundry, telephones, cable, and propane gas are available. There is a grocery store nearby.

Reservations, fee: Call ahead for space and fee.

Who to contact: Phone the park at (619)724-6654.

Location: From Interstate 15 northbound, take the Gopher Canyon Road exit. Turn left on East Vista Way. Turn right on Taylor and drive to 817 Taylor Street. From Interstate 15 southbound, take Highway 76. Turn right on East Vista Way. Turn right on Taylor Street and drive to 817 Taylor Street.

Trip note: This rural country park provides an overnight spot for highway cruisers. The San Diego Wild Animal Park is located about 20 miles southeast via Highway 15 and 78. Open year-round.

Map grid **b0**

GUAJOME COUNTY PARK

in Oceanside

Campsites, facilities: There are 17 motor home spaces with water and electrical hookups. Picnic tables and fireplaces are provided. Flush toilets, showers, a dump station, and a playground are available. A grocery store and propane gas are nearby. Pets are permitted on leashes.

Reservations, fee: Call for available space; $14 fee per night; pets $1.

Who to contact: Phone the County Parks Department at (619)565-3600 or (619694-3049.

Location: From Oceanside, drive seven miles east on Highway 76. Turn right on Guajome Lakes Road (Santa Fe Road) and drive to the entrance.

Trip note: This is one of the several options for motor home drivers cruising Highway 5 along the coast. It's not far from Mission San Luis Rey. Open year-round.

Map grid b5

CRESTLINE GROUP CAMP

near Palomar Observatory

CLEVELAND NATIONAL FOREST

Campsites, facilities: There is one group campsite for tents. Piped water, fireplaces, and picnic tables are provided, and vault toilets are available. A grocery store is nearby.

Reservations, fee: Reservations requested; $50 group fee per night.

Who to contact: Phone the Cleveland National Forest at (619)557-5050.

Location: From Interstate 15, turn east on Highway 76 and drive about 20 miles to County Road S6 (goes up to Palomar Mountain). Turn left (north) and drive 6.5 miles. The campground is at the junction of County Roads S6 and S7.

Trip note: This Forest Service camp is designed expressly for large groups planning to visit Palomar Observatory. The elevation is 4,800 feet. Open from May to November.

Map grid b5

OAK KNOLL CAMPGROUND

near Palomar Observatory

Campsites, facilities: There are 55 sites for tents or motor homes, many with full or partial hookups. Flush toilets, showers, a playground, a solar heated pool, a clubhouse, a baseball diamond, a dump station, laundry, propane gas, and groceries are available.

Reservations, fee: Call ahead for available space and fee.

Who to contact: Phone the park at (619)742-3437.

Location: From Interstate 15, turn east on Highway 76 and drive about 20 miles to County Road S6 (goes up to Palomar Mountain). Turn left (north) and drive one block to the campground.

Trip note: This is one in a series of camps where visitors can set up shop while visiting nearby Palomar Observatory, which houses the largest telescope in the world. The camp is set at 3,000 feet elevation in the San Diego County foothill country, among giant old California Oaks. Open year-round.

Map grid b8

INDIAN FLATS GROUP CAMP

near Pacific Crest Trail

CLEVELAND NATIONAL FOREST

Campsites, facilities: There are two group campsites for tents or motor homes. Piped water, fireplaces, and picnic tables are provided. Vault toilets are available.

Reservations, fee: Reserve through MISTIX at (800)283-CAMP ($6 MISTIX fee); $25 per night group fee.

Who to contact: Phone the Cleveland National Forest at (619)557-5050.

Location: From Warner Springs on Highway 79, drive two miles northwest on Highway 79. Turn right (north) on Forest Service Road 9S05 and drive six miles to the campground.

Trip note: This is a nearby option to the Oak Grove camp, expressly designed for groups who need some room and don't want to be bugged by anything. For side trip information, see that trip note. The elevation is 3,600 feet. Open from April to November.

Map grid b8

INDIAN FLATS CAMP

near Pacific Crest Trail
CLEVELAND NATIONAL FOREST

Campsites, facilities: There are 17 campsites for tents or motor homes. Piped water, fireplaces, and picnic tables are provided. Vault toilets are available. Pets are permitted on leashes.

Reservations, fee: No reservations; $6 fee per night.

Who to contact: Phone the Cleveland National Forest at (619)557-5050.

Location: From Warner Springs on Highway 79, drive two miles northwest on Highway 79. Turn right (north) on Forest Service Road 9S05 and drive six miles to the campground.

Trip note: The Pacific Crest Trail passes only two miles away, providing the opportunity for a day hike or a multi-day adventure for backpackers. A possible side trip is Lake Henshaw, about 15 miles away, where fishing for bass and catfish can be good and no waterskiers are allowed. Boat rentals are available from a resort on the south shore. The elevation is 3,600 feet. Open from April to November.

Map grid c2

DIXON LAKE RECREATION AREA

near Escondido

Campsites, facilities: There are 45 campsites for tents or motor homes, some with full hookups. Picnic tables, fireplaces, and piped water are provided. Flush toilets, showers, boat rentals, bait, ice, snack bar, and playground are available. Pets are not permitted.

Reservations, fee: Call for available space; $10-$14 fee per night.

Who to contact: Phone the park at (619)741-3328.

Location: In Escondido, drive four miles northeast on El Norte Parkway to La Honda Drive. Turn left and drive to 1700 North La Honda Drive at Dixon Lake.

Trip note: On this small lake, set near Escondido, boating is restricted to rental boats only. The lake is primarily used by anglers. Nearby Lake Hodges to the south is much bigger, has big bass, and no restrictions on boating. The elevation is 1,000 feet. Open year-round.

Map grid c3

WOODS VALLEY KAMPGROUND

near Lake Wohlford

Campsites, facilities: There are 59 motor home spaces and 30 campsites for tents or motor homes. Picnic tables, fireplaces, electrical connections, piped water, and, in some cases, sewer hookups are provided. Flush toilets, showers, a dump station, and a playground are available. Supplies and a laundromat are nearby. Pets are permitted on leashes.

Reservations, fee: Reservations accepted; $14-$23 fee per night; pets $1.

Who to contact: Phone the park at (619)749-2905.

Location: From Escondido on Interstate 15, turn east on County Road S6 and drive northeast to Valley Center. Turn right on Woods Valley Road and drive two miles east to 15236 Woods Valley Road.

Trip note: This privately-operated park is set up primarily for motor homes. It is a short drive from Lake Wohlford to the south. Other possible side trips include the San Pasqual Battlefield State Historic Park on Highway 78 to the south and big Lake Hodges, located south of Escondido. Open year-round.

Map grid c6

LAKE HENSHAW RESORT RV
near San Ysabel

Campsites, facilities: There are 164 campsites for tents or motor homes, many with full hookups. Flush toilets, showers, a swimming pool, a jacuzzi, a clubhouse, a playground, a dump station, laundry, propane gas, boat and motor rentals, a boat launch, a bait and tackle shop, a restaurant, and groceries are available. A golf course is nearby. Pets are permitted on leashes.

Reservations, fee: Reservations accepted; $10-$12 fee per night.

Who to contact: Phone (619)782-3487 or (619)782-3501.

Location: From San Ysabel, drive seven miles north on Highway 79. Turn left on Highway 76 and drive four miles to the campground.

Trip note: Lake Henshaw is the biggest lake in San Diego County, yet it only has one camp. This one is located on the southern corner of the lake. The lake is fed by several streams and provides good trout fishing in the winter and spring and good catfishing in the summer. It is stocked annually with 10,000 pounds—and sometimes more—of channel catfish and rainbow trout. The elevation is 2,700 feet. Open year-round.

Map grid d8

WILLIAM HEISE COUNTY PARK
near Julian

Campsites, facilities: There are 43 sites for tents only, 40 campsites for tents or motor homes, and several group sites. Fireplaces and picnic tables are provided. Piped water, flush toilets, showers, a dump station, and a playground are available. Supplies and laundromat are nearby in Julian. Pets are permitted on leashes.

Reservations, fee: Reservations needed; $11 fee per night; pets $1.

Who to contact: Phone the County Parks Department at (619)565-3600.

Location: From Highway 78 west of Julian, turn south on Pine Hills Road and drive two miles. Turn left on Frisius Drive and drive two miles to the park.

Trip note: This little-known spot, set at 4,200 feet elevation, offers hiking trails and a playground, and is surrounded by recreation options. They include Cleveland National Forest to the immediate south, Lake Cuyamaca and Cuyamaca State Park to the southeast, and the vast Anza-Borrego Desert State Park to the east. Open year-round.

Map grid e3

DOS PICOS COUNTY PARK
near Ramona

Campsites, facilities: There are 14 tent sites and 50 motor home spaces with water and electrical hookups. Picnic tables and fireplaces are provided. Flush toilets, showers, a playground, and a dump station are available. Supplies and a laundromat are nearby in Ramona. Pets are permitted on leashes.

Reservations, fee: Call for available space; $10-$14 fee per night; pets $1.

Who to contact: Phone the park at (619)565-3600.

Location: From Interstate 8 in El Cajon, drive 22 miles north on Highway 67. Make a sharp right on Mussey Grade Road and drive two miles to the park.

Trip note: As a county park, this camp is often missed by folks relying on less complete guides. Several nearby recreation options are in the area. San Vicente Lake is about 15 miles away, a prime bass lake open Thursday through Sunday from September through June. The Barona Ranch Indian Reservation and Barona Mission, also 15 miles from the park, are located to the southeast. The elevation is 1,500 feet. Open year-round.

Map grid fO

DE ANZA HARBOR RESORT

on Mission Bay

Campsites, facilities: There are 250 motor home spaces with full hookups and patios. Flush toilets, showers, a playground, a dump station, a laundromat, a recreation room, a jacuzzi, bike rentals, a boat ramp, propane gas, and a grocery store are available.

Reservations, fee: Call for available space; $27-$39 fee per night.

Who to contact: Phone the park at (619)273-3211.

Location: From southbound Interstate 5, take the Balboa-Garnet exit to Mission Bay Drive. Turn left and drive to North Mission Bay Drive. Turn right on De Anza Road and drive to 2727 De Anza Road.

Trip note: Location means everything in real estate and campgrounds, and this private park passes the test. It is set on a small peninsula that is surrounded on three sides by Mission Bay, Sea World, and the San Diego Zoo. Beaches and golf courses are nearby. Open year-round.

Map grid fO

CAMPLAND ON THE BAY

on Mission Bay

Campsites, facilities: There are 750 tent and motor home spaces, most with full or partial hookups. Picnic tables and fireplaces are provided. Flush toilets, showers, phone hookups, swimming pools, a jacuzzi, a recreation hall, a playground, a dump station, a laundromat, a grocery store, RV supplies, propane gas, a boat ramp, boat docks, boat and bike rentals, and groceries are available. Pets are permitted on leashes.

Reservations, fee: Reservations accepted; seasonal rates are $33.50-$43.50 fee per night; off-season rates are $24.50-$29.50 per night; pets $3.

Who to contact: Phone the park at (619)274-6260.

Location: From southbound Interstate 5 in San Diego, take the Balboa-Garnet exit. Drive straight on Mission Bay Drive to Grand Avenue. Turn right and drive one mile. Turn left on Olney Avenue and drive a short distance to the campground entrance. From northbound Interstate 5 in San Diego, take the Grand-Garnet exit. Stay in the left lane and turn left on Grand Avenue. Turn left on Olney Avenue as above.

Trip note: No kidding, this is one of the biggest campgrounds on this side of the galaxy. With space for both tenters and motor homes, you can usually find a spot to shoehorn your way into. It is set on Mission Bay, a beautiful spot. Sea World, located just north of San Diego, offers a premium side trip. Open year-round.

A

Map grid f0 SANTA FE TRAVEL TRAILER PARK
in San Diego

Campsites, facilities: There are 129 motor home spaces with full hookups. Flush toilets, showers, a playground, a swimming pool, a dump station and laundry facilities are available. Pets are permitted on leashes.

B

Reservations, fee: Call for available space; $22-$33 fee per night; pets $1.

Who to contact: Phone the park at (619)272-4051.

Location: In San Diego from Interstate 5, take the Balboa-Garnet exit (southbound). Drive straight (south) on Mission Drive for a short distance to Damon Street (2nd light). Go left and follow to Santa Fe Street. Turn left and drive to 5707 Santa Fe Street.

C

Trip note: This camp is a short drive from a variety of side trips, including the San Diego Zoo, Sea World, golf courses, beaches, sport fishing, and Tijuana. Open year-round.

Map grid f3 SANTEE LAKES REGIONAL PARK
near Santee

D

Campsites, facilities: There are 152 sites for motor homes with full hookups. There are 50 sites (out of the total 152) which can be used for tents. Some BBQ grills are provided. Flush toilets, showers, a dump station, boat rentals, a playground, a grocery store, and a laundromat are available. A snack bar is nearby. Pets are permitted in campground, but not in park.

E

Reservations, fee: Call for available space; $16 fee per night; pets $1.

Who to contact: Phone the park at (619)448-2482.

Location: From Interstate 8 in El Cajon, drive two miles north on Highway 67 to the town of Santee. Turn left on Mission Gorge Road and drive 2.5 miles to Carlton Hills Boulevard. Turn right and drive one mile to the park.

F

Trip note: This small regional park is located 20 miles east of San Diego. Low-key boating is the name of the game here. Rowboats, pedal boats, and canoes are available for rent. The camp is set at 400 feet elevation. Open year-round.

G

Map grid f4 RANCHO LOS COCHES RV PARK
near Lake Jennings

Campsites, facilities: There are 4 tent sites and 60 motor home spaces with full hookups. Flush toilets, showers, a dump station, and laundry facilities are available. A grocery store is nearby.

H

Reservations, fee: Call ahead for available space and fee.

Who to contact: Phone the park at (619)443-2025.

Location: From El Cajon, drive east on Interstate 8 to the Los Coches Road exit. Go under the freeway. Turn right on Olde 80 and drive to park entrance at 13468 Olde Highway 80.

I

Trip note: Nearby Lake Jennings provides an option for boaters and anglers and also has a less developed camp located on its northeast shore. Vista Point on the southeastern side of the lake provides a side trip.

Map grid f4 LAKE JENNINGS COUNTY PARK

J6

Campsites, facilities: There are 35 sites for tents only, 13 campsites for tents or motor homes, and 63 motor home spaces, most with full hookups. Picnic tables and fireplaces are provided. Flush toilets, showers, a playground, and a dump station are available. A grocery store is nearby. Pets are permitted on leashes.

Reservations, fee: Call for available space; $10-$16 fee per night; pets $1.

Who to contact: Phone the County Parks Department at (619)565-3600.

Location: From San Diego, drive 16 miles east on Interstate 8. Take Lake Jennings Park Road north to the park.

Trip note: Only one camp is available at little Lake Jennings and this is it. It is set on the northeastern shore at 800 feet elevation. Easy access from Highway 8 is a bonus. The lake is known for bass and catfish, and has a boat ramp and rentals available nearby on the east shore of the lake. Open year-round.

Map grid f6

ALPINE RV RESORT

near Lake Jennings

Campsites, facilities: There are 340 campsites for tents or motor homes, some with full or partial hookups. Picnic tables are provided. Flush toilets, showers, a dump station, a laundromat, a recreation room, and a swimming pool are available. No pets over 15 pounds are permitted.

Reservations, fee: Call for available space; $11-$14 fee per night.

Who to contact: Phone the park at (619)445-3162.

Location: From Interstate 8 just east of Alpine, take the East Willows exit. Cross over the freeway and drive one-third mile to 5635 Willows Drive.

Trip note: This is one of the few motor home parks in the area that welcomes tent campers. It is set in the foothill country in Alpine, eight miles from Lake Jennings to the west. The small lake has good fishing in the spring, (a boat ramp, boat rentals, and supplies are available). Other nearby lakes include larger El Capitan to the north and Loveland Reservoir to the south. Open year-round.

Map grid f7

PASO PICACHO

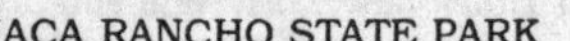

CUYAMACA RANCHO STATE PARK

Campsites, facilities: There are 85 campsites for tents or motor homes. Fireplaces and picnic tables are provided. Piped water, flush toilets, showers, and a dump station are available. Pets are permitted. Supplies are nearby in Cuyamaca.

Reservations, fee: Reserve through MISTIX at (800)444-PARK ($3.95 MISTIX fee); $12-$14 fee per night; pets $1.

Who to contact: Phone the Cuyamaca Rancho State Park at (619)765-0755.

Location: From Julian, drive 11 miles south on Highway 79 to the park entrance.

Trip note: This camp, in Cuyamaca State Park, is located just south of Lake Cuyamaca. It is set at 4,900 feet elevation, not far from the park headquarters, where exhibits about the area's Indians, goldmining, and natural history are available for your perusal. Perusal? That means for you to look at, podnah. Open year-round.

Map grid f7

GREEN VALLEY FALLS

CUYAMACA RANCHO STATE PARK

Campsites, facilities: There are 81 campsites for tents or motor homes. Piped water, fireplaces, and picnic tables are provided. Flush toilets and showers are available. Some of the campgrounds, picnic areas, and exhibits are wheelchair accessible. A grocery store and propane gas are nearby.

Reservations, fee: Reserve through MISTIX at (800)444-PARK ($3.95 MISTIX fee); $12-$14 fee per night; pets $1.

Who to contact: Phone the Cuyamaca Rancho State Park at (619)765-0755.

Location: From San Diego, drive approximately 40 miles east on Interstate 8 to Highway 79. Turn north and drive seven miles. Turn left (west) on Green Valley road, the entrance road into the park.

Trip note: This is the southernmost camp in Cuyamaca Rancho State Park. It is set at 3,900 feet, with Cuyamaca Mountain (6,512 feet) looming overhead to the northwest. Newcomers should visit the park headquarters, where there are exhibits detailing the natural history of the area. Open year-round.

Map grid f9

HORSE HEAVEN GROUP CAMP

near Pacific Crest Trail

CLEVELAND NATIONAL FOREST

Campsites, facilities: There are three group campsites for tents or motor homes. Piped water, fireplaces, and picnic tables are provided. Vault toilets are available. Supplies can be purchased in Mount Laguna.

Reservations, fee: Reserve through MISTIX at (800)283-CAMP ($6 MISTIX fee); $35-$75 fee per group per night.

Who to contact: Phone the Cleveland National Forest Headquarters at (619)557-5050.

Location: From San Diego, drive about 50 miles east on Interstate 8 to the Laguna Junction exit. Drive about 11 miles north on Sunrise Highway to the town of Mt. Laguna. Continue north for two miles on Sunrise Highway-Laguna Mountain Road to the campground entrance road on the left.

Trip note: Horse Heaven is set on the northeastern border of Cleveland National Forest at 5,500 feet elevation, near Mt. Laguna in the Laguna Recreation Area. The Pacific Crest Trail passes near the camp. Laguna and El Prado camps provide nearby options. Side trip possibilities include visiting Little Laguna Lake, to the immediate west, and Desert View Picnic Area, to the south at Mt. Laguna. Open from May to October.

Map grid f9

LAGUNA

near Little Laguna Lake

CLEVELAND NATIONAL FOREST

Campsites, facilities: There are 75 sites for tents only, 25 motor home spaces, and 20 campsites for tents or motor homes. Piped water, fireplaces, and picnic tables are provided. Vault toilets are available. A grocery store and propane gas are nearby.

Reservations, fee: Some sites by reservation only; phone MISTIX at (800)283-CAMP ($6 MISTIX fee); $8 fee per night.

Who to contact: Phone the Cleveland National Forest Headquarters at (619)557-5050.

Location: From San Diego, drive about 50 miles east on Interstate 8 to the Laguna Junction exit. Drive about 11 miles north on Sunrise Highway to the town of Mt. Laguna. Continue north for 2.5 miles on Sunrise Highway-Laguna Mountain Road to the campground entrance road on the left.

Trip note: Take your pick of the three camps in the immediate area, the others being El Prado Group Camp and Horse Heaven Group Camp. Little Laguna Lake is located to the southwest, and the Pacific Crest Trail passes near the camp. The elevation is 5,550 feet. Open year-round.

Map grid f9

EL PRADO GROUP CAMP
CLEVELAND NATIONAL FOREST

Campsites, facilities: There are five group campsites for tents or motor homes. Piped water, fireplaces, and picnic tables are provided. Vault toilets are available. Supplies can be purchased in Mt. Laguna.

Reservations, fee: Reserve through MISTIX at (800)283-CAMP ($6 MISTIX fee); $10 fee per group per night.

Who to contact: Phone the Cleveland National Forest Headquarters at (619)557-5050.

Location: From San Diego, drive about 50 miles east on Interstate 8 to the Laguna Junction exit. Drive about 11 miles north on Sunrise Highway to the town of Mt. Laguna. Continue north for 2.5 miles on Sunrise Highway-Laguna Mountain Road to the campground entrance road on the left.

Trip note: This is a nearby option to Horse Heaven Group Camp. See that trip note for recreation details. The elevation is 5,500 feet.Open from May to October.

Map grid f9

AGUA DULCE GROUP CAMP
near Pacific Crest Trail
CLEVELAND NATIONAL FOREST

Campsites, facilities: There are seven group campsites for tents. Piped water, fireplaces, and picnic tables are provided. Vault toilets are available. A grocery store is nearby.

Reservations, fee: Reserve through MISTIX at (800)283-CAMP ($6 MISTIX fee); $40 fee per group per night.

Who to contact: Phone the Cleveland National Forest Headquarters at (619)557-5050.

Location: From San Diego, drive approximately 50 miles east on Interstate 8 to the Laguna Junction exit. Drive about eight miles north on Sunrise Highway-Laguna Mountain Road to the campground entrance road on the left.

Trip note: This is one of the three camps that are set on the southern flanks of Mt. Laguna. Little Agua Dulce Creek runs nearby, and the Desert View Picnic Area, located two miles to the northwest, provides a side trip option. The Pacific Crest Trail passes nearby, running past the Burnt Rancheria camp. The elevation is 5,000 feet. Open from May to October.

Map grid g8

PINE VALLEY TRAILER PARK
near Cuyamaca Rancho State Park

Campsites, facilities: There are 85 motor home spaces with full hookups, including telephone. Laundromat facilities are available. Riding stables and a grocery store are nearby.

Reservations, fee: Call ahead for available space and fee.

Who to contact: Phone the park at (619)473-9040.

Location: From San Diego, drive 45 miles east on Interstate 8 to the Pine Valley exit. Go left and at the first stop sign go left again onto Olde Highway 80. Drive for about 3 miles to the park at 27521 Olde Highway 80.

Trip note: This privately-operated park provides a refined option to the more primitive camps located north in Cuyamaca Rancho State Park. It is set in a rustic area that is surrounded by National Forest land. Open year-round.

Map grid **g9**

CIBBETS FLAT
on Troy Canyon Creek
CLEVELAND NATIONAL FOREST

Campsites, facilities: There are 23 campsites for tents or small motor homes. Piped water, fireplaces, and picnic tables are provided. Vault toilets are available. Pets are permitted on leashes.

Reservations, fee: No reservations; $7 fee per night.

Who to contact: Phone the Cleveland National Forest Headquarters at (619)557-5050.

Location: From San Diego, drive about 53 miles east on Interstate 8 to the Kitchen Creek-Cameron Station exit. Turn north on Kitchen Creek Road and drive 4.5 miles to the campground entrance on the right.

Trip note: This small camp is set along Kitchen Creek, less than a mile from the Pacific Crest Trail. The elevation is 4,000 feet. Open from May to October.

Map grid **g9**

BURNT RANCHERIA
near Pacific Crest Trail
CLEVELAND NATIONAL FOREST

Campsites, facilities: There are 64 sites for tents only and 45 campsites for tents or motor homes. Piped water, fireplaces, and picnic tables are provided. Vault toilets and horseback riding facilities are available. Supplies are nearby in Mount Laguna.

Reservations, fee: Some sites by reservation only; reserve MISTIX at (800)283-CAMP ($6 MISTIX fee); $8 fee per night.

Who to contact: Phone the Cleveland National Forest Headquarters at (619)557-5050.

Location: From San Diego, drive approximately 50 miles east on Interstate 8 to the Laguna Junction exit. Drive about nine miles north on Sunrise Highway-Laguna Mountain Road to the campground entrance on the right.

Trip note: Set high (6,000 feet elevation) on the slopes of Mt. Laguna in Cleveland National Forest, the Pacific Crest Trail runs right alongside this camp. Desert View Picnic Area, a mile to the north, provides a good side trip. Open from May to October.

Map grid **g9**

WOODED HILL GROUP CAMP
near Pacific Crest Trail
CLEVELAND NATIONAL FOREST

Campsites, facilities: There are 22 campsites for tents or motor homes. Piped water, fireplaces, and picnic tables are provided. Vault toilets are available. A grocery store is nearby.

Reservations, fee: Reserve through MISTIX at (800)283-CAMP ($6 MISTIX fee); $85 group fee per night.

Who to contact: Phone the Cleveland National Forest Headquarters at (619)557-5050.

Location: From San Diego, drive approximately 50 miles east on Interstate 8 to the Laguna Junction exit. Drive about eight miles north on Sunrise Highway-Laguna Mountain Road to the campground entrance road on the left.

Trip note: This camp is set right along side Agua Dulce camp, on the southern flank of Mt. Laguna. The Pacific Crest Trail passes right by the Burnt Rancheria campground, located a mile up the road to the northwest. The elevation is 6,800 feet. Open from May to October.

Map grid h0 **INTERNATIONAL MOTOR INN RV PARK**
near Imperial Beach

Campsites, facilities: There are 42 motor home spaces with full hookups. Picnic tables and patios are provided. Flush toilets, showers, a swimming pool, a jacuzzi, and a laundromat are available. Pets are permitted on leashes.
Reservations, fee: Call for available space; $19 fee per night.
Who to contact: Phone the park at (619)428-4486.
Location: From Interstate 5, take the Via de San Ysidro exit and drive south on Calle Primera to 190 East Calle Primera, next to Motel 6.
Trip note: Easy access from Highway 5 is a big plus here, but be advised to call ahead for available space. Nearby side trips include west to Imperial Beach, south to Tijuana, and east to Otay Lake. Open year-round.

Map grid h1 **CHULA VISTA MARINA AND RV PARK** 
in Chula Vista

Campsites, facilities: There are 237 motor home spaces with full hookups. Flush toilets, showers, TV hookups, a playground, a heated pool and spa, a game room, a marina, a fishing pier, a free boat launch, free transportation to the San Diego Trolley, a laundromat, propane gas, and groceries are available. Some facilities are wheelchair accessible. Pets are permitted on leashes.
Reservations, fee: Call for available space; $25-$34 fee per night; pets $1.
Who to contact: Phone the park at (619)422-0111.
Location: From Interstate 5 in Chula Vista, take the J Street exit and drive west a short distance to Sandpiper. Go left and drive to 460 Sandpiper Way.
Trip note: This is one of two parks in Chula Vista. See the trip note for San Diego Metropolitan KOA for detailed trip options. Open year-round.

Map grid h1 **BORDER GATE RV PARK** 
in San Ysidro

Campsites, facilities: There are 179 motor home spaces with full hookups and individual lawns and patios. Flush toilets, showers, a playground, a heated pool, a dump station, laundry, propane gas, and groceries are available. Some facilities are wheelchair accessible. Pets are permitted on leashes.
Reservations, fee: Call for available space; $22-$25 fee per night; pets $1.
Who to contact: Phone the park at (619)428-4411.
Location: From Interstate 5 in San Ysidro, drive east on Dairymart Road to San Ysidro Boulevard. Turn left and drive to 1010 San Ysidro Boulevard.
Trip note: Border Gate is literally that. It is less than two miles from the Mexican border, with a regular Mexicoach bus service from the park to downtown Tijuana and back. Open year-round.

Map grid h1 **SAN DIEGO METROPOLITAN KOA** 
in Chula Vista

Campsites, facilities: There are 64 tent sites and 206 motor home spaces with full hookups. Picnic tables and BBQ grills are provided. Flush toilets, showers, a playground, a dump station, a laundromat, a swimming pool, a jacuzzi, bike rentals, propane gas, and groceries are available. Some facilities are wheelchair

accessible. Pets are permitted on leashes.
Reservations, fee: Reservations accepted; \$23-\$29 fee per night.
Who to contact: Phone the park at (619)427-3601.
Location: From Interstate 5 in Chula Vista, take the E Street exit and drive three miles east. Turn north on Second Street and drive to 111 North Second Street.
Trip note: This is one in a series of parks set up primarily for motor homes cruising Highway 5. Chula Vista is located between Mexico and San Diego, allowing visitors to make side trips east to Lower Otay Lake, north to the San Diego attractions, south to Tijuana, or "around the corner" on Highway 75 to Silver Strand State Beach. Open year-round.

A B

Map grid h2

OTAY LAKE COUNTY PARK
near Chula Vista

C

Campsites, facilities: There are 18 tent sites and 26 motor home spaces with partial hookups. Picnic tables and fireplaces are provided. Piped water, flush toilets, showers, and a playground are available. Pets are permitted on leashes.
Reservations, fee: Call for available space; \$10-\$12 fee per night; pets \$1.
Who to contact: Phone the County Parks Department at (619)565-3600.
Location: From Interstate 805 east of Chula Vista, take the Telegraph Canyon Road exit and drive east for five miles. Continue east on Otay Lakes Road. Turn right on Wueste Road and drive three miles to the park.
Trip note: This is an ideal base camp for campers and anglers in pursuit of Otay Lakes giant Florida strain of largemouth bass. I was fishing with Jack Neu the day he caught the California record for the largest five-fish limit of bass, 53 pounds, 14 ounces (using crawdads for bait). The camp is located at the southern tip of Lower Otay Lake. A paved boat ramp, boat rentals, tackle, a snack bar, and groceries are available on the west shore of the lake. The lake and its facilities are open Wednesdays, Saturdays, and Sundays, February through mid-October. Open year-round.

D E F

Map grid h5

BARRETT LAKE MOBILE HOME & RV PARK
north of Tecate

G

Campsites, facilities: There are 46 RV spaces with partial hookups and 10 with full hookups. Flush toilets, showers, picnic tables, a dump station, laundry, and two swimming pools are available.
Reservations, fee: Call ahead for available space and fee.
Who to contact: Phone the park at (619)468-3332.
Location: From Campo, drive 11 miles on Highway 94 to the junction of Highway 94 and Barrett Lake Road. Turn north on Barrett Lake Road and drive to the campground at 1250 Barrett Lake Road.
Trip note: This is just enough off the beaten path to get missed by a lot of folks. It is set near Barrett Lake amid the surrounding Cleveland National Forest. The lake, known for occasionally good fishing for bass and catfish, is only about ten miles north of the Mexican border. Open year-round.

H I

Map grid h7

POTRERO COUNTY PARK
near Mexican border

J6

Campsites, facilities: There are 32 campsites for tents or motor homes. Picnic tables, fireplaces, electrical hookups and piped water are provided. Flush toilets, showers, a playground, and a dump station are available. Supplies can be purchased in Potrero. Pets are permitted on leashes.

Reservations, fee: Call for available space; $12 fee per night; pets $1.

Who to contact: Phone the County Parks Department at (619)565-3600.

Location: From Potrero, drive two miles northeast on Highway 94.

Trip note: If you want to hole up for the night before getting through Customs, this is the place. It is set just a heartbeat away from the Customs inspection station in Tecate. A good side trip is to the nearby Tecate Mission Chapel, where you can pray the guards do not rip your car up in the search for contraband. It's a lot easier just to be clean, live clean. Open year-round.

Map grid h7

LAKE MORENA TRAILER RESORT
near Campo

Campsites, facilities: There are 42 motor home spaces with full hookups. Picnic tables are provided. Flush toilets, showers, propane gas, and a laundromat are available.

Reservations, fee: Call for available space; $16 fee per night; deposit required on three-day weekends.

Who to contact: Phone the park at (619)478-5677.

Location: From San Diego, drive approximately 53 miles east on Interstate 8. Take the Buckman Springs Road exit (County Road S1) and drive 5.5 miles south. Turn right (west) on Oak Drive and drive 2.5 miles. Turn left on Lake Morena Drive and drive to 2330 Lake Morena Drive. From Campo on Highway 94, turn north on County Road S1 and drive five miles to Oak Drive. Turn left on Oak Drive. Turn left on Lake Morena Drive and drive to 2330 Lake Morena Drive.

Trip note: The camp is set near the southern side of Lake Morena. It is one of the three camps near the lake and the best for motor homes. Lake Morena, at 3,200 feet elevation, is a large reservoir set in the San Diego County foothills and is known for the big bass. The lake record weighed 19 pounds, 2 ounces. The lake has a paved ramp and rowboat rentals. Open year-round.

Map grid h7

LAKE MORENA COUNTY PARK
near Campo

Campsites, facilities: There are 90 campsites for tents or motor homes, some with partial hookups. Picnic tables and fireplaces are provided. Piped water, chemical toilets,and showers are available. A grocery store, a boat ramp, and rowboat rentals are nearby. Pets are permitted on leashes.

Reservations, fee: Call for available space; $10-$12 fee per night; pets $1.

Who to contact: Phone the park at (619)565-3600 or (619)478-5473.

Location: From San Diego, drive approximately 53 miles east on Interstate 8. Take the Buckman Springs Road exit (County Road S1) and drive 5.5 miles south. Turn right (west) on Oak Drive and follow signs to the park. Turn left on Lake Morena Drive and drive to 2330 Lake Morena Drive.

Trip note: This camp is set along the southern shore of Lake Morena at 3,150 feet elevation. Morena is a large reservoir, not far from the California-Mexico border, that is known for occasionally producing giant bass. The lake record weighed 19 pounds, 2 ounces. Rowboat rentals are available nearby. Open year-round.

Map grid **h8**

BOULDER OAKS

A

near Lake Morena
CLEVELAND NATIONAL FOREST

Campsites, facilities: There are six sites for tents only, 12 campsites for tents or motor homes, and 14 equestrian sites. Picnic tables, fireplaces, and piped water are provided. Vault toilets are available. A grocery store is nearby.

B

Reservations, fee: Some sites by reservation only; phone MISTIX at (800)283-CAMP ($6 MISTIX fee); $7 fee per night.

Who to contact: Phone the Cleveland National Forest Headquarters at (619)557-5050.

Location: From San Diego, drive approximately 55 miles east on Interstate 8 to the Kitchen Creek-Cameron Station exit. Turn right on the southern frontage road and drive about one mile to the campground.

C

Trip note: This campground is about ten miles (by car) from Lake Morena, a large reservoir that is the home of some big bass in the 15-pound class, as elusive as they can often prove to be. Rowboat rentals are available. The Pacific Crest Trail passes nearby, the same trail that extends north for 2,700 miles to the Washington-Canada border. The elevation is 3,500 feet. Open year-round.

D

E

F

G

H

I

J6

◆ MAP J7 ◆

BEACH
TREES
5% CLUB
DESERT
URBAN
FOOTHILL
GRASSLAND
15 MILES

to Indio
to Cahuilla
to Julian to Warner Springs
to Campo to Pine Valley
to Niland
to Brawley
to Calexico

a b c d e f g h i j

0 1 2 3 4 5 6 7 8 9

195
111
86
CHOCOLATE MTN. IMPACT AREA
ANZA–
Desert Shores
SALTON SEA STATE REC. AREA
SALTON SEA BEACH
Borrego Springs
S22
BORREGO
Salton Sea
Salton Sea
SALTON SEA NAVAL TEST RANGE
S3
OCOTILLO WELLS ST. VEHICLE REC. AREA
78
Ocotilla Wells
DESERT
Agua Caliente Springs
STATE
Westmorland
Superstition Mtn. EL. 759
S2
US NAVAL AERIAL GUNNERY RANGES
S30
MANAZITA INDIAN RESERVATION
PARK
Carrizo Mtn. EL. 2,408
Imperial
8
Summit EL. 4,350
CAMPO INDIAN RES.
S80
Plaster City
Ocotillo
Seeley
El Centro
Boulevard
Mnt. Springs Pass EL. 3,241
S29
Jacumba
98
Mt. Signal
MEXICO
2
La Rumorosa
Colonia Progreso

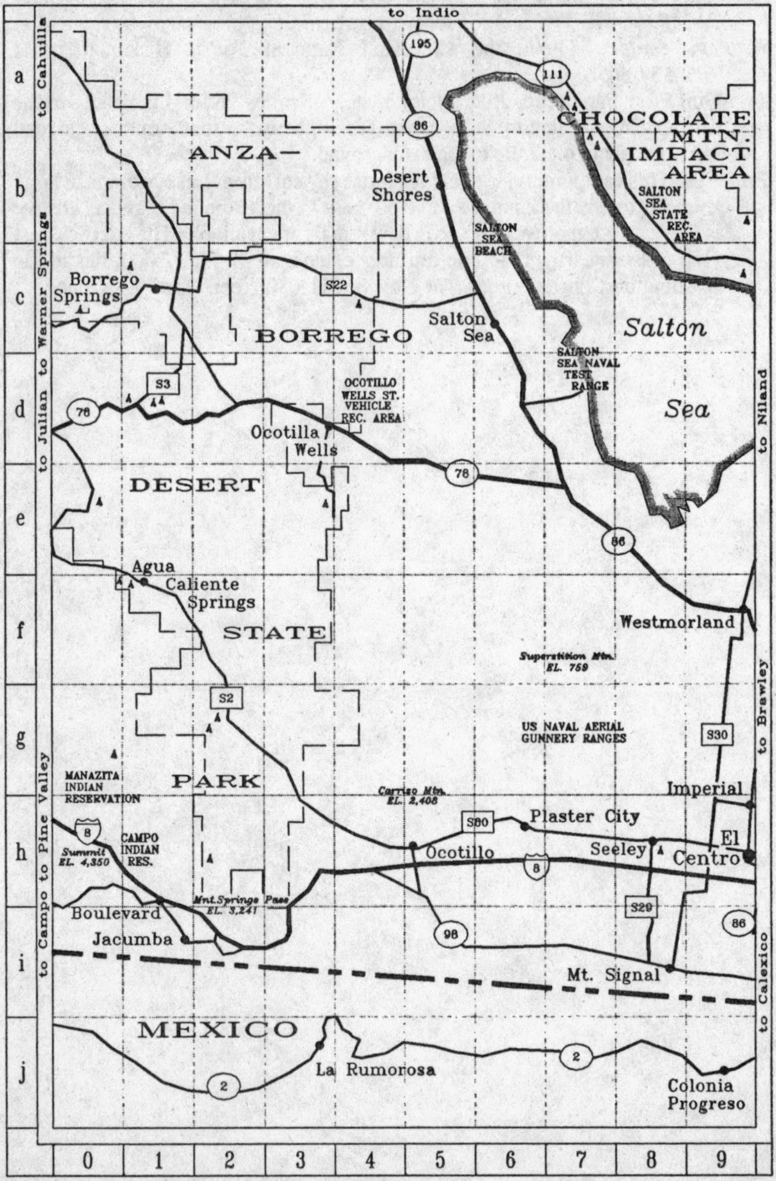

Map grid **a7**

HEADQUARTERS
SALTON SEA STATE RECREATION AREA

Campsites, facilities: There are 25 campsites for tents or motor homes up to 32 feet long. Piped water, fireplaces, and picnic tables are provided. Sixteen sites have electrical connections and sewer hookups. Rest rooms, showers, a dump station, a grocery store, and propane gas are available nearby. There is wheelchair access to camping, picnicking, boating, fishing and exhibit areas. Pets are permitted on leashes.
Reservations, fee: Reserve through MISTIX at (800)444-PARK ($3.95 MISTIX fee); $12-$16 fee per night; pets $1.
Who to contact: Phone Salton Sea State Recreation Area at (619)393-3052.
Location: From Mecca, drive ten miles southeast on Highway 111 to the entrance.
Trip note: This is the northernmost of the camps on the shore of the giant Salton Sea, that vast, shallow, and unique lake. It is set at the recreation area headquarters, just south of the town of Desert Beach at an elevation of 220 feet below sea level. Corvina fishing can be quite good at this lake. The best time to visit is from October through May. Summer is like visiting the devil, and spring and fall can be quite windy. If winds are hazardous, a red beacon on the northeast shore of the lake will flash. If you see it, it's time to flat git to the nearest shore. Open year-round.

Map grid **a7**

MECCA BEACH
SALTON SEA STATE RECREATION AREA

Campsites, facilities: There are 110 campsites for tents or motor homes up to 30 feet long. Piped water, fireplaces, and picnic tables are provided. Flush toilets, showers, groceries, and propane gas are available. Pets are permitted on leashes.
Reservations, fee: No reservations; $12 fee per night; pets $1.
Who to contact: Phone the Salton Sea State Recreation Area at (619)393-3052.
Location: From Mecca, drive 12 miles southeast on Highway 111 to the entrance.
Trip note: This is one of the camps set in the Salton Sea State Recreation Area on the northeastern shore of the lake. For details, see the trip note for Headquarters camp.

Map grid **b7**

CORVINA BEACH
SALTON SEA STATE RECREATION AREA

Campsites, facilities: There are 500 primitive campsites for tents or motor homes. Piped water is provided. Chemical toilets and a boat ramp are available. Groceries and propane gas are available nearby. Pets are permitted on leashes.
Reservations, fee: No reservations; $7 fee per night; pets $1.
Who to contact: Phone the Salton Sea State Recreation Area at (619)393-3052.
Location: From Mecca, drive 14 miles southeast on Highway 111 to the entrance.
Trip note: This is by far the biggest of the campgrounds on the Salton Sea. For details, see the trip note for Headquarters camp. Open year-round.

Map grid **b7**

SALT CREEK PRIMITIVE AREA
SALTON SEA STATE RECREATION AREA

Campsites, facilities: There are 150 primitive campsites for tents or motor homes. Chemical toilets are available, but **no piped water** is available, so bring your own. Pets are permitted on leashes.

Reservations, fee: No reservations; $7 fee per night; pets $1.

Who to contact: Phone the Salton Sea State Recreation Area at (619)393-3052.

Location: From Mecca, drive 17 miles southeast on Highway 111 to the entrance.

Trip note: Every camp has some claim to fame, however obscure. This one gets the award for the least likely place you want to visit on the Salton Sea. Why? No water. Even a water purifier won't work with the lake water, unless you're a corvina. For details on the area, see the trip note for Headquarters camp.

Map grid **b9**

FOUNTAIN OF YOUTH SPA

near Salton Sea

Campsites, facilities: There are 400 primitive sites and 546 motor home spaces with full hookups. Flush toilets, showers, natural artesian steam rooms, hydrojet pools, swimming pools, recreation centers, dump stations, laundry, a barber-shop, a beauty parlor, a masseur, church services, propane gas, and groceries are available.

Reservations, fee: Call ahead for available space and fee.

Who to contact: Phone the park at (619)354-1340.

Location: From Indio, drive 44 miles south on Highway 111 to Hot Mineral Spa Road. Or from Niland, drive 15 miles north on Highway 111 to Hot Mineral Spa Road. Turn north on Hot Mineral Spa Road and drive several miles to the park.

Trip note: Natural artesian steam rooms are the highlight here, but I didn't seem to get any younger. It is a vast private park, set near the Salton Sea. See the trip note for Red Hill County Park, located nearby, for side trip options.

Map grid **c0**

CULP VALLEY PRIMITIVE CAMP AREA

near Pena Springs

ANZA-BORREGO DESERT STATE PARK

Campsites, facilities: This is an open camping area in Anza-Borrego Desert State Park. It can be used for tents or motor homes. Open fires are not allowed and there is **no piped water,** so bring your own.

Reservations, fee: No reservations, no fee.

Who to contact: Phone the Anza-Borrego Desert State Park at (619)767-5311.

Location: From Borrego Springs, drive ten miles southwest on County Road S22.

Trip note: Culp Valley is set near Pena Spring and offers a trailhead for a hike that is routed to the northeast to the high desert. An advisable side trip is to the Panorama Outlook, located at the Visitor Center about a 15-minute drive north on County Road S22. The elevation is 3,400 feet. Open year-round.

Map grid **c1**

BORREGO PALM CANYON

ANZA-BORREGO DESERT STATE PARK

Campsites, facilities: There are 52 motor home spaces with full hookups and 65 campsites for tents or motor homes. Piped water, fireplaces, and picnic tables are provided. Flush toilets and showers are available. A grocery store, laundromat, and propane gas are nearby. There are also five group tent camps that can accommodate 10-24 people.

Reservations, fee: Phone MISTIX at (800)444-PARK ($3.95 MISTIX fee); $10-$18 fee per night; $36 group fee.

Who to contact: Phone the Anza-Borrego Desert State Park at (619)767-5311.

Location: From Borrego Springs, drive 2.5 miles west on County Road S22 and Palm Canyon Drive.

Trip note: This is the place to go for motor home cruisers. The Panorama Outlook trail starts here, and a Visitors Center is also available. The latter offers exhibits and a slide show. The elevation is 760 feet. Open year-round.

A

Map grid **c4** **ARROYO SALADO PRIMITIVE CAMP AREA**
ANZA-BORREGO DESERT STATE PARK

B

Campsites, facilities: This is an open camping area in the Anza-Borrego Desert State Park. It can be used for tents or motor homes. Open fires are not allowed and there is **no piped water,** so bring your own.

Reservations, fee: No reservations, no fee.

Who to contact: Phone the Anza-Borrego Desert State Park at (619)767-5311.

Location: From Borrego Springs, drive 16 miles east on County Road S22.

Trip note: The camp is a primitive spot set along (and named after) an ephemeral stream, the Arroyo Salado. A few miles to the west is the trailhead for the Thimble Trail, which is routed south into a wash in the Borrego Badlands. The elevation is 800 feet. Open year-round.

C

D

Map grid **c9** **BOMBAY BEACH**
SALTON SEA STATE RECREATION AREA

Campsites, facilities: There are 200 campsites for tents or motor homes. Piped water and chemical toilets are available. Pets are permitted on leashes.

E

Reservations, fee: No reservations; $7 fee per night; pets $1.

Who to contact: Phone the Salton Sea State Recreation Area at (619)393-3052.

Location: From Niland, drive 18 miles northwest on Highway 111 to the entrance.

Trip note: All in all, this is a strange looking place, the vast body of water surrounded by stark countryside. Salton Sea is the unique saltwater lake set below sea level, where corvina provide a lively sports fishery. This camp is set in a bay along the southeastern shoreline, where a beach and nature trails are available. Nearby, to the south, is the Wister Waterfowl Management Area. Open year-round.

F

G

Map grid **d1** **YAQUI WELL PRIMITIVE CAMP AREA**
ANZA-BORREGO DESERT STATE PARK

Campsites, facilities: This is an open camping area in Anza-Borrego Desert State Park. It can be used for tents or motor homes. Pit toilets are available. Open fires are not allowed and there is **no piped water,** so bring your own.

H

Reservations, fee: No reservations, no fee.

Who to contact: Phone the Anza-Borrego Desert State Park at (619)767-5311.

Location: From Borrego Springs, drive about five miles south on County Road S3. Turn right on Yaqui Pass Road (County Road S3) and drive about six miles to the camping area on the right.

I

Trip note: This camp is used primarily as an overflow area if the more developed Tamarisk Grove camp is full. A hiking trail, the Cactus Loop Trail, starts at Tamarisk Grove. The elevation is 1,400 feet. Open year-round.

Map grid **d1** **YAQUI PASS PRIMITIVE CAMP AREA**
ANZA-BORREGO DESERT STATE PARK

J7

Campsites, facilities: This is an open camping area in Anza-Borrego Desert State

Park. It can be used for tents or motor homes. There are no toilets. Open fires are not allowed and there is **no piped water,** so bring your own.

Reservations, fee: No reservations, no fee.

Who to contact: Phone the Anza-Borrego Desert State Park at (619)767-5311.

Location: From Borrego Springs, drive about five miles south on County Road S3. Turn right on Yaqui Pass Road (County Road S3) and drive about four miles to the camping area on the left.

Trip note: Set beside primitive Yaqui Pass Road, at 1730 feet elevation. The trailhead for the Kenyan Loop Trail, a side trip possibility, is located to the immediate south. This spot is often overlooked because the Tamarisk Grove camp nearby provides piped water. Open year-round.

Map grid d1 — TAMARISK GROVE

ANZA-BORREGO DESERT STATE PARK

Campsites, facilities: There are 27 campsites for tents or motor homes. Piped water, fireplaces, and picnic tables are provided. Flush toilets and showers are available. Pets are permitted on leashes.

Reservations, fee: Reserve through MISTIX at (800)444-PARK ($3.95 MISTIX fee); $10-$12 fee per night; pets $1.

Who to contact: Phone the Anza-Borrego Desert State Park at (619)767-5311.

Location: From Borrego Springs, drive 12 miles south on County Road S3 (which becomes Yaqui Pass Road) to the intersection with Highway 78.

Trip note: They've got piped water here, and right there is the number one reason that this is one of the most popular camps in this desert park. It is one of the three camps in the immediate area, so if this camp is full, primitive Yaqui Well to the immediate west and Yaqui Pass to the north on Yaqui Pass Road, provide options. The Cactus Loop Trail, with the trailhead just north of camp, provides a hiking option. The elevation is 1,400 feet. Open year-round.

Map grid e0 — BLAIR VALLEY ENVIRONMENTAL CAMPS

ANZA-BORREGO DESERT STATE PARK

Campsites, facilities: These campsites have been developed to offer maximum seclusion for the camper. The sites are walk-in and are about 100 yards from their parking areas. Each site has a cupboard and picnic table, but no toilet. **No piped water** is available, so bring your own.

Reservations, fee: Reservation requested, no fee.

Who to contact: Phone the Anza-Borrego Desert State Park at (619)767-5311.

Location: From Julian on Highway 78, drive 12 miles east. Turn right (south) on County Road S2 and drive about five miles to the campground entrance road.

Trip note: An attraction of this camp is the nearby hiking, with the Morteros Trail (drive three miles) and Pictograph Trail (drive six miles) located down the road—look for the trailheads on the right side. The elevation is 2,500 feet. Open year-round.

Map grid e3 — FISH CREEK

ANZA-BORREGO DESERT STATE PARK

Campsites, facilities: There are eight campsites for tents or motor homes. Pit toilets are available, but there is **no piped water,** so bring your own.

Reservations, fee: No reservations, no fee.

Who to contact: Phone the Anza Borrego State Park at (619)767-5311.

Location: From Highway 78 in Ocotillo Wells, drive 12 miles south on Split Mountain Road to the campground.

Trip note: This primitive camp is set just inside the eastern border of Anza-Borrego State Park, at the foot of the Vallecito Mountains to the west. A possible side trip is to hike the Elephant Trees Discovery Trail, located a few miles to the north. This is the closest camp to the Ocotillo Wells State Vehicular Recreation Area, which is located 12 miles to the north.

Map grid f0

VALLECITO COUNTY PARK

ANZA BORREGO DESERT STATE PARK

Campsites, facilities: There are 40 campsites for tents or motor homes. Fireplaces and picnic tables are provided. Piped water, flush toilets, and a playground are available. Pets are permitted on leashes.

Reservations, fee: No reservations; $8 fee per night; pets $1.

Who to contact: Phone the County Parks Department at (619)565-3600.

Location: From Julian, drive 12 miles east on Highway 78. Turn right (south) on County Road S2 and drive 18 miles to the park entrance on the right.

Trip note: This nice county park in the desert gets little attention in the face of the other nearby attractions. Nearby are the Agua Caliente Hot Springs, Anza-Borrego Desert State Park to the east, and Cuyamaca Reservoir and Cuyamaca Rancho State Park are about 35 miles away. The elevation is 1,500 feet. Open from October to June.

Map grid f1

AGUA CALIENTE COUNTY PARK

near Anza-Borrego Desert State Park

Campsites, facilities: There are 104 motor home spaces with full or partial hookups and 36 campsites for tents or motor homes. Piped water, fireplaces, and picnic tables are provided. Flush toilets, showers, and a playground are available. Groceries and propane gas are nearby.

Reservations, fee: Call for available space; $10-$14 fee per night.

Who to contact: Phone the County Parks Department at (619)565-3600.

Location: From Julian, drive 12 miles east on Highway 78. Turn right (south) on County Road S2 and drive 21 miles south to the park entrance road on the right.

Trip note: Everything is hot here. The weather is hot, the coffee is hot, and the water is hot, and hey, that's what "Agua Caliente" means. Hot water, named after the nearby hot springs. Anza-Borrego Desert State Park is also nearby. If you like to see some cold water, Cuyamaca Reservoir and Cuyamaca Rancho State Park are about 35 miles away. The elevation is 1,350 feet. Open year-round.

Map grid g0

COTTONWOOD

McCAIN VALLEY WILDLIFE MANAGEMENT AREA

Campsites, facilities: There are 24 campsites for tents or motor homes. Piped water, fireplaces, and picnic tables are provided. Vault toilets are available. Pets are permitted on leashes.

Reservations, fee: No reservations; $4 fee per night.

Who to contact: Phone the Bureau of Land Management at (714)276-6394 or (619)352-5842.

Location: From San Diego, drive approximately 70 miles east on Interstate 8 to the McCain Valley-Boulevard exit. Turn right, then left on the southern frontage (county) road and continue east for two miles to the intersection with McCain

Valley Road. Turn left (north) on McCain Valley Road and drive about 14 miles to the campground.

Trip note: This camp is set on the western edge of the McCain Valley National Cooperative Land and Wildlife Management Area. The area is not well known by out of towners. The elevation is 4,000 feet. Open year-round.

Map grid g2

BOW WILLOW

near Bow Willow Canyon

ANZA-BORREGO DESERT STATE PARK

Campsites, facilities: There are 14 campsites for tents or motor homes. Picnic tables and ramadas are provided. Piped water (limited) and vault toilets are available. Pets are permitted on leashes.

Reservations, fee: No reservations; $7-$9 fee per night; pets $1.

Who to contact: Phone the Anza Borrego Desert State Park at (619)767-5311.

Location: From Interstate 8 in Ocotillo, turn north on County Road S2 and drive 14 miles to the campground gravel entrance road on the left.

Trip note: Bow Willow Canyon is a rugged setting that can be explored by hiking the trail that starts at this camp. A short distance east of the camp, the trail forks to the south to Rockhouse Canyon. A good side trip is to drive back to County Road S2 and head south over Sweeney Pass for the view at the Carrizo Badlands Overlook. Open year-round.

Map grid g2

MOUNTAIN PALM SPRINGS PRIMITIVE CAMP AREA

ANZA-BORREGO DESERT STATE PARK

Campsites, facilities: This is an open camping area in Anza-Borrego Desert State Park. It can be used for tents or motor homes. Pit toilets are available. Open fires are not allowed and there is **no piped water,** so bring your own.

Reservations, fee: No reservations, no fee.

Who to contact: Phone the Anza-Borrego Desert State Park at (619)767-5311.

Location: From Interstate 8 in Ocotillo, turn north on County Road S2 and drive 15 miles to the camping entrance road on the left.

Trip note: Easy access from County Road S2 is a plus, but no water is a minus at this camp. Regardless of either, to get the full benefit of this camp, you need to get out and hoof it. A trail leads south to Bow Willow Creek (and Bow Willow camp) and onward into Bow Willow Canyon. The Carrizo Badlands Overlook is located on the southeast side of Sweeney Pass, about a ten-minute drive south on County Road S2. The elevation is 950 feet. Open year-round.

Map grid h2

LARK CANYON

McCAIN VALLEY WILDLIFE MANAGEMENT AREA

Campsites, facilities: There are 20 campsites for tents or motor homes. Fireplaces and picnic tables are provided. Piped water and pit toilets are available. Pets are permitted on leashes.

Reservations, fee: No reservations; $4 fee per night.

Who to contact: Phone the Bureau of Land Management at (714)276-6394 or (619) 352-5842.

Location: From San Diego, drive approximately 70 miles east on Interstate 8 to the McCain Valley-Boulevard exit. Turn right, then left on the frontage (county) road and continue east for two miles to the intersection with McCain Valley

Road. Turn left (north) on McCain Valley Road and drive seven miles to the campground.

Trip note: Here's a chance to join the Five Percent Club, that is, the five percent of campers who use the state's prettiest, little-known spots. This is a small camp that few know of, set at 4,000 feet in the McCain Valley National Cooperative and Wildlife Management Area. Open year-round.

◆ MAP J8 ◆

BEACH
TREES
5% CLUB
DESERT
URBAN
FOOTHILL
GRASSLAND

15 MILES

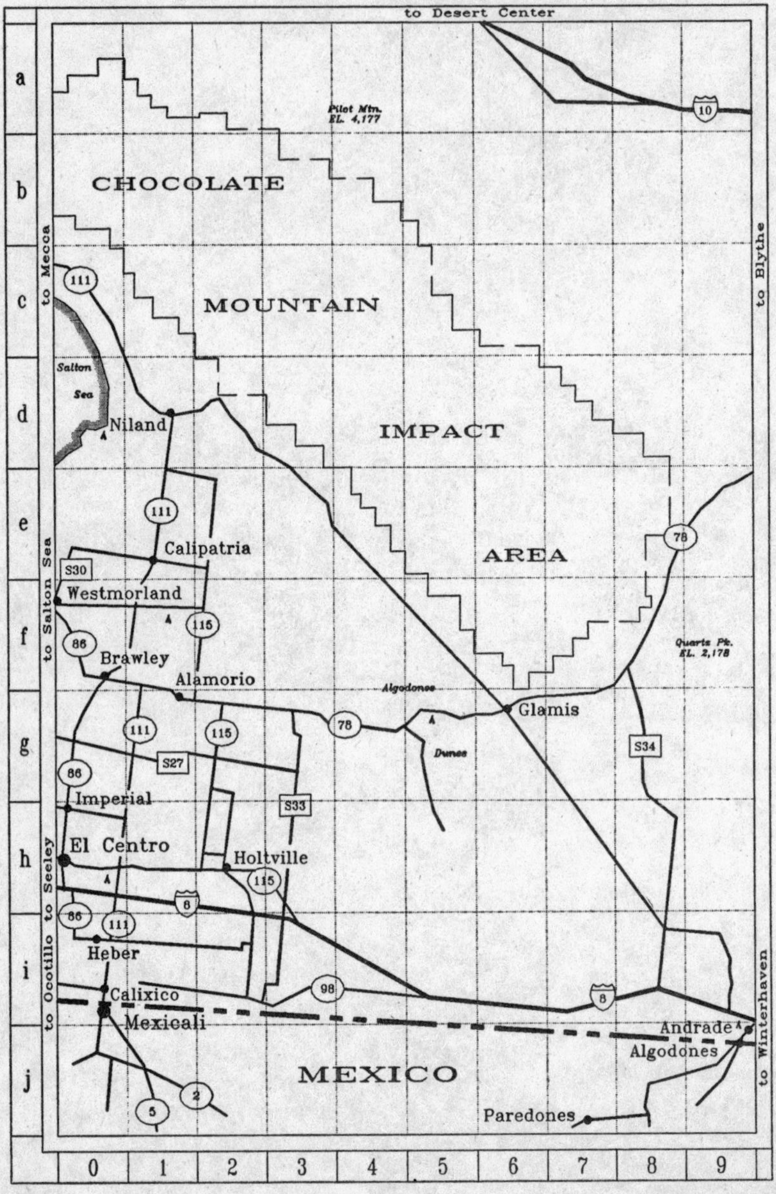

to Desert Center
Pilot Mtn. EL. 4,177
10
CHOCOLATE
MOUNTAIN
IMPACT
AREA
to Mecca
to Blythe
111
Salton Sea
Niland
111
Calipatria
S30
Westmorland
115
78
to Salton Sea
86
Brawley
Alamorio
Quartz Pk. EL. 2,178
Algodones
Dunes
Glamis
78
111
115
S27
S34
86
Imperial
S33
El Centro
Holtville
115
to Ocotillo to Seeley
8
86
111
Heber
Calixico
98
8
Mexicali
Andrade
Algodones
to Winterhaven
MEXICO
2
5
Paredones

a b c d e f g h i j
0 1 2 3 4 5 6 7 8 9

Map grid **d0**

RED HILL MARINA COUNTY PARK

near Salton Sea

Campsites, facilities: There are 400 campsites for tents or motor homes. Picnic tables, piped water, and, in some cases, electrical connections are provided. Flush toilets and showers are available.

Reservations, fee: No reservations; $5 fee per night.

Who to contact: Phone the park at (619)348-2310.

Location: From Niland, drive 5 miles south on Highway 111 to Sinclair Road. Turn right and drive to Garst Road. Go right and follow to end (about 1.5 miles). Go left on Red Hill Road and follow to marina and campground.

Trip note: This county park is set near the south end of the Salton Sea. Several wildlife refuges are in the immediate area, including two separate chunks of the Imperial Wildfowl Management Area, to the west and south, and the huge Wister Waterfowl Management Area, northwest of Niland. For side trip options, see the trip note for Bombay Beach.

Map grid **f1**

WIEST LAKE COUNTY PARK

on Wiest Lake

Campsites, facilities: There are 20 tent sites and 24 motor home spaces with full hookups. Picnic tables, fireplaces, piped water, and a dump station are provided. Flush toilets and showers are available. A grocery store, a laundromat, and propane gas are nearby.

Reservations, fee: No reservations; $9 fee per night.

Who to contact: Phone the park at (619)344-3712.

Location: From Brawley, drive approximately five miles north on Highway 111. Turn right (east) on Rutherford Road and drive two miles to the park entrance.

Trip note: This is a developed county park set along the southern shore of Wiest Lake, which adjoins the Imperial Wildfowl Management Area to the north. The park is actually below sea level. The Salton Sea, about a 20-minute ride to the northwest, provides a nearby side trip.

Map grid **g5**

GECKO

near Brawley

Campsites, facilities: There are many undesignated, dispersed campsites for tents or motor homes. Vault toilets and a sanitary disposal station are provided, but there is **no piped water,** so bring your own. Pets are permitted on leashes.

Reservations, fee: No reservations, no fee.

Who to contact: Phone the Bureau of Land Management at (619)352-5842.

Location: From Brawley, drive 27 miles east on Highway 78.

Trip note: There isn't a tree within a million miles of this camp. People who wind up here all have the same thing in common. They're ready to ride across the dunes in their dune buggies. Other recreation options include watching the sky and waiting for a cloud to show up. Open year-round.

Map grid **h0**

EL CENTRO KOA

near El Centro

Campsites, facilities: There are 30 tent sites and 175 motor home spaces with full hookups. Flush toilets, showers, swimming pool, spa, clubhouse, laundry, propane gas and groceries are available. Some facilities are wheelchair accessible. Pets are permitted on leashes.

Reservations, fee: Call ahead for available space; $12-$16 fee per night.

Who to contact: Phone the park at (619)353-1051.

Location: From Interstate 8 in El Centro, take the Highway 111 exit and drive one-quarter mile north. Turn left on Ross Road and drive a short distance to the campground entrance.

Trip note: You'd best have air conditioning. This is a motor home parking lot on the desert flats about a ten-minute drive north of the Mexican border. Nearby side trips include the Salton Sea to the north, little Sunbeam Lake County Park to the west, and, if you need to sober up, the border Customs to the south. Open year-round.

Map grid j9

PILOT KNOB CAMPGROUND

near Colorado River

Campsites, facilities: There are 105 RV spaces with full hookups and picnic tables. Flush toilets, showers, a recreation room, a swimming pool, a spa and a laundromat are available. Pets are permitted on leashes.

Reservations, fee: Call for available space; $16 fee per night.

Who to contact: Phone the park at (619)572-5232.

Location: From Interstate 8 in Winterhaven, take the Sidewinder Road exit and drive to the southern frontage road. Drive one-half mile west on the frontage road to the campground.

Trip note: They don't call the town Winterhaven for nothing. Just try visiting in the summer and you'll find out winter is preferred. This is a privately-operated motor home park that is a winter attraction for folks in the Pacific Northwest who are starting to rust from all the rain up there. The Colorado River and the Mexican border are to the south. Open year-round.

◆ MAP J9 ◆

BEACH
DESERT
FOOTHILL
TREES
URBAN
GRASSLAND
5% CLUB

15 MILES

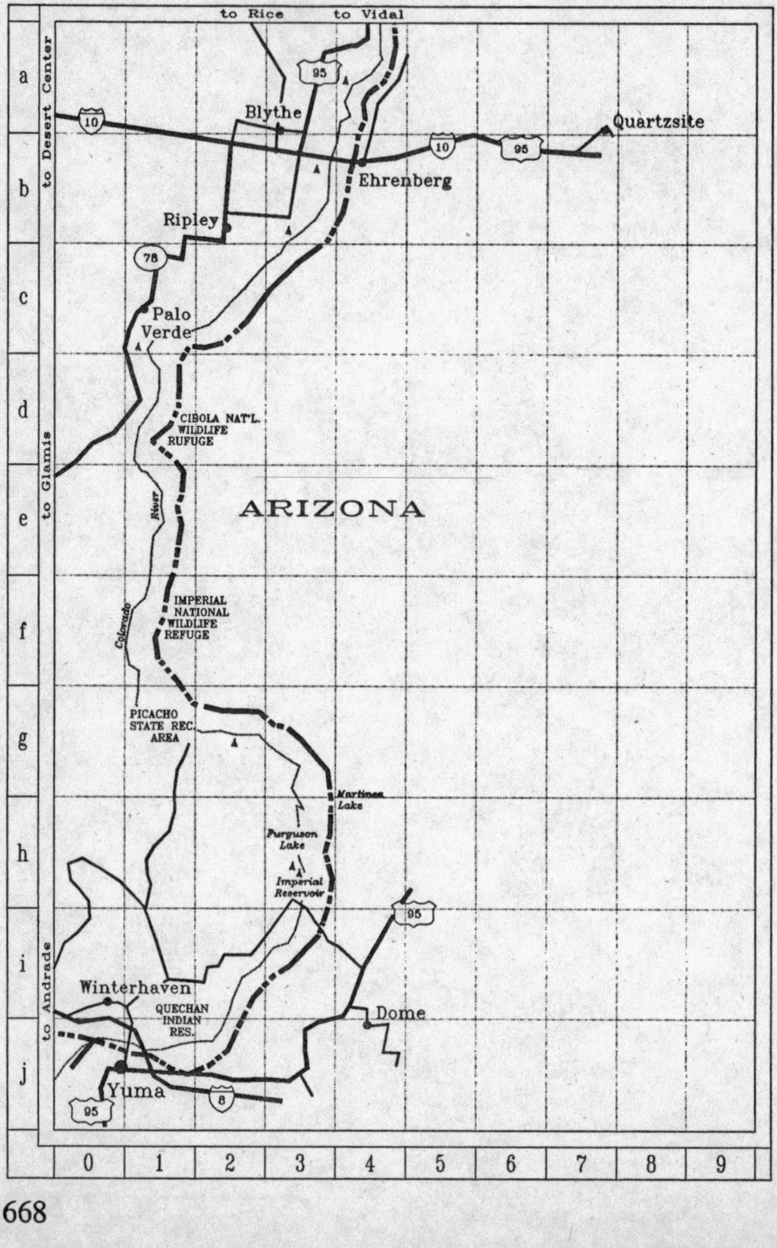

Map grid a4 — MAYFLOWER COUNTY PARK
on Colorado River

A

Campsites, facilities: There are 28 tent sites and 152 motor home spaces with piped water and electrical connections provided. There are picnic tables and fireplaces at the tent sites. Flush toilets, showers, a dump station, a playground, a snack bar, groceries and a boat ramp are available. Pets are permitted on leashes.

B

Reservations, fee: No reservations; $10-$12 fee per night; pets $1.
Who to contact: Phone the park at (619)922-4665.
Location: From Blythe, drive seven miles northeast on Intake Boulevard (US 95) to 6th Avenue and Colorado River Road.
Trip note: The Colorado River is the fountain of life around these parts, and for campers, it provides the main element that makes it an attraction. It is a popular spot for water skiing. Open year-round.

C

Map grid b3 — McINTYRE PARK
near Colorado River

D

Campsites, facilities: There are 140 tent sites and 160 motor home spaces, with picnic tables, piped water and electrical connections provided. Restrooms, showers, a dump station, propane gas, a snack bar, a grocery store, bait, ice, and a boat ramp are available. Some facilities are wheelchair accessible. Pets are not permitted.

E

Reservations, fee: No reservations; $11-$15 fee per night; pets $2.
Who to contact: Phone the park at (619)922-8205.
Location: From Blythe on Interstate 10, drive seven miles south on Intake Boulevard (Highway 95) to the foot of 26th Avenue.
Trip note: How you rate this place depends on whether you are coming or going to Las Vegas. If you are just arriving, you'll probably just keep on cruising to the bright lights. If you're coming back with darn near empty pockets, well, even a motor home park on the outskirts of Blythe starts to look good. The park is two miles from the Colorado River. Open year-round.

F

Map grid b3 — RIVIERA BLYTHE MARINA
near Colorado River

G

Campsites, facilities: There are 285 motor home spaces, many with full or partial hookups. Picnic tables are provided. Rest rooms, showers, a swimming pool, spa, cable TV, a laundromat, a store, a card room, a boat ramp and propane gas are available. A golf course is nearby.

H

Reservations, fee: Reservations accepted; $15-$25 fee per night.
Who to contact: Phone the park at (619)922-5350.
Location: From Blythe, drive two miles east on Interstate 10 to Riviera Drive exit. Follow to 14100 Riviera Drive.
Trip note: This motor home park is set up for camper-boaters who want to hunker down for awhile along the Colorado River and cool off. Open year-round.

I

Map grid c1 — PALO VERDE COUNTY PARK
near Colorado River

Campsites, facilities: There are an undesignated number of sites for tents or motor homes. Piped water, flush toilets and a playground are available. A boat ramp is available at the Palo Verde Oxbow BLM site five miles west on the Colorado

J9

River (see trip note for instructions). A grocery store, laundromat and propane gas are available in Palo Verde.

Reservations, fee: No reservations, no fee.

Who to contact: Phone the park at (619)339-4384.

Location: From Palo Verde, drive three miles south on Highway 78.

Trip note: Now that you're out here, don't start getting all picky. This is the only game in town, with no other camps for many miles. It is set near a bend in the Colorado River, not far from the Cibola National Wildlife Refuge. To get to the boat ramp, available at the Palo Verde Oxbow BLM site on the Colorado River, take the gravel road between mileposts 77 and 78 off Highway 78. Drive west for five miles to the river. Open year-round.

Map grid g2

PICACHO STATE RECREATION AREA

Taylor Lake on Colorado River

Campsites, facilities: There are 55 campsites for tents or small motor homes. Picnic tables and fireplaces are provided. There are several boat-in campsites available. Piped water, pit toilets, a sanitary disposal station, cold showers, and a boat launch are available. Pets are permitted.

Reservations, fee: No reservations; $12 fee per night; pets $1.

Who to contact: Phone (619)393-3052.

Location: From Interstate 5 in Winterhaven, take the Winterhaven-Fourth Avenue exit. Turn left on Fourth Avenue. Turn right on County Road S24. Turn left on Picacho Road and drive under the railroad tracks. Continue on Picacho Road. When you cross the American Canal the road becomes dirt. Continue north for 18 miles on the winding dirt road (not suitable for large motor homes) to the campground. This takes about one hour.

Trip note: To get here, you really have to want it. It's way out there, requiring a long drive north out of Winterhaven on a spindly little road. The camp is on the southern side of "Taylor Lake" on the Colorado River. The park is the best deal around for many miles though, with a boat ramp, water skiing, good bass fishing, and some occasional, crazy folks having the time of their life. The sun and water make a good combination. Open year-round.

Map grid h3

SENATOR WASH RECREATION AREA

near Senator Wash Reservoir

Campsites, facilities: There are an undesignated number of sites for tents or self-contained motor homes. There is **no piped water,** so bring your own. A boat ramp is available. No camping at boat ramp allowed.

Reservations, fee: No reservations, no fee.

Who to contact: Phone the Bureau of Land Management at (602)726-6300.

Location: From Yuma, Arizona, drive approximately 23 miles northeast on Imperial Highway (County Road S24) to Senator Wash Road. Turn left and drive about three miles to the campground.

Trip note: This campground is set in a large recreation area that borders the Colorado River. More specifically, it is nestled between Senator Wash Reservoir to the west and Squaw Lake (created by Imperial Dam on the Colorado River) to the southeast. It is a vast, virtually unmonitored area. Open year-round.

Map grid **h3**

SQUAW LAKE
near Colorado River

Campsites, facilities: There are 80 campsites for tents or motor homes. Picnic tables and fireplaces are provided. Piped water, flush toilets, cold showers, and a boat ramp are available. Some facilities are wheelchair accessible. Pets are permitted on leashes.

Reservations, fee: No reservations; $5 fee per night.

Who to contact: Phone the Bureau of Land Management at (602)726-6300.

Location: From Yuma, Arizona, drive approximately 23 miles northeast on Imperial Highway (County Road S24) to Senator Wash Road. Turn left and drive about three miles to the campground.

Trip note: Take your pick. There are two camps near the Colorado River in this area. This one is near Squaw Lake, created by the nearby Imperial Dam on the Colorado River. Open year-round.

INDEX KEY	
Campgrounds are indexed in capitals and followed by these codes	
B	boats without motors
BF	bass fishing
CP	county park
D	pets allowed
F	fishing
G	golf course nearby
H	hunting
I	hiking
M	motor home site
MB	motor boats allowed
N	no fee
NF	national forest
NM	national monument
NP	national park
P	primitive
R	horse corrals/riding
RP	regional park
S	swimming
SF	salmon fishing
SP	state park
T	tennis
TF	trout fishing
9	rafting

I N D E X

FIND YOUR IDEAL CAMPGROUND

You'll find every campground indexed here and set apart with capital letters. The codes that follow in the parenthesis show the type of park setting, available facilities and activities at each campground. Use the index key for easy reference.

You'll also find cities, parks, lakes, mountains, rivers, and other landmarks indexed. When the names match, for instance Big Bend (the town) and BIG BEND (the campground), the town comes first, the campground second. Remember, you can always find the campgrounds easily—they appear in capitals throughout. Learn your way around this simple index and you'll find the ideal site for every trip.

No.

A

B

INDEX KEY

Campgrounds are indexed in capitals and followed by these codes

B	boats without motors
BF	bass fishing
CP	county park
D	pets allowed
F	fishing
G	golf course nearby
H	hunting
I	hiking
M	motor home site
MB	motor boats allowed
N	no fee
NF	national forest
NM	national monument
NP	national park
P	primitive
R	horse corrals/riding
RP	regional park
S	swimming
SF	salmon fishing
SP	state park
T	tennis
TF	trout fishing
Q	rafting

C

INDEX KEY

Campgrounds are indexed in capitals and followed by these codes

B	boats without motors
BF	bass fishing
CP	county park
D	pets allowed
F	fishing
G	golf course nearby
H	hunting
I	hiking
M	motor home site
MB	motor boats allowed
N	no fee
NF	national forest
NM	national monument
NP	national park
P	primitive
R	horse corrals/riding
RP	regional park
S	swimming
SF	salmon fishing
SP	state park
T	tennis
TF	trout fishing
9	rafting

D

INDEX KEY

Campgrounds are indexed in capitals and followed by these codes

B	boats without motors
BF	bass fishing
CP	county park
D	pets allowed
F	fishing
G	golf course nearby
H	hunting
I	hiking
M	motor home site
MB	motor boats allowed
N	no fee
NF	national forest
NM	national monument
NP	national park
P	primitive
R	horse corrals/riding
RP	regional park
S	swimming
SF	salmon fishing
SP	state park
T	tennis
TF	trout fishing
9	rafting

E

F

INDEX KEY

Campgrounds are indexed in capitals and followed by these codes

B	boats without motors
BF	bass fishing
CP	county park
D	pets allowed
F	fishing
G	golf course nearby
H	hunting
I	hiking
M	motor home site
MB	motor boats allowed
N	no fee
NF	national forest
NM	national monument
NP	national park
P	primitive
R	horse corrals/riding
RP	regional park
S	swimming
SF	salmon fishing
SP	state park
T	tennis
TF	trout fishing
Q	rafting

H

I

J

INDEX KEY

Campgrounds are indexed in capitals and followed by these codes

B	boats without motors
BF	bass fishing
CP	county park
D	pets allowed
F	fishing
G	golf course nearby
H	hunting
I	hiking
M	motor home site
MB	motor boats allowed
N	no fee
NF	national forest
NM	national monument
NP	national park
P	primitive
R	horse corrals/riding
RP	regional park
S	swimming
SF	salmon fishing
SP	state park
T	tennis
TF	trout fishing
Ω	rafting

K

L

INDEX KEY

Campgrounds are indexed in capitals and followed by these codes

B boats without motors
BF bass fishing
CP county park
D pets allowed
F fishing
G golf course nearby
H hunting
I hiking
M motor home site
MB motor boats allowed
N no fee
NF national forest
NM national monument
NP national park
P primitive
R horse corrals/riding
RP regional park
S swimming
SF salmon fishing
SP state park
T tennis
TF trout fishing
9 rafting

M

INDEX KEY

Campgrounds are indexed in capitals and followed by these codes

B	boats without motors
BF	bass fishing
CP	county park
D	pets allowed
F	fishing
G	golf course nearby
H	hunting
I	hiking
M	motor home site
MB	motor boats allowed
N	no fee
NF	national forest
NM	national monument
NP	national park
P	primitive
R	horse corrals/riding
RP	regional park
S	swimming
SF	salmon fishing
SP	state park
T	tennis
TF	trout fishing
Q	rafting

N

O

P

INDEX KEY

Campgrounds are indexed in capitals and followed by these codes

B	boats without motors
BF	bass fishing
CP	county park
D	pets allowed
F	fishing
G	golf course nearby
H	hunting
I	hiking
M	motor home site
MB	motor boats allowed
N	no fee
NF	national forest
NM	national monument
NP	national park
P	primitive
R	horse corrals/riding
RP	regional park
S	swimming
SF	salmon fishing
SP	state park
T	tennis
TF	trout fishing
9	rafting

Q

R

S

INDEX KEY

Campgrounds are indexed in capitals and followed by these codes

B	boats without motors
BF	bass fishing
CP	county park
D	pets allowed
F	fishing
G	golf course nearby
H	hunting
I	hiking
M	motor home site
MB	motor boats allowed
N	no fee
NF	national forest
NM	national monument
NP	national park
P	primitive
R	horse corrals/riding
RP	regional park
S	swimming
SF	salmon fishing
SP	state park
T	tennis
TF	trout fishing
Q	rafting

INDEX KEY

Campgrounds are indexed in capitals and followed by these codes

B	boats without motors
BF	bass fishing
CP	county park
D	pets allowed
F	fishing
G	golf course nearby
H	hunting
I	hiking
M	motor home site
MB	motor boats allowed
N	no fee
NF	national forest
NM	national monument
NP	national park
P	primitive
R	horse corrals/riding
RP	regional park
S	swimming
SF	salmon fishing
SP	state park
T	tennis
TF	trout fishing
Q	rafting

T

U

V

INDEX KEY

Campgrounds are indexed in capitals and followed by these codes

B	boats without motors
BF	bass fishing
CP	county park
D	pets allowed
F	fishing
G	golf course nearby
H	hunting
I	hiking
M	motor home site
MB	motor boats allowed
N	no fee
NF	national forest
NM	national monument
NP	national park
P	primitive
R	horse corrals/riding
RP	regional park
S	swimming
SF	salmon fishing
SP	state park
T	tennis
TF	trout fishing
9	rafting

INDEX KEY

Campgrounds are indexed in capitals and followed by these codes

B	boats without motors
BF	bass fishing
CP	county park
D	pets allowed
F	fishing
G	golf course nearby
H	hunting
I	hiking
M	motor home site
MB	motor boats allowed
N	no fee
NF	national forest
NM	national monument
NP	national park
P	primitive
R	horse corrals/riding
RP	regional park
S	swimming
SF	salmon fishing
SP	state park
T	tennis
TF	trout fishing
g	rafting

1991-92 CALIFORNIA CAMPING COMMENT FORM

Foghorn Press invites you to share your comments on a campground included in this book and/or on the book itself:

PLEASE PRINT CLEARLY

Campground name: ______________________________

Page number of listing: ______________ **Date of trip:** __________

Your comments on this campground: ______________________

____

____

____

Are you a: ❒ car camper ❒ tent camper ❒ RV camper

Where did you purchase this book? ____________________

Please rate the usefulness of CALIFORNIA CAMPING (circle one):

(very) 1 2 3 4 5 (not at all)

Your comments on the book: ____________________________

____

____

Signature: ______________________ **Today's date:** __________

Address: ____________________________________

City, State, Zip: ______________________________

1991-92 CALIFORNIA CAMPING ALERT FORM

If you've camped at a spot not included in this book that you feel should be, please let us know.

PLEASE PRINT CLEARLY

Campground name: ______________________________

Mailing address: ______________________________

____

Nearest city: __________________________________

Phone number: ____________________ **Date opened:** __________

number of spaces: ________**Tent**________**RV**

Type of park ownership (circle one):

Private Federal State County City Other

Print name: ___________________________________

Signature: ____________________________________

Phone: ________________________ **Today's date:** __________

Address: ____________________________________

City, State, Zip: ______________________________

Detach and mail to:

Attn: CC Research Editor
Foghorn Press
P.O. Box 77845
San Francisco, CA 94107